# Get Connected.

## FEATURES

### Interactive Applications

Connect Management's **Interactive Applications** deliver the chapter's content through an engaging and interactive environment that allows students to apply the theory. Students will receive immediate feedback on how they are progressing.

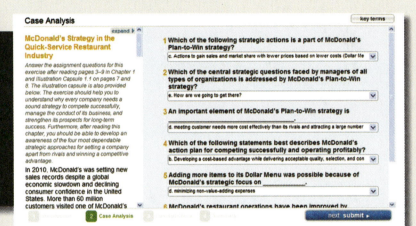

### Lecture Capture

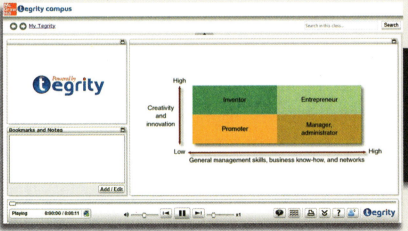

Make your classes available anytime, anywhere. With simple, one-click recording, students can search for a word or phrase and be taken to the exact place in your lecture that they need to review.

# Get Engaged.

## Case Exercises

The Connect® platform also includes author-developed case exercises for 14 of the 30 cases in this edition that require students to work through answers to a select number of the assignment questions for the case. These exercises have multiple components and can include calculating assorted financial ratios to assess a company's financial performance and balance sheet strength, identifying a company's strategy, doing five-forces and driving-forces analysis, doing a SWOT analysis, and recommending actions to improve company performance. The content of these case exercises is tailored to match the circumstances presented in each case, calling upon students to do whatever strategic thinking and strategic analysis is called for to arrive at pragmatic, analysis-based action recommendations for improving company performance.

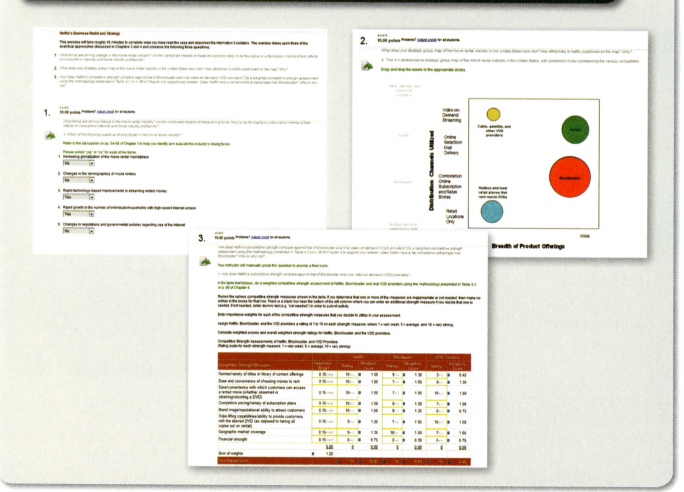

# Crafting and Executing Strategy

## THE QUEST FOR COMPETITIVE ADVANTAGE

### Concepts and Cases

# Crafting and Executing Strategy

## THE QUEST FOR COMPETITIVE ADVANTAGE

### Concepts and Cases

NINETEENTH EDITION

**Arthur A. Thompson**
*The University of Alabama*

**Margaret A. Peteraf**
*Dartmouth College*

**John E. Gamble**
*University of South Alabama*

**A. J. Strickland III**
*The University of Alabama*

McGraw-Hill Irwin

CRAFTING AND EXECUTING STRATEGY: THE QUEST FOR COMPETITIVE ADVANTAGE, CONCEPTS AND CASES, NINETEENTH EDITION

Published by McGraw-Hill/Irwin, a business unit of The McGraw-Hill Companies, Inc., 1221 Avenue of the Americas, New York, NY, 10020. Copyright © 2014 by The McGraw-Hill Companies, Inc. All rights reserved. Printed in the United States of America. Previous editions © 2012, 2010, and 2008. No part of this publication may be reproduced or distributed in any form or by any means, or stored in a database or retrieval system, without the prior written consent of The McGraw-Hill Companies, Inc., including, but not limited to, in any network or other electronic storage or transmission, or broadcast for distance learning.

Some ancillaries, including electronic and print components, may not be available to customers outside the United States.

This book is printed on acid-free paper.

3 4 5 6 7 8 9 0 QVS/QVS 1 0 9 8 7 6 5 4

ISBN 978-0-07-802950-9
MHID 0-07-802950-3

Senior vice president, products & markets: Kurt L. Strand
Vice president, general manager, products & markets: Brent Gordon
Vice president, content production & technology services: Kimberly Meriwether David
Managing director: Paul Ducham
Executive brand manager: Michael Ablassmeir
Executive director of development: Ann Torbert
Development editor II: Laura Griffin
Marketing manager : Elizabeth Trepkowski
Lead project manager: Harvey Yep

Senior buyer: Michael R. McCormick
Cover/interior designer: Cara Hawthorne, cara david DESIGN
Content licensing specialist: Joanne Mennemeier
Photo researcher: Bill VanWerden
Manager, content production: Mark Christianson
Senior media project manager: Susan Lombardi
Media project manager: Cathy L. Tepper
Typeface: 10.5/12 Minion Pro
Compositor: Laserwords Private Limited
Printer: Quad/Graphics

All credits appearing on page or at the end of the book are considered to be an extension of the copyright page.

**Library of Congress Cataloging-in-Publication Data**

Crafting and executing strategy : the quest for competitive advantage, concepts and cases / Arthur A. Thompson, The University of Alabama, Margaret A. Peteraf, Dartmouth College, John E. Gamble, University of South Alabama, A. J. Strickland III, The University of Alabama.—NINETEENTH EDITION.
    pages cm
  Includes index.
  ISBN 978-0-07-802950-9 (alk. paper)—ISBN 0-07-802950-3 (alk. paper)
  1.  Strategic planning. 2.  Strategic planning—Case studies.  I. Thompson, Arthur A., 1940-
HD30.28.T53 2014
658.4'012—dc23

                                                                            2012041878

The Internet addresses listed in the text were accurate at the time of publication. The inclusion of a website does not indicate an endorsement by the authors or McGraw-Hill, and McGraw-Hill does not guarantee the accuracy of the information presented at these sites.

To our families and especially our spouses:
Hasseline, Paul, and Kitty.

**A**rthur A. Thompson, Jr., earned his B.S. and Ph.D. degrees in economics from The University of Tennessee, spent three years on the economics faculty at Virginia Tech, and served on the faculty of The University of Alabama's College of Commerce and Business Administration for 24 years. In 1974 and again in 1982, Dr. Thompson spent semester-long sabbaticals as a visiting scholar at the Harvard Business School.

His areas of specialization are business strategy, competition and market analysis, and the economics of business enterprises. In addition to publishing over 30 articles in some 25 different professional and trade publications, he has authored or co-authored five textbooks and six computer-based simulation exercises. His textbooks and strategy simulations have been used at well over 1,000 college and university campuses worldwide.

Dr. Thompson and his wife of 51 years have two daughters, two grandchildren, and a Yorkshire Terrier.

**M**argaret A. Peteraf is the Leon E. Williams Professor of Management at the Tuck School of Business at Dartmouth College. She is an internationally recognized scholar of strategic management, with a long list of publications in top management journals. She has earned myriad honors and prizes for her contributions, including the 1999 Strategic Management Society Best Paper Award recognizing the deep influence of her work on the field of Strategic Management. Professor Peteraf is on the Board of Directors of the Strategic Management Society and has been elected as a Fellow of the Society. She served previously as a member of the Academy of Management's Board of Governors and as Chair of the Business Policy and Strategy Division of the Academy. She has also served in various editorial roles and is presently on numerous editorial boards, including the *Strategic Management Journal,* the *Academy of Management Review,* and *Organization Science.* She has taught in Executive Education programs in various programs around the world and has won teaching awards at the MBA and Executive level.

Professor Peteraf earned her Ph.D., M.A., and M.Phil. at Yale University and held previous faculty appointments at Northwestern University's Kellogg Graduate School of Management and at the University of Minnesota's Carlson School of Management.

**J**ohn E. Gamble is currently a Professor of Management in the Mitchell College of Business at the University of South Alabama. His teaching specialty at USA is strategic management and he also conducts a course in strategic management in Germany, which is sponsored by the University of Applied Sciences in Worms.

Dr. Gamble's research interests center on strategic issues in entrepreneurial, health care, and manufacturing settings. His work has been published in various scholarly journals and he is the author or co-author of more than 50 case studies published in an assortment of strategic management and strategic marketing texts. He has done consulting on industry and market analysis for clients in a diverse mix of industries.

Professor Gamble received his Ph.D. in management from The University of Alabama in 1995. Dr. Gamble also has a Bachelor of Science degree and a Master of Arts degree from The University of Alabama.

**D**r. A. J. (Lonnie) Strickland is the Thomas R. Miller Professor of Strategic Management at the Culverhouse School of Business at The University of Alabama. He is a native of north Georgia, and attended the University of Georgia, where he received a Bachelor of Science degree in math and physics; Georgia Institute of Technology, where he received a Master of Science in industrial management; and Georgia State University, where he received his Ph.D. in business administration.

Lonnie's experience in consulting and executive development is in the strategic management arena, with a concentration in industry and competitive analysis. He has developed strategic planning systems for numerous firms all over the world. He served as Director of Marketing and Strategy at Bell-South, has taken two companies to the New York Stock Exchange, is one of the founders and directors of American Equity Investment Life Holding (AEL), and serves on numerous boards of directors. He is a very popular speaker in the area of Strategic Management.

Lonnie and his wife, Kitty, have been married for 46 years. They have two children and two grandchildren. Each summer, Lonnie and his wife live on their private game reserve in South Africa where they enjoy taking their friends on safaris.

By offering the most engaging, clearly articulated, and conceptually sound text on strategic management, Crafting and Executing Strategy has been able to maintain its position as the leading textbook in strategic management for close to 30 years. With this latest edition, we build on this strong foundation, maintaining the attributes of the book that have long made it the most teachable text on the market, while updating the content, sharpening its presentation, and providing enlightening new illustrations and examples.

The distinguishing mark of the 19th edition is its enriched and enlivened presentation of the material in each of the 12 chapters, providing an as up-to-date and engrossing discussion of the core concepts and analytical tools as you will find anywhere. As with each of our new editions, there is an accompanying lineup of exciting new cases that bring the content to life and are sure to provoke interesting classroom discussions, deepening students' understanding of the material in the process.

While this 19th edition retains the 12-chapter structure of the prior edition, every chapter—indeed every paragraph and every line—has been reexamined, refined, and refreshed. New content has been added to keep the material in line with the latest developments in the theory and practice of strategic management. In other areas, coverage has been trimmed to keep the book at a more manageable size. Scores of new examples have been added, along with 16 new Illustration Capsules, to enrich understanding of the content and to provide students with a ringside view of strategy in action. The result is a text that cuts straight to the chase in terms of what students really need to know and gives instructors a leg up on teaching that material effectively. It remains, as always, solidly mainstream and balanced, mirroring *both* the penetrating insight of academic thought and the pragmatism of real-world strategic management.

A stand-out feature of this text has always been the tight linkage between the content of the chapters and the cases. The lineup of cases that accompany the 19th edition is outstanding in this respect—a truly appealing mix of strategically relevant and thoughtfully crafted cases, certain to engage students and sharpen their skills in applying the concepts and tools of strategic analysis. Many involve high-profile companies that the students will immediately recognize and relate to; all are framed around key strategic issues and serve to add depth and context to the topical content of the chapters. We are confident you will be impressed with how well these cases work in the classroom and the amount of student interest they will spark.

For some years now, growing numbers of strategy instructors at business schools worldwide have been transitioning from a purely text-case course structure to a more robust and energizing text-case-simulation course structure. Incorporating a competition-based strategy simulation has the strong appeal of providing class members with *an immediate and engaging opportunity to apply the concepts and analytical tools covered in the chapters and to become personally involved in crafting and executing a strategy for a virtual company that they have been assigned to manage and that competes head-to-head with companies run by other class members.* Two widely used and pedagogically effective online strategy simulations, *The Business Strategy Game* and *GLO-BUS,* are optional companions for this text. Both simulations were created by Arthur Thompson, one of the text authors, and, like the cases, are closely linked to the content of each chapter in the text. The Exercises for Simulation Participants, found at the end of each chapter, provide clear guidance to class members in applying the concepts and analytical tools covered in the chapters to the issues and decisions that they have to wrestle with in managing their simulation company.

To assist instructors assessing student achievement of program learning objectives, in line with new AACSB requirements, the 19th edition includes a set of Assurance of Learning Exercises at the end of each chapter that link to the specific learning objectives appearing at the beginning of each chapter and highlighted throughout the text. A new feature of the 19th edition is its more closely *integrated* linkage of selected chapter-end Assurance of Learning Exercises and cases to the publisher's web-based assignment and assessment platform called Connect.™ Your students will be able to use the online Connect™ supplement to (1) complete two or three of the Assurance of Learning Exercises appearing at the end of each of the 12 chapters, (2) complete chapter-end quizzes, and (3) enter their answers to a select number of the suggested assignment questions for 7 of the 30 cases in this edition. All of the Connect™ exercises are automatically graded, thereby enabling you to easily assess the learning that has occurred.

In addition, both of the companion strategy simulations have a built-in Learning Assurance Report that quantifies how well each member of your class performed on nine skills / learning measures *versus tens of thousands of other students worldwide* who completed the simulation in the past 12 months. We believe the chapter-end Assurance of Learning Exercises, the all-new online and automatically graded Connect™ exercises, and the Learning Assurance Report generated at the conclusion of *The Business Strategy Game* and *GLO-BUS* simulations provide you with easy-to-use, empirical measures of student learning in your course. All can be used in conjunction with other instructor-developed or school-developed scoring rubrics and assessment tools to comprehensively evaluate course or program learning outcomes and measure compliance with AACSB accreditation standards.

Taken together, the various components of the 19th-edition package and the supporting set of instructor resources provide you with enormous course design flexibility and a powerful kit of teaching/learning tools. We've done our very best to ensure that the elements constituting the 19th edition will work well for you in the classroom, help you economize on the time needed to be well prepared for each class, and cause students to conclude that your course is one of the very best they have ever taken—from the standpoint of both enjoyment and learning.

# DIFFERENTIATING FEATURES OF THE 19TH EDITION

Six standout features strongly differentiate this text and the accompanying instructional package from others in the field:

1. *Our integrated coverage of the two most popular perspectives on strategic management—positioning theory and resource-based theory—is unsurpassed by any other leading strategy text.* Principles and concepts from both the positioning perspective and the resource-based perspective are prominently and comprehensively integrated into our coverage of crafting both single-business and multibusiness strategies. By highlighting the relationship between a firm's resources and

capabilities to the activities it conducts along its value chain, we show explicitly how these two perspectives relate to one another. Moreover, in Chapters 3 through 8 it is emphasized repeatedly that a company's strategy must be matched *not only* to its external market circumstances *but also* to its internal resources and competitive capabilities.

2.   *Our coverage of cooperative strategies and the role that interorganizational activity can play in the pursuit of competitive advantage, is similarly distinguished.* The topics of strategic alliances, licensing, joint ventures, and other types of collaborative relationships are featured prominently in a number of chapters and are integrated into other material throughout the text. We show how strategies of this nature can contribute to the success of single-business companies as well as multibusiness enterprises, whether with respect to firms operating in domestic markets or those operating in the international realm.

3.   *With a stand-alone chapter devoted to this topic, our coverage of business ethics, corporate social responsibility, and environmental sustainability goes well beyond that offered by any other leading strategy text.* This chapter, "Ethics, Corporate Social Responsibility, Environmental Sustainability, and Strategy" fulfills the important functions of (1) alerting students to the role and importance of ethical and socially responsible decision making and (2) addressing the accreditation requirement of the AACSB International that business ethics be visibly and thoroughly embedded in the core curriculum. Moreover, discussions of the roles of values and ethics are integrated into portions of other chapters to further reinforce why and how considerations relating to ethics, values, social responsibility, and sustainability should figure prominently into the managerial task of crafting and executing company strategies.

4.   *Long known as an important differentiator of this text, the case collection in the 19th edition is truly unrivaled* from the standpoints of student appeal, teachability, and suitability for drilling students in the use of the concepts and analytical treatments in Chapters 1 through 12. The 30 cases included in this edition are the very latest, the best, and the most on target that we could find. The ample information about the cases in the Instructor's Manual makes it effortless to select a set of cases each term that will capture the interest of students from start to finish.

5.   *The text is now more tightly linked to the publisher's trailblazing web-based assignment and assessment platform called Connect.*™ This will enable professors to gauge class members' prowess in accurately completing (a) selected chapter-end exercises, (b) chapter-end quizzes, and (c) the creative author-developed exercises for seven of the cases in this edition.

6.   *Two cutting-edge and widely used strategy simulations—The Business Strategy Game and GLO-BUS—are optional companions to the 19th edition.* These give you an unmatched capability to employ a text-case-simulation model of course delivery.

# ORGANIZATION, CONTENT, AND FEATURES OF THE 19TH-EDITION TEXT CHAPTERS

- Chapter 1 serves as a brief, general introduction to the topic of strategy, focusing on the central questions of *"What is strategy?"* and *"Why is it important?"* As such, it serves as the perfect accompaniment for your opening-day lecture on what the course is all about and why it matters. Using the example of McDonald's to drive home the concepts in this chapter, we introduce students to what we mean by "competitive advantage" and the key features of business-level strategy. Describing strategy-making as a process, we explain why a company's strategy is partly planned and partly reactive and why a strategy tends to co-evolve with its environment over time. We show that a viable business model must provide both an attractive value proposition for the company's customers as well as a formula for making profits for the company, framing this discussion in terms of value, price, and cost. We show how the mark of a winning strategy is its ability to pass three tests: (1) the *fit test* (for internal and external fit), (2) the *competitive advantage test,* and (3) the *performance test.* And we explain why good company performance depends not only upon a sound strategy but upon solid strategy execution as well.

- Chapter 2 presents a more complete overview of the strategic management process, covering topics ranging from the role of vision, mission, and values to what constitutes good corporate governance. It makes a great assignment for the second day of class and provides a smooth transition into the heart of the course. It introduces students to such core concepts as strategic versus financial objectives, the balanced scorecard, strategic intent, and business-level versus corporate-level strategies. It explains why *all managers are on a company's strategy-making, strategy-executing team* and why a company's strategic plan is a collection of strategies devised by different managers at different levels in the organizational hierarchy. The chapter concludes with a section on the role of the board of directors in the strategy-making, strategy-executing process and examines the conditions that led to recent high-profile corporate governance failures.

- The next two chapters introduce students to the two most fundamental perspectives on strategy-making: the positioning view, exemplified by Michael Porter's "five forces model of competition" and the resource-based view. Chapter 3 provides *what has long been the clearest, most straightforward discussion of the five forces framework to be found in any text on strategic management.* It also offers a set of complementary analytical tools for conducting competitive analysis and demonstrates the importance of tailoring strategy to fit the circumstances of a company's industry and competitive environment. What's new in this edition is the inclusion of a framework for conducting competitor analysis that provides a window into a rival's probable moves and countermoves. There is also a more explicit use of the *PESTEL analysis* framework for assessing the *p*olitical, *e*conomic, *s*ocial, *t*echnological, *e*nvironmental, and *l*egal factors in a company's macro-environment.

- Chapter 4 presents the resource-based view of the firm, showing why resource and capability analysis is such a powerful tool for sizing up a company's competitive assets. It offers a simple framework for identifying a company's resources and capabilities and another for determining whether they can provide the company with a sustainable competitive advantage over its competitors. New to this edition is a more explicit reference to the widely used *VRIN framework.* Other topics covered in this chapter include dynamic capabilities, SWOT analysis, value chain analysis, benchmarking, and competitive strength assessments, thus enabling a solid appraisal of a company's relative cost position and customer value proposition vis-á-vis its rivals. *An important feature of this chapter is a table showing how key financial and operating ratios are calculated and how to interpret them.* Students will find this table handy in doing the number crunching needed to evaluate whether a company's strategy is delivering good financial performance.

- Chapter 5 sets forth the basic approaches available for competing and winning in the market-place in terms of the five generic competitive strategies—low-cost leadership, differentiation, best-cost provider, focused differentiation, and focused low cost. It describes when each of these approaches works best and what pitfalls to avoid. It explains the role of *cost drivers* and *uniqueness drivers* in reducing a company's costs and enhancing its differentiation, respectively.

- Chapter 6 focuses on *other strategic actions* a company can take to complement its competitive approach and maximize the power of its overall strategy. These include a variety of offensive or defensive competitive moves, and their timing, such as blue-ocean strategies and first-mover advantages and disadvantages. It also includes choices concerning the breadth of a company's activities (or its *scope* of operations along an industry's entire value chain), ranging from horizontal mergers and acquisitions, to vertical integration, outsourcing, and strategic alliances. This material serves to segue into that covered in the next two chapters on international and diversification strategies.

- Chapter 7 takes up the topic of how to compete in international markets. It begins with a discussion of why differing market conditions across countries must necessarily influence a company's strategic choices about how to enter and compete in foreign markets. It presents five major strategic options for expanding a company's geographic scope and competing in foreign markets: export strategies, licensing, franchising, establishing a wholly owned subsidiary via acquisition or "greenfield" venture, and alliance strategies. It includes coverage of topics such as Porter's Diamond of National Advantage, profit sanctuaries, and the choice between multidomestic, global, and transnational strategies. This chapter explains the impetus for sharing, transferring, or accessing valuable resources and capabilities across national borders in the quest for competitive advantage, connecting the material to that on the resource-based view from Chapter 4. The chapter concludes with a discussion of the unique characteristics of competing in developing-country markets.

- Chapter 8 concerns strategy-making in the multibusiness company, introducing the topic of corporate-level strategy with its special focus on diversification. The first portion of this chapter describes when and why diversification makes good strategic sense, the different means of diversifying a company's business lineup, and the pros and cons of related versus unrelated diversification strategies. The second part of the chapter looks at how to evaluate the attractiveness of a diversified company's business lineup, how to decide whether it has a good diversification strategy, and what the strategic options are for improving a diversified company's future performance. The evaluative technique integrates material concerning both industry analysis and the resource-based view, in that it considers the relative attractiveness of the various industries the company has diversified into, the company's competitive strength in each of its lines of business, and the extent to which its different businesses exhibit both *strategic fit* and *resource fit*.

- Although the topic of ethics and values comes up at various points in this textbook, Chapter 9 brings more direct attention to such issues and may be used as a stand-alone assignment in either the early, middle, or late part of a course. It concerns the themes of ethical standards in business, approaches to ensuring consistent ethical standards for companies with international operations, corporate social responsibility, and environmental sustainability. The contents of this chapter are sure to give students some things to ponder, rouse lively discussion, and help to make students more *ethically aware* and conscious of *why all companies should conduct their business in a socially responsible and sustainable manner.*

- The next three chapters (Chapters 10, 11, and 12) comprise a module on strategy execution that is presented in terms of a 10-step framework. Chapter 10 provides an overview of this framework and then explores the first three of these tasks: (1) staffing the organization with people capable of executing the strategy well, (2) building the organizational capabilities needed for successful strategy execution, and (3) creating an organizational structure supportive of the strategy execution process.

- Chapter 11 discusses five additional managerial actions that advance the cause of good strategy execution: (1) *allocating resources* to enable the strategy execution process, (2) ensuring that *policies and procedures* facilitate rather than impede strategy execution, (3) using *process management tools* and *best practices* to drive continuous improvement in the performance of value chain activities, (4) installing *information and operating systems* that help company personnel carry out their strategic roles, and (5) using *rewards and incentives* to encourage good strategy execution and the achievement of performance targets.

- Chapter 12 completes the framework with a consideration of the roles of corporate culture and leadership in promoting good strategy execution. The recurring theme throughout the final three chapters is that executing strategy involves deciding on the specific actions, behaviors, and conditions needed for a smooth strategy-supportive operation and then following through to get things done and deliver results. The goal here is to ensure that students understand that the strategy-executing phase is a *make-things-happen and make-them-happen-right* kind of managerial exercise—one that is critical for achieving operating excellence and reaching the goal of strong company performance.

In this latest edition, we have put our utmost effort into ensuring that the 12 chapters are consistent with the latest and best thinking of academics and practitioners in the field of strategic management and provide the topical coverage required for both undergraduate and MBA-level strategy courses. The ultimate test of the text, of course, is the positive pedagogical impact it has in the classroom. If this edition sets a more effective stage for your lectures and does a better job of helping you persuade students that the discipline of strategy merits their rapt attention, then it will have fulfilled its purpose.

# THE CASE COLLECTION

The 30-case lineup in this edition is flush with interesting companies and valuable lessons for students in the art and science of crafting and executing strategy. There's a good blend of cases from a length perspective—close to one-fifth are under 15 pages yet offer plenty for students to chew on; about one-fourth are medium-length cases; and the remainder are detail-rich cases that call for more sweeping analysis.

At least 26 of the 30 cases involve companies, products, people, or activities that students will have heard of, know about from personal experience, or can easily identify with. The lineup includes at least 15 cases that will deepen student understanding of the special demands of competing in industry environments where product life cycles are short and competitive maneuvering among rivals is quite active. Twenty-one of the cases involve situations in which company resources and competitive capabilities play as large a role in the strategy-making, strategy executing scheme of things as industry and competitive conditions do. Scattered throughout the lineup are nine cases concerning non-U.S. companies, globally competitive industries, and/or cross-cultural situations. These cases, in conjunction with the globalized content of the text chapters, provide abundant material for linking the study of strategic management tightly to the ongoing globalization of the world economy. You'll also find 6 cases dealing with the strategic problems of family-owned or relatively small entrepreneurial businesses and 21 cases involving public companies and situations where students can do further research on the Internet.

The "Guide to Case Analysis" follows the last case. It contains sections on what a case is, why cases are a standard part of courses in strategy, preparing a case for class discussion, doing a written case analysis, doing an oral presentation, and using financial ratio analysis to assess a company's financial condition. We suggest having students read this guide before the first class discussion of a case.

A number of cases have accompanying videotape segments on the DVD.

# THE TWO STRATEGY SIMULATION SUPPLEMENTS: THE BUSINESS STRATEGY GAME AND GLO-BUS

*The Business Strategy Game* and *GLO-BUS: Developing Winning Competitive Strategies*—two competition-based strategy simulations that are delivered online and that feature automated processing and grading of performance—are being marketed by the publisher as companion supplements for use with the 19th edition (and other texts in the field).

- *The Business Strategy Game* is the world's most popular strategy simulation, having been used by nearly 2,000 instructors in courses involving approximately 700,000 students on 900 university campuses in 60 countries.
- *GLO-BUS*, a somewhat simpler strategy simulation introduced in 2004, has been used by more than 1,100 instructors at more than 540 university campuses in 40 countries.

## How the Strategy Simulations Work

In both *The Business Strategy Game (BSG)* and *GLO-BUS*, class members are divided into teams of one to five persons and assigned to run a company that competes head-to-head against companies run by other class members.

- In *BSG*, team members run an athletic footwear company, producing and marketing both branded and private-label footwear.
- In *GLO-BUS*, team members operate a digital camera company that designs, assembles, and markets entry-level digital cameras and upscale, multifeatured cameras.

In both simulations, companies compete in a global market arena, selling their products in four geographic regions—Europe-Africa, North America, Asia-Pacific, and Latin America. Each management team is called upon to craft a strategy for their company and make decisions relating to plant operations, workforce compensation, pricing and marketing, social responsibility/citizenship, and finance.

Company co-managers are held accountable for their decision making. Each company's performance is scored on the basis of earnings per share, return-on-equity investment, stock price, credit rating, and image rating. Rankings of company performance, along with a wealth of industry and company statistics, are available to company co-managers after each decision round to use in making strategy adjustments and operating decisions for the next competitive round. You can be certain that the market environment, strategic issues, and operating challenges that company co-managers must contend with are *very tightly linked* to what your class members will be reading about in the text chapters. The circumstances that co-managers face in running their simulation company embrace the very concepts, analytical tools, and strategy options they encounter in the text chapters (this is something you can quickly confirm by skimming through some of the Exercises for Simulation Participants that appear at the end of each chapter).

We suggest that you schedule 1 or 2 practice rounds and anywhere from 4 to 10 regular (scored) decision rounds (more rounds are better than fewer rounds). Each decision round represents a year of company operations and will entail roughly two hours of time for company co-managers to complete. In traditional 13-week, semester-long courses, there is merit in scheduling one decision round per week. In courses that run 5 to 10 weeks, it is wise to schedule two decision rounds per week for the last several weeks of the term (sample course schedules are provided for courses of varying length and varying numbers of class meetings).

When the instructor-specified deadline for a decision round arrives, the simulation server automatically accesses the saved decision entries of each company, determines the competitiveness and buyer appeal of each company's product offering relative to the other companies being run by students in your class, and then awards sales and market shares to the competing companies, geographic region by geographic region. The unit sales volumes awarded to each company *are totally governed by:*

- How its prices compare against the prices of rival brands.
- How its product quality compares against the quality of rival brands.
- How its product line breadth and selection compare.
- How its advertising effort compares.
- And so on, for a total of 11 competitive factors that determine unit sales and market shares.

The competitiveness and overall buyer appeal of each company's product offering *in comparison to the product offerings of rival companies* is all-decisive—this algorithmic feature is what makes *BSG* and *GLO-BUS* "competition-based" strategy simulations. Once each company's sales and market shares are awarded based on the competitiveness of its respective overall product offering, the various company and industry reports detailing the outcomes of the decision round are then generated. Company co-managers can access the results of the decision round 15 to 20 minutes after the decision deadline.

## The Compelling Case for Incorporating Use of a Strategy Simulation

There are *three exceptionally important benefits* associated with using a competition-based simulation in strategy courses taken by seniors and MBA students:

- *A three-pronged text-case-simulation course model delivers significantly more teaching-learning power than the traditional text-case model.* Using *both* cases and a strategy simulation to drill students in thinking strategically and applying what they read in the text chapters is a stronger, more effective means of helping them connect theory with practice and develop better business judgment. What cases do that a simulation cannot is give class members broad exposure to a variety of companies and industry situations and insight into the kinds of strategy-related problems managers face. But what a competition-based strategy simulation does far better than case analysis is thrust class members squarely into *an active, hands-on managerial role* where they are totally responsible for assessing market conditions, determining how to respond to the actions of competitors, forging a long-term direction and strategy for their company, and making all kinds of operating decisions. Because they are held fully accountable for their decisions and their company's performance, *co-managers are strongly motivated* to dig deeply into company operations, probe for ways to be more cost-efficient and competitive, and ferret out strategic moves and decisions calculated to boost company performance. *Consequently, incorporating both case assignments and a strategy simulation to develop the skills of class members in thinking strategically and applying the concepts and tools of strategic analysis turns out to be more pedagogically powerful than relying solely on case assignments—there's stronger retention of the lessons learned and better achievement of course learning objectives.*

To provide you with quantitative evidence of the learning that occurs with using *The Business Strategy Game* or *GLO-BUS,* there is a built-in Learning Assurance Report showing how well each class member performs on nine skills/learning measures versus tens of thousands of students worldwide who have completed the simulation in the past 12 months.

- *The competitive nature of a strategy simulation arouses positive energy and steps up the whole tempo of the course by a notch or two.* Nothing sparks class excitement quicker or better than the concerted efforts on the part of class members at each decision round to achieve a high industry ranking and avoid the perilous consequences of being outcompeted by other class members. Students really enjoy taking on the role of a manager, running their own company, crafting strategies, making all kinds of operating decisions, trying to outcompete rival companies, and getting immediate feedback on the resulting company performance. Lots of back-and-forth chatter occurs when the results of the latest simulation round become available and co-managers renew their quest for strategic moves and actions that will strengthen company performance. Co-managers become *emotionally invested* in running their company and figuring out what strategic moves to make to boost their company's performance. Interest levels climb. All this stimulates learning and causes students to see the practical relevance of the subject matter and the benefits of taking your course.

  As soon as your students start to say "Wow! Not only is this fun but I am learning a lot," *which they will,* you have won the battle of engaging students in the subject matter and moved the value of taking your course to a much higher plateau in the business school curriculum. This translates into *a livelier, richer learning experience from a student perspective and better instructor-course evaluations.*

- *Use of a fully automated online simulation reduces the time instructors spend on course preparation, course administration, and grading.* Since the simulation exercise involves a 20- to 30-hour workload for student teams (roughly 2 hours per decision round times 10 to 12 rounds, plus optional assignments), simulation adopters often compensate by trimming the number of assigned cases from, say, 10 to 12 to perhaps 4 to 6. This significantly reduces the time instructors spend reading cases, studying teaching notes, and otherwise getting ready to lead class discussion of a case or grade oral team presentations. Course preparation time is further cut because you can use several class days to have students meet in the computer lab to work on upcoming decision rounds or a three-year strategic plan (in lieu of lecturing on a chapter or covering an additional assigned case). Not only does use of a simulation permit assigning fewer cases, but it also permits you to eliminate at least one assignment that entails considerable grading on your part. Grading one less written case or essay exam or other written assignment saves enormous time. With *BSG* and *GLO-BUS*, grading is effortless and takes only minutes; once you enter percentage weights for each assignment in your online grade book, a suggested overall grade is calculated for you. You'll be pleasantly surprised— and quite pleased—at how little time it takes to gear up for and administer *The Business Strategy Game* or *GLO-BUS*.

In sum, incorporating use of a strategy simulation turns out to be *a win–win proposition for both students and instructors.* Moreover, a very convincing argument can be made that a competition-based strategy simulation is *the single most effective teaching/ learning tool that instructors can employ to teach the discipline of business and competitive strategy, to make learning more enjoyable, and to promote better achievement of course learning objectives.*

## A Bird's-Eye View of *The Business Strategy Game*

The setting for *The Business Strategy Game (BSG)* is the global athletic footwear industry (there can be little doubt in today's world that a globally competitive strategy simulation is *vastly superior* to a simulation with a domestic-only setting). Global market demand for footwear grows at the rate of 7 to 9 percent annually for the first five years and 5 to 7 percent annually for the second five years. However, market growth rates vary by geographic region—North America, Latin America, Europe-Africa, and Asia-Pacific.

Companies begin the simulation producing branded and private-label footwear in two plants, one in North America and one in Asia. They have the option to establish production facilities in Latin America and Europe-Africa, either by constructing new plants or by buying previously constructed plants that have been sold by competing companies. Company co-managers exercise control over production costs on the basis of the styling and quality they opt to manufacture, plant location (wages and incentive compensation vary from region to region), the use of best practices and Six Sigma programs to reduce the production of defective footwear and to boost worker productivity, and compensation practices.

All newly produced footwear is shipped in bulk containers to one of four geographic distribution centers. All sales in a geographic region are made from footwear inventories in that region's distribution center. Costs at the four regional distribution centers are a function of inventory storage costs, packing and shipping fees, import tariffs paid on incoming pairs shipped from foreign plants, and exchange rate impacts. At the start of the simulation, import tariffs average $4 per pair in Europe-Africa, $6 per pair in Latin America, and $8 in the Asia-Pacific region. However, the Free Trade Treaty of the Americas allows tariff-free movement of footwear between North America and Latin America. Instructors have the option to alter tariffs as the game progresses.

Companies market their brand of athletic footwear to footwear retailers worldwide and to individuals buying online at the company's website. Each company's sales and market share in the branded footwear segments hinge on its competitiveness on 11 factors: attractive pricing, footwear styling and quality, product line breadth, advertising, use of mail-in rebates, appeal of celebrities endorsing a company's brand, success in convincing footwear retailers to carry its brand, number of weeks it takes to fill retailer orders, effectiveness of a company's online sales effort at its website, and customer loyalty. Sales of private-label footwear hinge solely on being the low-price bidder.

All told, company co-managers make as many as 53 types of decisions each period that cut across production operations (up to 10 decisions per plant, with a maximum of four plants), plant capacity additions/sales/upgrades (up to 6 decisions per plant), worker compensation and training (3 decisions per plant), shipping (up to 8 decisions per plant), pricing and marketing (up to 10 decisions in four geographic regions), bids to sign celebrities (2 decision entries per bid), financing of company operations (up to 8 decisions), and corporate social responsibility and environmental sustainability (up to 6 decisions).

Each time company co-managers make a decision entry, an assortment of on-screen calculations instantly shows the projected effects on unit sales, revenues, market shares, unit costs, profit, earnings per share, ROE, and other operating statistics. The on-screen calculations help team members evaluate the relative merits of one decision entry versus another and put together a promising strategy.

Companies can employ any of the five generic competitive strategy options in selling branded footwear—low-cost leadership, differentiation, best-cost provider, focused low cost, and focused differentiation. They can pursue essentially the same strategy worldwide or craft slightly or very different strategies for the Europe-Africa, Asia-Pacific, Latin America, and North America markets. They can strive for competitive advantage based on more advertising, a wider selection of models, more appealing styling/quality, bigger rebates, and so on.

*Any well-conceived, well-executed competitive approach is capable of succeeding, provided it is not overpowered by the strategies of competitors or defeated by the presence of too many copycat strategies that dilute its effectiveness.* The challenge for each company's management team is to craft and execute a competitive strategy that produces good performance on five measures: earnings per share, return on equity investment, stock price appreciation, credit rating, and brand image.

All activity for *The Business Strategy Game* takes place at www.bsg-online.com.

## A Bird's-Eye View of GLO-BUS

The industry setting for *GLO-BUS* is the digital camera industry. Global market demand grows at the rate of 8 to 10 percent annually for the first five years and 4 to 6 percent annually for the second five years. Retail sales of digital cameras are seasonal, with about 20 percent of consumer demand coming in each of the first three quarters of each calendar year and 40 percent coming during the big fourth-quarter retailing season.

Companies produce entry-level and upscale, multifeatured cameras of varying designs and quality in a Taiwan assembly facility and ship assembled cameras directly to retailers in North America, Asia-Pacific, Europe-Africa, and Latin America. All cameras are assembled as retail orders come in and are shipped immediately upon completion of the assembly process— companies maintain no finished-goods inventories, and all parts and components are delivered on a just-in-time basis (which eliminates the need to track inventories and simplifies the accounting for plant operations and costs). Company co-managers exercise control over production costs on the basis of the designs and components they specify for their cameras, workforce compensation and training, the length of warranties offered (which affects warranty costs), the amount spent for technical support provided to buyers of the company's cameras, and their management of the assembly process.

Competition in each of the two product market segments (entry-level and multi-featured digital cameras) is based on 10 factors: price, camera performance and quality, number of quarterly sales promotions, length of promotions in weeks, size of the promotional discounts offered, advertising, number of camera models, size of the retail dealer network, warranty period, and amount/caliber of technical support provided to camera buyers. Low-cost leadership, differentiation strategies, best-cost provider strategies, and focus strategies are all viable competitive options. Rival companies can strive to be the clear market leader in either entry-level cameras or upscale multifea-tured cameras or both. They can focus on one or two geographic regions or strive for geographic balance. They can pursue essentially the same strategy worldwide or craft slightly or very different strategies for the Europe-Africa, Asia-Pacific, Latin America, and North America markets. Just as with *The Business Strategy Game,* almost any well-conceived, well-executed competitive approach is capable of succeeding, *provided it is not overpowered by the strategies of competitors or defeated by the presence of too many copycat strategies that dilute its effectiveness.*

Company co-managers make 49 types of decisions each period, ranging from R&D, camera components, and camera performance (10 decisions) to production operations and worker compensation (15 decisions) to pricing and marketing (15 decisions) to the financing of company operations (4 decisions) to corporate social responsibility (5 decisions). *Each time participants make a decision entry, an assortment of on-screen calculations instantly shows the projected effects on unit sales, revenues, market shares, unit costs, profit, earnings per share, ROE, and other operating statistics. These on-screen calculations help team members evaluate the relative merits of one decision entry versus another and stitch the separate decisions into a cohesive and promising strategy.* Company performance is judged on five criteria: earnings per share, return on equity investment, stock price, credit rating, and brand image.

All activity for *GLO-BUS* occurs at www.glo-bus.com.

## Administration and Operating Features of the Two Simulations

The Internet delivery and user-friendly designs of both *BSG* and *GLO-BUS* make them incredibly easy to administer, even for first-time users. And the menus and controls are so similar that you can readily switch between the two simulations or use one in your undergraduate class and the other in a graduate class. If you have not yet used either of the two simulations, you may find the following of particular interest:

- Setting up the simulation for your course is done online and takes about 10 to 15 minutes. Once setup is completed, no other administrative actions are required beyond those of moving participants to a different team (should the need arise) and monitoring the progress of the simulation (to whatever extent desired).

- Participant's Guides are delivered electronically to class members at the website—students can read the guide on their monitors or print out a copy, as they prefer.

- There are 2- to 4-minute Video Tutorials scattered throughout the software (including each decision screen and each page of each report) that provide on-demand guidance to class members who may be uncertain about how to proceed.

- Complementing the Video Tutorials are detailed and clearly written Help sections explaining "all there is to know" about (a) each decision entry and the relevant cause-effect relationships, (b) the information on each page of the Industry Reports, and (c) the numbers presented in the Company Reports. *The Video Tutorials and the Help screens allow company co-managers to figure things out for themselves, thereby curbing the need for students to ask the instructor "how things work."*

- Team members running the same company who are logged-in simultaneously on different computers at different locations can click a button to enter Collaboration Mode, enabling them to work collaboratively from the same screen in viewing reports and making decision entries, and click a second button to enter Audio Mode, letting them talk to one another.

  ○ When in "Collaboration Mode," each team member sees the same screen at the same time as all other team members who are logged in and have joined Collaboration Mode. If one team member chooses to view a particular decision screen, that same screen appears on the monitors for all team members in Collaboration Mode.

  ○ Each team member controls their own color-coded mouse pointer (with their first-name appearing in a color-coded box linked to their mouse pointer) and can make a decision entry or move the mouse to point to particular on-screen items.

  ○ A decision entry change made by one team member is seen by all, in real time, and all team members can immediately view the on-screen calculations that result from the new decision entry.

  ○ If one team member wishes to view a report page and clicks on the menu link to the desired report, that same report page will immediately appear for the other team members engaged in collaboration.

  ○ Use of Audio Mode capability requires that each team member work from a computer with a built-in microphone (if they want to be heard by their team members) and speakers (so they may hear their teammates) or else have a headset with a microphone that they can plug into their desktop or laptop. A headset is recommended for best results, but most laptops now are equipped with a built-in microphone and speakers that will support use of our new voice chat feature.

  ○ Real-time VoIP audio chat capability among team members who have entered both the Audio Mode and the Collaboration Mode is a tremendous boost in functionality that enables team members to go online simultaneously on computers at different locations and conveniently and effectively collaborate in running their simulation company.

  ○ In addition, instructors have the capability to join the online session of any company and speak with team members, thus circumventing the need for team members to arrange for and attend a meeting in the instructor's office. Using the standard menu for administering a particular industry, instructors can connect with the company desirous of assistance. Instructors who wish not only to talk but also enter Collaboration (highly recommended because all attendees are then viewing the same screen) have a red-colored mouse pointer linked to a red box labeled Instructor.

    Without a doubt, the Collaboration and Voice-Chat capabilities are hugely valuable for students enrolled in online and distance-learning courses where meeting face-to-face is impractical or time-consuming. Likewise, the instructors of online and distance-learning courses will appreciate having the capability to join the online meetings of particular company teams when their advice or assistance is requested.

- Both simulations are quite suitable for use in distance-learning or online courses (and are currently being used in such courses on numerous campuses).

- Participants and instructors are notified via e-mail when the results are ready (usually about 15 to 20 minutes after the decision round deadline specified by the instructor/game administrator).

- Following each decision round, participants are provided with a complete set of reports—a six-page Industry Report, a one-page Competitive Intelligence report for each geographic region that includes strategic group maps and bulleted lists of competitive strengths and weaknesses, and a set of Company Reports (income statement, balance sheet, cash flow statement, and assorted production, marketing, and cost statistics).

- Two "open-book" multiple-choice tests of 20 questions are built into each simulation. The quizzes, which you can require or not as you see fit, are taken online and automatically graded, with scores reported instantaneously to participants and automatically recorded in the instructor's electronic grade book. Students are automatically provided with three sample questions for each test.

- Both simulations contain a three-year strategic plan option that you can assign. Scores on the plan are automatically recorded in the instructor's online grade book.

- At the end of the simulation, you can have students complete online peer evaluations (again, the scores are automatically recorded in your online grade book).

- Both simulations have a Company Presentation feature that enables each team of company co-managers to easily prepare PowerPoint slides for use in describing their strategy and summarizing their company's performance in a presentation to either the class, the instructor, or an "outside" board of directors.

- *A Learning Assurance Report provides you with hard data concerning how well your students performed vis-á-vis students playing the simulation worldwide over the past 12 months.* The report is based on nine measures of student proficiency, business know-how, and decision-making skill and can also be used in evaluating the extent to which your school's academic curriculum produces the desired degree of student learning insofar as accreditation standards are concerned.

For more details on either simulation, please consult Section 2 of the Instructor's Manual accompanying this text or register as an instructor at the simulation websites (**www.bsg-online.com** and **www.glo-bus.com**) to access even more comprehensive information. You should also consider signing up for one of the webinars that the simulation authors conduct several times each month (sometimes several times weekly) to demonstrate how the software works, walk you through the various features and menu options, and answer any questions. You have an open invitation to call the senior author of this text at (205) 722-9145 to arrange a personal demonstration or talk about how one of the simulations might work in one of your courses. We think you'll be quite impressed with the cutting-edge capabilities that have been programmed into *The Business Strategy Game* and *GLO-BUS,* the simplicity with which both simulations can be administered, and their exceptionally tight connection to the text chapters, core concepts, and standard analytical tools.

# RESOURCES AND SUPPORT MATERIALS FOR THE 19TH EDITION

## For Students

**Key Points Summaries**    At the end of each chapter is a synopsis of the core concepts, analytical tools, and other key points discussed in the chapter. These chapter-end synopses, along with the core concept definitions and margin notes scattered throughout each chapter, help students focus on basic strategy principles, digest the messages of each chapter, and prepare for tests.

**Two Sets of Chapter-End Exercises**    Each chapter concludes with two sets of exercises. The *Assurance of Learning Exercises* can be used as the basis for class discussion, oral presentation assignments, short written reports, and substitutes for case assignments. The *Exercises for Simulation Participants* are designed expressly for use by adopters who have incorporated use of a simulation and want to go a step further in tightly and explicitly connecting the chapter content to the simulation company their students are running. The questions in both sets of exercises (along with those Illustration Capsules that qualify as "mini-cases") can be used to round out the rest of a 75-minute class period should your lecture on a chapter last for only 50 minutes.

**A Value-Added Website**    The student section of the Online Learning Center (OLC) at website **www.mhhe.com/thompson** contains a number of helpful aids:

- Ten-question self-scoring chapter tests that students can take to measure their grasp of the material presented in each of the 12 chapters.
- PowerPoint slides for each chapter.
- Selected Case Video clips.

## The *Connect*™ *Management* Web-Based Assignment and Assessment Platform
Beginning with the 18th edition, we began taking advantage of the publisher's innovative *Connect*™ assignment and assessment platform and created several features that simplify the task of assigning and grading three types of exercises for students:

- There are self-scoring chapter tests consisting of 20 to 25 multiple-choice questions that students can take to measure their grasp of the material presented in each of the 12 chapters.
- There are two author-developed Interactive Application exercises for each of the 12 chapters that drill students in the use and application of the concepts and tools of strategic analysis.
- The *Connect*™ platform also includes author-developed Interactive Application exercises for 14 of the 30 cases in this edition that require students to work through answers to a select number of the assignment questions for the case. These exercises have multiple components and can include calculating assorted financial ratios to assess a company's financial performance and balance sheet strength, identifying a company's strategy, doing five-forces and driving-forces analysis, doing a SWOT analysis, and recommending actions to improve company performance. The

content of these case exercises is tailored to match the circumstances presented in each case, calling upon students to do whatever strategic thinking and strategic analysis are called for to arrive at pragmatic, analysis-based action recommendations for improving company performance.

All of the *Connect*™ exercises are automatically graded (with the exception of those exercise components that entail student entry of short answer and/or essay answers), thereby simplifying the task of evaluating each class member's performance and monitoring the learning outcomes. The progress-tracking function built into the *Connect*™ *Management* system enables you to:

- View scored work immediately and track individual or group performance with assignment and grade reports.
- Access an instant view of student or class performance relative to learning objectives.
- Collect data and generate reports required by many accreditation organizations, such as AACSB.

# For Instructors

### Online Learning Center (OLC)    In addition to the student resources, the instructor section of www.mhhe.com/thompson includes an Instructor's Manual and other support materials. Your McGraw-Hill representative can arrange delivery of instructor support materials in a format-ready Standard Cartridge for Blackboard, WebCT, and other web-based educational platforms.

### Instructor's Manual    The accompanying IM contains:

- A section on suggestions for organizing and structuring your course.
- Sample syllabi and course outlines.
- A set of lecture notes on each chapter.
- Answers to the chapter-end Assurance of Learning Exercises.
- A copy of the test bank.
- A comprehensive case teaching note for each of the 30 cases. These teaching notes are filled with suggestions for using the case effectively, have very thorough, analysis-based answers to the suggested assignment questions for the case, and contain an epilogue detailing any important developments since the case was written.

### Test Bank and EZ Test Online    There is a test bank containing over 900 multiple-choice questions and short-answer/essay questions. It has been tagged with AACSB and Bloom's Taxonomy criteria. All of the test bank questions are also accessible within a computerized test bank powered by McGraw-Hill's flexible electronic testing program EZ Test Online (www.eztestonline.com). Using EZ Test Online allows you to create paper and online tests or quizzes. With EZ Test Online, instructors can select questions from multiple McGraw-Hill test banks or author their own and then either print the test for paper distribution or give it online.

### PowerPoint Slides    To facilitate delivery preparation of your lectures and to serve as chapter outlines, you'll have access to approximately 500 colorful and

professional-looking slides displaying core concepts, analytical procedures, key points, and all the figures in the text chapters.

### *The Business Strategy Game* and *GLO-BUS Online Simulations*   Using one of the two companion simulations is a powerful and constructive way of emotionally connecting students to the subject matter of the course. We know of no more effective way to arouse the competitive energy of students and prepare them for the challenges of real-world business decision making than to have them match strategic wits with classmates in running a company in head-to-head competition for global market leadership.

# ACKNOWLEDGMENTS

We heartily acknowledge the contributions of the case researchers whose case-writing efforts appear herein and the companies whose cooperation made the cases possible. To each one goes a very special thank-you. We cannot overstate the importance of timely, carefully researched cases in contributing to a substantive study of strategic management issues and practices.

A great number of colleagues and students at various universities, business acquaintances, and people at McGraw-Hill provided inspiration, encouragement, and counsel during the course of this project. Like all text authors in the strategy field, we are intellectually indebted to the many academics whose research and writing have blazed new trails and advanced the discipline of strategic management. In addition, we'd like to thank the following reviewers who provided seasoned advice and splendid suggestions over the years for improving the chapters:

Joan H. Bailar, David Blair, Jane Boyland, William J. Donoher, Stephen A. Drew, Jo Anne Duffy, Alan Ellstrand, Susan Fox-Wolfgramm, Rebecca M. Guidice, Mark Hoelscher, Sean D. Jasso, Xin Liang, Paul Mallette, Dan Marlin, Raza Mir, Mansour Moussavi, James D. Spina, Monica A. Zimmerman, Dennis R. Balch, Jeffrey R. Bruehl, Edith C. Busija, Donald A. Drost, Randall Harris, Mark Lewis Hoelscher, Phyllis Holland, James W. Kroeger, Sal Kukalis, Brian W. Kulik, Paul Mallette, Anthony U. Martinez, Lee Pickler, Sabine Reddy, Thomas D. Schramko, V. Seshan, Charles Strain, Sabine Turnley, S. Stephen Vitucci, Andrew Ward, Sibin Wu, Lynne Patten, Nancy E. Landrum, Jim Goes, Jon Kalinowski, Rodney M. Walter, Judith D. Powell, Seyda Deligonul, David Flanagan, Esmerlda Garbi, Mohsin Habib, Kim Hester, Jeffrey E. McGee, Diana J. Wong, F. William Brown, Anthony F. Chelte, Gregory G. Dess, Alan B. Eisner, John George, Carle M. Hunt, Theresa Marron-Grodsky, Sarah Marsh, Joshua D. Martin, William L. Moore, Donald Neubaum, George M. Puia, Amit Shah, Lois M. Shelton, Mark Weber, Steve Barndt, J. Michael Geringer, Ming-Fang Li, Richard Stackman, Stephen Tallman, Gerardo R. Ungson, James Boulgarides, Betty Diener, Daniel F. Jennings, David Kuhn, Kathryn Martell, Wilbur Mouton, Bobby Vaught, Tuck Bounds, Lee Burk, Ralph Catalanello, William Crittenden, Vince Luchsinger, Stan Mendenhall, John Moore, Will Mulvaney, Sandra Richard, Ralph Roberts, Thomas Turk, Gordon Von Stroh, Fred Zimmerman, S. A. Billion, Charles Byles, Gerald L. Geisler, Rose Knotts, Joseph Rosenstein, James B. Thurman, Ivan Able, W. Harvey Hegarty, Roger Evered, Charles B. Saunders, Rhae M. Swisher, Claude I. Shell, R. Thomas Lenz, Michael C. White, Dennis Callahan, R. Duane Ireland, William E. Burr II, C. W. Millard, Richard Mann, Kurt Christensen, Neil W. Jacobs, Louis W. Fry, D. Robley Wood, George J. Gore, and William R. Soukup.

We owe a debt of gratitude to Professors Catherine A. Maritan, Jeffrey A. Martin, Richard S. Shreve, and Anant K. Sundaram for their helpful comments on various chapters. We'd also like to thank the following students of the Tuck School of Business for their assistance with the revisions: Kenneth P. Fraser, John L. Gardner, Dennis L. Huggins, Judith H. Lon, Margaret W. Macauley, Divya A. Mani, Avni V. Patel, Chris Pearson-Smith, Maximilian A. Pinto, Ross M. Templeton, C. David Morgan, Amy E. Florentino, and John R. Moran. And we'd like to acknowledge the help of Dartmouth students Jenna Pfeffer and Xuanyi Chen, as well as Tuck staff member Mary Biathrow.

As always, we value your recommendations and thoughts about the book. Your comments regarding coverage and contents will be taken to heart, and we always are grateful for the time you take to call our attention to printing errors, deficiencies, and other shortcomings. Please e-mail us at athompso@cba.ua.edu, margaret.a.peteraf@ tuck.dartmouth.edu, jgamble@usouthal.edu, or astrickl@cba.ua.edu.

Arthur A. Thompson

Margaret A. Peteraf

John E. Gamble

A. J. Strickland

## Chapter Structure and Organization

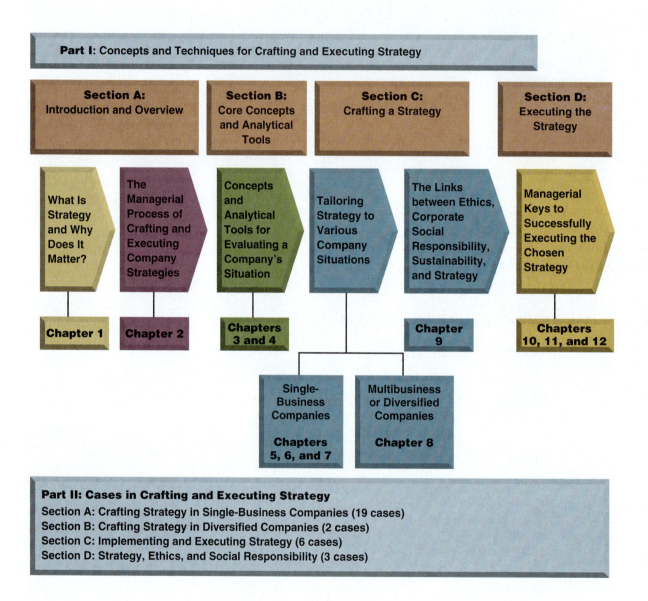

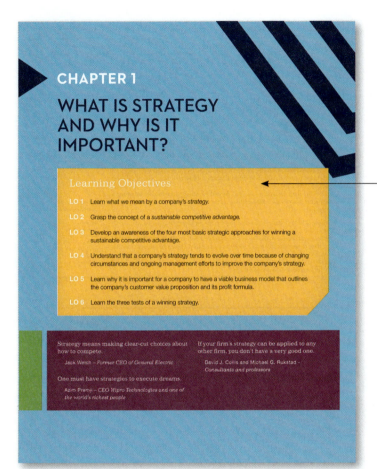

**CHAPTER 1**

## WHAT IS STRATEGY AND WHY IS IT IMPORTANT?

### Learning Objectives

**LO 1** Learn what we mean by a company's *strategy*.

**LO 2** Grasp the concept of a *sustainable competitive advantage*.

**LO 3** Develop an awareness of the four most basic strategic approaches for winning a sustainable competitive advantage.

**LO 4** Understand that a company's strategy tends to evolve over time because of changing circumstances and ongoing management efforts to improve the company's strategy.

**LO 5** Learn why it is important for a company to have a viable business model that outlines the company's customer value proposition and its profit formula.

**LO 6** Learn the three tests of a winning strategy.

Strategy means making clear-cut choices about how to compete.

*Jack Welch – Former CEO of General Electric*

One must have strategies to execute dreams.

*Azim Premji – CEO Wipro Technologies and one of the world's richest people*

If your firm's strategy can be applied to any other firm, you don't have a very good one.

*David J. Collis and Michael G. Rukstad – Consultants and professors*

**Learning Objectives** are listed at the beginning of each chapter; corresponding numbered indicators in the margins show where learning objectives are covered in the text.

**Illustration Capsules** appear in boxes throughout each chapter to provide in-depth examples, connect the text presentation to real-world companies, and convincingly demonstrate "strategy in action." Some are appropriate for use as mini-cases.

**ILLUSTRATION CAPSULE 9.4**

### Burt's Bees: A Strategy Based on Corporate Social Responsibility

Burt's Bees is a leading company in natural personal care, offering nearly 200 products including its popular beeswax lip balms and skin-care creams. The brand has enjoyed tremendous success as consumers have begun to embrace all-natural, environmentally friendly products, boosting Burt's Bees' revenues to over $250M by 2012. Much of Burt's Bees' success can be attributed to its skillful use of Corporate Social Responsibility (CSR) as a strategic tool to engage customers and differentiate itself from competitors.

While many companies have embraced Corporate Social Responsibility, few companies have managed to integrate CSR as fully and seamlessly throughout their organizations as Burt's Bees. The company's business model is centered on a principle they refer to as "The Greater Good," which specifies that all company practices must be socially responsible. The execution of this strategy is managed by a special committee dedicated to leading the organization to attain its CSR goals with respect to three primary areas: natural well-being, humanitarian responsibility, and environmental sustainability.

Natural well-being is focused on the ingredients used to create Burt's Bees products. Today, the average Burt's Bees product contains over 99 percent natural ingredients; by 2020, the brand expects to produce only 100 percent natural products.

Burt's Bees' humanitarian focus is centered on its relationships with employees and suppliers. A key part of this effort involves a mandatory employee training program that focuses on four key areas: outreach, wellness, world-class leadership, and the environment. Another is the company's Responsible Sourcing Mission, which lays out a carefully prescribed set of guidelines for sourcing responsible suppliers and managing supplier relationships.

A focus on caring for the environment is clearly interwoven into all aspects of Burt's Bees. By focusing on environmentally efficient processes, the company uses its in-house manufacturing capability as a point of

Burt's Bees faced some consumer backlash when it was purchased recently by The Clorox Company, whose traditional image is viewed in sharp contrast to Burt's Bees values. But while Burt's Bees is still only a small part of Clorox's total revenue, it has become its fastest-growing division.

**Margin Notes** define core concepts and call attention to important ideas and principles.

efficiently—whatever form it takes—nearly always requires performing value chain activities differently than rivals and building competencies and resource capabilities that are not readily matched. In Illustration Capsule 1.1, it's evident that McDonald's has gained a competitive advantage over its rivals in the fast-food industry through its efforts to minimize costs, ensure fast and consistent delivery of foods with wide appeal, and keep its prices low, thereby driving sales volume. A creative *distinctive* strategy such as that used by McDonald's is a company's most reliable ticket for developing a competitive advantage over its rivals. If a strategy is not distinctive, then there can be no competitive advantage, since no firm would be meeting customer needs better or operating more efficiently than any other.

If a company's competitive edge holds promise for being *sustainable* (as opposed to just temporary), then so much the better for both the strategy and the company's future profitability. What makes a competitive advantage **sustainable** (or durable), as opposed to temporary, are elements of the strategy that give buyers lasting reasons to prefer a company's products or services over those of competitors—*reasons that competitors are unable to nullify or overcome despite their best efforts*. In the case of McDonald's, the company's unparalleled name recognition, reputation for tasty, quick-service food, and formidable volume advantage make it difficult for competitors to weaken or overcome McDonald's competitive advantage. Not only has their strategy provided them with a sustainable competitive advantage, it has made them one of the most admired companies on the planet.

Four of the most frequently used and dependable strategic approaches to setting a company apart from rivals, building strong customer loyalty, and winning a competitive advantage are:

1.  *Striving to be the industry's low-cost provider, thereby aiming for a cost-based competitive advantage over rivals.* Walmart and Southwest Airlines have earned strong market positions because of the low-cost advantages they have achieved over their rivals and their consequent ability to underprice competitors. These advantages in meeting customer needs *efficiently* have translated into volume advantages, with Walmart as the world's largest discount retailer and Southwest as the largest U.S. air carrier, based on the number of domestic passengers.[4]

**LO 3**

Develop an awareness of the four most dependable strategic approaches for setting a company apart from rivals and winning a sustainable competitive advantage.

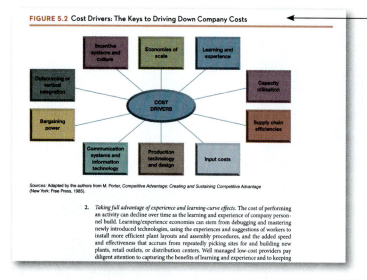

FIGURE 5.2 Cost Drivers: The Keys to Driving Down Company Costs

**COST DRIVERS**

Incentive systems and culture

Economies of scale

Learning and experience

Outsourcing or vertical integration

Capacity utilization

Bargaining power

Supply chain efficiencies

Communication systems and information technology

Production technology and design

Input costs

*Sources:* Adapted by the authors from M. Porter, *Competitive Advantage: Creating and Sustaining Competitive Advantage* (New York: Free Press, 1985).

**Figures** scattered throughout the chapters provide conceptual and analytical frameworks.

2.  *Taking full advantage of experience and learning-curve effects.* The cost of performing an activity can decline over time as the learning and experience of company personnel build. Learning/experience economies can stem from debugging and mastering newly introduced technologies, using the experiences and suggestions of workers to install more efficient plant layouts and assembly procedures, and the added speed and effectiveness that accrues from repeatedly picking sites for and building new plants, retail outlets, or distribution centers. Well managed low-cost providers pay diligent attention to capturing the benefits of learning and experience and to keeping

**Key Points** at the end of each chapter provide a handy summary of essential ideas and things to remember.

**KEY POINTS**

Thinking strategically about a company's external situation involves probing for answers to the following seven questions:

1.  *What are the strategically relevant factors in the macro-environment?* Industries differ significantly as to how they are affected by conditions in the broad macro-environment. Identifying which of these factors is strategically relevant is the first step to understanding how a company is situated in its external environment. PESTEL analysis of the political, economic, sociocultural, technological, environmental/ecological, and legal/regulatory factors provides a framework for approaching this issue systematically. Identifying the strategically relevant features of the macro-environment sets the stage for the analysis to come, since they play an important role in determining an industry's potential for attractive profits.

2.  *What kinds of competitive forces are industry members facing, and how strong is each force?* The strength of competition is a composite of five forces: (1) competitive pressures stemming from the competitive jockeying among industry rivals, (2) competitive pressures associated with the market inroads being made by the sellers of substitutes, (3) competitive pressures associated with the threat of new entrants into the market, (4) competitive pressures stemming from supplier bargaining power, and (5) competitive pressures stemming from buyer bargaining. The nature and strength of the competitive pressures have to be examined force by force, and their collective strength must be evaluated. One strong force, however, can be sufficient to keep average industry profitability low. Working through the five forces model aids strategy makers in assessing how to insulate the company from the strongest forces, identify attractive arenas for expansion, or alter the

**Exercises** at the end of each chapter, linked to learning objectives, provide a basis for class discussion, oral presentations, and written assignments. Several chapters have exercises that qualify as mini-cases.

**Thirty cases** detail the strategic circumstances of actual companies and provide practice in applying the concepts and tools of strategic analysis.

## CASE 10

# Chipotle Mexican Grill in 2012: Can It Hit a Second Home Run?

**connect**

Arthur A. Thompson
The University of Alabama

In early 2012, it was obvious that founder, co-CEO, and chairman Steve Ells's vision and strategy for Chipotle Mexican Grill had resulted in a home run. Ells's vision for Chipotle (pronounced chi-POAT-lay) was "to change the way people think about and eat fast food." Taking his inspiration from features commonly found in many fine-dining restaurants, Ells's strategy for Chipotle was predicated on five elements:

- Serving a focused menu of burritos, tacos, burrito bowls (a burrito without the tortilla), and salads.
- Using high-quality raw ingredients and classic cooking methods to create great tasting, reasonably priced dishes that were ready to be served to customers minutes after they were ordered.
- Creating an operationally efficient restaurant with an aesthetically pleasing and distinctive interior setting.
- Having friendly people take care of each customer.
- Doing all of this with increasing awareness and respect for the environment, the use of organically grown fresh produce, and meats raised in a humane manner without hormones and antibiotics.

Since 1993, the company had grown from a 1-unit operation in Denver into a 1,230-unit operation serving over 800,000 customers a day in 41 states, the District of Columbia, Canada, and the United Kingdom. In 2011, Chipotle reported revenues of $2.3 billion, net income of $214.9 million, and diluted earnings per share of $6.76. When the company went public in January 2006, the stock doubled on its first day of trading, jumping from the initial offering price of $22 per share to close at $44 per share. As of late February 2012, Chipotle Mexican Grill's stock price had climbed to record highs each of the past seven weeks and was trading in the $380–$385 range, up more than 80 percent since January 1, 2011 and up 334 percent since January 1, 2010.

But Steve Ells was not content to capitalize on the growing demand for healthier, more wholesome fast foods and rapidly open thousands of new domestic and international Chipotle Mexican Grill locations, perhaps eventually mounting a challenge to McDonald's, the solidly entrenched global leader of the fast-food industry and the company that had invented the fast-food concept in the 1950s—McDonald's currently had 33,000 company-owned and franchised restaurant locations serving about 64 million customers in 119 countries daily. In 2011–2012, Ells and other Chipotle executives were busily planning the launch of a second restaurant concept, ShopHouse Southeast Asian Kitchen, predicated on much the same strategic principles as Chipotle Mexican Grill but with a different menu. In announcing that Chipotle would open the first ShopHouse restaurant in Washington, D.C., in the summer of 2011, Ells said, "I have always believed that the Chipotle model could work well with a variety of different cuisines." A second ShopHouse unit opened in 2012 to further test and refine the concept. Many observers believed that Chipotle was likely to hit a second home run with ShopHouse, a rare and unusual feat for a young company still rounding the bases on its first home run. In February 2012, one Wall Street analyst called Chipotle Mexican Grill "the perfect stock," and another believed that Chipotle could well prove to be the next McDonald's.[1]

## CHIPOTLE MEXICAN GRILL'S EARLY YEARS

Steve Ells graduated from the Culinary Institute of America and then worked for two years at Stars Restaurant in San Francisco. Soon after moving to Denver,

# FOR STUDENTS: An Assortment of Support Materials

**Website:** **www.mhhe.com/thompson** The student portion of the website features 10-question self-scoring chapter tests, a select number of PowerPoint slides for each chapter, and selected video case clips.

 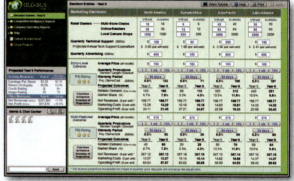

*The Business Strategy Game* or *GLO-BUS* **Simulation Exercises** Either one of these text supplements involves teams of students managing companies in a head-to-head contest for global market leadership. Company co-managers have to make decisions relating to product quality, production, workforce compensation and training, pricing and marketing, and financing of company operations. The challenge is to craft and execute a strategy that is powerful enough to deliver good financial performance despite the competitive efforts of rival companies. Each company competes in America, Latin America, Europe-Africa, and Asia-Pacific.

# BRIEF CONTENTS

*Section B: Crafting Strategy in Diversified Companies*

*Section C: Implementing and Executing Strategy*

# CONTENTS

# PART 1

## Concepts and Techniques for Crafting and Executing Strategy

# CHAPTER 1

# WHAT IS STRATEGY AND WHY IS IT IMPORTANT?

## Learning Objectives

**LO 1**   Learn what we mean by a company's *strategy.*

**LO 2**   Grasp the concept of a *sustainable competitive advantage.*

**LO 3**   Develop an awareness of the four most basic strategic approaches for winning a sustainable competitive advantage.

**LO 4**   Understand that a company's strategy tends to evolve over time because of changing circumstances and ongoing management efforts to improve the company's strategy.

**LO 5**   Learn why it is important for a company to have a viable business model that outlines the company's customer value proposition and its profit formula.

**LO 6**   Learn the three tests of a winning strategy.

---

Strategy means making clear-cut choices about how to compete.

> Jack Welch – *Former CEO of General Electric*

One must have strategies to execute dreams.

> Azim Premji – *CEO Wipro Technologies and one of the world's richest people*

If your firm's strategy can be applied to any other firm, you don't have a very good one.

> David J. Collis and Michael G. Rukstad – *Consultants and professors*

In any given year, a group of companies will stand out as the top performers, in terms of metrics such as profitability, sales growth, or growth in shareholder value. Some of these companies will find that their star status fades quickly, due to little more than a fortuitous constellation of circumstances, such as being in the right business at the right time. But other companies somehow manage to rise to the top and stay there, year after year, pleasing their customers, shareholders, and other stakeholders alike in the process. Companies such as Apple, Google, Coca-Cola, Procter & Gamble, McDonald's, Berkshire Hathaway, and General Electric come to mind—but long-lived success is not just the province of U.S. companies. Diverse kinds of companies, both large and small, from many different countries have been able to sustain strong performance records, including Singapore Airlines, Sweden's IKEA (in home furnishings), Korea's Hyundai Heavy Industries (in shipbuilding and construction), Mexico's America Movil (in telecommunications), and Japan's Nintendo (in video game systems).

What can explain the ability of companies like these to beat the odds and experience prolonged periods of profitability and growth? Why is it that some companies, like Southwest Airlines and Walmart, continue to do well even when others in their industry are faltering? Why can some companies survive and prosper even through economic downturns and industry turbulence?

Many factors enter into a full explanation of a company's performance, of course. Some come from the external environment; others are internal to the firm. But only one thing can account for the kind of long-lived success records that we see in the world's greatest companies—and that is a cleverly crafted and well executed *strategy*, one that facilitates the capture of emerging opportunities, produces enduringly good performance, is adaptable to changing business conditions, and can withstand the competitive challenges from rival firms.

In this opening chapter, we define the concept of strategy and describe its many facets. We will explain what is meant by a competitive advantage, discuss the relationship between a company's strategy and its business model, and introduce you to the kinds of competitive strategies that can give a company an advantage over rivals in attracting customers and earning above-average profits. We will look at what sets a winning strategy apart from others and why the caliber of a company's strategy determines whether it will enjoy a competitive advantage over other firms or be burdened by competitive disadvantage. By the end of this chapter, you will have a clear idea of why the tasks of crafting and executing strategy are core management functions and why excellent execution of an excellent strategy is the most reliable recipe for turning a company into a standout performer over the long term.

# WHAT DO WE MEAN BY *STRATEGY*?

A company's **strategy** is its action plan for outperforming its competitors and achieving superior profitability. In effect, it represents a managerial commitment to an integrated array of considered choices about how to compete.[1] These include choices about:

- *How* to attract and please customers.
- *How* to compete against rivals.
- *How* to position the company in the marketplace.
- *How* best to respond to changing economic and market conditions.
- *How* to capitalize on attractive opportunities to grow the business.
- *How* to achieve the company's performance targets.

The objective of a well-crafted strategy is not merely temporary competitive success and profits in the short run, but rather the sort of lasting success that can support growth and secure the company's future over the long term. In most industries, there are many different avenues for outcompeting rivals and boosting company performance.[2] Consequently, some companies strive to improve their performance by employing strategies aimed at achieving lower costs than rivals, while others pursue strategies aimed at achieving product superiority or personalized customer service or quality dimensions that rivals cannot match. Some companies opt for wide product lines, while others concentrate their energies on a narrow product lineup. Some competitors deliberately confine their operations to local or regional markets; others opt to compete nationally, internationally (several countries), or globally (all or most of the major country markets worldwide).

**Strategy Is about Competing Differently**    Every strategy needs a distinctive element that attracts customers and produces a competitive edge. But there is no shortage of opportunity to fashion a strategy that both tightly fits a company's own particular situation and is discernibly different from the strategies of rivals. In fact, competitive success requires a company's managers to make strategic choices about the key building blocks of its strategy that differ from the choices made by competitors—not 100 percent different, but at least different in several important respects. A strategy only stands a chance of succeeding when it is predicated on actions, business approaches, and competitive moves aimed at appealing to buyers *in ways that set a company apart from rivals*. Simply trying to mimic the strategies of the industry's successful companies never works. Rather, every company's strategy needs to have some distinctive element that draws in customers and produces a competitive edge. Strategy, at its essence, is about competing differently—doing what rival firms *don't* do or what rival firms *can't* do.[3]

A company's strategy provides direction and guidance, in terms of not only what the company *should* do but also what it *should not* do. Knowing what not to do can be as important as knowing what to do, strategically. At best, making the wrong strategic moves will prove a distraction and a waste of company resources. At worst, it can bring about unintended long-term consequences that put the company's very survival at risk.

Figure 1.1 illustrates the broad types of actions and approaches that often characterize a company's strategy in a particular business or industry. For a more concrete example of the specific actions constituting a firm's strategy, see Illustration Capsule 1.1, describing McDonald's strategy in the quick-service restaurant industry.

# Strategy and the Quest for Competitive Advantage

The heart and soul of any strategy are the actions and moves in the marketplace that managers are taking to gain a competitive advantage over rivals. A company achieves a competitive advantage whenever it has some type of edge over rivals in attracting buyers and coping with competitive forces. There are many routes to competitive advantage, but they all involve either giving buyers what they perceive as superior value compared to the offerings of rival sellers or giving buyers the same value as others at a lower cost to the firm. Superior value can mean a good product at a lower price, a superior product that is worth paying more for, or a best-value offering that represents an attractive combination of price, features, quality, service, and other appealing attributes. Delivering superior value or delivering value more

**LO 2**

Grasp the concept of a *sustainable competitive advantage.*

## FIGURE 1.1    Identifying a Company's Strategy—What to Look For

Actions to strengthen the firm's bargaining position with suppliers, distributors, and others

Actions to gain sales and market share via more performance features, more appealing design, better quality or customer service, wider product selection, or other such actions.

Actions to upgrade, build, or acquire competitively important resources and capabilities

Actions to gain sales and market share with lower prices based on lower costs

Actions and approaches used in managing R&D, production, sales and marketing, finance, and other key activities

THE PATTERN OF ACTIONS AND BUSINESS APPROACHES THAT DEFINE A COMPANY'S STRATEGY

Actions to enter new product or geographic markets or to exit existing ones

Actions to strengthen competitiveness via strategic alliances and collaborative partnerships

Actions to capture emerging market opportunities and defend against external threats to the company's business prospects

Actions to strengthen market standing and competitiveness by acquiring or merging with other companies

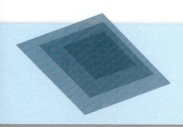

# McDonald's Strategy in the Quick-Service Restaurant Industry

In 2011, McDonald's was setting new sales records despite a global economic slowdown and declining consumer confidence in the United States. More than 64 million customers visited one of McDonald's 33,000 restaurants in 119 countries each day, which allowed the company to record 2011 revenues and earnings of more than $27 billion and $5.5 billion, respectively. McDonald's performance in the marketplace made it the top performing company on the Dow Jones Stock Market Index for 2011, with a 35 percent return to investors. The company's sales were holding up well amid the ongoing economic uncertainty in early 2012, with global sales as measured in constant currencies increasing by more than 4 percent in the first quarter. The company's success was a result of its well-conceived and executed Plan-to-Win strategy that focused on "being better, not just bigger." Key initiatives of the Plan-to-Win strategy included:

- *Improved restaurant operations.* McDonald's global restaurant operations improvement process involved employee training programs ranging from on-the-job training for new crew members to college-level management courses offered at the company's Hamburger University. The company sends nearly 200 high-potential employees annually to its McDonald's Leadership Institute to build leadership skills. The company trains its store managers to closely monitor labor, food, and utility costs. McDonald's excellence earned the company 10th place on *Fortune*'s list of the World's Most Admired Companies in 2011.

- *Affordable pricing.* McDonald's kept its prices low by scrutinizing restaurant operating costs, administrative costs, and other corporate expenses. McDonald's saw the poor economy in the United States as an opportunity to renegotiate its advertising contracts with newspapers and television networks. The company also began to replace its company-owned vehicles with more fuel-efficient models when gasoline prices escalated dramatically. However, McDonald's did not sacrifice product quality in order to offer lower prices. The company implemented extensive supplier monitoring programs to ensure that its suppliers did not change product specifications to lower costs.

- *Wide menu variety and beverage choices.* McDonald's has expanded its menu beyond the popular-selling Big Mac and Quarter Pounder to include new, healthy quick-service items. The company has also added an extensive line of premium coffees that include espressos, cappuccinos, and lattes sold in its McCafé restaurant locations in the United States, Europe, and the Asia/Pacific region.

- *Convenience and expansion of dining opportunities.* The addition of McCafés helped McDonald's increase same store sales by extending traditional dining hours. Customers wanting a midmorning coffee or an afternoon snack helped keep store traffic high after McDonald's had sold its last Egg McMuffin and before the lunch crowd arrived to order Big Macs. The company also extended its drive-thru hours to 24 hours in many cities where consumers tend to eat at all hours of the day and night.

- *Ongoing restaurant reinvestment and international expansion.* With more than 14,000 restaurants in the United States, the focus of McDonald's expansion of units was in rapidly growing emerging markets such as China. The company also intends to refurbish 90 percent of the interiors and 50 percent of the exteriors of its restaurants by the end of 2012 to make its restaurants a pleasant place for both customers and employees.

Developed with Jenna P. Pfeffer. *Sources:* Janet Adamy, "McDonald's Seeks Way to Keep Sizzling," *Wall Street Journal Online,* March 10, 2009; various annual reports; various company press releases.

efficiently—whatever form it takes—nearly always requires performing value chain activities differently than rivals and building competencies and resource capabilities that are not readily matched. In Illustration Capsule 1.1, it's evident that McDonald's has gained a competitive advantage over its rivals in the fast-food industry through its efforts to minimize costs, ensure fast and consistent delivery of foods with wide appeal, and keep its prices low, thereby driving sales volume. A creative *distinctive* strategy such as that used by McDonald's is a company's most reliable ticket for developing a competitive advantage over its rivals. If a strategy is not distinctive, then there can be no competitive advantage, since no firm would be meeting customer needs better or operating more efficiently than any other.

If a company's competitive edge holds promise for being *sustainable* (as opposed to just temporary), then so much the better for both the strategy and the company's future profitability. What makes a competitive advantage **sustainable** (or durable), as opposed to temporary, are elements of the strategy that give buyers lasting reasons to prefer a company's products or services over those of competitors—*reasons that competitors are unable to nullify or overcome despite their best efforts.* In the case of McDonald's, the company's unparalleled name recognition, reputation for tasty, quick-service food, and formidable volume advantage make it difficult for competitors to weaken or overcome McDonald's competitive advantage. Not only has their strategy provided them with a sustainable competitive advantage, it has made them one of the most admired companies on the planet.

Four of the most frequently used and dependable strategic approaches to setting a company apart from rivals, building strong customer loyalty, and winning a competitive advantage are:

1. *Striving to be the industry's low-cost provider, thereby aiming for a cost-based competitive advantage over rivals.* Walmart and Southwest Airlines have earned strong market positions because of the low-cost advantages they have achieved over their rivals and their consequent ability to underprice competitors. These advantages in meeting customer needs *efficiently* have translated into volume advantages, with Walmart as the world's largest discount retailer and Southwest as the largest U.S. air carrier, based on the number of domestic passengers.[4]

2. *Outcompeting rivals on the basis of differentiating features, such as higher quality, wider product selection, added performance, value-added services, more attractive styling, and technological superiority.* Successful adopters of differentiation strategies include Apple (innovative products), Johnson & Johnson in baby products (product reliability), Chanel and Rolex (luxury and prestige), and Mercedes and BMW (engineering design and performance). These companies have achieved a competitive advantage because of their ability to meet customer needs more effectively than rivals can, thus driving up their customers' willingness to pay higher prices. One way to sustain this type of competitive advantage is to be sufficiently innovative to thwart the efforts of clever rivals to copy or closely imitate the product offering.

3. *Developing an advantage based on offering more value for the money.* Giving customers more value for their money by satisfying buyers' expectations on key quality/features/performance/service attributes while beating their price expectations is known as a *best-cost provider strategy.* This approach is a hybrid strategy that blends elements of the previous approaches. Target is an example of a company that is known

**CORE CONCEPT**

A company achieves a **competitive advantage** when it provides buyers with superior value compared to rival sellers or offers the same value at a lower cost to the firm. The advantage is **sustainable** if it persists despite the best efforts of competitors to match or surpass this advantage.

**LO 3**

Develop an awareness of the four most dependable strategic approaches for setting a company apart from rivals and winning a sustainable competitive advantage.

for its hip product design (a reputation it built by featuring cheap-chic designers such as Isaac Mizrahi), as well as a more appealing shopping ambience for discount store shoppers. It offers the perfect illustration of a best-cost provider strategy.

4. *Focusing on a narrow market niche within an industry.* There are two types of strategies based on focus. The first aims to achieve an advantage through greater efficiency in serving a niche; the goal of the second is greater effectiveness in meeting the niche's special needs. Prominent companies that enjoy competitive success in a specialized market niche include eBay in online auctions, Jiffy Lube International in quick oil changes, McAfee in virus protection software, and The Weather Channel in cable TV.

**LO 4**

Understand that a company's strategy tends to evolve over time because of changing circumstances and ongoing management efforts to improve the company's strategy.

Winning a *sustainable* competitive edge over rivals with any of the preceding four strategies generally hinges as much on building competitively valuable expertise and capabilities that rivals cannot readily match as it does on having a distinctive product offering. Clever rivals can nearly always copy the attributes of a popular product or service, but for rivals to match the experience, know-how, and specialized capabilities that a company has developed and perfected over a long period of time is substantially harder to do and takes much longer. FedEx, for example, has superior capabilities in next-day delivery of small packages. Apple has demonstrated impressive product innovation capabilities in digital music players, smartphones, and e-readers. Hyundai has become the world's fastest-growing automaker as a result of its advanced manufacturing processes and unparalleled quality control system. Each of these capabilities has proved hard for competitors to imitate or best.

## Why a Company's Strategy Evolves over Time

Changing circumstances and ongoing management efforts to improve the strategy cause a company's strategy to evolve over time—a condition that makes the task of crafting strategy *a work in progress,* not a one-time event.

The appeal of a strategy that yields a sustainable competitive advantage is that it offers the potential for an enduring edge over rivals. However, managers of every company must be willing and ready to modify the strategy in response to changing market conditions, advancing technology, unexpected moves by competitors, shifting buyer needs, emerging market opportunities, and mounting evidence that the strategy is not working well. Most of the time, a company's strategy evolves incrementally from management's ongoing efforts to fine-tune the strategy and to adjust certain strategy elements in response to new learning and unfolding events.[5] But in industries where industry and competitive conditions change frequently and in sometimes dramatic ways, the life cycle of a given strategy is short. Industry environments characterized by high-velocity change require companies to repeatedly adapt their strategies.[6] For example, companies in industries with rapid-fire advances in technology like medical equipment, electronics, and wireless devices often find it essential to adjust key elements of their strategies several times a year, sometimes even finding it necessary to "reinvent" their approach to providing value to their customers.

A company's strategy is shaped partly by management analysis and choice and partly by the necessity of adapting and learning by doing.

Regardless of whether a company's strategy changes gradually or swiftly, the important point is that the task of crafting strategy is not a one-time event but always a work in progress. Adapting to new conditions and constantly evaluating what is working well enough to continue and what needs to be improved are normal parts of the strategy-making process, resulting in an *evolving strategy.*[7]

## A Company's Strategy Is Partly Proactive and Partly Reactive

The evolving nature of a company's strategy means that the typical company strategy is a blend of (1) *proactive,* planned initiatives to improve the company's financial performance and secure a competitive edge, and (2) *reactive* responses to unanticipated developments and fresh market conditions. The biggest portion of a company's current strategy flows from ongoing actions that have proven themselves in the marketplace and newly launched initiatives aimed at building a larger lead over rivals and further boosting financial performance. This part of management's action plan for running the company is its **deliberate strategy,** consisting of proactive strategy elements that are both planned and realized as planned (while other planned strategy elements may not work out)—see Figure 1.2.[8]

But managers must always be willing to supplement or modify the proactive strategy elements with as-needed reactions to unanticipated conditions. Inevitably, there will be occasions when market and competitive conditions take an unexpected turn that calls for some kind of strategic reaction. Hence, *a portion of a company's strategy is always developed on the fly,* coming as a response to fresh strategic maneuvers on the part of rival firms, unexpected shifts in customer requirements, fast-changing technological developments, newly appearing market opportunities, a changing political or economic climate, or other unanticipated happenings in the surrounding environment. These unplanned, reactive, and adaptive strategy adjustments make up the firm's **emergent strategy.** A company's strategy *in toto* (its **realized strategy**) thus tends to be a *combination* of proactive and reactive elements, with certain strategy elements being *abandoned* because they have become obsolete or ineffective. A company's realized strategy can be observed in the pattern of its actions over time, which is a far better indicator than any of its strategic plans on paper or any public pronouncements about its strategy.

> ### CORE CONCEPT
>
> A company's **deliberate strategy** consists of *proactive* strategy elements that are both planned and realized as planned; its **emergent strategy** consists of *reactive* strategy elements that emerge as changing conditions warrant.

**FIGURE 1.2   A Company's Strategy Is a Blend of Proactive Initiatives and Reactive Adjustments**

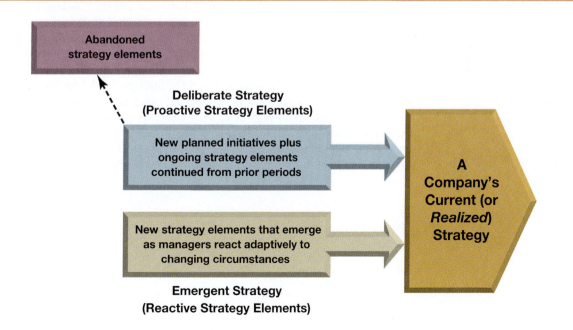

# A COMPANY'S STRATEGY AND ITS BUSINESS MODEL

**LO 5**

Learn why it is important for a company to have a viable business model that outlines the company's customer value proposition and its profit formula.

---

**CORE CONCEPT**

A company's **business model** sets forth the logic for how its strategy will create value for customers, while at the same time generate revenues sufficient to cover costs and realize a profit.

At the center of a company's strategy is the company's **business model.** A business model is management's blueprint for delivering a valuable product or service to customers in a manner that will generate revenues sufficient to cover costs and yield an attractive profit.[9] The two elements of a company's business model are (1) its *customer value proposition* and (2) its *profit formula.* The customer value proposition lays out the company's approach to satisfying buyer wants and needs at a price customers will consider a good value. Plainly, from a customer perspective, the greater the value delivered *(V)* and the lower the price *(P)*, the more attractive is the company's value proposition. The profit formula describes the company's approach to determining a cost structure that will allow for acceptable profits, given the pricing tied to its customer value proposition. The lower the costs *(C)*, given the customer value proposition *(V − P)*, the greater the ability of the business model to be a moneymaker. Thus the profit formula reveals how efficiently a company can meet customer wants and needs and deliver on the value proposition. The nitty-gritty issue surrounding a company's business model is whether it can execute its customer value proposition profitably. Just because company managers have crafted a strategy for competing and running the business, this does not automatically mean that the strategy will lead to profitability—it may or it may not.

Magazines and newspapers employ a business model keyed to delivering information and entertainment they believe readers will find valuable and a profit formula aimed at securing sufficient revenues from subscriptions and advertising to more than cover the costs of producing and delivering their products to readers. Mobile phone providers, satellite radio companies, and broadband providers also employ a subscription-based business model. The business model of network TV and radio broadcasters entails providing free programming to audiences but charging advertising fees based on audience size. Gillette's business model in razor blades involves selling a "master product"—the razor—at an attractively low price and then making money on repeat purchases of razor blades that can be produced very cheaply and sold at high profit margins. Printer manufacturers like Hewlett-Packard, Lexmark, and Epson pursue much the same business model as Gillette—selling printers at a low (virtually break-even) price and making large profit margins on the repeat purchases of printer supplies, especially ink cartridges. McDonald's invented the business model for fast food—providing value to customers in the form of economical quick-service meals at clean convenient locations. Its profit formula involves such elements as standardized cost-efficient store design, stringent specifications for ingredients, detailed operating procedures for each unit, and heavy reliance on advertising and in-store promotions to drive volume. Illustration Capsule 1.2 describes two contrasting business models in radio broadcasting.

## Sirius XM and Over-the-Air Broadcast Radio: Two Contrasting Business Models

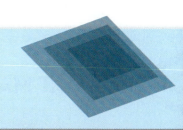

| | Sirius XM | Over-the-Air Radio Broadcasters |
|---|---|---|
| **Customer value proposition** | Digital music, news, national and regional weather, traffic reports in limited areas, and talk radio programming provided for a monthly subscription fee. Programming is interrupted only by brief occasional ads. | Free-of-charge music, national and local news, local traffic reports, national and local weather, and talk radio programming. Listeners can expect frequent programming interruption for ads. |
| **Profit formula** | ***Revenue generation:*** Monthly subscription fees, sales of satellite radio equipment, and advertising revenues.<br><br>***Cost structure:*** Fixed costs associated with operating a satellite-based music delivery service.<br><br>Fixed and variable costs related to programming and content royalties, marketing, and support activities. | ***Revenue generation:*** Advertising sales to national and local businesses.<br><br>***Cost structure:*** Fixed costs associated with terrestrial broadcasting operations.<br><br>Fixed and variable costs related to local news reporting, advertising sales operations, network affiliate fees, programming and content royalties, commercial production activities, and support activities. |
| | ***Profit margin:*** Sirius XM's profitability is dependent on attracting a sufficiently large number of subscribers to cover its costs and provide attractive profits. | ***Profit margin:*** The profitability of over-the-air radio stations was dependent on generating sufficient advertising revenues to cover costs and provide attractive profits. |

# WHAT MAKES A STRATEGY A WINNER?

**LO 6**

Learn the three tests of a winning strategy.

A **winning strategy** must pass three tests:
1. The Fit Test
2. The Competitive Advantage Test
3. The Performance Test

Three tests can be applied to determine whether a strategy is a *winning strategy:*

1. ***The Fit Test:*** *How well does the strategy fit the company's situation?* To qualify as a winner, a strategy has to be well matched to industry and competitive conditions, a company's best market opportunities, and other pertinent aspects of the business environment in which the company operates. No strategy can work well unless it exhibits good *external fit* and is in sync with prevailing market conditions. At the same time, a winning strategy must be tailored to the company's resources and competitive capabilities and be supported by a complementary set of functional activities (i.e., activities in the realms of supply chain management, operations, sales and marketing, and so on). That is, it must also exhibit *internal fit* and be compatible with a company's ability to execute the strategy in a competent manner. Unless a strategy exhibits good fit with both the external and internal aspects of a company's overall situation, it is likely to be an underperformer and fall short of producing winning results. Winning strategies also exhibit *dynamic fit* in the sense that they evolve over time in a manner that maintains close and effective alignment with the company's situation even as external and internal conditions change.[10]

2. ***The Competitive Advantage Test:*** *Can the strategy help the company achieve a sustainable competitive advantage?* Strategies that fail to achieve a durable competitive advantage over rivals are unlikely to produce superior performance for more than a brief period of time. Winning strategies enable a company to achieve a competitive advantage over key rivals that is long-lasting. The bigger and more durable the competitive advantage, the more powerful it is.

3. ***The Performance Test:*** *Is the strategy producing good company performance?* The mark of a winning strategy is strong company performance. Two kinds of performance indicators tell the most about the caliber of a company's strategy: (1) competitive strength and market standing and (2) profitability and financial strength. Above-average financial performance or gains in market share, competitive position, or profitability are signs of a winning strategy.

Strategies that come up short on one or more of the preceding tests are plainly less appealing than strategies passing all three tests with flying colors. Managers should use the same questions when evaluating either proposed or existing strategies. New initiatives that don't seem to match the company's internal and external situations should be scrapped before they come to fruition, while existing strategies must be scrutinized on a regular basis to ensure they have good fit, offer a competitive advantage, and are contributing to above-average performance or performance improvements.

# WHY CRAFTING AND EXECUTING STRATEGY ARE IMPORTANT TASKS

Crafting and executing strategy are top-priority managerial tasks for a very big reason. A clear and reasoned strategy is management's prescription for doing business, its road map to competitive advantage, its game plan for pleasing customers, and its formula for improving performance. High-achieving enterprises are nearly always the product of astute, creative, and proactive strategy making. Companies don't get to the top of the industry rankings or stay there with illogical strategies, copy-cat strategies, or timid attempts to try to do better. Only a handful of companies can boast of hitting home runs in the marketplace due to lucky breaks or the good fortune of having stumbled into the right market at the right time with the right product. And even then, unless they subsequently craft a strategy that capitalizes on their luck, building on what's working and discarding the rest, success of this sort will be fleeting. So there can be little argument that a company's strategy matters—and matters a lot.

The chief executive officer of one successful company put it well when he said:

> In the main, our competitors are acquainted with the same fundamental concepts and techniques and approaches that we follow, and they are as free to pursue them as we are. More often than not, the difference between their level of success and ours lies in the relative thoroughness and self-discipline with which we and they develop and execute our strategies for the future.

## Good Strategy + Good Strategy Execution = Good Management

Crafting and executing strategy are thus core management functions. Among all the things managers do, nothing affects a company's ultimate success or failure more fundamentally than how well its management team charts the company's direction, develops competitively effective strategic moves and business approaches, and pursues what needs to be done internally to produce good day-in, day-out strategy execution and operating excellence. Indeed, *good strategy and good strategy execution are the most telling signs of good management.* Managers don't deserve a gold star for designing a potentially brilliant strategy but failing to put the organizational means in place to carry it out in high-caliber fashion. Competent execution of a mediocre strategy scarcely merits enthusiastic applause for management's efforts either. The rationale for using the twin standards of good strategy making and good strategy execution to determine whether a company is well managed is therefore compelling: *The better conceived a company's strategy and the more competently it is executed, the more likely the company will be a standout performer in the marketplace.* In stark contrast, a company that lacks clear-cut direction, has a flawed strategy, or can't execute its strategy competently is a company whose financial performance is probably suffering, whose business is at long-term risk, and whose management is sorely lacking.

How well a company performs is directly attributable to the caliber of its strategy and the proficiency with which the strategy is executed.

# THE ROAD AHEAD

Throughout the chapters to come and in the accompanying case collection, the spotlight will be trained on the foremost question in running a business enterprise: *What must managers do, and do well, to make a company a winner in the marketplace?* The answer that emerges is that doing a good job of managing inherently requires good strategic thinking and good management of the strategy-making, strategy-executing process.

The mission of this book is to provide a solid overview of what every business student and aspiring manager needs to know about crafting and executing strategy. We will explore what good strategic thinking entails, describe the core concepts and tools of strategic analysis, and examine the ins and outs of crafting and executing strategy. The accompanying cases will help build your skills in both diagnosing how well the strategy-making, strategy-executing task is being performed and prescribing actions for how the strategy in question or its execution can be improved. The strategic management course that you are enrolled in may also include a strategy simulation exercise where you will run a company in head-to-head competition with companies run by your classmates. Your mastery of the strategic management concepts presented in the following chapters will put you in a strong position to craft a winning strategy for your company and figure out how to execute it in a cost-effective and profitable manner. As you progress through the chapters of the text and the activities assigned during the term, we hope to convince you that first-rate capabilities in crafting and executing strategy are essential to good management.

## KEY POINTS

1. A company's strategy is its action plan for outperforming its competitors and achieving superior profitability.

2. The central thrust of a company's strategy is undertaking moves to build and strengthen the company's long-term competitive position and financial performance by *competing differently* from rivals and gaining a sustainable competitive advantage over them.

3. A company achieves a **competitive advantage** when it provides buyers with superior value compared to rival sellers or offers the same value at a lower cost to the firm. The advantage is **sustainable** if it persists despite the best efforts of competitors to match or surpass this advantage.

4. A company's strategy typically evolves over time, emerging from a blend of (1) proactive deliberate actions on the part of company managers to improve the strategy, and (2) reactive emergent responses to unanticipated developments and fresh market conditions.

5. A company's business model sets forth the logic for how its strategy will create value for customers, while at the same time generate revenues sufficient to cover costs and realize a profit. Thus, it contains two crucial elements: (1) the *customer value proposition*—a plan for satisfying customer wants and needs at a price customers will consider good value, and (2) the *profit formula*—a plan for a cost structure that will enable the company to deliver the customer value proposition profitably.

6. A winning strategy will pass three tests: (1) *Fit* (external, internal, and dynamic consistency), (2) *Competitive Advantage* (durable competitive advantage), and (3) *Performance* (outstanding financial and market performance).

7. Crafting and executing strategy are core management functions. How well a company performs and the degree of market success it enjoys are directly attributable to the caliber of its strategy and the proficiency with which the strategy is executed.

## ASSURANCE OF LEARNING EXERCISES

**connect**

**LO 1, LO 2, LO 3**

1. Based on what you know about the quick-service restaurant industry, does McDonald's strategy (as described in Illustration Capsule 1.1) seem to be well-matched to industry and competitive conditions? Does the strategy seem to be keyed to a cost-based advantage, differentiating features, serving the unique needs of a niche, or some combination of these? What is there about McDonald's strategy that can lead to sustainable competitive advantage?

**connect**

**LO 4, LO 6**

2. Elements of Walmart's strategy have evolved in meaningful ways since the company's founding in 1962. Prepare a one- to two-page report that discusses how its strategy has evolved after reviewing all of the links at Walmart's About Us page, which can be found at walmartstores.com/AboutUs/. Your report should also assess how well Walmart's strategy passes the three tests of a winning strategy.

3. Go to **www.nytco.com/investors** and check whether *The New York Times'* recent financial reports indicate that its business model is working. Does the company's business model remain sound as more consumers go to the Internet to find general information and stay abreast of current events and news stories? Is its revenue stream from advertisements growing or declining? Are its subscription fees and circulation increasing or declining?

LO 5

## EXERCISE FOR SIMULATION PARTICIPANTS

Three basic questions must be answered by managers of organizations of all sizes as they begin the process of crafting strategy:

- What is our present situation?
- Where do we want to go from here?
- How are we going to get there?

After you have read the Participant's Guide or Player's Manual for the strategy simulation exercise that you will participate in this academic term, you and your co-managers should come up with brief one- or two-paragraph answers to these three questions *prior* to entering your first set of decisions. While your answers to the first of the three questions can be developed from your reading of the manual, the second and third questions will require a collaborative discussion among the members of your company's management team about how you intend to manage the company you have been assigned to run.

1. What is our company's current situation? A substantive answer to this question should cover the following issues:

LO 1, LO 2, LO 3

- Is your company in a good, average, or weak competitive position vis-à-vis rival companies?
- Does your company appear to be in a sound financial condition?
- Does it appear to have a competitive advantage and is it likely to be sustainable?
- What problems does your company have that need to be addressed?

2. Where do we want to take the company during the time we are in charge? A complete answer to this question should say something about each of the following:

LO 4, LO 6

- What goals or aspirations do you have for your company?
- What do you want the company to be known for?
- What market share would you like your company to have after the first five decision rounds?
- By what amount or percentage would you like to increase total profits of the company by the end of the final decision round?
- What kinds of performance outcomes will signal that you and your co-managers are managing the company in a successful manner?

3. How are we going to get there? Your answer should cover these issues:

LO 4, LO 5

- Which of the basic strategic and competitive approaches discussed in this chapter do you think makes the most sense to pursue?
- What kind of competitive advantage over rivals will you try to achieve?

- How would you describe the company's business model?
- What kind of actions will support these objectives?

## ENDNOTES

[1] Jan Rivkin, "An Alternative Approach to Making Strategic Choices," Harvard Business School, 9-702-433, 2001.

[2] Michael E. Porter, "What Is Strategy?" Harvard Business Review 74, no. 6 (November–December 1996).

[3] Ibid.

[4] Walmartstores.com/download/2230.pdf; Southwest Airlines Fact Sheet, July 16, 2009.

[5] Eric T. Anderson and Duncan Simester, "A Step-by-Step Guide to Smart Business Experiments," Harvard Business Review 89, no. 3 (March 2011).

[6] Shona L. Brown and Kathleen M. Eisenhardt, Competing on the Edge: Strategy as Structured Chaos (Boston, MA: Harvard Business School Press, 1998).

[7] Cynthia A. Montgomery, "Putting Leadership Back into Strategy," Harvard Business Review 86, no. 1 (January 2008).

[8] Henry Mintzberg and J. A. Waters, "Of Strategies, Deliberate and Emergent," Strategic Management Journal 6 (1985); Costas Markides, "Strategy as Balance: From 'Either-Or' to 'And,'" Business Strategy Review 12, no. 3 (September 2001).

[9] Mark W. Johnson, Clayton M. Christensen, and Henning Kagermann, "Reinventing Your Business Model," Harvard Business Review 86, no. 12 (December 2008); Joan Magretta, "Why Business Models Matter," Harvard Business Review 80, no. 5 (May 2002).

[10] Jan Rivkin, "An Alternative Approach to Making Strategic Choices."

# CHAPTER 2

# CHARTING A COMPANY'S DIRECTION: ITS VISION, MISSION, OBJECTIVES, AND STRATEGY

## Learning Objectives

**LO 1**   Grasp why it is critical for company managers to have a clear strategic vision of where a company needs to head and why.

**LO 2**   Understand the importance of setting both strategic and financial objectives.

**LO 3**   Understand why the strategic initiatives taken at various organizational levels must be tightly coordinated to achieve companywide performance targets.

**LO 4**   Become aware of what a company must do to achieve operating excellence and to execute its strategy proficiently.

**LO 5**   Become aware of the role and responsibility of a company's board of directors in overseeing the strategic management process.

> The vision we have . . . determines what we do and the opportunities we see or don't see.
>
> Charles G. Koch – *CEO of Koch Industries*

> I dream for a living.
>
> Steven Spielberg – *The most financially successful motion picture director in history*

> A good goal is like a strenuous exercise—it makes you stretch.
>
> Mary Kay Ash – *Founder of Mary Kay Cosmetics*

Crafting and executing strategy are the heart and soul of managing a business enterprise. But exactly what is involved in developing a strategy and executing it proficiently? What are the various components of the strategy-making, strategy-executing process and to what extent are company personnel—aside from senior management—involved in the process? In this chapter, we present an overview of the ins and outs of crafting and executing company strategies. Special attention will be given to management's direction-setting responsibilities—charting a strategic course, setting performance targets, and choosing a strategy capable of producing the desired outcomes. We will also explain why strategy making is a task for a company's entire management team and discuss which kinds of strategic decisions tend to be made at which levels of management. The chapter concludes with a look at the roles and responsibilities of a company's board of directors in the strategy-making, strategy-executing process and how good corporate governance protects shareholder interests and promotes good management.

# WHAT DOES THE STRATEGY-MAKING, STRATEGY-EXECUTING PROCESS ENTAIL?

The managerial process of crafting and executing a company's strategy consists of five integrated tasks:

1. *Developing a strategic vision* that charts the company's long-term direction, a *mission statement* that describes the company's purpose, and a set of *core values* to guide the pursuit of the vision and mission.
2. *Setting objectives* for measuring the company's performance and tracking its progress in moving in the intended long-term direction.
3. *Crafting a strategy* to move the company along the strategic course that management has charted and achieve the objectives.
4. *Executing the chosen strategy* efficiently and effectively.
5. *Monitoring developments, evaluating performance, and initiating corrective adjustments* in the company's vision and mission statement, objectives, strategy, or approach to strategy execution in light of actual experience, changing conditions, new ideas, and new opportunities.

**FIGURE 2.1**  The Strategy-Making, Strategy-Executing Process

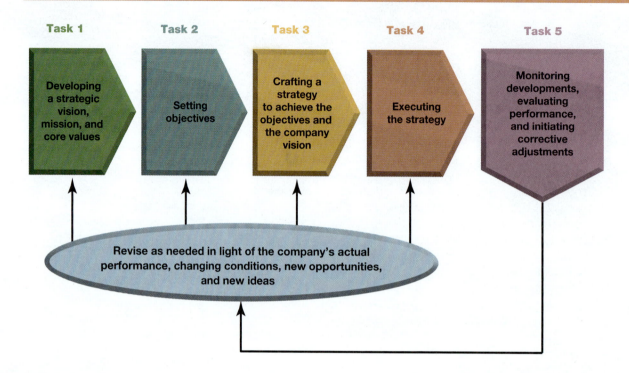

A company's **strategic plan** lays out its future direction, performance targets, and strategy.

Figure 2.1 displays this five-task process, which we examine next in some detail.

The first three tasks of the strategic management process make up a strategic plan. A **strategic plan** maps out where a company is headed, establishes strategic and financial targets, and outlines the competitive moves and approaches to be used in achieving the desired business results.[1]

# TASK 1: DEVELOPING A STRATEGIC VISION, A MISSION STATEMENT, AND A SET OF CORE VALUES

**LO 1**

Grasp why it is critical for company managers to have a clear strategic vision of where a company needs to head and why.

At the outset of the strategy-making process, a company's senior managers must wrestle with the issue of what directional path the company should take. Can the company's prospects be improved by changing its product offerings, or the markets in which it participates, or the customers it aims to serve? Deciding to commit the company to one path versus another pushes managers to draw some carefully reasoned conclusions about whether the company's present strategic course offers attractive opportunities for growth and profitability or whether changes of one kind or another in the company's strategy and long-term direction are needed.

# Developing a Strategic Vision

Top management's views and conclusions about the company's long-term direction and what product–market–customer mix seems optimal for the road ahead constitute a **strategic vision** for the company. A strategic vision delineates management's aspirations for the business, providing a panoramic view of "where we are going" and a convincing rationale for why this makes good business sense for the company. A strategic vision thus points an organization in a particular direction, charts a strategic path for it to follow in preparing for the future, and builds commitment to the future course of action. A clearly articulated strategic vision communicates management's aspirations to stakeholders and helps steer the energies of company personnel in a common direction. For instance, Henry Ford's vision of a car in every garage had power because it captured the imagination of others, aided internal efforts to mobilize the Ford Motor Company's resources, and served as a reference point for gauging the merits of the company's strategic actions.

Well-conceived visions are *distinctive* and *specific* to a particular organization; they avoid generic, feel-good statements like "We will become a global leader and the first choice of customers in every market we serve"—which could apply to hundreds of organizations.[2] A surprising number of the vision statements found on company websites and in annual reports are vague and unrevealing, saying very little about the company's future direction. Some could apply to almost any company in any industry. Many read like a public relations statement—high-sounding words that someone came up with because it is fashionable for companies to have an official vision statement.[3] But the real purpose of a vision statement is to serve as a management tool for giving the organization a sense of direction.

For a strategic vision to function as a valuable managerial tool, it must convey what management wants the business to look like and provide managers with a reference point in making strategic decisions and preparing the company for the future. It must say something definitive about how the company's leaders intend to position the company beyond where it is today. Table 2.1 provides some dos and don'ts in composing an effectively worded vision statement. Illustration Capsule 2.1 provides a critique of the strategic visions of several prominent companies.

# Communicating the Strategic Vision

A strategic vision has little value to the organization unless it's effectively communicated down the line to lower-level managers and employees. A vision cannot provide direction for middle managers nor can it inspire and energize employees unless everyone in the company is familiar with it and can observe management's commitment to the vision. It is particularly important for executives to provide a compelling rationale for a dramatically *new* strategic vision and company direction. When company personnel don't understand or accept the need for redirecting organizational efforts, they are prone to resist change. Hence, explaining the basis for the new direction, addressing employee concerns head-on, calming fears, lifting spirits, and providing updates and progress reports as events unfold all become part of the task in mobilizing support for the vision and winning commitment to needed actions.

Winning the support of organization members for the vision nearly always means putting "where we are going and why" in writing, distributing the statement organizationwide, and having executives personally explain the vision and its rationale to as

**TABLE 2.1    Wording a Vision Statement—the Dos and Don'ts**

| The Dos | The Don'ts |
| --- | --- |
| **Be graphic.** Paint a clear picture of where the company is headed and the market position(s) the company is striving to stake out. | **Don't be vague or incomplete.** Never skimp on specifics about where the company is headed or how the company intends to prepare for the future. |
| **Be forward-looking and directional.** Describe the strategic course that will help the company prepare for the future. | **Don't dwell on the present.** A vision is not about what a company once did or does now; it's about "where we are going." |
| **Keep it focused.** Focus on providing managers with guidance in making decisions and allocating resources. | **Don't use overly broad language.** All-inclusive language that gives the company license to pursue any opportunity must be avoided. |
| **Have some wiggle room.** Language that allows some flexibility allows the directional course to be adjusted as market–customer–technology circumstances change. | **Don't state the vision in bland or uninspiring terms.** The best vision statements have the power to motivate company personnel and inspire shareholder confidence about the company's future. |
| **Be sure the journey is feasible.** The path and direction should be within the realm of what the company can accomplish; over time, a company should be able to demonstrate measurable progress in achieving the vision. | **Don't be generic.** A vision statement that could apply to companies in any of several industries (or to any of several companies in the same industry) is not specific enough to provide any guidance. |
| **Indicate why the directional path makes good business sense.** The directional path should be in the long-term interests of stakeholders (especially shareowners, employees, and suppliers). | **Don't rely on superlatives.** Visions that claim the company's strategic course is one of being the "best" or "most successful" usually lack specifics about the path the company is taking to get there. |
| **Make it memorable.** To give the organization a sense of direction and purpose, the vision needs to be easily communicated. Ideally, it should be reducible to a few choice lines or a memorable "slogan." | **Don't run on and on.** A vision statement that is not short and to the point will tend to lose its audience. |

*Sources:* John P. Kotter, *Leading Change* (Boston: Harvard Business School Press, 1996), Hugh Davidson, *The Committed Enterprise* (Oxford: Butterworth Heinemann, 2002), and Michel Robert, *Strategy Pure and Simple II* (New York: McGraw-Hill, 1992).

many people as feasible. *A strategic vision can usually be stated adequately in one to two paragraphs, and managers should be able to explain it to company personnel and outsiders in 5 to 10 minutes.* Ideally, executives should present their vision for the company in a manner that reaches out and grabs people. An engaging and convincing strategic vision has enormous motivational value—for the same reason that a stonemason is more inspired by the opportunity to build a great cathedral for the ages. Thus executive ability to paint a convincing and inspiring picture of a company's journey and destination is an important element of effective strategic leadership.

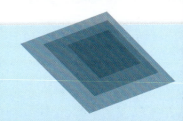

# Examples of Strategic Visions—How Well Do They Measure Up?

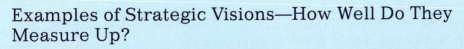

| Vision Statement | Effective Elements | Shortcomings |
|---|---|---|
| **Coca-Cola**<br>Our vision serves as the framework for our Roadmap and guides every aspect of our business by describing what we need to accomplish in order to continue achieving sustainable, quality growth.<br><br>• People: Be a great place to work where people are inspired to be the best they can be.<br><br>• Portfolio: Bring to the world a portfolio of quality beverage brands that anticipate and satisfy people's desires and needs.<br><br>• Partners: Nurture a winning network of customers and suppliers; together we create mutual, enduring value.<br><br>• Planet: Be a responsible citizen that makes a difference by helping build and support sustainable communities.<br><br>• Profit: Maximize long-term return to shareowners while being mindful of our overall responsibilities.<br><br>• Productivity: Be a highly effective, lean, and fast-moving organization. | • Graphic<br>• Focused<br>• Flexible<br>• Makes good business sense | • Long<br>• Not forward-looking |
| **Procter & Gamble**<br>We will provide branded products and services of superior quality and value that improve the lives of the world's consumers, now and for generations to come. As a result, consumers will reward us with leadership sales, profit and value creation, allowing our people, our shareholders and the communities in which we live and work to prosper. | • Forward-looking<br>• Flexible<br>• Feasible<br>• Makes good business sense | • Not graphic<br>• Not focused<br>• Not memorable |
| **Heinz**<br>We define a compelling, sustainable future and create the path to achieve it. | • Forward-looking<br>• Flexible | • Not graphic<br>• Not focused<br>• Confusing<br>• Not memorable<br>• Not necessarily feasible |

Developed with Jenna P. Pfeffer.

*Sources:* Company documents and websites (accessed June 6, 2010, February 4 and 12, 2012).

**Expressing the Essence of the Vision in a Slogan**    The task of effectively conveying the vision to company personnel is assisted when management can capture the vision of where to head in a catchy or easily remembered slogan. A number of organizations have summed up their vision in a brief phrase:

- Levi Strauss & Company: "We will clothe the world by marketing the most appealing and widely worn casual clothing in the world."
- Nike: "To bring innovation and inspiration to every athlete in the world."
- Mayo Clinic: "The best care to every patient every day."
- Scotland Yard: "To make London the safest major city in the world."
- Greenpeace: "To halt environmental abuse and promote environmental solutions."

Creating a short slogan to illuminate an organization's direction and purpose and using it repeatedly as a reminder of "where we are headed and why" helps rally organization members to hurdle whatever obstacles lie in the company's path and maintain their focus.

## Why a Sound, Well-Communicated Strategic Vision Matters

A well thought-out, forcefully communicated strategic vision pays off in several respects: (1) It crystallizes senior executives' own views about the firm's long-term direction; (2) it reduces the risk of rudderless decision making; (3) it is a tool for winning the support of organization members to help make the vision a reality; (4) it provides a beacon for lower-level managers in setting departmental objectives and crafting departmental strategies that are in sync with the company's overall strategy; and (5) it helps an organization prepare for the future. When management is able to demonstrate significant progress in achieving these five benefits, it can count its efforts to create an effective vision for the company as successful.

# Developing a Company Mission Statement

The defining characteristic of a strategic vision is what it says about the company's *future strategic course*—"the direction we are headed and what we want our business to look like in the future." It is aspirational. In contrast, a **mission statement** describes the enterprise's *present business and purpose*—"who we are, what we do, and why we are here." It is purely descriptive. Ideally, a company mission statement (1) identifies the company's products/services, (2) specifies the buyer needs that it seeks to satisfy and the customer groups or markets it serves, and (3) gives the company its own identity. The mission statements that one finds in company annual reports or posted on company websites are typically quite brief; some do a better job than others of conveying what the enterprise is all about.

The following three mission statements provide reasonably informative specifics about "who we are, what we do, and why we are here:"

- Trader Joe's (a specialty grocery chain): "The mission of Trader Joe's is to give our customers the best food and beverage values that they can find anywhere and to provide them with the information required for informed buying decisions. We provide these with a dedication to the highest quality of customer satisfaction delivered with a sense of warmth, friendliness, fun, individual pride, and company spirit.
- Occupational Safety and Health Administration (OSHA): "To assure the safety and health of America's workers by setting and enforcing standards; providing training, outreach, and education; establishing partnerships; and encouraging continual improvement in workplace safety and health."
- Google: "To organize the world's information and make it universally accessible and useful."

The distinction between a strategic vision and a mission statement is fairly clear-cut: A **strategic vision** portrays a company's aspirations for its *future* ("where we are going"), whereas a company's **mission** describes its *purpose* and its *present* business ("who we are, what we do, and why we are here").

An example of a not-so-revealing mission statement is that of Microsoft. "To help people and businesses throughout the world realize their full potential" says nothing about its products or business makeup and could apply to many companies in many different industries. A person unfamiliar with Microsoft could not discern from its mission statement that it is a globally known provider of PC software and a leading maker of video game consoles (the popular Xbox 360). Coca-Cola, which markets nearly 400 beverage brands in over 200 countries, also has an uninformative mission statement: "to benefit and refresh everyone it touches." The usefulness of a mission statement that blurs the essence of a company's business activities and purpose is unclear.

Occasionally, companies couch their mission in terms of making a profit. This, too, is flawed. Profit is more correctly an *objective* and a *result* of what a company does. Moreover, earning a profit is the obvious intent of every commercial enterprise. Such companies as BMW, Netflix, Shell Oil, Procter & Gamble, Google, and McDonald's are each striving to earn a profit for shareholders; but plainly the fundamentals of their businesses are substantially different when it comes to "who we are and what we do." It is management's answer to "make a profit doing what and for whom?" that reveals the substance of a company's true mission and business purpose.

## Linking the Vision and Mission with Company Values

The **values** of a company (sometimes called *core values*) are the beliefs, traits, and behavioral norms that management has determined should guide the pursuit of its vision and mission. They relate to such things as fair treatment, integrity, ethical behavior, innovativeness, teamwork, top-notch quality, superior customer service, social responsibility, and community citizenship. Many companies have developed a statement of values to emphasize the expectation that the values be reflected in the conduct of company operations and the behavior of company personnel.

> **CORE CONCEPT**
>
> A company's **values** are the beliefs, traits, and behavioral norms that company personnel are expected to display in conducting the company's business and pursuing its strategic vision and mission.

Most companies have articulated four to eight core values that company personnel are expected to display and that are supposed to be mirrored in how the company conducts its business. Kodak's core values are respect for the dignity of the individual, uncompromising integrity, unquestioned trust, constant credibility, continual improvement and personal renewal, and open celebration of individual and team achievements. At Foster Wheeler, a global engineering and construction firm, the four core values are integrity, accountability, high performance, valuing people, and teamwork. In its quest to be the world's leading home-improvement retail, Home Depot embraces eight values—entrepreneurial spirit, excellent customer service, giving back to the community, respect for all people, doing the right thing, taking care of people, building strong relationships, and creating shareholder value.

Do companies practice what they preach when it comes to their professed values? Sometimes no, sometimes yes—it runs the gamut. At one extreme are companies with window-dressing values; the values are given lip service by top executives but have little discernible impact on either how company personnel behave or how the company operates. Such companies have value statements because they are in vogue and make the company look good. At the other extreme are companies whose executives are committed to grounding company operations on sound values and principled ways of doing business. Executives at these companies deliberately seek to ingrain the designated core values into the corporate culture—the core values thus become an integral part of the company's DNA and what makes it tick. At such values-driven companies, executives "walk the talk" and company personnel are held accountable for embodying the stated values in their behavior.

## Zappos Family Mission and Core Values

We've been asked by a lot of people how we've grown so quickly, and the answer is actually really simple. . . . We've aligned the entire organization around one mission: *to provide the best customer service possible.* Internally, we call this our **WOW** philosophy.

These are the ten core values that we live by:

### DELIVER WOW THROUGH SERVICE.

At the Zappos Family of Companies, anything worth doing is worth doing with WOW. WOW is such a short, simple word, but it really encompasses a lot of things. To WOW, you must differentiate yourself, which means doing something a little unconventional and innovative. You must do something that's above and beyond what's expected. And whatever you do must have an emotional impact on the receiver. We are not an average company, our service is not average, and we don't want our people to be average. We expect every employee to deliver WOW.

### EMBRACE AND DRIVE CHANGE.

Part of being in a growing company is that change is constant. For some people, especially those who come from bigger companies, the constant change can be

somewhat unsettling at first. If you are not prepared to deal with constant change, then you probably are not a good fit for the company.

### CREATE FUN AND A LITTLE WEIRDNESS.

At Zappos, We're Always Creating Fun and A Little Weirdness! One of the things that makes our company different from a lot of other companies is that we value being fun and being a little weird. We don't want to become one of those big companies that feels corporate

At companies where the stated values are real rather than cosmetic, managers connect values to the pursuit of the strategic vision and mission in one of two ways. In companies with long-standing values that are deeply entrenched in the corporate culture, senior managers are careful to craft a vision, mission, and strategy that match established values; they also reiterate how the value-based behavioral norms contribute to the company's business success. If the company changes to a different vision or strategy, executives take care to explain how and why the core values continue to be relevant. In new companies, top management has to consider what values, behaviors, and business conduct should characterize the company and then draft a value statement that is circulated among managers and employees for discussion and possible modification. A final value statement that incorporates the desired behaviors and traits and that connects to the vision and mission is then officially adopted. Some companies combine their vision, mission, and values into a single statement or document, circulate it to all organization members, and in many instances post the vision, mission, and values statement on the company's website. Illustration Capsule 2.2 describes how core values drive the company's mission at the Zappos Family of Companies, a widely known and quite successful online shoe and apparel retailer.

and boring. We want to be able to laugh at ourselves. We look for both fun and humor in our daily work.

### BE ADVENTUROUS, CREATIVE, AND OPEN MINDED.

We think it's important for people and the company as a whole to be bold and daring (but not reckless). We do not want people to be afraid to take risks and make mistakes. We believe if people aren't making mistakes, then that means they're not taking enough risks. Over time, we want everyone to develop his/her gut about business decisions. We want people to develop and improve their decision-making skills. We encourage people to make mistakes as long as they learn from them.

### PURSUE GROWTH AND LEARNING.

We think it's important for employees to grow both personally and professionally. It's important to constantly challenge and stretch yourself and not be stuck in a job where you don't feel like you are growing or learning.

### BUILD OPEN AND HONEST RELATIONSHIPS WITH COMMUNICATION.

Fundamentally, we believe that openness and honesty make for the best relationships because that leads to trust and faith. We value strong relationships in all areas: with managers, direct reports, customers (internal and external), vendors, business partners, team members, and co-workers.

### BUILD A POSITIVE TEAM AND FAMILY SPIRIT.

At our company, we place a lot of emphasis on our culture because we are both a team and a family. We want to create an environment that is friendly, warm, and exciting. We encourage diversity in ideas, opinions, and points of view.

### DO MORE WITH LESS.

The Zappos Family of Companies has always been about being able to do more with less. While we may be casual in our interactions with each other, we are focused and serious about the operations of our business. We believe in working hard and putting in the extra effort to get things done.

### BE PASSIONATE AND DETERMINED.

Passion is the fuel that drives us and our company forward. We value passion, determination, perseverance, and the sense of urgency. We are inspired because we believe in what we are doing and where we are going. We don't take "no" or "that'll never work" for an answer because if we had, then our company would have never started in the first place.

### BE HUMBLE.

While we have grown quickly in the past, we recognize that there are always challenges ahead to tackle. We believe that no matter what happens we should always be respectful of everyone.

LO 2

Understand the importance of setting both strategic and financial objectives.

# TASK 2: SETTING OBJECTIVES

The managerial purpose of setting **objectives** is to convert the vision and mission into specific performance targets. Objectives reflect management's aspirations for company performance in light of the industry's prevailing economic and competitive conditions and the company's internal capabilities. Well-stated objectives are *quantifiable* or *measurable,* and contain a *deadline for achievement.* As Bill Hewlett, cofounder of Hewlett-Packard, shrewdly observed, "You cannot manage what you cannot measure. . . . And what gets measured gets done."[4] Concrete, measurable objectives are managerially valuable for three reasons: (1) They focus efforts and align actions throughout the organization, (2) they serve as *yardsticks* for tracking a company's performance and progress, and (3) they motivate employees to expend greater effort and perform at a high level.

## CORE CONCEPT

**Objectives** are an organization's performance targets—the specific results management wants to achieve.

## The Imperative of Setting Stretch Objectives

The experiences of countless companies and managers teach that one of the best ways to promote outstanding company performance is for managers to deliberately set performance targets high enough to *stretch an organization to perform at its full potential and deliver the best possible results.* Challenging company personnel to go all out and deliver "stretch" gains in performance pushes an enterprise to be more inventive, to exhibit more urgency in improving both its financial performance and its business position, and to be more intentional and focused in its actions. Stretch objectives spur exceptional performance and help build a firewall against contentment with modest gains in organizational performance. Manning Selvage & Lee (MS&L), a U.S. public relations firm, used ambitious stretch objectives to triple its revenues in three years. A company exhibits *strategic intent* when it relentlessly pursues an ambitious strategic objective, concentrating the full force of its resources and competitive actions on achieving that objective. MS&L's strategic intent was to become one of the leading global PR firms, which it achieved with the help of its stretch objectives. Honda's long-standing strategic intent of producing an ultra-light jet was finally realized in 2012 when the five-passenger plane dubbed the "Honda Civic of the sky" went into production.

## What Kinds of Objectives to Set

Two very distinct types of performance targets are required: those relating to financial performance and those relating to strategic performance. **Financial objectives** communicate management's goals for financial performance. **Strategic objectives** are goals concerning a company's marketing standing and competitive position. A company's set of financial and strategic objectives should include both near-term and longer-term performance targets. Short-term (quarterly or annual) objectives focus attention on delivering performance improvements in the current period and satisfy shareholder expectations for near-term progress. Longer-term targets (three to five years off) force managers to consider what to do *now* to put the company in position to perform better later. Long-term objectives are critical for achieving optimal long-term performance and stand as a barrier to a nearsighted management philosophy and an undue focus on short-term results. When trade-offs have to be made between achieving long-term objectives and achieving short-term objectives, long-term objectives should take precedence (unless the achievement of one or more short-term performance targets has unique importance). Examples of commonly used financial and strategic objectives include the following:

## The Need for a Balanced Approach to Objective Setting

The importance of setting and attaining financial objectives is obvious. Without adequate profitability and financial strength, a company's long-term health and ultimate survival are jeopardized. Furthermore, subpar earnings and a weak balance sheet alarm shareholders and creditors and put the jobs of senior executives at risk. However, good financial performance, by itself, is not enough. Of equal or greater importance is a company's strategic performance—outcomes that indicate whether a company's market position and competitiveness are deteriorating, holding steady, or improving. *A stronger market standing and greater competitive vitality is what enables a company to improve its financial performance.*

Moreover, a company's financial performance measures are really *lagging indicators* that reflect the results of past decisions and organizational activities.[5] But a company's past or current financial performance is not a reliable indicator of its future prospects—poor financial performers often turn things around and do better, while good financial

| Financial Objectives | Strategic Objectives |
|---|---|
| • An *x* percent increase in annual revenues <br> • Annual increases in after-tax profits *of x* percent <br> • Annual increases in earnings per share of *x* percent <br> • Annual dividend increases of *x* percent <br> • Profit margins of *x* percent <br> • An *x* percent return on capital employed (ROCE) or return on shareholders' equity investment (ROE) <br> • Increased shareholder value—in the form of an upward-trending stock price <br> • Bond and credit ratings of *x* <br> • Internal cash flows of *x* dollars to fund new capital investment | • Winning an *x* percent market share <br> • Achieving lower overall costs than rivals <br> • Overtaking key competitors on product performance or quality or customer service <br> • Deriving *x* percent of revenues from the sale of new products introduced within the past five years <br> • Having broader or deeper technological capabilities than rivals <br> • Having a wider product line than rivals <br> • Having a better-known or more powerful brand name than rivals <br> • Having stronger national or global sales and distribution capabilities than rivals <br> • Consistently getting new or improved products to market ahead of rivals |

performers can fall upon hard times. The best and most reliable *leading indicators* of a company's future financial performance and business prospects are strategic outcomes that indicate whether the company's competitiveness and market position are stronger or weaker. The accomplishment of strategic objectives signals that the company is well positioned to sustain or improve its performance. For instance, if a company is achieving ambitious strategic objectives such that its competitive strength and market position are on the rise, then there's reason to expect that its *future* financial performance will be better than its current or past performance. If a company begins to lose competitive strength and fails to achieve important strategic objectives, then its ability to maintain its present profitability is doubtful.

Consequently, it is important to utilize a performance measurement system that strikes a *balance* between financial objectives and strategic objectives.[6] The most widely used framework for balancing financial objectives with strategic objectives is known as the **Balanced Scorecard.**[7] This is a method for linking financial performance objectives to specific strategic objectives that derive from a company's business model. It provides a company's employees with clear guidelines about how their jobs are linked to the overall objectives of the organization, so they can contribute most productively and collaboratively to the achievement of these goals. In 2010, nearly 50 percent of global companies used a balanced-scorecard approach to measuring strategic and financial performance.[8] Examples of organizations that have adopted a balanced-scorecard approach to setting objectives and measuring performance include SAS Institute, UPS, Ann Taylor Stores, Fort Bragg Army Garrison, Caterpillar, Daimler AG, Hilton Hotels, Susan G. Komen for the Cure, and Siemens AG.[9] Illustration Capsule 2.3 provides selected strategic and financial objectives of three prominent companies.

### CORE CONCEPT

The **Balanced Scorecard** is a widely used method for combining the use of both strategic and financial objectives, tracking their achievement, and giving management a more complete and balanced view of how well an organization is performing.

## Setting Objectives for Every Organizational Level
Objective setting should not stop with top management's establishing of companywide performance targets. Company objectives need to be broken down into performance targets for each of the organization's separate businesses, product lines, functional departments, and

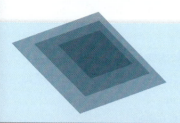

# Examples of Company Objectives

## NORDSTROM

Increase same store sales by 2–4 percent. Expand credit revenue by $25–$35 million while also reducing associated expenses by $10–$20 million as a result of lower bad debt expenses. Continue moderate store growth by opening three new Nordstrom stores, relocating one store and opening 17 Nordstrom Racks. Find more ways to connect with customers on a multichannel basis, including plans for an enhanced online experience, improved mobile shopping capabilities and better engagement with customers through social networking. Improve customer focus: "Most important, we continue to do everything in our power to elevate our focus on the customer. Our challenge is to keep building on this momentum. Our number one goal firmly remains improving customer service" (Blake Nordstrom, CEO).

## GOODYEAR

Increase operating income from $917 million in 2010 to $1.6 billion in 2013; increase operating income from international tire division from $899 in 2010 to $1,150 million in 2013; increase operating income from North American division from $18 million in 2010 to $450 million in 2013; reduce the percentage of non-branded replacement tires sold from 16 percent in 2010 to 9 percent in 2013; improve brand awareness in Mexico; increase number of retail outlets in China from 735 in 2010 to 1,555 in 2015; increase fuel efficiency of automobile and truck

tires; improve braking distance on new tire designs; improve treadlife on new tire designs; collaborate with regulatory agencies in the U.S. and Europe to develop tire labeling standards by 2013.

## PEPSICO

Accelerate top-line growth; Build and expand our better-for-you snacks and beverages and nutrition businesses; Improve our water use efficiency by 20 percent per unit of production by 2015; Reduce packaging weight by 350 million pounds by 2012; Improve our electricity use efficiency by 20 percent per unit of production by 2015; Maintain appropriate financial flexibility with ready access to global capital and credit markets at favorable interest rates.

Developed with C. David Morgan.

*Sources:* Thompson Reuters Street Events, "JWN – Q4 2009 Nordstrom Earnings Conference Call," www.streetevents.com, February 2010 (transcribed version of Webcast accessed April 30, 2010, through InvesText database); information posted on company websites, accessed May 27, 2011.

individual work units. Employees within various functional areas and operating levels will be guided much better by narrow objectives relating directly to their departmental activities than broad organizational level goals. Objective-setting is thus a *top-down process* that must extend to the lowest organizational levels. And it means that each organizational unit must take care to set performance targets that support—rather than conflict with or negate—the achievement of companywide strategic and financial objectives.

The ideal situation is a team effort in which each organizational unit strives to produce results that contribute to the achievement of the company's performance targets and strategic vision. Such consistency signals that organizational units know their strategic role and are on board in helping the company move down the chosen strategic path and produce the desired results.

# TASK 3: CRAFTING A STRATEGY

As indicated in Chapter 1, the task of stitching a strategy together entails addressing a series of "hows": *how* to attract and please customers, *how* to compete against rivals, *how* to position the company in the marketplace, *how* to respond to changing market conditions, *how* to capitalize on attractive opportunities to grow the business, and *how* to achieve strategic and financial objectives. Astute entrepreneurship is called for in choosing among the various strategic alternatives and in proactively searching for opportunities to do new things or to do existing things in new or better ways.[10] The faster a company's business environment is changing, the more critical it becomes for its managers to be good entrepreneurs in diagnosing the direction and force of the changes under way and in responding with timely adjustments in strategy. Strategy makers have to pay attention to early warnings of future change and be willing to experiment with dare-to-be-different ways to establish a market position in that future. When obstacles appear unexpectedly in a company's path, it is up to management to adapt rapidly and innovatively. *Masterful strategies come from doing things differently from competitors where it counts—out-innovating them, being more efficient, being more imaginative, adapting faster—rather than running with the herd.* Good strategy making is therefore inseparable from good business entrepreneurship. One cannot exist without the other.

LO 3

Understand why the strategic initiatives taken at various organizational levels must be tightly coordinated to achieve companywide performance targets.

## Strategy Making Involves Managers at All Organizational Levels

A company's senior executives obviously have lead strategy-making roles and responsibilities. The chief executive officer (CEO), as captain of the ship, carries the mantles of chief direction setter, chief objective setter, chief strategy maker, and chief strategy implementer for the total enterprise. Ultimate responsibility for *leading* the strategy-making, strategy-executing process rests with the CEO. And the CEO is always fully accountable for the results the strategy produces, whether good or bad. In some enterprises, the CEO or owner functions as chief architect of the strategy, personally deciding what the key elements of the company's strategy will be, although they may seek the advice of key subordinates and board members. A CEO-centered approach to strategy development is characteristic of small owner-managed companies and some large corporations that were founded by the present CEO or that have a CEO with strong strategic leadership skills. Steve Jobs at Apple, Andrea Jung at Avon, and Howard Schultz at Starbucks are prominent examples of corporate CEOs who have wielded a heavy hand in shaping their company's strategy.

In most corporations, however, strategy is the product of more than just the CEO's handiwork. Typically, other senior executives—business unit heads, the chief financial officer, and vice presidents for production, marketing, human resources, and other functional departments have influential strategy-making roles and help fashion the chief strategy components. Normally, a company's chief financial officer is in charge of devising and implementing an appropriate financial strategy; the production vice president takes the lead in developing the company's production strategy; the marketing vice president orchestrates sales and marketing strategy; a brand manager is in charge of the strategy for a particular brand in the company's product lineup, and so on. Moreover, the strategy-making efforts of top managers are complemented by advice and counsel from the company's board of directors and, normally, all major strategic decisions are submitted to the board of directors for review, discussion, and official approval.

In most companies, crafting and executing strategy is a *collaborative team effort* in which every manager has a role for the area he or she heads; it is rarely something that only high-level managers do.

But strategy making is by no means solely a *top* management function, the exclusive province of owner-entrepreneurs, CEOs, high-ranking executives, and board members. The more a company's operations cut across different products, industries, and geographic areas, the more that headquarters executives have little option but to delegate considerable strategy-making authority to down-the-line managers in charge of particular subsidiaries, divisions, product lines, geographic sales offices, distribution centers, and plants. On-the-scene managers who oversee specific operating units can be reliably counted on to have more detailed command of the strategic issues and choices for the particular operating unit under their supervision—knowing the prevailing market and competitive conditions, customer requirements and expectations, and all the other relevant aspects affecting the several strategic options available. Managers with day-to-day familiarity of, and authority over, a specific operating unit thus have a big edge over headquarters executives in making wise strategic choices for their operating unit. The result is that, in most of today's companies, crafting and executing strategy is a *collaborative team effort* in which *every company manager plays a strategy-making role*—ranging from minor to major—for the area he or she heads.

Take, for example, a company like General Electric, a $200 billion global corporation with 287,000 employees, operations in some 120 countries, and businesses that include jet engines, lighting, power generation, electric transmission and distribution equipment, housewares and appliances, medical equipment, media and entertainment, locomotives, security devices, water purification, and financial services. While top-level headquarters executives may well be personally involved in shaping GE's *overall* strategy and fashioning *important* strategic moves, it doesn't follow that a few senior executives in GE's headquarters have either the expertise or a sufficiently detailed understanding of all the relevant factors to wisely craft all the strategic initiatives taken for hundreds of subsidiaries and thousands of products. They simply cannot know enough about the situation in every GE organizational unit to decide on every strategy detail and direct every strategic move made in GE's worldwide organization. Rather, it takes involvement on the part of GE's whole management team—top executives, business group heads, the heads of specific business units and product categories, and key managers in plants, sales offices, and distribution centers—to craft the thousands of strategic initiatives that end up constituting the whole of GE's strategy.

## A Company's Strategy-Making Hierarchy

**CORE CONCEPT**

**Corporate strategy** is strategy at the *multi-business level,* concerning how to improve company performance or gain competitive advantage by managing a set of businesses simultaneously.

In diversified companies, where multiple and sometimes strikingly different businesses have to be managed (like at General Electric), crafting a full-fledged strategy involves four distinct types of strategic actions and initiatives. Each of these involves different facets of the company's overall strategy and calls for the participation of different types of managers, as shown in Figure 2.2. The pieces of a company's strategy up and down the strategy hierarchy should be cohesive and mutually reinforcing, fitting together like a jigsaw puzzle.

As shown in Figure 2.2, **corporate strategy** is orchestrated by the CEO and other senior executives and establishes an overall strategy for managing a *set of businesses* in a diversified, multibusiness company. Corporate strategy concerns how to boost the combined performance of the set of businesses the company has diversified into and the means of capturing cross-business synergies and turning them into competitive advantage. It addresses the questions of what businesses to hold or divest, which new markets to enter, and how to best enter new markets (by acquisition, creation of a strategic alliance, or through internal development, for example). Corporate strategy and business diversification are the subjects of Chapter 8, where they are discussed in detail.

**FIGURE 2.2** A Company's Strategy-Making Hierarchy

Orchestrated by the CEO and other senior executives.

**Corporate Strategy**
**(for the set of businesses as a whole)**
• How to gain advantage from managing a set of businesses

In the case of a single-business company, these two levels of the strategy-making hierarchy merge into one level— *Business strategy*—that is orchestrated by the company's CEO and other top executives.

Two-Way Influence

Orchestrated by the general managers of each of the company's different lines of business, often with advice and input from more senior executives and the heads of functional area activities within each business.

**Business Strategy**
**(one for each business the company has diversified into)**
• How to gain and sustain a competitive advantage for a single line of business

Two-Way Influence

Orchestrated by the heads of major functional activities within a particular business, often in collaboration with other key people.

**Functional Area Strategies**
**(within each business)**
• How to manage a particular activity within a business in ways that support the business strategy

Two-Way Influence

Orchestrated by brand managers, the operating managers of plants, distribution centers, and purchasing centers, and the managers of strategically important activities like website operations, often in collaboration with other key people.

**Operating Strategies**
**(within each functional area)**
• How to manage activities of strategic significance within each functional area, adding detail and completeness

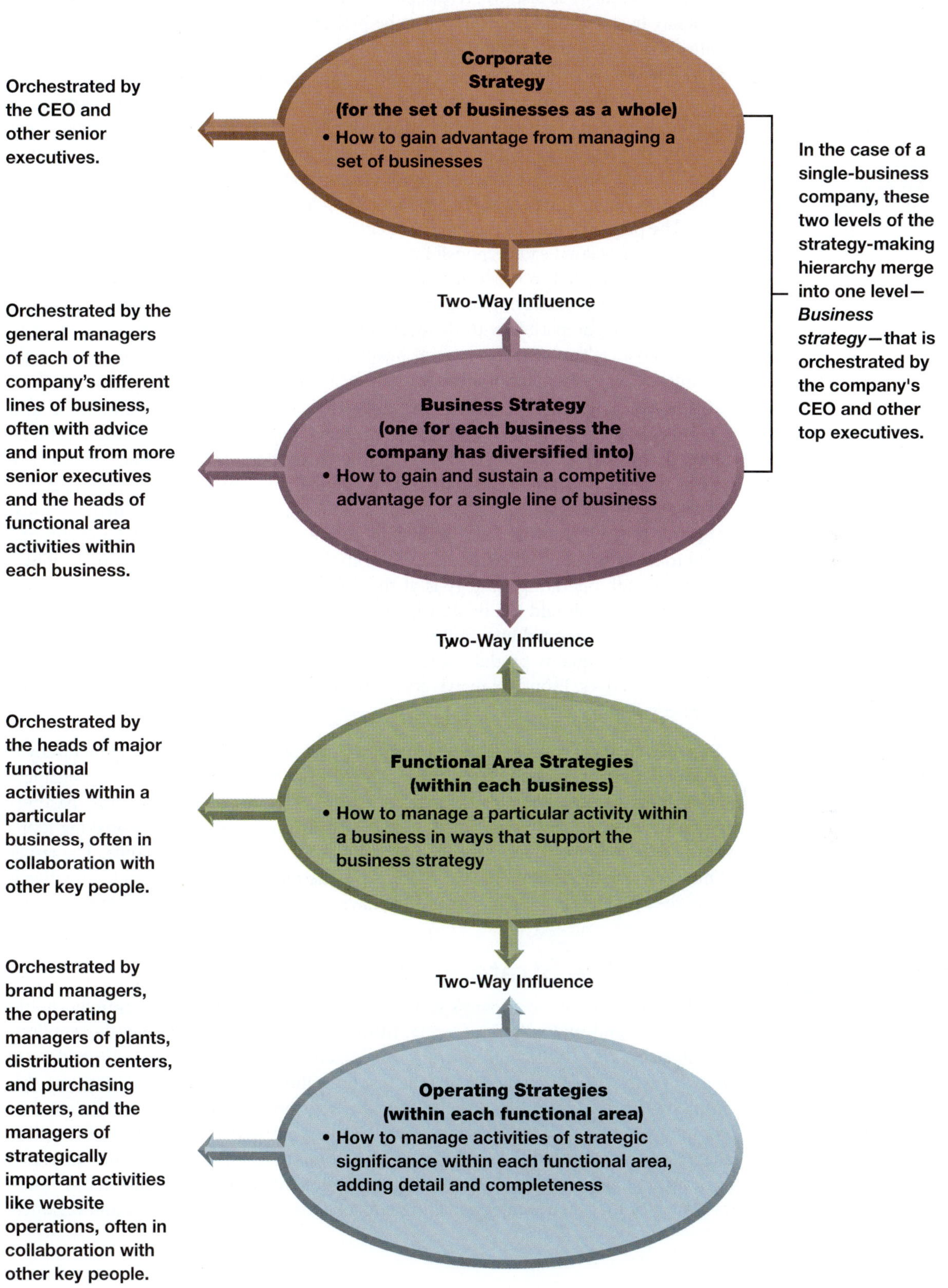

**Business strategy** is concerned with building competitive advantage in a single business unit of a diversified company or in a non-diversified single business company. Business strategy is also the responsibility of the CEO and other senior executives, but key business-unit heads may also be influential, especially in strategic decisions affecting the businesses they head.

**Functional-area strategies** concern the actions and approaches employed in managing particular functions within a business—like R&D, production, sales and marketing, customer service, and finance. A company's marketing strategy, for example, represents the managerial game plan for running the sales and marketing part of the business. A company's product development strategy represents the game plan for keeping the company's product lineup in tune with what buyers are looking for. The primary role of functional strategies is to flesh out the details of a company's business strategy. Lead responsibility for functional strategies within a business is normally delegated to the heads of the respective functions, with the general manager of the business having final approval. Since the different functional-level strategies must be compatible with the overall business strategy and with one another to have beneficial impact, the general business manager may at times exert stronger influence on the content of the functional strategies.

**Operating strategies** concern the relatively narrow strategic initiatives and approaches for managing key operating units (e.g., plants, distribution centers, purchasing centers) and specific operating activities with strategic significance (e.g., quality control, materials purchasing, brand management, Internet sales). A distribution center manager of a company promising customers speedy delivery must have a strategy to ensure that finished goods are rapidly turned around and shipped out to customers once they are received from the company's manufacturing facilities. Even though operating strategy is at the bottom of the strategy-making hierarchy, its importance should not be downplayed. A major plant that fails in its strategy to achieve production volume, unit cost, and quality targets can damage the company's reputation for quality products and undercut the achievement of company sales and profit objectives. Frontline managers are thus an important part of an organization's strategy-making team.

In single business companies, the uppermost level of the strategy-making hierarchy is the business strategy, so a single-business company has three levels of strategy: business strategy, functional-area strategies, and operating strategies. Proprietorships, partnerships, and owner-managed enterprises may have only one or two strategy-making levels since their strategy-making process can be handled by just a few key people. The larger and more diverse the operations of an enterprise, the more points of strategic initiative it has and the more levels of management that have a significant strategy-making role.

## Uniting the Strategy-Making Hierarchy

Ideally, the pieces of a company's strategy up and down the strategy hierarchy should be cohesive and mutually reinforcing, fitting together like a jigsaw puzzle. *Anything less than a unified collection of strategies weakens the overall strategy and is likely to impair company performance.*[11] It is the responsibility of top executives to achieve this unity by clearly communicating the company's vision, objectives, and major strategy components to down-the-line managers and key personnel. Midlevel and frontline managers cannot craft unified strategic moves without first understanding the company's long-term direction and knowing the major components of the corporate and/or business strategies that their strategy-making efforts are supposed to support and enhance.

Thus, as a general rule, strategy-making must start at the top of the organization and then proceed downward from the corporate level to the business level and then from the business level to the associated functional and operating levels.

Furthermore, once strategies up and down the hierarchy have been created, lower-level strategies must be scrutinized for consistency and support of higher-level strategies. Any strategy conflicts must be addressed and resolved, either by modifying the lower-level strategies with conflicting elements or by adapting the higher-level strategy to accommodate what may be more appealing strategy ideas and initiatives bubbling up from below.

## A Strategic Vision + Objectives + Strategy = A Strategic Plan

Developing a strategic vision and mission, setting objectives, and crafting a strategy are basic direction-setting tasks. They map out where a company is headed, its purpose, the targeted strategic and financial outcomes, the basic business model, and the competitive moves and internal action approaches to be used in achieving the desired business results. Together, they constitute a **strategic plan** for coping with industry conditions, outcompeting rivals, meeting objectives, and making progress toward the strategic vision.[12] Typically, a strategic plan includes a commitment to allocate resources to the plan and specifies a time period for achieving goals (usually three to five years).

In companies that do regular strategy reviews and develop explicit strategic plans, the strategic plan usually ends up as a written document that is circulated to most managers and perhaps selected employees. A number of companies summarize key elements of their strategic plans in the company's annual report to shareholders, in postings on their websites, or in statements provided to the business media, whereas others, perhaps for reasons of competitive sensitivity, make only vague, general statements about their strategic plans.[13] In small, privately owned companies, it is rare for strategic plans to exist in written form. Small-company strategic plans tend to reside in the thinking and directives of owners/executives, with aspects of the plan being revealed in conversations with company personnel about where to head, what to accomplish, and how to proceed.

# TASK 4: EXECUTING THE STRATEGY

Managing the implementation of a strategy is easily the most demanding and time-consuming part of the strategy management process. Converting strategic plans into actions and results tests a manager's ability to direct organizational action, motivate people, build and strengthen competitive capabilities, create and nurture a strategy-supportive work climate, and meet or beat performance targets. Initiatives to put the strategy in place and execute it proficiently have to be launched and managed on many organizational fronts.

Management's action agenda for executing the chosen strategy emerges from assessing what the company will have to do to achieve the targeted financial and strategic performance. Each company manager has to think through the answer to "What has to be done in my area to execute my piece of the strategic plan, and what actions should I take to get the process under way?" How much internal change is needed depends on how much of the strategy is new, how far internal practices and competencies deviate from what the strategy requires, and how well the present work culture supports good strategy execution. Depending on the amount of internal change involved, full implementation and proficient execution of the company strategy (or important new pieces thereof) can take several months to several years.

In most situations, managing the strategy execution process includes the following principal aspects:

- Staffing the organization to obtain needed skills and expertise.
- Developing and strengthening strategy-supporting resources and capabilities.
- Creating a strategy-supporting structure.
- Allocating ample resources to the activities critical to strategic success.
- Ensuring that policies and procedures facilitate effective strategy execution.
- Organizing the work effort along the lines of best practice.
- Installing information and operating systems that enable company personnel to perform essential activities.
- Motivating people and tying rewards directly to the achievement of performance objectives.
- Creating a company culture and work climate conducive to successful strategy execution.
- Exerting the internal leadership needed to propel implementation forward.

Good strategy execution requires diligent pursuit of operating excellence. It is a job for a company's whole management team. Success hinges on the skills and cooperation of operating managers who can push for needed changes in their organizational units and consistently deliver good results. Management's handling of the strategy implementation process can be considered successful if things go smoothly enough that the company meets or beats its strategic and financial performance targets and shows good progress in achieving management's strategic vision.

# TASK 5: EVALUATING PERFORMANCE AND INITIATING CORRECTIVE ADJUSTMENTS

The fifth component of the strategy management process—monitoring new external developments, evaluating the company's progress, and making corrective adjustments—is the trigger point for deciding whether to continue or change the company's vision and mission, objectives, strategy, and/or strategy execution methods.[14] As long as the company's strategy continues to pass the three tests of a winning strategy discussed in Chapter 1 (good fit, competitive advantage, strong performance), company executives may well decide to stay the course. Simply fine-tuning the strategic plan and continuing with efforts to improve strategy execution are sufficient.

But whenever a company encounters disruptive changes in its environment, questions need to be raised about the appropriateness of its direction and strategy. If a company experiences a downturn in its market position or persistent shortfalls in performance, then company managers are obligated to ferret out the causes—Do they relate to poor strategy, poor strategy execution, or both?—and take timely corrective action. A company's direction, objectives, and strategy have to be revisited anytime external or internal conditions warrant.

Likewise, managers are obligated to assess which of the company's operating methods and approaches to strategy execution merit continuation and which need improvement. Proficient strategy execution is always the product of much organizational learning. It is achieved unevenly—coming quickly in some areas and proving nettlesome in others. Consequently, top-notch strategy execution requires a company's

A company's vision and mission, as well as its objectives, strategy, and approach to strategy execution are never final; managing strategy is an ongoing process.

management team to scrutinize the entire strategy execution effort and proactively institute timely and effective adjustments that will move the company closer to operating excellence.

# CORPORATE GOVERNANCE: THE ROLE OF THE BOARD OF DIRECTORS IN THE STRATEGY-CRAFTING, STRATEGY-EXECUTING PROCESS

Although senior managers have the *lead responsibility* for crafting and executing a company's strategy, it is the duty of a company's board of directors to exercise strong oversight and see that the five tasks of strategic management are conducted in a manner that is in the best interests of shareholders and other stakeholders.[15] A company's board of directors has four important obligations to fulfill:

**LO 5**

Become aware of the role and responsibility of a company's board of directors in overseeing the strategic management process.

1.  *Oversee the company's financial accounting and financial reporting practices.* While top executives, particularly the company's CEO and CFO (chief financial officer), are primarily responsible for seeing that the company's financial statements fairly and accurately report the results of the company's operations, board members have a fiduciary duty to protect shareholders by exercising oversight of the company's financial practices. In addition, corporate boards must ensure that generally acceptable accounting principles (GAAP) are properly used in preparing the company's financial statements and determine whether proper financial controls are in place to prevent fraud and misuse of funds. Virtually all boards of directors monitor the financial reporting activities by appointing an audit committee, always composed entirely of *outside directors* (*inside directors* hold management positions in the company and either directly or indirectly report to the CEO). The members of the audit committee have the lead responsibility for overseeing the decisions of the company's financial officers and consulting with both internal and external auditors to ensure that financial reports are accurate and that adequate financial controls are in place. Faulty oversight of corporate accounting and financial reporting practices by audit committees and corporate boards during the early 2000s resulted in the federal investigation of more than 20 major corporations between 2000 and 2002. The investigations of such well-known companies as AOL Time Warner, Enron, Qwest Communications, and WorldCom found that upper management had employed fraudulent or unsound accounting practices to artificially inflate revenues, overstate assets, and reduce expenses. The scandals resulted in the conviction of a number of corporate executives and the passage of the Sarbanes–Oxley Act of 2002, which tightened financial reporting standards and created additional compliance requirements for public boards.

2.  *Critically appraise the company's direction, strategy, and business approaches.* Even though board members have a legal obligation to warrant the accuracy of the company's financial reports, directors must set aside time to guide management in choosing a strategic direction and to make independent judgments about the validity and wisdom of management's proposed strategic actions. This aspect of their duties takes on heightened importance when the company's strategy is failing or is plagued with faulty execution, and certainly when there is a precipitous collapse in profitability. But under more normal circumstances, many boards have found that meeting agendas become consumed by compliance matters with little time left to discuss matters of strategic importance. The board of directors and management at Philips Electronics

hold annual two- to three-day retreats devoted exclusively to evaluating the company's long-term direction and various strategic proposals. The company's exit from the semiconductor business and its increased focus on medical technology and home health care resulted from management-board discussions during such retreats.[16]

3. *Evaluate the caliber of senior executives' strategic leadership skills.* The board is always responsible for determining whether the current CEO is doing a good job of strategic leadership.[17] The board must also evaluate the leadership skills of other senior executives, since the board must elect a successor when the incumbent CEO steps down, either going with an insider or deciding that an outsider is needed. Evaluation of senior executives' skills is enhanced when outside directors visit company facilities and talk with company personnel personally to evaluate whether the strategy is on track, how well the strategy is being executed, and how well issues and problems are being addressed. Independent board members at GE visit operating executives at each major business unit once a year to assess the company's talent pool and stay abreast of emerging strategic and operating issues affecting the company's divisions.

4. *Institute a compensation plan for top executives that rewards them for actions and results that serve shareholder interests.* A basic principle of corporate governance is that the owners of a corporation (the shareholders) delegate operating authority and managerial control to top management in return for compensation. In their role as an *agent* of shareholders, top executives have a clear and unequivocal duty to make decisions and operate the company in accord with shareholder interests. (This does not mean disregarding the interests of other stakeholders—employees, suppliers, the communities in which the company operates, and society at large.) Most boards of directors have a compensation committee, composed entirely of directors from *outside* the company, to develop a salary and incentive compensation plan that rewards senior executives for boosting the company's *long-term* performance on behalf of shareholders. The compensation committee's recommendations are presented to the full board for approval. But during the past 10 to 15 years, many boards of directors have done a poor job of ensuring that executive salary increases, bonuses, and stock option awards are tied tightly to performance measures that are truly in the long-term interests of shareholders. Rather, compensation packages at many companies have increasingly rewarded executives for short-term performance improvements—most notably, achieving quarterly and annual earnings targets and boosting the stock price by specified percentages. This has had the perverse effect of causing company managers to become preoccupied with actions to improve a company's near-term performance, often motivating them to take unwise business risks to boost short-term earnings by amounts sufficient to qualify for multimillion dollar compensation packages (that, in the view of many people, were obscenely large). The focus on short-term performance has proved damaging to long-term company performance and shareholder interests—witness the huge loss of shareholder wealth that occurred at many financial institutions in 2008–2009 because of executive risk taking in subprime loans, credit default swaps, and collateralized mortgage securities in 2006–2007. As a consequence, the need to overhaul and reform executive compensation has become a hot topic in both public circles and corporate boardrooms. Illustration Capsule 2.4 discusses how weak governance at the mortgage companies Fannie Mae and Freddie Mac allowed opportunistic senior managers to secure exorbitant bonuses while making decisions that imperiled the futures of the companies they managed.

Effective corporate governance requires the board of directors to oversee the company's strategic direction, evaluate its senior executives, handle executive compensation, and oversee financial reporting practices.

Every corporation should have a strong independent board of directors that (1) is well informed about the company's performance, (2) guides and judges the CEO and other top executives, (3) has the courage to curb management actions the board

# Corporate Governance Failures at Fannie Mae and Freddie Mac

Excessive executive compensation in the financial services industry ranks high among examples of failed corporate governance. Corporate governance at the government-sponsored mortgage giants Fannie Mae and Freddie Mac was particularly weak. The politically appointed boards at both enterprises failed to understand the risks of the subprime loan strategies being employed, did not adequately monitor the decisions of the CEO, did not exercise effective oversight of the accounting principles being employed (which led to inflated earnings), and approved executive compensation systems that allowed management to manipulate earnings to receive lucrative performance bonuses. The audit and compensation committees at Fannie Mae were particularly ineffective in protecting shareholder interests, with the audit committee allowing the company's financial officers to audit reports prepared under their direction and used to determine performance bonuses. Fannie Mae's audit committee also was aware of management's use of questionable accounting practices that reduced losses and recorded one-time gains to achieve financial targets linked to bonuses. In addition, the audit committee failed to investigate formal charges of accounting improprieties filed by a manager in the Office of the Controller.

Fannie Mae's compensation committee was equally ineffective. The committee allowed the company's CEO, Franklin Raines, to select the consultant employed to design the mortgage firm's executive compensation plan and agreed to a tiered bonus plan that would permit Raines and other senior managers to receive maximum bonuses without great difficulty. The compensation plan allowed Raines to earn performance-based bonuses of $52 million and a total compensation of $90 million between 1999 and 2004. Raines was forced to resign in December 2004 when the Office of Federal Housing Enterprise Oversight found that Fannie Mae executives had fraudulently inflated earnings to receive bonuses linked to financial performance. Securities and Exchange Commission investigators also found evidence of improper accounting at Fannie Mae and required the company to restate its earnings between 2002 and 2004 by $6.3 billion.

Poor governance at Freddie Mac allowed its CEO and senior management to manipulate financial data

to receive performance-based compensation as well. Freddie Mac CEO Richard Syron received 2007 compensation of $19.8 million while the mortgage company's share price declined from a high of $70 in 2005 to $25 at year-end 2007. During Syron's tenure as CEO, the company became embroiled in a multibillion-dollar accounting scandal, and Syron personally disregarded internal reports dating to 2004 that cautioned of an impending financial crisis at the company. Forewarnings within Freddie Mac and by federal regulators and outside industry observers proved to be correct, with loan underwriting policies at Freddie Mac and Fannie Mae leading to combined losses at the two firms in 2008 of more than $100 billion. The price of Freddie Mac's shares had fallen to below $1 by the time of Syron's resignation in September 2008.

*(continued)*

Both organizations were placed into a conservatorship under the direction of the U.S. government in September 2008 and were provided bailout funds of more than $150 billion by early 2011. The U.S. Federal Housing Finance Agency estimated that the bailout of Fannie Mae and Freddie Mac would potentially reach $200 billion to $300 billion by 2013.

*Sources:* Chris Isidore, "Fannie, Freddie Bailout: $153 Billion. . .and Counting," CNNMoney, February 11, 2011; "Adding Up the Government's Total Bailout Tab," *New York Times Online,* February 4, 2009; Eric Dash, "Fannie Mae to Restate Results by $6.3 Billion because of Accounting," *New York Times Online,* www.nytimes.com, December 7, 2006; Annys Shin, "Fannie Mae Sets Executive Salaries," *Washington Post,* February 9, 2006, p. D4; and Scott DeCarlo, Eric Weiss, Mark Jickling, and James R. Cristie, *Fannie Mae and Freddie Mac: Scandal in U.S. Housing* (Nova Publishers, 2006), pp. 266–286.

believes are inappropriate or unduly risky, (4) certifies to shareholders that the CEO is doing what the board expects, (5) provides insight and advice to management, and (6) is intensely involved in debating the pros and cons of key decisions and actions.[18] Boards of directors that lack the backbone to challenge a strong-willed or "imperial" CEO or that rubber-stamp almost anything the CEO recommends without probing inquiry and debate (perhaps because the board is stacked with the CEO's cronies) abdicate their duty to represent and protect shareholder interests.

## KEY POINTS

The strategic management process consists of five interrelated and integrated tasks:

1. *Developing a strategic vision* of the company's future, a *mission statement* that defines the company's current purpose, and a set of *core values* to guide the pursuit of the vision and mission. This managerial task provides direction for the company, motivates and inspires company personnel, aligns and guides actions throughout the organization, and communicates to stakeholders management's aspirations for the company's future.

2. *Setting objectives* to convert the vision and mission into performance targets and using the targeted results as yardsticks for measuring the company's performance. Objectives need to spell out *how much* of *what kind* of performance *by when.* Two broad types of objectives are required: *financial objectives* and *strategic objectives.* A *balanced-scorecard* approach for measuring company performance entails setting both *financial objectives and strategic objectives.*

3. *Crafting a strategy* to achieve the objectives and move the company along the strategic course that management has charted. Masterful strategies come from doing things differently from competitors where it counts—out-innovating them, being more efficient, being more imaginative, adapting faster—rather than running with the herd. In large diversified companies, the strategy-making hierarchy consists of four levels, each of which involves a corresponding level of management: corporate strategy (multibusiness strategy), business strategy (strategy for individual businesses that compete in a single industry), functional-area strategies within each business (e.g., marketing, R&D, logistics), and operating strategies (for key operating units, such as manufacturing plants). Thus, strategy making is an inclusive collaborative activity involving not only senior company executives but also the heads of major business divisions, functional-area managers, and operating managers on the frontlines. The larger and more diverse the operations of an enterprise, the more points of strategic initiative it has and the more levels of management that play a significant strategy-making role.

4. *Executing the chosen strategy* and converting the strategic plan into action. Managing the execution of strategy is an operations-oriented, make-things-happen activity aimed at shaping the performance of core business activities in a strategy-supportive manner. Management's handling of the strategy implementation process can be considered successful if things go smoothly enough that the company meets or beats its strategic and financial performance targets and shows good progress in achieving management's strategic vision.

5. *Monitoring developments, evaluating performance, and initiating corrective adjustments* in light of actual experience, changing conditions, new ideas, and new opportunities. This task of the strategy management process is the trigger point for deciding whether to continue or change the company's vision and mission, objectives, strategy, and/or strategy execution methods.

The sum of a company's strategic vision and mission, objectives, and strategy constitutes a *strategic plan* for coping with industry conditions, outcompeting rivals, meeting objectives, and making progress toward the strategic vision. *Stretch objectives* spur exceptional performance and help build a firewall against contentment with modest gains in organizational performance. A company exhibits *strategic intent* when it relentlessly pursues an ambitious strategic objective, concentrating the full force of its resources and competitive actions on achieving that objective.

Boards of directors have a duty to shareholders to play a vigilant role in overseeing management's handling of a company's strategy-making, strategy-executing process. This entails four important obligations: (1) Ensure that the company issues accurate financial reports and has adequate financial controls, (2) critically appraise the company's direction, strategy, and strategy execution, (3) evaluate the caliber of senior executives' strategic leadership skills, and (4) institute a compensation plan for top executives that rewards them for actions and results that serve stakeholder interests—*especially those of shareholders.*

## ASSURANCE OF LEARNING EXERCISES

1. Using the information in Table 2.1, critique the adequacy and merit of the following vision statements, listing effective elements and shortcomings. Rank the vision statements from best to worst once you complete your evaluation.

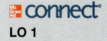
**LO 1**

| Vision Statement | Effective Elements | Shortcomings |
|---|---|---|
| **Amazon** <br> Our vision is to be earth's most customer centric company; to build a place where people can come to find and discover anything they might want to buy online. | | |
| **BASF** <br> We are "The Chemical Company" successfully operating in all major markets. <br> • Our customers view BASF as their partner of choice. <br> • Our innovative products, intelligent solutions and services make us the most competent worldwide supplier in the chemical industry. <br> • We generate a high return on assets. <br> • We strive for sustainable development. <br> • We welcome change as an opportunity. <br> • We, the employees of BASF, together ensure our success. | | |

*(continued)*

| Vision Statement | Effective Elements | Shortcomings |
|---|---|---|
| **MasterCard**<br>• A world beyond cash | | |
| **Hilton Hotels Corporation**<br>Our vision is to be the first choice of the world's travelers. Hilton intends to build on the rich heritage and strength of our brands by:<br>• Consistently delighting our customers<br>• Investing in our team members<br>• Delivering innovative products and services<br>• Continuously improving performance<br>• Increasing shareholder value<br>• Creating a culture of pride<br>• Strengthening the loyalty of our constituents | | |

*Source:* Company websites and annual reports.

**LO 2**    2. Go to the company websites for Intel (**http://www.intc.com**); Home Depot (**http://corporate.homedepot.com/wps/portal**); and Avon (**www.avoncompany.com/**) to find some examples of strategic and financial objectives. Make a list of four objectives for each company, and indicate which of these are strategic and which are financial.

**LO 3**    3. The primary strategic initiatives of Ford Motor Company's restructuring plan executed between 2005 and 2010 involved accelerating the development of new cars that customers would value, improving its balance sheet, working with its union employees to improve manufacturing competitiveness, reducing product engineering costs, reducing production capacity by approximately 40 percent, and reducing hourly headcount by 40–50 percent. At the conclusion of the restructuring plan in 2010, Ford was ranked first among U.S. automobile manufacturers by J.D. Power in initial quality and had earned more than $5.4 billion in pre-tax profit on net revenues of $64.4 billion. Explain why its strategic initiatives taken at various organizational levels and functions were necessarily tightly coordinated to achieve its commendable results.

**LO 4**    4. Go to the investor relations website for Walmart (**http://investors.walmartstores.com**) and review past presentations it has made during various investor conferences by clicking on the Events option in the navigation bar. Prepare a one- to two-page report that outlines what Walmart has said to investors about its approach to strategy execution. Specifically, what has management discussed concerning staffing, resource allocation, policies and procedures, information and operating systems, continuous improvement, rewards and incentives, corporate culture, and internal leadership at the company?

   5. Go to **www.dell.com/leadership**, and read the sections dedicated to Dell's board of directors and corporate governance. Is there evidence of effective governance at Dell in regard to (1) accurate financial reports and controls, (2) a critical appraisal of strategic action plans, (3) evaluation of the strategic leadership skills of the CEO, and (4) executive compensation?

**LO 5**    6. Based on the information provided in Illustration Capsule 2.4, explain how corporate governance at Freddie Mac failed the enterprise's shareholders and other stakeholders. Which important obligations to shareholders were fulfilled by Fannie Mae's board of directors? What is your assessment of how well Fannie Mae's compensation committee handled executive compensation at the government-sponsored mortgage giant?

## EXERCISE FOR SIMULATION PARTICIPANTS

1. Meet with your co-managers and prepare a strategic vision statement for your company. It should be at least one sentence long and no longer than a brief paragraph. When you are finished, check to see if your vision statement meets the conditions for an effectively worded strategic vision set forth in Table 2.1. If not, then revise it accordingly. What would be a good slogan that captures the essence of your strategic vision and that could be used to help communicate the vision to company personnel, shareholders, and other stakeholders?    **LO 1**

2. What are your company's financial objectives? What are your company's strategic objectives?    **LO 2**

3. What are the three to four key elements of your company's strategy?    **LO 3**

## ENDNOTES

[1] Gordon Shaw, Robert Brown, and Philip Bromiley, "Strategic Stories: How 3M Is Rewriting Business Planning," *Harvard Business Review* 76, no. 3 (May–June 1998); David J. Collins and Michael G. Rukstad, "Can You Say What Your Strategy Is?" *Harvard Business Review* 86, no. 4 (April 2008).

[2] Hugh Davidson, *The Committed Enterprise: How to Make Vision and Values Work* (Oxford: Butterworth Heinemann, 2002); W. Chan Kim and Renée Mauborgne, "Charting Your Company's Future," *Harvard Business Review* 80, no. 6 (June 2002), pp. 77–83; James C. Collins and Jerry I. Porras, "Building Your Company's Vision," *Harvard Business Review* 74, no. 5 (September–October 1996), pp. 65–77; Jim Collins and Jerry Porras, *Built to Last: Successful Habits of Visionary Companies* (New York: HarperCollins, 1994); Michel Robert, *Strategy Pure and Simple II: How Winning Companies Dominate Their Competitors* (New York: McGraw-Hill, 1998).

[3] Davidson, *The Committed Enterprise,* pp. 20 and 54.

[4] As quoted in Charles H. House and Raymond L. Price, "The Return Map: Tracking Product Teams," *Harvard Business Review* 60, no. 1 (January–February 1991), p. 93.

[5] Robert S. Kaplan and David P. Norton, *The Strategy-Focused Organization* (Boston: Harvard Business School Press, 2001); Robert S. Kaplan and David P. Norton, *The Balanced Scorecard: Translating Strategy into Action* (Boston: Harvard Business School Press, 1996).

[6] Kaplan and Norton; Kevin B. Hendricks, Larry Menor, and Christine Wiedman, "The Balanced Scorecard: To Adopt or Not to Adopt," *Ivey Business Journal* 69, no. 2 (November–December 2004), pp. 1–7; Sandy Richardson, "The Key Elements of Balanced Scorecard Success," *Ivey Business Journal* 69, no. 2 (November–December 2004), pp. 7–9.

[7] Kaplan and Norton, *The Balanced Scorecard.*

[8] Information posted on the website of Bain and Company, www.bain.com, accessed May 27, 2011.

[9] Information posted on the website of the Balanced Scorecard Institute, accessed May 27, 2011.

[10] Henry Mintzberg, Bruce Ahlstrand, and Joseph Lampel, *Strategy Safari: A Guided Tour through the Wilds of Strategic Management* (New York: Free Press, 1998); Bruce Barringer and Allen C. Bluedorn, "The Relationship between Corporate Entrepreneurship and Strategic Management," *Strategic Management Journal* 20 (1999), pp. 421–444; Jeffrey G. Covin and Morgan P. Miles, "Corporate Entrepreneurship and the Pursuit of Competitive Advantage," *Entrepreneurship: Theory and Practice* 23, no. 3 (Spring 1999), pp. 47–63; David A. Garvin and Lynned C. Levesque, "Meeting the Challenge of Corporate Entrepreneurship," *Harvard Business Review* 84, no. 10 (October 2006), pp. 102–112.

[11] Joseph L. Bower and Clark G. Gilbert, "How Managers' Everyday Decisions Create or Destroy Your Company's Strategy," *Harvard Business Review* 85, no. 2 (February 2007), pp. 72–79.

[12] Gordon Shaw, Robert Brown, and Philip Bromiley, "Strategic Stories: How 3M Is Rewriting Business Planning," *Harvard Business Review* 76, no. 3 (May–June 1998), pp. 41–50.

[13] David J. Collis and Michael G. Rukstad, "Can You Say What Your Strategy Is?" *Harvard Business Review* 86, no. 4 (April 2008), pp. 82–90.

[14] Cynthia A. Montgomery, "Putting Leadership Back into Strategy," *Harvard Business Review* 86, no. 1 (January 2008), pp. 54–60.

[15] Jay W. Lorsch and Robert C. Clark, "Leading from the Boardroom," *Harvard Business Review* 86, no. 4 (April 2008), pp. 105–111.

[16] Jay W. Lorsch and Robert C. Clark, "Leading from the Boardroom," *Harvard Business Review* 86, no. 4 (April 2008).

[17] Stephen P. Kaufman, "Evaluating the CEO," *Harvard Business Review* 86, no. 10 (October 2008), pp. 53–57.

[18] David A. Nadler, "Building Better Boards," *Harvard Business Review* 82, no. 5 (May 2004), pp. 102–105; Cynthia A. Montgomery and Rhonda Kaufman, "The Board's Missing Link," *Harvard Business Review* 81, no. 3 (March 2003), pp. 86–93; John Carver, "What Continues to Be Wrong with Corporate Governance and How to Fix It," *Ivey Business Journal* 68, no. 1 (September–October 2003), pp. 1–5. See also Gordon Donaldson, "A New Tool for Boards: The Strategic Audit," *Harvard Business Review* 73, no. 4 (July–August 1995), pp. 99–107.

# CHAPTER 3

# EVALUATING A COMPANY'S EXTERNAL ENVIRONMENT

## Learning Objectives

**LO 1** Become aware of factors in a company's broad macro-environment that may have strategic significance.

**LO 2** Gain command of the basic concepts and analytical tools widely used to diagnose the competitive conditions in a company's industry.

**LO 3** Become adept at mapping the market positions of key groups of industry rivals.

**LO 4** Learn how to use multiple frameworks to determine whether an industry's outlook presents a company with sufficiently attractive opportunities for growth and profitability.

Analysis is the critical starting point of strategic thinking.

Kenichi Ohmae – *Consultant and Author*

Things are always different—the art is figuring out which differences matter.

Laszlo Birinyi – *Investments Manager*

In essence, the job of a strategist is to understand and cope with competition.

Michael Porter – *Harvard Business School professor and Cofounder of Monitor Consulting*

The task of crafting strategy begins with an appraisal of the company's present situation. Two facets of a company's situation are especially pertinent: (1) the competitive conditions in the industry in which the company operates—its external environment; and (2) the company's resources and organizational capabilities—its internal environment.

Insightful diagnosis of a company's external and internal environments is a prerequisite for managers to succeed in crafting a strategy that is an excellent *fit* with the company's situation—the first test of a winning strategy. As depicted in Figure 3.1, strategic thinking begins with an appraisal of the company's external environment and internal environment (as a basis for deciding on a long-term direction and developing a strategic vision), then moves toward an evaluation of the most promising alternative strategies and business models, and culminates in choosing a specific strategy.

This chapter presents the concepts and analytical tools for zeroing in on those aspects of a company's external environment that should be considered in making strategic choices about

## FIGURE 3.1  From Thinking Strategically about the Company's Situation to Choosing a Strategy

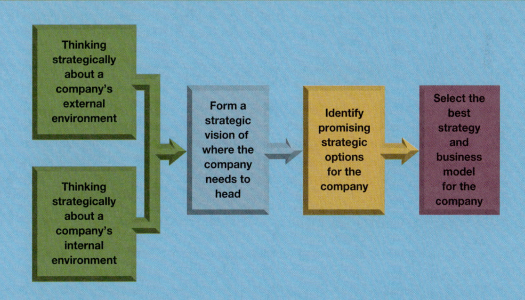

Thinking strategically about a company's external environment

Thinking strategically about a company's internal environment

Form a strategic vision of where the company needs to head

Identify promising strategic options for the company

Select the best strategy and business model for the company

where and how to compete. Attention centers on the broad environmental context, the narrower competitive arena in which a company operates, the drivers of market change, the market positions of rival companies, the moves and countermoves of rivals, and the factors that determine competitive success. In Chapter 4, we explore the methods of evaluating a company's internal circumstances and competitive capabilities. Here we begin with a set of questions that managers should address in analyzing and making strategic sense of their external situation.

# QUESTION 1: WHAT ARE THE STRATEGICALLY RELEVANT FACTORS IN THE MACRO-ENVIRONMENT?

**LO 1**

Become aware of factors in a company's broad macro-environment that may have strategic significance.

**CORE CONCEPT**

The **macro-environment** encompasses the broad environmental context in which a company's industry is situated.

**CORE CONCEPT**

**PESTEL analysis** focuses on the six principal components of strategic significance in the macro-environment: Political, Economic, Social, Technological, Environmental, and Legal forces.

Every company operates in a broad **"macro-environment"** that comprises six principal components: political factors, economic conditions in the firm's general environment (local, country, regional, worldwide), sociocultural forces, technological factors, environmental factors (concerning the natural environment), and legal/regulatory conditions. Each of these components has the potential to affect the firm's more immediate industry and competitive environment, although some are likely to have a more important effect than others (see Figure 3.2). An analysis of the impact of these factors is often referred to as **PESTEL analysis**, an acronym that serves as a reminder of the six components involved.

Since macroeconomic factors affect different industries in different ways and to different degrees, it is important for managers to determine which of these represent the most *strategically relevant factors* outside the firm's industry boundaries. By *strategically relevant,* we mean important enough to have a bearing on the decisions the company ultimately makes about its long-term direction, objectives, strategy, and business model. The impact of the outer-ring factors depicted in Figure 3.2 on a company's choice of strategy can range from big to small. But even if those factors change slowly or are likely to have a low impact on the company's business situation, they still merit a watchful eye.

For example, the strategic opportunities of cigarette producers to grow their businesses are greatly reduced by antismoking ordinances, the decisions of governments to impose higher cigarette taxes, and the growing cultural stigma attached to smoking. Motor vehicle companies must adapt their strategies to customer concerns about high gasoline prices and to environmental concerns about carbon emissions. Companies in the food processing, restaurant, sports, and fitness industries have to pay special attention to changes in lifestyles, eating habits, leisure-time preferences, and attitudes toward nutrition and fitness in fashioning their strategies. Table 3.1 provides a brief description of the components of the macro-environment and some examples of the industries or business situations that they might affect.

# FIGURE 3.2 The Components of a Company's Macro-Environment

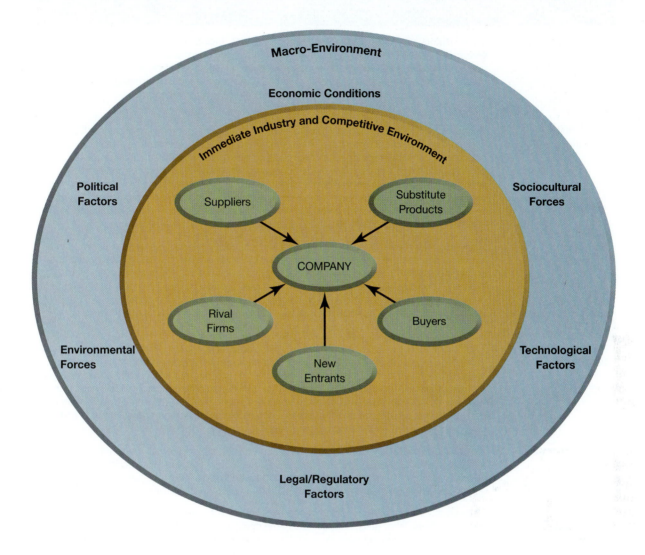

As company managers scan the external environment, they must be alert for potentially important outer-ring developments, assess their impact and influence, and adapt the company's direction and strategy as needed. However, the factors in a company's environment having the *biggest* strategy-shaping impact typically pertain to the company's immediate industry and competitive environment. Consequently, it is on a company's industry and competitive environment that we concentrate the bulk of our attention in this chapter.

**TABLE 3.1   The Six Components of the Macro-Environment**

| Component | Description |
| --- | --- |
| Political factors | These factors include political policies and processes, including the extent to which a government intervenes in the economy. They include such matters as tax policy, fiscal policy, tariffs, the political climate, and the strength of institutions such as the federal banking system. Some political factors, such as bailouts, are industry-specific. Others, such as energy policy, affect certain types of industries (energy producers and heavy users of energy) more than others. |
| Economic conditions | Economic conditions include the general economic climate and specific factors such as interest rates, exchange rates, the inflation rate, and the unemployment rate, the rate of economic growth, trade deficits or surpluses, savings rates, and per capita domestic product. Economic factors also include conditions in the markets for stocks and bonds, which can affect consumer confidence and discretionary income. Some industries, such as construction, are particularly vulnerable to economic downturns but are positively affected by factors such as low interest rates. Others, such as discount retailing, may benefit when general economic conditions weaken, as consumers become more price-conscious. |
| Sociocultural forces | Sociocultural forces include the societal values, attitudes, cultural factors, and lifestyles that impact businesses, as well as demographic factors such as the population size, growth rate and age distribution. Sociocultural forces vary by locale and change over time. An example is the trend toward healthier lifestyles, which can shift spending toward exercise equipment and health clubs and away from alcohol and snack foods. Population demographics can have large implications for industries such as health care, where costs and service needs vary with demographic factors such as age and income distribution. |
| Technological factors | Technological factors include the pace of technological change and technical developments that have the potential for wide-ranging effects on society, such as genetic engineering and nanotechnology. They include institutions involved in creating new knowledge and controlling the use of technology, such as R&D consortia, university-sponsored technology incubators, patent and copyright laws, and government control over the Internet. Technological change can encourage the birth of new industries, such as those based on nanotechnology, and disrupt others, such as the recording industry. |
| Environmental forces | This includes ecological and environmental forces such as weather, climate, climate change, and associated factors like water shortages. These factors can directly impact industries such as insurance, farming, energy production, and tourism. They may have an indirect but substantial effect on other industries such as transportation and utilities. |
| Legal and regulatory factors | These factors include the regulations and laws with which companies must comply such as consumer laws, labor laws, antitrust laws, and occupational health and safety regulation. Some factors, such as banking deregulation, are industry-specific. Others, such as minimum wage legislation, affect certain types of industries (low-wage, labor-intensive industries) more than others. |

# ASSESSING THE COMPANY'S INDUSTRY AND COMPETITIVE ENVIRONMENT

Thinking strategically about a company's industry and competitive environment entails using some well-validated concepts and analytical tools to get clear answers to six additional questions:

1. How strong are the industry's competitive forces?
2. What are the driving forces in the industry, and what impact will they have on competitive intensity and industry profitability?

3. What market positions do industry rivals occupy—who is strongly positioned and who is not?

4. What strategic moves are rivals likely to make next?

5. What are the industry's key success factors?

6. Is the industry outlook conducive to good profitability?

Analysis-based answers to these six questions provide managers with the understanding needed to craft a strategy that fits the company's external situation. The remainder of this chapter is devoted to describing the methods of obtaining solid answers to these questions and explaining how the nature of a company's industry and competitive environment weighs upon the strategic choices of company managers.

# QUESTION 2: HOW STRONG ARE THE INDUSTRY'S COMPETITIVE FORCES?

The character and strength of the competitive forces operating in an industry are never the same from one industry to another. Far and away the most powerful and widely used tool for diagnosing the principal competitive pressures in a market is the *five forces model of competition.*[1] This model, depicted in Figure 3.3, holds that competitive pressures on companies within an industry come from five sources. These include (1) competition from *rival sellers,* (2) competition from *potential new entrants* to the industry, (3) competition from producers of *substitute products,* (4) *supplier* bargaining power, and (5) *customer* bargaining power.

**LO 2**

Gain command of the basic concepts and analytical tools widely used to diagnose the competitive conditions in a company's industry.

In brief, using the five forces model to determine the nature and strength of competitive pressures in a given industry involves three steps:

- *Step 1:* For each of the five forces, identify the different parties involved, along with the specific factors that bring about competitive pressures.
- *Step 2:* Evaluate how strong the pressures stemming from each of the five forces are (strong, moderate, or weak).
- *Step 3:* Determine whether the strength of the five forces, overall, is conducive to earning attractive profits in the industry.

## Competitive Pressures Created by the Rivalry among Competing Sellers

The strongest of the five competitive forces is often the rivalry for buyer patronage among competing sellers of a product or service. The intensity of rivalry among competing sellers within an industry depends on a number of identifiable factors. Figure 3.4 summarizes these factors, identifying those that intensify or weaken rivalry among direct competitors in an industry. A brief explanation of why these factors affect the degree of rivalry is in order:

- *Rivalry increases when buyer demand is growing slowly or declining.* Rapidly expanding buyer demand produces enough new business for all industry members to grow without using volume-boosting sales tactics to draw customers away from rival enterprises. But in markets where buyer demand is growing only 1 to 2 percent or is shrinking, companies desperate to gain more business typically employ price discounts, sales promotions, and other tactics to boost their sales volumes, sometimes to the point of igniting a fierce battle for market share.

## FIGURE 3.3  The Five Forces Model of Competition: A Key Analytical Tool

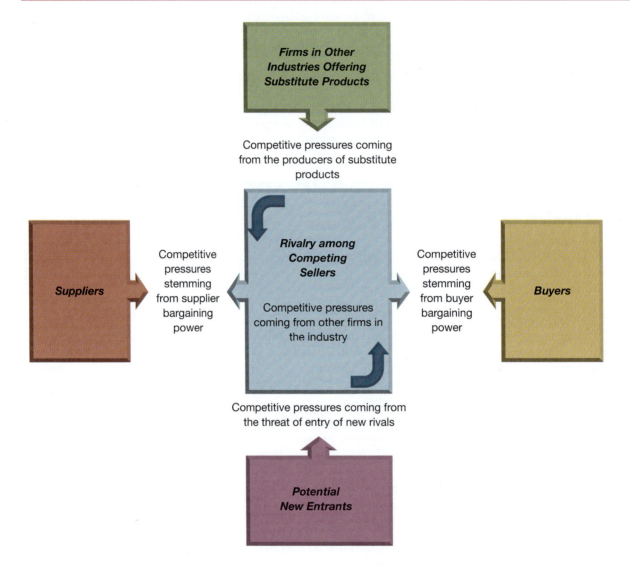

*Sources:* Adapted from Michael E. Porter, "How Competitive Forces Shape Strategy," *Harvard Business Review* 57, no. 2 (March–April 1979), pp. 137–145, and Michael E. Porter, "The Five Competitive Forces That Shape Strategy," *Harvard Business Review* 86, no. 1 (January 2008), pp. 80–86.

- *Rivalry increases as it becomes less costly for buyers to switch brands.* The less costly it is for buyers to switch their purchases from one seller to another, the easier it is for sellers to steal customers away from rivals. When the cost of switching brands is higher, buyers are less prone to brand switching. Switching costs include not only monetary costs but also the time, inconvenience, and psychological costs involved in switching brands. For example, distributors and retailers may not switch to the brands of rival manufacturers because they are hesitant to sever long-standing supplier relationships, incur any technical support costs or retraining expenses in making the switchover, or go to the trouble of testing the quality and reliability of the rival brand.

## FIGURE 3.4 Factors Affecting the Strength of Rivalry

**Substitutes**

*Suppliers*

*Buyers*

**Rivalry among Competing Sellers:**
**How strong are competitive pressures coming from industry rivals?**

*Rivalry is stronger when:*

- Buyer demand is growing slowly or delining
- Buyer costs to switch brands are low
- The products of industry members are commodities or else weakly differentiated
- The firms in the industry have high fixed costs or high storage costs
- Competitors are numerous or are of roughly equal size and competitive strength
- Rivals have diverse objectives, strategies, and/or countries of origin
- Rivals face high exit barriers

*Rivalry is weaker when:*

- Buyer demand is growing rapidly
- Buyer costs to switch brands are high
- The products of rival sellers are strongly differentiated and customer loyalty is high
- Fixed and storage costs are low
- Sales are concentrated among a few large sellers
- Rivals are similar in size, strength, objectives, strategy, and country of origin
- Exit barriers are low

**New Entrants**

- *Rivalry increases as the products of rival sellers become less strongly differentiated.* When the offerings of rivals are identical or weakly differentiated, buyers have less reason to be brand-loyal—a condition that makes it easier for rivals to convince buyers to switch to their offerings. Moreover, when the products of different sellers are virtually identical, shoppers will choose on the basis of price, which can result in fierce price competition among sellers. On the other hand, strongly differentiated product offerings among rivals breed high brand loyalty on the part of buyers—because many buyers view the attributes of certain brands as more appealing or better suited to their needs.

- *Rivalry is more intense when there is excess supply or unused production capacity, especially if the industry's product has high fixed costs or high storage costs.* Whenever a market has excess supply, rivalry intensifies as sellers cut prices in a desperate effort to cope with the unsold inventory. A similar effect occurs when a product is perishable or seasonal, since firms often engage in aggressive price cutting to ensure that everything is sold. Likewise, whenever fixed costs account for a large fraction of total cost so that unit costs are significantly lower at full capacity, firms come under significant pressure to cut prices whenever they are operating below full capacity. Unused capacity imposes a significant cost-increasing penalty because there are fewer units over which to spread fixed costs. The pressure of high fixed or high storage costs can push rival firms into price concessions, special discounts, rebates, and other volume-boosting competitive tactics.

- *Rivalry intensifies as the number of competitors increases and they become more equal in size and capability.* When there are many competitors in a market, companies eager to increase their meager market share often engage in price-cutting activities to drive sales, leading to intense rivalry. When there are only three or four competitors, companies are more wary of how their rivals may react to their attempts to take market share away from them. Fear of retaliation and a descent into a damaging price war leads to restrained competitive moves. Moreover, when rivals are of comparable size and competitive strength, they can usually compete on a fairly equal footing—an evenly matched contest tends to be fiercer than a contest in which one or more industry members have commanding market shares and substantially greater resources and capabilities than their much smaller rivals.

- *Rivalry becomes more intense as the diversity of competitors increases in terms of long-term directions, objectives, strategies, and countries of origin.* A diverse group of sellers often contains one or more mavericks willing to try novel or rule-breaking market approaches, thus generating a more volatile and less predictable competitive environment. Globally competitive markets are often more rivalrous, especially when aggressors have lower costs and are intent on gaining a strong foothold in new country markets.

- *Rivalry is stronger when high exit barriers keep unprofitable firms from leaving the industry.* In industries where the assets cannot easily be sold or transferred to other uses, where workers are entitled to job protection, or where owners are committed to remaining in business for personal reasons, failing firms tend to hold on longer than they might otherwise—even when they are bleeding red ink. This increases rivalry in two ways. Firms that are losing ground or in financial trouble often resort to deep price discounting that can trigger a price war and destabilize an otherwise attractive industry. In addition, high exit barriers result in an industry being more overcrowded than it would otherwise be, and this forces the weakest companies to engage in desperate maneuvers to win sufficient sales to stay in business.

Evaluating the strength of rivalry in an industry is a matter of determining whether the factors stated here, taken as a whole, indicate that the rivalry is relatively strong, moderate, or weak. When rivalry is *strong,* the battle for market share is generally so vigorous that the profit margins of most industry members are squeezed to bare-bones levels. When rivalry is *moderate,* a more normal state, the maneuvering among industry members, while lively and healthy, still allows most industry members to earn acceptable profits. When rivalry is *weak,* most companies in the industry are relatively well satisfied with their sales growth and market shares, rarely undertake offensives to steal customers away from one another, and—because of weak competitive forces—earn consistently good profits and returns on investment.

**The Choice of Competitive Weapons**   Competitive contests are ongoing and dynamic. Each competing company endeavors to deploy whatever means it believes will attract and retain buyers, strengthen its market position, and yield good profits. But when one firm makes a strategic move that produces good results, its rivals typically respond with offensive or defensive countermoves of their own. This pattern of action and reaction, move and countermove, produces a continually evolving competitive landscape where the market battle ebbs and flows and produces winners and losers.[2]

Competitive battles among rival sellers can assume many forms that extend well beyond lively price competition. For example, competitors may resort to such marketing tactics as special sales promotions, heavy advertising, rebates, or low-interest-rate financing to drum up additional sales. Rivals may race one another to differentiate their products by offering better performance features or higher quality or improved customer service or a wider product selection. They may also compete through the rapid introduction of next-generation products, the frequent introduction of new or improved products, and efforts to build stronger dealer networks, establish positions in foreign markets, or otherwise expand distribution capabilities and market presence. Table 3.2 provides a sampling of the types of competitive weapons available to rivals, along with their primary effects with respect to the price *(P)*, cost *(C)*, and value *(V)*—the elements of an effective business model, as discussed in Chapter 1.

## TABLE 3.2   Common "Weapons" for Competing with Rivals

| Types of Competitive Weapons | Primary Effects |
|---|---|
| Price discounting, clearance sales | Lowers price (*P*), acts to boost total sales volume and market share, lowers profit margins per unit sold when price cuts are big and/or increases in sales volume are relatively small |
| Couponing, advertising items on sale | Acts to increase unit sales volume and total revenues, lowers price (*P*), increases unit costs (*C*), may lower profit margins per unit sold (*P* − *C*) |
| Advertising product or service characteristics, using ads to enhance a company's image | Boosts buyer demand, increases product differentiation and perceived value (*V*), acts to increase total sales volume and market share, may increase unit costs (*C*) and/or lower profit margins per unit sold |
| Innovating to improve product performance and quality | Acts to increase product differentiation and value (*V*), boosts buyer demand, acts to boost total sales volume, likely to increase unit costs (*C*) |
| Introducing new or improved features, increasing the number of styles to provide greater product selection | Acts to increase product differentiation and value (*V*), strengthens buyer demand, acts to boost total sales volume and market share, likely to increase unit costs (*C*) |
| Increasing customization of product or service | Acts to increase product differentiation and value (*V*), increases switching costs, acts to boost total sales volume, often increases unit costs (*C*) |
| Building a bigger, better dealer network | Broadens access to buyers, acts to boost total sales volume and market share, may increase unit costs (*C*) |
| Improving warranties, offering low-interest financing | Acts to increase product differentiation and value (*V*), increases unit costs (*C*), increases buyer costs to switch brands, acts to boost total sales volume and market share |

# Competitive Pressures Associated with the Threat of New Entrants

New entrants to a market bring new production capacity, the desire to establish a secure place in the market, and sometimes substantial resources. Just how serious the competitive threat of entry is in a particular market depends on two classes of factors: the *expected reaction of incumbent firms to new entry* and what are known as *barriers to entry*.

Industry incumbents that are willing and able to launch strong defensive maneuvers to maintain their positions can make it hard for a new entrant to gain a sufficient market foothold to survive and eventually become profitable. Defensive maneuvers against potential entrants may include price discounts (especially to the very customer groups a newcomer is seeking to attract), ramped-up advertising, special sales promotions, new product features (to match or beat the newcomer's product offering), or additional customer services. Such defensive maneuvers on the part of incumbents raise an entrant's costs and risks and have to be considered likely if one or more incumbents have previously tried to strongly contest the entry of new firms into the marketplace.

A barrier to entry exists whenever it is hard for a newcomer to break into the market and/or the economics of the business put a potential entrant at a disadvantage. The most widely encountered barriers that entry candidates must hurdle include the following:[3]

- *Cost advantages enjoyed by industry incumbents.* Existing industry members frequently have costs that are hard for a newcomer to replicate. The cost advantages of industry incumbents can stem from (1) scale economies in production, distribution, advertising, or other activities, (2) the learning-based costs savings that accrue from experience in performing certain activities such as manufacturing or new product development or inventory management, (3) cost-savings accruing from patents or proprietary technology, (4) exclusive partnerships with the best and cheapest suppliers of raw materials and components, (5) favorable locations, and (6) low fixed costs (because they have older facilities that have been mostly depreciated). The bigger the cost advantages of industry incumbents, the riskier it becomes for outsiders to attempt entry (since they will have to accept thinner profit margins or even losses until the cost disadvantages can be overcome).

- *Strong brand preferences and high degrees of customer loyalty.* The stronger the attachment of buyers to established brands, the harder it is for a newcomer to break into the marketplace. In such cases, a new entrant must have the financial resources to spend enough on advertising and sales promotion to overcome customer loyalties and build its own clientele. Establishing brand recognition and building customer loyalty can be a slow and costly process. In addition, if it is difficult or costly for a customer to switch to a new brand, a new entrant may have to offer a discounted price or otherwise persuade buyers that its brand is worth the switching costs. Such barriers discourage new entry because they act to boost financial requirements and lower expected profit margins for new entrants.

- *Strong "network effects" in customer demand.* In industries where buyers are more attracted to a product when there are many other users of the product, there are said to be "network effects," since demand is higher the larger the network of users. Video game systems are an example, since users prefer to have the same systems as their friends so that they can play together on systems they all know and share games. When incumbents have a large existing base of users, new entrants with otherwise comparable products face a serious disadvantage in attracting buyers.

- *High capital requirements.* The larger the total dollar investment needed to enter the market successfully, the more limited the pool of potential entrants. The most obvious capital requirements for new entrants relate to manufacturing facilities and equipment, introductory advertising and sales promotion campaigns, working capital to finance inventories and customer credit, and sufficient cash to cover startup costs.

- *The difficulties of building a network of distributors or dealers and securing adequate space on retailers' shelves.* A potential entrant can face numerous distribution channel challenges. Wholesale distributors may be reluctant to take on a product that lacks buyer recognition. Retailers must be recruited and convinced to give a new brand ample display space and an adequate trial period. When existing sellers have strong, well-functioning distributor–dealer networks, a newcomer has an uphill struggle in squeezing its way into existing distribution channels. Potential entrants sometimes have to "buy" their way into wholesale or retail channels by cutting their prices to provide dealers and distributors with higher markups and profit margins or by giving them big advertising and promotional allowances. As a consequence, a potential entrant's own profits may be squeezed unless and until its product gains enough consumer acceptance that distributors and retailers are anxious to carry it.

- *Restrictive government policies.* Regulated industries like cable TV, telecommunications, electric and gas utilities, radio and television broadcasting, liquor retailing, and railroads entail government-controlled entry. Government agencies can also limit or even bar entry by requiring licenses and permits, such as the medallion required to drive a taxicab in New York City. Government-mandated safety regulations and environmental pollution standards also create entry barriers because they raise entry costs. In international markets, host governments commonly limit foreign entry and must approve all foreign investment applications. National governments commonly use tariffs and trade restrictions (antidumping rules, local content requirements, quotas, and so on) to raise entry barriers for foreign firms and protect domestic producers from outside competition.

Figure 3.5 summarizes the factors that cause the overall competitive threat from potential new entrants to be strong, moderate, or weak. An analysis of these factors can help managers determine whether the threat of entry into their industry is high or low, *in general.* But certain kinds of companies—those with sizable financial resources, proven competitive capabilities, and a respected brand name—may be able to hurdle an industry's entry barriers even when they are high.[4] For example, when Honda opted to enter the U.S. lawnmower market in competition against Toro, Snapper, Craftsman, John Deere, and others, it was easily able to hurdle entry barriers that would have been formidable to other newcomers because it had longstanding expertise in gasoline engines, and a reputation for quality and durability in automobiles that gave it instant credibility with homeowners. As a result, Honda had to spend relatively little on inducing dealers to handle the Honda lawnmower line or attracting customers. Companies already well-established in certain product categories or geographic areas often possess the resources, competencies, and competitive capabilities to hurdle the barriers of entering a different market segment or new geographic area. Thus, *the strongest competitive pressures associated with potential entry frequently come not from outsiders but from current industry participants looking for growth opportunities.*

It is also important to recognize that the threat of entry changes as the industry's prospects grow brighter or dimmer and as entry barriers rise or fall. For example, in the pharmaceutical industry the expiration of a key patent on a widely prescribed drug virtually guarantees that one or more drug makers will enter with generic offerings of their own. Use of the Internet for shopping has made it much easier for e-tailers to enter into competition against some of the best-known retail chains. Moreover, new strategic actions by incumbent firms to increase advertising, strengthen distributor–dealer relations, step up R&D, or improve product quality can erect higher roadblocks to entry.

Whether an industry's entry barriers ought to be considered high or low depends on the resources and capabilities possessed by the pool of potential entrants.

High entry barriers and weak entry threats today do not always translate into high entry barriers and weak entry threats tomorrow.

**FIGURE 3.5** Factors Affecting the Threat of Entry

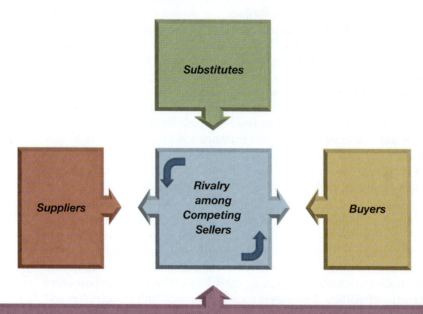

**Potential New Entrants**

**How strong are the competitive pressures coming from the threat of entry of new rivals?**

*Entry threats are stronger when:*
- Entry barriers are low
- Industry members are unwilling or unable to strongly contest the entry of newcomers
- There is a large pool of potential entrants, some of which have the capabilities to overcome high entry barriers
- Existing industry members are looking to expand their market reach by entering product segments or geographic areas where they do not have a presence
- Buyer demand is growing rapidly and newcomers can expect to earn attractive profits without inviting a strong reaction from incumbents

*Entry threats are weaker when:*
- Entry barriers are high since incumbents enjoy:
  - Cost advantages due to economies of scale, experience, low fixed cost, or access to lower cost inputs, technology, or location
  - Strong product differentiation and brand loyalty
  - Strong network effects
  - High capital requirements
  - Preferential access to distribution channels
  - Restrictive government policies
- Industry members are willing and able to contest new entry
- Industry outlook is risky and uncertain, discouraging entry

# Competitive Pressures from the Sellers of Substitute Products

Companies in one industry are vulnerable to competitive pressure from the actions of companies in a closely adjoining industry whenever buyers view the products of the two industries as good substitutes. For instance, the producers of sugar experience competitive pressures from the sales and marketing efforts of the makers of Equal, Splenda, and Sweet'N Low. Newspapers are struggling to maintain their relevance to subscribers who

**FIGURE 3.6** Factors Affecting Competition from Substitute Products

*Firms in Other Industries Offering Substitute Products*

*How strong are competitive pressures coming from substitute products from outside the industry?*

*Competitive pressures from substitutes are stronger when:*

- Good substitutes are readily available and attractively priced.
- Substitutes have comparable or better performance features.
- Buyers have low costs in switching to substitutes.

*Competitive pressures from substitutes are weaker when:*

- Good substitutes are not readily available or attractively priced.
- Substitutes' performance features are not comparable or better.
- Buyers have high costs in switching to substitutes.

**Signs that Competition from Substitutes Is Strong**

- Sales of substitutes are growing faster than sales of the industry being analyzed.
- Producers of substitutes are moving to add new capacity.
- Profits of the producers of substitutes are on the rise.

*Suppliers*

*Rivalry among Competing Sellers*

*Buyers*

*New Entrants*

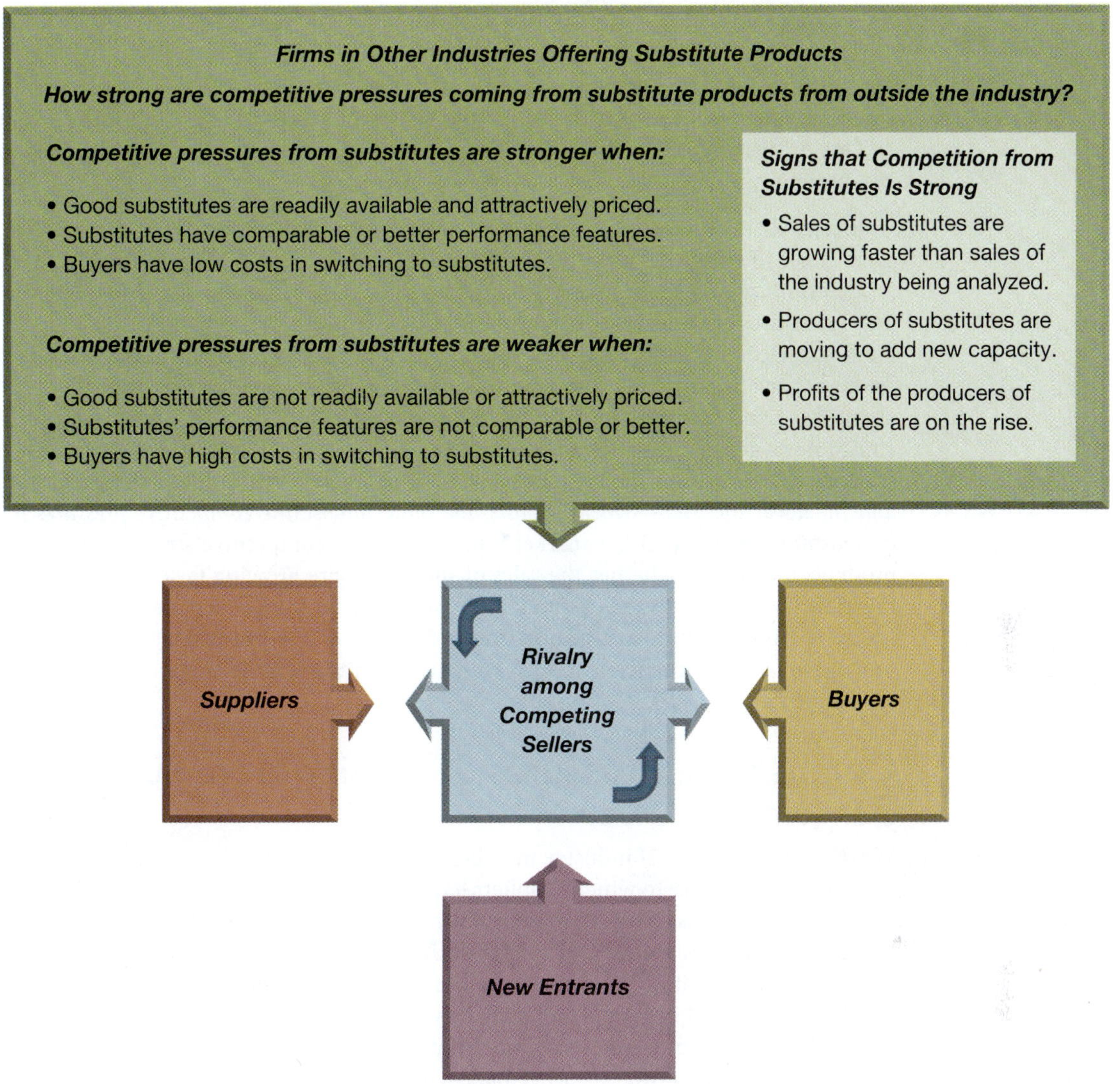

can watch the news on any of numerous TV channels and use Internet sources to get information about sports results, stock quotes, and job opportunities. Similarly, the producers of eyeglasses and contact lenses face competitive pressures from doctors who do corrective laser surgery.

As depicted in Figure 3.6, whether the competitive pressures from substitute products are strong, moderate, or weak depends on three factors:

1. *Whether substitutes are readily available and attractively priced.* The presence of readily available and attractively priced substitutes creates competitive pressure by placing a ceiling on the prices industry members can charge. This price ceiling, at the same time, puts a lid on the profits that industry members can earn unless they find ways to cut costs.

2. *Whether buyers view the substitutes as being comparable or better in terms of quality, performance, and other relevant attributes.* The availability of substitutes inevitably invites customers to compare performance, features, ease of use, and other attributes as well as price. The users of paper cartons constantly weigh the price/performance trade-offs with plastic containers and metal cans, for example.

3. *Whether the costs that buyers incur in switching to the substitutes are low or high.* Low switching costs make it easier for the sellers of attractive substitutes to lure buyers to their offerings; high switching costs deter buyers from purchasing substitute products.

Before assessing the competitive pressures coming from substitutes, company managers must identify the substitutes, which is less easy than it sounds since it involves (1) determining where the industry boundaries lie and (2) figuring out which other products or services can address the same basic customer needs as those produced by industry members. Deciding on the industry boundaries is necessary for determining which firms are direct rivals and which produce substitutes. This is a matter of perspective—there are no hard-and-fast rules, other than to say that other brands of the same basic product constitute rival products and not substitutes.

As a rule, *the lower the price of substitutes, the higher their quality and performance; and the lower the user's switching costs, the more intense the competitive pressures posed by substitute products.* Other market indicators of the competitive strength of substitute products include (1) whether the sales of substitutes are growing faster than the sales of the industry being analyzed (a sign that the sellers of substitutes may be drawing customers away from the industry in question), (2) whether the producers of substitutes are moving to add new capacity, and (3) whether the profits of the producers of substitutes are on the rise.

## Competitive Pressures Stemming from Supplier Bargaining Power

Whether the suppliers of industry members represent a weak or strong competitive force depends on the degree to which suppliers have sufficient *bargaining power* to influence the terms and conditions of supply in their favor. Suppliers with strong bargaining power can erode industry profitability by charging industry members higher prices, passing costs on to them, and limiting their opportunities to find better deals. For instance, Microsoft and Intel, both of whom supply PC makers with essential components, have been known to use their dominant market status not only to charge PC makers premium prices but also to leverage their power over PC makers in other ways. The bargaining power of these two companies over their customers is so great that both companies have faced antitrust charges on numerous occasions. Prior to a legal agreement ending the practice, Microsoft pressured PC makers to load only Microsoft products on the PCs they shipped. Intel has defended itself against similar antitrust charges, but continues to give PC makers who use the biggest percentages of Intel chips in their PC models top priority in filling orders for newly introduced Intel chips. Being on Intel's list of preferred customers helps a PC maker get an early allocation of Intel's latest chips and thus allows a PC maker to get new models to market ahead of rivals.

Small-scale retailers often must contend with the power of manufacturers whose products enjoy well-known brand names, since consumers expect to find these products on the shelves of the retail stores where they shop. This provides the manufacturer with a degree of pricing power and often the ability to push hard for favorable shelf displays. Supplier bargaining power is also a competitive factor in industries where unions have been able to organize the workforce (which supplies labor). Air pilot unions, for example, have employed their bargaining power to increase pilots' wages and benefits in the air transport industry.

As shown in Figure 3.7, a variety of factors determines the strength of suppliers' bargaining power:

- *Whether demand for suppliers' products is high and they are in short supply.* Suppliers of items in short supply have pricing power, whereas a surge in the available supply of particular items shifts the bargaining power to the industry members.

## FIGURE 3.7 Factors Affecting the Bargaining Power of Suppliers

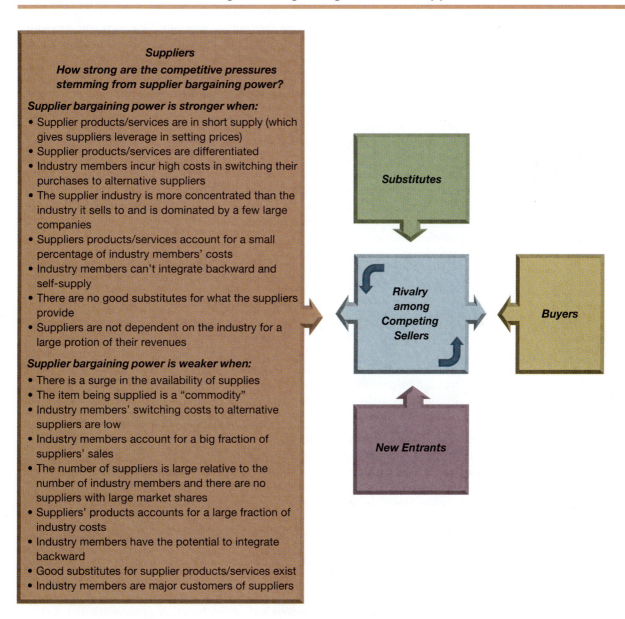

**Suppliers**
*How strong are the competitive pressures stemming from supplier bargaining power?*

*Supplier bargaining power is stronger when:*
- Supplier products/services are in short supply (which gives suppliers leverage in setting prices)
- Supplier products/services are differentiated
- Industry members incur high costs in switching their purchases to alternative suppliers
- The supplier industry is more concentrated than the industry it sells to and is dominated by a few large companies
- Suppliers products/services account for a small percentage of industry members' costs
- Industry members can't integrate backward and self-supply
- There are no good substitutes for what the suppliers provide
- Suppliers are not dependent on the industry for a large protion of their revenues

*Supplier bargaining power is weaker when:*
- There is a surge in the availability of supplies
- The item being supplied is a "commodity"
- Industry members' switching costs to alternative suppliers are low
- Industry members account for a big fraction of suppliers' sales
- The number of suppliers is large relative to the number of industry members and there are no suppliers with large market shares
- Suppliers' products accounts for a large fraction of industry costs
- Industry members have the potential to integrate backward
- Good substitutes for supplier products/services exist
- Industry members are major customers of suppliers

Substitutes

Rivalry among Competing Sellers

Buyers

New Entrants

- *Whether suppliers provide a differentiated input that enhances the performance of the industry's product.* The more valuable a particular input is in terms of enhancing the performance or quality of the products of industry members, the more bargaining leverage suppliers have. On the other hand, the suppliers of commodities are in a weak bargaining position, since industry members have no reason other than price to prefer one supplier over another.
- *Whether it is difficult or costly for industry members to switch their purchases from one supplier to another.* Low switching costs limit supplier bargaining power by enabling industry members to change suppliers if any one supplier attempts to raise prices by more than the costs of switching. Thus, the higher the switching costs of industry members, the stronger the bargaining power of their suppliers.
- *Whether the supplier industry is dominated by a few large companies and whether it is more concentrated than the industry it sells to.* Suppliers with sizable market shares and strong demand for the items they supply generally have sufficient bargaining power to charge high prices and deny requests from industry members for lower prices or other concessions.
- *Whether suppliers provide an item that accounts for a sizable fraction of the costs of the industry's product.* The bigger the cost of a particular part or component, the more industry members will be sensitive to the actions of suppliers to raise or lower their prices. As a result, they will bargain more aggressively.
- *Whether it makes good economic sense for industry members to integrate backward and self-manufacture items they have been buying from suppliers.* As a rule, suppliers are safe from the threat of self-manufacture by their customers until the volume of parts a customer needs becomes large enough for the customer to justify backward integration into self-manufacture of the component. When industry members can threaten credibly to self-manufacture suppliers' goods, their bargaining power over suppliers increases proportionately.
- *Whether there are good substitutes available for the suppliers' products.* The ready availability of substitute inputs lessens the bargaining power of suppliers by reducing the dependence of industry members on the suppliers. The better the price and performance characteristics of the substitute inputs, the weaker the bargaining power of suppliers.
- *Whether industry members are major customers of suppliers.* As a rule, suppliers have less bargaining leverage when their sales to members of the industry constitute a big percentage of their total sales. In such cases, the well-being of suppliers is closely tied to the well-being of their major customers. Suppliers have a big incentive to protect and enhance the competitiveness of their major customers via reasonable prices, exceptional quality, and ongoing advances in the technology of the items supplied.

In identifying the degree of supplier power in an industry, it is important to recognize that different types of suppliers are likely to have different amounts of bargaining power. Thus, the first step is for managers to identify the different types of suppliers, paying particular attention to those that provide the industry with important inputs. The next step is to assess the bargaining power of each type of supplier separately. Figure 3.7 summarizes the conditions that tend to make supplier bargaining power strong or weak.

## Competitive Pressures Stemming from Buyer Bargaining Power and Price Sensitivity

Whether buyers are able to exert strong competitive pressures on industry members depends on (1) the degree to which buyers have bargaining power and (2) the extent to which buyers are price-sensitive. Buyers with strong bargaining power can limit industry profitability by demanding price concessions, better payment terms, or additional features and services that increase industry members' costs. Buyer price sensitivity limits the profit potential of industry members by restricting the ability of sellers to raise prices without losing revenue.

The leverage that buyers have in negotiating favorable terms of the sale can range from weak to strong. Individual consumers, for example, rarely have much bargaining power in negotiating price concessions or other favorable terms with sellers. However, their price sensitivity varies by individual and by the type of product they are buying (whether it's a necessity or a discretionary purchase, for example). Business buyers, in contrast, can have considerable bargaining power. Retailers tend to have greater bargaining power over industry sellers if they have influence over the purchase decisions of the end user or if they are critical in providing sellers with access to the end user. For example, large retail chains like Walmart, Best Buy, Staples, and Home Depot typically have considerable negotiating leverage in purchasing products from manufacturers because of manufacturers' need for access to their broad base of customers. Major supermarket chains like Kroger, Safeway, Food Lion, and Publix have sufficient bargaining power to demand promotional allowances and lump-sum payments (called slotting fees) from food products manufacturers in return for stocking certain brands or putting them in the best shelf locations. Motor vehicle manufacturers have strong bargaining power in negotiating to buy original-equipment tires from tire makers not only because they buy in large quantities but also because consumers are more likely to buy replacement tires that match the tire brand on their vehicle at the time of purchase.

Figure 3.8 summarizes the factors determining the strength of buyer power in an industry. As described next, the first six factors are the mirror image of those determining the bargaining power of suppliers.

- *Buyer power increases when buyer demand is weak in relation to industry supply.* Weak or declining demand creates a "buyers' market," in which bargain-hunting buyers are able to press for better deals and special treatment; conversely, strong or rapidly growing demand creates a "sellers' market" and shifts bargaining power to sellers.
- *Buyer power increases when industry goods are standardized or differentiation is weak.* In such circumstances, buyers make their selections on the basis of price, which increases price competition among vendors.
- *Buyers' bargaining power is greater when their costs of switching to competing brands or substitutes are relatively low.* Switching costs put a cap on how much industry producers can raise prices or reduce quality before they will lose the buyer's business.
- *Buyers have more power when they are large and few in number relative to the number of sellers.* The larger the buyer, the more important their business is to the seller and the more sellers will be willing to grant concessions.
- *Buyers gain leverage if they are well informed about sellers' products, prices, and costs.* The more information buyers have, the better bargaining position they are in. The mushrooming availability of product information on the Internet is giving added bargaining power to consumers, since they can use this to find or negotiate for better deals.
- *Buyers' bargaining power is greater when they pose a credible threat of integrating backward into the business of sellers.* Companies like Anheuser-Busch, Coors, and Heinz have partially integrated backward into metal can manufacturing to gain bargaining power in obtaining the balance of their can requirements from otherwise powerful metal can manufacturers.

## FIGURE 3.8 Factors Affecting the Bargaining Power of Buyers

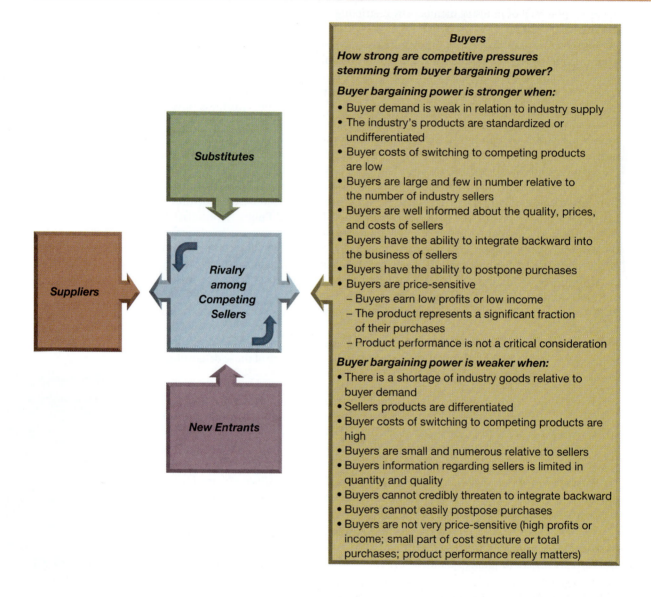

- *Buyer leverage increases if buyers have discretion to delay their purchases or perhaps even not make a purchase at all.* Consumers often have the option to delay purchases of durable goods, such as major appliances, or discretionary goods, such as hot tubs and home entertainment centers, if they are not happy with the prices offered. Business customers may also be able to defer their purchases of certain items, such as plant equipment or maintenance services. This puts pressure on sellers to provide concessions to buyers so that the sellers can keep their sales numbers from dropping off.
- *Buyer price sensitivity increases when buyers are earning low profits or have low income.* Price is a critical factor in the purchase decisions of low-income consumers and companies that are barely scraping by. In such cases, their high price sensitivity limits the ability of sellers to charge high prices.

- *Buyers are more price-sensitive if the product represents a large fraction of their total purchases.* When a purchase eats up a large portion of a buyer's budget or represents a significant part of his or her cost structure, the buyer cares more about price than might otherwise be the case.

The starting point for the analysis of buyers as a competitive force is to identify the different types of buyers along the value chain—then proceed to analyzing the bargaining power and price sensitivity of each type separately. It is important to recognize that *not all buyers of an industry's product have equal degrees of bargaining power with sellers,* and some may be less sensitive than others to price, quality, or service differences. For example, apparel manufacturers confront significant bargaining power when selling to big retailers like Target, Macy's, or L.L. Bean but they can command much better prices selling to small owner-managed apparel boutiques.

## Is the Collective Strength of the Five Competitive Forces Conducive to Good Profitability?

Assessing whether each of the five competitive forces gives rise to strong, moderate, or weak competitive pressures sets the stage for evaluating whether, overall, the strength of the five forces is conducive to good profitability. Are some of the competitive forces sufficiently powerful to undermine industry profitability? Can companies in this industry reasonably expect to earn decent profits in light of the prevailing competitive forces?

The most extreme case of a "competitively unattractive" industry occurs when all five forces are producing strong competitive pressures: Rivalry among sellers is vigorous, low entry barriers allow new rivals to gain a market foothold, competition from substitutes is intense, and both suppliers and buyers are able to exercise considerable leverage. Strong competitive pressures coming from all five directions drive industry profitability to unacceptably low levels, frequently producing losses for many industry members and forcing some out of business. But an industry can be competitively unattractive without all five competitive forces being strong. In fact, intense competitive pressures *from just one* of the five forces may suffice to destroy the conditions for good profitability and prompt some companies to exit the business.

As a rule, *the strongest competitive forces determine the extent of the competitive pressure on industry profitability.*[5] Thus, in evaluating the strength of the five forces overall and their effect on industry profitability, managers should look to the strongest forces. Having more than one strong force will not worsen the effect on industry profitability, but it does mean that the industry has multiple competitive challenges with which to cope. In that sense, an industry with three to five strong forces is even more "unattractive" as a place to compete. Especially intense competitive conditions seem to be the norm in tire manufacturing, apparel, and commercial airlines, three industries where profit margins have historically been thin.

> **CORE CONCEPT**
>
> The strongest of the five forces determines the extent of the downward pressure on an industry's profitability.

In contrast, when the overall impact of the five competitive forces is moderate to weak, an industry is "attractive" in the sense that the *average* industry member can reasonably expect to earn good profits and a nice return on investment. The ideal competitive environment for earning superior profits is one in which both suppliers and customers are in weak bargaining positions, there are no good substitutes, high barriers block further entry, and rivalry among present sellers is muted. Weak competition is the best of all possible worlds for also-ran companies because even they can usually eke out a decent profit—if a company can't make a decent profit when competition is weak, then its business outlook is indeed grim.

### Matching Company Strategy to Competitive Conditions

Working through the five forces model step by step not only aids strategy makers in assessing whether the intensity of competition allows good profitability but also promotes sound strategic thinking about how to better match company strategy to the specific competitive character of the marketplace. Effectively matching a company's business strategy to prevailing competitive conditions has two aspects:

1. Pursuing avenues that shield the firm from as many of the different competitive pressures as possible.
2. Initiating actions calculated to shift the competitive forces in the company's favor by altering the underlying factors driving the five forces.

But making headway on these two fronts first requires identifying competitive pressures, gauging the relative strength of each of the five competitive forces, and gaining a deep enough understanding of the state of competition in the industry to know which strategy buttons to push.

> A company's strategy is increasingly effective the more it provides some insulation from competitive pressures, shifts the competitive battle in the company's favor, and positions firms to take advantage of attractive growth opportunities.

# QUESTION 3: WHAT FACTORS ARE DRIVING INDUSTRY CHANGE, AND WHAT IMPACT WILL THEY HAVE?

While it is critical to understand the nature and intensity of the competitive forces in an industry, it is equally critical to understand that the intensity of these forces is fluid and subject to change. All industries are affected by new developments and ongoing trends that alter industry conditions, some more speedily than others. Any strategies devised by management will therefore play out in a dynamic industry environment, so it's imperative that managers consider the factors driving industry change and how they might affect the industry environment. Moreover, with early notice, managers may be able to influence the direction or scope of environmental change and improve the outlook.

## The Concept of Industry Driving Forces

Industry and competitive conditions change because forces are enticing or pressuring certain industry participants (competitors, customers, suppliers) to alter their actions in important ways. The most powerful of the change agents are called **driving forces** because they have the biggest influences in reshaping the industry landscape and altering competitive conditions. Some driving forces originate in the outer ring of the company's macro-environment (see Figure 3.2), but most originate in the company's more immediate industry and competitive environment.

> **CORE CONCEPT**
> **Driving forces** are the major underlying causes of change in industry and competitive conditions.

Driving forces analysis has three steps: (1) identifying what the driving forces are, (2) assessing whether the drivers of change are, on the whole, acting to make the industry more or less attractive, and (3) determining what strategy changes are needed to prepare for the impact of the driving forces. All three steps merit further discussion.

## Identifying an Industry's Driving Forces

Many developments can affect an industry powerfully enough to qualify as driving forces. Some drivers of change are unique and specific to a particular industry situation, but most drivers of industry and competitive change fall into one of the following categories:

- *Changes in an industry's long-term growth rate.* Shifts in industry growth up or down have the potential to affect the balance between industry supply and buyer demand, entry and exit, and the character and strength of competition. Whether demand is growing or declining is one of the key factors influencing the intensity of rivalry in an industry, as explained earlier. But the strength of this effect will depend on how changes in the industry growth rate affect entry and exit in the industry. If entry barriers are low, then growth in demand will attract new entrants, increasing the number of industry rivals. If exit barriers are low, then shrinking demand will induce exit, resulting in fewer remaining rivals. If demand for the industry's product continues to shrink, the remaining industry members may be forced to close inefficient plants and retrench to a smaller production base. Hence, whether industry growth turns up or down, the outcome is a much-changed competitive landscape.

- *Increasing globalization.* Competition begins to shift from primarily a regional or national focus to an international or global focus when industry members begin seeking out customers in foreign markets or when production activities begin to migrate to countries where costs are lowest. Globalization can also be precipitated by the blossoming of consumer demand in developing countries and by the actions of government officials in many countries to reduce trade barriers or open up once-closed markets to foreign competitors, as is occurring in many parts of Latin America and Asia. Significant differences in labor costs among countries give manufacturers a strong incentive to locate plants for labor-intensive products in low-wage countries and use these plants to supply market demand across the world. Wages in China, India, Singapore, Mexico, and Brazil, for example, are significantly less than those in the United States, Germany, and Japan. The forces of globalization are sometimes such a strong driver that companies find it highly advantageous, if not necessary, to spread their operating reach into more and more country markets. Globalization is very much a driver of industry change in such industries as motor vehicles, steel, petroleum, personal computers, video games, public accounting, and textbook publishing.

- *Emerging new Internet capabilities and applications.* Mushrooming use of high-speed Internet service and Voice-over-Internet-Protocol (VoIP) technology, growing acceptance of Internet shopping, and the exploding popularity of Internet applications ("apps") for cell phones and TVs have been major drivers of change in industry after industry. The ability of companies to reach consumers via the Internet increases the number of rivals a company faces and often escalates rivalry by pitting pure online sellers against brick-and-mortar sellers. Online course offerings, for example, are profoundly affecting higher education. The Internet of the future will feature faster speeds, dazzling applications, and over a billion connected gadgets performing an array of functions, thus driving further industry and competitive changes. But Internet-related impacts vary from industry to industry. The challenges here are to assess precisely how emerging Internet developments are altering a particular industry's landscape and to factor these impacts into the strategy-making equation.

- *Changes in who buys the product and how they use it.* Shifts in buyer demographics and the ways products are used can greatly alter industry and competitive conditions. Longer life expectancies and growing percentages of relatively well-to-do retirees, for example, are driving demand growth in such industries as health care, prescription drugs, recreational living, and vacation travel. Apple's iPod models have transformed how music is bought and listened to—album sales are dropping, downloads of single digital recordings are mushrooming, and iPods have become the device of choice for millions of music listeners. Smart cell phones, with their growing array of features, functions, and downloadable applications, have become multi-use devices that have totally transformed the user experience and attracted altogether new types of buyers.

- *Technological change and manufacturing process innovation.* Advances in technology can cause disruptive change in an industry by introducing substitutes that offer buyers an irresistible price/performance combination. They can also alter the industry landscape by opening up whole new industry frontiers. For instance, high-definition technology has revolutionized TV viewing and broadcasting. Advances in battery technology are beginning to change how motor vehicles are powered. Stem cell research holds promise for finding ways to cure or treat an array of diseases.

- *Product and marketing innovation.* An ongoing stream of product innovations tends to alter the pattern of competition in an industry by attracting more first-time buyers, rejuvenating industry growth, and/or increasing product differentiation, with concomitant effects on rivalry, entry threat, and buyer power. Product innovation has been a key driving force in such industries as digital cameras, golf clubs, video games, toys, and prescription drugs. Similarly, when firms are successful in introducing *new ways* to market their products, they can spark a burst of buyer interest, widen industry demand, increase or lower entry barriers, and increase product differentiation—any or all of which can alter the competitiveness of an industry.

- *Entry or exit of major firms.* The entry of one or more foreign companies into a geographic market once dominated by domestic firms nearly always shakes up competitive conditions. Likewise, when an established domestic firm from another industry attempts entry either by acquisition or by launching its own startup venture, it usually pushes competition in new directions. Entry by a major firm thus often produces a new ball game, not only with new key players but also with new rules for competing. Similarly, exit of a major firm changes the competitive structure by reducing the number of market leaders and increasing the dominance of the leaders who remain.

- *Diffusion of technical know-how across companies and countries.* As knowledge about how to perform a particular activity or execute a particular manufacturing technology spreads, products tend to become more commodity-like. Knowledge diffusion can occur through scientific journals, trade publications, onsite plant tours, word of mouth among suppliers and customers, employee migration, and Internet sources.

- *Changes in cost and efficiency.* Widening or shrinking differences in the costs among key competitors tend to dramatically alter the state of competition. Lower production costs and longer-life products have allowed the makers of super-efficient fluorescent-based spiral light bulbs to cut deeply into the sales of incandescent light bulbs. Lower-cost eBooks are cutting into sales of costlier hardcover books as increasing numbers of consumers opt to buy iPads, Kindles, and other brands of tablets.

- *Reductions in uncertainty and business risk.* Many companies are hesitant to enter industries with uncertain futures or high levels of business risk, and firms already in these industries may be cautious about making aggressive capital investments to expand—often because it is unclear how much time and money it will take to overcome various technological hurdles and achieve acceptable production costs (as is the case in the infant solar power industry). Likewise, firms entering foreign markets where demand is just emerging or where political conditions are volatile may be cautious and limit their downside exposure by using less risky strategies. Over time, however, diminishing risk levels and uncertainty tend to stimulate new entry and capital investments on the part of growth-minded companies seeking new opportunities, thus dramatically altering industry and competitive conditions.

- *Regulatory influences and government policy changes.* Government regulatory actions can often mandate significant changes in industry practices and strategic approaches—as has recently occurred in the world's banking industry. Deregulation has proved to be a potent pro-competitive force in the airline industry. New rules and regulations pertaining to government-sponsored health insurance programs are driving changes in the health care industry. In international markets, host governments can drive competitive changes by opening their domestic markets to foreign participation or closing them to protect domestic companies. Note that this driving force is spawned by forces in a company's macro-environment (Figure 3.2).

- *Changing societal concerns, attitudes, and lifestyles.* Emerging social issues as well as changing attitudes and lifestyles can be powerful instigators of industry change. Growing concerns about climate change have emerged as a major driver of change in the energy industry. Mounting consumer concerns about the use of chemical additives and the nutritional content of food products are driving changes in the restaurant and food industries. Shifting societal concerns, attitudes, and lifestyles alter the pattern of competition, favoring those players that respond with products targeted to the new trends and conditions. As with the preceding driving force, this driving force springs from factors at work in a company's macro-environment.

Table 3.3 lists these 12 most common drivers of change. That there are so many different *potential* drivers of change explains why a full understanding of all types of change drivers is a fundamental part of analyzing industry dynamics. However, for each industry no more than three or four of these drivers are likely to be powerful enough to qualify as the *major determinants* of why and how an industry's competitive conditions are changing. The true analytical task is to evaluate the forces of industry and competitive change carefully enough to separate major factors from minor ones.

## TABLE 3.3  The Most Common Drivers of Industry Change

| |
|---|
| 1.  Changes in the long-term industry growth rate |
| 2.  Increasing globalization |
| 3.  Emerging new Internet capabilities and applications |
| 4.  Changes in who buys the product and how they use it |
| 5.  Technological change and manufacturing process innovation |
| 6.  Product and marketing innovation |
| 7.  Entry or exit of major firms |
| 8.  Diffusion of technical know-how across companies and countries |
| 9.  Changes in cost and efficiency |
| 10.  Reductions in uncertainty and business risk |
| 11.  Regulatory influences and government policy changes |
| 12.  Changing societal concerns, attitudes, and lifestyles |

## Assessing the Impact of the Factors Driving Industry Change

The second step in driving forces analysis is to determine whether the prevailing change drivers, on the whole, are acting to make the industry environment more or less attractive. Answers to three questions are needed:

1. Are the driving forces as a whole causing demand for the industry's product to increase or decrease?
2. Is the collective impact of the driving forces making competition more or less intense?
3. Will the combined impacts of the driving forces lead to higher or lower industry profitability?

Getting a handle on the collective impact of the driving forces requires looking at the likely effects of each factor separately, since the driving forces may not all be pushing change in the same direction. For example, one driving force may be acting to spur demand for the industry's product while another is working to curtail demand. Whether the net effect on industry demand is up or down hinges on which driver of change is the more powerful.

## Adjusting Strategy to Prepare for the Impacts of Driving Forces

The third step in the strategic analysis of industry dynamics—where the real payoff for strategy making comes—is for managers to draw some conclusions about *what strategy adjustments will be needed to deal with the impacts of the driving forces.* But taking the "right" kinds of actions to prepare for the industry and competitive changes being wrought by the driving forces first requires accurate diagnosis of the forces driving industry change and the impacts these forces will have on both the industry environment and the company's business. To the extent that managers are unclear about the drivers of industry change and their impacts, or if their views are off-base, the chances of making astute and timely strategy adjustments are slim. So driving-forces analysis is not something to take lightly; it has practical value and is basic to the task of thinking strategically about where the industry is headed and how to prepare for the changes ahead.

# QUESTION 4: HOW ARE INDUSTRY RIVALS POSITIONED IN THE MARKET?

Within an industry, companies commonly sell in different price/quality ranges, appeal to different types of buyers, have different geographic coverage, and so on. Some are more attractively positioned than others. Understanding which companies are strongly positioned and which are weakly positioned is an integral part of analyzing an industry's competitive structure. The best technique for revealing the market positions of industry competitors is **strategic group mapping**.

# Using Strategic Group Maps to Assess the Market Positions of Key Competitors

A **strategic group** consists of those industry members with similar competitive approaches and positions in the market. Companies in the same strategic group can resemble one another in a variety of ways. For example, they may have comparable product-line breadth, emphasize the same distribution channels, depend on identical technological approaches, or offer buyers essentially the same product attributes or similar services and technical assistance.[6] An industry contains only one strategic group when all sellers pursue essentially identical strategies and have similar market positions. At the other extreme, an industry may contain as many strategic groups as there are competitors when each rival pursues a distinctively different competitive approach and occupies a substantially different market position. The number of strategic groups in an industry and their respective market positions can be displayed on a strategic group map.

> **CORE CONCEPT**
>
> A **strategic group** is a cluster of industry rivals that have similar competitive approaches and market positions.

The procedure for constructing a *strategic group map* is straightforward:

- Identify the competitive characteristics that delineate strategic approaches used in the industry. Typical variables used in creating strategic group maps are price/quality range (high, medium, low), geographic coverage (local, regional, national, global), product-line breadth (wide, narrow), degree of service offered (no frills, limited, full), use of distribution channels (retail, wholesale, Internet, multiple), degree of vertical integration (none, partial, full), and degree of diversification into other industries (none, some, considerable).
- Plot the firms on a two-variable map using pairs of these variables.
- Assign firms occupying about the same map location to the same strategic group.
- Draw circles around each strategic group, making the circles proportional to the size of the group's share of total industry sales revenues.

This produces a two-dimensional diagram like the one for the U.S. beer industry in Illustration Capsule 3.1.

Several guidelines need to be observed in creating strategic group maps. First, the two variables selected as axes for the map should *not* be highly correlated; if they are, the circles on the map will fall along a diagonal and reveal nothing more about the relative positions of competitors than would be revealed by comparing the rivals on just one of the variables. For instance, if companies with broad product lines use multiple distribution channels while companies with narrow lines use a single distribution channel, then looking at the differences in distribution channel approaches adds no new information about positioning. Second, the variables chosen as axes for the map should reflect important differences among rival approaches—when rivals differ on both variables, the locations of the rivals will be scattered, thus showing how they are positioned differently. Third, the variables used as axes don't have to be either quantitative or continuous; rather, they can be discrete variables, defined in terms of distinct classes and combinations. Fourth, drawing the sizes of the circles on the map proportional to the combined sales of the firms in each strategic group allows the map to reflect the relative sizes of each strategic group. Fifth, if more than two good variables can be used as axes for the map, then it is wise to draw several maps to give different exposures to the competitive positioning relationships present in the industry's structure—there is not necessarily one best map for portraying how competing firms are positioned.

# Comparative Market Positions of Producers in the U.S. Beer Industry: A Strategic Group Map Example

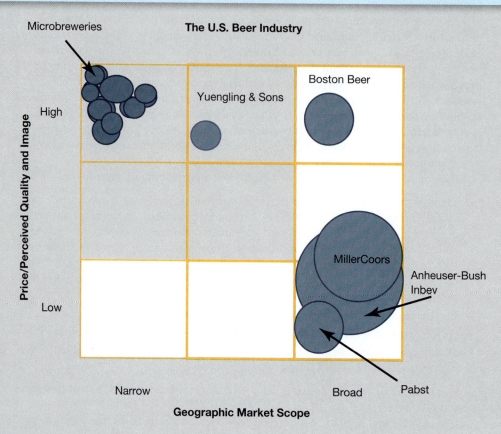

*Footnote:* Circles are drawn roughly proportional to the sizes of the chains, based on revenues.

## The Value of Strategic Group Maps?

Strategic group maps are revealing in several respects. The most important has to do with identifying which industry members are close rivals and which are distant rivals. Firms in the same strategic group are the closest rivals; the next closest rivals are in the immediately adjacent groups. Often, firms in strategic groups that are far apart on the map hardly compete at all. For instance, Walmart's clientele, merchandise selection, and pricing points are much too different to justify calling Walmart a close competitor of Neiman Marcus or Saks Fifth Avenue. For the same reason, Timex is not a meaningful competitive rival of Rolex.

The second thing to be gleaned from strategic group mapping is that *not all positions on the map are equally attractive.*[7] Two reasons account for why some positions can be more attractive than others:

1. *Prevailing competitive pressures from the industry's five forces may cause the profit potential of different strategic groups to vary.* The profit prospects of firms in different

> Strategic group maps reveal which companies are close competitors and which are distant competitors.

strategic groups can vary from good to poor because of differing degrees of competitive rivalry within strategic groups, differing pressures from potential entrants to each group, differing degrees of exposure to competition from substitute products outside the industry, and differing degrees of supplier or customer bargaining power from group to group. For instance, in the ready-to-eat cereal industry, there are significantly higher entry barriers (capital requirements, brand loyalty, and so on) for the strategic group comprising the large branded-cereal makers than for the group of generic-cereal makers or the group of small natural-cereal producers. Differences in differentiation among the branded rivals versus the generic cereal makers make rivalry stronger within the generic strategic group. In the retail chain industry, the competitive battle between Walmart and Target is more intense (with consequently smaller profit margins) than the rivalry among Versace, Chanel, Fendi, and other high-end fashion retailers.

> Some strategic groups are more favorably positioned than others because they confront weaker competitive forces and/ or because they are more favorably impacted by industry driving forces.

2. *Industry driving forces may favor some strategic groups and hurt others.* Likewise, industry driving forces can boost the business outlook for some strategic groups and adversely impact the business prospects of others. In the news industry, for example, Internet news services and cable news networks are gaining ground at the expense of newspapers and networks due to changes in technology and changing social lifestyles. Firms in strategic groups that are being adversely impacted by driving forces may try to shift to a more favorably situated position. If certain firms are known to be trying to change their competitive positions on the map, then attaching arrows to the circles showing the targeted direction helps clarify the picture of competitive maneuvering among rivals.

Thus, part of strategic group map analysis always entails drawing conclusions about where on the map is the "best" place to be and why. Which companies / strategic groups are destined to prosper because of their positions? Which companies / strategic groups seem destined to struggle? What accounts for why some parts of the map are better than others?

# QUESTION 5: WHAT STRATEGIC MOVES ARE RIVALS LIKELY TO MAKE NEXT?

Unless a company pays attention to the strategies and situations of competitors and has some inkling of what moves they will be making, it ends up flying blind into competitive battle. As in sports, scouting the opposition is an essential part of game plan development. Having good information about the strategic direction and likely moves of key competitors allows a company to prepare defensive countermoves, to craft its own strategic moves with some confidence about what market maneuvers to expect from rivals in response, and to exploit any openings that arise from competitors' missteps. The question is where to look for such information, since rivals rarely reveal their strategic intentions openly. If information is not directly available, what are the best indicators?

> Studying competitors' past behavior and preferences provides a valuable assist in anticipating what moves rivals are likely to make next and outmaneuvering them in the marketplace.

# A FRAMEWORK FOR COMPETITOR ANALYSIS

Michael Porter's **Framework for Competitor Analysis** points to four indicators of a rival's likely strategic moves and countermoves. These include a rival's *current strategy, objectives, capabilities,* and *assumptions* about itself and the industry, as shown in

**FIGURE 3.9** A Framework for Competitor Analysis

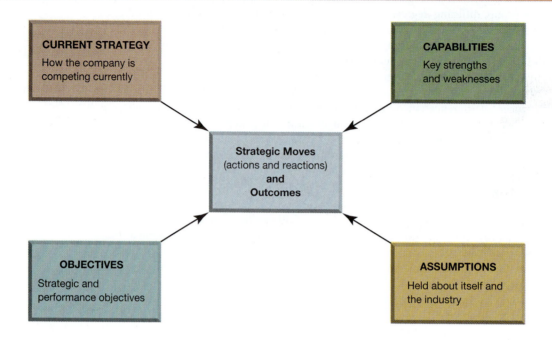

Figure 3.9. A strategic profile of a rival that provides good clues to their behavioral proclivities can be constructed by characterizing the rival along these four dimensions.

**Current Strategy**    To succeed in predicting a competitor's next moves, company strategists need to have a good understanding of each rival's current strategy, as an indicator of its pattern of behavior and best strategic options. Questions to consider include: How is the competitor positioned in the market? What is the basis for its competitive advantage (if any)? What kinds of investments is it making (as an indicator of its growth trajectory)?

**Objectives**    An appraisal of a rival's objectives should include not only its financial performance objectives, but strategic ones as well (such as those concerning market share). What is even more important is to consider the extent to which they are meeting these objectives and whether they are under pressure to improve. Rivals with good financial performance are likely to continue their present strategy with only minor fine-tuning. Poorly performing rivals are virtually certain to make fresh strategic moves.

**Capabilities**    A rival's strategic moves and countermoves are both enabled and constrained by the set of capabilities they have at hand. Thus a rival's capabilities (and efforts to acquire new capabilities) serve as a strong signal of future strategic actions (and reactions to your company's moves). Assessing a rival's capabilities involves sizing up not only their strengths in this respect, but their weaknesses as well.

# Business Ethics and Competitive Intelligence

Those who gather competitive intelligence on rivals can sometimes cross the fine line between honest inquiry and unethical or even illegal behavior. For example, calling rivals to get information about prices, the dates of new product introductions, or wage and salary levels is legal, but misrepresenting one's company affiliation during such calls is unethical. Pumping rivals' representatives at trade shows is ethical only if one wears a name tag with accurate company affiliation indicated.

Avon Products at one point secured information about its biggest rival, Mary Kay Cosmetics (MKC), by having its personnel search through the garbage bins outside MKC's headquarters. When MKC officials learned

of the action and sued, Avon claimed it did nothing illegal, since a 1988 Supreme Court case had ruled that trash left on public property (in this case, a sidewalk) was anyone's for the taking. Avon even produced a videotape of its removal of the trash at the MKC site. Avon won the lawsuit—but Avon's action, while legal, scarcely qualifies as ethical.

**Assumptions**   How a rival's top managers think about their strategic situation can have a big impact on how they behave. Banks that believe they are "too big to fail," for example, may take on more risk than is financially prudent. Assessing a rival's assumptions entails considering their assumptions about itself as well as the industry it participates in.

Information regarding these four analytical components can often be gleaned from company press releases, information posted on the company's website (especially the presentations management has recently made to securities analysts), and such public documents as annual reports and 10-K filings. Many companies also have a competitive intelligence unit that sifts through the available information to construct up-to-date strategic profiles of rivals. (See Illustration Capsule 3.2 for a discussion of the ethical limits to gathering competitive intelligence.)[8]

Doing the necessary detective work can be time-consuming, but scouting competitors well enough to anticipate their next moves allows managers to prepare effective countermoves (perhaps even beat a rival to the punch) and to take rivals' probable actions into account in crafting their own best course of action.

# QUESTION 6: WHAT ARE THE INDUSTRY'S KEY FACTORS?

An industry's **key success factors (KSFs)** are those competitive factors that most affect industry members' ability to survive and prosper in the marketplace—the particular strategy elements, product attributes, operational approaches, resources, and competitive capabilities that spell the difference between being a strong competitor and a weak competitor—and between profit and loss. KSFs by their very nature are so important to competitive success that *all firms* in the industry must pay close attention to them or risk becoming an industry laggard or failure. To indicate the significance of KSFs another way, how well the elements of a company's strategy measure up against an industry's KSFs determines whether it can meet the basic criteria for surviving and thriving in the industry. Identifying KSFs, in light of the prevailing and anticipated industry and competitive conditions, is therefore always a top priority in analytical and strategy-making considerations. Company strategists need to understand the industry landscape well enough to separate the factors most important to competitive success from those that are less important.

Key success factors vary from industry to industry, and even from time to time within the same industry, as drivers of change and competitive conditions change. But regardless of the circumstances, an industry's key success factors can always be deduced by asking the same three questions:

1.  On what basis do buyers of the industry's product choose between the competing brands of sellers? That is, what product attributes and service characteristics are crucial?

2.  Given the nature of competitive rivalry prevailing in the marketplace, what resources and competitive capabilities must a company have to be competitively successful?

3.  What shortcomings are almost certain to put a company at a significant competitive disadvantage?

Only rarely are there more than five key factors for competitive success. And even among these, two or three usually outrank the others in importance. Managers should therefore bear in mind the purpose of identifying key success factors—to determine which factors are most important to competitive success—and resist the temptation to label a factor that has only minor importance as a KSF. Compiling a list of every factor that matters even a little bit defeats the purpose of concentrating management attention on the factors truly critical to long-term competitive success.

In the beer industry, for example, although there are many types of buyers (whole-sale, retail, end consumer), it is most important to understand the preferences and buying behavior of the beer drinkers. Their purchase decisions are driven by price, taste, convenient access, and marketing. Thus the KSFs include a *strong network of wholesale distributors* (to get the company's brand stocked and favorably displayed in retail outlets, bars, restaurants, and stadiums, where beer is sold) and *clever advertising* (to induce beer drinkers to buy the company's brand and thereby pull beer sales through the established wholesale/retail channels). Because there is a potential for strong buyer power on the part of large distributors and retail chains, competitive success depends on some mechanism to offset that power, of which advertising (to create demand pull) is one. Thus the KSFs also include *superior product differentiation* (as in microbrews) or *superior firm size and branding capabilities* (as in national brands). The KSFs also include *full utilization of brewing capacity* (to keep manufacturing costs low and offset the high advertising, branding, and product differentiation costs).

Correctly diagnosing an industry's KSFs raises a company's chances of crafting a sound strategy. The key success factors of an industry point to those things that every firm in the industry needs to attend to in order to retain customers and weather the competition. If the company's strategy cannot deliver on the key success factors of its industry, it is unlikely to earn enough profits to remain a viable business. The goal of strategists, however, should be to do more than just meet the KSFs, since all firms in the industry need to clear this bar to survive. The goal of company strategists should be to design a strategy that allows it to compare favorably vis-à-vis rivals on each and every one of the industry's KSFs and that aims at being *distinctively better* than rivals on one (or possibly two) of the KSFs.

# QUESTION 7: IS THE INDUSTRY OUTLOOK CONDUCIVE TO GOOD PROFITABILITY?

Each of the frameworks presented in this chapter—PESTEL, five forces analysis, driving forces, strategy groups, competitor analysis, and key success factors—provides a useful perspective on an industry's outlook for future profitability. Putting them all together provides an even richer and more nuanced picture. Thus, the final step in evaluating the industry and competitive environment is to use the results of the analyses performed in answering Questions 1 to 6 to determine whether the industry presents the company with strong prospects for competitive success and attractive profits. The important factors on which to base a conclusion include:

LO 4

Learn how to use multiple frameworks to determine whether an industry's outlook presents a company with sufficiently attractive opportunities for growth and profitability.

- How the company is being impacted by the state of the macro-environment.
- Whether strong competitive forces are squeezing industry profitability to subpar levels.
- Whether industry profitability will be favorably or unfavorably affected by the prevailing driving forces.
- Whether the company occupies a stronger market position than rivals.
- Whether this is likely to change in the course of competitive interactions.
- How well the company's strategy delivers on the industry key success factors.

As a general proposition, *the anticipated industry environment is fundamentally attractive if it presents a company with good opportunity for above-average profitability; the industry outlook is fundamentally unattractive if a company's profit prospects are unappealingly low.*

However, it is a mistake to think of a particular industry as being equally attractive or unattractive to all industry participants and all potential entrants.[9] Attractiveness is relative, not absolute, and conclusions one way or the other have to be drawn from the perspective of a particular company. For instance, a favorably positioned competitor may see ample opportunity to capitalize on the vulnerabilities of weaker rivals even though industry conditions are otherwise somewhat dismal. At the same time, industries attractive to insiders may be unattractive to outsiders because of the difficulty of challenging current market leaders or because they have more attractive opportunities elsewhere.

When a company decides an industry is fundamentally attractive and presents good opportunities, a strong case can be made that it should invest aggressively to capture the opportunities it sees and to improve its long-term competitive position in the business. When a strong competitor concludes an industry is becoming less attractive, it may elect to simply protect its present position, investing cautiously—if at all—and looking for opportunities in other industries. A competitively weak company in an unattractive industry may see its best option as finding a buyer, perhaps a rival, to acquire its business.

The degree to which an industry is attractive or unattractive is not the same for all industry participants and all potential entrants.

Thinking strategically about a company's external situation involves probing for answers to the following seven questions:

1. *What are the strategically relevant factors in the macro-environment?* Industries differ significantly as to how they are affected by conditions in the broad macro-environment. Identifying which of these factors is strategically relevant is the first step to understanding how a company is situated in its external environment. PESTEL analysis of the political, economic, sociocultural, technological, environmental/ecological, and legal/regulatory factors provides a framework for approaching this issue systematically. Identifying the strategically relevant features of the macro-environment sets the stage for the analysis to come, since they play an important role in determining an industry's potential for attractive profits.

2. *What kinds of competitive forces are industry members facing, and how strong is each force?* The strength of competition is a composite of five forces: (1) competitive pressures stemming from the competitive jockeying among industry rivals, (2) competitive pressures associated with the market inroads being made by the sellers of substitutes, (3) competitive pressures associated with the threat of new entrants into the market, (4) competitive pressures stemming from supplier bargaining power, and (5) competitive pressures stemming from buyer bargaining. The nature and strength of the competitive pressures have to be examined force by force, and their collective strength must be evaluated. One strong force, however, can be sufficient to keep average industry profitability low. Working through the five forces model aids strategy makers in assessing how to insulate the company from the strongest forces, identify attractive arenas for expansion, or alter the competitive conditions so that they offer more favorable prospects for profitability.

3. *What factors are driving changes in the industry, and what impact will they have on competitive intensity and industry profitability?* Industry and competitive conditions change because certain forces are acting to create incentives or pressures for change. The most common driving forces include changes in the long-term industry growth rate, increasing globalization, Internet-related developments, changing buyer behavior, technological change and manufacturing process innovation, product and marketing innovation, the entry or exit of major firms, the diffusion of know-how, efficiency improvements in adjacent markets, reductions in uncertainty and business risk, regulatory and government policy changes, and changing societal factors. Once an industry's change drivers have been identified, the analytical task becomes one of determining whether they are acting, individually and collectively, to make the industry environment more or less attractive.

4. *What market positions do industry rivals occupy—who is strongly positioned and who is not?* Strategic group mapping is a valuable tool for understanding the similarities, differences, strengths, and weaknesses inherent in the market positions of rival companies. Rivals in the same or nearby strategic groups are close competitors, whereas companies in distant strategic groups usually pose little or no immediate threat. The lesson of strategic group mapping is that some positions on the map are more favorable than others. The profit potential of different strategic groups may not be the same because industry driving forces and competitive forces likely have varying effects on the industry's distinct strategic groups.

5. *What strategic moves are rivals likely to make next?* Scouting competitors well enough to anticipate their actions can help a company prepare effective countermoves (perhaps even beating a rival to the punch) and allows managers to take rivals' probable actions into

account in designing their own company's best course of action. Managers who fail to study competitors risk being caught unprepared by the strategic moves of rivals.

6. *What are the key factors for competitive success?* An industry's key success factors (KSFs) are the particular strategy elements, product attributes, operational approaches, resources, and competitive capabilities that all industry members must have in order to survive and prosper in the industry. KSFs by their very nature are so important to competitive success that *all firms* in the industry must pay close attention to them or risk being driven out of the industry. For any industry, however, they can be deduced by answering three basic questions: (1) On what basis do buyers of the industry's product choose between the competing brands of sellers, (2) what resources and competitive capabilities must a company have to be competitively successful, and (3) what shortcomings are almost certain to put a company at a significant competitive disadvantage? Correctly diagnosing an industry's KSFs raises a company's chances of crafting a sound strategy.

7. *Is the industry outlook conducive to good profitability?* The last step in industry analysis is summing up the results from applying each of the frameworks employed in answering questions 1 to 6: PESTEL, five forces analysis, driving forces, strategic group mapping, competitor analysis, and key success factors. Applying multiple lenses to the question of what the industry outlook looks like offers a more robust and nuanced answer. If the answers from each framework, seen as a whole, reveal that a company's profit prospects in that industry are above average, then the industry environment is basically attractive *for that company;* if industry profit prospects are below average, conditions are unattractive for them. What may look like an attractive environment for one company may appear to be unattractive from the perspective of a different company.

Clear, insightful diagnosis of a company's external situation is an essential first step in crafting strategies that are well matched to industry and competitive conditions. To do cutting-edge strategic thinking about the external environment, managers must know what questions to pose and what analytical tools to use in answering these questions. This is why this chapter has concentrated on suggesting the right questions to ask, explaining concepts and analytical approaches, and indicating the kinds of things to look for.

## ASSURANCE OF LEARNING EXERCISES

1. Prepare a brief analysis of the coffee industry using the information provided on the industry trade association websites. Of the list of macro-economic factors found in Table 3.1, which do you think might be strategically relevant for this industry? On the basis of information provided on the trade association websites, draw a five forces diagram for this industry and briefly discuss the nature and strength of each of the five competitive forces. What factors are driving change in the industry?

    **connect** 
    **LO 1, LO 2**

2. Based on the strategic group map in Illustration Capsule 3.1, who are Yuengling & Sons's closest competitors? Between which two strategic groups is competition the strongest? Why do you think no beer producers are positioned in the lower left corner of the map? Which company/strategic group faces the weakest competition from the members of other strategic groups?

    **connect** 
    **LO 1, LO 3**

3. The Snack Food Association publishes an annual State of the Industry report that can be found at www.sfa.org. Based on information in the latest State of the Industry report, does it appear that the economic characteristics of the industry will present industry participants with attractive opportunities for growth and profitability? Explain.

    **LO 1, LO 4**

**LO 1** 1. Which of the factors listed in Table 3.1 might have the most strategic relevance for your industry?

**LO 2** 2. Which of the five competitive forces is creating the strongest competitive pressures for your company?

3. What are the "weapons of competition" that rival companies in your industry can use to gain sales and market share? See Table 3.2 to help you identify the various competitive factors.

4. What are the factors affecting the intensity of rivalry in the industry in which your company is competing? Use Figure 3.4 and the accompanying discussion to help you in pinpointing the specific factors most affecting competitive intensity. Would you characterize the rivalry and jockeying for better market position, increased sales, and market share among the companies in your industry as fierce, very strong, strong, moderate, or relatively weak? Why?

**LO 4** 5. Are there any driving forces in the industry in which your company is competing? What impact will these driving forces have? Will they cause competition to be more or less intense? Will they act to boost or squeeze profit margins? List at least two actions your company should consider taking in order to combat any negative impacts of the driving forces.

**LO 3** 6. Draw a strategic group map showing the market positions of the companies in your industry. Which companies do you believe are in the most attractive position on the map? Which companies are the most weakly positioned? Which companies do you believe are likely to try to move to a different position on the strategic group map?

**LO 4** 7. What do you see as the key factors for being a successful competitor in your industry? List at least three.

8. Does your overall assessment of the industry suggest that industry rivals have sufficiently attractive opportunities for growth and profitability? Explain.

## ENDNOTES

[1] Michael E. Porter, "How Competitive Forces Shape Strategy," *Harvard Business Review* 57, no. 2 (March–April 1979), pp. 137–45; Porter, *Competitive Strategy,* Free Press, 1980; "The Five Competitive Forces That Shape Strategy," *Harvard Business Review* 86, no. 1 (January 2008), pp. 78–93.
[2] Pamela J. Derfus, Patrick G. Maggitti, Curtis M. Grimm, and Ken G. Smith, "The Red Queen Effect: Competitive Actions and Firm Performance," *Academy of Management Journal* 51, no. 1 (February 2008), pp. 61–80.
[3] J. S. Bain, *Barriers to New Competition* (Cambridge, MA: Harvard University Press, 1956); F. M. Scherer, *Industrial Market Structure and Economic Performance* (Chicago: Rand McNally, 1971); Porter, *Competitive Strategy;* Porter, "The Five Competitive Forces that Shape Strategy."
[4] C. A. Montgomery and S. Hariharan, "Diversified Expansion by Large Established Firms," *Journal of Economic Behavior & Organization* 15, no. 1 (January 1991), pp. 71–89.
[5] Porter, "The Five Competitive Forces that Shape Strategy."
[6] Mary Ellen Gordon and George R. Milne, "Selecting the Dimensions that Define Strategic Groups: A Novel Market-Driven Approach," *Journal of Managerial Issues* 11, no. 2 (Summer 1999), pp. 213–33.
[7] Avi Fiegenbaum and Howard Thomas, "Strategic Groups as Reference Groups: Theory, Modeling and Empirical Examination of Industry and Competitive Strategy," *Strategic Management Journal* 16 (1995), pp. 461–76; S. Ade Olusoga, Michael P. Mokwa, and Charles H. Noble, "Strategic Groups, Mobility Barriers, and Competitive Advantage," *Journal of Business Research* 33 (1995), pp. 153–64.
[8] Larry Kahaner, *Competitive Intelligence* (New York: Simon & Schuster, 1996).
[9] B. Wernerfelt and C. Montgomery, "What Is an Attractive Industry?" *Management Science* 32, no. 10 (October 1986), pp. 1223–30.

# CHAPTER 4

# EVALUATING A COMPANY'S RESOURCES, CAPABILITIES, AND COMPETITIVENESS

## Learning Objectives

**LO 1**   Learn how to assess how well a company's strategy is working.

**LO 2**   Understand why a company's resources and capabilities are central to its strategic approach and how to evaluate their potential for giving the company a competitive edge over rivals.

**LO 3**   Discover how to assess the company's strengths and weaknesses in light of market opportunities and external threats.

**LO 4**   Grasp how a company's value chain activities can affect the company's cost structure and customer value proposition.

**LO 5**   Understand how a comprehensive evaluation of a company's competitive situation can assist managers in making critical decisions about their next strategic moves.

Only firms who are able to continually build new strategic assets faster and cheaper than their competitors will earn superior returns over the long term.

*C. C. Markides and P. J. Williamson*
*– London Business School Professors and Consultants*

A new strategy nearly always involves acquiring new resources and capabilities.

*Laurence Capron and Will Mitchell*
*– INSEAD and University of Toronto Professors and Consultants*

You have to learn to treat people as a resource . . . you have to ask not what do they cost, but what is the yield, what can they produce?

*Peter F. Drucker – Business Thinker and Management Consultant*

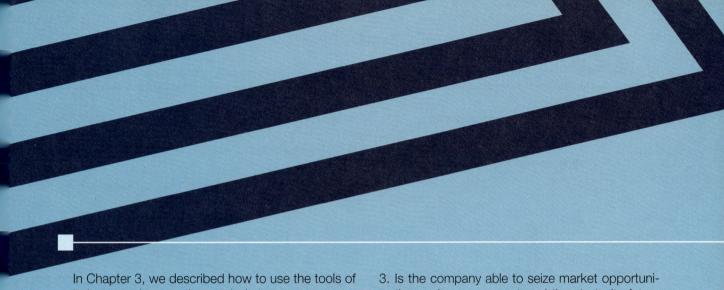

In Chapter 3, we described how to use the tools of industry and competitor analysis to assess a company's external environment and lay the groundwork for matching a company's strategy to its external situation. In this chapter, we discuss techniques for evaluating a company's internal situation, including its collection of resources and capabilities and the activities it performs along its value chain. Internal analysis enables managers to determine whether their strategy has appealing prospects for giving the company a significant competitive edge over rival firms. Combined with external analysis, it facilitates an understanding of how to reposition a firm to take advantage of new opportunities and to cope with emerging competitive threats. The analytical spotlight will be trained on six questions:

1. How well is the company's present strategy working?

2. What are the company's competitively important resources and capabilities?

3. Is the company able to seize market opportunities and overcome external threats to its future well-being?

4. Are the company's cost structure and customer value proposition competitive?

5. Is the company competitively stronger or weaker than key rivals?

6. What strategic issues and problems merit front-burner managerial attention?

In probing for answers to these questions, five analytical tools—resource and capability analysis, SWOT analysis, value chain analysis, benchmarking, and competitive strength assessment—will be used. All five are valuable techniques for revealing a company's competitiveness and for helping company managers match their strategy to the company's own particular circumstances.

# QUESTION 1: HOW WELL IS THE COMPANY'S PRESENT STRATEGY WORKING?

In evaluating how well a company's present strategy is working, the best way to start is with a clear view of what the strategy entails. Figure 4.1 shows the key components of a single-business company's strategy. The first thing to examine is the company's competitive approach. What moves has the company made recently to attract customers and improve its market position—for instance, has it cut prices, improved the design of its product, added new features, stepped up advertising, entered a new geographic market

**FIGURE 4.1** Identifying the Components of a Single-Business Company's Strategy

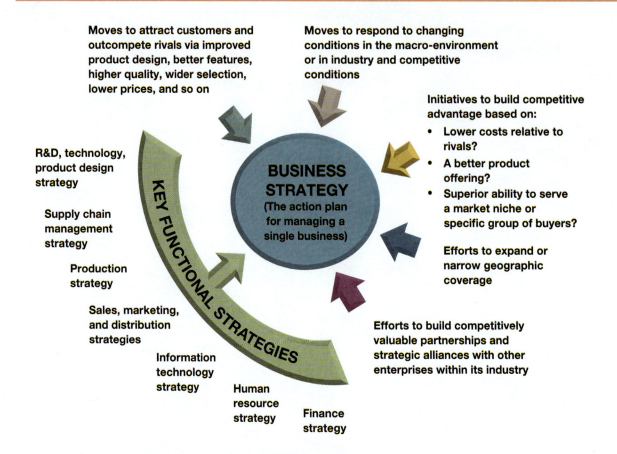

(domestic or foreign), or merged with a competitor? Is it striving for a competitive advantage based on low costs or a better product offering? Is it concentrating on serving a broad spectrum of customers or a narrow market niche? The company's functional strategies in R&D, production, marketing, finance, human resources, information technology, and so on further characterize company strategy, as do any efforts to establish competitively valuable alliances or partnerships with other enterprises.

The three best indicators of how well a company's strategy is working are (1) whether the company is achieving its stated financial and strategic objectives, (2) whether its financial performance is above the industry average, and whether it is gaining customers and increasing its market share. Persistent shortfalls in meeting company performance targets and weak marketplace performance relative to rivals are reliable warning signs that the company has a weak strategy or suffers from poor strategy execution or both. Specific indicators of how well a company's strategy is working include:

- Whether the firm's sales are growing faster than, slower than, or about the same pace as the market as a whole, thus resulting in a rising, eroding, or stable market share.
- Whether the company is acquiring new customers at an attractive rate as well as retaining existing customers.
- Whether the firm's image and reputation with its customers is growing stronger or weaker.

- Whether the firm's profit margins are increasing or decreasing and how well its margins compare to rival firms' margins.
- Trends in the firm's net profits and return on investment relative to those of other companies in the industry.
- Whether the company's overall financial strength and credit rating are improving or declining.
- How well the company stacks up against rivals on factors relevant to buyers' choices, such as price, product quality, innovative features, delivery time, and customer service.
- Whether key measures of operating performance (such as days of inventory, employee productivity, unit cost, defect rate, scrap rate, order-filling accuracy, delivery times, and warranty costs) are improving, remaining steady, or deteriorating.

The stronger a company's current overall performance, the more likely it has a well-conceived, well-executed strategy. The weaker a company's financial performance and market standing, the more its current strategy must be questioned and the more likely the need for radical changes.

Evaluating how well a company's strategy is working should include quantitative as well as qualitative assessments. Table 4.1 provides a compilation of the financial ratios most commonly used to evaluate a company's financial performance and balance sheet strength.

Sluggish financial performance and second-rate market accomplishments almost always signal weak strategy, weak execution, or both.

## TABLE 4.1   Key Financial Ratios: How to Calculate Them and What They Mean

| Ratio | How Calculated | What It Shows |
|---|---|---|
| **Profitability Ratios** | | |
| 1. Gross profit margin | $\dfrac{\text{Sales revenues} - \text{Cost of goods sold}}{\text{Sales revenues}}$ | Shows the percentage of revenues available to cover operating expenses and yield a profit. Higher is better, and the trend should be upward. |
| 2. Operating profit margin (or return on sales) | $\dfrac{\text{Sales revenues} - \text{Operating expenses}}{\text{Sales revenues}}$ or $\dfrac{\text{Operating income}}{\text{Sales revenues}}$ | Shows the profitability of current operations without regard to interest charges and income taxes. Earnings before interest and taxes is known as *EBIT* in financial and business accounting. |
| 3. Net profit margin (or net return on sales) | $\dfrac{\text{Profits after taxes}}{\text{Sales revenues}}$ | Shows after-tax profits per dollar of sales. |
| 4. Total return on assets | $\dfrac{\text{Profits after taxes} + \text{Interest}}{\text{Total assets}}$ | A measure of the return on total investment in the enterprise. Interest is added to after-tax profits to form the numerator, since total assets are financed by creditors as well as by stockholders. Higher is better, and the trend should be upward. |
| 5. Net return on total assets (ROA) | $\dfrac{\text{Profits after taxes}}{\text{Total assets}}$ | A measure of the return earned by stockholders on the firm's total assets. |

*(Continued)*

**TABLE 4.1**   *(Continued)*

| Ratio | How Calculated | What It Shows |
|---|---|---|
| 6. Return on stockholders' equity (ROE) | $$\frac{\text{Profits after taxes}}{\text{Total stockholders' equity}}$$ | The return stockholders are earning on their capital investment in the enterprise. A return in the 12–15% range is "average," and the trend should be upward. |
| 7. Return on invested capital (ROIC)—sometimes referred to as return on capital employed (ROCE) | $$\frac{\text{Profits after taxes}}{\text{Long-term debt} + \text{Total stockholders' equity}}$$ | A measure of the return that shareholders are earning on the long-term monetary capital invested in the enterprise. A higher return reflects greater bottom-line effectiveness in the use of long-term capital; the trend should be upward. |
| **Liquidity Ratios** | | |
| 1. Current ratio | $$\frac{\text{Current assets}}{\text{Current liabilities}}$$ | Shows a firm's ability to pay current liabilities using assets that can be converted to cash in the near term. Ratio should be higher than 1.0; a ratio of 2 or higher are better still. |
| 2. Working capital | Current assets − Current liabilities | The cash available for a firm's day-to-day operations. Larger amounts mean the company has more internal funds to (1) pay its current liabilities on a timely basis and (2) finance inventory expansion, additional accounts receivable, and a larger base of operations without resorting to borrowing or raising more equity capital. |
| **Leverage Ratios** | | |
| 1. Total debt-to-assets ratio | $$\frac{\text{Total debt}}{\text{Total assets}}$$ | Measures the extent to which borrowed funds (both short-term loans and long-term debt) have been used to finance the firm's operations. A low fraction or ratio is better—a high fraction indicates overuse of debt and greater risk of bankruptcy. |
| 2. Long-term debt-to-capital ratio | $$\frac{\text{Long-term debt}}{\text{Long-term debt} + \text{Total stockholders' equity}}$$ | An important measure of creditworthiness and balance sheet strength. It indicates the percentage of capital investment in the enterprise that has been financed by both long-term lenders and stockholders. A ratio below 0.25 is preferable since the lower the ratio, the greater the capacity to borrow additional funds. Debt-to-capital ratios above 0.50, and certainly above 0.75, indicate a heavy and perhaps excessive reliance on long-term borrowing, lower creditworthiness, and weak balance sheet strength. |

*(Continued)*

**TABLE 4.1**    *(Concluded)*

| Ratio | How Calculated | What It Shows |
|---|---|---|
| 3. Debt-to-equity ratio | $$\frac{\text{Total debt}}{\text{Total stockholders' equity}}$$ | Shows the balance between debt (funds borrowed both short term and long term) and the amount that stockholders have invested in the enterprise. The further the ratio is below 1.0, the greater the firm's ability to borrow additional funds. Ratios above 1.0, and definitely above 2.0, put creditors at greater risk, signal weaker balance sheet strength, and often result in lower credit ratings. |
| 4. Long-term debt-to-equity ratio | $$\frac{\text{Long-term debt}}{\text{Total stockholders' equity}}$$ | Shows the balance between long-term debt and stockholders' equity in the firm's *long-term* capital structure. Low ratios indicate a greater capacity to borrow additional funds if needed. |
| 5. Times-interest-earned (or coverage) ratio | $$\frac{\text{Operating income}}{\text{Interest expenses}}$$ | Measures the ability to pay annual interest charges. Lenders usually insist on a minimum ratio of 2.0, but ratios above 3.0 signal progressively better creditworthiness. |
| **Activity Ratios** | | |
| 1. Days of inventory | $$\frac{\text{Inventory}}{\text{Cost of goods sold} \div 365}$$ | Measures inventory management efficiency. Fewer days of inventory are usually better. |
| 2. Inventory turnover | $$\frac{\text{Cost of goods sold}}{\text{Inventory}}$$ | Measures the number of inventory turns per year. Higher is better. |
| 3. Average collection period | $$\frac{\text{Accounts receivable}}{\text{Total sales} \div 365}$$ *or* $$\frac{\text{Accounts receivable}}{\text{Average daily sales}}$$ | Indicates the average length of time the firm must wait after making a sale to receive cash payment. A shorter collection time is better. |
| **Other Important Measures of Financial Performance** | | |
| 1. Dividend yield on common stock | $$\frac{\text{Annual dividends per share}}{\text{Current market price per share}}$$ | A measure of the return that shareholders receive in the form of dividends. A "typical" dividend yield is 2–3%. The dividend yield for fast-growth companies is often below 1% (maybe even 0); the dividend yield for slow-growth companies can run 4–5%. |
| 2. Price-to-earnings ratio | $$\frac{\text{Current market price per share}}{\text{Earnings per share}}$$ | P/E ratios above 20 indicate strong investor confidence in a firm's outlook and earnings growth; firms whose future earnings are at risk or likely to grow slowly typically have ratios below 12. |

*(Continued)*

**TABLE 4.1** *(Continued)*

| Ratio | How Calculated | What It Shows |
|---|---|---|
| 3. Dividend payout ratio | $\dfrac{\text{Annual dividends per share}}{\text{Earnings per share}}$ | Indicates the percentage of after-tax profits paid out as dividends. |
| 4. Internal cash flow | After tax profits + Depreciation | A quick and rough estimate of the cash a company's business is generating after payment of operating expenses, interest, and taxes. Such amounts can be used for dividend payments or funding capital expenditures. |
| 5. Free cash flow | After tax profits + Depreciation − Capital Expenditures − Dividends | A quick and rough estimate of the cash a company's business is generating after payment of operating expenses, interest, taxes, dividends, and desirable reinvestments in the business. The larger a company's free cash flow, the greater is its ability to internally fund new strategic initiatives, repay debt, make new acquisitions, repurchase shares of stock, or increase dividend payments. |

# QUESTION 2: WHAT ARE THE COMPANY'S COMPETITIVELY IMPORTANT RESOURCES AND CAPABILITIES?

An essential element of deciding whether a company's overall situation is fundamentally healthy or unhealthy entails examining the attractiveness of its resources and capabilities. A company's resources and capabilities are its **competitive assets** and determine whether its competitive power in the marketplace will be impressively strong or disappointingly weak. Companies with second-rate competitive assets nearly always are relegated to a trailing position in the industry.

**Resource and capability analysis** provides managers with a powerful tool for sizing up the company's competitive assets and determining whether they can provide the foundation necessary for competitive success in the marketplace. This is a two-step process. The first step is to identify the company's resources and capabilities. The second step is to examine them more closely to ascertain which are the most competitively important and whether they can support a sustainable competitive advantage over rival firms.[1] This second step involves applying the *four tests of a resource's competitive power*.

## Identifying the Company's Resources and Capabilities

A firm's resources and capabilities are the fundamental building blocks of its competitive strategy. In crafting strategy, it is essential for managers to know how to take stock of the company's full complement of resources and capabilities. But before they can do so, managers and strategists need a more precise definition of these terms.

In brief, a **resource** is a productive input or competitive asset that is owned or controlled by the firm. Firms have many different types of resources at their disposal that vary not only in kind but in quality as well. Some are of a higher quality than others, and some are more competitively valuable, having greater potential to give a firm a competitive advantage over its rivals. For example, a company's brand is a resource, as is an R&D team—yet some brands such as Coca-Cola and Kleenex are well known, with enduring value, while others have little more name recognition than generic products. In similar fashion, some R&D teams are far more innovative and productive than others due to the outstanding talents of the individual team members, the team's composition, and its chemistry.

A **capability** is the capacity of a firm to perform some internal activity competently. Capabilities vary in form, quality, and competitive importance, with some being more competitively valuable than others. Apple's product innovation capabilities are widely recognized as being far superior to those of its competitors; Nordstrom is known for its superior incentive management capabilities; PepsiCo is admired for its marketing and brand management capabilities. *Organizational capabilities are developed and enabled through the deployment of a company's resources or some combination of its resources.*[2]

## Types of Company Resources

A useful way to identify a company's resources is to look for them within categories, as shown in Table 4.2. Broadly speaking, resources can be divided into two main categories: **tangible** and **intangible** resources. Although *human resources* make up one of the most important parts of a company's resource base, we include them in the intangible category to emphasize the role played by the skills, talents, and knowledge of a company's human resources.

Tangible resources are the most easily identified, since tangible resources are those that can be touched or quantified readily. Obviously, they include various types of *physical resources* such as manufacturing facilities and mineral resources, but they also include a company's *financial resources, technological resources,* and *organizational resources* such as the company's communication and control systems.

Intangible resources are harder to discern, but they are often among the most important of a firm's competitive assets. They include various sorts of *human assets and intellectual capital,* as well as a company's *brands, image, and reputational assets.* While intangible resources have no material existence on their own, they are often embodied in something material. Thus, the skills and knowledge resources of a firm are embodied in its managers and employees; a company's brand name is embodied in the company logo or product labels. Other important kinds of intangible resources include a company's *relationships* with suppliers, buyers, or partners of various sorts, and the *company's culture and incentive system.* A more detailed listing of the various types of tangible and intangible resources is provided in Table 4.2.

Listing a company's resources category by category can prevent managers from inadvertently overlooking some company resources that might be competitively important. At times, it can be difficult to decide exactly how to categorize certain types of resources. For example, resources such as a work group's specialized expertise in developing innovative products can be considered to be technological assets or human assets or intellectual capital and knowledge assets; the work ethic and drive of a company's workforce could be included under the company's human assets or its culture and incentive system. In this regard, it is important to remember that *it is not exactly how a resource is categorized that matters but, rather, that all of the company's different types of resources are included in the inventory.* The real purpose of using categories in identifying a company's resources is to ensure that none of a company's resources go unnoticed when sizing up the company's competitive assets.

**Resource and capability analysis** is a powerful tool for sizing up a company's competitive assets and determining if they can support a sustainable competitive advantage over market rivals.

## CORE CONCEPT

A **resource** is a competitive asset that is owned or controlled by a company; a **capability** or **competence** is the capacity of a firm to perform some internal activity competently. Capabilities are developed and enabled through the deployment of a company's resources.

**TABLE 4.2**  **Types of Company Resources**

| Tangible Resources |
| --- |
| • *Physical resources:* land and real estate; manufacturing plants, equipment, and/or distribution facilities; the locations of stores, plants, or distribution centers, including the overall pattern of their physical locations; ownership of or access rights to natural resources (such as mineral deposits) |
| • *Financial resources:* cash and cash equivalents; marketable securities; other financial assets such as a company's credit rating and borrowing capacity |
| • *Technological assets:* patents, copyrights, and trade secrets; production technology, innovation technologies, technological processes |
| • *Organizational resources:* IT and communication systems (satellites, servers, workstations, etc.); other planning, coordination, and control systems; the company's organizational design and reporting structure |

| Intangible Resources |
| --- |
| • *Human assets and intellectual capital:* the education, experience, knowledge, and talent of the workforce, cumulative learning, and tacit knowledge of employees; collective learning embedded in the organization, the intellectual capital and know-how of specialized teams and work groups; the knowledge of key personnel concerning important business functions; managerial talent and leadership skill; the creativity and innovativeness of certain personnel |
| • *Brands, company image, and reputational assets:* brand names, trademarks, product or company image, buyer loyalty and goodwill; company reputation for quality, service, and reliability; reputation with suppliers and partners for fair dealing |
| • *Relationships:* alliances, joint ventures, or partnerships that provide access to technologies, specialized know-how, or geographic markets; networks of dealers or distributors; the trust established with various partners |
| • *Company culture and incentive system:* the norms of behavior, business principles, and ingrained beliefs within the company; the attachment of personnel to the company's ideals; the compensation system and the motivation level of company personnel |

**Identifying Capabilities**   Organizational capabilities are more complex entities than resources; indeed, they are built up through the use of resources and draw on some combination of the firm's resources as they are exercised.[3] Virtually all organizational capabilities are *knowledge-based, residing in people and in a company's intellectual capital or in organizational processes and systems, which embody tacit knowledge.* For example, Procter & Gamble's brand management capabilities draw on the knowledge of the company's brand managers, the expertise of its marketing department, and the company's relationships with retailers, since brand building is a cooperative activity requiring retailer support. The capability in video game design for which Electronic Arts is known derives from the creative talents and technological expertise of its highly talented game developers, the company's culture of creativity, and a compensation system that generously rewards talented developers for creating best-selling video games.

Because of their complexity, capabilities are harder to categorize than resources and more challenging to search for as a result. There are, however, two approaches that can make the process of uncovering and identifying a firm's capabilities more systematic. The first method takes the completed listing of a firm's resources as its starting point. Since capabilities are built from resources and utilize resources as they are exercised, a firm's resources can provide a strong set of clues about the types of capabilities the firm is likely to have accumulated. This approach simply involves looking over the firm's resources and considering whether (and to what extent) the firm has built up any related capabilities. So, for example, a fleet of trucks, the latest RFID tracking technology, and a set of large automated distribution centers may be indicative of sophisticated capabilities in logistics and distribution. R&D teams composed of top scientists with expertise in genomics may suggest organizational capabilities in developing new gene therapies or in biotechnology more generally.

The second method of identifying a firm's capabilities takes a functional approach. Many capabilities relate to fairly specific functions; these draw on a limited set of resources and typically involve a single department or organizational unit. Capabilities in injection molding or continuous casting or metal stamping are manufacturing-related; capabilities in direct selling, promotional pricing, or database marketing all connect to the sales and marketing functions; capabilities in basic research, strategic innovation, or new product development link to a company's R&D function. This approach requires managers to survey the various functions a firm performs to find the different capabilities associated with each function.

A problem with this second method is that many of the most important capabilities of firms are inherently *cross-functional.* Cross-functional capabilities draw on a number of different kinds of resources and are multidimensional in nature—they spring from the effective collaboration among people with different types of expertise working in different organizational units. An example is Nike's cross-functional design process, spanning R&D activities, marketing research efforts, styling expertise, and manufacturing. Cross-functional capabilities and other complex capabilities involving numerous linked and closely integrated competitive assets are sometimes referred to as **resource bundles.**

It is important not to miss identifying a company's resource bundles, since they can be the most competitively important of a firm's competitive assets. Resource bundles can sometimes pass the four tests of a resource's competitive power even when the individual components of the resource bundle cannot. For example, although Callaway Golf Company's engineering capabilities and market research capabilities are matched relatively well by rivals Cobra Golf and Ping Golf, the company's bundling of resources used in its product development process (including cross-functional development systems, technological capabilities, knowledge of consumer preferences, and a collaborative organizational culture) gives it a competitive advantage that has allowed it to remain the largest seller of golf equipment for more than a decade.

> **CORE CONCEPT**
>
> A **resource bundle** is a linked and closely integrated set of competitive assets centered around one or more cross-functional capabilities.

## Assessing the Competitive Power of a Company's Resources and Capabilities

To assess their competitive power, one must go beyond merely identifying a company's resources and capabilities to probe their *caliber.*[4] Thus, the second step in resource and capability analysis is designed to ascertain which of a company's resources and capabilities are competitively superior and to what extent they can support a company's quest for a sustainable competitive advantage over market rivals. When a company has competitive assets that are central to its strategy and superior to those of rival firms, they can support a competitive advantage, as defined in Chapter 1. If this advantage proves durable despite the best efforts of competitors to overcome it, then the company is said to have a ***sustainable competitive advantage.*** While it may be difficult for a company to achieve a sustainable competitive advantage, it is an important strategic objective because it imparts a potential for attractive and long-lived profitability.

## The Four Tests of a Resource's Competitive Power

The competitive power of a resource or capability is measured by how many of the following four tests it can pass.[5] These tests are often referred to as the **VRIN tests for sustainable competitive advantage**—a short-hand reminder standing for *Valuable, Rare, Inimitable,* and *Non-substitutable.* The first two tests determine whether a resource or capability can support a competitive advantage. The last two determine whether the competitive advantage can be sustained in the face of active competition.

1. *Is the resource (or capability) competitively **Valuable**?* To be competitively valuable, a resource or capability must be directly relevant to the company's strategy, making the company a more effective competitor, able to exploit market opportunities and ward off external threats. Unless the resource contributes to the effectiveness of the company's strategy, it cannot pass this first test. An indicator of its effectiveness is whether the resource enables the company to strengthen its business model through a better customer value proposition and/or profit formula. Companies have to guard against contending that something they do well is necessarily competitively valuable. Apple's operating system for its PCs is by most accounts a world beater (compared to Windows Vista and Windows 7), but Apple has failed miserably in converting its strength in operating system design into competitive success in the global PC market—it is an also-ran with a only a 5 percent market share worldwide. Thus, although Apple has many competitively valuable resources (its design capabilities, for example), its operating system is not among them.

2. *Is the resource **Rare**—is it something rivals lack?* Resources and capabilities that are common among firms and widely available cannot be a source of competitive advantage. All makers of branded cereals have valuable marketing capabilities and brands, since the key success factors in the ready-to-eat cereal industry demand this. They are not rare. The brand strength of Cheerios, however, is uncommon and has provided General Mills with greater market share as well as the opportunity to benefit from brand extensions like Honey Nut Cheerios. A resource or capability is considered rare if it is held by only a small number of firms in an industry or specific competitive domain. Thus, while general management capabilities are not rare in an absolute sense, they are relatively rare in some of the less developed regions of the world and in some business domains.

3. *Is the resource hard to copy (**Inimitable**)?* If a resource or capability is both valuable and rare, it will be competitively superior to comparable resources of rival firms. As such, it is a source of competitive advantage for the company. The more difficult and more costly it is for competitors to imitate, the more likely that it can also provide a *sustainable* competitive advantage. Resources tend to be difficult to copy when they are unique (a fantastic real estate location, patent-protected technology, an unusually talented and motivated labor force), when they must be built over time in ways that are difficult to imitate (a well-known brand name, mastery of a complex process technology, years of cumulative experience and learning), and when they entail financial outlays or large-scale operations that few industry members can undertake (a global network of dealers and distributors). Imitation is also difficult for resources that reflect a high level of *social complexity* (company culture, interpersonal relationships among the managers or R&D teams, trust-based relations with customers or suppliers) and *causal ambiguity,* a term that signifies the hard-to-disentangle nature of the complex resources, such as a web of intricate processes enabling new drug discovery. Hard-to-copy resources and capabilities are important competitive assets, contributing to the longevity of a company's market position and offering the potential for sustained profitability.

4.  *Is the resource invulnerable to the threat of substitution from different types of resources and capabilities (**Non-substitutable**)?* Even resources and capabilities that are valuable, rare, and hard to copy can lose much of their competitive power if rivals have other types of resources and capabilities that are of equal or greater competitive power. A company may have the most technologically advanced and sophisticated plants in its industry, but any efficiency advantage it enjoys may be nullified if rivals are able to produce equally good products at lower cost by locating their plants in countries where wage rates are relatively low and a labor force with adequate skills is available.

The vast majority of companies are not well endowed with standout resources or capabilities, capable of passing all four tests with high marks. Most firms have a mixed bag of resources—one or two quite valuable, some good, many satisfactory to mediocre. Resources and capabilities that are valuable pass the first of the four tests. As key contributors to the effectiveness of the strategy, they are relevant to the firm's competitiveness but are no guarantee of competitive advantage. They may offer no more than competitive parity with competing firms.

Passing both of the first two tests requires more—it requires resources and capabilities that are not only valuable but also rare. This is a much higher hurdle that can be cleared only by resources and capabilities that are *competitively superior.* Resources and capabilities that are competitively superior are the company's true strategic assets. They provide the company with a competitive advantage over its competitors, if only in the short run.

To pass the last two tests, a resource must be able to maintain its competitive superiority in the face of competition. It must be resistant to imitative attempts and efforts by competitors to find equally valuable substitute resources. Assessing the availability of substitutes is the most difficult of all the tests since substitutes are harder to recognize, but the key is to look for resources or capabilities held by other firms that *can serve the same function* as the company's core resources and capabilities.[6]

Very few firms have resources and capabilities that can pass all four tests, but those that do enjoy a sustainable competitive advantage with far greater profit potential. Walmart is a notable example, with capabilities in logistics and supply chain management that have surpassed those of its competitors for over 30 years. Lincoln Electric Company, less well known but no less notable in its achievements, has been the world leader in welding products for over 100 years as a result of its unique piecework incentive system for compensating production workers and the unsurpassed worker productivity and product quality that this system has fostered.

## A Company's Resources and Capabilities Must Be Managed Dynamically

Even companies like Walmart and Lincoln Electric cannot afford to rest on their laurels. Rivals that are initially unable to replicate a key resource may develop better and better substitutes over time. Resources and capabilities can depreciate like other assets if they are managed with benign neglect. Disruptive changes in technology, customer preferences, distribution channels, or other competitive factors can also destroy the value of key strategic assets, turning resources and capabilities "from diamonds to rust."[7]

Resources and capabilities must be continually strengthened and nurtured to sustain their competitive power and, at times, may need to be broadened and deepened to allow the company to position itself to pursue emerging market opportunities.[8] Organizational resources and capabilities that grow stale can impair competitiveness unless they are refreshed, modified, or even phased out and replaced in response

A company requires a dynamically evolving portfolio of resources and capabilities to sustain its competitiveness and help drive improvements in its performance.

to ongoing market changes and shifts in company strategy. Management's challenge in managing the firm's resources and capabilities dynamically has two elements: (1) attending to the ongoing modification of existing competitive assets and (2) casting a watchful eye for opportunities to develop totally new kinds of capabilities.

**The Role of Dynamic Capabilities**    Companies that know the importance of recalibrating and upgrading their most valuable resources and capabilities ensure that these activities are done on a continual basis. By incorporating these activities into their routine managerial functions, they gain the experience necessary to be able to do them consistently well. At that point, their ability to freshen and renew their competitive assets becomes a capability in itself—a **dynamic capability.** A dynamic capability is the ability to modify, deepen, or augment the company's existing resources and capabilities.[9] This includes the capacity to improve existing resources and capabilities incrementally, in the way that 3M continually upgrades the R&D resources driving its product innovation strategy. It also includes the capacity to add new resources and capabilities to the company's competitive asset portfolio. An example is Pfizer's acquisition capabilities, which have enabled it to replace degraded resources such as expiring patents with newly acquired capabilities in biotechnology.

# QUESTION 3: IS THE COMPANY ABLE TO SEIZE MARKET OPPORTUNITIES AND NULLIFY EXTERNAL THREATS?

**LO 3**

Discover how to assess the company's strengths and weaknesses in light of market opportunities and external threats.

In evaluating a company's overall situation, a key question is whether the company is in a position to pursue attractive market opportunities and defend against external threats to its future well-being. The simplest and most easily applied tool for conducting this examination is widely known as *SWOT analysis,* so named because it zeros in on a company's internal **S**trengths and **W**eaknesses, market **O**pportunities, and external **T**hreats. A first-rate SWOT analysis provides the basis for crafting a strategy that capitalizes on the company's strengths, overcomes its weaknesses, aims squarely at capturing the company's best opportunities, and defends against competitive and environmental threats.

## Identifying a Company's Internal Strengths

A *strength* is something a company is good at doing or an attribute that enhances its competitiveness in the marketplace. A company's strengths depend on the quality of its resources and capabilities. Resource and capability analysis provides a way for managers to assess the quality objectively. While resources and capabilities that pass the VRIN tests of sustainable competitive advantage are among the company's greatest strengths, other types can be counted among the company's strengths as well. A capability that is not potent enough to produce a sustainable advantage over rivals may yet enable a series of temporary advantages if used as a basis for entry into a new market or market segment. A resource bundle that fails to match those of top-tier competitors may still allow a company to compete successfully against the second tier.

## Assessing a Company's Competencies—What Activities Does It Perform Well?

One way to appraise the degree of a company's strengths has to do with the company's skill level in performing key pieces of its business—such as supply chain management, R&D, production, distribution, sales and marketing, and customer service. A company's skill or proficiency in performing different facets of its operations can range from one of minimal ability to perform an activity (perhaps having just struggled to do it the first time) to the other extreme of being able to perform the activity better than any other company in the industry.

When a company's proficiency rises from that of mere ability to perform an activity to the point of being able to perform it consistently well and at acceptable cost, it is said to have a **competence**—a true *capability,* in other words. A **core competence** is a proficiently performed internal activity that is *central* to a company's strategy and competitiveness. A core competence is a more competitively valuable strength than a competence because of the activity's key role in the company's strategy and the contribution it makes to the company's market success and profitability. Often, core competencies can be leveraged to create new markets or new product demand, as the engine behind a company's growth. 3M Corporation has a core competence in product innovation—its record of introducing new products goes back several decades and new product introduction is central to 3M's strategy of growing its business.

A **distinctive competence** is a competitively valuable activity that a company *performs better than its rivals.* A distinctive competence thus signifies greater proficiency than a core competence. Because a distinctive competence represents a level of proficiency that rivals do not have, it qualifies as a *competitively superior strength* with competitive advantage potential. This is particularly true when the distinctive competence enables a company to deliver standout value to customers (in the form of lower prices, better product performance, or superior service). For instance, Walt Disney has a distinctive competence in feature film animation.

The conceptual differences between a competence, a core competence, and a distinctive competence draw attention to the fact that a company's strengths and competitive assets are not all equal.[10] All competencies have some value. But mere ability to perform an activity well does not necessarily give a company competitive clout. Some competencies merely enable market survival because most rivals also have them—indeed, not having a competence that rivals have can result in competitive disadvantage. An apparel manufacturer cannot survive without the capability to produce its apparel items very cost-efficiently, given the intensely price-competitive nature of the apparel industry. A maker of cell phones cannot survive without good product design and product innovation capabilities.

## Identifying Company Weaknesses and Competitive Deficiencies

A **weakness**, or *competitive deficiency,* is something a company lacks or does poorly (in comparison to others) or a condition that puts it at a disadvantage in the marketplace. A company's internal weaknesses can relate to (1) inferior or unproven skills, expertise, or intellectual capital in competitively important areas of the business; (2) deficiencies in competitively important physical, organizational, or intangible assets; or (3) missing or competitively inferior capabilities in key areas. *Company weaknesses*

---

Basing a company's strategy on its most competitively valuable strengths gives the company its best chance for market success.

**CORE CONCEPT**

A **competence** is an activity that a company has learned to perform with proficiency—a capability, in other words.

**CORE CONCEPT**

A **core competence** is an activity that a company performs proficiently that is also central to its strategy and competitive success.

**CORE CONCEPT**

A **distinctive competence** is a competitively important activity that a company performs better than its rivals—it thus represents *a competitively superior internal strength.*

**CORE CONCEPT**

A company's **strengths** represent its competitive assets; its **weaknesses** are shortcomings that constitute competitive liabilities.

*are thus internal shortcomings that constitute competitive liabilities.* Nearly all companies have competitive liabilities of one kind or another. Whether a company's internal weaknesses make it competitively vulnerable depends on how much they matter in the marketplace and whether they are offset by the company's strengths.

Table 4.3 lists many of the things to consider in compiling a company's strengths and weaknesses. Sizing up a company's complement of strengths and deficiencies is akin to constructing a *strategic balance sheet,* where strengths represent *competitive assets* and weaknesses represent *competitive liabilities.* Obviously, the ideal condition is for the company's competitive assets to outweigh its competitive liabilities by an ample margin—a 50-50 balance is definitely not the desired condition!

## Identifying a Company's Market Opportunities

Market opportunity is a big factor in shaping a company's strategy. Indeed, managers can't properly tailor strategy to the company's situation without first identifying its market opportunities and appraising the growth and profit potential each one holds. Depending on the prevailing circumstances, a company's opportunities can be plentiful or scarce, fleeting or lasting, and can range from wildly attractive (an absolute "must" to pursue) to marginally interesting (because of the high risks or questionable profit potentials) to unsuitable (because the company's strengths are ill-suited to successfully capitalizing on the opportunities). A sampling of potential market opportunities is shown in Table 4.3.

Newly emerging and fast-changing markets sometimes present stunningly big or "golden" opportunities, but it is typically hard for managers at one company to peer into "the fog of the future" and spot them much ahead of managers at other companies.[11] But as the fog begins to clear, golden opportunities are nearly always seized rapidly—and the companies that seize them are usually those that have been actively waiting, staying alert with diligent market reconnaissance, and preparing themselves to capitalize on shifting market conditions by patiently assembling an arsenal of competitively valuable resources—talented personnel, technical know-how, strategic partnerships, and a war chest of cash to finance aggressive action when the time comes. In mature markets, unusually attractive market opportunities emerge sporadically, often after long periods of relative calm—but future market conditions may be more predictable, making emerging opportunities easier for industry members to detect.

In evaluating a company's market opportunities and ranking their attractiveness, managers have to guard against viewing every *industry* opportunity as a *company* opportunity. Rarely does a company have the resource depth to pursue all available market opportunities simultaneously without spreading itself too thin. Some companies have resources and capabilities that are better-suited for pursuing some opportunities, and a few companies may be hopelessly outclassed in competing for any of an industry's attractive opportunities. *The market opportunities most relevant to a company are those that match up well with the company's competitive assets, offer the best prospects for growth and profitability, and present the most potential for competitive advantage.*

> A company is well advised to pass on a particular market opportunity unless it has or can acquire the resources and competencies needed to capture it.

## Identifying the Threats to a Company's Future Profitability

Often, certain factors in a company's external environment pose *threats* to its profitability and competitive well-being. Threats can stem from the emergence of cheaper or better technologies, the entry of lower-cost foreign competitors into a company's market stronghold,

**TABLE 4.3   What to Look for in Identifying a Company's Strengths, Weaknesses, Opportunities, and Threats**

| Potential Strengths and Competitive Assets | Potential Weaknesses and Competitive Deficiencies |
|---|---|
| • Competencies that are well matched to industry key success factors<br>• Ample financial resources to grow the business<br>• Strong brand-name image/company reputation<br>• Economies of scale and/or learning and experience curve advantages over rivals<br>• Other cost advantages over rivals<br>• Attractive customer base<br>• Proprietary technology, superior technological skills, important patents<br>• Strong bargaining power over suppliers or buyers<br>• Resources and capabilities that are valuable and rare<br>• Resources and capabilities that are hard to copy and for which there are no good substitutes<br>• Superior product quality<br>• Wide geographic coverage and/or strong global distribution capability<br>• Alliances / joint ventures that provide access to valuable technology, competencies, and/or attractive geographic markets | • No clear strategic vision<br>• No well-developed or proven core competencies<br>• No distinctive competencies or competitively superior resources<br>• Lack of attention to customer needs<br>• A product/service with features and attributes that are inferior to those of rivals<br>• Weak balance sheet, short on financial resources to grow the firm, too much debt<br>• Higher overall unit costs relative to those of key competitors<br>• Too narrow a product line relative to rivals<br>• Weak brand image or reputation<br>• Weaker dealer network than key rivals and/or lack of adequate distribution capability<br>• Lack of management depth<br>• Plagued with internal operating problems or obsolete facilities<br>• Too much underutilized plant capacity<br>• Resources that are readily copied or for which there are good substitutes |
| **Potential Market Opportunities** | **Potential External Threats to a Company's Future Profitability** |
| • Sharply rising buyer demand for the industry's product<br>• Serving additional customer groups or market segments<br>• Expanding into new geographic markets<br>• Expanding the company's product line to meet a broader range of customer needs<br>• Utilizing existing company skills or technological know-how to enter new product lines or new businesses<br>• Falling trade barriers in attractive foreign markets<br>• Acquiring rival firms or companies with attractive technological expertise or capabilities<br>• Entering into alliances or joint ventures to expand the firm's market coverage or boost its competitive capability | • Increasing intensity of competition among industry rivals—may squeeze profit margins<br>• Slowdowns in market growth<br>• Likely entry of potent new competitors<br>• Growing bargaining power of customers or suppliers<br>• A shift in buyer needs and tastes away from the industry's product<br>• Adverse demographic changes that threaten to curtail demand for the industry's product<br>• Adverse economic conditions that threaten critical suppliers or distributers<br>• Changes in technology—particularly disruptive technology that can undermine the company's distinctive competencies<br>• Restrictive foreign trade policies<br>• Costly new regulatory requirements<br>• Tight credit conditions<br>• Rising prices on energy or other key inputs |

Simply making lists of a company's strengths, weaknesses, opportunities, and threats is not enough; the payoff from SWOT analysis comes from the conclusions about a company's situation and the implications for strategy improvement that flow from the four lists.

new regulations that are more burdensome to a company than to its competitors, unfavorable demographic shifts, political upheaval in a foreign country where the company has facilities, and the like. A list of potential threats to a company's future profitability and market position is shown in Table 4.3.

External threats may pose no more than a moderate degree of adversity (all companies confront some threatening elements in the course of doing business), or they may be so imposing as to make a company's situation look quite tenuous. On rare occasions, market shocks can give birth to a *sudden-death* threat that throws a company into an immediate crisis and a battle to survive. Many of the world's major financial institutions were plunged into unprecedented crisis in 2008–2009 by the aftereffects of high-risk mortgage lending, inflated credit ratings on subprime mortgage securities, the collapse of housing prices, and a market flooded with mortgage-related investments (collateralized debt obligations) whose values suddenly evaporated. It is management's job to identify the threats to the company's future prospects and to evaluate what strategic actions can be taken to neutralize or lessen their impact.

## What Do the SWOT Listings Reveal?

SWOT analysis involves more than making four lists. The two most important parts of SWOT analysis are *drawing conclusions* from the SWOT listings about the company's overall situation and *translating these conclusions into strategic actions* to better match the company's strategy to its internal strengths and market opportunities, to correct important weaknesses, and to defend against external threats. Figure 4.2 shows the steps involved in gleaning insights from SWOT analysis.

Just what story the SWOT listings tell about the company's overall situation is often revealed in the answers to the following set of questions:

- What are the attractive aspects of the company's situation?
- What aspects are of the most concern?
- Are the company's internal strengths and competitive assets sufficiently strong to enable it to compete successfully?
- Are the company's weaknesses and competitive deficiencies of small consequence and readily correctable, or could they prove fatal if not remedied soon?
- Do the company's strengths outweigh its weaknesses by an attractive margin?
- Does the company have attractive market opportunities that are well suited to its internal strengths? Does the company lack the competitive assets to pursue the most attractive opportunities?
- All things considered, where on a scale of 1 to 10 (where 1 is alarmingly weak and 10 is exceptionally strong) do the company's overall situation and future prospects rank?

The final piece of SWOT analysis is to translate the diagnosis of the company's situation into actions for improving the company's strategy and business prospects. *A company's internal strengths should always serve as the basis of its strategy—placing heavy reliance on a company's best competitive assets is the soundest route to attracting customers and competing successfully against rivals.*[12] As a rule, strategies that place heavy demands on areas where the company is weakest or has unproven competencies should be avoided. Plainly, managers must look toward correcting competitive weaknesses that make the company vulnerable, hold down profitability, or disqualify it from pursuing an attractive opportunity. Furthermore, a company's strategy should be aimed squarely at capturing those market opportunities that are most attractive and suited to the company's collection

**FIGURE 4.2** The Steps Involved in SWOT Analysis: Identify the Four Components of SWOT, Draw Conclusions, Translate Implications into Strategic Actions

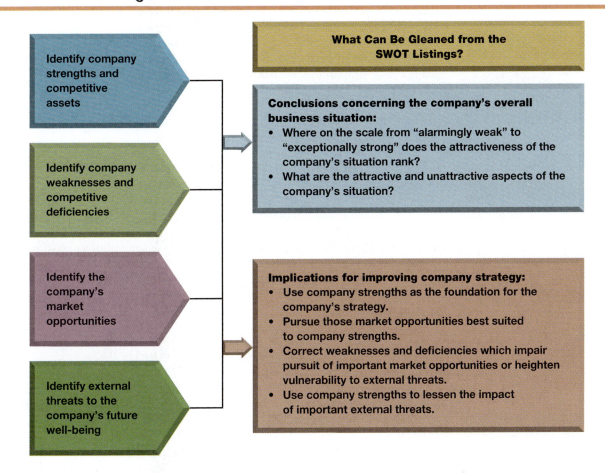

Identify company strengths and competitive assets

Identify company weaknesses and competitive deficiencies

Identify the company's market opportunities

Identify external threats to the company's future well-being

**What Can Be Gleaned from the SWOT Listings?**

**Conclusions concerning the company's overall business situation:**
- Where on the scale from "alarmingly weak" to "exceptionally strong" does the attractiveness of the company's situation rank?
- What are the attractive and unattractive aspects of the company's situation?

**Implications for improving company strategy:**
- Use company strengths as the foundation for the company's strategy.
- Pursue those market opportunities best suited to company strengths.
- Correct weaknesses and deficiencies which impair pursuit of important market opportunities or heighten vulnerability to external threats.
- Use company strengths to lessen the impact of important external threats.

of capabilities. How much attention to devote to defending against external threats to the company's future performance hinges on how vulnerable the company is, whether defensive moves can be taken to lessen their impact, and whether the costs of undertaking such moves represent the best use of company resources.

# QUESTION 4: ARE THE COMPANY'S COST STRUCTURE AND CUSTOMER VALUE PROPOSITION COMPETITIVE?

Company managers are often stunned when a competitor cuts its prices to "unbelievably low" levels or when a new market entrant comes on strong with a great new product offered at a surprisingly low price. Such competitors may not, however, be buying market positions with prices that are below costs. They may simply have substantially lower costs and therefore are able to offer prices that result in more appealing customer value propositions.

**LO 4**

Grasp how a company's value chain activities can affect the company's cost structure and customer value proposition.

While less common, new entrants can also storm the market with a product that ratchets the quality level up so high that customers will abandon competing sellers even if they have to pay more for the new product. With its vastly greater storage capacity and lightweight, cool design, Apple's iPod left other makers of portable digital music players in the dust when it was first introduced. Apple's new iPad appears to be doing the same in the market for e-readers and tablet PCs.

Regardless of where on the quality spectrum a company competes, it must remain competitive in terms of its customer value proposition in order to stay in the game. Tiffany's value proposition, for example, remains attractive to customers who want customer service, the assurance of quality, and a high-status brand despite the availability of cut-rate diamond jewelry online. Target's customer value proposition has withstood the Walmart low-price juggernaut by attention to product design, image, and attractive store layouts in addition to efficiency.

The value provided to the customer depends on how well a customer's needs are met for the price paid. How well customer needs are met depends on the perceived quality of a product or service as well as other, more tangible attributes. The greater the amount of customer value that the company can offer profitably compared to its rivals, the less vulnerable it will be to competitive attack. For managers, the key is to keep close track of how *cost effectively* the company can deliver value to customers relative to its competitors. If they can deliver the same amount of value with lower expenditures (or more value at the same cost), they will maintain a competitive edge.

Two analytical tools are particularly useful in determining whether a company's costs and customer value proposition are competitive: value chain analysis and benchmarking.

> The higher a company's costs are above those of close rivals, the more competitively vulnerable it becomes.

> The greater the amount of customer value that a company can offer profitably relative to close rivals, the less competitively vulnerable it becomes.

## The Concept of a Company Value Chain

Every company's business consists of a collection of activities undertaken in the course of producing, delivering, and supporting its product or service. All the various activities that a company performs internally combine to form a **value chain**—so-called because the underlying intent of a company's activities is to do things that ultimately *create value for buyers.*

As shown in Figure 4.3, a company's value chain consists of two broad categories of activities: the *primary activities* that are foremost in creating value for customers and the requisite *support activities* that facilitate and enhance the performance of the primary activities.[13] The exact natures of the primary and secondary activities that make up a company's value chain vary according to the specifics of a company's business; hence, the listing of the primary and support activities in Figure 4.3 is illustrative rather than definitive. For example, the primary activities at a hotel chain like Sheraton are mainly comprised of site selection and construction, reservations, and hotel operations (check-in and check-out, maintenance and housekeeping, dining and room service, and conventions and meetings); principal support activities that drive costs and impact customer value include hiring and training hotel staff, and general administration. Supply chain management is a crucial activity for Nissan and **Amazon.com** but is not a value chain component at Google or a radio broadcasting company. Sales and marketing are dominant activities at Procter & Gamble and Sony but have minor roles at oil drilling companies and natural gas pipeline companies.

With its focus on value-creating activities, the value chain is an ideal tool for examining how a company delivers on its customer value proposition. It permits a deep look at the company's cost structure and ability to offer low prices. It reveals the emphasis that a company places on activities that enhance differentiation and support higher

### CORE CONCEPT

A company's **value chain** identifies the primary activities and related support activities that create customer value.

## FIGURE 4.3 A Representative Company Value Chain

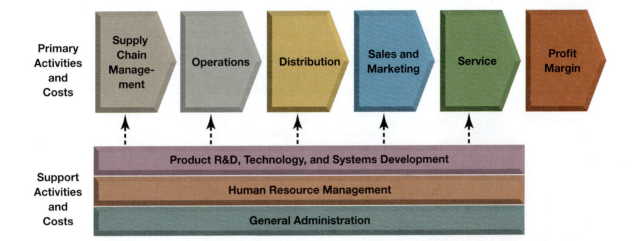

**PRIMARY ACTIVITIES**

- **Supply Chain Management**—Activities, costs, and assets associated with purchasing fuel, energy, raw materials, parts and components, merchandise, and consumable items from vendors; receiving, storing, and disseminating inputs from suppliers; inspection; and inventory management.

- **Operations**—Activities, costs, and assets associated with converting inputs into final product form (production, assembly, packaging, equipment maintenance, facilities, operations, quality assurance, environmental protection).

- **Distribution**—Activities, costs, and assets dealing with physically distributing the product to buyers (finished goods warehousing, order processing, order picking and packing, shipping, delivery vehicle operations, establishing and maintaining a network of dealers and distributors).

- **Sales and Marketing**—Activities, costs, and assets related to sales force efforts, advertising and promotion, market research and planning, and dealer/distributor support.

- **Service**—Activities, costs, and assets associated with providing assistance to buyers, such as installation, spare parts delivery, maintenance and repair, technical assistance, buyer inquiries, and complaints.

**SUPPORT ACTIVITIES**

- **Product R&D, Technology, and Systems Development**—Activities, costs, and assets relating to product R&D, process R&D, process design improvement, equipment design, computer software development, telecommunications systems, computer-assisted design and engineering, database capabilities, and development of computerized support systems.

- **Human Resources Management**—Activities, costs, and assets associated with the recruitment, hiring, training, development, and compensation of all types of personnel; labor relations activities; and development of knowledge-based skills and core competencies.

- **General Administration**—Activities, costs, and assets relating to general management, accounting and finance, legal and regulatory affairs, safety and security, management information systems, forming strategic alliances and collaborating with strategic partners, and other "overhead" functions.

*Source:* Based on the discussion in Michael E. Porter, *Competitive Advantage* (New York: Free Press, 1985), pp. 37–43.

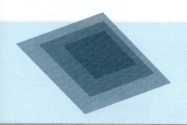
# The Value Chain for KP MacLane, a Producer of Polo Shirts

| Value Chain Activities and Costs in Producing and Selling a Women's Polo Shirt | |
|---|---:|
| 1. Cotton-blend fabric from France | $ 6.80 |
| 2. Fabric for placket and vent | $ 0.99 |
| 3. 4 buttons, including 1 extra | $ 0.12 |
| 4. Thread | $ 0.09 |
| 5. Labels | $ 1.10 |
| 6. Hang tag | $ 0.40 |
| 7. Waste fabric | $ 0.85 |
| 8. Labor | $ 11.05 |
| 9. Packing materials | $ 0.17 |
| 10. Shipping materials to factory; shirt to store | $ 5.00 |
| 11. Hand-embroidered linen bag | $ 3.00 |
| 12. Total company costs | $ 29.57 |
| 13. Wholesale markup over company costs (company operating profit) | $ 35.43 |
| 14. Wholesale price | $ 65.00 |
| 15. Retailer's markup | $ 90.00 |
| 16. Retail price | $155.00 |

*Source:* Christina Binkley, "What Goes Into a $155 Price Tag?" *The Wall St. Journal,* U.S Home Edition, On Style, 2/2/2012, Accessed 2/3/12 online at http://online.wsj .com/article_email/SB10001424052970204652904577195252388913754- IMyQjAxMTAyMDAwMzEwNDMyWj.html?mod=wsj_share_email.

prices, such as service and marketing. Note that there is also a profit margin component to the value chain; this is because profits are necessary to compensate the company's owners/shareholders and investors, who bear risks and provide capital. Tracking the profit margin along with the value-creating activities is critical because unless an enterprise succeeds in delivering customer value profitably (with a sufficient return on invested capital), it can't survive for long. Attention to a company's profit formula in addition to its customer value proposition is the essence of a sound business model, as described in Chapter 1.

Illustration Capsule 4.1 shows representative costs for various activities performed by KP MacLane, a maker of upscale polo shirts.

**Comparing the Value Chains of Rival Companies**   The primary purpose of value chain analysis is to facilitate a comparison, activity-by-activity, of how effectively and efficiently a company delivers value to its customers, relative to its competitors. Segregating the company's operations into different types of primary and secondary activities is the first step in this comparison. The next is to do the same for the company's most significant competitors.

Even rivals in the same industry may differ significantly in terms of the activities they perform. For instance, the "operations" component of the value chain for a manufacturer that makes all of its own parts and components and assembles them into a finished product differs from the "operations" of a rival producer that buys the needed parts and components from outside suppliers and only performs assembly operations. How each activity is performed may affect a company's relative cost position as well as its capacity for differentiation. Thus, even a simple comparison of how the activities of rivals' value chains differ can be revealing of competitive differences.

**A Company's Primary and Secondary Activities Identify the Major Components of Its Internal Cost Structure**   The combined costs of all the various primary and support activities comprising a company's value chain define its internal cost structure. Further, the cost of each activity contributes to whether the company's overall cost position relative to rivals is favorable or unfavorable. Key purposes of value chain analysis and benchmarking are to develop the data for comparing a company's costs activity by activity against the costs of key rivals and to learn which internal activities are a source of cost advantage or disadvantage.

Evaluating a company's cost-competitiveness involves using what accountants call *activity-based costing* to determine the costs of performing each value chain activity (and the assets required, including working capital).[14] The degree to which a company's total costs should be broken down into costs for specific activities depends on how valuable it is to know the costs of very specific activities versus broadly defined activities. At the very least, cost estimates are needed for each broad category of primary and support activities, but cost estimates for more specific activities within each broad category may be needed if a company discovers that it has a cost disadvantage vis-à-vis rivals and wants to pin down the exact source or activity causing the cost disadvantage. However, a company's own *internal costs* may be insufficient to assess whether its product offering and customer value proposition are competitive with those of rivals. Cost and price differences among competing companies can have their origins in activities performed by suppliers or by distribution allies involved in getting the product to the final customer or end user of the product, in which case the company's entire *value chain system* becomes relevant.

> A company's cost competitiveness depends not only on the costs of internally performed activities (its own value chain) but also on costs in the value chains of its suppliers and distribution channel allies.

# The Value Chain System

A company's value chain is embedded in a larger system of activities that includes the value chains of its suppliers and the value chains of whatever wholesale distributors and retailers it utilizes in getting its product or service to end users. This *value chain system* has implications that extend far beyond the company's costs. It can affect attributes like product quality that enhance differentiation and have importance for the company's customer value proposition, as well as its profitability.[15] Suppliers' value chains are relevant because suppliers perform activities and incur costs in creating and delivering the purchased inputs utilized in a company's own value-creating activities. The costs, performance features, and quality of these inputs influence a company's own costs and product differentiation capabilities. Anything a company can do to help its suppliers' drive down the costs of their value chain activities or improve the quality and performance of the items being supplied can enhance its own competitiveness—a powerful reason for working collaboratively with suppliers in managing supply chain activities.[16]

Similarly, the value chains of a company's distribution channel partners are relevant because (1) the costs and margins of a company's distributors and retail dealers are part of the price the ultimate consumer pays and (2) the activities that distribution allies perform affect sales volumes and customer satisfaction. For these reasons, companies normally work closely with their distribution allies (who are their direct customers) to perform value chain activities in mutually beneficial ways. For instance, motor vehicle manufacturers have a competitive interest in working closely with their automobile dealers to promote higher sales volumes and better customer satisfaction with dealers' repair and maintenance services. Producers of kitchen cabinets are heavily dependent on the sales and promotional activities of their distributors and building supply retailers and on whether distributors/retailers operate cost-effectively enough to be able to sell at prices that lead to attractive sales volumes.

As a consequence, *accurately assessing a company's competitiveness entails scrutinizing the nature and costs of value chain activities throughout the entire value chain system for delivering its products or services to end-use customers.* A typical value chain system that incorporates the value chains of suppliers and forward channel allies (if any) is shown in Figure 4.4. As was the case with company value chains, the specific activities constituting value chain systems vary significantly from industry to industry. The primary value chain system activities in the pulp and paper industry (timber farming, logging, pulp mills, and papermaking) differ from the primary value chain system activities in the home appliance industry (parts and components manufacture, assembly, wholesale distribution, retail sales). The value chain system in the soft-drink industry (syrup manufacture, bottling, wholesale distribution, advertising, and retail merchandising) differs from that in the computer software industry (programming, disk loading, marketing, distribution).

## FIGURE 4.4 A Representative Value Chain System

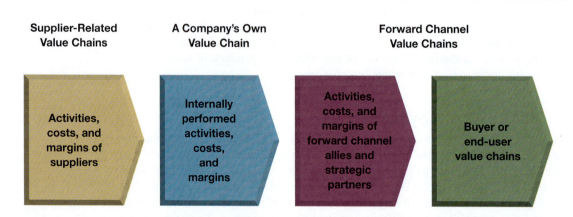

*Source:* Based in part on the single-industry value chain displayed in Michael E. Porter, *Competitive Advantage* (New York: Free Press, 1985), p. 35.

# Benchmarking: A Tool for Assessing Whether the Costs and Effectiveness of a Company's Value Chain Activities Are in Line

Once a company has developed good estimates for the costs and effectiveness of each of the major activities in its own value chain and has sufficient data relating to the value chain activities of suppliers and distribution allies, then it is ready to explore how it compares on these dimensions with key rivals. This is where benchmarking comes in. **Benchmarking** entails comparing how different companies perform various value chain activities—how materials are purchased, how inventories are managed, how products are assembled, how fast the company can get new products to market, how customer orders are filled and shipped—and then making cross-company comparisons of the costs and effectiveness of these activities.[17] The objectives of benchmarking are to identify the best practices in performing an activity and to emulate those best practices when they are possessed by others.

Xerox led the way in the use of benchmarking to become more cost-competitive, quickly deciding not to restrict its benchmarking efforts to its office equipment rivals but to extend them to any company regarded as "world class" in performing *any activity* relevant to Xerox's business. Other companies quickly picked up on Xerox's approach. Toyota managers got their idea for just-in-time inventory deliveries by studying how U.S. supermarkets replenished their shelves. Southwest Airlines reduced the turnaround time of its aircraft at each scheduled stop by studying pit crews on the auto racing circuit. Over 80 percent of Fortune 500 companies reportedly use benchmarking for comparing themselves against rivals on cost and other competitively important measures.

The tough part of benchmarking is not whether to do it but rather how to gain access to information about other companies' practices and costs. Sometimes benchmarking can be accomplished by collecting information from published reports, trade groups, and industry research firms or by talking to knowledgeable industry analysts, customers, and suppliers. Sometimes field trips to the facilities of competing or noncompeting companies can be arranged to observe how things are done, compare practices and processes, and perhaps exchange data on productivity and other cost components. However, such companies, even if they agree to host facilities tours and answer questions, are unlikely to share competitively sensitive cost information. Furthermore, comparing two companies' costs may not involve comparing apples to apples if the two companies employ different cost accounting principles to calculate the costs of particular activities.

However, a third and fairly reliable source of benchmarking information has emerged. The explosive interest of companies in benchmarking costs and identifying best practices has prompted consulting organizations (e.g., Accenture, A. T. Kearney, Benchnet—The Benchmarking Exchange, and Best Practices, LLC) and several associations (e.g., the Qualserve Benchmarking Clearinghouse, and the Strategic Planning Institute's Council on Benchmarking) to gather benchmarking data, distribute information about best practices, and provide comparative cost data without identifying the names of particular companies. Having an independent group gather the information and report it in a manner that disguises the names of individual companies protects competitively sensitive data and lessens the potential for unethical behavior on the part of company personnel in gathering their own data about competitors. Illustration Capsule 4.2 presents a widely recommended code of conduct for engaging in benchmarking.

## CORE CONCEPT

**Benchmarking** is a potent tool for improving a company's own internal activities that is based on learning how other companies perform them and borrowing their "best practices."

Benchmarking the costs of company activities against rivals provides hard evidence of whether a company is cost-competitive.

# Benchmarking and Ethical Conduct

Because discussions between benchmarking partners can involve competitively sensitive data, conceivably raising questions about possible restraint of trade or improper business conduct, many benchmarking organizations urge all individuals and organizations involved in benchmarking to abide by a code of conduct grounded in ethical business behavior. One of the most widely used codes of conduct is the one developed by APQC (formerly the American Productivity and Quality Center) and advocated by the Qualserve Benchmarking Clearinghouse; it is based on the following principles and guidelines:

- Avoid discussions or actions that could lead to or imply an interest in restraint of trade, market and/or customer allocation schemes, price fixing, dealing arrangements, bid rigging, or bribery. Don't discuss costs with competitors if costs are an element of pricing.

- Refrain from the acquisition of trade secrets from another by any means that could be interpreted as improper, including the breach of any duty to maintain secrecy. Do not disclose or use any trade secret that may have been obtained through improper means or that was disclosed by another in violation of duty to maintain its secrecy or limit its use.

- Be willing to provide to your benchmarking partner the same type and level of information that you request from that partner.

- Communicate fully and early in the relationship to clarify expectations, avoid misunderstanding, and establish mutual interest in the benchmarking exchange.

- Be honest and complete with the information submitted.

- The use or communication of a benchmarking partner's name with the data obtained or practices observed requires the prior permission of the benchmarking partner.

- Honor the wishes of benchmarking partners regarding how the information that is provided will be handled and used.

- In benchmarking with competitors, establish specific ground rules up front. For example, "We don't want to talk about things that will give either of us a competitive advantage, but rather we want to see where we both can mutually improve or gain benefit."

- Check with legal counsel if any information-gathering procedure is in doubt. If uncomfortable, do not proceed. Alternatively, negotiate and sign a specific nondisclosure agreement that will satisfy the attorneys representing each partner.

- Do not ask competitors for sensitive data or cause benchmarking partners to feel they must provide data to continue the process.

- Use an ethical third party to assemble and "blind" competitive data, with inputs from legal counsel in direct competitor sharing. (Note: When cost is closely linked to price, sharing cost data can be considered to be the same as sharing price data.)

- Any information obtained from a benchmarking partner should be treated as internal, privileged communications. If "confidential" or proprietary material is to be exchanged, then a specific agreement should be executed to specify the content of the material that needs to be protected, the duration of the period of protection, the conditions for permitting access to the material, and the specific handling requirements necessary for that material.

*Sources:* APQC, **www.apqc.org**; Qualserve Benchmarking Clearinghouse, **www.awwa.org** (accessed October 8, 2010).

# Strategic Options for Remedying a Cost or Value Disadvantage

The results of value chain analysis and benchmarking may disclose cost or value disadvantages relative to key rivals. Such information is vital in crafting strategic actions to eliminate any such disadvantages and improve profitability. Information of this nature can also help a company to recognize and reinforce activities in which it has a comparative advantage and to find new avenues for enhancing its competitiveness through lower costs or a more attractive customer value proposition. There are three main areas in a company's total value chain system where company managers can try to improve its efficiency and effectiveness in delivering customer value: (1) a company's own internal activities, (2) suppliers' part of the value chain system, and (3) the forward channel portion of the value chain system.

# Improving Internally Performed Value Chain Activities

Managers can pursue any of several strategic approaches to reduce the costs of internally performed value chain activities and improve a company's cost competitiveness:

- *Implement the use of best practices* throughout the company, particularly for high-cost activities.
- *Eliminate some cost-producing activities altogether* by revamping the value chain. Many retailers have found that donating returned items to charitable organizations and taking the appropriate tax deduction results in a smaller loss than incurring the costs of the value chain activities involved in reverse logistics.
- *Relocate high-cost activities* (such as manufacturing) to geographic areas like China, Latin America, or Eastern Europe where they can be performed more cheaply.
- *Outsource activities* from vendors or contractors if they can perform them more cheaply than can be done in-house.
- *Invest in productivity enhancing, cost-saving technological improvements* (robotics, flexible manufacturing techniques, state-of-the-art electronic networking).
- *Find ways to detour around the activities or items where costs are high*—computer chip makers regularly design around the patents held by others to avoid paying royalties; automakers have substituted lower-cost plastic for metal at many exterior body locations.
- Redesign the product and/or some of its components to facilitate speedier and more economical manufacture or assembly.

How successfully a company competes depends on more than low costs. It also depends on how effectively it delivers value to the customer and on its ability to differentiate itself from rivals. To improve the effectiveness of its customer value proposition and enhance differentiation, there are several approaches a manager can take:

- Implement the use of best practices for quality throughout the company, particularly for high-value activities (those that are important for creating value for the customer).
- Adopt best practices and technologies that spur innovation, improve design, and enhance creativity.
- Implement the use of best practices in providing customer service.
- Reallocate resources to activities that address buyers' most important purchase criteria, which will have the biggest impact on the value delivered to the customer.
- For intermediate buyers (distributors or retailers, for example), gain an understanding of how the activities the company performs impact the buyer's value chain and improve those that have the greatest impact.
- Adopt best practices for marketing, brand management, and enhancing customer perceptions.

## Improving Supplier-Related Value Chain Activities

Improving suppliers' performance of value chain activities can also remedy company disadvantages concerning costs and customer value. On the cost side, a company can gain savings in the suppliers' part of the overall value chain by pressuring those suppliers for lower prices, switching to lower-priced substitute inputs, and collaborating closely with suppliers to identify mutual cost-saving opportunities.[18] For example, just-in-time deliveries from suppliers can lower a company's inventory and internal logistics costs and may also allow suppliers to economize on their warehousing, shipping, and production scheduling costs—a win–win outcome for both. In a few instances, companies may find that it is cheaper to integrate backward into the business of high-cost suppliers and make the item in-house instead of buying it from outsiders.

Similarly, a company can enhance its customer value proposition by working with or through its suppliers to do so. Some methods include selecting and retaining suppliers who meet higher-quality standards, coordinating with suppliers to enhance design or other features desired by customers, providing incentives to encourage suppliers to meet higher-quality standards, and assisting suppliers in their efforts to improve. Fewer defects in parts from suppliers not only improve quality and enhance differentiation throughout the value chain system but can lower costs as well since there is less waste and disruption to the production processes.

### Improving Value Chain Activities of Forward Channel Allies

Any of three means can be used to achieve better cost competitiveness in the forward portion of the industry value chain: (1) pressure distributors, dealers, and other forward channel allies to reduce their costs and markups; (2) collaborate with forward channel allies to identify win–win opportunities to reduce costs—a chocolate manufacturer, for example, learned that by shipping its bulk chocolate in liquid form in tank cars instead of as 10-pound molded bars, it could not only save its candy bar manufacturing customers the costs associated with unpacking and melting but also eliminate its own costs of molding bars and packing them; and (3) change to a more economical distribution strategy, including switching to cheaper distribution channels (perhaps direct sales via the Internet) or perhaps integrating forward into company-owned retail outlets. Dell Computer's direct sales model eliminated all costs associated with distributors, dealers, and retailers by allowing buyers to purchase customized PCs directly from Dell.

The means to enhance differentiation through activities at the forward end of the value chain system include (1) engaging in cooperative advertising and promotions with forward allies (dealers, distributors, retailers, and so on), (2) creating exclusive arrangements with downstream sellers or other mechanisms that increase their incentives to enhance delivered customer value, and (3) creating and enforcing standards for downstream activities and assisting in training channel partners in business practices. Harley-Davidson, for example, enhances the shopping experience and perceptions of buyers by selling through retailers that sell Harley-Davidson motorcycles exclusively and meet Harley-Davidson standards.

## Translating Proficient Performance of Value Chain Activities into Competitive Advantage

Value chain analysis and benchmarking are not only useful for identifying and remedying competitive disadvantages; they can also be used to uncover and strengthen competitive advantages. A company's value-creating activities can offer a competitive advantage in one of two ways: (1) They can contribute to greater efficiency and lower costs relative to competitors, or (2) they can provide a basis for differentiation, so customers are willing to pay relatively more for the company's goods and services. A company that does a *first-rate job* of managing its value chain activities *relative to competitors* stands a good chance of profiting from its competitive advantage.

Achieving a cost-based competitive advantage requires determined management efforts to be cost-efficient in performing value chain activities. Such efforts have to be ongoing and persistent, and they have to involve each and every value chain activity. The goal must be continuous cost reduction, not a one-time or on-again–off-again effort. Companies like Dollar General, Nucor Steel, Irish airline Ryanair, Greyhound Lines, and

French discount retailer Carrefour have been highly successful in managing their value chains in a low-cost manner.

Ongoing and persistent efforts are also required for a competitive advantage based on differentiation. Superior reputations and brands are built up slowly over time, through continuous investment and activities that deliver consistent, reinforcing messages. Differentiation based on quality requires vigilant management of activities for quality assurance throughout the value chain. While the basis for differentiation (e.g., status, design, innovation, customer service, reliability, image) may vary widely among companies pursuing a differentiation advantage, companies that succeed do so on the basis of a commitment to coordinated value chain activities aimed purposefully at this objective. Examples include Grey Goose Vodka (status), IKEA (design), FedEx (reliability), 3M (innovation), and Nordstrom (customer service).

**How Activities Relate to Resources and Capabilities**   There is a close relationship between the value-creating activities that a company performs and its resources and capabilities. An organizational capability or competence implies a *capacity* for action; in contrast, a value-creating activity *initiates* the action. With respect to resources and capabilities, activities are "where the rubber hits the road." When companies engage in a value-creating activity, they do so by drawing on specific company resources and capabilities that underlie and enable the activity. For example, brand-building activities depend on human resources, such as experienced brand managers (including their knowledge and expertise in this arena), as well as organizational capabilities in advertising and marketing. Cost-cutting activities may derive from organizational capabilities in inventory management, for example, and resources such as inventory tracking systems.

Because of this correspondence between activities and supporting resources and capabilities, value chain analysis can complement resource and capability analysis as another tool for assessing a company's competitive advantage. Resources and capabilities that are *both valuable and rare* provide a company with *what it takes* for competitive advantage. For a company with competitive assets of this sort, the potential is there. When these assets are deployed in the form of a value-creating activity, that potential is realized due to their competitive superiority. Resource analysis is one tool for identifying competitively superior resources and capabilities. But their value and the competitive superiority of that value can only be assessed objectively *after* they are deployed. Value chain analysis and benchmarking provide the type of data needed to make that objective assessment.

There is also a dynamic relationship between a company's activities and its resources and capabilities. Value-creating activities are more than just the embodiment of a resource's or capability's potential. They also contribute to the formation and development of capabilities. The road to competitive advantage begins with management efforts to build organizational expertise in performing certain competitively important value chain activities. With consistent practice and continuous investment of company resources, these activities rise to the level of a reliable organizational capability or a competence. To the extent that top management makes the growing capability a cornerstone of the company's strategy, this capability becomes a core competence for the company. Later, with further organizational learning and gains in proficiency, the core competence may evolve into a distinctive competence, giving the company superiority over rivals in performing an important value chain activity. Such superiority, if it gives the company significant competitive clout in the marketplace, can produce an attractive competitive edge over rivals. Whether the resulting competitive advantage is on the cost side or on the differentiation side (or both) will depend on the company's choice of which types of competence-building activities to engage in over this time period, as shown in Figure 4.5.

Performing value chain activities with capabilities that permit the company to either outmatch rivals on differentiation or beat them on costs will give the company a competitive advantage.

**FIGURE 4.5** Translating Company Performance of Value Chain Activities into Competitive Advantage

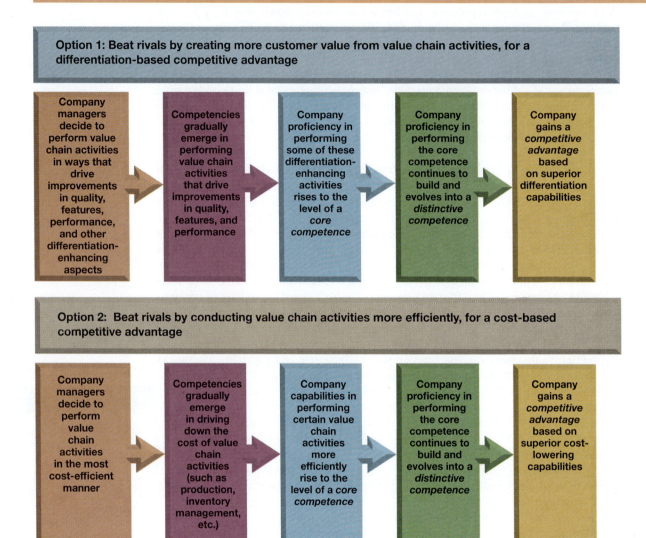

## QUESTION 5: IS THE COMPANY COMPETITIVELY STRONGER OR WEAKER THAN KEY RIVALS?

Using resource analysis, value chain analysis, and benchmarking to determine a company's competitiveness on value and cost is necessary but not sufficient. A more comprehensive assessment needs to be made of the company's *overall* competitive strength. The answers to two questions are of particular interest: First, how does the company rank relative to competitors on each of the important factors that determine market success? Second, all things considered, does the company have a *net* competitive advantage or disadvantage versus major competitors?

An easy-to-use method for answering these two questions involves developing quantitative strength ratings for the company and its key competitors on each industry key success factor and each competitively pivotal resource, capability, and value chain activity. Much of the information needed for doing a competitive strength assessment comes from previous analyses. Industry and competitive analyses reveal the key success factors and competitive forces that separate industry winners from losers. Benchmarking data and scouting key competitors provide a basis for judging the competitive strength of rivals on such factors as cost, key product attributes, customer service, image and reputation, financial strength, technological skills, distribution capability, and other factors. Resource and capability analysis reveals which of these are competitively important, given the external situation, and whether the company's competitive advantages are sustainable. SWOT analysis provides a more comprehensive and forward-looking picture of the company's overall situation.

Step 1 in doing a competitive strength assessment is to make a list of the industry's key success factors and other telling measures of competitive strength or weakness (6 to 10 measures usually suffice). Step 2 is to assign weights to each of the measures of competitive strength based on their perceived importance. (The sum of the weights for each measure must add up to 1.0.) Step 3 is to calculate weighted strength ratings by scoring each competitor on each strength measure (using a 1 to 10 rating scale where 1 is very weak and 10 is very strong) and multiplying the assigned rating by the assigned weight. Step 4 is to sum the weighted strength ratings on each factor to get an overall measure of competitive strength for each company being rated. Step 5 is to use the overall strength ratings to draw conclusions about the size and extent of the company's net competitive advantage or disadvantage and to take specific note of areas of strength and weakness.

Table 4.4 provides an example of competitive strength assessment in which a hypothetical company (ABC Company) competes against two rivals. In the example, relative cost is the most telling measure of competitive strength, and the other strength measures are of lesser importance. The company with the highest rating on a given measure has an implied competitive edge on that measure, with the size of its edge reflected in the difference between its weighted rating and rivals' weighted ratings. For instance, Rival 1's 3.00 weighted strength rating on relative cost signals a considerable cost advantage versus ABC Company (with a 1.50 weighted score on relative cost) and an even bigger cost advantage against Rival 2 (with a weighted score of 0.30). The measure-by-measure ratings reveal the competitive areas where a company is strongest and weakest, and against whom.

The overall competitive strength scores indicate how all the different strength measures add up—whether the company is at a net overall competitive advantage or disadvantage against each rival. The higher a company's *overall weighted strength rating*, the stronger its *overall competitiveness* versus rivals. The bigger the difference between a company's overall weighted rating and the scores of *lower-rated* rivals, the greater is its implied *net competitive advantage*. Thus, Rival 1's overall weighted score of 7.70 indicates a greater net competitive advantage over Rival 2 (with a score of 2.10) than over ABC Company (with a score of 5.95). Conversely, the bigger the difference between a company's overall rating and the scores of *higher-rated* rivals, the greater its implied *net competitive disadvantage*. Rival 2's score of 2.10 gives it a smaller net competitive disadvantage against ABC Company (with an overall score of 5.95) than against Rival 1 (with an overall score of 7.70).

## Strategic Implications of Competitive Strength Assessments

In addition to showing how competitively strong or weak a company is relative to rivals, the strength ratings provide guidelines for designing wise offensive and defensive strategies. For example, if ABC Co. wants to go on the offensive to win additional sales and market share,

High-weighted competitive strength ratings signal a strong competitive position and possession of competitive advantage; low ratings signal a weak position and competitive disadvantage.

## TABLE 4.4  A Representative Weighted Competitive Strength Assessment

| Key Success Factor / Strength Measure | Importance Weight | Competitive Strength Assessment (Rating scale: 1 = very weak; 10 = very strong) ABC Co. Strength Rating | ABC Co. Weighted Score | Rival 1 Strength Rating | Rival 1 Weighted Score | Rival 2 Strength Rating | Rival 2 Weighted Score |
|---|---|---|---|---|---|---|---|
| Quality/product performance | 0.10 | 8 | 0.80 | 5 | 0.50 | 1 | 0.10 |
| Reputation/image | 0.10 | 8 | 0.80 | 7 | 0.70 | 1 | 0.10 |
| Manufacturing capability | 0.10 | 2 | 0.20 | 10 | 1.00 | 5 | 0.50 |
| Technological skills | 0.05 | 10 | 0.50 | 1 | 0.05 | 3 | 0.15 |
| Dealer network / distribution capability | 0.05 | 9 | 0.45 | 4 | 0.20 | 5 | 0.25 |
| New product innovation capability | 0.05 | 9 | 0.45 | 4 | 0.20 | 5 | 0.25 |
| Financial resources | 0.10 | 5 | 0.50 | 10 | 1.00 | 3 | 0.30 |
| Relative cost position | 0.30 | 5 | 1.50 | 10 | 3.00 | 1 | 0.30 |
| Customer service capabilities | 0.15 | 5 | 0.75 | 7 | 1.05 | 1 | 0.15 |
| Sum of importance weights | **1.00** | | | | | | |
| **Overall weighted competitive strength rating** | | | **5.95** | | **7.70** | | **2.10** |

A company's competitive strength scores pinpoint its strengths and weaknesses against rivals and point directly to the kinds of offensive/defensive actions it can use to exploit its competitive strengths and reduce its competitive vulnerabilities.

such an offensive probably needs to be aimed directly at winning customers away from Rival 2 (which has a lower overall strength score) rather than Rival 1 (which has a higher overall strength score). Moreover, while ABC has high ratings for technological skills (a 10 rating), dealer network / distribution capability (a 9 rating), new product innovation capability (a 9 rating), quality/product performance (an 8 rating), and reputation/image (an 8 rating), these strength measures have low importance weights—meaning that ABC has strengths in areas that don't translate into much competitive clout in the marketplace. Even so, it outclasses Rival 2 in all five areas, plus it enjoys substantially lower costs than Rival 2 (ABC has a 5 rating on relative cost position versus a 1 rating for Rival 2)—and relative cost position carries the highest importance weight of all the strength measures. ABC also has greater competitive strength than Rival 3 as concerns customer service capabilities (which carries the second-highest importance weight). Hence, because ABC's strengths are in the very areas where Rival 2 is weak, ABC is in a good position to attack Rival 2. Indeed, ABC may well be able to persuade a number of Rival 2's customers to switch their purchases over to its product.

But ABC should be cautious about cutting price aggressively to win customers away from Rival 2, because Rival 1 could interpret that as an attack by ABC to win away Rival 1's customers as well. And Rival 1 is in far and away the best position to compete on the basis of low price, given its high rating on relative cost in an industry where low costs are competitively important (relative cost carries an importance weight of 0.30).

Rival 1's very strong relative cost position vis-à-vis both ABC and Rival 2 arms it with the ability to use its lower-cost advantage to thwart any price cutting on ABC's part. Clearly ABC is vulnerable to any retaliatory price cuts by Rival 1—Rival 1 can easily defeat both ABC and Rival 2 in a price-based battle for sales and market share. If ABC wants to defend against its vulnerability to potential price cutting by Rival 1, then it needs to aim a portion of its strategy at lowering its costs.

The point here is that a competitively astute company should utilize the strength scores in deciding what strategic moves to make. When a company has important competitive strengths in areas where one or more rivals are weak, it makes sense to consider offensive moves to exploit rivals' competitive weaknesses. When a company has important competitive weaknesses in areas where one or more rivals are strong, it makes sense to consider defensive moves to curtail its vulnerability.

# QUESTION 6: WHAT STRATEGIC ISSUES AND PROBLEMS MERIT FRONT-BURNER MANAGERIAL ATTENTION?

The final and most important analytical step is to zero in on exactly what strategic issues company managers need to address—and resolve—for the company to be more financially and competitively successful in the years ahead. This step involves drawing on the results of both industry analysis and the evaluations of the company's own competitiveness. The task here is to get a clear fix on exactly what strategic and competitive challenges confront the company, which of the company's competitive shortcomings need fixing, and what specific problems merit front-burner attention by company managers. *Pinpointing the precise things that management needs to worry about sets the agenda for deciding what actions to take next to improve the company's performance and business outlook.*

The "worry list" of issues and problems that have to be wrestled with can include such things as *how* to stave off market challenges from new foreign competitors, *how* to combat the price discounting of rivals, *how* to reduce the company's high costs, *how* to sustain the company's present rate of growth in light of slowing buyer demand, *whether* to correct the company's competitive deficiencies by acquiring a rival company with the missing strengths, *whether* to expand into foreign markets, *whether* to reposition the company and move to a different strategic group, *what to do* about growing buyer interest in substitute products, and *what to do* to combat the aging demographics of the company's customer base. The worry list thus always centers on such concerns as "how to . . .," "what to do about . . .," and "whether to . . ."—the purpose of the worry list is to identify the specific issues/problems that management needs to address, not to figure out what specific actions to take. Deciding what to do—which strategic actions to take and which strategic moves to make—comes later (when it is time to craft the strategy and choose among the various strategic alternatives).

If the items on the worry list are relatively minor—which suggests that the company's strategy is mostly on track and reasonably well matched to the company's overall situation—company managers seldom need to go much beyond fine-tuning the present strategy. If, however, the problems confronting the company are serious and indicate the present strategy is not well suited for the road ahead, the task of crafting a better strategy needs to be at the top of management's action agenda.

Zeroing in on the strategic issues a company faces and compiling a list of problems and roadblocks creates a strategic agenda of problems that merit prompt managerial attention.

A good strategy must contain ways to deal with all the strategic issues and obstacles that stand in the way of the company's financial and competitive success in the years ahead.

There are six key questions to consider in evaluating a company's ability to compete successfully against market rivals:

1.  *How well is the present strategy working?* This involves evaluating the strategy from a qualitative standpoint (completeness, internal consistency, rationale, and suitability to the situation) and also from a quantitative standpoint (the strategic and financial results the strategy is producing). The stronger a company's current overall performance, the less likely the need for radical strategy changes. The weaker a company's performance and/or the faster the changes in its external situation (which can be gleaned from industry and competitive forces analysis), the more its current strategy must be questioned.

2.  *Do the company's resources and capabilities have sufficient competitive power to give it a sustainable advantage over competitors?* The answer to this question comes from conducting the four tests of a resource's competitive power—the VRIN tests. If a company has resources and capabilities that are competitively *valuable* and *rare,* the firm will have a competitive advantage over market rivals. If its resources and capabilities are also hard to copy (*inimitable*), with no good substitutes (*non-substitutable*), then the firm may be able to sustain this advantage even in the face of active efforts by rivals to overcome it.

3.  *Is the company able to seize market opportunities and overcome external threats to its future well-being?* The answer to this question comes from performing a SWOT analysis. The two most important parts of SWOT analysis are (1) drawing conclusions about what story the compilation of strengths, weaknesses, opportunities, and threats tells about the company's overall situation and (2) acting on the conclusions to better match the company's strategy to its internal strengths and market opportunities, to correct the important internal weaknesses, and to defend against external threats. A company's strengths and competitive assets are strategically relevant because they are the most logical and appealing building blocks for strategy; internal weaknesses are important because they may represent vulnerabilities that need correction. External opportunities and threats come into play because a good strategy necessarily aims at capturing a company's most attractive opportunities and at defending against threats to its well-being.

4.  *Are the company's cost structure and value proposition competitive?* One telling sign of whether a company's situation is strong or precarious is whether its costs are competitive with those of industry rivals. Another sign is how it compares with rivals in terms of differentiation—how effectively it delivers on its customer value proposition. Value chain analysis and benchmarking are essential tools in determining whether the company is performing particular functions and activities well, whether its costs are in line with competitors, whether it is differentiating in ways that really enhance customer value, and whether particular internal activities and business processes need improvement. They complement resource and capability analysis by providing data at the level of individual activities that provides more objective evidence of whether individual resources and capabilities, or bundles of resources and linked activity sets, are competitively superior.

5.  *On an overall basis, is the company competitively stronger or weaker than key rivals?* The key appraisals here involve how the company matches up against key rivals on

industry key success factors and other chief determinants of competitive success and whether and why the company has a *net* competitive advantage or disadvantage. Quantitative competitive strength assessments, using the method presented in Table 4.4, indicate where a company is competitively strong and weak and provide insight into the company's ability to defend or enhance its market position. As a rule, a company's competitive strategy should be built around its competitive strengths and should aim at shoring up areas where it is competitively vulnerable. When a company has important competitive strengths in areas where one or more rivals are weak, it makes sense to consider offensive moves to exploit rivals' competitive weaknesses. When a company has important competitive weaknesses in areas where one or more rivals are strong, it makes sense to consider defensive moves to curtail its vulnerability.

6. *What strategic issues and problems merit front-burner managerial attention?* This analytical step zeros in on the strategic issues and problems that stand in the way of the company's success. It involves using the results of industry analysis as well as resource and value chain analysis of the company's competitive situation to identify a "worry list" of issues to be resolved for the company to be financially and competitively successful in the years ahead. Actually deciding on a strategy and what specific actions to take is what comes after the list of strategic issues and problems that merit front-burner management attention is developed.

*Solid analysis of the company's competitive situation vis-à-vis its key rivals, like good industry analysis, is a valuable precondition for good strategy making.* A competently done evaluation of a company's resources, capabilities, and value chain activities exposes strong and weak points in the present strategy and how attractive or unattractive the company's competitive position is and why. Managers need such understanding to craft a strategy that is well suited to the company's competitive circumstances.

## ASSURANCE OF LEARNING EXERCISES

1. Using the financial ratios provided in the Appendix and the following financial statement information for Avon Products, Inc., calculate the following ratios for Avon for both 2009 and 2010:

   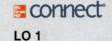

   **LO 1**

   a. Gross profit margin
   b. Operating profit margin
   c. Net profit margin
   d. Times interest earned coverage
   e. Return on shareholders' equity
   f. Return on assets
   g. Debt-to-equity ratio
   h. Days of inventory
   i. Inventory turnover ratio
   j. Average collection period

   Based on these ratios, did the Avon's financial performance improve, weaken, or remain about the same from 2009 to 2010?

## Consolidated Statements of Income for Avon Products, Inc., 2009–2010 (in millions, except per share data)

| Years ended December 31 | 2010 | 2009 |
|---|---|---|
| Net sales | $10,731.3 | $10,084.8 |
| Other revenue | 131.5 | 120.4 |
| Total revenue | 10,862.8 | 10,205.2 |
| Costs, expenses and other: | | |
| Cost of sales | 4,041.3 | 3,825.5 |
| Selling, general and administrative expenses | 5,748.4 | 5,374.1 |
| Operating profit | 1,073.1 | 1,005.6 |
| Interest expense | 87.1 | 104.8 |
| Interest income | (14.0) | (20.2) |
| Other expense, net | 54.6 | 7.3 |
| Total other expenses | 127.7 | 91.9 |
| Income from continuing operations, before taxes | 945.4 | 913.7 |
| Income taxes | 350.2 | 294.5 |
| Income from continuing operations, net of tax | 595.2 | 619.2 |
| Discontinued operations, net of tax | 14.1 | 9.0 |
| Net income | $ 609.3 | $ 628.2 |
| Earnings per share: | | |
| Basic from continuing operations | $ 1.37 | $ 1.43 |
| Diluted from continuing operations | $ 1.36 | $ 1.43 |
| Weighted-average shares outstanding: | | |
| Basic | 428.75 | 426.90 |
| Diluted | 431.35 | 428.54 |

## Consolidated Balance Sheets for Avon Products, Inc., 2009–2010

(in millions, except per share data)

| December 31 | 2010 | 2009 |
|---|---|---|
| **Assets** | | |
| **Current assets** | | |
| Cash, including cash equivalents of $572.0 and $670.5 | $ 1,179.9 | $1,298.1 |
| Accounts receivable (less allowances of $232.0 and $165.1) | 826.3 | 765.7 |
| Inventories | 1,152.9 | 1,049.8 |
| Prepaid expenses and other | 1,025.2 | 1,042.3 |
| Current assets of discontinued operations | – | 50.3 |
| Total current assets | 4,184.3 | 4,206.2 |
| Property, plant and equipment, at cost Land | 69.2 | 115.9 |
| Buildings and improvements | 1,140.2 | 954.2 |
| Equipment | 1,541.5 | 1,435.8 |
| | 2,750.9 | 2,505.9 |
| Less accumulated depreciation | (1,123.5) | (1,036.9) |
| | 1,627.4 | 1,469.0 |
| Goodwill | 675.1 | 215.5 |
| Other intangible assets, net | 368.3 | 13.8 |
| Other assets | 1,018.6 | 846.1 |
| Non-current assets of discontinued operations | – | 72.8 |
| Total assets | $7,873.7 | $6,823.4 |
| **Liabilities and Shareholders' Equity** | | |
| **Current liabilities** | | |
| Debt maturing within one year | $ 727.6 | $ 137.8 |
| Accounts payable | 809.8 | 739.0 |
| Accrued compensation | 293.2 | 282.6 |
| Other accrued liabilities | 771.6 | 706.3 |
| Sales and taxes other than income | 207.6 | 254.1 |
| Income taxes | 146.5 | 134.5 |
| Non-current liabilities of discontinued operations | – | 12.1 |
| Total current liabilities | 2,956.3 | 2,291.7 |

*(Continued)*

| | | |
|---|---|---|
| Long-term debt | 2,408.6 | 2,307.2 |
| Employee benefit plans | 561.3 | 577.8 |
| Long-term income taxes | 128.9 | 147.6 |
| Other liabilities | 146.0 | 186.5 |
| **Total liabilities** | $6,201.1 | $5,510.8 |
| Commitments and contingencies | | |
| Shareholders' equity | | |
| Common stock, par value $.25—authorized 1,500 shares; issued 743.3 and 740.9 shares | $ 186.6 | $ 186.1 |
| Additional paid-in capital | 2,024.2 | 1,941.0 |
| Retained earnings | 4,610.8 | 4,383.9 |
| Accumulated other comprehensive loss | (605.8) | (692.6) |
| Treasury stock, at cost − 313.8 and 313.4 shares | (4,559.3) | (4,545.8) |
| Noncontrolling interest | 16.1 | 40.0 |
| **Total shareholders' equity** | $1,672.6 | $1,312.6 |
| **Total liabilities and shareholders' equity** | $7,873.7 | $6,823.4 |

*Source:* Avon Products, Inc. 2010, 10-K.

**LO 2**   2.  Starbucks operates more than 17,000 stores in more than 50 countries. How many of the four tests of the competitive power of a resource does the store network pass? Explain your answer.

**LO 3**   3.  Using your general knowledge of the coffee take-out industry, perform a SWOT analysis for Starbucks.

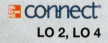

**LO 2, LO 4**   4.  Review the information in Illustration Capsule 4.1 concerning the value chain average costs of producing and selling an upscale polo shirt and compare this with the representative value chain depicted in Figure 4.3. Then answer the following questions:

   **a.** Which of the company's primary value chain activities account for the largest percentage of its operating expenses?

   **b.** What support activities described in Figure 4.3 would be necessary at KP MacLane?

   **c.** What value chain activities might be important in securing or maintaining a competitive advantage for a producer of upscale, branded shirts like KP MacLane?

**LO 5**   5.  Using the methodology illustrated in Table 4.3 and your knowledge as an automobile owner, prepare a competitive strength assessment for General Motors and its rivals Ford, Chrysler, Toyota, and Honda. Each of the five automobile manufacturers should be evaluated on the key success factors / strength measures of: cost competitiveness, product line breadth, product quality and reliability, financial resources and profitability, and customer service. What does your competitive strength assessment disclose about the overall competitiveness of each automobile manufacturer? What factors account most for Toyota's competitive success? Does Toyota have competitive weaknesses that were disclosed by your analysis? Explain.

1. Using the formulas in Table 4.1 and the data in your company's latest financial statements, calculate the following measures of financial performance for your company:

   **LO 1**

   a. Operating profit margin
   b. Return on total assets
   c. Current ratio
   d. Working capital
   e. Long-term debt-to-capital ratio
   f. Price-earnings ratio

2. On the basis of your company's latest financial statements and all the other available data regarding your company's performance that appear in the Industry Report, list the three measures of financial performance on which your company did "best" and the three measures on which your company's financial performance was "worst."

   **LO 1**

3. What hard evidence can you cite that indicates your company's strategy is working fairly well (or perhaps not working so well, if your company's performance is lagging that of rival companies)?

   **LO 1**

4. What internal strengths and weaknesses does your company have? What external market opportunities for growth and increased profitability exist for your company? What external threats to your company's future well-being and profitability do you and your co-managers see? What does the preceding SWOT analysis indicate about your company's present situation and future prospects—where on the scale from "exceptionally strong" to "alarmingly weak" does the attractiveness of your company's situation rank?

   **LO 2, LO 3**

5. Does your company have any core competencies? If so, what are they?

   **LO 2, LO 3**

6. What are the key elements of your company's value chain? Refer to Figure 4.3 in developing your answer.

   **LO 4**

7. Using the methodology presented in Table 4.4, do a weighted competitive strength assessment for your company and two other companies that you and your co-managers consider to be very close competitors.

   **LO 5**

## ENDNOTES

[1] Birger Wernerfelt, "A Resource-Based View of the Firm," *Strategic Management Journal* 5, no. 5 (September–October 1984), pp. 171–80; Jay Barney, "Firm Resources and Sustained Competitive Advantage," *Journal of Management* 17, no. 1 (1991), pp. 99–120; Margaret A. Peteraf, "The Cornerstones of Competitive Advantage: A Resource-Based View," *Strategic Management Journal* 14, no. 3 (March 1993), pp. 179–91.

[2] R. Amit and P. Schoemaker, "Strategic Assets and Organizational Rent," *Strategic Management Journal* 14, (1993).

[3] Ibid, pp. 33–46.

[4] Jay B. Barney, "Looking Inside for Competitive Advantage," *Academy of Management Executive* 9, no. 4 (November 1995), pp. 49–61; Christopher A. Bartlett and Sumantra Ghoshal, "Building Competitive Advantage through People," *MIT Sloan Management Review* 43, no. 2 (Winter 2002), pp. 34–41; Danny Miller, Russell Eisenstat, and Nathaniel Foote, "Strategy from the Inside Out: Building Capability-Creating Organizations," *California Management Review* 44, no. 3 (Spring 2002), pp. 37–54.

[5] Barney, "Firm Resources and Sustained Competitive Advantage," pp. 105–9; M. Peteraf and J. Barney, "Unraveling the Resource-Based Tangle," *Managerial and Decision Economics* 24, no. 4 (June–July 2003), pp. 309–23.

[6] Margaret A. Peteraf and Mark E. Bergen, "Scanning Dynamic Competitive Landscapes: A Market-Based and Resource-Based Framework," *Strategic Management Journal* 24 (2003), pp. 1027–42.

[7] C. Montgomery, "Of Diamonds and Rust: A New Look at Resources," in C. Montgomery (ed.), *Resource-Based and Evolutionary Theories of the Firm* (Boston: Kluwer Academic, 1995), pp. 251–68.

[8] David J. Teece, Gary Pisano, and Amy Shuen, "Dynamic Capabilities and Strategic Management," *Strategic Management Journal* 18, no. 7 (1997); and Constance E. Helfat and Margaret A. Peteraf, "The Dynamic Resource-Based View: Capability Lifecycles," *Strategic Management Journal* 24, no. 10 (2003).

[9] D. Teece, G. Pisano, and A. Shuen, "Dynamic Capabilities and Strategic Management," *Strategic Management Journal* 18, no. 7 (1997), pp. 509–33. K. Eisenhardt and J. Martin, "Dynamic Capabilities: What Are They?" *Strategic Management Journal* 21, nos. 10–11 (2000), pp. 1105–21; M. Zollo and S. Winter, "Deliberate Learning and the Evolution of Dynamic Capabilities,"

*Organization Science* 13 (2002), pp. 339–51; C. Helfat et al., *Dynamic Capabilities: Understanding Strategic Change in Organizations* (Malden, MA: Blackwell, 2007).

[10] David W. Birchall and George Tovstiga, "The Strategic Potential of a Firm's Knowledge Portfolio," *Journal of General Management* 25, no. 1 (Autumn 1999), pp. 1–16; Nick Bontis, Nicola C. Dragonetti, Kristine Jacobsen, and Goran Roos, "The Knowledge Toolbox: A Review of the Tools Available to Measure and Manage Intangible Resources," *European Management Journal* 17, no. 4 (August 1999), pp. 391–401; David Teece, "Capturing Value from Knowledge Assets: The New Economy, Markets for Know-How, and Intangible Assets," *California Management Review* 40, no. 3 (Spring 1998), pp. 55–79.

[11] Donald Sull, "Strategy as Active Waiting," *Harvard Business Review* 83, no. 9 (September 2005), pp. 121–26.

[12] M. Peteraf, "The Cornerstones of Competitive Advantage: A Resource-Based View," *Strategic Management Journal,* March 1993, pp. 179–91.

[13] Michael Porter in his 1985 best-seller, *Competitive Advantage* (New York: Free Press).

[14] For discussions of the accounting challenges in calculating the costs of value chain activities, see John K. Shank and Vijay Govindarajan, *Strategic Cost Management* (New York: Free Press, 1993), especially Chapters 2–6, 10, and 11; Robin Cooper and Robert S. Kaplan, "Measure Costs Right: Make the Right Decisions," *Harvard Business Review* 66, no. 5 (September–October, 1988), pp. 96–103; and Joseph A. Ness and Thomas G. Cucuzza, "Tapping the Full Potential of ABC," *Harvard Business Review* 73, no. 4 (July–August 1995), pp. 130–138.

[15] Porter, *Competitive Advantage,* p. 34.

[16] Hau L. Lee, "The Triple-A Supply Chain," *Harvard Business Review* 82, no. 10 (October 2004), pp. 102–12.

[17] Gregory H. Watson, *Strategic Benchmarking: How to Rate Your Company's Performance Against the World's Best* (New York: Wiley, 1993); Robert C. Camp, *Benchmarking: The Search for Industry Best Practices that Lead to Superior Performance* (Milwaukee: ASQC Quality Press, 1989); Dawn Iacobucci and Christie Nordhielm, "Creative Benchmarking," *Harvard Business Review* 78 no. 6 (November–December 2000), pp. 24–25.

[18] Reuben E. Stone, "Leading a Supply Chain Turnaround," *Harvard Business Review* 82, no. 10 (October 2004), pp. 114–21.

# CHAPTER 5

# THE FIVE GENERIC COMPETITIVE STRATEGIES

## Which One to Employ?

I'm spending my time trying to understand our competitive position and how we're serving customers.

**Lou Gerstner** – *Former CEO credited with IBM's turnaround*

It is much better to make your own products obsolete than allow a competitor to do it.

**Michael A. Cusamano and Richard W. Selby** – *Professors, authors, and consultants*

Competitive strategy is about being different. It means deliberately choosing to perform activities differently or to perform different activities than rivals to deliver a unique mix of value.

**Michael E. Porter** – *Professor and Cofounder of Monitor Consulting*

There are several basic approaches to competing successfully and gaining a competitive advantage over rivals, but they all involve delivering more value to the customer than rivals or delivering value more efficiently than rivals (or both). More value for the customer can mean a good product at a lower price, a superior product that is worth paying more for, or a best-value offering that represents an attractive combination of price, features, service, and other appealing attributes. Greater efficiency means delivering a given level of value to customers at a lower cost to the company. But whatever approach to delivering value the company takes, it nearly always requires performing value chain activities differently than rivals and building competitively valuable resources and capabilities that rivals cannot readily match or trump.

This chapter describes the five *generic competitive strategy options*. Which of the five to employ is a company's first and foremost choice in crafting an overall strategy and beginning its quest for competitive advantage.

# THE FIVE GENERIC COMPETITIVE STRATEGIES

A company's competitive strategy *deals exclusively with the specifics of management's game plan for competing successfully*—its specific efforts to please customers, strengthen its market position, counter the maneuvers of rivals, respond to shifting market conditions, and achieve a particular kind of competitive advantage. The chances are remote that any two companies—even companies in the same industry—will employ competitive strategies that are exactly alike in every detail. However, when one strips away the details to get at the real substance, the two biggest factors that distinguish one competitive strategy from another boil down to (1) whether a company's market target is broad or narrow, and (2) whether the company is pursuing a competitive advantage linked to lower costs or differentiation. These two factors give rise to five competitive strategy options, as shown in Figure 5.1 and listed next.[1]

1. *A low-cost provider strategy*—striving to achieve lower overall costs than rivals on comparable products that attract a broad spectrum of buyers.
2. *A broad differentiation strategy*—seeking to differentiate the company's product offering from rivals' with superior attributes that will appeal to a broad spectrum of buyers.

## FIGURE 5.1 The Five Generic Competitive Strategies

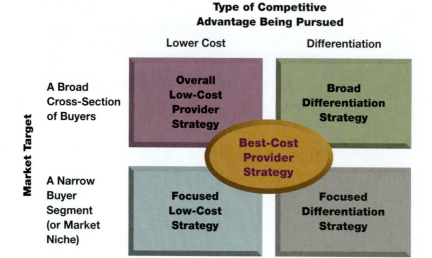

*Source:* This is an author-expanded version of a three-strategy classification discussed in Michael E. Porter, *Competitive Strategy* (New York: Free Press, 1980).

3. *A focused low-cost strategy*—concentrating on a narrow buyer segment (or market niche) and outcompeting rivals on costs, thus being able to serve niche members at a lower price.

4. *A focused differentiation strategy*—concentrating on a narrow buyer segment (or market niche) and outcompeting rivals with a product offering that meets the specific tastes and requirements of niche members better than the product offerings of rivals.

5. *A best-cost provider strategy*—giving customers *more value for their money* by satisfying buyers' expectations on key quality/features/performance/service attributes while beating their price expectations. This option is a *hybrid* strategy that blends elements of differentiation and low-cost strategies; the aim is to have the lowest (best) costs and prices among sellers offering products with comparable differentiating attributes.

The remainder of this chapter explores the ins and outs of these five generic competitive strategies and how they differ.

# LOW-COST PROVIDER STRATEGIES

Striving to be the industry's overall low-cost provider is a powerful competitive approach in markets with many price-sensitive buyers. A company achieves **low-cost leadership** when it becomes the industry's lowest-cost provider rather than just being one of perhaps several competitors with comparatively low costs. Successful low-cost providers boast meaningfully lower costs than rivals—but not necessarily the absolutely lowest possible cost. In striving for a cost advantage over rivals, company managers must take care to incorporate features and services that buyers consider essential. A product offering that is too frills-free can be viewed by consumers as offering little value even, regardless of its pricing.

A company has two options for translating a low-cost advantage over rivals into attractive profit performance. Option 1 is to use the lower-cost edge to underprice competitors and attract price-sensitive buyers in great enough numbers to increase total profits. Option 2 is to maintain the present price, be content with the present market share, and use the lower-cost edge to earn a higher profit margin on each unit sold, thereby raising the firm's total profits and overall return on investment.

While many companies are inclined to exploit a low-cost advantage by using option 1 (attacking rivals with lower prices), this strategy can backfire if rivals respond with retaliatory price cuts of their own (in order to protect their customer base) and the aggressor's price cuts fail to produce sales gains that are big enough to offset the profit erosion associated with charging a lower price. The bigger the risk that rivals will respond with matching price cuts, the more appealing it becomes to employ the second option for using a low-cost advantage to achieve higher profitability.

## The Two Major Avenues for Achieving a Cost Advantage

To achieve a low-cost edge over rivals, a firm's cumulative costs across its overall value chain must be lower than competitors' cumulative costs. There are two ways to accomplish this:[2]

1. Perform value chain activities more cost-effectively than rivals.
2. Revamp the firm's overall value chain to eliminate or bypass some cost-producing activities.

### Cost-Efficient Management of Value Chain Activities

For a company to do a more cost-efficient job of managing its value chain than rivals, managers must launch a concerted, ongoing effort to ferret out cost-saving opportunities in every part of the value chain. No activity can escape cost-saving scrutiny, and all company personnel must be expected to use their talents and ingenuity to come up with innovative and effective ways to keep costs down. Particular attention, however, needs to be paid to a set of factors known as **cost drivers**, which have an especially strong effect on a company's costs and which managers can use as levers to push costs down. (Figure 5.2 provides a list of important cost drivers.) Cost-cutting methods that demonstrate an effective use of the cost drivers include:

1. *Striving to capture all available economies of scale.* Economies of scale stem from an ability to lower unit costs by increasing the scale of operation. Many occasions arise when a large plant or distribution center is more economical to operate than a small one. In global industries, selling a mostly standard product worldwide tends to lower unit costs as opposed to making separate products for each country market where costs are typically higher due to an inability to reach the most economic scale of production for each country. There are economies of scale in advertising as well. For example, Anheuser-Busch could afford to pay the $3.5 million cost of a 30-second Super Bowl ad in 2012 because the cost could be spread out over the hundreds of millions of units of Budweiser that they sell.

**LO 2**

Gain command of the major avenues for achieving a competitive advantage based on lower costs.

**CORE CONCEPT**

A **low-cost provider's** basis for competitive advantage is lower overall costs than competitors. Successful **low-cost leaders,** who have the lowest industry costs, are exceptionally good at finding ways to drive costs out of their businesses and still provide a product or service that buyers find acceptable.

A low-cost advantage over rivals can translate into better profitability than rivals attain.

**CORE CONCEPT**

A **cost driver** is a factor that has a strong influence on a company's costs.

**FIGURE 5.2** Cost Drivers: The Keys to Driving Down Company Costs

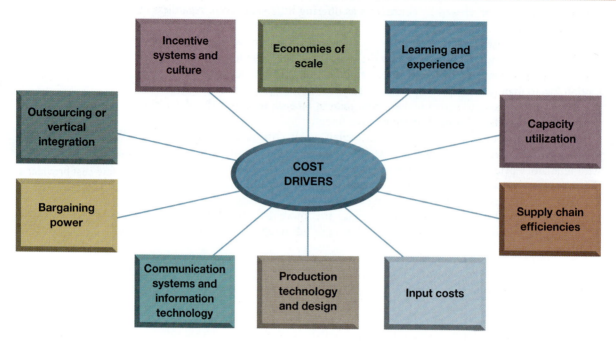

*Sources:* Adapted by the authors from M. Porter, *Competitive Advantage: Creating and Sustaining Competitive Advantage* (New York: Free Press, 1985).

2. *Taking full advantage of experience and learning-curve effects.* The cost of performing an activity can decline over time as the learning and experience of company personnel build. Learning/experience economies can stem from debugging and mastering newly introduced technologies, using the experiences and suggestions of workers to install more efficient plant layouts and assembly procedures, and the added speed and effectiveness that accrues from repeatedly picking sites for and building new plants, retail outlets, or distribution centers. Well managed low-cost providers pay diligent attention to capturing the benefits of learning and experience and to keeping these benefits proprietary to whatever extent possible.

3. *Trying to operate facilities at full capacity.* Whether a company is able to operate at or near full capacity has a big impact on units costs when its value chain contains activities associated with substantial fixed costs. Higher rates of capacity utilization allow depreciation and other fixed costs to be spread over a larger unit volume, thereby lowering fixed costs per unit. The more capital-intensive the business and the higher the fixed costs as a percentage of total costs, the greater the unit-cost penalty for operating at less than full capacity.

4. *Improving supply chain efficiency.* Partnering with suppliers to streamline the ordering and purchasing process, to reduce inventory carrying costs via just-in-time inventory practices, to economize on shipping and materials handling, and to ferret out other cost-saving opportunities is a much-used approach to cost reduction. A company with a distinctive competence in cost-efficient supply chain management, such as BASF (the world's leading chemical company), can sometimes achieve a sizable cost advantage over less adept rivals.

5. *Using lower cost inputs wherever doing so will not entail too great a sacrifice in quality.* Some examples include lower-cost raw materials or component parts, nonunion labor "inputs," and lower rental fees due to differences in location. If the costs of certain factors are "too high," a company may even design the high-cost inputs out of the product altogether.

6. *Using the company's bargaining power vis-à-vis suppliers or others in the value chain system to gain concessions.* Home Depot, for example, has sufficient bargaining clout with suppliers to win price discounts on large-volume purchases. PepsiCo similarly uses its bargaining power to win concessions from supermarkets, mass merchandisers, and other forward channel allies.

7. *Using communication systems and information technology to achieve operating efficiencies.* For example, sharing data and production schedules with suppliers, coupled with the use of enterprise resource planning (ERP) and manufacturing execution system (MES) software, can reduce parts inventories, trim production times, and lower labor requirements.

8. *Employing advanced production technology and process design to improve overall efficiency.* Often production costs can be cut by utilizing design for manufacture (DFM) procedures and computer-assisted design (CAD) techniques that enable more integrated and efficient production methods, investing in highly automated robotic production technology, and shifting to a production. Dell's highly automated PC assembly plant in Austin, Texas, is a prime example of the use of advanced product and process technologies. Many companies are ardent users of total quality management systems, business process reengineering, six sigma methodology, and other business process management techniques that aim at boosting efficiency and reducing costs.

9. *Being alert to the cost advantages of outsourcing or vertical integration.* Outsourcing the performance of certain value chain activities can be more economical than performing them in-house if outside specialists, by virtue of their expertise and volume, can perform the activities at lower cost. On the other hand, there can be times when integrating into the activities of either suppliers or distribution channel allies can lower costs through greater production efficiencies, reduced transaction costs, or a better bargaining position.

10. *Motivating employees through incentives and company culture.* A company's incentive system can encourage not only greater worker productivity but also cost-saving innovations that come from worker suggestions. The culture of a company can also spur worker pride in productivity and continuous improvement. Companies that are well known for their cost-reducing incentive systems and culture include Nucor Steel, which characterizes itself as a company of "11,900 teammates," Southwest Airlines, and Walmart.

## Revamping the Value Chain System to Lower Costs
Dramatic cost advantages can often emerge from redesigning the company's value chain system in ways that eliminate costly work steps and entirely bypass certain cost-producing value chain activities. Such value chain revamping can include:

- *Selling direct to consumers and bypassing the activities and costs of distributors and dealers.* To circumvent the need for distributors–dealers, a company can (1) create its own direct sales force (which adds the costs of maintaining and supporting a sales force but which may well be cheaper than utilizing independent distributors and dealers to access buyers) and/or (2) conduct sales operations at the company's website (costs for website operations and shipping may be a substantially cheaper way to make sales than going through distributor–dealer channels). Costs in the wholesale/retail portions of the value chain frequently represent 35 to 50 percent of the price final consumers pay, so establishing a direct sales force or selling online may offer big cost savings.

- *Streamlining operations by eliminating low value-added or unnecessary work steps and activities.* At Walmart, some items supplied by manufacturers are delivered directly to retail stores rather than being routed through Walmart's distribution centers and delivered by Walmart trucks. In other instances, Walmart unloads incoming shipments from manufacturers' trucks arriving at its distribution centers directly onto outgoing Walmart trucks headed to particular stores without ever moving the goods into the distribution center. Many supermarket chains have greatly reduced in-store meat butchering and cutting activities by shifting to meats that are cut and packaged at the meatpacking plant and then delivered to their stores in ready-to-sell form. Online systems allow warranty claims and product performance problems involving supplier components to be instantly relayed to the relevant suppliers so corrections can be expedited. New software has greatly reduced the time it takes to do product design and graphics design.

- *Reducing materials handling and shipping costs by having suppliers locate their plants or warehouses close to the company's own facilities.* Having suppliers locate their plants or warehouses very close to a company's own plant facilitates just-in-time deliveries of parts and components to the exact work station where thcy will be utilized in assembling the company's product. This not only lowers incoming shipping costs but also curbs or eliminates the need for a company to build and operate storerooms for incoming parts and components and have plant personnel move the inventories to the work stations as needed for assembly.

Illustration Capsule 5.1 describes how Walmart has managed its value chain in the retail grocery portion of its business to achieve a dramatic cost advantage over rival supermarket chains and become the world's biggest grocery retailer.

## Examples of Companies that Revamped Their Value Chains to Reduce Costs

Nucor Corporation, the most profitable steel producer in the United States and one of the largest steel producers worldwide, drastically revamped the value chain process for manufacturing steel products by using relatively inexpensive electric arc furnaces and continuous casting processes. Using electric arc furnaces to melt recycled scrap steel eliminated many of the steps used by traditional steel mills that made their steel products from iron ore, coke, limestone, and other ingredients using costly coke ovens, basic oxygen blast furnaces, ingot casters, and multiple types of finishing facilities—plus Nucor's value chain system required far fewer employees. As a consequence, Nucor produces steel with a far lower capital investment, a far smaller workforce, and far lower operating costs than traditional steel mills. Nucor's strategy to replace the traditional steelmaking value chain with its simpler quicker value chain approach has made it one of the world's lowest-cost producers of steel, allowing it to take a huge amount of market share away from traditional steel companies and earn attractive profits. (Nucor reported a profit in 176 out of 180 quarters during 1966–2011—a remarkable feat in a mature and cyclical industry notorious for roller-coaster bottom-line performance).

Southwest Airlines has achieved considerable cost savings by reconfiguring the traditional value chain of commercial airlines, thereby permitting it to offer travelers dramatically lower fares. Its mastery of fast turnarounds at the gates (about 25 minutes versus 45 minutes for rivals) allows its planes to fly more hours per day. This translates into being

# How Walmart Managed Its Value Chain to Achieve a Huge Low-Cost Advantage over Rival Supermarket Chains

Walmart has achieved a very substantial cost and pricing advantage over rival supermarket chains both by revamping portions of the grocery retailing value chain and by outmanaging its rivals in efficiently performing various value chain activities. Its cost advantage stems from a series of initiatives and practices:

• Instituting extensive information sharing with vendors via online systems that relay sales at its checkout counters directly to suppliers of the items, thereby providing suppliers with real-time information on customer demand and preferences (creating an estimated 6 percent cost advantage). It is standard practice at Walmart to collaborate extensively with vendors on all aspects of the purchasing and store delivery process to squeeze out mutually beneficial cost savings. Procter & Gamble, Walmart's biggest supplier, went so far as to integrate its enterprise resource planning (ERP) system with Walmart's.

• Pursuing global procurement of some items and centralizing most purchasing activities so as to leverage the company's buying power (creating an estimated 2.5 percent cost advantage).

• Investing in state-of-the-art automation at its distribution centers, efficiently operating a truck fleet that makes daily deliveries to Walmart's stores, and putting other assorted cost-saving practices into place at its headquarters, distribution centers, and stores (resulting in an estimated 4 percent cost advantage).

• Striving to optimize the product mix and achieve greater sales turnover (resulting in about a 2 percent cost advantage).

• Installing security systems and store operating procedures that lower shrinkage rates (producing a cost advantage of about 0.5 percent).

• Negotiating preferred real estate rental and leasing rates with real estate developers and owners of its store sites (yielding a cost advantage of 2 percent).

• Managing and compensating its workforce in a manner that produces lower labor costs (yielding an estimated 5 percent cost advantage).

Altogether, these value chain initiatives give Walmart an approximately 22 percent cost advantage over Kroger, Safeway, and other leading supermarket chains. With such a sizable cost advantage, Walmart has been able to underprice its rivals and rapidly become the world's leading supermarket retailer.

*Sources:* Developed by the authors from information at www.walmart.com and in Marco Iansiti and Roy Levien, "Strategy as Ecology," *Harvard Business Review* 82, no. 3 (March 2004), p. 70.

able to schedule more flights per day with fewer aircraft, allowing Southwest to generate more revenue per plane on average than rivals. Southwest does not offer assigned seating, baggage transfer to connecting airlines, or first-class seating and service, thereby eliminating all the cost-producing activities associated with these features. The company's fast and user-friendly online reservation system facilitates e-ticketing and reduces staffing requirements at telephone reservation centers and airport counters. Its use of automated check-in equipment reduces staffing requirements for terminal check-in. The company's carefully designed point-to-point route system minimized connections, delays, and total trip time for passengers, allowing about 75 percent of Southwest passengers to fly nonstop to their destinations and at the same time helping reduce Southwest's costs for flight operations.

# The Keys to Being a Successful Low-Cost Provider

Success in achieving a low-cost edge over rivals comes from out-managing rivals in finding ways to perform value chain activities faster, more accurately, and more cost-effectively.

While low-cost providers are champions of frugality, they seldom hesitate to spend aggressively on resources and capabilities *that promise to drive costs out of the business.* Indeed, having competitive assets of this type and ensuring that they remain competitively superior is essential for achieving competitive advantage as a low-cost provider. Walmart has been an early adopter of state-of-the-art technology throughout its operations, as Illustration Capsule 5.1 suggests; *however, Walmart carefully estimates the cost savings of new technologies before it rushes to invest in them.* By continuously investing in complex, cost-saving technologies that are hard for rivals to match, Walmart has sustained its low-cost advantage for over 30 years.

Other companies noted for their successful use of low-cost provider strategies include Vizio in big-screen TVs, Briggs & Stratton in small gasoline engines, Bic in ball-point pens, Stride Rite in footwear, Poulan in chain saws, and General Electric and Whirl-pool in major home appliances.

## When a Low-Cost Provider Strategy Works Best

A low-cost provider strategy becomes increasingly appealing and competitively powerful when:

1. *Price competition among rival sellers is vigorous.* Low-cost providers are in the best position to compete offensively on the basis of price, to use the appeal of lower price to grab sales (and market share) from rivals, to win the business of price-sensitive buyers, to remain profitable despite strong price competition, and to survive price wars.

2. *The products of rival sellers are essentially identical and readily available from many eager sellers.* Look-alike products and/or overabundant product supply set the stage for lively price competition; in such markets, it is the less efficient, higher-cost companies whose profits get squeezed the most.

3. *There are few ways to achieve product differentiation in ways that have value to buyers.* When the differences between product attributes or brands do not matter much to buyers, buyers are nearly always very sensitive to price differences, and industry-leading companies tend to be those with the lowest-priced brands.

4. *Most buyers use the product in the same ways.* With common user requirements, a standardized product can satisfy the needs of buyers, in which case low price, not features or quality, becomes the dominant factor in causing buyers to choose one seller's product over another's.

5. *Buyers incur low costs in switching their purchases from one seller to another.* Low switching costs give buyers the flexibility to shift purchases to lower-priced sellers having equally good products or to attractively priced substitute products. A low-cost leader is well positioned to use low price to induce potential customers to switch to its brand.

6. *The majority of industry sales are made to a few, large volume buyers.* Low-cost providers have partial profit-margin protection in bargaining with high-volume buyers, since powerful buyers are rarely able to bargain their price down past the survival level of the next most cost-efficient seller.

7. *Industry newcomers use introductory low prices to attract buyers and build a customer base.* A low-cost provider can use price cuts of its own to make it harder for a new rival to win customers. Moreover, the pricing power of a low-cost provider acts as a barrier for new entrants.

# Pitfalls to Avoid in Pursuing a Low-Cost Provider Strategy

Perhaps the biggest mistake a low-cost provider can make is getting carried away with *overly aggressive price cutting* and ending up with lower, rather than higher, profitability. A low-cost/low-price advantage results in superior profitability only if the added gains in unit sales are large enough to bring in a bigger total profit despite lower margins per unit sold. Thus, a company with a 5 percent per-unit cost advantage cannot cut prices 20 percent, end up with a volume gain of only 10 percent, and still expect to earn higher profits!

A second big pitfall is *relying on an approach to reduce costs that can be easily copied by rivals.* The value of a cost advantage depends on its sustainability. Sustainability, in turn, hinges on whether the company achieves its cost advantage in ways difficult for rivals to replicate or match. If rivals find it relatively easy or inexpensive to imitate the leader's low-cost methods, then the leader's advantage will be too short-lived to yield a valuable edge in the marketplace.

A third pitfall is becoming *too fixated on cost reduction.* Low costs cannot be pursued so zealously that a firm's offering ends up being too features-poor to gain the interest of buyers. Furthermore, a company driving hard to push its costs down has to guard against misreading or ignoring increased buyer interest in added features or service, declining buyer sensitivity to price, or new developments that alter how buyers use the product. Otherwise, it risks losing market ground if buyers start opting for more upscale or feature-rich products.

Even if these mistakes are avoided, a low-cost provider strategy still entails risk. An innovative rival may discover an even lower-cost value chain approach. Important cost-saving technological breakthroughs may suddenly emerge. And if a low-cost provider has heavy investments in its present means of operating, then it can prove very costly to quickly shift to the new value chain approach or a new technology.

> A low-cost provider is in the best position to win the business of price-sensitive buyers, set the floor on market price, and still earn a profit.

> Reducing price does not lead to higher total profits unless the added gains in unit sales are large enough to bring in a bigger total profit despite lower margins per unit sold.

> A low-cost provider's product offering must always contain enough attributes to be attractive to prospective buyers—low price, by itself, is not always appealing to buyers.

# BROAD DIFFERENTIATION STRATEGIES

Differentiation strategies are attractive whenever buyers' needs and preferences are too diverse to be fully satisfied by a standardized product offering. Successful product differentiation requires careful study of buyers' needs and behaviors to learn what buyers consider important, what they think has value, and what they are willing to pay for.[3] Then the company must include these desirable features to clearly set itself apart from rivals lacking such product or service attributes. A differentiation strategy calls for a customer value proposition that is *unique.* The strategy achieves its aim when an attractively large number of buyers find the customer value proposition appealing and become strongly attached to a company's differentiated attributes.

Successful differentiation allows a firm to do one or more of the following:

- Command a premium price for its product.
- Increase unit sales (because additional buyers are won over by the differentiating features).
- Gain buyer loyalty to its brand (because some buyers are strongly attracted to the differentiating features and bond with the company and its products).

**LO 3**

Learn the major avenues to a competitive advantage based on differentiating a company's product or service offering from the offerings of rivals.

Differentiation enhances profitability whenever a company's product can command a sufficiently higher price or produce sufficiently bigger unit sales *to more than cover the added costs of achieving the differentiation.* Company differentiation strategies fail when buyers don't value the brand's uniqueness sufficiently and/or when a company's approach to differentiation is easily matched by its rivals.

Companies can pursue differentiation from many angles: a unique taste (Red Bull, Listerine); multiple features (Microsoft Office, Apple iPad); wide selection and one-stop shopping (Home Depot, Amazon.com); superior service (Ritz-Carlton, Nordstrom); engineering design and performance (Mercedes, BMW); luxury and prestige (Rolex, Gucci); product reliability (Whirlpool and Bosch in large home appliances); quality manufacture (Michelin, Honda); technological leadership (3M Corporation in bonding and coating products); a full range of services (Charles Schwab); and wide product selection (Campbell's soups, Frito-Lay snack foods).

## Managing the Value Chain to Create the Differentiating Attributes

Differentiation is not something hatched in marketing and advertising departments, nor is it limited to the catchalls of quality and service. Differentiation opportunities can exist in activities all along an industry's value chain. The most systematic approach that managers can take, however, involves focusing on the **uniqueness drivers**, a set of factors—analogous to cost drivers—that are particularly effective in creating differentiation. Figure 5.3 contains a list of important uniqueness drivers. Ways that managers can enhance differentiation based on these drivers include the following:

**FIGURE 5.3** Uniqueness Drivers: The Keys to Creating a Differentiation Advantage

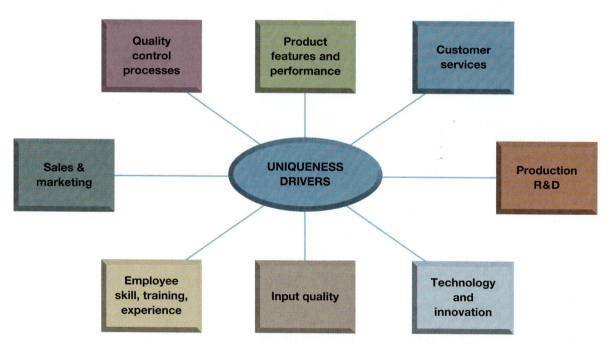

*Source:* Adapted from M. Porter, *Competitive Advantage: Creating and Sustaining Competitive Advantage* (New York: Free Press, 1985).

1. *Striving to create superior product features, design, and performance.* This applies to the physical as well as functional attributes of a product, including features such as expanded end uses and applications, added user safety, greater recycling capability, or enhanced environmental protection. Design features can be important in enhancing the aesthetic appeal of a product. Ducati's motorcycles, for example, are prized for their designs and have been exhibited in the Guggenheim art museum in New York City.[4]

> **CORE CONCEPT**
>
> A **uniqueness driver** is a factor that can have a strong differentiating effect.

2. *Improving customer service or adding additional services.* Better customer services, in areas such as delivery, returns, and repair, can be as important in creating differentiation as superior product features. Examples include superior technical assistance to buyers, higher-quality maintenance services, more and better product information provided to customers, more and better training materials for end users, better credit terms, quicker order processing, or greater customer convenience.

3. *Pursuing production R&D activities.* Engaging in production R&D may permit custom-order manufacture at an efficient cost, provide wider product variety and selection through product "versioning," improve product quality, or make production methods safer for the environment. Many manufacturers have developed flexible manufacturing systems that allow different models and product versions to be made on the same assembly line. Being able to provide buyers with made-to-order products can be a potent differentiating capability.

4. *Striving for innovation and technological advances.* Successful innovation is the route to more frequent first-on-the-market victories and is a powerful differentiator. If the innovation proves hard to replicate, through patent protection or other means, it can provide a company with a first mover advantage that is sustainable.

5. *Pursuing continuous quality improvement.* Quality control processes can be applied throughout the value chain, including postsale customer service activities. They can reduce product defects, prevent premature product failure, extend product life, make it economical to offer longer warranty coverage, improve economy of use, result in more end-user convenience, or enhance product appearance. Companies whose quality management systems meet certification standards, such as the ISO 9001 standards, can enhance their reputation for quality with customers.

6. *Increasing emphasis on marketing and brand-building activities.* Marketing and advertising can have a tremendous effect on the value perceived by buyers and therefore their willingness to pay more for the company's offerings. They can create differentiation even when little tangible differentiation exists otherwise. For example, blind taste tests show that even the most loyal Pepsi or Coke drinkers have trouble telling one cola drink from another.[5] Brands create customer loyalty, which increases the perceived "cost" of switching to another product.

7. *Seeking out high-quality inputs.* Input quality can ultimately spill over to affect the performance or quality of the company's end product. Starbucks, for example, gets high ratings on its coffees partly because it has very strict specifications on the coffee beans purchased from suppliers.

8. *Emphasizing human resource management activities that improve the skills, expertise, and knowledge of company personnel.* A company with high-caliber intellectual capital often has the capacity to generate the kinds of ideas that drive product innovation, technological advances, better product design and product performance, improved production techniques, and higher product quality. Well-designed incentive compensation systems can often unleash the efforts of talented personnel to develop and implement new and effective differentiating attributes.

**Revamping the Value Chain System to Increase Differentiation**     Just as pursuing a cost advantage can involve the entire value chain system, the same is true for a differentiation advantage. Activities performed upstream by suppliers or downstream by distributors and retailers can have a meaningful effect on customers' perceptions of a company's offerings and its value proposition. Approaches to enhancing differentiation through changes in the value chain system include:

- *Coordinating with channel allies to enhance customer perceptions of value.* Coordinating with downstream partners such as distributors, dealers, brokers, and retailers can contribute to differentiation in a variety of ways. Methods that companies use to influence the value chain activities of their channel allies include setting standards for downstream partners to follow, providing them with templates to standardize the selling environment or practices, training channel personnel, or cosponsoring promotions and advertising campaigns. Coordinating with retailers is important for enhancing the buying experience and building a company's image. Coordinating with distributors or shippers can mean quicker delivery to customers, more accurate order filling, and/or lower shipping costs. The Coca-Cola Company considers coordination with its bottler/distributors so important that it has at times taken over a troubled bottler for the purpose of improving its management and upgrading its plant and equipment before releasing it again.[6]

- *Coordinating with suppliers to better address customer needs.* Collaborating with suppliers can also be a powerful route to a more effective differentiation strategy. Coordinating and collaborating with suppliers can improve many dimensions affecting product features and quality. This is particularly true for companies that only engage in assembly operations, such as Dell in PCs and Ducati in motorcycles. Close coordination with suppliers can also enhance differentiation by speeding up new product development cycles or speeding delivery to end customers. Strong relationships with suppliers can also mean that the company's supply requirements are prioritized when industry supply is insufficient to meet overall demand.

## Delivering Superior Value via a Broad Differentiation Strategy

Differentiation strategies depend on meeting customer needs in unique ways or creating new needs, through activities such as innovation or persuasive advertising. The objective is to offer customers something that rivals can't—at least in terms of the level of satisfaction. There are four basic routes to achieving this aim.

The first route is to incorporate product attributes and user features that *lower the buyer's overall costs* of using the company's product. This is the least obvious and most overlooked route to a differentiation advantage. It is a differentiating factor since it can help business buyers be more competitive in their markets and more profitable. Producers of materials and components often win orders for their products by reducing a buyer's raw-material waste (providing cut-to-size components), reducing a buyer's inventory requirements (providing just-in-time deliveries), using online systems to reduce a buyer's procurement and order processing costs, and providing free technical support. This route to differentiation can also appeal to individual consumers who are looking to economize on their overall costs of consumption. Making a company's product more economical for a buyer to use can be done by incorporating energy-efficient features (energy-saving appliances and lightbulbs help cut buyers' utility bills; fuel-efficient vehicles cut buyer costs for gasoline) and/or by increasing maintenance intervals and product reliability so as to lower buyer costs for maintenance and repairs.

A second route is to incorporate *tangible* features that increase customer satisfaction with the product, such as product specifications, functions, and styling. This can be accomplished by including attributes that add functionality, enhance the design, save time for the user, are more reliable, or make the product cleaner, safer, quieter, simpler to use, more portable, more convenient, or longer-lasting than rival brands. Cell phone manufacturers are in a race to introduce next-generation devices capable of being used for more purposes and having simpler menu functionality.

A third route to a differentiation-based competitive advantage is to incorporate *intangible* features that enhance buyer satisfaction in noneconomic ways. Toyota's Prius appeals to environmentally conscious motorists not only because these drivers want to help reduce global carbon dioxide emissions but also because they identify with the image conveyed. Rolls-Royce, Ralph Lauren, Tiffany, Bugatti, and Prada have differentiation-based competitive advantages linked to buyer desires for status, image, prestige, upscale fashion, superior craftsmanship, and the finer things in life. Intangibles that contribute to differentiation can extend beyond product attributes to the reputation of the company and to customer relations or trust.

The fourth route is to *signal the value* of the company's product offering to buyers. Typical signals of value include a high price (in instances where high price implies high quality and performance), more appealing or fancier packaging than competing products, ad content that emphasizes a product's standout attributes, the quality of brochures and sales presentations, and the luxuriousness and ambience of a seller's facilities (important for high-end retailers and for offices or other facilities frequented by customers). They make potential buyers aware of the professionalism, appearance, and personalities of the seller's employees and/or make potential buyers realize that a company has prestigious customers. Signaling value is particularly important (1) when the nature of differentiation is based on intangible features and is therefore subjective or hard to quantify, (2) when buyers are making a first-time purchase and are unsure what their experience with the product will be, and (3) when repurchase is infrequent, and (4) when buyers are unsophisticated.

> Differentiation can be based on *tangible* or *intangible* attributes.

Regardless of the approach taken, achieving a successful differentiation strategy requires, first, that the company have capabilities in areas such as customer service, marketing, brand management, and technology that can create and support differentiation. That is, the resources, competencies, and value chain activities of the company must be well matched to the requirements of the strategy. For the strategy to result in competitive advantage, the company's competencies must also be sufficiently unique in delivering value to buyers that they help set its product offering apart from those of rivals. They must be competitively superior. There are numerous examples of companies that have differentiated themselves on the basis of distinctive capabilities. When a major new event occurs, many people turn to Fox News and CNN because they have the capability to devote more airtime to breaking news stories and get reporters on the scene very quickly. Avon and Mary Kay Cosmetics have differentiated themselves from other cosmetics and personal care companies by assembling a sales force numbering in the hundreds of thousands that gives them a direct sales capability—their sales associates personally demonstrate products to interested buyers, take their orders on the spot, and deliver the items to buyers' homes.

The most successful approaches to differentiation are those that are difficult for rivals to duplicate. Indeed, this is the route to a sustainable differentiation advantage. While resourceful competitors can, in time, clone almost any tangible product attribute, socially complex intangible attributes, such as company reputation, long-standing relationships with buyers, and image are much harder to imitate. Differentiation that creates switching costs that lock in buyers also provides a route to sustainable advantage. For example, if a buyer makes a substantial investment in learning to use one type of system, that buyer is less likely to switch to a competitor's system. (This has kept many users from switching away from Microsoft Office products, despite the fact that there are other applications with superior features.) As a rule, differentiation yields a longer-lasting and more profitable competitive edge when it is based on a well-established brand image, patent-protected product innovation, complex technical superiority, a reputation for superior product quality and reliability, relationship-based customer service, and unique competitive capabilities.

## When a Differentiation Strategy Works Best

Differentiation strategies tend to work best in market circumstances where:

- *Buyer needs and uses of the product are diverse.* Diverse buyer preferences present competitors with a bigger window of opportunity to do things differently and set themselves apart with product attributes that appeal to particular buyers. For instance, the diversity of consumer preferences for menu selection, ambience, pricing, and customer service gives restaurants exceptionally wide latitude in creating a differentiated product offering. Other industries with diverse buyer needs include magazine publishing, automobile manufacturing, footwear, and kitchen appliances.
- *There are many ways to differentiate the product or service that have value to buyers.* Industries that offer opportunities for competitors to add features to products and services are well suited to differentiation strategies. For example, hotel chains can differentiate on such features as location, size of room, range of guest services, in-hotel dining, and the quality and luxuriousness of bedding and furnishings. Similarly, cosmetics producers are able to differentiate based upon prestige and image, formulations that fight the signs of aging, UV light protection, exclusivity of retail locations, the inclusion of antioxidants and natural ingredients, or prohibitions against animal testing. Basic commodities, such as chemicals, mineral deposits, and agricultural products, provide few opportunities for differentiation.
- *Few rival firms are following a similar differentiation approach.* The best differentiation approaches involve trying to appeal to buyers on the basis of attributes that rivals are not emphasizing. A differentiator encounters less head-to-head rivalry when it goes its own separate way in creating uniqueness and does not try to outdifferentiate rivals on the very same attributes. When many rivals base their differentiation efforts on the same attributes, the most likely result is weak brand differentiation and "strategy overcrowding"—competitors end up chasing much the same buyers with much the same product offerings.
- *Technological change is fast-paced and competition revolves around rapidly evolving product features.* Rapid product innovation and frequent introductions of next-version products heighten buyer interest and provide space for companies to pursue distinct differentiating paths. In video game hardware and video games, golf equipment, mobile phones, and big-screen TVs, competitors are locked into an ongoing battle to set themselves apart by introducing the best next-generation products. Companies that fail to come up with new and improved products and distinctive performance features quickly lose out in the marketplace.

## Pitfalls to Avoid in Pursuing a Differentiation Strategy

Differentiation strategies can fail for any of several reasons. *A differentiation strategy keyed to product or service attributes that are easily and quickly copied is always doomed.* Rapid imitation means that no rival achieves differentiation, since whenever one firm introduces some aspect of uniqueness that strikes the fancy of buyers, fast-following copycats quickly reestablish parity. This is why a firm must seek out sources of uniqueness that are time-consuming or burdensome for rivals to match if it hopes to use differentiation to win a sustainable competitive edge.

*A second pitfall is that the company's attempt at differentiation produces an unenthusiastic response on the part of buyers.* Thus even if a company succeeds in setting its product apart from those of rivals, its strategy can result in disappointing sales and profits if buyers find other brands more appealing. Any time many potential buyers look at a company's differentiated product offering with indifference, the company's differentiation strategy is in deep trouble.

*The third big pitfall is overspending on efforts to differentiate the company's product offering, thus eroding profitability.* Company efforts to achieve differentiation nearly always raise costs—often substantially, since marketing and R&D are expensive undertakings. The key to profitable differentiation is either to keep the unit cost of achieving differentiation below the price premium that the differentiating attributes can command (thus increasing the profit margin per unit sold) or to offset thinner profit margins per unit by selling enough additional units to increase total profits. If a company goes overboard in pursuing costly differentiation, it could be saddled with unacceptably thin profit margins or even losses.

Other common mistakes in crafting a differentiation strategy include:

- *Offering only trivial improvements in quality, service, or performance features vis-à-vis the products of rivals.* Tiny differences between rivals' product offerings may not be visible or important to buyers. If a company wants to generate the fiercely loyal customer following needed to earn superior profits and open up a differentiation-based competitive advantage over rivals, then its strategy must result in *strong rather than weak product differentiation.* In markets where differentiators do no better than achieve weak product differentiation, customer loyalty is weak, the costs of brand switching are low, and no one company has enough of a market edge to command a price premium over rival brands.

- *Adding so many frills and extra features that the product exceeds the needs and use patterns of most buyers.* A dazzling array of features and options not only drives up product price but also runs the risk that many buyers will conclude that a less deluxe and lower-priced brand is a better value, since they have little occasion to use the deluxe attributes.

- *Charging too high a price premium.* While buyers may be intrigued by a product's deluxe features, they may nonetheless see it as being overpriced relative to the value delivered by the differentiating attributes. A company must guard against turning off would-be buyers with what is perceived as "price gouging." Normally, the bigger the price premium for the differentiating extras, the harder it is to keep buyers from switching to the lower-priced offerings of competitors.

> Overdifferentiating and overcharging are fatal strategy mistakes.

*A low-cost provider strategy can defeat a differentiation strategy when buyers are satisfied with a basic product and don't think "extra" attributes are worth a higher price.*

# FOCUSED (OR MARKET NICHE) STRATEGIES

What sets focused strategies apart from low-cost provider and broad differentiation strategies is concentrated attention on a narrow piece of the total market. The target segment, or niche, can be defined by geographic uniqueness, by specialized requirements in using the product, or by special product attributes that appeal only to niche members.

Community Coffee, the largest family-owned specialty coffee retailer in the United States, has a geographic focus on the state of Louisiana and communities across the Gulf of Mexico. Community holds only a 1.1 percent share of the national coffee market but has recorded sales in excess of $100 million and has won a 50 percent share of the coffee business in the 11-state region where it is distributed. Examples of firms that concentrate on a well-defined market niche keyed to a particular product or buyer segment include Animal Planet and the History Channel (in cable TV), Cartier (in high-end jewelry), Ferrari (in sports cars), and CGA, Inc. (a specialist in providing insurance to cover the cost of lucrative hole-in-one prizes at golf tournaments). Microbreweries, local bakeries, bed-and-breakfast inns, and local owner-managed retail boutiques are all good examples of enterprises that have scaled their operations to serve narrow or local customer segments.

## A Focused Low-Cost Strategy

A focused strategy based on low cost aims at securing a competitive advantage by serving buyers in the target market niche at a lower cost and lower price than those of rival competitors. This strategy has considerable attraction when a firm can lower costs significantly by limiting its customer base to a well-defined buyer segment. The avenues to achieving a cost advantage over rivals also serving the target market niche are the same as those for low-cost leadership—outmanage rivals in keeping the costs of value chain activities contained to a bare minimum and search for innovative ways to bypass nonessential activities. The only real difference between a low-cost provider strategy and a focused low-cost strategy is the size of the buyer group to which a company is appealing—the former involves a product offering that appeals broadly to almost all buyer groups and market segments, whereas the latter aims at just meeting the needs of buyers in a narrow market segment.

Focused low-cost strategies are fairly common. Producers of private-label goods are able to achieve low costs in product development, marketing, distribution, and advertising by concentrating on making generic items imitative of name-brand merchandise and selling directly to retail chains wanting a low-priced store brand. The Perrigo Company has become a leading manufacturer of over-the-counter health care products, with 2011 sales of more than $2.7 billion, by focusing on producing private-label brands for retailers such as Walmart, CVS, Walgreens, Rite-Aid, and Safeway. Budget motel chains, like Motel 6, Sleep Inn, and Super 8, cater to price-conscious travelers who just want to pay for a clean, no-frills place to spend the night. Illustration Capsule 5.2 describes how Aravind's focus on lowering the costs of cataract removal allowed it to address the needs of the "bottom of the pyramid" in India's population where blindness due to cataracts is an endemic problem.

## A Focused Differentiation Strategy

Focused differentiation strategies are keyed to offering products or services designed to appeal to the unique preferences and needs of a narrow, well-defined group of buyers. Successful use of a focused differentiation strategy depends on the existence of a buyer segment that is looking for special product attributes or seller capabilities and on a firm's ability to stand apart from rivals competing in the same target market niche.

Companies like Godiva Chocolates, Rolls-Royce, Louis Vuitton, and W. L. Gore (the maker of GORE-TEX) employ successful differentiation-based focused strategies targeted at upscale buyers wanting products and services with world-class attributes. Indeed, most markets contain a buyer segment willing to pay a big price premium for the very finest items available, thus opening the strategic window for some competitors to

# Aravind Eye Care System's Focused Low-Cost Strategy

Cataracts, the largest cause of preventable blindness, can be treated with a quick surgical procedure that restores sight; however, poverty and limited access to care prevent millions worldwide from obtaining surgery. The Aravind Eye Care System has found a way to address this problem, with a *focused low-cost strategy* that has made cataract surgery not only affordable for more people in India, but free for the very poorest. On the basis of this strategy, Aravind has achieved world renown and become the largest provider of eye care in the world.

High volume and high efficiency are at the cornerstone of Aravind's strategy. The Aravind network with its five eye hospitals in India has become one of the most productive systems in the world, conducting about 300,000 surgeries a year in addition to seeing over 2.6 million outpatients each year. Using the unique model of screening eye camps all over the country, Aravind reaches a broader cross-section of the market for surgical treatment. Additionally, Aravind attains very high staff productivity with each surgeon performing more than 2,500 surgeries annually, compared to 125 for a comparable American surgeon.

What enabled this level of productivity (with no loss in quality of care) was the development of a standardized system of surgical treatment, capitalizing on the fact that cataract removal was already a fairly routine process. Aravind streamlined as much of the process as possible, reducing discretionary elements to a minimum, and tracking outcomes to ensure continuous process improvement. At Aravind's hospitals, there is no wasted

time between surgeries as different teams of support-staff prepare patients for surgery and bring them to the operating theater so that surgeons simply need to turn from one table to another to perform surgery on the next prepared patient. Aravind also drove costs down through the creation of its own manufacturing division, Aurolab, to produce intraocular lenses, suture needles, pharmaceuticals, and surgical blades in India.

Aravind's low costs allow them to keep their prices for cataract surgery very low at Rs. 500.00 ($10) per patient, compared to an average cost of $1500 for surgery in the US. Nevertheless, the system provides surgical outcomes and quality comparable to clinics in the United States. As a result of its unique fee system and effective management, Aravind is also able to provide free eye care to 60 percent of its patients from the revenue generated from paying.

Developed with Avni V. Patel.

*Sources:* G. Natchiar, A. L. Robin, R. Thulasiraj, et al., "Attacking the Backlog of India's Curable Blind; The Aravind Eye Hospital Model," *Arch Ophthalmol* (1994) 112:987–93; D. F. Chang, "Tackling the Greatest Challenge in Cataract Surgery," *Br J Ophthalmol.,* (2005) 89:1073–7; "Driving Down the Cost of High Quality Care," *McKinsey Health International,* December 2011.

pursue differentiation-based focused strategies aimed at the very top of the market pyramid. Another successful focused differentiator is "fashion food retailer" Trader Joe's, a 369-store, 33-state chain that is a combination gourmet deli and food warehouse. Customers shop Trader Joe's as much for entertainment as for conventional grocery items—the store stocks out-of-the-ordinary culinary treats like raspberry salsa, salmon burgers, and jasmine fried rice, as well as the standard goods normally found in supermarkets. What sets Trader Joe's apart is not just its unique combination of food novelties and competitively priced grocery items but also its capability to turn an otherwise mundane grocery excursion into a whimsical treasure hunt that is just plain fun. Illustration Capsule 5.3 describes how Popchips has been grabbing market share with a focused differentiation strategy.

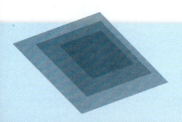

## Popchips's Focused Differentiation Strategy

Potato chips are big business: Americans consume $7B worth annually. But the industry is a hard one to break into since it's a mature, slow-growth industry, dominated by a few large competitors. Frito-Lay alone (maker of Lays and Ruffles) has a commanding 60 percent market share. These characteristics are enough to dissuade most potential entrants, but not Popchips, a small potato chip startup. Despite difficult odds, Popchips has made impressive inroads into the industry over the last five years, with the help of a *focused differentiation strategy*.

Popchips was founded in 2007 by Keith Belling, a serial entrepreneur, and Pat Turpin, a former Costco snack executive. Their idea was simple: take advantage of high-income purchasers' growing desire for tasty, low-fat snacks. Using an innovative cooking method, they found a way to halve the fat content in potato chips while preserving flavor. Popchips has a differentiated product. But its real point of differentiation is in its brand and distribution strategy. Most potato chips have mass distribution and a broad buyer base. Belling and Turpin decided from the outset to narrow their distribution and narrow their targeted buyers. They hoped that focusing on a market niche would allow their product to stand out from the bags of *Lays* and cans of *Pringles* in aisles all over America. Popchips's target: upper income, health-conscious urban and suburban consumers.

To that end, the firm has signed distribution deals with Whole Foods, Target, and, reflecting Turpin's roots, Costco. Popchips's marketing emphasizes social marketing and word of mouth recommendations. The company sends out samples to key tastemakers who tweet, blog, or recommend the product in traditional media. Ashton Kutcher, MTV's former Punk'd host, was so impressed with the chips that he volunteered to promote them. Like Punk'd, Popchips's advertising is similarly irreverent, with taglines like, "love. without the handles."

Popchips's differentiation strategy is succeeding. Between 2009–2011, the company's sales accounted for

nearly all potato chip sales growth at natural supermarket stores, like Whole Foods. Popchips now has nearly 15 percent market share in this niche distribution channel. The company's 2010 sales were $45.7M, over double the 2009 figure. That's particularly impressive given that the industry growth rate has been a paltry 4 percent. In 2011, Forbes put Popchips on its list of America's Most Promising Companies.

Developed with Dennis L. Huggins.

*Sources:* Molly Maier, "Chips, Pretzels and Corn Snacks - US - January 2012," *Mintel,* January 2012, www.oxygen.mintel.com (accessed on February 1, 2012); Lindsay Blakely and Caitlin Elsaesser, "One Snacker at a Time: How Popchips Grew Without Losing Its Character," *CBS News,* January 2011, (accessed at www.cbsnews.com on February 1, 2012); Laura Petrecca, "Popchips CEO Keith Belling is 'Poptimist' on Healthy Snacks," *USA Today,* March 2010 (accessed at www.usatoday.com on February 13, 2012); http://www.forbes.com/, accessed February 28, 2012; Popchips website.

# When a Focused Low-Cost or Focused Differentiation Strategy Is Attractive

A focused strategy aimed at securing a competitive edge based either on low cost or differentiation becomes increasingly attractive as more of the following conditions are met:

- The target market niche is big enough to be profitable and offers good growth potential.
- Industry leaders have chosen not to compete in the niche—in which case focusers can avoid battling head to head against the industry's biggest and strongest competitors.
- It is costly or difficult for multisegment competitors to meet the specialized needs of niche buyers and at the same time satisfy the expectations of their mainstream customers.
- The industry has many different niches and segments, thereby allowing a focuser to pick the niche best suited to its resources and capabilities. Also, with more niches there is more room for focusers to avoid each other in competing for the same customers.
- Few if any rivals are attempting to specialize in the same target segment—a condition that reduces the risk of segment overcrowding.

The advantages of focusing a company's entire competitive effort on a single market niche are considerable, especially for smaller and medium-sized companies that may lack the breadth and depth of resources to tackle going after a broad customer base with a "something for everyone" lineup of models, styles, and product selection. YouTube has become a household name by concentrating on short video clips posted online. Papa John's and Domino's Pizza have created impressive businesses by focusing on the home delivery segment.

# The Risks of a Focused Low-Cost or Focused Differentiation Strategy

Focusing carries several risks. One is the chance that competitors will find effective ways to match the focused firm's capabilities in serving the target niche—perhaps by coming up with products or brands specifically designed to appeal to buyers in the target niche or by developing expertise and capabilities that offset the focuser's strengths. In the lodging business, large chains like Marriott have launched multibrand strategies that allow them to compete effectively in several lodging segments simultaneously. Marriott has flagship J.W. Marriot and Ritz-Carlton hotels with deluxe accommodations for business travelers and resort vacationers. Its Courtyard by Marriott and SpringHill Suites brands cater to business travelers looking for moderately priced lodging, while Marriott Residence Inns and TownePlace Suites are designed as a "home away from home" for travelers staying five or more nights, and the 670 Fairfield Inn & Suite locations are intended to appeal to travelers looking for quality lodging at an "affordable" price. Multibrand strategies are attractive to large companies like Marriott precisely because they enable a company to enter a market niche and siphon business away from companies that employ a focused strategy.

A second risk of employing a focused strategy is the potential for the preferences and needs of niche members to shift over time toward the product attributes desired by the majority of buyers. An erosion of the differences across buyer segments lowers entry barriers into a focuser's market niche and provides an open invitation for rivals in adjacent segments to begin competing for the focuser's customers. A third risk is that the segment may become so attractive that it is soon inundated with competitors, intensifying rivalry and splintering segment profits. And there is always the risk for segment growth to slow to such a small rate that a focusers' prospects for future sales and profit gains become unacceptably dim.

# BEST-COST PROVIDER STRATEGIES

As Figure 5.1 indicates, **best-cost provider strategies** stake out a middle ground between pursuing a low-cost advantage and a differentiation advantage, and between appealing to the broad market as a whole and a narrow market niche. Companies pursuing best-cost strategies aim squarely at the sometimes great mass of value-conscious buyers looking for a good-to-very-good product or service at an economical price. Value-conscious buyers frequently shy away from both cheap low-end products and expensive high-end products, but they are quite willing to pay a "fair" price for extra features and functionality they find appealing and useful. The essence of a best-cost provider strategy is giving customers more *value for the money* by satisfying buyer desires for appealing features/performance/quality/service and charging a lower price for these attributes compared to rivals with similar caliber product offerings.[7] From a competitive-positioning standpoint, best-cost strategies are thus a *hybrid,* balancing a strategic emphasis on low cost against a strategic emphasis on differentiation (desirable features delivered at a relatively low price).

> ## CORE CONCEPT
>
> **Best-cost provider strategies** are a *hybrid* of low-cost provider and differentiation strategies that aim at providing desired quality/features/performance/service attributes while beating rivals on price.

> ### LO 4
>
> Recognize the attributes of a best-cost provider strategy—a hybrid of low-cost provider and differentiation strategies.

To profitably employ a best-cost provider strategy, a company *must have the resources and capabilities to incorporate attractive or upscale attributes into its product offering at a lower cost than rivals.* When a company can incorporate appealing features, good to excellent product performance or quality, or more satisfying customer service into its product offering *at a lower cost than rivals,* then it enjoys "best-cost" status—it is the low-cost provider of a product or service with *upscale attributes.* A best-cost provider can use its low-cost advantage to underprice rivals whose products or services have similarly upscale attributes and still earn attractive profits.

Being a best-cost provider is different from being a low-cost provider because the additional attractive attributes entail additional costs (which a low-cost provider can avoid by offering buyers a basic product with few frills). Moreover, the two strategies aim at a distinguishably different market target. *The target market for a best-cost provider is value-conscious buyers*—buyers who are looking for appealing extras and functionality at a comparatively low price. Value-hunting buyers (as distinct from *price-conscious buyers* looking for a basic product at a bargain-basement price) often constitute a very sizable part of the overall market for a product or service.

## When a Best-Cost Provider Strategy Works Best

A best-cost provider strategy works best in markets where product differentiation is the norm and an attractively large number of value-conscious buyers can be induced to purchase midrange products rather than cheap, basic products or expensive top-of-the-line products. A best-cost provider needs to position itself near the middle of the market with either a medium-quality product at a below-average price or a high-quality product at an average or slightly higher price. Best-cost provider strategies also work well in recessionary times when great masses of buyers become value-conscious and are attracted to economically priced products and services with appealing attributes. But unless a

# Toyota's Best-Cost Provider Strategy for Its Lexus Line

Toyota Motor Company is widely regarded as a low-cost producer among the world's motor vehicle manufacturers. Despite its emphasis on product quality, Toyota has achieved low-cost leadership because it has developed considerable skills in efficient supply chain management and low-cost assembly capabilities and because its models are positioned in the low-to-medium end of the price spectrum, where high production volumes are conducive to low unit costs. But when Toyota decided to introduce its new Lexus models to compete in the luxury-car market segment, it employed a classic best-cost provider strategy. Toyota took the following four steps in crafting and implementing its Lexus strategy:

- Designing an array of high-performance characteristics and upscale features into the Lexus models to make them comparable in performance and luxury to other high-end models and attractive to Mercedes, BMW, Audi, Jaguar, Cadillac, and Lincoln buyers.

- Transferring its capabilities in making high-quality Toyota models at low cost to making premium-quality Lexus models at costs below other luxury-car makers. Toyota's supply chain capabilities and low-cost assembly know-how allowed it to incorporate high-tech performance features and upscale quality into Lexus models at substantially less cost than comparable Mercedes and BMW models.

- Using its relatively lower manufacturing costs to underprice comparable Mercedes and BMW models. With its cost advantage, Toyota could price attractively equipped Lexus cars low enough to draw price-conscious buyers away from comparable high-end brands. Toyota's pricing policy also allowed it to induce Honda, Ford, or GM owners desiring more luxury to switch to a Lexus. Lexus's pricing advantage over Mercedes and BMW was sometimes quite significant. For example, in 2012 the Lexus RX 350, a mid-sized SUV, carried a sticker price in the $39,000–$54,000 range (depending on how it was equipped), whereas variously equipped Mercedes ML 350 SUVs had price tags from $48,000 to over $92,000 and a BMW X5 SUV could range anywhere from $46,000 to $94,000, depending on the optional equipment chosen.

- Establishing a new network of Lexus dealers, separate from Toyota dealers, dedicated to providing a level of personalized, attentive customer service unmatched in the industry.

Toyota's best-cost strategy for its Lexus line succeeded in making Lexus the best-selling luxury car brand worldwide from 1999 through 2010.

---

company has the resources, know-how, and capabilities to incorporate upscale product or service attributes at a lower cost than rivals, adopting a best-cost strategy is ill-advised—*a winning strategy must always be matched to a company's resources and capabilities.*

Illustration Capsule 5.4 describes how Toyota has applied the principles of the best-cost provider strategy in producing and marketing its Lexus brand.

## The Big Risk of a Best-Cost Provider Strategy

A company's biggest vulnerability in employing a best-cost provider strategy is getting squeezed between the strategies of firms using low-cost and high-end differentiation strategies. Low-cost providers may be able to siphon customers away with the appeal of a lower price (despite less appealing product attributes). High-end differentiators may be able to steal customers away with the appeal of better product attributes (even though their products carry a higher price tag). Thus, to be successful, a best-cost provider has to achieve significantly lower costs in providing upscale features so it can outcompete high-end differentiators on the basis of a *significantly* lower price. Likewise, it must offer buyers *significantly* better product attributes in order to justify a price above what low-cost leaders are charging.

# THE CONTRASTING FEATURES OF THE FIVE GENERIC COMPETITIVE STRATEGIES: A SUMMARY

Deciding which generic competitive strategy should serve as the framework on which to hang the rest of the company's strategy is not a trivial matter. Each of the five generic competitive strategies *positions* the company differently in its market and competitive environment. Each establishes a central theme for how the company will endeavor to out-compete rivals. Each creates some boundaries or guidelines for maneuvering as market circumstances unfold and as ideas for improving the strategy are debated. Each entails differences in terms of product line, production emphasis, marketing emphasis, and means of maintaining the strategy, as shown in Table 5.1.

Thus a choice of which generic strategy to employ spills over to affect many aspects of how the business will be operated and the manner in which value chain activities must

**TABLE 5.1    Distinguishing Features of the Five Generic Competitive Strategies**

|  | Low-Cost Provider | Broad Differentiation | Focused Low-Cost Provider | Focused Differentiation | Best-Cost Provider |
|---|---|---|---|---|---|
| **Strategic target** | • A broad cross-section of the market. | • A broad cross-section of the market. | • A narrow market niche where buyer needs and preferences are distinctively different. | • A narrow market niche where buyer needs and preferences are distinctively different. | • Value-conscious buyers.<br>• A middle market range. |
| **Basis of competitive strategy** | • Lower overall costs than competitors. | • Ability to offer buyers something attractively different from competitors' offerings. | • Lower overall cost than rivals in serving niche members. | • Attributes that appeal specifically to niche members. | • Ability to offer better goods at attractive prices. |
| **Product line** | • A good basic product with few frills (acceptable quality and limited selection). | • Many product variations, wide selection; emphasis on differentiating features. | • Features and attributes tailored to the tastes and requirements of niche members. | • Features and attributes tailored to the tastes and requirements of niche members. | • Items with appealing attributes; assorted features; better quality, not best. |
| **Production emphasis** | • A continuous search for cost reduction without sacrificing acceptable quality and essential features. | • Build in whatever differentiating features buyers are willing to pay for; strive for product superiority. | • A continuous search for cost reduction for products that meet basic needs of niche members. | • Small-scale production or custom-made products that match the tastes and requirements of niche members. | • Build in appealing features and better quality at lower cost than rivals. |

*(Continued)*

**TABLE 5.1**    *(Concluded)*

|  | Low-Cost Provider | Broad Differentiation | Focused Low-Cost Provider | Focused Differentiation | Best-Cost Provider |
|---|---|---|---|---|---|
| **Marketing emphasis** | • Low prices, good value.<br>• Try to make a virtue out of product features that lead to low cost. | • Tout differentiating features.<br>• Charge a premium price to cover the extra costs of differentiating features. | • Communicate attractive features of a budget-priced product offering that fits niche buyers' expectations. | • Communicate how product offering does the best job of meeting niche buyers' expectations. | • Tout delivery of *best* value.<br>• Either deliver comparable features at a lower price than rivals or else match rivals on prices and provide better features. |
| **Keys to maintaining the strategy** | • Economical prices, good value.<br>• Strive to manage costs down, year after year, in every area of the business. | • Stress constant innovation to stay ahead of imitative competitors.<br>• Concentrate on a few key differentiating features. | • Stay committed to serving the niche at the lowest overall cost; don't blur the firm's image by entering other market segments or adding other products to widen market appeal. | • Stay committed to serving the niche better than rivals; don't blur the firm's image by entering other market segments or adding other products to widen market appeal. | • Unique expertise in simultaneously managing costs down while incorporating upscale features and attributes. |
| **Resources and capabilities required** | • Capabilities for driving costs out of the value chain system.<br>• *Examples:* large-scale automated plants, an efficiency-oriented culture, bargaining power. | • Capabilities concerning quality, design, intangibles, and innovation.<br>• *Examples:* marketing capabilities, R&D teams, technology. | • Capabilities to lower costs on niche goods.<br>• *Examples:* lower input costs for the specific product desired by the niche, batch production capabilities. | • Capabilities to meet the highly specific needs of niche members.<br>• *Examples:* custom production, close customer relations. | • Capabilities to simultaneously deliver lower cost and higher-quality/differentiated features.<br>• *Examples:* TQM practices, mass customization. |

be managed. Deciding which generic strategy to employ is perhaps the most important strategic commitment a company makes—it tends to drive the rest of the strategic actions a company decides to undertake.

# Successful Competitive Strategies Are Resource-Based

For a company's competitive strategy to succeed in delivering good performance and the intended competitive edge over rivals, it has to be well-matched to a company's internal situation and underpinned by an appropriate set of resources, know-how, and competitive capabilities. To succeed in employing a low-cost provider strategy, a company must have the resources and capabilities to keep its costs below those of its competitors.

A company's competitive strategy should be well-matched to its internal situation and predicated on leveraging its collection of competitively valuable resources and capabilities.

This means having the expertise to cost-effectively manage value chain activities better than rivals and/or having the innovative capability to bypass certain value chain activities being performed by rivals. To succeed in a differentiation strategy, a company must have the resources and capabilities to incorporate unique attributes into its product offering that a broad range of buyers will find appealing and worth paying for. Successful focused strategies require the capability to do an outstanding job of satisfying the needs and expectations of niche buyers. Success in employing a best-cost strategy requires the resources and capabilities to incorporate upscale product or service attributes at a lower cost than rivals. For all types of generic strategies, success in sustaining the competitive edge depends on resources and capabilities that rivals have a hard time duplicating and for which there are no good substitutes.

## KEY POINTS

The key points to take away from this chapter include the following:

1.  Deciding which of the five generic competitive strategies to employ—overall low-cost, broad differentiation, focused low-cost, focused differentiation, or best-cost—is perhaps the most important strategic commitment a company makes. It tends to drive the remaining strategic actions a company undertakes and sets the whole tone for pursuing a competitive advantage over rivals.

2.  In employing a low-cost provider strategy and trying to achieve a low-cost advantage over rivals, a company must do a better job than rivals of cost-effectively managing value chain activities and/or it must find innovative ways to eliminate cost-producing activities. Low-cost provider strategies work particularly well when price competition is strong and the products of rival sellers are virtually identical, when there are not many ways to differentiate, when buyers are price-sensitive or have the power to bargain down prices, when buyer switching costs are low, and when industry newcomers are likely to use a low introductory price to build market share.

3.  Broad differentiation strategies seek to produce a competitive edge by incorporating tangible and intangible attributes that set a company's product/service offering apart from rivals in ways that buyers consider valuable and worth paying for. Successful differentiation allows a firm to (1) command a premium price for its product, (2) increase unit sales (if additional buyers are won over by the differentiating features), and/or (3) gain buyer loyalty to its brand (because some buyers are strongly attracted to the differentiating features and bond with the company and its products). Differentiation strategies work best when buyers have diverse product preferences, when few other rivals are pursuing a similar differentiation approach, and when technological change is fast-paced and competition centers on rapidly evolving product features. A differentiation strategy is doomed when competitors are able to quickly copy most or all of the appealing product attributes a company comes up with, when a company's differentiation efforts fail to interest many buyers, and when a company overspends on efforts to differentiate its product offering or tries to overcharge for its differentiating extras.

4.  A focused strategy delivers competitive advantage either by achieving lower costs than rivals in serving buyers constituting the target market niche or by developing a specialized ability to offer niche buyers an appealingly differentiated offering that meets their needs better than rival brands do. A focused strategy based on either low

cost or differentiation becomes increasingly attractive when the target market niche is big enough to be profitable and offers good growth potential, when it is costly or difficult for multisegment competitors to meet the specialized needs of the target market niche and at the same time satisfy the expectations of their mainstream customers, when there are one or more niches that present a good match for a focuser's resources and capabilities, and when few other rivals are attempting to specialize in the same target segment.

5. Best-cost strategies stake out a middle ground between pursuing a low-cost advantage and a differentiation-based advantage and between appealing to the broad market as a whole and a narrow market niche. The aim is to create competitive advantage by giving buyers *more value for the money*—satisfying buyer expectations on key quality/features/performance/service attributes while beating customer expectations on price. To profitably employ a best-cost provider strategy, a company *must have the capability to incorporate attractive or upscale attributes at a lower cost than rivals.* A best-cost provider strategy works best in markets with large numbers of value-conscious buyers desirous of purchasing good products and services for less money.

6. In all cases, competitive advantage depends on having competitively superior resources and capabilities that are a good match for the chosen generic strategy. A sustainable advantage depends on maintaining that competitive superiority with resources, capabilities, and value chain activities that rivals have trouble matching and for which there are no good substitutes.

## ASSURANCE OF LEARNING EXERCISES

1. Best Buy is the largest consumer electronics retailer in the United States, with 2011 sales of more than $50 billion. The company competes aggressively on price with such rivals as Costco Wholesale, Sam's Club, Walmart, and Target, but it is also known by consumers for its first-rate customer service. Best Buy customers have commented that the retailer's sales staff is exceptionally knowledgeable about the company's products and can direct them to the exact location of difficult-to-find items. Best Buy customers also appreciate that demonstration models of PC monitors, digital media players, and other electronics are fully powered and ready for in-store use. Best Buy's Geek Squad tech support and installation services are additional customer service features that are valued by many customers. How would you characterize Best Buy's competitive strategy? Should it be classified as a low-cost provider strategy? A differentiation strategy? A best-cost strategy? Explain your answer.

   **LO 1, LO 2, LO 3, LO 4**

2. Illustration Capsule 5.1 discusses Walmart's low-cost position in the supermarket industry. Based on information provided in the capsule, explain how Walmart has built its low-cost advantage in the industry and why a low-cost provider strategy is well-suited to the industry.

   **connect**

   **LO1, LO2**

3. Stihl is the world's leading manufacturer and marketer of chain saws with annual sales exceeding $2 billion. With innovations dating to its 1929 invention of the gasoline-powered chain saw, the company holds over 1,000 patents related to chain saws and outdoor power tools. The company's chain saws, leaf blowers, and hedge trimmers sell at price points well above competing brands and are sold only by its network of over 8,000 independent dealers.

   **LO1, LO2, LO3, LO4**

How would you characterize Stihl's competitive strategy? Should it be classified as a low-cost provider strategy? A differentiation strategy? A best-cost strategy? Also, has the company chosen to focus on a narrow piece of the market or does it appear to pursue a broad market approach? Explain your answer.

**connect**

**LO1, LO3, LO4**

4. Explore BMW's website at **www.bmwgroup.com** and see if you can identify at least three ways in which the company seeks to differentiate itself from rival automakers. Is there reason to believe that BMW's differentiation strategy has been successful in producing a competitive advantage? Why or why not?

## EXERCISE FOR SIMULATION PARTICIPANTS

**LO 1, LO 2, LO 3, LO 4**

1. Which one of the five generic competitive strategies best characterize your company's strategic approach to competing successfully?

2. Which rival companies appear to be employing a low-cost provider strategy?

3. Which rival companies appear to be employing a broad differentiation strategy?

4. Which rival companies appear to be employing a best-cost provider strategy?

5. Which rival companies appear to be employing some type of focused strategy?

6. What is your company's action plan to achieve a sustainable competitive advantage over rival companies? List at least three (preferably more than three) specific kinds of decision entries on specific decision screens that your company has made or intends to make to win this kind of competitive edge over rivals.

## ENDNOTES

[1]Michael E. Porter, *Competitive Strategy: Techniques for Analyzing Industries and Competitors* (New York: Free Press, 1980), Chapter 2; Michael E. Porter, "What Is Strategy?" *Harvard Business Review* 74, no. 6 (November–December 1996).
[2]M. Porter, *Competitive Advantage: Creating and Sustaining Superior Performance* (New York: Free Press, 1985).

[3]Richard L. Priem, "A Consumer Perspective on Value Creation," *Academy of Management Review* 32, no. 1 (2007), pp. 219–35.
[4]G. Gavetti, "Ducati," Harvard Business School case 9-701-132, rev. March 8, 2002.
[5]http://jrscience.wcp.muohio.edu/nsfall01/FinalArticles/Final-IsitWorthitBrandsan.html.
[6]D. Yoffie, "Cola Wars Continue: Coke and Pepsi in 2006," Harvard Business School case 9-706-447.

[7]Peter J. Williamson and Ming Zeng, "Value-for-Money Strategies for Recessionary Times," *Harvard Business Review* 87, no. 3 (March 2009), pp. 66–74.

# CHAPTER 6

# STRENGTHENING A COMPANY'S COMPETITIVE POSITION

## Strategic Moves, Timing, and Scope of Operations

## Learning Objectives

**LO 1**  Learn whether and when to pursue offensive or defensive strategic moves to improve a company's market position.

**LO 2**  Recognize when being a first mover or a fast follower or a late mover is most advantageous.

**LO 3**  Become aware of the strategic benefits and risks of expanding a company's horizontal scope through mergers and acquisitions.

**LO 4**  Learn the advantages and disadvantages of extending the company's scope of operations via vertical integration.

**LO 5**  Become aware of the conditions that favor farming out certain value chain activities to outside parties.

**LO 6**  Understand when and how strategic alliances can substitute for horizontal mergers and acquisitions or vertical integration and how they can facilitate outsourcing.

> Competing in the marketplace is like war. You have injuries and casualties, and the best strategy wins.
>
> John Collins – *NHL executive*

> In the virtual economy, collaboration is a new competitive imperative.
>
> Michael Dell – *CEO of Dell Inc.*

> Our success has really been based on partnerships from the very beginning.
>
> Bill Gates – *Founder and CEO of Microsoft*

> Don't form an alliance to correct a weakness . . . The only result from a marriage of weaknesses is the creation of even more weaknesses.
>
> Michel Robert – *Author and consultant*

Once a company has settled on which of the five generic competitive strategies to employ, attention turns to what *other strategic actions* it can take to complement its competitive approach and maximize the power of its overall strategy. The first set of decisions concerns whether to undertake offensive or defensive competitive moves, and the timing of such moves. The second set concerns the breadth of a company's activities (or its *scope* of operations along an industry's entire value chain). All in all, the following measures to strengthen a company's competitive position must be considered:

- Whether to go on the offensive and initiate aggressive strategic moves to improve the company's market position.
- Whether to employ defensive strategies to protect the company's market position.

- When to undertake strategic moves—whether advantage or disadvantage lies in being a first mover, a fast follower, or a late mover.
- Whether to bolster the company's market position by merging with or acquiring another company in the same industry.
- Whether to integrate backward or forward into more stages of the industry value chain system.
- Which value chain activities, if any, should be outsourced.
- Whether to enter into strategic alliances or partnership arrangements with other enterprises.

This chapter presents the pros and cons of each of these measures.

# GOING ON THE OFFENSIVE—STRATEGIC OPTIONS TO IMPROVE A COMPANY'S MARKET POSITION

No matter which of the five generic competitive strategies a firm employs, there are times when it makes sense for the company to *go on the offensive* to improve its market position and business performance. Strategic offensives are called for when a company spots opportunities to gain profitable market share at the expense of rivals or when a company has no choice but to try to whittle away at a strong rival's competitive advantage. Companies like Exxon Mobil, Amazon, Walmart, and Microsoft play hardball, aggressively pursuing competitive advantage and trying to reap the benefits a competitive edge offers—a

Sometimes a company's best strategic option is to seize the initiative, go on the attack, and launch a strategic offensive to improve its market position.

leading market share, excellent profit margins, and rapid growth.[1] The best offensives tend to incorporate several principles: (1) focusing relentlessly on building competitive advantage and then striving to convert it into a sustainable advantage, (2) applying resources where rivals are least able to defend themselves, (3) employing the element of surprise as opposed to doing what rivals expect and are prepared for, and (4) displaying a strong bias for swift, decisive, and overwhelming actions to overpower rivals.[2]

## Choosing the Basis for Competitive Attack

Challenging rivals on competitive grounds where they are strong is an uphill struggle.[3] Offensive initiatives that exploit competitor weaknesses stand a better chance of succeeding than do those that challenge competitor strengths, especially if the weaknesses represent important vulnerabilities and weak rivals can be caught by surprise with no ready defense.

*Strategic offensives should, as a general rule, be based on a company's strongest competitive assets*—its most valuable resources and capabilities such as a better-known brand name, a more efficient production or distribution system, greater technological capability, or a superior reputation for quality. But a consideration of the company's strengths should not be made without also considering the rival's strengths and weaknesses. A strategic offensive should be based on those areas of strength where the company has its greatest competitive advantage over the targeted rivals. If a company has especially good customer service capabilities, it can make special sales pitches to the customers of those rivals that provide subpar customer service. Likewise, it may be attractive to pay special attention to buyer segments that a rival is neglecting or is weakly equipped to serve.

The best offensives use a company's most powerful resources and capabilities to attack rivals in the areas where they are weakest.

Ignoring the need to tie a strategic offensive to a company's competitive strengths and what it does best is like going to war with a popgun—the prospects for success are dim. For instance, it is foolish for a company with relatively high costs to employ a price-cutting offensive. Price-cutting offensives are best left to financially strong companies whose costs are relatively low in comparison to those of the companies being attacked.

The principal offensive strategy options include the following:

1. *Offering an equally good or better product at a lower price.* Lower prices can produce market share gains if competitors don't respond with price cuts of their own and if the challenger convinces buyers that its product is just as good or better. However, such a strategy increases total profits only if the gains in additional unit sales are enough to offset the impact of lower prices and thinner margins per unit sold. Price-cutting offensives are best initiated by companies that have *first achieved a cost advantage.*[4] Irish airline Ryanair used this strategy successfully against rivals such

as British Air and Aer Lingus, by first cutting costs to the bone and then targeting leisure passengers who care more about low price than in-flight amenities and service.[5]

2.  *Leapfrogging competitors by being first to market with next-generation products.* In technology-based industries, the opportune time to overtake an entrenched competitor is when there is a shift to the next generation of the technology. Microsoft got its next-generation Xbox 360 to market a full 12 months ahead of Sony's PlayStation 3 and Nintendo's Wii, helping it build a sizeable market share and develop a reputation for cutting-edge innovation in the video game industry.

3.  *Pursuing continuous product innovation to draw sales and market share away from less innovative rivals.* Ongoing introductions of new and improved products can put rivals under tremendous competitive pressure, especially when rivals' new product development capabilities are weak. But such offensives can be sustained only if a company can keep its pipeline full and maintain buyer enthusiasm for its new and better product offerings.

4.  *Adopting and improving on the good ideas of other companies (rivals or otherwise).* The idea of warehouse-type home improvement centers did not originate with Home Depot cofounders Arthur Blank and Bernie Marcus; they got the "big-box" concept from their former employer Handy Dan Home Improvement. But they were quick to improve on Handy Dan's business model and take Home Depot to the next plateau in terms of product line breadth and customer service. Offense-minded companies are often quick to adopt any good idea (not nailed down by a patent or other legal protection) and build upon it to create competitive advantage for themselves.

5.  *Using hit-and-run or guerrilla warfare tactics to grab market share from complacent or distracted rivals.* Options for "guerrilla offensives" include occasional lowballing on price (to win a big order or steal a key account from a rival), surprising rivals with sporadic but intense bursts of promotional activity (offering a special trial offer to draw customers away from rival brands), or undertaking special campaigns to attract the customers of rivals plagued with a strike or problems in meeting buyer demand.[6] Guerrilla offensives are particularly well suited to small challengers that have neither the resources nor the market visibility to mount a full-fledged attack on industry leaders.

6.  *Launching a preemptive strike to secure an advantageous position that rivals are prevented or discouraged from duplicating.*[7] What makes a move preemptive is its one-of-a-kind nature—whoever strikes first stands to acquire competitive assets that rivals can't readily match. Examples of preemptive moves include (1) securing the best distributors in a particular geographic region or country, (2) moving to obtain the most favorable site at a new interchange or intersection, in a new shopping mall, and so on, (3) tying up the most reliable, high-quality suppliers via exclusive partnerships, long-term contracts, or acquisition, and (4) moving swiftly to acquire the assets of distressed rivals at bargain prices. To be successful, a preemptive move doesn't have to totally block rivals from following; it merely needs to give a firm a prime position that is not easily circumvented.

How long it takes for an offensive to yield good results varies with the competitive circumstances.[8] It can be short if buyers respond immediately (as can occur with a dramatic cost-based price cut, an imaginative ad campaign, or an especially appealing new product). Securing a competitive edge can take much longer if winning consumer acceptance of an innovative product will take some time or if the firm may need several years to debug a new technology or put a new production capacity in place. But how long it takes for an offensive move to improve a company's market standing (and whether it can do so) also depends on whether market rivals recognize the threat and begin a counterresponse. And whether rivals will respond depends on whether they are capable of making an effective response and if they believe that a counterattack is worth the expense and the distraction.[9]

## Choosing Which Rivals to Attack

Offensive-minded firms need to analyze which of their rivals to challenge as well as how to mount the challenge. The following are the best targets for offensive attacks:[10]

- *Market leaders that are vulnerable.* Offensive attacks make good sense when a company that leads in terms of market share is not a true leader in terms of serving the market well. Signs of leader vulnerability include unhappy buyers, an inferior product line, a weak competitive strategy with regard to low-cost leadership or differentiation, aging technology or outdated plants and equipment, a preoccupation with diversification into other industries, and financial problems. Toyota's massive product recalls in 2009 and 2010 due to safety concerns presented other car companies with a prime opportunity to attack a vulnerable and distracted market leader. GM and Ford used incentives and low-financing offers aimed at winning over Toyota buyers to increase their market share during this period.

- *Runner-up firms with weaknesses in areas where the challenger is strong.* Runner-up firms are an especially attractive target when a challenger's resources and capabilities are well suited to exploiting their weaknesses.

- *Struggling enterprises that are on the verge of going under.* Challenging a hard-pressed rival in ways that further sap its financial strength and competitive position can weaken its resolve and hasten its exit from the market. In this type of situation, it makes sense to attack the rival in the market segments where it makes the most profits, since this will threaten its survival the most.

- *Small local and regional firms with limited capabilities.* Because small firms typically have limited expertise and resources, a challenger with broader and/or deeper capabilities is well positioned to raid their biggest and best customers—particularly those that are growing rapidly, have increasingly sophisticated requirements, and may already be thinking about switching to a supplier with a more full-service capability.

## CORE CONCEPT

A **blue-ocean strategy** offers growth in revenues and profits by discovering or inventing new industry segments that create altogether new demand.

## Blue-Ocean Strategy—A Special Kind of Offensive

A **blue-ocean strategy** seeks to gain a dramatic and durable competitive advantage by abandoning efforts to beat out competitors in existing markets and, instead, *inventing a new industry or distinctive market segment that renders existing competitors largely irrelevant and allows a company to create and capture altogether new demand.*[11] This strategy views the business universe as consisting of two distinct types of market space. One is where industry boundaries are defined and accepted, the competitive rules of the game are well understood by all industry members, and companies try to outperform rivals by capturing a bigger share of existing demand. In such markets, lively competition constrains a company's prospects for rapid growth and superior profitability since rivals move quickly to either imitate or counter the successes of competitors. The second type of market space is a "blue ocean," where the industry does not really exist yet, is untainted by competition, and offers wide-open opportunity for profitable and rapid growth if a company can create new demand with a new type of product offering.

A terrific example of such wide-open or blue-ocean market space is the online auction industry that eBay created and now dominates. Other examples of companies that

# Gilt Groupe's Blue-Ocean Strategy in the U.S. Flash Sale Industry

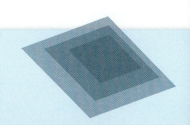

Luxury fashion flash sales exploded onto the U.S. e-commerce scene when Gilt Groupe launched its business in 2007. Flash sales offer limited quantities of high-end designer brands at steep discounts to site members over a very narrow timeframe: the opportunity to snap up an incredible bargain is over in a "flash." The concept of online time-limited, designer-brand sale events, available to members only, had been invented six years earlier by the French company, Vente Privée. But since Vente Privée operated in Europe and the UK, the U.S. market represented a wide-open, blue ocean of uncontested opportunity. Gilt Groupe's only rival was Ideeli, another U.S. startup that had launched in the same year.

Gilt Groupe thrived and grew rapidly in the calm waters of the early days of the U.S. industry. Its tremendous growth stemmed from its recognition of an underserved segment of the population—the web-savvy, value-conscious fashionista—and also from fortuitous timing. The Great Recession hit the U.S. in December 2007, causing a sharp decline in consumer buying and leaving designers with unforeseen quantities of luxury items they could not sell. The fledgling flash sale industry was the perfect channel to offload some of the excess inventory since it still maintained the cachet of exclusivity, with members-only sales and limited-time availability.

Gilt's revenue grew exponentially from $25 million in 2008 to upwards of $600 million by 2011. But their success prompted an influx of fast followers into the luxury flash sale industry, including Hautelook and RueLaLa, who were able to enter the market in December 2007 and April 2008, respectively. The new rivals not only competed for online customers, who could switch costlessly from site to site (since memberships were free), but they also competed for unsold designer inventory. As the U.S. economy came out of the recession, much less of this type of inventory was available. Larger players had also begun to enter the flash sales market in the U.S., with Nordstrom's acquisition of Hautelook, eBay's

purchase of RueLaLa, and Amazon's 2011 acquisition of MyHabit.com. In late 2011, Vente Privée announced the launch of their U.S. online site, via a joint venture with American Express.

As the competitive waters have begun to roil and turn increasingly red, Gilt Groupe has been looking for new ways to compete, expanding into a variety of online luxury product and services niches and venturing overseas. They have been successful in getting new rounds of venture capital, but as of early 2012 had not yet become profitable. Can they survive and prosper in a more crowded competitive space? Only time will tell.

Developed with Judith H. Lin.

*Sources:* Matthew Carroll, "The Rise of Gilt Groupe," *Forbes.com*, January 2012; Mark Brohan, "The Top 500 Guide," *Internet Retailer,* June 2011; Colleen Debaise, "Launching Gilt Groupe, A Fashionable Enterprise," *The Wall Street Journal,* October 2010 (all accessed at www.wsj.com on February 26, 2012); and http://about.americanexpress.com/news/pr/2011/vente_usa.aspx, accessed March 3, 2012.

have achieved competitive advantages by creating blue-ocean market spaces include Starbucks in the coffee shop industry, The Weather Channel in cable TV, FedEx in overnight package delivery, and Cirque du Soleil in live entertainment. Cirque du Soleil "reinvented the circus" by pulling in a whole new group of customers—adults and corporate clients—who not only were noncustomers of traditional circuses (like Ringling Brothers), but were also willing to pay several times more than the price of a conventional circus ticket to have a "sophisticated entertainment experience" featuring stunning visuals and star-quality acrobatic acts. Zipcar Inc. is presently using a blue-ocean strategy to compete against entrenched rivals in the rental-car industry. It rents cars by the hour or day (rather than by the week) to members who pay a yearly fee for access to cars parked in designated spaces located conveniently throughout large cities. By allowing drivers under 25 years of age to rent cars and by targeting city dwellers who need to supplement their use of public transportation with short-term car rentals, Zipcar entered uncharted waters in the rental-car industry, growing rapidly in the process.

Blue-ocean strategies provide a company with a great opportunity in the short run. But they don't guarantee a company's long-term success, which depends more on whether a company can protect the market position they opened up and sustain their early advantage. See Illustration Capsule 6.1 for an example of a company that opened up new competitive space in online luxury retailing only to see their blue ocean waters ultimately turn red.

> Good defensive strategies can help protect a competitive advantage but rarely are the basis for creating one.

# DEFENSIVE STRATEGIES—PROTECTING MARKET POSITION AND COMPETITIVE ADVANTAGE

In a competitive market, all firms are subject to offensive challenges from rivals. The purposes of defensive strategies are to lower the risk of being attacked, weaken the impact of any attack that occurs, and influence challengers to aim their efforts at other rivals. While defensive strategies usually don't enhance a firm's competitive advantage, they can definitely help fortify the firm's competitive position, protect its most valuable resources and capabilities from imitation, and defend whatever competitive advantage it might have. Defensive strategies can take either of two forms: actions to block challengers and actions to signal the likelihood of strong retaliation.

## Blocking the Avenues Open to Challengers

The most frequently employed approach to defending a company's present position involves actions that restrict a challenger's options for initiating a competitive attack. There are any number of obstacles that can be put in the path of would-be challengers. A defender can introduce new features, add new models, or broaden its product line to close off gaps and vacant niches to opportunity-seeking challengers. It can thwart the efforts of rivals to attack with a lower price by maintaining economy-priced options of its own. It can try to

> There are many ways to throw obstacles in the path of would-be challengers.

discourage buyers from trying competitors' brands by lengthening warranties, offering free training and support services, and providing coupons and sample giveaways to buyers most prone to experiment. It can make early announcements about impending new products or price changes to induce potential buyers to postpone switching. It can challenge the quality or safety of rivals' products. Finally, a defender can grant volume discounts or better financing terms to dealers and distributors to discourage them from experimenting with other suppliers, or it can convince them to handle its product line *exclusively* and force competitors to use other distribution outlets.

## Signaling Challengers that Retaliation Is Likely

The goal of signaling challengers that strong retaliation is likely in the event of an attack is either to dissuade challengers from attacking at all or to divert them to less threatening options. Either goal can be achieved by letting challengers know the battle will cost more than it is worth. Signals to would-be challengers can be given by:

- Publicly announcing management's commitment to maintain the firm's present market share.
- Publicly committing the company to a policy of matching competitors' terms or prices.
- Maintaining a war chest of cash and marketable securities.
- Making an occasional strong counterresponse to the moves of weak competitors to enhance the firm's image as a tough defender.

Signaling is most likely to be an effective defensive strategy if the signal is accompanied by a credible commitment to follow through.

# ➤ TIMING A COMPANY'S OFFENSIVE AND DEFENSIVE STRATEGIC MOVES

*When* to make a strategic move is often as crucial as *what* move to make. Timing is especially important when **first-mover advantages** or **disadvantages** exist. Under certain conditions, being first to initiate a strategic move can have a high payoff in the form of a competitive advantage that later movers can't dislodge. Moving first is no guarantee of success, however, since first movers also face some significant disadvantages. Indeed, there are circumstances in which it is more advantageous to be a fast follower or even a late mover. Because the timing of strategic moves can be consequential, it is important for company strategists to be aware of the nature of first-mover advantages and disadvantages and the conditions favoring each type.[12]

## The Potential for First-Mover Advantages

Market pioneers and other types of first movers typically bear greater risks and greater development costs than firms that move later. If the market responds well to its initial move, the pioneer will benefit from a monopoly position (by virtue of being first to market) that enables it to recover its investment costs and make an attractive profit. If the firm's pioneering move gives it a competitive advantage that can be sustained even after other firms enter the market space, its first-mover advantage will be greater still. The extent of this type of advantage, however, will depend on whether and how fast follower firms can piggyback on the pioneer's success and either imitate or improve on its move.

The conditions that favor first-mover advantages, then, are those that slow the moves of follower firms or prevent them from imitating the success of the first mover. There are six such conditions in which first-mover advantages are most likely to arise:

1.  *When pioneering helps build a firm's reputation and creates strong brand loyalty.* Customer loyalty to an early mover's brand can create a tie that binds, limiting the success of later entrants' attempts to poach from the early mover's customer base and steal market share.

**LO 2**

Recognize when being a first mover or a fast follower or a late mover is most advantageous.

2.  *When a first-mover's customers will thereafter face significant switching costs.* Switching costs can protect first movers when consumers make large investments in learning how to use a specific company's product or in complementary products that are also brand-specific. Switching costs can also arise from loyalty programs or long-term contracts that give customers incentives to remain with an initial provider.

3.  *When property rights protections thwart rapid imitation of the initial move.* In certain types of industries, property rights protections in the form of patents, copyrights, and trademarks prevent the ready imitation of an early mover's initial moves. First-mover advantages in pharmaceuticals, for example, are heavily dependent on patent protections, and patent races in this industry are common. In other industries, however, patents provide limited protection and can frequently be circumvented. Property rights protections also vary among nations, since they are dependent on a country's legal institutions and enforcement mechanisms.

4.  *When an early lead enables the first mover to move down the learning curve ahead of rivals.* When there is a steep learning curve and when learning can be kept proprietary, a first mover can benefit from volume-based cost advantages that grow ever larger as its experience accumulates and its scale of operations increases. This type of first-mover advantage is self-reinforcing and, as such, can preserve a first-mover's competitive advantage over long periods of time. Honda's advantage in small multiuse motorcycles has been attributed to such an effect.

5.  *When a first mover can set the technical standard for the industry.* In many technology-based industries, the market will converge around a single technical standard. By establishing the industry standard, a first mover can gain a powerful advantage that, like experienced-based advantages, builds over time. The lure of such an advantage, however, can result in standard wars among early movers, as each strives to set the industry standard. The key to winning such wars is to enter early on the basis of strong fast-cycle product development capabilities, gain the support of key customers and suppliers, employ penetration pricing, and make allies of the producers of complementary products.

Illustration Capsule 6.2 describes how **Amazon.com** achieved a first-mover advantage in online retailing.

## The Potential for Late-Mover Advantages or First-Mover Disadvantages

There are instances when there are advantages *to being an adept follower* rather than a first mover. Late-mover advantages (or *first-mover disadvantages*) arise in four instances:

- When pioneering is more costly than imitative following, and only negligible learning-curve benefits accrue to the leader—a condition that allows a follower to end up with lower costs than the first-mover.

- When the products of an innovator are somewhat primitive and do not live up to buyer expectations, thus allowing a follower with better-performing products to win disenchanted buyers away from the leader.

- When rapid market evolution (due to fast-paced changes in either technology or buyer needs) gives second-movers the opening to leapfrog a first-mover's products with more attractive next-version products.

- When market uncertainties make it difficult to ascertain what will eventually succeed, allowing late movers to wait until these needs are clarified.

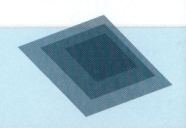

## Amazon.com's First-Mover Advantage in Online Retailing

Amazon.com's path to becoming the world's largest online retailer began in 1994 when Jeff Bezos, a Manhattan hedge fund analyst at the time, noticed that the number of Internet users was increasing by 2,300 percent annually. Bezos saw the tremendous growth as an opportunity to sell products online that would be demanded by a large number of Internet users and could be easily shipped. Bezos launched the online bookseller Amazon.com in 1995. The startup's revenues soared to $148 million in 1997, $610 million in 1998, and $1.6 billion in 1999. Bezos's business plan—hatched while on a cross-country trip with his wife in 1994—made him *Time* magazine's Person of the Year in 1999.

The volume-based and reputational benefits of Amazon.com's early entry into online retailing had delivered a first-mover advantage, but between 2000 and 2011 Bezos undertook a series of additional strategic initiatives to solidify the company's number-one ranking in the industry. Bezos undertook a massive building program in the late-1990s that added five new warehouses and fulfillment centers totaling $300 million. The additional warehouse capacity was added years before it was needed, but Bezos wanted to move preemptively against potential rivals and ensure that, as demand continued to grow, the company could continue to offer its customers the best selection, the lowest prices, and the cheapest and most convenient delivery. The company also expanded its product line to include sporting goods, tools, toys, grocery items, electronics, and digital music downloads, giving it another means of maintaining its experience and scale-based

advantages. Amazon.com's 2010 revenues of $34.2 billion made it the world's largest Internet retailer and Jeff Bezos's shares in Amazon.com made him the 12th wealthiest person in the United States with an estimated net worth of $12.6 billion.

Moving down the learning curve in Internet retailing was not an entirely straightforward process for Amazon.com. Bezos commented in a *Fortune* article profiling the company, "We were investors in every bankrupt, 1999-vintage e-commerce startup. Pets.com, living.com, kozmo.com. We invested in a lot of high-profile flameouts." He went on to specify that although the ventures were a "waste of money," they "didn't take us off our own mission." Bezos also suggested that gaining advantage as a first mover is "taking a million tiny steps—and learning quickly from your missteps."

*Sources:* Mark Brohan, "The Top 500 Guide," *Internet Retailer,* June 2009 (accessed at www.internetretailer.com on June 17, 2009); Josh Quittner, "How Jeff Bezos Rules the Retail Space," *Fortune,* May 5, 2008, pp. 126–34; company website.

## To Be a First Mover or Not

In weighing the pros and cons of being a first mover versus a fast follower versus a late mover, it matters whether the race to market leadership in a particular industry is a marathon or a sprint. In marathons, a slow mover is not unduly penalized—first-mover advantages can be fleeting, and there's ample time for fast followers and sometimes even late movers to catch up.[13] Thus the speed at which the pioneering innovation is likely to catch on matters considerably as companies struggle with whether to pursue an emerging market opportunity aggressively (as a first mover or fast follower) or cautiously (as a late mover). For instance, it took 5.5 years for worldwide mobile phone use to grow from 10 million to 100 million worldwide and close to 10 years for the number of at-home broadband subscribers to grow to 100 million worldwide. The lesson here is that there is a market penetration curve for every emerging opportunity. Typically, the curve has an inflection point at which all the pieces of the business model fall into place, buyer demand explodes, and the market takes off. The inflection point can come early on a fast-rising curve (like the use of e-mail) or farther on up a slow-rising curve (like the use of broadband). Any company that seeks competitive advantage by being a first mover thus needs to ask some hard questions:

- Does market takeoff depend on the development of complementary products or services that currently are not available?
- Is new infrastructure required before buyer demand can surge?
- Will buyers need to learn new skills or adopt new behaviors?
- Will buyers encounter high switching costs in moving to the newly introduced product or service?
- Are there influential competitors in a position to delay or derail the efforts of a first mover?

When the answers to any of these questions are yes, then a company must be careful not to pour too many resources into getting ahead of the market opportunity—the race is likely going to be more of a 10-year marathon than a 2-year sprint.[14] On the other hand, if the market is a winner-take-all type of market, where powerful first-mover advantages insulate early entrants from competition and prevent later movers from making any headway, then it may be best to move quickly despite the risks.

# STRENGTHENING A COMPANY'S MARKET POSITION VIA ITS SCOPE OF OPERATIONS

Apart from considerations of competitive moves and their timing, there is another set of managerial decisions that can affect the strength of a company's market position. These decisions concern the scope of a company's operations—the breadth of its activities and the extent of its market reach. Decisions regarding the **scope of the firm** focus on which activities a firm will perform internally and which it will not. For example, should Panera Bread Company produce the fresh dough that its company-owned and franchised bakery-cafés use in making baguettes, pastries, bagels, and other types of bread, or should it obtain its dough from outside suppliers? Scope decisions also concern which segments of the market to serve—decisions that can include geographic market segments as well as product and service segments. Should Panera expand its menu to include light dinner entrées? Should it offer delivery or drive-through service? Should it expand into all 50 states or concentrate on strengthening its market presence regionally?

Decisions such as these, in essence, determine where the boundaries of a firm lie and the degree to which the operations within those boundaries cohere. They also have much to do with the direction and extent of a business's growth. In this chapter, we introduce the topic of company scope and discuss different types of scope decisions in relation to a company's business-level strategy. In the next two chapters, we develop two additional dimensions of a firm's scope. Chapter 7 focuses on international expansion—a matter of extending the company's geographic scope into foreign markets. Chapter 8 takes up the topic of corporate strategy, which concerns diversifying into a mix of different businesses. Scope issues are at the very heart of corporate-level strategy.

Several dimensions of firm scope have relevance for business-level strategy in terms of their capacity to strengthen a company's position in a given market. These include the firm's **horizontal scope,** which is the range of product and service segments that the firm serves within its product or service market. Mergers and acquisitions involving other market participants provide a means for a company to expand its horizontal scope. Expanding the firm's vertical scope by means of vertical integration can also affect the success of its market strategy. **Vertical scope** is the extent to which the firm engages in the various activities that make up the industry's entire value chain system, from initial activities such as raw-material production all the way to retailing and after-sales service activities. Outsourcing decisions concern another dimension of scope since they involve narrowing the firm's boundaries with respect to its participation in value chain activities. We discuss the pros and cons of each of these options in the sections that follow. Since strategic alliances and partnerships provide an alternative to vertical integration and acquisition strategies and are sometimes used to facilitate outsourcing, we conclude this chapter with a discussion of the benefits and challenges associated with cooperative arrangements of this nature.

> ### CORE CONCEPT
>
> **Horizontal scope** is the range of product and service segments that a firm serves within its focal market.

> ### CORE CONCEPT
>
> **Vertical scope** is the extent to which a firm's internal activities encompass one, some, many, or all of the activities that make up an industry's entire value chain system, ranging from raw-material production to final sales and service activities.

# HORIZONTAL MERGER AND ACQUISITION STRATEGIES

Mergers and acquisitions are much-used strategic options to strengthen a company's market position. A *merger* is the combining of two or more companies into a single corporate entity, with the newly created company often taking on a new name. An *acquisition* is a combination in which one company, the acquirer, purchases and absorbs the operations of another, the acquired. The difference between a merger and an acquisition relates more to the details of ownership, management control, and financial arrangements than to strategy and competitive advantage. The resources and competitive capabilities of the newly created enterprise end up much the same whether the combination is the result of an acquisition or merger.

> **LO 3**
>
> Become aware of the strategic benefits and risks of expanding a company's horizontal scope through mergers and acquisitions.

Horizontal mergers and acquisitions, which involve combining the operations of firms within the same product or service market, provide an effective means for firms to rapidly increase the scale and horizontal scope of their core business. For example, Microsoft has used an aggressive acquisition strategy to extend its software business into new segments and strengthen its technological capabilities in this domain. Mergers between airlines, such as the recent United–Continental merger, have increased their scale of operations and extended their reach geographically.

Merger and acquisition strategies typically set sights on achieving any of five objectives:[15]

1.  *Creating a more cost-efficient operation out of the combined companies.* Many mergers and acquisitions are undertaken with the objective of transforming two or more high-cost companies into one lean competitor with significantly lower costs. When a company acquires another company in the same industry, there's usually enough

overlap in operations that less efficient plants can be closed or distribution and sales activities partly combined and downsized. Likewise, it is usually feasible to squeeze out cost savings in administrative activities, again by combining and downsizing such administrative activities as finance and accounting, information technology, human resources, and so on. The combined companies may also be able to reduce supply chain costs because of greater bargaining power over common suppliers and closer collaboration with supply chain partners. By helping to consolidate the industry and remove excess capacity, such combinations can also reduce industry rivalry and improve industry profitability.

2.  *Expanding a company's geographic coverage.* One of the best and quickest ways to expand a company's geographic coverage is to acquire rivals with operations in the desired locations. Since a company's size increases with its geographic scope, another benefit is increased bargaining power with the company's suppliers or buyers. Greater geographic coverage can also contribute to product differentiation by enhancing a company's name recognition and brand awareness. Banks like Wells Fargo and Bank of America have used acquisition strategies to establish a market presence and gain name recognition in an ever-growing number of states and localities.

3.  *Extending the company's business into new product categories.* Many times a company has gaps in its product line that need to be filled in order to offer customers a more effective product bundle or the benefits of one-stop-shopping. For example, customers might prefer to acquire a suite of software applications from a single vendor that can offer more integrated solutions to the company's problems. Acquisition can be a quicker and more potent way to broaden a company's product line than going through the exercise of introducing a company's own new product to fill the gap. Coca-Cola has increased the effectiveness of the product bundle it provides to retailers by acquiring beverage makers Minute Maid, Odwalla, Hi-C, and Glaceau.

4.  *Gaining quick access to new technologies or complementary resources and capabilities.* Making acquisitions to bolster a company's technological know-how or to expand its skills and capabilities allows a company to bypass a time-consuming and expensive internal effort to build desirable new resources and capabilities. From 2000 through April 2011, Cisco Systems purchased 97 companies to give it more technological reach and product breadth, thereby enhancing its standing as the world's largest provider of hardware, software, and services for building and operating Internet networks.

5.  *Leading the convergence of industries whose boundaries are being blurred by changing technologies and new market opportunities.* In fast-cycle industries or industries whose boundaries are changing, companies can use acquisition strategies to hedge their bets about the direction that an industry will take, to increase their capacity to meet changing demands, and to respond flexibly to changing buyer needs and technological demands. News Corporation has prepared for the convergence of media services with the purchase of satellite TV companies to complement its media holdings in TV broadcasting (the Fox network and TV stations in various countries), cable TV (Fox News, Fox Sports, and FX), filmed entertainment (Twentieth Century Fox and Fox studios), newspapers, magazines, and book publishing.

Numerous companies have employed a horizontal acquisition strategy to catapult themselves from the ranks of the unknown into positions of market leadership. Wells Fargo began as a small regional bank and grew via acquisition, transforming itself into a nationwide bank with global presence. By 2011, it still lagged behind the largest banks in terms of assets, but far outclassed them in terms of efficiency, profitability, and market value.[16] Moreover, it was also listed by *Fortune* magazine in 2011 as among the world's "Most Admired Companies."

## ILLUSTRATION CAPSULE 6.3

# Bristol-Myers Squibb's "String-of-Pearls" Horizontal Acquisition Strategy

Back in 2007, the pharmaceutical company Bristol-Myers Squibb had a problem: its top-selling drugs, Plavix and Abilify, would go off patent by 2012 and its drug pipeline was nearly empty. Together these drugs (the first for heart attacks, the second for depression) accounted for nearly half of the company's sales. Not surprisingly, the company's stock price had stagnated and was underperforming that of its peers.

Developing new drugs is difficult: new drugs must be identified, tested in increasingly sophisticated trials and approved by the Food and Drug Administration. On average, this process takes 13 years and costs $2B. The success rate is low: only one drug in eight manages to pass through clinical testing. In 2007, Bristol-Myers Squibb had only six new drugs at the clinical testing stage.

At the time, many drug companies were diversifying into new markets like over-the-counter drugs to better manage drug development risk. Bristol-Myers Squibb's management pursued a different strategy: product diversification through horizontal acquisitions. Bristol-Myers Squibb targeted small companies in new treatment areas, with the objective of reducing new product development risk by betting on pre-identified drugs. The small companies it targeted, with one or two drugs in development, needed cash; Bristol-Myers Squibb needed new drugs. The firm's management called this its "string-of-pearls" strategy.

To implement its approach and obtain the cash it needed, Bristol-Myers Squibb sold its stake in Mead

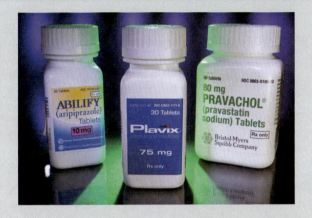

Johnson, a nutritional supplement manufacturer. Then, it went on a shopping spree. Starting in 2007, the company spent over $8B on 18 transactions, including 12 horizontal acquisitions. In the process, the company acquired many promising new drug candidates for common diseases such as cancer, cardiovascular disease, rheumatoid arthritis, and Hepatitis C.

By early 2012, the company's string-of-pearls acquisitions were estimated to have added over $4B of new revenue to the company's coffers. Analysts reported that Bristol-Myers Squibb had one of the best pipelines among drug makers. Investors agreed: between 2007 and 2012, the company's stock price climbed 20 percent, substantially outperforming that of its peers.

Developed with Dennis L. Huggins.

*Sources:* D. Armstrong and M. Tirrell, "Bristol's Buy of Inhibitex for Hepatitis Drug Won't Be Last," *Bloomberg Businessweek,* January 2012 (accessed at **www.bloomberg.com** on January 30, 2012); S. M. Paul, et al., "How to Improve R&D Productivity: the Pharmaceutical Industry's Grand Challenge," *Nature Reviews,* March 2010, pp. 203–214; Bristol-Myers Squibb 2007 and 2011 Annual Reports.

Illustration Capsule 6.3 describes how Bristol-Myers Squibb developed its "string-of-pearls" horizontal acquisition strategy to fill in its pharmaceutical product development gaps.

# Why Mergers and Acquisitions Sometimes Fail to Produce Anticipated Results

Despite many successes, mergers and acquisitions do not always produce the hoped-for outcomes.[17] Cost savings may prove smaller than expected. Gains in competitive capabilities may take substantially longer to realize or, worse, may never materialize at all. Efforts to mesh the corporate cultures can stall due to formidable resistance from organization members. Key employees at the acquired company can quickly become disenchanted and leave; the morale of company personnel who remain can drop to disturbingly low levels because they disagree with newly instituted changes. Differences in management styles and operating procedures can prove hard to resolve. In addition, the managers appointed to oversee the integration of a newly acquired company can make mistakes in deciding which activities to leave alone and which activities to meld into their own operations and systems.

A number of mergers/acquisitions have been notably unsuccessful. eBay's $2.6 billion acquisition of Skype in 2005 proved to be a mistake—eBay wrote off $900 million of its Skype investment in 2007 and sold 70 percent of its ownership in Skype in September 2009 to a group of investors. While the company finally found a white knight in Microsoft in 2011, the jury is out as to whether or not Microsoft can make this acquisition work. A number of recent mergers and acquisitions have yet to live up to expectations—prominent examples include Oracle's acquisition of Sun Microsystems, the Fiat–Chrysler deal, and Bank of America's acquisition of Countrywide Financial.

# VERTICAL INTEGRATION STRATEGIES

Learn the advantages and disadvantages of extending the company's scope of operations via vertical integration.

**CORE CONCEPT**

A **vertically integrated firm** is one that performs value chain activities along more than one stage of an industry's value chain system.

Expanding the firm's vertical scope by means of a vertical integration strategy provides another way to strengthen the company's position in its core market. A **vertically integrated firm** is one that participates in multiple segments or stages of an industry's value chain system. A good example of a vertically integrated firm is Maple Leaf Foods, a major Canadian producer of fresh and processed meats whose best-selling brands include Maple Leaf and Schneiders. Maple Leaf Foods participates in hog and poultry production, with company-owned hog and poultry farms; it has its own meat-processing and rendering facilities; it packages its products and distributes them from company-owned distribution centers; and it conducts marketing, sales, and customer service activities for its wholesale and retail buyers but does not otherwise participate in the final stage of the meat processing vertical chain—the retailing stage.

A vertical integration strategy can expand the firm's range of activities *backward* into sources of supply and/or *forward* toward end users. When Tiffany & Co, a manufacturer and retailer of fine jewelry, began sourcing, cutting, and polishing its own diamonds, it integrated backward along the diamond supply chain. Mining giant De Beers Group and Canadian miner Aber Diamond integrated forward when they entered the diamond retailing business.

A firm can pursue vertical integration by starting its own operations in other stages of the vertical activity chain or by acquiring a company already performing the activities it wants to bring in-house. Vertical integration strategies can aim at *full integration* (participating in all stages of the vertical chain) or *partial integration* (building positions in selected stages of the vertical chain). Firms can also engage in *tapered integration* strategies, which involve a mix of in-house and outsourced activity in any given stage of the vertical chain. Oil companies, for instance, supply their refineries with oil from their own wells as well as with oil that they purchase from other producers—they engage in tapered backward integration. Boston Beer Company, the maker of Samuel Adams, engages in tapered forward integration, since it operates brew-pubs, but sells the majority of its products through third-party distributors.

## The Advantages of a Vertical Integration Strategy

Under the right conditions, a vertical integration strategy can add materially to a company's technological capabilities, strengthen the firm's competitive position, and boost its profitability.[18] But it is important to keep in mind that vertical integration has no real payoff strategywise or profitwise unless the extra investment can be justified by compensating improvements in company costs, differentiation, or competitive strength.

## Integrating Backward to Achieve Greater Competitiveness

It is harder than one might think to generate cost savings or improve profitability by integrating backward into activities such as parts and components manufacture (which could otherwise be purchased from suppliers with specialized expertise in making these parts and components). For **backward integration** to be a cost-saving and profitable strategy, a company must be able to (1) achieve the same scale economies as outside suppliers and (2) match or beat suppliers' production efficiency with no drop-off in quality. Neither outcome is a slam dunk. To begin with, a company's in-house requirements are often too small to reach the optimum size for low-cost operation. Furthermore, matching the production efficiency of suppliers is fraught with problems when suppliers have considerable production experience of their own, when the technology they employ has elements that are hard to master, and/or when substantial R&D expertise is required to develop next-version components or keep pace with advancing technology in components production.

**CORE CONCEPT**

**Backward integration** involves entry into activities previously performed by suppliers or other enterprises positioned along earlier stages of the industry value chain system; **forward integration** involves entry into value chain system activities closer to the end user.

That said, occasions still arise when a company can improve its cost position and competitiveness by performing a broader range of industry value chain activities in-house rather than having such activities performed by outside suppliers. When suppliers have outsized profit margins or when there is a sole supplier, vertical integration can lower costs by limiting supplier power. Vertical integration can also lower costs by facilitating the coordination of production flows and avoiding bottleneck problems. Furthermore, when a company has proprietary know-how that it wants to keep from rivals, then in-house performance of value-adding activities related to this know-how is beneficial even if such activities could be performed by outsiders. Apple recently decided to integrate backward into producing its own chips for iPhones, chiefly because chips are a major cost component, they have big profit margins, and in-house production would help coordinate design tasks and protect Apple's proprietary iPhone technology. International Paper Company backward integrates into pulp mills that it sets up near its paper mills (outside suppliers are generally unwilling to make a site-specific investment for a buyer) and reaps the benefits of coordinated production flows, energy savings, and transportation economies.

Backward vertical integration can produce a differentiation-based competitive advantage when performing activities internally contributes to a better quality product/service offering, improves the caliber of customer service, or in other ways enhances the performance of the final product. On occasion, integrating into more stages along the industry value chain system can add to a company's differentiation capabilities by allowing it to build or strengthen its core competencies, better master key skills or strategy-critical technologies, or add features that deliver greater customer value. Spanish clothing maker Inditex has backward integrated into fabric making, as well as garment design and manufacture, for its successful Zara brand. By tightly controlling the process and postponing dyeing until later stages, Zara can respond quickly to changes in fashion trends and supply its customers with the hottest items. NewsCorp backward integrated into film studios (Twentieth Century Fox) and TV program production to ensure access to high-quality content for its TV stations (and to limit supplier power).

## Integrating Forward to Enhance Competitiveness
Like backward integration, **forward integration** can lower costs by increasing efficiency and bargaining power. In addition, it can allow manufacturers to gain better access to

end users, improve market visibility, and include the end user's purchasing experience as a differentiating feature. For example, Ducati and Harley motorcycles both have company-owned retail stores that are essentially little museums, filled with iconography, that provide an environment conducive to selling not only motorcycles and gear but also memorabilia, clothing, and other items featuring the brand. Insurance companies and brokerages have the ability to make consumers' interactions with local agents and office personnel a differentiating feature by focusing on building relationships.

In many industries, independent sales agents, wholesalers, and retailers handle competing brands of the same product and have no allegiance to any one company's brand—they tend to push whatever offers the biggest profits. An independent insurance agency, for example, represents a number of different insurance companies. Under this arrangement, there's plenty of opportunity for independent agents to promote the policies of favored insurers over others. An insurance company may conclude, therefore, that it is better off integrating forward and setting up its own local offices, as State Farm and Allstate have done. Likewise, it can be advantageous for a manufacturer to integrate forward into wholesaling or retailing rather than depend on the sales efforts of independent distributors/retailers that stock multiple brands and steer customers to the brands on which they earn the highest profit margins. To avoid dependence on distributors/dealers with divided loyalties, Goodyear has integrated forward into company-owned and franchised retail tire stores. Consumer-goods companies like Bath & Body Works, Tommy Hilfiger, Chico's, and Polo Ralph Lauren have integrated forward into retailing and operate their own branded stores in factory outlet malls, enabling them to move overstocked items, slow-selling items, and seconds.

Some producers have opted to integrate forward by selling directly to customers at the company's website. Bypassing regular wholesale/retail channels in favor of direct sales and Internet retailing can have appeal if it reinforces the brand and enhances consumer satisfaction or if it lowers distribution costs, produces a relative cost advantage over certain rivals, and results in lower selling prices to end users. In addition, sellers are compelled to include the Internet as a retail channel when a sufficiently large number of buyers in an industry prefer to make purchases online. However, a company that is vigorously pursuing online sales to consumers at the same time that it is also heavily promoting sales to consumers through its network of wholesalers and retailers is *competing directly against its distribution allies*. Such actions constitute *channel conflict* and create a tricky route to negotiate. A company that is actively trying to expand online sales to consumers is signaling a weak strategic commitment to its dealers *and* a willingness to cannibalize dealers' sales and growth potential. The likely result is angry dealers and loss of dealer goodwill. Quite possibly, a company may stand to lose more sales by offending its dealers than it gains from its own online sales effort. Consequently, in industries where the strong support and goodwill of dealer networks is essential, companies may conclude that it is important to avoid channel conflict and that *their websites should be designed to partner with dealers rather than compete against them*.

## The Disadvantages of a Vertical Integration Strategy

Vertical integration has some substantial drawbacks beyond the potential for channel conflict.[19] The most serious drawbacks to vertical integration include the following concerns:

- Vertical integration raises a firm's capital investment in the industry, thereby *increasing business risk*.

- Vertically integrated companies are often *slow to embrace technological advances* or more efficient production methods when they are saddled with older technology or facilities. A company that obtains parts and components from outside suppliers can always shop the market for the newest, best, and cheapest parts, whereas a vertically integrated firm saddled with older technology or facilities may choose to continue making suboptimal parts rather than face the high costs of premature abandonment.

- Vertical integration can result in *less flexibility in accommodating shifting buyer preferences* when a new product design doesn't include parts and components that the company makes in-house. It is one thing to design out a component made by a supplier and another to design out a component being made in-house (which can mean laying off employees and writing off the associated investment in equipment and facilities). Integrating forward or backward locks a firm into relying on its own in-house activities and sources of supply.

- Vertical integration *may not enable a company to realize economies of scale* if its production levels are below the minimum efficient scale. Small companies in particular are likely to suffer a cost disadvantage by producing in-house when suppliers that serve many small companies can realize scale economies that a small company cannot attain on its own.

- Vertical integration poses all kinds of *capacity matching problems*. In motor vehicle manufacturing, for example, the most efficient scale of operation for making axles is different from the most economic volume for radiators, and different yet again for both engines and transmissions. Consequently, integrating across several production stages in ways that achieve the lowest feasible costs can be a monumental challenge.

- Integration forward or backward often *calls for developing different types of resources and capabilities*. Parts and components manufacturing, assembly operations, wholesale distribution and retailing, and direct sales via the Internet represent different kinds of businesses, operating in different types of industries, with different key success factors. Many manufacturers learn the hard way that company-owned wholesale/retail networks present many headaches, fit poorly with what they do best, and don't always add the kind of value to their core business they thought they would.

In today's world of close working relationships with suppliers and efficient supply chain management systems, *very few businesses can make a case for integrating backward into the business of suppliers* to ensure a reliable supply of materials and components or to reduce production costs. The best materials and components suppliers stay abreast of advancing technology and are adept in improving their efficiency and keeping their costs and prices as low as possible. A company that pursues a vertical integration strategy and tries to produce many parts and components in-house is likely to find itself very hard-pressed to keep up with technological advances and cutting-edge production practices for each part and component used in making its product.

# Weighing the Pros and Cons of Vertical Integration

All in all, therefore, a strategy of vertical integration can have both important strengths and weaknesses. The tip of the scales depends on (1) whether vertical integration can enhance the performance of strategy-critical activities in ways that lower cost, build expertise, protect proprietary know-how, or increase differentiation, (2) the impact of vertical integration on investment costs, flexibility, and response times, (3) the administrative costs of coordinating operations across more vertical chain activities, and (4) how difficult it will be for the company to acquire the set of skills and capabilities needed to operate in another stage of the vertical chain. *Vertical integration strategies have merit*

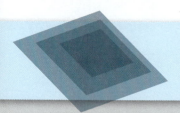
## American Apparel's Vertical Integration Strategy

American Apparel, known for its hip line of basic garments and its provocative advertisements, is no stranger to the concept of "doing it all." The Los Angeles–based casual wear company has made both forward and backward vertical integration a central part of its strategy, making American Apparel a rarity in the U.S. fashion industry. Not only does it do all its own fabric cutting and sewing, but it also owns several knitting and dyeing facilities in southern California, as well as a distribution warehouse, a wholesale operation, and over 270 retail stores in 20 countries. American Apparel even does its own clothing design, marketing, and advertising, often using its employees as photographers and clothing models.

Founder and CEO Dov Charney claims that the company's vertical integration strategy lets American Apparel respond more quickly to rapid market changes, allowing the company to bring an item from design to its stores worldwide in the span of a week. End-to-end coordination also improves inventory control, helping prevent common problems in the fashion business such as stockouts and steep markdowns. The company capitalizes on its California-based vertically integrated operations by using taglines such as "Sweatshop Free. Made in the USA" to bolster its "authentic" image.

However, this strategy is not without risks and costs. In an industry where 97 percent of goods are imported, American Apparel pays its workers wages and benefits

above the relatively high mandated American minimum. Furthermore, operating in so many key vertical chain activities makes it impossible to be expert in all of them and creates optimal scale and capacity mismatches—problems with which the firm has partly dealt by tapering its backward integration into knitting and dyeing. Lastly, while the company can respond quickly to new fashion trends, its vertical integration strategy may make it more difficult for the company to scale back in an economic downturn or respond to radical change in the industry environment. Ultimately, only time will tell whether American Apparel will dilute or capitalize on its vertical integration strategy in its pursuit of profitable growth.

Developed with John R. Moran.

*Sources:* American Apparel website, www.americanapparel.net (accessed June 16, 2010); American Apparel investor presentation, June 2009, http://files.shareholder.com/downloads/APP/938846703x0x300331/3dd0b7ca-e458-45b8-8516-e25ca272016d/NYC%20JUNE%202009.pdf; Dov Charney, "American Apparel—Dov Charney Interview," *YouTube,* 2007, http://youtube.com/watch?v=hYqR8UII8A4; Christopher Palmeri, "Living on the Edge at American Apparel," *BusinessWeek,* June 27, 2005.

*according to which capabilities and value-adding activities truly need to be performed in-house and which can be performed better or cheaper by outsiders.* Without solid benefits, integrating forward or backward is not likely to be an attractive strategy option.

American Apparel, the largest U.S. clothing manufacturer, has made vertical integration a central part of its strategy, as described in Illustration Capsule 6.4.

# OUTSOURCING STRATEGIES: NARROWING THE SCOPE OF OPERATIONS

In contrast to vertical integration strategies, outsourcing strategies narrow the scope of a business's operations (and the firm's boundaries, in terms of what activities are performed internally). **Outsourcing** involves a conscious decision to abandon attempts to perform certain value chain activities internally and instead to farm them out to outside specialists.[20] Many PC makers, for example, have shifted from assembling units in-house to outsourcing the entire assembly process to manufacturing specialists, which can operate more efficiently due to their greater scale, experience, and bargaining power over components makers. Nike has outsourced most of its manufacturing-related value chain activities so it can concentrate on marketing and managing its brand.

Outsourcing certain value chain activities makes strategic sense whenever:

CORE CONCEPT

**Outsourcing** involves contracting out certain value chain activities to outside vendors.

- *An activity can be performed better or more cheaply by outside specialists.* A company should generally *not* perform any value chain activity internally that can be performed more efficiently or effectively by outsiders—the chief exception occurs when a particular activity is strategically crucial and internal control over that activity is deemed essential.

- *The activity is not crucial to the firm's ability to achieve sustainable competitive advantage.* Outsourcing of support activities such as maintenance services, data processing, data storage, fringe-benefit management, and website operations has become commonplace. Colgate-Palmolive, for instance, has been able to reduce its information technology operational costs by more than 10 percent per year through an outsourcing agreement with IBM.

- *It improves organizational flexibility and speeds time to market.* Outsourcing gives a company the flexibility to switch suppliers in the event that its present supplier falls behind competing suppliers. Moreover, seeking out new suppliers with the needed capabilities already in place is frequently quicker, easier, less risky, and cheaper than hurriedly retooling internal operations to replace obsolete capabilities or trying to install and master new technologies.

- *It reduces the company's risk exposure to changing technology or buyer preferences.* When a company outsources certain parts, components, and services, its suppliers must bear the burden of incorporating state-of-the-art technologies and/or undertaking redesigns and upgrades to accommodate a company's plans to introduce next-generation products. If what a supplier provides falls out of favor with buyers, or is rendered unnecessary by technological change, it is the supplier's business that suffers rather than the company's.

- *It allows a company to assemble diverse kinds of expertise speedily and efficiently.* A company can nearly always gain quicker access to first-rate capabilities and expertise by employing suppliers who already have them in place than by trying to build them from scratch internally.

- *It allows a company to concentrate on its core business, leverage its key resources, and do even better what it already does best.* A company is better able to enhance its own competitively valuable capabilities when it concentrates its full resources and energies on performing only those activities. Coach, for example, devotes its energies to designing new styles of ladies handbags and leather accessories, opting to outsource handbag production to 40 contract manufacturers in 15 countries. Hewlett-Packard, IBM, and others have sold their manufacturing plants to outsiders and contracted to repurchase the output from the new owners.

LO 5

Become aware of the conditions that favor farming out certain value chain activities to outside parties.

## The Big Risk of Outsourcing Value Chain Activities

*The biggest danger of outsourcing is that a company will farm out too many or the wrong types of activities and thereby hollow out its own capabilities.*[21] In such cases, a company loses touch with the very activities and expertise that over the long run determine its success. But most companies are alert to this danger and take actions to protect against

A company must guard against outsourcing activities that hollow out the resources and capabilities that it needs to be a master of its own destiny.

being held hostage by outside suppliers. Cisco Systems guards against loss of control and protects its manufacturing expertise by designing the production methods that its contract manufacturers must use. Cisco keeps the source code for its designs proprietary, thereby controlling the initiation of all improvements and safeguarding its innovations from imitation. Further, Cisco uses the Internet to monitor the factory operations of contract manufacturers around the clock, and can therefore know immediately when problems arise and decide whether to get involved.

Another risk of outsourcing comes from the lack of direct control. It may be difficult to monitor, control, and coordinate the activities of outside parties via contracts and arm's-length transactions alone. Unanticipated problems may arise that cause delays or cost overruns and become hard to resolve amicably. Moreover, contract-based outsourcing can be problematic because outside parties lack incentives to make investments specific to the needs of the outsourcing company's internal value chain.

# STRATEGIC ALLIANCES AND PARTNERSHIPS

**LO 6**

Understand when and how strategic alliances can substitute for horizontal mergers and acquisitions or vertical integration and how they can facilitate outsourcing.

Strategic alliances and cooperative partnerships provide one way to gain some of the benefits offered by vertical integration, outsourcing, and horizontal mergers and acquisitions while minimizing the associated problems. Companies frequently engage in cooperative strategies as an alternative to vertical integration or horizontal mergers and acquisitions. Increasingly, companies are also employing strategic alliances and partnerships to extend their scope of operations via international expansion and diversification strategies, as we describe in Chapters 7 and 8. Strategic alliances and cooperative arrangements are now a common means of narrowing a company's scope of operations as well, serving as a useful way to manage outsourcing (in lieu of traditional, purely price-oriented contracts).

For example, oil and gas companies engage in considerable vertical integration—but Shell Oil Company and Pemex (Mexico's state-owned petroleum company) have found that joint ownership of their Deer Park Refinery in Texas lowers their investment costs and risks in comparison to going it alone. The colossal failure of the Daimler-Chrysler merger formed an expensive lesson for Daimler AG about what can go wrong with horizontal mergers and acquisitions; its 2010 strategic alliance with Renault-Nissan may allow the two companies to achieve jointly the global scale required for cost competitiveness in cars and trucks while avoiding the type of problems that so plagued Daimler-Chrysler. Many companies employ strategic alliances to manage the problems that might otherwise occur with outsourcing—Cisco's system of alliances guards against loss of control, protects its proprietary manufacturing expertise, and enables the company to monitor closely the assembly operations of its partners while devoting its energy to designing new generations of the switches, routers, and other Internet-related equipment for which it is known.

## CORE CONCEPT

A **strategic alliance** is a formal agreement between two or more separate companies in which they agree to work cooperatively toward some common objective.

Companies in all types of industries have elected to form strategic alliances and partnerships to complement their own strategic initiatives and strengthen their competitiveness—the very same goals that motivate vertical integration, horizontal mergers and acquisitions, and outsourcing initiatives. A **strategic alliance** is a formal agreement between two or more separate companies in which they agree to work collaboratively toward some strategically relevant objective. Typically, they involve shared financial responsibility, joint contribution of resources and capabilities, shared risk, shared control, and mutual dependence. They may be characterized by cooperative marketing, sales or distribution, joint production, design collaboration, or projects to jointly develop new technologies or products. They can vary in terms of their duration and the extent of the collaboration; some are intended as long-term arrangements, involving an extensive set of cooperative activities, while others are designed to accomplish more limited, short-term objectives.

Collaborative arrangements may entail a contractual agreement, but they commonly stop short of formal ownership ties between the partners (although sometimes an alliance member will secure minority ownership of another member). A special type of strategic alliance involving ownership ties is the **joint venture**. A joint venture entails forming a new corporate entity that is jointly owned by two or more companies that agree to share in the revenues, expenses, and control of the newly formed entity. Since joint ventures involve setting up a mutually owned business, they tend to be more durable but also riskier than other arrangements. In other types of strategic alliances, the collaboration between the partners involves a much less rigid structure in which the partners retain their independence from one another. If a strategic alliance is not working out, a partner can choose to simply walk away or reduce its commitment to collaborating at any time.

> **CORE CONCEPT**
>
> A **joint venture** is a partnership involving the establishment of an independent corporate entity that the partners own and control jointly, sharing in its revenues and expenses.

An alliance becomes "strategic," as opposed to just a convenient business arrangement, when it serves any of the following purposes:[22]

1.  It facilitates achievement of an important business objective (like lowering costs or delivering more value to customers in the form of better quality, added features, and greater durability).
2.  It helps build, sustain, or enhance a core competence or competitive advantage.
3.  It helps block a competitive threat.
4.  It helps remedy an important resource deficiency or competitive weakness.
5.  It increases the bargaining power of alliance members over suppliers or buyers.
6.  It helps open up important new market opportunities.
7.  It mitigates a significant risk to a company's business.

Strategic cooperation is a much-favored approach in industries where new technological developments are occurring at a furious pace along many different paths and where advances in one technology spill over to affect others (often blurring industry boundaries). Whenever industries are experiencing high-velocity technological advances in many areas simultaneously, firms find it virtually essential to have cooperative relationships with other enterprises to stay on the leading edge of technology, even in their own area of specialization.

It took a $3.2 billion joint venture involving the likes of Sprint-Nextel, Clearwire, Intel, Time Warner Cable, Google, Comcast, and Bright House Networks to roll out next-generation 4G wireless services based on Sprint's and Clearwire's WiMax mobile networks. WiMax was an advanced Wi-Fi technology that allowed people to browse the Internet at speeds as great as 10 times faster than other cellular Wi-Fi technologies. The venture was a necessity for Sprint-Nextel and Clearwire since they lacked the financial resources to handle the rollout on their own. The appeal of the partnership for Time Warner, Comcast, and Bright House was the ability to bundle the sale of wireless services to their cable customers, while Intel had the chip sets for WiMax and hoped that WiMax would become the dominant wireless Internet format. Google's interest in the alliance was to strengthen its lead in desktop search on wireless devices.

Clear Channel Communications has entered into a series of partnerships to provide a multiplatform launchpad for artists like Taylor Swift, Phoenix, and Sara Bareilles. In 2010, they partnered with MySpace, Hulu, and the artist management company 19 Entertainment for *If I Can Dream,* an original reality series where unsigned musicians and actors share a "real world"–style house in Los Angeles and document their attempts at stardom.

Clear Channel has helped promote the show by conducting exclusive radio interviews and performances with the talent, which in turn has helped the show become a top-30 weekly program on Hulu.[23]

Because of the varied benefits of strategic alliances, many large corporations have become involved in 30 to 50 alliances, and a number have formed hundreds of alliances. Genentech, a leader in biotechnology and human genetics, has formed R&D alliances with over 30 companies to boost its prospects for developing new cures for various diseases and ailments. Most automakers have forged a variety of long-term strategic partnerships with suppliers of automotive parts and components, both to achieve lower costs and to improve the quality and reliability of their vehicles. Daimler AG has been entering a number of alliances to lower its risks and improve its prospects in electric cars, where

> Companies that have formed a host of alliances need to manage their alliances like a portfolio.

it lacks key capabilities. Its equity-based strategic partnership with Tesla Motors, for example, will allow Daimler to use proven technology to bring its electric vehicles to market quickly, while helping Tesla learn how to mass produce its electric cars. Daimler's 2010 joint venture with Chinese car maker BYD is intended to help Daimler make and sell electric cars for the Chinese market. Companies that have formed a host of alliances need to manage their alliances like a portfolio—terminating those that no longer serve a useful purpose or that have produced meager results, forming promising new alliances, and restructuring existing alliances to correct performance problems and/or redirect the collaborative effort.

## Why and How Strategic Alliances Are Advantageous

The most common reasons companies enter into strategic alliances are to expedite the development of promising new technologies or products, to overcome deficits in their own expertise and capabilities, to improve supply chain efficiency, to share the risks of high-stake, risky ventures, to gain economies of scale in production and/or marketing, and to obtain market access through joint marketing agreements.[24] When a company needs to correct particular resource gaps or deficiencies, it may be faster and cheaper to partner with other enterprises that have the missing know-how and capabilities. Manufacturers frequently pursue alliances with parts and components suppliers to gain the efficiencies of better supply chain management and to speed new products to market. Allies can learn much from one another in performing joint research, sharing technological know-how, and collaborating on complementary new technologies and products—sometimes enough to enable them to pursue other new opportunities on their own.[25] In industries where technology is advancing rapidly, alliances are all about fast cycles of learning, staying abreast of the latest developments, gaining quick access to the latest round of technological know-how, and developing dynamic capabilities. In bringing together firms with different skills and knowledge bases, alliances open up learning opportunities that help partner firms better leverage their own resources and capabilities.[26]

> The best alliances are highly selective, focusing on particular value chain activities and on obtaining a specific competitive benefit. They enable a firm to build on its strengths and to learn.

There are several other instances in which companies find strategic alliances particularly valuable. A company that is racing to *stake out a strong position in an industry of the future* needs alliances to:

- *Establish a stronger beachhead* for participating in the target industry.
- *Master new technologies and build new expertise and competencies* faster than would be possible through internal efforts.
- *Open up broader opportunities* in the target industry by melding the firm's own capabilities with the expertise and resources of partners.

# Capturing the Benefits of Strategic Alliances

The extent to which companies benefit from entering into alliances and partnerships seems to be a function of six factors:[27]

1.  *Picking a good partner.* A good partner must bring complementary strengths to the relationship. To the extent that alliance members have nonoverlapping strengths, there is greater potential for synergy and less potential for coordination problems and conflict. In addition, a good partner needs to share the company's vision about the overall purpose of the alliance and to have specific goals that either match or complement those of the company. Strong partnerships also depend on good chemistry among key personnel and compatible views about how the alliance should be structured and managed.

2.  *Being sensitive to cultural differences.* Cultural differences among companies can make it difficult for their personnel to work together effectively. Cultural differences can be problematic among companies from the same country, but when the partners have different national origins, the problems are often magnified. Unless there is respect among all the parties for company cultural differences, including those stemming from different local cultures and local business practices, productive working relationships are unlikely to emerge.

3.  *Recognizing that the alliance must benefit both sides.* Information must be shared as well as gained, and the relationship must remain forthright and trustful. If either partner plays games with information or tries to take advantage of the other, the resulting friction can quickly erode the value of further collaboration. Open, trustworthy behavior on both sides is essential for fruitful collaboration.

4.  *Ensuring that both parties live up to their commitments.* Both parties have to deliver on their commitments for the alliance to produce the intended benefits. The division of work has to be perceived as fairly apportioned, and the caliber of the benefits received on both sides has to be perceived as adequate.

5.  *Structuring the decision-making process so that actions can be taken swiftly when needed.* In many instances, the fast pace of technological and competitive changes dictates an equally fast decision-making process. If the parties get bogged down in discussions or in gaining internal approval from higher-ups, the alliance can turn into an anchor of delay and inaction.

6.  *Managing the learning process and then adjusting the alliance agreement over time to fit new circumstances.* One of the keys to long-lasting success is adapting the nature and structure of the alliance to be responsive to shifting market conditions, emerging technologies, and changing customer requirements. Wise allies are quick to recognize the merit of an evolving collaborative arrangement, where adjustments are made to accommodate changing market conditions and to overcome whatever problems arise in establishing an effective working relationship.

Most alliances that aim at sharing technology or providing market access turn out to be temporary, lasting only a few years. This is not necessarily an indicator of failure, however. Strategic alliances can be terminated after a few years simply because they have fulfilled their purpose; indeed, many alliances are intended to be of limited duration, set up to accomplish specific short-term objectives. Longer-lasting collaborative arrangements, however, may provide even greater strategic benefits. Alliances are more likely to be long-lasting when (1) they involve collaboration with partners that do not compete directly, (2) a trusting relationship has been established, and (3) both parties conclude that continued collaboration is in their mutual interest, perhaps because new opportunities for learning are emerging.

# The Drawbacks of Strategic Alliances and Partnerships

While strategic alliances provide a way of obtaining the benefits of vertical integration, mergers and acquisitions, and outsourcing, they also suffer from some of the same drawbacks. Anticipated gains may fail to materialize due to an overly optimistic view of the synergies or a poor fit in terms of the combination of resources and capabilities. When outsourcing is conducted via alliances, there is no less risk of becoming dependent on other companies for essential expertise and capabilities—indeed, this may be the Achilles' heel of such alliances. Moreover, there are additional pitfalls to collaborative arrangements. The greatest danger is that a partner will gain access to a company's proprietary knowledge base, technologies, or trade secrets, enabling the partner to match the company's core strengths and costing the company its hard-won competitive advantage. This risk is greatest when the alliance is among industry rivals or when the alliance is for the purpose of collaborative R&D, since this type of partnership requires an extensive exchange of closely held information.

The question for managers is when to engage in a strategic alliance and when to choose an alternative means of meeting their objectives. The answer to this question depends on the relative advantages of each method and the circumstances under which each type of organizational arrangement is favored.

The principle advantages of strategic alliances over vertical integration or horizontal mergers/acquisitons are threefold:

1. They lower investment costs and risks for each partner by facilitating resource pooling and risk sharing. This can be particularly important when investment needs and uncertainty are high, such as when a dominant technology standard has not yet emerged.

2. They are more flexible organizational forms and allow for a more adaptive response to changing conditions. Flexibility is essential when environmental conditions or technologies are changing rapidly. Moreover, strategic alliances under such circumstances may enable the development of each partner's dynamic capabilities.

3. They are more rapidly deployed—a critical factor when speed is of the essence. Speed is of the essence when there is a winner-take-all type of competitive situation, such as the race for a dominant technological design or a race down a steep experience curve, where there is a large first-mover advantage.

The key advantages of using strategic alliances rather than arm's-length transactions to manage outsourcing are (1) the increased ability to exercise control over the partners' activities and (2) a greater willingness for the partners to make relationship-specific investments. Arm's-length transactions discourage such investments since they imply less commitment and do not build trust.

On the other hand, there are circumstances when other organizational mechanisms are preferable to alliances and partnering. Mergers and acquisitions are especially suited for situations in which strategic alliances or partnerships do not go far enough in providing a company with access to needed resources and capabilities. Ownership ties are more permanent than partnership ties, allowing the operations of the merger/acquisition participants to be tightly integrated and creating more in-house control and autonomy. Other organizational mechanisms are also preferable to alliances when there is limited property rights protection for valuable know-how and when companies fear being taken advantage of by opportunistic partners.

While it is important for managers to understand when strategic alliances and partnerships are most likely (and least likely) to prove useful, it is also important to know how to manage them.

## How to Make Strategic Alliances Work

A surprisingly large number of alliances never live up to expectations. Even though the number of strategic alliances increases by about 25 percent annually, about 60 to 70 percent of alliances continue to fail each year. The success of an alliance depends on how well the partners work together, their capacity to respond and adapt to changing internal and external conditions, and their willingness to renegotiate the bargain if circumstances so warrant. A successful alliance requires real in-the-trenches collaboration, not merely an arm's-length exchange of ideas. Unless partners place a high value on the skills, resources, and contributions each brings to the alliance and the cooperative arrangement results in valuable win–win outcomes, it is doomed to fail.

While the track record for strategic alliances is poor on average, many companies have learned how to manage strategic alliances successfully and routinely defy these averages. Samsung Group, which includes Samsung Electronics, successfully manages an ecosystem of over 1,300 partnerships that enable productive activities from global procurement to local marketing to collaborative R&D. Companies that have greater success in managing their strategic alliances and partnerships often credit the following factors:

- *They create a system for managing their alliances.* Companies need to manage their alliances in a systematic fashion, just as they manage other functions. This means setting up a process for managing the different aspects of alliance management from partner selection to alliance termination procedures. To ensure that the system is followed on a routine basis by all company managers, many companies create a set of explicit procedures, process templates, manuals, or the like.

- *They build relationships with their partners and establish trust.* Establishing strong interpersonal relationships is a critical factor in making strategic alliances work since they facilitate opening up channels of communication, coordinating activity, aligning interests, and building trust.

- *They protect themselves from the threat of opportunism by setting up safeguards.* There are a number of means for preventing a company from being taken advantage of by an untrustworthy partner or unwittingly losing control over key assets. Cisco Systems, for example, does not divulge the source code for its designs to its alliance partners, thereby controlling the initiation of all improvements and safeguarding its innovations from imitation. Contractual safeguards, including noncompete clauses, can provide other forms of protection.

- *They make commitments to their partners and see that their partners do the same.* When partners make credible commitments to a joint enterprise, they have stronger incentives for making it work and are less likely to "free-ride" on the efforts of other partners. Because of this, equity-based alliances tend to be more successful than nonequity alliances.[28]

- *They make learning a routine part of the management process.* There are always opportunities for learning from a partner, but organizational learning does not take place automatically. Whatever learning occurs cannot add to a company's knowledge base unless the learning is incorporated systematically into the company's routines and practices.

Finally, managers should realize that alliance management is an organizational capability, much like any other. It develops over time, out of effort, experience, and learning. For this reason, it is wise to begin slowly, with simple alliances, designed to meet limited, short-term objectives. Short-term partnerships that are successful often become the basis for much more extensive collaborative arrangements. Even when strategic alliances are set up with the hope that they will become long-term engagements, they have a better chance of succeeding if they are phased in, so that the partners can learn how they can work together most fruitfully.

## KEY POINTS

1. Once a company has settled on which of the five generic competitive strategies to employ, attention turns to how strategic choices regarding (1) competitive actions, (2) timing of those actions, and (3) scope of operations can complement its competitive approach and maximize the power of its overall strategy.

2. Strategic offensives should, as a general rule, be grounded in a company's strategic assets and employ a company's strengths to attack rivals in the competitive areas where they are weakest.

3. Companies have a number of offensive strategy options for improving their market positions: using a cost-based advantage to attack competitors on the basis of price or value, leapfrogging competitors with next-generation technologies, pursuing continuous product innovation, adopting and improving the best ideas of others, using hit-and-run tactics to steal sales away from unsuspecting rivals, and launching preemptive strikes. A blue-ocean type of offensive strategy seeks to gain a dramatic new competitive advantage by abandoning efforts to beat out competitors in existing markets and, instead, inventing a new industry or distinctive market segment that renders existing competitors largely irrelevant and allows a company to create and capture altogether new demand.

4. The purposes of defensive strategies are to lower the risk of being attacked, weaken the impact of any attack that occurs, and influence challengers to aim their efforts at other rivals. Defensive strategies to protect a company's position usually take one of two forms: (1) actions to block challengers and (2) actions to signal the likelihood of strong retaliation.

5. The timing of strategic moves also has relevance in the quest for competitive advantage. Company managers are obligated to carefully consider the advantages or disadvantages that attach to being a first mover versus a fast follower versus a wait-and-see late mover.

6. Decisions concerning the scope of a company's operations—which activities a firm will perform internally and which it will not—can also affect the strength of a company's market position. The *scope of the firm* refers to the range of its activities, the breadth of its product and service offerings, the extent of its geographic market presence, and its mix of businesses. Companies can expand their scope horizontally (more broadly within their focal market) or vertically (up or down the industry value chain system that starts with raw-materials production and ends with sales and service to the end consumer). Horizontal mergers and acquisitions (combinations of market rivals) provide a means for a company to expand its horizontal scope. Vertical integration expands a firm's vertical scope.

7. Horizontal mergers and acquisitions can strengthen a firm's competitiveness in five ways: (1) by improving the efficiency of its operations, (2) by heightening its product differentiation, (3) by reducing market rivalry, (3) by increasing the company's bargaining power over suppliers and buyers, and (5) by enhancing its flexibility and dynamic capabilities.

8. Vertical integration, forward or backward, makes strategic sense only if it strengthens a company's position via either cost reduction or creation of a differentiation-based advantage. Otherwise, the drawbacks of vertical integration (increased investment, greater business risk, increased vulnerability to technological changes, less flexibility in making product changes, and the potential for channel conflict) are likely to outweigh any advantages.

9. Outsourcing involves contracting out pieces of the value chain formerly performed in-house to outside vendors, thereby narrowing the scope of the firm. Outsourcing can enhance a company's competitiveness whenever (1) an activity can be performed better or more cheaply by outside specialists; (2) having the activity performed by others won't hollow out the outsourcing company's core competencies; (3) it streamlines company operations in ways that improve organizational flexibility, speed decision making, and cut cycle time; (4) it reduces the company's risk exposure; (5) it allows a company to access capabilities more quickly and improves its ability to innovate; and (6) it permits a company to concentrate on its core business and focus on what it does best.

10. Strategic alliances and cooperative partnerships provide one way to gain some of the benefits offered by vertical integration, outsourcing, and horizontal mergers and acquisitions while minimizing the associated problems. They serve as an alternative to vertical integration and mergers and acquisitions; they serve as a supplement to outsourcing, allowing more control relative to outsourcing via arm's-length transactions.

11. Companies that manage their alliances well generally (1) create a system for managing their alliances, (2) build relationships with their partners and establish trust, (3) protect themselves from the threat of opportunism by setting up safeguards, (4) make commitments to their partners and see that their partners do the same, and (5) make learning a routine part of the management process.

## ASSURANCE OF LEARNING EXERCISES

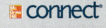

1. Does it appear that Nintendo relies more heavily on offensive or defensive strategies as it competes in the video game industry? Has Nintendo's timing of strategic moves made it an early mover or a fast follower? Could Nintendo's introduction of the Wii be characterized as a blue-ocean strategy? You may rely on your knowledge of the video game industry and information provided at Nintendo's Investor Relations website (www.nintendo.co.jp) to provide justification for your answers to these questions.

**LO 1, LO 2**

2. Using your university library's subscription to Lexis-Nexis, EBSCO, or a similar database, identify at least two companies in different industries that are using mergers and acquisitions to strengthen their market positions. How have these mergers and acquisitions enhanced the acquiring companies' resources and competitive capabilities?

**LO 3**

**LO 4**    3. American Apparel, known for its hip line of basic garments and its provocative advertisements, is no stranger to the concept of "doing it all." Illustration Capsule 6.4 describes how American Apparel has made vertical integration a central part of its strategy. What value chain segments has American Apparel chosen to enter and perform internally? How has vertical integration aided the company in building competitive advantage? Has vertical integration strengthened its market position? Explain why or why not.

**connect**    4. Perform an Internet search to identify at least two companies in different industries that have entered into outsourcing agreements with firms with specialized services. In addition, describe what value chain activities the companies have chosen to outsource. Do any of these outsourcing agreements seem likely to threaten any of the companies' competitive capabilities?

**LO 5**

**LO 6**    5. Using your university library's subscription to Lexis-Nexis, EBSCO, or a similar database, find two examples of how companies have relied on strategic alliances or joint ventures to substitute for horizontal or vertical integration.

## EXERCISE FOR SIMULATION PARTICIPANTS

**LO 1, LO 2**    1. Has your company relied more on offensive or defensive strategies to achieve your rank in the industry? What options for being a first mover does your company have? Do any of these first-mover options hold competitive advantage potential?

**LO 3**    2. Does your company have the option to merge with or acquire other companies? If so, which rival companies would you like to acquire or merge with?

**LO 4**    3. Is your company vertically integrated? Explain.

**LO 5, LO 6**    4. Is your company able to engage in outsourcing? If so, what do you see as the pros and cons of outsourcing? Are strategic alliances involved? Explain.

## ENDNOTES

[1] George Stalk, Jr., and Rob Lachenauer, "Hardball: Five Killer Strategies for Trouncing the Competition," *Harvard Business Review* 82, no. 4 (April 2004); Richard D'Aveni, "The Empire Strikes Back: Counterrevolutionary Strategies for Industry Leaders," *Harvard Business Review* 80, no. 11 (November 2002); David J. Bryce and Jeffrey H. Dyer, "Strategies to Crack Well-Guarded Markets," *Harvard Business Review* 85, no. 5 (May 2007).

[2] George Stalk, "Playing Hardball: Why Strategy Still Matters," *Ivey Business Journal* 69, no.2 (November–December 2004), pp. 1–2; K. G. Smith, W. J. Ferrier, and C. M. Grimm, "King of the Hill: Dethroning the Industry Leader," *Academy of Management Executive* 15, no. 2 (May 2001), pp. 59–70; W. J. Ferrier, K. G. Smith, and C. M. Grimm, "The Role of Competitive Action in Market Share Erosion and Industry Dethronement: A Study of Industry Leaders and Challengers," *Academy of Management Journal* 42, no. 4 (August 1999), pp. 372–88.

[3] David B. Yoffie and Mary Kwak, "Mastering Balance: How to Meet and Beat a Stronger Opponent," *California Management Review* 44, no. 2 (Winter 2002), pp. 8–24.

[4] Ian C. MacMillan, Alexander B. van Putten, and Rita Gunther McGrath, "Global Gamesmanship," *Harvard Business Review* 81, no. 5 (May 2003); and Ashkay R. Rao, Mark E. Bergen, and Scott Davis, "How to Fight a Price War," *Harvard Business Review* 78, no. 2 (March–April, 2000).

[5] D. B. Yoffie and M. A. Cusumano, "Judo Strategy—The Competitive Dynamics of Internet Time," *Harvard Business Review* 77, no. 1 (January–February 1999), pp. 70–81;

[6] Ming-Jer Chen and Donald C. Hambrick, "Speed, Stealth, and Selective Attack: How Small Firms Differ from Large Firms in Competitive Behavior," *Academy of Management Journal* 38, no. 2 (April 1995), pp. 453–82; Ian MacMillan, "How Business Strategists Can Use Guerrilla Warfare Tactics," *Journal of Business Strategy* 1, no. 2 (Fall 1980), pp. 63–65; William

E. Rothschild, "Surprise and the Competitive Advantage," *Journal of Business Strategy* 4, no. 3 (Winter 1984), pp. 10–18; Kathryn R. Harrigan, *Strategic Flexibility* (Lexington, MA: Lexington Books, 1985); Liam Fahey, "Guerrilla Strategy: The Hit-and-Run Attack," in Liam Fahey (ed.), *The Strategic Management Planning Reader* (Englewood Cliffs, NJ: Prentice Hall, 1989), pp. 194–97.

[7] Ian MacMillan, "Preemptive Strategies," *Journal of Business Strategy* 14, no. 2 (Fall 1983), pp. 16–26.

[8] Ian C. MacMillan, "How Long Can You Sustain a Competitive Advantage?" in Liam Fahey (ed.), *The Strategic Planning Management Reader* (Englewood Cliffs, NJ: Prentice Hall, 1989), pp. 23–24.

[9] Kevin P. Coyne and John Horn, "Predicting Your Competitor's Reactions," *Harvard Business Review* 87 no. 4 (April 2009), pp. 90–97.

[10] Philip Kotler, *Marketing Management,* 5th ed. (Englewood Cliffs, NJ: Prentice Hall, 1984).

[11] W. Chan Kim and Renée Mauborgne, "Blue Ocean Strategy," *Harvard Business Review* 82, no. 10 (October 2004), pp. 76–84.

[12] Jeffrey G. Covin, Dennis P. Slevin, and Michael B. Heeley, "Pioneers and Followers: Competitive Tactics, Environment, and Growth," *Journal of Business Venturing* 15, no. 2 (March 1999), pp. 175–210; Christopher A. Bartlett and Sumantra Ghoshal, "Going Global: Lessons from Late-Movers," *Harvard Business Review* 78, no. 2 (March–April 2000), pp. 132–45.

[13] Costas Markides and Paul A. Geroski, Racing to be 2nd: Conquering the Industries of the Future," *Business Strategy Review* 15, no. 4 (Winter 2004), pp. 25–31.

[14] Fernando Suarez and Gianvito Lanzolla, "The Half-Truth of First-Mover Advantage," *Harvard Business Review* 83, no. 4 (April 2005), pp. 121–27.

[15] Joseph L. Bower, "Not All M&As Are Alike—and That Matters," *Harvard Business Review* 79, no. 3 (March 2001); O. Chatain and P Zemsky, "The Horizontal Scope of the Firm: Organizational Tradeoffs vs. Buyer–Supplier Relationships," *Management Science* 53, no. 4 (April 2007), pp. 550–65.

[16] M. Schiffrin and H. Touryalai, "The Bank that Works," Forbes, February 13, 2012, pp. 66–73.

[17] Jeffrey H. Dyer, Prashant Kale, and Harbir Singh, "When to Ally and When to Acquire," *Harvard Business Review* 82, no. 4 (July–August 2004), pp. 109–10.

[18] Kathryn R. Harrigan, "Matching Vertical Integration Strategies to Competitive Conditions," *Strategic Management Journal* 7, no. 6 (November–December 1986), pp. 535–56; John Stuckey and David White, "When and When Not to Vertically Integrate," *Sloan Management Review* (Spring 1993), pp. 71–83.

[19] Thomas Osegowitsch and Anoop Madhok, "Vertical Integration Is Dead, or Is It?" *Business Horizons* 46, no. 2 (March–April 2003), pp. 25–35.

[20] Ronan McIvor, "What Is the Right Outsourcing Strategy for Your Process?" *European Management Journal* 26, no. 1 (February 2008), pp. 24–34.

[21] Gary P. Pisano and Willy C. Shih, "Restoring American Competitiveness," *Harvard Business Review* 87, no. 7–8 (July–August 2009), pp. 114–25; Jérôme Barthélemy, "The Seven Deadly Sins of Outsourcing," *Academy of Management Executive* 17, no. 2 (May 2003), pp. 87–100.

[22] Jason Wakeam, "The Five Factors of a Strategic Alliance," *Ivey Business Journal* 68, no 3 (May–June 2003), pp. 1–4.

[23] *Advertising Age,* May 24, 2010, p. 14.

[24] Michael E. Porter, *The Competitive Advantage of Nations* (New York: Free Press, 1990; Nancy J. Kaplan and Jonathan Hurd, "Realizing the Promise of Partnerships," *Journal of Business Strategy* 23, no. 3 (May–June 2002), pp. 38–42; Parise and Sasson, "Leveraging Knowledge Management across Strategic Alliances," pp. 41–47; Jonathan Hughes and Jeff Weiss, "Simple Rules for Making Alliances Work," *Harvard Business Review* 85, no. 11 (November 2007), pp. 122–31.

[25] M. Koza and A. Lewin, "Managing Partnerships and Strategic Alliances: Raising the Odds of Success," *European Management Journal* 18, no. 2 (April 2000), pp. 146–51.

[26] A. Inkpen, "Learning, Knowledge Acquisition, and Strategic Alliances," *European Management Journal* 16, no. 2 (April 1998), pp. 223–29.

[27] Patricia Anslinger and Justin Jenk, "Creating Successful Alliances," *Journal of Business Strategy* 25, no. 2 (2004), pp. 18–23; Rosabeth Moss Kanter, "Collaborative Advantage: The Art of the Alliance," *Harvard Business Review* 72, no. 4 (July–August 1994), pp. 96–108; Joel Bleeke and David Ernst, "The Way to Win in Cross-Border Alliances," *Harvard Business Review* 69, no. 6 (November–December 1991), pp. 127–35; Gary Hamel, Yves L. Doz, and C. K. Prahalad, "Collaborate with Your Competitors—and Win," *Harvard Business Review* 67, no. 1 (January–February 1989), pp. 133–39.

[28] Y. G. Pan and D. K. Tse, "The Hierarchical Model of Market Entry Modes," *Journal of International Business Studies* 31, no. 4 (2000), pp. 535–54.

# CHAPTER 7

# STRATEGIES FOR COMPETING IN INTERNATIONAL MARKETS

## Learning Objectives

**LO 1**  Develop an understanding of the primary reasons companies choose to compete in international markets.

**LO 2**  Learn how and why differing market conditions across countries influence a company's strategy choices in international markets.

**LO 3**  Learn about the five major strategic options for entering foreign markets.

**LO 4**  Gain familiarity with the three main strategic approaches for competing internationally.

**LO 5**  Understand how multinational companies are able to use international operations to improve overall competitiveness.

**LO 6**  Gain an understanding of the unique characteristics of competing in developing-country markets.

Globalization is forcing companies to do things in new ways.

Bill Gates – *Founder and Chairman of Microsoft*

Globalization has changed us into a company that searches the world, not just to sell or to source, but to find intellectual capital—the world's best talents and greatest ideas.

Jack Welch – *Former Chairman and CEO of GE*

We must ensure that the global market is embedded in broadly shared values and practices that reflect global social needs, and that all the world's people share the benefits of globalization.

Kofi Annan – *Nobel Peace Prize Winner, former Secretary-General of the United Nations*

Any company that aspires to industry leadership in the 21st century must think in terms of global, not domestic, market leadership. The world economy is globalizing at an accelerating pace as countries previously closed to foreign companies open up their markets, as countries with previously planned economies embrace market or mixed economies, as information technology shrinks the importance of geographic distance, and as growth-minded companies race to build stronger competitive positions in the markets of more and more countries. The forces of globalization are changing the competitive landscape in many industries, offering companies attractive new opportunities but at the same time introducing new competitive threats. Companies in industries where these forces are greatest are therefore under considerable pressure to come up with a strategy for competing successfully in foreign markets.

This chapter focuses on strategy options for expanding beyond domestic boundaries and competing in the markets of either a few or a great many countries. In the process of exploring these options, we will introduce such concepts as multidomestic, transnational, and global strategies, the Porter diamond of national competitive advantage, and profit sanctuaries. The chapter also includes sections on cross-country differences in cultural, demographic, and market conditions, strategy options for entering in foreign markets, the importance of locating value chain operations in the most advantageous countries; and the special circumstances of competing in developing markets as those in China, India, Brazil, Russia, and Eastern Europe.

# WHY COMPANIES DECIDE TO ENTER FOREIGN MARKETS

A company may opt to expand outside its domestic market for any of five major reasons:

1. *To gain access to new customers.* Expanding into foreign markets offers potential for increased revenues, profits, and long-term growth and becomes an especially attractive option when a company encounters dwindling growth opportunities in its home market. Companies often expand internationally to extend the life cycle of their products, as Honda has done with its classic 50-cc motorcycle, the Honda cub (which is still selling well in developing markets, more than 50 years after it was first introduced in Japan). A larger target market also offers companies the opportunity to earn a return on large investments more rapidly. This can be particularly important in R&D-intensive industries, where development is fast-paced or competitors imitate innovations rapidly.

2. *To achieve lower costs through economies of scale, experience, and increased purchasing power.* Many companies are driven to seek out foreign buyers for their products and services because they cannot capture a large enough sales volume domestically to fully capture economies of scale in product development, manufacturing, or marketing. Similarly, firms expand internationally to increase the rate at which they accumulate experience and move down the learning curve. International expansion can also lower a company's input costs through greater pooled purchasing power. The relatively small size of country markets in Europe and limited domestic volume explains why companies like Michelin, BMW, and Nestlé long ago began selling their products all across Europe and then moved into markets in North America and Latin America.

3. *To further exploit its core competencies.* A company with competitively valuable resources and capabilities may be able to extend a market-leading position in its domestic market into a position of regional or global market leadership by leveraging these resources further. Walmart is capitalizing on its considerable expertise in discount retailing to expand into China, Latin America, Japan, South Korea, and the United Kingdom; Walmart executives believe the company has tremendous growth opportunities in China. Companies can often leverage their resources internationally by replicating a successful business model, using it as a basic blueprint for international operations, as Starbucks and McDonald's have done.[1]

4. *To gain access to resources and capabilities located in foreign markets.* An increasingly important motive for entering foreign markets is to acquire resources and capabilities that cannot be accessed as readily in a company's home market. Companies often enter into cross-border alliances or joint ventures, for example, to gain access to resources and capabilities that complement their own or to learn from their partners.[2] Cross-border acquisitions are commonly made for similar reasons.[3] In other cases, companies choose to establish operations in other countries to utilize local distribution networks, employ low-cost human resources, or acquire technical knowledge. In a few cases, companies in industries based on natural resources (e.g., oil and gas, minerals, rubber, and lumber) find it necessary to operate in the international arena because attractive raw-material supplies are located in many different parts of the world.

5. *To spread its business risk across a wider market base.* A company spreads business risk by operating in many different countries rather than depending entirely on operations in its domestic market. Then, when it encounters an economic downturn in its home market, its performance may be bolstered by buoyant sales elsewhere.

In addition, companies that are the suppliers of other companies often expand internationally when their major customers do so, to meet their needs abroad and retain their position as a key supply chain partner. Automotive parts suppliers, for example, have followed automobile manufacturers abroad, and retail goods suppliers, such as Newell-Rubbermaid, have followed their discount retailer customers, such as Walmart, into foreign markets.

# WHY COMPETING ACROSS NATIONAL BORDERS MAKES STRATEGY-MAKING MORE COMPLEX

Crafting a strategy to compete in one or more countries of the world is inherently more complex for five reasons. First, different countries have different home-country advantages in different industries. This is due to four sets of factors that can be analyzed using Porter's Diamond Framework of National Competitive Advantage. Second, there are location-based advantages to conducting particular value chain activities in different parts of the world. Third, different government policies, tax rates, inflation rates, and other economic conditions make the general business climate more favorable in some countries than in others. Fourth, companies face risk due to adverse shifts in currency exchange rates when operating in foreign markets. And fifth, differences in buyer tastes and preferences present a challenge for companies concerning customizing versus standardizing their products and services.

**LO 2**

Learn how and why differing market conditions across countries influence a company's strategy choices in international markets.

## Porter's Diamond of National Competitive Advantage

Certain countries are known for their strengths in particular industries. For example, Chile has competitive strengths in industries such as copper, fruit, fish products, paper and pulp, chemicals, and wine. Japan is known for competitive strength in consumer electronics, automobiles, semiconductors, steel products, and specialty steel. Where industries are more likely to develop competitive strength depends on a set of factors that describe the nature of each country's business environment and vary from country to country. Because strong industries are made up of strong firms, the strategies of firms that expand internationally are usually grounded in one or more of these factors. The four major factors are summarized in a framework developed by Michael Porter known as the *Diamond of National Competitive Advantage* (see Figure 7.1).[4]

**Demand Conditions**   The demand conditions in an industry's home market include the relative size of the market, its growth potential, and the nature of domestic buyers' needs and wants. Differing population sizes, income levels, and other demographic factors give rise to considerable differences in market size and growth rates from country to country. Industry sectors that are larger and more important in their home market tend to attract more resources and grow faster than others. For example, owing to widely differing population demographics and income levels, there is a far bigger market for luxury automobiles in the United States and Germany than in Argentina, India, Mexico, and China. At the same time, in developing markets like India, China, Brazil, and Malaysia, market growth potential is far higher than it is in the more mature economies of Britain, Denmark, Canada, and Japan. The potential for market growth in automobiles is explosive in China, where 2010 sales of new vehicles amounted to 18 million, surpassing U.S. sales of 11.6 million and making China the world's largest market for the second year in a row.[5] Demanding domestic buyers for an industry's products spur greater innovativeness and improvements in quality. Such conditions foster the development of stronger industries, with firms that are capable of translating a home-market advantage into a competitive advantage in the international arena.

**Factor Conditions**   Factor conditions describe the availability, quality, and cost of raw materials and other inputs (called *factors*) that firms in an industry require to produce their products and services. The relevant factors vary from industry to industry but can include different types of labor, technical or managerial knowledge, land, financial capital, and natural resources. Elements of a country's infrastructure may be included as well, such as its transportation, communication, and banking system. For instance, in India there are efficient, well-developed national channels for distributing trucks, scooters, farm equipment, groceries, personal care items, and other packaged products to the country's 3 million retailers, whereas in China distribution is primarily local and there is a limited national network for distributing most products. Competitively strong industries and firms develop where relevant factor conditions are favorable.

**FIGURE 7.1**   The Diamond of National Competitive Advantage

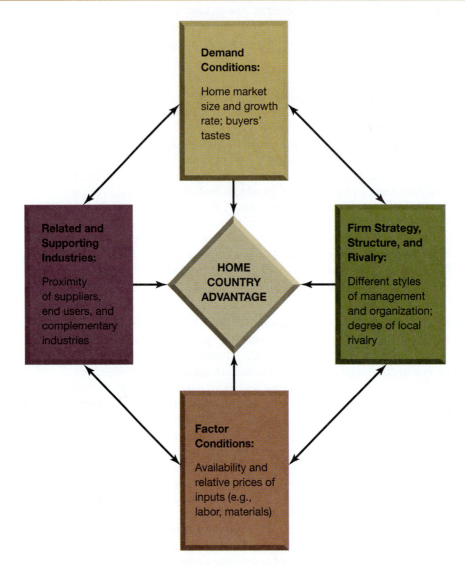

*Source:* Adapted from M. Porter, "The Competitive Advantage of Nations," *Harvard Business Review,* March–April 1990, pp. 73–93.

**Related and Supporting Industries**   Robust industries often develop as part of a cluster of related industries, including suppliers of components and capital equipment, end users, and the makers of complementary products, including those that are technologically related. The sports car makers Ferrari and Maserati, for example, are located in an area of Italy known as the "engine technological district" that includes other firms involved in racing, such as Ducati Motorcycles, along with hundreds of small suppliers. The advantage to firms that develop as part of a related-industry cluster comes from the close collaboration with key suppliers and the greater knowledge sharing throughout the cluster, resulting in greater efficiency and innovativeness.

**Firm Strategy, Structure, and Rivalry**    Different country environments foster the development of different styles of management, organization, and strategy. For example, strategic alliances are a more common strategy for firms from Asian or Latin American countries, which emphasize trust and cooperation in their organizations, than for firms from North America, where individualism is more influential. In addition, countries vary in terms of the competitive rivalry of their industries. Fierce rivalry in home markets tends to hone domestic firms' competitive capabilities and ready them for competing internationally.

For an industry in a particular country to become competitively strong, all four factors must be favorable for that industry. When they are, the industry is likely to contain firms that are capable of competing successfully in the international arena. Thus the diamond framework can be used to reveal the answers to several questions that are important for competing on an international basis. First, it can help predict where foreign entrants into an industry are most likely to come from. This can help managers prepare to cope with new foreign competitors, since the framework also reveals something about the basis of the new rivals' strengths. Second, it can reveal the countries in which foreign rivals are likely to be weakest and thus help managers decide which foreign markets to enter first. And third, because it focuses on the attributes of a country's business environment that allow firms to flourish, it reveals something about the advantages of conducting particular business activities in that country. Thus the diamond framework is an aid to deciding where to locate different value chain activities most beneficially—a topic that we address next.

## Locating Value Chain Activities Advantageously

Increasingly, companies are locating different value chain activities in different parts of the world to exploit location-based advantages that vary from country to country. This is particularly evident with respect to the location of manufacturing activities. Differences in wage rates, worker productivity, energy costs and the like, create sizable variations in manufacturing costs from country to country. By locating its plants in certain countries, firms in some industries can reap major manufacturing cost advantages because of lower input costs (especially labor), relaxed government regulations, the proximity of suppliers and technologically related industries, or unique natural resources. In such cases, the low-cost countries become principal production sites, with most of the output being exported to markets in other parts of the world. Companies that build production facilities in low-cost countries (or that source their products from contract manufacturers in these countries) gain a competitive advantage over rivals with plants in countries where costs are higher. The competitive role of low manufacturing costs is most evident in low-wage countries like China, India, Pakistan, Cambodia, Vietnam, Mexico, Brazil, Guatemala, the Philippines, and several countries in Africa and eastern Europe that have become production havens for manufactured goods with high labor content (especially textiles and apparel). Hourly compensation for manufacturing workers in 2009 averaged about $1.36 in China, $1.50 in the Philippines, $5.38 in Mexico, $5.96 in Brazil, $7.76 in Taiwan, $8.62 in Hungary, $11.95 in Portugal, $14.20 in South Korea, $30.36 in Japan, $33.53 in the U.S., $29.60 in Canada, $46.52 in Germany, and $53.89 in Norway.[6] Not surprisingly, China has emerged as the manufacturing capital of the world—virtually all of the world's major manufacturing companies now have facilities in China.

For other types of value chain activities, input quality or availability are more important considerations. Tiffany entered the mining industry in Canada to access diamonds that could be certified as "conflict free" and not associated with either the funding of African wars or unethical mining conditions. Many U.S. companies locate call centers in countries such as India and Ireland, where English is spoken and the workforce is well educated. Other companies locate R&D activities in countries where there are prestigious research institutions and well-trained scientists and engineers. Likewise, concerns about short delivery times and low shipping costs make some countries better locations than others for establishing distribution centers.

## The Impact of Government Policies and Economic Conditions in Host Countries

Cross-country variations in government policies and economic conditions affect both the opportunities available to a foreign entrant and the risks of operating within that country. The governments of some countries are anxious to attract foreign investments and go all out to create a business climate that outsiders will view as favorable. Governments anxious to spur economic growth, create more jobs, and raise living standards for their citizens usually enact policies aimed at stimulating business innovation and capital investment. They may provide such incentives as reduced taxes, low-cost loans, site location and site development assistance, and government-sponsored training for workers to encourage companies to construct production and distribution facilities. When new business-related issues or developments arise, pro-business governments make a practice of seeking advice and counsel from business leaders. When tougher business-related regulations are deemed appropriate, they endeavor to make the transition to more costly and stringent regulations somewhat business-friendly rather than adversarial.

On the other hand, governments sometimes enact policies that, from a business perspective, make locating facilities within a country's borders less attractive. For example, the nature of a company's operations may make it particularly costly to achieve compliance with a country's environmental regulations. Some governments, desirous of discouraging foreign imports, provide subsidies and low-interest loans to domestic companies (to enable them to better compete against foreign companies), enact deliberately burdensome procedures and requirements for imported goods to pass customs inspection (to make it harder for imported goods to compete against the products of local businesses), and impose tariffs or quotas on the imports of certain goods (also to help protect local businesses from foreign competition). Additionally, they may specify that a certain percentage of the parts and components used in manufacturing a product be obtained from local suppliers, require prior approval of capital spending projects, limit withdrawal of funds from the country, and require minority (sometimes majority) ownership of foreign company operations by local companies or investors. There are times when a government may place restrictions on exports to ensure adequate local supplies and regulate the prices of imported and locally produced goods. Such government actions make a country's business climate less attractive and in some cases may be sufficiently onerous as to discourage a company from locating production or distribution facilities in that country or maybe even selling its products in that country.

A country's business climate is also a function of the political and economic risks associated with operating within its borders. **Political risks** have to do with the instability of weak governments, the likelihood of new onerous legislation or regulations on foreign-owned businesses, and the potential for future elections to produce corrupt or tyrannical government leaders. In industries that a government deems critical to the national welfare, there is sometimes a risk that the government will nationalize the industry and expropriate the assets of foreign companies. In 2010, for example, Ecuador threatened to expropriate the holdings of all foreign oil companies that refused to sign new contracts giving the state control of all production. Other political risks include the loss of investments due to war or political unrest, regulatory changes that create operating uncertainties, security risks due to terrorism, and corruption. **Economic risks** have to do with the stability of a country's economy—whether inflation rates might skyrocket or whether uncontrolled deficit-spending on the part of government could lead to a breakdown of the country's monetary system and prolonged economic distress. The threat of piracy and lack of protection for intellectual property are also sources of economic risk. Another is fluctuations in the value of different currencies—a factor that we discuss in more detail next.

## The Risks of Adverse Exchange Rate Shifts

When companies produce and market their products and services in many different countries, they are subject to the impacts of sometimes favorable and sometimes unfavorable changes in currency exchange rates. The rates of exchange between different currencies can vary by as much as 20 to 40 percent annually, with the changes occurring sometimes gradually and sometimes swiftly. Sizable shifts in exchange rates, which tend to be hard to predict because of the variety of factors involved and the uncertainties surrounding when and by how much these factors will change, shuffle the global cards of which countries represent the low-cost manufacturing locations and which rivals have the upper hand in the marketplace.

To understand the economic risks associated with fluctuating exchange rates, consider the case of a U.S. company that has located manufacturing facilities in Brazil (where the currency is *reals*—pronounced "ray-alls") and that exports most of the Brazilian-made goods to markets in the European Union (where the currency is euros). To keep the numbers simple, assume that the exchange rate is 4 Brazilian reals for 1 euro and that the product being made in Brazil has a manufacturing cost of 4 Brazilian reals (or 1 euro). Now suppose that for some reason the exchange rate shifts from 4 reals per euro to 5 reals per euro (meaning that the real has declined in value and that the euro is stronger). Making the product in Brazil is now more cost-competitive because a Brazilian good costing 4 reals to produce has fallen to only 0.8 euro at the new exchange rate (4 reals divided by 5 reals per euro = 0.8 euro) and this clearly puts the producer of the Brazilian-made good *in a better position to compete* against the European makers of the same good. On the other hand, should the value of the Brazilian real grow stronger in relation to the euro—resulting in an exchange rate of 3 reals to 1 euro—the same Brazilian-made good formerly costing 4 reals (or 1 euro) to produce now has a cost of 1.33 euros (4 reals divided by 3 reals per euro = 1.33 euros) and this puts the producer of the Brazilian-made good in a weaker competitive position vis-à-vis European producers of the same good. Clearly, the attraction of manufacturing a good in Brazil and selling it in Europe is far greater when the euro is strong (an exchange rate of 1 euro for 5 Brazilian reals) than when the euro is weak and exchanges for only 3 Brazilian reals.

But there is one more piece to the story. When the exchange rate changes from 4 reals per euro to 5 reals per euro, not only is the cost competitiveness of the Brazilian manufacturer stronger relative to European manufacturers of the same item but the Brazilian-made good that formerly cost 1 euro and now costs only 0.8 euros can also be sold to consumers in the European Union for a lower euro price than before. In other words, the combination of a stronger euro and a weaker real acts to *lower the price of Brazilian-made goods* in all the countries that are members of the European Union, and this is likely to *spur sales of the Brazilian-made good in Europe and boost Brazilian exports to Europe.* Conversely, should the exchange rate shift from 4 reals per euro to 3 reals per euro—which makes the Brazilian manufacturer less cost competitive with European manufacturers of the same item—the Brazilian-made good that formerly cost 1 euro and now costs 1.33 euros will sell for a higher price in euros than before, thus weakening the demand of European consumers for Brazilian-made goods and acting to reduce Brazilian exports to Europe. Thus Brazilian exporters are likely to experience (1) rising demand for their goods in Europe whenever the Brazilian real grows weaker relative to the euro and (2) falling demand for their goods in Europe whenever the real grows stronger relative to the euro. Consequently, from the standpoint of a company with Brazilian manufacturing plants, *a weaker Brazilian real is a favorable exchange rate shift* and *a stronger Brazilian real is an unfavorable exchange rate shift.*

It follows from the previous discussion that shifting exchange rates have a big impact on the ability of domestic manufacturers to compete with foreign rivals. For example, U.S.-based manufacturers locked in a fierce competitive battle with low-cost foreign imports benefit from a *weaker* U.S. dollar. There are several reasons why this is so:

- Declines in the value of the U.S. dollar against foreign currencies have the effect of raising the U.S. dollar–costs of goods manufactured by foreign rivals at plants located in the countries whose currencies have grown stronger relative to the U.S. dollar. A weaker dollar acts to reduce or eliminate whatever cost advantage foreign manufacturers may have had over U.S. manufacturers (and helps protect the manufacturing jobs of U.S. workers).

- A *weaker* dollar makes foreign-made goods more expensive in dollar terms to U.S. consumers—this acts to curtail U.S. buyer demand for foreign-made goods, stimulate greater demand on the part of U.S. consumers for U.S.-made goods, and reduce U.S. imports of foreign-made goods.

- A *weaker* U.S. dollar has the effect of enabling the U.S.-made goods to be sold at lower prices to consumers in those countries whose currencies have grown stronger relative to the U.S. dollar—such lower prices boost foreign buyer demand for the now relatively cheaper U.S.-made goods, thereby stimulating exports of U.S.-made goods to foreign countries and perhaps creating more jobs in U.S.-based manufacturing plants.

- A *weaker* dollar has the effect of increasing the dollar value of profits a company earns in those foreign country markets where the local currency is stronger relative to the dollar. For example, if a U.S.-based manufacturer earns a profit of €10 million on its sales in Europe, those €10 million convert to a larger number of dollars when the dollar grows weaker against the euro.

Fluctuating exchange rates pose significant economic risks to a company's competitiveness in foreign markets. Exporters are disadvantaged when the currency of the country where goods are being manufactured grows stronger relative to the currency of the importing country.

*A weaker U.S. dollar is therefore an economically favorable exchange rate shift for manufacturing plants based in the United States.* A decline in the value of the U.S. dollar strengthens the cost-competitiveness of U.S.-based manufacturing plants and boosts buyer demand for U.S.-made goods. When the value of the U.S. dollar is expected to remain weak for some time to come, foreign companies have an incentive to build manufacturing facilities in the U.S. to make goods for U.S. consumers rather than export the same goods to the U.S. from foreign plants where production costs in dollar terms have been driven up by the decline in the value of the dollar. Conversely, a *stronger* U.S. dollar is an *unfavorable exchange rate shift* for U.S.-based manufacturing plants because it makes such plants less cost-competitive with foreign plants and weakens foreign demand for U.S.-made goods. A strong dollar also weakens the incentive of foreign companies to locate manufacturing facilities in the U.S. to make goods for U.S. consumers. The same reasoning applies to companies who have plants in countries in the European Union where euros are the local currency. A weak euro versus other currencies enhances the cost-competitiveness of companies manufacturing goods in Europe vis-à-vis foreign rivals with plants in countries whose currencies have grown stronger relative to the euro; a strong euro versus other currencies weakens the cost-competitiveness of companies with plants in the European Union.

Insofar as U.S.-based manufacturers are concerned, declines in the value of the U.S. dollar against foreign currencies act to reduce or eliminate whatever cost advantage foreign manufacturers might have over U.S. manufacturers and can even prompt foreign companies to establish production plants in the United States. Likewise, a weak euro versus other currencies enhances the cost competitiveness of companies manufacturing goods in Europe for export to foreign markets; a strong euro versus other currencies weakens the cost competitiveness of European plants that manufacture goods for export. The growing strength of the euro relative to the U.S. dollar has encouraged a number of European manufacturers such as Volkswagen, Fiat, and Airbus to shift production from European factories to new facilities in the United States. Also, the weakening dollar caused Chrysler to discontinue its contract manufacturing agreement with an Austrian firm for assembly of minivans and Jeeps sold in Europe. Beginning in 2008, Chrysler's vehicles sold in Europe were exported from its factories in Illinois and Missouri. The weak dollar was also a factor in Ford's and GM's recent decisions to begin exporting U.S.-made vehicles to China and Latin America.

> Domestic companies facing competitive pressure from lower-cost imports benefit when their government's currency grows *weaker* in relation to the currencies of the countries where the lower-cost imports are being made.

It is important to note that *currency exchange rates are rather unpredictable,* swinging first one way and then another way, so the competitiveness of any company's facilities in any country is partly dependent on whether exchange rate changes over time have a favorable or unfavorable cost impact. Companies producing goods in one country for export abroad always improve their cost competitiveness when the country's currency grows weaker relative to currencies of the countries where the goods are being exported to, and they find their cost competitiveness eroded when the local currency grows stronger. On the other hand, domestic companies that are under pressure from lower-cost imported goods become more cost competitive when their currency grows weaker in relation to the currencies of the countries where the imported goods are made—in other words, a U.S. manufacturer views a weaker U.S. dollar as a *favorable exchange rate shift* because such shifts help make its costs more competitive than those of foreign rivals.

## Cross-Country Differences in Demographic, Cultural, and Market Conditions

Buyer tastes for a particular product or service sometimes differ substantially from country to country. In France, consumers prefer top-loading washing machines, while in most other European countries consumers prefer front-loading machines. Soups that appeal to Swedish consumers are not popular in Malaysia. Italian coffee drinkers prefer espressos, but in North America the preference is for mild-roasted coffees. Sometimes, product designs suitable in one country are inappropriate in another because of differing local standards—for example, in the United States electrical devices run on 110-volt electric systems, but in some European countries the standard is a 240-volt electric system, necessitating the use of different electrical designs and components. Cultural influences can also affect consumer demand for a product. For instance, in South Korea, many parents are reluctant to purchase PCs even when they can afford them because of concerns that their children will be distracted from their schoolwork by surfing the Web, playing PC-based video games, and becoming Internet "addicts."[7]

Consequently, companies operating in an international marketplace have to wrestle with *whether and how much to customize their offerings in each different country market to match the tastes and preferences of local buyers or whether to pursue a strategy of offering a mostly standardized product worldwide.* While making products that are closely matched to local tastes makes them more appealing to local buyers, customizing a company's products country by country may have the effect of raising production and distribution costs due to the greater variety of designs and components, shorter production runs, and the complications of added inventory handling and distribution logistics. Greater standardization of a multinational company's product offering, on the other hand, can lead to scale economies and learning curve effects, thus contributing to the achievement of a low-cost advantage. *The tension between the market pressures to localize a company's product offerings country by country and the competitive pressures to lower costs is one of the big strategic issues that participants in foreign markets have to resolve.*

# STRATEGIC OPTIONS FOR ENTERING AND COMPETING IN INTERNATIONAL MARKETS

Once a company decides to expand beyond its domestic borders, it must consider the question of how to enter foreign markets. There are six primary strategic options for doing so:

1. Maintain a national (one-country) production base and export goods to foreign markets.
2. License foreign firms to produce and distribute the company's products abroad.
3. Employ a franchising strategy.
4. Establish a subsidiary in a foreign market via acquisition or internal development.
5. Rely on strategic alliances or joint ventures with foreign companies.

Which option to employ depends on a variety of factors, including the nature of the firm's strategic objectives, whether the firm has the full range of resources and capabilities needed to operate abroad, country-specific factors such as trade barriers, and the transaction costs involved (the costs of contracting with a partner and monitoring its compliance with the terms of the contract, for example). The options vary considerably regarding the level of investment required and the associated risks, but higher levels of investment and risk generally provide the firm with the benefits of greater ownership and control.

## Export Strategies

Using domestic plants as a production base for exporting goods to foreign markets is an excellent initial strategy for pursuing international sales. It is a conservative way to test the international waters. The amount of capital needed to begin exporting is often quite minimal; existing production capacity may well be sufficient to make goods for export. With an export-bases entry strategy, a manufacturer can limit its involvement in foreign markets by contracting with foreign wholesalers experienced in importing to handle the entire distribution and marketing function in their countries or regions of the world. If it is more advantageous to maintain control over these functions, however, a manufacturer can establish its own distribution and sales organizations in some or all of the target foreign markets. Either way, a home-based production and export strategy helps the firm minimize its direct investments in foreign countries.

Whether an export strategy can be pursued successfully over the long run hinges on whether its advantages for the company continue to outweigh its disadvantages. This depends in part on the relative cost competitiveness of the home-country production base. In some industries, firms gain additional scale economies and learning curve benefits from centralizing production in one or several giant plants whose output capability exceeds demand in any one country market; exporting is one obvious way to capture such economies. However, an export strategy is vulnerable when (1) manufacturing costs in the home country are substantially higher than in foreign countries where rivals have plants, (2) the costs of shipping the product to distant foreign markets are relatively high, (3) adverse shifts occur in currency exchange rates, and (4) importing countries impose tariffs or erect other trade barriers. Unless an exporter can both keep its production and shipping costs competitive with rivals, secure adequate local distribution and marketing support of its products, and successfully hedge against unfavorable changes in currency exchange rates, its success will be limited.

## Licensing Strategies

Licensing as an entry strategy makes sense when a firm with valuable technical know-how, an appealing brand, or a unique patented product has neither the internal organizational capability nor the resources to enter foreign markets. Licensing also has the advantage of avoiding the risks of committing resources to country markets that are unfamiliar, politically volatile, economically unstable, or otherwise risky. By licensing the technology, trademark, or production rights to foreign-based firms, the firm does not have to bear the costs and risks of entering foreign markets on its own, yet it is able to generate income from royalties. The big disadvantage of licensing is the risk of providing valuable technological know-how to foreign companies and thereby losing some degree of control over its use. Monitoring licensees and safeguarding the company's proprietary know-how can prove quite difficult in some circumstances. But if the royalty potential is considerable and the companies to whom the licenses are being granted are trustworthy and reputable, then licensing can be a very attractive option. Many software and pharmaceutical companies use licensing strategies to compete in foreign markets.

## Franchising Strategies

While licensing works well for manufacturers and owners of proprietary technology, franchising is often better suited to the international expansion efforts of service and retailing enterprises. McDonald's, Yum! Brands (the parent of A&W, Pizza Hut, KFC, Long John Silver's, and Taco Bell), the UPS Store, Roto-Rooter, 7-Eleven, and Hilton Hotels have all used franchising to build a presence in foreign markets. Franchising has much the same advantages as licensing. The franchisee bears most of the costs and risks of establishing foreign locations; a franchisor has to expend only the resources to recruit, train, support, and monitor franchisees. The big problem a franchisor faces is maintaining quality control; foreign franchisees do not always exhibit strong commitment to consistency and standardization, especially when the local culture does not stress the same kinds of quality concerns. Another problem that can arise is whether to allow foreign franchisees to make modifications in the franchisor's product offering so as to better satisfy the tastes and expectations of local buyers. Should McDonald's give franchisees in each nation some leeway in what products they put on their menus? Should the franchised KFC units in China be permitted to substitute spices that appeal to Chinese consumers? Or should the same menu offerings be rigorously and unvaryingly required of all franchisees worldwide?

## Foreign Subsidiary Strategies

While exporting, licensing, and franchising rely upon the resources and capabilities of allies in international markets to deliver goods or services to buyers, companies pursuing international expansion may elect to take responsibility for the performance of all essential value chain activities in foreign markets. Companies that prefer direct control over all aspects of operating in a foreign market can establish a wholly owned subsidiary, either by acquiring a foreign company or by establishing operations from the ground up via internal development. A subsidiary business that is established by setting up the entire operation from the ground up is called a **greenfield venture**.

> **CORE CONCEPT**
>
> A **greenfield venture** is a subsidiary business that is established by setting up the entire operation from the ground up.

Acquisition is the quicker of the two options, and it may be the least risky and cost-efficient means of hurdling such entry barriers as gaining access to local distribution channels, building supplier relationships, and establishing working relationships with key government officials and other constituencies. Buying an ongoing operation allows the acquirer to move directly to the task of transferring resources and personnel to the newly acquired business, integrating and redirecting the activities of the acquired business into its own operation, putting its own strategy into place, and accelerating efforts to build a strong market position.[8]

The big issue an acquisition-minded firm must consider is whether to pay a premium price for a successful local company or to buy a struggling competitor at a bargain price. If the buying firm has little knowledge of the local market but ample capital, it is often better off purchasing a capable, strongly positioned firm—unless the acquisition price is prohibitive. However, when the acquirer sees promising ways to transform a weak firm into a strong one and has the resources and managerial know-how to do it, a struggling company can be the better long-term investment.

Entering a new foreign country via a greenfield venture strategy makes sense when a company already operates in a number of countries, has experience in getting new subsidiaries up and running and overseeing their operations, and has a sufficiently large pool of resources and competencies to rapidly equip a new subsidiary with the personnel and capabilities it needs to compete successfully and profitably. Four other conditions make an internal startup strategy appealing:

- When creating an internal startup is cheaper than making an acquisition.
- When adding new production capacity will not adversely impact the supply–demand balance in the local market.
- When a startup subsidiary has the ability to gain good distribution access (perhaps because of the company's recognized brand name).
- When a startup subsidiary will have the size, cost structure, and resource strengths to compete head-to-head against local rivals.

Greenfield ventures in foreign markets can also pose problems, just as other entry strategies do. They represent a costly capital investment, subject to a high level of risk. They require numerous other company resources as well, diverting them from other uses. They do not work well in countries without strong, well-functioning markets and institutions that protect the rights of foreign investors and provide other legal protections. Moreover, an important disadvantage of greenfield ventures relative to other means of international expansion is that they are the slowest entry route—particularly if the objective is to achieve a sizable market share. On the other hand, successful greenfield ventures may offer higher returns to compensate for their high risk and slower path.

## Alliance and Joint Venture Strategies

Collaborative strategies involving alliances or joint ventures with foreign partners are a popular way for companies to edge their way into the markets of foreign countries.

Strategic alliances, joint ventures, and other cooperative agreements with foreign companies are a widely used means of entering foreign markets.[9] A company can benefit immensely from a foreign partner's familiarity with local government regulations, its knowledge of the buying habits and product preferences of consumers, its distribution channel relationships, and so on.[10] Both Japanese and American companies are actively forming alliances with European companies to better compete in the 27-nation European Union and to capitalize on emerging opportunities in the countries of Eastern Europe. Many U.S. and European companies are allying with Asian companies in their efforts to enter markets in China, India, Thailand, Indonesia, and other Asian countries. Many foreign companies, of course, are particularly interested in strategic partnerships that will strengthen their ability to gain a foothold in the U.S. market.

A second big appeal of cross-border alliances is to capture economies of scale in production and/or marketing. By joining forces in producing components, assembling models, and marketing their products, companies can realize cost savings not achievable with their own small volumes. A third motivation for entering into a cross-border alliance is to fill gaps in technical expertise and/or knowledge of local markets (buying habits and product preferences of consumers, local customs, and so on). Allies learn much from one another in performing joint research, sharing technological know-how, studying one another's manufacturing methods, and understanding how to tailor sales and marketing approaches to fit local cultures and traditions. Indeed, one of the win–win benefits of an alliance is to learn from the skills, technological know-how, and capabilities of alliance partners and implant the knowledge and know-how of these partners in personnel throughout the company.

A fourth motivation for cross-border alliances is to share distribution facilities and dealer networks, and to mutually strengthen each partner's access to buyers. A fifth benefit is that cross-border allies can direct their competitive energies more toward mutual rivals and less toward one another; teaming up may help them close the gap on leading companies. A sixth driver of cross-border alliances comes into play when companies wanting to enter a new foreign market conclude that alliances with local companies are an effective way to establish working relationships with key officials in the host-country government.[11] And, finally, alliances can be a particularly useful way for companies across the world to gain agreement on important technical standards—they have been used to arrive at standards for assorted PC devices, Internet-related technologies, high-definition televisions, and mobile phones.

What makes cross-border alliances an attractive strategic means of gaining the aforementioned types of benefits (as compared to acquiring or merging with foreign-based companies) is that entering into alliances and strategic partnerships allows a company to preserve its independence and avoid using perhaps scarce financial resources to fund acquisitions. Furthermore, an alliance offers the flexibility to readily disengage once its purpose has been served or if the benefits prove elusive, whereas an acquisition is a more permanent sort of arrangement.[12]

Illustration Capsule 7.1 shows how California-based Solazyme, a maker of biofuels and other green products, has used cross-border strategic alliances to fuel its growth.

> Cross-border alliances enable a growth-minded company to widen its geographic coverage and strengthen its competitiveness in foreign markets; at the same time, they offer flexibility and allow a company to retain some degree of autonomy and operating control.

## The Risks of Strategic Alliances with Foreign Partners

Alliances and joint ventures with foreign partners have their pitfalls, however. Sometimes the knowledge and expertise of local partners turns out to be less valuable than expected (because their knowledge is rendered obsolete by fast-changing market conditions or because their operating practices are archaic). Cross-border allies typically must overcome language and cultural barriers and figure out how to deal with diverse (or perhaps conflicting) operating practices. The transaction costs of working out a mutually agreeable arrangement and monitoring partner compliance with the terms of the arrangement can be high. The communication, trust building, and coordination costs are not trivial in terms of management time.[13] Often, partners soon discover they have conflicting objectives and strategies and/or deep differences of opinion about how to proceed, and/or important differences in corporate values and ethical standards. It is not unusual for there to be little personal chemistry among some of the key people on whom success or failure of the alliance depends—the rapport such personnel need to work well together may never emerge. And even if allies are able to develop productive personal relationships, they can still have trouble reaching mutually agreeable ways to deal with key issues or resolve differences. Occasionally, the egos of corporate executives can clash. An alliance between Northwest Airlines and KLM Royal Dutch Airlines resulted in a bitter feud among both companies' top officials (who, according to some reports, refused

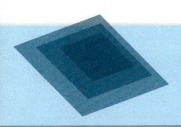
## Solazyme's Cross-Border Alliances with Unilever, Sephora, Qantas, and Roquette

Solazyme, a California-based company that produces oils for nutritional, cosmetic, and biofuel products from algae, was named "America's Fastest-Growing Manufacturing Company" by *Inc. Magazine* in 2011. The company has fueled its rapid growth through a variety of cross-border strategic alliances with much larger partners. These partnerships have not only facilitated Solazyme's entry into new markets, they have also created value through resource sharing and risk spreading.

Its partnership with Unilever, a British–Dutch consumer goods company, has focused on collaborative R&D. Projects underway are aimed at meeting the growing demand for completely renewable, natural, and sustainable personal care products through the use of algal oils. By further developing Solazyme's technology platform, the partnership will enable the production of Solazyme's oils and other biomaterials efficiently and at large scale.

Solazyme has entered into a variety of marketing and distribution agreements with French cosmetics company Sephora (now part of LVMH). In March 2011, Solazyme launched its luxury skin care brand, Algenist, with Sephora's help. Sephora has also agreed to distribute Solazyme's anti-aging skincare line, making it available in Sephora stores and at **Sephora.com**.

In 2011, Solazyme also signed a contract with Australian airline Qantas to supply, test, and refine Solazyme's jet fuel product, SolaJet. Solazyme stands to gain valuable input on how to design and distribute its product while receiving media attention and the marketing advantage of a well-known customer. On the other hand, Qantas hopes to better understand how it will achieve its sustainability goals while building its reputation as a sustainability leader in the airline industry.

Because its algae require sugar to produce oil, Solazyme has an interest in securing a stable supply of this feedstock. For this purpose, Solazyme created a 50/50 joint venture with French starch processor Roquette to develop, produce, and market food products globally. By working with Roquette to source feedstock and manufacture final food products, Solazyme lowered its exposure to sugar price fluctuations while taking advantage of Roquette's manufacturing infrastructure and expertise. In return, Roquette gained access to Solazyme's innovative technological resources.

*Developed with John L. Gardner.*

*Sources:* Company website; **http://gigaom.com/**; **http://www.businessgreen.com/**; **http://www.reuters.com/**; **http://www.foodnavigator-usa.com/** (all accessed March 4, 2012).

to speak to each other).[14] Plus there is the thorny problem of getting alliance partners to sort through issues and reach decisions fast enough to stay abreast of rapid advances in technology or fast-changing market conditions.

One worrisome problem with alliances or joint ventures is that a firm may risk losing some of its competitive advantage if an alliance partner is given full access to its proprietary technological expertise or other unique and competitively valuable capabilities.

There is a natural tendency for allies to struggle to collaborate effectively in competitively sensitive areas, thus spawning suspicions on both sides about forthright exchanges of information and expertise. It requires many meetings of many people working in good faith over a period of time to iron out what is to be shared, what is to remain proprietary, and how the cooperative arrangements will work.

Even if a collaborative arrangement proves to be a win–win proposition for both parties, a company must guard against becoming overly dependent on foreign partners for essential expertise and competitive capabilities. Companies aiming for global market leadership often need to develop their own resource capabilities in order to be masters of their destiny. Frequently, experienced multinational companies operating in 50 or more countries across the world find less need for entering into cross-border alliances than do companies in the early stages of globalizing their operations.[15] Companies with global operations make it a point to develop senior managers who understand how "the system" works in different countries, plus they can avail themselves of local managerial talent and know-how by simply hiring experienced local managers and thereby detouring the hazards of collaborative alliances with local companies. One of the lessons about cross-border partnerships is that they are more effective in helping a company establish a beachhead of new opportunity in world markets than they are in enabling a company to achieve and sustain global market leadership.

# COMPETING INTERNATIONALLY: THE THREE MAIN STRATEGIC APPROACHES

Broadly speaking, a firm's **international strategy** is simply its strategy for competing in two or more countries simultaneously. Typically, a company will start to compete internationally by entering just one or perhaps a select few foreign markets—selling its products or services in countries where there is a ready market for them. But as it expands further internationally, it will have to confront head-on the conflicting pressures of local responsiveness versus efficiency gains from standardizing its product offering globally. Deciding upon the degree to vary its competitive approach to fit the specific market conditions and buyer preferences in each host country is perhaps the foremost strategic issue that must be addressed when operating in two or more foreign markets.[16] Figure 7.2 shows a company's three options for resolving this issue: choosing a *multidomestic, global,* or *transnational* strategy.

**LO 4**

Gain familiarity with the three main strategic approaches for competing internationally.

**CORE CONCEPT**

An **international strategy** is a strategy for competing in two or more countries simultaneously.

## Multidomestic Strategy—Think Local, Act Local

A **multidomestic strategy** is one in which a company varies its product offering and competitive approach from country to country in an effort to meet differing buyer needs and to address divergent local market conditions. It involves having plants produce different product versions for different local markets and adapting marketing and distribution to fit local customs, cultures, regulations, and market requirements. The strength of employing a multidomestic strategy is that the company's actions and business approaches are deliberately crafted to appeal to the tastes and expectations of buyers in each country and to stake out the most attractive market positions vis-à-vis local competitors.[17] Castrol, a specialist in oil lubricants, produces over 3,000 different formulas of lubricants to meet the requirements of different climates, vehicle types and uses, and equipment applications that characterize different country markets. In the food products industry, it is common for companies to vary the ingredients in their products and sell

## FIGURE 7.2  Three Approaches for Competing Internationally

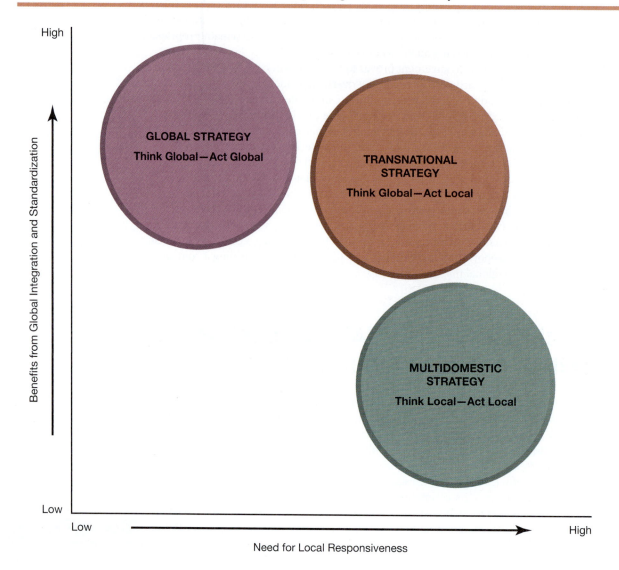

the localized versions under local brand names to cater to country-specific tastes and eating preferences.

In essence, a multidomestic strategy represents a **think-local, act-local** approach to international strategy. A think-local, act-local approach is possible only when decision making is decentralized, giving local managers considerable latitude for crafting and executing strategies for the country markets they are responsible for. Giving local managers decision-making authority allows them to address specific market needs and respond swiftly to local changes in demand. It also enables them to focus their competitive efforts, stake out attractive market positions vis-à-vis local competitors, react to rivals' moves in a timely fashion, and target new opportunities as they emerge.

A think-local, act-local approach to strategy making is most appropriate when the need for local responsiveness is high due to significant cross-country differences in demographic, cultural, and market conditions and when the potential for efficiency gains from standardization is limited, as depicted in Figure 7.2. Consider, for example, the wide variation in refrigerator usage and preference around the world. Northern Europeans want large refrigerators because they tend to shop once a week in supermarkets; southern Europeans prefer small refrigerators because they shop daily. In parts of Asia, refrigerators are a status symbol and may be placed in the living room, leading to preferences for stylish designs and colors—in India, bright blue and red are popular colors. In other Asian countries, household space is constrained, and many refrigerators are only 4 feet high so that the top can be used for storage. If the minimum efficient scale for producing refrigerators is relatively low, there would be little reason to forgo the benefits of meeting these varying needs precisely in favor of a standardized, one-size-fits-all approach to production.

Despite their obvious benefits, think-local, act-local strategies have three big drawbacks:

1. They hinder transfer of a company's capabilities, knowledge, and other resources across country boundaries, since the company's efforts are not integrated or coordinated across country boundaries. This can make the company less innovative overall.

2. They raise production and distribution costs due to the greater variety of designs and components, shorter production runs for each product version, and complications of added inventory handling and distribution logistics.

3. They are not conducive to building a single, worldwide competitive advantage. When a company's competitive approach and product offering vary from country to country, the nature and size of any resulting competitive edge also tends to vary. At the most, multidomestic strategies are capable of producing a group of local competitive advantages of varying types and degrees of strength.

> **CORE CONCEPT**
>
> A **multidomestic strategy** is one in which a company varies its product offering and competitive approach from country to country in an effort to be responsive to differing buyer preferences and market conditions. It is a **think-local, act-local** type of international strategy, facilitated by decision making decentralized to the local level.

## Global Strategy—Think Global, Act Global

A **global strategy** contrasts sharply with a multidomestic strategy in that it takes a standardized, globally integrated approach to producing, packaging, selling, and delivering the company's products and services worldwide. Companies employing a global strategy sell the same products under the same brand names everywhere, utilize much the same distribution channels in all countries, and compete on the basis of the same capabilities and marketing approaches worldwide. Although the company's strategy or product offering may be adapted in very minor ways to accommodate specific situations in a few host countries, the company's fundamental competitive approach (low cost, differentiation, best cost, or focused) remains very much intact worldwide and local managers stick close to the global strategy.

A **think-global, act-global** strategic theme prompts company managers to integrate and coordinate the company's strategic moves worldwide and to expand into most, if not all, nations where there is significant buyer demand. It puts considerable strategic emphasis on building a *global* brand name and aggressively pursuing opportunities to transfer ideas, new products, and capabilities from one country to another. Global strategies are characterized by relatively centralized value chain activities, such as production and distribution. While there may be more than one manufacturing plant and distribution center to minimize transportation costs, for example, they tend to be few in number. Achieving the efficiency potential of a global strategy requires that resources and best practices be shared, value chain activities be integrated, and capabilities be transferred from one location to another as they are developed. These objectives are best facilitated through centralized decision making and strong headquarters control.

> **CORE CONCEPT**
>
> A **global strategy** is one in which a company employs the same basic competitive approach in all countries where it operates, sells much the same products everywhere, strives to build global brands, and coordinates its actions worldwide with strong headquarters control. It represents a **think-global, act-global** approach.

Because a global strategy cannot accommodate varying local needs, it is an appropriate strategic choice when there are pronounced efficiency benefits from standardization and when buyer needs are relatively homogeneous across countries and regions. A globally standardized and integrated approach is especially beneficial when high volumes significantly lower costs due to economies of scale or added experience (moving the company further down a learning curve). It can also be advantageous if it allows the firm to replicate a successful business model on a global basis efficiently or engage in higher levels of R&D by spreading the fixed costs and risks over a higher-volume output. It is a fitting response to industry conditions marked by global competition.

Ford's global design strategy is a move toward a think global, act global strategy by the company. It involves the development and production of standardized models with country-specific modifications limited primarily to what is required to meet local country emission and safety standards. The 2010 Ford Fiesta and 2011 Ford Focus were the company's first global design models to be marketed in Europe, North America, Asia, and Australia. Whenever country-to-country differences are small enough to be accommodated within the framework of a global strategy, a global strategy is preferable to localized strategies because a company can more readily unify its operations and focus on establishing a brand image and reputation that is uniform from country to country. Moreover, with a global strategy a company is better able to focus its full resources on securing a sustainable low-cost or differentiation-based competitive advantage over both domestic rivals and global rivals.

There are, however, several drawbacks to global strategies: (1) They do not enable firms to address local needs as precisely as locally based rivals can, (2) they are less responsive to changes in local market conditions, either in the form of new opportunities or competitive threats, (3) they raise transportation costs and may involve higher tariffs, and (4) they involve higher coordination costs due to the more complex task of managing a globally integrated enterprise.

# Transnational Strategy—Think Global, Act Local

A **transnational strategy** (sometimes called *glocalization*) incorporates elements of both a globalized and a localized approach to strategy making. This type of middle-ground strategy is called for when there are relatively high needs for local responsiveness as well as appreciable benefits to be realized from standardization, as Figure 7.2 suggests. A transnational strategy encourages a company to **think global, act local** to balance these competing objectives.

Often, companies implement a transnational strategy with mass-customization techniques that enable them to address local preferences in an efficient, semistandardized manner. Both McDonald's and KFC have discovered ways to customize their menu offerings in various countries without compromising costs, product quality, and operating effectiveness. When it first opened Disneyland Paris, Disney learned the hard way that a global approach to its international theme parks would not work; it has since adapted elements of its strategy to accommodate local preferences even though much of its strategy still derives from a globally applied formula. Otis Elevator found that a transnational strategy delivers better results than a global strategy when competing in countries like China where local needs are highly differentiated. In 2000, it switched from its customary single-brand approach to a multibrand strategy aimed at serving different segments of the market. By 2009, it had doubled its market share in China and increased its revenues sixfold.[18]

As a rule, most companies that operate multinationally endeavor to employ as global a strategy as customer needs and market conditions permit. Electronic Arts has two major design studios—one in Vancouver, British Columbia, and one in Los Angeles—and smaller design studios in San Francisco, Orlando, London, and Tokyo. This dispersion of design studios helps EA to design games that are specific to different cultures—for example, the London studio took the lead in designing the popular FIFA Soccer game to suit European tastes and to replicate the stadiums, signage, and team rosters; the U.S. studio took the lead in designing games involving NFL football, NBA basketball, and NASCAR racing.

A transnational strategy is far more conducive than other strategies to transferring and leveraging subsidiary skills and capabilities. But, like other approaches to competing internationally, transnational strategies also have significant drawbacks:

1. They are the most difficult of all multinational strategies to implement due to the added complexity of varying the elements of the strategy to situational conditions.

2. They place large demands on the organization due to the need to pursue conflicting objectives simultaneously.

3. Implementing the strategy is likely to be a costly and time-consuming enterprise, with an uncertain outcome.

Table 7.1 provides a summary of the pluses and minuses of the three approaches to competing internationally.

## TABLE 7.1  Advantages and Disadvantages of Multidomestic, Global, and Transnational Approaches

| | Advantages | Disadvantages |
|---|---|---|
| **Multidomestic** (think local, act local) | • Can meet the specific needs of each market more precisely<br>• Can respond more swiftly to localized changes in demand<br>• Can target reactions to the moves of local rivals<br>• Can respond more quickly to local opportunities and threats | • Hinders resource and capability sharing or cross-market transfers<br>• Higher production and distribution costs<br>• Not conducive to a worldwide competitive advantage |
| **Transnational** (think global, act local) | • Offers the benefits of both local responsiveness and global integration<br>• Enables the transfer and sharing of resources and capabilities across borders<br>• Provides the benefits of flexible coordination | • More complex and harder to implement<br>• Conflicting goals may be difficult to reconcile and require trade-offs<br>• Implementation more costly and time-consuming |
| **Global** (think global, act global) | • Lower costs due to scale and scope economies<br>• Greater efficiencies due to the ability to transfer best practices across markets<br>• More innovation from knowledge sharing and capability transfer<br>• The benefit of a global brand and reputation | • Unable to address local needs precisely<br>• Less responsive to changes in local market conditions<br>• Higher transportation costs and tariffs<br>• Higher coordination and integration costs |

# THE QUEST FOR COMPETITIVE ADVANTAGE IN THE INTERNATIONAL ARENA

**LO 5**

Understand how multinational companies are able to use international operations to improve overall competitiveness.

There are three important ways in which a firm can gain competitive advantage (or offset domestic disadvantages) by expanding outside its domestic market. First, it can use location to lower costs or achieve greater product differentiation. Second, it can transfer competitively valuable resources and capabilities from one country to another or share them across international borders to extend its competitive advantages. And third, it can benefit from cross-border coordination opportunities that are not open to domestic-only competitors.

## Using Location to Build Competitive Advantage

To use location to build competitive advantage, a company must consider two issues: (1) whether to concentrate each activity it performs in a few select countries or to disperse performance of the activity to many nations, and (2) in which countries to locate particular activities.

Companies that compete internationally can pursue competitive advantage in world markets by locating their value chain activities in whatever nations prove most advantageous.

**When to Concentrate Activities in a Few Locations**    It is advantageous for a company to concentrate its activities in a limited number of locations in the following circumstances:

- *When the costs of manufacturing or other activities are significantly lower in some geographic locations than in others.* For example, much of the world's athletic footwear is manufactured in Asia (China and Korea) because of low labor costs; much of the production of circuit boards for PCs is located in Taiwan because of both low costs and the high-caliber technical skills of the Taiwanese labor force.
- *When there are significant scale economies in production or distribution.* The presence of significant economies of scale in components production or final assembly means that a company can gain major cost savings from operating a few superefficient plants as opposed to a host of small plants scattered across the world. Makers of digital cameras and LCD TVs located in Japan, South Korea, and Taiwan have used their scale economies to establish a low-cost advantage in this way. Achieving low-cost provider status often requires a company to have the largest worldwide manufacturing share (as distinct from brand share or market share), with production centralized in one or a few world-scale plants. Some companies even use such plants to manufacture units sold under the brand names of rivals to further boost production-related scale economies. Likewise, a company may be able to reduce its distribution costs by establishing large-scale distribution centers to serve major geographic regions of the world market (for example, North America, Latin America, Europe–Middle East, and Asia-Pacific).
- *When there are sizable learning and experience benefits associated with performing an activity in a single location.* In some industries, learning curve effects can allow a manufacturer to lower unit costs, boost quality, or master a new technology more quickly by concentrating production in a few locations. The key to riding down the learning curve is to concentrate production in a few locations to increase the accumulated volume at a plant (and thus the experience of the plant's workforce) as rapidly as possible.

- *When certain locations have superior resources, allow better coordination of related activities, or offer other valuable advantages.* A research unit or a sophisticated production facility may be situated in a particular nation because of the nation's pool of technically trained personnel. Samsung became a leader in memory chip technology by establishing a major R&D facility in Silicon Valley and transferring the know-how it gained back to headquarters and its plants in South Korea. Where just-in-time inventory practices yield big cost savings and/or where an assembly firm has long-term partnering arrangements with its key suppliers, parts manufacturing plants may be located close to final assembly plants. A customer service center or sales office may be opened in a particular country to help cultivate strong relationships with pivotal customers located nearby.

**When to Disperse Activities across Many Locations**   In some instances, dispersing activities across locations is more advantageous than concentrating them. Buyer-related activities—such as distribution to dealers, sales and advertising, and after-sale service—usually must take place close to buyers. This means physically locating the capability to perform such activities in every country market where a firm has major customers (unless buyers in several adjoining countries can be served quickly from a nearby central location). For example, firms that make mining and oil-drilling equipment maintain operations in many locations around the world to support customers' needs for speedy equipment repair and technical assistance. Large public accounting firms have offices in numerous countries to serve the foreign operations of their multinational corporate clients. Dispersing activities to many locations is also competitively advantageous when high transportation costs, diseconomies of large size, and trade barriers make it too expensive to operate from a central location. Many companies distribute their products from multiple locations to shorten delivery times to customers. In addition, dispersing activities helps hedge against the risks of fluctuating exchange rates, supply interruptions (due to strikes, mechanical failures, and transportation delays), and adverse political developments. Such risks are usually greater when activities are concentrated in a single location.

Even though multinational and global firms have strong reason to disperse buyer-related activities to many international locations, such activities as materials procurement, parts manufacture, finished-goods assembly, technology research, and new product development can frequently be decoupled from buyer locations and performed wherever advantage lies. Components can be made in Mexico; technology research done in Frankfurt; new products developed and tested in Phoenix; and assembly plants located in Spain, Brazil, Taiwan, or South Carolina. Capital can be raised in whatever country it is available on the best terms.

## Sharing and Transferring Resources and Capabilities across Borders to Build Competitive Advantage

When a company has competitively valuable resources and capabilities, it may be able to mount a resource-based strategic offensive to enter additional country markets. If its resources retain their value in foreign contexts, then entering new markets can extend the company's resource-based competitive advantage over a broader domain. For example, companies like Armani, Burberry, and Cartier have utilized their powerful brand names to extend their differentiation-based competitive advantages into markets far beyond their home-country origins. In each of these cases, the luxury brand name represents a valuable resource that can readily be *shared* by all of the company's international operations, enabling the company to gain a higher degree of market penetration over a wider geographic area than would otherwise be possible.

*Transferring* resources and capabilities across borders provides another means to extend a company's competitive advantage internationally. For instance, if a company discovers ways to assemble a product faster and more cost-effectively at one plant, then that know-how can be transferred to its assembly plants in other countries. Whirlpool, the leading global manufacturer of home appliances, with 69 manufacturing and technology research centers around the world, uses an online global information technology platform to quickly and effectively transfer key product innovations and improved production techniques both across national borders and across various appliance brands.

Sharing or transferring resources and capabilities across borders provides a way for a company to leverage its core competencies more fully and extend its competitive advantages into a wider array of geographic markets. Thus a technology-based differentiation advantage in one country market may provide a similar basis for advantage in other country markets (depending on local market conditions). But since sharing or transferring valuable resources across borders is a very cost-effective means of extending a company's competitive advantage, these activities can also contribute to a company's competitive advantage on the costs side, giving multinational companies a powerful edge over domestic-only rivals. Since valuable resources and capabilities (such as brands, technologies, and production capabilities) are often developed at very high cost, deploying them abroad spreads the fixed development cost over greater output, thus lowering the company's unit costs. The cost of transferring already developed resources and capabilities is low by comparison. And even if the resources and capabilities need to be fully replicated in the foreign market or adapted to local conditions, this can usually be done at low additional cost relative to the initial investment in capability building.

Consider the case of Walt Disney's theme parks as an example. The success of the theme parks in the United States derives in part from core resources such as the Disney brand name, and characters like Mickey Mouse that have universal appeal and worldwide recognition. These resources can be freely shared with new theme parks as Disney expands internationally. Disney can also replicate its theme parks in new countries cost-effectively since it has already borne the costs of developing its core resources, park attractions, basic park design, and operating capabilities. The cost of replicating its theme parks abroad should be relatively low, even if they need to be adapted to a variety of local country conditions. By expanding internationally, Disney is able to enhance its competitive advantage over local theme park rivals. It does so by leveraging the differentiation advantage conferred by resources such as the Disney name and the park attractions. And by moving into new foreign markets, it augments its competitive advantage worldwide through the efficiency gains that come from cross-border resource sharing and low-cost capability transfer and business model replication.

Sharing and transferring resources and capabilities across country borders may also contribute to the development of broader or deeper competencies and capabilities—helping a company achieve *dominating depth* in some competitively valuable area. For example, the reputation for quality that Honda established worldwide began in motorcycles but enabled the company to command a position in both automobiles and outdoor power equipment in multiple-country markets. A one-country customer base is often too small to support the resource buildup needed to achieve such depth; this is particularly true in a developing or protected market, where competitively powerful resources are not required. By deploying capabilities across a larger international domain, a company can gain the experience needed to upgrade them to a higher performance standard. And by facing a more challenging set of international competitors, a company may be spurred to develop a stronger set of competitive capabilities. Moreover, by entering international markets, firms may be able to augment their capability set by learning from international rivals, cooperative partners, or acquisition targets.

However, cross-border resource-sharing and transfers of capabilities are not guaranteed recipes for competitive success. Because lifestyles and buying habits differ internationally, resources and capabilities that are valuable in one country may not have value in another. For example, brands that are popular in one country may not transfer well or may lack recognition in the new context and thus offer no advantage against an established local brand. In addition, whether a resource or capability can confer a competitive advantage abroad depends on the conditions of rivalry in each particular market. If the rivals in a foreign country market have superior resources and capabilities, then an entering firm may find itself at a competitive disadvantage even if it has a resource-based advantage domestically and can transfer the resources at low cost.

## Benefiting from Cross-Border Coordination

Companies that compete on an international basis have another source of competitive advantage relative to their purely domestic rivals: They are able to benefit from coordinating activities across different countries' domains.[19] For example, an international manufacturer can shift production from a plant in one country to a plant in another to take advantage of exchange rate fluctuations, to cope with components shortages, or to profit from changing wage rates or energy costs. Production schedules can be coordinated worldwide; shipments can be diverted from one distribution center to another if sales rise unexpectedly in one place and fall in another. By coordinating their activities, multinational companies may also be able to enhance their leverage with host-country governments or respond adaptively to changes in tariffs and quotas. Efficiencies can also be achieved by shifting workloads from where they are unusually heavy to locations where personnel are underutilized.

# PROFIT SANCTUARIES AND CROSS-BORDER STRATEGIC MOVES

**Profit sanctuaries** are country markets (or geographic regions) in which a company derives substantial profits because of a strong or protected market position. In most cases, a company's biggest and most strategically crucial profit sanctuary is its home market, but international and global companies may also enjoy profit sanctuary status in other nations where they have a strong position based on some type of competitive advantage. Companies that compete globally are likely to have more profit sanctuaries than companies that compete in just a few country markets; a domestic-only competitor, of course, can have only one profit sanctuary (see Figure 7.3).

Nike, which markets its products in 160 countries, has three major profit sanctuaries: North America (where it earned $1.5 billion in operating profits in 2010), Western Europe (where it had $856 million in operating earnings in 2010), and Greater China (where it reported $637 million in operating earnings in 2010). McDonald's serves more than 62 million customers daily at 32,000 locations in 117 countries on five

## FIGURE 7.3  Profit Sanctuary Potential of Domestic-Only, International, and Global Competitors

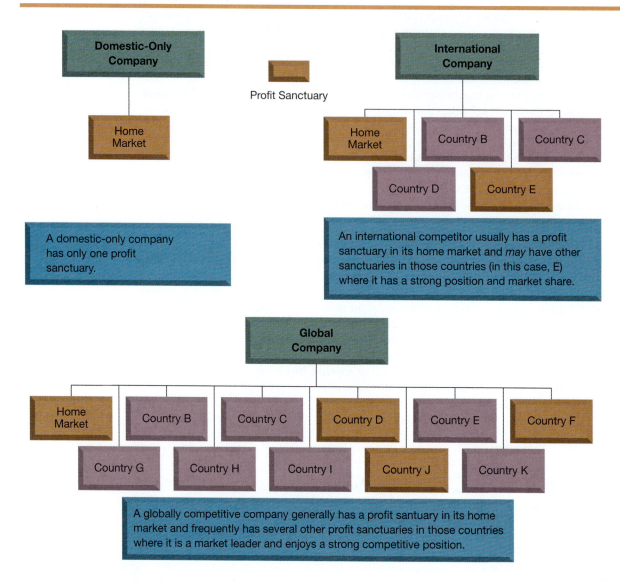

continents. Its biggest profit sanctuary is the United States, which generated 46.1 percent of 2010 profits despite accounting for just 33.6 percent of 2010 revenues. Japan is the chief profit sanctuary for most Japanese companies because trade barriers erected by the Japanese government effectively block foreign companies from competing for a large share of Japanese sales. Protected from the threat of foreign competition in their home market, Japanese companies can safely charge somewhat higher prices to their Japanese customers and thus earn attractively large profits on sales made in Japan. Japanese companies such as Cannon, Honda, Mitsubishi, Sony, Ricoh, Sharp, NEC, Fujitsu, and Toyota, however, enjoy unassailable market positions within their profit sanctuaries (and elsewhere) due to their unrivaled and inimitable capabilities.

# Using Profit Sanctuaries to Wage a Strategic Offensive

Profit sanctuaries are valuable competitive assets, providing the financial strength to support strategic offensives in selected country markets and fuel a company's race for world-market leadership. The added financial capability afforded by multiple profit sanctuaries gives a multinational competitor the financial strength to wage a market offensive against a domestic competitor whose only profit sanctuary is its home market. The multinational company has the flexibility of lowballing its prices or launching high-cost marketing campaigns in the domestic company's home market and grabbing market share at the domestic company's expense. Razor-thin margins or even losses in these markets can be subsidized with the healthy profits earned in its profit sanctuaries—a practice called **cross-market subsidization**. The multinational company can adjust the depth of its price cutting to move in and capture market share quickly, or it can shave prices slightly to make gradual market inroads (perhaps over a decade or more) so as not to threaten domestic firms precipitously and trigger protectionist government actions. If the domestic company retaliates with matching price cuts or increased marketing expenses, it thereby exposes its entire revenue stream and profit base to erosion; its profits can be squeezed substantially and its competitive strength sapped, even if it is the domestic market leader.

> **CORE CONCEPT**
>
> **Cross-market subsidization**—supporting competitive offensives in one market with resources and profits diverted from operations in another market—can be a powerful competitive weapon.

When taken to the extreme, cut-rate pricing attacks by international competitors may draw charges of unfair dumping. A company is said to be dumping when it sells its goods in foreign markets at prices that are (1) well below the prices at which it normally sells in its home market or (2) well below its full costs per unit. Almost all governments can be expected to retaliate against perceived dumping practices by imposing special tariffs on goods being imported from the countries of the guilty companies. Indeed, as the trade among nations has mushroomed over the past 10 years, most governments have joined the World Trade Organization (WTO), which promotes fair-trade practices among nations and actively polices dumping. Companies deemed guilty of dumping frequently come under pressure from their government to cease and desist, especially if the tariffs adversely affect innocent companies based in the same country or if the advent of special tariffs raises the specter of an international trade war.

# Using Profit Sanctuaries to Defend against International Rivals

Cross-border tactics involving profit sanctuaries can also be used as a means of defending against the strategic moves of rivals with multiple profit sanctuaries of their own. If a company finds itself under competitive attack by a multinational rival in one country market, one way to respond is with a counterattack against one of the rival's key markets in a different country—preferably where the rival is least protected and has the most to lose. This is a possible option when rivals compete against one another in much the same markets around the world.

For companies with at least one profit sanctuary, having a presence in a rival's key markets can be enough to deter the rival from making aggressive attacks. The reason for this is that the combination of market presence in the rival's key markets and a profit sanctuary elsewhere can send a signal to the rival that the company could quickly ramp up production (funded by the profit sanctuary) to mount a competitive counterattack if the rival attacks one of the company's key markets.

When multinational rivals compete against one another in multiple-country markets, this type of deterrence effect can restrain them from taking aggressive action

> **CORE CONCEPT**
>
> When the same companies compete against one another in multiple geographic markets, the threat of cross-border counterattacks may be enough to deter aggressive competitive moves and encourage **mutual restraint** among international rivals.

against one another, due to the fear of a retaliatory response that might escalate the battle into a cross-border competitive war. **Mutual restraint** of this sort tends to stabilize the competitive position of multimarket rivals against one another. And while it may prevent each firm from making any major market share gains at the expense of its rival, it also protects against costly competitive battles that would be likely to erode the profitability of both companies without any compensating gain.

# STRATEGIES FOR COMPETING IN THE MARKETS OF DEVELOPING COUNTRIES

**LO 6**

Gain an understanding of the unique characteristics of competing in developing-country markets.

Companies racing for global leadership have to consider competing in developing-economy markets like China, India, Brazil, Indonesia, Thailand, and Russia—countries where the business risks are considerable but where the opportunities for growth are huge, especially as their economies develop and living standards climb toward levels in the industrialized world.[20] With the world now comprising nearly 7 billion people—fully 40 percent of whom live in India and China, and hundreds of millions more live in other, less developed countries in Asia and Latin America—a company that aspires to world market leadership (or to sustained rapid growth) cannot ignore the market opportunities or the base of technical and managerial talent such countries offer. For example, in 2010 China was the world's second-largest economy (behind the United States), as measured by purchasing power. Its population of 1.4 billion people now consumes a quarter of the world's luxury products, due to the rapid growth of a wealthy class.[21] China is also the world's largest consumer of many commodities. China's growth in demand for consumer goods had made it the world's largest market for vehicles by 2009 and put it on track to become the world's largest market for luxury goods by 2014.[22] Thus, no company that aspires to global market leadership can afford to ignore the strategic importance of establishing competitive market positions in the so-called BRIC countries (Brazil, Russia, India, and China), as well as in other parts of the Asia-Pacific region, Latin America, and Eastern Europe. Illustration Capsule 7.2 describes Yum! Brands's strategy to increase its sales and market share in China.

Tailoring products to fit market conditions in developing countries, however, often involves more than making minor product changes and becoming more familiar with local cultures. Ford's attempt to sell a Ford Escort in India at a price of $21,000—a luxury-car price, given that India's best-selling Maruti-Suzuki model sold at the time for $10,000 or less and that fewer than 10 percent of Indian households had an annual purchasing power greater than $20,000—met with a less-than-enthusiastic market response. Kellogg has struggled to introduce its cereals successfully because consumers in many less developed countries do not eat cereal for breakfast. Single-serving packages of detergents, shampoos, pickles, cough syrup, and cooking oils are very popular in India because they allow buyers to conserve cash by purchasing only what they need immediately. Thus, many companies find that trying to employ a strategy akin to that used in the markets of developed countries is hazardous.[23] Experimenting with some, perhaps many, local twists is usually necessary to find a strategy combination that works.

## Strategy Options for Competing in Developing-Country Markets

There are several options for tailoring a company's strategy to fit the sometimes unusual or challenging circumstances presented in developing-country markets:

# Yum! Brands's Strategy for Becoming the Leading Food Service Brand in China

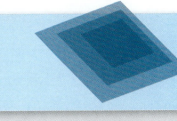

In 2012, Yum! Brands operated more than 37,000 restaurants in more than 117 countries. Its best-known brands were KFC, Taco Bell, Pizza Hut, A&W, and Long John Silver's. In 2011, its fastest growth in revenues came from its 4,500 restaurants in China, which recorded operating profits of $908 million during the year. KFC was the largest quick-service chain in China, with 3,700 units in 2011, while Pizza Hut was the largest casual-dining chain, with 630 units. Yum! Brands planned to open at least 500 new restaurant locations annually in China, including new Pizza Hut home delivery units and East Dawning units, which had a menu offering traditional Chinese food. All of Yum! Brands's menu items for China were developed in its R&D facility in Shanghai.

In addition to adapting its menu to local tastes and adding new units at a rapid pace, Yum! Brands also adapted the restaurant ambience and decor to appeal to local consumer preferences and behavior. The company changed its KFC store formats to provide educational displays that supported parents' priorities for their children and to make KFC a fun place for children to visit. The typical KFC outlet in China averaged two birthday parties per day.

In 2011, Yum! Brands operated 60 KFC, Taco Bell, Pizza Hut, A&W, and Long John Silver's restaurants for every 1 million Americans. The company's more than 4,500 units in China represented only three restaurants per 1 million Chinese. Yum! Brands management believed that its strategy keyed to continued expansion in the number of units in China, and additional menu refinements would allow its operating profits from restaurants located in China to account for 40 percent of systemwide operating profits by 2017.

*Sources:* http://www.brandchannel.com/home/post/2011/01/13/International-Expansion-Looks-Yummy-for-Yum!-Brands-Inc.aspx and other information posted at www.yum.com, accessed March 28, 2012.

- *Prepare to compete on the basis of low price.* Consumers in developing markets are often highly focused on price, which can give low-cost local competitors the edge unless a company can find ways to attract buyers with bargain prices as well as better products. For example, in order to enter the market for laundry detergents in India, Unilever had to develop a low-cost detergent (named Wheel), construct new low-cost production facilities, package the detergent in single-use amounts so that it could be sold at a very low unit price, distribute the product to local merchants by handcarts, and craft an economical marketing campaign that included painted signs on buildings and demonstrations near stores. The new brand quickly captured $100 million in sales and was the number-one detergent brand in India based on 2011 dollar sales. Unilever later replicated the strategy in India with low-priced packets of shampoos and deodorants and in South America with a detergent brand named Ala.

- *Modify aspects of the company's business model to accommodate local circumstances (but not to such an extent that the company loses the advantage of global scale and branding).* For instance, when Dell entered China, it discovered that individuals and businesses were not accustomed to placing orders through the Internet. To adapt,

Dell modified its direct sales model to rely more heavily on phone and fax orders and decided to be patient in getting Chinese customers to place Internet orders. Further, because numerous Chinese government departments and state-owned enterprises insisted that hardware vendors make their bids through distributors and systems integrators (as opposed to dealing directly with Dell salespeople), Dell opted to use third parties in marketing its products to this buyer segment. But Dell was careful not to abandon the parts of its business model that gave it a competitive edge over rivals. Similarly, when McDonald's moved into Russia in the 1990s, it was forced to alter its practice of obtaining supplies from outside vendors because capable local suppliers were not available. In order to supply its Russian outlets and stay true to its core principle of serving consistent-quality fast food, McDonald's set up its own vertically integrated supply chain—cattle were imported from Holland and russet potatoes were imported from the United States. McDonald's management also worked with a select number of Russian bakers for its bread, brought in agricultural specialists from Canada and Europe to improve the management practices of Russian farmers, built its own 100,000-square-foot McComplex to produce hamburgers, French fries, ketchup, mustard, and Big Mac sauce, and set up a trucking fleet to move supplies to restaurants.

- *Try to change the local market to better match the way the company does business elsewhere.* A multinational company often has enough market clout to drive major changes in the way a local country market operates. When Hong Kong–based STAR launched its first satellite TV channel in 1991, it generated profound impacts on the TV marketplace in India. The Indian government lost its monopoly on TV broadcasts, several other satellite TV channels aimed at Indian audiences quickly emerged, and the excitement of additional TV channels in India triggered a boom in TV manufacturing in India. When Japan's Suzuki entered India, it triggered a quality revolution among Indian auto parts manufacturers. Local component suppliers teamed up with Suzuki's vendors in Japan and worked with Japanese experts to produce higher-quality products. Over the next two decades, Indian companies became proficient in making top-notch components for vehicles, won more prizes for quality than companies in any country other than Japan, and broke into the global market as suppliers to many automakers in Asia and other parts of the world. Mahindra and Mahindra, one of India's premier automobile manufacturers, has been recognized by a number of organizations for its product quality.

- *Stay away from developing markets where it is impractical or uneconomic to modify the company's business model to accommodate local circumstances.* Home Depot expanded into Mexico in 2001 and China in 2006, but it has avoided entry into other developing countries because its value proposition of good quality, low prices, and attentive customer service relies on (1) good highways and logistical systems to minimize store inventory costs, (2) employee stock ownership to help motivate store personnel to provide good customer service, and (3) high labor costs for housing construction and home repairs that encourage homeowners to engage in do-it-yourself projects. Relying on these factors in the U.S. and Canadian markets has worked spectacularly for Home Depot, but the company has found that it cannot count on these factors in nearby Latin America.

> Profitability in developing markets rarely comes quickly or easily—new entrants have to adapt their business models to local conditions and be patient in earning a profit.

Company experiences in entering developing markets like Argentina, Vietnam, Malaysia, and Brazil indicate that profitability seldom comes quickly or easily. Building a market for the company's products can often turn into a long-term process that involves re-education of consumers, sizable investments in advertising to alter tastes and buying habits, and upgrades of the local infrastructure (transportation systems, distribution channels, etc.). In such cases, a company must be patient, work within the system to improve the infrastructure, and lay the foundation for generating sizable revenues and profits once conditions are ripe for market takeoff.

# DEFENDING AGAINST GLOBAL GIANTS: STRATEGIES FOR LOCAL COMPANIES IN DEVELOPING COUNTRIES

If opportunity-seeking, resource-rich multinational companies are looking to enter developing-country markets, what strategy options can local companies use to survive? As it turns out, the prospects for local companies facing global giants are by no means grim. Studies of local companies in developing markets have disclosed five strategies that have proved themselves in defending against globally competitive companies.[24] Illustration Capsule 7.3 discusses how a travel agency in China used a combination of these strategies to become that country's largest travel consolidator and online travel agent.

1.  *Develop business models that exploit shortcomings in local distribution networks or infrastructure.* In many instances, the extensive collection of resources possessed by the global giants is of little help in building a presence in developing markets. The lack of well-established wholesaler and distributor networks, telecommunication systems, consumer banking, or media necessary for advertising makes it difficult for large internationals to migrate business models proved in developed markets to emerging markets. Such markets sometimes favor local companies whose managers are familiar with the local language and culture and are skilled in selecting large numbers of conscientious employees to carry out labor-intensive tasks. Shanda, a Chinese producer of massively multiplayer online role-playing games (MMORPG), has overcome China's lack of an established credit card network by selling prepaid access cards through local merchants. The company's focus on online games also addresses shortcomings in China's software piracy laws. An India-based electronics company has been able to carve out a market niche for itself by developing an all-in-one business machine designed especially for India's 1.2 million small shopkeepers that tolerates the frequent power outages in that country.[25]

2.  *Utilize keen understanding of local customer needs and preferences to create customized products or services.* When developing-country markets are largely made up of customers with strong local needs, a good strategy option is to concentrate on customers who prefer a local touch and to accept the loss of the customers attracted to global brands.[26] A local company may be able to astutely exploit its local orientation—its familiarity with local preferences, its expertise in traditional products, its long-standing customer relationships. A small Middle Eastern cell phone manufacturer competes successfully against industry giants Nokia, Samsung, and Motorola by selling a model designed especially for Muslims—it is loaded with the Koran, alerts people at prayer times, and is equipped with a compass that points them toward Mecca. Shenzhen-based Tencent has become the leader in instant messaging in China through its unique understanding of Chinese behavior and culture.

3.  *Take advantage of aspects of the local workforce with which large multinational companies may be unfamiliar.* Local companies that lack the technological capabilities of foreign entrants may be able to rely on their better understanding of the local labor force

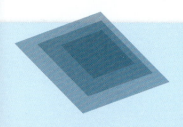

## ILLUSTRATION CAPSULE 7.3

# How Ctrip Successfully Defended against International Rivals to Become China's Largest Online Travel Agency

Ctrip has utilized a business model tailored to the Chinese travel market, its access to low-cost labor, and its unique understanding of customer preferences and buying habits to build scale rapidly and defeat foreign rivals such as Expedia and Travelocity in becoming the largest travel agency in China. The company was founded in 1999 with a focus on business travelers, since corporate travel accounts for the majority of China's travel bookings. The company also placed little emphasis on online transactions, since at the time there was no national ticketing system in China, most hotels did not belong to a national or international chain, and most consumers preferred paper tickets to electronic tickets. To overcome this infrastructure shortcoming, the company established its own central database of 5,600 hotels located throughout China and flight information for all major airlines operating in China. Ctrip set up a call center of 3,000 representatives that could use its proprietary database to provide travel information for up to 100,000 customers per day. Because most of its transactions were not done over the Internet, the company hired couriers in all major cities in China to ride by bicycle or scooter to collect payments and deliver tickets to Ctrip's corporate customers. Ctrip also initiated a loyalty program that provided gifts and incentives to the administrative personnel who arranged travel for business executives. By 2011, **Ctrip.com** held 60 percent of China's online travel market, having grown 40 percent every year since 1999. As of March 2012, its market cap reached $3.1 billion and was creeping up rapidly on Expedia's market cap of over $4 billion.

*Sources:* Arindam K. Bhattacharya and David C. Michael, "How Local Companies Keep Multinationals at Bay," *Harvard Business Review* 86, no. 3 (March 2008), pp. 85–95; http://www.thatsmags.com/shanghai/article/detail/480/a-journey-with-ctrip; http://money.cnn.com/quote/quote.html?symb=EXPE, accessed March 28, 2012.

to offset any disadvantage. Focus Media is China's largest outdoor advertising firm and has relied on low-cost labor to update its 130,000 LCD displays and billboards in 90 cities in a low-tech manner, while multinational companies operating in China use electronically networked screens that allow messages to be changed remotely. Focus uses an army of employees who ride to each display by bicycle to change advertisements with programming contained on a USB flash drive or DVD. Indian information technology firms such as Infosys Technologies and Satyam Computer Services have been able to keep their personnel costs lower than those of international competitors EDS and Accenture because of their familiarity with local labor markets. While the large internationals have focused recruiting efforts in urban centers like Bangalore and Delhi, driving up engineering and computer science salaries in such cities, local companies have shifted recruiting efforts to second-tier cities that are unfamiliar to foreign firms.

4. *Use acquisition and rapid-growth strategies to better defend against expansion-minded internationals.* With the growth potential of developing markets such as China, Indonesia, and Brazil obvious to the world, local companies must attempt to develop scale and upgrade their competitive capabilities as quickly as possible to defend against the stronger international's arsenal of resources. Most successful companies

in developing markets have pursued mergers and acquisitions at a rapid-fire pace to build first a nationwide and then an international presence. Hindalco, India's largest aluminum producer, has followed just such a path to achieve its ambitions for global dominance. By acquiring companies in India first, it gained enough experience and confidence to eventually acquire much larger foreign companies with world-class capabilities.[27] When China began to liberalize its foreign trade policies, Lenovo (the Chinese PC maker) realized that its long-held position of market dominance in China could not withstand the onslaught of new international entrants such as Dell and HP. Its acquisition of IBM's PC business allowed Lenovo to gain rapid access to IBM's globally recognized PC brand, its R&D capability, and its existing distribution in developed countries. This has allowed Lenovo not only to hold its own against the incursion of global giants into its home market but to expand into new markets around the world.[28]

5. *Transfer company expertise to cross-border markets and initiate actions to contend on an international level.* When a company from a developing country has resources and capabilities suitable for competing in other country markets, launching initiatives to transfer its expertise to foreign markets becomes a viable strategic option. Televisa, Mexico's largest media company, used its expertise in Spanish culture and linguistics to become the world's most prolific producer of Spanish-language soap operas. By continuing to upgrade its capabilities and learn from its experience in foreign markets, a company can sometimes transform itself into one capable of competing on a worldwide basis, as an emerging global giant. Sundaram Fasteners of India began its foray into foreign markets as a supplier of radiator caps to GM—an opportunity it pursued when GM first decided to outsource the production of this part. As a participant in GM's supplier network, the company learned about emerging technical standards, built its capabilities, and became one of the first Indian companies to achieve QS 9000 quality certification. With the expertise it gained and its recognition for meeting quality standards, Sundaram was then able to pursue opportunities to supply automotive parts in Japan and Europe.

## KEY POINTS

1. Competing in international markets allows companies to (1) gain access to new customers, (2) achieve lower costs through greater scale economies, learning curve effects, or purchasing power, (3) leverage core competencies developed domestically in additional country markets, (4) gain access to resources and capabilities located outside a company's domestic market, and (5) spread business risk across a wider market base.

2. Strategy making is more complex for five reasons: (1) different countries have *home-country advantages* in different industries; (2) there exist location-based advantages to performing different value chain activities in different parts of the world; (3) varying political and economic risks make the business climate of some countries more favorable than others; (4) companies face the risk of adverse shifts in exchange rates when operating in foreign countries; and (5) differences in buyer tastes and preferences present a conundrum concerning the trade-off between customizing and standardizing products and services.

3. The strategies of firms that expand internationally are usually grounded in home-country advantages concerning demand conditions, factor conditions, related and supporting industries, and firm strategy, structure, and rivalry, as described by the Diamond of National Competitive Advantage framework.

4. There are five strategic options for entering foreign markets. These include maintaining a national (one-country) production base and *exporting* goods to foreign markets, *licensing* foreign firms to produce and distribute the company's products abroad, employing a *franchising* strategy, establishing a foreign *subsidiary via acquisition or greenfield venture,* and using *strategic alliances or other collaborative partnerships.*

5. A company must choose among three alternative approaches for competing internationally: (1) a *multidomestic strategy* or *think-local, act-local* approach to crafting international strategy; (2) a *global strategy*—a *think-global, act-global* approach; and (3) a combination *think-global, act-local* approach, known as a *transnational strategy.* A "think-local, act-local," or multidomestic, strategy is appropriate for industries or companies that must vary their product offerings and competitive approaches from country to country in order to accommodate different buyer preferences and market conditions. The "think-global, act-global" approach (or global strategy) works best when there are substantial cost benefits to be gained from taking a standardized and globally integrated approach and little need for local responsiveness. A transnational approach (think global, act local) is called for when there is a high need for local responsiveness as well as substantial benefits from taking a globally integrated approach. In this approach, a company strives to employ the same basic competitive strategy in all markets but still customize its product offering and some aspect of its operations to fit local market circumstances.

6. There are three general ways in which a firm can gain competitive advantage (or offset domestic disadvantages) in international markets. One way involves locating various value chain activities among nations in a manner that lowers costs or achieves greater product differentiation. A second way draws on a multinational competitor's ability to extend its competitive advantage by cost-effectively sharing, replicating, or transferring its most valuable resources and capabilities across borders. A third concerns benefiting from cross-border coordination in ways that are unavailable to domestic-only competitors.

7. Profit sanctuaries are country markets in which a company derives substantial profits because of its strong or protected market position. They are a source of financial strength for mounting strategic offensives in selected country markets or for making defensive moves that can ward off mutually destructive competitive battles. They are useful in waging strategic offenses in international markets through *cross-subsidization*—a practice of supporting competitive offensives in one market with resources and profits diverted from operations in another market. They may be used defensively to encourage *mutual restraint* among competitors when there is international *multimarket competition* by signaling that each company has the financial capability for mounting a strong counterattack if threatened. For companies with at least one profit sanctuary, having a presence in a rival's key markets can be enough to deter the rival from making aggressive attacks.

8. Companies racing for global leadership have to consider competing in developing markets like the BRIC countries, Brazil, Russia, India, and China—countries where the business risks are considerable but the opportunities for growth are huge. To succeed in these markets, companies often have to (1) compete on the basis of low price, (2) modify aspects of the company's business model or strategy to accommodate local circumstances (but not so much that the company loses the advantages of global scale and branding), and/or (3) try to change the local market to better match the way the company does business elsewhere. Profitability is unlikely to come quickly or easily in developing markets, typically because of the investments needed to alter buying habits and tastes, the increased political and economic risk,

and/or the need for infrastructure upgrades. And there may be times when a company should simply stay away from certain developing markets until conditions for entry are better suited to its business model and strategy.

9. Local companies in developing-country markets can seek to compete against large multinational companies by (1) developing business models that exploit shortcomings in local distribution networks or infrastructure, (2) utilizing a superior understanding of local customer needs and preferences or local relationships, (3) taking advantage of competitively important qualities of the local workforce with which large multinational companies may be unfamiliar, (4) using acquisition strategies and rapid-growth strategies to better defend against expansion-minded multinational companies, or (5) transferring company expertise to cross-border markets and initiating actions to compete on an international level.

## ASSURANCE OF LEARNING EXERCISES

1. Chile's largest producer of wine, Concha y Toro, chooses to compete in Europe, North America, the Caribbean, and Asia using an export strategy. Go to the Investor Relations section of the company's website (http://www.conchaytoro.com/the-company/investor-relations/) to review the company's press releases, annual reports, and presentations. Why does it seem that the company has avoided developing vineyards and wineries in wine-growing regions outside of South America? What reasons does Concha y Toro likely have to pursue exporting rather than stick to a domestic-only sales and distribution strategy?

**LO 1, LO 3**

2. Collaborative agreements with foreign companies in the form of strategic alliances or joint ventures are widely used as a means of entering foreign markets. They are also used as a means of acquiring resources and capabilities by learning from foreign partners. And they are used to put together powerful combinations of complementary resources and capabilities by accessing the complementary resources and capabilities of a foreign partner. Illustration Capsule 7.1 provides examples of four cross-border strategic alliances that Solazyme has participated in. What were each of these partnerships (with Unilever, Sephora, Qantas, and Roquette) designed to achieve and why would they make sense for a company like Solazyme. (Analyze each partnership separately based on the information provided in the capsule.)

**LO 1, LO 3**

3. Assume you are in charge of developing the strategy for a multinational company selling products in some 50 different countries around the world. One of the issues you face is whether to employ a multicountry strategy, a transnational, or a global strategy.

**LO 2, LO 4**

   a. If your company's product is mobile phones, do you think it would make better strategic sense to employ a multidomestic strategy, a transnational strategy, or a global strategy? Why?

   b. If your company's product is dry soup mixes and canned soups, would a multidomestic strategy seem to be more advisable than a transnational or global strategy? Why?

   c. If your company's product is large home appliances such as washing machines, ranges, ovens, and refrigerators, would it seem to make more sense to pursue a multidomestic strategy, a transnational strategy, or a global strategy? Why?

   d. If your company's product is apparel and footwear, would a multidomestic strategy, a transnational strategy, or a global strategy seem to have more appeal? Why?

**LO 5, LO 6**    4.   Using your university library's subscription to Lexis-Nexis, EBSCO, or a similar database, identify and discuss three key strategies that Volkswagen is using to compete in China.

## EXERCISES FOR SIMULATION PARTICIPANTS

The following questions are for simulation participants whose companies operate in an international market arena. If your company competes only in a single country, then skip the questions in this section.

**LO 2**    1.   To what extent, if any, have you and your co-managers adapted your company's strategy to take shifting exchange rates into account? In other words, have you undertaken any actions to try to minimize the impact of adverse shifts in exchange rates?

**LO 2**    2.   To what extent, if any, have you and your co-managers adapted your company's strategy to take geographic differences in import tariffs or import duties into account?

**LO 4**    3.   Which one of the following best describes the strategic approach your company is taking in trying to compete successfully on an international basis?

- Multidomestic or think local, act local approach
- Global or think global, act local approach
- Transnational or think global, act global approach

Explain your answer and indicate two or three chief elements of your company's strategy for competing in two or more different geographic regions.

## ENDNOTES

[1] Sidney G. Winter and Gabriel Szulanski, "Replication as Strategy," *Organization Science* 12, no. 6 (November–December 2001), pp. 730–43; Sidney G. Winter and Gabriel Szulanski, "Getting It Right the Second Time," *Harvard Business Review* 80, no. 1 (January 2002), pp. 62–69.

[2] A. C. Inkpen and A. Dinur, "Knowledge Management Processes and International Joint Ventures," *Organization Science* 9, no. 4 (July–August 1998), pp. 454–68; P. Dussauge, B. Garrette, and W. Mitchell, "Learning from Competing Partners: Outcomes and Durations of Scale and Link Alliances in Europe, North America and Asia," *Strategic Management Journal* 21, no. 2 (February 2000), pp. 99–126; C. Dhanaraj, M. A. Lyles, H. K. Steensma, et al., "Managing Tacit and Explicit Knowledge Transfer in IJVs: The Role of Relational Embeddedness and the Impact on Performance," *Journal of International Business Studies* 35, no. 5 (September 2004), pp. 428–42; K. W. Glaister and P. J. Buckley, "Strategic Motives for International Alliance Formation," *Journal of Management Studies* 33, no. 3 (May 1996), pp. 301–32.

[3] J. Anand and B. Kogut, "Technological Capabilities of Countries, Firm Rivalry

and Foreign Direct Investment," *Journal of International Business Studies* 28, no. 3 (1997), pp. 445–65; J. Anand and A. Delios, "Absolute and Relative Resources as Determinants of International Acquisitions," *Strategic Management Journal* 23, no. 2 (February 2002), pp. 119–35; A. Seth, K. Song, and A. Pettit, "Value Creation and Destruction in Cross-Border Acquisitions: An Empirical Analysis of Foreign Acquisitions of U.S. Firms," *Strategic Management Journal* 23, no. 10 (October 2002), pp. 921–40; J. Anand, L. Capron, and W. Mitchell, "Using Acquisitions to Access Multinational Diversity: Thinking beyond the Domestic versus Cross-Border M&A Comparison," *Industrial & Corporate Change* 14, no. 2 (April 2005), pp. 191–224.

[4] M. Porter, "The Competitive Advantage of Nations," *Harvard Business Review,* March–April 1990, pp. 73–93.

[5] "China Car Sales 'Overtook the US' in 2009," *BBC News,* January 11, 2010, http://news.bbc.co.uk/2/hi/8451887.stm.

[6] New release by U.S. Department of Labor, Bureau of Labor Statistics, "International Comparisons of Hourly Compensation Costs in Manufacturing, 2009," March 8, 2011, pp. 3–6.

[7] Sangwon Yoon, "South Korea Targets Internet Addicts; 2 Million Hooked," *Valley News,* April 25, 2010, p. C2.

[8] E. Pablo, "Determinants of Cross-Border M&As in Latin America," *Journal of Business Research* 62, no. 9 (2009); R. Olie, "Shades of Culture and Institutions in International Mergers," *Organization Studies* 15, no. 3 (1994); K. E. Meyer, M. Wright, and S. Pruthi, "Institutions, Resources, and Entry Strategies in Emerging Economies," *Strategic Management Journal* 30, no. 5 (2009).

[9] Yves L. Doz and Gary Hamel, *Alliance Advantage* (Boston: Harvard Business School Press, 1998); Joel Bleeke and David Ernst, "The Way to Win in Cross-Border Alliances," *Harvard Business Review* 69, no. 6 (November –December 1991), pp. 127–33; Gary Hamel, Yves L. Doz, and C. K. Prahalad, "Collaborate with Your Competitors—and Win," *Harvard Business Review* 67, no. 1 (January–February 1989), pp. 134–35.

[10] K. W. Glaister and P. J. Buckley, "Strategic Motives for International Alliance Formation," *Journal of Management Studies* 33, no. 3 (May 1996), pp. 301–32.

[11] H. Kurt Christensen, "Corporate Strategy: Managing a Set of Businesses," in *The*

*Portable MBA in Strategy,* ed. Liam Fahey and Robert M. Randall (New York: Wiley, 2001).

[12] Jeffrey H. Dyer, Prashant Kale, and Harbir Singh, "When to Ally and When to Acquire," *Harvard Business Review* 82, no. 7/8 (July–August 2004).

[13] Doz and Hamel, *Alliance Advantage,* chaps. 2–7; Rosabeth Moss Kanter, "Collaborative Advantage: The Art of the Alliance," *Harvard Business Review* 72, no. 4 (July–August 1994), pp. 96–108.

[14] Shawn Tully, "The Alliance from Hell," *Fortune,* June 24, 1996, pp. 64–72.

[15] C. K. Prahalad and Kenneth Lieberthal, "The End of Corporate Imperialism," *Harvard Business Review* 76, no. 4 (July–August, 2004), p. 77.

[16] Pankaj Ghemawat, "Managing Differences: The Central Challenge of Global Strategy," *Harvard Business Review* 85, no. 3 (March 2007).

[17] C. A. Bartlett and S. Ghoshal, *Managing Across Borders: The Transnational Solution,* 2nd ed. (Boston: Harvard Business School Press, 1998).

[18] Lynn S. Paine, "The China Rules," *Harvard Business Review* 88, no. 6 (June 2010) pp. 103–8.

[19] C. K. Prahalad and Yves L. Doz, *The Multinational Mission* (New York: Free Press).

[20] David J. Arnold and John A. Quelch, "New Strategies in Emerging Markets," *Sloan Management Review* 40, no. 1 (Fall 1998), pp. 7–20; C. K. Prahalad, *The Fortune at the Bottom of the Pyramid: Eradicating Poverty through Profits* (Upper Saddle River, NJ: Wharton, 2005).

[21] "Is a Luxury Good Consumption Tax Useful?" *Beijing Review.com.cn,* June 18, 2010, www.bjreview.com.cn/print/txt/2010-06/18/content_280191.htm; "GM's First-Half China Sales Surge Past the U.S.," *Bloomberg Businessweek,* July 2, 2010, http://businessweek.com/news/2010-07-02/gm-s-first-half-china-sales-surge-past-the-u-s-.html.

[22] Joanne Muller, "Can China Save GM?" *Forbes.com,* May 10, 2010, www.forbes.com/forbes/2010/0510/global-2000-10-automobiles-china-detroit-whitacre-save-gm.html.

[23] Tarun Khanna, Krishna G. Palepu, and Jayant Sinha, "Strategies That Fit Emerging Markets," *Harvard Business Review* 83, no. 6 (June 2005), p. 63; Arindam K. Bhattacharya and David C. Michael, "How Local Companies Keep Multinationals at Bay,"

*Harvard Business Review* 86, no. 3 (March 2008), pp. 94–95.

[24] Tarun Khanna and Krishna G. Palepu, "Emerging Giants: Building World-Class Companies in Developing Countries," *Harvard Business Review* 84, no. 10 (October 2006), pp. 60–69.

[25] Steve Hamm, "Tech's Future," *BusinessWeek,* September 27, 2004, p. 88.

[26] Niroj Dawar and Tony Frost, "Competing with Giants: Survival Strategies for Local Companies in Emerging Markets," *Harvard Business Review* 77, no. 1 (January–February 1999), p. 122; Guitz Ger, "Localizing in the Global Village: Local Firms Competing in Global Markets," *California Management Review* 41, no. 4 (Summer 1999), pp. 64–84.

[27] N. Kumar, "How Emerging Giants Are Rewriting the Rules of M&A," *Harvard Business Review,* May 2009, pp. 115–21.

[28] H. Rui and G. Yip, "Foreign Acquisitions by Chinese Firms: A Strategic Intent Perspective," *Journal of World Business* 43 (2008), pp. 213–26.

# CHAPTER 8

# CORPORATE STRATEGY
## Diversification and the Multibusiness Company

## Learning Objectives

**LO 1** Understand when and how business diversification can enhance shareholder value.

**LO 2** Gain an understanding of how related diversification strategies can produce cross-business strategic fit capable of delivering competitive advantage.

**LO 3** Become aware of the merits and risks of corporate strategies keyed to unrelated diversification.

**LO 4** Gain command of the analytical tools for evaluating a company's diversification strategy.

**LO 5** Understand a diversified company's four main corporate strategy options for solidifying its diversification strategy and improving company performance.

---

I think our biggest achievement to date has been bringing back to life an inherent Disney synergy that enables each part of our business to draw from, build upon, and bolster the others.

**Michael Eisner** – *Former CEO, Walt Disney Company*

Make winners out of every business in your company. Don't carry losers.

**Jack Welch** – *Former CEO, General Electric*

How many senior executives discuss the crucial distinction between competitive strategy at the level of a business and competitive strategy at the level of an entire company?

**C. K. Prahalad and Gary Hamel** – *Professors, authors, and consultants*

In this chapter, we move up one level in the strategy-making hierarchy, from strategy making in a single-business enterprise to strategy making in a diversified enterprise. Because a diversified company is a collection of individual businesses, the strategy-making task is more complicated. In a one-business company, managers have to come up with a plan for competing successfully in only a single industry environment—the result is what we labeled in Chapter 2 as *business-level strategy.* But in a diversified company, the strategy-making challenge involves assessing multiple industry environments and developing *a set of business strategies,* one for each industry arena in which the diversified company operates. And top executives at a diversified company must still go one step further and devise a companywide or *corporate strategy* for improving the performance of the company's overall business lineup and for making a rational whole out of its collection of individual businesses.

In the first portion of this chapter, we describe when and why diversification makes good strategic sense, the different means of diversifying a company's business lineup, and the pros and cons of related versus unrelated diversification strategies. The second part of the chapter looks at how to evaluate the attractiveness of a diversified company's business lineup, how to decide whether it has a good diversification strategy, and what the strategic options are for improving a diversified company's future performance.

## WHAT DOES CRAFTING A DIVERSIFICATION STRATEGY ENTAIL?

The task of crafting a diversified company's overall *corporate strategy* falls squarely in the lap of top-level executives and involves four distinct facets:

1. *Picking new industries to enter and deciding on the means of entry.* The decision to pursue business diversification requires that management decide which new industries to enter and whether to enter by starting a new business from the ground up, acquiring a company already in the target industry, or forming a joint venture or strategic alliance with another company.

2. *Pursuing opportunities to leverage cross-business value chain relationships and strategic fit into competitive advantage.* The task here is to determine whether there are opportunities to strengthen a diversified company's businesses by such means as transferring competitively valuable resources and capabilities from one business to another, combining the related value chain activities of different businesses to achieve lower costs, sharing the use of a powerful and well-respected brand name across multiple businesses, and encouraging knowledge-sharing and collaborative activity among the businesses.

3. *Establishing investment priorities and steering corporate resources into the most attractive business units.* Typically, this translates into pursuing rapid-growth strategies in its most promising businesses, initiating profit improvement or turnaround strategies in weak-performing businesses with potential, and divesting businesses that are no longer attractive or that don't fit into management's long-range plans.

4. *Initiating actions to boost the combined performance of the corporation's collection of businesses.* Strategic options for improving the corporations overall performance include (a) sticking closely with the existing business lineup and pursuing opportunities presented by these businesses, (b) broadening the scope of diversification by entering additional industries, (c) divesting some businesses and retrenching to a narrower collection of diversified businesses with better overall performance prospects, and (d) restructuring the entire company by divesting some businesses and acquiring others so as to put a whole new face on the company's business lineup.

The demanding and time-consuming nature of these four tasks explains why corporate executives generally refrain from becoming immersed in the details of crafting and executing business-level strategies, preferring instead to delegate lead responsibility for business strategy and business-level operations to the heads of each business unit. Rather, the normal procedure is to delegate lead responsibility for business strategy to the heads of each business, giving them the latitude to craft strategies suited to their particular industry and competitive circumstances while holding them accountable for producing good results.

# WHEN BUSINESS DIVERSIFICATION BECOMES A CONSIDERATION

As long as a company has plentiful opportunities for profitable growth in its present industry, there is no urgency to pursue diversification. But growth opportunities are often limited in mature industries and declining markets. A company may also encounter diminishing market opportunities and stagnating sales if demand for the industry's product is eroded by the appearance of alternative technologies, substitute products, or fast-shifting buyer preferences. Consider, for example, what the growing use of debit cards and online bill payment have done to the check printing business and what mobile phone companies and marketers of Voice over Internet Protocol (VoIP) have done to the revenues of long-distance providers such as AT&T, British Telecommunications, and NTT in Japan.

Thus, *diversifying into new industries always merits strong consideration whenever a single-business company encounters diminishing market opportunities and stagnating sales in its principal business.* But there are four other instances in which a company becomes a prime candidate for diversifying:[1]

1. When it spots opportunities for expanding into industries whose technologies and products complement its present business.

2. When it can leverage its collection of resources and capabilities by expanding into businesses where these resources and capabilities are valuable competitive assets.

3. When diversifying into additional businesses opens new avenues for reducing costs.

4. When it has a powerful and well-known brand name that can be transferred to the products of other businesses.

The decision to diversify presents wide-ranging possibilities. A company can diversify into closely related businesses or into totally unrelated businesses. It can diversify its present revenue and earnings base to a small or major extent. It can move into one or two large new businesses or a greater number of small ones. It can achieve diversification by acquiring an existing company, starting up a new business from scratch, or forming a joint venture with one or more companies to enter new businesses.

# BUILDING SHAREHOLDER VALUE: THE ULTIMATE JUSTIFICATION FOR DIVERSIFYING

Diversification must do more for a company than simply spread its business risk across various industries. In principle, diversification cannot be considered a success unless it results in *added long-term economic value for shareholders*—value that shareholders cannot capture on their own by purchasing stock in companies in different industries or investing in mutual funds so as to spread their investments across several industries.

LO 1

Understand when and how business diversification can enhance shareholder value.

For there to be reasonable expectations of producing added long-term shareholder value, a move to diversify into a new business must pass three tests:[2]

1.  *The industry attractiveness test*—The industry to be entered through diversification must offer an opportunity for profits and return on investment that is equal to or better than that of the company's present business(es).

2.  *The cost-of-entry test*—The cost to enter the target industry must not be so high as to exceed the potential for good profitability. A catch-22 can prevail here, however. The more attractive an industry's prospects are for growth and good long-term profitability, the more expensive it can be to enter. Entry barriers for startup companies are likely to be high in attractive industries—were barriers low, a rush of new entrants would soon erode the potential for high profitability. And buying a well-positioned company in an appealing industry often entails a high acquisition cost that makes passing the cost-of-entry test less likely. Since the owners of a successful and growing company usually demand a price that reflects their business's profit prospects, it's easy for such an acquisition to fail the cost-of-entry test.

3.  *The better-off test.*—Diversifying into a new business must offer potential for the company's existing businesses and the new business to perform better together under a single corporate umbrella than they would perform operating as independent, stand-alone businesses—an effect known as **synergy**. For example, let's say that company A diversifies by purchasing company B in another industry. If A and B's consolidated profits in the years to come prove no greater than what each could have earned on its own, then A's diversification won't provide its shareholders with any added value. Company A's shareholders could have achieved the same $1 + 1 = 2$ result by merely purchasing stock in company B. Diversification does not result in added long-term value for shareholders unless it produces a $1 + 1 = 3$ effect whereby sister businesses *perform better together* as part of the same firm than they could have performed as independent companies.

**CORE CONCEPT**

Creating added value for shareholders via diversification requires building a multibusiness company where the whole is greater than the sum of its parts—an outcome known as **synergy**.

Diversification moves must satisfy all three tests to grow shareholder value over the long term. Diversification moves that can pass only one or two tests are suspect.

# APPROACHES TO DIVERSIFYING THE BUSINESS LINEUP

The means of entering new businesses can take any of three forms: acquisition, internal startup, or joint ventures with other companies.

## Diversification by Acquisition of an Existing Business

Acquisition is a popular means of diversifying into another industry. Not only is it quicker than trying to launch a brand-new operation, but it also offers an effective way to hurdle such entry barriers as acquiring technological know-how, establishing supplier relationships, achieving scale economies, building brand awareness, and securing adequate distribution. Acquisitions are also commonly employed to access resources and capabilities that are complementary to those of the acquiring firm and that cannot be developed readily internally. Buying an ongoing operation allows the acquirer to move directly to the task of building a strong market position in the target industry, rather than getting bogged down in trying to develop the knowledge, experience, scale of operation, and market reputation necessary for a startup entrant to become an effective competitor.

However, acquiring an existing business can prove quite expensive. The costs of acquiring another business include not only the acquisition price but also the costs of performing the due diligence to ascertain the worth of the other company, negotiating and completing the purchase transaction, and the costs of integrating the business into the diversified company's portfolio. If the company to be acquired is a successful company, the acquisition price will include a hefty *premium* over the preacquisition value of the company. For example, the $5.8 billion that Xerox paid to acquire Affiliated Computer Services in 2010 included a 38 percent premium over the service company's market value.[3] Premiums are paid in order to convince the shareholders and managers of the target company that it is in their financial interests to approve the deal. The average premium in deals between U.S. companies rose to 55 percent in 2010, but it is more often in the 30 to 40 percent range.[4]

The big dilemma an acquisition-minded firm faces is whether to pay a premium price for a successful company or to buy a struggling company at a bargain price.[5] If the buying firm has little knowledge of the industry but ample capital, it is often better off purchasing a capable, strongly positioned firm—even if its current owners demand a premium price. However, when the acquirer sees promising ways to transform a weak firm into a strong one and has the resources, the know-how, and the patience to do it, a struggling company can be the better long-term investment.

While acquisitions offer an enticing means for entering a new business, many fail to deliver on their promise.[6] Realizing the potential gains from an acquisition requires a successful integration of the acquired company into the culture, systems, and structure of the acquiring firm. This can be a costly and time-consuming operation. Acquisitions can also fail to deliver long-term shareholder value if the acquirer overestimates the potential gains and pays a premium in excess of the realized gains. High integration costs and excessive price premiums are two reasons that an acquisition might fail the cost-of-entry test. Firms with significant experience in making acquisitions are better able to avoid these types of problems.[7]

> ### CORE CONCEPT
>
> An **acquisition premium** is the amount by which the price offered exceeds the preacquisition market value of the target company.

# Entering a New Line of Business through Internal Development

Internal development of new businesses has become an increasingly important means for companies to diversify and is often referred to as **corporate venturing** or *new venture development*. It involves building a new business from scratch. Although building a new business from the ground up is generally a time-consuming and uncertain process, it avoids the pitfalls associated with entry via acquisition and may allow the firm to realize greater profits in the end. It may offer a viable means of entering a new or emerging industry where there are no good acquisition candidates.

Entering a new business via internal development also poses some significant hurdles. An internal new venture not only has to overcome industry entry barriers but also must invest in new production capacity, develop sources of supply, hire and train employees, build channels of distribution, grow a customer base, and so on, unless the new business is quite similar to the company's existing business. The risks associated with internal startups can be substantial, and the likelihood of failure is often high. Moreover, the culture, structures, and organizational systems of some companies may impede innovation and make it difficult for corporate entrepreneurship to flourish.

Generally, internal development of a new business has appeal only when (1) the parent company already has in-house most of the skills and resources it needs to piece together a new business and compete effectively; (2) there is ample time to launch the business; (3) the internal cost of entry is lower than the cost of entry via acquisition; (4) the targeted industry is populated with many relatively small firms such that the new startup does not have to compete head to head against larger, powerful rivals; (5) adding new production capacity will not adversely impact the supply-demand balance in the industry; and (6) incumbent firms are likely to be slow or ineffective in responding to a new entrant's efforts to crack the market.[8]

## CORE CONCEPT

**Corporate venturing** (or *new venture development*) is the process of developing new businesses as an outgrowth of a company's established business operations. It is also referred to as *corporate entrepreneurship* or *intrapreneurship* since it requires entrepreneurial-like qualities within a larger enterprise.

# Joint Ventures

Entering a new business via a joint venture can be useful in at least three types of situations.[9] First, a joint venture is a good vehicle for pursuing an opportunity that is too complex, uneconomical, or risky for one company to pursue alone. Second, joint ventures make sense when the opportunities in a new industry require a broader range of competencies and know-how than a company can marshal. Many of the opportunities in satellite-based telecommunications, biotechnology, and network-based systems that blend hardware, software, and services call for the coordinated development of complementary innovations and the tackling of an intricate web of financial, technical, political, and regulatory factors simultaneously. In such cases, pooling the resources and competencies of two or more companies is a wiser and less risky way to proceed. Third, companies sometimes use joint ventures to diversify into a new industry when the diversification move entails having operations in a foreign country—several governments require foreign companies operating within their borders to have a local partner that has minority, if not majority, ownership in the local operations. Aside from fulfilling host-government ownership requirements, companies usually seek out a local partner with expertise and other resources that will aid the success of the newly established local operation. However, as discussed in Chapters 6 and 7, partnering with another company has significant drawbacks due to the potential for conflicting objectives, disagreements over how to best operate the venture, culture clashes, and so on. Joint ventures are generally the least durable of the entry options, usually lasting only until the partners decide to go their own ways.

# Choosing a Mode of Entry

The choice of how best to enter a new business—whether through internal development, acquisition, or joint venture—depends on the answers to four important questions:

- Does the company have all of the resources and capabilities it requires to enter the business through internal development or is it lacking some critical resources?
- Are there entry barriers to overcome?
- Is speed an important factor in the firm's chances for successful entry?
- Which is the least costly mode of entry, given the company's objectives?

**The Question of Critical Resources and Capabilities**    If a firm has all the resources it needs to start up a new business or will be able to easily purchase or lease any missing resources, it may choose to enter the business via internal development. However, if missing critical resources cannot be easily purchased or leased, a firm wishing to enter a new business must obtain these missing resources through either acquisition or joint venture. Bank of America acquired Merrill Lynch in 2008 to obtain critical investment banking resources and capabilities that it lacked. The acquisition of these additional capabilities complemented Bank of America's strengths in corporate banking and opened up new business opportunities for Bank of America. Firms often acquire other companies as a way to enter foreign markets where they lack local marketing knowledge, distribution capabilities, and relationships with local suppliers or customers. McDonald's acquisition of Burghy, Italy's only national hamburger chain, offers an example.[10] If there are no good acquisition opportunities or if the firm wants to avoid the high cost of acquiring and integrating another firm, it may choose to enter via joint venture. This type of entry mode has the added advantage of spreading the risk of entering a new business, which is particularly attractive when uncertainty is high. DeBeers's joint venture with the luxury goods company LVMH provided DeBeers with the complementary marketing capabilities it needed to enter the diamond retailing business, as well as a partner to share the risk.

**The Question of Entry Barriers**    The second question to ask is whether entry barriers would prevent a new entrant from gaining a foothold and succeeding in the industry. If entry barriers are low and the industry is populated by small firms, internal development may be the preferred mode of entry. If entry barriers are high, the company may still be able to enter with ease if it has the requisite resources and capabilities for overcoming high barriers. For example, entry barriers due to reputational advantages may be surmounted by a diversified company with a widely known and trusted corporate name. But if the entry barriers cannot be overcome readily, then the only feasible entry route may be through acquisition of a well-established company. While entry barriers may also be overcome with a strong complementary joint venture, this mode is the more uncertain choice due to the lack of industry experience.

**The Question of Speed**    Speed is another determining factor in deciding how to go about entering a new business. Acquisition is a favored mode of entry when speed is of the essence, as is the case in rapidly changing industries where fast movers can secure long-term positioning advantages. Speed is important in industries where early movers gain experience-based advantages that grow ever larger over time as they move down the learning curve and in technology-based industries where there is a race to establish an industry standard or leading technological platform. But in other cases it can be better to enter a market after the uncertainties about technology or consumer preferences have been resolved and learn from the missteps of early entrants. In these cases, joint venture or internal development may be preferred.

**The Question of Comparative Cost**   The question of which mode of entry is most cost-effective is a critical one, given the need for a diversification strategy to pass the cost-of-entry test. Acquisition can be a high-cost mode of entry due to the need to pay a premium over the share price of the target company. When the premium is high, the price of the deal will exceed the worth of the acquired company as a stand-alone business by a substantial amount. Whether it is worth it to pay that high a price will depend on how much extra value will be created by the new combination of companies. Moreover, the true cost of an acquisition must include the **transaction costs** of identifying and evaluating potential targets, negotiating a price, and completing other aspects of deal making. In addition, the true cost must take into account the costs of integrating the acquired company into the parent company's portfolio of businesses.

Joint ventures may provide a way to conserve on such entry costs. But even here, there are organizational coordination costs and transaction costs that must be considered, including settling on the terms of the arrangement. If the partnership doesn't proceed smoothly and is not founded on trust, these costs may be significant.

> **CORE CONCEPT**
>
> **Transaction costs** are the costs of completing a business agreement or deal of some sort, over and above the price of the deal. They can include the costs of searching for an attractive target, the costs of evaluating its worth, bargaining costs, and the costs of completing the transaction.

# CHOOSING THE DIVERSIFICATION PATH: RELATED VERSUS UNRELATED BUSINESSES

Once a company decides to diversify, it faces the choice of whether to diversify into **related businesses, unrelated businesses,** or some mix of both. *Businesses are said to be related when their value chains exhibit competitively important cross-business relationships.* By this, we mean that there is a close correspondence between the businesses in terms of how they perform *key* value chain activities and the resources and capabilities each needs to perform those activities. The big appeal of related diversification is to build shareholder value by leveraging these cross-business relationships into competitive advantages, thus allowing the company as a whole to perform better than just the sum of its individual businesses. *Businesses are said to be unrelated when the resource requirements and key value chain activities are so dissimilar that no competitively important cross-business relationships exist.*

The next two sections explore the ins and outs of related and unrelated diversification.

> **CORE CONCEPT**
>
> **Related businesses** possess competitively valuable cross-business value chain and resource matchups; **unrelated businesses** have dissimilar value chains and resource requirements, with no competitively important cross-business relationships at the value chain level.

# DIVERSIFYING INTO RELATED BUSINESSES

A related diversification strategy involves building the company around businesses with *strategic fit with respect to key value chain activities and competitive assets.* **Strategic fit** exists whenever one or more activities constituting the value chains of different businesses are sufficiently similar as to present opportunities for cross-business sharing or

**CORE CONCEPT**

**Strategic fit** exists whenever one or more activities constituting the value chains of different businesses are sufficiently similar as to present opportunities for cross-business sharing or transferring of the resources and capabilities that enable these activities.

transferring of the resources and capabilities that enable these activities.[11] Prime examples of such opportunities include:

- *Transferring specialized expertise, technological know-how, or other valuable resources and capabilities from one business's value chain to another's.* Google's ability to transfer software developers and other information technology specialists from other business applications to the development of its Android mobile operating system and Chrome operating system for PCs aided considerably in the success of these new internal ventures.

- *Cost sharing between businesses by combining their related value chain activities into a single operation.* For instance, it is often feasible to manufacture the products of different businesses in a single plant, use the same warehouses for shipping and distribution, or have a single sales force for the products of different businesses if they are marketed to the same types of customers.

- *Exploiting common use of a well-known brand name.* For example, Yamaha's name in motorcycles gave the company instant credibility and recognition in entering the personal-watercraft business, allowing it to achieve a significant market share without spending large sums on advertising to establish a brand identity for the WaveRunner. Likewise, Apple's reputation for producing easy-to-operate computers was a competitive asset that facilitated the company's diversification into digital music players and smartphones.

- *Sharing other resources (besides brands) that support corresponding value chain activities across businesses.* After acquiring Marvel Comics in 2009, the Walt Disney Company saw to it that Marvel's iconic characters, such as Spiderman, Iron Man, and the Black Widow, were shared with many of the other Disney businesses, including its theme parks, retail stores, and video game business. (Disney's characters, starting with Mickey Mouse, have always been among the most valuable of its resources.) Automobile companies like Ford share resources such as their relationships with suppliers and dealer networks across their lines of business.

- *Engaging in cross-business collaboration and knowledge sharing to create new competitively valuable resources and capabilities.*

Related diversification is based on value chain matchups with respect to *key* value chain activities—those that play a central role in each business's strategy and that link to its industry's key success factors. Such matchups facilitate the sharing or transfer of the competitively important resources and capabilities that enable the performance of these activities and underlie each business's quest for competitive advantage. By facilitating the sharing or transferring of such important competitive assets, related diversification can boost each business's prospects for competitive success.

The resources and capabilities that are leveraged in related diversification are *specialized resources and capabilities.* By this, we mean that they have very *specific* applications; their use is restricted to a limited range of business contexts in which these applications are competitively relevant. Because they are adapted for particular applications, specialized resources and capabilities must be utilized by particular types of businesses operating in specific kinds of industries to have value; they have limited utility outside this specific range of industry and business applications. This is in contrast to *generalized resources and capabilities* (such as general management capabilities, human resource management capabilities, and general accounting services), which can be applied usefully across a wide range of industry and business types.

L'Oréal is the world's largest beauty products company, with more than $25 billion in revenues and a successful strategy of related diversification built upon leveraging a highly specialized set of resources and capabilities. These include 18 dermatologic and cosmetic research centers, R&D capabilities and scientific knowledge concerning skin and hair care, patents and secret formulas for hair and skin care products, and robotic applications developed specifically for testing the safety of hair and skin care products. These resources and capabilities are highly valuable for businesses focused on products for human skin and hair—they are *specialized* to such applications, and, in consequence, they are of little or no value beyond this restricted range of applications. To leverage these resources in a way that maximizes their potential value, L'Oréal has diversified into cosmetics, hair care products, skin care products, and fragrances (but not food, transportation, industrial services, or any application area far from the narrow domain in which its specialized resources are competitively relevant). L'Oréal's businesses are related to one another on the basis of its value-generating specialized resources and capabilities and the cross-business linkages among the value chain activities that they enable.

Corning's most competitively valuable resources and capabilities are specialized to applications concerning fiber optics and specialty glass and ceramics. Over the course of its 150-year history, it has developed an unmatched understanding of fundamental glass science and related technologies in the field of optics. Its capabilities now span a variety of sophisticated technologies and include expertise in domains such as custom glass composition, specialty glass melting and forming, precision optics, high-end transmissive coatings, and opto-mechanical materials. Corning has leveraged these specialized capabilities into a position of global leadership in five related market segments: display technologies based on glass substrates, environmental technologies using ceramic substrates and filters, optical fibers and cables for telecommunications, optical biosensors for drug discovery, and specialty materials employing advanced optics and specialty glass solutions. The market segments into which Corning has diversified are all related by their reliance on Corning's specialized capability set and by the many value chain activities that they have in common as a result.

General Mills has diversified into a closely related set of food businesses on the basis of its capabilities in the realm of "kitchen chemistry" and food production technologies. Its businesses include General Mills cereals, Pillsbury and Betty Crocker baking products, yogurts, organic foods, dinner mixes, canned goods, and snacks. Earlier it had diversified into restaurant businesses on the mistaken notion that all food businesses were related. As a result of exiting these businesses in the mid-1990s, the company was able to improve its overall profitability and strengthen its position in its remaining businesses. The lesson from its experience—and a takeaway for the managers of any diversified company—is that *it is not product relatedness that defines a well-crafted related diversification strategy*. Rather, the businesses must be related in terms of their key value chain activities and the specialized resources and capabilities that enable these activities.[12] An example is Citizen Holdings Company, whose products appear to be different (watches, miniature card calculators, handheld televisions) but are related in terms of their common reliance on miniaturization know-how and advanced precision technologies.[13]

While companies pursuing related diversification strategies may also have opportunities to share or transfer their *generalized* resources and capabilities (e.g., information systems; human resource management practices; accounting and tax services; budgeting, planning, and financial reporting systems; expertise in legal and regulatory affairs; and fringe-benefit management systems), *the most competitively valuable opportunities for resource sharing or transfer always come from leveraging their specialized resources and capabilities*. The reason for this is that specialized resources and capabilities drive the key value-creating activities that both connect the businesses (at points where there is strategic fit) and link to the key success factors in the markets

---

## CORE CONCEPT

Related diversification involves sharing or transferring *specialized* resources and capabilities. **Specialized resources and capabilities** have very specific applications and their use is limited to a restricted range of industry and business types, in contrast to **generalized resources and capabilities** that can be widely applied and can be deployed across a broad range of industry and business types.

where they are competitively relevant. Figure 8.1 illustrates the range of opportunities to share and/or transfer specialized resources and capabilities among the value chain activities of related businesses. It is important to recognize that *even though generalized resources and capabilities may be shared by multiple business units, such resource sharing alone cannot form the backbone of a strategy keyed to related diversification.*

## Identifying Cross-Business Strategic Fit along the Value Chain

Cross-business strategic fit can exist anywhere along the value chain—in R&D and technology activities, in supply chain activities and relationships with suppliers, in manufacturing, in sales and marketing, in distribution activities, or in customer service activities.[14]

**Strategic Fit in Supply Chain Activities**    Businesses with strategic fit with respect to their supply chain activities can perform better together because of the potential for skills transfer in procuring materials, the sharing of resources and capabilities in logistics, the benefits of added collaboration with common supply chain partners, and/or added leverage with shippers in securing volume discounts on incoming parts and components. Dell Computer's strategic partnerships with leading suppliers of microprocessors, circuit boards, disk drives, memory chips, flat-panel displays, wireless

**FIGURE 8.1**    Related Businesses Provide Opportunities to Benefit from Competitively Valuable Strategic Fit

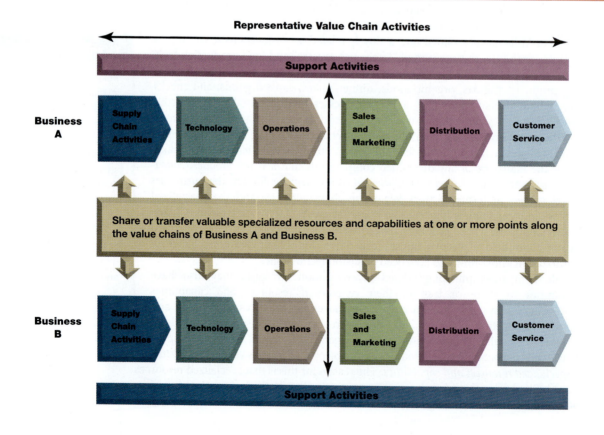

capabilities, long-life batteries, and other PC-related components have been an important element of the company's strategy to diversify into servers, data storage devices, networking components, and LCD TVs—products that include many components common to PCs and that can be sourced from the same strategic partners that provide Dell with PC components.

**Strategic Fit in R&D and Technology Activities**    Businesses with strategic fit in R&D or technology activities perform better together than apart because of potential cost savings in R&D, potentially shorter times in getting new products to market, and more innovative products or processes. Moreover, technological advances in one business can lead to increased sales for both. Technological innovations have been the driver behind the efforts of cable TV companies to diversify into high-speed Internet access (via the use of cable modems) and, further, to explore providing local and long-distance telephone service to residential and commercial customers either through a single wire or by means of VoIP (Voice over Internet Protocol) technology.

**Manufacturing-Related Strategic Fit**    Cross-business strategic fit in manufacturing-related activities can be exploited when a diversifier's expertise in quality manufacture and cost-efficient production methods can be transferred to another business. When Emerson Electric diversified into the chain-saw business, it transferred its expertise in low-cost manufacture to its newly acquired Beaird-Poulan business division. The transfer drove Beaird-Poulan's new strategy—to be the low-cost provider of chain-saw products—and fundamentally changed the way Beaird-Poulan chain saws were designed and manufactured. Another benefit of production-related value chain match-ups is the ability to consolidate production into a smaller number of plants and significantly reduce overall production costs. When snowmobile maker Bombardier diversified into motorcycles, it was able to set up motorcycle assembly lines in the same manufacturing facility where it was assembling snowmobiles. When Smucker's acquired Procter & Gamble's Jif peanut butter business, it was able to combine the manufacture of its own Smucker's peanut butter products with those of Jif, plus it gained greater leverage with vendors in purchasing its peanut supplies.

**Strategic Fit in Sales and Marketing Activities**    Various cost-saving opportunities spring from diversifying into businesses with closely related sales and marketing activities. When the products are sold directly to the same customers, sales costs can often be reduced by using a single sales force and avoiding having two different salespeople call on the same customer. The products of related businesses can be promoted at the same website and included in the same media ads and sales brochures. There may be opportunities to reduce costs by consolidating order processing and billing and using common promotional tie-ins. When global power-tool maker Black & Decker acquired Vector Products, it was able to use its own global sales force to sell the newly acquired Vector power inverters, vehicle battery chargers, and rechargeable spotlights because the types of customers that carried its power tools (discounters like Walmart and Target, home centers, and hardware stores) also stocked the types of products produced by Vector.

A second category of benefits arises when different businesses use similar sales and marketing approaches. In such cases, there may be competitively valuable opportunities to transfer selling, merchandising, advertising, and product differentiation skills from one business to another. Procter & Gamble's product lineup includes Folgers coffee, Tide laundry detergent, Crest toothpaste, Ivory soap, Charmin toilet tissue, Gillette razors and blades, Duracell batteries, Oral-B toothbrushes, and Head & Shoulders shampoo. All of these have different competitors and different supply chain and production requirements, but they all move through the same wholesale distribution systems, are sold in common retail settings to the same shoppers, are advertised and promoted in many of the same ways, and require the same marketing and merchandising skills.

**Distribution-Related Strategic Fit**   Businesses with closely related distribution activities can perform better together than apart because of potential cost savings in sharing the same distribution facilities or using many of the same wholesale distributors and retail dealers to access customers. When Conair Corporation acquired Allegro Manufacturing's travel bag and travel accessory business, it was able to consolidate its own distribution centers for hair dryers and curling irons with those of Allegro, thereby generating cost savings for both businesses. Likewise, since Conair products and Allegro's neck rests, ear plugs, luggage tags, and toiletry kits were sold by the same types of retailers (discount stores, supermarket chains, and drugstore chains), Conair was able to convince many of the retailers not carrying Allegro products to take on the line.

**Strategic Fit in Customer Service Activities**   Cost savings from sharing resources or for greater differentiation through skills transfer can come from strategic fit with respect to customer service activities, just as they do along other points of the value chain. For example, cost savings may come from consolidating after-sale service and repair organizations for the products of closely related businesses into a single operation. Likewise, different businesses can often use the same customer service infrastructure. For instance, an electric utility that diversifies into natural gas, water, appliance sales and repair services, and home security services can use the same customer data network, the same customer call centers and local offices, the same billing and customer accounting systems, and the same customer service infrastructure to support all of its products and services. Through the transfer of best practices in customer service across a set of related businesses or through sharing resources such as proprietary information about customer preferences, a multibusiness company can create a differentiation advantage through higher-quality customer service.

## Strategic Fit, Economies of Scope, and Competitive Advantage

What makes related diversification an attractive strategy is the opportunity to convert cross-business strategic fit into a competitive advantage over business rivals whose operations do not offer comparable strategic-fit benefits. The greater the relatedness among a diversified company's businesses, the bigger a company's window for converting strategic fit into competitive advantage via (1) transferring skills or knowledge, (2) combining related value chain activities to achieve lower costs, (3) leveraging the use of a well-respected brand name or other differentiation-enhancing resources, and (4) using cross-business collaboration and knowledge sharing to create new resources and capabilities and drive innovation.

**Strategic Fit and Economies of Scope**   Strategic fit in the value chain activities of a diversified corporation's different businesses opens up opportunities for economies of scope—a concept distinct from *economies of scale*. Economies of *scale* are cost savings that accrue directly from a larger-sized operation—for example, unit costs may be lower in a large plant than in a small plant. Economies of *scope*, however, *stem directly from strategic fit along the value chains of related businesses,* which in turn enables the businesses to share resources and transfer them from business to business at low cost. Such economies are open only to firms engaged in related diversification, since they are the result of sister businesses performing R&D together, transferring managers from one business to another, using common manufacturing or distribution facilities, sharing a common sales force or dealer network, using the same established brand name, and the like. *The greater the cross-business economies associated with resource sharing and transfer, the greater the potential for a related diversification strategy to give a multibusiness enterprise a cost advantage over rivals.*

### From Strategic Fit to Competitive Advantage, Added Profitability, and Gains in Shareholder Value

The cost advantage from economies of scope is due to the fact that resource sharing allows a multibusiness firm to spread resource costs across its businesses and to avoid the expense of having to acquire and maintain duplicate sets of resources—one for each business. But related diversified companies can benefit from strategic fit in other ways as well.

Sharing or transferring valuable specialized assets among the company's businesses can help each business perform its value chain activities more proficiently. This translates into competitive advantage for the businesses in one or two basic ways: (1) The businesses can contribute to greater efficiency and lower costs relative to their competitors, and/or (2) they can provide a basis for differentiation so that customers are willing to pay relatively more for the businesses' goods and services. In either or both of these ways, a firm with a well-executed related diversification strategy can boost the chances of its businesses attaining a competitive advantage.

The competitive advantage potential that flows from economies of scope and the capture of other strategic-fit benefits is what enables a company pursuing related diversification to achieve $1 + 1 = 3$ financial performance and the hoped-for gains in shareholder value. The strategic and business logic is compelling: Capturing the benefits of strategic fit along the value chains of its related businesses gives a diversified company a clear path to achieving competitive advantage over undiversified competitors and competitors whose own diversification efforts don't offer equivalent strategic-fit benefits.[15] Such competitive advantage potential provides a company with a dependable basis for earning profits and a return on investment that exceeds what the company's businesses could earn as stand-alone enterprises. Converting the competitive advantage potential into greater profitability is what fuels $1 + 1 = 3$ gains in shareholder value—the necessary outcome for satisfying *the better-off test* and proving the business merit of a company's diversification effort.

There are four things to bear in mind here:

1. Capturing cross-business strategic-fit benefits via a strategy of related diversification builds shareholder value in ways that shareholders cannot undertake by simply owning a portfolio of stocks of companies in different industries.

2. The capture of cross-business strategic-fit benefits is possible only via a strategy of related diversification.

3. The benefits of cross-business strategic fit come from the transferring or sharing of competitively valuable resources and capabilities among the businesses—resources and capabilities that are *specialized* to certain applications and have value only in specific types of industries and businesses.

4. The benefits of cross-business strategic fit are not automatically realized when a company diversifies into related businesses; *the benefits materialize only after management has successfully pursued internal actions to capture them.*

# DIVERSIFICATION INTO UNRELATED BUSINESSES

**LO 3**

Become aware of the merits and risks of corporate strategies keyed to unrelated diversification.

Unrelated diversification strategies discount the merits of pursuing cross-business strategic fit and, instead, focuses squarely on entering and operating businesses in industries that allow the company as a whole to increase its earnings. Companies that pursue a strategy of unrelated diversification generally exhibit a willingness to diversify into *any industry* where senior managers see an opportunity to realize consistently good financial results. Such companies are frequently labeled *conglomerates* because their business interests range broadly across diverse industries. Companies that pursue unrelated diversification nearly always enter new businesses by acquiring an established company rather than by forming a startup subsidiary within their own corporate structures or participating in joint ventures.

With a strategy of unrelated diversification, an acquisition is deemed to have potential if it passes the industry attractiveness and cost-of-entry tests and if it has good prospects for attractive financial performance. Thus, with an unrelated diversification strategy, company managers spend much time and effort screening acquisition candidates and evaluating the pros and cons of keeping or divesting existing businesses, using such criteria as:

- Whether the business can meet corporate targets for profitability and return on investment.
- Whether the business is in an industry with attractive growth potential.
- Whether the business is big enough to contribute *significantly* to the parent firm's bottom line.

But the key to successful unrelated diversification is to go beyond these considerations and ensure that the strategy passes the better-off test as well. This test requires more than just growth in revenues; it requires *growth in profits*—beyond what could be achieved by a mutual fund or a holding company that owns the businesses without adding any value. Unless the different businesses are more profitable together under the corporate umbrella than they are apart as independent businesses, *the strategy cannot create economic value for shareholders.* And unless it does so, there is *no real justification for unrelated diversification,* since top executives have a fiduciary responsibility to maximize long-term shareholder value.

## Building Shareholder Value via Unrelated Diversification

Given the absence of cross-business strategic fit with which to create competitive advantages, building economic shareholder value via unrelated diversification ultimately hinges on the ability of the parent company to improve its businesses via other means. Critical to this endeavor is the role that the parent company plays *as a corporate parent.*[16] To the extent that a company has strong *parenting capabilities*—capabilities that involve nurturing, guiding, grooming, and governing constituent businesses—a corporate parent can propel its businesses forward and help them gain ground over their market rivals. Corporate parents also contribute to the competitiveness of their unrelated businesses by sharing or transferring *generalized resources and capabilities* across the businesses— competitive assets that have utility in *any type* of industry and that can be leveraged across a wide range of business types as a result. Examples of the kinds of generalized resources that a corporate parent leverages in unrelated diversification include the corporation's reputation, credit rating, and access to financial markets, governance mechanisms, a corporate ethics program, a central data and communications center, shared administrative resources such as public relations and legal services, and common systems for functions such as budgeting, financial reporting, and quality control.

### The Benefits of Astute Corporate Parenting

One of the most important ways that corporate parents contribute to the success of their businesses is by offering high-level oversight and guidance.[17] The top executives of a large diversified corporation have among them many years of accumulated experience in a variety of business settings and can often contribute expert problem-solving skills, creative strategy suggestions, and first-rate advice and guidance on how to improve competitiveness and financial performance to the heads of the company's various business subsidiaries. This is especially true in the case of newly acquired businesses. Particularly astute high-level guidance from corporate executives can help the subsidiaries perform better than they would otherwise be able to do through the efforts of the business-unit heads alone.[18] The outstanding leadership of Royal Little, the founder of Textron, was a major reason that the company became an exemplar of the unrelated diversification strategy while he was CEO. Little's bold moves transformed the company from its origins as a small textile manufacturer into a global powerhouse known for its Bell helicopters, Cessna aircraft, and host of other strong brands in a wide array of industries. Norm Wesley, CEO of the conglomerate Fortune Brands from 1999 to 2007, is similarly credited with driving the sharp rise in the company's stock price while he was at the helm. Fortune Brands became the $7 billion maker of products ranging from spirits (e.g., Jim Beam bourbon and rye, Gilbey's gin and vodka, Courvoisier cognac) to golf products (e.g., Titleist golf balls and clubs, FootJoy golf shoes and apparel, Scotty Cameron putters) to hardware (e.g., Moen faucets, American Lock security devices). (In 2011, Fortune Brands was converted into two separate entities, Beam Inc. and Fortune Brands Home & Security).

Corporate parents can also create added value for their businesses by providing them with other types of generalized or parenting resources that lower the operating costs of the individual businesses or that enhance their operating effectiveness. The administrative resources located at a company's corporate headquarters are a prime example. They typically include legal services, accounting expertise and tax services, and other elements of the administrative infrastructure, such as risk management capabilities, information technology resources, and public relations capabilities. Providing individual business with generalized support resources such as these creates value by lowering companywide overhead costs, since each business would otherwise have to duplicate the centralized activities.

Corporate brands that do not connote any specific type of product are another type of generalized corporate resource that can be shared among unrelated businesses. GE's brand is an example, having been applied to businesses as diverse as financial services (GE Capital), medical imaging (GE medical diagnostics), and lighting (GE lightbulbs). Corporate brands that are applied in this fashion are sometimes called *umbrella brands.* Utilizing a well-known corporate name (GE) in a diversified company's individual businesses has potential not only to lower costs (by spreading the fixed cost of developing and maintaining the brand over many businesses) but also to enhance each business's customer value proposition by linking its products to a name that consumers trust. In similar fashion, a corporation's reputation for well-crafted products, for product reliability, or for trustworthiness can lead to greater customer willingness to purchase the products of a wider range of a diversified company's businesses. Incentive systems,

**CORE CONCEPT**

**Corporate parenting** refers to the role that a diversified corporation plays in nurturing its component businesses through the provision of top management expertise, disciplined control, financial resources, and other types of generalized resources and capabilities such as long-term planning systems, business development skills, management development processes, and incentive systems.

financial control systems, and a company's culture are other types of generalized corporate resources that may prove useful in enhancing the daily operations of a diverse set of businesses.

Two other commonly employed ways for corporate parents to add value to their unrelated businesses are discussed next.

## Judicious Cross-Business Allocation of Financial Resources

An umbrella brand is a corporate brand name that can be applied to a wide assortment of business types. As such, it is a generalized resource that can be leveraged in unrelated diversification.

By reallocating surplus cash flows from some businesses to fund the capital requirements of other businesses—in essence, having the company serve as an internal capital market—corporate parents may also be able to create value. Such actions can be particularly important when interest rates are high or credit is unusually tight (such as in the wake of the worldwide banking crisis that began in 2008) or in economies with less well developed capital markets. Under these conditions, with strong financial resources a corporate parent can add value by shifting funds from business units generating excess cash (more than they need to fund their own operating requirements and new capital investment opportunities) to other, cash-short businesses with appealing growth prospects. A parent company's ability to function as its own internal capital market enhances overall corporate performance and boosts shareholder value to the extent that its top managers have better access to information about investment opportunities internal to the firm than do external financiers and can avoid the costs of external borrowing.

## Acquiring and Restructuring Undervalued Companies

**CORE CONCEPT**

**Restructuring** refers to overhauling and streamlining the activities of a business—combining plants with excess capacity, selling off underutilized assets, reducing unnecessary expenses, and otherwise improving the productivity and profitability of a company.

Another way for parent companies to add value to unrelated businesses is by acquiring weakly performing companies at a bargain price and then *restructuring* their operations in ways that produce sometimes dramatic increases in profitability. **Restructuring** refers to overhauling and streamlining the operations of a business—combining plants with excess capacity, selling off underutilized assets, reducing unnecessary expenses, revamping its product offerings, consolidating administrative functions to reduce overhead costs, and otherwise improving the operating efficiency and profitability of a company. Restructuring generally involves transferring seasoned managers to the newly acquired business, either to replace the top layers of management or to step in temporarily until the business is returned to profitability or is well on its way to becoming a major market contender.

Restructuring is often undertaken when a diversified company acquires a new business that is performing well below levels that the corporate parent believes are achievable. Diversified companies that have capabilities in restructuring (sometimes called *turnaround capabilities*) are able to significantly boost the performance of weak businesses in a relatively wide range of industries. Newell Rubbermaid (whose diverse product line includes Sharpie pens, Levolor window treatments, Goody hair accessories, Calphalon cookware, and Lenox power and hand tools) developed such a strong set of turnaround capabilities that the company was said to "Newellize" the businesses it acquired.

Successful unrelated diversification strategies based on restructuring require the parent company to have considerable expertise in identifying underperforming target companies and in negotiating attractive acquisition prices so that each acquisition passes the cost-of-entry test. The capabilities in this regard of Lords James Hanson and Gordon White, who headed up the storied British conglomerate Hanson Trust, played a large part in Hanson's impressive record of profitability through the early 1990s.

# The Path to Greater Shareholder Value through Unrelated Diversification

For a strategy of unrelated diversification to produce companywide financial results above and beyond what the businesses could generate operating as stand-alone entities, corporate executives must do three things:

1. Diversify into businesses that can produce consistently good earnings and returns on investment (to satisfy the attractiveness test).
2. Negotiate favorable acquisition prices (to satisfy the cost-of-entry test).
3. Do a superior job of corporate parenting via high-level managerial oversight and resource sharing, financial resource allocation and portfolio management, or restructuring underperforming businesses (to satisfy the better-off test).

The best corporate parents understand the nature and value of the kinds of resources at their command and know how to leverage them effectively across their businesses. Those that are able to create more value in their businesses than other diversified companies have what is called a **parenting advantage**.[19] When a corporation has a parenting advantage, its top executives have the best chance of being able to craft and execute an unrelated diversification strategy that can satisfy all three tests and truly enhance long-term economic shareholder value.

## CORE CONCEPT

A diversified company has a parenting advantage when it is more able than other companies to boost the combined performance of its individual businesses through high-level guidance, general oversight, and other corporate-level contributions.

# The Drawbacks of Unrelated Diversification

Unrelated diversification strategies have two important negatives that undercut the pluses: very demanding managerial requirements and limited competitive advantage potential.

### Demanding Managerial Requirements

Successfully managing a set of fundamentally different businesses operating in fundamentally different industry and competitive environments is a very challenging and exceptionally difficult proposition.[20] Consider, for example, that corporations like General Electric and Berkshire Hathaway have dozens of business subsidiaries making hundreds and sometimes thousands of products. While headquarters executives can glean information about the industry from third-party sources, ask lots of questions when making occasional visits to the operations of the different businesses, and do their best to learn about the company's different businesses, they still remain heavily dependent on briefings from business-unit heads and on "managing by the numbers"—that is, keeping a close track on the financial and operating results of each subsidiary. Managing by the numbers works well enough when business conditions are normal and the heads of the various business units are capable of consistently meeting their numbers. But problems arise if things start to go awry in a business and corporate management has to get deeply involved in the problems of a business it does not know all that much about. Because every business tends to encounter rough sledding at some juncture, unrelated diversification is thus a somewhat risky strategy from a managerial perspective.[21] Just one or two unforeseen problems or big strategic mistakes can cause a precipitous drop in corporate earnings and crash the parent company's stock price.

Hence, competently overseeing a set of widely diverse businesses can turn out to be much harder than it sounds. In practice, comparatively few companies have proved that they have top management capabilities that are up to the task. There are far more companies whose corporate executives have failed at delivering consistently good financial results with an unrelated diversification strategy than there are companies with corporate executives who have been successful.[22] Unless a company truly has a parenting advantage, the odds are that the result of unrelated diversification will be $1 + 1 = 2$ or even less.

**Limited Competitive Advantage Potential**   The second big negative is that *unrelated diversification offers a limited potential for competitive advantage beyond what each individual business can generate on its own.* Unlike a related diversification strategy, unrelated diversification provides no cross-business strategic-fit benefits that allow each business to perform its key value chain activities in a more efficient and effective manner. A cash-rich corporate parent pursuing unrelated diversification can provide its subsidiaries with much-needed capital, may achieve economies of scope in activities relying on generalized corporate resources, and may even offer some managerial know-how to help resolve problems in particular business units, but otherwise it has little to offer in the way of enhancing the competitive strength of its individual business units. In comparison to the highly specialized resources that facilitate related diversification, the generalized resources that support unrelated diversification tend to be relatively low value, for the simple reason that they are more common. Unless they are of exceptionally high quality (such as GE's world-renowned general management capabilities), resources and capabilities that are generalized in nature are less likely to provide a source of competitive advantage for diversified companies. Without the competitive advantage potential of strategic fit in strategically important value chain activities, consolidated performance of an unrelated group of businesses stands to be little more than the sum of what the individual business units could achieve if they were independent, in most circumstances.

> Relying solely on leveraging generalized resources and the expertise of corporate executives to wisely manage a set of unrelated businesses is *a much weaker foundation for enhancing shareholder value* than is a strategy of related diversification.

## Misguided Reasons for Pursuing Unrelated Diversification

Companies sometimes pursue unrelated diversification for reasons that are misguided. These include the following:

- *Risk reduction.* Spreading the company's investments over a set of diverse industries to spread risk cannot create long-term shareholder value since the company's shareholders can more flexibly (and more efficiently) reduce their exposure to risk by investing in a diversified portfolio of stocks and bonds.
- *Growth.* While unrelated diversification may enable a company to achieve rapid or continuous growth, firms that pursue growth for growth's sake are unlikely to maximize shareholder value. Only *profitable growth*—the kind that comes from creating added value for shareholders—can justify a strategy of unrelated diversification.
- *Stabilization.* Managers sometimes pursue broad diversification in the hope that market downtrends in some of the company's businesses will be partially offset by cyclical upswings in its other businesses, thus producing somewhat less earnings volatility. In actual practice, however, there's no convincing evidence that the consolidated profits of firms with unrelated diversification strategies are more stable or less subject to reversal in periods of recession and economic stress than the profits of firms with related diversification strategies.
- *Managerial motives.* Unrelated diversification can provide benefits to managers such as higher compensation (which tends to increase with firm size and degree of diversification) and reduced employment risk. Pursuing diversification for these reasons will likely reduce shareholder value and violate managers' fiduciary responsibilities.

Because unrelated diversification strategies *at their best* have only a limited potential for creating long-term economic value for shareholders, it is essential that managers not compound this problem by taking a misguided approach toward unrelated diversification, in pursuit of objectives that are more likely to destroy shareholder value than create it.

> Only *profitable growth*— the kind that comes from creating added value for shareholders—can justify a strategy of unrelated diversification.

# COMBINATION RELATED-UNRELATED DIVERSIFICATION STRATEGIES

There's nothing to preclude a company from diversifying into both related and unrelated businesses. Indeed, in actual practice the business makeup of diversified companies varies considerably. Some diversified companies are really *dominant-business enterprises*—one major "core" business accounts for 50 to 80 percent of total revenues and a collection of small related or unrelated businesses accounts for the remainder. Some diversified companies are *narrowly diversified* around a few (two to five) related or unrelated businesses. Others are *broadly diversified* around a wide-ranging collection of related businesses, unrelated businesses, or a mixture of both. A number of multibusiness enterprises have diversified into unrelated areas but have a collection of related businesses within each area—thus giving them a business portfolio consisting of *several unrelated groups of related businesses.* There's ample room for companies to customize their diversification strategies to incorporate elements of both related and unrelated diversification, as may suit their own competitive asset profile and strategic vision. *Combination related-unrelated diversification strategies have particular appeal for companies with a mix of valuable competitive assets, covering the spectrum from generalized to specialized resources and capabilities.*

Figure 8.2 shows the range of alternatives for companies pursuing diversification.

# EVALUATING THE STRATEGY OF A DIVERSIFIED COMPANY

Strategic analysis of diversified companies builds on the concepts and methods used for single-business companies. But there are some additional aspects to consider and a couple of new analytical tools to master. The procedure for evaluating the pluses and minuses of a diversified company's strategy and deciding what actions to take to improve the company's performance involves six steps:

> **LO 4**
>
> Gain command of the analytical tools for evaluating a company's diversification strategy.

1. Assessing the attractiveness of the industries the company has diversified into, both individually and as a group.
2. Assessing the competitive strength of the company's business units.
3. Evaluating the extent of cross-business strategic fit along the value chains of the company's various business units.
4. Checking whether the firm's resources fit the requirements of its present business lineup.
5. Ranking the performance prospects of the businesses from best to worst and determining a priority for allocating resources.
6. Crafting new strategic moves to improve overall corporate performance.

**FIGURE 8.2** Three Strategy Alternatives for Pursuing Diversification

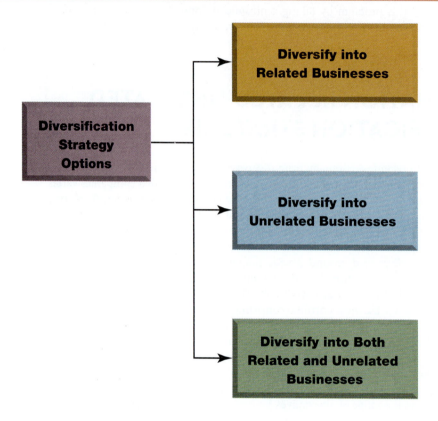

The core concepts and analytical techniques underlying each of these steps merit further discussion.

## Step 1: Evaluating Industry Attractiveness

A principal consideration in evaluating a diversified company's business makeup and the caliber of its strategy is the attractiveness of the industries in which it has business operations. Several questions need to be answered:

1. *Does each industry the company has diversified into represent a good market for the company to be in—does it pass the industry attractiveness test?*
2. *Which of the company's industries are most attractive, and which are least attractive?*
3. *How appealing is the whole group of industries in which the company has invested?*

The more attractive the industries (both individually and as a group) a diversified company is in, the better its prospects for good long-term performance.

**Calculating Industry Attractiveness Scores for Each Industry into Which the Company Has Diversified**    A simple and reliable analytical tool for gauging industry attractiveness involves calculating quantitative industry attractiveness scores based on a variety of factors. First comes a consideration of the conditions of each business's macro-environment as well as its competitive environment—the very same factors that are used to evaluate the strategy of a single-business company, as discussed in Chapter 3. Key indicators of industry attractiveness thus include:

- Social, political, regulatory, and environmental factors
- Seasonal and cyclical factors
- Industry uncertainty and business risk
- Market size and projected growth rate
- Industry profitability
- The intensity of competition (five forces)
- Emerging opportunities and threats

Next, it is critically important to consider those aspects of industry attractiveness that pertain *specifically* to a company's diversification strategy. This involves looking at all the industries in which the company has invested to assess their resource requirements and to consider whether there is good cross-industry strategic fit. The following two measures are typically used to gauge industry attractiveness from this multibusiness perspective:

- *The presence of cross-industry strategic fit.* The more an industry's value chain and resource requirements match up well with the value chain activities of other industries in which the company has operations, the more attractive the industry is to a firm pursuing related diversification.
- *Matching resource requirements.* Industries having resource requirements that match those of the parent company or are otherwise within the company's reach are more attractive than industries in which capital and other resource requirements could strain corporate financial resources and organizational capabilities.

Each attractiveness measure is then assigned a weight reflecting its relative importance in determining an industry's attractiveness, since not all attractiveness measures are equally important. The intensity of competition in an industry should nearly always carry a high weight (say, 0.20 to 0.30). Strategic-fit considerations should be assigned a high weight in the case of companies with related diversification strategies; but for companies with an unrelated diversification strategy, strategic fit with other industries may be dropped from the list of attractiveness measures altogether. The importance weights must add up to 1.

Finally, each industry is rated on each of the chosen industry attractiveness measures, using a rating scale of 1 to 10 (where a *high* rating signifies *high* attractiveness, and a *low* rating signifies *low* attractiveness). *Keep in mind here that the more intensely competitive an industry is, the lower the attractiveness rating for that industry.* Likewise, the more the resource requirements associated with being in a particular industry are beyond the parent company's reach, the lower the attractiveness rating. On the other hand, the presence of good cross-industry strategic fit should be given a very high attractiveness rating, since there is good potential for competitive advantage and added shareholder value. Weighted attractiveness scores are then calculated by multiplying the industry's rating on each measure by the corresponding weight. For example, a rating of 8 times a weight of 0.25 gives a weighted attractiveness score of 2.00. The sum of the weighted scores for all the attractiveness measures provides an overall industry attractiveness score. This procedure is illustrated in Table 8.1.

### Interpreting the Industry Attractiveness Scores
Industries with a score much below 5 probably do not pass the attractiveness test. If a company's industry attractiveness scores are all above 5, it is probably fair to conclude that the group

## TABLE 8.1    Calculating Weighted Industry Attractiveness Scores

| Industry Attractiveness Measures | Importance Weight | Industry A | | Industry B | | Industry C | |
|---|---|---|---|---|---|---|---|
| | | Attractiveness Rating | Weighted Score | Attractiveness Rating | Weighted Score | Attractiveness Rating | Weighted Score |
| Market size and projected growth rate | 0.10 | 8 | 0.80 | 3 | 0.30 | 5 | 0.50 |
| Intensity of competition | 0.25 | 8 | 2.00 | 2 | 0.50 | 5 | 1.25 |
| Emerging opportunities and threats | 0.10 | 6 | 0.60 | 5 | 0.50 | 4 | 0.40 |
| Cross-industry strategic fit | 0.20 | 8 | 1.60 | 2 | 0.40 | 3 | 0.60 |
| Resource requirements | 0.10 | 6 | 0.60 | 5 | 0.50 | 4 | 0.40 |
| Seasonal and cyclical influences | 0.05 | 9 | 0.45 | 5 | 0.25 | 10 | 0.50 |
| Social, political, regulatory, and environmental factors | 0.05 | 8 | 0.40 | 3 | 0.15 | 7 | 0.35 |
| Industry profitability | 0.10 | 5 | 0.50 | 3 | 0.30 | 6 | 0.60 |
| Industry uncertainty and business risk | 0.05 | 5 | 0.25 | 1 | 0.05 | 10 | 0.50 |
| **Sum of importance weights** | **1.00** | | | | | | |
| **Weighted overall industry attractiveness scores** | | | **7.20** | | **2.95** | | **5.10** |

[Rating scale: 1 = Very unattractive to company; 10 = Very attractive to company]

of industries the company operates in is attractive as a whole. But the group of industries takes on a decidedly lower degree of attractiveness as the number of industries with scores below 5 increases, especially if industries with low scores account for a sizable fraction of the company's revenues.

For a diversified company to be a strong performer, a substantial portion of its revenues and profits must come from business units with relatively high attractiveness scores. It is particularly important that a diversified company's principal businesses be in industries with a good outlook for growth and above-average profitability. Having a big fraction of the company's revenues and profits come from industries with slow growth, low profitability, or intense competition tends to drag overall company performance down. Business units in the least attractive industries are potential candidates for divestiture, unless they are positioned strongly enough to overcome the unattractive aspects of their industry environments or they are a strategically important component of the company's business makeup.

## Step 2: Evaluating Business-Unit Competitive Strength

The second step in evaluating a diversified company is to appraise how strongly positioned each of its business units is in its respective industry. Doing an appraisal of each business unit's strength and competitive position in its industry not only reveals its chances for industry success but also provides a basis for ranking the units from competitively strongest to weakest.

### Calculating Competitive Strength Scores for Each Business

**Unit** Quantitative measures of each business unit's competitive strength can be calculated using a procedure similar to that for measuring industry attractiveness. The following factors are used in quantifying the competitive strengths of a diversified company's business subsidiaries:

> Using relative market share to measure competitive strength is analytically superior to using straight-percentage market share.

- Relative market share—A business unit's *relative market share* is defined as the ratio of its market share to the market share held by the largest rival firm in the industry, with market share measured in unit volume, not dollars. For instance, if business A has a market-leading share of 40 percent and its largest rival has 30 percent, A's relative market share is 1.33. (Note that only business units that are market share leaders in their respective industries can have relative market shares greater than 1.0.) If business B has a 15 percent market share and B's largest rival has 30 percent, B's relative market share is 0.5. *The further below 1.0 a business unit's relative market share is, the weaker its competitive strength and market position vis-à-vis rivals.*

- Costs relative to competitors' costs—There's reason to expect that business units with higher relative market shares have lower unit costs than competitors with lower relative market shares because of the possibility of scale economies and experience or learning-curve effects.

- Ability to match or beat rivals on key product attributes—A company's competitiveness depends in part on being able to satisfy buyer expectations with regard to features, product performance, reliability, service, and other important attributes.

- Brand image and reputation—A widely known and respected brand name is a valuable competitive asset in most industries.

- Other competitively valuable resources and capabilities—Valuable resources and capabilities, including those accessed through alliances and collaborative partnerships, enhance a company's ability to compete successfully and perhaps contend for industry leadership.

- Ability to benefit from strategic fit with the company's other businesses—Strategic fit with other businesses within the company enhance a business unit's competitive strength and may provide a competitive edge.

- Ability to exercise bargaining leverage with key suppliers or customers—Having bargaining leverage signals competitive strength and can be a source of competitive advantage.

- Profitability relative to competitors—Above-average profitability is a signal of competitive advantage, while below-average profitability usually denotes competitive disadvantage.

After settling on a set of competitive strength measures that are well matched to the circumstances of the various business units, weights indicating each measure's importance need to be assigned. As in the assignment of weights to industry attractiveness measures, the importance weights must add up to 1.0. Each business unit is then rated on each of the chosen strength measures, using a rating scale of 1 to 10 (where a *high* rating signifies competitive *strength* and a *low* rating signifies competitive *weakness*). In the event that the available information is too skimpy to confidently assign a rating value to a business unit on a particular strength measure, it is usually best to use a score of 5, which avoids biasing the overall score either up or down. Weighted strength ratings are calculated by multiplying the business unit's rating on each strength measure by the assigned weight. For example, a strength score of 6 times a weight of 0.15 gives a weighted strength rating of 0.90. The sum of the weighted ratings across all the strength measures provides a quantitative measure of a business unit's overall market strength and competitive standing. Table 8.2 provides sample calculations of competitive strength ratings for three businesses.

**TABLE 8.2**  **Calculating Weighted Competitive Strength Scores for a Diversified Company's Business Units**

| | | Competitive Strength Assessments | | | | | |
| | | Business A in Industry A | | Business B in Industry B | | Business C in Industry C | |
| Competitive Strength Measures | Importance Weight | Strength Rating | Weighted Score | Strength Rating | Weighted Score | Strength Rating | Weighted Score |
|---|---|---|---|---|---|---|---|
| Relative market share | 0.15 | 10 | 1.50 | 2 | 0.30 | 6 | 0.90 |
| Costs relative to competitors' costs | 0.20 | 7 | 1.40 | 4 | 0.80 | 5 | 1.00 |
| Ability to match or beat rivals on key product attributes | 0.05 | 9 | 0.45 | 5 | 0.25 | 8 | 0.40 |
| Ability to benefit from strategic fit with sister businesses | 0.20 | 8 | 1.60 | 4 | 0.80 | 8 | 0.80 |
| Bargaining leverage with suppliers/customers | 0.05 | 9 | 0.45 | 2 | 0.10 | 6 | 0.30 |
| Brand image and reputation | 0.10 | 9 | 0.90 | 4 | 0.40 | 7 | 0.70 |
| Competitively valuable capabilities | 0.15 | 7 | 1.05 | 2 | 0.30 | 5 | 0.75 |
| Profitability relative to competitors | 0.10 | 5 | 0.50 | 2 | 0.20 | 4 | 0.40 |
| **Sum of importance weights** | **1.00** | | | | | | |
| **Weighted overall competitive strength scores** | | | **7.85** | | **3.15** | | **5.25** |

[Rating scale: 1 = Very weak; 10 = Very strong]

**Interpreting the Competitive Strength Scores**    Business units with competitive strength ratings above 6.7 (on a scale of 1 to 10) are strong market contenders in their industries. Businesses with ratings in the 3.3-to-6.7 range have moderate competitive strength vis-à-vis rivals. Businesses with ratings below 3.3 are in competitively weak market positions. If a diversified company's business units all have competitive strength scores above 5, it is fair to conclude that its business units are all fairly strong market contenders in their respective industries. But as the number of business units with scores below 5 increases, there's reason to question whether the company can perform well with so many businesses in relatively weak competitive positions. This concern takes on even more importance when business units with low scores account for a sizable fraction of the company's revenues.

**Using a Nine-Cell Matrix to Simultaneously Portray Industry Attractiveness and Competitive Strength**    The industry attractiveness and business strength scores can be used to portray the strategic positions of each business in a diversified company. Industry attractiveness is plotted on the vertical axis and competitive strength on the horizontal axis. A nine-cell grid emerges from dividing the vertical axis into three regions (high, medium, and low attractiveness) and the horizontal axis into three regions (strong, average, and weak competitive strength). *Each business unit is plotted on the nine-cell matrix according to its overall attractiveness score and strength score, and then it is shown as a "bubble."* The size of each bubble is scaled to the percentage of revenues the business generates relative to total corporate revenues. The bubbles in Figure 8.3 were located on the grid using the three industry attractiveness scores from Table 8.1 and the strength scores for the three business units in Table 8.2.

The locations of the business units on the attractiveness–strength matrix provide valuable guidance in deploying corporate resources. In general, *a diversified company's best prospects for good overall performance involve concentrating corporate resources on business units having the greatest competitive strength and industry attractiveness.* Businesses plotted in the three cells in the upper left portion of the attractiveness–strength matrix have both favorable industry attractiveness and competitive strength and should receive a high investment priority. Business units plotted in these three cells (like business A) are referred to as "grow and build" businesses because of their capability to drive future increases in shareholder value.

Next in priority come businesses positioned in the three diagonal cells stretching from the lower left to the upper right (like business C in Figure 8.3). Such businesses usually merit intermediate priority in the parent's resource allocation ranking. However, some businesses in the medium-priority diagonal cells may have brighter or dimmer prospects than others. For example, a small business in the upper right cell of the matrix, despite being in a highly attractive industry, may occupy too weak a competitive position in its industry to justify the investment and resources needed to turn it into a strong market contender.

Businesses in the three cells in the lower right corner of the matrix (like business B in Figure 8.3) have comparatively low industry attractiveness and minimal competitive strength, making them weak performers with little potential for improvement. At best, they have the lowest claim on corporate resources and often are good candidates for being divested (sold to other companies). However, there are occasions when a business located in the three lower-right cells generates sizable positive cash flows. It may make sense to retain such businesses and manage them in a manner calculated to squeeze out the maximum cash flows from operations—the cash flows from

## FIGURE 8.3 A Nine-Cell Industry Attractiveness–Competitive Strength Matrix

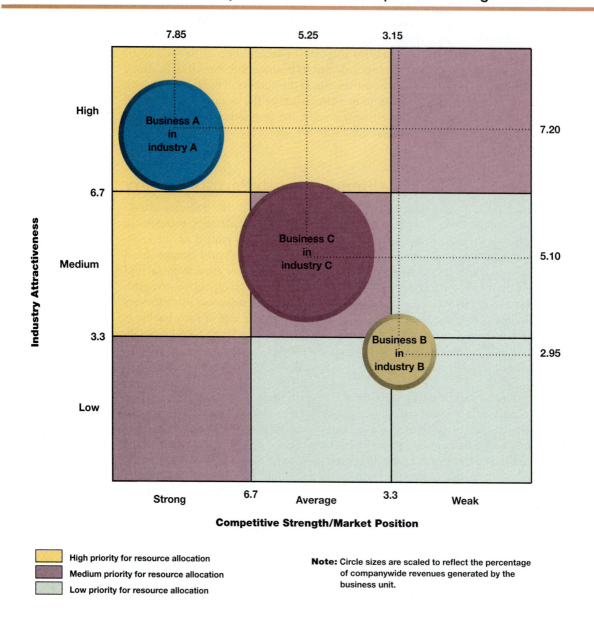

low-performing/low-potential businesses can then be diverted to financing expansion of business units with greater potential for revenue and profit growth.

The nine-cell attractiveness–strength matrix provides clear, strong logic for why a diversified company needs to consider both industry attractiveness and business strength in allocating resources and investment capital to its different businesses. A good case can be made for concentrating resources in those businesses that enjoy higher degrees of attractiveness and competitive strength, being very selective in making investments in businesses with intermediate positions on the grid, and withdrawing resources from businesses that are lower in attractiveness and strength unless they offer exceptional profit or cash flow potential.

# Step 3: Determining the Competitive Value of Strategic Fit in Diversified Companies

While this step can be bypassed for diversified companies whose businesses are all unrelated (since, by design, strategic fit is lacking), assessing the degree of strategic fit across its businesses is central to evaluating a company's related diversification strategy. *But more than just strategic-fit identification is needed. The real test is what competitive value can be generated from strategic fit.* To what extent can cost savings be realized? How much competitive value will come from the cross-business transfer of skills, technology, or intellectual capital? Will transferring a potent brand name to the products of other businesses increase sales significantly? Will cross-business collaboration to create or strengthen competitive capabilities lead to significant gains in the marketplace or in financial performance? Without significant strategic fit and dedicated company efforts to capture the benefits, one has to be skeptical about the potential for a diversified company's businesses to perform better together than apart.

Figure 8.4 illustrates the process of comparing the value chains of a company's businesses and identifying opportunities to exploit competitively valuable cross-business strategic fit.

> The greater the value of cross-business strategic fit in enhancing a company's performance in the marketplace or on the bottom line, the more competitively powerful is its strategy of related diversification.

**FIGURE 8.4** Identifying the Competitive Advantage Potential of Cross-Business Strategic Fit

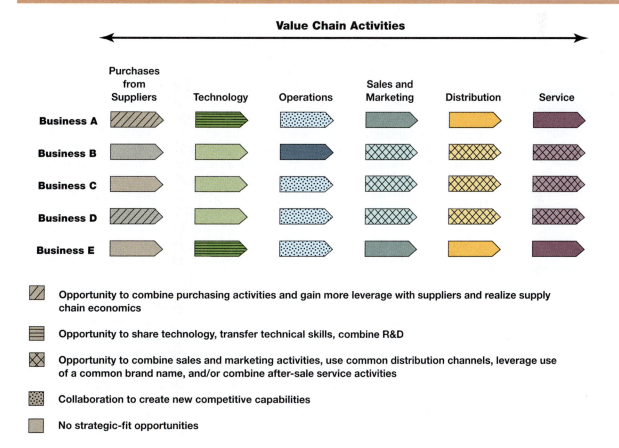

**Value Chain Activities**

|  | Purchases from Suppliers | Technology | Operations | Sales and Marketing | Distribution | Service |
|---|---|---|---|---|---|---|
| **Business A** |  |  |  |  |  |  |
| **Business B** |  |  |  |  |  |  |
| **Business C** |  |  |  |  |  |  |
| **Business D** |  |  |  |  |  |  |
| **Business E** |  |  |  |  |  |  |

Opportunity to combine purchasing activities and gain more leverage with suppliers and realize supply chain economics

Opportunity to share technology, transfer technical skills, combine R&D

Opportunity to combine sales and marketing activities, use common distribution channels, leverage use of a common brand name, and/or combine after-sale service activities

Collaboration to create new competitive capabilities

No strategic-fit opportunities

# Step 4: Checking for Resource Fit

The businesses in a diversified company's lineup need to exhibit good **resource fit**. In firms with a related diversification strategy, resource fit exists *when the firm's businesses have matching resource requirements at points along their value chains* that are critical for the businesses' market success. Matching resource requirements are important in related diversification because they facilitate resource sharing and low-cost transfer. In companies pursuing unrelated diversification, resource fit exists when the company has solid *parenting capabilities or resources of a general nature that it can share or transfer to its component businesses*. Firms pursuing related diversification and firms with combination related-unrelated diversification strategies can also benefit from leveraging corporate parenting capabilities and other general resources. Another dimension of resource fit that concerns all types of multibusiness firms is whether they have resources sufficient to support their group of businesses without being spread too thin.

## Financial Resource Fit

**Financial Resource Fit**    One dimension of resource fit concerns whether a diversified company can generate the internal cash flows sufficient to fund the capital requirements of its businesses, pay its dividends, meet its debt obligations, and otherwise remain financially healthy. (Financial resources, including the firm's ability to borrow or otherwise raise funds, are a generalized type of resource.) While additional capital can usually be raised in financial markets, it is important for a diversified firm to have a healthy **internal capital market** that can support the financial requirements of its business lineup. The greater the extent to which a diversified company is able to fund investment in its businesses through internally generated cash flows rather than from equity issues or borrowing, the more powerful its financial resource fit and the less dependent the firm is on external financial resources. This can provide a competitive advantage over single business rivals when credit market conditions are tight, as they have been in the United States and abroad in recent years.

A **portfolio approach** to ensuring financial fit among a firm's businesses is based on the fact that different businesses have different cash flow and investment characteristics. For example, business units in rapidly growing industries are often **cash hogs**—so labeled because the cash flows they are able to generate from internal operations aren't big enough to fund their expansion. To keep pace with rising buyer demand, rapid-growth businesses frequently need sizable annual capital investments—for new facilities and equipment, for new product development or technology improvements, and for additional working capital to support inventory expansion and a larger base of operations. A business in a fast-growing industry becomes an even bigger cash hog when it has a relatively low market share and is pursuing a strategy to become an industry leader.

In contrast, business units with leading market positions in mature industries are frequently **cash cows**—businesses that generate substantial cash surpluses over what is needed to adequately fund their operations. Market leaders in slow-growth industries often generate sizable positive cash flows *over and above what is needed for growth and reinvestment* because their industry-leading positions tend to generate attractive earnings and because the slow-growth nature of their industry often entails relatively modest annual investment requirements. Cash cows, although not always attractive from a growth standpoint, are valuable businesses from a financial resource perspective. The surplus cash flows they generate can be used to pay corporate dividends, finance acquisitions, and provide funds for investing in the company's promising cash hogs. It makes good financial and strategic sense for diversified companies to keep cash cows in a healthy condition, fortifying and defending their market position so as to preserve their cash-generating capability and have an ongoing source of financial resources to deploy elsewhere. General Electric considers its advanced materials, equipment services, and appliance and lighting businesses to be cash cow businesses.

Viewing a diversified group of businesses as a collection of cash flows and cash requirements (present and future) is a major step forward in understanding what the financial ramifications of diversification are and why having businesses with good financial resource fit can be important. For instance, *a diversified company's businesses exhibit good financial resource fit when the excess cash generated by its cash cow businesses is sufficient to fund the investment requirements of promising cash hog businesses.* Ideally, investing in promising cash hog businesses over time results in growing the hogs into self-supporting *star businesses* that have strong or market-leading competitive positions in attractive, high-growth markets and high levels of profitability. Star businesses are often the cash cows of the future. When the markets of star businesses begin to mature and their growth slows, their competitive strength should produce self-generated cash flows that are more than sufficient to cover their investment needs. The "success sequence" is thus cash hog to young star (but perhaps still a cash hog) to self-supporting star to cash cow. While the practice of viewing a diversified company in terms of cash cows and cash hogs has declined in popularity, it illustrates one approach to analyzing financial resource fit and allocating financial resources across a portfolio of different businesses.

Aside from cash flow considerations, there are two other factors to consider in assessing whether a diversified company's businesses exhibit good financial fit:

- *Do each of the individual businesses adequately contribute to achieving companywide performance targets?* A business exhibits poor financial fit if it soaks up a disproportionate share of the company's financial resources, while making subpar or insignificant contributions to the bottom line. Too many underperforming businesses reduce the company's overall performance and ultimately limit growth in shareholder value.
- *Does the corporation have adequate financial strength to fund its different businesses and maintain a healthy credit rating?* A diversified company's strategy fails the resource fit test when the resource needs of its portfolio unduly stretch the company's financial health and threaten to impair its credit rating. Many of the world's largest banks (e.g., Royal Bank of Scotland, Citigroup, HSBC) recently found themselves so undercapitalized and financially overextended that they were forced to sell off some of their business assets to meet regulatory requirements and restore public confidence in their solvency.

## Nonfinancial Resource Fit
Just as a diversified company must have adequate financial resources to support its various individual businesses, it must also have a big enough and deep enough pool of managerial, administrative, and competitive capabilities to support all of its different businesses. The following two questions help reveal whether a diversified company has sufficient nonfinancial resources:

- *Does the company have (or can it develop) the specific resources and capabilities needed to be successful in each of its businesses?*[23] Sometimes a diversified company's resources and capabilities are poorly matched to the resource requirements of one or more businesses it has diversified into. For instance, BTR, a multibusiness company in Great Britain, discovered that the company's resources and managerial skills were quite well suited for parenting its industrial manufacturing businesses but not for parenting its distribution businesses (National Tyre Services and Texas-based Summers Group). As a result, BTR decided to divest its distribution businesses and focus exclusively on diversifying around small industrial manufacturing.[24] For companies pursuing related diversification strategies, a mismatch between the company's competitive assets and the key success factors of an industry can be serious enough to warrant divesting businesses in that industry or not acquiring a new business. In contrast, when a company's resources and capabilities are a good match with the key success factors of industries it is not presently in, it makes sense to take a hard look at acquiring companies in these industries and expanding the company's business lineup.

- *Are the company's resources being stretched too thinly by the resource requirements of one or more of its businesses?* A diversified company must guard against overtaxing its resources and capabilities, a condition that can arise when (1) it goes on an acquisition spree and management is called on to assimilate and oversee many new businesses very quickly or (2) it lacks sufficient resource depth to do a creditable job of transferring skills and competencies from one of its businesses to another. The broader the diversification, the greater the concern about whether the company has sufficient managerial depth to cope with the diverse range of operating problems its wide business lineup presents. Plus, the more a company's diversification strategy is tied to transferring its existing know-how or technologies to new businesses, the more it has to develop a big-enough and deep-enough resource pool to supply these businesses with sufficient capability to create competitive advantage.[25] Otherwise, its competitive assets end up being thinly spread across many businesses, and the opportunity for competitive advantage slips through the cracks.

## Step 5: Ranking Business Units and Assigning a Priority for Resource Allocation

Once a diversified company's strategy has been evaluated from the perspective of industry attractiveness, competitive strength, strategic fit, and resource fit, the next step is to use this information to rank the performance prospects of the businesses from best to worst. Such ranking helps top-level executives assign each business a priority for resource support and capital investment.

The locations of the different businesses in the nine-cell industry attractiveness/competitive strength matrix provide a solid basis for identifying high-opportunity businesses and low-opportunity businesses. Normally, competitively strong businesses in attractive industries have significantly better performance prospects than competitively weak businesses in unattractive industries. Also, the revenue and earnings outlook for businesses in fast-growing businesses is normally better than for businesses in slow-growing businesses. As a rule, *business subsidiaries with the brightest profit and growth prospects, attractive positions in the nine-cell matrix, and solid strategic and resource fit should receive top priority for allocation of corporate resources.* However, in ranking the prospects of the different businesses from best to worst, it is usually wise to also take into account each business's past performance as concerns sales growth, profit growth, contribution to company earnings, return on capital invested in the business, and cash flow from operations. While past performance is not always a reliable predictor of future performance, it does signal whether a business already has good to excellent performance or has problems to overcome.

**Allocating Financial Resources**   Figure 8.5 shows the chief strategic and financial options for allocating a diversified company's financial resources. Divesting

**FIGURE 8.5** The Chief Strategic and Financial Options for Allocating a Diversified Company's Financial Resources

businesses with the weakest future prospects and businesses that lack adequate strategic fit and/or resource fit is one of the best ways of generating additional funds for redeployment to businesses with better opportunities and better strategic and resource fit. Free cash flows from cash cow businesses also add to the pool of funds that can be usefully redeployed. *Ideally,* a diversified company will have sufficient financial resources to strengthen or grow its existing businesses, make any new acquisitions that are desirable, fund other promising business opportunities, pay off existing debt, and periodically increase dividend payments to shareholders and/or repurchase shares of stock. But, as a practical matter, a company's financial resources are limited. Thus for top executives to make the best use of the available funds, they must steer resources to those businesses with the best opportunities and performance prospects and allocate little if any resources to businesses with marginal or dim prospects—this is why ranking the performance prospects of the various businesses from best to worst is so crucial. Strategic uses of corporate financial resources (see Figure 8.5) should usually take precedence unless there is a compelling reason to strengthen the firm's balance sheet or better reward shareholders.

## Step 6: Crafting New Strategic Moves to Improve Overall Corporate Performance

The conclusions flowing from the five preceding analytical steps set the agenda for crafting strategic moves to improve a diversified company's overall performance. The strategic options boil down to four broad categories of actions (see Figure 8.6):

1. Sticking closely with the existing business lineup and pursuing the opportunities these businesses present.

2. Broadening the company's business scope by making new acquisitions in new industries.

**LO 5**

Understand a diversified company's four main corporate strategy options for solidifying its diversification strategy and improving company performance.

## FIGURE 8.6 A Company's Four Main Strategic Alternatives after It Diversifies

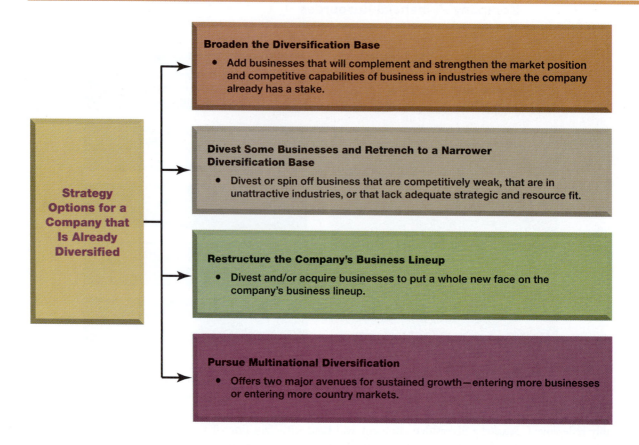

**Strategy Options for a Company that Is Already Diversified**

**Broaden the Diversification Base**
- Add businesses that will complement and strengthen the market position and competitive capabilities of business in industries where the company already has a stake.

**Divest Some Businesses and Retrench to a Narrower Diversification Base**
- Divest or spin off business that are competitively weak, that are in unattractive industries, or that lack adequate strategic and resource fit.

**Restructure the Company's Business Lineup**
- Divest and/or acquire businesses to put a whole new face on the company's business lineup.

**Pursue Multinational Diversification**
- Offers two major avenues for sustained growth—entering more businesses or entering more country markets.

3. Divesting some businesses and retrenching to a narrower base of business operations.
4. Restructuring the company's business lineup and putting a whole new face on the company's business makeup.

**Sticking Closely with the Existing Business Lineup**    The option of sticking with the current business lineup makes sense when the company's present businesses offer attractive growth opportunities and can be counted on to create economic value for shareholders. As long as the company's set of existing businesses puts it in good position for the future and these businesses have good strategic and resource fit, then major changes in the company's business mix are unnecessary. Corporate executives can concentrate their attention on getting the best performance from each of the businesses, steering corporate resources into areas of greatest potential and profitability. The specifics of "what to do" to wring better performance from the present business lineup have to be dictated by each business's circumstances and the preceding analysis of the corporate parent's diversification strategy.

However, in the event that corporate executives are not entirely satisfied with the opportunities they see in the company's present set of businesses and conclude that changes in the company's direction and business makeup are in order, they can opt for any of the three other strategic alternatives that follow.

**Broadening a Diversified Company's Business Base**    Diversified companies sometimes find it desirable to build positions in new industries, whether related or unrelated. There are several motivating factors. One is the potential for transferring resources and capabilities to other related or complementary businesses. A second is rapidly changing conditions in one or more of a company's core businesses brought on by technological, legislative, or new product innovations that alter buyer preferences and resource requirements. For instance, the passage of legislation in the United States allowing banks, insurance companies, and stock brokerages to enter each other's businesses spurred a raft of acquisitions and mergers to create full-service financial enterprises capable of meeting the multiple financial needs of customers. A third, and very important, motivating factor for adding new businesses is to complement and strengthen the market position and competitive capabilities of one or more of the company's present businesses. Procter & Gamble's acquisition of Gillette strengthened and extended P&G's reach into personal care and household products—Gillette's businesses included Oral-B toothbrushes, Gillette razors and razor blades, Duracell batteries, and Braun shavers and small appliances.

Another important avenue for expanding the scope of a diversified company is to grow by extending the operations of existing businesses into additional country markets, as discussed in Chapter 7. Expanding a company's geographic scope may offer an exceptional competitive advantage potential by facilitating the full capture of economies of scale and learning/experience curve effects. In some businesses, the volume of sales needed to realize full economies of scale and/or benefit fully from experience and learning curve effects exceeds the volume that can be achieved by operating within the boundaries of just one or several country markets, especially small ones.

Illustration Capsule 8.1 describes how Johnson & Johnson has used acquisitions to diversify far beyond its well-known Band-Aid and baby care businesses and become a major player in pharmaceuticals, medical devices, and medical diagnostics.

**Divesting Businesses and Retrenching to a Narrower Diversification Base**    A number of diversified firms have had difficulty managing a diverse group of businesses and have elected to get out of some of them. Selling a business outright to another company is far and away the most frequently used option for divesting a business. Sara Lee Corporation sold its International Coffee and Tea business to J.M. Smucker in 2012; it sold Ambi Pur Air Care to Procter & Gamble in 2010. But sometimes a business selected for divestiture has ample resources and capabilities to compete successfully on its own. In such cases, a corporate parent may elect to spin the unwanted business off as a financially and managerially independent company, either by selling shares to the public via an initial public offering or by distributing shares in the new company to shareholders of the corporate parent. Online travel company Expedia, Inc. spun off TripAdvisor as a public company in 2011, distributing shares to its shareholders. Expedia itself was spun off from IAC/InterActiveCorp (IACI) in 2005.

A **spinoff** is an independent company created when a corporate parent divests a business by distributing to its stockholders new shares in this business.

Retrenching to a narrower diversification base is usually undertaken when top management concludes that its diversification strategy has ranged too far afield and that the company can improve long-term performance by concentrating on a smaller number of businesses. But there are other important reasons for divesting one or more of a company's present businesses. Sometimes divesting a business has to be considered because market conditions in a once-attractive industry have badly deteriorated. A business can become a prime candidate for divestiture because it lacks adequate strategic or resource fit, because it is a cash hog with questionable long-term potential, or because it is weakly

# Managing Diversification at Johnson & Johnson: The Benefits of Cross-Business Strategic Fit

Johnson & Johnson (J&J), once a consumer products company known for its Band-Aid line and its baby care products, has evolved into a $65 billion diversified enterprise consisting of some 250-plus operating companies organized into three divisions: pharmaceuticals, medical devices and diagnostics, and consumer health care products. Over the past decade, J&J has made acquisitions totaling more than $50 billion; about 10 to 15 percent of J&J's annual growth in revenues has come from acquisitions. Much of the company's recent growth has been in the pharmaceutical division, which in 2011 accounted for 37 percent of J&J's revenues and 47 percent of its operating profits.

While each of J&J's business units sets its own strategies and operates with its own finance and human resource departments, corporate management strongly encourages cross-business cooperation and collaboration, believing that many of the advances in 21st-century medicine will come from applying advances in one discipline to another. J&J's drug-coated stent grew out of a discussion between a drug researcher and a researcher in the company's stent business. The innovative product helps prevent infection after cardiac procedures. (When stents are inserted to prop open arteries following angioplasty, the drug coating helps prevent infection.) A gene technology database compiled by the company's gene research lab was shared with personnel from the diagnostics division, who developed a test that the drug researchers used to predict which patients would most benefit from an experimental cancer therapy. J&J's liquid Band-Aid product (a liquid coating applied to hard-to-cover places like fingers and knuckles) is based on a material used in a wound-closing product sold by the company's hospital products company. Scientists from three separate business units worked collaboratively toward the development of an absorbable patch that would stop bleeding on contact. The development of the instant clotting patch was expected to save the lives of thousands of accident victims since uncontrolled bleeding was the number-one cause of death due to injury.

J&J's corporate management maintains that close collaboration among people in its diagnostics, medical devices, and pharmaceutical businesses—where numerous examples of cross-business strategic fit exist—gives J&J an edge on competitors, most of whom cannot match the company's breadth and depth of expertise.

*Sources:* Amy Barrett, "Staying on Top," *BusinessWeek,* May 5, 2003, pp. 60–68; Johnson & Johnson 2007 Annual Report; www.jnj.com (accessed July 29, 2010); http://www.mergentonline.com/companydetail.php?pagetype=businesssegments&compnumber=4593, accessed March 28, 2012.

positioned in its industry. Sometimes a company acquires businesses that, down the road, just do not work out as expected even though management has tried its best. Subpar performance by some business units is bound to occur, thereby raising questions of whether to divest them or keep them and attempt a turnaround. Other business units, despite adequate financial performance, may not mesh as well with the rest of the firm as was originally thought. For instance, PepsiCo divested its group of fast-food restaurant businesses to focus on its core soft-drink and snack-food businesses, where their resources and capabilities could add more value.

On occasion, a diversification move that seems sensible from a strategic-fit standpoint turns out to be a poor *cultural fit.*[26] When several pharmaceutical companies diversified into cosmetics and perfume, they discovered their personnel had little respect for the "frivolous" nature of such products compared to the far nobler task of developing miracle drugs to cure the ill. The absence of shared values and cultural compatibility between the medical research and chemical-compounding expertise of the pharmaceutical companies and the fashion/marketing orientation of the cosmetics business was the undoing of what otherwise was diversification into businesses with technology-sharing potential, product-development fit, and some overlap in distribution channels.

A useful guide to determine whether or when to divest a business subsidiary is to ask, "If we were not in this business today, would we want to get into it now?"[27] When the answer is no or probably not, divestiture should be considered. Another signal that a business should be divested is when it is worth more to another company than to the present parent; in such cases, shareholders would be well served if the company sells the business and collects a premium price from the buyer for whom the business is a valuable fit.[28]

Diversified companies need to divest low-performing businesses or businesses that don't fit in order to concentrate on expanding existing businesses and entering new ones where opportunities are more promising.

## Restructuring a Diversified Company's Business Lineup

Restructuring a diversified company on a companywide basis *(corporate restructuring)* involves making major changes by divesting some businesses and/or acquiring others, so as to put a whole new face on the company's business lineup.[29] Performing radical surgery on a company's group of businesses is appealing when its financial performance is being squeezed or eroded by:

- A serious mismatch between the company's resources and capabilities and the type of diversification that it has pursued.
- Too many businesses in slow-growth, declining, low-margin, or otherwise unattractive industries.
- Too many competitively weak businesses.
- Ongoing declines in the market shares of one or more major business units that are falling prey to more market-savvy competitors.
- An excessive debt burden with interest costs that eat deeply into profitability.
- Ill-chosen acquisitions that haven't lived up to expectations.

Companywide restructuring can also be mandated by the emergence of new technologies that threaten the survival of one or more of a diversified company's important businesses. On occasion, corporate restructuring can be prompted by special circumstances—such as when a firm has a unique opportunity to make an acquisition so big and important that it has to sell several existing business units to finance the new acquisition or when a company needs to sell off some businesses in order to raise the cash for entering a potentially big industry with wave-of-the-future technologies or products.

Candidates for divestiture in a corporate restructuring effort typically include not only weak performers or those in unattractive industries but also business units that lack strategic fit with the businesses to be retained, businesses that are cash hogs or that lack other types of resource fit, and businesses incompatible with the company's revised diversification strategy (even though they may be profitable or in an attractive industry). As businesses are divested, corporate restructuring generally involves aligning the remaining business units into groups with the best strategic fit and then redeploying the cash flows from the divested business to either pay down debt or make new acquisitions to strengthen the parent company's business position in the industries it has chosen to emphasize.[30]

Over the past decade, corporate restructuring has become a popular strategy at many diversified companies, especially those that had diversified broadly into many different

# Growth through Restructuring at Kraft Foods

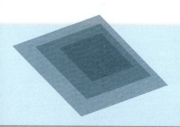

In 2012, Kraft Foods, the 90-year-old darling of the Consumer Packaged Goods industry, moved to improve its long-term performance by *restructuring* the corporation—the latest move in a series by CEO Irene Rosenfeld who was brought in to turn around the company's performance. In addition to trimming operations, the restructuring plan called for dividing the enterprise into two separate units: a $32B fast-growing global snacks business that included Oreo and Cadbury (the British confectionary acquired in 2010) and a North American grocery unit that included Kraft Macaroni and Cheese,

Oscar Meyer, and other non-snack brands. With this radical new operational structure in place, Kraft hoped to improve its ability focus on new opportunities and pursue profitable growth.

Managing these two large and very different businesses jointly had made it difficult for Kraft to act nimbly and adapt to changing market conditions. It also inhibited the company from executing new strategies free from significant portfolio-wide considerations. In announcing her intention to split the company in September 2011, CEO Irene Rosenfeld said, "Simply put, we have now reached a point where North American grocery and global snacks will each benefit from standing on its own and focusing on its unique drivers for success." She noted that as separate businesses, "each will have the leadership, resources, and mandate to realize its full potential."

Prior to the split, Kraft plans additional restructuring efforts in its U.S. sales operations, including reducing the number of management centers and selling off some underperforming brands. Although in refashioning the company Kraft loses some of the operational benefits it enjoyed as a single entity, managers and investors hope the move will ultimately improve the company's ability to sustain profitable growth and increase shareholder value.

*Developed with Maximilian A. Pinto.*

*Sources:* Sam Webb, "New Reality Makes Kraft Split Vital," *Food Global News,* September 2011; E. J. Schultz, "Could Kraft Split Be a Blueprint for Blue Chips?" *Advertising Age,* August 2011, vol. 82, iss. 29; http://www.nytimes.com/2007/02/21/business/21kraft.html, accessed March 2, 2012; http://stocks.investopedia.com/, accessed March 2, 2012.

industries and lines of business. VF Corporation, maker of North Face and other popular "lifestyle" apparel brands, has used a restructuring strategy to provide its shareholders with returns that are more than five times greater than shareholder returns for competing apparel makers. Since its acquisition and turnaround of North Face in 2000, VF has spent nearly $5 billion to acquire 19 additional businesses, including about $2 billion in 2011 for Timberland. New apparel brands acquired by VF Corporation include 7 For All Mankind sportswear, Vans skateboard shoes, Nautica, John Varvatos, Reef surf wear, and Lucy athletic wear. By 2011, VF Corporation had become one of the most profitable apparel and footwear companies in the world, with net earnings of $913 million on revenues of $9.5 billion. It was listed as number 310 on *Fortune*'s 2011 list of the 500 largest U.S. companies.

Illustration Capsule 8.2 discusses how Kraft Foods has been pursuing long-term growth and increased shareholder value by restructuring their operations.

1.  The purpose of diversification is to build shareholder value. Diversification builds shareholder value when a diversified group of businesses can perform better under the auspices of a single corporate parent than they would as independent, stand-alone businesses—the goal is to achieve not just a $1 + 1 = 2$ result but, rather, to realize important $1 + 1 = 3$ performance benefits. Whether getting into a new business has the potential to enhance shareholder value hinges on whether a company's entry into that business can pass the attractiveness test, the cost-of-entry test, and the better-off test.

2.  Entry into new businesses can take any of three forms: acquisition, internal startup, or joint venture. The choice of which is best depends on the firm's resources and capabilities, the industry's entry barriers, the importance of speed, and the relative costs.

3.  There are two fundamental approaches to diversification—into related businesses and into unrelated businesses. The rationale for *related* diversification is to benefit from *strategic fit:* Diversify into businesses with matchups along their respective value chains, and then capitalize on the strategic fit by sharing or transferring the resources and capabilities across matching value chain activities to gain competitive advantage.

4.  *Unrelated* diversification strategies surrender the competitive advantage potential of strategic fit at the value chain level in return for the potential that can be realized from superior corporate parenting or the sharing and transfer of generalized resources and capabilities. An outstanding corporate parent can benefit its businesses through (1) providing high-level oversight and making available other corporate resources, (2) allocating financial resources across the business portfolio, and (3) restructuring underperforming acquisitions.

5.  Related diversification provides a stronger foundation for creating shareholder value than unrelated diversification, since the *specialized resources and capabilities* that are leveraged in related diversification tend to be more valuable competitive assets than the *generalized resources and capabilities* underlying unrelated diversification, which in most cases are relatively common and easier to imitate.

6.  Analyzing how good a company's diversification strategy is consists of a six-step process:

    **Step 1:** *Evaluate the long-term attractiveness of the industries into which the firm has diversified.* Industry attractiveness needs to be evaluated from three angles: the attractiveness of each industry on its own, the attractiveness of each industry relative to the others, and the attractiveness of all the industries as a group.

    **Step 2:** *Evaluate the relative competitive strength of each of the company's business units.* The purpose of rating the competitive strength of each business is to gain a clear understanding of which businesses are strong contenders in their industries, which are weak contenders, and the underlying reasons for their strength or weakness. The conclusions about industry attractiveness can be joined with the conclusions about competitive strength by drawing a nine-cell industry attractiveness–competitive strength matrix that helps identify the prospects of each business and what priority each business should be given in allocating corporate resources and investment capital.

**Step 3:** *Check for cross-business strategic fit.* A business is more attractive strategically when it has value chain relationships with the sister business units that offer potential to (1) realize economies of scope, (2) transfer technology, skills, know-how, or other resource capabilities from one business to another, (3) leverage use of a trusted brand name or other resources that enhance differentiation, and (4) build new resources and competitive capabilities via cross-business collaboration. Cross-business strategic fit represents a significant avenue for producing competitive advantage beyond what any one business can achieve on its own.

**Step 4:** *Check whether the firm's resources fit the resource requirements of its present business lineup.* In firms with a related diversification strategy, resource fit exists when the firm's businesses have matching resource requirements at points along their value chains that are critical for the businesses' market success. In companies pursuing unrelated diversification, resource fit exists when the company has solid parenting capabilities or resources of a general nature that it can share or transfer to its component businesses. When there is financial resource fit among the businesses of any type of diversified company, the company can generate internal cash flows sufficient to fund the capital requirements of its businesses, pay its dividends, meet its debt obligations, and otherwise remain financially healthy.

**Step 5:** *Rank the performance prospects of the businesses from best to worst, and determine what the corporate parent's priority should be in allocating resources to its various businesses.* The most important considerations in judging business-unit performance are sales growth, profit growth, contribution to company earnings, and the return on capital invested in the business. Normally, strong business units in attractive industries should head the list for corporate resource support.

**Step 6:** *Crafting new strategic moves to improve overall corporate performance.* This step entails using the results of the preceding analysis as the basis for selecting one of four different strategic paths for improving a diversified company's performance: (a) Stick closely with the existing business lineup and pursue opportunities presented by these businesses, (b) broaden the scope of diversification by entering additional industries, (c) retrench to a narrower scope of diversification by divesting poorly performing businesses, and (d) broadly restructure the business lineup with multiple divestitures and/or acquisitions.

## ASSURANCE OF LEARNING EXERCISES

**LO 1, LO 2, LO 3**

1. See if you can identify the value chain relationships that make the businesses of the following companies related in competitively relevant ways. In particular, you should consider whether there are cross-business opportunities for (1) transferring skills/technology, (2) combining related value chain activities to achieve economies of scope, and/or (3) leveraging the use of a well-respected brand name or other resources that enhance differentiation.

### OSI Restaurant Partners

- Outback Steakhouse
- Carrabba's Italian Grill
- Roy's Restaurant (Hawaiian fusion cuisine)
- Bonefish Grill (market-fresh fine seafood)
- Fleming's Prime Steakhouse & Wine Bar

- Lee Roy Selmon's (Southern comfort food)
- Cheeseburger in Paradise
- Blue Coral Seafood & Spirits (Fine seafood)

## L'Oréal

- Maybelline, Lancôme, Helena Rubinstein, Kiehl's, Garner, and Shu Uemura cosmetics
- L'Oréal and Soft Sheen/Carson hair care products
- Redken, Matrix, L'Oréal Professional, and Kerastase Paris professional hair care and skin care products
- Ralph Lauren and Giorgio Armani fragrances
- Biotherm skincare products
- La Roche–Posay and Vichy Laboratories dermocosmetics

## Johnson & Johnson

- Baby products (powder, shampoo, oil, lotion)
- Band-Aids and other first-aid products
- Women's health and personal care products (Stayfree, Carefree, Sure & Natural)
- Neutrogena and Aveeno skin care products
- Nonprescription drugs (Tylenol, Motrin, Pepcid AC, Mylanta, Monistat)
- Prescription drugs
- Prosthetic and other medical devices
- Surgical and hospital products
- Acuvue contact lenses

2. Peruse the business group listings for United Technologies shown next and listed at its website (www.utc.com). How would you characterize the company's corporate strategy? Related diversification, unrelated diversification, or a combination related-unrelated diversification strategy? Explain your answer.

**LO 1, LO 2, LO 3**

- Carrier—the world's largest provider of air-conditioning, heating, and refrigeration solutions.
- Hamilton Sundstrand—technologically advanced aerospace and industrial products.
- Otis—the world's leading manufacturer, installer, and maintainer of elevators, escalators, and moving walkways.
- Pratt & Whitney—designs, manufactures, services, and supports aircraft engines, industrial gas turbines, and space propulsion systems.
- Sikorsky—a world leader in helicopter design, manufacture, and service.
- UTC Fire & Security—fire and security systems developed for commercial, industrial, and residential customers.
- UTC Power—a full-service provider of environmentally advanced power solutions.

3. The Walt Disney Company is in the following businesses:

**LO 1, LO 2, LO 3**

- Theme parks
- Cruise lines (Disney Cruise Line)
- Resort properties

- Movies, videos, and theatrical productions (for both children and adults)
- Television broadcasting (ABC, Disney Channel, Toon Disney, Classic Sports Network, ESPN and ESPN2, e!, Lifetime, and A&E networks)
- Radio broadcasting (Disney Radio)
- Musical recordings and sales of animation art
- Baseball teams (the Anaheim Angels Major League Baseball franchise—25 percent ownership)
- Books and magazine publishing
- Interactive software and Internet sites
- Retail shops (The Disney Store)

Based on the preceding list, would you say that Walt Disney's business lineup reflects a strategy of related diversification, unrelated diversification, or a combination related-unrelated diversification? What benefits are generated from any strategic fit existing between Disney's businesses? Also what types of companies should Walt Disney Company consider acquiring that might improve shareholder value? Justify your answer.

**LO 4, LO 5**    4.   ITT Corporation has had a long history as a conglomerate enterprise. In recent years, however, the company has undergone some significant changes. How would you describe these changes and what do you think were the drivers? Explain. (You can find lots of information about this company and its recent strategic moves on the Web.)

## EXERCISES FOR SIMULATION PARTICIPANTS

**LO 1, LO 2, LO 3**    1.   In the event that your company has the opportunity to diversify into other products or businesses of your choosing, would you opt to pursue related diversification, unrelated diversification, or a combination of both? Explain why.

**LO 1, LO 2**    2.   What specific resources and capabilities does your company possess that would make diversifying into related businesses attractive? Indicate what kinds of strategic-fit benefits could be captured by transferring these resources and competitive capabilities to newly acquired related businesses.

**LO 1, LO 2**    3.   If your company opted to pursue a strategy of related diversification, what industries or product categories could it diversify into that would allow it to achieve economies of scope? Name at least two or three such industries or product categories, and indicate the specific kinds of cost savings that might accrue from entry into each.

**LO 1, LO 2**    4.   If your company opted to pursue a strategy of related diversification, what industries or product categories could it diversify into that would allow it to capitalize on using its present brand name and corporate image to good advantage in the newly entered businesses or product categories? Name at least two or three such industries or product categories, and indicate *the specific benefits* that might be captured by transferring your company's brand name to each.

## ENDNOTES

[1] Constantinos C. Markides, "To Diversify or Not to Diversify," *Harvard Business Review* 75, no. 6 (November–December 1997).
[2] Michael E. Porter, "From Competitive Advantage to Corporate Strategy," *Harvard*
*Business Review* 45, no. 3 (May–June 1987), pp. 46–49.
[3] Rita Nazareth, "CEOs Paying 56% M&A Premium Shows Stocks May Be Cheap (Update3)," *Bloomberg.com*, December
21, 2009, www.bloomberg.com/apps/news?pid=20603037&sid=ahPolYY.zgQ.
[4] Ibid.
[5] Michael E. Porter, *Competitive Strategy: Techniques for Analyzing Industries and*

*Competitors* (New York: Free Press, 1980), pp. 354–55.

[6] A. Shleifer and R. Vishny, "Takeovers in the 60s and the 80s—Evidence and Implications," *Strategic Management Journal* 12 (Winter 1991), pp. 51–59; T. Brush, "Predicted Change in Operational Synergy and Post-Acquisition Performance of Acquired Businesses," *Strategic Management Journal* 17, no. 1 (1996), pp. 1–24; J. P. Walsh, "Top Management Turnover Following Mergers and Acquisitions," *Strategic Management Journal* 9, no. 2 (1988), pp. 173–83; A. Cannella and D. Hambrick, "Effects of Executive Departures on the Performance of Acquired Firms," *Strategic Management Journal* 14 (Summer 1993), pp. 137–52; R. Roll, "The Hubris Hypothesis of Corporate Takeovers," *Journal of Business* 59, no. 2 (1986), pp. 197–216; P. Haspeslagh and D. Jemison, *Managing Acquisitions* (New York: Free Press, 1991).

[7] M.L.A. Hayward, "When Do Firms Learn from Their Acquisition Experience? Evidence from 1990–1995," *Strategic Management Journal* 23, no. 1 (2002), pp. 21–29; G. Ahuja and R. Katila, "Technological Acquisitions and the Innovation Performance of Acquiring Firms: A Longitudinal Study," *Strategic Management Journal* 22, no. 3 (2001), pp. 197–220; H. Barkema and F. Vermeulen, "International Expansion through Start-Up or Acquisition: A Learning Perspective," *Academy of Management Journal* 41, no. 1 (1998), pp. 7–26.

[8] Haspeslagh and Jemison, *Managing Acquisitions*, pp. 344–45.

[9] Yves L. Doz and Gary Hamel, *Alliance Advantage: The Art of Creating Value through Partnering* (Boston: Harvard Business School Press, 1998), chaps. 1 and 2.

[10] J. Glover, "The Guardian," March 23, 1996, www.mcspotlight.org/media/press/guardpizza_23mar96.html.

[11] Michael E. Porter, *Competitive Advantage* (New York: Free Press, 1985), pp. 318–19 and pp. 337–53; Porter, "From Competitive Advantage to Corporate Strategy,"

pp. 53–57. For an empirical study supporting the notion that strategic fit enhances performance (provided the resulting combination is competitively valuable and difficult to duplicate by rivals), see Constantinos C. Markides and Peter J. Williamson, "Corporate Diversification and Organization Structure: A Resource-Based View," *Academy of Management Journal* 39, no. 2 (April 1996), pp. 340–67.

[12] David J. Collis and Cynthia A. Montgomery, "Creating Corporate Advantage," *Harvard Business Review* 76, no. 3 (May–June 1998), pp. 72–80; Markides and Williamson, "Corporate Diversification and Organization Structure."

[13] Markides and Williamson, "Corporate Diversification and Organization Structure."

[14] Jeanne M. Liedtka, "Collaboration across Lines of Business for Competitive Advantage," *Academy of Management Executive* 10, no. 2 (May 1996), pp. 20–34.

[15] For a discussion of what is involved in actually capturing strategic-fit benefits, see Kathleen M. Eisenhardt and D. Charles Galunic, "Coevolving: At Last, a Way to Make Synergies Work," *Harvard Business Review* 78, no. 1 (January–February 2000), pp. 91–101; Constantinos C. Markides and Peter J. Williamson, "Related Diversification, Core Competences and Corporate Performance," *Strategic Management Journal* 15 (Summer 1994), pp. 149–65.

[16] A. Campbell, M. Goold, and M. Alexander, "Corporate Strategy: The Quest for Parenting Advantage," *Harvard Business Review* 73, no. 2 (March–April 1995), pp. 120–32.

[17] C. Montgomery and B. Wernerfelt, "Diversification, Ricardian Rents, and Tobin-Q," *RAND Journal of Economics* 19, no. 4 (1988), pp. 623–32.

[18] Ibid.

[19] Ibid.

[20] For a review of the experiences of companies that have pursued unrelated diversification successfully, see Patricia L. Anslinger and Thomas E. Copeland, "Growth through Acquisitions: A Fresh

Look," *Harvard Business Review* 74, no. 1 (January–February 1996), pp. 126–35.

[21] M. Lubatkin and S. Chatterjee, "Extending Modern Portfolio Theory," *Academy of Management Journal* 37, no.1 (February 1994), pp. 109–36.

[22] For research evidence of the failure of broad diversification and trend of companies to focus their diversification efforts more narrowly, see Lawrence G. Franko, "The Death of Diversification? The Focusing of the World's Industrial Firms, 1980–2000," *Business Horizons* 47, no. 4 (July–August 2004), pp. 41–50.

[23] For an excellent discussion of what to look for in assessing this type of strategic fit, see Campbell, Goold, and Alexander, "Corporate Strategy: The Quest for Parenting Advantage."

[24] Ibid., p. 128.

[25] A good discussion of the importance of having adequate resources, as well as upgrading corporate resources and capabilities, can be found in David J. Collis and Cynthia A. Montgomery, "Competing on Resources: Strategy in the 90s," *Harvard Business Review* 73, no. 4 (July–August 1995), pp. 118–28.

[26] Peter F. Drucker, *Management: Tasks, Responsibilities, Practices* (New York: Harper & Row, 1974), p. 709.

[27] Ibid., p. 94.

[28] Collis and Montgomery, "Creating Corporate Advantage."

[29] For a discussion of why divestiture needs to be a standard part of any company's diversification strategy, see Lee Dranikoff, Tim Koller, and Anton Schneider, "Divestiture: Strategy's Missing Link," *Harvard Business Review* 80, no. 5 (May 2002), pp. 74–83.

[30] Evidence that restructuring strategies tend to result in higher levels of performance is contained in Markides, "Diversification, Restructuring, and Economic Performance."

# CHAPTER 9

# ETHICS, CORPORATE SOCIAL RESPONSIBILITY, ENVIRONMENTAL SUSTAINABILITY, AND STRATEGY

## Learning Objectives

**LO 1** Understand how the standards of ethical behavior in business are no different from the ethical standards and norms of the larger society and culture in which a company operates.

**LO 2** Recognize conditions that can give rise to unethical business strategies and behavior.

**LO 3** Gain an understanding of the costs of business ethics failures.

**LO 4** Learn the concepts of corporate social responsibility and environmental sustainability and how companies balance these duties with economic responsibilities to shareholders.

> Business is the most important engine for social change in our society.
>
> Lawrence Perlman – *Former CEO of Ceridian Corporation*

> Companies have to be socially responsible or shareholders pay eventually.
>
> Warren Shaw – *Former CEO of LGT Asset Management*

> After all, sustainability means running the global environment—Earth Inc.—like a corporation. In other words, keeping the asset whole, rather than undermining your natural capital.
>
> Maurice Strong – *Canadian entrepreneur, former CEO of Petro-Canada and Ontario Hydro*

In capitalistic or market economies, management has a fiduciary duty to create value for the company's shareholders by operating profitably and growing the business. Clearly, a company and its personnel also have a duty to obey the laws and comply with government regulations. But does a company have a duty to go beyond legal requirements and conform to the ethical norms of the societies in which it operates—should it play by the rules of fair competition? And does a company have an obligation to contribute to the betterment of society independent of the needs and preferences of the customers it serves? Should a company display a social conscience and devote a portion of its resources to bettering society? Should companies be obligated to protect the environment, conserve natural resources for use by future generations, and ensure that its operations do not ultimately endanger the planet?

This chapter focuses on whether a company, in the course of trying to craft and execute a strategy that delivers value to both customers and shareholders, also has a duty to (1) act in an ethical and fair-dealing manner, (2) demonstrate socially responsible behavior by being a committed corporate citizen and directing corporate resources to the betterment of employees, the communities in which it operates, and society as a whole, and (3) adopt business practices that conserve natural resources, protect the interests of future generations, and preserve the well-being of the planet.

## WHAT DO WE MEAN BY *BUSINESS ETHICS?*

Ethics concerns principles of right or wrong conduct. **Business ethics** is the application of ethical principles and standards to the actions and decisions of business organizations and the conduct of their personnel.[1] *Ethical principles in business are not materially different from ethical principles in general.* Why? Because business actions have to be judged in the context of society's standards of right and wrong, not by a special set of ethical standards applicable only to business situations. If dishonesty is considered unethical and immoral, then dishonest behavior in business—whether it relates to customers, suppliers, employees, shareholders, competitors, or government—qualifies as equally unethical and immoral. If being ethical entails not deliberately harming others, then failing to recall a defective or unsafe product swiftly, regardless of the cost, is likewise unethical. If society deems bribery unethical, then it is unethical for company personnel to bestow favors on government officials or prospective customers to win or retain business. In short, ethical behavior in business situations requires adhering to generally accepted norms about right or wrong conduct. As a consequence, company managers have an obligation—indeed, a duty—to observe ethical norms when crafting and executing strategy.

> ### CORE CONCEPT
>
> **Business ethics** involves the application of general ethical principles to the actions and decisions of businesses and the conduct of their personnel.

# WHERE DO ETHICAL STANDARDS COME FROM—ARE THEY UNIVERSAL OR DEPENDENT ON LOCAL NORMS?

**LO 1**

Understand how the standards of ethical behavior in business are no different from the ethical standards and norms of the larger society and culture in which a company operates.

Notions of right and wrong, fair and unfair, are present in all societies and cultures. But there are three distinct schools of thought about the extent to which ethical standards travel across cultures and whether multinational companies can apply the same set of ethical standards in any and all locations where they operate. Illustration Capsule 9.1 describes the difficulties Apple has faced in trying to enforce a common set of ethical standards across its vast global supplier network.

## The School of Ethical Universalism

According to the school of **ethical universalism,** the most fundamental conceptions of right and wrong are *universal* and transcend culture, society, and religion.[2] For instance, being truthful (or not being deliberately deceitful) strikes a chord of what's right in the peoples of all nations. Likewise, demonstrating integrity of character, not cheating or harming people, and treating others with decency are concepts that resonate with people of virtually all cultures and religions.

> **CORE CONCEPT**
>
> The school of **ethical universalism** holds that the most fundamental conceptions of right and wrong are *universal* and apply to members of all societies, all companies, and all businesspeople.

Common moral agreement about right and wrong actions and behaviors across multiple cultures and countries gives rise to universal ethical standards that apply to members of all societies, all companies, and all businesspeople. These universal ethical principles set forth the traits and behaviors that are considered virtuous and that a good person is supposed to believe in and to display. Thus, adherents of the school of ethical universalism maintain it is entirely appropriate to expect all businesspeople to conform to these universal ethical standards.[3] For example, people in most societies would concur that it is unethical for companies to knowingly expose workers to toxic chemicals and hazardous materials or to sell products known to be unsafe or harmful to the users.

The strength of ethical universalism is that it draws on the collective views of multiple societies and cultures to put some clear boundaries on what constitutes ethical and unethical business behavior, regardless of the country or culture in which a company's personnel are conducting activities. This means that in those instances where basic moral standards really do not vary significantly according to local cultural beliefs, traditions, or religious convictions, a multinational company can develop a code of ethics that it applies more or less evenly across its worldwide operations. It can avoid the slippery slope that comes from having different ethical standards for different company personnel depending on where in the world they are working.

> **CORE CONCEPT**
>
> The school of **ethical relativism** holds that differing religious beliefs, customs, and behavioral norms across countries and cultures give rise to *multiple sets of standards concerning what is ethically right or wrong.* These differing standards mean that whether business-related actions are right or wrong depends on the prevailing local ethical standards.

## The School of Ethical Relativism

While undoubtedly there are some universal moral prescriptions (like being truthful), there are also observable variations from one society to another as to what constitutes ethical or unethical behavior. Indeed, differing religious beliefs, social customs, traditions, core values, and behavioral norms frequently give rise to different standards about what is fair or unfair, moral or immoral, and ethically right or wrong. For instance, European and American managers often establish standards of business conduct and ethical behavior that protect personal human rights as freedom of movement

# Apple's Failures in Enforcing Its Supplier Code of Conduct

Apple requires its suppliers to comply with the company's Supplier Code of Conduct as a condition of being awarded contracts. To ensure compliance, Apple has a supplier monitoring program that includes audits of supplier factories, corrective action plans, and verification measures. In the company's 27-page 2011 Progress Report on Supplier Responsibility, Apple reported that in 2011 it conducted 229 audits of supplier facilities in such countries as China, the Czech Republic, Malaysia, the Philippines, Singapore, South Korea, Taiwan, Thailand, and the United States. More than 100 of these audits were first-time audits.

Apple distinguishes among the seriousness of infractions, designating "core violations" as those that go directly against the core principles of its Supplier Code of Conduct and must be remedied immediately. During the 2011 audits, core violations were discovered in 35 facilities, including cases of underage labor, excessive recruitment fees, improper hazardous waste disposal, and deliberately falsified audit records. Apple responded by ensuring that immediate corrective actions were taken, placing violators on probation, and planning to audit them again in a year's time.

While Apple's final assembly manufacturers had high compliance scores for most categories, suppliers did not fare very well in terms of working hours. At 93 of the audited facilities, workers were required to work more than 60 hours per week—Apple sets a maximum of 60 hours per week (except in unusual or emergency circumstances). In 90 of the audited facilities, workers were found to have been required to work more than six consecutive days a week at least once per month—Apple requires at least one day of rest per seven days of work (except in unusual or emergency circumstances). At 108 facilities, Apple also found that overtime wages

had been calculated improperly, resulting in underpayment of overtime compensation.

Apple requires suppliers to provide a safe working environment and to eliminate physical hazards to employees where possible. But the 2011 audits revealed that workers were not wearing appropriate protective personal equipment at 58 facilities. Violations were found at 126 facilities where unlicensed workers were operating equipment. Moreover, the audits revealed that 74 supplier facilities did not have any personnel assigned to ensuring compliance with Apple's Supplier Code of Conduct.

For Apple, the audits represent a starting point for bringing its suppliers into compliance, through greater scrutiny, education and training of suppliers' personnel, and incentives. Apple collects quarterly data to hold its suppliers accountable for their actions and makes procurement decisions based, in part, on these numbers. Suppliers that are unable to meet Apple's high standards of conduct ultimately end up losing Apple's business.

*Sources:* Apple, *Apple Supplier Responsibility 2012 Progress Report,* January 13, 2012. **http://images.apple.com/supplierresponsibility/ pdf/Apple_SR_2012_Progress_Report.pdf** (accessed March 2, 2012); Nick Wingfield and Charles Duhigg, "Apple Lists Its Suppliers for 1st Time," *Nytimes.com,* January 13, 2012. **http://www.nytimes.com/** (accessed March 2, 2012).

and residence, freedom of speech and political opinion, and the right to privacy. In Japan, managers believe that showing respect for the collective good of society is a more important ethical consideration. In Muslim countries, managers typically apply ethical standards compatible with the teachings of Mohammed. Consequently, the school of **ethical relativism** holds that a "one-size-fits-all" template for judging the ethical appropriateness of business actions and the behaviors of company personnel is totally inappropriate. Rather, the underlying thesis of ethical relativism is that when there are cross-country or cross-cultural differences in ethical standards, it is appropriate for *local ethical standards to take precedence over what the ethical standards may be in a company's home market.*[4] In a world of ethical relativism, there are few absolutes when it comes to business ethics, and thus few ethical absolutes for consistently judging the ethical correctness of a company's conduct in various countries and markets.

While the ethical relativism rule of "When in Rome, do as the Romans do" appears reasonable, it leads to the conclusion that what prevails as local morality is an adequate and definitive guide to ethical behavior. But this poses some challenging ethical dilemmas. Consider the following two examples.

### The Use of Underage Labor

In industrialized nations, the use of underage workers is considered taboo. Social activists are adamant that child labor is unethical and that companies should neither employ children under the age of 18 as full-time employees nor source any products from foreign suppliers that employ underage workers. Many countries have passed legislation forbidding the use of underage labor or, at a minimum, regulating the employment of people under the age of 18. However, in India, Bangladesh, Botswana, Sri Lanka, Ghana, Somalia, Turkey, and more than 50 other countries, it is customary to view children as potential, even necessary, workers.[5] As of 2012, the International Labor Organization estimated that 215 million children, from age 5 to 14, were working around the world.[6]

While exposing children to hazardous work and long work hours is unquestionably deplorable, the fact remains that poverty-stricken families in many poor countries cannot subsist without the work efforts of young family members; sending their children to school instead of having them work is not a realistic option. If such children are not permitted to work (especially those in the 12–17 age group)—due to pressures imposed by activist groups in industrialized nations—they may be forced to go out on the streets begging or to seek work in parts of the "underground" economy such as drug trafficking and prostitution.[7] So if all businesses in countries where employing underage workers is common succumb to the pressures to stop employing underage labor, then have they served the best interests of the underage workers, their families, and society in general?

### The Payment of Bribes and Kickbacks

A particularly thorny area facing multinational companies is the degree of cross-country variability in paying bribes.[8] In many countries in eastern Europe, Africa, Latin America, and Asia, it is customary to pay bribes to government officials in order to win a government contract, obtain a license or permit, or facilitate an administrative ruling.[9] In some developing nations, it is difficult for any company, foreign or domestic, to move goods through customs without paying off low-level officials.[10] Senior managers in China often use their power to obtain kickbacks when they purchase materials or other products for their companies.[11] Likewise, in many countries it is normal to make payments to prospective customers in order to win or retain their business. In some developing nations, it is difficult for any company, foreign or domestic, to move goods through customs without paying off low-level officials. A *Wall Street Journal* article reported that 30 to 60 percent of all business transactions in eastern Europe involved paying bribes and the costs of bribe payments averaged 2 to 8 percent of revenues.[12] Some people stretch to justify the payment of bribes and kickbacks on grounds that bribing government officials to get goods through customs or giving kickbacks to customers to retain their business or win new orders is simply a payment for services rendered, in the same way that people tip for service at restaurants.[13] But while this is a clever rationalization, it rests on moral quicksand.

Companies that forbid the payment of bribes and kickbacks in their codes of ethical conduct and that are serious about enforcing this prohibition face a particularly vexing problem in countries where bribery and kickback payments are an entrenched local custom. Complying with the company's code of ethical conduct in these countries is very often tantamount to losing business to competitors that have no such scruples—an outcome that penalizes ethical companies and ethical company personnel (who may suffer lost sales commissions or bonuses). On the other hand, the payment of bribes or kickbacks not only undercuts the company's code of ethics but also risks breaking the law. U.S. companies are prohibited by the Foreign Corrupt Practices Act (FCPA) from paying bribes to government officials, political parties, political candidates, or others in all countries where they do business. The Organization for Economic Cooperation and Development (OECD) has anti-bribery standards that criminalize the bribery of foreign public officials in international business transactions—as of 2009, the 30 OECD members and 8 nonmember countries had adopted these standards.[14]

Despite laws forbidding bribery to secure sales and contracts, the practice persists. In 2010, there were some 345 cases in various stages of investigation for bribery and corruption. In 2010, Hewlett-Packard (HP) agreed to pay $16.25 million to settle allegations that it bribed Texas school officials with expensive gifts in exchange for federally funded contracts that paid for Internet connections for schools and libraries. In 2011, Daimler AG, the maker of Mercedes-Benz vehicles, paid $185 million in fines to settle charges that it used secret bank accounts to make 200 illicit payments totaling more than $56 million to foreign officials in 22 countries between 1998 and 2008. Daimler's kickback scheme of cash and gifts enabled it to secure sales of about 6,300 commercial vehicles and 500 passenger cars worth $1.9 billion and earn an estimated $91.4 million in profits. In recognition of such problems, penalizing companies for overseas bribes is becoming more widespread internationally.

> Under ethical relativism, there can be no one-size-fits-all set of authentic ethical norms against which to gauge the conduct of company personnel.

### Basing Ethical Standards on Ethical Relativism Is Problematic for Multinational Companies

From a global markets perspective, ethical relativism results in a maze of conflicting ethical standards for multinational companies wanting to address the very real issue of which ethical standards to enforce companywide. It is a slippery slope indeed to resolve such ethical diversity without any kind of higher-order moral compass. Consider, for example, the ethical inconsistency of a multinational company that, in the name of ethical relativism, declares it impermissible to engage in bribery and kickbacks, unless such payments are customary and generally overlooked by legal authorities. It is likewise problematic for a multinational company to declare it ethically acceptable to use underage labor in its plants in those countries where child labor is allowed but ethically inappropriate to employ underage labor at its plants elsewhere. If a country's culture is accepting of environmental degradation or exposing workers to dangerous conditions (toxic chemicals or bodily harm), then should a multinational company lower its ethical bar in that country and deem such actions within ethical bounds but raise the ethical bar and rule the very same actions to be ethically wrong in other countries?

Company managers who rely upon the principle of ethical relativism to justify conflicting ethical standards for operating in different countries have little moral basis for establishing or enforcing ethical standards companywide. Rather, when a company's ethical standards vary from country to country, the clear message being sent to employees is that the company has no ethical standards or convictions of its own and prefers to let its standards of ethically right and wrong be governed by the customs and practices of the countries in which it operates. Applying multiple sets of ethical standards without some kind of higher-order moral compass is scarcely a basis for holding company personnel to high standards of ethical behavior.

> Codes of conduct based on ethical relativism can be *ethically dangerous* for multinational companies by creating a maze of conflicting ethical standards.

# Ethics and Integrative Social Contracts Theory

**Integrative social contracts theory** provides a middle position between the opposing views of universalism and relativism.[15] According to this theory, the ethical standards a company should try to uphold are governed by both (1) a limited number of universal ethical principles that are widely recognized as putting legitimate ethical boundaries on behaviors in *all* situations and (2) the circumstances of local cultures, traditions, and values that further prescribe what constitutes ethically permissible behavior. The universal ethical principles are based on the collective views of multiple cultures and societies and combine to form a "social contract" that all individuals, groups, organizations, and businesses in all situations have a duty to observe. *Within the boundaries of this social contract,* local cultures or groups can specify what other actions may or may not be ethically permissible. While this system leaves some "moral free space" for the people in a particular country (or local culture, or profession, or even a company) to make specific interpretations of what other actions may or may not be permissible, *universal ethical norms always take precedence.* Thus, local ethical standards can be *more* stringent than the universal ethical standards, but never less so. For example, both the legal and medical professions have standards regarding what kinds of advertising are ethically permissible that extend beyond the universal norm that advertising not be false or misleading.

The strength of integrated social contracts theory is that it accommodates the best parts of ethical universalism and ethical relativism. Moreover, integrative social contracts theory offers managers in multinational companies clear guidance in resolving cross-country ethical differences: Those parts of the company's code of ethics that involve universal ethical norms must be enforced worldwide, but within these boundaries there is room for ethical diversity and the opportunity for host country cultures to exert *some* influence over the moral and ethical standards of business units operating in that country. Such an approach avoids the discomforting case of a self-righteous multinational company trying to operate as the standard bearer of moral truth and imposing its interpretation of its code of ethics worldwide no matter what. And it avoids the equally disturbing case for a company's ethical conduct to be no higher than local ethical norms in situations where local ethical norms permit practices that are generally considered immoral or when local norms clearly conflict with a company's code of ethical conduct.

A good example of the application of integrative social contracts theory to business involves the payment of bribes and kickbacks. Yes, bribes and kickbacks seem to be common in some countries, but does this justify paying them? Just because bribery flourishes in a country does not mean it is an authentic or legitimate ethical norm. Virtually all of the world's major religions (e.g., Buddhism, Christianity, Confucianism, Hinduism, Islam, Judaism, Sikhism, and Taoism) and all moral schools of thought condemn bribery and corruption.[16] Therefore, a multinational company might reasonably conclude that there is a universal ethical principle to be observed in this case—one of refusing to condone bribery and kickbacks on the part of company personnel no matter what the local custom is and no matter what the sales consequences are.

# HOW AND WHY ETHICAL STANDARDS IMPACT THE TASKS OF CRAFTING AND EXECUTING STRATEGY

Many companies have acknowledged their ethical obligations in official codes of ethical conduct. In the United States, for example, the Sarbanes–Oxley Act, passed in 2002, requires that companies whose stock is publicly traded have a code of ethics or else explain in writing to the Securities and Exchange Commission (SEC) why they do not. But there's a big difference between having a code of ethics because it is mandated and having ethical standards that truly provide guidance for a company's strategy and business conduct.[17] *The litmus test of whether a company's code of ethics is cosmetic is the extent to which it is embraced in crafting strategy and in operating the business day to day.*

It is up to senior executives to lead the way on compliance with the company's ethical code of conduct. They can do so by making a point to consider three sets of questions whenever a new strategic initiative is under review:

- Is what we are proposing to do fully compliant with our code of ethical conduct? Are there any areas of ambiguity that may be of concern?
- Is it apparent that this proposed action is in harmony with our code? Are any conflicts or potential problems evident?
- Is there anything in the proposed action that could be considered ethically objectionable? Would our customers, employees, suppliers, stockholders, competitors, communities, the SEC, or the media view this action as ethically objectionable?

Unless questions of this nature are posed—either in open discussion or by force of habit in the minds of strategy makers—there's room for strategic initiatives to become disconnected from the company's code of ethics. If a company's executives believe strongly in living up to the company's ethical standards, they will unhesitatingly reject strategic initiatives and operating approaches that don't measure up. However, in companies with a cosmetic approach to ethics, any strategy–ethics linkage stems mainly from a desire to avoid the risk of embarrassment and possible disciplinary action for approving a strategic initiative that is deemed by society to be unethical and perhaps illegal.

While most company managers are careful to ensure that a company's strategy is within the bounds of what is legal, evidence indicates they are not always so careful to ensure that all elements of their strategies and operating activities are within the bounds of what is considered ethical. In recent years, there have been revelations of ethical misconduct on the part of managers at such companies as Goldman Sachs, Halliburton, Fannie Mae, Freddie Mac, BP, Deepwater Horizon, Royal Dutch/Shell, Rite Aid, Mexican oil giant Pemex, AIG, several leading brokerage houses, mutual fund companies, investment banking firms, and a host of mortgage lenders. The consequences of crafting strategies that cannot pass the test of moral scrutiny are manifested in sizable fines, devastating public relations hits, sharp drops in stock prices that cost shareholders billions of dollars, and criminal indictments and convictions of company executives. The fallout from all these scandals has resulted in heightened management attention to legal and ethical considerations in crafting strategy.

# WHAT ARE THE DRIVERS OF UNETHICAL STRATEGIES AND BUSINESS BEHAVIOR?

Apart from "the business of business is business, not ethics" kind of thinking apparent in recent high-profile business scandals, three other main drivers of unethical business behavior also stand out:[18]

- Faulty oversight, enabling the unscrupulous pursuit of personal gain and self-interest.
- Heavy pressures on company managers to meet or beat short-term performance targets.
- A company culture that puts profitability and business performance ahead of ethical behavior.

**LO 2**

Recognize conditions that can give rise to unethical business strategies and behavior.

## Faulty Oversight, Enabling the Unscrupulous Pursuit of Personal Gain and Self-Interest

People who are obsessed with wealth accumulation, power, status, and their own self-interest often push ethical principles aside in their quest for personal gain. Driven by greed and ambition, they exhibit few qualms in skirting the rules or doing whatever is necessary to achieve their goals. A general disregard for business ethics can prompt all kinds of unethical strategic maneuvers and behaviors at companies. The U.S. government has been conducting a multiyear investigation of "inside trading," the illegal practice of exchanging confidential information to gain an advantage in the stock market. Focusing on the hedge fund industry and nicknamed "Operation Perfect Hedge," the investigation has brought to light scores of violations and led to more than 60 guilty pleas or convictions by early 2012. Among the most prominent of those convicted was Raj Rajarathnam, the former head of Galleon Group, who was sentenced to 11 years in prison and fined $10 million. In January 2012, seven hedge fund managers, described as a "circle of friends who formed a criminal club" were charged with reaping nearly $62 million in illegal profits on trades of Dell Inc.[19]

Responsible corporate governance and oversight by the company's corporate board is necessary to guard against self-dealing and the manipulation of information to disguise such actions by a company's managers. **Self-dealing** occurs when managers take advantage of their position to further their own private interests rather than those of the firm. As discussed in Chapter 2, the duty of the corporate board (and its compensation and audit committees in particular) is to guard against such actions. A strong, independent board is necessary to have proper oversight of the company's financial practices and to hold top managers accountable for their actions.

> ### CORE CONCEPT
>
> **Self-dealing** occurs when managers take advantage of their position to further their own private interests rather than those of the firm.

A particularly egregious example of the lack of proper oversight is the scandal over mortgage lending and banking practices that resulted in a crisis for the U.S. residential real estate market and heartrending consequences for many home buyers. This scandal stemmed from consciously unethical strategies at many banks and mortgage companies to boost the fees they earned on home mortgages by deliberately lowering lending standards to approve so-called "subprime loans" for home buyers whose incomes were insufficient to make their monthly mortgage payments. Once these lenders earned their fees on these loans, they repackaged the loans to hide their true nature and auctioned them off to unsuspecting investors, who later suffered huge losses when the high-risk borrowers began to default on their loan payments. (Government authorities later forced some of the firms that auctioned off these packaged loans to repurchase them at the auction price and bear the losses themselves.) A lawsuit by the attorneys general of 49 states charging widespread and systematic fraud ultimately resulted in a $26 billion settlement by the five largest U.S. banks (Bank of America, Citigroup, JPMorgan Chase, Wells Fargo, and Ally Financial). Included in the settlement were new rules designed to increase oversight and reform policies and practices among the mortgage companies. The settlement includes what are believed to be a set of robust monitoring and enforcement mechanisms that should help prevent such abuses in the future.[20]

Illustration Capsule 9.2 discusses the high-profile multibillion-dollar Ponzi schemes perpetrated at Bernard L. Madoff Investment Securities and alleged at Stanford Financial Group.

## Heavy Pressures on Company Managers to Meet Short-Term Earnings Targets

When key personnel find themselves scrambling to meet the quarterly and annual sales and profit expectations of investors and financial analysts, they often feel enormous pressure to *do whatever it takes* to protect their reputation for delivering good results. Executives at high-performing companies know that investors will see the slightest sign of a slowdown in earnings growth as a red flag and drive down the

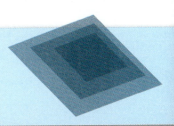

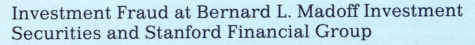

# Investment Fraud at Bernard L. Madoff Investment Securities and Stanford Financial Group

Bernard Madoff engineered the largest investment scam in history to accumulate a net worth of more than $820 million and build a reputation as one of Wall Street's most savvy investors. Madoff deceived investors with a simple Ponzi scheme that promised returns that would beat the market by 400 to 500 percent. The hedge funds, banks, and wealthy individuals that sent Bernard L. Madoff Investment Securities billions to invest on their behalf were quite pleased when their statements arrived showing annual returns as high as 45 percent. But, in fact, the portfolio gains shown on these statements were fictitious. Funds placed with Bernard Madoff were seldom, if ever, actually invested in any type of security—the money went to cover losses in his legitimate stock-trading business, fund periodic withdrawals of investors' funds, and support Madoff's lifestyle (including three vacation homes and a $7 million Manhattan condominium.

For decades, the Ponzi scheme was never in danger of collapse because most Madoff investors were so impressed with the reported returns that they seldom made withdrawals from their accounts, and when they did withdraw funds Madoff used new investors' deposits to cover the payments. Madoff's deception came to an end in late 2008 when the dramatic drop in world stock prices caused so many of Madoff's investors to request withdrawals of their balances that there was not nearly enough new money coming in to cover the amounts being withdrawn. As with any Ponzi scheme, the first investors to ask Madoff for their funds were paid, but those asking later were left empty-handed. All told, more than 1,300 account holders lost about $65 billion when Bernard Madoff admitted to the scam in December 2008. As of October 2011, investigators had located assets of only about $9 billion to return to Madoff account holders. Madoff was sentenced to 150 years in prison for his crimes.

Increased oversight at the Securities and Exchange Commission after the December 2008 Madoff confession led to the indictment of R. Allen Stanford and five others who were accused of running an investment scheme similar to that perpetrated by Bernard Madoff. Stanford was alleged to have defrauded more than 30,000 Stanford Financial Group account holders out of $7.2 billion through the sale of spurious certificates of deposit (CDs). Federal prosecutors alleged that deposits of at least $1.6 billion were diverted into undisclosed personal loans to Allen Stanford.

At the time of Stanford's indictment, he ranked 605th on *Forbes* magazine's list of the world's wealthiest persons, with an estimated net worth of $2.2 billion. He was also a notable sports enthusiast and philanthropist, having contributed millions to the St. Jude Children's Research Hospital and museums in Houston and Miami. After his indictment, he was denied bail and sent to jail to await trial, where he was badly beaten by prison inmates. In March 2012, he was convicted of money laundering and fraud in a Ponzi scheme.

*Sources:* James Bandler, Nicholas Varchaver, and Doris Burke, "How Bernie Did It," *Fortune Online,* April 30, 2009 (accessed July 7, 2009); Alyssa Abkowitz, "The Investment Scam-Artist's Playbook," *Fortune Online,* February 25, 2009 (accessed July 9, 2009); Jane J. Kim, "The Madoff Fraud: SIPC Sets Payouts in Madoff Scandal," *The Wall Street Journal* (Eastern Edition), October 29, 2009, p. C4; http://www.dailymail.co.uk/, accessed March 3, 2012; D. Gilbert, "Stanford Guilty in Ponzi Scheme," *WSJ online,* Markets, March 6, 2012.

company's stock price. In addition, slowing growth or declining profits could lead to a downgrade of the company's credit rating if it has used lots of debt to finance its growth. The pressure to "never miss a quarter"—so as not to upset the expectations of analysts, investors, and creditors—prompts nearsighted managers to engage in short-term maneuvers to make the numbers, regardless of whether these moves are really in the best long-term interests of the company. Sometimes the pressure induces company personnel to continue to stretch the rules until the limits of ethical conduct are overlooked.[21] Once ethical boundaries are crossed in efforts to "meet or beat their numbers," the threshold for making more extreme ethical compromises becomes lower.

In 2010, ATM maker Diebold, Inc. agreed to pay $25 million to settle a case brought by the Securities and Exchange Commission alleging that Diebold engaged in a fraudulent accounting scheme to inflate the company's earnings. Three of Diebold's former financial executives were also charged with manipulating the company's books to meet earnings forecasts. As Robert Khuzami, Director of the SEC's Division of Enforcement noted, "When executives disregard their professional obligations to investors, both they and their companies face significant legal consequences.[22] More recently, an investigation into a decade-long cover-up of investment losses by the Japanese camera maker Olympus resulted in the 2012 arrest of seven executives on suspicion of violation of Japanese securities laws. The share price of Olympus collapsed when the scandal broke, and the company now faces a daunting battle to regain its credibility along with its financial footing.

Company executives often feel pressured to hit financial performance targets because their compensation depends heavily on the company's performance. Over the last two decades, it has become fashionable for boards of directors to grant lavish bonuses, stock option awards, and other compensation benefits to executives for meeting specified performance targets. So outlandishly large were these rewards that executives had strong personal incentives to bend the rules and engage in behaviors that allowed the targets to be met. Much of the accounting manipulation at the root of recent corporate scandals has entailed situations in which executives benefited enormously from misleading accounting or other shady activities that allowed them to hit the numbers and receive incentive awards ranging from $10 million to more than $1 billion dollars for hedge fund managers.

The fundamental problem with **short-termism**—the tendency for managers to focus excessive attention on short-term performance objectives—is that it doesn't create value for customers or improve the firm's competitiveness in the marketplace; that is, it sacrifices the activities that are the most reliable drivers of higher profits and added shareholder value in the long run. Cutting ethical corners in the name of profits carries exceptionally high risk for shareholders—the steep stock price decline and tarnished brand image that accompany the discovery of scurrilous behavior leave shareholders with a company worth much less than before—and the rebuilding task can be arduous, taking both considerable time and resources.

> **CORE CONCEPT**
>
> **Short-termism** is the tendency for managers to focus excessively on short-term performance objectives at the expense of longer-term strategic objectives. It has negative implications for the likelihood of ethical lapses as well as company performance in the longer run.

## A Company Culture that Puts Profitability and Business Performance Ahead of Ethical Behavior

When a company's culture spawns an ethically corrupt or amoral work climate, people have a company-approved license to ignore "what's right" and employ any strategy they think they can get away with. Such cultural norms as "everyone else does it" and "it is okay to bend the rules to get the job done" permeate the work environment. At such companies, ethically immoral people are certain to play down observance of ethical strategic actions and business conduct. Moreover, cultural pressures to utilize unethical means if circumstances become challenging can prompt otherwise honorable people to behave unethically. A perfect example of a company culture gone awry on ethics is Enron, a now-defunct company found guilty of one of the most sprawling business frauds in U.S. history.[23]

Enron's leaders encouraged company personnel to focus on the current bottom line and to be innovative and aggressive in figuring out how to grow current earnings—regardless of the methods. Enron's annual "rank and yank" performance evaluation process, in which the lowest-ranking 15 to 20 percent of employees were let go, made it abundantly clear that bottom-line results were what mattered most. The name of the game at Enron became devising clever ways to boost revenues and earnings, even if this sometimes meant operating outside established policies. In fact, outside-the-lines behavior was celebrated if it generated profitable new business.

A high-performance/high-rewards climate came to pervade the Enron culture, as the best workers (determined by who produced the best bottom-line results) received

# How Novo Nordisk Puts Its Ethical Principles into Practice

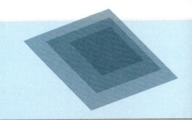

Novo Nordisk is a $12B global pharmaceutical company, known for its innovation and leadership in diabetes treatments. It is also known for its dedication to ethical business practices. In 2009, Novo Nordisk was declared one of the world's most ethical companies by the U.S. business ethics think tank *Ethicsphere*. In 2012, the company was listed as the global leader in business ethics by *Corporate Knights*, a corporate social responsibility advisory firm.

Novo Nordisk's company policies are explicit in their attention to both bioethics and business ethics. In the realm of bioethics, the company is committed to conducting its research involving people, animals, and gene technology in accordance with the highest global ethical standards. Moreover, the company requires that all of their suppliers and other external partners also adhere to Novo Nordisk's bioethical standards. In the realm of business ethics, the policies dictate: (1) that high ethical standards be applied consistently across the company's value chain, (2) that all ethical dilemmas encountered be addressed transparently, and (3) that company officers and employees be held accountable for complying with all laws, regulations, and company rules.

Novo Nordisk's strong culture of responsibility helps to translate the company's policies into practice. At Novo Nordisk, every employee pledges to conduct themselves according to the Novo Nordisk Way, a set of behavioral norms that has come to define the company's culture. It's a culture that promotes teamwork, cooperation, respect for others, and fairness. The commitment to business ethics grew out of those values, which are promoted throughout the company by hiring practices, management leadership, and employee mobility to foster a global one-company culture.

As part of this process, Novo Nordisk has set up a business ethics board, composed of senior management. The board identifies key ethical challenges for the company, drafting guidelines and developing training programs. Those training programs are rigorous: all Novo Nordisk employees are trained annually in business ethics. The board is also responsible for ensuring

compliance. It has set up an anonymous hotline and conducts ethics audits. During 2011, 43 audits were conducted. The goal of these audits is to maintain a culture that promotes the principles of the Novo Nordisk Way.

Implementing a code of ethics across an organization of 26,000 employees is very difficult and lapses do occur. But such incidents are exceptional and are swiftly addressed by the company. For example, when insider trading allegations came to light against a corporate executive in 2008, the company immediately suspended and subsequently fired the employee.

Developed with Dennis L. Huggins.

*Sources:* Jim Edwards, "Novo Nordisk Exec Charged with Insider Trading; Cash Stashed in Caribbean," *CBS News,* September 2008 (accessed at **www.cbsnews.com** on February 19, 2012); company website, accessed February 19, 2012; Corporate Knights, "The 8th Annual Global 100," (accessed at **http://global100.org/** on February 20, 2012).

impressively large incentives and bonuses. On Car Day at Enron, an array of luxury sports cars arrived for presentation to the most successful employees. Understandably, employees wanted to be seen as part of Enron's star team and partake in the benefits granted to Enron's best and brightest employees. The high monetary rewards, the ambitious and hard-driving people whom the company hired and promoted, and the competitive, results-oriented culture combined to give Enron a reputation not only for trampling competitors but also for internal ruthlessness. The company's win-at-all-costs mindset nurtured a culture that gradually and then more rapidly fostered the erosion of ethical standards, eventually making a mockery of the company's stated values of integrity and respect. When it became evident in fall of 2001 that Enron was a house of cards propped up by deceitful accounting and myriad unsavory practices, the company imploded in a matter of weeks—one of the biggest bankruptcies of all time, costing investors $64 billion in losses.

In contrast, when high ethical principles are deeply ingrained in the corporate culture of a company, culture can function as a powerful mechanism for communicating ethical behavioral norms and gaining employee buy-in to the company's moral standards, business principles, and corporate values. In such cases, the ethical principles embraced in the company's code of ethics and/or in its statement of corporate values are seen as integral to the company's identity, self-image, and ways of operating. The message that ethics matters—and matters a lot—resounds loudly and clearly throughout the organization and in its strategy and decisions. Illustration Capsule 9.3 discusses Novo Nordisk's approach to building an ethical culture and putting its ethical principles into practice.

# WHY SHOULD COMPANY STRATEGIES BE ETHICAL?

There are two reasons why a company's strategy should be ethical: (1) because a strategy that is unethical is morally wrong and reflects badly on the character of the company personnel and (2) because an ethical strategy can be good business and serve the self-interest of shareholders.

## The Moral Case for an Ethical Strategy

Managers do not dispassionately assess what strategic course to steer. Ethical strategy making generally begins with managers who themselves have strong moral character (i.e., who are trustworthy, have integrity, and truly care about conducting the company's business in an honorable manner). Managers with high ethical principles are usually advocates of a corporate code of ethics and strong ethics compliance, and they are genuinely committed to upholding corporate values and ethical business principles. They demonstrate their commitment by displaying the company's stated values and living up to its business principles and ethical standards. They understand there's a big difference between adopting value statements and codes of ethics and ensuring that they are followed strictly in a company's actual strategy and business conduct. As a consequence, ethically strong managers consciously opt for strategic actions that can pass the strictest moral scrutiny—they display no tolerance for strategies with ethically controversial components.

**LO 3**

Gain an understanding of the costs of business ethics failures.

## The Business Case for Ethical Strategies

In addition to the moral reasons for adopting ethical strategies, there may be solid business reasons. Pursuing unethical strategies and tolerating unethical conduct not only damages a company's reputation but also may result in a wide-ranging set of other costly consequences. Figure 9.1 shows the wide-ranging costs a company can incur when unethical behavior on its part is discovered, the wrongdoings of company personnel are headlined in the media, and it is forced to make amends for its behavior. The more egregious are a company's ethical violations, the higher the costs and the bigger the damage to its reputation (and to the reputations of the company personnel involved). In high-profile instances, the costs of ethical misconduct can easily run into the hundreds of millions and even billions of dollars, especially if they provoke widespread public outrage and many people were harmed. The penalties levied on executives caught in wrongdoing can skyrocket as well, as the 150-year prison term sentence of financier Bernie Madoff illustrates.

The fallout of ethical misconduct on the part of a company goes well beyond the costs of making amends for the misdeeds. Rehabilitating a company's shattered reputation is time-consuming and costly. Customers shun companies known for their shady behavior. Companies known to have engaged in unethical conduct have difficulty in recruiting and retaining talented employees.[24] Most ethically upstanding people don't want to get entrapped in a compromising situation, nor do they want their personal reputations tarnished by the actions of an unsavory employer. Creditors are unnerved by the unethical actions of a borrower because of the potential business fallout and subsequent risk of default on loans.

All told, a company's unethical behavior risks doing considerable damage to shareholders in the form of lost revenues, higher costs, lower profits, lower stock prices, and a diminished business reputation. To a significant degree, therefore, ethical strategies and ethical

> Conducting business in an ethical fashion is not only morally right—it is in a company's enlightened self-interest.

> Shareholders suffer major damage when a company's unethical behavior is discovered. Making amends for unethical business conduct is costly, and it takes years to rehabilitate a tarnished company reputation.

**FIGURE 9.1** The Costs Companies Incur When Ethical Wrongdoing Is Discovered

| Visible Costs | Internal Administrative Costs | Intangible or Less Visible Costs |
|---|---|---|
| • Government fines and penalties<br>• Civil penalties arising from class-action lawsuits and other litigation aimed at punishing the company for its offense and the harm done to others<br>• The costs to shareholders in the form of a lower stock price (and possibly lower dividends) | • Legal and investigative costs incurred by the company<br>• The costs of providing remedial education and ethics training to company personnel<br>• Costs of taking corrective actions<br>• Administrative costs associated with ensuring future compliance | • Customer defections<br>• Loss of reputation<br>• Lost employee morale and higher degrees of employee cynicism<br>• Higher employee turnover<br>• Higher recruiting costs and difficulty in attracting talented employees<br>• Adverse effects on employee productivity<br>• The costs of complying with often harsher government regulations |

*Source:* Adapted from Terry Thomas, John R. Schermerhorn, and John W. Dienhart, "Strategic Leadership of Ethical Behavior," *Academy of Management Executive* 18, no. 2 (May 2004), p. 58.

conduct are *good business.* Most companies understand the value of operating in a manner that wins the approval of suppliers, employees, investors, and society at large. Most business-people recognize the personal risks and adverse fallout attached to the discovery of unethical behavior. Hence, companies have an incentive to employ strategies that can pass the test of being ethical. Even if a company's managers are not of strong moral character and personally committed to high ethical standards, they have good reason to operate within ethical bounds, if only to avoid the risk of embarrassment, scandal, disciplinary action, fines, and possible jail-time for unethical conduct on their part.

# STRATEGY, CORPORATE SOCIAL RESPONSIBILITY, AND ENVIRONMENTAL SUSTAINABILITY

The idea that businesses have an obligation to foster social betterment, a much-debated topic in the past 50 years, took root in the 19th century when progressive companies in the aftermath of the industrial revolution began to provide workers with housing and other amenities. The notion that corporate executives should balance the interests of all stakeholders—shareholders, employees, customers, suppliers, the communities in which they operated, and society at large—began to blossom in the 1960s. Some years later, a group of chief executives of America's 200 largest corporations, calling themselves the Business Roundtable, came out in strong support of the concept of **corporate social responsibility:**[25]

> Balancing the shareholder's expectations of maximum return against other priorities is one of the fundamental problems confronting corporate management. The shareholder must receive a good return but the legitimate concerns of other constituencies (customers, employees, communities, suppliers and society at large) also must have the appropriate attention. . . . [Leading managers] believe that by giving enlightened consideration to balancing the legitimate claims of all its constituents, a corporation will best serve the interest of its shareholders.

Today, corporate social responsibility (CSR) is a concept that resonates in western Europe, the United States, Canada, and such developing nations as Brazil and India.

## What Do We Mean by Corporate Social Responsibility?

The essence of socially responsible business behavior is that a company should balance strategic actions to benefit shareholders against the *duty* to be a good corporate citizen. The underlying thesis is that company managers should display a *social conscience* in operating the business and specifically take into account how management decisions and company actions affect the well-being of employees, local communities, the environment, and society at large.[26] Acting in a socially responsible manner thus encompasses more than just participating in community service projects and donating monies to charities and other worthy social causes. Demonstrating social responsibility also entails undertaking actions that earn trust and respect from all stakeholders—operating in an honorable and ethical manner, striving to make the company a great place to work, demonstrating genuine respect for the environment, and trying to make a difference in bettering society. As depicted in Figure 9.2, corporate responsibility programs commonly include the following elements:

- *Making efforts to employ an ethical strategy and observe ethical principles in operating the business.* A sincere commitment to observing ethical principles is a necessary component of a CSR strategy simply because unethical conduct is incompatible with the concept of good corporate citizenship and socially responsible business behavior.

**FIGURE 9.2**  The Five Components of a Corporate Social Responsibility Strategy

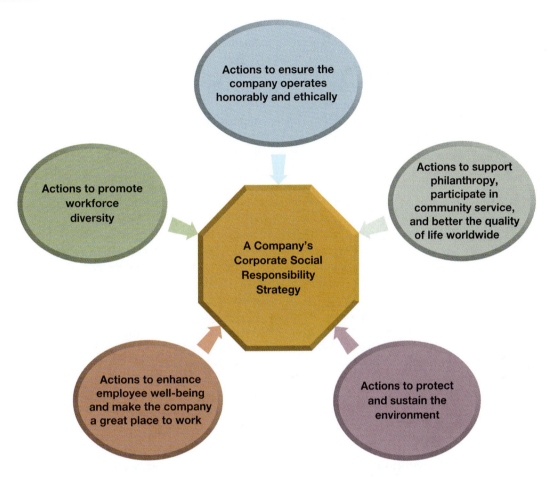

*Source:* Adapted from material in Ronald Paul Hill, Debra Stephens, and Iain Smith, "Corporate Social Responsibility: An Examination of Individual Firm Behavior," *Business and Society Review* 108, no. 3 (September 2003), p. 348.

- *Making charitable contributions, supporting community service endeavors, engaging in broader philanthropic initiatives, and reaching out to make a difference in the lives of the disadvantaged.* Some companies fulfill their philanthropic obligations by spreading their efforts over a multitude of charitable and community activities—for instance, Microsoft and Johnson & Johnson support a broad variety of community, art, and social welfare programs. Others prefer to focus their energies more narrowly. McDonald's, for example, concentrates on sponsoring the Ronald McDonald House program (which provides a home away from home for the families of seriously ill children receiving treatment at nearby hospitals). British Telecom gives 1 percent of its profits directly to communities, largely for education—teacher training, in-school workshops, and digital technology. Leading prescription drug maker GlaxoSmith-Kline and other pharmaceutical companies either donate or heavily discount medicines for distribution in the least developed nations. Companies frequently reinforce their philanthropic efforts by encouraging employees to support charitable causes and participate in community affairs, often through programs that match employee contributions.

- *Taking actions to protect the environment and, in particular, to minimize or eliminate any adverse impact on the environment stemming from the company's own business activities.* Corporate social responsibility as it applies to environmental protection entails actively striving to be a good steward of the environment. This means using the best available science and technology to reduce environmentally harmful aspects of the company's operations *below the levels required by prevailing environmental regulations.* It also means putting time and money into improving the environment in ways that extend past a company's own industry boundaries—such as participating in recycling projects, adopting energy conservation practices, and supporting efforts to clean up local water supplies. Retailers like Walmart and Home Depot in the United States and B&Q in the United Kingdom have pressured their suppliers to adopt stronger environmental protection practices in order to lower the carbon footprint of their entire supply chains.[27]

- *Taking actions to create a work environment that enhances the quality of life for employees.* Numerous companies exert extra effort to enhance the quality of life for their employees, both at work and at home. This can include onsite day care, flexible work schedules, workplace exercise facilities, special leaves for employees to care for sick family members, work-at-home opportunities, career development programs and education opportunities, special safety programs, and the like.

- *Taking actions to build a workforce that is diverse with respect to gender, race, national origin, and other aspects that different people bring to the workplace.* Most large companies in the United States have established workforce diversity programs, and some go the extra mile to ensure that their workplaces are attractive to ethnic minorities and inclusive of all groups and perspectives. At some companies, the diversity initiative extends to suppliers—sourcing items from small businesses owned by women or ethnic minorities, for example. The pursuit of workforce diversity can also be good business. At Coca-Cola, where strategic success depends on getting people all over the world to become loyal consumers of the company's beverages, efforts to build a public persona of inclusiveness for people of all races, religions, nationalities, interests, and talents have considerable strategic value.

The particular combination of socially responsible endeavors a company elects to pursue defines its **corporate social responsibility (CSR) strategy.** Illustration Capsule 9.4 describes Burt's Bees' approach to corporate social responsibility—an approach that ensures that social responsibility is reflected in all of the company's actions and endeavors. As the Burt's Bees example shows, the specific components emphasized in a CSR strategy vary from company to company and are typically linked to a company's core values. General Mills, for example, builds its CSR strategy around the theme of "nourishing lives" to emphasize its commitment to good nutrition as well as philanthropy, community building, and environmental protection.[28] Starbucks's CSR strategy includes four main elements (ethical sourcing, community service, environmental stewardship, and farmer support), all of which have touch points with the way that the company procures its coffee—a key aspect of its product differentiation strategy.[29] Some companies use other terms, such as *corporate citizenship, corporate responsibility,* or *sustainable responsible business (SRB)* to characterize their CSR initiatives.

Although there is wide variation in how companies devise and implement a CSR strategy, communities of companies concerned with corporate social responsibility (such as CSR Europe) have emerged to help companies share best CSR practices. Moreover, a number of reporting standards have been developed, including ISO 26000—a new internationally recognized standard for social responsibility produced by the International Standards Organization (ISO).[30] Companies that exhibit a strong commitment to

> **CORE CONCEPT**
>
> A company's **CSR strategy** is defined by the specific combination of socially beneficial activities the company opts to support with its contributions of time, money, and other resources.

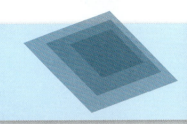

# Burt's Bees: A Strategy Based on Corporate Social Responsibility

Burt's Bees is a leading company in natural personal care, offering nearly 200 products including its popular beeswax lip balms and skin-care creams. The brand has enjoyed tremendous success as consumers have begun to embrace all-natural, environmentally friendly products, boosting Burt's Bees' revenues to over $250M by 2012. Much of Burt's Bees' success can be attributed to its skillful use of Corporate Social Responsibility (CSR) as a strategic tool to engage customers and differentiate itself from competitors.

While many companies have embraced Corporate Social Responsibility, few companies have managed to integrate CSR as fully and seamlessly throughout their organizations as Burt's Bees. The company's business model is centered on a principle they refer to as "The Greater Good," which specifies that all company practices must be socially responsible. The execution of this strategy is managed by a special committee dedicated to leading the organization to attain its CSR goals with respect to three primary areas: natural well-being, humanitarian responsibility, and environmental sustainability.

Natural well-being is focused on the ingredients used to create Burt's Bees products. Today, the average Burt's Bees product contains over 99 percent natural ingredients; by 2020, the brand expects to produce only 100 percent natural products.

Burt's Bees' humanitarian focus is centered on its relationships with employees and suppliers. A key part of this effort involves a mandatory employee training program that focuses on four key areas: outreach, wellness, world-class leadership, and the environment. Another is the company's Responsible Sourcing Mission, which lays out a carefully prescribed set of guidelines for sourcing responsible suppliers and managing supplier relationships.

A focus on caring for the environment is clearly interwoven into all aspects of Burt's Bees. By focusing on environmentally efficient processes, the company uses its in-house manufacturing capability as a point of strategic differentiation.

Burt's Bees faced some consumer backlash when it was purchased recently by The Clorox Company, whose traditional image is viewed in sharp contrast to Burt's Bees values. But while Burt's Bees is still only a small part of Clorox's total revenue, it has become its fastest-growing division.

Developed with Ross M. Templeton.

*Sources:* Company websites; Louise Story, "Can Burt's Bees Turn Clorox Green?" (*The New York Times,* January 6, 2008); Bill Chameides, "Burt's Bees Are Busy on the Sustainability Front" (*Huffington Post,* June 25, 2010); Katie Bird, "Burt's Bees' International Performance Weaker than Expected" (*CosmeticsDesign.com,* January 6, 2011); "Burt's Bees, Marks & Spencer Share Staff Engagement Tactics" (*EnvironmentalLeader.com,* May 31, 2011); http://blogs.newsobserver.com/, accessed March 1, 2012.

corporate social responsibility are often recognized by being included on lists such as *Corporate Responsibility* magazine's "100 Best Corporate Citizens" or *Corporate Knights* magazine's "Global 100 Most Sustainable Corporations."

## Corporate Social Responsibility and the Triple Bottom Line

CSR initiatives undertaken by companies are frequently directed at improving the company's "triple bottom line"—a reference to three types of performance metrics: *economic, social, environmental.* The goal is for a company to succeed simultaneously in all three dimensions, as illustrated in Figure 9.3.[31] The three dimensions of performance are often referred to in terms of the "three pillars" of "people, planet, and profit." The term *people* refers to the various social initiatives that make up CSR strategies, such as corporate giving, community involvement, and company efforts to improve the lives of its internal and external stakeholders. *Planet* refers to a firm's ecological impact and environmental practices. The term *profit* has a broader meaning with respect to the triple bottom line than it does otherwise. It encompasses not only the profit a firm earns for its shareholders but also the economic impact that the company has on society more generally, in terms of the overall value that it creates and the overall costs that it imposes on society. For example, Procter & Gamble's Swiffer cleaning system, one of the company's best-selling products, not only offers an earth-friendly design but also outperforms less ecologically friendly alternatives in terms of its broader economic impact: It reduces demands on municipal water sources, saves electricity that would be needed to heat mop water, and doesn't add to the amount of detergent making its way into waterways and waste treatment facilities. Nike sees itself as bringing people, planet, and profits into balance by producing

## FIGURE 9.3  The Triple Bottom Line: Excelling on Three Measures of Company Performance

*Source:* Developed with help from Amy E. Florentino.

innovative new products in a more sustainable way, recognizing that sustainability is key to its future profitability.

Many companies now make a point of citing the beneficial outcomes of their CSR strategies in press releases and issue special reports for consumers and investors to review. Staples, the world's largest office products company, makes reporting an important part of its commitment to corporate responsibility; the company posts a "Staples Soul Report" on its website that describes its initiatives and accomplishments in the areas of diversity, environment, community, and ethics. Triple-bottom-line (TBL) reporting is emerging as an increasingly important way for companies to make the results of their CSR strategies apparent to stakeholders and for stakeholders to hold companies accountable for their impact on society. The use of standard reporting frameworks and metrics, such as those developed by the Global Reporting Initiative, promotes greater transparency and facilitates benchmarking CSR efforts across firms and industries.

Investment firms have created mutual funds comprised of companies that are excelling on the basis of the triple bottom line in order to attract funds from environmentally and socially aware investors. The Dow Jones Sustainability World Index is made up of the top 10 percent of the 2,500 companies listed in the Dow Jones World Index in terms of economic performance, environmental performance, and social performance. Companies are evaluated in these three performance areas, using indicators such as corporate governance, climate change mitigation, and labor practices. Table 9.1 shows a sampling of the companies selected for the Dow Jones Sustainability World Index in 2011.

## What Do We Mean by *Sustainability* and *Sustainable Business Practices*?

The term *sustainability* is used in a variety of ways. In many firms, it is synonymous with corporate social responsibility; it is seen by some as a term that is gradually replacing CSR in the business lexicon. Indeed, sustainability reporting and TBL reporting are often one and the same, as illustrated by the Dow Jones Sustainability Index, which tracks the same three types of performance measures that constitute the triple bottom line.

More often, however, the term takes on a more focused meaning, concerned with the relationship of a company to its *environment* and its use of *natural resources,* including land, water, air, plants, animals, minerals, fossil fuels, and biodiversity. It is widely recognized that the world's natural resources are finite and are being consumed and degraded at rates that threaten their capacity for renewal. Since corporations are the biggest users of natural resources, managing and maintaining these resources is critical for the long-term economic interests of corporations.

For some companies, this issue has direct and obvious implications for the continued viability of their business model and strategy. Pacific Gas and Electric has begun measuring the full carbon footprint of its supply chain to become not only "greener" but a more efficient energy producer.[32] Beverage companies such as Coca-Cola and PepsiCo are having to rethink their business models because of the prospect of future worldwide water shortages. For other companies, the connection is less direct, but all companies are part of a business ecosystem whose economic health depends on the availability of natural resources. In response, most major companies have begun to change *how* they do business, emphasizing the use of **sustainable business practices,** defined as those capable of meeting the needs of the present without compromising the ability to meet the needs of the future.[33] Many have also begun to incorporate a consideration of environmental sustainability into their strategy-making activities.

**Environmental sustainability strategies** entail deliberate and concerted actions to operate businesses in a manner that protects natural resources and ecological support

### CORE CONCEPT

**Sustainable business practices** are those that meet the needs of the present without compromising the ability to meet the needs of the future.

### CORE CONCEPT

A company's **environmental sustainability strategy** consists of its deliberate actions to protect the environment, provide for the longevity of natural resources, maintain ecological support systems for future generations, and guard against ultimate endangerment of the planet.

**TABLE 9.1**    A Selection of Companies Recognized for Their Triple-Bottom-Line Performance in 2011

| Name | Market Sector | Country |
| --- | --- | --- |
| Air France-KLM | Travel & Leisure | France |
| BMW AG | Automobiles & Parts | Germany |
| Enagas S.A. | Utilities | Spain |
| Hyundai Engineering & Construction Co. Ltd. | Construction & Materials | Korea |
| Itausa-Investimentos Itau S/A | Financial Services | Brazil |
| Koninklijke DSM N.V. | Chemicals | Netherlands |
| Koninklijke Philips Electronics N.V. | Personal & Household Goods | Netherlands |
| KT Corp. | Telecommunications | Korea |
| Lotte Shopping Co. Ltd. | Retail | Korea |
| Pearson PLC | Media | UK |
| PepsiCo Inc. | Food & Beverage | United States |
| PostNL N.V. | Industrial Goods & Services | Netherlands |
| Repsol YPF S.A. | Oil & Gas | Spain |
| Roche Holding AG | Health Care | Switzerland |
| Samsung Electronics Co. Ltd. | Technology | Korea |
| Stockland | Real Estate | Australia |
| Swiss Re Limited | Insurance | UK |
| Westpac Banking Corp. | Banks | Australia |
| Xstrata PLC | Basic Resources | Switzerland |

*Sources:* Dow Jones indexes, STOXX Limited, and SAM Group, http://www.sustainability-index.com/djsi_pdf/news/PressReleases/110908-djsi-review-2011-e-vdef.pdf (accessed February 13, 2012).

systems, guards against outcomes that will ultimately endanger the planet, and is therefore sustainable for centuries.[34] One aspect of environmental sustainability is keeping use of the Earth's natural resources within levels that can be replenished via the use of sustainable business practices. In the case of some resources (like crude oil, fresh water, and the harvesting of edible fish from the oceans), scientists say that use levels either are already unsustainable or will be soon, given the world's growing population and propensity to consume additional resources as incomes and living standards rise. Another aspect of sustainability concerns containing the adverse effects of greenhouse gases and other forms of air pollution so as to reduce their impact on undesirable climate and atmospheric changes. Other aspects of sustainability include greater reliance on sustainable energy sources, greater use of recyclable materials, the use of sustainable methods of growing foods (so as to reduce topsoil depletion and the use of pesticides, herbicides, fertilizers, and other chemicals that may be harmful to human health or ecological systems), habitat protection, environmentally sound waste management practices, and increased attempts to decouple environmental degradation and economic growth (according to many scientists, economic growth has historically been accompanied by declines in the well-being of the environment).

Unilever, a diversified producer of processed foods, personal care, and home cleaning products, is among the many committed corporations pursuing sustainable business practices. The company tracks 11 sustainable agricultural indicators in its processed-foods business and has launched a variety of programs to improve the environmental performance of its suppliers. Examples of such programs include special low-rate financing for tomato suppliers choosing to switch to water-conserving irrigation systems and training programs in India that have allowed contract cucumber growers to reduce pesticide use by 90 percent while improving yields by 78 percent. Unilever has also reengineered many internal processes to improve the company's overall performance on sustainability measures. For example, the company's factories have reduced water usage by 63 percent and total waste by 67 percent since 1995 through the implementation of sustainability initiatives. Unilever has also redesigned packaging for many of its products to conserve natural resources and reduce the volume of consumer waste. For example, the company's Suave shampoo bottles were reshaped to save almost 150 tons of plastic resin per year, which is the equivalent of 15 million fewer empty bottles making it to landfills annually. As the producer of Lipton Tea, Unilever is the world's largest purchaser of tea leaves; the company has committed to sourcing all of its tea from Rainforest Alliance Certified farms by 2015, due to their comprehensive triple-bottom-line approach toward sustainable farm management.

## Crafting Corporate Social Responsibility and Sustainability Strategies

While CSR and environmental sustainability strategies take many forms, those that both provide valuable social benefits *and* fulfill customer needs in a superior fashion may also contribute to a company's competitive advantage.[35] For example, while carbon emissions may be a generic social concern for financial institutions such as Wells Fargo, Toyota's sustainability strategy for reducing carbon emissions has produced both competitive advantage and environmental benefits. Its Prius hybrid electric/gasoline-powered automobile is not only among the least polluting automobiles but is also the best-selling hybrid vehicle in the United States; it has earned the company the loyalty of fuel-conscious buyers and given Toyota a green image. Green Mountain Coffee Roasters' commitment to protect the welfare of coffee growers and their families (in particular, making sure they receive a fair price) also meets its customers' wants and needs. In its dealings with suppliers at small farmer cooperatives in Peru, Mexico, and Sumatra, Green Mountain pays "fair-trade" prices for coffee beans (in 2011, the fair-trade prices were a minimum of $1.26 per pound for conventional coffee versus market prices of $0.70 per pound). Green Mountain also purchases about 29 percent of its coffee directly from farmers so as to cut out intermediaries and see that farmers realize a higher price for their efforts—coffee is the world's second most heavily traded commodity after oil, requiring the labor of some 20 million people, most of whom live at the poverty level.[36] Its consumers are aware of these efforts and purchase Green Mountain coffee, in part, to encourage such practices.

CSR strategies and environmental sustainability strategies are more likely to contribute to a company's competitive advantage if they are linked to a company's competitively important resources and capabilities or value chain activities. Thus, it is common for companies engaged in natural resource extraction, electric power production, forestry

> CSR strategies and environmental sustainability strategies that both provide valuable social benefits *and* fulfill customer needs in a superior fashion can lead to competitive advantage. Corporate social agendas that address only social issues may help boost a company's reputation for corporate citizenship but are unlikely to improve its competitive strength in the marketplace.

and paper products, motor vehicles, and chemical production to place more empha-sis on addressing environmental concerns than, say, software and electronics firms or apparel manufacturers. Companies whose business success is heavily dependent on high employee morale or attracting and retaining the best and brightest employees are some-what more prone to stress the well-being of their employees and foster a positive, high-energy workplace environment that elicits the dedication and enthusiastic commitment of employees, thus putting real meaning behind the claim "Our people are our greatest asset." Ernst & Young, one of the four largest global accounting firms, stresses its "People First" workforce diversity strategy that is all about respecting differences, fostering indi-viduality, and promoting inclusiveness so that its more than 152,000 employees in 140 countries can feel valued, engaged, and empowered in developing creative ways to serve the firm's clients. As a service business, Marriot's most competitively important resource is also people. Thus its social agenda includes providing 180 hours of paid classroom and on-the-job training to the chronically unemployed. Ninety percent of the graduates from the job training program take jobs with Marriott, and about two-thirds of those remain with Marriott for more than a year. At Whole Foods Market, an $11.1 billion supermarket chain specializing in organic and natural foods, its environmental sustainability strategy is evident in almost every segment of its company value chain and is a big part of its dif-ferentiation strategy. The company's procurement policies encourage stores to purchase fresh fruits and vegetables from local farmers and screen processed-food items for more than 400 common ingredients that the company considers unhealthy or environmentally unsound. Spoiled food items are sent to regional composting centers rather than landfills, and all cleaning products used in its stores are biodegradable. The company also has cre-ated the Animal Compassion Foundation to develop natural and humane ways of raising farm animals and has converted all of its vehicles to run on biofuels.

Not all companies choose to link their corporate environmental or social agendas to their value chain, their business model, or their industry. For example, Chick-Fil-A, an Atlanta-based fast-food chain with over 1,500 outlets in 39 states, has a charitable foundation that funds two scholarship programs and supports 14 foster homes as well as a summer camp for some 1,900 campers.[37] However, unless a company's social responsi-bility initiatives become part of the way it operates its business every day, the initiatives are unlikely to catch fire and be fully effective. As an executive at Royal Dutch/Shell put it, corporate social responsibility "is not a cosmetic; it must be rooted in our values. It must make a difference to the way we do business."[38] The same is true for environmental sustainability initiatives.

## The Moral Case for Corporate Social Responsibility and Environmentally Sustainable Business Practices

The moral case for why businesses should act in a manner that benefits all of the compa-ny's stakeholders—not just shareholders—boils down to "It's the right thing to do." Ordi-nary decency, civic-mindedness, and contributions to the well-being of society should be expected of any business.[39] In today's social and political climate, most business leaders can be expected to acknowledge that socially responsible actions are important and that businesses have a duty to be good corporate citizens. But there is a comple-mentary school of thought that business operates on the basis of an implied social contract with the members of society. According to this contract, society grants a busi-ness the right to conduct its business affairs and agrees not to unreasonably restrain its pursuit of a fair profit for the goods or services it sells. In return for this "license to

Every action a company takes can be interpreted as a statement of what it stands for.

operate," a business is obligated to act as a responsible citizen, do its fair share to promote the general welfare, and avoid doing any harm. Such a view clearly puts a moral burden on a company to take corporate citizenship into consideration and do what's best for shareholders within the confines of discharging its duties to operate honorably, provide good working conditions to employees, be a good environmental steward, and display good corporate citizenship.

# The Business Case for Corporate Social Responsibility and Environmentally Sustainable Business Practices

Whatever the moral arguments for socially responsible business behavior and environmentally sustainable business practices, there are definitely good business reasons why companies should be public-spirited and devote time and resources to social responsibility initiatives, environmental sustainability, and good corporate citizenship:

- *Such actions can lead to increased buyer patronage.* A strong visible social responsibility or environmental sustainability strategy gives a company an edge in appealing to consumers who prefer to do business with companies that are good corporate citizens. Ben & Jerry's, Whole Foods Market, Stonyfield Farm, and The Body Shop have definitely expanded their customer bases because of their visible and well-publicized activities as socially conscious companies. More and more companies are also recognizing the cash register payoff of social responsibility strategies that reach out to people of all cultures and demographics (women, retirees, and ethnic groups).

- *A strong commitment to socially responsible behavior reduces the risk of reputation-damaging incidents.* Companies that place little importance on operating in a socially responsible manner are more prone to scandal and embarrassment. Consumer, environmental, and human rights activist groups are quick to criticize businesses whose behavior they consider to be out of line, and they are adept at getting their message into the media and onto the Internet. Pressure groups can generate widespread adverse publicity, promote boycotts, and influence like-minded or sympathetic buyers to avoid an offender's products. Research has shown that product boycott announcements are associated with a decline in a company's stock price.[40] When a major oil company suffered damage to its reputation on environmental and social grounds, the CEO repeatedly said that the most negative impact the company suffered—and the one that made him fear for the future of the company—was that bright young graduates were no longer attracted to working for the company. For many years, Nike received stinging criticism for not policing sweatshop conditions in the Asian factories that produced Nike footwear, causing Nike cofounder and former CEO Phil Knight to observe that "Nike has become synonymous with slave wages, forced overtime, and arbitrary abuse."[41] In 1997, Nike began an extensive effort to monitor conditions in the 800 factories of the contract manufacturers that produced Nike shoes. As Knight said, "Good shoes come from good factories and good factories have good labor relations." Nonetheless, Nike has continually been plagued by complaints from human rights activists that its monitoring procedures are flawed and that it is not doing enough to correct the plight of factory workers. As this suggests, a damaged reputation is not easily repaired.

- *Socially responsible actions and sustainable business practices can lower costs and enhance employee recruiting and workforce retention.* Companies with deservedly good

> The higher the public profile of a company or its brand, the greater the scrutiny of its activities and the higher the potential for it to become a target for pressure group action.

reputations for social responsibility and sustainable business practices are better able to attract and retain employees, compared to companies with tarnished reputations. Some employees just feel better about working for a company committed to improving society.[42] This can contribute to lower turnover and better worker productivity. Other direct and indirect economic benefits include lower costs for staff recruitment and training. For example, Starbucks is said to enjoy much lower rates of employee turnover because of its full benefits package for both full-time and part-time employees, management efforts to make Starbucks a great place to work, and the company's socially responsible practices. Sustainable business practices are often concomitant with greater operational efficiencies. For example, when a U.S. manufacturer of recycled paper, taking eco-efficiency to heart, discovered how to increase its fiber recovery rate, it saved the equivalent of 20,000 tons of waste paper—a factor that helped the company become the industry's lowest-cost producer. By helping two-thirds of its employees stop smoking and investing in a number of wellness programs for employees, Johnson & Johnson has saved $250 million on its health care costs over the past decade.[43]

- *Opportunities for revenue enhancement may also come from CSR and environmental sustainability strategies.* The drive for sustainability and social responsibility can spur innovative efforts that in turn lead to new products and opportunities for revenue enhancement. Electric cars such as the Chevy Volt and the Tesla Roadster are one example. In many cases, the revenue opportunities are tied to a company's core products. PepsiCo and Coca-Cola, for example, have expanded into the juice business to offer a healthier alternative to their carbonated beverages. GE has created a profitable new business in wind turbines. In other cases, revenue enhancement opportunities come from innovative ways to reduce waste and use the by-products of a company's production. Tyson Foods now produces jet fuel for B52 bombers from the vast amount of animal waste resulting from its meat product business. Staples has become one of the largest nonutility corporate producers of renewable energy in the United States due to its installation of solar power panels in all of its outlets (and the sale of what it does not consume in renewable energy credit markets).

- *Well-conceived CSR strategies and sustainable business practices are in the best long-term interest of shareholders.* When CSR and sustainability strategies increase buyer patronage, offer revenue-enhancing opportunities, lower costs, increase productivity, and reduce the risk of reputation-damaging incidents, they contribute to the total value created by a company and improve its profitability. A two-year study of leading companies found that improving environmental compliance and developing environmentally friendly products can enhance earnings per share, profitability, and the likelihood of winning contracts. The stock prices of companies that rate high on social and environmental performance criteria have been found to perform 35 to 45 percent better than the average of the 2,500 companies comprising the Dow Jones Global Index.[44] A review of 135 studies indicated there is a positive, but small, correlation between good corporate behavior and good financial performance; only 2 percent of the studies showed that dedicating corporate resources to social responsibility harmed the interests of shareholders.[45] Furthermore, socially responsible business behavior helps avoid or preempt legal and regulatory actions that could prove costly and otherwise burdensome. In some cases, it is possible to craft corporate social responsibility strategies that contribute to competitive advantage and, at the same time, deliver greater value to society. For instance, Walmart, by working with its suppliers to reduce the use of packaging materials and revamping the routes of its delivery trucks to cut out 100 million miles of travel, saved $200 million in costs

Socially responsible strategies that create value for customers and lower costs can improve company profits and shareholder value at the same time that they address other stakeholder interests.

in 2009 (which enhanced its cost competitiveness vis-à-vis rivals) and lowered carbon emissions.[46] Thus, a social responsibility strategy that packs some punch and is more than rhetorical flourish can produce outcomes that are in the best interest of shareholders.

In sum, companies that take social responsibility and environmental sustainability seriously can improve their business reputations and operational efficiency while also reducing their risk exposure and encouraging loyalty and innovation. Overall, companies that take special pains to protect the environment (beyond what is required by law), are active in community affairs, and are generous supporters of charitable causes and projects that benefit society are more likely to be seen as good investments and as good companies to work for or do business with. Shareholders are likely to view the business case for social responsibility as a strong one, particularly when it results in the creation of more customer value, greater productivity, lower operating costs, and lower business risk—all of which should increase firm profitability and enhance shareholder value even as the company's actions address broader stakeholder interests.

Companies are, of course, sometimes rewarded for bad behavior—a company that is able to shift environmental and other social costs associated with its activities onto society as a whole can reap large short-term profits. The major cigarette producers for many years were able to earn greatly inflated profits by shifting the health-related costs of smoking onto others and escaping any responsibility for the harm their products caused to consumers and the general public. Only recently have they been facing the prospect of having to pay high punitive damages for their actions. Unfortunately, the cigarette makers are not alone in trying to evade paying for the social harms of their operations for as long as they can. Calling a halt to such actions usually hinges on (1) the effectiveness of activist social groups in publicizing the adverse consequences of a company's social irresponsibility and marshaling public opinion for something to be done, (2) the enactment of legislation or regulations to correct the inequity, and (3) decisions on the part of socially conscious buyers to take their business elsewhere.

> There's little hard evidence indicating shareholders are disadvantaged in any meaningful way by a company's actions to be socially responsible.

# KEY POINTS

1. Ethics concerns standards of right and wrong. Business ethics concerns the application of ethical principles to the actions and decisions of business organizations and the conduct of their personnel. Ethical principles in business are not materially different from ethical principles in general.

2. There are three schools of thought about ethical standards for companies with international operations:

   - According to the *school of ethical universalism,* common understandings across multiple cultures and countries about what constitutes right and wrong behaviors give rise to universal ethical standards that apply to members of all societies, all companies, and all businesspeople.

   - According to the *school of ethical relativism,* different societal cultures and customs have divergent values and standards of right and wrong. Thus, what is ethical or unethical must be judged in the light of local customs and social mores and can vary from one culture or nation to another.

- According to the *integrated social contracts theory,* universal ethical principles based on the collective views of multiple cultures and societies combine to form a "social contract" that all individuals in all situations have a duty to observe. Within the boundaries of this social contract, local cultures or groups can specify what additional actions are not ethically permissible. However, universal norms always take precedence over local ethical norms.

3. Apart from "the business of business is business, not ethics" kind of thinking, three other factors contribute to unethical business behavior: (1) faulty oversight that enables the unscrupulous pursuit of personal gain, (2) heavy pressures on company managers to meet or beat short-term earnings targets, and (3) a company culture that puts profitability and good business performance ahead of ethical behavior. In contrast, culture can function as a powerful mechanism for promoting ethical business conduct when high ethical principles are deeply ingrained in the corporate culture of a company.

4. Business ethics failures can result in three types of costs: (1) visible costs, such as fines, penalties, and lower stock prices, (2) internal administrative costs, such as legal costs and costs of taking corrective action, and (3) intangible costs, such as customer defections and damage to the company's reputation.

5. The term *corporate social responsibility* concerns a company's *duty* to operate in an honorable manner, provide good working conditions for employees, encourage workforce diversity, be a good steward of the environment, and support philanthropic endeavors in local communities where it operates and in society at large. The particular combination of socially responsible endeavors a company elects to pursue defines its corporate social responsibility (CSR) strategy.

6. The triple bottom line refers to company performance in three realms: economic, social, environmental. Increasingly, companies are reporting their performance with respect to all three performance dimensions.

7. *Sustainability* is a term that is used in various ways, but most often it concerns a firm's relationship to the environment and its use of natural resources. Sustainable business practices are those capable of meeting the needs of the present without compromising the world's ability to meet future needs. A company's environmental sustainability strategy consists of its deliberate actions to protect the environment, provide for the longevity of natural resources, maintain ecological support systems for future generations, and guard against ultimate endangerment of the planet.

8. CSR strategies and environmental sustainability strategies that both provide valuable social benefits *and* fulfill customer needs in a superior fashion can lead to competitive advantage.

9. The moral case for corporate social responsibility and environmental sustainability boils down to a simple concept: It's the right thing to do. There are also solid reasons why CSR and environmental sustainability strategies may be good business—they can be conducive to greater buyer patronage, reduce the risk of reputation-damaging incidents, provide opportunities for revenue enhancement, and lower costs. Well-crafted CSR and environmental sustainability strategies are in the best long-term interest of shareholders, for the reasons just mentioned and because they can avoid or preempt costly legal or regulatory actions.

# ASSURANCE OF LEARNING EXERCISES

1. Ikea is widely known for its commitment to business ethics and environmental sustainability. After reviewing its About Ikea section of its website (**http://www.ikea.com/ms/en_US/about_ikea/index.html**), prepare a list of 10 specific policies and programs that help the company achieve its vision of creating a better everyday life for people around the world.

   **LO 1, LO 4**

2. Prepare a one- to two-page analysis of a recent ethics scandal using your university library's access to Lexis-Nexis or other Internet resources. Your report should (1) discuss the conditions that gave rise to unethical business strategies and behavior and (2) provide an overview of the costs resulting from the company's business ethics failure.

   **LO 2, LO 3**

3. Based on information provided in Illustration Capsule 9.3, discuss the actions taken by top management at Novo Nordisk that have allowed the company to be considered a global leader in business ethics. Also, explain how the company's values encourage employees to act in an ethical manner. What role does the company's culture have in promoting ethical business behavior? Explain.

   **connect**

   **LO 2**

4. Review Microsoft's statements about its corporate citizenship programs at **www.microsoft.com/about/corporatecitizenship**. How does the company's commitment to CSR provide positive benefits for its stakeholders?

   **LO 4**

5. Go to **www.nestle.com** and read the company's latest sustainability report. What are Nestlé's key environmental sustainable environmental policies? How do these initiatives relate to the company's principles, values, and culture and its approach to competing in the food industry?

   **connect**

   **LO 4**

# EXERCISES FOR SIMULATION PARTICIPANTS

1. Is your company's strategy ethical? Why or why not? Is there anything that your company has done or is now doing that could legitimately be considered as "shady" by your competitiors?

   **LO 1**

2. In what ways, if any, is your company exercising corporate social responsibility? What are the elements of your company's CSR strategy? Are there any changes to this strategy that you would suggest?

   **LO 4**

3. If some shareholders complained that you and your co-managers have been spending too little or too much on corporate social responsibility, what would you tell them?

   **LO 3, LO 4**

4. Is your company striving to conduct its business in an environmentally sustainable manner? What specific *additional* actions could your company take that would make an even greater contribution to environmental sustainability?

   **LO 4**

5. In what ways is your company's environmental sustainability strategy in the best long-term interest of shareholders? Does it contribute to your company's competitive advantage or profitability?

   **LO 4**

# ENDNOTES

[1] James E. Post, Anne T. Lawrence, and James Weber, *Business and Society: Corporate Strategy, Public Policy, Ethics,* 10th ed. (Burr Ridge, IL: McGraw-Hill Irwin, 2002).

[2] Mark S. Schwartz, "Universal Moral Values for Corporate Codes of Ethics," *Journal of Business Ethics* 59, no. 1 (June 2005), pp. 27–44.

[3] Mark. S. Schwartz, "A Code of Ethics for Corporate Codes of Ethics," *Journal of Business Ethics* 41, nos. 1–2 (November–December 2002), pp. 27–43.

[4] T. L. Beauchamp and N. E. Bowie, *Ethical Theory and Business* (Upper Saddle River, NJ: Prentice-Hall, 2001).

[5] U.S. Department of Labor, "The Department of Labor's 2002 Findings on the Worst Forms of Child Labor," 2003, accessible at www.dol.gov/ILAB/media/reports.

[6] U.S. Department of Labor, "The Department of Labor's 2006 Findings on the Worst Forms of Child Labor," 2006, www.dol.gov/ilab/programs/ocft/PDF/2006OCFTreport.pdf.

[7] W. M. Greenfield, "In the Name of Corporate Social Responsibility," *Business Horizons* 47, no. 1 (January–February 2004), p. 22.

[8] Rajib Sanyal, "Determinants of Bribery in International Business: The Cultural and Economic Factors," *Journal of Business Ethics* 59, no. 1 (June 2005), pp. 139–45.

[9] Transparency International, *2007 Global Corruption Report,* p. 332, and *2008 Global Corruption Report,* p. 306, www.globalcorruptionreport.org.

[10] Thomas Donaldson and Thomas W. Dunfee, "When Ethics Travel: The Promise and Peril of Global Business Ethics," *California Management Review* 41, no. 4 (Summer 1999), p. 53.

[11] Roger Chen and Chia-Pei Chen, "Chinese Professional Managers and the Issue of Ethical Behavior," *Ivey Business Journal* 69, no. 5 (May/June 2005), p. 1.

[12] John Reed and Erik Portanger, "Bribery, Corruption Are Rampant in Eastern Europe, Survey Finds," *The Wall Street Journal,* November 9, 1999, p. A21.

[13] Antonio Argandoa, "Corruption and Companies: The Use of Facilitating Payments," *Journal of Business Ethics* 60, no. 3 (September 2005), pp. 251–64.

[14] "OECD Convention on Combating Bribery of Foreign Public Officials in International Business Transactions," www.oecd.org/document/21/0,3343,en_2649_34859_2017813_1_1_1_1,00.html (accessed May 22, 2009).

[15] Thomas Donaldson and Thomas W. Dunfee, "Towards a Unified Conception of Business Ethics: Integrative Social Contracts Theory," *Academy of Management Review* 19, no. 2 (April 1994), pp. 252–84; Andrew Spicer, Thomas W. Dunfee, and Wendy J. Bailey, "Does National Context Matter in Ethical Decision Making? An Empirical Test of Integrative Social Contracts Theory," *Academy of Management Journal* 47, no. 4 (August 2004), p. 610.

[16] P. M. Nichols, "Outlawing Transnational Bribery through the World Trade Organization," *Law and Policy in International Business* 28, no. 2 (1997), pp. 321–22.

[17] Lynn Paine, Rohit Deshpandé, Joshua D. Margolis, and Kim Eric Bettcher, "Up to Code: Does Your Company's Conduct Meet World-Class Standards?" *Harvard Business Review* 83, no. 12 (December 2005), pp. 122–33.

[18] John F. Veiga, Timothy D. Golden, and Kathleen Dechant, "Why Managers Bend Company Rules," *Academy of Management Executive* 18, no. 2 (May 2004).

[19] Basil Katz and Grant McCool, "US charges 7 in $62 million Dell insider-trading case," Reuters, January 18, 2012, accessed on February 15, 2012 at http://www.reuters.com/article/2012/01/18/us-insidertrading-arrests-idUSTRE80H18920120118.

[20] Lorin Berlin and Emily Peck, "National Mortgage Settlement: States, Big Banks Reach $25 Billion Deal," *Huff Post Business,* February 09, 2012, accessed at http://www.huffingtonpost.com/2012/02/09/national-mortgage-settlement_n_1265292.html on February 15, 2012.

[21] Ronald R. Sims and Johannes Brinkmann, "Enron Ethics (Or: Culture Matters More than Codes)," *Journal of Business Ethics* 45, no. 3 (July 2003), pp. 244–46.

[22] Marcy Gordon, "Diebold-SEC Fraud Settlement Reached: Former Voting Machine Maker to Pay $25 Million," *Huff Post Business,* 06/2/10, accessed at http://www.huffingtonpost.com/2010/06/02/dieboldsec-fraud-settleme_n_598627.html on February 16, 2012.

[23] Kurt Eichenwald, *Conspiracy of Fools: A True Story* (New York: Broadway Books, 2005).

[24] Archie B. Carroll, "The Four Faces of Corporate Citizenship," *Business and Society Review* 100/101 (September 1998), p. 6.

[25] Business Roundtable, "Statement on Corporate Responsibility," October 1981, p. 9.

[26] Timothy M. Devinney, "Is the Socially Responsible Corporation a Myth? The Good, the Bad, and the Ugly of Corporate Social Responsibility," *Academy of Management Perspectives* 23, no. 2 (May 2009), pp. 44–56.

[27] Sarah Roberts, Justin Keeble, and David Brown, "The Business Case for Corporate Citizenship" (study conducted by Arthur D. Little for the World Economic Forum), p. 3, www.afic.am (accessed June 9, 2009). A revised and more wide-ranging version of this study can be found at www.bitc.org.uk/document.rm?id=5253.

[28] "General Mills' 2010 Corporate Social Responsibility Report Highlights New and Longstanding Achievements in the Areas of Health, Community, and Environment" (CSR press release), *CSRwire,* April 15, 2010, www.csrwire.com/press_releases/29347-General-Mills-2010-Corporate-Social-Responsibility-report-now-available.html.

[29] Arthur A. Thompson and Amit J. Shah, "Starbucks' Strategy and Internal Initiatives to Return to Profitable Growth," a case study appearing in the Cases section of this text.

[30] Adrian Henriques, "ISO 26000: A New Standard for Human Rights?" Institute for Human Rights and Business, March 23, 2010, www.institutehrb.org/blogs/guest/iso_26000_a_new_standard_for_human_rights.html?gclid=CJih7NjN2aICFVs65Qodr VOdyQ (accessed July 7, 2010).

[31] Gerald I.J.M. Zetsloot and Marcel N. A. van Marrewijk, "From Quality to Sustainability," *Journal of Business Ethics* 55 (2004), pp. 79–82.

[32] Tilde Herrera, "PG&E Claims Industry First with Supply Chain Footprint Project," GreenBiz.com, June 30, 2010, www.greenbiz.com/news/2010/06/30/pge--claims-industry-first-supply-chain-carbon-footprint-project.

[33] This definition is based on the Brundtland Commission's report, which described sustainable development in a like manner: United Nations General Assembly, "Report of the World Commission on Environment and Development: Our Common Future," 1987, www.un-documents.net/wced-ocf.htm, transmitted to the General Assembly as an annex to document A/42/427—"Development and International Co-operation: Environment" (retrieved February 15, 2009).

[34] Robert Goodland, "The Concept of Environmental Sustainability," *Annual Review of Ecology and Systematics* 26 (1995), pp. 1–25; J. G. Speth, *The Bridge at the End of the World: Capitalism, the Environment, and Crossing from Crisis to Sustainability* (New Haven, CT: Yale University Press, 2008).

[35] Michael E. Porter and Mark R. Kramer, "Strategy & Society: The Link between Competitive Advantage and Corporate Social Responsibility," *Harvard Business Review* 84, no. 12 (December 2006), pp. 78–92.

[36] World Business Council for Sustainable Development, "Corporate Social Responsibility: Making Good Business Sense," January 2000, p. 7, www.wbscd.ch (accessed October 10, 2003). David Hess, Nikolai Rogovsky, and Thomas W. Dunfee, "The Next Wave of Corporate Community Involvement: Corporate Social Initiatives," *California Management Review* 44, no. 2 (Winter 2002), pp. 110–25; Susan Ariel Aaronson, "Corporate Responsibility in the Global Village: The British Role Model and the American Laggard," *Business and Society Review* 108, no. 3 (September 2003), p. 323.

[37] www.chick-fil-a.com (accessed June 1, 2009).

[38] N. Craig Smith, "Corporate Responsibility: Whether and How," *California Management Review* 45, no. 4 (Summer 2003), p. 63.

[39] Jeb Brugmann and C. K. Prahalad, "Cocreating Business's New Social Compact," *Harvard Business Review* 85, no. 2 (February 2007), pp. 80–90.

[40] Wallace N. Davidson, Abuzar El-Jelly, and Dan L. Worrell, "Influencing Managers to Change Unpopular Corporate Behavior through Boycotts and Divestitures: A Stock Market Test," *Business and Society* 34, no. 2 (1995), pp. 171–96.

[41] Tom McCawley, "Racing to Improve Its Reputation: Nike Has Fought to Shed Its Image as an Exploiter of Third-World Labor Yet It Is Still a Target of Activists," *Financial Times,* December 2000, p. 14.

[42] World Economic Forum, "Findings of a Survey on Global Corporate Leadership," www.weforum.org/corporatecitizenship (accessed October 11, 2003).

[43] Michael E. Porter and Mark Kramer, "Creating Shared Value," *Harvard Business Review* 89, no. 1/2 (January-February 2011).

[44] James C. Collins and Jerry I. Porras, *Built to Last: Successful Habits of Visionary Companies,* Third Edition (London: Harper-Business, 2002).

[45] Joshua D. Margolis and Hillary A. Elfenbein, "Doing Well by Doing Good: Don't Count on It," *Harvard Business Review* 86, no. 1 (January 2008), pp. 19–20; Lee E. Preston and Douglas P. O'Bannon, "The Corporate Social-Financial Performance Relationship," *Business and Society* 36, no. 4 (December 1997), pp. 419–29; Ronald M. Roman, Sefa Hayibor, and Bradley R. Agle, "The Relationship between Social and Financial Performance: Repainting a Portrait," *Business and Society* 38, no. 1 (March 1999), pp. 109–25; Joshua D. Margolis and James P. Walsh, *People and Profits* (Mahwah, NJ: Lawrence Erlbaum, 2001).

[46] Leonard L. Berry, Ann M. Mirobito, and William B. Baun, "What's the Hard Return on Employee Wellness Programs?" *Harvard Business Review* 88, no. 12 (December 2010), pp. 105.

# CHAPTER 10

# BUILDING AN ORGANIZATION CAPABLE OF GOOD STRATEGY EXECUTION

## People, Capabilities, and Structure

### Learning Objectives

**LO 1**  Gain command of what managers must do to execute strategy successfully.

**LO 2**  Learn why hiring, training, and retaining the right people constitute a key component of the strategy execution process.

**LO 3**  Understand that good strategy execution requires continuously building and upgrading the organization's resources and capabilities.

**LO 4**  Recognize what issues to consider in establishing a strategy-supportive organizational structure and organizing the work effort.

**LO 5**  Become aware of the pros and cons of centralized and decentralized decision making in implementing the chosen strategy.

> Of all the things I've done, the most vital is coordinating the talents of those who work for us and pointing them toward a certain goal.
>
> Walt Disney – *Founder of the Disney Company*

> Management of many is the same as management of few. It is a matter of organization.
>
> Sun Tzu – *Ancient Chinese general, strategist, and philosopher*

> Any strategy, however brilliant, needs to be implemented properly if it is to deliver the desired results.
>
> Costas Markides – *London Business School professor and consultant*

Once managers have decided on a strategy, the emphasis turns to converting it into actions and good results. Putting the strategy into place and getting the organization to execute it well call for different sets of managerial skills. Whereas crafting strategy is largely a market-driven and resource-driven activity, executing strategy is an operations-driven activity revolving around the management of people and business processes. Successful strategy execution depends on doing a good job of working with and through others; building and strengthening competitive capabilities; creating an appropriate organizational structure; allocating resources, instituting strategy-supportive policies, processes, and systems; motivating and rewarding people; and instilling a discipline of getting things done. Executing strategy is an action-oriented, make-things-happen task that tests a manager's ability to achieve continuous improvement in operations and business processes, create and nurture a strategy-supportive culture, and consistently meet or beat performance targets.

Experienced managers are well aware that it is a whole lot easier to develop a sound strategic plan than it is to execute the plan and achieve the desired outcomes. According to one executive, "It's been rather easy for us to decide where we wanted to go. The hard part is to get the organization to act on the new priorities."[1] *Just because senior managers announce a new strategy doesn't mean that organization members will embrace it and move forward enthusiastically to implement it.* It takes adept managerial leadership to convincingly communicate a new strategy and the reasons for it, overcome pockets of doubt, secure the commitment of key personnel, gain agreement on how to implement the strategy, and move forward to get all the pieces into place. Company personnel must understand—in their heads and hearts—why a new strategic direction is necessary and where the new strategy is taking them.[2] Instituting change is, of course, easier when the problems with the old strategy have become obvious and/or the company has spiraled into a financial crisis.

But the challenge of successfully implementing new strategic initiatives goes well beyond managerial adeptness in overcoming resistance to change. What really makes executing strategy a tougher, more time-consuming management challenge than crafting strategy are the wide array of managerial activities that must be attended to, the many ways to put new strategic initiatives in place and keep things moving, and the number of bedeviling issues that always crop up and have to be resolved. It takes first-rate "managerial smarts" to zero in on what exactly needs to be done to put new strategic initiatives in place and, further, how to get good results in a timely manner. Excellent people-management skills and perseverance are required to get a variety of initiatives launched and to integrate the efforts of many different work groups into a smoothly functioning whole. Depending on how much consensus building and organizational change is involved, the process of implementing strategy changes can take several months to several years. To achieve *real proficiency* in executing the strategy can take even longer.

Like crafting strategy, *executing strategy is a job for a company's whole management team—not* *just a few senior managers.* While the chief executive officer and the heads of major units (business divisions, functional departments, and key operating units) are ultimately responsible for seeing that strategy is executed successfully, the process typically affects every part of the firm—all value chain activities and all work groups. Top-level managers must rely on the active support of middle and lower managers to institute whatever new operating practices are needed in the various operating units to achieve the desired results. Middle and lower-level managers must ensure that frontline employees perform strategy-critical value chain activities well and produce operating results that allow companywide performance targets to be met. In consequence, *all company personnel are actively involved in the strategy execution process in one way or another.*

# A FRAMEWORK FOR EXECUTING STRATEGY

**LO 1**

Gain command of what managers must do to execute strategy successfully.

Executing strategy entails figuring out the specific actions, and behaviors that are needed to get things done and deliver good results. The exact items that need to be placed on management's action agenda always have to be customized to fit the particulars of a company's situation. The techniques for successfully executing a low-cost provider strategy are different from those for executing a high-end differentiation strategy. Implementing a new strategy for a struggling company in the midst of a financial crisis is a different job from that of making minor improvements to strategy execution in a company that is doing relatively well. Moreover, some managers are more adept than others at using particular approaches to achieving the desired kinds of organizational changes. Hence, there's no definitive managerial recipe for successful strategy execution that cuts across all company situations and all types of strategies or that works for all types of managers. Rather, the specific actions required to execute a strategy—the "to-do list" that constitutes management's action agenda—always represent management's judgment about how best to proceed in light of prevailing circumstances.

## The Principal Components of the Strategy Execution Process

Despite the need to tailor a company's strategy-executing approaches to the particulars of its situation, certain managerial bases must be covered no matter what the circumstances. These include ten basic managerial tasks (see Figure 10.1):

1.  Staff the organization with managers and employees capable of executing the strategy well.
2.  Build the organizational capabilities required for successful strategy execution.
3.  Create a strategy-supportive organizational structure.

## FIGURE 10.1    The 10 Basic Tasks of the Strategy Execution Process

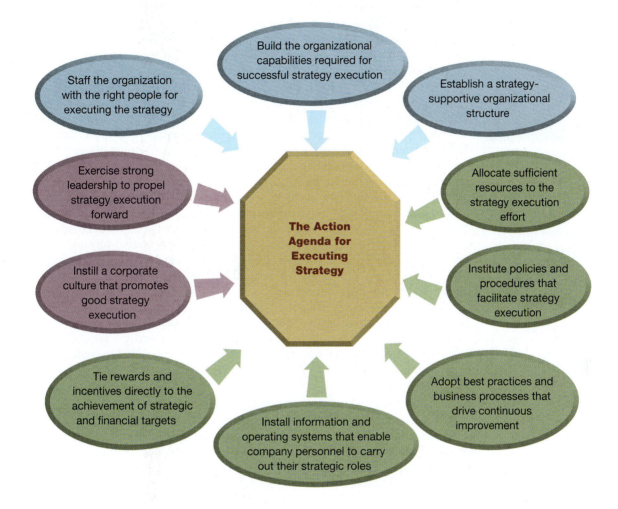

4. Allocate sufficient resources (budgetary and otherwise) to the strategy execution effort.

5. Institute policies and procedures that facilitate strategy execution.

6. Adopt best practices and business processes that drive continuous improvement in strategy execution activities.

7. Install information and operating systems that enable company personnel to carry out their strategic roles proficiently.

8. Tie rewards and incentives directly to the achievement of strategic and financial targets.

9. Instill a corporate culture that promotes good strategy execution.

10. Exercise the internal leadership needed to propel strategy implementation forward.

How well managers perform these 10 tasks has a decisive impact on whether the outcome of the strategy execution effort is a spectacular success, a colossal failure, or something in between.

When strategies fail, it is often because of poor execution. Strategy execution is therefore a critical managerial endeavor.

The two best signs of good strategy execution are whether a company is meeting or beating its performance targets and whether they are performing value chain activities in a manner that is conducive to companywide operating excellence.

In devising an action agenda for executing strategy, the place for managers to start is with *a probing assessment of what the organization must do differently to carry out the strategy successfully.* Each manager needs to ask the question "What needs to be done in my area of responsibility to implement our part of the company's strategy and what should I do to get these things accomplished?" It is then incumbent on every manager to determine *precisely how to make the necessary internal changes.* Successful strategy implementers are masters in promoting results-oriented behaviors on the part of company personnel and following through on making the right things happen in a timely fashion.[3]

In big organizations with geographically scattered operating units, the action agenda of senior executives mostly involves communicating the case for change, building consensus for how to proceed, installing strong managers to move the process forward in key organizational units, directing resources to the right places, establishing deadlines and measures of progress, rewarding those who achieve implementation milestones, and personally leading the strategic change process. Thus, the bigger the organization, the more that successful strategy execution depends on the cooperation and implementing skills of operating managers who can promote needed changes at the lowest organizational levels and deliver results. In small organizations, top managers can deal directly with frontline managers and employees, personally orchestrating the action steps and implementation sequence, observing firsthand how implementation is progressing, and deciding how hard and how fast to push the process along. Regardless of the organization's size and whether strategy implementation involves sweeping or minor changes, the most important leadership trait is a strong, confident sense of what to do and how to do it. Having a strong grip on these two things comes from understanding the circumstances of the organization and the requirements for effective strategy execution. Then it remains for company personnel in strategy-critical areas to step up to the plate and produce the desired results.

**What's Covered in Chapters 10, 11, and 12**    In the remainder of this chapter and in the next two chapters, we will discuss what is involved in performing the 10 key managerial tasks that shape the process of executing strategy. This chapter explores the first three of these tasks (highlighted in blue in Figure 10.1): (1) staffing the organization with people capable of executing the strategy well, (2) building the organizational capabilities needed for successful strategy execution, and (3) creating an organizational structure supportive of the strategy execution process. Chapter 11 concerns the tasks of allocating resources, instituting strategy-facilitating policies and procedures, employing business process management tools and best practices, installing operating and information systems, and tying rewards to the achievement of good results (highlighted in green in Figure 10.1). Chapter 12 deals with the two remaining tasks: creating a strategy-supportive corporate culture and exercising the leadership needed to drive the execution process forward (highlighted in purple).

# BUILDING AN ORGANIZATION CAPABLE OF GOOD STRATEGY EXECUTION: THREE KEY ACTIONS

Proficient strategy execution depends foremost on having in place an organization capable of the tasks demanded of it. Building an execution-capable organization is thus always a top priority. As shown in Figure 10.2, three types of organization-building actions are paramount:

1. *Staffing the organization*—Putting together a strong management team, and recruiting and retaining employees with the needed experience, technical skills, and intellectual capital.

2. *Acquiring, developing, and strengthening strategy-supportive resources and capabilities*—Accumulating the required resources, developing proficiencies in performing strategy-critical value chain activities, and updating the company's capabilities to match changing market conditions and customer expectations.

3. *Structuring the organization and work effort*—Organizing value chain activities and business processes, establishing lines of authority and reporting relationships, and deciding how much decision-making authority to delegate to lower-level managers and frontline employees.

Implementing a strategy depends critically on ensuring that strategy-supportive resources and capabilities are in place, ready to be deployed. These include the skills, talents, experience, and knowledge of the company's human resources (managerial and otherwise)—see Figure 10.2. Proficient strategy execution depends heavily on competent personnel of

**FIGURE 10.2** Building an Organization Capable of Proficient Strategy Execution: Three Key Actions

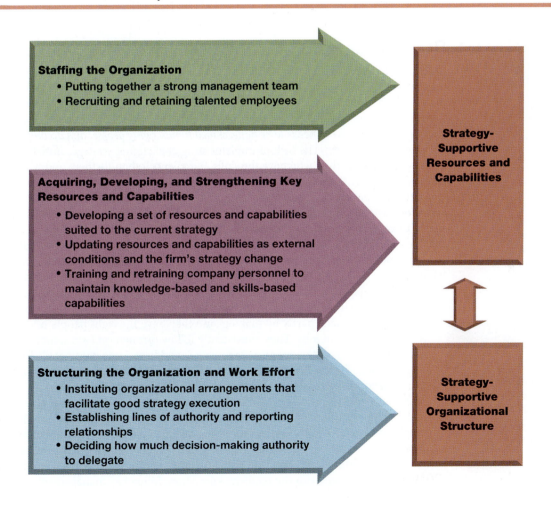

all types, but because of the many managerial tasks involved and the role of leadership in strategy execution, assembling a strong management team is especially important.

If the strategy being implemented is a new strategy, the company may need to add to its resource and capability mix in other respects as well. But renewing, upgrading, and revising the organization's resources and capabilities is a part of the strategy execution process even if the strategy is fundamentally the same, since resources depreciate and conditions are always changing. Thus, augmenting and strengthening the firm's core competencies and seeing that they are suited to the current strategy are also top priorities.

Structuring the organization and work effort is another critical aspect of building an organization capable of good strategy execution. An organization structure that is well matched to the strategy can help facilitate its implementation; one that is not well suited can lead to higher bureaucratic costs and communication or coordination breakdowns.

# STAFFING THE ORGANIZATION

**LO 2**

Learn why hiring, training, and retaining the right people constitute a key component of the strategy execution process.

No company can hope to perform the activities required for successful strategy execution without attracting and retaining talented managers and employees with suitable skills and intellectual capital.

## Putting Together a Strong Management Team

Assembling a capable management team is a cornerstone of the organization-building task.[4] While different strategies and company circumstances sometimes call for different mixes of backgrounds, experiences, management styles, and know-how, *the most important consideration is to fill key managerial slots with smart people who are clear thinkers, good at figuring out what needs to be done, skilled in managing people, and accomplished in delivering good results.*[5] The task of implementing challenging strategic initiatives must be assigned to executives who have the skills and talents to handle them and who can be counted on to get the job done well. Without a capable, results-oriented management team, the implementation process is likely to be hampered by missed deadlines, misdirected or wasteful efforts, and managerial ineptness. Weak executives are serious impediments to getting optimal results because they are unable to differentiate between ideas that have merit and those that are misguided. In contrast, managers with strong strategy-implementation capabilities have a talent for asking tough, incisive questions. They know enough about the details of the business to be able to ensure the soundness of the decisions of the people around them, and they can discern whether the resources people are asking for to put the strategy in place make sense. They are good at getting things done through others, partly by making sure they have the right people under them, assigned to the right jobs. They consistently follow through on issues, monitor progress carefully, make adjustments when needed, and keep important details from slipping through the cracks. In short, they understand how to drive organizational change, and they have the managerial discipline requisite for first-rate strategy execution.

Sometimes a company's existing management team is up to the task. At other times it may need to be strengthened by promoting qualified people from within or by bringing in outsiders whose experiences, talents, and leadership styles better suit the situation. In turnaround and rapid-growth situations, and in instances when a company doesn't have insiders with the requisite know-how, filling key management slots from

*Putting together a talented management team with the right mix of experiences, skills, and abilities to get things done is one of the first steps to take in launching the strategy-executing process.*

the outside is a fairly standard organization-building approach. In addition, it is important to identify and replace managers who are incapable, for whatever reason, of making the required changes in a timely and cost-effective manner. For a management team to be truly effective at strategy execution, it must be composed of managers who recognize that organizational changes are needed and who are ready to get on with the process.

The overriding aim in building a management team should be to assemble a *critical mass* of talented managers who can function as agents of change and oversee top-notch strategy execution. Every manager's success is enhanced (or limited) by the quality of his or her managerial colleagues and the degree to which they freely exchange ideas, debate ways to make operating improvements, and join forces to tackle issues and solve problems. When a first-rate manager enjoys the help and support of other first-rate managers, it's possible to create a managerial whole that is greater than the sum of individual efforts—talented managers who work well together as a team can produce organizational results that are dramatically better than what one or two star managers acting individually can achieve.[6]

Illustration Capsule 10.1 describes Procter & Gamble's widely acclaimed approach to developing a top-caliber management team.

## Recruiting, Training, and Retaining Capable Employees

Assembling a capable management team is not enough. Staffing the organization with the right kinds of people must go much deeper than managerial jobs in order for strategy-critical value chain activities to be performed competently. *The quality of an organization's people is always an essential ingredient of successful strategy execution—knowledgeable, engaged employees are a company's best source of creative ideas for the nuts-and-bolts operating improvements that lead to operating excellence.* Companies like Google, Edward Jones, Mercedes-Benz, Intuit, McKinsey & Company, REI, Goldman Sachs, DreamWorks Animation, and Boston Consulting Group make a concerted effort to recruit the best and brightest people they can find and then retain them with excellent compensation packages, opportunities for rapid advancement and professional growth, and interesting assignments. Having a pool of "A players" with strong skill sets and lots of brainpower is essential to their business.

Facebook makes a point of hiring the very brightest and most talented programmers it can find and motivating them with both good monetary incentives and the challenge of working on cutting-edge technology projects. McKinsey & Company, one of the world's premier management consulting firms, recruits only cream-of-the-crop MBAs at the nation's top-10 business schools; such talent is essential to McKinsey's strategy of performing high-level consulting for the world's top corporations. The leading global accounting firms screen candidates not only on the basis of their accounting expertise but also on whether they possess the people skills needed to relate well with clients and colleagues. Southwest Airlines goes to considerable lengths to hire people who can have fun and be fun on the job; it uses special interviewing and screening methods to gauge whether applicants for customer-contact jobs have outgoing personality traits that match its strategy of creating a high-spirited, fun-loving, in-flight atmosphere for passengers. Southwest Airlines is so selective that only about 3 percent of the people who apply are offered jobs.

In high-tech companies, the challenge is to staff work groups with gifted, imaginative, and energetic people who can bring life to new ideas quickly and inject into the organization what one Dell executive calls "hum."[7] The saying "People are our most

In many industries, adding to a company's talent base and building intellectual capital are more important to good strategy execution than additional investments in capital projects.

# "Build From Within": P&G's Approach to Management Development

Procter and Gamble takes a systematic approach to management development with its "Build From Within" program—a mutually reinforcing set of policies and practices designed to nurture home-grown managerial talent. Ninety-five percent of P&G's managers (including its 12 past and present CEOs) first joined the company at the entry level. The promote-from-within approach has paid off: P&G regularly tops lists of "Best Companies for Leaders" and is a well-known breeding ground for future general managers. To ensure a pipeline of committed, high-quality leaders, P&G invests in each stage of the management development life cycle:

- **Rigorous recruiting process.** P&G hires less than 1 percent of applicants each year. The recruiting process includes multiple rounds of tests that assess leadership, logical and numerical abilities, as well as interviews to test candidates' intellectual, interpersonal, and executional fit.

- **Extensive on-the-job and formal training opportunities.** P&G rotates employees through a series of challenging 18–24 month "Accelerator Experiences" that build collaborative, project management, and customer-facing skills. The company has also developed a world-class training curriculum; each employee logs nearly 70 hours per year in required courses and seminars.

- **Detailed development and career planning.** The company's Work and Development Planning (W&DP) system tracks each employee's development in terms of: (1) previous year's plan versus results; (2) areas for further growth; (3) near- and long-term career goals; (4) development targets for the coming year. Monthly, quarterly, and annual talent reviews serve as a consistent mechanism for identifying and investing in top talent.

- **Clear path to leadership.** P&G was the first consumer packaged goods company to develop and implement the Brand Manager (BM) position, a role requiring cross-functional relationships, deep business knowledge, and an ability to synthesize complex data into pithy recommendations. Though the path is demanding (requiring, on average, two to three rotations in an entry level role), it is the only track to company leadership.

- **Actively managed succession planning.** At P&G, developing future leaders is everyone's responsibility: managers seek feedback from cross-functional partners in making promotion and compensation decisions. Most importantly, senior leaders play an active role, meeting regularly to review P&G's talent pipeline. As a result, the company always has replacement candidates lined up for key managerial positions.

Developed with Divya A. Mani.

*Sources:* company websites; *Winning with the P&G 99,* Charles L. Decker, 1998; "100 Best Companies to Work For," Fortune, 2007; "Some Firms' Fertile Soil Grows Crop of Future CEOs," *USA Today,* January 9, 2008; "P&G's Leadership Machine," *Fortune,* May 20, 2009; "How Companies Develop Great Leaders," *Bloomberg Businessweek,* February 16, 2010; "25 Top Companies for Leaders," *Fortune,* November 4, 2011.

important asset" may seem trite, but it fits high-technology companies precisely. Besides checking closely for functional and technical skills, Dell tests applicants for their tolerance of ambiguity and change, their capacity to work in teams, and their ability to learn on-the-fly. Companies like **Amazon.com**, Google, and Cisco Systems have broken new ground in recruiting, hiring, cultivating, developing, and retaining talented employees—almost all of whom are in their 20s and 30s. Cisco goes after the top 10 percent, raiding other companies and endeavoring to retain key people at the companies it acquires. Cisco executives believe that a cadre of star engineers, programmers, managers, salespeople, and support personnel is the backbone of the company's efforts to execute its strategy and remain the world's leading provider of Internet infrastructure products and technology.

The practices listed next are common among companies dedicated to staffing jobs with the most capable people they can find:

1. Putting forth considerable effort on screening and evaluating job applicants—selecting only those with suitable skill sets, energy, initiative, judgment, aptitude for learning, and personality traits that mesh well with the company's work environment and culture.

2. Providing employees with training programs that continue throughout their careers.

3. Offering promising employees challenging, interesting, and skill-stretching assignments.

4. Rotating people through jobs that span functional and geographic boundaries. Providing people with opportunities to gain experience in a variety of international settings is increasingly considered an essential part of career development in multinational companies.

5. Making the work environment stimulating and engaging so that employees will consider the company a great place to work.

6. Encouraging employees to challenge existing ways of doing things, to be creative and innovative in proposing better ways of operating, and to push their ideas for new products or businesses. Progressive companies work hard at creating an environment in which employees are made to feel that their views and suggestions count.

7. Striving to retain talented, high-performing employees via promotions, salary increases, performance bonuses, stock options and equity ownership, fringe-benefit packages, and other perks.

8. Coaching average performers to improve their skills and capabilities, while weeding out underperformers and benchwarmers.

> The best companies make a point of recruiting and retaining talented employees—the objective is to make the company's entire workforce (managers and rank-and-file employees) a genuine competitive asset.

# ACQUIRING, DEVELOPING, AND STRENGTHENING KEY RESOURCES AND CAPABILITIES

High among the organization-building priorities in the strategy execution process is the need to build and strengthen competitively valuable resources and capabilities. As explained in Chapter 4, a company's ability to perform value-creating activities and realize its strategic objectives depends upon its resources and capabilities. In the course of crafting strategy, it is important for managers to identify the resources and capabilities that will enable the firm's strategy to succeed. Good strategy execution requires putting those resources and capabilities into place, strengthening them as needed, and then modifying them as market conditions evolve.

If the strategy being implemented is new, company managers may have to acquire new resources, significantly broaden or deepen certain capabilities, or even add entirely new competencies in order to put the strategic initiatives in place and execute them proficiently. But even if the strategy has not changed materially, good strategy execution involves refreshing and strengthening the firm's resources and capabilities to keep them in top form.

**LO 3**

Understand that good strategy execution requires continuously building and upgrading the organization's resources and capabilities.

# Three Approaches to Building and Strengthening Capabilities

Building core competencies and competitive capabilities is a time-consuming, managerially challenging exercise. While some assist can be gotten from discovering how best-in-industry or best-in-world companies perform a particular activity, trying to replicate and then improve on the capabilities of others is, however, much easier said than done—for the same reasons that one is unlikely to ever become a world-class moguls skier just by studying what Olympic gold medal winner Hannah Kearney does.

With deliberate effort, well-orchestrated organizational actions, and continued practice, however, it is possible for a firm to become proficient at capability building despite the difficulty. Indeed, by making capability-building activities a routine part of their strategy execution endeavors, some firms are able to develop *dynamic capabilities* that assist them in managing resource and capability change, as discussed in Chapter 4. The most common approaches to capability building include (1) internal development, (2) acquiring capabilities through mergers and acquisitions, and (3) accessing capabilities via collaborative partnerships.[8]

**Developing Capabilities Internally**    Capabilities develop incrementally along an evolutionary development path as organizations search for solutions to their problems. The process is a complex one, since capabilities are the product of bundles of skills and know-how that are integrated into organizational routines and deployed within activity systems through the combined efforts of teams that are often cross-functional in nature, spanning a variety of departments and locations. For instance, the capability of speeding new products to market involves the collaborative efforts of personnel in R&D, engineering and design, purchasing, production, marketing, and distribution. Similarly, the capability to provide superior customer service is a team effort among people in customer call centers (where orders are taken and inquiries are answered), shipping and delivery, billing and accounts receivable, and after-sale support. The process of building a capability begins when managers set an objective of developing a particular capability and organize activity around that objective.[9] Managers can ignite the process by having high aspirations and setting "stretch objectives" for the organization, as described in Chapter 2.[10]

Because the process is incremental, the first step is to develop the *ability* to do something, however imperfectly or inefficiently. This entails selecting people with the requisite skills and experience, upgrading or expanding individual abilities as needed, and then molding the efforts of individuals into a collaborative effort to create an organizational ability. At this stage, progress can be fitful since it depends on experimentation, active search for alternative solutions, and learning through trial and error.[11]

As experience grows and company personnel learn how to perform the activities consistently well and at an acceptable cost, the ability evolves into a tried-and-true competence. Getting to this point requires a continual investment of resources and systematic efforts to improve processes and solve problems creatively as they arise. Improvements in the functioning of a capability come from task repetition and the resulting learning by doing of individuals and teams. But the process can be accelerated by making learning a more deliberate endeavor and providing the incentives that will motivate company personnel to achieve the desired ends.[12] This can be critical to successful strategy execution when market conditions are changing rapidly.

> Building new competencies and capabilities is a multistage process that occurs over a period of months and years. It is not something that is accomplished overnight.

> A company's capabilities must be continually refreshed and renewed to remain aligned with changing customer expectations, altered competitive conditions, and new strategic initiatives.

It is generally much easier and less time-consuming to update and remodel a company's existing capabilities as external conditions and company strategy change than it is to create them from scratch. Maintaining capabilities in top form may simply require exercising them continually and fine-tuning them as necessary. Refreshing and updating capabilities require only a limited set of modifications to a set of routines that is otherwise in place. Phasing out an existing capability takes significantly less effort than adding a brand new one. Replicating a company capability, while not an easy process, still begins with an established template.[13] Even the process of augmenting a capability may require less effort if it involves the recombination of well-established company capabilities and draws on existing company resources.[14] Companies like Cray in large computers and Honda in gasoline engines, for example, have leveraged the expertise of their talent pool by frequently re-forming high-intensity teams and reusing key people on special projects designed to augment their capabilities. Canon combined miniaturization capabilities that it developed in producing calculators with its existing capabilities in precision optics to revolutionize the 35-mm camera market.[15] Toyota, en route to overtaking General Motors as the global leader in motor vehicles, aggressively upgraded its capabilities in fuel-efficient hybrid engine technology and constantly fine-tuned its famed Toyota Production System to enhance its already proficient capabilities in manufacturing top-quality vehicles at relatively low costs—see Illustration Capsule 10.2.

Managerial actions to develop core competencies and competitive capabilities generally take one of two forms: either strengthening the company's base of skills, knowledge, and experience or coordinating and integrating the efforts of the various work groups and departments. Actions of the first sort can be undertaken at all managerial levels, but actions of the second sort are best orchestrated by senior managers who not only appreciate the strategy-executing significance of strong capabilities but also have the clout to enforce the necessary cooperation and coordination among individuals, groups, and departments.[16]

## Acquiring Capabilities through Mergers and Acquisitions

Sometimes a company can refresh and strengthen its competencies by acquiring another company with attractive resources and capabilities.[17] An acquisition aimed at building a stronger portfolio of resources and capabilities can be every bit as valuable as an acquisition aimed at adding new products or services to the company's lineup of offerings. The advantage of this mode of acquiring new capabilities is primarily one of speed, since developing new capabilities internally can take many years of effort. Capabilities-motivated acquisitions are essential (1) when a market opportunity can slip by faster than a needed capability can be created internally and (2) when industry conditions, technology, or competitors are moving at such a rapid clip, that time is of the essence.

At the same time, acquiring capabilities in this way is not without difficulty. Capabilities involve tacit knowledge and complex routines that cannot be transferred readily from one organizational unit to another. This may limit the extent to which the new capability can be utilized. For example, the Newell Company acquired Rubbermaid in part for its famed product innovation capabilities. Transferring these capabilities to other parts of the Newell organization proved easier said than done, however, contributing to a slump in the firm's stock prices that lasted for some time. Integrating the capabilities of two firms involved in a merger or acquisition may pose an additional challenge, particularly if there are underlying incompatibilities in their supporting systems or processes.

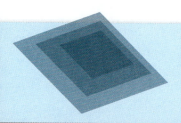
# Toyota's Legendary Production System: A Capability that Translates into Competitive Advantage

The heart of Toyota's strategy in motor vehicles is to out-compete rivals by manufacturing world-class, quality vehicles at lower costs and selling them at competitive price levels. To achieve this result, Toyota began efforts to improve its manufacturing competence over 50 years ago. Through tireless trial and error, the company gradually took what started as a loose collection of techniques and practices and integrated them into a full-fledged process now known as the Toyota Production System (TPS). TPS is grounded in the following principles, practices, and techniques:

- *Use just-in-time delivery of parts and components to the point of vehicle assembly.* The idea here is to stop transferring materials from place to place and to discontinue all activities on the part of workers that don't add value.

- *Develop people who can come up with unique ideas for production improvements.* Toyota encourages employees at all levels to question existing ways of doing things—even if this means challenging a boss on the soundness of a directive. Also, Toyota gives workers training to become better problem solvers.

- *Emphasize continuous improvement.* Workers are expected to develop better ways of doing things. Toyota managers tout messages such as "Never be satisfied." Another mantra is that the *T* in TPS also stands for "Thinking."

- *Empower workers to stop the assembly line when there's a problem or a defect is spotted.* Toyota views worker efforts to purge defects and sort out the problem immediately as critical to the whole concept of building quality into the production process.

- *Deal with defects only when they occur.* TPS philosophy holds that when things are running smoothly, they should not be subject to control; if attention is directed to fixing problems that are found, quality control can be handled with fewer personnel.

- *Ask yourself "Why?" five times.* The value of asking "Why?" five times enables identifying the root cause of the error and correcting it so that the error won't recur.

- *Organize all jobs around human motion to create a production/assembly system with no wasted effort.* Work organized in this fashion is called "standardized work" and people are trained to observe standardized work procedures so workers can do their jobs continuously in a set sequence of subprocesses.

- *Find where a part is made cheaply, and use that price as a benchmark.*

There's widespread agreement that Toyota's ongoing effort to refine and improve on its renowned TPS gives it manufacturing capabilities that others envy. Not only have auto manufacturers attempted to emulate key elements of TPS, but elements of Toyota's production philosophy have been adopted by hospitals and postal services.

*Sources:* Information posted at www.toyotageorgetown.com; Hirotaka Takeuchi, Emi Osono, and Norihiko Shimizu, "The Contradictions That Drive Toyota's Success," *Harvard Business Review* 86, no. 6 (June 2008), pp. 96–104; Taiichi Ohno, *Toyota Production System: Beyond Large-Scale Production* (New York: Sheridan, 1988).

Moreover, since internal fit is important, there is always the risk that under new management the acquired capabilities may not be as productive as they had been. In a worst-case scenario, the acquisition process may end up damaging or destroying the very capabilities that were the object of the acquisition in the first place.

## Accessing Capabilities through Collaborative Partnerships

Another method of acquiring capabilities from an external source is to access them via collaborative partnerships with suppliers, competitors, or other companies having the cutting-edge expertise. There are three basic ways to pursue this course of action:

1. *Outsource the function requiring the capabilities to a key supplier or another provider.* Whether this is a wise move depends on what can be safely delegated to outside suppliers or allies and which internal capabilities are key to the company's long-term success. As discussed in Chapter 6, outsourcing has the advantage of conserving resources so that the firm can focus its energies on those activities most central to its strategy. It may be a good choice for firms that are too small and resource-constrained to execute all the parts of their strategy internally.

2. *Collaborate with a firm that has complementary resources and capabilities in a joint venture, strategic alliance, or other type of partnership established for the purpose of achieving a shared strategic objective.* This requires launching initiatives to identify the most attractive potential partners and to establish collaborative working relationships. Since the success of the venture will depend on how well the partners work together, potential partners should be selected as much for their management style, culture, and goals as for their resources and capabilities.

3. *Engage in a collaborative partnership for the purpose of learning how the partner does things, internalizing its methods and thereby acquiring its capabilities.* This may be a viable method when each partner has something to learn from the other. But in other cases, it involves an abuse of trust. In consequence, it not only puts the cooperative venture at risk but also encourages the firm's partner to treat the firm similarly or refuse further dealings with the firm.

# The Strategic Role of Employee Training

Training and retraining are important when a company shifts to a strategy requiring different skills, competitive capabilities, and operating methods. Training is also strategically important in organizational efforts to build skills-based competencies. And it is a key activity in businesses where technical know-how is changing so rapidly that a company loses its ability to compete unless its employees have cutting-edge knowledge and expertise. Successful strategy implementers see to it that the training function is both adequately funded and effective. If the chosen strategy calls for new skills, deeper technological capability, or the building and using of new capabilities, training efforts need to be placed near the top of the action agenda.

The strategic importance of training has not gone unnoticed. Over 600 companies have established internal "universities" to lead the training effort, facilitate continuous organizational learning, and upgrade their company's knowledge resources. Many companies conduct orientation sessions for new employees, fund an assortment of competence-building training programs, and reimburse employees for tuition and other expenses associated with obtaining additional college education, attending professional development courses, and earning professional certification of one kind or another. A number of companies offer online, just-in-time training courses to employees around the clock. Increasingly, employees at all levels are expected to take an active role in their own professional development and assume responsibility for keeping their skills up to date and in sync with the company's needs.

## Strategy Execution Capabilities and Competitive Advantage

As firms get better at executing their strategies, they develop capabilities in the domain of strategy execution much as they build other organizational capabilities. Superior strategy execution capabilities allow companies to get the most from their organizational resources and competitive capabilities. In this way they contribute to the success of a firm's business model. But excellence in strategy execution can also be a more direct source of competitive advantage, since more efficient and effective strategy execution can lower costs and permit firms to deliver more value to customers. Superior strategy execution capabilities may also enable a company to react more quickly to market changes and beat other firms to the market with new products and services. This can allow a company to profit from a period of uncontested market dominance.

Because strategy execution capabilities are socially complex capabilities that develop with experience over long periods of time, they are hard to imitate. And there is no substitute for good strategy execution. (Recall the tests of resource advantage from Chapter 4.) As such, they may be as important a source of sustained competitive advantage as the capabilities that drive a firm's strategies. Indeed, they may be a far more important avenue for securing a competitive edge over rivals in situations where it is relatively easy for rivals to copy promising strategies. In such cases, the only way for firms to achieve lasting competitive advantage is to outexecute their competitors.

# MATCHING ORGANIZATIONAL STRUCTURE TO THE STRATEGY

**LO 4**

Recognize what issues to consider in establishing a strategy-supportive organizational structure and organizing the work effort.

While there are few hard-and-fast rules for organizing the work effort to support good strategy execution, there is one: a firm's organizational structure should be matched to the particular requirements of implementing the firm's strategy. Every company's strategy is grounded in its own set of organizational capabilities and value chain activities. Moreover, every firm's organization chart is partly a product of its particular situation, reflecting prior organizational patterns, varying internal circumstances, executive judgments about reporting relationships, and the politics of who gets which assignments. Thus, the determinants of the fine details of each firm's organizational structure are unique. But some considerations in organizing the work effort are common to all companies. These are summarized in Figure 10.3 and discussed in the following sections.

## Deciding Which Value Chain Activities to Perform Internally and Which to Outsource

Aside from the fact that an outsider may be able to perform certain value chain activities better or cheaper than a company can perform them internally (as discussed in Chapter 6), outsourcing can also sometimes make a positive contribution to strategy execution. Outsourcing the performance of selected value chain activities to outside vendors enables a company to heighten its strategic focus and *concentrate its full energies on performing those value chain activities that are at the core of its strategy, where it can create unique value.* For example, E. & J. Gallo Winery outsources 95 percent of its grape production, letting farmers take on weather-related and other grape-growing risks while it concentrates its full energies on wine production and sales.[18] Broadcom, a global leader in chips for broadband communication systems, outsources the manufacture of its chips to Taiwan

**FIGURE 10.3**  **Structuring the Work Effort to Promote Successful Strategy Execution**

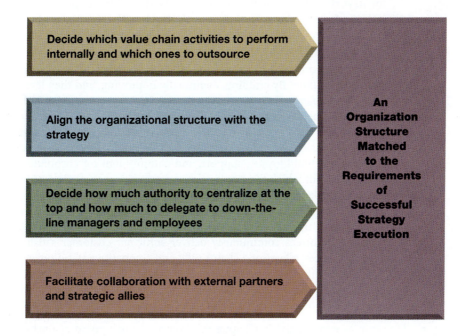

Semiconductor, thus freeing company personnel to focus their efforts on R&D, new chip design, and marketing. Nike concentrates on design, marketing, and distribution while outsourcing virtually all production of its shoes and sporting apparel. Illustration Capsule 10.3 describes Apple's decisions about which activities to outsource and which to perform in-house.

Such heightened focus on performing strategy-critical activities can yield three important execution-related benefits:

- *The company improves its chances for outclassing rivals in the performance of strategy-critical activities and turning a competence into a distinctive competence.* At the very least, the heightened focus on performing a select few value chain activities should promote more effective performance of those activities. This could materially enhance competitive capabilities by either lowering costs or improving quality. Whirlpool, ING Insurance, Hugo Boss, Japan Airlines, and Chevron have outsourced their data processing activities to computer service firms, believing that outside specialists can perform the needed services at lower costs and equal or better quality. A relatively large number of companies outsource the operation of their websites to web design and hosting enterprises. Many businesses that get a lot of inquiries from customers or that have to provide 24/7 technical support to users of their products around the world have found that it is considerably less expensive to outsource these functions to specialists (often located in foreign countries where skilled personnel are readily available and worker compensation costs are much lower) than to operate their own call centers.

- *The streamlining of internal operations that flows from outsourcing often acts to decrease internal bureaucracies, flatten the organizational structure, speed internal decision making, and shorten the time it takes to respond to changing market conditions.*[19] In consumer electronics, where advancing technology drives new product

Wisely choosing which activities to perform internally and which to outsource can lead to several strategy-executing advantages—lower costs, heightened strategic focus, less internal bureaucracy, speedier decision making, and a better arsenal of organizational capabilities.

innovation, organizing the work effort in a manner that expedites getting next-generation products to market ahead of rivals is a critical competitive capability. The world's motor vehicle manufacturers have found that they can shorten the cycle time for new models by outsourcing the production of many parts and components to independent suppliers. They then work closely with the suppliers to swiftly incorporate new technology and to better integrate individual parts and components to form engine cooling systems, transmission systems, and electrical systems.

- *Partnerships can add to a company's arsenal of capabilities and contribute to better strategy execution.* By building, continually improving, and then leveraging partnerships, a company enhances its overall organizational capabilities and strengthens its competitive assets—assets that deliver more value to customers and consequently pave the way for competitive success. Soft-drink and beer manufacturers cultivate their relationships with their bottlers and distributors to strengthen access to local markets and build loyalty, support, and commitment for corporate marketing programs, without which their own sales and growth are weakened. Similarly, fast-food enterprises like Wendy's and Burger King find it essential to work hand in hand with franchisees on outlet cleanliness, consistency of product quality, in-store ambience, courtesy and friendliness of store personnel, and other aspects of store operations. Unless franchisees continuously deliver sufficient customer satisfaction to attract repeat business, a fast-food chain's sales and competitive standing will suffer quickly. Companies like Boeing, Aerospatiale, Verizon Communications, and Dell have learned that their central R&D groups cannot begin to match the innovative capabilities of a well-managed network of supply chain partners.

However, as emphasized in Chapter 6, a company must guard against going overboard on outsourcing and becoming overly dependent on outside suppliers. A company cannot be the master of its own destiny unless it maintains expertise and resource depth in performing those value chain activities that underpin its long-term competitive success.[20] As a general rule, therefore, it is the strategically less important activities—like handling customer inquiries and providing technical support, doing the payroll, administering employee benefit programs, providing corporate security, maintaining fleet vehicles, operating the company's website, conducting employee training, and managing an assortment of information and data processing functions—where outsourcing is likely to make the most strategic sense.

## Aligning the Firm's Organizational Structure with Its Strategy

The design of the firm's **organizational structure** is a critical aspect of the strategy execution process. The organizational structure comprises the formal and informal arrangement of tasks, responsibilities, and lines of authority and communication by which the firm is administered.[21] It specifies the linkages among parts of the organization, the reporting relationships, the direction of information flows, and the decision-making processes. It is a key factor in strategy implementation since it exerts a strong influence on how well managers can coordinate and control the complex set of activities involved.[22]

A well-designed organizational structure is one in which the various parts (e.g., decision-making rights, communication patterns) are aligned with one another and also matched to the requirements of the strategy. With the right structure in place, managers can orchestrate the various aspects of the implementation process with an even hand and a light touch. Without a supportive structure, strategy execution is more likely to become bogged down by administrative confusion, political maneuvering, and bureaucratic waste.

# Which Value Chain Activities Does Apple Outsource and Why?

Innovation and design are core competencies for Apple and the drivers behind the creation of winning products such as the iPod, iPhone, and iPad. In consequence, all activities directly related to new product development and product design are performed internally. For example, Apple's Industrial Design Group is responsible for creating the look and feel of all Apple products—from the Mac mini to the iPad Touch.

Producing a continuing stream of great new products and product versions is key to the success of Apple's strategy. But executing this strategy takes more than innovation and design capabilities. Manufacturing flexibility and speed are imperative in the production of Apple products to ensure that the latest ideas are reflected in the products and that the company meets the high demand for their products—especially around launch.

For these capabilities, Apple turns to outsourcing, like the majority of its competitors in the consumer electronics space. Apple outsources the manufacturing of products like its iPhone to Asia, where Contract Manufacturing Organizations (CMOs) create value through their vast scale, high flexibility, and low cost. Perhaps no company better epitomizes the Asian CMO value proposition than FoxConn, a company that assembles not only for Apple, but for Hewlett-Packard,

Motorola, Amazon, and Samsung as well. FoxConn's scale is incredible, with their largest facility (FoxConn City in Shenzhen, China) employing over 230,000 workers. Such scale offers companies a significant degree of flexibility as FoxConn has the ability to hire 3,000 employees on practically a moment's notice. Apple, more so than their competitors, is able to capture CMO value creation by leveraging their immense sales volume and strong cash position to receive preferred treatment.

Developed with Margaret W. Macauley.

*Sources:* Company website; Charles Duhigg, "How the U.S. Lost Out on iPhone Work," *The New York Times,* January 22, 2012. Web: February 19, 2012, accessed March 5, 2012.

*Good organizational design may even contribute to the firm's ability to create value for customers and realize a profit.* By enabling lower bureaucratic costs and facilitating operational efficiency, it can lower a firm's operating costs. By facilitating the coordination of activities within the firm, it can improve the capability-building process, leading to greater differentiation and/or lower costs. Moreover, by improving the speed with which information is communicated and activities are coordinated, it can enable the firm to beat rivals to the market and profit from a period of unrivaled advantage.

## Making Strategy-Critical Activities the Main Building Blocks of the Organizational Structure
In any business, some activities in the value chain are always more critical to successful strategy execution than others. For instance, a ski apparel company like Spyder must be good at styling and design, low-cost manufacturing, distribution (convincing an attractively large number of dealers to stock and promote the company's brand), and marketing and advertising (building a brand

image that generates buzz and appeal among ski enthusiasts). For discount stock brokers, like Scottrade and TDAmeritrade, the strategy-critical activities are fast access to information, accurate order execution, efficient record keeping and transactions processing, and good customer service. Where such is the case, it is important for management to build its organizational structure around proficient performance of these activities, making them the centerpieces or main building blocks in the enterprise's organizational structure.

The rationale for making strategy-critical activities the main building blocks in structuring a business is compelling: If activities crucial to strategic success are to have the resources, decision-making influence, and organizational impact they need, they have to be centerpieces in the organizational scheme. Making them the focus of structuring efforts will also facilitate their coordination and promote good internal fit—an essential attribute of a winning strategy, as summarized in Chapter 1 and elaborated in Chapter 4. To the extent that implementing a new strategy entails new or altered key activities or capabilities, different organizational arrangements may be required.

## Matching Type of Organizational Structure to Strategy Execution Requirements

Organizational structures can be classified into a limited number of standard types. The type that is most suitable for a given firm will depend on the firm's size and complexity as well as its strategy. As firms grow and their needs for structure evolve, their structural form is likely to evolve from one type to another. The four basic types are the *simple structure*, the *functional structure*, the *multidivisional structure*, and the *matrix structure*, as described next.

*1. Simple Structure*    A **simple structure** is one in which a central executive (often the owner-manager) handles all major decisions and oversees the operations of the organization with the help of a small staff.[23] Simple structures are also known as *line-and-staff structures*, since a central administrative staff supervises line employees who conduct the operations of the firm, or *flat structures*, since there are few levels of hierarchy. It is characterized by limited task specialization; few rules; informal relationships; minimal use of training, planning, and liaison devices; and a lack of sophisticated support systems. It has all the advantages of simplicity, including low administrative costs, ease of coordination, flexibility, quick decision making, adaptability, and responsiveness to change. Its informality and lack of rules may foster creativity and heightened individual responsibility.

Simple organizational structures are typically employed by small firms and entrepreneurial startups. The simple structure is the most common type of organizational structure since small firms are the most prevalent type of business. As an organization grows, however, this structural form becomes inadequate to the demands that come with size and complexity. In response, growing firms tend to alter their organizational structure from a simple structure to a *functional structure*.

*2. Functional Structure*    A **functional structure** is one that is organized along functional lines, where a function represents a major component of the firm's value chain, such as R&D, engineering and design, manufacturing, sales and marketing, logistics, and customer service. Each functional unit is supervised by functional line managers who report to the chief executive officer and a corporate staff. This arrangement allows functional managers to focus on their area of responsibility, leaving it to the CEO and headquarters to provide direction and ensure that their activities are coordinated and integrated. Functional structures are also known as *departmental structures*, since the functional units are commonly called departments, and *unitary structures* or *U-forms*, since a single unit is responsible for each function.

In large organizations, functional structures lighten the load on top management, relative to simple structures, and make for a more efficient use of managerial resources. Their primary advantage, however, is due to greater task specialization, which promotes learning, enables the realization of scale economies, and offers productivity advantages not otherwise available. Their chief disadvantage is that the departmental boundaries can inhibit the flow of information and limit the opportunities for cross-functional cooperation and coordination.

It is generally agreed that some type of functional structure is the best organizational arrangement when a company is in just one particular business (irrespective of which of the five generic competitive strategies it opts to pursue). For instance, a technical instruments manufacturer may be organized around research and development, engineering, supply chain management, assembly, quality control, marketing, and technical services. A discount retailer, such as Dollar General or Kmart, may organize around such functional units as purchasing, warehousing, distribution logistics, store operations, advertising, merchandising and promotion, and customer service. Functional structures can also be appropriate for firms with high-volume production, products that are closely related, and a limited degree of vertical integration. For example, General Motors now manages all of its brands (e.g., Cadillac, GMC, Chevrolet, Buick) under a common functional structure designed to promote technical transfer and capture economies of scale.

As firms continue to grow, they often become more diversified and complex, placing a greater burden on top management. At some point, the centralized control that characterizes the functional structure becomes a liability, and the advantages of functional specialization begin to break down. To resolve these problems and address a growing need for coordination across functions, firms generally turn to the *multidivisional structure.*

**3. *Multidivisional Structure***   A **multidivisional structure** is a decentralized structure consisting of a set of operating divisions organized along market, customer, product, or geographic lines, along with a central corporate headquarters, which monitors divisional activities, allocates resources, performs assorted support functions, and exercises overall control. Since each division is essentially a business (often called *single business units* or *SBUs*), the divisions typically operate as independent profit centers (i.e., with profit/loss responsibility) and are organized internally along functional lines. Division managers oversee day-to-day operations and the development of business-level strategy, while corporate executives attend to overall performance and corporate strategy, the elements of which were described in Chapter 8. Multidivisional structures are also called *divisional structures* or *M-forms,* in contrast with U-form (functional) structures.

Multidivisional structures are common among companies pursuing some form of diversification strategy or multinational strategy, with operations in a number of businesses or countries. When the strategy is one of unrelated diversification, as in a conglomerate or holding company, the divisions generally represent businesses in separate industries. When the strategy is based on related diversification, the divisions may be organized according to markets, customer groups, product lines, geographic regions, or technologies. In this arrangement, the decision about where to draw the divisional lines depends foremost on the nature of the relatedness and the strategy-critical building blocks, in terms of which businesses have key value chain activities in common. For example, a company selling closely related products to business customers as well as two types of end consumers—online buyers and in-store buyers—may organize its divisions according to customer groups since the value chains involved in serving the three groups differ. Another company may organize by product line due to commonalities in product development and production within each product line. Multidivisional structures are also

> ### CORE CONCEPT
>
> A **multidivisional structure** is a decentralized structure consisting of a set of operating divisions organized along business, product, customer group, or geographic lines, and a central corporate headquarters that allocates resources, provides support functions, and monitors divisional activities. Multidivisional structures are also called *divisional* structures or *M-forms.*

common among vertically integrated firms. There the major building blocks are often divisional units performing one or more of the major processing steps along the value chain (e.g., raw-material production, components manufacture, assembly, wholesale distribution, retail store operations).

Multidivisional structures offer significant advantages over functional structures in terms of facilitating the management of a complex and diverse set of operations.[24] Putting business-level strategy in the hands of division managers while leaving corporate strategy to top executives reduces the potential for information overload and improves the quality of decision making in each domain. This also minimizes the costs of coordinating divisionwide activities while enhancing top management's ability to control a diverse and complex operation. Moreover, multidivisional structures can help align individual incentives with the goals of the corporation and spur productivity by encouraging competition for resources among the different divisions.

But a divisional business-unit structure can also present some problems to a company pursuing related diversification, because having independent business units—each running its own business in its own way—inhibits cross-business collaboration and the capture of cross-business synergies. To solve this type of problem, firms turn to more complex structures, such as the matrix structure.

**CORE CONCEPT**

A **matrix structure** is a structure that combines two or more organizational forms, with multiple reporting relationships. It is used to foster cross-unit collaboration. Matrix structures are also called *composite* structures or *combination* structures.

**4. Matrix Structure**    A **matrix structure** is a combination structure in which the organization is organized along two or more dimensions at once (e.g., business, geographic area, value chain function) for the purpose of enhancing cross-unit communication, collaboration, and coordination. In essence, it overlays one type of structure onto another type. Matrix structures are managed through multiple reporting relationships, so a middle manager may report to several bosses. For instance, in a matrix structure based on product line, region, and function, a sales manager for plastic containers in Georgia might report to the manager of the plastics division, the head of the southeast sales region, and the head of marketing.

Matrix organizational structures have evolved from the complex, overformalized structures that were popular in the 1960s, '70s, and '80s but often produced inefficient, unwieldy bureaucracies. The modern incarnation of the matrix structure is generally a more flexible arrangement, with a single primary reporting relationship that can be overlaid with a temporary secondary reporting relationship as need arises. For example, a software company that is organized into functional departments (software design, quality control, customer relations) may assign employees from those departments to different projects on a temporary basis, so an employee reports to a project manager as well as to his or her primary boss (the functional department head) for the duration of a project.

Matrix structures are also called *composite structures* or *combination structures*. They are often used for project-based, process-based, or team-based management. Such approaches are common in businesses involving projects of limited duration, such as consulting, architecture, and engineering services. The type of close cross-unit collaboration that a flexible matrix structure supports is also needed to build competitive capabilities in strategically important activities, such as speeding new products to market, that involve employees scattered across several organizational units.[25] Capabilities-based matrix structures that combine process departments (like new product development) with more traditional functional departments provide a solution.

An advantage of matrix structures is that they facilitate the sharing of plant and equipment, specialized knowledge, and other key resources. Thus, they lower costs by enabling the realization of economies of scope. They also have the advantage of flexibility in form and may allow for better oversight since supervision is provided from more than one perspective. A disadvantage is that they add an additional layer of management, thereby increasing bureaucratic costs and possibly decreasing response time to new situations.[26] In addition, there is a potential for confusion among employees due to dual reporting relationships and divided loyalties. While there is some controversy over the utility of matrix structures, the modern approach to matrix structures does much to minimize their disadvantages.[27]

# Determining How Much Authority to Delegate

Under any organizational structure, there is room for considerable variation in how much authority top managers retain and how much is delegated to down-the-line managers and employees. In executing strategy, companies must decide how much authority to delegate to the managers of each organizational unit—especially the heads of divisions, functional departments, and other operating units—and how much decision-making latitude to give individual employees in performing their jobs. The two extremes are to *centralize decision making* at the top or to *decentralize decision making* by giving middle managers and front-line employees considerable decision-making latitude in their areas of responsibility. As shown in Table 10.1, the two approaches are based on sharply different underlying principles and beliefs, with each having its pros and cons.

**LO 5**

Become aware of the pros and cons of centralized and decentralized decision making in implementing the chosen strategy.

**Centralized Decision Making: Pros and Cons**   In a highly centralized organizational structure, *top executives retain authority for most strategic and operating decisions* and keep a tight rein on business-unit heads, department heads, and the managers of key operating units. Comparatively little discretionary authority is granted to frontline supervisors and rank-and-file employees. The command-and-control paradigm of centralized structures is based on the underlying assumptions that frontline personnel have neither the time nor the inclination to direct and properly control the work they are performing and that they lack the knowledge and judgment to make wise decisions about how best to do it—hence the need for managerially prescribed policies and procedures, close supervision, and tight control. The thesis underlying centralized structures is that strict enforcement of detailed procedures backed by rigorous managerial oversight is the most reliable way to keep the daily execution of strategy on track.

One advantage of a centralized structure is tight control by the manager in charge—it is easy to know who is accountable when things do not go well. This structure can also reduce the potential for conflicting decisions and actions among lower-level managers who may have differing perspectives and ideas about how to tackle certain tasks or resolve particular issues. For example, a manager in charge of an engineering department may be more interested in pursuing a new technology than is a marketing manager who doubts that customers will value the technology as highly. Another advantage of a command-and-control structure is that it can enable a more uniform and swift response to a crisis situation that affects the organization as a whole.

But there are some serious disadvantages as well. Hierarchical command-and-control structures can make a large organization with a complex structure sluggish in responding to changing market conditions because of the time it takes for the review/approval process to run up all the layers of the management bureaucracy. Furthermore, to work well centralized decision making requires top-level managers to gather and process whatever information is relevant to the decision. When the relevant knowledge resides at lower organizational levels (or is technical, detailed, or hard to express in words), it is difficult and time-consuming to get all the facts and nuances in front of a high-level executive located far from the scene of the action—full understanding of the situation cannot be readily copied from one mind to another. Hence, centralized decision making is often impractical—the larger the company and the more scattered its operations, the more that decision-making authority must be delegated to managers closer to the scene of the action.

**TABLE 10.1  Advantages and Disadvantages of Centralized versus Decentralized Decision Making**

| Centralized Organizational Structures | Decentralized Organizational Structures |
|---|---|
| **Basic Tenets**<br><br>• Decisions on most matters of importance should be in the hands of top-level managers who have the experience, expertise, and judgment to decide what is the best course of action<br><br>• Lower-level personnel have neither the knowledge, the time, nor the inclination to properly manage the tasks they are performing<br><br>• Strong control from the top is a more effective means for coordinating company actions | **Basic Tenets**<br><br>• Decision-making authority should be put in the hands of the people closest to, and most familiar with, the situation<br><br>• Those with decision-making authority should be trained to exercise good judgment<br><br>• A company that draws on the combined intellectual capital of all its employees can outperform a command-and-control company |
| **Chief Advantages**<br><br>• Fixes accountability through tight control from the top<br><br>• Eliminates potential for conflicting goals and actions on the part of lower-level managers<br><br>• Facilitates quick decision making and strong leadership under crisis situations | **Chief Advantages**<br><br>• Encourages company employees to exercise initiative and act responsibly<br><br>• Promotes greater motivation and involvement in the business on the part of more company personnel<br><br>• Spurs new ideas and creative thinking<br><br>• Allows for fast response to market change<br><br>• Entails fewer layers of management |
| **Primary Disadvantages**<br><br>• Lengthens response times by those closest to the market conditions because they must seek approval for their actions<br><br>• Does not encourage responsibility among lower-level managers and rank-and-file employees<br><br>• Discourages lower-level managers and rank-and-file employees from exercising any initiative | **Primary Disadvantages**<br><br>• Higher-level managers may be unaware of actions taken by empowered personnel under their supervision<br><br>• Puts the organization at risk if empowered employees happen to make "bad" decisions<br><br>• Can impair cross-unit collaboration |

**Decentralized Decision Making: Pros and Cons**    In a highly decentralized organization, *decision-making authority is pushed down to the lowest organizational level capable of making timely, informed, competent decisions.* The objective is to put adequate decision-making authority in the hands of the people closest to and most familiar with the situation and train them to weigh all the factors and exercise good judgment. Decentralized decision making means that the managers of each organizational unit are delegated lead responsibility for deciding how best to execute strategy. At Starbucks, for example, employees are encouraged to exercise initiative in promoting customer satisfaction—there's the oft-repeated story of a store employee who, when the computerized cash register system went offline, enthusiastically offered free coffee to waiting customers.[28]

The case for empowering down-the-line managers and employees to make decisions related to daily operations and strategy execution is based on the belief that a company that draws on the combined intellectual capital of all its employees can outperform

> The ultimate goal of decentralized decision making is to put authority in the hands of those persons closest to and most knowledgeable about the situation.

a command-and-control company.[29] The challenge in a decentralized system is in maintaining adequate control. With decentralized decision making, top management maintains control by placing limits on the authority granted to company personnel, installing companywide strategic control systems, holding people accountable for their decisions, instituting compensation incentives that reward people for doing their jobs well, and creating a corporate culture where there's strong peer pressure on individuals to act responsibly.[30]

Decentralized organization structures have much to recommend them. Delegating authority to lower-level managers and rank-and-file employees encourages them to take responsibility and exercise initiative. It shortens organizational response times to market changes and spurs new ideas, creative thinking, innovation, and greater involvement on the part of all company personnel. In worker-empowered structures, jobs can be defined more broadly, several tasks can be integrated into a single job, and people can direct their own work. Fewer layers of managers are needed because deciding how to do things becomes part of each person's or team's job. Further, today's online communication systems and smart phones make it easy and relatively inexpensive for people at all organizational levels to have direct access to data, other employees, managers, suppliers, and customers. They can access information quickly (via the Internet or company network), readily check with superiors or whomever else as needed, and take responsible action. Typically, there are genuine gains in morale and productivity when people are provided with the tools and information they need to operate in a self-directed way.

But decentralization also has some disadvantages. Top managers lose an element of control over what goes on and may thus be unaware of actions being taken by personnel under their supervision. Such lack of control can put a company at risk in the event that empowered employees happen to make unwise decisions. Moreover, because decentralization gives organizational units the authority to act independently, there is risk of too little collaboration and coordination between different organizational units.

Many companies have concluded that the advantages of decentralization outweigh the disadvantages. Over the past 15 to 20 years, there's been a decided shift from centralized, hierarchical structures to flatter, more decentralized structures that stress employee empowerment. This shift reflects a strong and growing consensus that authoritarian, hierarchical organizational structures are not well suited to implementing and executing strategies in an era when extensive information and instant communication are the norm and when a big fraction of the organization's most valuable assets consists of intellectual capital and resides in the knowledge and capabilities of its employees.

## Capturing Cross-Business Strategic Fit in a Decentralized Structure
Diversified companies striving to capture the benefits of synergy between separate businesses have to beware of giving business-unit heads full rein to operate independently. Cross-business strategic fit typically must be captured either by enforcing close cross-business collaboration or by centralizing performance of functions requiring close coordination at the corporate level.[31] For example, if businesses with overlapping process and product technologies have their own independent R&D departments—each pursuing its own priorities, projects, and strategic agendas—it's hard for the corporate parent to prevent duplication of effort, capture either economies of scale or economies of scope, or encourage more collaborative R&D efforts. Where cross-business strategic fit with respect to R&D is important, the best solution is usually to centralize the R&D function and have a coordinated corporate R&D effort that serves both the interests of individual businesses and the company as a whole. Likewise, centralizing the related

activities of separate businesses makes sense when there are opportunities to share a common sales force, use common distribution channels, rely on a common field service organization, use common e-commerce systems, and so on.

## Facilitating Collaboration with External Partners and Strategic Allies

Organizational mechanisms—whether formal or informal—are also required to ensure effective working relationships with each major outside constituency involved in strategy execution. Strategic alliances, outsourcing arrangements, joint ventures, and cooperative partnerships can contribute little of value without active management of the relationship. Unless top management sees that constructive organizational bridge-building with external partners occurs and that productive working relationships emerge, the potential value of cooperative relationships is lost and the company's power to execute its strategy is weakened. For example, if close working relationships with suppliers are crucial, then supply chain management must enter into considerations regarding how to create an effective organizational structure. If distributor/dealer/franchisee relationships are important, then someone must be assigned the task of nurturing the relationships with forward channel allies.

Building organizational bridges with external partners and strategic allies can be accomplished by appointing "relationship managers" with responsibility for making particular strategic partnerships generate the intended benefits. Relationship managers have many roles and functions: getting the right people together, promoting good rapport, facilitating the flow of information, nurturing interpersonal communication and cooperation, and ensuring effective coordination.[32] Multiple cross-organization ties have to be established and kept open to ensure proper communication and coordination. There has to be enough information sharing to make the relationship work and periodic frank discussions of conflicts, trouble spots, and changing situations.

Organizing and managing a network structure provides another mechanism for encouraging more effective collaboration and cooperation among external partners. A **network structure** is the arrangement linking a number of independent organizations involved in some common undertaking. A well-managed network structure typically includes one firm in a more central role, with the responsibility of ensuring that the right partners are included and the activities across the network are coordinated. The high-end Italian motorcycle company Ducati operates in this manner, assembling its motorcycles from parts obtained from a hand-picked integrated network of parts suppliers.

## Further Perspectives on Structuring the Work Effort

All organization designs have their strategy-related strengths and weaknesses. To do a good job of matching structure to strategy, strategy implementers first have to pick a basic organizational design and modify it as needed to fit the company's particular business lineup. They must then (1) supplement the design with appropriate coordinating mechanisms (cross-functional task forces, special project teams, self-contained work teams, and so on) and (2) institute whatever networking and communications arrangements it takes to support effective execution of the firm's strategy. Some companies may avoid setting up "ideal" organizational arrangements because they do not want to disturb existing reporting relationships or because they need to accommodate other situational idiosyncrasies, yet they must still work toward the goal of building a competitively capable organization.

---

Efforts to decentralize decision making and give company personnel some leeway in conducting operations must be tempered with the need to maintain adequate control and cross-unit coordination.

---

**CORE CONCEPT**

A **network structure** is the arrangement linking a number of independent organizations involved in some common undertaking.

What can be said unequivocally is that building a capable organization entails a process of consciously knitting together the efforts of individuals and groups. Organizational capabilities emerge from establishing and nurturing cooperative working relationships among people and groups to perform activities in a more efficient, value-creating fashion. While an appropriate organizational structure can facilitate this, organization building is a task in which senior management must be deeply involved. Indeed, effectively managing both internal organization processes and external collaboration to create and develop competitively valuable organizational capabilities remains a top challenge for senior executives in today's companies.

## KEY POINTS

1. Executing strategy is an action-oriented, operations-driven activity revolving around the management of people and business processes. In devising an action agenda for executing strategy, the place for managers to start is with a probing assessment of what the organization must do differently to carry out the strategy successfully. They should then consider precisely *how* to make the necessary internal changes.

2. Good strategy execution requires a *team effort*. All managers have strategy-executing responsibility in their areas of authority, and all employees are active participants in the strategy execution process.

3. Ten managerial tasks are part of every company effort to execute strategy: (1) staffing the organization with the right people, (2) building the necessary organizational capabilities, (3) creating a supportive organizational structure, (4) allocating sufficient resources, (5) instituting supportive policies and procedures, (6) adopting processes for continuous improvement, (7) installing systems that enable proficient company operations, (8) tying incentives to the achievement of desired targets, (9) instilling the right corporate culture, and (10) exercising internal leadership to propel strategy execution forward.

4. The two best signs of good strategy execution are whether a company is meeting or beating its performance targets and performing value chain activities in a manner that is conducive to companywide operating excellence. *Shortfalls in performance signal weak strategy, weak execution, or both.*

5. Building an organization capable of good strategy execution entails three types of actions: (1) *staffing the organization*—assembling a talented management team, and recruiting and retaining employees with the needed experience, technical skills, and intellectual capital; (2) a*cquiring, developing, and strengthening strategy-supportive resources and capabilities*—accumulating the required resources, developing proficiencies in performing strategy-critical value chain activities, and updating the company's capabilities to match changing market conditions and customer expectations; and (3) *structuring the organization and work effort*—instituting organizational arrangements that facilitate good strategy execution, deciding how much decision-making authority to delegate, and managing external relationships.

6. Building core competencies and competitive capabilities is a time-consuming, managerially challenging exercise that can be approached in three ways: (1) developing capabilities internally, (2) acquiring capabilities through mergers and acquisitions, and (3) accessing capabilities via collaborative partnerships.

7. In building capabilities internally, the first step is to develop the *ability* to do something, through experimentation, active searches for alternative solutions, and

learning by trial and error. As experience grows and company personnel learn how to perform the activities consistently well and at an acceptable cost, the ability evolves into a tried-and-true capability. The process can be accelerated by making learning a more deliberate endeavor and providing the incentives that will motivate company personnel to achieve the desired ends.

8. As firms get better at executing their strategies, they develop capabilities in the domain of strategy execution. Superior strategy execution capabilities allow companies to get the most from their organizational resources and competitive capabilities. But excellence in strategy execution can also be a more direct source of competitive advantage, since more efficient and effective strategy execution can lower costs and permit firms to deliver more value to customers. Because they are socially complex capabilities, superior strategy execution capabilities are hard to imitate and have no good substitutes. As such, they can be an important source of *sustainable* competitive advantage. Any time rivals can readily duplicate successful strategies, making it impossible to *outstrategize* rivals, the chief way to achieve lasting competitive advantage is to *outexecute* them.

9. Structuring the organization and organizing the work effort in a strategy-supportive fashion has four aspects: (1) deciding which value chain activities to perform internally and which ones to outsource; (2) aligning the firm's organizational structure with its strategy; (3) deciding how much authority to centralize at the top and how much to delegate to down-the-line managers and employees; and (4) facilitating the necessary collaboration and coordination with external partners and strategic allies.

10. To align the firm's organizational structure with its strategy, it is important to make strategy-critical activities the main building blocks. There are four basic types of organizational structures: the simple structure, the functional structure, the multidivisional structure, and the matrix structure. Which is most appropriate depends on the firm's size, complexity, and strategy.

## ASSURANCE OF LEARNING EXERCISES

**LO 1**

1. The heart of Toyota's strategy in motor vehicles is to out-compete rivals by manufacturing world-class, quality vehicles at lower costs and selling them at competitive price levels. Executing this strategy requires top-notch manufacturing capability and super-efficient management of people, equipment, and materials. Illustration Capsule 10.2 discusses the principles, practices, and techniques grounded in Toyota's famed Toyota Production System. How does Toyota's philosophy of dealing with defects, empowering employees, and developing capabilities impact strategy execution? Why are its slogans such as "Never be satisfied" and "Ask yourself 'Why?' five times" important?

**LO 2**

2. Procter and Gamble's systematic approach to management development is discussed in Illustration Capsule 10.1. Based upon the information provided in the capsule, explain how the company's approach to recruiting and its promotion from within policy helps build managerial talent. Explain why its formal training opportunities and career planning efforts help the company retain its most valuable employees. How does Procter and Gamble make sure that its managers are good at knowing what needs to be done and are skilled in "making it happen."

**LO 2, LO 3**

3. Review the Careers link on L'Oréal's worldwide corporate website (go to **www.loreal.com** and click on the company's worldwide corporate website option). The section provides extensive information about personal development, international learning

opportunities, integration of new hires into existing teams, and other areas of management development. How do the programs discussed help L'Oréal hire good people and build core competencies and competitive capabilities? Please use the chapter's discussions of recruiting, training, and retaining capable employees and building core competencies and competitive capabilities as a guide for preparing your answer.

4. Examine the overall corporate organizational structure chart for Exelon Corporation. The chart can be found by going to **www.exeloncorp.com** and using the website search feature to locate "organizational charts." Does it appear that strategy-critical activities are the building blocks of Exelon's organizational arrangement? Is its organizational structure best characterized as a departmental structure tied to functional, process, or geographic departments? Is the company's organizational structure better categorized as a divisional structure? Would you categorize Exelon's organizational structure as a matrix arrangement? Explain your answer. **LO 4**

5. Using Google Scholar or your university library's access to EBSCO, InfoTrac, or other online databases, do a search for recent writings on decentralized decision making and employee empowerment. According to the articles you find in the various management journals, what are the conditions under which decision making should be pushed down to lower levels of management? **LO 5**

## EXERCISES FOR SIMULATION PARTICIPANTS

1. How would you describe the organization of your company's top management team? Is some decision making decentralized and delegated to individual managers? If so, explain how the decentralization works. Or are decisions made more by consensus, with all co-managers having input? What do you see as the advantages and disadvantages of the decision-making approach your company is employing? **LO 5**

2. What specific actions have you and your co-managers taken to develop core competencies or competitive capabilities that can contribute to good strategy execution and potential competitive advantage? If no actions have been taken, explain your rationale for doing nothing. **LO 3**

3. What value chain activities are most crucial to good execution of your company's strategy? Does your company have the ability to outsource any value chain activities? If so, have you and your co-managers opted to engage in outsourcing? Why or why not? **LO 1, LO 4**

## ENDNOTES

[1] Steven W. Floyd and Bill Wooldridge, "Managing Strategic Consensus: The Foundation of Effective Implementation," *Academy of Management Executive* 6, no. 4 (November 1992), p. 27.
[2] Jack Welch with Suzy Welch, *Winning* (New York: HarperBusiness, 2005).
[3] Larry Bossidy and Ram Charan, *Execution: The Discipline of Getting Things Done* (New York: Crown Business, 2002).
[4] Christopher A. Bartlett and Sumantra Ghoshal, "Building Competitive Advantage through People," *MIT Sloan Management Review* 43, no. 2 (Winter 2002), pp. 34–41.

[5] Justin Menkes, "Hiring for Smarts," *Harvard Business Review* 83, no. 11 (November 2005), pp. 100–9; Justin Menkes, *Executive Intelligence* (New York: HarperCollins, 2005).
[6] Jim Collins, *Good to Great* (New York: HarperBusiness, 2001).
[7] John Byrne, "The Search for the Young and Gifted," *BusinessWeek,* October 4, 1999, p. 108.
[8] Helfat et al., *Dynamic Capabilities: Understanding Strategic Change in Organizations* (Malden, MA: Blackwell, 2007); R. Grant, *Contemporary Strategy Analysis,* 6th ed. (Malden, MA: Blackwell, 2008).

[9] C. Helfat and M. Peteraf, "The Dynamic Resource-Based View: Capability Life-Cycles," *Strategic Management Journal,* 24, no. 10 (October 2003), pp. 997–1010.
[10] G. Hamel and C. K. Prahalad, "Strategy as Stretch and Leverage," *Harvard Business Review* 71, no. 2 (March/April 1993), pp. 75–84.
[11] G. Dosi, R. Nelson, and S. Winter (eds.), *The Nature and Dynamics of Organizational Capabilities* (Oxford, England: Oxford University Press, 2001).
[12] S. Winter, "The Satisficing Principle in Capability Learning," *Strategic Management Journal* 21, nos. 10/11 (October/November

2000), pp. 981–96; M. Zollo and S. Winter, "Deliberate Learning and the Evolution of Dynamic Capabilities," *Organization Science* 13, no. 3 (May/June 2002), pp. 339–51.

[13] G. Szulanski and S. Winter, "Getting It Right the Second Time," *Harvard Business Review* 80 (January 2002), pp. 62–69; S. Winter and G. Szulanski, "Replication as Strategy," *Organization Science* 12, no. 6 (November/December 2001), pp. 730–43.

[14] B. Kogut and U. Zander, "Knowledge of the Firm, Combinative Capabilities, and the Replication of Technology," *Organization Science* 3, no. 3 (August 1992), pp. 383–97.

[15] C. Helfat and R. Raubitschek, "Product Sequencing: Co-Evolution of Knowledge, Capabilities and Products," *Strategic Management Journal* 21, nos. 10/11 (October/November 2000), pp. 961–80.

[16] Robert H. Hayes, Gary P. Pisano, and David M. Upton, *Strategic Operations: Competing through Capabilities* (New York: Free Press, 1996); Jonas Ridderstrale, "Cashing In on Corporate Competencies," *Business Strategy Review* 14, no. 1 (Spring 2003), pp. 27–38; Danny Miller, Russell Eisenstat, and Nathaniel Foote, "Strategy from the Inside Out: Building Capability-Creating Organizations," *California Management Review* 44, no. 3 (Spring 2002), pp. 37–55.

[17] S. Karim and W. Mitchell, "Path-Dependent and Path-Breaking Change: Reconfiguring Business Resources Following Business," *Strategic Management Journal* 21, nos. 10/11 (October/November 2000), pp. 1061–82; L. Capron, P. Dussauge, and W. Mitchell, "Resource Redeployment Following Horizontal Acquisitions in Europe and North America, 1988–1992," *Strategic Management Journal* 19, no. 7 (July 1998), pp. 631–62.

[18] J. B. Quinn, *Intelligent Enterprise* (New York: Free Press, 1992).

[19] J. B. Quinn and F. Hilmer, "Strategic Outsourcing," *McKinsey Quarterly* 1 (1995), pp. 48–70; Jussi Heikkilä and Carlos Cordon, "Outsourcing: A Core or Non-Core Strategic Management Decision," *Strategic Change* 11, no. 3 (June–July 2002), pp. 183–93; J. B. Quinn, "Strategic Outsourcing: Leveraging Knowledge Capabilities," *Sloan Management Review* 40, no. 4 (Summer 1999), pp. 9–2; C. K. Prahalad, "The Art of Outsourcing," *The Wall Street Journal*, June 8, 2005, p. A13; Jérôme Barthélemy, "The Seven Deadly Sins of Outsourcing," *Academy of Management Executive* 17, no. 2 (May 2003), pp. 87–98.

[20] Gary P. Pisano and Willy C. Shih, "Restoring American Competitiveness," *Harvard Business Review* 87, nos. 7–8 (July–August 2009), pp. 114–25.

[21] A. Chandler, *Strategy and Structure* (Cambridge, MA: MIT Press, 1962).

[22] E. Olsen, S. Slater, and G. Hult, "The Importance of Structure and Process to Strategy Implementation," *Business Horizons* 48, no. 1 (2005), pp. 47–54; H. Barkema, J. Baum, and E. Mannix, "Management Challenges in a New Time," *Academy of Management Journal* 45, no. 5 (October 2002), pp. 916–30.

[23] H. Mintzberg, *The Structuring of Organizations* (Englewood Cliffs, NJ: Prentice Hall, 1979); C. Levicki, *The Interactive Strategy Workout,* 2nd ed. (London: Prentice Hall, 1999).

[24] O. Williamson, *Market and Hierarchies* (New York: Free Press, 1975); R. M. Burton and B. Obel, "A Computer Simulation Test of the M-Form Hypothesis," *Administrative Science Quarterly* 25 (1980), pp. 457–76.

[25] J. Baum and S. Wally, "Strategic Decision Speed and Firm Performance," *Strategic Management Journal* 24 (2003), pp. 1107–29.

[26] C. Bartlett and S. Ghoshal, "Matrix Management: Not a Structure, a Frame of Mind," *Harvard Business Review,* July–August 1990, pp. 138–45.

[27] M. Goold and A. Campbell, "Structured Networks: Towards the Well Designed Matrix," *Long Range Planning* 36, no. 5 (2003), pp. 427–39.

[28] Iain Somerville and John Edward Mroz, "New Competencies for a New World," in Frances Hesselbein, Marshall Goldsmith, and Richard Beckard (eds.), *The Organization of the Future* (San Francisco: Jossey-Bass, 1997), p. 70.

[29] Stanley E. Fawcett, Gary K. Rhoads, and Phillip Burnah, "People as the Bridge to Competitiveness: Benchmarking the 'ABCs' of an Empowered Workforce," *Benchmarking: An International Journal* 11, no. 4 (2004), pp. 346–60.

[30] Robert Simons, "Control in an Age of Empowerment," *Harvard Business Review* 73 (March–April 1995), pp. 80–88.

[31] Jeanne M. Liedtka, "Collaboration across Lines of Business for Competitive Advantage," *Academy of Management Executive* 10, no. 2 (May 1996), pp. 20–34.

[32] Rosabeth Moss Kanter, "Collaborative Advantage: The Art of the Alliance," *Harvard Business Review* 72, no. 4 (July–August 1994), pp. 96–108.

# CHAPTER 11

# MANAGING INTERNAL OPERATIONS

## Actions that Promote Good Strategy Execution

### Learning Objectives

**LO 1** Learn why resource allocation should always be based on strategic priorities.

**LO 2** Understand how well-designed policies and procedures can facilitate good strategy execution.

**LO 3** Learn how best practices and process management tools drive continuous improvement in the performance of value chain activities and promote superior strategy execution.

**LO 4** Recognize the role of information and operating systems in enabling company personnel to carry out their strategic roles proficiently.

**LO 5** Comprehend how and why the use of well-designed incentives and rewards can be management's single most powerful tool for promoting adept strategy execution.

The achievements of an organization are the results of the combined effort of each individual.

> Vince Lombardi – *American football coach, famed for his ability to win*

Note to salary setters: Pay your people the least possible and you'll get the same from them.

> Malcolm Forbes – *Late publisher of Forbes magazine*

Great companies don't focus on information. They focus on turning information into information that cannot be ignored.

> Jim Collins – *Author and management consultant*

Decision making is the all-important intermediate step between knowledge and action, between strategy and execution.

> —American Management Association (AMA)

In Chapter 10, we emphasized the importance of building an organization capable of proficient strategy execution through three key actions: staffing the organization with the right people, acquiring, developing, and strengthening the firm's resources and capabilities, and structuring the organization in a manner supportive of the strategy-execution effort.

In this chapter, we discuss five additional managerial actions that advance the cause of good strategy execution:

- Allocating resources to the drive for good strategy execution.

- Ensuring that policies and procedures facilitate rather than impede strategy execution.

- Using process management tools to drive continuous improvement in how value chain activities are performed.

- Installing information and operating systems that enable company personnel to carry out their strategic roles proficiently.

- Using rewards and incentives to promote better strategy execution and the achievement of strategic and financial targets.

# ALLOCATING RESOURCES TO THE STRATEGY EXECUTION EFFORT

**LO 1**

Learn why resource allocation should always be based on strategic priorities.

Early in the strategy implementation process, managers need to determine what resources (in terms of funding, people, and so on) will be required and how they should be distributed across the company's various organizational units. Plainly, organizational units must have the operating budgets and resources for executing their respective parts of the strategic plan effectively and efficiently. Too little funding and an insufficiency of other types of resources slow progress and impede the efforts of organizational units to execute their pieces of the strategic plan proficiently. Too much funding and an overabundance of other resources waste organizational resources and reduce financial performance. Both outcomes argue for managers to be deeply involved in reviewing budget proposals and directing the proper kinds and amounts of resources to strategy-critical organizational units. This includes carefully screening requests for more people and new facilities and equipment, approving those that will contribute to the strategy execution effort, and turning down those that don't. Should internal cash flows prove insufficient to fund the planned strategic initiatives, then management must raise additional funds through borrowing or selling additional shares of stock to willing investors.

A change in strategy nearly always calls for budget reallocations and resource shifting. Previously important units that are less important to the new strategy may need downsizing. Units that now have a bigger strategic role may need more people, new equipment, additional facilities, and above-average increases in their operating budgets. Implementing a new strategy requires managers to take an active and sometimes forceful role in shifting resources, not only to amply support activities with a critical role in the new strategy but also to find opportunities to execute the strategy more cost-effectively. This requires putting enough resources behind new strategic initiatives to fuel their success and making the tough decisions to kill projects and activities that are no longer justified. Honda's strong support of R&D activities allowed it to develop the first motorcycle airbag, the first low-polluting four-stroke outboard marine engine, a wide range of ultra-low-emission cars, the first hybrid car (Honda Insight) in the U.S. market, and the first hydrogen fuel cell car (Honda Clarity). However, Honda managers had no trouble stopping production of the Honda Insight in 2006 when its sales failed to take off and then shifting resources to the development and manufacture of other promising hybrid models, including a totally redesigned Insight that was launched in the United States in 2009.

The funding requirements of good strategy execution must drive how capital allocations are made and the size of each unit's operating budget. Underfunding organizational units and activities pivotal to the strategy impedes successful strategy implementation.

Visible actions to reallocate operating funds and move people into new organizational units signal a determined commitment to strategic change. Such actions can catalyze the implementation process and give it credibility. Microsoft has made a practice of regularly shifting hundreds of programmers to new high-priority programming initiatives within a matter of weeks or even days. At Harris Corporation, where the strategy was to diffuse research ideas into areas that were commercially viable, top management regularly moved groups of engineers out of low-opportunity activities into its most promising new commercial venture divisions. Fast-moving developments in many markets are prompting companies to abandon traditional annual budgeting and resource allocation cycles in favor of resource allocation processes supportive of more rapid adjustments in strategy.

A company's operating budget must be both *strategy-driven* (in order to amply fund the performance of key value chain activities) and *lean* (in order to operate as cost-effectively as possible).

Merely fine-tuning the execution of a company's existing strategy seldom requires big shifts of resources from one area to another. In contrast, new strategic initiatives generally require not only big shifts in resources but a larger allocation of resources to the effort as well. However, there are times when strategy changes or new execution initiatives need to be made without adding to total company expenses. In such circumstances, managers have to work their way through the existing budget line by line and activity by activity, looking for ways to trim costs and shift resources to activities that are higher-priority in the strategy execution effort. In the event that a company needs to make significant cost cuts during the course of launching new strategic initiatives, then managers have to be especially creative in finding ways to do more with less. Indeed, it is not unusual for strategy changes and the drive for good strategy execution to be conducted in a manner that entails achieving considerably higher levels of operating efficiency and, at the same time, making sure key activities are performed as effectively as possible.

# INSTITUTING POLICIES AND PROCEDURES THAT FACILITATE STRATEGY EXECUTION

A company's policies and procedures can either support or hinder good strategy execution. Any time a company moves to put new strategy elements in place or improve its strategy execution capabilities, some changes in work practices are usually required. Managers are thus well advised to carefully review existing policies and procedures and to proactively revise or abandon those that are out of sync.

> **LO 2**
>
> Understand how well-designed policies and procedures can facilitate good strategy execution.

As shown in Figure 11.1, well-conceived policies and operating procedures facilitate strategy execution in three ways:

1. *They provide top-down guidance regarding how things need to be done.* Policies and procedures provide company personnel with a set of guidelines for how to perform organizational activities, conduct various aspects of operations, solve problems as they arise, and accomplish particular tasks. In essence, they represent a store of organizational or managerial knowledge about efficient and effective ways of doing things. They clarify uncertainty about how to proceed in executing strategy and align the actions and behavior of company personnel with the requirements for good strategy execution. Moreover, they place limits on ineffective independent action. When they are well matched with the requirements of the strategy implementation plan, they channel the efforts of individuals along a path that supports the plan. When existing ways of doing things pose a barrier to strategy execution initiatives, actions, and behaviors have to be changed. Under these conditions, the managerial role is to establish and enforce new policies and operating practices that are more conducive to executing the strategy appropriately. Policies are a particularly useful way to counteract tendencies for some people to resist change. People generally refrain from violating company policy or going against recommended practices and procedures without gaining clearance or having strong justification.

> Well-conceived policies and procedures aid strategy execution; out-of-sync ones hinder effective execution.

2. *They help ensure consistency in how execution-critical activities are performed.* Policies and procedures serve to standardize the way that activities are performed. This can be important for ensuring the quality and reliability of the strategy execution process. It helps align and coordinate the strategy execution efforts of individuals and groups throughout the organization—a feature that is particularly beneficial when there are geographically scattered operating units. For example, eliminating significant differences in the operating practices of different plants, sales regions, customer service

**FIGURE 11.1** How Policies and Procedures Facilitate Good Strategy Execution

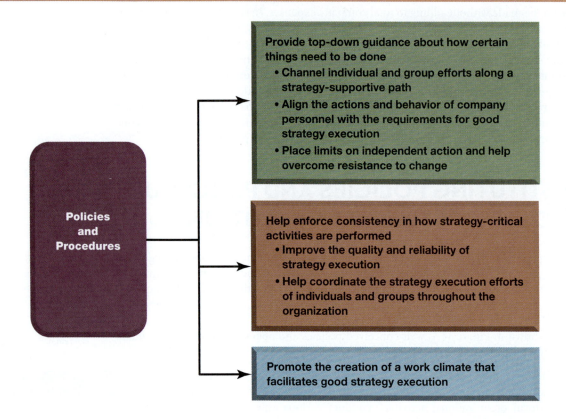

**Policies and Procedures**

**Provide top-down guidance about how certain things need to be done**
- Channel individual and group efforts along a strategy-supportive path
- Align the actions and behavior of company personnel with the requirements for good strategy execution
- Place limits on independent action and help overcome resistance to change

**Help enforce consistency in how strategy-critical activities are performed**
- Improve the quality and reliability of strategy execution
- Help coordinate the strategy execution efforts of individuals and groups throughout the organization

**Promote the creation of a work climate that facilitates good strategy execution**

centers, or the individual outlets in a chain operation helps a company deliver consistent product quality and service to customers. Good strategy execution nearly always entails an ability to replicate product quality and the caliber of customer service at every location where the company does business—anything less blurs the company's image and lowers customer satisfaction.

3.  *They promote the creation of a work climate that facilitates good strategy execution.* A company's policies and procedures help to set the tone of a company's work climate and contribute to a common understanding of "how we do things around here." Because abandoning old policies and procedures in favor of new ones invariably alters the internal work climate, managers can use the policy-changing process as a powerful lever for changing the corporate culture in ways that produce a stronger fit with the new strategy. The trick here, obviously, is to come up with new policies or procedures that catch the immediate attention of company personnel and which quickly shift their actions and behavior—eventually becoming embedded in how things are done.

To ensure consistency in product quality and service behavior patterns, McDonald's policy manual spells out detailed procedures that personnel in each McDonald's unit are expected to observe. For example, "Cooks must turn, never flip, hamburgers. If they haven't been purchased, Big Macs must be discarded in 10 minutes after being cooked and French fries in 7 minutes. Cashiers must make eye contact with and smile at every customer."

Nordstrom has a company policy of promoting only those people whose personnel records contain evidence of "heroic acts" to please customers—especially customers who may have made "unreasonable requests" that require special efforts. This induces store personnel to dedicate themselves to outstanding customer service, consistent with the requirements of executing a strategy based on exceptionally high service quality. To ensure that its R&D activities are responsive to customer needs and expectations, Hewlett-Packard requires its R&D people to make regular visits to customers to learn about their problems and learn their reactions to HP's latest new products.

One of the big policy-making issues concerns what activities need to be rigidly prescribed and what activities ought to allow room for independent action on the part of empowered personnel. Few companies need thick policy manuals to direct the strategy execution process or prescribe exactly how daily operations are to be conducted. Too much policy can be as obstructive as wrong policy and as confusing as no policy. There is wisdom in a middle approach: *Prescribe enough policies to give organization members clear direction and to place reasonable boundaries on their actions; then empower them to act within these boundaries in pursuit of company goals.* Allowing company personnel to act with some degree of freedom is especially appropriate when individual creativity and initiative are more essential to good strategy execution than standardization and strict conformity. Instituting policies that facilitate strategy execution can therefore mean policies that require things be done according to a strictly defined standard or policies that give employees substantial leeway to do activities the way they think best.

# INSTITUTING BEST PRACTICES AND EMPLOYING PROCESS MANAGEMENT TOOLS

Company managers can significantly advance the cause of superior strategy execution by employing best practices and process management tools to drive continuous improvement in how internal operations are conducted. One of the most widely used methods for gauging how well a company is executing its strategy entails benchmarking the company's performance of particular activities and business processes against "best-in-industry" and "best-in-world" performers.[1] It can also be useful to look at "best-in-company" performers of an activity if a company has a number of different organizational units performing much the same function at different locations. Identifying, analyzing, and understanding how top-performing companies or organizational units conduct particular value chain activities and business processes provides useful yardsticks for judging the effectiveness and efficiency of internal operations and setting performance standards for organizational units to meet or beat.

LO 3

Learn how best practices and process management tools drive continuous improvement in the performance of value chain activities and promote superior strategy execution.

## How the Process of Identifying and Incorporating Best Practices Works

A **best practice** is a method of performing an activity or business process that consistently delivers superior results compared to other approaches.[2] To qualify as a legitimate best practice, the method must have been employed by at least one enterprise and shown to be *unusually effective* in lowering costs, improving quality or performance, shortening time requirements, enhancing safety, or achieving some other highly positive operating outcome. Best practices thus identify a path to operating excellence.

**CORE CONCEPT**

A **best practice** is a method of performing an activity that consistently delivers superior results compared to other approaches.

As discussed in Chapter 4, *benchmarking* is the backbone of the process of identifying, studying, and implementing best practices. The role of benchmarking is to look outward to find best practices and then to develop the data for measuring how well a company's own performance of an activity stacks up against the best-practice standard. However, benchmarking is more complicated than simply identifying which companies are the best performers of an activity and then trying to imitate their approaches—especially if these companies are in other industries. Normally, the best practices of other organizations must be *adapted* to fit the specific circumstances of a company's own business, strategy, and operating requirements. Since each organization is unique, the telling part of any best-practice initiative is how well the company puts its own version of the best practice into place and makes it work. Indeed, a best practice remains little more than another company's interesting success story unless company personnel buy into the task of translating what can be learned from other companies into real action and results. The agents of change must be frontline employees who are convinced of the need to abandon the old ways of doing things and switch to a best-practice mindset.

> The more that organizational units use best practices in performing their work, the closer a company comes to achieving effective and efficient strategy execution.

As shown in Figure 11.2, to the extent that a company is able to successfully adapt a best practice pioneered elsewhere to fit its circumstances, it is likely to improve its performance of the activity, perhaps dramatically—an outcome that promotes better strategy execution. It follows that a company can make giant strides toward excellent strategy execution by adopting a best-practices mindset and successfully *implementing the use of best practices across more of its value chain activities.* The more that organizational units use best practices in performing their work, the closer a company moves toward performing its value chain activities more effectively and efficiently. This is what operational excellence in strategy execution is all about. Employing best practices to improve internal operations has powerful appeal—legions of companies across the world are now making concerted efforts to employ best practices in performing many value chain activities, and they regularly benchmark their performance of these activities against best-in industry or best-in-world performers.

**FIGURE 11.2** From Benchmarking and Best-Practice Implementation to Operational Excellence in Strategy Execution

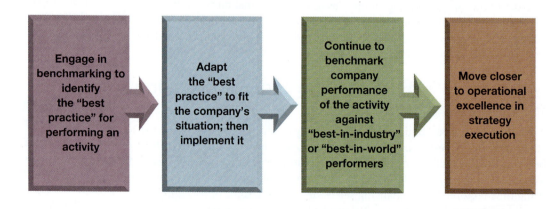

# Business Process Reengineering, Total Quality Management, and Six Sigma Quality Programs: Tools for Promoting Operating Excellence

Three other potent management tools for promoting operating excellence and better strategy execution are business process reengineering, total quality management (TQM) programs, and Six Sigma quality control techniques. Each of these merits discussion because, in recent years, many companies around the world have begun using them to help execute strategies keyed to cost reduction, defect-free manufacture, superior product quality, superior customer service, and total customer satisfaction.

**Business Process Reengineering**   Companies searching for ways to improve their operations have sometimes discovered that the execution of strategy-critical activities is hampered by a disconnected organizational arrangement whereby pieces of an activity are performed in several different functional departments, with no one manager or group being accountable for optimal performance of the entire activity. This can easily occur in such inherently cross-functional activities as customer service (which can involve personnel in order filling, warehousing and shipping, invoicing, accounts receivable, after-sale repair, and technical support), particularly for companies with a functional organizational structure.

To address the suboptimal performance problems that can arise from this type of situation, a company can *reengineer the work effort*, pulling the pieces of an activity out of different departments and creating a single department or cross-functional work group to take charge of the whole process. The use of cross-functional teams has been popularized by the practice of **business process reengineering**, which involves radically redesigning and streamlining the workflow (often enabled by cutting-edge use of online technology and information systems), with the goal of achieving quantum gains in performance of the activity.[3]

The reengineering of value chain activities has been undertaken at many companies in many industries all over the world, with excellent results being achieved at some firms.[4] Hallmark reengineered its process for developing new greeting cards, creating teams of mixed-occupation personnel (artists, writers, lithographers, merchandisers, and administrators) to work on a single holiday or greeting card theme. The reengineered process speeded development times for new lines of greeting cards by up to 24 months, was more cost-efficient, and increased customer satisfaction.[5] In the order-processing section of General Electric's circuit breaker division, elapsed time from order receipt to delivery was cut from three weeks to three days by consolidating six production units into one, reducing a variety of former inventory and handling steps, automating the design system to replace a human custom-design process, and cutting the organizational layers between managers and workers from three to one. Productivity rose 20 percent in one year, and unit manufacturing costs dropped 30 percent. Northwest Water, a British utility, used process reengineering to eliminate 45 work depots that served as home bases to crews who installed and repaired water and sewage lines and equipment. Under the reengineered arrangement, crews worked directly from their vehicles, receiving assignments and reporting work completion from computer terminals in their trucks. Crew members became contractors to Northwest Water rather than employees, a move that not only eliminated the need for the work depots but also allowed Northwest Water to eliminate a big percentage of the bureaucratic personnel and supervisory organization that managed the crews.[6]

## CORE CONCEPT

**Business process reengineering** involves radically redesigning and streamlining how an activity is performed, with the intent of achieving quantum improvements in performance.

While business process reengineering has been criticized for its use by some companies as an excuse for downsizing, it has nonetheless proved itself a useful tool for streamlining a company's work effort and moving closer to operational excellence. It has also inspired more technologically based approaches to integrating and streamlining business processes, such as *Enterprise Resource Planning,* a software-based system implemented with the help of consulting companies such as SAP (the leading provider of business software).

## Total Quality Management Programs

Total quality management (TQM) is a philosophy of managing a set of business practices that emphasizes continuous improvement in all phases of operations, 100 percent accuracy in performing tasks, involvement and empowerment of employees at all levels, team-based work design, benchmarking, and total customer satisfaction.[7] While TQM concentrates on producing quality goods and fully satisfying customer expectations, it achieves its biggest successes when it is extended to employee efforts in *all departments*—human resources, billing, accounting, and information systems—that may lack pressing, customer-driven incentives to improve. It involves reforming the corporate culture and shifting to a continuous improvement business philosophy that permeates every facet of the organization.[8] TQM aims at instilling enthusiasm and commitment to doing things right from the top to the bottom of the organization. Management's job is to kindle an organizationwide search for ways to improve—a search that involves all company personnel exercising initiative and using their ingenuity. TQM doctrine preaches that there's no such thing as "good enough" and that everyone has a responsibility to participate in continuous improvement. TQM is thus a race without a finish. Success comes from making little steps forward each day, a process that the Japanese call *kaizen.*

TQM takes a fairly long time to show significant results—very little benefit emerges within the first six months. The long-term payoff of TQM, if it comes, depends heavily on management's success in implanting a culture within which the TQM philosophy and practices can thrive. But it is a management tool that has attracted numerous users and advocates over several decades, and it can deliver good results when used properly.

## Six Sigma Quality Control Programs

Six Sigma programs offer another way to drive continuous improvement in quality and strategy execution. This approach entails the use of advanced statistical methods to identify and remove the causes of defects (errors) and variability in performing an activity or business process. When performance of an activity or process reaches "Six Sigma quality," there are *no more than 3.4 defects per million iterations* (equal to 99.9997 percent accuracy).[9]

There are two important types of Six Sigma programs. The Six Sigma process of define, measure, analyze, improve, and control (DMAIC, pronounced *De-may-ic*) is an improvement system for existing processes falling below specification and needing incremental improvement. The Six Sigma process of define, measure, analyze, design, and verify (DMADV, pronounced *De-mad-vee*) is used to develop *new* processes or products at Six Sigma quality levels. DMADV is sometimes referred to as Design for Six Sigma, or DFSS. Both Six Sigma programs are overseen by personnel who have completed Six Sigma "master black belt" training and are executed by personnel who have earned Six Sigma "green belts" and Six Sigma "black belts." According to the Six Sigma Academy, personnel with black belts can save companies approximately $230,000 per project and can complete four to six projects a year.[10]

The statistical thinking underlying Six Sigma is based on the following three principles: (1) all work is a process, (2) all processes have variability, and (3) all processes create data that explain variability.[11] Six Sigma's DMAIC process is a particularly good vehicle for improving performance when there are *wide variations* in how well an activity is performed. For instance, airlines striving to improve the on-time performance of their flights have more to gain from actions to curtail the number of flights that are late by more than 30 minutes than from actions to reduce the number of flights that are late by less than 5 minutes. It is also of particular interest for large companies, which are better able to shoulder the cost of the large investment required in employee training, organizational infrastructure, and consulting services. For example, to realize a cost savings of $4.4 billion from rolling out its Six Sigma program during 1996–1999, GE had to invest $1.6 billion and suffer losses from the program during its first year.[12]

Since the mid-1990s, thousands of companies and nonprofit organizations around the world have used Six Sigma programs to promote operating excellence. For companies at the forefront of this movement, such as Motorola, GE, Ford, and Honeywell (Allied Signal), the cost savings as a percentage of revenue varied from 1.2 percent to 4.5 percent, according to data analysis conducted by iSixSigma (an organization that provides free articles, tools, and resources concerning Six Sigma).[13] More recently, there has been a resurgence of interest in Six Sigma practices, with companies such as Merck, Dunkin Brands (donuts), Capital One, and Target turning to Six Sigma as a vehicle to boost their bottom lines. Best Buy's director of their Six Sigma program credits the program with helping them weather the 2007–2009 recession by removing the inefficiencies from their system.[14]

Six Sigma has also been used to improve processes in health care. A Milwaukee hospital used Six Sigma to improve the accuracy of administering the proper drug doses to patients. DMAIC analysis of the three-stage process by which prescriptions were written by doctors, filled by the hospital pharmacy, and then administered to patients by nurses revealed that most mistakes came from misreading the doctors' handwriting. The hospital implemented a program requiring doctors to enter the prescription on the hospital's computers, which slashed the number of errors dramatically. In 2009, Pfizer embarked on 85 Six Sigma projects to streamline its R&D process and lower the cost of delivering medicines to patients in its pharmaceutical sciences division.[15]

Illustration Capsule 11.1 describes Whirlpool's use of Six Sigma in its appliance business.

Despite its potential benefits, Six Sigma is not without its problems. There is evidence, for example, that Six Sigma techniques can stifle innovation and creativity.[16] The essence of Six Sigma is to reduce variability in processes, but creative processes, by nature, include quite a bit of variability. In many instances, breakthrough innovations occur only after thousands of ideas have been abandoned and promising ideas have gone through multiple iterations and extensive prototyping. Google CEO Eric Schmidt has commented that the innovation process is "anti–Six Sigma" and that applying Six Sigma principles to those performing creative work at Google would choke off innovation at the company.[17]

A blended approach to Six Sigma implementation that is gaining in popularity pursues incremental improvements in operating efficiency, while R&D and other processes that allow the company to develop new ways of offering value to customers are given freer rein. Managers of these *ambidextrous organizations* are adept at employing continuous improvement in operating processes but allowing R&D to operate under a set of rules that allows for the development of breakthrough innovations. However, the two distinctly different approaches to managing employees must be carried out by tightly integrated senior managers to ensure that the separate and diversely oriented units operate with a common purpose. Ciba Vision, a global leader in contact lenses, has dramatically reduced operating expenses through the use of continuous improvement programs, while simultaneously and harmoniously developing a new series of contact lens products that have

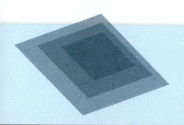

## Whirlpool's Use of Six Sigma to Promote Operating Excellence

Top management at Whirlpool Corporation (with 66 manufacturing and technology centers around the globe and sales in some 170 countries totaling $19 billion in 2011) has a vision of Whirlpool appliances in "Every Home ... Everywhere with Pride, Passion, and Performance." One of management's chief objectives in pursuing this vision is to build unmatched customer loyalty to the Whirlpool brand. Whirlpool's strategy to win the hearts and minds of appliance buyers the world over has been to produce and market appliances with top-notch quality and innovative features that users will find appealing. In addition, Whirlpool's strategy has been to offer a wide selection of models (recognizing that buyer tastes and needs differ) and to strive for low-cost production efficiency, thereby enabling Whirlpool to price its products very competitively. Executing this strategy at Whirlpool's operations in North America (where it is the market leader), Latin America (where it is also the market leader), Europe (where it ranks third), and Asia (where it is number one in India and has a foothold with huge growth opportunities elsewhere) has involved a strong focus on continuous improvement, lean manufacturing capabilities, and a drive for operating excellence. To marshal the efforts of its 68,000 employees in executing the strategy successfully, management developed a comprehensive Operational Excellence program with Six Sigma as one of the centerpieces.

The Operational Excellence initiative, which began in the 1990s, incorporated Six Sigma techniques to improve the quality of Whirlpool products and, at the same time, lower costs and trim the time it took to get product innovations into the marketplace. The Six Sigma program helped Whirlpool save $175 million in manufacturing costs in its first three years.

To sustain the productivity gains and cost savings, Whirlpool embedded Six Sigma practices within each of its manufacturing facilities worldwide and instilled a culture based on Six Sigma and lean manufacturing skills and capabilities. In 2002, each of Whirlpool's operating units began taking the Six Sigma initiative to a higher level by first placing the needs of the customer at the center of every function—R&D, technology, manufacturing, marketing, and administrative support—and then striving to consistently improve quality levels while eliminating all unnecessary costs. The company systematically went through every aspect of its business with the view that company personnel should perform every activity at every level in a manner that delivers value to the customer and leads to continuous improvement on how things are done.

Whirlpool management believes that the company's Operational Excellence process has been a major contributor in sustaining the company's position as the leading global manufacturer and marketer of home appliances.

*Source:* www.whirlpool.com, accessed April 3, 2012; Lexis-Nexis-Edgar Online, exhibit type: exhibit 99 - additional exhibits, filing date: June 21, 2010.

allowed its revenues to increase by 300 percent over a 10-year period.[18] An enterprise that systematically and wisely applies Six Sigma methods to its value chain, activity by activity, can make major strides in improving the proficiency with which its strategy is executed without sacrificing innovation. As is the case with TQM, obtaining managerial commitment, establishing a quality culture, and fully involving employees are all of critical importance to the successful implementation of Six Sigma quality programs.[19]

## The Difference between Business Process Reengineering and Continuous Improvement Programs like Six Sigma and TQM

Business process reengineering and continuous improvement efforts like TQM and Six Sigma both aim at improved productivity and reduced costs, better product quality, and greater customer satisfaction. The essential difference between business process reengineering and continuous improvement programs is that reengineering aims at *quantum gains* on the order of 30 to 50 percent or more, whereas programs like TQM and Six Sigma stress *incremental progress,* striving for inch-by-inch gains again and again, in a never-ending stream. The two approaches to improved performance of value chain activities and operating excellence are not mutually exclusive; it makes sense to use them in tandem. Reengineering can be used first to produce a good basic design that yields quick, dramatic improvements in performing a business process. Total quality or Six Sigma programs can then be used as a follow-on to reengineering and best-practice implementation to deliver continuing improvements over a longer period of time.

> Business process reengineering aims at one-time quantum improvement, while continuous improvement programs like TQM and Six Sigma aim at ongoing incremental improvements.

## Capturing the Benefits of Initiatives to Improve Operations

The biggest beneficiaries of benchmarking and best-practice initiatives, reengineering, TQM, and Six Sigma are companies that view such programs not as ends in themselves but as tools for implementing company strategy more effectively. The least rewarding payoffs occur when company managers seize on them as novel ideas that might be worth a try. In most such instances, they result in strategy-blind efforts to simply manage better.

There's an important lesson here. Business process management tools all need to be linked to a company's strategic priorities to contribute effectively to improving the strategy's execution. Only strategy can point to which value chain activities matter and what performance targets make the most sense. Without a strategic framework, managers lack the context in which to fix things that really matter to business-unit performance and competitive success.

To get the most from initiatives to execute strategy more proficiently, managers must have a clear idea of what specific outcomes really matter. Is it high on-time delivery, lower overall costs, fewer customer complaints, shorter cycle times, a higher percentage of revenues coming from recently introduced products, or what? Benchmarking best-in-industry and best-in-world performance of targeted value chain activities provides a realistic basis for setting internal performance milestones and longer-range targets. Once initiatives to improve operations are linked to the company's strategic priorities, then comes the managerial task of building a total quality culture that is genuinely committed to achieving the performance outcomes that strategic success requires.[20]

Managers can take the following action steps to realize full value from TQM or Six Sigma initiatives and promote a culture of operating excellence:[21]

1. Demonstrating visible, unequivocal, and unyielding commitment to total quality and continuous improvement, including specifying measurable objectives for increasing quality and making continual progress.
2. Nudging people toward quality-supportive behaviors by:
   a. Screening job applicants rigorously and hiring only those with attitudes and aptitudes right for quality-based performance.
   b. Providing quality training for most employees.

    *c.*   Using teams and team-building exercises to reinforce and nurture individual effort (the creation of a quality culture is facilitated when teams become more cross-functional, multitask-oriented, and increasingly self-managed).

    *d.*   Recognizing and rewarding individual and team efforts to improve quality regularly and systematically.

    *e.*   Stressing prevention (doing it right the first time), not correction (instituting ways to undo or overcome mistakes).

**3.**   Empowering employees so that authority for delivering great service or improving products is in the hands of the doers rather than the overseers—*improving quality has to be seen as part of everyone's job.*

**4.**   Using online systems to provide all relevant parties with the latest best practices, thereby speeding the diffusion and adoption of best practices throughout the organization. Online systems can also allow company personnel to exchange data and opinions about how to upgrade the prevailing best-in-company practices.

**5.**   Emphasizing that performance can and must be improved, because competitors are not resting on their laurels and customers are always looking for something better.

The purpose of using benchmarking, best practices, business process reengineering, TQM, and Six Sigma programs is to improve the performance of strategy-critical activities and thereby enhance strategy execution.

In sum, benchmarking, the adoption of best practices, business process reengineering, TQM, and Six Sigma techniques all need to be seen and used as part of a bigger-picture effort to execute strategy proficiently. Used properly, all of these tools are capable of improving the proficiency with which an organization performs its value chain activities. Not only do improvements from such initiatives add up over time and strengthen organizational capabilities, but they also help build a culture of operating excellence. All this lays the groundwork for gaining a competitive advantage.[22] While it is relatively easy for rivals to also implement process management tools, it is much more difficult and time-consuming for them to instill a deeply ingrained culture of operating excellence (as occurs when such techniques are religiously employed and top management exhibits lasting commitment to operational excellence throughout the organization).

# INSTALLING INFORMATION AND OPERATING SYSTEMS

**LO 4**

Recognize the role of information and operating systems in enabling company personnel to carry out their strategic roles proficiently.

Company strategies can't be executed well without a number of internal systems for business operations. Qantas Airways, JetBlue, Ryanair, British Airways, and other successful airlines cannot hope to provide passenger-pleasing service without a user-friendly online reservation system, an accurate and speedy baggage handling system, and a strict aircraft maintenance program that minimizes problems requiring at-the-gate service that delay departures. FedEx has internal communication systems that allow it to coordinate its over 90,000 vehicles in handling a daily average of 8.5 million shipments to 220 countries. Its leading-edge flight operations systems allow a single controller to direct as many as 200 of FedEx's 690 aircraft simultaneously, overriding their flight plans should weather problems or other special circumstances arise. In addition, FedEx has created a series of e-business tools for customers that allow them to ship and track packages online, create address books, review shipping history, generate custom reports, simplify customer billing, reduce internal warehousing and inventory management costs, purchase goods and services from suppliers, and respond to quickly changing customer demands. All of

FedEx's systems support the company's strategy of providing businesses and individuals with a broad array of package delivery services and enhancing its competitiveness against United Parcel Service, DHL, and the U.S. Postal Service.

**Amazon.com** ships customer orders of books, CDs, and myriad other items from 53 fully computerized warehouses with a capacity of over 24.5 million square feet in 2011. The warehouses are so technologically sophisticated that they require about as many lines of code to run as Amazon's website does. Using complex picking algorithms, computers initiate the order-picking process by sending signals to workers' wireless receivers, telling them which items to pick off the shelves in which order. Computers also generate data on misboxed items, chute backup times, line speed, worker productivity, and shipping weights on orders. Systems are upgraded regularly, and productivity improvements are aggressively pursued. Amazon's warehouse efficiency and cost per order filled are so low that one of the fastest-growing and most profitable parts of Amazon's business is using its warehouses to run the e-commerce operations of large retail chains such as Target.

Otis Elevator, the world's largest manufacturer of elevators, with more than 2.4 million elevators and escalators installed worldwide, has a 24-hour remote electronic monitoring system that can detect when an elevator or escalator installed on a customer's site has any of 325 problems.[23] If the monitoring system detects a problem, it analyzes and diagnoses the cause and location, then makes the service call to an Otis mechanic at the nearest location, and helps the mechanic (who is equipped with a web-enabled cell phone) identify the component causing the problem. The company's maintenance system helps keep outage times under three hours. All trouble-call data are relayed to design and manufacturing personnel, allowing them to quickly alter design specifications or manufacturing procedures when needed to correct recurring problems. All customers have online access to performance data on each of their Otis elevators and escalators.

Well-conceived state-of-the-art operating systems not only enable better strategy execution but also strengthen organizational capabilities—enough at times to provide a competitive edge over rivals. For example, a company with a differentiation strategy based on superior quality has added capability if it has systems for training personnel in quality techniques, tracking product quality at each production step, and ensuring that all goods shipped meet quality standards. If the systems it employs are advanced systems that have not yet been adopted by rivals, the systems may provide the company with a competitive advantage as long as the costs of deploying the systems do not outweigh their benefits. Similarly, a company striving to be a low-cost provider is competitively stronger if it has an unrivaled benchmarking system that identifies opportunities to implement best practices and drive costs out of the business faster than others can. Fast-growing companies get an important assist from having capabilities in place to recruit and train new employees in large numbers and from investing in infrastructure that gives them the capability to handle rapid growth as it occurs, rather than having to scramble to catch up to customer demand.

# Instituting Adequate Information Systems, Performance Tracking, and Controls

Accurate and timely information about daily operations is essential if managers are to gauge how well the strategy execution process is proceeding. Information systems need to cover five broad areas: (1) customer data, (2) operations data, (3) employee data, (4) supplier/strategic partner data, and (5) financial performance data. All key strategic performance indicators must be tracked and reported in real time whenever possible. Long the norm, monthly profit-and-loss statements and monthly statistical summaries are fast being replaced with daily statistical updates and even up-to-the-minute performance monitoring, made possible by online technology. Most retail companies have automated online systems that generate daily sales reports for each store and maintain up-to-the-minute inventory and sales records on each item. Manufacturing plants typically generate daily production reports and track labor productivity on every shift. Many retailers and manufacturers have online data systems connecting them with their suppliers that monitor the status of inventories, track shipments and deliveries, and measure defect rates.

Real-time information systems permit company managers to stay on top of implementation initiatives and daily operations and to intervene if things seem to be drifting off course. Tracking key performance indicators, gathering information from operating personnel, quickly identifying and diagnosing problems, and taking corrective actions are all integral pieces of the process of managing strategy execution and overseeing operations. A number of companies have recently begun creating "electronic scorecards" for senior managers that gather daily or weekly statistics from different databases about inventory, sales, costs, and sales trends; such information enables these managers to easily stay abreast of what's happening and make better on-the-spot decisions. Telephone companies have elaborate information systems to measure signal quality, connection times, interrupts, wrong connections, billing errors, and other measures of reliability that affect customer service and satisfaction. British Petroleum (BP) has outfitted rail cars carrying hazardous materials with sensors and global-positioning systems (GPSs) so it can track the status, location, and other information about these shipments via satellite and relay the data to its corporate intranet. Companies that rely on empowered customer-contact personnel to act promptly and creatively in pleasing customers have installed online information systems that make essential customer data accessible to such personnel through a few keystrokes; this enables them to respond more effectively to customer inquiries and to deliver personalized customer service.

> Having state-of-the-art operating systems, information systems, and real-time data is integral to superior strategy execution and operating excellence.

Statistical information gives managers a feel for the numbers, briefings and meetings provide a feel for the latest developments and emerging issues, and personal contacts add a feel for the people dimension. All are good barometers. Managers must identify problem areas and deviations from plans before they can take action to get the organization back on course, by either improving the approaches to strategy execution or fine-tuning the strategy. Jeff Bezos, Amazon's CEO, is an ardent proponent of managing by the numbers. As he puts it, "Math-based decisions always trump opinion and judgment. The trouble with most corporations is that they make judgment-based decisions when data-based decisions could be made."[24]

**Monitoring Employee Performance**    Information systems also provide managers with a means for monitoring the performance of empowered workers to see that they are acting within the specified limits.[25] Leaving empowered employees to their own devices in meeting performance standards without appropriate checks and balances can expose an organization to excessive risk.[26] Instances abound of employees' decisions or behavior going awry, sometimes costing a company huge sums or producing lawsuits and reputation-damaging publicity.

Scrutinizing daily and weekly operating statistics is one of the ways in which managers can monitor the results that flow from the actions of subordinates without resorting to constant over-the-shoulder supervision; if the operating results look good, then it is reasonable to assume that empowerment is working. But close monitoring of operating performance is only one of the control tools at management's disposal. Another valuable lever of control in companies that rely on empowered employees, especially in those that use self-managed work groups or other such teams, is peer-based control. Because peer evaluation is such a powerful control device, companies organized into teams can remove some layers of the management hierarchy and rely on strong peer pressure to keep team members operating between the white lines. This is especially true when a company has the information systems capability to monitor team performance daily or in real time.

# USING REWARDS AND INCENTIVES TO PROMOTE BETTER STRATEGY EXECUTION

It is essential that company personnel be enthusiastically committed to executing strategy successfully and achieving performance targets. Enlisting such organization commitment typically requires use of an assortment of motivational techniques and rewards. Indeed, *a properly designed reward structure is management's most powerful tool for mobilizing organizational commitment to successful strategy execution.* But incentives and rewards do more than just strengthen the resolve of company personnel to succeed—they also focus their attention on the accomplishment of specific strategy execution objectives. Not only do they spur the efforts of individuals to achieve those aims, but they also help to coordinate the activities of individuals throughout the organization by aligning their personal motives with the goals of the organization. In this manner, reward systems serve as an indirect type of control mechanism that conserves on the more costly control mechanism of supervisory oversight.

To win employees' sustained, energetic commitment to the strategy execution process, management must be resourceful in designing and using motivational incentives—both monetary and nonmonetary. The more a manager understands what motivates subordinates and the more he or she relies on motivational incentives as a tool for achieving the targeted strategic and financial results, the greater will be employees' commitment to good day-in, day-out strategy execution and the achievement of performance targets.[27]

## Incentives and Motivational Practices that Facilitate Good Strategy Execution

Financial incentives generally head the list of motivating tools for gaining wholehearted employee commitment to good strategy execution and focusing attention on strategic priorities. They provide *high-powered* motivation for individuals to increase their efforts when rewards are tied to specific outcome objectives. A company's package of monetary rewards typically includes some combination of base-pay increases, performance bonuses, profit-sharing plans, stock awards, company contributions to employee 401(k) or retirement plans, and piecework incentives (in the case of production workers). But most successful companies and managers also make extensive use of nonmonetary incentives. Some of the most important nonmonetary approaches companies can use to enhance motivation are listed next:[28]

- *Providing attractive perks and fringe benefits.* The various options include coverage of health insurance premiums, college tuition reimbursement, generous paid vacation time, onsite child care, onsite fitness centers, opportunities for getaways at company-owned recreational facilities, personal concierge services, subsidized cafeterias and free lunches, casual dress every day, personal travel services, paid sabbaticals, maternity and paternity leaves, paid leaves to care for ill family members, telecommuting, compressed workweeks (four 10-hour days instead of five 8-hour days), flextime (variable work schedules that accommodate individual needs), college scholarships for children, and relocation services.

- *Giving awards and other forms of public recognition to high performers, and celebrating the achievement of organizational goals.* Many companies hold award ceremonies to honor top-performing individuals, teams, and organizational units and to showcase company successes. This can help create healthy competition among units and teams within the company, but it can also create a positive esprit de corps among the organization as a whole. Other examples include providing special recognition at informal company gatherings or in the company newsletter, offering tangible tokens of appreciation for jobs well done, and giving frequent words of praise.

- *Relying on promotion from within whenever possible.* This practice helps bind workers to their employer, and employers to their workers. Moreover, it provides strong incentives for good performance. Promoting from within also helps ensure that people in positions of responsibility have knowledge specific to the business, technology, and operations they are managing.

- *Inviting and acting on ideas and suggestions from employees.* Many companies find that their best ideas for nuts-and-bolts operating improvements come from the suggestions of employees. Moreover, research indicates that the moves of many companies to push decision making down the line and empower employees increases employees' motivation and satisfaction as well as their productivity. The use of self-managed teams has much the same effect.

- *Creating a work atmosphere in which there is genuine caring and mutual respect among workers and between management and employees.* A "family" work environment where people are on a first-name basis and there is strong camaraderie promotes teamwork and cross-unit collaboration.

- *Stating the strategic vision in inspirational terms that make employees feel they are a part of something very worthwhile in a larger social sense.* There's strong motivating power associated with giving people a chance to be part of something exciting and personally satisfying. Jobs with a noble purpose tend to inspire employees to give their all. As described in Chapter 9, this not only increases productivity but reduces turnover and lowers costs for staff recruitment and training as well.

- *Sharing information with employees about financial performance, strategy, operational measures, market conditions, and competitors' actions.* Broad disclosure and prompt communication send the message that managers trust their workers and regard them as valued partners in the enterprise. Keeping employees in the dark denies them information useful to performing their jobs, prevents them from being intellectually engaged, saps their motivation, and detracts from performance.

- *Providing a comfortable and attractive working environment.* An appealing workplace environment can have decidedly positive effects on employee morale and productivity. Providing a comfortable work environment, designed with ergonomics in mind, is particularly important when workers are expected to spend long hours at work.

For specific examples of the motivational tactics employed by several prominent companies (many of which appear on *Fortune*'s list of the 100 best companies to work for in America), see Illustration Capsule 11.2.

## Striking the Right Balance between Rewards and Punishment

Decisions on salary increases, incentive compensation, promotions, key assignments, dismissals and layoffs, and the ways and means of awarding praise and recognition are potent attention-getting, commitment-generating devices. Such decisions seldom escape

# What Companies Do to Motivate and Reward Employees

Companies have come up with an impressive variety of motivational and reward practices to help create a work environment that energizes employees and promotes better strategy execution. Here's a sampling of what companies are doing:

- Google has a sprawling 20-building headquarters complex known as the Googleplex where its several thousand employees have access to 19 cafes and 60 snack centers, unlimited ice cream, four gyms, heated swimming pools, ping-pong and pool tables, and community bicycles to go from building to building. Management built the Googleplex to be "a dream workplace" and a showcase for environmentally correct building design and construction.

- Lincoln Electric, widely known for its piecework pay scheme and incentive bonus plan, rewards individual productivity by paying workers for each nondefective piece produced. Workers have to correct quality problems on their own time—defects in products used by customers can be traced back to the worker who caused them. Lincoln's piecework plan motivates workers to pay attention to both quality and volume produced. In addition, the company sets aside a substantial portion of its profits above a specified base for worker bonuses. To determine bonus size, Lincoln Electric rates each worker on four equally important performance measures: (1) dependability, (2) quality, (3) output, and (4) ideas and cooperation. The higher a worker's merit rating, the higher the incentive bonus earned; the highest-rated workers in good profit years receive bonuses of as much as 110 percent of their piecework compensation.

- At JM Family Enterprises, a Toyota distributor in Florida, employees get attractive lease options on new Toyotas and enjoy onsite amenities such as a heated lap pool, a fitness center, a free nail salon, free prescriptions delivered by a "pharmacy concierge," and professionally made take-home dinners. The most exceptional performers are flown to the Bahamas for cruises on the 172-foot company yacht.

- Wegmans, a family-owned grocer with 75 stores on the East Coast of the United States, provides employees with flexible schedules and benefits that include onsite fitness centers. The company's approach to managing people allows it to provide a very high level of customer service not found in other grocery chains. Employees ranging from cashiers to butchers to store managers are all treated equally and viewed as experts in their jobs. Employees receive 50 hours of formal training per year and are allowed to make decisions that they believe are appropriate for their jobs. The company's 2011 annual turnover rate is only 7 percent, which is less than one-half the 19 percent average turnover rate in the U.S. supermarket industry.

- Nordstrom, widely regarded for its superior in-house customer service experience, typically pays its retail salespeople an hourly wage higher than the prevailing rates paid by other department store chains plus a commission on each sale. Spurred by a culture that encourages salespeople to go all out to satisfy customers and to seek out and promote new fashion ideas, Nordstrom salespeople earn nearly 65 percent more than the average sales employee at competing stores. The typical Nordstrom salesperson earns nearly $40,000 per year, but top performers can earn salaries in the six figures.[29] Nordstrom's rules for employees are simple: "Rule #1: Use your good judgment in all situations. There will be no additional rules."

- At W. L. Gore (the maker of GORE-TEX), employees get to choose what project/team they work on, and each team member's compensation is based on other team members' rankings of his or her contribution to the enterprise.

- At Ukrop's Super Markets, a family-owned chain, stores stay closed on Sunday; the company pays out 20 percent of pre-tax profits to employees in the form of quarterly bonuses; and the company picks up the membership tab for employees if they visit their health club 30 times a quarter.

- At biotech leader Amgen, employees get 16 paid holidays, generous vacation time, tuition reimbursements up to $10,000, onsite massages, discounted car-wash services, and the convenience of shopping at onsite farmers' markets.

*Sources: Fortune's* lists of the 100 best companies to work for in America, 2011; http://www.careerbliss.com/, accessed April 3, 2012; Jefferson Graham, "The Search Engine That Could," *USA Today,* August 26, 2003, p. B3; company websites (accessed June 2010).

the closest employee scrutiny, thus saying more about what is expected and who is considered to be doing a good job than virtually any other factor. While most approaches to motivation, compensation, and people management accentuate the positive, companies also hold out the possibility of positive for non-compliance with directives or unsatisfactory performance. At General Electric, McKinsey & Company, several global public accounting firms, and other companies that look for and expect top-notch individual performance, there's an "up-or-out" policy—managers and professionals whose performance is not good enough to warrant promotion are first denied bonuses and stock awards and eventually weeded out. A number of companies deliberately give employees heavy workloads and tight deadlines to test their metal—personnel are pushed hard to achieve "stretch" objectives and are expected to put in long hours (nights and weekends if need be). At most companies, senior executives and key personnel in underperforming units are pressured to raise performance to acceptable levels and keep it there or risk being replaced.

As a general rule, it is unwise to take off the pressure for good performance or play down the adverse consequences of shortfalls in performance. There is no evidence that a no-pressure/no-adverse-consequences work environment leads to superior strategy execution or operating excellence. As the CEO of a major bank put it, "There's a deliberate policy here to create a level of anxiety. Winners usually play like they're one touchdown behind."[30] High-performing organizations nearly always have a cadre of ambitious people who relish the opportunity to climb the ladder of success, love a challenge, thrive in a performance-oriented environment, and find some competition and pressure useful to satisfy their own drives for personal recognition, accomplishment, and self-satisfaction.

However, if an organization's motivational approaches and reward structure induce too much stress, internal competitiveness, job insecurity, and fear of unpleasant consequences, the impact on workforce morale and strategy execution can be counterproductive. Evidence shows that managerial initiatives to improve strategy execution should incorporate more positive than negative motivational elements because when cooperation is positively enlisted and rewarded, rather than coerced by orders and threats (implicit or explicit), people tend to respond with more enthusiasm, dedication, creativity, and initiative.[31]

## Linking Rewards to Achieving the Right Outcomes

To create a strategy-supportive system of rewards and incentives, a company must reward people for accomplishing results, not for just dutifully performing assigned tasks. Showing up for work and attending to one's job assignment does not, by itself, guarantee results. To make the work environment results-oriented, managers need to focus jobholders' attention and energy on what to *achieve* as opposed to what to *do*.[32] Employee productivity among employees at Best Buy's corporate headquarters rose by 35 percent after the company began to focus on the results of each employee's work rather than on employees' willingness to come to work early and stay late.

Ideally, every organization unit, every manager, every team or work group, and perhaps every employee should be held accountable for achieving outcomes that contribute to good strategy execution and business performance. If the company's strategy is to be a low-cost provider, the incentive system must reward actions and achievements that result in lower costs. If the company has a differentiation strategy focused on delivering superior quality and service, the incentive system must reward such outcomes as Six Sigma defect rates, low numbers of customer complaints, speedy order processing and delivery, and high levels of customer satisfaction. If a company's

Incentives must be based on accomplishing the right results, not on dutifully performing assigned tasks.

The key to creating a reward system that promotes good strategy execution is to make measures of good business performance and good strategy execution the *dominating basis* for designing incentives, evaluating individual and group efforts, and handing out rewards.

growth is predicated on a strategy of new product innovation, incentives should be tied to such factors as the percentages of revenues and profits coming from newly introduced products.

Incentive compensation for top executives is typically tied to such financial measures as revenue and earnings growth, stock price performance, return on investment, and creditworthiness, or to strategic measures such as market share growth. However, incentives for department heads, teams, and individual workers may be tied to performance outcomes more closely related to their strategic area of responsibility. In manufacturing, incentive compensation may be tied to unit manufacturing costs, on-time production and shipping, defect rates, the number and extent of work stoppages due to equipment breakdowns, and so on. In sales and marketing, there may be incentives for achieving dollar sales or unit volume targets, market share, sales penetration of each target customer group, the fate of newly introduced products, the frequency of customer complaints, the number of new accounts acquired, and customer satisfaction. Which performance measures to base incentive compensation on depends on the situation—the priority placed on various financial and strategic objectives, the requirements for strategic and competitive success, and what specific results are needed to keep strategy execution on track.

Illustration Capsule 11.3 provides a vivid example of how one company has designed incentives linked directly to outcomes reflecting good execution.

## Guidelines for Designing Incentive Compensation Systems

The first principle in designing an effective incentive compensation system is to tie rewards to performance outcomes directly linked to good strategy execution and targeted strategic and financial objectives, as explained earlier. But for a company's reward system to truly motivate organization members, inspire their best efforts, and sustain high levels of productivity, it is equally important to observe the following additional guidelines in designing and administering the reward system:

> The first principle in designing an effective incentive compensation system is to tie rewards to performance outcomes directly linked to good strategy execution and the achievement of financial and strategic objectives.

- *Make the performance payoff a major, not minor, piece of the total compensation package.* Performance bonuses must be at least 10 to 12 percent of base salary to have much impact. Incentives that amount to 20 percent or more of total compensation are big attention-getters, likely to really drive individual or team efforts. Incentives amounting to less than 5 percent of total compensation have a comparatively weak motivational impact. Moreover, the payoff for high-performing individuals and teams must be meaningfully greater than the payoff for average performers, and the payoff for average performers meaningfully bigger than that for below-average performers.

- *Have incentives that extend to all managers and all workers, not just top management.* It is a gross miscalculation to expect that lower-level managers and employees will work their hardest to hit performance targets just so a few senior executives can get lucrative rewards.

- *Administer the reward system with scrupulous objectivity and fairness.* If performance standards are set unrealistically high or if individual/group performance evaluations are not accurate and well documented, dissatisfaction with the system will overcome any positive benefits.

- *Ensure that the performance targets set for each individual or team involve outcomes that the individual or team can personally affect.* The role of incentives is to enhance individual commitment and channel behavior in beneficial directions. This role is not well served when the performance measures by which company personnel are judged are outside their arena of influence.

# Nucor Corporation: Tying Incentives Directly to Strategy Execution

The strategy at Nucor Corporation, one of the three largest steel producers in the United States, is to be *the* low-cost producer of steel products. Because labor costs are a significant fraction of total cost in the steel business, successful implementation of Nucor's low-cost leadership strategy entails achieving lower labor costs per ton of steel than competitors' costs. Nucor management uses an incentive system to promote high worker productivity and drive labor costs per ton below rivals'. Each plant's workforce is organized into production teams (each assigned to perform particular functions), and weekly production targets are established for each team. Base-pay scales are set at levels comparable to wages for similar manufacturing jobs in the local areas where Nucor has plants, but workers can earn a 1 percent bonus for each 1 percent that their output exceeds target levels. If a production team exceeds its weekly production target by 10 percent, team members receive a 10 percent bonus in their next paycheck; if a team exceeds its quota by 20 percent, team members earn a 20 percent bonus. Bonuses, paid every two weeks, are based on the prior two weeks' actual production levels measured against the targets.

Nucor's piece-rate incentive plan has produced impressive results. The production teams put forth exceptional effort; it is not uncommon for most teams to beat their weekly production targets anywhere from 20 to 50 percent. When added to their base pay, the bonuses earned by Nucor workers make Nucor's workforce among the highest-paid in the U.S. steel industry. From a management perspective, the incentive system has resulted in Nucor having labor productivity levels 10 to 20 percent above the average of the unionized

workforces at several of its largest rivals, which in turn has given Nucor a significant labor cost advantage over most rivals.

After years of record-setting profits, Nucor struggled in the economic downturn of 2008–2010, along with the manufacturers and builders who buy its steel. But while bonuses have dwindled, Nucor showed remarkable loyalty to its production workers, avoiding layoffs by having employees get ahead on maintenance, perform work formerly done by contractors, and search for cost savings. Morale at the company has remained high and Nucor's CEO Daniel DiMicco has been inducted into *IndustryWeek* magazine's Manufacturing Hall of Fame because of his no-layoff policies. As industry growth resumes, Nucor will have a well-trained workforce still in place, more committed than ever to achieving the kind of productivity for which Nucor is justifiably famous. When the turnaround comes, DiMicco has good reason to expect Nucor to be "first out of the box."

*Sources:* Company website (accessed March 2012); N. Byrnes, "Pain, but No Layoffs at Nucor," *Bloomberg Businessweek,* March 26, 2009.

- *Keep the time between achieving the performance target and receiving the reward as short as possible.* Nucor, a leading producer of steel products, has achieved high labor productivity by paying its workers weekly bonuses based on prior-week production levels. To limit the problem of late-arriving flights, Continental pays employees a bonus whenever actual on-time flight performance meets or beats the monthly on-time target. Annual bonus payouts work best for higher-level managers and for situations where the outcome target relates to overall company profitability.

- *Avoid rewarding effort rather than results.* While it is tempting to reward people who have tried hard, gone the extra mile, and yet fallen short of achieving performance targets because of circumstances beyond their control, it is ill advised to do so. The problem with making exceptions for unknowable, uncontrollable, or unforeseeable circumstances is that once "good excuses" start to creep into justifying rewards for subpar results, the door opens to all kinds of reasons as to why actual performance has failed to match targeted performance. A "no excuses" standard is more even-handed, easier to administer, and more conducive to creating a results-oriented work climate.

For an organization's incentive system to work well, the details of the reward structure must be communicated and explained. Everybody needs to understand how their incentive compensation is calculated and how individual/group performance targets contribute to organizational performance targets. The pressure to achieve the specified financial and strategic performance objectives and continuously improve on strategy execution should be unrelenting. People at all levels must be held accountable for carrying out their assigned parts of the strategic plan, and they must understand that their rewards are based on the caliber of results achieved. But with the pressure to perform should come meaningful rewards. Without an ample payoff, the system breaks down, and managers are left with the less workable options of issuing orders, trying to enforce compliance, and depending on the goodwill of employees.

> The unwavering standard for judging whether individuals, teams, and organizational units have done a good job must be whether they meet or beat performance targets that reflect good strategy execution.

## KEY POINTS

1. Implementing a new or different strategy calls for managers to identify the resource requirements of each new strategic initiative and then consider whether the current pattern of resource allocation and the budgets of the various subunits are suitable.

2. Company policies and procedures facilitate strategy execution when they are designed to fit the strategy and its objectives. Anytime a company alters its strategy, managers should review existing policies and operating procedures and replace those that are out of sync. Well-conceived policies and procedures aid the task of strategy execution by (1) providing top-down guidance to company personnel regarding how certain things need to be done and what the limits are on independent actions, (2) enforcing consistency in the performance of strategy-critical activities, thereby improving the quality of the strategy execution effort and coordinating the efforts of company personnel, however widely dispersed, and (3) promoting the creation of a work climate conducive to good strategy execution.

3. Competent strategy execution entails visible unyielding managerial commitment to best practices and continuous improvement. Benchmarking, best-practice adoption, business process reengineering, total quality management (TQM), and Six Sigma programs are important process management tools for promoting better strategy execution.

4. Company strategies can't be implemented or executed well without a number of support systems to carry on business operations. Real-time information systems and control systems further aid the cause of good strategy execution.

5. Strategy-supportive motivational practices and reward systems are powerful management tools for gaining employee commitment and focusing their attention on the strategy execution goals. The key to creating a reward system that promotes good strategy execution is to make measures of good business performance and good strategy execution the *dominating basis* for designing incentives, evaluating individual and group efforts, and handing out rewards. Positive motivational practices generally

work better than negative ones, but there is a place for both. While financial rewards provide high-powered incentives, nonmonetary incentives are also important. For an incentive compensation system to work well, (1) the performance payoff should be a major percentage of the compensation package, (2) the use of incentives should extend to all managers and workers, (3) the system should be administered with objectivity and fairness, (4) each individual's performance targets should involve outcomes the person can personally affect, (5) rewards should promptly follow the achievement of performance targets, and (6) rewards should be given for results and not just effort.

## ASSURANCE OF LEARNING EXERCISES

**LO 1**    **1.** Implementing and executing a new or different strategy calls for new resource allocations. Using your university's access to Lexis-Nexis or EBSCO, search for recent articles that discuss how a company has revised its pattern of resource allocation and divisional budgets to support new strategic initiatives.

**LO 2**    **2.** Policies and procedures facilitate strategy execution when they are designed to fit the company's strategy and objectives. Using your university's access to Lexis-Nexis or EBSCO, search for recent articles that discuss how a company has revised its policies and procedures to provide better top-down guidance to company personnel about how certain things should be done.

**LO 3**    **3.** Illustration Capsule 11.1 discusses Whirlpool Corporation's Operational Excellence initiative and its use of Six Sigma practices. How did the implementation of the program change the culture and mindset of the company's personnel? List three tangible benefits provided by the program. Explain why a commitment to quality control is important in the appliance industry?

**LO 3**    **4.** Read some of the recent Six Sigma articles posted at isixsigma.com. Prepare a one-page report to your instructor detailing how Six Sigma is being used in various companies and what benefits these companies are reaping from Six Sigma implementation.

**LO 4**    **5.** Company strategies can't be implemented or executed well without a number of support systems to carry on business operations. Using your university's access to Lexis-Nexis or EBSCO, search for recent articles that discuss how a company has used real-time information systems and control systems to aid the cause of good strategy execution.

**LO 5**    **6.** Illustration Capsule 11.2 on pages 333 provides a sampling of motivational tactics employed by several prominent companies (many of which appear on *Fortune*'s list of the 100 best companies to work for in America). Discuss how rewards at Google, Lincoln Electric, Nordstrom, W. L. Gore, and Amgen aid in the strategy execution efforts of each company.

## EXERCISE FOR SIMULATION PARTICIPANTS

**LO 1**    **1.** Have you and your co-managers allocated ample resources to strategy-critical areas? If so, explain how these investments have contributed to good strategy execution and improved company performance.

**LO 2, LO 3, LO 4**    **2.** What actions, if any, is your company taking to pursue continuous improvement in how it performs certain value chain activities?

3. Is benchmarking data available in the simulation exercise in which you are participating? If so, do you and your co-managers regularly study the benchmarking data to see how well your company is doing? Do you consider the benchmarking information provided to be valuable? Why or why not? Cite three recent instances in which your examination of the benchmarking statistics has caused you and your co-managers to take corrective actions to boost company performance. **LO 3**

4. What hard evidence can you cite that indicates your company's management team is doing a *better* or *worse* job of achieving operating excellence and executing your strategy than are the management teams at rival companies? **LO 3**

5. Are you and your co-managers consciously trying to achieve "operating excellence"? What are the indicators of operating excellence at your company? Based on these indicators, how well does your company measure up? **LO 2, LO 3, LO 4**

6. Does your company have opportunities to use incentive compensation techniques? If so, explain your company's approach to incentive compensation. Is there any hard evidence you can cite that indicates your company's use of incentive compensation techniques has worked? For example, have your company's compensation incentives actually increased productivity? Can you cite evidence indicating that the productivity gains have resulted in lower labor costs? If the productivity gains have *not* translated into lower labor costs, is it fair to say that your company's use of incentive compensation is a failure? **LO 5**

## ENDNOTES

[1] Christopher E. Bogan and Michael J. English, *Benchmarking for Best Practices: Winning through Innovative Adaptation* (New York: McGraw-Hill, 1994); Mustafa Ungan, "Factors Affecting the Adoption of Manufacturing Best Practices," *Benchmarking: An International Journal* 11, no. 5 (2004), pp. 504–20; Paul Hyland and Ron Beckett, "Learning to Compete: The Value of Internal Benchmarking," *Benchmarking: An International Journal* 9, no. 3 (2002), pp. 293–304; Yoshinobu Ohinata, "Benchmarking: The Japanese Experience," *Long-Range Planning* 27, no. 4 (August 1994), pp. 48–53.

[2] www.businessdictionary.com/definition/best-practice.html (accessed December 2, 2009).

[3] M. Hammer and J. Champy, *Reengineering the Corporation: A Manifesto for Business Revolution* (New York: Harper Collins Publishers, 1993).

[4] James Brian Quinn, *Intelligent Enterprise* (New York: Free Press, 1992); Ann Majchrzak and Qianwei Wang, "Breaking the Functional Mind-Set in Process Organizations," *Harvard Business Review* 74, no. 5 (September–October 1996), pp. 93–99; Stephen L. Walston, Lawton R. Burns, and John R. Kimberly, "Does Reengineering Really Work? An Examination of the Context and Outcomes of Hospital Reengineering Initiatives," *Health Services Research* 34, no. 6 (February 2000), pp. 1363–1388; Allessio Ascari, Melinda Rock, and Soumitra Dutta, "Reengineering and Organizational Change: Lessons from a Comparative Analysis of Company Experiences," *European Management Journal* 13, no. 1 (March 1995), pp. 1–13; Ronald J. Burke, "Process Reengineering: Who Embraces It and Why?" *The TQM Magazine* 16, no. 2 (2004), pp. 114–19.

[5] www.answers.com (accessed July 8, 2009); "Reengineering: Beyond the Buzzword," *BusinessWeek,* May 24, 1993, www.businessweek.com (accessed July 8, 2009).

[6] Gene Hall, Jim Rosenthal, and Judy Wade, "How to Make Reengineering Really Work," *Harvard Business Review* 71, no. 6 (November–December 1993), pp. 119–31.

[7] M. Walton, *The Deming Management Method* (New York: Pedigree, 1986); J. Juran, *Juran on Quality by Design* (New York: Free Press, 1992); Philip Crosby, *Quality Is Free: The Act of Making Quality Certain* (New York: McGraw-Hill, 1979); S. George, *The Baldrige Quality System* (New York: Wiley, 1992); Mark J. Zbaracki, "The Rhetoric and Reality of Total Quality Management," *Administrative Science Quarterly* 43, no. 3 (September 1998), pp. 602–36.

[8] Robert T. Amsden, Thomas W. Ferratt, and Davida M. Amsden, "TQM: Core Paradigm Changes," *Business Horizons* 39, no. 6 (November–December 1996), pp. 6–14.

[9] Peter S. Pande and Larry Holpp, *What Is Six Sigma?* (New York: McGraw-Hill, 2002); Jiju Antony, "Some Pros and Cons of Six Sigma: An Academic Perspective," *TQM Magazine* 16, no. 4 (2004), pp. 303–6; Peter S. Pande, Robert P. Neuman, and Roland R. Cavanagh, *The Six Sigma Way: How GE, Motorola and Other Top Companies Are Honing Their Performance* (New York: McGraw-Hill, 2000); Joseph Gordon and M. Joseph Gordon, Jr., *Six Sigma Quality for Business and Manufacture* (New York: Elsevier, 2002); Godecke Wessel and Peter Burcher, "Six Sigma for Small and Medium-Sized Enterprises," *TQM Magazine* 16, no. 4 (2004), pp. 264–72.

[10] www.isixsigma.com (accessed November 4, 2002) and http://www.villanovau.com/certificate-programs/six-sigma-training.aspx, accessed February 16, 2012.

[11] Kennedy Smith, "Six Sigma for the Service Sector," *Quality Digest Magazine,* May 2003; www.qualitydigest.com (accessed September 28, 2003).

[12] http://www.isixsigma.com/implementation/financial-analysis/six-sigma-costs-and-savings/, accessed February 23, 2012.

[13] Ibid.

[14] Brian Burnsed and Emily Thornton, "Six Sigma Makes a Comeback," *Bloomberg Businessweek,* Management & Leadership, September 10, 2009, accessed at http://www.businessweek.com/magazine/content/09_38/b4147064137002.htm on February 23, 2012.

[15] Ibid.

[16] "A Dark Art No More," *Economist* 385, no. 8550 (October 13, 2007), p. 10; Brian Hindo, "At 3M, a Struggle between Efficiency and Creativity," *BusinessWeek,* June 11, 2007, pp. 8–16.

[17] As quoted in "A Dark Art No More."

[18] Charles A. O'Reilly and Michael L. Tushman, "The Ambidextrous Organization," *Harvard Business Review* 82, no. 4 (April 2004), pp. 74–81.

[19] Terry Nels Lee, Stanley E. Fawcett, and Jason Briscoe, "Benchmarking the Challenge to Quality Program Implementation," *Benchmarking: An International Journal* 9, no. 4 (2002), pp. 374–87.

[20] Milan Ambrož, "Total Quality System as a Product of the Empowered Corporate Culture," *TQM Magazine* 16, no. 2 (2004), pp. 93–104; Nick A. Dayton, "The Demise of Total Quality Management," *TQM Magazine* 15, no. 6 (2003), pp. 391–96.

[21] Judy D. Olian and Sara L. Rynes, "Making Total Quality Work: Aligning Organizational Processes, Performance Measures, and Stakeholders," *Human Resource Management* 30, no. 3 (Fall 1991), pp. 310–11; Paul S. Goodman and Eric D. Darr, "Exchanging Best Practices Information through Computer-Aided Systems," *Academy of Management Executive* 10, no. 2 (May 1996), p. 7.

[22] Thomas C. Powell, "Total Quality Management as Competitive Advantage," *Strategic Management Journal* 16 (1995), pp. 15–37; Richard M. Hodgetts, "Quality Lessons from America's Baldrige Winners," *Business Horizons* 37, no. 4 (July–August 1994), pp. 74–79; Richard Reed, David J. Lemak, and Joseph C. Montgomery, "Beyond Process: TQM Content and Firm Performance," *Academy of Management Review* 21, no. 1 (January 1996), pp. 173–202.

[23] www.otiselevator.com (accessed February 16, 2012).

[24] Fred Vogelstein, "Winning the Amazon Way," *Fortune* 147, no. 10 (May 26, 2003), pp. 60–69.

[25] Robert Simons, "Control in an Age of Empowerment," *Harvard Business Review* 73 (March–April 1995), pp. 80–88.

[26] David C. Band and Gerald Scanlan, "Strategic Control through Core Competencies," *Long Range Planning* 28, no. 2 (April 1995), pp. 102–14.

[27] Stanley E. Fawcett, Gary K. Rhoads, and Phillip Burnah, "People as the Bridge to Competitiveness: Benchmarking the 'ABCs' of an Empowered Workforce," *Benchmarking: An International Journal* 11, no. 4(2004), pp. 346–60.

[28] Jeffrey Pfeffer and John F. Veiga, "Putting People First for Organizational Success," *Academy of Management Executive* 13, no. 2 (May 1999), pp. 37–45; Linda K. Stroh and Paula M. Caliguiri, "Increasing Global Competitiveness through Effective People Management," *Journal of World Business* 33, no. 1 (Spring 1998), pp. 1–16; articles in *Fortune* on the 100 best companies to work for (various issues).

[29] Jenni Mintz, "Nordstrom Opening in Three Weeks: Company Plans 'Tailgate Party for Women' and Other Events," *Ventura County Star* (California), *McClatchy-Tribune Regional News,* August 12, 2008.

[30] As quoted in John P. Kotter and James L. Heskett, *Corporate Culture and Performance* (New York: Free Press, 1992), p. 91.

[31] Clayton M. Christensen, Matt Marx, and Howard Stevenson, "The Tools of Cooperation and Change," *Harvard Business Review* 84, no. 10 (October 2006), pp. 73–80.

[32] Steven Kerr, "On the Folly of Rewarding A While Hoping for B," *Academy of Management Executive* 9, no. 1 (February 1995), pp. 7–14; Doran Twer, "Linking Pay to Business Objectives," *Journal of Business Strategy* 15, no. 4 (July–August 1994), pp. 15–18.

# CHAPTER 12

# CORPORATE CULTURE AND LEADERSHIP

## Keys to Good Strategy Execution

### Learning Objectives

**LO 1**  Be able to identify the key features of a company's corporate culture and appreciate the role of a company's core values and ethical standards in building corporate culture.

**LO 2**  Gain an understanding of how and why a company's culture can aid the drive for proficient strategy execution.

**LO 3**  Learn the kinds of actions management can take to change a problem corporate culture.

**LO 4**  Understand what constitutes effective managerial leadership in achieving superior strategy execution.

The thing I have learned at IBM is that culture is everything.

> Louis V. Gerstner, Jr. – *Former CEO of IBM*

Management is doing things right; leadership is doing the right things.

> Peter Drucker – *Author and management consultant*

If your actions inspire others to dream more, learn more, do more and become more, you are a leader.

> John Quincy Adams – *6th President of the United States*

In the previous two chapters, we examined eight of the managerial tasks that drive good strategy execution: staffing the organization, acquiring the needed resources and capabilities, designing the organizational structure, allocating resources, establishing policies and procedures, employing process management tools, installing operating systems, and providing the right incentives. In this chapter, we explore the two remaining managerial tasks that contribute to good strategy execution: creating a strategy-supportive corporate culture and exerting the internal leadership needed to drive the implementation of strategic initiatives forward.

# INSTILLING A CORPORATE CULTURE CONDUCIVE TO GOOD STRATEGY EXECUTION

Every company has its own **corporate culture**—the shared values, ingrained attitudes, and company traditions that determine norms of behavior, accepted work practices, and styles of operating.[1] The character of a company's culture is a product of the core values and beliefs that executives espouse, the standards of what is ethically acceptable and what is not, the "chemistry" and the "personality" that permeates the work environment, the company's traditions, and the stories that get told over and over to illustrate and reinforce the company's shared values, business practices, and traditions. In a very real sense, the culture is the company's automatic, self-replicating "operating system" that defines "how we do things around here."[2] It can be thought of as the company's psyche or *organizational DNA*.[3] A company's culture is important because it influences the organization's actions and approaches to conducting business. As such, it plays an important role in strategy execution and may have an appreciable effect on business performance as well.

Corporate cultures vary widely. For instance, the bedrock of Walmart's culture is dedication to the zealous pursuit of low costs and frugal operating practices, a strong work ethic, ritualistic headquarters meetings to exchange ideas and review problems, and company executives' commitment to visiting stores, listening to customers, and soliciting suggestions from employees. General Electric's culture is founded on a hard-driving, results-oriented atmosphere; extensive cross-business sharing of ideas, best practices, and learning; reliance on "workout sessions" to identify, debate, and resolve burning issues; a commitment to Six Sigma quality; and a globalized approach to operations. At Nordstrom, the corporate culture is centered on delivering exceptional service to customers, where the company's motto is "Respond to unreasonable customer requests," and each out-of-the-ordinary request is seen as an opportunity for a "heroic" act by an employee that can further the company's reputation for unparalleled customer service. Nordstrom makes a point of promoting employees noted for their heroic acts and dedication to outstanding service. The company motivates its salespeople with a commission-based compensation system that enables Nordstrom's best salespeople to earn more than double what other department stores pay. Illustration Capsule 12.1 describes the corporate culture at W. L. Gore & Associates—the inventor of GORE-TEX.

# Identifying the Key Features of a Company's Corporate Culture

**LO 1**

Be able to identify the key features of a company's corporate culture and appreciate the role of a company's core values and ethical standards in building corporate culture.

A company's corporate culture is mirrored in the character or "personality" of its work environment—the features that describe how the company goes about its business and the workplace behaviors that are held in high esteem. Some of these features are readily apparent, and others operate quite subtly. The chief things to look for include the following:

- The values, business principles, and ethical standards that management preaches and *practices*—these are the key to a company's culture, but actions speak much louder than words here.
- The company's approach to people management and the official policies, procedures, and operating practices that provide guidelines for the behavior of company personnel.
- The atmosphere and spirit that pervades the work climate—whether competitive and political, vibrant and fun, methodical and all business, and the like.
- The way managers and employees interact and relate to one another—the reliance on teamwork and open communication, the extent to which there is good camaraderie, whether people are called by their first names, whether co-workers spend little or lots of time together outside the workplace, and the dress code.
- The strength of peer pressure to do things in particular ways and conform to expected norms.
- The actions and behaviors that are explicitly encouraged and rewarded by management in the form of compensation and promotion.
- The company's revered traditions and oft-repeated stories about "heroic acts" and "how we do things around here."
- The manner in which the company deals with external stakeholders—whether it treats suppliers as business partners or prefers hard-nosed, arm's-length business arrangements, and the strength and genuineness of the commitment to corporate citizenship and environmental sustainability.

The values, beliefs, and practices that undergird a company's culture can come from anywhere in the organizational hierarchy, most often representing the business philosophy and managerial style of influential executives but also resulting from exemplary actions

# The Culture that Drives Innovation at W. L. Gore & Associates

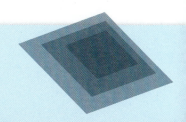

W. L. Gore & Associates is best known for GORE-TEX, the waterproof/breathable fabric so highly prized by outdoor enthusiasts. But the company has developed a wide variety of other revolutionary products, including Elixir guitar strings, Ride-On bike cables, and a host of medical devices such as cardiovascular patches and synthetic blood vessels. As a result, it is now one of the largest privately held companies in the United States, with roughly $3B in revenue and more than 9,500 employees in 30 countries worldwide.

When Gore developed the core technology on which most of its more than 2,000 worldwide patents is based, the company's unique culture played a crucial role in allowing it to pursue multiple end-market applications simultaneously, enabling rapid growth from a niche business into a diversified multinational company. The company's culture is team-based and designed to foster personal initiative. It is described on the company's website as follows:

> There are no traditional organizational charts, no chains of command, nor predetermined channels of communication. Instead, we communicate directly with each other and are accountable to fellow members of our multi-discipline teams. We encourage hands-on innovation, involving those closest to a project in decision making. Teams organize around opportunities and leaders emerge.

Personal stories posted on the website describe the discovery process behind a number of breakthrough products developed by particular teams at W. L. Gore & Associates. Employees are encouraged to use 10 percent of their time to tinker with new ideas and to take the long view regarding the idea's development. Promising ideas attract more people who are willing to work on them without orders from higher-ups. Instead, self-managing associates operating in self-developed teams are simply encouraged to pursue novel applications of Gore technology until these applications are fully commercialized or have had their potential exhausted. The encouragement comes from both the culture (norms and practices) of the organization and from a profit-sharing arrangement that allows employees to benefit directly from their successes.

This approach makes Gore a great place to work and has helped it attract, retain, and motivate top talent globally. Gore has been on *Fortune* magazine's list of the "100 Best Companies to Work For" in the United States for the last 14 years. Gore places similarly on the lists of other countries in which it operates, such as the United Kingdom, Germany, France, Italy, and Sweden.

Developed with Kenneth P. Fraser.

*Sources:* Company websites; http://www.gore.com/en_xx/news/FORTUNE-2011.html; http://www.director.co.uk/magazine/2010/2_Feb/WLGore_63_06.html; http://www.fastcompany.com/magazine/89/open_gore.html; accessed March 10, 2012.

on the part of company personnel and consensus agreement about appropriate norms of behavior.[4] Typically, key elements of the culture originate with a founder or certain strong leaders who articulated them as a set of business principles, company policies, operating approaches, and ways of dealing with employees, customers, vendors, shareholders, and local communities where the company has operations. Over time, these cultural underpinnings take root, become embedded in how the company conducts its business, come to be accepted by company managers and employees alike, and then persist as new employees are encouraged to embrace the company values and adopt the implied attitudes, behaviors, and work practices.

**The Role of Core Values and Ethics**    The foundation of a company's corporate culture nearly always resides in its dedication to certain core values and the bar it sets for ethical behavior. The culture-shaping significance of core values and ethical behaviors accounts for one reason why so many companies have developed a formal values statement and a code of ethics. Of course, sometimes a company's stated core values and code of ethics are cosmetic, existing mainly to impress outsiders and help create a positive company image. But more usually they have been developed to mold the culture and communicate what kinds of actions and behavior are expected of all company personnel. Many executives want the work climate at their companies to mirror certain values and ethical standards, not only because of personal convictions, but also because they are convinced that adherence to such principles will promote better strategy execution, make the company a better performer, and improve its image.[5] Not incidentally, strongly ingrained values and ethical standards reduce the likelihood of lapses in ethical and socially approved behavior that mar a company's reputation and put its financial performance and market standing at risk.

> A company's culture is grounded in and shaped by its core values and ethical standards.

As depicted in Figure 12.1, a company's stated core values and ethical principles have two roles in the culture-building process. First, a company that works hard at putting its stated core values and ethical principles into practice fosters a work climate in which company personnel share strongly held convictions about how the company's business is to be conducted. Second, the stated values and ethical principles provide company personnel with guidance about the manner in which they are to do their jobs—which behaviors and ways of doing things are approved (and expected) and which are out-of-bounds. These values-based and ethics-based cultural norms serve as yardsticks for gauging the appropriateness of particular actions, decisions, and behaviors, thus helping steer company personnel toward both doing things right and doing the right thing.

**FIGURE 12.1**    The Two Culture-Building Roles of a Company's Core Values and Ethical Standards

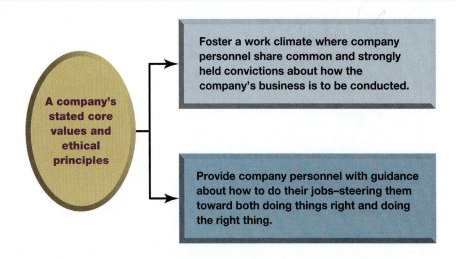

# Transforming Core Values and Ethical Standards into Cultural Norms

Once values and ethical standards have been formally adopted, they must be institutionalized in the company's policies and practices and embedded in the conduct of company personnel. This can be done in a number of different ways.[6] Tradition-steeped companies with a rich folklore rely heavily on word-of-mouth indoctrination and the power of tradition to instill values and enforce ethical conduct. But most companies employ a variety of techniques, drawing on some or all of the following:

> A company's values statement and code of ethics communicate expectations of how employees should conduct themselves in the workplace.

1. Giving explicit attention to values and ethics in recruiting and hiring to screen out applicants who do not exhibit compatible character traits.

2. Incorporating a discussion of the company's values and code of ethics into orientation programs for new employees and training courses for managers and employees.

3. Having senior executives frequently reiterate the importance and role of company values and ethical principles at company events and in internal communications to employees.

4. Using values statements and codes of ethical conduct as benchmarks for judging the appropriateness of company policies and operating practices.

5. Making the display of core values and ethical principles a factor in evaluating each person's job performance.

6. Making sure that managers from the CEO down to front-line supervisors stress the importance of ethical conduct and that line managers at all levels give serious and continuous attention to the task of explaining how the values and ethical code apply in their areas.

7. Encouraging everyone to use his or her influence in helping enforce observance of core values and ethical standards.

8. Periodically having ceremonial occasions to recognize individuals and groups who display the company values and ethical principles.

9. Instituting ethics monitoring and enforcement procedures.

To deeply ingrain the stated core values and high ethical standards, companies must turn them into *strictly enforced cultural norms*. They must make it unequivocally clear that living up to the company's values and ethical standards has to be "a way of life" at the company and that there will be little toleration for errant behavior.

# The Role of Stories

Frequently, a significant part of a company's culture is captured in the stories that get told over and over again to illustrate to newcomers the importance of certain values and the depth of commitment that various company personnel have displayed. One of the folktales at FedEx, world renowned for the reliability of its next-day package delivery guarantee, is about a deliveryman who had been given the wrong key to a FedEx drop box. Rather than leave the packages in the drop box until the next day when the right key was available, the deliveryman unbolted the drop box from its base, loaded it into the truck, and took it back to the station. There, the box was pried open and the contents removed and sped on their way to their destination the next day. Nordstrom keeps a scrapbook commemorating the heroic acts of its employees and uses it as a regular reminder of the above-and-beyond-the-call-of-duty behaviors that employees are encouraged to display. When a customer was unable to find a shoe she was looking for at Nordstrom, a salesman found the shoe at a competing store and had it shipped to her, at Nordstrom's expense. At Frito-Lay, there are dozens of stories about truck drivers who went to extraordinary lengths in overcoming adverse weather conditions in order to make scheduled deliveries to retail customers and keep store shelves stocked with Frito-Lay products. Such stories serve the valuable purpose of illustrating the kinds of behavior the company reveres and inspiring company personnel to perform similarly. Moreover, each retelling of a legendary story puts a bit more peer pressure on company personnel to display core values and do their part in keeping the company's traditions alive.

**Forces that Cause a Company's Culture to Evolve**   Despite the role of time-honored stories and long-standing traditions in perpetuating a company's culture, cultures are far from static—just like strategy and organization structure, they evolve. New challenges in the marketplace, revolutionary technologies, and shifting internal conditions—especially an internal crisis, a change in company direction, or top executive turnover—tend to breed new ways of doing things and, in turn, drive cultural evolution. An incoming CEO who decides to shake up the existing business and take it in new directions often triggers a cultural shift, perhaps one of major proportions. Likewise, diversification into new businesses, expansion into foreign countries, rapid growth that brings an influx of new employees, and the merger with or acquisition of another company can all precipitate significant cultural change.

## Strong vs. Weak Cultures

Company cultures vary widely in strength and influence. Some are strongly embedded and have a big influence on a company's operating practices and the behavior of company personnel. Others are weakly ingrained and have little effect on behaviors and how company activities are conducted.

> **CORE CONCEPT**
>
> In a **strong-culture company,** deeply rooted values and norms of behavior are widely shared and regulate the conduct of the company's business.

**Strong-Culture Companies**   The hallmark of a **strong-culture company** is the dominating presence of certain deeply rooted values and behavioral norms that "regulate" the conduct of company personnel as they go about the company's business.[7] Strong cultures enable a company to operate like a well-oiled machine, smoothly operating without a lot of intervention from management. Senior managers in strong-culture companies embody the cultural norms in their own actions and expect the same of others within the company. An unequivocal expectation that company personnel will act and behave in accordance with the adopted values and ways of doing business leads to two important outcomes: (1) Over time, the values come to be widely shared by rank-and-file employees—people who dislike the culture tend to leave—and (2) individuals encounter strong peer pressure from co-workers to observe the culturally approved norms and behaviors. Hence, a strongly implanted corporate culture ends up having a powerful influence on behavior because so many company personnel are accepting of cultural traditions and because this acceptance is reinforced by both management expectations and co-worker peer pressure to conform to cultural norms.

Strong cultures emerge over a period of years (sometimes decades) and are never an overnight phenomenon. Two factors contribute to the development of strong cultures: (1) a founder or strong leader who established core values, principles, and practices that are viewed as having contributed to the success of the company, and (2) a sincere, long-standing company commitment to operating the business according to these established traditions and values. Continuity of leadership, low workforce turnover, geographic concentration, and considerable organizational success all contribute to the emergence and sustainability of a strong culture.[8]

In strong-culture companies, values and behavioral norms are so ingrained that they can endure leadership changes at the top—although their strength can erode over time if new CEOs cease to nurture them or move aggressively to institute cultural adjustments. The cultural norms in a strong-culture company typically do not change much as strategy evolves, either because the culture constrains the choice of new strategies or because the dominant traits of the culture are somewhat strategy-neutral and compatible with evolving versions of the company's strategy. As a consequence, *strongly implanted cultures provide a huge assist in executing strategy* because company managers can use the traditions, beliefs, values, common bonds, or behavioral norms as levers to mobilize commitment to executing the chosen strategy.

**Weak-Culture Companies**    In direct contrast to strong-culture companies, weak-culture companies lack widely shared and strongly held values and principles. As a result, they also lack cultural mechanisms for aligning, constraining, and regulating the actions, decisions, and behaviors of company personnel. In weak-culture companies, few widely revered traditions and few culture-induced norms are evident in employee behavior or operating practices. Because top executives at a weak-culture company don't repeatedly espouse any particular business philosophy or exhibit long-standing commitment to particular values or behavioral norms, individuals encounter little pressure to do things in particular ways. A weak company culture breeds no strong employee allegiance to what the company stands for or to operating the business in well-defined ways. While individual employees may well have some bonds of identification with and loyalty toward their department, their colleagues, their union, or their immediate boss, there's neither passion about the company nor emotional commitment to what it is trying to accomplish—a condition that often results in many employees viewing their company as just a place to work and their job as just a way to make a living.

As a consequence, *weak cultures provide little or no assistance in executing strategy* because there are no traditions, beliefs, values, common bonds, or behavioral norms that management can use as levers to mobilize commitment to executing the chosen strategy. Without a work climate that channels organizational energy in the direction of good strategy execution, managers are left with the options of either using compensation incentives and other motivational devices to mobilize employee commitment, supervising and monitoring employee actions more closely, or trying to establish cultural roots that will in time start to nurture the strategy execution process.

## Why Corporate Cultures Matter to the Strategy Execution Process

Even if a company has a strong culture, the culture and work climate may or may not be compatible with what is needed for effective implementation of the chosen strategy. When a company's present culture promotes attitudes, behaviors, and ways of doing things that are *in sync with the chosen strategy* and conducive to first-rate strategy execution, the culture functions as a valuable ally in the strategy execution process. For example, a corporate culture characterized by frugality and thrift prompts employee actions to identify cost-saving opportunities—the very behavior needed for successful execution of a low-cost leadership strategy. A culture which celebrates taking initiative, exhibiting creativity, taking risks, and embracing change is conducive to successful execution of product innovation and technological leadership strategies.[9]

**LO 2**

Gain an understanding of how and why a company's culture can aid the drive for proficient strategy execution.

A strong culture that encourages actions, behaviors, and work practices that are in sync with the chosen strategy and conducive to good strategy execution is a valuable ally in the strategy execution process.

A culture that is grounded in actions, behaviors, and work practices that are conducive to good strategy implementation assists the strategy execution effort in three ways:

1. *A culture that is well matched to the chosen strategy and the requirements of the strategy execution effort focuses the attention of employees on what is most important to this effort.* Moreover, it directs their behavior and serves as a guide to their decision making. In this manner, it can align the efforts and decisions of employees throughout the firm and minimize the need for direct supervision.

2. *Culture-induced peer pressure further induces company personnel to do things in a manner that aids the cause of good strategy execution.* The stronger the culture (the more widely shared and deeply held the values), the more effective peer pressure is in shaping and supporting the strategy execution effort. Research has shown that strong group norms can shape employee behavior even more powerfully than can financial incentives.

3. *A company culture that is consistent with the requirements for good strategy execution can energize employees, deepen their commitment to execute the strategy flawlessly, and enhance worker productivity in the process.* When a company's culture is grounded in many of the needed strategy-executing behaviors, employees feel genuinely better about their jobs, the company they work for, and the merits of what the company is trying to accomplish. As a consequence, greater numbers of company personnel exhibit passion in their work and exert their best efforts to execute the strategy and achieve performance targets.

In sharp contrast, when a culture is in conflict with the chosen strategy or what is required to execute the company's strategy well, the culture becomes a stumbling block.[10] Some of the very behaviors needed to execute the strategy successfully run contrary to the attitudes, behaviors, and operating practices embedded in the prevailing culture. Such a clash poses a real dilemma for company personnel. Should they be loyal to the culture and company traditions (to which they are likely to be emotionally attached) and thus resist or be indifferent to actions that will promote better strategy execution—a choice that will certainly weaken the drive for good strategy execution? Alternatively, should they go along with the strategy execution effort and engage in actions that run counter to the culture—a choice that will likely impair morale and lead to a less-than-wholehearted commitment to management's strategy execution efforts? Neither choice leads to desirable outcomes. Culture-bred resistance to the actions and behaviors needed for good strategy execution, particularly if strong and widespread, poses a formidable hurdle that must be cleared for a strategy's execution to get very far.

It is in management's best interest to dedicate considerable effort to establishing a corporate culture that encourages behaviors and work practices conducive to good strategy execution.

This says something important about the task of managing the strategy execution process: *Closely aligning corporate culture with the requirements for proficient strategy execution merits the full attention of senior executives.* The culture-building objective is to create a work climate and style of operating that mobilize the energy of company personnel squarely behind efforts to execute strategy competently. The more deeply management can embed execution-supportive ways of doing things, the more management can rely on the culture to automatically steer company personnel toward behaviors and work practices that aid good strategy execution and veer from doing things that impede it. Moreover, culturally astute managers understand that nourishing the right cultural environment not only adds power to their push for proficient strategy execution but also promotes strong employee identification with, and commitment to, the company's vision, performance targets, and strategy.

# Healthy Cultures that Aid Good Strategy Execution

A strong culture, provided it fits the chosen strategy and embraces execution-supportive attitudes, behaviors, and work practices, is definitely a healthy culture. Two other types of cultures exist that tend to be healthy and largely supportive of good strategy execution: high-performance cultures and adaptive cultures.

**High-Performance Cultures**    Some companies have so-called high-performance cultures where the standout traits are a "can-do" spirit, pride in doing things right, no-excuses accountability, and a pervasive results-oriented work climate in which people go all out to meet or beat stretch objectives.[11] In high-performance cultures, there's a strong sense of involvement on the part of company personnel and emphasis on individual initiative and effort. Performance expectations are clearly delineated for the company as a whole, for each organizational unit, and for each individual. Issues and problems are promptly addressed; there's a razor-sharp focus on what needs to be done. The clear and unyielding expectation is that all company personnel, from senior executives to frontline employees, will display high-performance behaviors and a passion for making the company successful. Such a culture—permeated by a spirit of achievement and constructive pressure to meet or beat performance targets—is a valuable contributor to good strategy execution and operating excellence.[12]

The challenge in creating a high-performance culture is to inspire high loyalty and dedication on the part of employees, such that they are energized to put forth their very best efforts. Managers have to take pains to reinforce constructive behavior, reward top performers, and purge habits and behaviors that stand in the way of high productivity and good results. They must work at knowing the strengths and weaknesses of their subordinates, so as to better match talent with task and enable people to make meaningful contributions by doing what they do best. They have to stress learning from mistakes and must put an unrelenting emphasis on moving forward and making good progress—in effect, there has to be a disciplined, performance-focused approach to managing the organization.

**Adaptive Cultures**    The hallmark of adaptive corporate cultures is a willingness on the part of organization members to accept change and take on the challenge of introducing and executing new strategies. Company personnel share a feeling of confidence that the organization can deal with whatever threats and opportunities arise; they are receptive to risk taking, experimentation, innovation, and changing strategies and practices. The work climate is supportive of managers and employees who propose or initiate useful change. Internal entrepreneurship on the part of individuals and groups is encouraged and rewarded. Senior executives seek out, support, and promote individuals who exercise initiative, spot opportunities for improvement, and display the skills to implement them. Managers openly evaluate ideas and suggestions, fund initiatives to develop new or better products, and take prudent risks to pursue emerging market opportunities. As in high-performance cultures, the company exhibits a proactive approach to identifying issues, evaluating the implications and options, and moving ahead quickly with workable solutions. Strategies and traditional operating practices are modified as needed to adjust to, or take advantage of, changes in the business environment.

But why is change so willingly embraced in an adaptive culture? Why are organization members not fearful of how change will affect them? Why does an adaptive culture not break down from the force of ongoing changes in strategy, operating practices, and approaches to strategy execution? The answers lie in two distinctive and dominant

As a company's strategy evolves, an adaptive culture is a definite ally in the strategy-implementing, strategy-executing process as compared to cultures that are resistant to change.

traits of an adaptive culture: (1) Any changes in operating practices and behaviors must *not* compromise core values and long-standing business principles (since they are at the root of the culture), and (2) the changes that are instituted must satisfy the legitimate interests of stakeholders—customers, employees, shareowners, suppliers, and the communities where the company operates. In other words, what sustains an adaptive culture is that organization members perceive the changes that management is trying to institute as *legitimate,* in keeping with the core values, and in the overall best interests of key constituencies.[13] Not surprisingly, company personnel are usually more receptive to change when their employment security is not threatened and when they view new duties or job assignments as part of the process of adapting to new conditions. Should workforce downsizing be necessary, it is important that layoffs be handled humanely and employee departures be made as painless as possible.

Technology companies, software companies, and Internet-based companies are good illustrations of organizations with adaptive cultures. Such companies thrive on change—driving it, leading it, and capitalizing on it. Companies like Facebook, Twitter, Groupon, LinkedIn, Apple, Google, and Intel cultivate the capability to act and react rapidly. They are avid practitioners of entrepreneurship and innovation, with a demonstrated willingness to take bold risks to create altogether new products, new businesses, and new industries. To create and nurture a culture that can adapt rapidly to shifting business conditions, they make a point of staffing their organizations with people who are flexible, who rise to the challenge of change, and who have an aptitude for adapting well to new circumstances.

In fast-changing business environments, a corporate culture that is receptive to altering organizational practices and behaviors is a virtual necessity. However, adaptive cultures work to the advantage of all companies, not just those in rapid-change environments. Every company operates in a market and business climate that is changing to one degree or another and that, in turn, requires internal operating responses and new behaviors on the part of organization members.

# Unhealthy Cultures that Impede Good Strategy Execution

The distinctive characteristic of an unhealthy corporate culture is the presence of counterproductive cultural traits that adversely impact the work climate and company performance. Five particularly unhealthy cultural traits are hostility to change, heavily politicized decision making, insular thinking, unethical and greed-driven behaviors, and the presence of incompatible, clashing subcultures.

### Change-Resistant Cultures
Change-resistant cultures—where skepticism about the importance of new developments and a fear of change are the norm—place a premium on not making mistakes, prompting managers to lean toward safe, conservative options intended to maintain the status quo, protect their power base, and guard their immediate interests. When such companies encounter business environments with accelerating change, going slow on altering traditional ways of doing things can be a serious liability. Under these conditions, change-resistant cultures encourage a number of unhealthy behaviors—avoiding risks, not capitalizing on emerging opportunities, taking a lax approach to both product innovation and continuous improvement in performing value chain activities, and responding more slowly than is warranted to market change. In change-resistant cultures, word quickly gets around that proposals to do things differently face an uphill battle and that people who champion them may be seen as something

of a nuisance or a troublemaker. Executives who don't value managers or employees with initiative and new ideas put a damper on product innovation, experimentation, and efforts to improve.

Hostility to change is most often found in companies with stodgy bureaucracies that have enjoyed considerable market success in years past and that are wedded to the "We have done it this way for years" syndrome. General Motors, IBM, Sears, and Eastman Kodak are classic examples of companies whose change-resistant bureaucracies have damaged their market standings and financial performance; clinging to what made them successful, they were reluctant to alter operating practices and modify their business approaches when signals of market change first sounded. As strategies of gradual change won out over bold innovation, all four lost market share to rivals that quickly moved to institute changes more in tune with evolving market conditions and buyer preferences. While IBM has made strides in building a culture needed for market success, Sears, GM, and Kodak are still struggling to recoup lost ground.

**Politicized Cultures**    What makes a politicized internal environment so unhealthy is that political infighting consumes a great deal of organizational energy, often with the result that what's best for the company takes a backseat to political maneuvering. In companies where internal politics pervades the work climate, empire-building managers pursue their own agendas and operate the work units under their supervision as autonomous "fiefdoms." The positions they take on issues are usually aimed at protecting or expanding their own turf. Collaboration with other organizational units is viewed with suspicion, and cross-unit cooperation occurs grudgingly. The support or opposition of politically influential executives or coalitions among departments with vested interests in a particular outcome tends to shape what actions the company takes. All this political maneuvering takes away from efforts to execute strategy with real proficiency and frustrates company personnel who are less political and more inclined to do what is in the company's best interests.

**Insular, Inwardly Focused Cultures**    Sometimes a company reigns as an industry leader or enjoys great market success for so long that its personnel start to believe they have all the answers or can develop them on their own. There is a strong tendency to neglect what customers are saying and how their needs and expectations are changing. Such confidence in the correctness of how it does things and an unflinching belief in the company's competitive superiority breeds arrogance, prompting company personnel to discount the merits of what outsiders are doing and to see little payoff from studying best-in-class performers. Insular thinking, internally driven solutions, and a must-be-invented-here mindset come to permeate the corporate culture. An inwardly focused corporate culture gives rise to managerial inbreeding and a failure to recruit people who can offer fresh thinking and outside perspectives. The big risk of insular cultural thinking is that the company can underestimate the capabilities and accomplishments of rival companies and overestimate its own progress—all of which diminishes a company's competitiveness over time.

**Unethical and Greed-Driven Cultures**    Companies that have little regard for ethical standards or that are run by executives driven by greed and ego gratification are scandals waiting to happen. Executives exude the negatives of arrogance, ego, greed, and an "ends-justify-the-means" mentality in pursuing overambitious revenue and profitability targets.[14] Senior managers wink at unethical behavior and may cross over the line to unethical (and sometimes criminal) behavior themselves. They are prone to adopt accounting principles that make financial performance look better than it really is. Legions of companies have fallen prey to unethical behavior and greed, most notably WorldCom, Enron, Quest, HealthSouth, Adelphia, Tyco, Parmalat, Rite Aid, Hollinger International, Refco, Marsh & McLennan, Siemens, Countrywide Financial, and Stanford Financial Group, with executives being indicted and/or convicted of criminal behavior.

**Incompatible Subcultures**   Although it is common to speak about corporate culture in the singular, it is not unusual for companies to have multiple cultures (or subcultures). Values, beliefs, and practices within a company sometimes vary significantly by department, geographic location, division, or business unit. As long as the subcultures are compatible with the overarching corporate culture and are supportive of the strategy execution efforts, this is not problematic. Multiple cultures pose an unhealthy situation when they are composed of incompatible subcultures that embrace conflicting business philosophies, support inconsistent approaches to strategy execution, and encourage incompatible methods of people management. Clashing subcultures can prevent a company from coordinating its efforts to craft and execute strategy and can distract company personnel from the business of business. Internal jockeying among the subcultures for cultural dominance impedes teamwork among the company's various organizational units and blocks the emergence of a collaborative approach to strategy execution. Such a lack of consensus about how to proceed is likely to result in fragmented or inconsistent approaches to implementing new strategic initiatives and limited success in executing the company's overall strategy.

# Changing a Problem Culture

*When a strong culture is unhealthy or otherwise out of sync with the actions and behaviors needed to execute the strategy successfully, the culture must be changed as rapidly as can be managed.* This means eliminating any unhealthy or dysfunctional cultural traits as fast as possible and aggressively striving to ingrain new behaviors and work practices that will enable first-rate strategy execution. The more entrenched the mismatched or unhealthy aspects of a company culture, the more likely the culture will impede strategy execution and the greater the need for change.

Changing a problem culture is among the toughest management tasks because of the heavy anchor of ingrained behaviors and attitudes. It is natural for company personnel to cling to familiar practices and to be wary, if not hostile, to new approaches of how things are to be done. Consequently, it takes concerted management action over a period of time to root out certain unwanted behaviors and replace an out-of-sync culture with more effective ways of doing things. *The single most visible factor that distinguishes successful culture-change efforts from failed attempts is competent leadership at the top.* Great power is needed to force major cultural change and overcome the "springback" resistance of entrenched cultures—and great power is possessed only by the most senior executives, especially the CEO. However, while top management must be out front leading the effort, the tasks of marshaling support for a new culture and instilling the desired cultural behaviors must involve the whole management team. Middle managers and frontline supervisors play a key role in implementing the new work practices and operating approaches, helping win rank-and-file acceptance of and support for changes, and instilling the desired behavioral norms.

As shown in Figure 12.2, the first step in fixing a problem culture is for top management to identify those facets of the present culture that pose obstacles to executing

**FIGURE 12.2    Changing a Problem Culture**

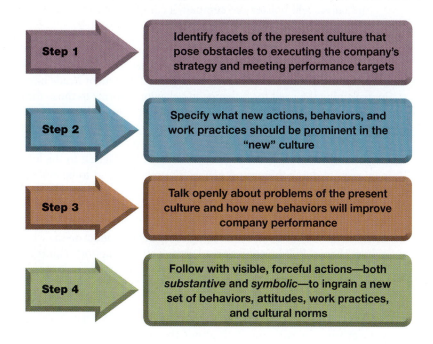

**Step 1** — Identify facets of the present culture that pose obstacles to executing the company's strategy and meeting performance targets

**Step 2** — Specify what new actions, behaviors, and work practices should be prominent in the "new" culture

**Step 3** — Talk openly about problems of the present culture and how new behaviors will improve company performance

**Step 4** — Follow with visible, forceful actions—both *substantive* and *symbolic*—to ingrain a new set of behaviors, attitudes, work practices, and cultural norms

new strategic initiatives and meeting company performance targets. Second, managers must clearly define the desired new behaviors and features of the culture they want to create. Third, managers have to convince company personnel of why the present culture poses problems and why and how new behaviors and operating approaches will improve company performance—the case for cultural reform has to be persuasive. Fourth, and most important, all the talk about remodeling the present culture has to be followed swiftly by visible, forceful actions to promote the desired new behaviors and work practices—actions that company personnel will interpret as a determined top management commitment to bringing about a different work climate and new ways of operating. The actions to implant the new culture must be both substantive and symbolic.

**Making a Compelling Case for Culture Change**    The way for management to begin a major remodeling of the corporate culture is by selling company personnel on the need for new-style behaviors and work practices. This means making a compelling case for why the culture-remodeling efforts are in the organization's best interests and why company personnel should wholeheartedly join the effort to doing things somewhat differently. This can be done by:

- Explaining why and how certain behaviors and work practices in the current culture pose obstacles to good strategy execution.
- Explaining how new behaviors and work practices will be more advantageous and produce better results. Effective culture-change leaders are good at telling stories to describe the new values and desired behaviors and connect them to everyday practices.

- Citing reasons why the current strategy has to be modified, if the need for cultural change is due to a change in strategy. This includes explaining why the new strategic initiatives will bolster the company's competitiveness and performance and how a change in culture can help in executing the new strategy.

It is essential for the CEO and other top executives to talk personally to company personnel all across the company about the reasons for modifying work practices and culture-related behaviors. Senior officers and department heads have to play a lead role in explaining the need for a change in behavioral norms to those they manage—and the explanations will likely have to be repeated many times. For the culture-change effort to be successful, frontline supervisors and employee opinion leaders must be won over to the cause, which means convincing them of the merits of *practicing* and *enforcing* cultural norms at every level of the organization, from the highest to the lowest. Arguments for new ways of doing things and new work practices tend to be embraced more readily if employees understand how they will benefit company stakeholders (particularly customers, employees, and shareholders). Until a large majority of employees accept the need for a new culture and agree that different work practices and behaviors are called for, there's more work to be done in selling company personnel on the whys and wherefores of culture change. Building widespread organizational support requires taking every opportunity to repeat the message of why the new work practices, operating approaches, and behaviors are good for company stakeholders.

**Substantive Culture-Changing Actions**    No culture change effort can get very far with just talk about the need for different actions, behaviors, and work practices. Company executives must give the culture-change effort some teeth by initiating *a series of actions* that company personnel will see as credible and unmistakably indicative of the seriousness of management's commitment to cultural change. The strongest signs that management is truly committed to instilling a new culture include:

- Replacing key executives who are resisting and obstructing needed organizational and cultural changes.
- Promoting individuals who have stepped forward to spearhead the shift to a different culture and who can serve as role models for the desired cultural behavior.
- Appointing outsiders with the desired cultural attributes to high-profile positions—bringing in new-breed managers sends an unmistakable message that a new era is dawning.
- Screening all candidates for new positions carefully, hiring only those who appear to fit in with the new culture.
- Mandating that all company personnel attend culture-training programs to better understand the culture-related actions and behaviors that are expected.
- Designing compensation incentives that boost the pay of teams and individuals who display the desired cultural behaviors. Company personnel are much more inclined to exhibit the desired kinds of actions and behaviors when it is in their financial best interest to do so.
- Revising policies and procedures in ways that will help drive cultural change.

Executives must take care to launch enough companywide culture-change actions at the outset so as to leave no room for doubt that management is dead serious about changing the present culture and that a cultural transformation is inevitable. The series of actions initiated by top management must create lots of hallway talk across the whole company, get the change process off to a fast start, and be followed by unrelenting efforts to firmly establish the new work practices, desired behaviors, and style of operating as "standard."

**Symbolic Culture-Changing Actions**   There's also an important place for symbolic managerial actions to alter a problem culture and tighten the strategy-culture fit. The most important symbolic actions are those that top executives take to *lead by example.* For instance, if the organization's strategy involves a drive to become the industry's low-cost producer, senior managers must display frugality in their own actions and decisions: inexpensive decorations in the executive suite, conservative expense accounts and entertainment allowances, a lean staff in the corporate office, scrutiny of budget requests, few executive perks, and so on. At Walmart, all the executive offices are simply decorated; executives are habitually frugal in their own actions, and they are zealous in their efforts to control costs and promote greater efficiency. At Nucor, one of the world's low-cost producers of steel products, executives fly coach class and use taxis at airports rather than limousines. Top executives must be alert to the fact that company personnel will be watching their behavior to see if their actions match their rhetoric. Hence, they need to make sure their current decisions and actions will be construed as consistent with the new-culture values and norms.[15]

Another category of symbolic actions includes holding ceremonial events to single out and honor people whose actions and performance exemplify what is called for in the new culture. In addition, each culture-change success needs to be celebrated. Executives sensitive to their role in promoting strategy-culture fit make a habit of appearing at ceremonial functions to praise individuals and groups that exemplify the desired behaviors. They show up at employee training programs to stress strategic priorities, values, ethical principles, and cultural norms. Every group gathering is seen as an opportunity to repeat and ingrain values, praise good deeds, expound on the merits of the new culture, and cite instances of how the new work practices and operating approaches have worked to good advantage.

The use of symbols in culture building is widespread. Numerous businesses have employee-of-the-month awards. The military has a long-standing custom of awarding ribbons and medals for exemplary actions. Mary Kay Cosmetics awards an array of prizes ceremoniously to its beauty consultants for reaching various sales plateaus.

**How Long Does It Take to Change a Problem Culture?**   Planting and growing the seeds of a new culture require a determined effort by the chief executive and other senior managers. It demands a sustained and persistent effort to reinforce the culture at every opportunity through both word and deed. Changing a problem culture is never a short-term exercise. It takes time for a new culture to emerge and prevail; overnight transformations simply don't occur. And it takes even longer for a new culture to become deeply embedded. The bigger the organization and the greater the cultural shift needed to produce an execution-supportive fit, the longer it takes. In large companies, fixing a problem culture and instilling a new set of attitudes and behaviors can take two to five years. In fact, it is usually tougher to reform an entrenched problematic culture than it is to instill a strategy-supportive culture from scratch in a brand new organization.

Illustration Capsule 12.2 discusses the approaches used at Chrysler in 2009–2010 to change a culture that was grounded in a 1970s view of the automobile industry.

## Changing the "Old Detroit" Culture at Chrysler

When Chrysler Group LLC emerged from bankruptcy in June 2009, its road to recovery was far from certain. "It was questionable whether they'd survive 2010," said Michelle Krebs, an analyst with auto information provider Edmunds.com. One thing that was holding Chrysler back was its culture—a legacy of "the Old Detroit," which was characterized by finger-pointing and blame shifting whenever problems arose.[a]

Chrysler's management had long been aware of its culture problem. In 2008, Robert Nardelli, Chrysler's autocratic new CEO, placed himself in charge of a wide-ranging culture-change program designed to break the ingrained behaviors that had damaged the company's reputation for quality. Chrysler's slide into bankruptcy was hardly the comeback that the controversial Nardelli envisioned when he was hired for the job by private-equity firm Cerberus Capital Management (which controlled Chrysler from 2007 until 2009).

A strategic partnership ceding management control to Italian automaker Fiat SpA was part of the deal for Chrysler's bankruptcy reorganization, with Fiat's CEO, Sergio Marchionne, becoming Chrysler's CEO as well. In discussing his five-year plan for Chrysler, Marchionne remarked, "What I've learned as a CEO is that culture is not part of the game—it is the game!"[b]

Marchionne put Doug Betts, a veteran of Toyota Motor Corp. and Nissan Motor Co., in charge of a systematic overhaul of Chrysler quality, with cultural change as the fundamental driver. Betts began by creating new

cross-functional teams designed to break down Chrysler's balkanized silos of manufacturing and engineering. Whereas problems were formerly handed off from one department to another, delaying action for an average of 71 days, quality teams are now encouraged to take ownership of solutions. Betts has also taken aim at the climate of fear, replacing concerns over recrimination and retribution with a positive focus on team empowerment and problem solving. By the end of 2009, Betts was saying, "It's different now. People are talking openly about problems now and how to fix [them]."[d] By August 2011, confidence in Chrysler had increased and U.S. sales were up by 42 percent over the same period in the previous year, resulting in the best August sales since 2007. This marked the 17th month of year-over-year gains for Chrysler.

[a] Jerry Hirsch, "Chrysler Performance Exceeds Expectations: The Fiat-Managed Company Cut Its Losses to $197 Million and Recorded a $143-Million Operating Profit in the First Quarter of the Year," *Los Angeles Times,* April 22, 2010, http://articles.latimes.com/2010/apr/22/business/la-fi-chrysler-20100422.

[b] Daniel Howes, "Chrysler's Last Chance to Get It Right," *Detroit News,* Business section, 1-dot edition, p. 4B.

[d] Alisa Priddle, "'Different' Chrysler Zeroes In on Quality," *Detroit News,* Business section, 2-dot edition, p. 1A. Developed with Amy Florentino.

*Sources:* Company website, accessed April 3, 2012; http://topics.nytimes.com/top/reference/timestopics/people/n/robert_l_nardelli/index.html, updated May 1, 2009; Neal E. Boudette, "Nardelli Tries to Shift Chrysler's Culture," *The Wall Street Journal,* June 18, 2008, p. B1.

# LEADING THE STRATEGY EXECUTION PROCESS

**LO 4**

Understand what constitutes effective managerial leadership in achieving superior strategy execution.

For an enterprise to execute its strategy in truly proficient fashion and approach operating excellence, top executives have to take the lead in the strategy implementation process and personally drive the pace of progress. They have to be out in the field, seeing for themselves how well operations are going, gathering information firsthand, and gauging the progress being made. Proficient strategy execution requires company managers to be diligent and adept in spotting problems, learning what obstacles lay in the path of good execution, and then clearing the way for progress—the goal must be to produce better results speedily and productively. There must be constructive, but unrelenting, pressure on organizational units to (1) demonstrate excellence in all dimensions of strategy execution and (2) do so on a consistent basis—ultimately, that's what will enable a well-crafted strategy to achieve the desired performance results.

For the most part, leading the strategy execution process must be done top-down and be driven by mandates to get things on the right track and show good results. The specifics of how to implement a strategy and deliver the intended results must start with understanding the requirements for good strategy execution. Afterward comes a diagnosis of the organization's preparedness to execute the strategic initiatives and decisions as to how to move forward and achieve the targeted results.[16] In general, leading the drive for good strategy execution and operating excellence calls for three actions on the part of the manager-in-charge:

- Staying on top of what is happening and closely monitoring progress.
- Putting constructive pressure on the organization to execute the strategy well and achieve operating excellence.
- Initiating corrective actions to improve strategy execution and achieve the targeted performance results.

## Staying on Top of How Well Things Are Going

To stay on top of how well the strategy execution process is going, senior executives have to tap into information from a wide range of sources. In addition to communicating regularly with key subordinates and reviewing the latest operating results, watching the competitive reactions of rival firms, and visiting with key customers and suppliers to get their perspectives, they usually visit various company facilities and talk with many different company personnel at many different organization levels—a technique often labeled **managing by walking around (MBWA).** Most managers attach great importance to spending time with people at company facilities, asking questions, listening to their opinions and concerns, and gathering firsthand information about how well aspects of the strategy execution process are going. Facilities tours and face-to-face contacts with operating-level employees give executives a good grasp of what progress is being made, what problems are being encountered, and whether additional resources or different approaches may be needed. Just as important, MBWA provides opportunities to give encouragement, lift spirits, shift attention from the old to the new priorities, and create some excitement—all of which generate positive energy and help boost strategy execution efforts.

Jeff Bezos, **Amazon.com's** CEO, is noted for his practice of MBWA, firing off a battery of questions when he tours facilities and insisting that Amazon managers spend time in the trenches with their people to prevent getting disconnected from the reality of what's happening.[17] Walmart executives have had a long-standing practice of spending two to three days every week visiting Walmart's stores and talking with store managers and employees. Sam Walton, Walmart's founder, insisted, "The key is to get out into the store and listen to what the associates have to say." Jack Welch, the highly effective CEO of General Electric (GE) from 1980 to 2001, not only spent several days each month personally visiting GE operations and talking with major customers but also arranged his schedule so that he could spend time exchanging information and ideas with GE managers from all over the world who were attending classes at the company's leadership development center near GE's headquarters.

Many manufacturing executives make a point of strolling the factory floor to talk with workers and meeting regularly with union officials. Some managers operate out of open

**CORE CONCEPT**

**Management by walking around (MBWA)** is one of the techniques that effective leaders use to stay informed about how well the strategy execution process is progressing.

cubicles in big spaces populated with open cubicles for other personnel so that they can interact easily and frequently with co-workers. Managers at some companies host weekly get-togethers (often on Friday afternoons) to create a regular opportunity for information to flow freely between executives and down-the-line employees.

# Mobilizing the Effort for Excellence in Strategy Execution

Managers have to be out front in mobilizing the effort for good strategy execution and operating excellence. Part of the leadership task entails nurturing a results-oriented work climate, where performance standards are high and a spirit of achievement is pervasive. Successfully leading the effort to foster a results-oriented, high-performance culture generally entails such leadership actions and managerial practices as:

- *Treating employees as valued partners.* Some companies symbolize the value of individual employees and the importance of their contributions by referring to them as cast members (Disney), crew members (McDonald's), job owners (Graniterock), partners (Starbucks), or associates (Walmart, LensCrafters, W. L. Gore, Edward Jones, Publix Supermarkets, and Marriott International). Very often, there is a strong company commitment to training each employee thoroughly, offering attractive compensation and career opportunities, emphasizing promotion from within, providing a high degree of job security, and otherwise making employees feel well treated and valued.

- *Fostering an esprit de corps that energizes organization members.* The task here is to skillfully use people-management practices calculated to build morale, foster pride in doing things right, promote teamwork, create a strong sense of involvement on the part of company personnel, win their emotional commitment, and inspire them to do their best.[18]

- *Using empowerment to help create a fully engaged workforce.* Top executives—and, to some degree, the enterprise's entire management team—must seek to engage the full organization in the strategy execution effort. A fully engaged workforce, one where individuals bring their best to work every day, is necessary to produce great results.[19] So is having a group of dedicated managers committed to making a difference in their organization. The two best things top-level executives can do to create a fully engaged organization are (1) delegate authority to middle and lower-level managers to get the strategy execution process moving and (2) empower rank-and-file employees to act on their own initiative. Operating excellence requires that everybody contribute ideas, exercise initiative and creativity in performing his or her work, and have a desire to do things in the best possible manner.

- *Setting stretch objectives and clearly communicating an expectation that company personnel are to give their best in achieving performance targets.* Stretch objectives—those beyond an organization's current capacities—can sometimes spur organization members to increase their resolve and redouble their efforts to execute the strategy flawlessly and ultimately reach the stretch objectives. When stretch objectives are met, the satisfaction of achievement and boost to employee morale can result in an even higher level of organizational drive.

- *Using the tools of benchmarking best practices, business process reengineering, TQM, and Six Sigma to focus attention on continuous improvement.* These are proven approaches to getting better operating results and facilitating better strategy execution.

- *Using the full range of motivational techniques and compensation incentives to inspire company personnel, nurture a results-oriented work climate, and reward high-performance.* Managers cannot mandate innovative improvements by simply exhorting people to "be creative," nor can they make continuous progress toward operating excellence with directives to "try harder." Rather, they must foster a culture where innovative ideas and experimentation with new ways of doing things can blossom and thrive. Individuals and groups should be strongly encouraged to brainstorm, let their imaginations fly in all directions, and come up with proposals for improving how things are done. This means giving company personnel enough autonomy to stand out, excel, and contribute. And it means that the rewards for successful champions of new ideas and operating improvements should be large and visible.

- *Celebrating individual, group, and company successes.* Top management should miss no opportunity to express respect for individual employees and appreciation of extraordinary individual and group effort.[20] Companies like Mary Kay Cosmetics, Tupperware, and McDonald's actively seek out reasons and opportunities to give pins, ribbons, buttons, badges, and medals for good showings by average performers— the idea being to express appreciation and give a motivational boost to people who stand out in doing ordinary jobs. General Electric and 3M Corporation make a point of ceremoniously honoring individuals who believe so strongly in their ideas that they take it on themselves to hurdle the bureaucracy, maneuver their projects through the system, and turn them into improved services, new products, or even new businesses.

While leadership efforts to instill a results-oriented, high-performance culture usually accentuate the positive, negative consequences for poor performance must be in play as well. Managers whose units consistently perform poorly must be replaced. Low-performing workers and people who reject the results-oriented cultural emphasis must be weeded out or at least employed differently. Average performers should be candidly counseled that they have limited career potential unless they show more progress in the form of additional effort, better skills, and improved ability to execute the strategy well and deliver good results.

## Leading the Process of Making Corrective Adjustments

There comes a time at every company when managers have to fine-tune or overhaul the approaches to strategy execution since no action plan for executing strategy can foresee all the problems that will arise. Clearly, when a company's strategy execution effort is not delivering good results, it is the leader's responsibility to step forward and initiate corrective actions, although sometimes it must be recognized that unsatisfactory performance may be due as much or more to flawed strategy as weak strategy execution.[21]

Success in making corrective actions hinges on (1) a thorough analysis of the situation, (2) the exercise of good business judgment in deciding what actions to take, and (3) good implementation of the corrective actions that are initiated. Successful managers are skilled in getting an organization back on track rather quickly. They (and their staffs) are good at discerning what actions to take and in bringing them to a successful conclusion. Managers who struggle to show measurable progress in implementing corrective actions in a timely fashion are often candidates for being replaced.

The process of making corrective adjustments in strategy execution varies according to the situation. In a crisis, taking remedial action fairly quickly is of the essence. But it still takes time to review the situation, examine the available data, identify and evaluate options (crunching whatever numbers may be appropriate to determine which options are likely to generate the best outcomes), and decide what to do. When the situation allows managers to proceed more deliberately in deciding when to make changes and what changes to make, most managers seem to prefer a process of incrementally solidifying commitment to a particular course of action.[22] The process that managers go through in deciding on corrective adjustments is essentially the same for both proactive and reactive changes: They sense needs, gather information, broaden and deepen their understanding of the situation, develop options and explore their pros and cons, put forth action proposals, strive for a consensus, and finally formally adopt an agreed-on course of action. The time frame for deciding what corrective changes to initiate can be a few hours, a few days, a few weeks, or even a few months if the situation is particularly complicated.

The challenges of making the right corrective adjustments and leading a successful strategy execution effort are, without question, substantial.[23] Because each instance of executing strategy occurs under different organizational circumstances, the managerial agenda for executing strategy always needs to be situation-specific—there's no generic procedure to follow. But the job is definitely doable. Although there is no prescriptive answer to the question of exactly what to do, any of several courses of action may produce good results. And, as we said at the beginning of Chapter 10, executing strategy is an action-oriented, make-the-right-things-happen task that challenges a manager's ability to lead and direct organizational change, create or reinvent business processes, manage and motivate people, and achieve performance targets. If you now better understand what the challenges are, what tasks are involved, what tools can be used to aid the managerial process of executing strategy, and why the action agenda for implementing and executing strategy sweeps across so many aspects of administrative and managerial work, then the discussions in Chapters 10, 11, and 12 have been a success.

# A FINAL WORD ON LEADING THE PROCESS OF CRAFTING AND EXECUTING STRATEGY

In practice, it is hard to separate leading the process of executing strategy from leading the other pieces of the strategy process. As we emphasized in Chapter 2, the job of crafting, implementing, and executing strategy consists of five interrelated and linked stages, with much looping and recycling to fine-tune and adjust the strategic vision, objectives, strategy, and implementation approaches to fit one another and to fit changing circumstances. The process is continuous, and the conceptually separate acts of crafting and executing strategy blur together in real-world situations. The best tests of good strategic leadership are whether the company has a good strategy and business model, whether the strategy is being competently executed, and whether the enterprise is meeting or beating its performance targets. If these three conditions exist, then there is every reason to conclude that the company has good strategic leadership and is a well-managed enterprise.

1. Corporate culture is the character of a company's internal work climate—the shared values, ingrained attitudes, core beliefs and company traditions that determine norms of behavior, accepted work practices, and styles of operating. A company's culture is important because it influences the organization's actions and approaches to conducting business. It can be thought of as the company's organizational DNA.

2. The key features of a company's culture include the company's values and ethical standards, its approach to people management, its work atmosphere and company spirit, how its personnel interact, the strength of peer pressure to conform to norms, the behaviors awarded through incentives (both financial and symbolic), the traditions and oft-repeated "myths," and its manner of dealing with stakeholders.

3. A company's culture is grounded in and shaped by its core values and ethical standards. Core values and ethical principles serve two roles in the culture-building process: (1) They foster a work climate in which employees share common and strongly held convictions about how company business is to be conducted, and (2) they provide company personnel with guidance about the manner in which they are to do their jobs—which behaviors and ways of doing things are approved (and expected) and which are out-of-bounds. They serve as yardsticks for gauging the appropriateness of particular actions, decisions, and behaviors.

4. Company cultures vary widely in strength and influence. Some cultures are strong and have a big impact on a company's practices and behavioral norms. Others are weak and have comparatively little influence on company operations.

5. Strong company cultures can have either positive or negative effects on strategy execution. When they are in sync with the chosen strategy and well matched to the behavioral requirements of the company's strategy implementation plan, they can be a powerful aid to strategy execution. A culture that is grounded in the types of actions and behaviors that are conducive to good strategy execution assists the effort in three ways:

    - By focusing employee attention on the actions that are most important in the strategy execution effort.
    - Through culture-induced peer pressure for employees to contribute to the success of the strategy execution effort.
    - By energizing employees, deepening their commitment to the strategy execution effort, and increasing the productivity of their efforts

    It is thus in management's best interest to dedicate considerable effort to establishing a strongly implanted corporate culture that encourages behaviors and work practices conducive to good strategy execution.

6. Strong corporate cultures that are conducive to good strategy execution are healthy cultures. So are high-performance cultures and adaptive cultures. The latter are particularly important in dynamic environments. Strong cultures can also be unhealthy. The five types of unhealthy cultures are those that are (1) change-resistant, (2) heavily politicized, (3) insular and inwardly focused, (4) ethically unprincipled and infused with greed, and (5) composed of incompatible subcultures. All five impede good strategy execution.

7. Changing a company's culture, especially a strong one with traits that don't fit a new strategy's requirements, is a tough and often time-consuming challenge. Changing a culture requires competent leadership at the top. It requires making a compelling case for cultural change and employing both symbolic actions and substantive actions that unmistakably indicate serious commitment on the part of top management. The more that culture-driven actions and behaviors fit what's needed for good strategy execution, the less managers must depend on policies, rules, procedures, and supervision to enforce what people should and should not do.

8. Leading the drive for good strategy execution and operating excellence calls for three actions on the part of the manager in charge:

- Staying on top of what is happening and closely monitoring progress. This is often accomplished through managing by walking around (MBWA).

- Mobilizing the effort for excellence in strategy execution by putting constructive pressure on the organization to execute the strategy well.

- Initiating corrective actions to improve strategy execution and achieve the targeted performance results.

## ASSURANCE OF LEARNING EXERCISES

**LO 1**
1. Go to the company page for John Deere at http://www.deere.com/wps/dcom/en_US/corporate/our_company/our_company.page?
Click through several of the tabs provided there (about us, citizenship, careers, etc.) to see what they reveal about the company's culture. What do you think are the key features of their culture and why? How do they link to the company's core values and ethical standards?

**LO 2**
2. Based on what you learned about John Deere from answering the previous question, how do you think their culture affects their ability to execute strategy and operate with excellence?

**LO 3**
3. Using Google Scholar or your university library's access to EBSCO, Lexis-Nexis, or other databases, search for recent articles in business publications on "culture change." Give examples of two companies that have recently undergone culture-change initiatives. What are the key features of each company's culture-change program? What results did management achieve at each company?

**LO 1**
4. Go to www.jnj.com, the website of Johnson & Johnson, and read the J&J Credo, which sets forth the company's responsibilities to customers, employees, the community, and shareholders. Then read the "Our Company" section. Why do you think the credo has resulted in numerous awards and accolades that recognize the company as a good corporate citizen?

**LO 4**
5. In recent years, Liz Claiborne, Inc., has been engaged in efforts to turn around its faltering Mexx chain. Use your favorite browser to search for information on the turnaround plan at Mexx, and read at least two articles or reports on this subject. Describe in one to two pages the approach being taken to turn around the Mexx chain. In your opinion, have the managers involved been demonstrating the kind of internal leadership needed for superior strategy execution at Mexx? Explain your answer.

6. Illustration Capsule 12.1 discusses W. L. Gore's strategy-supportive corporate culture. What are the standout features of Gore's corporate culture? How does W. L. Gore's culture contribute to innovation and creativity at the company? How does the company's culture make W. L. Gore a good place to work?

**LO 1, LO 2**

## EXERCISE FOR SIMULATION PARTICIPANTS

1. If you were making a speech to company personnel, what would you tell them about the kind of corporate culture you would like to have at your company? What specific cultural traits would you like your company to exhibit? Explain.

   **LO 1, LO 2**

2. What core values would you want to ingrain in your company's culture? Why?

   **LO 1**

3. Following each decision round, do you and your co-managers make corrective adjustments in either your company's strategy or how well the strategy is being executed? List at least three such adjustments you made in the most recent decision round. What hard evidence (in the form of results relating to your company's performance in the most recent year) can you cite that indicates the various corrective adjustments you made either succeeded or failed to improve your company's performance?

   **LO 3, LO 4**

4. What would happen to your company's performance if you and your co-managers stick with the status quo and fail to make any corrective adjustments after each decision round?

   **LO 4**

## ENDNOTES

[1] Jennifer A. Chatham and Sandra E. Cha, "Leading by Leveraging Culture," *California Management Review* 45, no. 4 (Summer 2003), pp. 20–34; Edgar Shein, *Organizational Culture and Leadership: A Dynamic View* (San Francisco, CA: Jossey-Bass, 1992).

[2] T. E. Deal and A. A. Kennedy, *Corporate Cultures: The Rites and Rituals of Corporate Life* (Harmondsworth, UK: Penguin Books, 1982).

[3] Joanne Reid and Victoria Hubbell, "Creating a Performance Culture," *Ivey Business Journal* 69, no. 4 (March–April 2005), p. 1.

[4] John P. Kotter and James L. Heskett, *Corporate Culture and Performance* (New York: Free Press, 1992); Robert Goffee and Gareth Jones, *The Character of a Corporation* (New York: HarperCollins, 1998).

[5] Joseph L. Badaracco, *Defining Moments: When Managers Must Choose between Right and Wrong* (Boston: Harvard Business School Press, 1997); Joe Badaracco and Allen P. Webb. "Business Ethics: A View from the Trenches," *California Management Review* 37, no. 2 (Winter 1995), pp. 8–28; Patrick E. Murphy, "Corporate Ethics Statements: Current Status and Future Prospects," *Journal of Business Ethics* 14 (1995), pp. 727–40; Lynn Sharp Paine, "Managing for Organizational Integrity,"

*Harvard Business Review* 72, no. 2 (March–April 1994), pp. 106–17.

[6] Emily F. Carasco and Jang B. Singh, "The Content and Focus of the Codes of Ethics of the World's Largest Transnational Corporations," *Business and Society Review* 108, no. 1 (January 2003), pp. 71–94; Patrick E. Murphy, "Corporate Ethics Statements: Current Status and Future Prospects," *Journal of Business Ethics* 14 (1995), pp. 727–40; John Humble, David Jackson, and Alan Thomson, "The Strategic Power of Corporate Values," *Long Range Planning* 27, no. 6 (December 1994), pp. 28–42; Mark S. Schwartz, "A Code of Ethics for Corporate Codes of Ethics," *Journal of Business Ethics* 41, nos. 1–2 (November–December 2002), pp. 27–43.

[7] Terrence E. Deal and Allen A. Kennedy, *Corporate Cultures* (Reading, MA: Addison-Wesley, 1982); Terrence E. Deal and Allen A. Kennedy, *The New Corporate Cultures: Revitalizing the Workplace after Downsizing, Mergers, and Reengineering* (Cambridge, MA: Perseus Publishing, 1999).

[8] Vijay Sathe, *Culture and Related Corporate Realities* (Homewood, IL: Irwin, 1985).

[9] Avan R. Jassawalla and Hemant C. Sashittal, "Cultures That Support Product-Innovation Processes," *Academy of Management*

*Executive* 16, no. 3 (August 2002), pp. 42–54.

[10] Kotter and Heskett, *Corporate Culture and Performance*, p. 5.

[11] Joanne Reid and Victoria Hubbell, "Creating a Performance Culture," *Ivey Business Journal* 69, no. 4 (March/April 2005), pp. 1–5.

[12] Jay B. Barney and Delwyn N. Clark, *Resource-Based Theory: Creating and Sustaining Competitive Advantage* (New York: Oxford University Press, 2007), ch. 4.

[13] Rosabeth Moss Kanter, "Transforming Giants," *Harvard Business Review* 86, no. 1 (January 2008), pp. 43–52.

[14] Kurt Eichenwald, *Conspiracy of Fools: A True Story* (New York: Broadway Books, 2005).

[15] Judy D. Olian and Sara L. Rynes, "Making Total Quality Work: Aligning Organizational Processes, Performance Measures, and Stakeholders," *Human Resource Management* 30, no. 3 (Fall 1991), p. 324.

[16] Larry Bossidy and Ram Charan, *Confronting Reality: Doing What Matters to Get Things Right* (New York: Crown Business, 2004); Larry Bossidy and Ram Charan, *Execution: The Discipline of Getting Things Done* (New York: Crown Business, 2002); John P. Kotter, "Leading Change: Why Transformation Efforts Fail," *Harvard*

*Business Review* 73, no. 2 (March–April 1995), pp. 59–67; Thomas M. Hout and John C. Carter, "Getting It Done: New Roles for Senior Executives," *Harvard Business Review* 73, no. 6 (November–December 1995), pp. 133–45; Sumantra Ghoshal and Christopher A. Bartlett, "Changing the Role of Top Management: Beyond Structure to Processes," *Harvard Business Review* 73, no. 1 (January–February 1995), pp. 86–96.

[17] Fred Vogelstein, "Winning the Amazon Way," *Fortune,* May 26, 2003, p. 64.

[18] Benjamin Schneider, Sarah K. Gunnarson, and Kathryn Niles-Jolly, "Creating the Climate and Culture of Success" *Organizational Dynamics,* Summer 1994, pp. 17–29.

[19] Michael T. Kanazawa and Robert H. Miles, *Big Ideas to Big Results* (Upper Saddle River, NJ: FT Press, 2008).

[20] Jeffrey Pfeffer, "Producing Sustainable Competitive Advantage through the Effective Management of People," *Academy of Management Executive* 9, no.1 (February 1995), pp. 55–69.

[21] Cynthia A. Montgomery, "Putting Leadership Back into Strategy," *Harvard Business Review* 86, no. 1 (January 2008), pp. 54–60.

[22] James Brian Quinn, *Strategies for Change: Logical Incrementalism* (Homewood, IL: Richard D. Irwin, 1980).

[23] Daniel Goleman, "What Makes a Leader," *Harvard Business Review* 76, no. 6 (November–December 1998), pp. 92–102; Ronald A. Heifetz and Donald L. Laurie, "The Work of Leadership," *Harvard Business Review* 75, no. 1 (January–February 1997), pp. 124–34; Charles M. Farkas and Suzy Wetlaufer, "The Ways Chief Executive Officers Lead," *Harvard Business Review* 74, no. 3 (May–June 1996), pp. 110–22; Michael E. Porter, Jay W. Lorsch, and Nitin Nohria, "Seven Surprises for New CEOs," *Harvard Business Review* 82, no. 10 (October 2004), pp. 62–72.

# PART 2

## Cases in Crafting and Executing Strategy

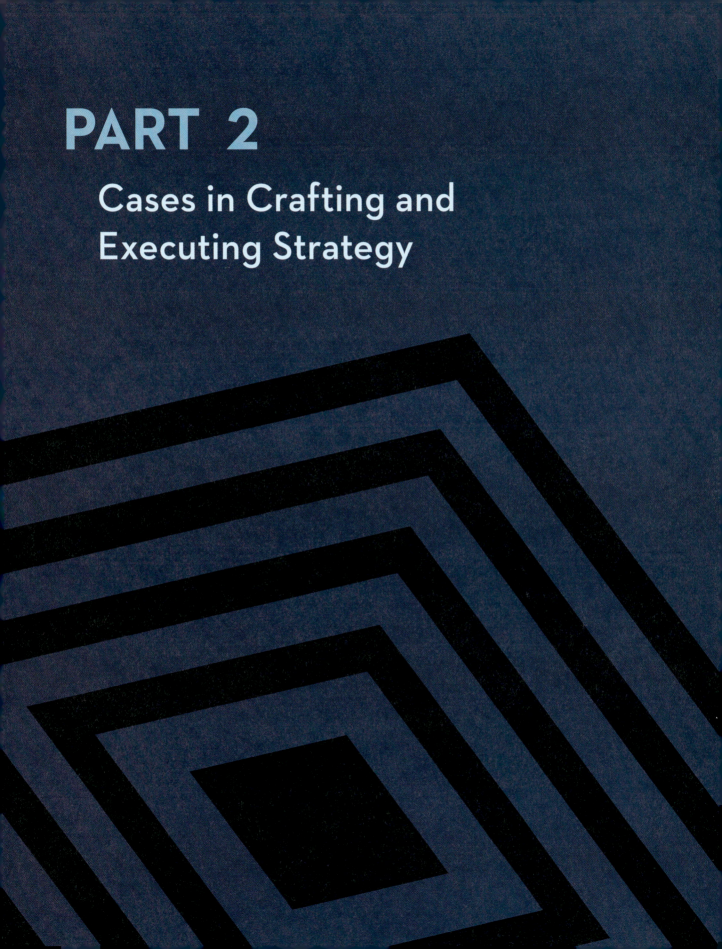

# Mystic Monk Coffee

### David L. Turnipseed
University of South Alabama

As Father Daniel Mary, the prior of the Carmelite Order of monks in Clark, Wyoming, walked to chapel to preside over Mass, he noticed the sun glistening across the four-inch snowfall from the previous evening. Snow in June was not unheard of in Wyoming, but the late snowfall and the bright glow of the rising sun made him consider the opposing forces accompanying change and how he might best prepare his monastery to achieve his vision of creating a new Mount Carmel in the Rocky Mountains. His vision of transforming the small brotherhood of 13 monks living in a small home used as makeshift rectory into a 500-acre monastery that would include accommodations for 30 monks, a Gothic church, a convent for Carmelite nuns, a retreat center for lay visitors, and a hermitage presented a formidable challenge. However, as a former high school football player, boxer, bull rider, and man of great faith, Father Prior Daniel Mary was unaccustomed to shrinking from a challenge.

Father Prior had identified a nearby ranch for sale that met the requirements of his vision perfectly, but its current listing price of $8.9 million presented a financial obstacle to creating a place of prayer, worship, and solitude in the Rockies. The Carmelites had received a $250,000 donation that could be used toward the purchase, and the monastery had earned nearly $75,000 during the first year of its Mystic Monk coffee-roasting operations, but more money would be needed. The coffee roaster used to produce packaged coffee sold to Catholic consumers at the Mystic Monk Coffee website was reaching its capacity, but a larger roaster could be purchased for $35,000. Also, local Cody, Wyoming, business owners had begun a foundation for those wishing to donate to the monks' cause. Father Prior Daniel Mary did not have a great deal of experience in business matters but considered to what extent the monastery could rely on its Mystic Monk Coffee operations to fund the purchase of the ranch. If Mystic Monk Coffee was capable of making the vision a reality, what were the next steps in turning the coffee into land?

## THE CARMELITE MONKS OF WYOMING

Carmelites are a religious order of the Catholic Church that was formed by men who traveled to the Holy Land as pilgrims and crusaders and had chosen to remain near Jerusalem to seek God. The men established their hermitage at Mount Carmel because of its beauty, seclusion, and biblical importance as the site where Elijah stood against King Ahab and the false prophets of Jezebel to prove Jehovah to be the one true God. The Carmelites led a life of solitude, silence, and prayer at Mount Carmel before eventually returning to Europe and becoming a recognized order of the Catholic Church. The size of the Carmelite Order varied widely throughout the centuries with its peak in the 1600s and stood at approximately 2,200 friars living on all inhabited continents at the beginning of the 21st century.

The Wyoming Carmelite monastery was founded by Father Daniel Mary who lived as a Carmelite hermit in Minnesota before moving to Clark, Wyoming, to establish the new monastery. The Wyoming Carmelites were a cloistered order and were allowed to leave the monastery only by permission of the bishop for medical needs or the death of a family member. The Wyoming monastery's abbey bore little resemblance to the great stone cathedrals and monasteries of Europe and was confined to a rectory that had once been a four-bedroom ranch-style home and an adjoining 42 acres of land that had been donated to the monastery.

There were 13 monks dedicated to a life of prayer and worship in the Wyoming Carmelite monastery. Since the founding of the monastery six years ago, there had been more than 500 inquiries from young men considering becoming a Wyoming Carmelite. Father Prior Daniel Mary wished to eventually have 30 monks who would join the brotherhood at age 19 to 30 and live out their lives in the monastery. However, the selection criteria for acceptance into the monastery were rigorous, with the monks making certain that applicants understood the reality of the vows of obedience, chastity, and poverty and the sacrifices associated with living a cloistered religious life.

## The Daily Activities of a Carmelite Monk

The Carmelite monks' day began at 4:10 a.m., when they arose and went to chapel for worship wearing traditional brown habits and handmade sandals. At about 6:00 a.m., the monks rested and contemplated in silence for one hour before Father Prior began morning Mass. After Mass, the monks went about their manual labors. In performing their labors, each brother had a special set of skills that enabled the monastery to independently maintain its operations. Brother Joseph Marie was an excellent mechanic, Brother Paul was a carpenter, Brother Peter Joseph (Brother Cook) worked in the kitchen, and five-foot, four-inch Brother Simon Mary (Little Monk) was the secretary to Father Daniel Mary. Brother Elias, affectionately known as Brother Java, was Mystic Monk Coffee's master roaster, although he was not a coffee drinker.

Each monk worked up to six hours per day; however, the monks' primary focus was spiritual, with eight hours of each day spent in prayer. At 11:40 a.m., the monks stopped work and went to Chapel. Afterward they had lunch, cleaned the dishes, and went back to work. At 3:00 p.m., the hour that Jesus was believed to have died on the cross, work stopped again for prayer and worship. The monks then returned to work until the bell was rung for Vespers (evening prayer). After Vespers, the monks had an hour of silent contemplation, an evening meal, and more prayers before bedtime.

## The New Mount Carmel

Soon after arriving in Wyoming, Father Daniel Mary had formed the vision of acquiring a large parcel of land—a new Mount Carmel—and building a monastery with accommodations for 30 monks, a retreat center for lay visitors, a Gothic church, a convent for Carmelite nuns, and a hermitage. In a letter to supporters posted on the monastery's website, Father Daniel Mary succinctly stated his vision: "We beg your prayers, your friendship and your support that this vision, our vision may come to be that Mount Carmel may be refounded in Wyoming's Rockies for the glory of God."

The brothers located a 496-acre ranch for sale that would satisfy all of the requirements to create a new Mount Carmel. The Irma Lake Ranch was located about 21 miles outside Cody, Wyoming, and included a remodeled 17,800-square-foot residence, a 1,700-square-foot caretaker house, a 2,950-square-foot guesthouse, a hunting cabin, a dairy and horse barn, and forested land. The ranch was at the end of a seven-mile-long private gravel road and was bordered on one side by the private Hoodoo Ranch (100,000 acres) and on the other by the Shoshone National Park (2.4 million acres). Although the asking price was $8.9 million, the monks believed they would be able to acquire the property through donations and the profits generated by the monastery's Mystic Monk Coffee operations. The $250,000 donation they had received from an individual wishing to support the Carmelites could be applied toward whatever purpose the monks chose. Additionally, a group of Cody business owners had formed the New Mount Carmel Foundation to help the monks raise funds.

## OVERVIEW OF THE COFFEE INDUSTRY

About 150 million consumers in the United States drank coffee, with 89 percent of U.S. coffee drinkers brewing their own coffee at home rather than purchasing ready-to-drink coffee at coffee shops and restaurants such as Starbucks, Dunkin' Donuts, or McDonald's. Packaged coffee for home brewing was easy to find in any grocery store and typically carried a retail price of $4 to $6 for a 12-ounce package. About 30 million coffee drinkers in the United States preferred premium-quality specialty coffees that sold for $7 to $10 per 12-ounce package. Specialty coffees are made from high-quality Arabica beans instead of the mix of low-quality Arabica beans and bitter, less flavorful Robusta beans that makers of value brands use. The wholesale price of Robusta coffee beans averaged $1.15 per pound, while mild Columbian Arabica wholesale prices averaged $1.43 per pound.

Prior to the 1990s, the market for premium-quality specialty coffees barely existed in the United States, but Howard Schultz's vision for Starbucks of bringing the Italian espresso bar experience to America helped specialty coffees become a large and thriving segment of the industry. The company's pursuit of its mission "To inspire and nurture the human spirit—one person, one cup, and one neighborhood at a time" had allowed Starbucks to become an iconic brand in most parts of the world. The company's success had given rise to a number of competing specialty coffee shops and premium brands of packaged specialty coffee, including Seattle's Best, Millstone, Green Mountain Coffee Roasters, and First Colony Coffee and Tea. Some producers such as First Colony had difficulty gaining shelf space in supermarkets and concentrated on private-label roasting and packaging for fine department stores and other retailers wishing to have a proprietary brand of coffee.

Specialty coffees sold under premium brands might be made from shade-grown or organically grown coffee beans, or have been purchased from a grower belonging to a World Fair Trade Organization (WFTO) cooperative. WFTO cooperative growers were paid above-market prices to better support the cost of operating their farms—for example, WFTO-certified organic wholesale prices averaged $1.55 per pound. Many consumers who purchased specialty coffees were willing to pay a higher price for organic, shade-grown, or fair trade coffee because of their personal health or social concerns—organic coffees are grown without the use of synthetic fertilizers or pesticides, shade-grown coffee plants are allowed to grow beneath the canopies of larger indigenous trees, and fair trade pricing makes it easier for farmers in developing countries to pay workers a living wage. The specialty coffee segment of the retail coffee industry had grown dramatically in the United States, with retail sales increasing from $8.3 billion to $13.5 billion during the last seven years. The retail sales of organic coffee accounted for about $1 billion of industry sales and had grown at an annual rate of 32 percent for each of the last seven years.

# MYSTIC MONK COFFEE

Mystic Monk Coffee was produced using high-quality fair trade Arabica and fair trade/organic Arabica beans. The monks produced whole-bean and ground caffeinated and decaffeinated varieties in dark, medium, and light roasts and in different flavors. The most popular Mystic Monk flavors were Mystical Chants of Carmel, Cowboy Blend, Royal Rum Pecan, and Mystic Monk Blend. With the exception of sample bags, which carried a retail price of $2.99, all varieties of Mystic Monk Coffee were sold via the monastery's website (**www.mysticmonkcoffee.com**) in 12-ounce bags at a price of $9.95. All purchases from the website were delivered by United Parcel Service (UPS) or the U.S. Postal Service. Frequent customers were given the option of joining a "coffee club," which offered monthly delivery of one to six bags of preselected coffee. Purchases of three or more bags qualified for free shipping. The Mystic Monk Coffee website also featured T-shirts, gift cards, CDs featuring the monastery's Gregorian chants, and coffee mugs.

Mystic Monk Coffee's target market was the segment of the U.S. Catholic population who drank coffee and wished to support the monastery's mission. More than 69 million Americans were members of the Catholic Church—making it four times larger than the second-largest Christian denomination in the United States. An appeal to Catholics to "use their Catholic coffee dollar for Christ and his Catholic church" was published on the Mystic Monk Coffee website.

## Mystic Monk Coffee-Roasting Operations

After the morning religious services and breakfast, Brother Java roasted the green coffee beans delivered each week from a coffee broker in Seattle, Washington. The monks paid the Seattle broker the prevailing wholesale price per pound, which fluctuated daily with global supply and demand. The capacity of Mystic Monk Coffee's roaster limited production to 540 pounds per day; production was also limited by time devoted to prayer, silent meditation, and worship. Demand for Mystic Monk Coffee had not yet exceeded the roaster's capacity, but the monastery planned to purchase a larger, 130-pound-per-hour-roaster when demand further approached the current roaster's capacity. The monks had received a quote of $35,000 for the new larger roaster.

# Marketing and Website Operations

Mystic Monk Coffee was promoted primarily by word of mouth among loyal customers in Catholic parishes across the United States. The majority of Mystic Monk's sales were made through its website, but on occasion telephone orders were placed with the monks' secretary, who worked outside the cloistered part of the monastery. Mystic Monk also offered secular website operators commissions on its sales through its Mystic Monk Coffee Affiliate Program, which placed banner ads and text ads on participating websites. Affiliate sites earned an 18 percent commission on sales made to customers who were directed to the Mystic Monk site from their site. The affiliate program's ShareASale participation level allowed affiliates to refer new affiliates to Mystic Monk and earn 56 percent of the new affiliate's commission. The monks had also just recently expanded Mystic Monk's business model to include wholesale sales to churches and local coffee shops.

# Mystic Monk's Financial Performance

At the conclusion of Mystic Monk Coffee's first year in operation, its sales of coffee and coffee accessories averaged about $56,500 per month. Its cost of sales averaged about 30 percent of revenues, inbound shipping costs accounted for 19 percent of revenues, and broker fees were 3 percent of revenues—for a total cost of goods sold of 52 percent. Operating expenses such as utilities, supplies, telephone, and website maintenance averaged 37 percent of revenues. Thus, Mystic Monk's net profit margin averaged 11 percent of revenues.

# REALIZING THE VISION

During a welcome period of solitude before his evening meal, Father Prior Daniel Mary again contemplated the purchase of the Irma Lake Ranch. He realized that his vision of purchasing the ranch would require careful planning and execution. For the Wyoming Carmelites, coffee sales were a means of support from the outside world that might provide the financial resources to purchase the land. Father Prior understood that the cloistered monastic environment offered unique challenges to operating a business enterprise, but it also provided opportunities that were not available to secular businesses. He resolved to develop an execution plan that would enable Mystic Monk Coffee to minimize the effect of its cloistered monastic constraints, maximize the potential of monastic opportunities, and realize his vision of buying the Irma Lake Ranch.

# Costco Wholesale in 2012: Mission, Business Model, and Strategy

## Arthur A. Thompson
The University of Alabama

Jim Sinegal, co-founder and long-time CEO of Costco Wholesale, was the driving force behind Costco's 29-year march to become the third largest retailer in the United States, the seventh largest retailer in the world, and the clear leader of the discount warehouse and wholesale club segment of the North American retailing industry. Sinegal was far from the stereotypical CEO. Grandfatherly and in his 70s, he dressed casually and unpretentiously, often going to the office or touring Costco stores wearing an open-collared cotton shirt that came from a Costco bargain rack and sporting a standard employee name tag that said, simply, "Jim." His informal dress, mustache, gray hair, and unimposing appearance made it easy for Costco shoppers to mistake him for a store clerk. He answered his own phone, once telling ABC News reporters, "If a customer's calling and they have a gripe, don't you think they kind of enjoy the fact that I picked up the phone and talked to them?"[1]

Sinegal spent considerable time touring Costco stores, using the company plane to fly from location to location and sometimes visiting 8 to 10 stores daily (the record for a single day was 12). Treated like a celebrity when he appeared at a store (the news "Jim's in the store" spread quickly), Sinegal made a point of greeting store employees. He observed, "The employees know that I want to say hello to them, because I like them. We have said from the very beginning: 'We're going to be a company that's on a first-name basis with everyone.'"[2] Employees genuinely seemed to like Sinegal. He talked quietly, in a commonsensical manner that suggested what he was saying was no big deal.[3] He came across as kind yet stern, but he was prone to display irritation when he disagreed sharply with what people were saying to him.

In touring a Costco store with the local store manager, Sinegal was very much the person-in-charge. He functioned as producer, director, and knowledgeable critic. He cut to the chase quickly, exhibiting intense attention to detail and pricing, wandering through store aisles firing a barrage of questions at store managers about sales volumes and stock levels of particular items, critiquing merchandising displays or the position of certain products in the stores, commenting on any aspect of store operations that caught his eye, and asking managers to do further research and get back to him with more information whenever he found their answers to his questions less than satisfying. Sinegal had tremendous merchandising savvy, demanded much of store managers and employees, and definitely set the tone for how the company operated its discounted retailing business. Knowledgeable observers regarded Jim Sinegal's merchandising expertise as being on a par with Walmart's legendary founder, Sam Walton.

In January 2012, Costco had a total of 598 warehouses in 40 states and Puerto Rico (433 locations), nine Canadian provinces (82 locations), the United Kingdom (22 locations), Korea (7 locations), Taiwan (8 locations, through a 55 percent–owned subsidiary), Japan (11 locations), Australia (3 locations), and 32 warehouses in Mexico through a 50 percent–owned joint venture. Costco's fiscal 2011 total revenues were a record high of $88.9 billion and net income was a record high of $1.46 billion. About 25 million households and 6.4 million businesses had membership cards entitling them to shop at Costco, generating nearly $1.9 billion in membership fees for the company. Annual sales per store averaged about $146 million, about 85 percent higher than the $78 million figure for Sam's Club, Costco's chief competitor. In fiscal 2011, 93 of Costco's warehouses generated sales exceeding $200 million annually, up from 56 in 2010 and four stores had sales exceeding $300 million, including one that had more than $400 million in sales.

## COMPANY BACKGROUND

The membership warehouse concept was pioneered by discount merchandising sage Sol Price, who opened the first Price Club in a converted airplane hangar on Morena Boulevard in San Diego in 1976. Price Club lost $750,000 in its first year of operation, but by 1979 it had two stores, 900 employees, 200,000 members, and a $1 million profit. Years earlier, Sol Price had experimented with discount retailing at a San Diego store called Fed-Mart. Jim Sinegal got his start in retailing there at the age of 18, loading mattresses for $1.25 an hour while attending San Diego Community College. When Sol Price sold Fed-Mart, Sinegal left with Price to help him start the San Diego Price Club store; within a few years, Sol Price's Price Club emerged as the unchallenged leader in member warehouse retailing, with stores operating primarily on the West Coast.

Although he originally conceived Price Club as a place where small local businesses could obtain needed merchandise at economical prices, Sol Price soon concluded that his fledgling operation could achieve far greater sales volumes and gain buying clout with suppliers by also granting membership to individuals—a conclusion that launched the deep-discount warehouse club industry on a steep growth curve.

When Sinegal was 26, Sol Price made him the manager of the original San Diego store, which had become unprofitable. Price saw that Sinegal had a special knack for discount retailing and for spotting what a store was doing wrong (usually either not being in the right merchandise categories or not selling items at the right price points)—the very things that Sol Price was good at and that were at the root of Price Club's growing success in the marketplace. Sinegal soon got the San Diego store back into the black. Over the next several years, Sinegal continued to build his prowess and talents for discount merchandising. He mirrored Sol Price's attention to detail and absorbed all the nuances and subtleties of his mentor's style of operating—constantly improving store operations, keeping operating costs and overhead low, stocking items that moved quickly, and charging ultra-low prices that kept customers coming back to shop. Realizing that he had mastered the tricks of running a successful membership warehouse business from Sol Price, Sinegal decided to leave Price Club and form his own warehouse club operation.

Sinegal and Seattle entrepreneur Jeff Brotman (now chairman of Costco's board of directors) founded Costco, and the first Costco store began operations in Seattle in 1983, the same year that Walmart launched its warehouse membership format, Sam's Club. By the end of 1984, there were nine Costco stores in five states serving over 200,000 members. In December 1985, Costco became a public company, selling shares to the public and raising additional capital for expansion. Costco became the first ever U.S. company to reach $1 billion in sales in less than six years. In October 1993, Costco merged with Price Club. Jim Sinegal became CEO of the merged company, presiding over 206 PriceCostco locations, with total annual sales of $16 billion. Jeff Brotman, who had functioned as Costco's chairman since the company's founding, became vice chairman of PriceCostco in 1993 and was elevated to chairman in December 1994. Brotman kept abreast of operations but stayed in the background and concentrated on managing the company's extensive real estate investment in land and buildings.

In January 1997, after the spin-off of most of its non-warehouse assets to Price Enterprises Inc., PriceCostco changed its name to Costco Companies Inc. When the company reincorporated from Delaware to Washington in August 1999, the name was changed to Costco Wholesale Corporation. The company's headquarters was in Issaquah, Washington, not far from Seattle.

In September 2011, Jim Sinegal informed Costco's Board of Directors of his intention to step down as Chief Executive Officer of the Company effective January 2012. The Board elected Craig Jelinek, President and Chief Operating Officer since February 2010, to succeed Sinegal and hold the titles of both President and Chief Executive Officer. Jelinek was a highly experienced retail executive with 37 years in the industry, 28 of them at Costco, where he started as one of the Company's first warehouse managers in 1984. He had served in every major role related to Costco's business operations and merchandising activities during his tenure. Sinegal was to remain with Costco through January 2013, serving in an advisory role and assisting Jelinek during the transition; he also remained a member of the company's board of directors.

Exhibit 1 contains a financial and operating summary for Costco for fiscal years 2000–2011.

## EXHIBIT 1    Selected Financial and Operating Data for Costco Wholesale Corp., Fiscal Years 2000–2011 ($ in millions, except for per share data)

| Selected Income Statement Data | Fiscal years ending on Sunday closest to August 31 | | | | | |
|---|---|---|---|---|---|---|
| | 2011 | 2010 | 2009 | 2008 | 2005 | 2000 |
| Net sales | $87,048 | $76,255 | $69,889 | $70,977 | $51,862 | $31,621 |
| Membership fees | 1,867 | 1,691 | 1,533 | 1,506 | 1,073 | 544 |
| Total revenue | 88,915 | 77,946 | 71,422 | 72,483 | 52,935 | 32,164 |
| Operating expenses | | | | | | |
| Merchandise costs | 77,739 | 67,995 | 62,335 | 63,503 | 46,347 | 28,322 |
| Selling, general, and administrative | 8,682 | 7,840 | 7,252 | 6,954 | 5,044 | 2,755 |
| Preopening expenses | 46 | 26 | 41 | 57 | 53 | 42 |
| Provision for impaired assets and store closing costs | 9 | 8 | 17 | 0 | 16 | 7 |
| Operating income | 2,439 | 2,077 | 1,777 | 1,969 | 1,474 | 1,037 |
| Other income (expense) | | | | | | |
| Interest expense | (116) | (111) | (108) | (103) | (34) | (39) |
| Interest income and other | 60 | 88 | 45 | 133 | 109 | 54 |
| Income before income taxes | 2,383 | 2,054 | 1,714 | 1,999 | 1,549 | 1,052 |
| Provision for income taxes | 841 | 731 | 628 | 716 | 486 | 421 |
| Net income | $ 1,462 | $ 1,303 | $ 1,086 | $ 1,283 | $ 1,063 | $ 631 |
| Diluted net income per share | $3.30 | $2.92 | $2.47 | $2.89 | $2.18 | $1.35 |
| Dividends per share | $0.89 | $0.77 | $0.68 | $0.61 | $0.43 | $0.00 |
| Millions of shares used in per share calculations | 443.1 | 446.0 | 440.5 | 444.2 | 492.0 | 475.7 |
| **Balance Sheet Data** | | | | | | |
| Cash and cash equivalents | $4,009 | $3,214 | $3,157 | $2,619 | $2,063 | $525 |
| Merchandise inventories | 6,638 | 5,638 | 5,405 | 5,039 | 4,015 | 2,490 |
| Current assets | 13,706 | 11,708 | 10,337 | 9,462 | 8,238 | 3,470 |
| Current liabilities | 12,050 | 10,063 | 9,281 | 8,874 | 6,761 | 3,404 |
| Net property and equipment | 12,432 | 11,314 | 10,900 | 10,355 | 7,790 | 4,834 |
| Total assets | 26,761 | 23,815 | 21,979 | 20,682 | 16,514 | 8,634 |
| Short-term borrowings | 0 | 26 | 16 | 134 | 54 | 10 |
| Long-term debt | 2,153 | 2,141 | 2,206 | 2,206 | 711 | 790 |
| Stockholders' equity | 12,573 | 10,829 | 10,018 | 9,192 | 8,881 | 4,240 |
| **Cash Flow Data** | | | | | | |
| Net cash provided by operating activities | $3,198 | $2,780 | $2,092 | $2,206 | $1,773 | $1,070 |
| **Warehouse Operations** | | | | | | |
| Warehouses at beginning of year[a] | 572 | 527 | 512 | 488 | 417 | 292 |
| New warehouses opened (including relocations) | 24 | 14 | 19 | 34 | 21 | 25 |
| Existing warehouses closed (including relocations) | (4) | (1) | (4) | (10) | (5) | (4) |
| Warehouses at end of year | 592 | 540 | 527 | 512 | 433 | 313 |
| Net sales per warehouse open at year-end (in millions)[b] | $147.1 | $141.3 | $132.6 | $138.6 | $119.8 | $101.0 |
| Average annual growth at warehouses open more than a year | 10% | 7% | −4% | 8% | 7% | 11% |

(Continued)

**EXHIBIT 1**   (*Concluded*)

| Members at Year-End[c] | Fiscal years ending on Sunday closest to August 31 | | | | | |
|---|---|---|---|---|---|---|
| | **2011** | **2010** | **2009** | **2008** | **2005** | **2000** |
| Businesses (000s) | 6,300 | 5,800 | 5,700 | 5,600 | 5,000 | 4,200 |
| Gold Star members (000s) | 25,000 | 22,500 | 21,500 | 20,200 | 16,200 | 10,500 |
| Add-on cardholders (employees of business members, spouses of members) | 32,700 | 29,700 | 28,800 | 27,700 | n.a. | n.a. |
| Total cardholders | 64,000 | 58,000 | 56,000 | 48,460 | — | — |

[a] Excludes, for years 2008–2010, those warehouses operated in Mexico through a 50 percent–owned joint venture. Mexico opened 30 of these warehouses in 2007, one in 2008, and one in 2009. However, due to an accounting change that became effective at the beginning of fiscal 2011, the 32 Mexico warehouses were consolidated and reported as part of Costco's total operations at the beginning of the fiscal year.
[b] This number is "biased downward" because new warehouses opened during the year had net sales for less than 12 full months.
[c] Membership numbers do not include Costco Mexico cardholders of approximately 2,900,000 in 2010 and 2,800,000 in 2009.
*Note:* Some totals may not add due to rounding and the fact that some line items in the company's statement of income were not included in this summary, for reasons of simplicity.

*Sources:* Company 10-K reports for fiscal years 2000, 2005, 2009, 2010, and 2011.

# COSTCO'S MISSION, BUSINESS MODEL, AND STRATEGY

Numerous company documents stated that Costco's mission in the membership warehouse business was: "To continually provide our members with quality goods and services at the lowest possible prices."[4] However, in their "Letter to Shareholders" in the company's 2011 Annual Report, Costco's three top executives—Jeff Brotman, Jim Sinegal, and Craig Jelinek—provided a more expansive view of Costco's mission, stating:[5]

> The company will continue to pursue its mission of bringing the highest quality goods and services to market at the lowest possible prices while providing excellent customer service and adhering to a strict code of ethics that includes taking care of our employees and members, respecting our suppliers, rewarding our shareholders, and seeking to be responsible corporate citizens and environmental stewards in our operations around the world.

The centerpiece of Costco's business model entailed generating high sales volumes and rapid inventory turnover by offering fee-paying members attractively low prices on a limited selection of nationally branded and selected private-label products in a wide range of merchandise categories. Rapid inventory turnover—when combined with the low operating costs achieved by volume purchasing, efficient distribution, and reduced handling of merchandise in no-frills, self-service warehouse facilities—enabled Costco to operate profitably at significantly lower gross margins than traditional wholesalers, mass merchandisers, supermarkets, and supercenters. Membership fees were a critical element of Costco's business model because they provided sufficient supplemental revenues to boost the company's overall profitability to acceptable levels.

A second important business model element was that Costco's high sales volume and rapid inventory turnover generally allowed it to sell and receive cash for inventory before it had to pay many of its merchandise vendors, even when vendor payments were made in time to take advantage of early payment discounts. Thus, Costco was able to finance a big percentage of its merchandise inventory through the payment terms provided by vendors rather than by having to maintain sizable working capital (defined as current assets minus current liabilities) to facilitate timely payment of suppliers.

## Costco's Strategy

The key elements of Costco's strategy were ultra-low prices, a limited selection of nationally branded and private-label products, a "treasure hunt" shopping environment, strong emphasis on low operating costs, and geographic expansion.

**Pricing**   Costco's philosophy was to keep customers coming in to shop by wowing them with low prices. The company stocked only those items that could be priced at bargain levels and thus provide members with significant cost savings; this was true even if an item was often requested by customers. For many years, a key element of Costco's pricing strategy had been to cap its markup on brand-name merchandise at 14 percent (compared to 20- to 50-percent markups at other discounters and many supermarkets). Markups on Costco's private-label Kirkland Signature items were a maximum of 15 percent, but the sometimes fractionally higher markups still resulted in Kirkland Signature items being priced about 20 percent below comparable name-brand items. Kirkland Signature products—which included vitamins, juice, bottled water, coffee, spices, olive oil, canned salmon and tuna, nuts, laundry detergent, baby products, dog food, luggage, cookware, trash bags, batteries, wines and spirits, paper towels and toilet paper, and clothing—were designed to be of equal or better quality than national brands.

As a result of these low markups, Costco's prices were just fractionally above breakeven levels, producing net sales revenues (not counting membership fees) that barely covered all operating expenses and generated only a modest contribution to operating profits. As can be verified from Exhibit 1, in 2005 and every year during 2008–2011, over 70 percent of Costco's operating profits were attributable to membership fees and, in fact, membership fees were larger than Costco's net income in every year shown in Exhibit 1 (or to put it another way, without the revenues from membership fees, Costco's net income after taxes would be miniscule because of its ultra-low pricing strategy and practice of capping the margins on branded goods at 14 percent and private-label goods at 15 percent).

Jim Sinegal explained the company's approach to pricing:

> We always look to see how much of a gulf we can create between ourselves and the competition. So that the competitors eventually say, "These guys are crazy. We'll compete somewhere else." Some years ago, we were selling a hot brand of jeans for $29.99. They were $50 in a department store. We got a great deal on them and could have sold them for a higher price but we went down to $29.99. Why? We knew it would create a riot.[6]

At another time, he said:

> We're very good merchants, and we offer value. The traditional retailer will say: "I'm selling this for $10. I wonder whether we can get $10.50 or $11." We say: "We're selling this for $9. How do we get it down to $8?" We understand that our members don't come and shop with us because of the window displays or the Santa Claus or the piano player. They come and shop with us because we offer great values.[7]

Indeed, Costco's markups and prices were so fractionally above the level needed to cover companywide operating costs and interest expenses that Wall Street analysts had criticized Costco management for going all out to please customers at the expense of increasing profits for shareholders. One retailing analyst said, "They could probably get more money for a lot of the items they sell."[8] Sinegal was unimpressed with Wall Street calls for Costco to abandon its ultra-low pricing strategy, commenting: "Those people are in the business of making money between now and next Tuesday. We're trying to build an organization that's going to be here 50 years from now."[9] He went on to explain why Costco's approach to pricing would remain unaltered during his tenure:

> When I started, Sears, Roebuck was the Costco of the country, but they allowed someone else to come in under them. We don't want to be one of the casualties. We don't want to turn around and say, "We got so fancy we've raised our prices, and all of a sudden a new competitor comes in and beats our prices."[10]

**Product Selection**    Whereas typical supermarkets stocked about 40,000 items and a Walmart Supercenter or a SuperTarget might have 125,000 to 150,000 items for shoppers to choose from, Costco's merchandising strategy was to provide members with a selection of approximately 3,600 active items. Of these, about 85 percent were quality brand-name products and 15 percent carried the company's private-label Kirkland Signature brand—however, Kirkland Signature items accounted for 20 percent of sales in fiscal 2011. Management believed that there were opportunities to increase the number of Kirkland Signature selections and build sales penetration of Kirkland Signature products to 30 percent of total sales over the next several years.

Costco's product range covered a broad spectrum—rotisserie chicken, all types of fresh meats, seafood, fresh and canned fruits and vegetables, paper products, cereals, coffee, dairy products, cheeses, frozen foods, flat-screen televisions, iPods, digital cameras, fresh flowers, fine wines, caskets, baby strollers, toys and games, musical instruments, ceiling fans, vacuum cleaners, books, apparel, cleaning supplies, DVDs, light bulbs, batteries, cookware, electric toothbrushes, vitamins, and washers and dryers—but the selection in each product category was deliberately limited to fast-selling models, sizes, and colors. Many consumable products like detergents, canned goods, office supplies, and soft drinks were sold only in big-container, case, carton, or multiple-pack quantities only.

But the selection within each product category was restricted, in some cases to a single offering. For example, Costco stocked only a 325-count bottle of Advil—a

## EXHIBIT 2    Costco's Sales by Major Product Category, 2003–2011

| Major Product Category | 2011 | 2010 | 2009 | 2007 | 2005 | 2003 |
|---|---|---|---|---|---|---|
| **Food** (fresh produce, meats and fish, bakery and deli products, and dry and institutionally packaged foods) | 33% | 33% | 33% | 31% | 30% | 30% |
| **Sundries** (candy, snack foods, tobacco, alcoholic and nonalcoholic beverages, and cleaning and institutional supplies) | 22% | 23% | 23% | 23% | 25% | 26% |
| **Hardlines** (major appliances, electronics, health and beauty aids, hardware, office supplies, garden and patio, sporting goods, furniture, cameras, and automotive supplies) | 17% | 18% | 19% | 21% | 20% | 20% |
| **Softlines** (including apparel, domestics, jewelry, housewares, books, movie DVDs, video games and music, home furnishings, and small appliances) | 10% | 10% | 10% | 11% | 12% | 14% |
| **Ancillary and Other** (gasoline, pharmacy, food court, optical, one-hour photo, hearing aids, and travel) | 18% | 16% | 15% | 14% | 13% | 10% |

*Source:* Company 10-K reports, 2005, 2007, 2009, and 2011.

size many shoppers might find too large for their needs. Sinegal explained why selections were limited:

> If you had ten customers come in to buy Advil, how many are not going to buy any because you just have one size? Maybe one or two. We refer to that as the intelligent loss of sales. We are prepared to give up that one customer. But if we had four or five sizes of Advil, as most grocery stores do, it would make our business more difficult to manage. Our business can only succeed if we are efficient. You can't go on selling at these margins if you are not.[11]

The approximate percentage of net sales accounted for by each major category of items stocked by Costco is shown in Exhibit 2.

As a means of giving members reasons to shop at Costco more frequently and make Costco more of a one-stop shopping destination, the company had opened ancillary departments within or next to most Costco warehouses, as shown just below:

Sales in Costco's ancillary businesses increased by 24 percent in 2011. Gasoline sales alone totaled nearly $9 billion, an increase of 40 percent over fiscal 2010. Only members were eligible to buy gasoline at Costco's discounted gasoline prices. Costco management believed that the availability of attractively priced gasoline at Costco warehouses acted to boost the frequency with which members shopped at Costco and made in-store purchases. Costco's pharmacies were highly regarded by members because of the low prices. A factor contributing to Costco's low prescription prices was its three central fill facilities that cut the cost of filling a prescription by about 50 percent; these three facilities serviced most of Costco's West Coast warehouses. Both prescription and over-the-counter drugs had strong sales and profit increases in fiscal 2011.

**Treasure-Hunt Merchandising**    While Costco's product line consisted of approximately 3,600 active

| | 2011 | 2010 | 2009 | 2008 | 2007 |
|---|---|---|---|---|---|
| Total number of warehouses | 592 | 540 | 527 | 512 | 488 |
| Warehouses having stores with | | | | | |
| Food Court | 586 | 534 | 521 | 506 | 482 |
| One-Hour photo centers | 581 | 530 | 518 | 504 | 480 |
| Optical dispensing centers | 574 | 523 | 509 | 496 | 472 |
| Pharmacies | 529 | 480 | 464 | 451 | 429 |
| Gas stations | 368 | 343 | 323 | 307 | 279 |
| Hearing aid centers | 427 | 357 | 303 | 274 | 237 |
| Print shops and copy centers | 10 | 10 | 10 | 8 | 8 |
| Car washes | 7 | 7 | 2 | — | — |

*Note:* The numbers for 2009 and 2011 exclude the 32 warehouses operated in Mexico.

items, some 20 to 25 percent of its product offerings were constantly changing. Costco's merchandise buyers were continuously making one-time purchases of items that would appeal to the company's clientele and that would sell out quickly. A sizable number of these items were high-end or name-brand products that carried big price tags—like $1,000–$2,500 big-screen HDTVs, $800 espresso machines, expensive jewellery and diamond rings (priced from $50,000 to as high as $250,000), Movado watches, exotic cheeses, Coach bags, $5,000 necklaces, cashmere sports coats, $1,500 digital pianos, and Dom Perignon champagne. Dozens of featured specials came and went quickly, sometimes in several days or a week—like Italian-made Hathaway shirts priced at $29.99 and $800 leather sectional sofas. The strategy was to entice shoppers to spend more than they might by offering irresistible deals on big-ticket items or name-brand specials and, further, to keep the mix of featured and treasure-hunt items constantly changing so that bargain-hunting shoppers would go to Costco more frequently than for periodic "stock up" trips.

Costco members quickly learned that they needed to go ahead and buy treasure-hunt specials that interested them because the items would very likely not be available on their next shopping trip. In many cases, Costco did not obtain its upscale treasure hunt items directly from high-end manufacturers like Calvin Klein or Waterford (who were unlikely to want their merchandise marketed at deep discounts at places like Costco); rather, Costco buyers searched for opportunities to source such items legally on the gray market from other wholesalers or distressed retailers looking to get rid of excess or slow-selling inventory.

Management believed that these practices kept its marketing expenses low relative to those at typical retailers, discounter, and supermarkets.

**Low-Cost Emphasis**    Keeping operating costs at a bare minimum was a major element of Costco's strategy and a key to its low pricing. As Jim Sinegal explained:[12]

> Costco is able to offer lower prices and better values by eliminating virtually all the frills and costs historically associated with conventional wholesalers and retailers, including salespeople, fancy buildings, delivery, billing, and accounts receivable. We run a tight operation with extremely low overhead which enables us to pass on dramatic savings to our members.

While Costco management made a point of locating warehouses on high-traffic routes in or near upscale suburbs that were easily accessible by small businesses and residents with above-average incomes, it avoided prime real estate sites in order to contain land costs. Because shoppers were attracted principally by Costco's low prices and merchandise selection, most warehouses were of a metal pre-engineered design, with concrete floors and minimal interior décor. Floor plans were designed for economy and efficiency in use of selling space, the handling of merchandise, and the control of inventory. Merchandise was generally stored on racks above the sales floor and displayed on pallets containing large quantities of each item, thereby reducing labor required for handling and stocking. In-store signage was done mostly on laser printers; there were no shopping bags at the checkout counter—merchandise was put directly into the shopping cart or sometimes loaded into empty boxes. Costco warehouses ranged in size from 70,000 to 205,000 square feet; the average size was 143,000 square feet. Newer units were usually in the 150,000- to 205,000-square-foot range. Images of Costco's warehouses are shown in Exhibit 3.

Warehouses generally operated on a seven-day, 69-hour week, typically being open between 10:00 a.m. and 8:30 p.m. weekdays, with earlier closing hours on the weekend; the gasoline operations outside many stores usually had extended hours. The shorter hours of operation as compared to those of traditional retailers, discount retailers, and supermarkets resulted in lower labor costs relative to the volume of sales.

**Growth Strategy**    Costco's growth strategy was to increase sales at existing stores by 5 percent or more annually and to open additional warehouses, both domestically and internationally. In fiscal 2011, sales at Costco's existing warehouses grew by an average of 10 percent, chiefly because members shopped Costco warehouses an average of four percent more often and spent about five percent more per visit than they did in fiscal 2010 (see Exhibit 1 for recent average annual sales increases at existing stores). In recent years, Costco had opened between 14 and 34 new locations annually (Exhibit 1); most were in the United States, but expansion was under way internationally as well. In fiscal 2011, Costco spent nearly $1.3 billion to open 20 new locations, two newly relocated warehouses, and several

## EXHIBIT 3   Images of Costco's Warehouses

*Source:* Costco management presentation, May 29, 2008 and March 2010.

distribution depots. Average annualized sales for these newly opened warehouses was $103 million per warehouse, the highest-ever number in the company's history.

Costco opened 4 new warehouses in the United States and 2 new warehouses in Japan in first four months of fiscal 2012 (between August 28 and December 31, 2011), and management planned to open an additional 12 new warehouses (including reopening the Tamasakai, Japan, warehouse damaged by the tsunami in early 2011,

and relocating one Canadian warehouse) by the end of its fiscal year on September 2, 2012.

Exhibit 4 shows a breakdown of Costco's geographic operations for fiscal years 2005–2011.

## Marketing and Advertising

Costco's low prices and its reputation for making shopping at Costco something of a treasure-hunt made it unnecessary to engage in extensive advertising or sales campaigns. Marketing and promotional

## EXHIBIT 4    Selected Geographic Operating Data, Costco Wholesale Corporation, Fiscal Years 2005–2011 ($ in millions)

| | United States Operations | Canadian Operations | Other International Operations | Total |
|---|---|---|---|---|
| **Year Ended August 28, 2011** | | | | |
| Total revenue (including membership fees) | $64,904 | $14,020 | $9,991 | $88,915 |
| Operating income | 1,395 | 621 | 423 | 2,439 |
| Capital expenditures | 876 | 144 | 270 | 1,290 |
| Number of warehouses | 429 | 82 | 81 | 592 |
| **Year Ended August 29, 2010** | | | | |
| Total revenue (including membership fees) | $59,624 | $12,501 | $6,271 | $77,946 |
| Operating income | 1,310 | 547 | 220 | 2,077 |
| Capital expenditures | 804 | 162 | 89 | 1,055 |
| Number of warehouses | 416 | 79 | 45 | 540 |
| **Year Ended August 30, 2009** | | | | |
| Total revenue (including membership fees) | $56,548 | $ 9,737 | $5,137 | $71,442 |
| Operating income | 1,273 | 354 | 150 | 1,777 |
| Capital expenditures | 904 | 135 | 211 | 1,250 |
| Number of warehouses | 406 | 77 | 44 | 527 |
| **Year Ended September 2, 2007** | | | | |
| Total revenue (including membership fees) | $51,532 | $ 8,724 | $4,144 | $64,400 |
| Operating income | 1,217 | 287 | 105 | 1,609 |
| Capital expenditures | 1,104 | 207 | 74 | 1,386 |
| Number of warehouses | 383 | 71 | 34 | 488 |
| **Year Ended August 28, 2005** | | | | |
| Total revenue (including membership fees) | $43,064 | $ 6,732 | $3,155 | $52,952 |
| Operating income | 1,168 | 242 | 65 | 1,474 |
| Capital expenditures | 734 | 140 | 122 | 995 |
| Number of warehouses | 338 | 65 | 30 | 433 |

*Note:* The dollar numbers shown for "Other" countries represent only Costco's ownership share, since all foreign operations were joint ventures (although Costco was the majority owner of these ventures); the warehouses operated by Costco Mexico in which Costco was a 50-percent joint venture partner were not included in the data for the "Other" countries until Fiscal Year 2011.

*Source:* Company 10-K reports, 2011, 2010, 2009, and 2007.

activities were generally limited to monthly coupon mailers to members, weekly e-mails to members from **Costco.com**, occasional direct mail to prospective new members, and regular direct marketing programs (such as The Costco Connection, a magazine published for members), in-store product sampling, and special campaigns for new warehouse openings.

For new warehouse openings, marketing teams personally contacted businesses in the area that were potential wholesale members; these contacts were supplemented with direct mailings during the period immediately prior to opening. Potential Gold Star (individual) members were contacted by direct mail or by promotions at local employee associations and businesses with large numbers of employees. After a membership base was established in an area, most new memberships came from word of mouth (existing members telling friends and acquaintances about their shopping experiences at Costco), follow-up messages distributed through regular payroll or other organizational communications to employee groups, and ongoing direct solicitations to prospective business and Gold Star members.

## Website Sales

Costco operated two websites—**www.costco.com** in the United States and **www.costco.ca** in Canada— both to enable members to shop for many in-store products online and to provide members with a means of obtaining a much wider variety of value-priced products and services that were not practical to stock at the company's warehouses. Examples of items that members could buy online at low Costco prices included sofas, beds, entertainment centers and TV lift cabinets, outdoor furniture, office furniture, kitchen appliances, billiard tables, and hot tubs. Members could also use the company's websites for such services as digital photo processing, prescription fulfillment, travel, the Costco auto program (for purchasing selected new vehicles with discount prices through participating dealerships), and other membership services. At Costco's online photo center, customers could upload images and pick up the prints at their local warehouse in little over an hour.

## Supply Chain and Distribution

Costco bought the majority of its merchandise directly from manufacturers, routing it either directly to its warehouse stores or to one of the company's cross-docking depots that served as distribution points for nearby stores. Depots received container-based shipments from manufacturers and reallocated these goods for combined shipment to individual warehouses, generally in less than 24 hours. This maximized freight volume and handling efficiencies. Going into 2012, Costco had 12 regional cross-docking depots in the United States, 4 such depots in Canada, and 4 depots at various other international locations, which had a combined space of 8.3 million square feet. When merchandise arrived at a warehouse, it was moved straight to the sales floor; very little was stored in locations off the sales floor in order to minimize receiving and handling costs.

Costco had direct buying relationships with many producers of national brand-name merchandise (including Canon, Casio, Coca-Cola, Colgate-Palmolive, Dell, Fuji, Hewlett-Packard, Kimberly-Clark, Kodak, Levi Strauss, Michelin, Nestlé, Panasonic, Procter & Gamble, Samsung, Sony, KitchenAid, and Jones of New York) and with manufacturers that supplied its Kirkland Signature products. No one manufacturer supplied a significant percentage of the merchandise that Costco stocked. Costco had not experienced difficulty in obtaining sufficient quantities of merchandise, and management believed that if one or more of its current sources of supply became unavailable, the company could switch its purchases to alternative manufacturers without experiencing a substantial disruption of its business.

Costco's merchandise buyers were always alert for opportunities to add products of top quality manufacturers and vendors. In fiscal 2011, the company established new relationships with Precor (a maker of premium fitness equipment), Cannon Gun Safes, Stanley Tools, Craftsman, Asics, Hartmann, Hurley (a popular maker of youth apparel and a Nike subsidiary), and Spanx (a well-known maker of body-slimming undergarments). Additionally, the company introduced a co-branded product with both the Kirkland Signature and the Cinnabon names on the package of cinnamon rolls sold in Costco bakeries; a co-branded turkey breast with Foster Farms; a new ready-to-drink green tea in partnership with Ito En, a leading Japanese food company; and finally, an assortment of canned soups that were co-branded with the Campbell Soup Company.

## Costco's Membership Base and Member Demographics

Costco attracted the most affluent customers in discount retailing—the average income of individual members was about $75,000, with over 30 percent of members having annual incomes of $100,000 or more. Many members were affluent urbanites, living in nice neighborhoods not far from Costco warehouses. One loyal Executive member, a criminal defense lawyer, said, "I think I spend over $20,000–$25,000 a year buying all my products here from food to clothing—except my suits. I have to buy them at the Armani stores."[13] Another Costco loyalist said, "This is the best place in the world. It's like going to church on Sunday. You can't get anything better than this. This is a religious experience."[14]

Costco had two primary types of memberships: Business and Gold Star (individual). Gold Star memberships were for individuals who did not qualify for a Business membership. Businesses—including individuals with a business license, retail sales license, or other evidence of business existence—qualified as Business members. Beginning in November 2011, business members in the United States and Canada paid an annual membership fee of $55 for the primary membership card, which also included a household membership card. These members could also purchase add-on membership cards for an annual fee of $55 each for partners or associates in the business. A significant number of business members also shopped at Costco for their personal needs.

Individuals in the United States and Canada who did not qualify for business membership could purchase a Gold Star membership for an annual fee of $55, which included a household card for another family member. In addition, both business and individual (Gold Star) members could upgrade to an Executive membership for an annual fee of $110. Executive members were entitled to an additional 2 percent savings on qualified purchases at Costco (redeemable at Costco warehouses), up to a maximum rebate of $750 per year. Executive members also were eligible for savings and benefits on various business and consumer services offered by Costco, including merchant credit card processing, small-business loans, auto and home insurance, long-distance telephone service, check printing, and real estate and mortgage services; these services were mostly offered by third-party providers and varied by state. In fiscal 2011, Executive members represented 38 percent of Costco's primary membership base and generally spent more than other members. Recent trends in membership are shown at the bottom of Exhibit 1. Members could shop at any Costco warehouse. Member renewal rates were about 89 percent in the U.S. and Canada, and approximately 86 percent on a worldwide basis.

Costco warehouses accepted cash, checks, most debit cards, American Express, and a private-label Costco credit card. Costco accepted merchandise returns when members were dissatisfied with their purchases. Losses associated with dishonored checks were minimal because any member whose check had been dishonored was prevented from paying by check or cashing a check at the point of sale until restitution was made. The membership format facilitated strictly controlling the entrances and exits of warehouses, resulting in limited inventory losses of less than two-tenths of 1 percent of net sales—well below those of typical discount retail operations.

## Warehouse Management

Costco warehouse managers were delegated considerable authority over store operations. In effect, warehouse managers functioned as entrepreneurs running their own retail operation. They were responsible for coming up with new ideas about what items would sell in their stores, effectively merchandising the ever-changing lineup of treasure-hunt products, and orchestrating in-store product locations and displays to maximize sales and quick turnover. In experimenting with what items to stock and what in-store merchandising techniques to employ, warehouse managers had to know the clientele who patronized their locations—for instance, big-ticket diamonds sold well at some warehouses but not at others. Costco's best managers kept their finger on the pulse of the members who shopped their warehouse location to stay in sync with what would sell well, and they had a flair for creating a certain element of excitement, hum, and buzz in their warehouses. Such managers spurred above-average sales volumes—sales at Costco's top-volume warehouses ran about $4 million to $7 million a week, with sales exceeding $1 million on many days. Successful managers also thrived on the rat race of running a high-traffic store and solving the inevitable crises of the moment.

## Compensation and Workforce Practices

In September 2011, Costco had 92,000 full-time employees and 72,000 part-time employees, including approximately 9,000 people employed by Costco Mexico, whose operations were not consolidated in Costco's financial and operating results. Approximately 13,600 hourly employees at locations in California, Maryland, New Jersey, and New York, as well as at one warehouse in Virginia, were represented by the International Brotherhood of Teamsters. All remaining employees were non-union.

Starting wages for new Costco employees were in the $10–$12 range in 2011; hourly pay scales for warehouse jobs ranged from $12 to $23, depending on the type of job. Salaried employees in Costco warehouses could earn anywhere from $30,000 to $125,000 annually.[15] For example, salaries for merchandise managers were in the $58,000 to $68,000 range; salaries for supervisors ranged from $45,000 to $73,000; and salaries for general managers of warehouses were in the $90,000 to $125,000 range. Employees enjoyed the full spectrum of benefits. Salaried employees were eligible for benefits on the first of the month after the date of hire. Full-time hourly employees were eligible for benefits starting the first of the month after working a probationary 90 days; part-time hourly employees became benefit-eligible on the first of the month after working 180 days. The benefit package included the following:

- Health and dental care plans. Full-time employees could choose from two different health care plans (a freedom-of-choice health care plan and a choice-plus plan) and two dental plans (a core dental plan and a premium dental plan). A choice-plus health care and a core dental plan were available for part-time employees.

- Convenient prescription pickup at Costco's pharmacies, with co-payments of $3 for generic drugs and 15 percent for brand-name drugs, subject to a minimum co-pay of $10 for brand-name drugs and a maximum co-pay of $50.

- A vision program that paid up to $60 for a refraction eye exam (the amount charged at Costco's optical centers) and had $150 annual allowances for the purchase of glasses and contact lenses at Costco Optical departments or $100 annual allowances if purchased elsewhere.

- A 401(k) plan in which Costco matched hourly employee contributions by 50 cents on the dollar for the first $1,000 annually to a maximum company match of $500 per year. Eligible employees qualified for additional company contributions based on the employee's years of service and eligible earnings. The company's union employees on the West Coast qualified for matching contributions of 50 cents on the dollar to a maximum company match of $250 a year; eligible union employees qualified for additional company contributions based on straight-time hours worked. Company contributions to employee 410(k) plans were $287 million in fiscal 2009, $313 million in fiscal 2010, and $345 million in fiscal 2011.

- A dependent care reimbursement plan in which Costco employees whose families qualified could pay for day care for children under 13 or adult day care with pretax dollars and realize savings of anywhere from $750 to $2,000 per year.

- Confidential professional counseling services.

- Company-paid long-term disability coverage equal to 60 percent of earnings if out for more than 180 days on a non–worker's compensation leave of absence.

- All employees who passed their 90-day probation period and were working at least 10 hours per week were automatically enrolled in a short-term disability plan covering non-work-related injuries or illnesses for up to 26 weeks. Weekly short-term disability payments equaled 60 percent of average weekly wages up to a maximum of $1,000.

- Generous life insurance and accidental death and dismemberment coverage, with benefits based on years of service and whether the employee worked full-time or part-time. Employees could elect to purchase supplemental coverage for themselves, their spouses, or their children.

- An employee stock purchase plan allowing all employees to buy Costco stock via payroll deduction so as to avoid commissions and fees.

- A health care reimbursement plan in which benefit eligible employees could arrange to have pretax money automatically deducted from their paychecks and deposited in a health care reimbursement account that could be used to pay medical and dental bills.

- A long-term care insurance plan for employees with 10 or more years of service. Eligible employees could purchase a basic or supplemental policy for nursing home care for themselves, their spouses, or their parents (including in-laws) or grandparents (including in-laws).

Although admitting that paying good wages and good benefits was contrary to conventional wisdom in discount retailing, Jim Sinegal was convinced that having a well-compensated workforce was very important to executing Costco's strategy successfully. He said, "Imagine that you have 120,000 loyal ambassadors out there who are constantly saying good things about Costco. It has to be a significant advantage for you. . . . Paying good wages and keeping your people working with you is very good business."[16] When a reporter asked him about why Costco treated its workers so well compared to other retailers (particularly Walmart, which paid lower wages and had a skimpier benefits package), Sinegal replied: "Why shouldn't employees have the right to good wages and good careers. . . . It absolutely makes good business sense. Most people agree that we're the lowest-cost producer. Yet we pay the highest wages. So it must mean we get better productivity. Its axiomatic in our business—you get what you pay for."[17]

Good wages and benefits were said to be why employee turnover at Costco typically ran under 6 to 7 percent after the first year of employment. Some Costco employees had been with the company since its founding in 1983. Many others had started working part-time at Costco while in high school or college and opted to make a career at the company. One Costco employee told an ABC *20/20* reporter, "It's a good place to work; they take good care of us."[18] A Costco vice president and head baker said working for Costco was a family affair: "My whole family works for Costco, my husband does, my daughter does, my new son-in-law does."[19] Another employee, a receiving clerk who made about $40,000 a year, said, "I want to retire here. I love it here."[20] An employee with over two years of service could not be fired without the approval of a senior company officer.

## Selecting People for Open Positions

Costco's top management wanted employees to feel that they could have a long career at Costco. It was company policy to fill the vast majority of its higher-level openings by promotions from within; at one recent point, the percentage ran close to 98 percent, which meant that the majority of Costco's management team members (including warehouse, merchandise, administrative, membership, front end, and receiving managers) had come up through the ranks. Many of the company's vice presidents had started in entry-level jobs. According to Jim Sinegal, "We have guys who started pushing shopping carts out on the parking lot for us who are now vice presidents of our company."[21] Costco made a point of recruiting at local universities; Sinegal explained why: "These people are smarter than the average person, hardworking, and they haven't made a career choice."[22] On another occasion, he said, "If someone came to us and said he just got a master's in business at Harvard, we would say fine, would you like to start pushing carts."[23] Those employees who demonstrated smarts and strong people management skills moved up through the ranks.

But without an aptitude for the details of discount retailing, even up-and-coming employees stood no chance of being promoted to a position of warehouse manager. Sinegal and other top Costco executives who oversaw warehouse operations insisted that candidates for warehouse managers be top-flight merchandisers with a gift for the details of making items fly off the shelves. Sinegal said, "People who have a feel for it just start to get it. Others, you look at them and it's like staring at a blank canvas. I'm not trying to be unduly harsh, but that's the way it works."[24] Most newly appointed warehouse managers at Costco came from the ranks of assistant warehouse managers who had a track record of being shrewd merchandisers and tuned into what new or different products might sell well given the clientele that patronized their particular warehouse. Just having the requisite skills in people management, crisis management, and cost-effective warehouse operations was not enough.

**Executive Compensation** Executives at Costco did not earn the outlandish salaries that had become customary over the past decade at most large corporations. In fiscal 2011, both Jeff Brotman and Jim Sinegal each received a salary of $350,000 and a bonus of $198,400 (as compared to salaries of $350,000 and bonuses of $190,400 in fiscal 2010).

As of late 2011, Brotman owned or had exercisable options for about 550,000 shares of Costco stock; Sinegal owned or had exercisable options for 2.35 million shares of Costco stock. Craig Jelinek's salary as President and Chief Operating Officer in fiscal 2011 was 649,999, and he received a bonus of $99,200. Other high-paid officers at Costco received salaries in the $575,000–$645,000 range and bonuses of $79,000–$89,000. Sinegal explained why executive compensation at Costco was only a fraction of the amounts typically paid to top-level executives at other corporations with annual sales of $75 billion to $90 billion: "I figured that if I was making something like 12 times more than the typical person working on the floor, that that was a fair salary."[25] To another reporter, he said: "Listen, I'm one of the founders of this business. I've been very well rewarded. I don't require a salary that's 100 times more than the people who work on the sales floor."[26] Sinegal's employment contract was only a page long and provided that he could be terminated for cause.

## Costco's Business Philosophy, Values, and Code of Ethics

Jim Sinegal, who was the son of a steelworker, had ingrained five simple and down-to-earth business principles into Costco's corporate culture and the manner in which the company operated. The following are excerpts of these principles and operating approaches:[27]

1. **Obey the law**—The law is irrefutable! Absent a moral imperative to challenge a law, we must conduct our business in total compliance with the laws of every community where we do business. We pledge to:

   - Comply with all laws and other legal requirements.
   - Respect all public officials and their positions.
   - Comply with safety and security standards for all products sold.
   - Exceed ecological standards required in every community where we do business.
   - Comply with all applicable wage and hour laws.
   - Comply with all applicable antitrust laws.
   - Conduct business in and with foreign countries in a manner that is legal and proper under United States and foreign laws.

- Not offer, give, ask for, or receive any form of bribe or kickback to or from any person or pay to expedite government action or otherwise act in violation of the Foreign Corrupt Practices Act or the laws of other countries.
- Promote fair, accurate, timely, and understandable disclosure in reports filed with the Securities and Exchange Commission and in other public communications by the Company.

2. **Take care of our members**—Costco membership is open to business owners, as well as individuals. Our members are our reason for being—the key to our success. If we don't keep our members happy, little else that we do will make a difference. There are plenty of shopping alternatives for our members, and if they fail to show up, we cannot survive. Our members have extended a trust to Costco by virtue of paying a fee to shop with us. We will succeed only if we do not violate the trust they have extended to us, and that trust extends to every area of our business. We pledge to:

- Provide top-quality products at the best prices in the market.
- Provide high-quality, safe, and wholesome food products by requiring that both vendors and employees be in compliance with the highest food safety standards in the industry.
- Provide our members with a 100 percent satisfaction guaranteed warranty on every product and service we sell, including their membership fee.
- Assure our members that every product we sell is authentic in make and in representation of performance.
- Make our shopping environment a pleasant experience by making our members feel welcome as our guests.
- Provide products to our members that will be ecologically sensitive.
- Provide our members with the best customer service in the retail industry.
- Give back to our communities through employee volunteerism and employee and corporate contributions to United Way and Children's Hospitals.

3. **Take care of our employees**—Our employees are our most important asset. We believe we have the very best employees in the warehouse club industry, and we are committed to providing them with

rewarding challenges and ample opportunities for personal and career growth. We pledge to provide our employees with:

- Competitive wages.
- Great benefits.
- A safe and healthy work environment.
- Challenging and fun work.
- Career opportunities.
- An atmosphere free from harassment or discrimination.
- An Open Door Policy that allows access to ascending levels of management to resolve issues.
- Opportunities to give back to their communities through volunteerism and fundraising.

4. **Respect our suppliers**—Our suppliers are our partners in business and for us to prosper as a company, they must prosper with us. To that end, we strive to:

- Treat all suppliers and their representatives as we would expect to be treated if visiting their places of business.
- Honor all commitments.
- Protect all suppliers' property assigned to Costco as though it were our own.
- Not accept gratuities of any kind from a supplier.
- Avoid actual or apparent conflicts of interest, including creating a business in competition with the Company or working for or on behalf of another employer in competition with the Company.
- If in doubt as to what course of action to take on a business matter that is open to varying ethical interpretations, TAKE THE HIGH ROAD AND DO WHAT IS RIGHT.

If we do these four things throughout our organization, then we will achieve our ultimate goal, which is to:

5. **Reward our shareholders**—As a company with stock that is traded publicly on the NASDAQ stock exchange, our shareholders are our business partners. We can only be successful so long as we are providing them with a good return on the money they invest in our company. . . . We pledge to operate our company in such a way that our present and future stockholders, as well as our employees, will be rewarded for our efforts.

## Environmental Sustainability

In recent years, Costco management had undertaken several initiatives to reduce the company's carbon footprint by investing in various environmental and energy saving systems. Going into 2012, Costco had rooftop solar photovoltaic systems in operation at 60 of its facilities, which were projected to generate 55 million kWh of electricity per year. Costco's metal warehouse design, one of several warehouse design styles the company had utilized over the past several years, was consistent with the requirements of the Silver Level LEED Standard—the certification standards of the organization Leadership in Energy and Environmental Design (LEED) were nationally accepted as a benchmark green building design and construction. Costco's metal building envelopes were all insulated to meet or exceed current energy code requirements, and the main building structure used 100 percent recycled steel material. The roof materials used on Costco metal pre-engineered warehouses were 100 percent recycled standing seam metal panels, designed to maximize efficiency for spanning the structure; and the exterior skin of the building was also 100 percent recycled metal.

Costco was continuing to expand the use of non-chemical water treatment systems used in warehouse cooling towers to reduce the amount of chemicals going into sewer systems. In addition, the tons of trash that warehouses generated each week, much of which was once sent to landfills, was being recycled into usable products. Grease recovery systems had been installed in 257 warehouses, resulting in the recovery of more than four million pounds of grease from the waste stream.

Costco had been an active member of the Environmental Protection Agency's Energy Star and Climate Protection Partnerships since 2002 and was a major retailer of Energy Star qualified compact florescent lamp (CFL) bulbs. Costco sold more than 35 million energy-saving CFL bulbs and 9 million LED light bulbs in the U.S. during 2011; since 2005, Costco had sold over 204 million energy-saving light bulbs.

## COMPETITION

The wholesale club and warehouse segment of retailing in North America was a $155 billion business in 2011, and it was growing 15–20 percent faster than retailing as a whole. There were three main competitors—Costco Wholesale, Sam's Club, and BJ's Wholesale Club. In early 2012, there were about 1,400 warehouse locations across the United States and Canada; most every major metropolitan area had one, if not several, warehouse clubs. Costco had just over a 57 percent share of warehouse club sales across the United States and Canada, with Sam's Club (a division of Walmart) having roughly a 35 percent share and BJ's Wholesale Club and several small warehouse club competitors about an 8 percent share.

Competition among the warehouse clubs was based on such factors as price, merchandise quality and selection, location, and member service. However, warehouse clubs also competed with a wide range of other types of retailers, including retail discounters like Walmart and Dollar General, supermarkets, general merchandise chains, specialty chains, gasoline stations, and Internet retailers. Not only did Walmart, the world's largest retailer, compete directly with Costco via its Sam's Club subsidiary, but its Walmart Supercenters sold many of the same types of merchandise at attractively low prices as well. Target, Kohl's, and Amazon.com had emerged as significant retail competitors in certain general merchandise categories. Low-cost operators selling a single category or narrow range of merchandise—such as Trader Joe's, Lowe's, Home Depot, Office Depot, Staples, Best Buy, Circuit City, PetSmart, and Barnes & Noble—had significant market share in their respective product categories. Notwithstanding the competition from other retailers and discounters, the low prices and merchandise selection found at Costco, Sam's Club, and BJ's Wholesale were attractive to small business owners, individual households (particularly bargain-hunters and those with large families), churches and non-profit organizations, caterers, and small restaurants. The internationally located warehouses faced similar types of competitors.

Brief profiles of Costco's two primary competitors in North America are presented in the following sections.

## Sam's Club

The first Sam's Club opened in 1984, and Walmart management in the ensuing years proceeded to grow the warehouse membership club concept into a significant business and major Walmart division. The concept of the Sam's Club format was to sell merchandise at very low profit margins, resulting in low prices to members. The mission of Sam's Club was "to make savings simple for members by providing them with exciting, quality merchandise and a superior shopping experience, all at a great value."[28]

In early 2012, there were 611 Sam's Club locations in the United States with 49 million members and record-high fiscal 2012 sales of $53.8 billion; many Sam's Club locations in the United States were adjacent to Walmart Supercenters. There were an additional 140 Sam's Club locations in Mexico, Brazil, and China, and plans called for Sam's Club to open 10 to 15 additional locations by January 2013. Sam's Clubs ranged between 70,000 and 190,000 square feet, with the average being about 133,000 square feet.

All Sam's Club warehouses had concrete floors, sparse décor, and goods displayed on pallets, simple wooden shelves, or racks in the case of apparel. In 2009–2010, Sam's Club began a long-term warehouse remodeling program; 52 remodels were completed in 2009 and about 70 more remodels were completed in 2010. Additional remodels were undertaken in fiscal years 2011 and 2012, with more scheduled for fiscal year 2013.

Exhibit 5 provides financial and operating highlights for selected years during 2001–2012.

## Merchandise Offerings

Sam's Club warehouses stocked about 4,000 items, a big fraction of which were standard and a small fraction of which represented special buys and one-time offerings. The treasure-hunt items at Sam's Club tended to be less upscale and carry lower price tags than those at Costco. The merchandise selection included brand-name merchandise in a variety of categories: canned goods, cereals, spices, packaged foods, paper products, detergents and cleaning supplies, health and wellness, apparel, electronics, software, small appliances, DVDs, books and games, jewelry, sporting goods, toys, tires and batteries, office supplies, restaurant supplies, institutional foods, and a selection of private-label items sold under the "Member's Mark,"

"Bakers & Chefs," and "Sam's Club" brands. Most club locations had fresh-foods departments that included bakery, meat, produce, floral products, and a Sam's Café. A significant number of clubs had a one-hour photo processing department, a pharmacy that filled prescriptions, an optical department, and self-service gasoline pumps. Sam's Club guaranteed it would beat any price for branded prescriptions. In 2010, Sam's Club pharmacies received the highest score in the Prescription Ordering and Pickup Process factor in a J.D. Power and Associates study. Members could shop for a wider assortment of merchandise and services online at www.samsclub.com. The percentage composition of sales across major merchandise categories is shown in the table at the bottom of this page.

In February 2012, there were media reports that Apple and Sam's Club were exploring the expansion of Apple's presence at as many as 50 Sam's Club locations. It was as yet unclear whether the expansion would take the form of a mini-Apple store in the electronics section of a Sam's Club warehouse or whether the partnership would just entail expanding the lineup of iPhones, iPods, and iPads that Sam's Club already had to include selected Mac computer models. In December 2010, Apple and Costco agreed that Apple products would no longer be sold at Costco, due (in part) to a restriction that kept Costco from being able to sell Apple's products online.

### Membership and Hours of Operation

The annual fee for Sam's Club business members was $35 for the primary membership card, with a spouse card available at no additional cost. Business members could add up to eight business associates for $35 each. The annual membership fee for an individual

| Merchandise Category | Fiscal Year Ending January 31 | | |
| --- | --- | --- | --- |
| | 2012 | 2011 | 2010 |
| Grocery and consumables (dairy, meat, bakery, deli, produce, dry, chilled or frozen packaged foods, alcoholic and nonalcoholic beverages, floral, snack foods, candy, other grocery items, health and beauty aids, paper goods, laundry and home care, baby care, pet supplies, and other consumable items and grocery items) | 55% | 55% | 56% |
| Fuel and other categories (tobacco, snack foods, tools and power equipment, sales of gasoline, and tire and battery centers) | 24% | 23% | 21% |
| Technology, office and entertainment (electronics, wireless, software, video games, movies, books, music, toys, office supplies, office furniture and photo processing) | 8% | 9% | 10% |
| Home and apparel (home improvement, outdoor living, grills, gardening, furniture, apparel, jewelry, house wares, seasonal items, mattresses, and small appliances) | 8% | 8% | 8% |
| Health and wellness (pharmacy and optical services, and over-the-counter drugs) | 5% | 5% | 5% |

**EXHIBIT 5**  Selected Financial and Operating Data for Sam's Club, Fiscal
Years 2001–2012

| Sam's Club | Fiscal Years Ending January 31 | | | | | | |
|---|---|---|---|---|---|---|---|
| | 2012 | 2011 | 2010 | 2009 | 2008 | 2007 | 2001 |
| Sales in U.S.[a] (millions of $) | $53,795 | $49,459 | $47,806 | $47,976 | $44,336 | $41,582 | $26,798 |
| Operating income in U.S. (millions of $) | 1,865 | 1,711 | 1,515 | 1,649 | 1,648 | 1,480 | 942 |
| Assets in U.S.(millions of $) | 12,823 | 12,531 | 12,073 | 12,388 | 11,722 | 11,448 | 3,843 |
| Number of locations at year-end | ~751 | ~746 | 729 | 727 | 713 | 693 | 564 |
| U.S. | 611 | 609 | 605 | 611 | 600 | 588 | 475 |
| International (Mexico, Brazil, and China) | ~140 | ~137 | 133 | 125 | 122 | 114 | 64 |
| Average sales per U.S. location (in millions of $) | $88.0 | $81.2 | $79.0 | $78.5 | $73.9 | $70.7 | $56.4 |
| Sales growth at existing U.S. warehouses open more than 12 months: | | | | | | | |
| Including gasoline sales | 8.4% | 3.7% | −1.4% | 4.9% | 4.9% | 2.5% | n.a. |
| Not including gasoline sales | 5.2% | 1.7% | 0.7% | 3.7% | 4.2% | 2.9% | n.a. |
| Average warehouse size in U.S. (square feet) | 133,000 | 133,000 | 133,000 | 133,000 | 132,000 | 132,000 | 122,100 |

[a]The sales figure includes membership fees and is for United States warehouses only. For financial reporting purposes, Walmart consolidates the operations of all foreign-based stores into a single "international" segment figure. Thus, separate financial information for only the foreign-based Sam's Club locations in Mexico, China, and Brazil is not separately available.

*Source:* Walmart's 10-K reports and annual reports, fiscal years 2012, 2011, 2010, 2008, and 2001.

Advantage member was $40, which included a spouse card. A Sam's Club Plus premium membership cost $100 and included health care insurance, merchant credit card processing, website operation, personal and financial services, and an auto, boat, and recreational vehicle program. When combined with a Sam's Club Discover card, Plus members could earn up to 2 percent cash back on a variety of purchases.

Regular hours of operations were Monday through Friday from 10:00 a.m. to 8:30 p.m., Saturday from 9:00 a.m. to 8:30 p.m., and Sunday from 10:00 a.m. to 6:00 p.m. All club locations offered a Gold Key program that permitted business members and Plus members to shop before the regular operating hours Monday through Saturday, starting at 7:00 a.m. All club members could use a variety of payment methods, including debit cards, certain types of credit cards, and a private label and co-branded Discover credit cards issued by a third-party provider. The pharmacy and optical departments accepted payments for products and services through members' health benefit plans.

**Distribution**  Approximately 65 percent of the non-fuel merchandise at Sam's Club was shipped from some 25 distribution facilities dedicated to Sam's Club operations that were strategically located across the continental United States, and in the case of perishable items, from nearby Walmart grocery distribution centers; the balance was shipped by suppliers direct to Sam's Club locations. Of these 25 distribution facilities, 8 were owned and operated by Sam's Club and 17 were owned and operated by third parties. Like Costco, Sam's Club distribution centers employed cross-docking techniques whereby incoming shipments were transferred immediately to outgoing trailers destined for Sam's Club locations; shipments typically spent less than 24 hours at a cross-docking facility and in some instances were there only an hour. In 2012, the Sam's Club distribution center network consisted of 8 company-owned-and-operated distribution facilities and 17 third-party-owned-and-operated facilities. A combination of company-owned trucks and independent trucking companies were used to transport merchandise from distribution centers to club locations.

**Employment**   In 2011, Sam's Club employed more than 100,000 people across all aspects of its operations in the United States. While the people who worked at Sam's Club warehouses were in all stages of life, a sizable fraction had accepted job offers because they had minimal skill levels and were looking for their first job, or needed only a part-time job, or were wanting to start a second career. More than 60 percent of managers of Sam's Club warehouses had begun their careers at Sam's as hourly warehouse employees and had moved up through the ranks to their present positions.

## BJ's Wholesale Club

BJ's Wholesale Club introduced the member warehouse concept to the northeastern United States in the mid-1980s and, as of mid-2011, had a total of 195 warehouses in 15 eastern states extending from Maine to Florida—173 of these facilities were full-sized warehouse clubs that averaged about 114,000 square feet and 22 smaller format warehouse clubs that averaged approximately 73,000 square feet and were located in markets too small to support a full-sized warehouse. Approximately 85 percent of BJ's full-sized warehouse clubs had at least one Costco or Sam's Club warehouse operating in their trading areas (within a distance of ten miles or less). Only one of the smaller BJ's clubs faced competition from a Costco or Sam's Club located within 10 miles it. In late June 2011, BJ's Wholesale agreed to a buyout offer from two private equity firms and shortly thereafter became a privately held company. Exhibit 6 shows selected financial and operating data for BJ's for fiscal years 2007 though 2011.

### Product Offerings and Merchandising
Like Costco and Sam's, BJ's Wholesale sold high-quality, brand-name merchandise at prices that were significantly lower than the prices found at supermarkets, discount retail chains, department stores, drugstores, and specialty retail stores like Best Buy. Its merchandise lineup of about 7,000 items included consumer electronics, prerecorded media, small appliances, tires, jewelry, health and beauty aids, household products, computer software, books, greeting cards, apparel, furniture, toys, seasonal items, frozen foods, fresh meat and dairy products, beverages, dry grocery items, fresh produce, flowers, canned goods, and household products. About 70 percent of BJ's product line could be found in supermarkets. Food and household paper products categories accounted for approximately 66 percent of merchandise sales in 2010.

The remaining 34 percent consisted of a wide variety of general merchandise items. BJ's private brand products were primarily premium quality and generally were priced below the top branded competing product. In recent years, BJ's had pruned its private label offerings by about 12 percent, opting to focus on those items having the highest margins and biggest sales volumes. Private label goods accounted for approximately 10 percent of food and general merchandise sales in both 2009 and 2010, versus 11 percent in 2008 and 13 percent in 2007. Members could purchase thousands of additional products at the company's website, www.bjs.com.

BJ's warehouses had a number of specialty services that were designed to enable members to complete more of their shopping at BJ's and to encourage more frequent trips to the clubs. Like Costco, BJ's sold gasoline at a discounted price as a means of displaying a favorable price image to prospective members and providing added value to existing members; in 2012, there were gas station operations at 107 BJ's locations. Other specialty services included full-service optical centers (more than 150 locations), food courts, full-service Verizon Wireless centers, vacation and travel packages, garden and storage sheds, patios and sunrooms, a propane tank filling service, an automobile buying service, a car rental service, muffler and brake services operated in conjunction with Monro Muffler Brake, and electronics and jewelry protection plans. Most of these services were provided by outside operators in space leased from BJ's. In early 2007, BJ's abandoned prescription filling and closed all of its 46 in-club pharmacies.

### Strategy Features that Differentiated BJ's
BJ's had developed a strategy and operating model that management believed differentiated the company from Costco and Sam's Club:

- Offering a wide range of choice—7,000 items versus 3,600 to 4,000 items at Costco and Sam's Club.

- Focusing on the individual consumer via merchandising strategies that emphasized a customer-friendly shopping experience.

- Clustering club locations to achieve the benefit of name recognition and maximize the efficiencies of management support, distribution, and marketing activities.

- Trying to establish and maintain the first or second industry leading position in each major market where it operated.

## EXHIBIT 6    Selected Financial and Operating Data, BJ's Wholesale Club, Fiscal Years 2007 thru 2011

| | Jan. 29 2011 | Jan. 30 2010 | Jan. 31 2009 | Feb. 2 2008 | Feb. 3 2007 (53 weeks) |
|---|---|---|---|---|---|
| **Selected Income Statement Data (in millions, except per share data)** | | | | | |
| Net sales | $10,633 | $9,954 | $9,802 | $8,792 | $8,280 |
| Membership fees | 191 | 182 | 178 | 176 | 162 |
| Other revenues | 53 | 51 | 48 | 47 | 54 |
| Total revenues | 10,877 | 10,187 | 10,027 | 9,014 | 8,497 |
| Cost of sales, including buying and occupancy costs | 9,697 | 9,081 | 9,004 | 8,091 | 7,601 |
| Selling, general and administrative expenses | 934 | 875 | 799 | 724 | 740 |
| Operating income | 208 | 224 | 221 | 195 | 144 |
| Net income | $   95 | $  132 | $  135 | $  123 | $   72 |
| Diluted earnings per share: | $1.77 | $2.42 | $2.28 | $1.90 | $1.08 |
| **Balance Sheet and Cash Flow Data (in millions)** | | | | | |
| Cash and cash equivalents | $  101 | $   59 | $   51 | $   97 | $   56 |
| Current assets | 1,292 | 1,173 | 1,076 | 1,145 | 1,070 |
| Current liabilities | 987 | 1,006 | 909 | 946 | 867 |
| Working capital | 305 | 167 | 167 | 199 | 203 |
| Merchandise inventories | 981 | 930 | 860 | 877 | 851 |
| Total assets | 2,322 | 2,166 | 2,021 | 2,047 | 1,993 |
| Long-term debt | — | 1 | 1 | 2 | 2 |
| Stockholders' equity | 1,144 | 1,033 | 985 | 980 | 1,020 |
| Cash flow from operations | 229 | 298 | 224 | 305 | 173 |
| Capital expenditures | 188 | 176 | 138 | 90 | 191 |
| **Selected Operating Data** | | | | | |
| Clubs open at end of year | 189 | 187 | 180 | 177 | 172 |
| Number of members (in thousands) | 9,600 | 9,400 | 9,000 | 8,800 | 8,700 |
| Average sales per club location (in millions) | $56.3 | $53.2 | $54.6 | $49.7 | $48.1 |
| Sales growth at existing clubs open more than 12 months | 4.4% | −1.9% | 9.4% | 3.7% | 1.2% |

*Source:* Company 10-K reports for 2011, 2010, 2008, and 2007.

- Creating an exciting shopping experience for members with a constantly changing mix of food and general merchandise items and carrying a broader product assortment than competitors.

- Supplementing the warehouse format with aisle markers, express checkout lanes, self-checkout lanes and low-cost video-based sales aids to make shopping more efficient for members.

- Being open longer hours than competitors; typical hours of operation were 9 a.m. to 7 p.m. Monday through Friday and 9 a.m. to 6 p.m. Saturday and Sunday.

- Offering smaller package sizes of many items.

- Accepting manufacturers' coupons.
- Accepting more credit card payment options.

**Membership**    BJ's Wholesale Club had about 9.6 million members in 2011 (see Exhibit 6). It charged $50 per year for a primary Inner Circle membership that included one free supplemental membership; members in the same household could purchase additional supplemental memberships for $25 each. A business membership also cost $50 per year, which included one free supplemental membership and the ability to purchase additional supplemental memberships for $25. BJ's launched a membership rewards program in 2003 that offered members a 2 percent rebate, capped at $500 per year, on most all in-club purchases; members who paid the $100 annual fee to enroll in the rewards program accounted for 7.8 percent of primary members and about 17 percent of total merchandise and food sales in early 2011. Purchases with a co-branded BJ's Visa earned a 1.5 percent rebate. BJ's accepted MasterCard, Visa, Discover, and American Express cards at all locations; members could also pay for purchases by cash, check, and debit cards. BJ's accepted returns of most merchandise within 30 days after purchase.

**Marketing and Promotion**   BJ's increased customer awareness of its clubs primarily through direct mail, public relations efforts, marketing programs for newly opened clubs, and a publication called *BJ's Journal,* which was mailed to members throughout the year. During the holiday season, BJ's engaged in radio and TV advertising, a portion of which was funded by vendors.

**Warehouse Club Operations**   BJ's warehouses were located in both free-standing locations and shopping centers. Construction and site development costs for a full-sized owned BJ's club were in the $6 million to $10 million range; land acquisition costs ranged from $3 million to $10 million but could be significantly higher in some locations. Each warehouse generally had an investment of $3 to $4 million for fixtures and equipment. Pre-opening

expenses at a new club ran $1.0 to $2.0 million. Including space for parking, a typical full-sized BJ's club required 13 to 14 acres of land; smaller clubs typically required about 8 acres. During recent years, the company had financed all of its club expansions, as well as all other capital expenditures, with internally generated funds.

Merchandise purchased from manufacturers was routed either to a BJ's cross-docking facility or directly to clubs. Personnel at the cross-docking facilities broke down truckload quantity shipments from manufacturers and reallocated goods for shipment to individual clubs, generally within 24 hours. BJ's worked closely with manufacturers to minimize the amount of handling required once merchandise is received at a club. Merchandise was generally displayed on pallets containing large quantities of each item, thereby reducing labor required for handling, stocking, and restocking. Backup merchandise was generally stored in steel racks above the sales floor. Most merchandise was pre-marked by the manufacturer so it did not require ticketing at the club. Full-sized clubs had approximately $2 million in inventory. Management had been able to limit inventory shrinkage to no more than 0.20 percent of net sales in each of the last three fiscal years (a percentage well below those of other types of retailers) by strictly controlling the exits of clubs, by generally limiting customers to members, and by using state-of-the-art electronic article surveillance technology.

## ENDNOTES

[1] As quoted in Alan B. Goldberg and Bill Ritter, "Costco CEO Finds Pro-Worker Means Profitability," an ABC News original report on *20/20,* August 2, 2006, http://abcnews.go.com/2020/Business/story?id=1362779 (accessed November 15, 2006).

[2] Ibid.

[3] As described in Nina Shapiro, "Company for the People," *Seattle Weekly,* December 15, 2004, www.seattleweekly.com (accessed November 14, 2006).

[4] See, for example, Costco's "Code of Ethics," posted in the investor relations section of Costco's website under a link entitled "Corporate Governance and Citizenship," accessed by the case author on February 24, 2012.

[5] Costco Wholesale, 2011 Annual Report for the year ended August 28, 2011, p. 5.

[6] As quoted in ibid., pp. 128–29.

[7] Steven Greenhouse, "How Costco Became the Anti-Wal-Mart," *The New York Times,* July

17, 2005, www.wakeupwalmart.com/news (accessed November 28, 2006).

[8] As quoted in Greenhouse, "How Costco Became the Anti-Wal-Mart."

[9] As quoted in Shapiro, "Company for the People."

[10] As quoted in Greenhouse, "How Costco Became the Anti-Wal-Mart."

[11] Boyle, "Why Costco Is So Damn Addictive," p. 132.

[12] Costco's 2005 Annual Report.

[13] As quoted in Goldberg and Ritter, "Costco CEO Finds Pro-Worker Means Profitability."

[14] Ibid.

[15] Based on information posted at www.glassdoor.com, accessed February 28, 2012.

[16] Ibid.

[17] Shapiro, "Company for the People."

[18] As quoted in Goldberg and Ritter, "Costco CEO Finds Pro-Worker Means Profitability."

[19] Ibid.

[20] As quoted in Greenhouse, "How Costco Became the Anti-Wal-Mart."

[21] As quoted in Goldberg and Ritter, "Costco CEO Finds Pro-Worker Means Profitability."

[22] Boyle, "Why Costco Is So Damn Addictive," p. 132.

[23] As quoted in Shapiro, "Company for the People."

[24] Ibid.

[25] As quoted in Goldberg and Ritter, "Costco CEO Finds Pro-Worker Means Profitability."

[26] As quoted in Shapiro, "Company for the People."

[27] Costco Code of Ethics, posted in the investor relations section of Costco's website, accessed March 1, 2012.

[28] Walmart 2010 Annual Report, p. 8.

# Harry Lindsol's Textbook Decision: An Ebook or a Traditional College Textbook

## A. J. Strickland
The University of Alabama

## Samantha Lindsay
The University of Alabama,
2012 MBA Student

In early 2012, professor Harry Lindsol noticed a trend. He saw that the Internet had taken over the way Americans purchased music, clothes, shoes, and more. No longer did people call a ticket office to purchase tickets to a concert or ball game—instead, they went to a ticket website. People researched important purchases (e.g., for computers) online for days or weeks, and then had them shipped to their homes. When he saw Amazon begin to edge out brick-and-mortar competitors like Barnes & Noble and local bookstores, he waited for the inevitable takeover of other book retailers in his local town, which was home to a university. He expected that online marketers such as Amazon would make the local college bookstore obsolete. However, as of late 2011, this had still not occurred, and Dr. Lindsol began to wonder why.

He found that while students were indeed purchasing some textbooks online, they often found it just as convenient to go to the local store and purchase all their books in one location without having to wait on shipping times. In addition, he found that students could sell those textbooks back to the store after their classes were finished. During his time observing students' purchasing habits, one significant trend emerged: Students were constantly connected to the Internet. They owned smartphones and carried laptops in their backpacks. Many also had devices known as ereaders, or electronic tablets that could hold many books for the purpose of leisure reading. Given this, Dr. Lindsol recognized an opportunity. If students' textbooks were available on their computers and ereaders, would an online company be able to beat out the local bookstores? Lindsol decided to analyze the textbook industry (from both the retailing and

publishing sides) to see if it would be feasible to create a publishing company that sold only etextbooks.

## PUBLISHERS: THE BUSINESS MODEL

Only a few companies in the United States are involved in large-scale textbook publishing. These companies, like McGraw-Hill and Pearson, have been in the industry for many years and have deep pockets. Lindsol knew that beating these industry giants would be a difficult task. Lindsol decided that if he opted to create his own company to compete against them, he needed to understand their business model.

An important part of the textbook publishers' business model was the use of acquisition editors who recruited professors to write textbooks for their publishing company. The acquisition editors were charged with identifying prospective authors who would write textbooks that would have broad market appeal and signing them to contracts. These editors were compensated based on the authors and textbooks they brought in to the company, similar to a commission-based pay system. In addition, there were incentives for acquisition editors based on the success of the textbooks—the better the textbook's sales, the bigger bonus they would receive. Before the advent of the Internet, textbook publishing companies had two main ways to convince college professors to use their textbooks—the books themselves and their book representatives. Companies relied on their representatives to make contact with professors and publicize their textbooks. For example, a representative would call a professor of marketing and offer to take him/her to lunch to discuss the merits of his company's marketing textbook versus the marketing texts of rival publishers. Professors typically adopted whichever one of the available textbooks for their course that appealed to him/her most. It was not uncommon for a professor to choose a book simply because it came from the publisher with whom he normally dealt. On other occasions, professors would choose a less expensive book so their students had to pay less money. However, on many occasions after committing to a textbook, professors would discover that they did not like the book for various reasons—some of the material was outdated, there was not enough information covered, only half of the book was relevant to the course, and so on.

The representative business model was heavily cost-intensive for publishing companies since they had to pay for the salaries of the sales representatives as well as any travel expenses, plus the cost of entertaining professors. In addition, it was not necessarily the best way to market textbooks. The majority of the success of a publisher depended on which company had the better authors and titles, along with professors' personal preferences for certain representatives. This business model had been very successful for 40 years. However, in light of ever-advancing technology, some publishers realized that it was possible to differentiate themselves from the competition.

## THE PLATFORM

 When the Internet became more popular among students, publishers began making PDF versions of their textbooks available online. However, these versions never became very popular with students for a variety of reasons. They were cumbersome to use, and students could not highlight or take notes in the margins of their books. Publishers began trying to find a way to make their virtual textbooks more appealing to both professors and students.

One of the ways they accomplished this was by creating online "platforms," or interactive online software that would encourage a professor to use their product instead of a competitor's. These platforms varied by company, but they generally included an interactive online homework "lab," as well as tutorials and quizzes. McGraw-Hill's version of this, called Connect™, was released in late 2011. This platform allowed professors to pick and choose from many available options—including online homework, notes, progress reports, and quizzes—to create a one-stop platform for students to use. This was appealing to professors because they had the option to assign online homework from a bank of end-of-chapter questions, choose online grading, or receive progress reports for each individual student, among a plethora of other options.

In addition, McGraw-Hill claimed that its Connect platform could interactively *teach* students through a component called LearnSmart™. If quiz results showed that a student did not grasp a particular concept, the platform would take students back to the concept he/she did not understand. In addition, LearnSmart was designed to adapt to each individual student's learning style and ability. In real time, it was able to diagnose students' progress and move them along at an appropriate pace. McGraw-Hill felt that by using LearnSmart, students would be able to study more efficiently and truly learn information rather than just memorize it.

The flexibility provided by platforms such as Connect allowed professors to see which students were struggling, which were excelling, and which were not reaching their potential. In addition, McGraw-Hill offered ConnectPlus ebooks, which was an interactive ebook program that integrated with the Connect platform. Pearson, McGraw-Hill's biggest competitor, had a similar platform called myLab™.

These platforms completely changed the way in which publishers interacted with professors. Instead of presenting the merits of the books themselves, representatives began to promote the superiority of their company's platform. Despite many students' beliefs, professors truly cared about their students' understanding of their class material. University students paid to take college courses—if professors could enhance students' learning experience simply by choosing a textbook that came with an online platform, why not do it? Another benefit of the platforms was that it gave acquisition agents another tool with which to approach professors. While convincing professors to write a textbook for their company, acquisition agents could point to the features of their interactive platform and show professors how it could complement their textbook.

# THE COMPETITORS: USED BOOKS

The used textbook market has severely cut into the profits and market share of publishers like McGraw-Hill. McGraw-Hill only received money from the initial sale of one of its textbooks: For all subsequent sales, all revenues and profits sent the sellers of used books, from on-campus bookstores to websites like half.com. Neither publishers nor authors made any additional revenue from the sale of used books. By making a profit on only one of these semesters, they could generate no more than 17–25 percent of their potential revenue. Textbook publishers generally came out with a new edition of a textbook every two to three years in order to undermine the sales of old editions.

Part of the reason that the used textbook industry was such a big competitor was the fact that most students sold their textbooks at the end of the term. Most college towns had an on-campus bookstore that repurchased textbooks, as well as several other off-campus stores that did the same. In addition to this, there was a blossoming online market for used textbooks. If students couldn't find a used book at their campus store, they could either search other local bookstores or order the book online and have it in a matter of days. Traditional publishers could not compete effectively with the sellers of used textbooks because used books were priced at a big discount to new books.

## Rental Textbooks

Used bookstores also began to rent textbooks to students. Usually rental textbooks were brand new, and students were expected to keep them in excellent condition. To rent a textbook, a student would pay a reduced price (for example, half the price of the textbook) and use the textbook as if he owned it. Students were expected not to write in textbooks or damage them in any other way, although normal wear and tear was acceptable. At the end of the semester, the student returned the book to the bookstore.

This option was attractive to many students because the difference in the price of the purchased textbook and the profit the student would gain from reselling it at the end of the semester was often less than the rental price. In other words, it was cheaper in the long run for the student to rent the book and give it back at the end of the semester. This was also attractive because of the cyclical nature of textbook editions.

When students needed to purchase a textbook that was on its "last leg"—that would not be used again—it was much more economical to rent the textbook since no bookstore at that particular college/university would buy it back. It was usually possible to sell a textbook online, but many students either did not think of this option, or did not think it worth the effort.

## New Editions

Publishers tried to combat the problem of used and rented textbooks with the frequent release of new editions (every two to four years). New editions could entail substantial revisions with all-new or significantly modified chapters and chapter organization, or the books might be much the same as their prior edition excepting minor changes and updates (particularly examples), somewhat different charts and graphs, a fresh cover, and a new interior design and look. Minor changes were fairly common in subjects like medieval history, calculus, or Spanish. Publishers felt compelled to regularly introduce new textbook editions in subjects where the edition-to-edition changes were minor in order to combat the revenue erosion that occurred when the same textbook was bought, used, and then resold term after term. In some disciplines, astute students recognized that an older edition was not much different from the latest one and opted to buy its older incarnation for discounted prices online.

However, in rapidly evolving subjects such as computer science, new editions every two years were not arriving rapidly enough to keep pace with industry changes. The knowledge base of these subjects was growing so rapidly that the two-year revision cycles were not entirely satisfactory. The lag between editions was caused by many things—the time it took authors to make changes (which could take six to eight months, if not more), the five to eight months it took publishers to go through the production cycle of copyediting, obtaining needed permissions, preparing the artwork, setting the pages, proofreading, getting the books printed and into the distribution warehouse, sending out sample copies to potential adopters, securing orders for the next term in which the course was used, shipping new books to bookstores, and so on.

Dr. Lindsol saw an opportunity in this market—if ebooks could be a viable product, the need for new hardcopy editions of old textbooks would be greatly diminished. One student would purchase one textbook and own it forever. There would be no used-books market, because the student could not sell a digital copy to a used bookstore. Therefore, the publishing company would make revenue on each sale of a textbook, instead of only the first sale. In addition, Lindsol realized that with ebooks, the process of updating textbooks in evolving subjects would become much simpler. An author would write new content, the new material would be edited and formatted properly, and then the content could be uploaded and instantly available to customers. No shipping would be necessary, and university bookstores would no longer have to purchase the books—they would be directly available to the students themselves.

## International Editions

Yet another problem publishers encountered was caused by the presence of the Internet. As with any manufacturer, textbook companies price their products so that people in certain markets can afford them. In many countries outside the U.S., a $200 textbook was simply too expensive, and deep price discounting was essential in order to gain adoptions by professors and enable sales to students. To avoid the need for deep price discounting, many publishers had opted to produce and market lower-cost paperback "international" editions—editions that originally were virtually identical to the premium-priced hardback edition, but were printed on cheaper paper, avoided the use of color, and came with fewer extras. These editions were often sold at one-quarter of the normal book price in the North American market. While this seemed sensible, it did not take long for this approach to lose much of its appeal and to backfire. Students in North America soon learned they could purchase these low-cost international editions online. To combat the flow of copies of international editions back into the North American marketplace, publishers recently began making the content of the International edition significantly different from the North American edition and essentially publishing two versions of their textbooks around the world. This was especially true when it came to textbooks for high-enrollment courses that commanded big sales volumes.

## The Amazon Kindle

In 2007, Amazon introduced the Amazon Kindle, a device that allowed readers to download digital copies of books. When it was first introduced, Amazon's Kindle Library (its collection of books for the Kindle) totaled 88,000 books. As of 2012, the Kindle Store

had over 1.3 million titles, and offered over 1 million other titles for free through various third parties, such as lending libraries. The original Kindle had a full keyboard, and users used arrow keys to change pages. However, as technology continued to develop, Amazon came out with new improved versions of the Kindle, including the Kindle Touch (which had only one button and used touchscreen technology) and the Kindle Fire, which was a color tablet that could run apps, view movies, and still have direct access to Amazon's vast library of ebooks. The Kindle was popular with avid readers for many reasons; the two most important of which were convenience and the books' cheap price.

Ebooks were less expensive than traditional physical books. This made sense, because the publishing company no longer had to pay for the materials of the actual books themselves. There was no cost for paper, binding materials, ink, or any other inputs. This saved consumers even more money when it came to hardback books, given that they were significantly more expensive to produce. The publisher was then able to pass these savings on to Amazon, who could still have a significant markup and yet offer books for a cheaper price than those in bookstores.

As mentioned, the other appeal for Kindle users was convenience. The Kindle weighed less than a pound and easily fit into a briefcase or purse. In addition, Kindles downloaded books wirelessly from Amazon at the click of a button. No longer did users need to drive to the bookstore, park, and search through shelves only to find that a certain book

wasn't available, or it cost too much, or didn't really appeal to them anyway. With the Kindle, they could read the description, summary, and user reviews for the book, click "Buy" and have the book in minutes. They then would have the book on a device that they could take anywhere (because it was lightweight and portable), that could even be read in bright sunlight, which was unique among tablets. Though Amazon did not disclose its Kindle sales numbers, in 2011 it was announced that Amazon was selling over one million Kindles per week after the release of Kindle Fire.

## iBooks

When Apple released its iPad in 2010, it created an app called iBooks that allowed readers to download digital copies of books from its online store, the

iBookstore. The iPad offered the same benefits as the Kindle when it came to reading. However, many consumers preferred the iPad because it had more uses than simply reading. As a full-sized tablet, it was large enough to have a full-size keyboard, display documents at near-actual size, and run any app created for the iPhone or iPod Touch. It was, however, significantly more expensive than the Kindle.

As reading on devices such as the Kindle and iPad (referred to as ereaders) became more and more prevalent, textbook publishers began to take notice. For years, many publishers had offered textbooks online, either in an interactive format on their websites or even downloadable as PDF files. However, students generally did not prefer this to a physical textbook because of a few factors: (1) The inability to take notes/highlight sections in a digital format; (2) the need for the Internet and a computer to access the book, and (3) the inability to have a copy of the book in their library—usually these books were accessible only through the Internet.

Though ereaders could not completely fix these issues, they did improve them drastically. Both the Kindle and iPad offered the ability to highlight passages and take notes that would pop up when a user clicked on them. Users could search for keywords to conveniently jump to a certain section. In addition,

the devices themselves contained the books, so students no longer needed to carry around a heavy computer or laptop in order to access them. The iPad was ideal for textbooks—its high-quality graphics and colorful screen were perfectly suited for displaying digital textbooks. A major weakness of the Amazon Kindle when it came to textbooks was its inability to display color and its relatively small screen. However, with the release of the Kindle Fire, which was very similar to an iPad, this became less of an issue.

In 2012, Apple introduced its iTextbooks program. This program began by offering a few textbooks available in the iBookstore. Many were interactive and were much more convenient for students to purchase. In addition, Apple created Study Cards. Whenever a student took notes or highlighted a passage, a virtual "note card" was created containing the notes, along with a link to the original passage. These cards were similar to flashcards, which were a traditional favorite student study method. Five of the original textbooks available were from McGraw-Hill and two were from Pearson, a competing publisher. However, these textbooks were geared toward high school students. No college textbooks had been made available at the time Harry Lindsol began studying the publishing industry. However, he was aware that iTextbooks would be a formidable opponent in the future should he decide to enter the etextbook industry.

## THE ECONOMICS OF EBOOKS

A major issue facing all book publishers was how to balance the production of ebooks and traditional bound books. Because no paper, ink, or binding materials were used to produce ebooks, they were cheaper to produce, while generally having a higher profit margin. Information on the cost of college textbooks is a closely guarded secret, but it is well known that college textbooks are the most profitable sector of the publishing business. The following costs are for a traditional novel, but the cost structure is similar for a college textbook, and yet textbook margins are far higher. It is estimated that the cost to print a book—be it hardcover, paperback, or other format—is about 10 percent of the selling price. For example, if a book retails for $25, it costs the company $2.50 to print. Of course, there are other costs associated with books, such as shipping and warehousing.

Book retailers (the campus bookstores) generally pay publishers about half of the selling price. In the previous example of a $25 book, the publisher would get $12.50 from the local bookstore. Of this, $2.50 goes to pay for printing. It is important to note that this 10 percent is the main cost difference between printed and virtual books. Authors typically get a 15 percent royalty (so around $3.75).

Ebooks, on the other hand, have prices set by the publishing company. Of this, publishers typically get about 70 percent of the selling price. For this example, let's use an ebook priced at $13. A publisher would get $9.10, which then is paid out to different departments such as editing, layout, and marketing. Of this $9.10, roughly 25 percent goes to the author as royalties (or roughly $2.28). On the surface, this higher royalty percentage sounds like a huge incentive for authors to switch to ebooks. However, when authors examined the actual profits they were making, they found they were receiving far less ($3.75 for a hardback book versus $2.28 for an ebook). This is because authors are making 25 percent of the 70 percent that publishers make—about 17 percent of the selling price. The increased royalty percentage (15 percent for hardcover books, but 25 percent for ebooks) was yet another tool that acquisition editors were able to use to attract the best authors. Though it may have resulted in a lower actual revenue per book, the higher percentage was an incentive acquisition editors used to appeal to professors.

However, ebooks are priced at a much lower price point than physical books. If ebooks were priced the same as hardcover books, authors would indeed be making a good financial decision by switching. The problem lies in the fact that consumers do not want to pay the same price for an ebook that they do for a hardcover book. In consumers' minds, the reason hardback books are so expensive is because of the expensive printing materials. In reality, the printing materials are only a small fraction of the cost of the book. The real markup comes from the privilege of buying the book first, before paperback editions come out. This deception on the part of publishers has hurt them when it comes to consumers' perceptions—according to consumers, ebooks should be cheaper than hardback and even paperback books because there is no cost to print. Consumers are not concerned with the other costs, such as editing, marketing, and even author royalties, especially when it comes to textbooks.

## Ebook Pricing—Agency vs. Retail Pricing

In early 2012, Apple and several book publishers had a lawsuit brought against them that alleged that Apple and the publishers had conspired to fix the prices of ebooks. As mentioned, Amazon.com was able to sell a huge number of ebooks. So many, in fact, that they were rapidly becoming the go-to ebook retailer and were in effect creating a monopoly in the market. This happened because Amazon priced many of its most popular ebooks at $9.99. This low price was likely causing them to lose money on book sales, but pick up a huge market share. This practice, known as predatory pricing, almost certainly resulted in huge losses for Amazon. It was expected, however, that once Amazon gained a truly large share of the market (and drove many competitors out of business) they would be able to return prices to where they should be—around $15.

In order to understand how Amazon was selling at a loss, one must understand the pricing model of the industry. Under the normal pricing model, publishers provided a "suggested" retail price for the book—for example, $20. The retailer (Amazon, Apple, or Barnes & Noble) would pay 50 percent of the suggested price to the publisher. In this example, that would be equal to $10. This amount covered all the publishers' expenses and left room for a profit. After purchasing the book, retailers had the option to price it however they wished—they could charge the suggested $20, mark it up to $25, or (as Amazon did with ebooks) sell the book at a loss by pricing it at $9.99.

Amazon's system did not bode well for Apple and many publishers. Apple was upset because no one wanted to buy iBooks at the regular price point of $15 when they could have one for $10. Likewise, publishers did not enjoy seeing their customers' valuation of their books drop so low. Because of this, Apple and several major publishing houses allegedly conspired together to fix prices and drive Amazon's prices back up. This became known as the agency model.

Under the agency model, a publisher was able to set the final retail price of the book. This meant that publishers could decide that ebook prices should be $15, for example. They made 70 percent of this revenue, which they used to cover their own expenses, such as in editing, marketing, and author royalties. The rest was kept as profit. The retailer (for instance, Apple or Amazon) kept the remaining 30 percent to cover any expenses and profit. No one publisher was able to force Amazon to accept the model—Amazon simply would have dropped that one publisher. However, by allegedly banding together and all stating the same terms, the publishers forced Amazon to accept their new pricing model.

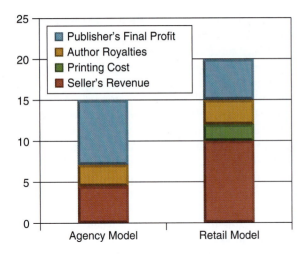

## The Benefits of Ebooks

One important change from the age of physical textbooks to ebooks was the problem of editions. In subjects that changed frequently—such as Business Intelligence, for example—publishers no longer had to wait the standard two years to update a textbook. Instead of waiting for printing and shipping lead times for a new book to reach the market, all the company had to do was edit the new content and format it into the existing textbook. This is an oversimplification of the process, of course, but the process for updating information became much shorter. Instead of having Editions 1, 2, and 3 of the same textbook published over a span of six years, the publishers could update editions at their discretion. McGraw-Hill called this new model "evergreen editions," where information could be updated as frequently or infrequently as possible.

Another benefit of ebooks was that they completely bypassed the used bookstore market. If a student bought a textbook on his Kindle or iPad, he would not be able to sell it to a used bookstore, which could in turn not resell it. Ebooks required that each student purchase his own textbook. When Harry Lindsol realized this fact, he understood why the big players in the textbook industry were eager to move toward ebooks. However, in early 2012 ebooks had not yet become a standard in college classrooms—he still had time to be a first mover in the market.

Because of the higher percentage returns authors received on ebooks, Lindsol believed that he might be able to approach professors and convince them to switch to the strictly-ebooks publishing company that he planned to start. He believed that, though ebooks currently were not the best-selling product in the textbook industry, they were the fastest growing segment and soon would overtake physical textbooks. He hoped that prominent textbook authors would agree with him and be excited to join his team.

## ENDNOTES

http://www.nytimes.com/2010/03/01/business/media/01ebooks.html?_r=1

http://online.wsj.com/article/SB10001424052748703369704575461542987870022.html

Special thanks to McGraw-Hill.

# Sift Cupcake and Dessert Bar

**Rui Gregorio**
Sonoma State University

**Andy Kiehl**
Sonoma State University

**Mark Mathewson**
Sonoma State University

**Meredith Nicklas**
Sonoma State University

**Cynthia Riggs**
Sonoma State University

**Armand Gilinsky**
Sonoma State University

In late October 2010, Sift founder, Andrea Ballus, her husband, Jeff, and manager, Corey Fanfa, gathered around a bright pink table in the party room of Ballus's third successful cupcake shop in Santa Rosa, California, to discuss Sift's future. There, Ballus stated:

> We pride ourselves on the fact that we are very team-oriented, more like a family, and that we develop from within, yet I want to be the premier cupcake shop in the San Francisco Bay Area. To do this, we need to hire smart experienced people to help us grow beyond the capacity of the three of us. How do we do this and continue to deliver the "OMG" experience every day?

As they reflected on their past successes, another issue loomed: Sift's line of credit (LOC) was maxed out and Sift had burned through the money that it had saved to pay income taxes. Jeff and Andrea had recently asked their banker for an increase in the company's LOC; however, the loan officer recommended against this idea. Instead, he offered to float their cash flow shortages in the short term, explaining that increasing Sift's current LOC could negatively impact their ultimate success in securing a much-needed $340,000 Small Business Administration (SBA) loan. To obtain the SBA loan and realize Andrea's dream of becoming the premier cupcake shop in the San Francisco Bay Area, they needed to create both a business plan and a strategic plan for 2011.

## THE SPECIALTY BAKING MARKET

With the exception of cakes and cupcakes, all other categories of bakery products declined in 2009.[1] In spite of negative factors facing the baking industry, such as grocery and "big box" in-store bakeries, high unemployment, and a sputtering economy, retail bakery sales had expected to grow 8.1 percent per year on average through 2014.[2]

Capitalizing on a national trend started at New York's Magnolia Bakery in 2005 and popularized on the hit television program *Sex and the City*, specialty cupcake bakeries had been opening up across the country. According to the market research firm, Mintel, nationwide cupcake sales were projected to rise another 20 percent between 2009 and 2014.[3] The specialty cupcake trend is so popular it has spawned its own Food Network show, Cupcake Wars, where top cupcake bakers around the country competed. According to Pam Nelson, owner of Butter Lane Bakery in New York:

> People still want a cupcake. I think it's kind of an indulgence and the price point is still low. For three dollars people can buy something for themselves instead of spending 100 bucks on a dinner and still feel like they are treating themselves.[4]

Consumer trends shifting toward more healthful choices could pose a risk to specialty cupcake bakeries. However, the National Association for the Specialty Food Trade (NASFT) reported that the next big food trend would be "Back to the future—a reaction against organic/healthful, etc. and a realization that old fashioned in moderation is a joy. Food will play the role of a necessity, a pleasure and an indulgence."[5] The NASFT also reported that consumers were responding to an improving economy by purchasing specialty foods. According to the 2010 research, 63 percent of consumers had purchased a specialty food product in the last six months. This compared with 46 percent in 2009, which was approaching the pre-recession specialty food consumption levels of 2005.[6] One of the benefits of cupcakes was that they came in relatively small portions and were a good snack for getting a sugar fix while assisting with portion control.[7]

According to the Bureau of Labor Statistics, in 2009 the 35-to-44– and the 45-to-54–year-old age brackets spent the most on bakery products, averaging $357 and $346, respectively, per person per year. (See Exhibit 1.) In November 2010, Sift conducted an online survey of 1,629 customers that resulted in a 32 percent response rate. Of the respondents, the majority fell within the higher spending age brackets (see Exhibit 2), as well as higher income brackets. (See Exhibit 3.) Of the customer respondents, 93.4 percent were women, and 6.6 percent were men. When sorted by parenting groups, 28.2 percent of Sift's customers had children under 10, while 35.8 percent had no children at all. (See Exhibit 4.) Specialty food consumers also

**EXHIBIT 2** Sift's Customers by Age Group, November 2010

| Age Group | % of Sift Customers | 2009 Bakery Product Spending |
|---|---|---|
| Under 25 | 9.9% | $167.75 |
| 25–34 | 35.3% | $269.75 |
| 35–44 | 26.5% | $357.00 |
| 45–54 | 18.0% | $346.00 |
| 55–64 | 8.7% | $313.50 |
| 65 and over | 1.7% | $275.25 |

*Source:* Sift Customer Survey, Bureau of Labor Statistics, and Sundale Research

**EXHIBIT 3** Sift's Customers by Family Income, November 2010

| Total Family Income | % of Sift Customers | 2009 Bakery Product Spending |
|---|---|---|
| Under $15,000 | 2.7% | Not available |
| $15,000–$29,999 | 5.9% | $201.25 |
| $30,000–$39,999 | 5.7% | $249.75 |
| $40,000–$49,000 | 7.0% | $290.50 |
| $50,000–$69,999 | 14.9% | $332.00 |
| $70,000–$79,999 | 6.3% | $355.50 |
| $80,000–$99,999 | 10.7% | $404.75 |
| $100,000 and over | 20.6% | $473.75 |

*Source:* Sift, Bureau of Labor Statistics, and Sundale Research

**EXHIBIT 1** U.S. Annual Consumer Spending on Bakery Products

| Age Group | 2009 Actual | 2014 Projected | % Change |
|---|---|---|---|
| Under 25 | 167.75 | $213.75 | 27% |
| 25–34 | 269.75 | $218.00 | (19%) |
| 35–44 | 357.00 | $404.50 | 13% |
| 45–54 | 346.00 | $394.25 | 14% |
| 55–64 | 313.50 | $361.75 | 15% |
| 65 and over | 275.25 | $322.75 | 17% |
| All consumers | $303.75 | $351.50 | 16% |

*Source:* Bureau of Labor Statistics and Sundale Research

**EXHIBIT 4** Sift's Customers by Parenting Group, November 2010

| Parenting Group | % of Sift Customers |
|---|---|
| Pregnant – no children | 1.9% |
| Children under 10 | 28.2% |
| Children 10–18 | 17.0% |
| Children over 18 living at home | 6.1% |
| Children over 18 not at home | 11.0% |
| No children | 35.8% |

*Source:* Sift Customer Survey

## EXHIBIT 5    U.S. Consumer Internet and Social Media Use in the Specialty Food Segment

| | % All Consumers | % Specialty Food Consumers |
|---|---|---|
| Online at least two hours per day away from work | 90% | 91% |
| Facebook | 59% | 65% |
| YouTube | 26% | 33% |
| Twitter | 14% | 17% |
| LinkedIn | 8% | 11% |
| Other | 8% | 9% |
| None | 32% | 24% |

*Base:* 1,500 adults aged 18+ with Internet access

*Source:* Mintel

spent a lot of time online, with more than 90 percent online two hours per day away from work.[8] (See Exhibit 5.)

## COMPANY HISTORY

In 2006, Andrea became obsessed with cupcakes. As a high-energy, successful sales rep for Nestlé Waters, Andrea sold San Pellegrino products to fine dining establishments in the greater Las Vegas area. She found that cupcakes provided the perfect "Wow" factor—getting her in the door of high-end dining establishments and taking her directly to decision makers.

When planning her northern California wine country wedding the next year, serving cupcakes rather than the traditional wedding cake seemed an obvious choice. However, she found the area disappointingly void of "designer" cupcakes, forcing her to drive her wedding cupcakes from Las Vegas to California. This got Andrea thinking . . .

In December 2007, Andrea and Jeff decided to move back to California to be closer to their families. Jeff's company was willing to transfer him to California, yet Andrea's was not. With the wedding experience fresh in her mind, Andrea leveraged her enterprising nature and decided to open a cupcake shop somewhere in Wine Country. Not knowing where to start, she found a "good opportunity" and began there.

Searching online, she found her first location. Site unseen, Andrea purchased an existing 1,000-square-foot coffee shop, located in a small strip mall in the college town of Cotati, California. Her friend, Corey, sent pictures of the location from California. Andrea soon closed the deal—again, without ever visiting the location—negotiating the purchase price from $13K down to $9K. Using a $15,000 bonus from her job at Nestlé, $14,000 from Jeff's 401(k), and a $20,000 investment by Andrea's mother as startup money, the three became shareholders of Sift a Cupcakery, LLC in early 2008. In March of that year, Andrea moved back to California and the Cotati store opened six weeks later. Andrea was the baker, the decorator, the "everything" gal. She relied heavily on family, friends, and her best friend Corey, who became a Sift employee and ultimately their first manager. In 2009, Jeff left his sales job to join Sift. He taught himself what he needed to learn in order to fill the much-needed role of working out logistics, addressing supply chain issues, as well as assisting with the day-to-day financial management of the company.

The company was profitable during its first year of operation and retained earnings from initial operations made it possible for Andrea to achieve her goal of opening a store in Napa during their second year. The 500-square-foot Napa store occupied sublet space in a women's clothing store operating under the name Cake Plate, providing retail sales without onsite baking.

During their third year of operation, Sift internally financed the opening of a third 2,260-square-foot full-service bakery with a party room in downtown Santa Rosa. The 200-square-foot party room introduced a new concept to the Sift business model and an additional revenue stream by providing decorating classes and parties for children and adults. The Santa Rosa kitchen was set up for production baking and supplied product to the Napa location. None of the three stores were exactly alike: each location adapted to the environment and opportunity available in the market at the time.

## MARKETING STRATEGY

Given her background in radio advertising sales, and because their print advertising results had proved disappointing, Andrea preferred to use local radio to promote the business. In addition, Sift used social media platforms like Facebook and Twitter as

## EXHIBIT 6    Sift's Mission and Values

| Sift Mission Statement |
| --- |
| At Sift Cupcake and Dessert Bar we do what it takes to deliver the OMG factor to all our customers. Our unique variety of outstanding house made treats is accompanied with exceptional customer service and a bright trendy décor. This provides our customers with their most positive and memorable cupcake and dessert experience. We want our customers to fall in love with us and will do whatever it takes to make that happen. |

| Sift Core Values |
| --- |
| 1.  Deliver the OMG factor every day. |
| 2.  Smile and be kind to everyone . . . ALWAYS! |
| 3.  Quality products, a clean environment, and OVER THE TOP customer service rule! |
| 4.  Create a fun place to work, learn, and grow. |
| 5.  Be innovative, creative, and passionate. |
| 6.  Build team spirit through open and honest communication. |
| 7.  Be accountable and learn from mistakes. |
| 8.  Be empowered. YOU have the power to create loyal Sift customers. |
| 9.  Challenge yourself to get 1 percent better each day. |
| 10. Support our community. |

communication and promotional tools. Sift already had close to 5,000 "fans" on Facebook and ran weekly Facebook promotions to drive traffic to the stores.

In addition to radio and social media, Sift was very active within the community. In exchange for promotional benefits, Sift donated to local school fundraisers and non-profit organizations. Sift also participated in large local community events, such as Levi's Grand Fondo and the Relay for Life, to help build brand recognition. Sift's management team saw growth potential in developing the wedding side of the business in both Napa and Sonoma. To take advantage of this opportunity, Sift secured booth space at seasonal wedding expos to promote cupcakes as a replacement for the traditional wedding cake.

In the early stages of her business, Andrea created a website for Sift. As the company grew, both Andrea and Jeff recognized they needed a more polished representation of the business. To that end, they hired a professional marketing company to develop a new website and assist with branding and promotional material development.

In October 2010, Andrea and Jeff decided to shift their strategy, focusing not only on cupcakes but also on a variety of complimentary desserts in hopes of creating even broader appeal. They rebranded the business from "Sift a Cupcakery" to "Sift Cupcake and Dessert Bar." The repositioning allowed for the creation of new desserts such as cruffles and whoopie cookies, ice cream sandwiches, macaroons and profiteroles, in addition to cupcakes and frosting shots. Andrea and Jeff believed that repositioning the business would establish Sift as a family dessert destination, the likes of which did not exist in the local marketplace.

## HUMAN RESOURCE ISSUES

Most of Andrea's employees were high school and college students, with an average age of 20 years old. Many employees had been with Sift from the beginning. Her employees were excited about working at Sift and indicated that they looked forward to working there for the foreseeable future. As Andrea commented:

> We have many long-term employees. Our turnover is very low compared to other retailers. If our turnover had been higher, it would not have allowed our growth. So my employees are important to me and we work hard to create a family culture among us.

Andrea believed that a happy employee equaled a happy customer. She sought to nurture her employees through hiring and promoting from within. She supported staff in learning new skills and provided them with opportunities for individual growth. (See Sift's Mission and Values Statement in Exhibit 6.) Although Andrea desired to promote from within, training employees for new positions presented challenges.

Sometimes an individual staff member just didn't possess the necessary skills for a position. The chain of command and effective communication about processes and their implementation also proved to be problematic. While everyone was eager to get things accomplished, there were no processes in place to guide decisions, so more work was created.

In 2010, Andrea hired Robert, a former store manager from Peet's Coffee—a nationwide chain of coffee emporia founded in Berkeley, California—to oversee Sift's Santa Rosa location. With his experience in a related industry, Robert took over certain daily tasks from Andrea so she could devote her time to larger business objectives. Andrea hoped Robert would also create a more efficient baking space and streamline Sift's processes.

Employing Robert signaled a change in Andrea's hiring policy—helping her improve her "business IQ" with each new hire. Andrea and her management team admitted that finding the right people for the job was a daunting task, and being able to offer enough compensation to attract that talent and finding the right incentives to motivate both new and existing employees was one of their biggest challenges. While their cupcake business was profitable and employees were making more than the California minimum wage, there was not enough revenue to support manager wages. However, with expansion, additional store managers would be necessary. (See Exhibit 7.)

## COMPETITION

There was no specialty cupcake trade association tracking the industry as it expanded across the United States. The industry segment relied on passionate cupcake bloggers such as cupcaketakesthecake.**blogspot. com**, and **allthingscupcake.com**, or the review site **Yelp.com** to stay up with industry trends and keep an eye on the competition.

As of November 1, 2010, there were 106 known "cupcakeries" in the bay area according to **Yelp.com**. Most of them were single-store operations. Hundreds of additional bakeries, dessert bars, and other commercial venues were also selling cupcakes. (See Exhibit 8.) Andrea and Jeff viewed Kara's Cupcakes as their primary competitor. Kara's had six Bay Area locations: two in San Francisco, and one each in Palo Alto, San Jose, Napa, and Walnut Creek. On a national level, Sprinkles® had emerged as the retail specialty cupcake leader. With ten locations in major metropolitan areas around the U.S., one of which was in Palo Alto, Sprinkles announced plans to open 15 more locations in 2011, including a store in San Francisco.

## SIFT FINANCIALS

Andrea started Sift with relatively little capital, founding the business with what she and Jeff could piece together, plus a small seed money investment from Andrea's mother, who remained a silent partner. The company grew by reinvesting its earnings, sweat equity, and Andrea's ability to find a "good deal." Financial statements for Sift's first three years of operation are shown in Exhibit 9.

Despite the fact that Sift had been profitable from its opening year, store managers were still expected to control their costs and payroll. However, store managers were not trained to read and utilize the new point of sale (POS) reports and had not been given clear financial guidelines to follow. Day-to-day financial monitoring seldom took place, negatively impacting profitability.

## FUTURE PLANS

At the end of their October 2010 meeting, Andrea, Jeff, and Corey agreed that a clear growth strategy must be developed to continue moving forward. Sift was in the process of relocating the Napa Store to a larger location with more foot traffic in a nearby shopping center. Sift was simultaneously in expansion mode and in the process of rebranding. Doing both had increased expenses, and for the first time since opening the business, Sift had begun to experience

## EXHIBIT 7   Sift's Store Staffing Levels, November 2010

| Job Title | Cotati | Santa Rosa | Napa | Total |
|---|---|---|---|---|
| Manager | 1 | 1 | 0 | 2 |
| Assistant manager | 1 | 0 | 1 | 2 |
| Bakers | 2 | 1 | 0 | 3 |
| Bakers' assistant | 0 | 2 | 0 | 2 |
| Frosting maker | 0 | 1 | 0 | 1 |
| Counter staff/decorator | 7 | 7 | 4 | 18 |
| Delivery driver | 0 | 1 | 0 | 1 |
| Wedding coordinator | 0 | 1 | 0 | 1 |
| Total staff | 11 | 14 | 5 | 30 |

## EXHIBIT 8    Current and Proposed San Francisco Bay Area Locations for Sift, November 2010

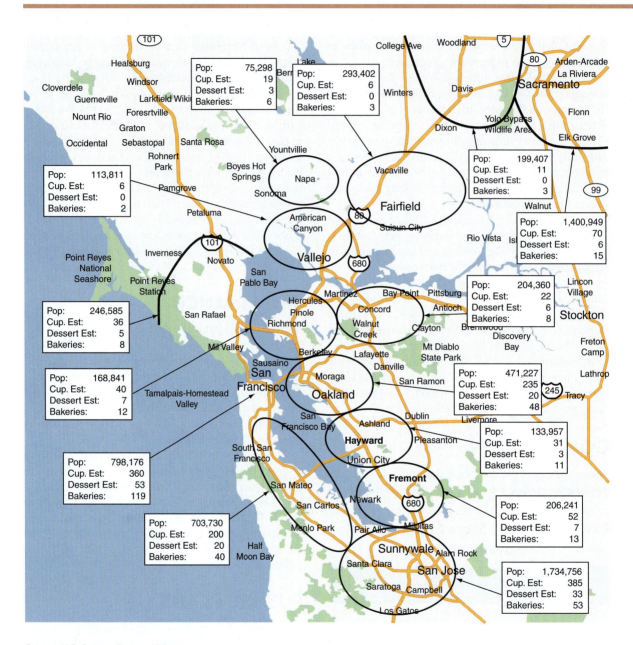

Source: U.S. Census Bureau, Yelp.com

Pop: Population of area indicated

Cup Est.: Any retailer that sells cupcakes

Dessert Est.: Retailers specializing in desserts

Bakeries: Stand-alone bakeries

## EXHIBIT 9   Sift Cupcake and Dessert Bar Financial Statements, 2008–2010

| Year Ending Dec. 31 | 2008 | 2009 | 2010** |
|---|---|---|---|
| Net sales | $220,904.46 | $508,357.99 | $961,118.23 |
| Cost of goods sold* | 58,067.35 | 137,036.98 | 607,085.68 |
| Gross profit | 162,837.11 | 371,321.01 | 354,032.56 |
| Operating expenses (exc. depreciation) | 155,667.77 | 335,257.86 | 190,843.67 |
| Depreciation | 0 | 0 | 0 |
| EBIT | 7,169.34 | 36,063.15 | 163,188.89 |
| Interest expenses | 0 | 0 | 0 |
| Income before taxes | 7,169.34 | 36,063.15 | 163,188.89 |
| Federal income taxes | 994.94 | 5,673.91 | 26,110.22 |
| Net Income | $   6,174.40 | $  30,389.25 | $137,078.67 |

*In 2010, Labor expense was moved from the Operating Expense line to Cost of Goods Sold
**Full Year forecast based on Actuals through October 2010

| Balance Sheet at Dec. 31 | 2008 | 2009 | 2010 |
|---|---|---|---|
| *Assets* | | | |
| Cash | $29,507 | $ 27,175 | $ 46,474 |
| Accounts receivable | 0 | 0 | 185 |
| Inventories | 185 | 15,757 | 17,669 |
| Total current assets | 29,692 | 42,932 | 64,328 |
| Net fixed assets | 29,917 | 93,433 | 215,341 |
| Total assets | 59,609 | 136,365 | 279,669 |
| *Liabilities and Stockholders' Equity* | | | |
| Notes payable—banks | 0 | 0 | 0 |
| Accounts payable | 4,452 | 1,950 | 17,473 |
| Accrued expenses and taxes | 1,307 | 11,138 | 28,455 |
| Total current liabilities | 5,760 | 13,088 | 45,928 |
| Long-term debt | 0 | 11,654 | 88,122 |
| Stockholders' equity/Retained earnings | 53,849 | 111,622 | 145,619 |
| Total liabilities and stockholders' equity | $59,609 | $136,365 | $279,669 |

serious cash flow challenges. To prepare a business plan for the SBA loan application, Andrea hired a consultant to help her prepare a formal three-year financial forecast for three separate scenarios, as described next and as detailed in Exhibit 10.

*Option 1: Maintaining Current Locations*—Maintain current stores and small business model while improving operational issues and strengthening infrastructure. Further develop brand identity and own the local marketplace.

*Option 2: Rapid Expansion with Retail-Only Stores/ Commissary*—Open a central baking commissary

along the I-80 freeway corridor. This commissary would service four additional 500- to 600-square-foot storefront locations in 2011 in affluent communities without existing specialty cupcake shops. Additional storefronts would be added at a rate of two storefronts per year. These storefronts will only decorate and sell cupcakes; all baking will be completed at the central commissary.

*Option 3: Expansion with Retail/Baking Stores*— Expand on current business model of baking, decorating, and selling in each new 1,500–2,000-square-foot store. Move into targeted locations as the opportunity

**EXHIBIT 10** Sift's Growth Options and Forecasted Income Statements for Each
Option, 2011–2013

## Option 1: Maintain Current Locations

| Ending Dec. 31 | Forecast 2011 | Forecast 2012 | Forecast 2013 |
|---|---|---|---|
| Net sales | $1,057,230 | $1,162,953 | $1,279,248 |
| Cost of goods sold | 667,794 | 734,574 | 808,031 |
| Gross profit | 389,436 | 428,379 | 471,217 |
| Operating expense (excl. dep.) | 194,661 | 198,554 | 202,525 |
| Depreciation | 0 | 0 | 0 |
| EBIT | 194,775 | 229,826 | 268,693 |
| Interest expense | 0 | 0 | 0 |
| Income before taxes | 194,775 | 229,826 | 268,693 |
| Federal income taxes @ 20% | 38,955 | 45,965 | 53,739 |
| Net income | $  155,820 | $  183,861 | $  214,954 |

## Option 2: Rapid Expansion with Retail-Only Stores/Commissary

| Ending Dec. 31 | Forecast 2011 | Forecast 2012 | Forecast 2013 |
|---|---|---|---|
| Net sales | $2,122,136 | $4,250,723 | $7,068,337 |
| Cost of goods sold | 1,363,216 | 2,028,020 | 3,123,599 |
| Gross profit | 758,920 | 2,222,703 | 3,944,738 |
| Operating expense (excl. dep.) | 574,641 | 1,166,407 | 2,170,779 |
| Depreciation | 53,321 | 94,892 | 140,378 |
| EBIT | 131,258 | 961,404 | 1,633,581 |
| Interest expense | 18,802 | 13,579 | 2,748 |
| Income before taxes | 112,456 | 947,825 | 1,630,833 |
| Federal income taxes @ 20% | 22,491 | 189,565 | 326,167 |
| Net income | $   89,965 | $  758,260 | $1,304,666 |

## Option 3: Expansion with Retail/Baking Stores

| Ending Dec. 31 | Forecast 2011 | Forecast 2012 | Forecast 2013 |
|---|---|---|---|
| Net sales | $1,691,730 | $2,283,903 | $2,935,293 |
| Cost of goods sold | 1,068,573 | 1,442,616 | 1,854,064 |
| Gross profit | 623,157 | 841,287 | 1,081,230 |
| Operating expense (excl. dep.) | 194,661 | 198,554 | 202,525 |
| Depreciation | 0 | 0 | 0 |
| EBIT | 428,496 | 642,733 | 878,705 |
| Interest expense | 18,802 | 13,579 | 2,748 |
| Income before taxes | 409,694 | 629,154 | 875,957 |
| Federal income taxes @ 20% | 81,939 | 125,831 | 175,191 |
| Net income | $  327,756 | $  503,323 | $  700,765 |

arises, with controlled growth based on the financial health of the business.

The plan was based on three stores opening in the last three quarters of 2011, followed by two additional stores opening each year following.

Back in 2010, Andrea wondered if it was the right time to establish a mail-order division as well. Many of Sift's competitors had already diversified into similar operations. Developing this new channel could expand Sift's potential customer base well beyond the reach of its brick-and-mortar stores.

## ENDNOTES

[1] Sundale Research U.S. Department of Commerce Data.

[2] Ibid.

[3] Elizabeth Olson, "The Latest Entrepreneurial Fantasy Is Selling Cupcakes," The New York Times. http://www.nytimes.com/2009/11/26/business/smallbusiness/26cupcake.html.

[4] "New York City's Cupcake Economy," The Wall Street Journal, July 16, 2010. http://blogs.wsj.com/metropolis/2010/07/16/new-york-citys-cupcake-economy/.

[5] "Today's Specialty Food Consumer Report 2010," Specialty Food Magazine.

[6] Ibid.

[7] Hubert Vigilla, "Let Them Eat Cupcakes: Why Cupcakes Are Such Trendy Snacks," October 1, 2008. http://www.docshop.com/2008/10/01/let-them-eat-cupcakes-why-cupcakes-are-such-trendy-snacks.

[8] Ibid.

# Under Armour—Challenging Nike in Sports Apparel

## Arthur A. Thompson
The University of Alabama

Founded in 1996 by former University of Maryland football player Kevin Plank, Under Armour was the originator of performance apparel—gear engineered to keep athletes cool, dry, and light throughout the course of a game, practice, or workout. It started with a simple plan to make a T-shirt that provided compression and "wicked" perspiration from the wearer's skin, thereby regulating body temperature and avoiding the discomfort of sweat-absorbed apparel.

Fifteen years later, with 2011 sales of nearly $1.5 billion, Under Armour had a growing brand presence in the roughly $60 billion multisegment retail market for sports apparel and active wear in the United States. Its interlocking "U" and "A" logo had become almost as familiar and well-known as industry-leader Nike's swoosh. The company had boosted its market share from 0.6 percent in 2003 to an estimated 2.8 percent in 2011, which compared quite favorably with Nike's industry-leading market share of 7.0 percent and the 5.4 percent share of second-ranked adidas.[1]

Founder and CEO Kevin Plank believed Under Armour's potential for long-term growth was exceptional for three reasons: (1) the company had built an incredibly powerful and authentic brand in a relatively short time, (2) there were significant opportunities to expand the company's narrow product lineup and brand name appeal into product categories where it currently had little or no market presence, and (3) the company was only in the early stages of establishing its brand and penetrating markets outside North America.

## COMPANY BACKGROUND

Kevin Plank honed his competitive instinct growing up with four older brothers and playing football. As a young teenager, he squirmed under the authority of his mother, who was the town mayor of Kensington, Maryland. When he was a high-school sophomore, he was tossed out of Georgetown Prep for poor academic performance and ended up at Fork Union Military Academy, where he learned to accept discipline and resumed playing high-school football. After graduation, Plank became a walk-on special-teams football player for the University of Maryland in the early 1990s, ending his college career as the special-teams' captain in 1995. Throughout his football career, he regularly experienced the discomfort of practicing on hot days and the unpleasantness of peeling off sweat-soaked cotton T-shirts after practice. At the University of Maryland, Plank sometimes changed the cotton T-shirt under his jersey as it became wet and heavy during the course of a game.

During his later college years and in classic entrepreneurial fashion, Plank hit upon the idea of using newly available moisture-wicking, polyester-blend fabrics to create next-generation, tighter-fitting shirts and undergarments that would make it cooler and more comfortable to engage in strenuous activities during high-temperature conditions.[2] While Plank had a job offer from Prudential Life Insurance at the end of his college days in 1995, he couldn't see himself being happy working in a corporate environment. As he told the author of a 2011 *Fortune* article on Under Armour, "I would have killed myself." Despite a lack of business training, Plank opted to try to make a living selling high-tech microfiber shirts. Plank's vision was to sell innovative, technically advanced apparel products engineered with a special fabric construction that provided supreme moisture management. A year of fabric and product testing produced a synthetic compression T-shirt that was suitable for wear beneath an athlete's uniform or equipment, provided a snug fit (like a second skin) and remained drier and lighter than a traditional cotton shirt. Plank formed KP Sports as a subchapter S corporation in Maryland in 1996 and commenced selling the shirt to athletes and sports teams.

## The Company's Early Years

Plank's former teammates at high school, military school, and the University of Maryland included some 40 NFL players that he knew well enough to call and offer them the shirt he had come up with. He worked the phone and, with a trunk full of shirts in the back of his car, visited schools and training camps in person to show his products. Within a short time, Plank's sales successes were good enough that he convinced Kip Fulks, who played lacrosse at Maryland, to become a partner in his enterprise. Fulks' initial role was to leverage his connections to promote use of the company's shirts by lacrosse players. Their sales strategy was predicated on networking and referrals. But Fulks had another critical role—he had good credit and was able to obtain 17 credit cards that were used to make purchases from suppliers and charge expenses.[3] Operations were conducted on a shoestring budget out of the basement of Plank's grandmother's house in Georgetown, a Washington, D.C. suburb. Plank and Fulks generated sufficient cash from their sales efforts and Fulks never missed a minimum payment on any of his credit cards. When cash flows became particularly tight, Plank's older brother Scott made loans to the company to help keep KP Sports afloat (in 2011, Scott owned 4 percent of the company's stock). It didn't take long for Plank and Fulks to learn that it was more productive to direct their sales efforts more toward equipment managers than to individual players. Getting a whole team to adopt use of the T-shirts that KP Sports was marketing meant convincing equipment managers that it was more economical to provide players with a pricey $25 high-performance T-shirt that would hold up better in the long-run than a cheap cotton T-shirt.

In 1998, the company's sales revenues and growth prospects were sufficient to secure a $250,000 small-business loan from a tiny bank in Washington, D.C.; the loan enabled the company to move its basement operation to a facility on Sharp Street in nearby Baltimore.[4] As sales continued to gain momentum, the D.C. bank later granted KP Sports additional small loans from time to time to help fund its needs for more working capital. Then Ryan Wood, one of Plank's acquaintances from high school, joined the company in 1999 and became a partner. The company consisted of three jocks trying to gain a foothold in a growing, highly competitive industry against some 25 + brands, including those of Nike, adidas, Columbia, and Patagonia. Plank functioned as president and CEO, Kip Fulks was vice president of sourcing and quality assurance, and Ryan Wood was vice president of sales.

Nonetheless, KP Sports' sales grew briskly as it expanded its product line to include high-tech undergarments tailored for athletes in different sports and for cold temperatures as well as hot temperatures, plus jerseys, team uniforms, socks, and other accessories. Increasingly, the company was able to secure deals not just to provide gear for a particular team but for most or all of a school's sports teams. However, the company's partners came to recognize the merits of tapping the retail market for high-performance apparel and began making sales calls on sports apparel retailers. In 2000, Galyan's, a large retail chain since acquired by Dick's Sporting Goods, signed on to carry KP Sports's expanding line of performance apparel for men, women, and youths. Sales to other sports apparel retailers began to explode, quickly making the retail segment of the sports apparel market the biggest component of the company's revenue stream. Revenues totaled $5.3 million in 2000, with an operating income of $0.7 million. The company's products were available in some 500 retail stores. Beginning in 2000, Scott Plank joined the company as vice president of finance, with operational and strategic responsibilities as well.

## Rapid Growth Ensues

Over the next 11 years, the company's product line evolved to include a widening variety of shirts, shorts, underwear, outerwear, gloves, and other offerings. The strategic intent was to grow the business by replacing products made with cotton and other traditional fabrics with innovatively designed performance products that incorporated a variety of technologically advanced fabrics and specialized manufacturing techniques, all in an attempt to make the wearer feel "drier, lighter, and more comfortable." In 1999, the company began selling its products in Japan through a licensee. On January 1, 2002, prompted by growing operational complexities, increased financial requirements, and plans for further geographic expansion, KP Sports revoked its "S" corporation status and became a "C" corporation. The company opened a Canadian sales office in 2003 and began efforts to grow its market presence in Canada. In 2004, KP Sports became the outfitter of the University of Maryland football team and was a supplier to some 400 women's sports teams at NCAA Division 1-A colleges and universities. The company used independent sales agents to begin selling its products in the United Kingdom in 2005. SportsScanINFO estimated that as of 2004, KP Sports had a 73 percent share of the U.S. market for compression tops and bottoms, more than seven times that of its nearest competitor.[5]

Broadening demand for the company's product offerings among professional, collegiate, and Olympic teams and athletes, active outdoor enthusiasts, elite tactical professionals and consumers with active lifestyles propelled revenue growth from $5.3 million in 2000 to $263.4 million for the 12 months ending September 30, 2005, equal to a compound annual growth rate of 127 percent. Operating income increased from $0.7 million in 2000 to $32.7 million during the same period, a compound annual growth rate of 124 percent. About 90 percent of the company revenues came from sales to some 6,000 retail stores in the United States and 2,000 stores in Canada, Japan, and the United Kingdom. In addition, sales were being made to high-profile athletes and teams, most notably in the National Football League, Major League Baseball, the National Hockey League, and major collegiate and Olympic sports. KP Sports had 574 employees at the end of September 2005.

Throughout 2005, KP Sports increased its offerings to include additional men's and women's performance products and, in particular, began entry into such off-field outdoor sports segments as hunting, fishing, running, mountain sports, skiing, and golf. Management expected that its new product offerings in 2006 would include football cleats.

## KP Sports Is Renamed Under Armour

In late 2005, the company changed its name to Under Armour and became a public company with an initial public offering of 9.5 million shares of Class A common stock that generated net proceeds of approximately $114.9 million. Simultaneously, existing stockholders sold 2.6 million shares of Class A stock from their personal holdings. The shares were all sold at just above the offer price of $13 per share. On the first day of trading after the IPO, the shares closed at $25.30, after opening at $31 per share. Following these initial sales of Under Armour stock to the general public, Under Armour's outstanding shares of common stock consisted of two classes: Class A common stock and Class B common stock; both classes were identical in all respects except for voting and conversion rights. Holders of Class A common stock were entitled to one vote per share, and holders of Class B common stock were entitled to 10 votes per share, on all matters to be voted on by common stockholders. Shares of Class A and Class B common stock voted together as a single class on all matters submitted to a vote of stockholders. All of the Class B common stock was beneficially owned by Kevin Plank, which represented 83.0 percent of the combined voting power of all of the outstanding common stock. As a result, Plank was able to control the outcome of substantially all matters submitted to a stockholder vote, including the election of directors, amendments to Under Armour's charter, and mergers or other business combinations.

At the time of Under Armour's IPO, Kevin Plank, Kip Fulks, and Ryan Wood were all 33 years old; Scott Plank was 39 years old. After the IPO, Kevin Plank owned 15.2 million shares of Under Armour's Class A shares (and all of the Class B shares); Kip Fulks owned 2.125 million Class A shares, Ryan Wood owned 2.142 million Class A shares, and Scott Plank owned 3.95 million Class A shares. All four had opted to sell a small fraction of their common shares at the time of the IPO—these accounted for a combined 1.83 million of the 2.6 million shares sold from the holdings of various directors, officers, and other entities. Ryan Wood decided to leave his position as senior vice president of sales at Under Armour in 2007 to run a cattle farm. Kip Fulks assumed the position of chief operating officer at Under Armour in September 2011, after moving up the executive ranks in several capacities, chiefly those related to sourcing, quality assurance, product development, and product innovation. In 2011, Scott Plank was the company's executive vice president of business development and focused on domestic and international business development opportunities. Prior to that, he served as senior vice president of retail from March 2006 to July 2009 with responsibility for retail outlet and specialty stores and e-commerce, as chief administrative officer from January 2004 to February 2006, and vice president of finance from 2000 to 2003.

**EXHIBIT 1**   Selected Financial Data for Under Armour, Inc., 2006–2011 (in 000s, except per-share amounts)

| | Years Ending December 31 | | | | |
|---|---|---|---|---|---|
| Selected Income Statement Data | 2011 | 2010 | 2009 | 2008 | 2006 |
| Net revenues | $1,472,684 | $1,063,927 | $856,411 | $725,244 | $430,689 |
| Cost of goods sold | 759,848 | 533,420 | 446,286 | 372,203 | 216,753 |
| Gross profit | 712,836 | 530,507 | 410,125 | 353,041 | 213,936 |
| Selling, general and administrative expenses | 550,069 | 418,152 | 324,852 | 276,116 | 157,018 |
| Income from operations | 162,767 | 112,355 | 85,273 | 76,925 | 56,918 |
| Interest expense, net | (3,841) | (2,258) | (2,344) | (850) | 1,457 |
| Other expense, net | (2,064) | (1,178) | (511) | (6,175) | 712 |
| Income before income taxes | 156,862 | 108,919 | 82,418 | 69,900 | 59,087 |
| Provision for income taxes | 59,943 | 40,442 | 35,633 | 31,671 | 20,108 |
| Net income | $  96,919 | $  68,477 | $ 46,785 | $ 38,229 | $ 38,979 |
| Net income per common share | | | | | |
| Basic | $1.88 | $1.35 | $0.94 | $0.78 | $0.82 |
| Diluted | 1.85 | 1.34 | 0.92 | 0.76 | 0.78 |
| Weighted average common shares outstanding | | | | | |
| Basic | 51,570 | 50,798 | 49,848 | 49,086 | 47,291 |
| Diluted | 52,526 | 51,282 | 50,650 | 50,342 | 49,676 |
| **Selected Balance Sheet Data (in 000s)** | | | | | |
| Cash and cash equivalents | $175,384 | $203,870 | $187,297 | $102,042 | $70,655 |
| Working capital[*] | 506,056 | 406,703 | 327,838 | 263,313 | 173,389 |
| Inventories at year-end | 324,409 | 215,355 | 148,488 | 182,232 | 81,031 |
| Total assets | 919,210 | 675,378 | 545,588 | 487,555 | 289,368 |
| Total debt and capital lease obligations, including current maturities | 77,724 | 15,942 | 20,223 | 45,591 | 6,257 |
| Total stockholders' equity | 636,432 | 496,966 | 399,997 | 331,097 | 214,388 |
| **Selected Cash Flow Data** | | | | | |
| Net cash provided by operating activities | $15,218 | $50,114 | $119,041 | $69,516 | $10,701 |

\* Working capital is defined as current assets minus current liabilities.

*Source:* Company 10-K reports 2011, 2010, and 2008.

Exhibit 1 summarizes Under Armour's financial performance in the six years following the company's 2005 IPO. The company stock was trading in the $72 to $78 range in January 2012. Following the announcement of better-than-expected first quarter 2012 earnings and management forecasts of full-year 2012 revenues of $1.78 to $1.80 billion, Under Armour's stock climbed to $102.70 per share in the last week of April 2012.

# UNDER ARMOUR'S STRATEGY

Under Armour's mission was "to make all athletes better through passion, design, and the relentless pursuit of innovation." The company's principal business activities in 2012 were the development, marketing, and distribution of branded performance apparel, footwear, and accessories for men, women, and youths. The brand's moisture-wicking fabrications were engineered

## EXHIBIT 2  Composition of Under Armour's Revenues, 2009–2011

### A. Net revenues by product category (in thousands of $)

| | 2011 | | 2010 | | 2009 | |
|---|---|---|---|---|---|---|
| | Dollars | Percent | Dollars | Percent | Dollars | Percent |
| Apparel | $1,122,031 | 76.2% | $ 853,493 | 80.2% | $651,779 | 76.1% |
| Footwear | 181,684 | 12.3 | 127,175 | 12.0 | 136,224 | 15.9 |
| Accessories | 132,400 | 9.0 | 43,882 | 4.1 | 35,077 | 4.1 |
| Total net sales | 1,436,115 | 97.5% | $1,024,550 | 96.3% | $823,080 | 96.1% |
| License revenues | 36,569 | 2.5 | 39,377 | 3.7 | 33,331 | 3.9 |
| Total net revenues | $1,472,684 | 100.0% | $1,063,927 | 100.0% | $856,411 | 100.0% |

### B. Net revenues by geographic region (in thousands of $)

| | 2011 | | 2010 | | 2009 | |
|---|---|---|---|---|---|---|
| | Dollars | Percent | Dollars | Percent | Dollars | Percent |
| North America | $1,383,346 | 93.9% | $ 997,816 | 93.7% | $808,020 | 94.3% |
| Other foreign countries | 89,338 | 6.1 | 66,111 | 6.3 | 48,391 | 5.7 |
| Total net revenues | $1,472,684 | 100.0% | $1,063,927 | 100.0% | $856,411 | 100.0% |

*Source:* Company 10-K reports, 2011 and 2010.

in many designs and styles for wear in nearly every climate to provide a performance alternative to traditional products. Its products were worn by athletes at all levels, from youth to professional, and by consumers with active lifestyles. Over 90 percent of Under Armour's sales were in North America, but international sales to distributors and retailers outside North America were growing. Exhibit 2 shows the composition of Under Armour's revenues.

## Growth Strategy

Under Armour's growth strategy in early 2012 consisted of several strategic initiatives:

- Continuing to broaden the company's product offerings to men, women, and youths for wear in a widening variety of sports and recreational activities.
- Targeting additional consumer segments for the company's ever-expanding lineup of performance products.
- Securing additional distribution of Under Armour products in the retail marketplace in North America via not only store retailers and catalog retailers but also through Under Armour factory outlet and specialty stores and sales at the company's website.

- Expanding the sale of Under Armour products in foreign countries and becoming a global competitor in the world market for sports apparel and performance products.
- Growing global awareness of the Under Armour brand name and strengthening the appeal of Under Armour products worldwide.

## Product Line Strategy

Under Armour's diverse product offerings in 2012 consisted of apparel, footwear, and accessories for men, women, and youths marketed at multiple price levels in a variety of styles and fits intended to regulate body temperature and enhance comfort, mobility, and performance regardless of weather conditions.

**Apparel**  The company designed and merchandised three lines of apparel gear: HeatGear® for hot weather conditions; ColdGear® for cold weather conditions; and AllSeasonGear® for temperature conditions between the extremes.

*HeatGear*  HeatGear was designed to be worn in warm to hot temperatures under equipment or as a single layer. The company's first compression T-shirt was the original HeatGear product and remained its signature style in 2012. In sharp contrast to a sweat-soaked cotton T-shirt that could weigh two to three pounds, HeatGear was engineered with a microfiber blend featuring what Under Armour termed a "Moisture Transport System" that ensured the body will stay cool, dry, and light. HeatGear was offered in a variety of tops and bottoms in a broad array of colors and styles for wear in the gym or outside in warm weather. Compression-fit HeatGear reduced muscle fatigue, was particularly popular for training sessions and competition, and was the company's top-selling gear line year-round.

*ColdGear*  Under Armour high-performance fabrics were appealing to people participating in cold-weather sports and vigorous recreational activities like snow skiing who needed both warmth and moisture-wicking protection from a sometimes overheated body. ColdGear was designed to wick moisture from the body while circulating body heat from hotspots to maintain a core body temperature. All ColdGear apparel provided dry warmth in a single light layer that could be worn beneath a jersey, uniform, protective gear or ski-vest, or other cold weather outerwear. ColdGear products generally were sold at higher price levels than other Under Armour gear lines.

*AllSeasonGear*  AllSeasonGear was designed to be worn in changing temperatures and used technical fabrics to keep the wearer cool and dry in warmer temperatures while preventing a chill in cooler temperatures.

Each of the three apparel lines contained three fit types: compression (tight fit), fitted (athletic fit) and loose (relaxed).

**Footwear**  Under Armour began marketing footwear products for men, women, and youths in 2006 and had expanded its footwear line every year since. Currently, its offerings included football, baseball, lacrosse, softball and soccer cleats, slides, performance training footwear, running footwear, basketball footwear, and hunting boots. Under Armour's athletic footwear was innovatively designed to provide stabilization, directional cushioning, and moisture management, and was engineered to be light and breathable and to maximize the athlete's comfort and control.

**Accessories**  Under Armour's accessory line in 2012 included gloves, socks, headwear, bags, knee-pads, custom-molded mouth guards, and eyewear designed to be used and worn before, during, and after competition.

All of these featured performance advantages and functionality similar to other Under Armour products. For instance, the company's baseball batting, football, golf, and running gloves included Heat-Gear and ColdGear technologies and were designed with advanced fabrications to provide various high-performance attributes that differentiated its gloves from those of rival brands.

Under Armour had entered into licensing agreements with a number of firms to produce and market some of its accessories (bags, headgear, and socks). In these instances, Under Armour product, marketing, and sales teams were actively involved in all steps of the design process in order to maintain brand standards and consistency. By 2011, however, Under Armour had developed its own headwear and bag accessories and began selling them itself rather than through licensees. Revenues generated from the sale of all licensed accessories are included in the licensing revenue amounts shown in Exhibit 2A.

## Marketing, Promotion, and Brand Management Strategies

Under Armour had an in-house marketing and promotions department that designed and produced most of its advertising campaigns to drive consumer demand for its products and build awareness of Under Armour as a leading performance athletic brand. The company's total marketing expenses, including endorsements and advertising, were $167.9 million in 2011, $128.2 million in 2010, and $108.9 million in 2009. These totals included the costs of sponsoring events and various sports teams, the costs of athlete endorsements, and advertising expenses.

**Sports Marketing**  A key element of Under Armour's marketing and promotion strategy was to promote the sales and use of its products to high-performing athletes and teams on the high school, collegiate, and professional levels. This strategy included entering into outfitting agreements with a variety of collegiate and professional sports teams, sponsoring an assortment of collegiate and professional sports events, and selling Under Armour products directly to team equipment managers and to individual athletes.

Management believed that having audiences see Under Armour products (with the interlocking UA logo prominently displayed) being worn by athletes on the playing field helped the company establish on-field authenticity of the Under Armour brand with consumers. Considerable effort went into giving

**EXHIBIT 3**    The Under Armour Logo and Its Use on Selected
Under Armour Products

Under Armour products broad exposure at live sporting events, as well as on television, in magazines, and on a wide variety of Internet sites. Exhibit 3 shows a sampling of the Under Armour logo and its use on Under Armour products.

In 2011, Under Armour was the official outfitter of *all* the athletic teams at Boston College, Texas Tech University, the University of Maryland, the University of South Carolina, Auburn University, and the University of South Florida and *selected* sports teams at the University of Illinois, Northwestern University, the University of Delaware, the University of Hawaii,

Southern Illinois University, Wagner College, Whittier College, and La Salle University. All told, it was the official outfitter of over 100 Division I men's and women's collegiate athletic teams, rapidly growing numbers (over 40) of high school athletic teams, and several Olympic sports teams; and it supplied sideline apparel and fan gear for many collegiate teams as well. In addition, Under Armour sold products to high profile professional athletes and teams, most notably in the National Football League, Major League Baseball, and the National Hockey League. Since 2006, Under Armour had been an official supplier of football cleats to the National Football League (NFL). In 2010, it signed an agreement to become an official supplier of gloves to the NFL beginning in 2011 and to supply the NFL with training apparel for athletes attending NFL tryout camps beginning in 2012.

Internationally, Under Armour was building its brand image by selling products to European soccer and rugby teams. It was the official supplier of performance apparel to the Hannover 96 football club and the Welsh Rugby Union, among others. In addition, it was an official supplier of performance apparel to Hockey Canada, had advertising rights at many locations in the Air Canada Center during the Toronto Maple Leafs' home games, and was the Official Performance Product Sponsor of the Toronto Maple Leafs.

Under Armour also had sponsorship agreements with individual athletes. Its strategy was to secure the endorsement of such newly emerging sports stars as Milwaukee Bucks point guard Brandon Jennings, U.S. professional skier and Olympic gold medal winner Lindsey Vonn, professional lacrosse player Paul Rabil, Baltimore Orioles catcher Matthew Wieters, 2010 National League Rookie of the Year Buster Posey, UFC Welterweight Champion Georges St-Pierre, the number one pick in the 2010 Major League Baseball Draft (Bryce Harper of the Washington Nationals), NBA rookie Kemba Walker, and the number 2 pick in the 2001 NBA draft (Derrick Williams). In addition, the company's roster of athletes included established stars: NFL football players Tom Brady, Ray Lewis, Brandon Jacobs, Miles Austin, Vernon Davis, and Anquan Boldin; triathlon champion Chris "Macca" McCormack; professional baseball players Ryan Zimmerman and Jose Reyes; U.S. Women's National Soccer Team players Heather Mitts and Lauren Cheney; U.S. Olympic and professional volleyball player Nicole Branagh; U.S. Olympic swimmer Michael Phelps; and professional golfer Hunter Mahan.

In 2010, Under Armour hosted over 50 combines, camps, and clinics for male and female athletes in many sports at various regional sites in the United States. It sponsored American Youth Football ( an organization that promoted the development of youth), the Under Armour All-America Football Game (a nationally televised annual competition between the top seniors in high school football), the Under Armour Senior Bowl (a televised annual competition between the top seniors in college football), The Under Armour (Baltimore) Marathon, The Under Armour All-America Lacrosse Classic, and the All-America games in softball and volleyball for elite high school athletes. Under Armour had partnered with Ripken Baseball to outfit some 35,000 Ripken Baseball participants and to be the title sponsor for all 25 Ripken youth baseball tournaments. It had partnered with the Baseball Factory to outfit top high school baseball athletes from head to toe and serve as the title sponsor for nationally recognized baseball tournaments and teams. In addition, it was the presenting sponsor for the 2010 NFL Scouting Combine and, beginning with the 2011 season, Under Armour became the Official Footwear Supplier of Major League Baseball.

Under Armour spent approximately $43.5 million in 2011 for athlete endorsements and various sponsorships, compared to about $29.4 million in 2010. The company was contractually obligated to spend a *minimum* of $52.9 million for endorsements and sponsorships during 2012, and at least an additional $115.7 million during 2013–2017.[6] The company did not know precisely what its future sponsorship costs for individual athletes would be because its contractual agreements with these athletes were subject to certain performance-based variables.

## Retail Marketing and Product Presentation
The primary thrust of Under Armour's retail marketing strategy was to increase the floor space *exclusively* dedicated to Under Armour products in the stores of its major retail accounts. The key initiative here was to design and fund Under Armour "concept shops"—including flooring, in-store fixtures, product displays, life-size athlete mannequins, and lighting—within the stores of its major retail customers. This shop-in-shop approach was seen as an effective way to gain the placement of Under Armour products in prime floor space, educate consumers about Under Armour products, and create a more engaging and sales-producing way for consumers to shop for Under Armour products.

In stores that did not have Under Armour concept shops, Under Armour worked with retailers to establish optimal placement of its products. In "big-box" sporting goods stores, it was important to be sure that the growing variety of Under Armour products was represented in all of the various departments (hunting apparel in the hunting goods department, footwear and socks in the footwear department, and so on). Except for the retail stores with Under Armour concept shops, company personnel worked with retailers to employ in-store fixtures and displays that highlighted the UA logo and conveyed a performance-oriented, athletic look (chiefly through the use of life-size athlete mannequins). The idea was not only to enhance the visibility of Under Armour products but also reinforce the message that the company's brand was distinct from those of competitors.

**Media and Promotion**    Under Armour advertised in a variety of national digital, broadcast, and print media outlets and its advertising campaigns included a variety of lengths and formats. The company's "Protect this House" and "Click-Clack" campaigns featured several NFL players, and its "Protect this House" campaign had been used in several NFL and collegiate stadiums during games as a crowd prompt. A related ad campaign, "Protect this House.® I Will," focused heavily on the training aspect of sports. On several occasions, the company had secured the use of Under Armour products in movies, television shows, and video games; management believed the appearance of Under Armour products in these media reinforced authenticity of the brand and provided brand exposure to audiences that may not have seen Under Armour's other advertising campaigns. In 2011, Under Armour significantly grew the company's "fan base" via social sites like Facebook and Twitter, surpassing the million-fan mark and bringing attention to what management considered as the company's most compelling brand stories.

## Distribution Strategy

Under Armour products were available in over 25,000 retail stores worldwide at the end of 2011, of which about 18,000 retail stores were in North America. Under Armour also sold its products directly to consumers through its own factory outlet and specialty stores, website, and catalogs.

**Wholesale Distribution**    In 2011, 70 percent of Under Armour's net revenues were generated from sales to retailers. The company's principal customers included Dick's Sporting Goods, about 18 percent of sales), The Sports Authority (about 8 percent of sales), Academy Sports and Outdoors, Hibbett Sporting Goods, Modell's Sporting Goods, Bass Pro Shops, Cabela's, Footlocker, Finish Line, and The Army and Air Force Exchange Service. In Canada, the company's biggest customers were Sportchek International and Sportman International. Roughly 75 percent of all sales made to retailers were to large-format national and regional retail chains. The remaining 25 percent of wholesale sales were to lesser-sized outdoor and other specialty retailers, institutional athletic departments, leagues, teams, and fitness specialists. Independent

and specialty retailers were serviced by a combination of in-house sales personnel and third-party commissioned manufacturer's representatives.

**Direct-to-Consumer Sales**    In late 2007, Under Armour opened its first company-owned retail location at the Westfield Annapolis mall in Annapolis, Maryland. In May 2008, Under Armour also opened a larger 6,000-square-foot store at Westfield Fox Valley in Aurora, Illinois (a Chicago suburb). Going into 2012, the company had five Under Armour specialty stores (in Annapolis; Aurora; Natick, Massachusetts—a Boston suburb; Bethesda, Maryland; and Vail, Colorado) and 80 factory outlet locations in 34 states. The first Under Armour specialty store outside of North America was opened in Edinburgh, Scotland—it was owned and operated by First XV, a rugby store that was situated next door. In 2012, Under Armour opened a 25,000-square-foot showroom and retail store at its Tide Point headquarters in Baltimore, Maryland. In 2011, 27 percent of Under Armour's net revenues were generated through direct-to-consumer sales, including discounted sales at its factory outlet stores and sales through its specialty stores, global website (**www.ua.com**), and catalog.

**Product Licensing**    About 3 percent of the company's net revenues came from licensing arrangements to manufacture and distribute Under Armour branded products. Under Armour pre-approved all products manufactured and sold by its licensees, and the company's quality assurance team strived to ensure that licensed products met the same quality and compliance standards as company-sold products. In 2012, Under Armour had relationships with several licensees for team uniforms, eyewear, and custom-molded mouth guards, as well as the distribution of Under Armour products to college bookstores and golf pro shops. In addition, Under Armour had a relationship with a Japanese licensee, Dome Corporation, that had the exclusive rights to distribute Under Armour products in Japan. Dome sold Under Armour products to professional baseball and soccer teams (including Omiya Ardija, a professional soccer club in Saitama, Japan) and to over 2,000 independent specialty stores and large sporting goods retailers, such as Alpen, Himaraya, The Sports Authority, and Xebio. Under Armour made a minority equity investment in Dome Corporation in January 2011.

**Distribution Outside North America**    Because Under Armour management was convinced that the trend toward using performance products was global, it had begun entering foreign country markets as rapidly as was prudent. A European headquarters was opened in 2006 in Amsterdam, The Netherlands, to conduct and oversee sales, marketing, and logistics activities across Europe. The strategy was to first sell Under Armour products directly to teams and athletes and then leverage visibility in the sports segment to access broader audiences of potential consumers. By 2011, Under Armour had succeeded in selling products to Premier League Football clubs and multiple running, golf, and cricket clubs in the United Kingdom, soccer teams in France, Germany, Greece, Ireland, Italy, Spain, and Sweden, as well as First Division Rugby clubs in France, Ireland, Italy, and the United Kingdom.

Sales to European retailers quickly followed on the heels of gains being made in the sports team segment. In 2012, Under Armour had 4,000 retail customers in Austria, France, Germany, Ireland, and the United Kingdom and was generating revenues from third-party distributors who sold Under Armour products to retailers in Australia, Italy, Greece, Scandinavia, and Spain. In 2010–2011, sales efforts commenced in Latin America and Asia. In Latin America, Under Armour sold directly to retailers in some countries and in other countries sold its products to independent distributors who then were responsible for securing sales to retailers. In 2011, Under Armour opened a specialty store in Shanghai, China, to begin learning about Chinese consumers.

## Product Design and Development

UA products were manufactured with technical fabrications produced by third parties and developed in collaboration with the company's product development team. Under Armour favored the use of superior, technically advanced fabrics, produced to its specifications, and focused its product development efforts on design, fit, climate, and product end-use. The company regularly upgraded its products as next-generation fabrics when better performance characteristics became available and as the needs of athletes changed. Product development efforts also aimed at broadening the company's product offerings in both new and existing product categories and market segments. An effort was made to design products with "visible technology," utilizing color, texture, and fabrication that would enhance customers' perception and understanding of the use and benefits of Under Armour products.

Under Armour's product development team had significant prior industry experience at leading fabric and other raw material suppliers and branded athletic apparel and footwear companies throughout the world. The team worked closely with Under Armour's sports marketing and sales teams as well as professional and collegiate athletes to identify product trends and determine market needs. Collaboration among the company's product development, sales, and sports marketing team had proved important in identifying the opportunity and market for the recently introduced Catalyst products (made from 100 percent recycled plastic bottles) that were the cornerstone of the Under Armour Green Collection.

## Sourcing, Manufacturing, and Quality Assurance

Many of the technically advanced specialty fabrics and other raw materials used in UA products were developed by third parties and, typically, were available only from a limited number of sources. In 2011, approximately 50 to 55 percent of the fabric used in UA products came from six suppliers, with locations in Malaysia, Mexico, Peru, Taiwan, and the United States. Because a big fraction of the materials used in UA products were petroleum-based synthetics, the costs of the fabrics sourced from suppliers were subject to crude oil price fluctuations. Beginning in 2011, Under Armour introduced a line of Charged Cotton™ products that incorporated cotton fabrics subject to price fluctuations and varying cotton harvests.

In 2011, substantially all UA products were manufactured by 23 primary manufacturers, operating in 16 countries; seven manufacturers produced approximately 45 percent of UA's products. Approximately 60 percent were manufactured in Asia, 22 percent in Central and South America, 8 percent in Mexico, and 8 percent in the Middle East. All manufacturers used only fabrics preapproved by Under Armour, and all were evaluated for quality systems, social compliance, and financial strength by Under Armour's quality assurance team, prior to being selected and also on an ongoing basis. Under Armour required its contract manufacturers to adhere to a code of conduct regarding quality of manufacturing, working conditions, and other social concerns. The company strived to qualify multiple manufacturers for particular product types and fabrications and to seek out vendors that could perform multiple manufacturing stages, such as procuring raw materials and providing finished products, which helped UA control its cost of goods sold. The company had an office in Hong Kong to support its manufacturing, quality assurance, and sourcing efforts for apparel, and offices in Guangzhou, China, to support its manufacturing, quality assurance, and sourcing efforts for footwear.

Under Armour had a 17,000-square-foot Special Make-Up Shop located at one of its distribution facilities in Maryland where it had the capability to make and ship customized apparel products on tight deadlines for high-profile athletes, leagues, and teams. While these apparel products represented a tiny fraction of Under Armour's revenues, management believed the facility helped provide superior service to an important customer segment.

## Distribution Facilities and Inventory Management

Under Armour packaged and shipped the majority of its products for the North American market at two distribution facilities located approximately 15 miles from its Baltimore, Maryland, headquarters. One was a 359,000-square-foot facility built in 2000 and the other was a 308,000-square-foot facility; both were leased. In addition, the company utilized the services of a third-party logistics provider with primary locations in California and in Florida; the company's agreement with this provider was set to expire in December 2013. Distribution to European customers was handled by a third-party logistics provider based in Venlo, The Netherlands. Under Armour had contracted with a third-party logistics provider to handle packing and shipment to customers in Asia. Management expected that the company would add additional distribution facilities in the future.

Under Armour based the amount of inventory it needed to have on hand for each item in its product line on existing orders, anticipated sales, and the need to rapidly deliver orders to customers. Its inventory strategy was focused on (1) having sufficient inventory to fill incoming orders promptly and (2) putting strong systems and procedures in place to improve the efficiency with which it managed its inventories of individual products and total inventory. The amounts of seasonal products it ordered from manufacturers were based on current bookings, the need to ship seasonal items at the start of the shipping window in order to maximize the floor space productivity of retail customers, and the need to adequately stock its factory outlet stores. Excess inventories of particular products were either shipped to its factory outlet stores or earmarked for sale to third-party liquidators.

However, the growing number of individual items in UA's product line and uncertainties surrounding upcoming consumer demand for individual items made it difficult to accurately forecast how many units to order from manufacturers and what the appropriate stocking requirements were for many items. Under Armour's year-end inventories rose from $148.4 million in 2009 to $215.4 million in 2010 to $324.4 million in 2011—percentage increases that exceeded the gains in companywide revenues and that caused days of inventories to climb from 121.4 days in 2009 to 148.4 days in 2010 and to 155.8 days in 2011. The increases were due, in part, to long lead-times for design and production of some products and from having to begin manufacturing many products before receiving any orders for them. In January 2012, management announced that because inventory growth of 118 percent over the past two years had outstripped revenue growth of 72 percent, it was instituting a review of UA's entire product line and was contemplating cutbacks in the number of products offered, perhaps by as much as 20 percent.

## COMPETITION

The multisegment global market for sports apparel, athletic footwear, and related accessories was fragmented among some 25 brand-name competitors with diverse product lines and varying geographic coverage and numerous small competitors with specialized-use apparel lines that usually operated within a single country or geographic region. Industry participants included athletic and leisure shoe companies, athletic and leisure apparel companies, sports equipment companies, and large companies having diversified lines of athletic and leisure shoes, apparel, and equipment. In 2011, the global market for athletic footwear was about $65 billion, and the global market for sports apparel was approximately $125 billion. Nike was the clear market leader, with a footwear market share of about 17 percent and a sports apparel share of about 4.4 percent. Other prominent competitors besides Under Armour included adidas, Puma, Columbia, Fila, and Polo Ralph Lauren. Exhibit 4 shows a representative sample of the best-known companies and brands.

Competition was intense and revolved around performance and reliability, new product development, price, product identity through marketing and promotion, and customer support and service. It was common for the leading companies to actively sponsor sporting events and clinics and to contract with prominent and influential athletes, coaches, teams,

**EXHIBIT 4**   Major Competitors and Brands in Selected Segments of the Sports Apparel, Athletic Footwear, and Accessory Industry, 2012

| Performance Apparel for Sports (baseball, football, basketball, softball, volleyball, hockey, lacrosse, soccer, track & field, and other action sports) | Performance-Driven Athletic Footwear | Training/Fitness Clothing |
|---|---|---|
| • Nike<br>• Under Armour<br>• Eastbay<br>• adidas<br>• Russell | • Nike<br>• Reebok<br>• adidas<br>• New Balance<br>• Saucony<br>• Puma<br>• Rockport<br>• Converse<br>• Ryka<br>• Asics | • Nike<br>• Under Armour<br>• Eastbay<br>• adidas<br>• Puma<br>• Fila<br>• Lululemon athletica<br>• Champion<br>• Asics<br>• SUGOI |

| Performance Activewear and Sports-Inspired Lifestyle Apparel | Performance Skiwear | Performance Golf Apparel |
|---|---|---|
| • Polo Ralph Lauren<br>• Lacoste<br>• Izod<br>• Cutter & Buck<br>• Timberland | • Salomon<br>• North Face<br>• Descente<br>• Columbia<br>• Patagonia<br>• Marmot<br>• Helly Hansen<br>• Bogner<br>• Spyder<br>• Many others | • Footjoy<br>• Polo Golf<br>• Nike<br>• adidas<br>• Puma<br>• Under Armour<br>• Ashworth<br>• Cutter & Buck<br>• Greg Norman<br>• Many others |

colleges, and sports leagues to endorse their brands and use their products.

## Nike, Inc.

Incorporated in 1968, Nike was engaged in the design, development, and worldwide marketing and selling of footwear, sports apparel, sports equipment, and accessory products. Its principal businesses in 2012 are shown in the table at the bottom of this page.

Total companywide sales were $20.9 billion in fiscal 2011. Nike was the world's largest seller of athletic footwear and athletic apparel, with over 40,000

| Businesses | Fiscal 2011 Sales |
|---|---|
| Nike Brand footwear (over 800 models and styles) | $11,493 million |
| Nike Brand apparel | 5,475 |
| Nike Brand equipment for a wide variety of sports | 1,013 |
| Converse (a designer and marketer of athletic footwear, apparel, and accessories) | 1,130 |
| Nike Golf (footwear, apparel, golf equipment, accessories) | 623 |
| Cole Haan (a designer and marketer of dress and casual footwear, apparel, and accessories for men and women) | 518 |
| Hurley (a designer and marketer of action sports and youth lifestyle footwear and apparel, including shorts, tees, tanks, hoodies, and swimwear) | 252 |
| Umbro (a prominent British-based global provider of soccer apparel and equipment) | 224 |

## EXHIBIT 5    Nike's Worldwide Retail and Distribution Network, 2011

| United States | Foreign Countries |
|---|---|
| • ~20,000 retail accounts<br>• 150 Nike factory outlet stores<br>• 16 Nike stores<br>• 9 NIKETOWN stores<br>• 3 distribution centers<br>• Company website (www.nikestore.com) | • More than 20,000 retail accounts<br>• 243 Nike factory outlet stores<br>• 50 Nike stores<br>• 3 NIKETOWN stores<br>• 16 distribution centers<br>• Independent distributors and licensees in over 170 countries<br>• Company website (www.nikestore.com) |

retail accounts, over 470 company-owned stores, 19 distribution centers, and selling arrangements with independent distributors and licensees in over 170 countries (see Exhibit 5). About 57 percent of Nike's sales came from outside the United States. Nike's retail account base in the U.S. included a mix of footwear stores, sporting goods stores, athletic specialty stores, department stores, skate, tennis and golf shops, and other retail accounts. During fiscal 2011, Nike's three largest customers accounted for approximately 23 percent of U.S. sales in the United States; its three largest customers outside the U.S. accounted for 9 percent of total non-U.S. sales. In fiscal 2011, Nike had sales of $3.2 billion at its company-owned stores and website.

**Principal Products** Nike's athletic footwear models and styles were designed primarily for specific athletic use, although many were worn for casual or leisure purposes. Running, training, basketball, soccer, sport-inspired casual shoes, and kids' shoes were the company's top-selling footwear categories. It also marketed footwear designed for baseball, cheerleading, football, golf, lacrosse, outdoor activities, skateboarding, tennis, volleyball, walking, and wrestling. The company designed and marketed Nike-branded sports apparel and accessories for most all of these same sports categories, as well as sports-inspired lifestyle apparel, athletic bags, and accessory items. Footwear, apparel, and accessories were often marketed in "collections" of similar design or for specific purposes. It also marketed apparel with licensed college and professional team and league logos. Nike-brand offerings in sporting equipment included bags, socks, sport balls, eyewear, timepieces, electronic devices, bats, gloves, protective equipment, and golf clubs.

Exhibit 6 shows a breakdown of Nike's sales of footwear, apparel, and equipment by geographic region for fiscal years 2009–2011.

**Marketing, Promotions, and Endorsements** Nike responded to trends and shifts in consumer preferences by (1) adjusting the mix of existing product offerings, (2) developing new products, styles, and categories, and (3) striving to influence sports and fitness preferences through aggressive marketing, promotional activities, sponsorships, and athlete endorsements. Nike spent $2.45 billion in fiscal 2011, $2.36 billion in fiscal 2010, and $2.35 billion for what it termed "demand creation expenses" that included advertising and promotion expenses and the costs of endorsement contracts. Well over 500 professional, collegiate, club, and Olympic sports teams in football, basketball, baseball, ice hockey, soccer, rugby, speed skating, tennis, swimming, and other sports wore Nike uniforms with the Nike swoosh prominently visible. There were over 1,000 prominent professional athletes with Nike endorsement contracts in 2011–2012, including NFL players Drew Brees, Tim Tebow, Tony Romo, Aaron Rodgers, and Clay Mathews; Major League Baseball players Albert Pujols and Alex Rodriguez; NBA players LeBron James and Dwayne Wade; professional golfers Tiger Woods and Michelle Wie; and professional tennis players Victoria Azarenka, Maria Sharapova, Venus and Serena Williams, Roger Federer, and Rafael Nadal. When Tiger Woods turned pro, Nike signed him to a five-year $100 million endorsement contract and made him the centerpiece of its campaign to make Nike a factor in the golf equipment and golf apparel marketplace. LeBron James's recent endorsement deal with Nike was said to be worth $120 million. Because soccer was such a popular sport globally, Nike had more endorsement contracts with soccer athletes than with athletes in any other sport; track and field athletes had the second-largest number of endorsement contracts.

**EXHIBIT 6**  Nike's Sales of Nike Brand Footwear, Apparel, and Equipment, by Geographic Region, Fiscal Years 2009–2011

| | Fiscal Years Ending May 31 | | |
|---|---|---|---|
| **Sales Revenues and Earnings (in millions)** | **2011** | **2010** | **2009** |
| **North America** | | | |
| Revenues—Nike Brand footwear | $ 5,109 | $ 4,610 | $ 4,694 |
| Nike Brand apparel | 2,105 | 1,740 | 1,740 |
| Nike Brand equipment | 364 | 346 | 344 |
| Total Nike Brand revenues | $ 7,578 | $ 6.696 | $ 6,778 |
| Earnings before interest and taxes | $ 1,750 | $ 1,538 | $ 1,429 |
| Profit margin | 23.0% | 23.0% | 21.1% |
| **Western Europe** | | | |
| Revenues—Nike Brand footwear | $ 2,327 | $ 2,320 | $ 2,385 |
| Nike Brand apparel | 1,266 | 1,325 | 1,463 |
| Nike Brand equipment | 217 | 247 | 291 |
| Total Nike Brand revenues | $ 3,810 | $ 3,892 | $ 4,139 |
| Earnings before interest and taxes | $ 721 | $ 856 | $ 939 |
| Profit margin | 18.9% | 22.0% | 22.7% |
| **Central & Eastern Europe** | | | |
| Revenues—Nike Brand footwear | $ 600 | $ 558 | $ 673 |
| Nike Brand apparel | 356 | 354 | 468 |
| Nike Brand equipment | 75 | 81 | 106 |
| Total Nike Brand revenues | $ 1,031 | $ 993 | $ 1,247 |
| Earnings before interest and taxes | $ 233 | $ 253 | $ 394 |
| Profit margin | 22.6% | 25.5% | 31.6% |
| **Greater China** | | | |
| Revenues—Nike Brand footwear | $ 1,164 | $ 953 | $ 940 |
| Nike Brand apparel | 789 | 684 | 700 |
| Nike Brand equipment | 107 | 105 | 103 |
| Total Nike Brand revenues | $ 2,060 | $ 1,742 | $ 1,743 |
| Earnings before interest and taxes | $ 777 | $ 637 | $ 575 |
| Profit margin | 37.7% | 36.6% | 33.0% |
| **Japan** | | | |
| Revenues—Nike Brand footwear | $ 396 | $ 433 | $ 430 |
| Nike Brand apparel | 302 | 357 | 397 |
| Nike Brand equipment | 68 | 92 | 99 |
| Total Nike Brand revenues | $ 766 | $ 882 | $ 926 |
| Earnings before interest and taxes | $ 114 | $ 180 | $ 205 |
| Profit margin | 14.9% | 20.4% | 22.1% |
| **Emerging Markets** | | | |
| Revenues—Nike Brand footwear | $ 1,897 | $ 1,458 | $ 1,185 |
| Nike Brand apparel | 657 | 577 | 477 |
| Nike Brand equipment | 182 | 164 | 166 |

*(Continued)*

**EXHIBIT 6**    *(Continued)*

| Sales Revenues and Earnings (in millions) | Fiscal Years Ending May 31 | | |
|---|---|---|---|
| | 2011 | 2010 | 2009 |
| Total Nike Brand revenues | $ 2,736 | $ 2,199 | $ 1,828 |
| Earnings before interest and taxes | $ 688 | $ 521 | $ 364 |
| Profit margin | 25.1% | 23.7% | 19.9% |
| **All Regions** | | | |
| Revenues—Nike Brand footwear | $11,493 | $10,332 | $10,307 |
| Nike Brand apparel | 5,475 | 5,037 | 5,245 |
| Nike Brand equipment | 1,013 | 1,035 | 1,109 |
| Total Nike Brand revenues | $17,981 | $16,404 | $16,661 |
| Earnings before interest and taxes | $ 4,283 | $ 3,985 | $ 3,906 |
| Profit margin | 23.8% | 24.3% | 23.4% |

*Note 1:* Nike Brand data does not include Nike Golf and other Nike-owned businesses such as Converse, Cole-Haan, and Hurley, all of which are separately organized and do not break their activities down by geographic region for reporting purposes. Nike Golf had revenues of $623 million in fiscal 2011, $638 million in fiscal 2010, and $648 million in fiscal 2009.

*Note 2:* The revenue and earnings figures for all geographic regions include the effects of currency exchange fluctuations.

*Source:* Nike's 10-K Report for Fiscal 2011, pp. 21–24.

**Research and Development** Nike management believed R&D efforts had been and would continue to be a key factor in the company's success. Technical innovation in the design of footwear, apparel, and athletic equipment received ongoing emphasis in an effort to provide products that helped reduce injury, enhance athletic performance, and maximize comfort.

In addition to Nike's own staff of specialists in the areas of biomechanics, chemistry, exercise physiology, engineering, industrial design, and related fields, the company utilized research committees and advisory boards made up of athletes, coaches, trainers, equipment managers, orthopedists, podiatrists, and other experts who reviewed designs, materials, concepts for product improvements, and compliance with product safety regulations around the world. Employee athletes, athletes engaged under sports marketing contracts, and other athletes wear-tested and evaluated products during the design and development process.

**Manufacturing** About 98 percent of Nike's footwear was produced by contract manufacturers in Vietnam, China, Indonesia, and India, but the company had manufacturing agreements with independent factories in Argentina, Brazil, India, and Mexico to manufacture footwear for sale primarily within those countries. Nike-branded apparel was manufactured outside of the United States by independent contract manufacturers located in 33 countries; most production occurred in China, Thailand, Vietnam, Malaysia, Sri Lanka, Indonesia, Turkey, Cambodia, El Salvador, and Mexico.

In 2011, Nike established a fiscal 2015 revenue target of $28–$30 billion and reaffirmed its ongoing target of annual earnings per share growth in the 14–16 percent range.

## The adidas Group

The mission of The adidas Group is to be the global leader in the sporting goods industry with brands built on a passion for sports and a sporting lifestyle. Headquartered in Germany, its businesses and brands consist of:

- **adidas**—a designer and marketer of active sportswear, uniforms, footwear, and sports products in football, basketball, soccer, running, training, outdoor, and six other categories (74.0 percent of Group sales in 2011).

- **Reebok**—a well-known global provider of athletic footwear for multiple uses, sports and fitness apparel, and accessories (14.7 percent of Group sales in 2011).

- **TaylorMade-adidas Golf**—a designer and marketer of TaylorMade golf equipment, adidas golf shoes and golf apparel, and Ashworth golf apparel (7.8 percent of Group sales in 2011).

- **Rockport**—a designer and marketer of dress, casual, and outdoor footwear that largely targeted

## EXHIBIT 7   Financial Highlights for The adidas Group, 2006–2011 (in millions of €)

| Income Statement Data | 2011 | 2010 | 2009 | 2008 |
|---|---|---|---|---|
| Net sales | €13,334 | €11,990 | €10,381 | €10,799 |
| Gross profit | 6,344 | 5,730 | 4,712 | 5,256 |
| Gross profit margin | 47.5% | 47.8% | 45.4% | 48.7% |
| Operating profit | 1,011 | 894 | 508 | 1,070 |
| Operating profit margin | 7.6% | 7.5% | 4.9% | 9.9% |
| Net income | 670 | 567 | 245 | 642 |
| Net profit margin | 5.0% | 4.7% | 2.4% | 5.9% |
| **Balance Sheet Data** | | | | |
| Inventories | € 2,482 | € 2,119 | € 1,471 | € 1,995 |
| Working capital | 2,154 | 1,972 | 1,649 | 1,290 |
| **Net Sales by Brand** | | | | |
| adidas | € 9,867 | € 8,714 | € 7,520 | € 7,821 |
| Reebok | 1,962 | 1,913 | 1,603 | 1,717 |
| TaylorMade-adidas Golf | 1,044 | 909 | 831 | 812 |
| Rockport | 261 | 252 | 232 | 243 |
| Reebok-CCM Hockey | 210 | 200 | 177 | 188 |
| **Net Sales by Product** | | | | |
| Footwear | € 6,275 | € 5,389 | € 4,642 | € 4,919 |
| Apparel | 5,734 | 5,380 | 4,663 | 4,775 |
| Equipment | 1,335 | 1,221 | 1,076 | 1,105 |
| **Net Sales by Region** | | | | |
| Western Europe | € 3,922 | € 3,543 | € 3,261 | € 3,527 |
| European emerging markets | 1,596 | 1,385 | 1,122 | 1,179 |
| North America | 3,102 | 2,805 | 2,362 | 2,520 |
| Greater China | 1,229 | 1,000 | 967 | 1,077 |
| Other Asian markets | 2,125 | 1,972 | 1,647 | 1,585 |
| Latin America | 1,368 | 1,285 | 1,006 | 893 |

*Source:* Company annual reports, 2011, 2010, and 2009.

metropolitan professional consumers (2.0 percent of Group sales in 2011).

- **Reebok CCM Hockey**—one of the world's largest designers, makers, and marketers of hockey equipment and apparel under the brand names Reebok Hockey and CCM Hockey (1.6 percent of Group sales in 2011).

In 2011, The adidas Group produced record sales of €13.3 billion, increased profits to €670 (from €567 million in 2010), and significantly reduced long-term

borrowings from €1,337 million to €991 million. Exhibit 7 shows the company's financial highlights for 2008–2011.

The company sold products in virtually every country of the world. In 2011, its extensive product offerings were marketed through third-party retailers (sporting goods chains, department stores, independent sporting goods retailer buying groups, lifestyle retailing chains, and Internet retailers), 1,355 company-owned and franchised adidas and Reebok "concept" stores, 734 company-owned adidas and Reebok factory outlet stores, 312 other adidas and Reebok stores with varying formats, and various company websites (such as **www.adidas.com**, **www.reebok.com**, and **www.taylormadegolf.com**).

Like Under Armour and Nike, both adidas and Reebok were actively engaged in sponsoring major sporting events, teams, and leagues and in using athlete endorsements to promote their products. Recent high-profile sponsorships and promotional partnerships included Official Sportwear Partner of the 2012 Olympic Games (adidas), outfitting all volunteers, technical staff, and officials as well as all the athletes in Team Great Britain; Official Sponsors and ball supplier of the 2010 FIFA World Cup, the 2011 FIFA Women's World Cup Germany, and numerous other important soccer tournaments held by FIFA and the Union of European Football Associations or UEFA (adidas); Official Outfitters of NHL (Reebok), NFL (Reebok), NBA (adidas), WNBA (adidas), and NBA-Development League (adidas); Official Apparel and Footwear Outfitter for Boston Marathon (adidas); Official Licensee of Major League Baseball fan and lifestyle apparel (Reebok). Athletes that were under contract to endorse some of the company's brands included NBA players Derrick Rose, Tim Duncan, and John Wall; professional golfers Paula Creamer (LPGA), Jim Furyk, Sergio Garcia, Retief Goosen, Dustin Johnson, Kenny Perry, Justin Rose, and Mike Weir; soccer player David Beckham; and various participants in the 2012 Summer Olympics in London. In 2003, David Beckham, who had been wearing adidas products since the age of 12, signed a $160 million lifetime endorsement deal with adidas that called for an immediate payment of $80 million and subsequent payments said to be worth an average of $2 million annually for the next 40 years.[7] adidas was anxious to sign Beckham to a lifetime deal not only to prevent Nike from trying to sign him but also because soccer was considered the world's most lucrative sport and adidas management believed that Beckham's endorsement of adidas products resulted in more sales than all of the company's other athlete endorsements combined. In 2011, the company launched its biggest-ever global advertising campaign for adidas-brand products. Companywide expenditures for advertising, event sponsorships, athlete endorsements, and other marketing activities were €1.36 billion in 2011, up from €1.29 billion in 2010.

Research and development activities commanded considerable emphasis at The adidas Group. Management had long stressed the critical importance of innovation in improving the performance characteristics of its products. New apparel and footwear collections featuring new fabrics, colors, and the latest fashion were introduced on an ongoing basis to heighten consumer interest, as well as to provide performance enhancements—35 "major product launches" were conducted in 2009, 39 in 2010, and 48 in 2011. About 1,000 people were employed in R&D activities at 11 locations, of which 5 were devoted to adidas products, 3 to Reebok products, and 1 each for TaylorMade-adidas Golf, Rockport, and Reebok-CCM Hockey. In addition to its own internal activities, the company drew upon the services of well-regarded researchers at universities in Canada, England, and Germany. R&D expenditures in 2011 were €115 million, up from €81 million in 2008, €86 million in 2009, and €102 million in 2010.

Over 95 percent of production was outsourced to 308 independent contract manufacturers located in China and other Asian countries (77 percent), the Americas (15 percent), Europe (7 percent), and Africa (1 percent). The Group operated 9 relatively small production and assembly sites of its own in Germany (1), Sweden (1), Finland (1), the United States (4), Canada (3), and China (1). Close to 97 percent of the Group's production of footwear was performed in Asia; annual volume sourced from footwear suppliers had ranged from a low of 191 million pairs to a high of 245 million pairs during 2007–2011. During the same time frame, apparel production ranged from 239 million to 321 million units and the production of hardware products ranged from 34 million to 51 million units.

## ENDNOTES

[1] Daniel Roberts, "Under Armour Gets Serious," *Fortune,* November 7, 2011, p. 153.
[2] Ibid., p. 156.
[3] Ibid.
[4] Ibid.

[5] As stated on p. 53 of Under Armour's Prospectus for its Initial Public Offering of common stock, dated November 17, 2005.
[6] Company 10-K reports, 2009, 2010, and 2011.

[7] Steve Seepersaud, "5 of the Biggest Athlete Endorsement Deals," posted at **www.askmen.com**, accessed February 5, 2012.

# lululemon athletica, Inc.

## Arthur A. Thompson
### The University of Alabama

In early 2012, investor interest in lululemon athletica—a designer and retailer of high-end, yoga-inspired athletic apparel under the lululemon athletica and ivivva athletica brand names—was surging. Over the past 30 months, growing numbers of female shoppers were patronizing the company's stores to pay premium prices for lululemon-branded items that offered performance, fit, and comfort and were stylish as well. The company's functional and stylish apparel had taken on "must have" status among growing numbers of fitness-conscious women. People were flocking to lululemon stores not only because of the fashionable products but also because of the store ambience and attentive, knowledgeable store personnel. The company had responded by opening additional stores—35 in 2010 and 40 in 2011—and embellishing its product offerings to create a comprehensive line of apparel and accessories designed for athletic pursuits such as yoga, running, and general fitness; technical clothing for active female youths; and athletic products for men.

As lululemon's sales revenues climbed rapidly toward $1 billion annually, the company's stock price had risen from $2.25 per share on March 9, 2009 to close at $64.58 per share on February 3, 2012. Business analysts were speculating how long the lululemon athletica phenomenon would last and whether the company could carve out a sustainable market position for itself in the fitness and athletic apparel industry against such competing names as Nike, Under Armour, adidas, and Reebok.

In 2012, the company's products could be bought at its 174 retail stores in the United States, Canada, Australia, and New Zealand, and at the company's website, www.lululemon.com. For the fiscal year ending January 29, 2012, lululemon reported net revenues of $1.0 billion and net earnings of $184.1 million. Retail store sales accounted for 81.7 percent of company revenues, website sales accounted for 10.6 percent, and other (including wholesale sales to franchised stores, showroom sales, and sales at outlet centers) accounted for 7.7 percent.

## COMPANY BACKGROUND

A year after selling his eight-store surf-, skate-, and snowboard-apparel chain called Westbeach Sports, Chip Wilson took the first commercial yoga class offered in Vancouver, British Columbia, and found the result exhilarating. But he found the cotton clothing used for sweaty, stretchy power yoga completely inappropriate. Wilson's passion was technical athletic fabrics and in 1998 he opened a design studio for yoga clothing that also served as a yoga studio at night to help pay the rent. He began offering upscale yoga clothing made of performance fabrics and asked local yoga instructors to wear the products and give him feedback. Gratified by the positive response to yoga apparel, Wilson opened lululemon's first real store in the beach area of Vancouver, called Kitsilano, in November of 2000.

While the store featured Wilson-designed yoga clothing, Chip Wilson's vision was for the store to be a community hub where people could learn and discuss the physical aspects of healthy living—from yoga and diet to running and cycling, plus the yoga-related mental aspects of living a powerful life of possibilities. But the store's clothing selections proved so popular that dealing with customers crowded out the community-based discussions and training about the merits of living healthy lifestyles. Nonetheless, Chip Wilson and store personnel were firmly committed to healthy, active lifestyles, and Wilson soon came to the conclusion that for the store to provide staff members with the salaries and opportunities to experience fulfilling lives, the one-store company needed to expand into a multistore enterprise. Wilson believed that the increasing number of women participating in sports, and specifically yoga, provided ample room for expansion, and he saw lululemon athletica's yoga-inspired performance apparel as a way to address a void in the women's athletic apparel market. Wilson also saw the company's mission as one of providing people with the components to live a longer, healthier, and more fun life.

Several new stores were opened in the Vancouver area, with operations conducted through a Canadian operating company, initially named Lululemon Athletica, Inc. and later renamed lululemon canada inc. In 2002, the company expanded into the United States and formed a sibling operating company, Lululemon Athletica USA Inc. (later renamed as lululemon usa, inc), to conduct its U.S. operations. Both operating companies were wholly owned by affiliates of Chip Wilson. In 2004, the company opened a franchised store in Australia as a means of more quickly disseminating the lululemon athletica brand name, conserving on capital expenditures for store expansion, and boosting revenues and profits. The company wound up its fiscal year ending January 31, 2005 with 14 company-owned stores, 1 franchised store, and net revenues of $40.7 million. A second franchised store was opened in Japan later in 2005. Franchisees paid lululemon a one-time franchise fee and an ongoing royalty based on a specified percentage of net revenues; lululemon supplied franchised stores with garments at a discount to the suggested retail price.

Five years after opening the first retail store, it was apparent that lululemon apparel was fast becoming something of a cult phenomenon and a status symbol among yoga fans in areas where lululemon stores had opened. Avid yoga exercisers were not hesitating to purchase $120 color-coordinated lululemon yoga outfits that felt comfortable and made them look good. Mall developers and mall operators knew what lululemon was and had begun actively recruiting lululemon to locate stores in their malls.

In December 2005, with 27 company-owned stores, 2 franchised stores, and record sales en route to $85 million annually, Chip Wilson sold 48 percent of his interest in the company's capital stock to a group of private equity investors led by Advent International Corporation, which purchased 38.1 percent of the stock, and Highland Capital Partners, which purchased a 9.6 percent ownership interest. In connection with the transaction, the owners formed lululemon athletica inc. to serve as a holding company for all of the company's related entities, including the two operating subsidiaries, lululemon canada inc. and lululemon usa inc. Robert Meers, who had 15 years experience at Reebok and was Reebok's CEO from 1996–1999, joined lululemon as CEO in December 2005. Chip Wilson headed the company's design team and played a central role in developing the company's strategy and nurturing the company's distinctive corporate culture; he was also chairman of the company's board of directors, a position he had held since founding the company in 1998. Wilson and Meers assembled a management team with a mix of retail, design, operations, product sourcing, and marketing experience from such leading apparel and retail companies as Abercrombie & Fitch, Limited Brands, Nike, and Reebok.

Brisk expansion ensued. The company ended fiscal 2006 with 41 company-owned stores, 10 franchised stores, net revenues of $149 million, and net income of $7.7 million.

In 2007, the company's owners elected to take the company public. The initial public offering took place on August 2, 2007, with the company selling 2,290,909 shares to the public and various stockholders selling 15,909,091 shares of their personal holdings. Shares began trading on the NASDAQ under the symbol LULU and on the Toronto Exchange under the symbol LLL.

The company's announced growth strategy had five key elements:

1. *Grow the company's store base in North America.* The strategic objective was to add new stores to strengthen the company's presence in locations where it had existing stores and then selectively enter new geographic markets in the United States and Canada. Management believed that the company's strong sales in U.S. stores demonstrated the portability of the lululemon brand and retail concept. Plans were to open 20 to 25 stores in fiscal 2007 and 30 to 35 stores in fiscal 2008 in the United States and Canada.

2. *Increase brand awareness.* This initiative entailed leveraging the publicity surrounding the opening of new stores with grassroots marketing programs

that included organizing events and partnering with local fitness practitioners.

3. *Introduce new product technologies.* Management intended to continue to focus on developing and offering products that incorporated technology-enhanced fabrics and performance features that differentiated lululemon apparel and helped broaden the company's customer base.

4. *Broaden the appeal of lululemon products.* This initiative entailed (1) adding a number of apparel items for men, (2) expanding product offerings for women and young females in such categories as athletic bags, undergarments, outerwear, and sandals, and (3) adding products suitable for additional sports and athletic activities.

5. *Expand beyond North America.* In the near term, the company planned to expand its presence in Australia and Japan and then, over time, pursue opportunities in other Asian and European markets that offered similar, attractive demographics.

The company's growth and success over the next five years were impressive by any standard. Exhibit 1 summarizes the company's recent performance. In March 2012, top management projected that lululemon's full-year fiscal 2012 net revenues would be in the range of $1.3 billion to $1.325 billion and that diluted earnings per share would be in the range of $1.50 to $1.57. In early May 2012, lululemon's stock traded in the $75 to $80 price range, up from $15 per share at the beginning of 2010.

In January 2008, Christine M. Day joined the company as executive vice president, retail operations. Previously, she had worked at Starbucks, functioning in a variety of capacities and positions, including president, Asia Pacific Group (July 2004—February 2007), co-president for Starbucks Coffee International (July 2003 to October 2003), senior vice president, North American Finance & Administration; and vice president of sales and operations for Business Alliances. In April 2008, Day was appointed as lululemon's president and chief operating officer, and was named chief executive officer and member of the board of directors in July 2008. She held those positions in early 2012. During her tenure as CEO, Day had expanded and strengthened the company's management team to support its expanding operating activities and geographic scope, favoring the addition of people with relevant backgrounds and experiences at such companies as Nike, Abercrombie & Fitch, The Gap, and Speedo International. She also spent a number of hours each week in the company's stores observing how customers shopped, listening to their comments and complaints, and using the information to tweak product offerings, merchandising, and store operations.

Company founder Chip Wilson stepped down from his executive position as lululemon's chief innovation and branding officer effective January 29, 2012, but continued in his role of chairman of the company's board of directors.

## EXHIBIT 1 Financial and Operating Highlights, lululemon athletica, Fiscal Years 2007–2012 (in millions of $)

| | Fiscal Year Ending Jan, 29, 2012 | Fiscal Year Ending Jan. 30, 2011 | Fiscal Year Ending Jan. 31, 2010 | Fiscal Year Ending Feb. 1, 2009 | Fiscal Year Ending Jan. 31, 2007 |
|---|---|---|---|---|---|
| **Selected Income Statement Data** | | | | | |
| Net revenues | $1,000.8 | $711.7 | $452.9 | $353.5 | $148.0 |
| Cost of goods sold | 431.6 | 316.8 | 229.8 | 174.4 | 72.2 |
| Gross profit | 569.3 | 394.9 | 223.1 | 179.1 | 75.7 |
| Selling, general, and administrative expenses | 282.3 | 212.8 | 136.2 | 118.1 | 51.9 |
| Operating profit | 287.0 | 180.4 | 86.5 | 56.6 | 16.6 |
| Net profit (loss) | 185.0 | 121.8 | 58.3 | 39.4 | 7.7 |
| Earnings per share | | | | | |
| Basic | $1.29 | $0.86 | $0.41 | $0.29 | $0.06 |
| Diluted | 1.27 | 0.85 | 0.41 | 0.28 | 0.06 |

*(Continued)*

**EXHIBIT 1**    *(Concluded)*

|  | Fiscal Year Ending Jan, 29, 2012 | Fiscal Year Ending Jan. 30, 2011 | Fiscal Year Ending Jan. 31, 2010 | Fiscal Year Ending Feb. 1, 2009 | Fiscal Year Ending Jan. 31, 2007 |
|---|---|---|---|---|---|
| **Balance Sheet Data** | | | | | |
| Cash and cash equivalents | $409.4 | $316.3 | $159.6 | $56.8 | $15.5 |
| Inventories | 104.1 | 57.5 | 44.1 | | 26.6 |
| Total assets | 734.6 | 499.3 | 307.3 | 211.6 | 71.3 |
| Stockholders' equity | 606.2 | 394.3 | 233.1 | 154.8 | 37.4 |
| **Cash Flow and Other Data** | | | | | |
| Net cash provided by operating activities | $203.6 | $180.0 | $118.0 | $45.4 | 25.4 |
| Capital expenditures | 116.9 | 30.4 | 15.5 | 40.5 | 13.3 |
| **Store Data** | | | | | |
| Number of corporate-owned stores open at end of period | 174 | 133 | 110 | 103 | 41 |
| Number of franchised stores open at end of period | 0 | 4 | 14 | 10 | 10 |
| Sales per gross square foot at corporate-owned stores open at least one full year | $2,004 | $1,726 | $1,318 | $1,450 | $1,411 |
| Average sales at corporate-owned stores open at least one year | $5.33 million | $4.96 million | $3.76 million | $4.06 million | $4.93 million |

*Source:* Company 10-K reports for fiscal years ending, January 31, 2008, February 1, 2009, January 30, 2011, and January 31, 2012.

# LULULEMON'S STRATEGY AND BUSINESS IN 2012

In 2012, lululemon athletica continued to view its core mission as "providing people with the components to live a longer, healthier and more fun life." Its primary target market was:

> "a sophisticated and educated woman who understands the importance of an active, healthy lifestyle. She is increasingly tasked with the dual responsibilities of career and family and is constantly challenged to balance her work, life, and health. We believe she pursues exercise to achieve physical fitness and inner peace."

Management believed that other athletic apparel companies were not effectively addressing the unique style, fit, and performance needs of women who were embracing yoga and a variety of other fitness and athletic activities. lululemon sought to address this void in the marketplace by incorporating style, feel-good comfort, and functionality into its apparel products and using its retail store network to market directly to these women. Almost 16 million Americans, of which nearly 73 percent were women, spent an estimated $5.7 billion on yoga classes and products in 2011.[1] However, while the company was founded to address the unique needs and preferences of women, management recognized the merits of broadening the company's market target to include other population segments. Recently, it had begun designing and marketing products for men and athletic female youths who appreciated the technical rigor and premium quality of athletic and fitness apparel. Management also believed that participation in athletic and fitness activities was destined to climb as people over 60 years of age became increasingly focused on living longer, healthier, active lives in their retirement years and engaged in regular exercise and recreational activities. Another demand-enhancing factor was that consumer decisions to purchase athletic, fitness, and recreational apparel were being driven not only by an actual need for functional products but also by a desire to create a particular lifestyle perception through the apparel they wore. Consequently, senior executives were positioning the company to capitalize on the broadening market potential for lululemon apparel that loomed ahead.

The chief components of the business strategy that top management had launched when lululemon athletica became a public company in mid-2007 remained largely intact in 2012:

- Grow the store base in North America, primarily the United States.
- Open additional stores outside of North America.
- Increase awareness of the lululemon brand and apparel line.
- Incorporate next-generation fabrics and technologies in the company's products to strengthen consumer association of the lululemon brand with technically advanced apparel products and enable lululemon to command higher prices for its apparel products compared to the prices of traditional athletic apparel.
- Broaden the product line by designing lululemon products for a bigger range of athletic activities.
- Provide a distinctive in-store shopping experience, complemented with strong ties to fitness instructors and fitness establishments, local athletes and fitness-conscious people, and various community-based athletic and fitness events.

Perhaps the two biggest strategic adjustments since 2007 had been to discontinue and reverse the use of franchising as a component of the company's retailing and store expansion strategy and to launch a direct-to-consumer strategic initiative whose principal thrust was selling apparel at the company's website, www.lululemon.com.

## Retail Distribution and Store Expansion Strategy

After several years of experience in establishing and working with franchised stores in the United States, Australia, Japan, and Canada, top management in 2010 determined that having franchised stores was not in the company's best long-term strategic interests. A strategic initiative was begun to either acquire the current stores of franchisees and operate them as company stores or convert the franchised stores to a joint venture arrangement where lululemon owned the controlling interest in the store and the former franchisee owned a minority interest. In some cases, contracts with franchisees contained a clause allowing lululemon to acquire a franchised store at a specified percentage of trailing 12-month sales. The three franchised stores in Canada became company-owned in 2009 and 2010. The franchise rights of nine store locations in Australia, in which lululemon already had an ownership interest, were acquired during 2010; five of nine franchised stores in the United States were converted to company-owned in 2010 and 2011. The franchised store established in Japan in 2005 was converted to a company-owned store months after it opened. The last four franchised stores—three in Colorado and one in California—were reacquired in 2011.

As of February 2012, lululemon's retail footprint included:

- 47 stores in Canada scattered across seven provinces, but mainly located in British Columbia, Alberta, and Ontario.
- 108 company-owned stores in the United States (27 states and the District of Columbia).
- 18 stores in Australia.
- 1 store in New Zealand (opened in 2011).

Virtually all stores were branded lululemon athletica, but five company-owned stores were branded ivivva athletica and specialized in dance-inspired apparel for female youths.

Current store expansion efforts were concentrated mainly in the United States. The company's plans for 2012 called for opening 30 new stores in the U.S., 2 ivivva athletica–branded stores in Canada, and 5 new stores in Australia and New Zealand. Over time, management expected to expand into additional countries, primarily Asia and Europe, either by opening company-owned stores or by entering into joint ventures with experienced and capable retail partners.

Lululemon management undertook ongoing evaluations of the company's portfolio of company-owned store locations. Underperforming store locations were closed. One California store was closed in 2009. In 2010, one corporate-owned ivivva athletica store in British Columbia and one corporate-owned lululemon athletica store in Australia were closed. No stores were closed in 2011.

In fiscal year 2011 ending January 31, 2012, the company's retail stores that had been open at least one year had average sales of $2,004 per square foot, versus average sales per square foot of $1,726 in fiscal 2010 and $1,318 in fiscal 2009 (Exhibit 1). Management believed its sales-per-square-foot performance had consistently been the best in the retail apparel sector—for example, the stores of specialty fashion retailers like J Crew and Abercrombie & Fitch typically had annual sales averaging $600–$700 per square foot.

## Lululemon's Store Showroom Strategy

In 2012 lululemon had "showrooms" in 35 locations in the United States, 4 Australian locations, 2 New Zealand locations, and 1 location in Hong Kong. Showrooms functioned as a means of introducing the lululemon brand and culture to a community, developing relationships with fitness instructors and fitness enthusiasts, and hosting community-related fitness events, all in preparation for the likely opening of a new lululemon athletica retail store in the near future. Showroom personnel worked with local athletes, recruited fitness instructors to be ambassadors for lululemon products and lululemon-sponsored fitness events, hosted get-acquainted parties for fitness instructors and fitness enthusiasts, and acted as local experts on where to find great yoga or Pilates classes, fitness centers, and health and wellness information and events. Showrooms were only open part of the week so that personnel could be out in the community meeting people, participating in local yoga and fitness classes, and promoting attendance at various fitness activities and wellness events. In addition, showroom personnel began the process of recruiting well-regarded local yoga studios, health clubs, and fitness centers to stock and retail a selection of lululemon's products.

## Wholesale Sales Strategy

Lululemon marketed its products to select yoga studios, health clubs, and fitness centers as a way to gain the implicit endorsement of local fitness instructors and personnel for lululemon branded apparel, familiarize the customers of these establishments with the lululemon brand, and give them an opportunity to conveniently purchase lululemon apparel. There was no intent to grow wholesale sales to these types of establishments into a significant revenue contributor. Rather, the strategic objective was to build brand awareness, especially in new geographic locales.

## Website Sales Strategy

In 2009, lululemon launched its e-commerce website to enable customers to make online purchases and supplement its already-functioning phone sales activities. Management saw online sales as having three strategic benefits: (1) providing added convenience for core customers, (2) making lululemon products in geographic markets where there were no lululemon stores, and (3) helping build brand awareness, especially in new markets, including those outside of North America. The company's direct-to-consumer channel (online and phone sales) quickly became an increasingly substantial part of the company's business, accounting for revenues of $57.3 million in fiscal 2010 (8.1 percent of net revenue) and $106.3 million in fiscal 2011 (10.6 percent of net revenue). lululemon provided free shipping on all orders.

In addition to making purchases, website visitors could browse information about what yoga was, what the various types of yoga were, and their benefits; learn about fabrics and technologies used in lululemon's products; read recent posts on lululemon's yoga blog; and stay abreast of lululemon activities in their communities.

## Retail Stores

The company's retail stores were located primarily on street locations, in upscale strip shopping centers, in lifestyle centers, and in malls. Typically, stores were leased and were 2,500 to 3,000 square feet in size. Most all stores included space for product display and merchandising, checkout, fitting rooms, a restroom, and an office/storage area. While the leased nature of the store spaces meant that each store had its own customized layout and arrangement of fixtures and displays, each store was carefully decorated and laid out in a manner that projected the ambience and feel of a homespun local apparel boutique rather than the more impersonal, cookie-cutter atmosphere of many apparel chain stores.

One unique feature of lululemon's retail stores was that the floor space allocated to merchandising displays and customer shopping could be sufficiently cleared to enable the store to hold an in-store yoga class before or after regular shopping hours. Every store hosted a complimentary yoga class each week, complete with yoga mats and a professional yoga instructor; when the class concluded, the attendees were given a 15 percent–off coupon to use in shopping for products in the store. From time to time, yoga ambassadors demonstrated their moves in the store windows and on the sales floor. Exhibit 2 shows the exteriors and interiors of representative lululemon athletica stores.

The company's goal was to sell all of its products at full price.[2] Special colors and seasonal items were in stores for only a limited time—such products were on 3, 6, or 12-week life cycles so that frequent shoppers could always find something new. Store inventories of short-cycle products were deliberately limited to help

## EXHIBIT 2   Representative Exterior and Interior Scenes at lululemon Stores

foster a sense of scarcity, condition customers to buy when they saw an item rather than wait, and avoid any need to discount unsold items. In one instance, a hot-pink color that launched in December was supposed to have a two-month shelf life, but supplies sold out in the first week. However, supplies of core products that did not change much from season to season were more ample to minimize the risk of lost sales due to items being out-of-stock. Approximately 95 percent of the merchandise in lululemon stores was sold at full price.[3]

| Women | | Men |
|---|---|---|
| • Sports bras | • Skirts and dresses | • Tops |
| • Tanks | • Socks and underwear | • Jackets and hoodies |
| • Tops | • Gear bags | • Shorts |
| • Jackets | • Caps and headbands | • Pants |
| • Hoodies | • Sweat cuffs and gloves | • Gear bags |
| • Pants | • Water bottles | • Socks and underwear |
| • Crops | • Yoga mats and props | • Caps and gloves |
| • Shorts | • Instructional yoga DVDs | • Yoga mats, props, and instructional DVDs |

## Product Line

In 2012, lululemon offered a diverse and growing selection of premium-priced performance apparel and accessories (see the table above) for women, men, and female youths that were designed for healthy lifestyle activities such as yoga, running, and general fitness. While many of its products were specifically intended for the growing number of people that participated in yoga, the company had for some years been broadening its product range to address the needs of other activities.

Exhibit 3 shows a sampling of lululemon's garment offerings.

## Product Design and Development

Lululemon's product design efforts were led by a team of designers based in Vancouver and headed by the company's founder, Chip Wilson. The team collaborated closely with various international designers. The lululemon design team included athletes and users of the company's products who embraced lululemon's design philosophy and dedication to premium quality. Input was also actively sought from the fitness ambassadors recruited by store personnel and store customers—ambassadors had become an integral part of the product design process, testing and evaluating products and providing real-time feedback on performance and functionality. Design team members regularly worked at stores to interact with and receive direct feedback from customers. In addition, the design team used various market intelligence sources to identify and track market trends. Plus, the team hosted meetings each year in several geographic markets to discuss the company's products with local athletes, trainers, yogis, and members of the fitness industry and gather their ideas for product improvements and new products. The design team incorporated all of this input to make fabric selections,

develop new products, and make adjustments in the fit, style, and function of existing products.

The design team worked closely with its apparel manufacturers to incorporate innovative fabrics that gave lululemon garments such characteristics as stretch ability, moisture-wicking capability, color fastness, feel-good comfort, and durability. Fabric quality was evaluated via actual wear tests and by a leading testing facility. Before bringing out new products with new fabrics, lululemon used the services of a leading independent inspection, verification, testing, and certification company to conduct a battery of tests on fabrics for such performance characteristics as pilling, shrinkage, abrasion resistance, and colorfastness. Lastly, lululemon design personnel worked with leading fabric suppliers to identify opportunities to develop fabrics that lululemon could trademark and thereby gain added brand recognition and brand differentiation. Trademarked fabrics currently incorporated in lululemon products included:

- *Luon*—a fabric that was designed to wick away moisture, move with the body, and eliminate irritation (was included in more than half of the company's products).
- *Luxtreme*—a wicking fabric that was silky and lightweight and primarily used in running products.
- *Silverescent*—a fabric that reduced odors as a result of the antibacterial properties of the silver in the fabric.

Where appropriate, product designs incorporated convenience features, such as pockets to hold credit cards, keys, digital audio players, and clips for heart rate monitors, and long sleeves that covered the hands for cold-weather exercising. Product specifications called for the use of advanced sewing techniques, such as flat seaming, that increased comfort and functionality, reduced chafing and skin irritation, and strengthened important seams. All of these design elements

## EXHIBIT 3    Examples of lululemon Apparel Items

*Source:* www.lululemon.com, accessed February 13, 2012.

and fabric technologies were factors in enabling lululemon to price its high-quality technical athletic apparel at prices above those of traditional athletic apparel.

Typically, it took 8 to 10 months for lululemon products to move from the design stage to availability in its retail stores; however, the company had the capability to bring select new products to market in as little as two months. Management believed its lead times were shorter than those of most apparel brands due to the company's streamlined design and development process, the real-time input received from customers and ambassadors at its store locations, and the short times it took to receive and approve samples from manufacturing suppliers. Short lead times facilitated quick responses to emerging trends or shifting market conditions.

## Sourcing and Manufacturing

Production was the only value chain activity that lululemon did not perform internally. lululemon did not own or operate any manufacturing facilities to produce fabrics or make garments. All of its products were sourced from a group of 45 manufacturers, five of which produced approximately 67 percent of the company's products in fiscal 2011. However, the company deliberately refrained from entering into long-term contracts with any of its manufacturing suppliers, preferring instead to transact business on an order-by-order basis and rely on the close working relationships it had developed with its suppliers over the years. The fabrics used in lululemon products were sourced by the manufacturers from a limited number of pre-approved suppliers. During the fiscal year ending January 31, 2012, approximately 49 percent of lululemon's apparel products were produced in China, approximately 41 percent in South/South East Asia, approximately 3 percent in Canada, and the remainder in the United States, Israel, Peru, Egypt, and other countries.

Lululemon took great care to ensure that its manufacturing suppliers shared lululemon's commitment to quality and ethical business conduct. All manufacturers were required to adhere to a code of conduct regarding quality of manufacturing, working conditions, environmental responsibility, fair wage practices, and compliance with child labor laws, among others. lululemon utilized the services of a leading inspection and verification firm to closely monitor each supplier's compliance with applicable law, lululemon's workplace code of conduct, and other business practices that could reflect badly on lululemon's choice of suppliers.

The company's North American manufacturers were the reason lululemon had the capability to speed select products to market and respond quickly to changing trends and unexpectedly high buyer demand for certain products. While management expected to utilize manufacturers outside of North America to supply the bulk of its apparel requirement in the years to come, it intended to maintain production in Canada and the United States whenever possible.

## Distribution Facilities

Lululemon shipped products to its stores in North America from a leased 102,000-square-foot facility in Vancouver, British Columbia, and a leased 82,000-square-foot facility in Sumner, Washington. Both were modern and cost-efficient. In 2011, the company began operations at a leased 54,000-square-foot distribution center in Melbourne, Australia, to supply its stores in Australia and New Zealand. Management believed these three facilities would be sufficient to accommodate its expected store growth and expanded product offerings over the next several years. Merchandise was typically shipped to retail stores through third-party delivery services multiple times per week, providing them with a steady flow of new inventory.

## Community-Based Marketing

One of lululemon's differentiating characteristics was its community-based approach to building brand awareness and customer loyalty. Local fitness practitioners chosen to be ambassadors introduced their fitness class attendees to the lululemon brand, thereby leading to interest in the brand, store visits, and word-of-mouth marketing. Each yoga-instructor ambassador was also called upon to conduct a complimentary yoga class every four to six weeks at the local lululemon store they were affiliated with. In return for helping drive business to lululemon stores and conducting classes, ambassadors were periodically given bags of free products, and billboard-size portraits of each ambassador wearing lululemon products and engaging in physical activity at a local landmark were posted in their local lululemon store, which helped them expand their clientele.

Every lululemon store had a dedicated community coordinator who developed a customized plan for organizing, sponsoring, and participating in athletic, fitness, and philanthropic events in the local area. In addition, each store had a community events bulletin board for posting announcements of upcoming activities, providing fitness education information and brochures, and promoting the local yoga studios and fitness centers of ambassadors. There was also a chalkboard in each store's fitting room area where customers could scribble comments about lululemon products or their yoga class experiences or store personnel; these comments were relayed to lululemon headquarters every two weeks. Customers could use a lululemon micro website to track their progress regarding fitness or progress toward life goals.

lululemon made little use of traditional advertising print or television advertisements, preferring instead to rely on its various grassroots, community-based marketing efforts.

## Store Personnel

As part of the company's commitment to providing customers with an inviting and educational store environment, lululemon's store sales associates, who the company referred to as educators, were coached to personally engage and connect with each guest who entered the store. Educators, many of whom had prior experience as a fitness practitioner or were avid runners or yoga enthusiasts, received approximately 30 hours of in-house training within the first three months of their employment. Training was focused on teaching educators about leading a healthy and balanced life, exercising self-responsibility, and setting lifestyle goals, and preparing them to explain the technical features of all lululemon products and to serve as knowledgeable references for customers seeking information on fitness classes, instructors, and events in the community. New hires that lacked knowledge about the intricacies of yoga were given subsidies to attend yoga classes so they could understand the activity and better explain the benefits of lululemon's yoga apparel.

People who shopped at lululemon stores were called "guests," and store personnel were taught how to "educate" guests about lululemon apparel, not sell to them. To provide a personalized, welcoming, and relaxed experience, store educators referred to their guests on a first-name basis in the fitting and changing area, allowed them to use store restrooms, and offered them complimentary fresh-filtered water. Management believed that such a soft-sell, customer-centric environment encouraged product trial, purchases, and repeat visits.

As of January 29, 2012, lululemon had 5,807 employees, of which 4,872 were employed in the company's retail stores, 157 were employed in distribution, 132 were employed in design, merchandise, and production, and the remaining 646 performed selling, general and administrative tasks, and other functions. None of the company's employees were covered by a collective bargaining agreement and there had been no labor-related work stoppages. Management believed its relations with employees were excellent.

## Core Values and Culture

Consistent with the company's mission of "providing people with the components to live a longer, healthier and more fun life," lululemon executives sought to promote and ingrain a set of core values centered on developing the highest-quality products, operating with integrity, leading a healthy balanced life, self-empowerment and self-responsibility, positive inner development, and individual goal-setting. The company sought to provide employees with a supportive and goal-oriented work environment; all employees were encouraged to set goals aimed at reaching their full professional, health, and personal potential. The company offered personal development workshops and goal-coaching to assist employees in achieving their goals. Many lululemon employees had a written set of professional, health, and personal goals. All employees had access to a "learning library" of personal development books that included Steven Covey's *The Seven Habits of Highly Effective People,* Rhonda Byrne's *The Secret,* and Brian Tracy's *The Psychology of Achievement.* To celebrate their first anniversary as a lululemon employee, staff members and store educators were rewarded with company-paid admission to a three-day weekend Landmark Forum seminar, a transformative workshop intended to help people think and act outside existing limits, act responsibly, and put themselves on a path to realizing their potential. lululemon's CEO, who had attended this Landmark Forum seminar, said, "We feel like Landmark is a tool. It has created a culture of accountability."[4]

All of this culture-related training was a direct result of Chip Wilson's long-term efforts to help employees live healthy, active, and fun lives. From the company's earliest days, Chip Wilson had maintained he didn't start lululemon just to sell premium-priced apparel; he believed an integral part of the company's mission was to give employees and customers a proactive assist on their journey to self-esteem, empowerment, and a fulfilling lifestyle. In the "Chip's Musings" section of the company website, Wilson said "The law of attraction"—(that visualizing goals is the key to attaining them, a central tenet of *The Secret*)—"is the fundamental law that lululemon was built on from its 1998 inception."[5] He went on to say that "Our vision is 'to elevate the world from mediocrity to greatness,' and we are growing so we can train more people and spread the word of *The Secret*—which to us at lululemon is not so secret."[6] Wilson, who was the chairman of lululemon's board of directors and owned 35 percent of the company's stock in 2012, was the principal architect of the company's culture and core values, and the company's work climate reflected his business and lifestyle philosophy. He had digested much of his

## EXHIBIT 4   The lululemon Manifesto

| The lululemon Manifesto |
|---|

- Drink FRESH water and as much water as you can. Water flushes unwanted toxins from your body and keeps your brain sharp.
- A daily hit of athletic-induced endorphins gives you the power to make better decisions, helps you be at peace with yourself, and offsets stress.
- Do one thing a day that scares you.
- Listen, listen, listen, and then ask strategic questions.
- Write down your short- and long-term GOALS four times a year. Two personal, two business and two health goals for the next 1, 5, and 10 years. Goal setting triggers your subconscious computer.
- Life is full of setbacks. Success is determined by how you handle setbacks.
- Your outlook on life is a direct reflection of how much you like yourself.
- That which matters the most should never give way to that which matters the least.
- Stress is related to 99 percent of all illness.
- Jealousy works the opposite way you want it to.
- The world is changing at such a rapid rate that waiting to implement changes will leave you two steps behind. DO IT NOW, DO IT NOW, DO IT NOW!
- Friends are more important than money.
- Breathe deeply and appreciate the moment. Living in the moment could be the meaning of life.
- Take various vitamins. You never know what small mineral can eliminate the bottleneck to everlasting health.
- Don't trust that an old age pension will be sufficient.
- Visualize your eventual demise. It can have an amazing effect on how you live for the moment.
- The conscious brain can only hold one thought at a time. Choose a positive thought.
- Live near the ocean and inhale the pure salt air that flows over the water. Vancouver will do nicely.
- Observe a plant before and after watering and relate these benefits to your body and brain.
- Practice yoga so you can remain active in physical sports as you age.
- Dance, sing, floss, and travel.
- Children are the orgasm of life. Just like you did not know what an orgasm was before you had one, nature does not let you know how great children are until you have them.
- Successful people replace the words "wish," "should," and "try," with "I will."
- Creativity is maximized when you're living in the moment.
- Nature wants us to be mediocre because we have a greater chance to survive and reproduce. Mediocre is as close to the bottom as it is to the top, and will give you a lousy life.
- lululemon athletica creates components for people to live longer, healthier, and more fun lives. If we can produce products to keep people active and stress-free, we believe the world will become a much better place.
- Do not use cleaning chemicals on your kitchen counters? Someone will inevitably make a sandwich on your counter.
- SWEAT once a day to regenerate your skin.
- Communication is COMPLICATED. We are all raised in a different family with slightly different definitions of every word. An agreement is an agreement only if each party knows the conditions for satisfaction and a time is set for satisfaction to occur.
- What we do to the earth we do to ourselves.
- The pursuit of happiness is the source of all unhappiness.

*Source:* www.lululemon.com, accessed February 12, 2012.

philosophy about life in general and personal development into a set of statements and prescriptions that he called "the lululemon manifesto" (see Exhibit 4). The manifesto was a core element of lululemon's culture.

Senior executives believed the company's work climate and core values attracted passionate and motivated employees who were driven to succeed, and they viewed the lululemon workforce as a valuable resource in enabling the company to successfully execute its business strategy, develop brand loyalty, connect with customers, and achieve strong financial performance. Moreover, many customers reacted quite positively to the educational emphasis store personnel placed on health, wellness, and personal development and to what they had seen or heard about lululemon's manifesto, corporate philosophy, and business mission.

## COMPETITION

Competition in the athletic apparel industry is principally centered on product quality, performance features, innovation, fit and style, distribution capabilities, brand image and recognition, and price. Rivalry among competing brands is vigorous, involving both established companies who were expanding their production and the marketing of performance products and recent entrants attracted by the growth opportunities.

Lululemon competed with wholesalers and direct sellers of technical athletic apparel, most especially Nike, The adidas Group AG (which marketed athletic and sports apparel under its adidas, Reebok, and Ashworth brands), and Under Armour. Nike had a powerful and well-known global brand name, an extensive and diverse line of athletic and sports apparel, 2011 apparel sales of $5.5 billion, and 2011 total revenues (footwear, apparel, and equipment) of $20.9 billion. Nike was the world's largest seller of athletic footwear and athletic apparel, with over 40,000 retail accounts, and over 470 company-owned stores, 19 distribution centers, and selling arrangements with independent distributors and licensees in over 170 countries; its retail account base for sports apparel in the U.S. included a mix of sporting goods stores, athletic specialty stores, department stores, and skate, tennis, and golf shops.

Adidas and Reebok were both global brands that produced worldwide sports apparel revenues of approximately $7.5 billion in 2011; their product lines consisted of high-tech performance garments for a wide variety of sports and fitness activities, as well as recreational sportswear. The adidas Group sold products in virtually every country of the world. In 2011, its extensive product offerings were marketed through third-party retailers (sporting goods chains, department stores, independent sporting goods retailer buying groups, lifestyle retailing chains, and Internet retailers), 1,355 company-owned and franchised adidas and Reebok "concept" stores, 734 company-owned adidas and Reebok factory outlet stores, 312 other adidas and Reebok stores with varying formats, and

various company websites (including **www.adidas .com** and **www.reebok.com**).

Under Armour, an up-and-coming designer and marketer of performance sports apparel, had apparel sales totaling $1.0 billion in 2011; as of early 2012, Under Armour products were available in 25,000 retail stores worldwide, 18,000 of which were in Canada and the United States. Under Armour also sold its products directly to consumers through its own factory outlet and specialty stores, website, and catalogs.

Nike, The adidas Group, and Under Armour all aggressively marketed and promoted their high-performance apparel products and spent heavily to grow consumer awareness of their brands and build brand loyalty. All three sponsored numerous athletic events, provided uniforms and equipment with their logos to collegiate and professional sports teams, and paid millions of dollars annually to numerous high-profile male and female athletes to endorse their products. Like lululemon, they designed their own products but outsourced the production of their garments to contract manufacturers.

Lululemon also competed with specialty department store retailers that carried women's athletic apparel, including:

- **The Gap**—a specialty fashion chain with more than 1,100 stores in North America and a product line that included its Bodyfit collection of performance and lifestyle products.

- **Athleta**—a new 10-store chain and online retailer that specialized in comfortable, fashionable, high-performance women's apparel for workouts, sports, physically active recreational activities, and leisure wear. Athleta was a subsidiary of Gap, Inc. and plans called for more than tripling the number of Athleta store locations in upscale metropolitan shopping areas across the U.S. over the next several years. In 2012, Athleta initiated its first national advertising campaign, "Power to the She," to promote the Athleta brand.

- **Nordstrom**—a nationally-respected retailer that had recently introduced its own Zella line of attire for yoga, other fitness activities, and leisure wear; many of the initial products in the Zella collection were designed by a former member of lululemon's design team. In 2012, Zella-branded items could be purchased online at Nordstrom's website and at some 200 Nordstrom full-line department stores (typically 140,000 to 250,000 square-feet in size) and Nordstrom Rack stores (typically 30,000 to 50,000 square-feet in size) in 28 states.

- **Lucy**—Lucy was a women's activewear brand designed for style, performance, and fit that was intended for yoga, running, training, and other fitness and active recreational activities; the product offerings included tops, bottoms, skirts, dresses, jackets, hoodies, sports bras, socks, caps, headbands, and bags/totes. Lucy-branded performance apparel was sold at 65 company-owned Lucy stores across the United States and at www.lucy.com. Lucy was a wholly owned subsidiary of VF Corp., a designer, marketer, wholesaler, and retailer of 23 brands of apparel and footwear, with 2011 sales of $9 billion.

- **bebe stores**—a 200+ store and online retailer of women's apparel; the company's BEBE SPORT collection was targeted for a variety of fitness and sports activities and included sports bras, tops, pants, shorts, jackets, hoodies, and tennis outfits.

The items in the Gap Bodyfit, Athleta, Zella, Lucy, and BEBE SPORT collections were typically priced 10 percent to 25 percent below similar kinds of lululemon products. Gap's Athleta stores also offered free yoga classes, sold direct to consumers at www.athleta.com (with free shipping), and was sponsoring 20 female athletes in 2012 (the group included yoga teachers, a karate instructor, a mountain climber, a skier, runners, and a mountain bike racer). In addition, Athleta had a special social media website, www.athleta.net/chi, that connected women with interests in sports and fitness, nutrition and health, tutorials and training plans, and travel and adventure.

## ENDNOTES

[1] "Yoga in America," *Yoga Journal,* January 27, 2012, posted at http://yogawithgaileee.blogspot.com/2010/01/yoga-in-america-study-by-yoga-journal.html, and accessed February 12, 2012.

[2] Dana Mattioli, "Lululemon's Secret Sauce," *The Wall Street Journal,* March 22, 2012, pp. B1–B2.

[3] Ibid.

[4] As quoted in Danielle Sacks, "Lululemon's Cult of Selling," *Fast Company,* April 1, 2009, posted at www.fastcompany.com and accessed on February 12, 2012.

[5] Ibid.

[6] Ibid.

# Coach Inc. in 2012: Its Strategy in the "Accessible" Luxury Goods Market

**John E. Gamble**
University of South Alabama

**Ronald W. Eastburn**
University of South Alabama

Coach Inc.'s strategy that created the "accessible" luxury market in ladies handbags made it among the best-known luxury brands in North America and Asia and had allowed its sales to grow at an annual rate of 20 percent between 2000 and 2011, reaching $4.2 billion. During that period, the company's net income increased from $16.7 million to $880 million. In 2012, Coach Inc. designed and marketed women's and men's bags, leather accessories, leather apparel items, business cases, footwear, jewelry, travel bags, watches, and fragrances. All of the company's leather products were manufactured by third-party suppliers in Asia, while Coach-branded footwear, eyewear, watches, and fragrances were made available through licensing agreements.

Coach's strategy, which focused on matching key luxury rivals in quality and styling while beating them on price by 50 percent or more, yielded a competitive advantage in attracting not only middle-income consumers desiring a taste of luxury, but also affluent and wealthy consumers with the means to spend considerably more on a handbag. Another distinctive element of the company's strategy was its multichannel distribution model, which included indirect wholesale sales to third-party retailers but focused primarily on direct-to-consumer sales. In 2012, Coach operated 345 full-price retail stores and 143 factory outlets in North America, 169 stores in Japan, and 66 stores in China, along with Internet and catalog sales. The direct-to-consumer segment accounted for 87 percent of the company's 2011 net sales. Coach's indirect wholesaler segment had 2011 net sales of $540 million, with the U.S. wholesale segment serving about 970 department store locations and the Coach International group supplying 211 department store locations in 20 countries.

The company's two primary strategic priorities in 2012 were to increase global distribution and improve same-store sales productivity. The company's strategy focused on five key initiatives:

- Build market share in North America by opening approximately 15 new full-price retail stores and 25 factory outlets.
- Build market share in Japan through the addition of 15 new locations.
- Raise brand awareness and build share in under-penetrated markets, including Europe and South America and, most notably Asia, with 30 new locations planned in the region.
- Increase sales of products targeted toward men. Specifically, new store openings in North America and Japan would focus on men's products, while the new shops in China would offer dual-gender product lines.
- Raise brand awareness and build market share through coach.com, global e-commerce sites, and social networking initiatives.

While the company's performance was commendable and its strategy seemed to have merit, the company's profit margins were still below the levels achieved prior to the onset of a slowing economy in 2007. In addition, its share price had experienced a sharp decline during the first six months of 2012. Going into fiscal 2013, it was undecided if the company's recent growth could be sustained and its competitive advantage would hold in the face of new accessible luxury lines launched by such aggressive and successful luxury brands as Michael Kors, Salvatore Ferragamo, Prada Giorgio Armani, Dolce & Gabbana, and Versace.

# COMPANY HISTORY

Coach was founded in 1941 when Miles Cahn, a New York City leather artisan, began producing ladies handbags. The handbags crafted by Cahn and his family in their SoHo loft were simple in style and extremely resilient to wear and tear. Coach's classic styling and sturdy construction proved popular with discriminating consumers, and the company's initial line of 12 unlined leather bags soon developed a loyal following. Over the next 40 years, Coach was able to grow at a steady rate by setting prices about 50 percent lower than those of more luxurious brands, adding new models, and establishing accounts with retailers such as Bloomingdale's and Saks Fifth Avenue. The Cahn family also opened company-owned stores that sold Coach handbags and leather accessories. After 44 years of family management, Coach was sold to diversified food and consumer goods producer, Sara Lee.

Sara Lee's 1985 acquisition of Coach left the handbag manufacturer's strategy and approach to operations more-or-less intact. The company continued to build a strong reputation for long-lasting, classic handbags. However, by the mid-1990s the company's performance began to decline as consumers developed a stronger preference for stylish French and Italian designer brands such as Gucci, Prada, Louis Vuitton, Dolce & Gabbana, and Ferragamo. By 1995, annual sales growth in Coach's best-performing stores declined from 40 percent to 5 percent as the company's traditional leather bags fell out of favor with consumers.

In 1996, Sara Lee made 18-year-Coach-veteran Lew Frankfort head of its languishing handbag division. Frankfort's first move was to hire Reed Krakoff, a top Tommy Hilfiger designer, as Coach's new creative director. Krakoff believed new products should be based upon market research rather than designers' instincts about what would sell. Under Krakoff, Coach conducted extensive consumer surveys and held focus groups to ask customers about styling, comfort, and functionality preferences. The company's research found that consumers were looking for edgier styling, softer leathers, and leather-trimmed fabric handbags. Once prototypes had been developed by a team of designers, merchandisers, and sourcing specialists, hundreds of previous customers were asked to rate prototype designs against existing handbags. The prototypes that made it to production were then tested in selected Coach stores for six months before a launch was announced. The design process developed by Krakoff also allowed Coach to launch new collections every month. Prior to Krakoff's arrival, Coach introduced only two collections per year.

Frankfort's turnaround plan also included a redesign of the company's flagship stores to complement Coach's contemporary new designs. Frankfort abandoned the stores' previous dark, wood-paneled interiors in favor of minimalist architectural features that provided a bright and airy ambiance. The company also improved the appearance of its factory stores, which carried test models, discontinued models, and special lines that sold at discounts ranging from 15 percent to 50 percent. Such discounts were made possible by the company's policy of outsourcing production to 40 suppliers in 15 countries. The outsourcing agreements allowed Coach to maintain a sizeable pricing advantage relative to other luxury handbag brands in its full-price stores as well. Handbags sold in Coach full-price stores ranged from $200 to $500, which was well below the $700 to $800 entry-level price charged by other luxury brands.

Coach's attractive pricing enabled it to appeal to consumers who would not normally consider luxury brands, while the quality and styling of its products were sufficient to satisfy traditional luxury consumers. In fact, a *Women's Wear Daily* survey found that Coach's quality, styling, and value mix was so powerful that affluent women in the U.S. ranked Coach ahead of much more expensive luxury brands like Hermes, Ralph Lauren, Prada, and Fendi.[1]

By 2000, the changes to Coach's strategy and operations allowed the brand to build a sizeable lead in the "accessible luxury" segment of the leather handbags and accessories industry and made it a solid performer in Sara Lee's business lineup. With the turnaround successfully executed, Sara Lee management elected to spin off Coach through an IPO in October 2000 as part of a restructuring initiative designed to focus the corporation on food and beverages.

Coach Inc.'s financial results and stock price performance proved to be stellar, as evidenced by its quadrupled growth in annual sales from $555 million in 1999 to more than $4.2 billion in 2012, reflecting their success in identifying and capitalizing quickly on opportunities for growth. This was translated into earnings over the same timeframe from $16.7 million to $880 million. Though Coach Inc.'s share price had fallen dramatically at the beginning of the economic slowdown in 2007, it rebounded after its profitability improved in 2010.

Exhibit 1 presents Coach's income statements for fiscal 2007 through fiscal 2011. Exhibit 2 presents the company's balance sheets for fiscal 2010 and fiscal 2011. Exhibit 3 provides a review of Coach's stock price performance since October 2000.

**EXHIBIT 1 Coach Inc.'s Consolidated Statements of Income, Fiscal 2007–Fiscal 2011 (in thousands, except share amounts)**

| | 2011 | 2010 | 2009 | 2008 | 2007 |
|---|---|---|---|---|---|
| Net sales | $4,158,507 | $3,607,636 | $3,230,468 | $3,180,757 | $2,612,456 |
| Cost of goods sold | 1,134,966 | 973,945 | 907,858 | 773,654 | 589,470 |
| Gross profit | 3,023,541 | 2,633,691 | 2,322,610 | 2,407,103 | 2,022,986 |
| Selling, general, and administrative expenses | 1,718,617 | 1,483,520 | 1,350,697 | 1,259,974 | 1,029,589 |
| Operating income | 1,304,924 | 1,150,171 | 971,913 | 1,147,129 | 993,397 |
| Interest income | 1,031 | 7,961 | 10,779 | 44,639 | 41,273 |
| Income tax | 425,155 | 423,192 | 359,323 | 408,729 | 398,141 |
| Net income | $ 880,800 | $ 734,940 | $ 623,369 | $ 783,039 | $ 636,529 |
| Dividends declared per common share | $0.68 | $0.38 | $0.08 | $0.00 | $0.00 |
| Net income per share | | | | | |
| Basic shares | $2.99 | $2.36 | $1.93 | $2.20 | $1.72 |
| Diluted shares | $2.92 | $2.33 | $1.91 | $2.17 | $1.69 |
| Shares | | | | | |
| Basic shares outstanding | 294,877 | 311,413 | 323,714 | 355,731 | 369,661 |
| Diluted shares outstanding | 301,558 | 315,848 | 325,620 | 360,332 | 377,356 |

*Source:* Coach Inc. 10Ks, various years.

**EXHIBIT 2 Coach Inc.'s Balance Sheets, Fiscal 2010–Fiscal 2011 (in thousands)**

| | July 2, 2011 | July 3, 2010 |
|---|---|---|
| **ASSETS** | | |
| Current assets: | | |
| Cash and cash equivalents | $ 699,782 | $ 596,470 |
| Short-term investments | 2,256 | 99,928 |
| Trade accounts receivable (less allowances of $9,544 and $6,374, respectively) | 142,898 | 109,068 |
| Inventories | 421,831 | 363,285 |
| Deferred income taxes | 93,902 | 77,355 |
| Prepaid expenses | 38,203 | 30,375 |
| Other current assets | 53,516 | 26,160 |
| Total current assets | 1,452,388 | 1,302,641 |
| Long-term investments | | |
| Property and equipment, net | 582,348 | 548,474 |
| Goodwill and intangible assets | 340,792 | 315,649 |
| Deferred income taxes | 103,657 | 156,465 |
| Other assets | 155,931 | 143,886 |
| Total assets | $2,635,116 | $2,467,115 |
| **LIABILITIES AND STOCKHOLDERS' EQUITY** | | |
| Current liabilities: | | |
| Accounts payable | $ 118,612 | $ 105,569 |
| Accrued liabilities | 473,610 | 422,725 |
| Revolving credit facilities | | |
| Current portion of long-term debt | 795 | 742 |
| Total current liabilities | 593,017 | 529,036 |
| Deferred income taxes | | |
| Long-term debt | 23,360 | 24,159 |

*(Continued)*

**EXHIBIT 2**   *(Concluded)*

|  | July 2, 2011 | July 3, 2010 |
|---|---|---|
| Other liabilities | 406,170 | 408,627 |
|    Total liabilities | 1,022,547 | 961,822 |
| Stockholders' equity: | | |
| Preferred stock: (auth. 25,000,000 shares; $0.01 par value) none issued | – | |
| Common stock: (authorized 1,000,000,000 shares; $0.01 par value) | 2,886 | 2,969 |
|    Issued and outstanding 288,514,529 and 296,867,247, respectively | | |
| Additional paid-in capital | 2,000,426 | 150,2982 |
| Accumulated deficit | (445,654) | (30,053) |
| Accumulated other comprehensive income | 54,911 | 29395 |
|      Total stockholders' equity | 1,612,569 | 1,505,293 |
|      Total liabilities and stockholders' equity | $2,635,116 | $2,467,115 |

*Source:* Coach Inc. 2011 10-K.

**EXHIBIT 3**   Performance of Coach Inc.'s Stock Price, October 2000–June 2011

**(a) Trend in Coach Inc.'s Common Stock Price**

**(b) Performance of Coach Inc.'s Stock Price versus the S&P 500 Index**

# OVERVIEW OF THE GLOBAL LUXURY GOODS INDUSTRY IN 2012

According to a 2011 Bank of America/Merrill Lynch study, the world's most well-to-do consumers spent more than $224 billion on luxury goods in 2010. The U.S. represented 30 percent of industry sales, Europe accounted for 30 percent, 20 percent of industry sales were made in China, and Japan was responsible for 11 percent of total industry sales. Italian companies commanded 27 percent of industry sales, while French companies held a 22 percent share, Swiss companies possessed a 19 percent share, and U.S. companies accounted for 14 percent of industry sales. The most valuable luxury brands in terms of annual revenues in 2011 were Louis Vuitton, Gucci, Hermes, and Cartier. The handbag and leather accessories segment of the industry was estimated at $28 billion in 2010 (see Exhibit 4).

The global luxury goods retail market was significantly affected by the economic slowdown and financial crisis of 2007–2009 as consumers in most income categories cut back on discretionary purchases. The poor general economic conditions created a 0.6 percent annual decline in industry sales between 2006 and 2010. However, while sales declined in the United States, Japan, and Europe, emerging markets, and especially China, became a key growth driver for the industry from 2006 to 2009. Continued growth in China and other emerging markets was expected to allow luxury goods sales to increase by 7.8 percent annually through 2015 to reach a staggering $350 billion.

Luxury brands, in general, relied on creative designs, high quality, and brand reputation to attract customers and build brand loyalty. Price sensitivity for luxury goods was driven by brand exclusivity, customer-centric marketing, and to a large extent some emotional sense of status and value. The market for luxury goods was divided into three main categories: haute-couture, traditional luxury, and the growing submarket "accessible luxury." At the apex of the market was haute couture with its very high-end "custom" product offering that catered to the extremely wealthy. Leading brands in the traditional luxury category included such fashion design houses as Prada, Burberry, Hermes, Gucci, Polo Ralph Lauren, Calvin Klein, and Louis Vuitton. Some of these luxury goods makers also broadened their appeal with diffusion lines in the accessible luxury market to compete with Coach, DKNY, and other lesser luxury brands. For example, while Dolce & Gabbana dresses might sell at price points between $1,000 and $1,500, under their D&G affordable luxury brand—dresses of similar appearance were priced at $400 to $600. Giorgio Armani's Emporio Armani line and Gianni Versace's Versus lines typically sold at price points about 50 percent less than similar-looking items carrying the marquee labels. Profit margins on marquee brands approximated 40–50 percent, while most diffusion brands carried profit margins of about 20 percent. Luxury goods manufacturers believed diffusion brands' lower profit margins were offset by the opportunity for increased sales volume and the growing size of the accessible luxury market and protected margins on such products by sourcing production to low-wage countries.

Industry sales in the United States had become more dependent on the success of diffusion lines in the accessible luxury category. Although primary traditional luxury consumers in the U.S. comprised the top one percent of wage earners with household

## EXHIBIT 4  The Global Handbag and Accessories Market (dollar amounts in billions)

| | U.S. | Japan | China | Asia (Including Japan) | Other/Europe | Total |
|---|---|---|---|---|---|---|
| **Sales** | $10.0 | $4.4 | $3.2 | $12.0 | $6.0 | $28.0 |
| **Share of market** | 36% | 16% | 11% | 43% | 21% | 100% |
| **Gender Mix Estimates** | | | | | | |
| **Men's** | 15% | 20% | 45% | 25% | 15% | 15% |
| **Women's** | 85% | 80% | 55% | 75% | 85% | 85% |

*Source:* J.P. Morgan Analyst Report and Coach reports.

incomes of $300,000 or better, those consumers that earned substantially less also aspired to own products with higher levels of quality and styling. The growing desire for luxury goods by middle-income consumers was thought to be a result of a wide range of factors, including effective advertising and television programming that promoted conspicuous consumption. The demanding day-to-day rigor of a two-income household was another factor suggested to urge middle-income consumers to reward themselves with luxuries. An additional factor contributing to rising sales of luxury goods in the United States was the "Trade up, trade down"[2] shopping strategy, whereby consumers would balance their spending by offsetting gains made with lower-priced necessities purchased at major retailers (e.g., Walmart and Target) to enable more discretionary spending available for indulgences on high-end product purchases.

## The Growing Demand for Luxury Goods in Emerging Markets

Emerging markets, especially China and India, were expected to provide a major boost to the luxury goods market because of rapidly increasing wealth levels and standard of living gains. In 2012, 2.7 million individuals in China had a net worth of more than $1 million, and 63,500 individuals had net worths of more than $15 million. Luxury goods were also highly demanded by China's middle class, which allowed it to become the world's third-largest luxury market in 2010, with sales of luxury goods approaching $32 billion. Luxury goods spending in China was expected to overtake that of Japan and the United States, making China the world's largest market for luxury goods by 2015.

This is a remarkable outcome considering the luxury market has only been in existence there since the 1990s. Prior to this time, market entry by outsiders was restricted by the Chinese government despite the so-called open-door policy and economic reform. However, this all changed around 2000, along with the rapid economic and social developments occurring in China, and a group of luxury brands, such as Chanel, Prada, and Dolce & Gabbana, entered the market. Others, like Coach entered with local distributors. From 2007 to 2010, the Chinese luxury goods market was one of the key growth drivers to the global luxury goods market, and the competition of luxury brands gradually moved from major cities to smaller-tier ones. In 2012, close to 1,000 store locations operated within the Chinese market under the brands of approximately 25 leading luxury marketers. Leading the charge was Hugo Boss with 114 stores, followed by Armani with 104 stores. Coach was ranked eighth in luxury goods store locations in China with 52 stores.

Luxury goods producers were also opening retail stores in India, which was another rapidly growing market for luxury goods. India's booming economy had created a new class of "business maharajahs"—highly affluent and globalized professionals. To serve this consumer segment, some 60 global luxury fashion and accessories brands had begun selling their products in India, mainly through local franchise partners who manage the brand. However, this opportunity came with some distinct challenges. For example, sales of western women's clothing had struggled because Indian women still consider elaborate, highly crafted saris and other traditional items the garments of choice for formal occasions. Also, local designers such as Tarun Tahiliani and Satya Paul had more local brand recognition than some European or U.S. fashion houses. Watches, jewelry, and handbags, most of which have immediate brand recognition, fared better and accounted for the largest portion of luxury good sales in India.

## Counterfeiting

It was estimated that between $300 and $600 billion worth of counterfeit goods were sold in countries throughout the world. European and American companies that produced highly sought after branded products were most vulnerable to counterfeiting, with fakes plaguing almost every industry. Fake Rolex watches or Ralph Lauren Polo shirts had long been a problem, but by the mid-2000s, counterfeiters were even making knockoffs of branded auto parts and prescription drugs. Counterfeiting had become so prevalent that the Global Congress on Combating Counterfeiting estimated that 9 percent of all goods sold worldwide were not genuine. About two-thirds of all counterfeit goods were produced by manufacturers in China and Asian countries.

Luxury brands have found it financially and operationally beneficial to team up to combat counterfeiters. Luxury brands such as LVMH and Estee Lauder had collaborated to develop best practices for measuring and implementing international piracy enforcement. LVMH and Apple teamed up and shared enforcement costs once it was discovered that counterfeit iPhone and iPad covers with LV logos were being produced—mutually gaining from their partnership.

# COACH'S STRATEGY AND INDUSTRY POSITIONING

Coach offered distinctive, easily recognizable luxury products that were extremely well made and provided excellent value. The company's array of products included ladies handbags, leather accessories such as key fobs, belts, electronic accessories, and cosmetics cases, and outerwear such as gloves, hats, and scarves. Also, Coach designed and marketed leather business cases and luggage. It also expanded its accessories product offerings through licensing agreements with the Movado Group for Coach-branded watches in 1998, the Jimlar Corporation for Coach-branded ladies footwear in 1999, and Marchon Eyewear, Inc. for Coach eyewear in 2003. However, Coach entered into a licensing agreement with Luxottica in 2010 that would transition its eyewear products business beginning in the second half of 2012. The new agreement would expand its collection of prescription glasses and sunglasses marketed in Coach retail stores, at coach.com, in department stores, and select sunglass retailers and optical retailers in major markets. In spring 2010, Estee Lauder agreed to produce a fragrance for Coach that would be distributed through Coach retail stores, coach.com, and about 3,000 U.S. department stores. Coach offered four women's fragrances and one men's fragrance.

Handbags accounted for 63 percent of Coach's 2011 sales of $4.2 billion, while accessories made up 27 percent. All other products accounted for 10 percent of company sales, which reflected a slight product mix change favoring the other product groupings since 2007, where the sales mix was 64 percent, 28 percent, and 8 percent, respectively. Royalties from Coach's licensing agreements with Movado, Jimlar, and Marchon accounted for approximately 1 percent of sales and was not a major contributor to overall earnings.

Coach positioned its brand in the lower part of the accessible or affordable luxury pyramid. This particular market provides a larger opportunity relative to that of more exclusive brands. Coach targeted the top 20 percent of Americans by household income, as opposed to the top 3 to 5 percent targeted by most European luxury brands. Coach had focused on sales in China, Japan, and the United States because these three countries lead global luxury goods spending. The company's sales in Japan had increased from $144 million in 2002 to $748 million in 2011, and its market share in the U.S. had nearly doubled since 2002.

During 2011, roughly 84 percent of Coach's total net sales (up from 75 percent in 2010) were generated from products introduced within the year. Given that the collections are seasonal and are planned to be sold in stores for short promotional periods of time, production quantities are limited, and are designed to minimize risks associated with owning inventory. Sales of Coach's products for men grew from about 2.5 percent to nearly 5 percent of its global business, increasing to more than $200 million by 2011. Over time, Coach expected men's products to account for 15 percent or more of its global sales. The company's emphasis on dual-gender product offerings reflects the uptrend in the men's luxury goods market.

## Flexible Sourcing

All of Coach's production was outsourced to contract manufacturers, with vendors in China accounting for 85 percent of its production requirements. Vendors located in Vietnam and India produced the remaining 15 percent of Coach's product requirements. Management controlled quality throughout the process with product development offices in Hong Kong, China, South Korea, India, and Vietnam. This broad-based, global manufacturing strategy was designed to optimize the mix of cost, lead times, and construction capabilities.

## Approach to Differentiation

The market research design process developed by Executive Creative Director Reed Krakoff provided the basis of Coach's differentiated product line: Each quarter, major consumer research is undertaken to define product trends, selections, and consumer desires. This, together with the company's procurement process that selected only the highest-quality leathers and its sourcing agreements with quality offshore manufacturers, contributed to the company's reputation for high quality and value. Monthly product launches enhanced the company's voguish image and gave consumers reason to make purchases on a regular basis. The company's market research found its best customers visited a Coach store once every two months and made a purchase every seven months. Research in 2006 suggested the average Coach customer purchased four handbags per year. Lew Frankfort said the increase was attributable to monthly product launches that "increase the frequency of consumer visits" and women's changing style preference of "using bags to complement their wardrobes in the same way they used to use shoes."[3] A retail analyst agreed with Frankfort's assessment of the importance of frequent product introductions, calling it "a huge driver of traffic and sales and has enabled them to capture the . . . customer who wants the newest items and fashions."[4] Seventy percent of Coach's sales came from products introduced within the fiscal year. However, the company's Coach Classics collection, which was made up of lighter-weight, updated versions of iconic Coach handbag designs from the 1970s and 1980s, was among its best-selling lines in 2012.

The aesthetic attractiveness of Coach's full-price stores, which were designed by an in-house architectural group under the direction of Krakoff, further enhanced the company's luxury image. The company's stores significantly enhanced the Coach brand and was consistent with its strategy of raising awareness and aggressively growing market share, For example, a 9,400-square-foot store opened in 2012 featured an impressive four-story glass and stainless steel back-lit facade, as well as the Coach Horse and Carriage logo. Coach sought to make customer service experiences an additional differentiating aspect of the brand. It had agreed since its founding to refurbish or replace damaged handbags, regardless of the age of the bag. The company provided store employees with regular customer service training programs and scheduled additional personnel during peak shopping periods to ensure all customers were attended to satisfactorily. Through the company's Special Request service, customers were allowed to order merchandise for home delivery if the particular handbag or color wasn't available during a visit to a Coach store.

Coach also saw its communications with its customers as an opportunity for further differentiation. It communicated with customers through a wide range of direct marketing activities that included email contacts, websites, catalogs, and brochures. In fiscal 2011, Coach reported that consumer contacts increased 52 percent to over 625 million and was primarily driven by increased email communications. The company contact list included approximately 19 million active households in North America and 4.2 million active households in Japan. Also in 2011, Coach distributed approximately a million catalogs in its stores in Japan, Hong Kong, Macau, and mainland China

## Retail Distribution

Coach channels of distribution involved direct-to-consumer channels and indirect channels. Direct-to-consumer channels included full-price stores in the

**EXHIBIT 5**   Coach Inc.'s Retail Stores by Geographic Region, 2007–2011

| | 2007 | 2008 | 2009 | 2010 | 2011 |
|---|---|---|---|---|---|
| North American retail stores | 259 | 297 | 330 | 342 | 345 |
| North American factory stores | 93 | 102 | 111 | 121 | 143 |
| Coach Japan locations | 137 | 149 | 155 | 161 | 169 |
| Coach China locations | 16 | 24 | 28 | 41 | 66 |
| Total stores | 505 | 572 | 624 | 665 | 723 |

Source: Coach Inc., 10-K.

U.S., factory stores in the U.S., Internet sales, catalog sales, and stores in both Japan and China. Indirect sales included wholesale accounts with department stores in the U.S. and other international markets. Exhibit 5 provides the number of Coach retail stores by geographic region for 2007 through 2011. Exhibit 6 presents Coach's net sales and operating income by channel of distribution for 2009 through 2011.

**Full-Price Stores**   In 2011, Coach had 345 full-price retail stores in the United States, which comprised 70 percent of its total U.S. outlets. Full-price stores were divided into three categories—core locations, fashion locations, and flagship stores. Under Coach's tiered merchandising strategy, the company's flagship stores carried the most sophisticated and highest-priced items, while core stores carried widely demanded lines. The company's fashion locations tended to stock a blend of Coach's best-selling lines and chic specialty bags.

Coach's site selection process placed its core and fashion stores in upscale shopping centers and downtown shopping areas, while flagship stores were restricted to high-profile fashion districts in cities such as New York, Chicago, Beverly Hills, and San Francisco. Even though flagship stores were "a beacon for the brand"[5] as Frankfort described them, the company had been very prudent in the number of flagship stores it operated since such stores, by definition, were required to be located on the world's most expensive parcels of real estate.

A further advance launched in 2010 was the Coach brand "Reed Krakoff," created as a standalone entity with higher average price points than the Coach brand, with store openings initially planned for North

**EXHIBIT 6   Selected Financial Data for Coach Inc. by Channel of Distribution, Fiscal 2009–Fiscal 2011 (in thousands)**

|  | Direct-to-Consumer | Indirect Corporate | Unallocated | Total |
|---|---|---|---|---|
| **FISCAL 2011** | | | | |
| Net sales | $3,621,886 | $536,621 | | $4,158,507 |
| Operating income (loss) | 1,423,191 | 296,032 | $(414,299) | 1,304,924 |
| **FISCAL 2010** | | | | |
| Net sales | 3,155,860 | 451,776 | | 3,607,636 |
| Operating income (loss) | 1,245,400 | 256,637 | (351,866) | 1,150,171 |
| **FISCAL 2009** | | | | |
| Net sales | 2,726,891 | 503,577 | | 3,230,468 |
| Operating income (loss) | 996,285 | 290,981 | (315,353) | 971,913 |

*Source:* Coach Inc., 2011 10-K.

America and Japan to bridge the more traditional luxury market.

**Factory Stores**   Coach had 143 factory stores by 2011. The company had placed an additional emphasis on factory stores since the onset of the economic downturn, with the number of factory stores increasing by about 9 annually between 2007 and 2011. Coach's factory stores in the U.S. were generally located 40 or more miles from its full-price stores. About 75 percent of factory store inventory was produced specifically for Coach's factory stores, while the remaining 25 percent was made up of overstocked items and discontinued models. Coach's 10 to 50 percent discounts offered in factory stores allowed the company to maintain a year round full-price policy in full-price stores. Coach CEO Lew Frankfort believed discounted prices were critical to success in retailing since 80 percent of women's apparel sold in the U.S. was bought on sale or in a discount store. "Women in the U.S. have been trained to expect to be able to find a bargain if they either go through the hunt . . . or are willing to buy something after the season," said Frankfort.[6]

Therefore, Coach's factory stores target value-oriented customers who might not otherwise buy a Coach product. Both factory store customers and full-price customers were equally brand loyal, but there was a distinct demographic difference between the shopper segments. The company's market research found the typical full-price store shopper was a 35-year-old,

college-educated, single or newly married working woman. The typical factory store shopper was a 45-year-old, college-educated, married, professional woman with children. The average annual spending in a Coach store by full-price shoppers was $1,100. Factory store shoppers spent about $770 annually on Coach products, with 80 percent spent in factory stores and 20 percent spent in a full-price store.

The factory store strategy capitalized on the brand's lead luxury image projected at their flagship and retail stores, and ensured it maintained its own individual identity so as not to dilute the foundation of the Coach brand. While the company had accelerated factory store openings, Frankfort did not want factory outlet stores to grow too rapidly since "Our destiny lies in our ability to grow full-price stores."[7] Some analysts were worried that Coach's highly successful factory stores might someday dilute its image. A Luxury Institute analyst described the dilemma faced by Coach and luxury diffusion brands by commenting "To be unique and exclusive you cannot be ubiquitous."[8]

**Coach Japan**   Coach sold their products in Japan in shop-in-shop department store locations, Coach full-price retail stores, and Coach factory outlets. The company had 169 retail locations in Japan in 2011, which generated $748 million in sales. The company's management believed Japan could support as many as 180 Coach retail outlets. The Japanese luxury goods market has been flat to slightly growing over the last several years, but Coach planed to drive growth in Japan by focusing on the market for men's luxury goods, which represented 25 percent of sales in the market in 2011.

**Coach China**    Coach had 66 stores in China in 2012, up from 41 stores in 2011. The company had targeted 120 cities in China with populations of at least 1 million for future store openings. The majority of Coach's stores in China carried dual-gender product lines since about 45 percent of China's luxury market was men's products. The market for men's luxury goods represented about 15 percent of sales in the United States and 20 percent of sales in Japan.

Rivalry in the luxury goods industry in China was very intense, with 26 luxury goods brands operating 969 retail stores in the market in 2011. Hugo Boss had the largest number of stores in China with 114 stores, followed by Armani with 104 stores. In 2011, Gucci operated 45 stores in China, Prada had 14 stores, and Kate Spade had 5 stores in China. Coach anticipated recording fiscal 2012 revenues in China of approximately $300 million.

**U.S. Wholesale**    Coach's products were sold in approximately 970 wholesale locations in the U.S. and Canada. The most significant U.S. wholesale customers included Macy's (including Bloomingdale's), Dillard's, Nordstrom, Lord & Taylor, and Saks Fifth Avenue. Wholesale sales of Coach products to U.S. department stores increased by 5 percent per year during 2006 to 2011 to reach approximately $300 million. However, department stores were becoming less relevant in the U.S. retailing industry with the average consumer spending less time in malls and shopping in fewer stores during visits to malls. The share of the U.S. retail market held by department stores declined from about 30 percent in 1990 to less than 20 percent in 2011.

**International Wholesale**    Coach's wholesale distribution in international markets involved department stores, freestanding retail locations, shop-in-shop locations, and specialty retailers in 18 countries. The company's largest international wholesale accounts were the DFS Group, Lotte Group, Shila Group, Tasa Meng Corporation, and Imaginex. The largest portion of sales by these companies was to traveling affluent Chinese and Japanese consumers. Coach's largest wholesale country markets were Korea, Hong Kong, Taiwan, Singapore, Japan, Saudi

**EXHIBIT 7**    Breakdown of Coach Inc.'s Selling, General, and Administrative Expenses, Fiscal 2007–Fiscal 2011 (in thousands)

| | 2011 | 2010 | 2009 | 2008 | 2007 |
|---|---|---|---|---|---|
| Selling | $1,180 | $1,049 | $ 981 | $ 865 | $ 718 |
| Advertising | 224 | 179 | 164 | 148 | 120 |
| Distribution | 58 | 48 | 52 | 48 | 53 |
| Administration | 204 | 153 | 130 | 167 | 139 |
| Administration adjustment | 51 | 54 | 24 | 32 | 0 |
| Total | 1,718 | 1,483 | 1,351 | 1,260 | 1,030 |

*Source:* Coach Inc. 10-K.

Arabia, Australia, Mexico, Thailand, Malaysia, the Caribbean, China, New Zealand, and France. In 2006, international wholesale accounts amounted to $147 million and have grown some 7.8 percent per year to reach approximately $230 million in 2011. A breakdown of the company's selling, general, and administrative expenses for 2007 through 2011 are presented in Exhibit 7.

# COACH'S STRATEGIC OPTIONS IN 2012

In 2012, Coach was evolving into more of a global growth–oriented company. Lew Frankfort's key growth initiatives involved store expansion in the U.S., Japan, Hong Kong, and mainland China; increasing sales to existing customers to drive comparable store growth, building market share in the men's market by introducing men's-only stores and building on the dual-gender store concept, and creating alliances to exploit the Coach brand in additional luxury categories. In addition, Coach was also considering opportunities to expand into the European luxury goods market. However, the company faced threats from prestigious European and North American luxury goods brands that had developed diffusion lines that carried price points similar to those offered by Coach. In addition, all of the world's major luxury brands were racing to establish a retail presence and brand loyalty in China, India, and other developing countries that would soon account for a large percentage of industry sales. In addition to market-related threats, Coach management also needed to consider how best to boost its profit margins to levels achieved in previous years and stabilize its stock price, which fell by nearly $20 during the first six months of 2012.

## ENDNOTES

[1] "How Coach Got Hot," *Fortune,* Vol. 146, Issue 8, October 28, 2002.

[2] As quoted in "Stores Dancing Chic to Chic," *Houston Chronicle,* May 6, 2000.

[3] As quoted in "Fashions Keep Retailer Busy," *Investor's Business Daily,* February 10, 2005, p. A04.

[4] Ibid.

[5] As quoted in "Coach's Split Personality," *BusinessWeek,* November 7, 2005.

[6] As quoted in "Coach Sales Strategy Is in the Bag," *Financial Times,* April 18, 2006.

[7] Ibid.

[8] As quoted in "Expansion into U.S.: Extending the Reach of the Exclusive Lifestyle Brands," *Financial Times,* July 8, 2006, p. 17.

# Tiffany's Little Blue Box: Does It Have Any Strategic Significance?

A. J. Strickland
The University of Alabama

Morgan Solomon
The University of Alabama,
2012 MBA Student

What is it about that little blue box from Tiffany & Co. that tells a recipient they are about to receive an elegant and perhaps quintessential gift? Does that blue box add significantly to the value of what it contains? And just how does that box fit into Tiffany's overall strategy?

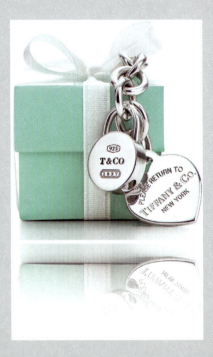

From sales of only $4.98 on its opening day in 1837 to becoming one of the most well-known jewelers in the world, Tiffany & Co. has long been viewed as a premier retailer of distinctive and luxurious jewelry, chiefly for very well-to-do consumers. But according to some analysts, both the Internet and big-box retailers have forever impacted the way many consumers shop for jewelry, and there are signs that the lingering effects of the global recession may have diminished the appeal of powerful global brand names because budget-conscious consumers have increasingly begun seeking out products that deliver more value for their money. Given this, could it be that the old saying "don't judge a book by its cover" is coming back in style where high-end jewelry is concerned? Can Tiffany confidently count upon customers concluding that a one-carat diamond ring in a Tiffany blue box delivers more value than, say, a comparably priced three-carat diamond ring from Costco Wholesale or an Internet jewelry retailer like Blue Nile? Might recessionary or slow-growth economic conditions precipitate such significant and sweeping shifts in consumer preferences and buying habits for jewelry that it will become difficult for Tiffany to sustain its plans for international expansion and continue with its premium-priced differentiation strategy of producing and marketing distinctive jewelry for the affluent?

## COMPANY BACKGROUND

Tiffany & Co. was founded in New York City in 1837 by Charles Lewis Tiffany and John Young. The company, which was then called Tiffany & Young was originally set up as a "stationery and fine goods emporium" that sold a variety of fine stationery and costume jewelry. It wasn't until 1845 that the company began selling everyday fine jewelry. In the 1840s, the company also published its first mail-order catalog,

"The Blue Book," and also added timepieces, silverware, perfumes, and other luxury goods to its product line. Throughout the 1800s, Lewis and Young quickly and greatly expanded their company and business operations. In 1851, Lewis and Young bought out the city's silversmith operations and added the design and manufacture of silver to their business. With the new manufacturing capabilities, Tiffany & Co. became the first company to institute the 925/1000 silver standard, which later was adopted as the silver standard for the U.S. Shortly after in 1853, Charles Lewis bought out his two partners, John Young and J. L. Ellis, and renamed the company to what we know it as today: Tiffany & Co. Tiffany & Co. found its main consumer base to be wealthy Americans who desired the finer things in life. It won multiple awards at jewelry and silverware conventions, which only further solidified the Tiffany & Co. name in the ever-growing jewelry industry. In 1878, the company acquired the Tiffany Diamond, one of the largest yellow diamonds in the world, weighing in at 287 carats. In 1886, Lewis introduced the signature Tiffany engagement ring setting, which is still a best-seller at Tiffany & Co. By 1887, the company had more than $40 million dollars of precious stones. In 1902, Charles Lewis Tiffany passed away and his son Louis Comfort Tiffany joined the firm and became the company's first design director. Louis later died in 1933.

Following the Great Depression, the company moved into its famous flagship store on 5th Avenue in the heart of Manhattan, where it remains today. In 1955, the Tiffany heirs sold their interest in the company to Walter Hoving, who became the new CEO and opened stores in San Francisco and Beverly Hills, California, as well as Houston, Texas. Sales continued to grow in the 1970s and the company was then sold to Avon Cosmetics in 1979. Avon increased Tiffany & Co.'s line of less expensive items, which was criticized by many as turning the store into an average department store rather than a fine jewelry and silver retailer. In 1984, the company was then sold again to a group of investors, including then-CEO William Chaney. Chaney immediately began trying to reinstate the exclusivity and luxury that once was Tiffany & Co.

In 1986, the company expanded into Europe, and in 1987 it went public with approximately 30 retail locations worldwide. The 1990s proved to be a decade of expansion for Tiffany & Co. as well. They opened over 20 new retail stores nationwide. In 1999, Michael Kolwaski became CEO and the company bought stakes in a diamond supplier, Aber Diamonds. Tiffany & Co.

also launched their first online store and website in 1999. In 2000, the company founded the Tiffany & Co. Foundation, which provides grants to nonprofit organizations working in the environment and the arts. The company also discontinued sales to retailers in the U.S. and Europe in order to try to regain control of their image and pristine brand name. In 2010, the company continued to expand into the Asia-Pacific region, opening eight stores, and then another three stores in Europe. In 2012, Tiffany & Co. celebrated 175 years of excellence with sales worldwide totaling over $3 billion.

## COMPANY STRATEGY

Tiffany & Co. has made it a priority to maintain the luxury brand and service that Charles Lewis Tiffany founded the company on in 1837. It still targets the more affluent population and still maintains their no-haggling policy, something which dates back to the original store. Today, its mission statement remains the same: "to be the world's most respected jeweler." Focused on customer service, Tiffany & Co. abides by strict hiring standards. Every employee must complete six to eight weeks of training in knowledge, skills, and product training, as well as pass a written test before they are allowed to meet with customers and work on the Tiffany & Co. sales floor. The company is also very proud of the high-quality standards instilled in its culture since its founding by Charles Lewis. The blue box created by Charles Lewis Tiffany himself is still given to each customer upon the purchase of a product. To the company, the little blue box is a symbol of Tiffany's high-quality products, its commitment to excellence, solid tradition and consistency, its respect for customers and their needs, and of course Tiffany's pristine reputation.

Over the years, Tiffany has insisted on opening its doors to all types of buyers. It has vastly expanded its product offering, and even added low-priced "tourist" items, such as a deck of cards for those individuals just looking for a glimpse of the Tiffany experience. Approximately 90 percent of its overall sales, however, comes from its jewelry selection. The sale of silver and gold items makes up about a third of the company's revenues. Another third of its revenue stream comes from their quintessential engagement rings and wedding bands. Although a large portion of Tiffany's sales are generated from jewelry, much of their revenue also comes from their ever-expanding product line. Currently, its main business strategy is to continue expanding that product line, but in a way that does not diminish Tiffany's prestigious brand name. In order to achieve this goal, the company is very selective in the types of products it chooses to carry, while continuing to expand its target market through its Blue Book Catalog, website, and new retail markets. In expanding its accessories line, Tiffany & Co. acquired the luxury handbag and footwear line Lambertson Truex from Samsonite in 2009. Previously, in 2006, Tiffany linked with luxury eyewear company Luxottica to begin production of a Tiffany-branded ophthalmic and sun eyewear collection. Starting in 2008, this eyewear collection was carried in all of Tiffany's retail stores. In addition, Tiffany's product line includes a variety of men's and women's jewelry, as well as key chains, handbags, eyewear, scarves, leather goods, table wear, vases, and other items.

Tiffany & Co. isn't just about jewelry, however. Since 1860, the company has also made a variety of silver products for multiple sporting event awards. For instance, in 1909 Tiffany created an eight-foot trophy for the Indianapolis 500 and continues to make the NASCAR Sprint Cup today. Tiffany has also created the NFL Vince Lombardi Super Bowl Trophy since 1967, the first world championship baseball trophy since 1988, and has produced the World Series Trophy since 2000. Tiffany also makes trophies for the U.S. Tennis Association and PGA Tour championships, along with a variety of other sporting tournaments.

## TIFFANY FINANCIALS

Tiffany & Co.'s U.S. retail stores account for 50 percent of the company's overall revenue, and the company spends roughly 6 percent of its revenues on advertising and marketing. It also manufactures 60 percent of its jewelry in order to maintain its high-quality standards, while typically outsourcing the non-jewelry items in its product line.

Like many businesses in the U.S., Tiffany & Co. suffered a financial downturn during the most recent recession, with U.S. sales declining in both 2008 and 2009. In 2007 and 2006, the company increased their retail prices due to the rising costs of gold and diamonds, sporting an average sales price of $3,400. With higher prices, the company was able to drastically increase their net income, showing a growth of 18.5 percent from 2006 to 2007. It was not until 2008 that the company began to feel the effects of the recession on their profit and growth. In 2009, company sales were down 4.9 percent from 2008. Although Tiffany & Co. definitely felt the effects of the recession in the U.S., it fared much better than many of its competitors, with its overall revenue decreasing only 2.7 percent. However, in 2010 the company rebounded and outperformed the market with a growth of 10.9 percent. This spurt in growth was mainly due to the increased prices of their jewelry. Since 2010, the company has shown strong growth potential for the future. For instance, the company's U.S. sales grew 15 percent to $1.8 billion by fiscal year-end 2011, and overall net sales rose 18 percent to $3.6 billion. The company's net earnings also increased 19 percent to $439 million.

Although Tiffany took a hit from the U.S. recession, the company was able to rebound by increasing prices and continuing with their original strategy of attracting and marketing to the more affluent consumers. It was also able to remain one of the top high-quality players (along with companies like Bulgari and Cartier) mainly due to the fact that all these companies were also impacted by the recession in some manner.

**EXHIBIT 1    Financial Performance Summary for Tiffany & Company's U.S. Segment, 2006–2011**

| Year | Revenue ($ million) | % Change | EBIT ($ million) | % Change |
|------|---------------------|----------|------------------|----------|
| 2006 | $1,560.9 | 8.0% | $250.3 | 0.7% |
| 2007 | 1,734.1 | 11.1 | 343.4 | 37.2 |
| 2008 | 1,547.0 | −10.8 | 228.3 | −33.5 |
| 2009 | 1,338.2 | −13.5 | 226.4 | −0.8 |
| 2010 | 1,484.5 | 10.9 | 352.1 | 55.5 |
| 2011 | 1,764.2 | 18.8 | 477.1 | 35.5 |

*Note:* EBIT = Earnings before interest and taxes.

\* *Source:* http://clients.ibisworld.com.libdata.lib.ua.edu/industryus/Majorcompanies.aspx?indid51075#MP8953.

# THE 4 C'S OF DIAMONDS

When it comes to choosing a diamond, there are a few things consumers need to be aware of before entering a store or purchasing items online. These characteristics are referred to as the 4 C's: carat, color, clarity, and cut. Created by the GIA, the Gemological Institute of America, the 4 C's are the international standard for describing the quality of the diamond. The creation of the 4 C's permitted universal communication when describing diamonds and also provided customers with a way of understanding what they were looking at in jewelry stores.

The first C, *carat,* refers to the actual weight of the diamond. One carat is equal to 200 milligrams, and each carat can be subdivided into 100 points. This allows for very precise measurements, to the hundredth decimal place. Diamond weights greater than one carat are expressed in carats and decimals, such as 1.25 carats or one point twenty-five carats. The greater the carat weight, the more expensive the diamond. This being said, two diamonds of the same weight can have very different values depending on the other three C's.

The second C, *color,* actually refers to the diamond's *lack* of color. A chemically and structurally perfect diamond is completely absent of color. Consequently, the clearer the diamond, the greater its value. GIA developed a color rating system ranked from D–Z, with D being colorless. This color rating system measures the degree of colorlessness by comparing a diamond under both controlled lighting and viewing conditions to a "master" diamond that has a perfect established color. Color differences can be almost indeterminable using the naked eye; however, a minor difference in color rating can create a large difference in value.

The third C, *clarity,* refers to the purity of the diamond and its absence of natural inclusions and blemishes. Determining a diamond's clarity is based on evaluating the number, size, relief, nature, and position of these defects, as well as how they affect the overall appearance of the stone. The greater the clarity of the diamond, the greater its value. The GIA clarity scale includes six different categories: *flawlessness (FL),* no inclusions or blemishes under 10x magnification; *internally flawless (IF),* no inclusions visible under 10x magnification; *very very slightly included (VVS1 and VVS2),* inclusions so slight that they are difficult for a skilled grader to see under 10x magnification; *very slightly included (VS1 and VS2),* inclusions are clearly visible under 10x magnification, but can be characterized as minor; *slightly included (S1 and S2),* inclusions are noticeable under 10x magnification; and *included (I1, I2, I3),* inclusions are obvious under 10x magnification, which may affect transparency and brilliance. Identifying blemishes and inclusions can be very difficult to see with the naked eye, but make an enormous difference in the value of the diamond. This is why it is so important for consumers to receive a professional appraisal.

To many people, the fourth C, *cut,* refers to the shape (round, princess, emerald, pearl) of the diamond. In truth, the cut of the diamond actually refers to how the diamond's facets interact with light—in essence, how it sparkles. The cut determines a diamond's final beauty and ultimately its value. In determining the cut of a diamond, GIA calculates the proportions of the facets that influence the diamond's face-up appearance, which lets an expert determine how the diamond interacts with light to create the most visually appealing diamond. The brightness of a diamond is also considered, which is how internal and external white light reflects from a diamond. Fire is also taken into consideration, which is how the diamond scatters white light into all the colors of the rainbow. Scintillation is the final characteristic considered, which is the amount of sparkle a diamond produces and the pattern of light and dark areas caused by reflections within the diamond. The cut is measured using a scale of five, from excellent to poor.

Considering the way the diamond industry is changing, with the ability to purchase items online and at big-box stores, consumers need to be aware now more than ever what constitutes a good quality diamond. GIA gives guidelines for consumers on how someone should go about purchasing a diamond:

- Choose a jeweler that has training from an accredited diploma program that can answer questions clearly and effectively, as well as explain the 4 C's.
- The consumer should understand what the 4 C's mean.
- Insist on being presented with a grading report of the chosen diamond.
- Protect the purchase by having your diamond appraised and insured.

## PURCHASING A DIAMOND

Thanks to the growing power of the Internet, the way consumers purchase goods is changing drastically. This includes how people buy diamonds. There is a multitude of retail jewelers, fine jewelers such as Tiffany & Co., online jewelers, and big-box warehouse jewelers.

Online stores, such as Blue Nile, have many advantages in the eyes of consumers. Buying online not only provides convenience, but also allows consumers the greatest selection of retailers and merchandise. Diamonds can be found in all shapes and sizes at all different price points, allowing the consumer to customize their shopping experience. Online shoppers are also able to easily compare prices from retailer to retailer. Online retailers also offer reasonable return policies in case the consumer is not satisfied with their original purchase. Though consumers are able to purchase diamonds without ever leaving their couch, the downside of online buying is

the customization factor. If a buyer purchases a diamond in a store, they are able to have a one-on-one discussion about the diamond's 4 C's and pick a specific setting for it. So although online retailers are becoming more and more popular, many consumers still feel more comfortable making such a large purchase at a brick-and-mortar jeweler.

People purchase jewelry for many reasons, one of the biggest being its status affect. Jewelry has always denoted wealth, class, and status and is synonymous with affluent individuals. According to *JCK* magazine, 67 percent of all jewelry is a planned purchase, making price the most important factor to consumers. More than 50 percent of responders to *JCK*'s survey reported that product quality, a salesperson's honesty, the service they received in the store, the store's reputation, and the salesperson's knowledge were the most important factors when purchasing jewelry. Less than 50 percent of respondents ranked store display, brand name, store location, the recommendation of another shopper, advertising, and store hours as the most important factors. Although many high-end brands exist, such as Tiffany & Co, Harry Winston, and David Yurman, many more unbranded stores make up a large chunk of the jewelry market. However, given the magnitude of a jewelry purchase, a well-known brand can give the consumer confidence in the purchase and more willingness to purchase jewelry based upon brand rather than price point.

For Tiffany & Co., the brand is everything. When Charles Lewis Tiffany permanently took over the company in 1853, he defined the Tiffany brand as one of prestige and wealth, making the Tiffany name and the little blue box that accompanied it something that people not only coveted, but that many couldn't afford. This set Tiffany & Co. apart from other jewelry companies and elevated them into the upper echelon of fine jewelry and silver. It is easy to see that Tiffany takes pride in its brand and the quality of their products. In 2004, Tiffany & Co. sued eBay for alleged trademark infringement, trademark dilution, and false advertising, given that the majority of Tiffany items on eBay being sold were counterfeits. The courts ruled in eBay's favor, and in 2010 Tiffany appealed to the U.S. Supreme Court, saying that eBay should be held liable for trademark infringement on Tiffany's brand. However, the Supreme Court rejected Tiffany & Co.'s appeal and eBay was not held liable for any charges of fraud or trademark infringement. When it comes to jewelry, Tiffany believes that cost

**EXHIBIT 2**   Jewelry Sales by Income Segment, 2011

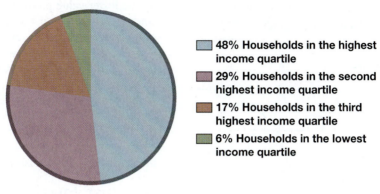

**Major Market Segmentation (2011)**

☐ **48% Households in the highest income quartile**

☐ **29% Households in the second highest income quartile**

☐ **17% Households in the third highest income quartile**

☐ **6% Households in the lowest income quartile**

**Total $30.2bn**

*Source:* www.ibisworld.com.

does not matter when you are getting a well-known, high-quality brand that will last a lifetime.

The largest segment of consumers in the jewelry market tends to be more affluent individuals. According to Exhibit 2, households are the primary market for jewelry purchases, because most jewelry is purchased as a gift. Therefore, sales tend to fluctuate around holidays such as Christmas and Valentine's Day. Medium-high-income households make up the largest market segment for jewelry retailers at 48 percent of total industry revenue. The top 50 percent of all income-producing households accounts for 70 percent of industry revenue, while the lowest 25 percent of income-producing households only makes up 6 percent of industry revenue. The revenues generated by the medium-high-income households showed signs of increasing during the recessionary period, because the recession tended to impact lower-income households more dramatically than higher-income individuals. Therefore, jewelry retailers tend to aim to gain the most revenue from the top 20 percent of premier customers. As far as age, individuals between the ages of 45 and 64 make up the majority of jewelry sales because they have established disposable incomes. Due to the aging population, jewelry purchases in this segment are expected to increase in the future. The next largest market segment is individuals between the ages of 20 and 30 years old, most likely due to the increased marriage rate in that age segment.

# THE U.S. JEWELRY INDUSTRY

The U.S. jewelry industry is a 30-billion-dollar industry made up of over 56,000 different businesses, with an annual growth rate of 3.1 percent. Although the jewelry industry has had positive growth as of 2011, the industry took a hit due to the recession that began in 2006. The effects of the recession on the jewelry industry began to show in 2008 when luxury spending started to drop. As household earnings and expenditures tightened, the sale of luxury goods declined as well. This drop in consumer expenditures caused the sales revenue of the industry to decline at an estimated annual rate of 2.7 percent over five years from 2006 to 2011.

The jewelry industry saw a slow recovery following the economic downturn in 2008. In 2010, the annual growth rate declined 1.7 percent. However, some larger companies like Signet and Tiffany & Co. proved to be outliers and showed positive sales growth in 2010. Due to the strong brands and image ratings of the larger fine jewelry retailers, they were able to weather the effects of the recession and became leading indicators of recovery in the industry.

In addition to the reduction in consumer spending, the jewelry industry was also affected by the rising price of gold. Exhibit 3 displays the effects that the increased price of gold had on the overall jewelry industry revenue. The price of gold increased from $604.71 per ounce in 2006 to $1564.91 per ounce in

**EXHIBIT 3**    The Effects of Changes in Gold Prices on U.S. Jewelry Industry Revenues, Actual and Projected, 2003–2017

**Industry Revenue**

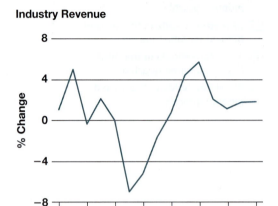

* *Source:* http://clients.ibisworld.com.libdata.lib.ua.edu/industryus/Majorcompanies.aspx?indid=1075#MP8952.

2011. The increased cost of gold pushed up a jeweler's overhead costs, which caused their profit to drop by 5.1 percent from 2006 to 2011. With the increased price of gold, it has become imperative for jewelry stores to manage their purchasing and overhead costs. Purchases account for over 50 percent of a firm's cost structure. Many stores had to employ budget-cutting measures in order to remain profitable. One popular tactic used by jewelry companies was to cut wages. Industry wages dropped from $5.2 billion in 2006 to $4.6 billion in 2011. Firms also suffered from default loans from borrowers, which led to sunk costs and increased debt for some firms. Harsh credit conditions as a result of the recession even caused some companies to file for bankruptcy, such as Friedman's Jewelers, which filed for bankruptcy in 2008. Some luckier firms were able to close retail locations in order to save on costs and avoid bankruptcy. This caused a large decrease in the number of operating firms in the U.S. during the recessionary period. For example, the number of retail firms in the U.S. in 2007 was 62,005, which then dropped to 56,007 by 2011.

Jewelry companies also began to face increased competition from non-jewelry outlets, such as supercenters and online retailers. These companies threatened the profits of firms like Tiffany & Co. because they offered lower prices and one-stop shopping for consumers. Threats from these competitors tended to be more intense and have a greater effect on the lower-value product segments. This increased competition from non-traditional jewelry retailers has caused size, sales growth, and profitability to slow.

The latest recession has also taken its toll on the industry, but estimated revenue growth is still predicted to be 3.1 percent per year through 2016. The number of retail stores is also expected to increase through 2016 to 70,013 stores nationwide. Although the industry is in the mature stage, the forecasted growth potential and the increasing consumer sentiment will keep this industry in working order.

## Not Just Jewelry

The jewelry industry is made up of a plethora of products, and has evolved from gemstones and diamonds to expanded product lines that include everything from accessories to luggage. However, the most common jewelry sold is still diamonds and gold. According to the product segmentation in Exhibit 4, diamond jewelry makes up the largest amount of jewelry products, accounting for 48 percent of industry revenue. This is most likely due to the increasing marriage rate, although during the recessionary period the marriage rate dropped slightly as couples postponed weddings due to lagging disposable incomes. The diamond segment of the industry includes bracelets, rings, necklaces, and so on in which diamonds make up 50 percent of the items value. Although the disposable income has decreased since the recession, the diamond segment has slightly increased due to the overall rise in personal wealth.

Gold makes up the second-largest segment of the product market. Many consumers purchase gold items because of the investment value since the price of gold has shown steady increases. The gold product segment is made up of all gold jewelry items, while diamonds, gems, and other items constitute less than 50 percent of the final items' value. Although gold makes up a large revenue segment for the industry, there has been a switch in consumer purchasing trends. For example, over the years there has been a shift from gold rings to more favorable platinum rings. This has caused yellow gold to lose market share due to the fact that gold jewelry has become less desirable for consumers. Watches make up the next largest product segment at 13.9 percent of the industry revenue. However, the demand for watches is in decline due to the increased number

**EXHIBIT 4**   **U.S. Jewelry Industry Sales, by Product Segment, 2011**

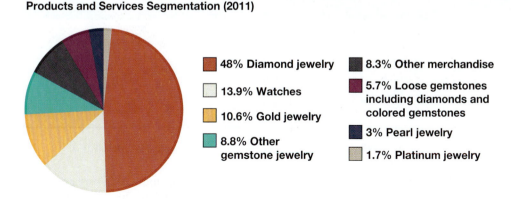

**Products and Services Segmentation (2011)**

- 48% Diamond jewelry
- 13.9% Watches
- 10.6% Gold jewelry
- 8.8% Other gemstone jewelry
- 8.3% Other merchandise
- 5.7% Loose gemstones including diamonds and colored gemstones
- 3% Pearl jewelry
- 1.7% Platinum jewelry

**Total $30.2bn**

*Source:* www.ibisworld.com.

of smartphones and PDAs that have built-in clocks. Besides silver and gold, jewelry stores offer a wide variety of gemstones, pearls, silverware and tableware, and other accessories, ranging from eyewear to luggage, depending on the size of the retailer.

## COMPETITION

The U.S. jewelry industry is mainly concentrated in the Southeast and Mid-Atlantic regions, which account for 45 percent of total industry sales. The concentration is highly dependent on population as well as per capita income. The higher the population and per capita income, the more concentrated the retail merchants in that particular area.

The four largest players in the jewelry industry have 20 percent of the total jewelry market. The jewelry industry is highly fragmented with no single dealer owning in excess of 10 percent of the total market. This is due to the high volume of retail jewelry stores and the vast availability of jewelry products and merchants. Therefore, over time, concentration in the jewelry industry has steadily increased and is expected to increase through 2016. With low barriers to entry, the jewelry industry is highly competitive and constantly growing. Due to the discretionary nature of jewelry purchases, the economy and disposable income of consumers greatly influence the competitive landscape in the jewelry industry.

Jewelry companies try to create stores in high-traffic retail areas that are near the more affluent areas

of a city. The depth of the product line a company offers can differentiate them from other competitors, and a signature trademark and reputable brand name, such as Tiffany & Co.'s blue box, can give a company a leg up on its competition. With the recent recession, price has become a more important factor than ever, which has increased the pressure on big-box stores and supercenters that carry a large selection of low-priced jewelry.

## Signet Group, PLC

The Signet Group is one of the largest jewelry retailers in the world with a 9.7 percent market share in the industry. Originally founded in the United Kingdom in 1862, the Signet Group operates in the jewelry retail segment through its Kay Jewelers locations, as well as Jared the Galleria of Jewelry. The company currently has more than 1,300 stores in the U.S., and the U.S. accounts for more than 75 percent of its overall sales. Signet built its empire on superb customer service, a value-driven product line, strategic marketing plans, and onsite customer financing.

Kay Jewelers is a subset of Signet based in mall locations and targets households that have a median annual income between $35,000 and $100,000. Due to the recession in 2006, Kay was forced to lower its prices in order to cater to more value-conscious customers. The division also enhanced its web presence to help boost sales and gain new customers. In addition, Signet operates other mall retail stores in order to meet a wide range of price points for customers.

## EXHIBIT 5   Financial Summary for Signet Group's U.S. Operations, 2006–2011

| Year | Revenue ($ million) | % Change | EBIT ($ million) | % Change |
|---|---|---|---|---|
| 2006 | $2,652.1 | 14.9% | $326.7 | 18.3% |
| 2007 | 2,705.7 | 2.0 | 262.2 | −19.7 |
| 2008 | 2,519.8 | −6.9 | −250.7 | N/C |
| 2009 | 2,540.4 | 0.8 | 224.5 | N/C |
| 2010 | 2,744.2 | 8.0 | 342.7 | 52.7 |
| 2011 | 2,929.3 | 6.7 | 423.7 | 23.6 |

\* *Source:* http://clients.ibisworld.com.libdata.lib.ua.edu/industryus/Majorcompanies.aspx?indid=1075#MP8952.

Jared the Galleria of Jewelry is the more higher-end U.S. retail segment of Signet and targets households with a median annual income between $50,000 and $150,000. Jared is an off-mall retailer that has a higher price point than Kay Jewelers at an average price of $713. Jared is more focused on providing customer service, knowledge about the products, as well as the onsite design and repair of jewelry.

Like many U.S. jewelers, Signet Group felt the effects of the recent recession. The company had decreases in revenue in 2008 and 2009, as shown in Exhibit 5; however, its revenue has increased since then. Prior to the recession, both Kay and Jared performed well, with increasing revenues and more store locations. Signet suffered the most in 2008 and 2009, with sales dropping 6.9 percent in 2008 alone. In 2009, the company weathered the storm by shifting its focus onto its more value-driven brand, Kay. The recession forced the company to eliminate new store openings, cut advertising budgets, and lay off workers. In 2010, Signet showed signs of improving growth (8 percent) due to targeted marketing strategies and the lowering of prices in its mall-based stores. Kay was also able to reach out to the "penny pinching" consumer through their popular and inexpensive charm bracelet line. As the economy improved, the company continued to show positive growth through 2011, and had plans to continue the expansion of their Jared store locations.

## Bulgari S.p.A

Bulgari is one of the top luxury goods and jewelry retailers in the world. The Bulgari Group has 41 companies in 21 different countries, 295 retail stores, and over 3,800 employees worldwide. The company offers many products, including jewelry, watches, accessories, perfumes, skin care products, and leather goods, and even has a line of hotels.

In 1884, a descendant of Greek silversmiths, Sotirio Bulgari opened his first jewelry store in Rome, Italy, where he began selling fine jewelry and antiquities. In 1905, with the help of his two sons Constantino and Georgio, he opened up what today is the flagship store in Via Condotti, Rome. In the early 20th century, Bulgari's two sons began to take an interest in precious stones, gems, jewelry, and watches. With much enthusiasm for the jewelry business, the two sons gradually took over their father's management position in the company. They then introduced a new, unique Greco-Roman style of jewelry to the store's product line. The exquisite jewelry caught the eye of many affluent and famous individuals, and by the 1950s and 1960s got Bulgari noticed as a fine luxury jewelry retailer. With the fast growth of the brand, Bulgari was soon able to expand internationally, opening stores in New York, Geneva, Paris, and Monte Carlo in the 1970s. In 1977, Bulgari's most famous watch was introduced, Bulgari-Bulgari, which remains the company's best-selling watch today. With the popularity of the company's watches, Bulgari founded the company's watch division in the early 1980s: Bulgari Time in Switzerland. In 1993, Bulgari expanded its product line and began offering fragrances along with their fine jewelry. The company went public in 1995 and was listed on the Italian Stock Exchange and the international SEAQ of London. In 1994, it expanded its product line as a luxury goods retailer further with the introduction of silk scarves. This was followed later in the decade with silk ties for men, eyewear, leather goods, and a multitude of other accessories. In 1997, in keeping with expanding the company's prestigious brand name, Bulgari joined with Ferragamo to market and distribute Ferragamo and Ungaro perfumes. The following year, Bulgari entered into the housewares market, partnering with Rosenthal to sell fine china, crystal, tableware, and stemware.

In the late 1990s and early 2000s, Bulgari continued expanding their product line and the company as a whole. In 2000, the company licensed its brand name to luggage and accessories for Cadillac's retro car, the Imaj. Shortly thereafter, Bulgari bought three Swiss watch-making units from The Hour Glass Ltd. Then in 2001 the company signed a license agreement with Marriot International to create a chain of Bulgari-branded hotels. The following year it opened its first store in Russia, and in 2007 opened its largest store ever, an 11-story building in Tokyo. This was followed by its largest store in Europe, opened in Paris, France. In 2010, Bulgari signed a contract with Hengdeli Holdings in China that will expand the company's watch lines there. In 2011, Bulgari was taken over by the French luxury goods company LVMH (Louis Vuitton Moet Hennesy).

Very much like Tiffany & Co., Bulgari prides itself on the superior quality of its products and customer service. Throughout all of the company's expansion ventures, it has still been able to maintain its sophisticated and luxurious brand name. Bulgari's main business goal today is to achieve full customer satisfaction through excellence in every aspect of their business structure. As the company states: "Excellence to Bulgari means the perfect balance between the highest quality products and impeccable service worldwide." From every aspect of the business, whether it be design, production, or distribution, Bulgari makes it a priority to instill the highest quality standards and specifications in each process, resulting in only the finest quality goods.

## Blue Nile, Inc.

Founded in 1999, Blue Nile is now the largest online retailer of diamonds and fine jewelry. Based in Seattle, Washington, this online retailer competes with the most distinguished brands in the business, such as Tiffany & Co., Cartier, and many more. The company offers a variety of luxury jewelry items, including loose diamonds, settings, engagement rings, gold, silver, and platinum jewelry set with a variety of gemstones and pearls. Blue Nile has made choosing a diamond or a piece of jewelry a completely different, and for many, a more convenient experience. Being able to browse through thousands of diamonds and compare the 4 C's, settings, and prices, all with the click of a button

or swipe of a finger, is what sets this company apart from their brick-and-mortar competitors. Many consumers find this terrifying when making such expensive purchases, but Blue Nile prides itself on educating first-time buyers and giving consumers the knowledge they need to make a well-educated purchase. In fact, Blue Nile's business model is built around the notion that "choosing an engagement ring doesn't have to be complicated." It offers over 60,000 gemologist-certified diamonds, providing all of the amenities that a brick-and-mortar retailer offers, such as sizing, gift wrapping, financing, insurance, and appraisals. The company has based its merchandising strategy on a "just-in-time" method that allows the e-tailer to save on inventory costs by advertising the diamonds on their website, and then purchasing them once the customer has actually made the order online.

Blue Nile recently expanded its website to include mobile devices. In 2010, the company launched a mobile website for users that is a scaled-down version of their main website, but that still enables consumers to browse thousands of diamonds and jewelry from anywhere they choose. This lets customers enter a brick-and-mortar firm like Tiffany & Co. and compare their prices to Blue Nile's while standing in the store. The company reported in 2011 that approximately 20 percent of their customers were using the mobile site. In 2011, the mobile site proved to have paid off when Blue Nile sold a $300,000 diamond through the iPhone application.

Like most jewelers, Blue Nile suffered from the recession. However, the company did have a slight increase in sales of 10 percent from 2009 to 2010, with international sales increasing 30 percent. With this large increase in international sales, as well as the fact that half the world's diamonds lie outside U.S. borders, Blue Nile has made it a company focus to continue expanding internationally. The company also plans to redirect its strategy and focus on non-bridal jewelry moving forward. According to Exhibit 6, the number of formal weddings in the U.S. is in decline. This is most likely an effect of the recession, as well as changing societal beliefs about marriage. Couples are also choosing to get married later in life, which has an impact on whether or not they have a wedding or buy an engagement ring. Although two-thirds of Blue Nile's sales come from engagement rings, due to the declining sales margins of the item the company has chosen to focus their strategy on other forms of jewelry, such as earrings and necklaces.

**EXHIBIT 6**   Number of Weddings in the United States, 2001–2010

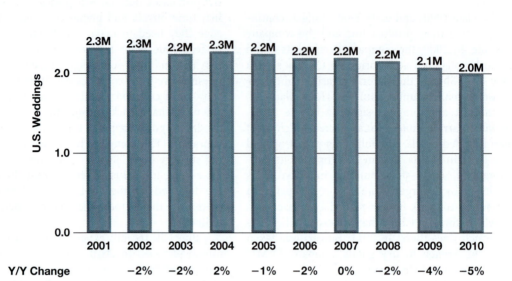

| Y/Y Change | | –2% | –2% | 2% | –1% | –2% | 0% | –2% | –4% | –5% |
|---|---|---|---|---|---|---|---|---|---|---|

\* *Source:* http://files.shareholder.com/downloads/NILE/1718335619x0x543349/f146dfde-e306-41b6-b851-81536ee8367a/Analyst_Day_February_16_2012_FINAL.pdf.

## Costco

Founded in 1983 in Seattle, Washington, Costco is now the largest membership warehouse chain in the United States with sales of over $87 billion in 2011. Costco provides customers with a one-stop discounted shopping experience. The company's product line ranges from everyday grocery and bakery items to electronics and treasure hunt items. But like many discount retailers and warehouse stores, the company also has a wide range of jewelry and diamonds for consumers to choose from. In 2011, Costco sold 103,000 carats of diamonds, with their largest diamond purchase being a 3.43-carat pink diamond ring worth $255,000. Among their other large diamond purchases was a pair of 6.56-carat diamond earrings priced at $67,900, as well as a 3.07-carat round diamond ring that sold for $67,300. Although consumers must purchase a membership to reap the benefits of Costco, upfront savings on large purchases such as diamonds and electronics seems to be worth the yearly fee.

Many big-box stores seem to be gaining market share on the diamond industry every year. With the ever-recovering economy, the definition of value has changed for many consumers. Why buy a one- to two-carat diamond ring at a high-end retailer such as Tiffany or Cartier, when the consumer can go to Walmart or Costco and get a three- to four-carat diamond ring of the same quality for the same price.

Even though companies like Tiffany are some of the most well-known and well-respected companies in the industry, the discount powerhouse retailer Walmart has the largest market share in the diamond industry. This is most likely due to their everyday low prices and one-stop-shopping atmosphere. Due to the highly fragmented industry, the top 20 jewelry retailers only make up 28.1 percent of the total market share, as seen in Exhibit 7. With this small percentage, big-box stores have the opportunity to take advantage of recessionary times, further penetrate the industry, and continue to take market share away from designer retailers such as Tiffany & Co.

## DOES BRAND REALLY MATTER?

In the mid-2000s, as the economy recovered from a mild recession, consumers began making more discerning purchases and holding on to their disposable income. With more penny-pinching consumers in the marketplace, a new version of retail jewelry

**EXHIBIT 7**   Percentage of Total Retail Jewelry Sales in the United States, by Major Retailer, 2011

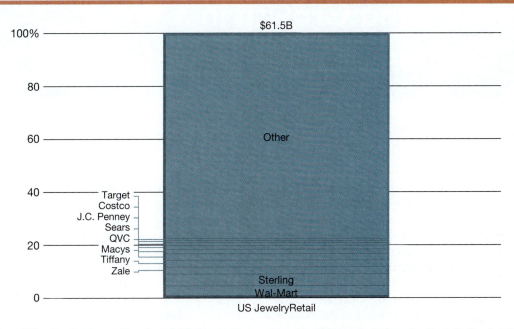

* *Source:* http://files.shareholder.com/downloads/NILE/1718335619x0x543349/f146dfde-e306-41b6-b851-81536ee8367a/Analyst_Day_February_16_2012_FINAL.pdf.

emerged. People became less discerning about where they bought their jewelry and more concerned about getting the biggest bang for their buck. This new phenomenon made retailers start asking, "Does brand really matter anymore? Or is it all about price and value?"

Consumers began to realize that they were paying a premium simply for the brand name attached to each jewelry item. In hard economic times, the pride that comes from a purchase with a fine retail jeweler may not be as important as the actual quality and size of the diamond. In 2006, ABC's *Good Morning, America* did a study on the differences in price and quality between a diamond from Tiffany & Co. versus a diamond from Costco. Although Costco did not have the high-quality customer service that a retailer like Tiffany has, Costco's prices far undercut those of a luxury jeweler. Where Tiffany & Co.'s jewelry started at $1,200, Costco's started as low as $500, ranging all the way up to $23,000. Although shopping for jewelry and diamonds amidst groceries and patio furniture may not be the ideal atmosphere for consumers, many people are willing to sacrifice the luxurious

ambiance and service of a high-end retail store for a lower-priced, larger-carat diamond. ABC's research found that a nearly flawless, one-carat diamond with a color grade of F (colorless) was $16,600, including the famous Tiffany & Co. engagement setting. The gemologist hired by ABC also noted that a diamond of the same exact quality—without the prestigious brand name—cost approximately $10,500. This puts a value of $6,100 on the Tiffany brand name and little blue box alone. The same consultant then ventured to Costco and purchased a round diamond, just over a carat in size with a color grade of H (nearly colorless) and paid $6,600, which was $10,000 less than an almost identical diamond at Tiffany & Co. Certainly, some may say that the Tiffany brand name is worth the extra $6,000, and many consumers make the choice every day to buy a name-brand product versus a no-name one, whether it be jeans, handbags, or jewelry due to quality concerns or simply to have the logo stitched on their pocket or hanging from their arm. But will the benefits of a designer name like Tiffany & Co. continue to be as prominent as it once was?

# Panera Bread Company in 2012— Pursuing Growth in a Weak Economy

McGraw Hill connect®

## Arthur A. Thompson
### The University of Alabama

In Spring 2012, the two core elements of Panera Bread Company's strategy were to aggressively expand its market presence across North America and improve the quality of the dining experience it provided to customers. It already operated 1,541 company-owned and franchised bakery-cafés in 42 states, the District of Columbia, and Ontario, Canada, under the Panera Bread, Saint Louis Bread Co., and Paradise Bakery & Café names. The number of locations was up from 1,027 units in 36 states at the end of 2006, but well short of the ambitious target the company set in 2006 to have 2,000 outlets in operation by the end of 2010. The Great Recession of 2008–2009 had forced management to scale back Panera's expansion plans, but the company then accelerated its growth by opening 76 new company-operated and franchised units in 2010 and another 88 new units in 2011. Plans called for opening 115 to 120 new company-operated and franchised units in 2012. Management was confident that Panera Bread's attractive menu and the dining ambiance of its bakery-cafés provided significant growth opportunity—despite the weak economic recovery, a stubbornly high 8 percent unemployment rate, and the fiercely competitive nature of the restaurant industry—and that the company's targeted long-term EPS growth rate of 15 to 20 percent annually was achievable.

Panera Bread baked more specialty breads daily than any other bakery-café enterprise in North America, and it was widely regarded as the clear leader of the "fast-casual" segment of the restaurant industry. In 2011, it had corporate revenues of $1.8 billion, systemwide store revenues of $3.4 billion, and average sales of $2.3 million per store location. On average, nearly 6.5 million customers patronized Panera locations systemwide each week.

The company was the recipient of many honors and awards. It had scored the highest level of customer loyalty among quick-casual restaurants, according to a 2011 research study conducted by TNS Intersearch.[1] In a 2011 Harris Poll EquiTrend® study, Panera Bread was named Casual Dining Brand of the Year. Additionally, in 2011, Zagat, a highly regarded restaurant review service, awarded Panera Bread #1 rankings for Best Salads and Top Rated Facilities (for chain restaurants with less than 5,000 outlets); in 2010, Zagat named Panera as Most Popular among chains with fewer than 5,000 locations and also gave Panera #1 rankings for Best Salad and Best Facilities and #2 rankings for Healthy Options, Best Value, and Best Breakfast Sandwich. Panera Bread was named to *BusinessWeek*'s 2010 list of the top 25 "Customer Service Champs" and to *Fortune* magazine's 2010 list of the 100 Fastest-Growing Companies. For eight consecutive years (2002–2009), customers had rated Panera Bread tops among chain restaurants in Sandleman & Associates Quick-Track "Awards of Excellence."

## COMPANY BACKGROUND

In 1981, Louis Kane and Ron Shaich founded a bakery-café enterprise named Au Bon Pain Co., Inc. Units were opened in malls, shopping centers, and airports along the east coast of the United States and internationally throughout the 1980s and 1990s; the company prospered and became the dominant operator within the bakery-café category. In 1993, Au Bon Pain Co. purchased Saint Louis Bread Company, a chain of 20 bakery-cafés located in the St. Louis area. Ron Shaich and a team of Au Bon Pain managers then spent considerable time in 1994 and 1995 traveling the country and studying the market for fast food and quick-service meals. They concluded that many patrons of fast-food chains like McDonald's, Wendy's, Burger King, Subway, Taco Bell, Pizza Hut, and KFC could be attracted to a higher-quality quick dining experience. Top management at Au Bon Pain then instituted a comprehensive overhaul of the newly acquired Saint Louis Bread locations, altering the menu and the dining atmosphere. The vision was to create a specialty café anchored by an authentic, fresh dough, artisan bakery, and upscale, quick-service menu selections. Between 1993 and 1997, average unit volumes at the revamped Saint Louis Bread units increased by 75 percent, and over 100 additional Saint Louis Bread units were opened. In 1997, the Saint Louis Bread bakery-cafés were renamed Panera Bread in all markets outside St. Louis.

By 1998, it was clear the re-concepted Panera Bread units had connected with consumers. Au Bon Pain management concluded the Panera Bread format had broad market appeal and could be rolled-out nationwide. Ron Shaich believed Panera Bread had the potential to become one of the leading "fast-casual" restaurant chains in the nation. Shaich also believed that growing Panera Bread into a national chain required significantly more management attention and financial resources than the company could marshal if it continued to pursue expansion of both the Au Bon Pain and Panera Bread chains. He convinced the Au Bon Pain board of directors that the best course of action was for the company to go exclusively with the Panera Bread concept and divest the Au Bon Pain cafés. In August 1998, the company announced the sale of its Au Bon Pain bakery-café division for $73 million in cash to ABP Corp.; the transaction was completed in May 1999. With the sale of the Au Bon Pain division, the company changed its name to Panera Bread Company. The restructured company had 180 Saint Louis and Panera Bread bakery-cafés and a debt-free balance sheet.

Between January 1999 and December 2006, close to 850 additional Panera Bread bakery-cafés were opened, some company-owned and some franchised. As of December 27, 2011, Panera had 740 company-owned and 801 franchised bakery-cafés in operation. In February 2007, Panera purchased a 51 percent interest in Arizona-based Paradise Bakery & Café, which operated 70 company-owned and franchised units in 10 states (primarily in the west and southwest) and had sales close to $100 million. At the time, Paradise Bakery units had average weekly sales of about $40,000 and an average check size of

$8 to $9. Panera purchased the remaining 49 percent ownership of Paradise Bakery in June 2009. In 2008, Panera expanded into Canada, opening two locations in Ontario; since then, an additional unit in Canada had been opened.

In May 2010, William W. Moreton, Panera's executive vice president and co-chief operating officer, was appointed president and chief executive officer and a member of the company's board. Ron Shaich, who had served as Panera's president and CEO since 1994 and as chairman or co-chairman of the board of directors since 1988, transitioned to the role of executive chairman of the board. In addition to the normal duties of board chairman, Shaich maintained an active strategic role, with a particular focus on how Panera Bread could continue to be the best competitive alternative in the market segments the company served. However, on March 15, 2012, the company announced that Ron Shaich and Bill Moreton would become co-CEOs, effective immediately; Shaich's formal title was changed to chairman of the board and co-CEO and Moreton's title became president and co-CEO. According to the company's press release, this new arrangement formalized a working relationship that had evolved over the last year and reflected how Shaich and Moreton actually operated as a top executive team.

A summary of Panera Bread's recent financial performance is shown in Exhibit 1. Exhibit 2 provides selected operating statistics for Panera's company-owned and franchise d bakery-cafes.

## PANERA BREAD'S CONCEPT AND STRATEGY

Panera Bread's identity was rooted in its fresh-baked artisan breads made with a craftsman's attention to quality and detail, and its breads and baked products were the platform for the dining experience at its bakery-cafés and a major basis for differentiating Panera from its competitors. The featured menu offerings at Panera locations included breads and pastries baked in-house, breakfast items and smoothies, made-to-order sandwiches, signature soups and salads, and café beverages. Recognizing that diners chose a dining establishment based on individual food preferences and mood, Panera strived to be the first choice for diners craving fresh-baked goods, a sandwich, soup, a salad, or a beverage served in a warm, friendly, comfortable dining environment. Its target market was urban workers and suburban dwellers looking for a

**EXHIBIT 1** Selected Consolidated Financial Data for Panera Bread, 2002–2011 (in thousands, except for per-share amounts)

|  | 2011 | 2010 | 2009 | 2007 | 2002 |
|---|---|---|---|---|---|
| **Income Statement Data** | | | | | |
| Revenues: | | | | | |
| Bakery-café sales | $1,592,951 | $1,321,162 | $1,153,255 | $ 894,902 | $212,645 |
| Franchise royalties and fees | 92,793 | 86,195 | 78,367 | 67,188 | 27,892 |
| Fresh dough and other product sales to franchisees | 136,288 | 135,192 | 121,872 | 104,601 | 41,688 |
| Total revenues | 1,822,032 | 1,542,489 | 1,353,494 | 1,066,691 | 282,225 |
| Bakery-café expenses: | | | | | |
| Food and paper products | 470,398 | 374,816 | 337,599 | 271,442 | 63,370 |
| Labor | 484,014 | 419,140 | 370,595 | 286,238 | 63,172 |
| Occupancy | 115,290 | 100,970 | 95,996 | 70,398 | 15,408 |
| Other operating expenses | 216,237 | 177,059 | 155,396 | 121,325 | 27,971 |
| Total bakery-café expenses | 1,285,939 | 1,071,985 | 959,586 | 749,403 | 169,921 |
| Fresh dough and other product costs of sales to franchisees | 116,267 | 110,986 | 100,229 | 92,852 | 38,432 |
| Depreciation and amortization | 79,899 | 68,673 | 67,162 | 57,903 | 13,794 |
| General and administrative expenses | 113,083 | 101,494 | 83,169 | 68,966 | 24,986 |
| Pre-opening expenses | 6,585 | 4,282 | 2,451 | 8,289 | 1,051 |
| Total costs and expenses | 1,601,773 | 1,357,420 | 1,212,597 | 977,413 | 248,184 |
| Operating profit | 220,259 | 185,069 | 140,897 | 89,278 | 34,041 |
| Interest expense | 822 | 675 | 700 | 483 | 32 |
| Other (income) expense, net | (466) | 4,232 | 273 | 333 | 467 |
| Income taxes | 83,951 | 68,563 | 53,073 | 31,434 | 12,242 |
| Less net income (loss) attributable to non-controlling interest | — | (267) | 801 | (428) | — |
| Net income to shareholders | $ 135,952 | $ 111,866 | $ 86,050 | $ 57,456 | $ 21,300 |
| Earnings per share | | | | | |
| Basic | $4.59 | $3.65 | $2.81 | $1.81 | $0.74 |
| Diluted | 4.55 | 3.62 | 2.78 | 1.79 | 0.71 |
| Weighted average shares outstanding | | | | | |
| Basic | 29,601 | 30,614 | 30,667 | 31,708 | 28,923 |
| Diluted | 29,903 | 30,922 | 30,979 | 32,178 | 29,891 |
| **Balance Sheet Data** | | | | | |
| Cash and cash equivalents | $ 222,640 | $ 229,299 | $ 246,400 | $ 68,242 | $ 29,924 |
| Short-term investments | 186 | 152 | — | 23,198 | 9,149 |
| Current assets | 353,119 | 330,685 | 322,084 | 152,121 | 59,262 |
| Total assets | 1,027,322 | 924,581 | 837,165 | 698,752 | 195,431 |
| Current liabilities | 238,334 | 211,516 | 142,259 | 127,766 | 32,325 |
| Total liabilities | 372,246 | 328,973 | 240,129 | 250,573 | 32,587 |
| Stockholders' equity | 655,076 | 595,608 | 597,036 | 446,164 | 151,503 |
| **Cash Flow Data** | | | | | |
| Net cash provided by operating activities | $ 236,889 | $ 237,634 | $ 214,904 | $ 154,014 | $ 46,323 |
| Net cash used in investing activities | (152,194) | (132,199) | (49,219) | (197,262) | (40,115) |
| Net cash (used in) provided by financing activities | (91,354) | (122,536) | 6,005 | 59,393 | 5,664 |
| Net (decrease) increase in cash and cash equivalents | (6,659) | (17,101) | 171,690 | 16,145 | 11,872 |

*Sources:* 2011 10-K report, pp. 41–43; 2010 10-K report, pp. 29–30, 46–48; 2008 10-K report, pp. 48–50; and 2003 10-K report, pp. 29–31.

## EXHIBIT 2   Selected Operating Statistics, Panera Bread Company, 2002–2011

| | 2011 | 2010 | 2009 | 2007 | 2002 |
|---|---|---|---|---|---|
| Revenues at company-operated stores (in millions) | $1,593.0 | $1,321.2 | $1,153.3 | $ 894.9 | $ 212.6 |
| Revenues at franchised stores (in millions) | $1,828.2 | $1,802.1 | $1,640.3 | $1,376.4 | $ 542.6 |
| Systemwide store revenues (in millions) | 3,421.2 | $3,123.3 | $2,793.6 | $2,271.3 | $ 755.2 |
| Average annualized revenues per company-operated bakery-café (in millions) | $ 2.292 | $ 2.179 | $ 2.031 | $ 1.952 | $ 1.764 |
| Average annualized revenues per franchised bakery-café (in millions) | $ 2.315 | $ 2.266 | $ 2.109 | $ 2.051 | $ 1.872 |
| Average weekly sales, company-owned cafés | $ 44,071 | $ 41,899 | $ 39,050 | $ 37,548 | $33,924 |
| Average weekly sales, franchised cafés | $ 44,527 | $ 43,578 | $ 40,566 | $ 39,438 | $35,997 |
| Comparable bakery-café sales percentage increases* | | | | | |
|   Company-owned outlets | 4.9% | 7.5% | 2.4% | 1.7% | 4.1% |
|   Franchised outlets | 3.4% | 8.2% | 2.0% | 1.7% | 6.1% |
| Company-owned bakery-cafés open at year-end | 740 | 662 | 585 | 532 | 132 |
| Franchised bakery-cafés open at year-end | 801 | 791 | 795 | 698 | 346 |
|   Total bakery-cafés open | 1,541 | 1,453 | 1,380 | 1,230 | 478 |

*The percentages for comparable store sales are based on annual changes at stores that were first opened prior to the first day of the previous fiscal year (meaning that a store had to be open for all 12 months of the year to be included in this statistic).

*Sources:* Company 10-K reports for 2011, 2010, 2008, and 2003.

quick service meal or light snack and an aesthetically pleasing dining experience. Management's long-term objective and strategic intent was to make Panera Bread a nationally recognized brand name and to be the dominant restaurant operator in upscale, quick-service dining. Top management believed that success depended on "being better than the guys across the street" and making the experience of dining at Panera so attractive that customers would be willing to pass by the outlets of other fast-casual restaurant competitors to dine at a nearby Panera Bread bakery-café.[2]

Panera management's blueprint for attracting and retaining customers was called Concept Essence. Concept Essence underpinned Panera's strategy and embraced several themes that, taken together, acted to differentiate Panera from its competitors:

- Offering an appealing selection of artisan breads, bagels, and pastry products that were handcrafted and baked daily at each café location.
- Serving high-quality food at prices that represented a good value.
- Developing a menu with sufficiently diverse offerings to enable Panera to draw customers from breakfast through the dinner hours each day.
- Providing courteous, capable, and efficient customer service.

- Designing bakery cafés that were aesthetically pleasing and inviting.
- Offering patrons such a sufficiently satisfying dining experience that they were induced to return again and again.

Panera Bread's menu, store design and ambiance, and unit location strategies enabled it to compete successfully in multiple segments of the restaurant business: breakfast, AM "chill" (when customers visited to take a break from morning-hour activities), lunch, PM "chill" (when customers visited to take a break from afternoon activities), dinner, and take home, through both on-premise sales and off-premise catering. It competed with a wide assortment of specialty food, casual dining, and quick-service establishments operating nationally, regionally, and locally. Its close competitors varied according to the menu item, meal, and time of day. For example, breakfast and AM "chill" competitors included Starbucks and McDonald's; close lunch and dinner competitors included such chains as Chili's, Applebee's, California Pizza Kitchen, Jason's Deli, Cracker Barrel, Ruby Tuesday, T.G.I. Friday's, Chipotle Mexican Grill, and Five Guys Burgers and Fries. In the bread and pastry segment, Panera competed with Corner Bakery Café, Atlanta Bread Company, Au Bon Pain, local bakeries, and supermarket bakeries.

Except for bread and pastry products, Panera's strongest competitors were dining establishments in the so-called "fast casual" restaurant category. Fast casual restaurants filled the gap between fast-food outlets and casual, full table service restaurants. A fast casual restaurant provided quick-service dining (much like fast-food enterprises) but was distinguished by enticing menus, higher food quality, and more inviting dining environments; typical meal costs per guest were in the $7–$12 range. Some fast casual restaurants had full table service, some had partial table service (with orders being delivered to the table after ordering and paying at the counter), and some were self-service (like fast-food establishments, with orders being taken and delivered at the counter). Exhibit 3 provides information on prominent national and regional dining chains that competed against Panera Bread in some or many geographical locations.

**EXHIBIT 3**  Representative Fast-Casual Restaurant Chains and Selected Full-Service Restaurant Chains in the U.S., 2010–2011

| Company | Number of Locations, 2011 | Select 2010–2011 Financial Data | Key Menu Categories |
|---|---|---|---|
| Atlanta Bread Company | ~100 bakery-cafés mainly in the southeastern U.S. | Not available (privately held company) | Fresh-baked breads, salads, sandwiches, soups, wood-fired pizza and pasta (select locations only), baked goods, desserts |
| Applebee's Neighborhood Grill and Bar* (a subsidiary of DineEquity) | 2,019 locations in 49 states, one U.S. territory, and 15 countries outside the U.S. | 2011 average annual sales of about $2.2 million per location | Beef, chicken, pork, seafood, and pasta entrees, plus appetizers, salads, sandwiches, a selection of under-500 calorie Weight Watchers–branded menu alternatives, desserts, and alcoholic beverages (about 12 percent of total sales) |
| Au Bon Pain | 200+ company-owned and franchised bakery-cafés in 23 states, South Korea, Thailand, and Taiwan | Not available (privately held company) | Baked goods (with a focus on croissants and bagels), soups, salads, sandwiches and wraps, and coffee drinks |
| Bruegger's | 300+ bakery-cafés in 26 states, the District of Columbia, and Canada | 2010 revenues of $254.5 million | Fresh-baked bagels and breads, sandwiches, salads, soups, and desserts |
| California Pizza Kitchen* (a subsidiary of Golden Gate Capital) | 265 locations in 32 states and 10 other countries | Average annual sales of about $3.2 million per location | Signature California-style hearth-baked pizzas, plus salads, pastas, soups, sandwiches, appetizers, desserts, beer, wine, coffees, teas, and assorted beverages |
| Chili's Grill and Bar* (a subsidiary of Brinker International) | 1,300 locations in 50 states and 241 locations in 30 foreign countries and two U.S. territories | 2011 average revenues of ~$3.0 million per location; average check size per customer of $13.52 | Chicken, beef, and seafood entrees, steaks, appetizers, salads, sandwiches, desserts, and alcoholic beverages (13.6 percent of sales) |
| Chipotle Mexican Grill | 1,230+ units | 2011 revenues of $2.3 billion; average unit sales of $2.0 million | Gourmet burritos and tacos, salads, beverages (including margaritas and beers) |
| Corner Bakery Café (a subsidiary of Roark Capital Group) | 130 locations in 10 states and the District of Columbia (planning to double number of locations by 2015) | Menu price range: $0.99 to $7.99 | Specialty breads, hot breakfasts, signature sandwiches, grilled panini, pastas, soups and chili, salads, sweets, coffees, and teas |
| Cracker Barrel* | 604 combination retail stores and restaurants in 42 states | Restaurant-only sales of $1.9 billion in 2011; average restaurant sales of $3.2 million; | Two menus (breakfast and lunch/dinner); rated in *Zagat's 2010 Consumer Survey* as "Best |

## EXHIBIT 3   (Continued)

| Company | Number of Locations, 2011 | Select 2010–2011 Financial Data | Key Menu Categories |
|---|---|---|---|
| | | average guest check of $9.22; serves an average of ~6,800 customers per week per location | Breakfast" among family dining chains and by *Technomics* as "Top of the Full-Service Restaurants in family and casual dining" |
| Culver's | 428 locations in 19 states | Not available (a privately held company) | Signature hamburgers served on buttered buns, fried battered cheese curds, value dinners (chicken, shrimp, cod with potato and slaw), salads, frozen custard, milkshakes, sundaes, and fountain drinks |
| Einstein Bros. Bagels (a unit of the Einstein Noah Restaurant Group) | ~330 company-owned and 100 licensed locations in ~35 states | Annual sales revenues per unit of ~$1.0 million | Fresh-baked bagels, hot breakfast sandwiches, made-to-order lunch sandwiches, creamed cheeses and other spreads, salads, soups, and gourmet coffees and teas |
| Fazoli's (a subsidiary of Sun Capital Partners) | 230 locations in 26 states | Not available (a privately held company) | Spaghetti and meatballs, fettuccine alfredo, lasagna, ravioli, submarinos and panini sandwiches, pizza, entrée salads, garlic breadsticks, and desserts |
| Firehouse Subs | ~500 locations in 29+ states | Average unit sales of $657,000 | Hot and cold subs, salads, sides, drinks, catering |
| Five Guys Burgers and Fries | 725+ locations in 46 states and six Canadian provinces | Not available (a privately held company) | Hamburgers (with choice of 15 toppings), hot dogs, fries, Coca-Cola, and beverages |
| Fuddruckers | ~200 locations in 32 states, the District of Columbia, Puerto Rico, and Canada | Not available (a privately held company) | Exotic hamburgers (the feature menu item), chicken and fish sandwiches, French fries and other sides, soups, salads, desserts |
| Jason's Deli | 230+ locations in 28 states | Not available (a privately held company) | Sandwiches, extensive salad bar, soups, loaded potatoes, desserts, catering services, party trays, and box lunches |
| Moe's Southwest Grill (a subsidiary of Roark Capital Group) | 420 locations in 26 states and the District of Columbia | Not available (a privately held company) | Burritos, quesadillas, fajitas, tacos, nachos, rice bowls (chicken, pork, or tofu), salads with a choice of two homemade dressings, a kid's menu, five side items (including queso and guacamole), two desserts (cookie or brownie), soft drinks, iced tea, bottled water, and catering |
| McAlister's Deli (a subsidiary of Roark Capital Group) | 200+ locations in 22 states | Not available (a privately held company) | Deli sandwiches, loaded baked potatoes, soups, salads, and desserts, plus sandwich trays, lunch boxes, and catering |
| Noodles & Company | 260+ urban and suburban locations in 22 states | Not available (a privately held company); designated by *Parents* magazine as one of the 10 best restaurant chains in 2011; typical price point of $7 | Asian, Mediterranean, and American noodle/pasta entrees, soups, salads, sandwiches, alcoholic beverages |

(Continued)

**EXHIBIT 3**   (*Concluded*)

| Company | Number of Locations, 2011 | Select 2010–2011 Financial Data | Key Menu Categories |
|---|---|---|---|
| Qdoba Mexican Grill (a subsidiary of Jack-in-the-Box, Inc.) | 583+ locations in 42 states and the District of Columbia | Average unit sales of $961,000 in 2011 | Signature burritos, tacos, taco salads, quesadillas, three-cheese nachos, Mexican gumbo, tortilla soup, five signature salsas, and breakfast selections at some locations |
| Ruby Tuesday* | 779 company-owned and franchised locations in 45 states and 46 franchised locations in 14 foreign countries and Guam | Fiscal 2011 sales of $1.26 billion; average revenues of ~$1.1 million per company-operated unit in 2011; entrée price ranges of $6.99 to $18.99 | Appetizers, handcrafted burgers, 40-item salad bar, steaks, fresh chicken, crab cakes, lobster, salmon, tilapia, ribs, desserts, non-alcoholic and alcoholic beverages, and catering |
| Starbucks | ~10,800 company-operated and licensed locations in the U.S. and 6,200+ international locations | 2011 revenues of $11.7 billion; estimated retail sales of $1.2 million per company-operated location in the U.S. | Italian-style espresso beverages, teas, sodas, juices, assorted pastries and confections; some locations offer sandwiches and salads |
| T.G.I. Friday's* (a subsidiary of Carlson's Restaurants) | 588 company-owned and franchised locations in 44 states and 341 locations in 60 foreign countries | Not available (a privately held company) | Appetizers, salads, soups, burgers and other sandwiches, chicken, seafood, steaks, pasta, desserts, non-alcoholic and alcoholic beverages, party platters |

*Denotes a full-service restaurant.

*Sources:* Company websites and FastCasual.com's "Top 100 2011 Movers and Shakers"; accessed at www.fastcasual.com on July 17, 2011.

Panera Bread's growth strategy was to capitalize on Panera's market potential by opening both company-owned and franchised Panera Bread locations as fast as was prudent. So far, working closely with franchisees to open new locations had been a key component of the company's efforts to broaden its market penetration. Panera Bread had organized its business around company-owned bakery-café operations, franchise operations, and fresh dough operations; the fresh bread unit supplied dough and other products to all Panera Bread stores, both company-owned and franchised.

## PANERA BREAD'S PRODUCT OFFERINGS AND MENU

Panera Bread's artisan signature breads were made from four ingredients—water, natural yeast, flour, and salt; no preservatives or chemicals were used.

Carefully trained bakers shaped every step of the process, from mixing the ingredients, to kneading the dough, to placing the loaves on hot stone slabs to bake in a traditional European-style stone deck bakery oven. Breads, as well as bagels, muffins, cookies, and other pastries, were baked fresh throughout the day at each café location. Exhibit 4 shows Panera's lineup of breads.

The Panera Bread menu was designed to provide target customers with products built on the company's bakery expertise, particularly its varieties of breads and bagels baked fresh throughout the day at each café location. The key menu groups were fresh baked goods, hot breakfast selections, bagels and cream cheese spreads, hot Panini, made-to-order sandwiches and salads, soups, fruit smoothies, frozen drinks, beverages, and Espresso bar selections. Exhibit 5 summarizes the menu offerings at Panera Bread locations as of April 2012.

## EXHIBIT 4   Panera's Line of Fresh-Baked Breads, April 2012

| Artisan Breads | Specialty Breads |
|---|---|
| **Country**<br>A crisp crust and nutty flavor. *Available in Loaf, Miche.*<br><br>**French**<br>Slightly blistered crust, wine-like aroma. *Available in Baguette, Miche.*<br><br>**Ciabatta**<br>A moist, chewy crumb with a thin crust and light olive oil flavor. *Available in Loaf.*<br><br>**Focaccia**<br>Italian flatbread baked with olive oil and topped with salt; two varieties—Asiago Cheese and Sea Salt. *Available in Loaf.*<br><br>**Stone-Milled Rye**<br>With chopped rye kernels and caraway seeds. *Available in Loaf, Miche.*<br><br>**Three Cheese**<br>Made with Parmesan, Romano, and Asiago cheeses. *Available in Demi, Loaf, Miche.*<br><br>**Three Seed**<br>Sesame, poppy, and fennel seeds. *Available in Demi.*<br><br>**Whole Grain**<br>Moist and hearty, sweetened with honey. *Available in Loaf, Miche, Baguette.*<br><br>**Sesame Semolina**<br>Delicate and moist, topped with sesame seeds. *Available in Loaf, Miche.* | **Sourdough**<br>Panera's signature sourdough bread that featured a golden crackled crust and a firm moderately structured crumb with a satisfying, tangy flavor. *Available in Loaf, XL Loaf, Roll, Bread Bowl.*<br><br>**Asiago Cheese**<br>Chunks of Asiago cheese were added to the standard sourdough recipe and baked right in, with more Asiago cheese sprinkled on top. *Available in Demi, Loaf.*<br><br>**Honey Wheat**<br>A mild wheat bread with tastes of honey and molasses; the soft crust and crumb made it great for sandwiches. *Available in Loaf.*<br><br>**White Whole Grain**<br>A thin crust and a soft crumb sweetened with honey and molasses. *Available in Loaf.*<br><br>**Tomato Basil**<br>Sourdough bread made with tomatoes and basil, topped with a sweet streusel topping. *Available in Loaf.*<br><br>**Cinnamon Raisin**<br>Made from sweet dough, egg, Korintge cinnamon, plump raisins, and brown sugar, topped with Panera's cinnamon crunch topping. *Available in Loaf.* |

*Source:* www.panerabread.com, accessed April 5, 2012.

Menu offerings were regularly reviewed and revised to sustain the interest of regular customers, satisfy changing consumer preferences, and be responsive to various seasons of the year. Special soup offerings, for example, appeared seasonally. Product development was focused on providing food that customers would crave and trust to be tasty. New menu items were developed in test kitchens and then introduced in a limited number of the bakery-cafés to determine customer response and verify that preparation and operating procedures resulted in product consistency and high-quality standards. If successful, they were then rolled out systemwide. New product introductions were integrated into periodic or seasonal menu rotations, referred to as "Celebrations." Ten new menu items were introduced in 2010, 14 new or improved items appeared on the menu in 2011, and 8 different selections (5 new ones and 3 that had been put back on the menu after being removed in prior periods) were being featured on Panera's menu as of April 2012.

Over the past eight years, Panera had responded to growing consumer interest in healthier, more nutritious menu offerings. In 2004, whole grain breads were introduced, and in 2005 Panera switched to the use of natural antibiotic chicken in all of Panera's chicken-related sandwiches and salads. Other recent health-related changes included using organic and all-natural ingredients in selected items, using unbleached flours in its breads, adding a yogurt-granola-fruit parfait and reduced-fat spreads for bagels to the menu, introducing fruit smoothies, increasing the use of fresh ingredients (like fresh-from-the-farm lettuces and tomatoes) and revising

## EXHIBIT 5    Panera Bread's Menu Selections, April 2012

**Bakery**
Artisan and Specialty Breads (15 varieties) – Bagels (10 varieties) – Scones (4 varieties) – Sweet Rolls (4 varieties) – Cinnamon Crumb Coffee Cake – Muffins and Muffies (7 varieties) Artisan Pastries (4 varieties) – Brownies – Cookies (6 varieties)

**Bagels & Cream Cheese Spreads** (10 varieties of bagels, 6 varieties of spreads)

**Hot Breakfast**
Signature Breakfast Sandwiches (4 varieties)
Baked Egg Soufflés (4 varieties)
Breakfast Power Sandwich on Whole Grain
Ciabatta Breakfast Sandwiches (2 varieties)

**Strawberry Granola Parfait**

**Steel Cut Oatmeal**

**Fruit Smoothies** (4 varieties)

**Signature Hot Paninis**
Steakhouse and White Cheddar – Turkey Artichoke – Frontega Chicken – Cuban Chicken – Smokehouse Turkey – Tomato and Mozzarella

**Signature Sandwiches**
Napa Almond Chicken Salad – Asiago Roast Beef – Italian Combo – Bacon Turkey Bravo – Chicken Caesar – Salmon Club

**Café Sandwiches**
Smoked Ham and Swiss – Smoked Turkey Breast – Tuna Salad – Mediterranean Veggie – Sierra Turkey

**Signature Pastas**
Mac & Cheese

**Soups (5 selections varying daily, plus seasonal specialties)**
Options include:  Broccoli Cheddar – French Onion – Baked Potato – Low Fat All-Natural Chicken Noodle – Cream of Chicken and Wild Rice – New England Clam Chowder – Low Fat Vegetarian Garden Vegetable with Pesto – Low Fat Vegetarian Black Bean – Low Fat Chicken Tortilla – Vegetarian Creamy Tomato

**Signature Salads**
Mediterranean Salmon – Salmon Caesar – Roasted Turkey Fuji Apple – Steak and Blue Cheese – BBQ Chopped Chicken – Chopped Chicken Cobb – Grilled Chicken Caesar – Asian Sesame Chicken – Fuji Apple Chicken – Thai Chopped Chicken

**Café Salads**
Chicken – Caesar – Classic

**Panera Kids**
Grilled Cheese – Peanut Butter and Jelly – Mac & Cheese – Kid's Deli (Organic American cheese and choice of smoked ham, turkey breast, or roast beef)

**Beverages**
Coffee (4 varieties) – Hot Teas – Iced Tea – Iced Green Tea – Pepsi beverages – Bottled Water – Organic Milk or Chocolate Milk – Orange Juice – Organic Apple Juice – Lemonade

**Frozen Drinks** (3 varieties)

**Espresso Bar**
Espresso – Cappuccino – Caffe Latte – Caffe Mocha – Caramel Latte – Chai Tea Latte (hot or iced) – Hot Chocolate

*Source:* Menu posted at www.panerabread.com, accessed April 5, 2012.

ingredients and preparation methods to yield 0 grams of artificial trans fat per serving. Panera's website had detailed nutritional information for individual products and a nutritional calculator that could be used to determine the nutritional content of an entire meal or combination of menu selections.

**Off-Premises Catering**    In 2004–2005, Panera Bread introduced a catering program to extend its market reach into the workplace, schools, and parties and gatherings held in homes, and grow their breakfast-, lunch-, and dinner-hour sales without making capital investments in additional physical facilities. A catering menu, that drew upon items appearing on the regular menu, was created and posted for viewing at the company's website. Selections included an assortment of bagels and morning pastries (with butter, cream cheeses, and preserves), a fruit bowl, individual servings of steel cut oatmeal, hot breakfast sandwiches and baked egg soufflés, sandwich assortments, boxed lunches, salads and soups for a group, and beverages. A catering coordinator was available to help customers make menu selections, choose between assortments or boxed meals, determine appropriate order quantities, and arrange pick-up or delivery times. Orders came complete with plates, napkins, and utensils, all packaged and presented in convenient, ready-to-serve-from packaging.

In 2010, Panera boosted the size of its catering sales staff and introduced sales training programs and other tools—factors that helped drive a 26 percent increase in catering sales in 2010. In 2011, Panera introduced an online catering system that catering customers could use to view the catering menu, place orders, and pay for purchases. Going forward, top executives at Panera believed that continuing to develop the company's off-premise catering capabilities and provide even more convenient catering options for customers would lead to significantly higher catering revenues at both company-operated and franchised locations.

**The MyPanera Loyalty Program**   In 2010, Panera initiated a loyalty program to reward customers who dined frequently at Panera Bread locations. The introduction of the MyPanera program was completed systemwide in November and, by the end of December, some 4.5 million customers had signed up and become registered card members. Members presented their MyPanera card when ordering. When the card was swiped, the specific items being purchased were automatically recorded to learn what items a member liked. As Panera got an idea of a member's preferences over the course of several visits, a member's card was "loaded" with such "surprises" as complimentary bakery-café items, exclusive previews and tastings, cooking and baking tips, invitations to special events, ideas for entertaining, or recipe books. On a member's next visit, when an order was placed and the card swiped, order-taking personnel informed the member of the surprise award. Members could also go online at www.MyPanera.com and see if a reward was waiting on their next visit. Going into 2012, the company's MyPanera program had over nine million members.

Management believed that the loyalty program had two primary benefits. One was to entice members to dine at Panera more frequently and thereby deepen the bond between Panera Bread and its most loyal customers. The second was to provide Panera management with better marketing research data on the purchasing behavior of customers and enable Panera to "get as close to one on one marketing with our customers as possible."[3]

**Panera's Non-Profit Pay-What-You-Want Bakery-Café Locations**   In May 2010, Panera Bread converted one of its restaurants in a wealthy St. Louis suburb into a non-profit pay-what-you-want Saint Louis Bread Cares bakery-café with the idea of helping to feed the needy and raising money for charitable work. A sign in the bakery-café said, "We

encourage those with the means to leave the requested amount or more if you're able. And we encourage those with a real need to take a discount." The menu board listed "suggested funding levels," not prices. Payments went into a donation box, with the cashiers providing change and handling credit card payments. The hope was that enough generous customers would donate money above and beyond the menu's suggested funding levels to subsidize discounted meals for those who were experiencing economic hardship and needed help. The restaurant was operated by Panera's charitable Panera Bread Foundation; all profits from the store were donated to community programs.

After several months of operation, the Saint Louis Bread Cares store was judged to be successful enough that Ron Shaich, who headed the Panera Bread Foundation, opted to open two similar Panera Cares cafés—one in the Detroit suburb of Dearborn, Michigan, and one in Portland, Oregon. At one juncture, Panera statistics indicated that roughly 60 percent of store patrons left the suggested amount; 20 percent left more, and 20 percent less.[4] Of course, there were occasional instances where a patron tried to game the system. Ron Shaich cited the case of a college student who ordered more than $40 worth of food and charged only $3 to his father's credit card; Shaich, who happened to be working in the store behind the counter, had to restrain himself, saying "I wanted to jump over the counter."[5] One person paid $500 for a meal, the largest single payment. Although in May 2011 Panera had intentions to open a new pay-what-you-want store every three months or so, the company still had only three pay-what-you-want café locations as of April 2012.

## MARKETING

In the company's early years, marketing had played only a small role in Panera's success. Brand awareness had been built on customers' satisfaction with their dining experience at Panera and their tendency to share their positive experiences with friends and neighbors. From time to time, Panera had utilized focus groups to determine customer food and drink preferences and price points. In 2006, Panera's marketing research indicated that about 85 percent of consumers who were aware that there was a Panera Bread bakery-café in their community or neighborhood had dined at Panera on at least one occasion; 57 percent of consumers who had "ever tried" dining at

Panera Bread had been customers in the past 30 days.[6] Panera's research also showed that people who dined at Panera Bread very frequently or moderately frequently did so for only one part of the day, although 81 percent indicated a "considerable willingness" to try dining at Panera Bread at other parts of the day.

This data prompted management to pursue three marketing initiatives during 2006–2007. One aimed at raising the quality of awareness about Panera by continuing to feature the caliber and appeal of its breads and baked goods, by hammering home the theme "food you crave, food you can trust," and by enhancing the appeal of its bakery-cafés as a neighborhood gathering place. A second initiative sought to raise awareness and boost customer trials of dining at Panera Bread at multiple meal times (breakfast, lunch, "chill out" times, and dinner). The third initiative was to increase perception of Panera Bread as a viable evening meal option by introducing a number of new entrée menu selections. Panera avoided hard-sell or "in your face" marketing approaches, preferring instead to employ a range of ways to softly drop the Panera Bread name into the midst of consumers as they moved through their lives and let them "gently collide" with the brand. The idea was to let consumers "discover" Panera Bread and then convert them into loyal repeat customers by providing a very satisfying dining experience when they tried Panera bakery-cafés for the first time or opted to try dining at Panera at a different part of the day, particularly during breakfast or dinner as opposed to the busier lunchtime hours. These initiatives were only partially successful, partly because of the difficult economic environment that emerged in 2008–2009 and partly because the new dinner entrées that were introduced did not prove popular enough to significantly boost dinner-hour traffic and were dropped from the menu—in 2011–2012, the only hot entrée on the menu was Mac & Cheese (see Exhibit 5).

Panera management was committed to growing sales at existing and new unit locations, continuously improving the customer experience at its restaurants, and encouraging more frequent customer visits via the newly instituted MyPanera loyalty programs and efforts to build a deeper and lasting relationship with customers who, management believed, would then recommend dining at Panera to their friends and acquaintances.

To reach target customer groups, Panera employed a mix of radio, billboards, social networking, television, print, and in-store sampling days. Much effort went into improving Panera's advertising messages to better capture the points of difference and the soul of the Panera concept and doing a better job of optimizing the media mix in each geographic market. Advertising expenses totaled $33.2 million in 2011, $27.4 million in 2010, $15.3 million in 2009, and $14.2 million in 2008. Whereas Panera spent only about 1 percent of systemwide sales on direct media advertising in 2010–2011 (and only about 0.6 percent in 2008–2009), it was the practice at many national restaurant chains to spend 3 to 5 percent of revenues on media advertising. In 2012, management planned to:

- Launch a new advertising campaign on selected cable channels to reach a broader audience.

- Continue efforts to gain increased audience exposure to the ads it placed in various media.

- Increase overall advertising expenditures.

Franchise-operated bakery-cafés were required, as part of their franchising agreement, to contribute 1.2 percent of their sales to a national advertising fund and 0.4 percent of their sales as a marketing administration fee, and were also required to spend 2.0 percent of their sales in their local markets on advertising. Panera contributed similar amounts from company-owned bakery-cafés toward the national advertising fund and marketing administration. The national advertising fund contribution of 1.2 percent had been increased from 0.7 percent starting in July 2010; the 0.7 percent contribution became effective in January 2006 when it was raised from 0.4 percent. According to the franchise agreement, Panera could opt to raise the national advertising fund contributions as high as 2.6 percent of sales.

Panera had recently hired a new chief marketing officer and a new vice president of marketing. Both had considerable consumer marketing experience and were playing an important role in crafting the company's long-term marketing strategy to boost customer traffic and grow revenues at all of Panera's restaurant locations. Efforts were underway to refine marketing initiatives aimed at increasing brand awareness, continuously improving the customer experience at the company's restaurants, expanding customer participation in the MyPanera loyalty program, and developing and promoting appealing new menu selections.

# FRANCHISE OPERATIONS

Opening additional franchised bakery-cafés was a core element of Panera Bread's strategy and management's initiatives to achieve the company's revenue growth and earnings targets. Panera Bread did not grant single-unit franchises, so a prospective franchisee could not open just one bakery-café. Rather, Panera Bread's franchising strategy was to enter into franchise agreements that required the franchise developer to open a number of units, typically 15 bakery-cafés in a period of six years. Franchisee candidates had to be well-capitalized, have a proven track record as excellent multi-unit restaurant operators, and agree to meet an aggressive development schedule. Applicants had to meet eight stringent criteria to gain consideration for a Panera Bread franchise:

- Experience as a multi-unit restaurant operator
- Recognition as a top restaurant operator
- Net worth of $7.5 million
- Liquid assets of $3 million
- Infrastructure and resources to meet Panera's development schedule for the market area the franchisee was applying to develop
- Real estate experience in the market to be developed
- Total commitment to the development of the Panera Bread brand
- Cultural fit and a passion for fresh bread

Exhibit 6 shows estimated costs of opening a new franchised Panera Bread bakery-café. The franchise agreement typically required the payment of a $5,000 development fee for each bakery-café contracted for in a franchisee's "area development agreement," a franchise fee of $30,000 per bakery-café (payable in a lump sum at least 30 days prior to the scheduled opening of a new bakery-café), and continuing royalties of 5 percent on gross sales at each franchised bakery-café.

**EXHIBIT 6**  Estimated Initial Investment for a Franchised Panera Bread Bakery-Café, 2012

| Investment Category | Actual or Estimated Amount | To Whom Paid |
|---|---|---|
| Development fee | $5,000 per bakery-café contracted for in the franchisee's Area Development Agreement | Panera |
| Franchise fee | $35,000 ($5,000 of the development fee was applied to the $35,000 franchise fee when a new bakery-café was opened) | Panera |
| Real property | Varies according to site and local real estate market conditions | |
| Leasehold improvements | $334,000 to $938,500 | Contractors |
| Equipment | $198,000 to $310,000 | Equipment vendors, Panera |
| Fixtures | $32,000 to $54,000 | Vendors |
| Furniture | $28,500 to $62,000 | Vendors |
| Consultant fees and municipal impact fees (if any) | $51,500 to $200,250 | Architect, engineer, expeditor, others |
| Supplies and inventory | $19,150 to $24,350 | Panera, other suppliers |
| Smallwares | $24,000 to $29,000 | Suppliers |
| Signage | $15,000 to $84,000 | Suppliers |
| Additional funds (for working capital and general operating expenses for 3 months) | $175,000 to $245,000 | Vendors, suppliers, employees, utilities, landlord, others |
| **Total** | **$917,150 to $1,987,000, plus real estate and related costs** | |

*Source:* **www.panerabread.com**, accessed April 5, 2012.

Franchise-operated bakery-cafés followed the same standards for in-store operating standards, product quality, menu, site selection, and bakery-café construction as did company-owned bakery-cafés. Franchisees were required to purchase all of their dough products from sources approved by Panera Bread. Panera's fresh dough facility system supplied fresh dough products to substantially all franchise-operated bakery-cafés. Panera did not finance franchisee construction or area development agreement payments or hold an equity interest in any of the franchise-operated bakery-cafés. All area development agreements executed after March 2003 included a clause allowing Panera Bread the right to purchase all bakery-cafés opened by the franchisee at a defined purchase price, at any time five years after the execution of the franchise agreement. In 2010, Panera purchased 37 bakery-cafés from the franchisee in the New Jersey market and sold 3 bakery-cafés in the Mobile, Alabama, market to an existing franchisee. In 2011, Panera completed the purchase of 25 bakery-cafés owned by its Milwaukee franchisee, 5 bakery-cafés owned by an Indiana franchisee, 37 bakery-cafés owned by a New Jersey franchisee. Also in 2011, Panera sold two Paradise Bakery & Café units to a Texas franchisee and terminated the franchise agreements for 13 Paradise bakery-cafes that were subsequently re-branded by the former franchisee.

As of January 2012, Panera Bread had agreements with 40 franchise groups that operated 801 bakery-cafés. Panera's largest franchisee operated nearly 200 bakery-cafés in Ohio, Pennsylvania, West Virginia, Kentucky, and Florida. The company's franchise groups had committed to open an additional 195 bakery-cafés. If a franchisee failed to develop bakery-cafés on schedule, Panera had the right to terminate the franchise agreement and develop its own company-operated locations or develop locations through new franchisees in that market. However, Panera from time to time agreed to modify the commitments of franchisees to open new locations when unfavorable market conditions or other circumstances warranted the postponement or cancellation of new unit openings.

The typical franchise-operated bakery-café averaged somewhat higher average weekly and annual sales volumes than company-operated cafés (see Exhibit 2). Also, franchised cafés tended to be equal to or slightly more profitable than company-operated locations and produced a slightly higher return on equity investment than company-operated cafés (partly because many franchisees made greater use of long-term debt in financing their operations than did Panera).[7] In 2010, annual sales at franchised bakery-cafés ranged from a low of $759,524 to a high of $4,559,121, with an average of $2,285,605; this compared very favorably with the sales range of $1,081,574 to $3,988,001 and the unit average of $2,191,072 for company-operated bakery-cafés.[8]

Panera provided its franchisees with support in a number of areas: market analysis and site selection assistance, lease review, design services and new store opening assistance, a comprehensive 10-week initial training program, a training program for hourly employees, manager and baker certification, bakery-café certification, continuing education classes, benchmarking data regarding costs and profit margins, access to company-developed marketing and advertising programs, neighborhood marketing assistance, and calendar planning assistance.

# SITE SELECTION AND CAFÉ ENVIRONMENT

Bakery-cafés were typically located in suburban, strip mall, and regional mall locations. In evaluating a potential location, Panera studied the surrounding trade area, demographic information within that area, and information on nearby competitors. Based on analysis of this information, including utilization of predictive modeling using proprietary software, Panera developed projections of sales and return on investment for candidate sites. Cafés had proven successful as free-standing units and as both in-line and end-cap locations in strip malls and large regional malls.

The average Panera bakery-café size was approximately 4,600 square feet. With the exception of two bakery-cafés, all company-operated locations were leased. Lease terms were typically for 10 years with one, two, or three 5-year renewal option periods at most locations. Leases typically entailed charges for minimum base occupancy, a proportionate share of building and common area operating expenses and real estate taxes, and a contingent percentage rent based on sales above a stipulated amount. Some lease agreements provided for scheduled rent increases during the lease term. The average construction, equipment, furniture and fixture, and signage cost for the 53 company-owned bakery-cafés opened in 2011 was $950,000 (net of landlord allowances and capitalized development overhead expenses), compared to average costs of $750,000 for 42 company-owned bakery-cafés opened in 2010 and $920,000 for 66 company-owned bakery-cafés opened in 2005.

Each bakery-café sought to provide a distinctive and engaging environment (what management referred to as "Panera Warmth"), in many cases using fixtures and materials complementary to the neighborhood location of the bakery-café. All Panera cafés used real china and stainless silverware, instead of paper plates and plastic utensils. In 2005–2006, the company had introduced a new café design aimed at further refining and enhancing the appeal of Panera bakery-cafés as a warm and appealing neighborhood gathering place. The design incorporated higher-quality furniture, cozier seating, comfortable gathering areas, and relaxing décor. A number of locations had fireplaces to further create an alluring and hospitable atmosphere that patrons would flock to on a regular basis, sometimes for a meal with or without friends and acquaintances and sometimes to take a break for a light snack or beverage. Many locations had outdoor seating, and all company-operated and most franchised locations had free wireless Internet to help make the bakery-cafés community gathering places where people could catch up on some work, hang out with friends, read the paper, or just relax (a strategy that Starbucks had used with great success).

In 2006, Panera began working on store designs and operating systems that would enable free standing and end-cap locations to incorporate a drive-thru window. In 2010–2011, increasing numbers of newly opened locations, both company-owned and franchised, featured drive-thru windows. Some existing units had undergone renovation to add a drive-thru window. Going into 2012, about 50 Panera Bread locations had drive-thru windows. Sales at these locations were running about 20 percent higher on average than units without drive-thru capability.

## BAKERY-CAFÉ OPERATIONS

Panera's top executives believed that operating excellence was the most important element of Panera Warmth and that without strong execution and operational skills and energized café personnel who were motivated to provide pleasing service, it would be difficult to build and maintain a strong relationship with the customers patronizing its bakery-cafés. Additionally, top management believed high-quality restaurant management was critical to the company's long-term success. Bakery-café managers were provided with detailed operations manuals and all café personnel received hands-on training, both in small group and individual settings. The company had created systems to educate

and prepare café personnel to respond to a customer's questions and do their part to create a better dining experience. Management strived to maintain adequate staffing at each café and had instituted competitive compensation for café managers and both full-time and part-time café personnel (who were called associates).

Going into 2011, Panera Bread had approximately 900 full-time associates (defined as associates who worked an average of 25 hours or more per week) employed in general or administrative functions, principally at the company's support centers; approximately 1,300 employed in fresh dough facility operations; approximately 15,800 full-time people employed in company-operated bakery-cafés as bakers, managers, and associates; and approximately 14,600 part-time hourly associates that worked at its bakery-cafés. Panera had no collective bargaining agreements with its associates and considered its employee relations to be good.

## PANERA'S BAKERY-CAFÉ SUPPLY CHAIN

Panera operated a network of 24 facilities (22 company-owned and 2 franchise-operated) to supply fresh dough for breads and bagels on a daily basis to almost all of its company-owned and franchised bakery-cafés—one of the company's 22 facilities was a limited production operation co-located at a company-owned bakery-café in Ontario, Canada, that supplied dough to all three of Panera's bakery-cafés in that market. All of the company's facilities were leased. Most of the 1,300 employees at these facilities were engaged in preparing dough for breads and bagels, a process that took about 48 hours. The dough-making process began with the preparation and mixing of starter dough, which then was given time to rise; other all-natural ingredients were then added to create the dough for each of the different bread and bagel varieties (no chemicals or preservatives were used). Another period of rising then took place. Next, the dough was cut into pieces, shaped into loaves or bagels, and readied for shipment in fresh dough form. There was no freezing of the dough, and no partial baking was done at the fresh dough facilities. Trained bakers at each bakery-café performed all of the baking activities, using the fresh doughs delivered daily.

Distribution of the fresh bread and bagel doughs (along with tuna, cream cheese spreads, and certain fresh fruits and vegetables) was accomplished through a leased fleet of about 200 temperature-controlled trucks operated by Panera personnel. The optimal maximum distribution route was approximately 300 miles; however, routes as long as 500 miles were sometimes necessary to supply cafés in outlying locations with only a few Panera restaurants. New regional facilities and trucks were added once the number of locations in an area was sufficient to support efficient production and distribution of fresh dough and other products to surrounding bakery-cafés. In 2010–2011, the various distribution routes for regional facilities entailed making daily deliveries to an average of seven bakery-cafés.

Panera obtained ingredients for its doughs and other products manufactured at its regional facilities. While some ingredients used at these facilities were sourced from a single supplier, there were numerous suppliers of each needed fresh dough and cheese spread ingredient and Panera could obtain ingredients from another supplier when necessary. Panera contracted externally for the manufacture and distribution of sweet goods to its bakery-cafés. After delivery, sweet good products were finished with fresh toppings and other ingredients (based on Panera's own recipes) and baked to Panera's artisan standards by professionally trained bakers at each café location.

Panera had arrangements with several independent distributors to handle the delivery of sweet goods products and other items to its bakery-cafés, but the company had contracted with a single supplier to deliver the majority of ingredients and other products to its bakery-cafés two or three times weekly. Virtually all other food products and supplies for their bakery-cafés, including paper goods, coffee, and smallwares, were contracted for by Panera and delivered by the vendors to designated independent distributors for delivery to the bakery-cafés. Individual bakery-cafés placed orders for the needed supplies directly with a distributor; distributors made deliveries to bakery-cafés two or three times per week. Panera maintained a list of approved suppliers and distributors that all company-owned and franchised cafés could select from in obtaining food products and other supplies not sourced from the company's regional facilities or delivered directly by contract suppliers.

Although many of the ingredients and menu items sourced from outside vendors were prepared to Panera's specifications, the ingredients for a big majority of menu selections were generally available and could be obtained from alternative sources when necessary. In a number of instances, Panera had entered into annual and multiyear contracts for certain ingredients in order to decrease the risks of supply interruptions

and cost fluctuation. Antibiotic-free chicken was currently obtained from three different suppliers; however, alternative sources of antibiotic-free chicken—as well as certain other organically grown items—in the quantities needed were limited.

Management believed the company's fresh dough-making capability provided a competitive advantage by ensuring consistent quality and dough-making efficiency (it was more economical to concentrate the dough-making operations in a few facilities dedicated to that function than it was to have each bakery-café equipped and staffed to do all of its baking from scratch). Management also believed that the company's growing size and scale of operations gave it increased bargaining power and leverage with suppliers to improve ingredient quality and cost and that its various supply-chain arrangements entailed little risk that its bakery-cafés would experience significant delivery interruptions from weather conditions or other factors that would adversely affect café operations.

The fresh dough made at the regional facilities was sold to both company-owned and franchised bakery-cafés at a delivered cost not to exceed 27 percent of the retail value of the product. Exhibit 7 provides financial data relating to each of Panera's three business segments: company-operated bakery-cafés, franchise operations, and the operations of the regional facilities that supplied fresh dough and other products. The sales and operating profits of the fresh dough and other products segment shown in Exhibit 7 represent only those transactions with franchised bakery-cafés. The company classified any operating profit of the regional facilities stemming from supplying fresh dough and other products to company-owned bakery-cafés as a reduction in the cost of food and paper products. The costs of food and paper products for company-operated bakery-cafés are shown in Exhibit 1.

## PANERA BREAD'S MANAGEMENT INFORMATION SYSTEMS

Each company-owned bakery-café had programmed point-of-sale registers that collected transaction data used to generate transaction counts, product mix, average check size, and other pertinent statistics. The prices of menu selections at all company-owned bakery-cafés were programmed into the point-of-sale registers from the company's data support centers. Franchisees were allowed access to certain parts of

## EXHIBIT 7   Business Segment Information, Panera Bread Company, 2009–2011 (in thousands of dollars)

| | 2011 | 2010 | 2009 |
|---|---|---|---|
| **Segment revenues:** | | | |
| Company bakery-café operations | $1,592,951 | $1,321,162 | $1,153,255 |
| Franchise operations | 92,793 | 86,195 | 78,367 |
| Fresh dough and other product operations at regional facilities | 275,096 | 252,045 | 216,116 |
| Intercompany sales eliminations | (138,808) | (116,913) | (94,244) |
| Total revenues | $1,822,032 | $1,542,489 | $1,353,494 |
| **Segment operating profit:** | | | |
| Company bakery-café operations | $ 307,012 | $ 249,177 | $ 193,669 |
| Franchise operations | 86,148 | 80,397 | 72,381 |
| Fresh dough and other product operations at regional facilities | 20,021 | 24,146 | 21,643 |
| Total segment operating profit | $ 413,181 | $ 353,720 | $ 287,693 |
| **Depreciation and amortization:** | | | |
| Company bakery-café operations | $ 68,651 | $ 57,031 | $ 55,726 |
| Fresh dough and other product operations at regional facilities | 6,777 | 7,495 | 7,620 |
| Corporate administration | 4,471 | 4,147 | 3,816 |
| Total | $ 79,899 | $ 68,673 | $ 67,162 |
| **Capital expenditures:** | | | |
| Company bakery-café operations | $ 94,873 | $ 66,961 | $ 46,408 |
| Fresh dough and other product operations at regional facilities | 6,483 | 6,452 | 3,681 |
| Corporate administration | 6,576 | 8,813 | 4,595 |
| Total capital expenditures | $ 107,932 | $ 82,226 | $ 54,684 |
| **Segment assets:** | | | |
| Company bakery-café operations | $ 682,246 | $ 581,193 | $ 498,806 |
| Franchise operations | 7,502 | 6,679 | 3,850 |
| Fresh dough and other product operations at regional facilities | 47,710 | 48,393 | 48,616 |
| Total segment assets | $ 737,458 | $ 636,265 | $ 551,272 |

*Source:* Panera's 2011 10-K Report, p. 69.

Panera's proprietary bakery-café systems and systems support. Franchisees were responsible for providing the appropriate menu prices, discount rates, and tax rates for system programming.

The company used in-store enterprise application tools to (1) assist café managers in scheduling work hours for café personnel and controlling food costs, in order to provide corporate and retail operations management with quick access to retail data, (2) enable café managers to place online orders with distributors, and to reduce the time café managers spent on administrative activities. The information collected electronically at café registers was used to generate daily and weekly consolidated reports regarding sales, transaction counts, average check size, product mix, sales trends, and other operating metrics, as well as detailed profit-and-loss statements for company-owned bakery-cafés. This data was incorporated into the company's "exception-based reporting" tools.

Panera's regional facilities had software that accepted electronic orders from bakery-cafés and monitored delivery of the ordered products back to the bakery-cafés. Panera also had developed proprietary digital software to provide online training to employees at bakery-cafés, and online baking instructions for the baking personnel at each café.

Most of Panera's bakery-cafés provided customers with free Internet access through a managed WiFi network that was among the largest free public WiFi networks in the United States.

# THE RESTAURANT INDUSTRY IN THE UNITED STATES

According to the National Restaurant Association, total food-and-drink sales at all types of foodservice locations in the United States were projected to reach a record $632 billion in 2012, up 3.5 percent over 2011 and up from $379 billion in 2000 and $239 billion in 1990. [9] Of the projected $632 billion in food-and-drink sales industry-wide in 2011, about $570 billion were expected to occur in commercial establishments of various kinds. The nation's 970,000 eating place establishments were expected to account for around $425 billion in sales, with the remainder divided among bars and taverns, lodging place restaurants, managed food service locations, and other types of retail, vending, recreational, and mobile operations with foodservice capability. Quick-service restaurants were expected to grow slightly faster than full-service restaurants, reaching sales of about $175 billion versus sales of just over $200 billion. In 2008, unit sales averaged $862,000 at full-service restaurants and $737,000 at quick-service restaurants; however, very popular restaurant locations achieved annual sales volumes in the $2.5 million to $5 million range. Annual sales at most full-service and quick-service restaurants were in the $750,000 to $900,000 range; however, very popular restaurant locations achieved annual sales volumes in the $2.5 million to $5 million range.

Restaurants were the nation's second largest private employer in 2012 with about 12.9 million employees. While the restaurant industry had shed 366,000 jobs from January 2008 to January 2010 because of the effects of recessionary forces, the industry was on track to reach pre-recession employment levels in early 2012. Nearly half of all adults in the United States had worked in the restaurant industry at some point in their lives, and close to one out of three adults got their first job experience in a restaurant. About 93 percent of all eating-and-drinking place businesses had fewer than 50 employees.

Even though the average U.S. consumer ate 76 percent of their meals at home, on a typical day, about 130 million U.S. consumers were foodservice patrons at an eating establishment—sales at commercial eating places averaged about $1.65 billion daily in 2011. Average household expenditures for food away from home in 2011 were $2,505, equal to about 48 percent of total household expenditures for food and drink.

The restaurant business was labor-intensive, extremely competitive, and risky. Industry members pursued differentiation strategies of one variety or another, seeking to set themselves apart from rivals via pricing, food quality, menu theme, signature menu selections, dining ambiance and atmosphere, service, convenience, and location. To further enhance their appeal, some restaurants tried to promote greater customer traffic via happy hours, lunch and dinner specials, children's menus, innovative or trendy dishes, diet-conscious menu selections, and beverage/appetizer specials during televised sporting events (important at restaurants/bars with big-screen TVs). Most restaurants were quick to adapt their menu offerings to changing consumer tastes and eating preferences, frequently featuring heart-healthy, vegetarian, organic, low-calorie, and/or low-carb items on their menus. Research conducted by the Natural Restaurant Industry in 2010–2011 indicated that:

- 75 percent of adults were trying to eat healthier at restaurants than they did two years earlier.
- 75 percent of adults were more likely to visit a restaurant that offered locally produced food items.
- More than half of all restaurants offered locally sourced produce.
- 60 percent were more likely to visit a restaurant that offered food that was grown in an organic or environmentally friendly way.
- 57 percent of adult consumers were more likely to choose restaurants that offered loyalty rewards.

It was the norm at many restaurants to rotate some menu selections seasonally and to periodically introduce creative dishes in an effort to keep regular patrons coming back, attract more patrons, and remain competitive.

The profitability of a restaurant location ranged from exceptional to good to average to marginal to money-losing. Consumers (especially those that ate out often) were prone to give newly opened eating establishments a trial, and if they were pleased with their experience might return, sometimes frequently—loyalty to existing restaurants was low when consumers perceived there were better dining alternatives. It was also common for a once-hot restaurant to lose favor and confront the stark realities of a dwindling clientele, forcing it to either re-concept its menu and dining environment or go out of business. Many restaurants had fairly short lives. There were multiple causes for a restaurant's failure—a lack of enthusiasm for the menu or dining experience, inconsistent food quality, poor service, a poor location, meal prices that patrons deemed too high, and being outcompeted by rivals with comparable menu offerings.

# PANERA BREAD'S PERFORMANCE IN THE FIRST QUARTER OF 2012

Panera Bread reported strong financial and operating results for the first two quarters of 2011. Highlights for the first 26 weeks of 2011 included the following:

- An 18 percent increase in sales revenues, from $743.3 million to $873.2 million.
- A 30 percent increase in net income, from $52.5 million to $68.5 million.
- A 36 percent increase in diluted earnings per share, from $1.67 to $2.27. (The 39 percent gain in diluted EPS reported for the second quarter of 2011 marked the 12th out of the last 13 quarters that diluted EPS had grown more than 20 percent.)
- Second-quarter sales increases of 4.4 percent at existing company-owned bakery-cafés, 3.6 percent at existing franchise-operated bakery-cafés, and 3.9 percent at bakery-cafés systemwide—all as compared to the second quarter of 2010. First-quarter 2011 sales increases (compared to the first quarter of 2010) averaged 3.3 percent at existing company-owned bakery-cafés, 3.4 percent at existing franchise-operated bakery-cafés, and 3.3 percent at existing bakery-cafés systemwide.
- The 4.4 percent sales increase at company-owned bakery-cafés' sales in the second quarter of 2011 was comprised of a year-over-year transaction growth of 2.9 percent and an average check growth of 1.5 percent.

Since January 1, 2011, a net of 40 new company-operated and franchised bakery-cafés were opened, boosting the systemwide total of bakery-cafés from 1,453 locations to 1,493 locations. Management expected that a net of 100 to 105 new bakery-cafés would be opened in 2011.In its second-quarter 2011 release, Panera Bread management announced that it was raising targeted earnings per diluted share for full-year 2011 to the $4.54 to $4.58 range; if the Company met its target, it would generate diluted earnings per share growth of 25 to 26 percent in fiscal 2011. Management also said that it was lowering its full-year 2011 forecast of average sales growth at existing bakery-café locations to 4.5 percent, chiefly because of weaker economic conditions than previously anticipated.

During the first three weeks of July 2011, Panera Bread's stock price traded between $129 and $132 per share, up from a closing price of $101.21 on December 31, 2010 and a closing price of $66.94 on December 31, 2009. However, in the days following the release of the company's second-quarter 2011 performance (which happened to coincide with a 7 percent decline in the S&P 500 and the Dow-Jones Industrial Average), Panera's stock price dropped sharply and traded in the $112 to $115 range.

For 2012, top management at Panera expected to open a net of 100 to 110 new bakery-cafés systemwide, achieve average sales gains at existing locations of 4 to 5 percent, and grow diluted earnings per share at the low end of its long-term target of 15 to 20 percent.

## ENDNOTES

[1] According to information posted at Panera Bread's website, www.panerabread.com, accessed March 30, 2012.

[2] As stated in a presentation to securities analysts, May 5, 2006.

[3] CEO William Moreton's letter to the stockholders, Panera's 2010 Annual Report, April 18, 2011.

[4] Ron Ruggless, "Panera Cares: One Year Later," Nation's Restaurant News, May 16,

2011, posted at www.nrn.com (accessed July 19, 2011).

[5] Sean Gregory-Clayton, "Sandwich Philanthropy," Time Magazine, August 2, 2010, posted at www.time.com (accessed July 19, 2011).

[6] As cited in Panera Bread's presentation to securities analysts on May 5, 2006.

[7] Ibid.

[8] Information posted in the franchise section at www.panerabread.com, accessed April 5, 2012.

[9] The statistical data in this section is based on information posted at www.restaurant.org, accessed July 26, 2011 and April 8, 2012.

# Chipotle Mexican Grill in 2012: Can It Hit a Second Home Run?

McGraw Hill connect®

## Arthur A. Thompson
### The University of Alabama

In early 2012, it was obvious that founder, co-CEO, and chairman Steve Ells's vision and strategy for Chipotle Mexican Grill had resulted in a home run. Ells's vision for Chipotle (pronounced chi-POAT-lay) was "to change the way people think about and eat fast food." Taking his inspiration from features commonly found in many fine-dining restaurants, Ells's strategy for Chipotle was predicated on five elements:

- Serving a focused menu of burritos, tacos, burrito bowls (a burrito without the tortilla), and salads.
- Using high-quality raw ingredients and classic cooking methods to create great tasting, reasonably priced dishes that were ready to be served to customers minutes after they were ordered.
- Creating an operationally efficient restaurant with an aesthetically pleasing and distinctive interior setting.
- Having friendly people take care of each customer.
- Doing all of this with increasing awareness and respect for the environment, the use of organically grown fresh produce, and meats raised in a humane manner without hormones and antibiotics.

Since 1993, the company had grown from a 1-unit operation in Denver into a 1,230-unit operation serving over 800,000 customers a day in 41 states, the District of Columbia, Canada, and the United Kingdom. In 2011, Chipotle reported revenues of $2.3 billion, net income of $214.9 million, and diluted earnings per share of $6.76. When the company went public in January 2006, the stock doubled on its first day of trading, jumping from the initial offering price of $22 per share to close at $44 per share. As of late February 2012, Chipotle Mexican Grill's stock price had climbed to record highs each of the past seven weeks and was trading in the $380–$385 range, up more than 80 percent since January 1, 2011 and up 334 percent since January 1, 2010.

But Steve Ells was not content to capitalize on the growing demand for healthier, more wholesome fast foods and rapidly open thousands of new domestic and international Chipotle Mexican Grill locations, perhaps eventually mounting a challenge to McDonald's, the solidly entrenched global leader of the fast-food industry and the company that had invented the fast-food concept in the 1950s—McDonald's currently had 33,000 company-owned and franchised restaurant locations serving about 64 million customers in 119 countries daily. In 2011–2012, Ells and other Chipotle executives were busily planning the launch of a second restaurant concept, ShopHouse Southeast Asian Kitchen, predicated on much the same strategic principles as Chipotle Mexican Grill but with a different menu. In announcing that Chipotle would open the first ShopHouse restaurant in Washington, D.C., in the summer of 2011, Ells said, "I have always believed that the Chipotle model could work well with a variety of different cuisines." A second ShopHouse unit opened in 2012 to further test and refine the concept. Many observers believed that Chipotle was likely to hit a second home run with ShopHouse, a rare and unusual feat for a young company still rounding the bases on its first home run. In February 2012, one Wall Street analyst called Chipotle Mexican Grill "the perfect stock," and another believed that Chipotle could well prove to be the next McDonald's.[1]

## CHIPOTLE MEXICAN GRILL'S EARLY YEARS

Steve Ells graduated from the Culinary Institute of America and then worked for two years at Stars Restaurant in San Francisco. Soon after moving to Denver, he began working on plans to open his own restaurant. Guided by a conviction that food served fast did not have to be low quality and that delicious food did not have to be expensive, he came up with the concept of Chipotle Mexican Grill. When the first Chipotle restaurant opened in Denver in 1993, it became an instant hit. Patrons were attracted by the experience of getting better-quality food served fast and dining in a restaurant setting that was more upscale and appealing than those of traditional fast-food enterprises. Over the next several years, Ells opened new Chipotle restaurants in Denver and other Colorado locations.

In 1998, intrigued by what it saw happening at Chipotle, McDonald's first acquired an initial ownership stake in the fledgling company, then acquired a controlling interest in early 2000. But McDonald's recognized the value of Ells's visionary leadership and kept him in the role of Chipotle's chief executive after it gained majority ownership. Drawing upon the investment capital provided by McDonald's and its decades of expertise in supply chain logistics, expanding a restaurant chain, and operating restaurants efficiently, Chipotle—under Ells's watchful and passionate guidance—embarked on a long-term strategy to open new restaurants and expand its market coverage. By year-end 2005, Chipotle had 489 locations in 24 states. As 2005 drew to a close, in somewhat of a surprise move, McDonald's top management determined that instead of continuing to parent Chipotle's growth, it would take the company public and give Chipotle management a free rein in charting the company's future growth and strategy. An initial public offering of shares was held in January 2006, and Steve Ells was designated as Chipotle's CEO and chairman of the board. During 2006, through the January IPO, a secondary offering in May 2006, and a tax-free exchange offer in October 2006, McDonald's disposed of its entire ownership interest in Chipotle Mexican Grill.

When Chipotle became an independent enterprise, Steve Ells and the company's other top executives kept the company squarely on a path of rapid expansion and continued to employ the same basic strategy elements that were the foundation of the company's success. Steve Ells functioned as the company's principal driving force for ongoing innovation and constant improvement. He pushed especially hard for new ways to boost "throughput"—the number of customers whose orders could be taken, prepared, and served per hour.[2] By 2012, Ells's mantra of "slow food, fast" had resulted in throughputs of 300 customers per hour at Chipotle's best restaurants.

During 2007–2011, Chipotle's revenues grew at a robust compound average rate of 20.2 percent. Net income grew at a compound rate of 32.1 percent, due to gains in operating efficiency that boosted profit margins. Average annual sales for restaurants open at least 12 full calendar months climbed from $1,085,000 in 2007 to $2,013,000 in 2011, owing to increased customer traffic and to higher expenditures per customer. The average tab per customer was about $9 in 2011.[3] Exhibit 1 presents recent financial and operating data for Chipotle Mexican Grill.

## EXHIBIT 1  Financial and Operating Highlights for Chipotle Mexican Grill, 2007–2011 (in 000s of dollars)

| | 2011 | 2010 | 2009 | 2008 | 2007 |
|---|---|---|---|---|---|
| **Income Statement Data:** | | | | | |
| Total revenue | $2,269,548 | $1,835,922 | $1,518,417 | $1,331,968 | $1,085,782 |
| Food, beverage and packaging costs | 738,720 | 561,107 | 466,027 | 431,947 | 346,393 |
| As a % of total revenue | 32.5% | 30.6% | 30.7% | 32.4% | 31.9% |
| Labor costs | 543,119 | 453,573 | 385,072 | 351,005 | 289,417 |
| As a % of total revenue | 23.9% | 24.7% | 25.4% | 26.4% | 26.7% |
| Occupancy costs | 147,274 | 128,933 | 114,218 | 98,071 | 75,891 |
| As a % of total revenue | 6.5% | 7.0% | 7.5% | 7.4% | 7.0% |
| Other operating costs | 251,208 | 202,904 | 174,581 | 164,018 | 131,512 |
| As a % of total revenue | 11.1% | 11.1% | 11.5% | 12.3% | 12.1% |
| General and administrative expenses | 149,426 | 118,590 | 99,149 | 89,155 | 75,038 |
| As a % of total revenue | 6.6% | 6.5% | 6.5% | 6.7% | 6.9% |
| Depreciation and amortization | 74,938 | 68,921 | 61,308 | 52,770 | 43,595 |
| Pre-opening costs | 8,495 | 7,767 | 8,401 | 11,624 | 9,585 |

*(Continued)*

## EXHIBIT 1    (Concluded)

| | 2011 | 2010 | 2009 | 2008 | 2007 |
|---|---|---|---|---|---|
| Loss on disposal of assets | 5,806 | 6,296 | 5,956 | 9,339 | 6,168 |
| Total operating expenses | 1,918,986 | 1,548,091 | 1,314,712 | 1,207,929 | 977,599 |
| Operating income | 350,562 | 287,831 | 203,705 | 124,039 | 108,183 |
| Interest and other income | 2,088 | 1,499 | 925 | 3,469 | 6,115 |
| Interest and other expense | (2,945) | (269) | (405) | (302) | (296) |
| Income before income taxes | 349,705 | 289,061 | 204,225 | 127,206 | 114,002 |
| Provision for income taxes | (134,760) | (110,080) | (77,380) | (49,004) | (43,439) |
| Net income | $ 214,945 | $ 178,981 | $ 126,845 | $ 78,202 | $ 70,563 |
| Earnings per share | | | | | |
| Basic | $6.89 | $5.73 | $3.99 | $2.39 | $2.16 |
| Diluted | 6.76 | 5.64 | 3.95 | 2.36 | 2.13 |
| Weighted average common shares outstanding | | | | | |
| Basic | 31,217 | 31,234 | 31,766 | 32,766 | 32,672 |
| Diluted | 31,775 | 31,735 | 32,102 | 33,146 | 33,146 |
| **Selected Balance Sheet Data:** | | | | | |
| Total current assets | $501,192 | $406,221 | $297,454 | $211,072 | $201,844 |
| Total assets | 1,425,308 | 1,121,605 | 961,505 | 824,985 | 722,115 |
| Total current liabilities | 157,453 | 123,054 | 102,153 | 76,788 | 73,301 |
| Total liabilities | 381,082 | 310,732 | 258,044 | 202,395 | 160,005 |
| Total shareholders' equity | 1,044,226 | 810,873 | 703,461 | 622,590 | 562,110 |
| **Other Financial Data:** | | | | | |
| Net cash provided by operating activities | $411,096 | $289,191 | $260,673 | $198,507 | $146,923 |
| Capital expenditures | 151,100 | 113,200 | 117,200 | 152,100 | 141,000 |
| **Restaurant Operations Data:** | | | | | |
| Restaurants open at year-end | 1,230 | 1,084 | 956 | 837 | 704 |
| Average annual sales for restaurants open at least 12 full calendar months (in 000s) | $2,013 | $1,840 | $1,728 | $1,332 | $1,085 |
| Comparable restaurant sales increases | 11.2% | 9.4% | 2.2% | 5.8% | 10.8% |
| Development and construction costs per newly opened restaurant (in 000s) | $800 | $795 | $850 | $916 | $880 |

*Note:* Comparable restaurant sales increases represent the change in period-over-period sales for restaurants beginning in their 13th full calendar month of operation.

*Source:* Company 10-K report, 2011 and 2008.

# MENU AND FOOD PREPARATION

The menu at Chipotle Mexican Grill restaurants was unusually limited: burritos, burrito bowls, tacos, and salads, plus soft drinks, fruit drinks, and milk. Except in restaurants where there were restrictions on serving alcoholic beverages, the drink options also included a selection of beers and margaritas. However, customers could customize their burritos, burrito bowls, tacos, and salads to their liking. Options included four different meats—marinated and grilled chicken and steak, carnitas (seasoned and braised pork), and barbacoa (spicy shredded beef), pinto beans, vegetarian black beans, rice tossed with lime juice and fresh-chopped cilantro, and such extras as sautéed peppers and onions, salsas, guacamole, sour cream, shredded cheese, lettuce, and tortilla chips seasoned with fresh lime and salt. In addition, it was restaurant policy to make special dishes for customers if the requested dish could be made from the ingredients on hand. Exhibit 2 describes the favorite dishes of some

**EXHIBIT 2    Examples of Favorite Menu Items and Meals of Chipotle Mexican Grill Employees**

- Chicken burrito with cilantro lime rice, vegetarian black beans, roasted chili corn salsa, green tomatillo salsa, sour cream, and cheese.
- A pair of soft corn tacos, one chicken or carnitas and one steak, both with green tomatillo salsa, fresh tomato salsa, a little sour cream and lettuce. Some chips and a side of sour cream, corn salsa, and green salsa mixed together.
- Steak fajita burrito with brown rice, red hot tomatillo salsa, sour cream, cheese, guacamole, and lettuce.
- The soft corn barbacoa tacos with cilantro and some fresh squeezed lime juice.
- The veggie bowl with brown rice, pinto beans, corn salsa, green tomatillo salsa, red tomatillo salsa, cheese, and guacamole.
- The barbacoa burrito with cilantro lime rice, pinto beans, two scoops of red tomatillo salsa, cheese, and a touch of guacamole.

*Source:* Information posted in the careers section at www.chipotle.com; accessed on February 19, 2012.

of Chipotle's employees. Exhibit 3 shows some of the menu dishes served at Chipotle.

From the outset, Chipotle's menu strategy had been to keep it simple, do a few things exceptionally well, and not include menu selections (like coffee and desserts) that complicated store operations and impaired efficiency. While it was management practice to consider menu additions, the menu offerings had remained fundamentally the same for many years. So far, Steve Ells had rejected the idea of commencing breakfast operations.

The food preparation area of each restaurant was equipped with stoves and grills, pots and pans, and an assortment of cutting knives, wire whisks, and other kitchen utensils. There was a walk-in refrigerator stocked with ingredients, and supplies of herbs, spices, and dry goods such as rice. The work space more closely resembled the layout of the kitchen in a fine dining restaurant than the cooking area of a typical fast food restaurant that made extensive use of automated cooking equipment and microwaves. All of the menu selections and optional extras were prepared from scratch—hours went into preparing food onsite, but some items were prepared from fresh ingredients in nearby commissaries. Kitchen crews used classic cooking methods: They marinated and grilled the chicken and steak, hand-cut produce and herbs, made fresh salsa and guacamole, and cooked rice in small batches throughout the day. While the food preparation methods were labor-intensive, the limited menu created efficiencies that helped keep costs down.

## Serving Orders Quickly

One of Chipotle's biggest innovations had been creating the ability to have a customer's order ready quickly.

**EXHIBIT 3    Representative Dishes Served at Chipotle Mexican Grill Restaurants**

As customers moved along the serving line, customers selected exactly what they wanted and how they wanted it by speaking directly to the employees that prepared the food and were assembling the order behind the counter. Much experimentation and fine-tuning had gone into creating a restaurant layout and serving line design that made the food-ordering and dish-creation process intuitive and time-efficient, thereby enabling a high rate of customer throughput. The low-end throughput target was 300 customers per hour, which kept the numbers of customers waiting in line at peak hours to a tolerable minimum. Management was focused on further improving the speed at which customers moved through the service line in all restaurants, so that orders placed by fax, online, or via an iPhone ordering app could be accommodated without slowing service to in-store customers and compromising the interactions between customers and crew members on the service line. The attention to serving orders quickly was motivated by management's belief that while customers returned because of the great-tasting food they also liked their orders served fast without having a "fast-food" experience (even when they were not in a hurry).

## The Commitment to "Food With Integrity"

Beginning in 2003–2004, Chipotle began a move to make increasing use of organically grown local produce, organic beans, organic dairy products, and meats from animals that were raised in accordance with animal welfare standards and were never given feeds containing antibiotics and growth hormones to speed weight gain. This shift in ingredient usage was part of a long-term management campaign to use top-quality, nutritious ingredients and improve "the Chipotle experience"—an effort that Chipotle management designated as "Food With Integrity." The company began working with experts in the areas of animal ethics to try to support more humane farming environments, and it started visiting the farms and ranches from which it obtained ingredients. It also began investigating using more produce supplied by farmers who respected the environment, avoided use of chemical fertilizers and pesticides, followed U.S. Department of Agriculture standards for growing organic products, and used agriculturally sustainable methods like conservation tillage methods that improved soil conditions and reduced erosion. Simultaneously, efforts were made to source a greater

portion of products locally (within 350 miles of the restaurants where they were used) while in season.

The transition to using organically grown local produce and naturally raised meats occurred gradually rather than being an all-at-once 100 percent switch because it took time for Chipotle to develop sufficient sources of supply to accommodate the requirements of all of its restaurants. Supplies of organic products, locally grown produce, and naturally raised meats were constrained because consumers were purchasing growing volumes of these items at their local farmers markets and supermarkets and because the chefs at many fine-dining establishments were making concerted efforts to incorporate organic, locally grown produce and natural meats into their dishes. Organic farmers and the growers of animals that were fed only vegetarian diets containing no antibiotics or hormones—both of whom raised animals in a humane fashion (what Chipotle called naturally raised meats)—were having difficulty keeping up with growing market demand for their products. Frequent supply–demand imbalances had resulted in market conditions where certain organic products and natural meats were sometimes either unavailable or prohibitively expensive.

As of December 31, 2011, all of the sour cream and cheese Chipotle purchased was made from milk that came from cows that were not given rBGH (recombinant bovine growth hormone). The milk used to make much of the purchased cheese and a portion of the purchased sour cream was sourced from dairies that provided pasture access for their cows rather than housing them in confined spaces. A portion of the beans the company used was organically grown and a portion was being grown by farmers who used sustainable agricultural practices. In addition, Chipotle was serving exclusively naturally raised meats in all of its restaurants in the U.S., although there were ongoing challenges regarding both the price and availability of adequate meat supplies and organic vegetables. Some Chipotle restaurants were forced to serve conventionally raised chicken or steak for much of 2011. Chipotle restaurants in a few markets reverted to the use of conventionally raised beef in early 2012. While adequate supplies of organic produce and organically grown beans were normally available, prices in some instances had crept upward because of cost pressures—organic and sustainable crops often took longer to grow and crop yields could be lower for organically or sustainably grown produce. Rising market prices for organically grown ingredients and naturally raised meats largely accounted for why

Chipotle's costs for food, beverages, and packing rose from 30.6 percent of revenues in 2010 to 32.5 percent of revenues in 2011 (see Exhibit 1).

Going forward, Chipotle executives were firmly committed to continuing the Food With Integrity initiative, despite the attendant price-cost challenges and supply chain complications. They wanted Chipotle to be at the forefront in responding to mounting consumer concerns about food nutrition, where their food came from, how fruits and vegetables were grown, and how animals used for meat were raised. And they wanted customers to view Chipotle Mexican Grill as a place that used high-quality, "better for you" ingredients in its dishes. Nonetheless, top management expected that there would be times when the prices of certain organic products and naturally raised meats would mean that some Chipotle restaurants would temporarily revert to using conventional produce and meats in its dishes in the interest of preserving the company's reputation for providing great food at reasonable prices and protecting profit margins. Over the longer term, top executives anticipated that the price volatility and shortages of organically grown ingredients and natural meats would gradually dissipate as growing demand for such products attracted more small farmers and larger agricultural enterprises to boost supplies. But it was also anticipated that most of these organic and natural meat ingredients would remain more expensive than conventionally raised, commodity-priced equivalents.

## Supply Chain Management Practices

Top executives were acutely aware that maintaining high levels of food quality in its restaurants depended in part on acquiring high-quality, fresh ingredients and other necessary supplies that met company specifications. However, Chipotle did not purchase ingredients for its dishes directly from farmers, nor purchase paper products, plastic ware, and other restaurant supplies directly from manufacturers. Rather, over the years, the company had developed long-term relationships with a number of reputable food industry suppliers that could provide high-quality, fresh ingredients and other products that met Chipotle's specifications. It then worked with these suppliers on an ongoing basis to establish and implement a set of forward, fixed, and formula pricing protocols for determining the prices that suppliers charged Chipotle for various items. Reliable suppliers that could meet Chipotle's quality specifications and were willing to comply with Chipotle's set of forward, fixed, and formula-pricing protocols and guidelines for certain products were put on Chipotle's list of approved suppliers. The number of approved suppliers was small for such key ingredients as beef, pork, chicken, beans, rice, sour cream, and tortillas. Recently, however, Chipotle had strived to increase the number of approved suppliers for ingredients subject to volatile prices and short supplies.

Instead of making purchases directly from approved suppliers, Chipotle utilized the services of 22 independently owned and operated regional distribution centers to purchase and deliver ingredients and other supplies to Chipotle restaurants. These distribution centers were required to make all purchases from Chipotle's list of approved suppliers in accordance with the agreed-upon pricing guidelines and protocols. As Chipotle continued to expand geographically, Chipotle management planned to add more regional distribution centers.

In addition, Chipotle personnel diligently monitored industry news, trade issues, weather, exchange rates, foreign demand, crises, and other world events so as to better anticipate potential impacts on ingredient prices.

## Quality Assurance and Food Safety

Chipotle had a quality assurance department that established and monitored quality and food safety throughout the company's supply chain and all the way through the serving lines at restaurants. There were quality and food safety standards for certain farms that grew ingredients used by company restaurants, approved suppliers, and the regional distribution centers that purchased and delivered products to the restaurants. Chipotle's training and risk management departments developed and implemented operating standards for food quality, preparation, cleanliness, and safety in company restaurants. The food safety programs for suppliers and restaurants were designed to ensure compliance with applicable federal, state, and local food safety regulations.

## Restaurant Management and Operations

Each Chipotle Mexican Grill typically had a general manager (a position top management characterized as the most important in the company), an apprentice manager (in about 75 percent of the restaurants), one or two hourly service managers, one or two hourly kitchen managers, and an average of 20 full- and part-time crew members. Busier restaurants had more crew members. Chipotle generally had two shifts at its restaurants, which simplified scheduling and facilitated assigning hourly employees with a regular number of work hours each week. Most employees were trained to work at a variety of stations, both to provide people with a variety of skills and to boost labor efficiency during busy periods. Personnel were empowered to make decisions within their assigned areas of responsibility. Restaurant managers and crew members were expected to welcome and interact with customers throughout the day. The designs of the open kitchen and service line placed crew members up front where they could speak to customers in a personal and hospitable manner, whether preparing food items or customizing the dish ordered by a customer moving along the service line. Crew members were expected to deliver a customer-pleasing experience "one burrito at a time," give each customer individual attention, and make every effort to respond positively to customer requests and suggestions.

The general managers of Chipotle restaurants sought to hire and retain crew members and other employees who had a strong work ethic, took pride in preparing food items correctly, enjoyed interacting with other people, exhibited enthusiasm in serving customers, and were team players in striving to operate the restaurant in accordance with the high standards expected by management. A sizable number of Chipotle's crew members had been attracted to apply for a job at Chipotle because of either encouragement from an acquaintance who worked at Chipotle or their own favorable impressions of the work atmosphere while going through the serving line and dining at a Chipotle Mexican Grill. New crew members received hands-on, shoulder-to-shoulder training. In 2012, full-time crew members had average earnings of nearly $18,250 (regular compensation and bonuses), plus benefits of about $2,830 (clothes, meals, insurance, and 401(k) contributions).[4] Total earnings and benefits averaged $27,000 for hourly managers, $50,000 for apprentice managers, and $63,000 for general managers. Top-performing employees and crew members could expect to be promoted because of the company's unusually heavy reliance on promotion from within—almost 98 percent of salaried managers

and more than 98 percent of hourly managers had been promoted from positions as crew members. In several instances, a newly hired crew member had risen rapidly through the ranks to become the general manager of a restaurant in 9 to 12 months; many more high-performing crew members had been promoted to general managers within two to four years. The long-term career opportunities for Chipotle employees were quite attractive because of the company's rapid growth and the speed with which it was opening new stores in both new and existing markets.

Chipotle executives sought to build and nurture a people-oriented, performance-based culture in each Chipotle restaurant, believing that such a culture led to the best possible experience for both customers and employees. The foundation of that culture started with hiring good people to manage and staff the company's restaurants. The general managers of restaurants that were especially successful in developing a high-performing team of hourly managers and crew members were promoted to Restaurateur, a position which entailed an average total compensation of $99,000 companywide in 2012. The most outstanding Restaurateurs were given the responsibility of mentoring one or more nearby restaurants, thus providing an opportunity for Restaurateurs to develop field leadership roles and also earn up to $129,000 annually. Restaurateurs whose mentoring efforts resulted in high-performing teams at four restaurants and the promotion of at least one of the four restaurant managers to Restaurateur could themselves be promoted to the position of Apprentice Team Leader and become a full-time member of the company's field support staff.

The field support staff included apprentice team leaders, team leaders or area managers, team directors, and a regional director. The principal task of people in these positions was to foster a culture of high standards, constant improvement, and employee empowerment in each of Chipotle's restaurants. One of Chipotle's field support staff members in 2012 had been hired as a crew member in 2003, promoted to General Manager in 12 months, and—nine years after starting with Chipotle—held the position of Team Director, with responsibilities for 53 restaurants and 1400+ employees.[5]

## Marketing

Chipotle's advertising and marketing costs totaled $31.9 million in 2011, versus $26.2 million in 2010 and $21.0 million in 2009 (these costs were included in "Other operating costs" in Exhibit 1). Chipotle utilized print, outdoor, transit, theaters, radio, and online ads. In February 2012, Chipotle Mexican Grill ran its first-ever national TV commercial during the broadcast of the Grammy Awards. The commercial was actually a short film, "Back to the Start," that Chipotle had shown in 2011 in theaters and online and was an unusually long commercial for a national broadcast. In addition, Chipotle generated considerable media coverage from scores of publications that had largely favorable articles describing Chipotle's food, restaurant concept, and business; the company had also been featured in a number of television programs.

Recently, Chipotle had been testing use of more "owned media," including new video and music programs, and a more visible event strategy that included the launch of the company's first festival of food, music, and ideas, "Cultivate Chicago," and participation in community events in markets where the company had restaurants or was opening new restaurants. Management believed these newer programs allowed the company to forge stronger emotional connections with customers and communicate its story better and with more nuance than it could through traditional advertising. The company was also increasing its use of digital, mobile, and social media in its overall marketing mix because it gave customers a greater opportunity to access Chipotle in ways that were convenient for them and that broadened Chipotle's ability to engage with its customers individually.

Chipotle executives were of the opinion that the best and most recognizable brands were built through all of the ways people experienced the brand as well as through advertising or promotional campaigns. Marketing personnel paid close attention to presenting the Chipotle brand consistently and keeping advertising and promotional programs, in-store communications, and menus closely aligned with who Chipotle was and what the Chipotle experience was all about.

When Chipotle opened restaurants in new markets, it initiated a range of promotional activities to introduce Chipotle to the local community and to create interest in the restaurant. In markets where there were existing Chipotle restaurants, newly opened restaurants typically attracted customers in volumes at or near market averages without having to initiate special promotions or advertising to support a new opening.

In September 2011, Chipotle launched an invitation-only rewards program, the "Farm Team," whereby it invited "loyal and passionate customers" to join a program that educated them about many of the things that made Chipotle special and rewarded them for expanding and sharing their knowledge of Chipotle Mexican Grill. Unlike other rewards programs, it was not intended to reward frequent customers. According to Chipotle's communications director:[6]

> Farm Team is, for now, an invitation-only program we created for some of our best customers. This is a passion program. Through Farm Team, we are looking to identify our most loyal and passionate customers and give them tools to share their passion for Chipotle. It's much more about building evangelism than it is about rewarding frequency.

Invitations to join the Farm Team were usually issued by a restaurant manager and sometimes by other Chipotle employees that had close contact with customers. Customers who accepted the invitation were provided access to a special member-only Chipotle website where they were educated about the full spectrum of farming, from very industrialized farming to more sustainable methods. They learned where Chipotle's food came from as it pertained to quality ingredients and its respect for the environment, took quizzes and polls, played games, and watched videos about the company. As Farm Team members made their way through the website to different levels, they earned points that could be exchanged for meals at Chipotle and other prizes.

Chipotle's collective marketing efforts, together with the considerable word-of-mouth publicity from customers telling others about their favorable experiences at Chipotle restaurants, had enabled the company to build good brand awareness among consumers with relatively low advertising expenditures—even in the highly competitive fast food and fast-casual segments of the restaurant industry—and to differentiate Chipotle from its competitors.

## Restaurant Site Selection

Chipotle had an internal team of real estate managers that devoted substantial time and effort to evaluating potential locations for new restaurants. The site selection process entailed studying the surrounding trade area, demographic and business information within that area, and available information on competitors. In addition, advice and recommendations were solicited from external real estate brokers with expertise in specific markets. Locations proposed by the internal real estate team were visited by a team of operations and development management as part of a formal site ride. A model based on proprietary formulas was used to determine projected sales and the targeted return on investment. Chipotle Mexican Grills had proved successful in a number of different types of locations, including in-line or end-cap locations in strip or power centers, regional malls, downtown business districts, free-standing buildings, and even a location at Dulles International Airport outside Washington, D.C.

## Development and Construction Costs for New Restaurants

Chipotle opened 150 restaurants in 2011 and planned to open between 155 and 165 restaurants in 2012, including one in Paris, France. Roughly 30 percent of the 2012 openings were scheduled to be slightly scaled-back "A Model" restaurants located primarily in secondary trade areas with attractive demographics. A Model restaurants typically had lower investment and occupancy costs than the restaurants that Chipotle had traditionally opened. In order to lower the average development costs for new restaurants, Chipotle had recently begun using a new, simpler design for its restaurants that incorporated some A Model design elements. Exhibit 4 shows the interiors and exteriors of several Chipotle Mexican Grills.

The company's average development and construction costs per restaurant decreased from about $850,000 in 2009 to about $800,000 in 2011

**EXHIBIT 4    Representative Interiors and Exteriors of Chipotle Mexican Grills**

(see Exhibit 1), due to cost savings realized from building more lower-cost A Model restaurants and the growing use of its new simpler restaurant design. Chipotle anticipated that average development costs for new restaurants to be opened in 2012 would be similar to 2011. In 2012, senior Chipotle executives expected that the company's annual cash flows from operations, together with current cash on hand, would be adequate to meet ongoing capital expenditures, working capital requirements, and other cash needs for the foreseeable future.

## The ShopHouse Test Concept

The ShopHouse Southeast Asia Kitchen format being tested grew out of Steve Ells's belief that the fundamental principles on which Chipotle Mexican Grill restaurants were based—finding the very best sustainably raised ingredients, prepared and cooked using classical methods in front of the customer, and served in an interactive format by special people dedicated to providing a great dining experience—could be adapted to other cuisines. To test the Chipotle model with different ingredients and a different style of food, the company opened its first ShopHouse Southeast Asian Kitchen on DuPont Circle in Washington, D.C., in September 2011. ShopHouse served a focused menu consisting of rice bowls, noodle bowls, and banh mi sandwiches, made with a choice of grilled steak, grilled chicken satay, pork and chicken meatballs, or organic tofu. In addition to a choice of meats or tofu, the rice and noodle bowls included choices of four fresh vegetables, a sauce (red or green curry or tamarind vinaigrette), and a garnish and topping (including chili-jam marmalade, roast corn with scallions, Chinese broccoli, pickled vegetables, and assorted aromatic herbs). Customers could have their dishes made anywhere from mega-spicy to mild. The flavors were a blend of Thai, Vietnamese, and Malaysian.

As was the case at Chipotle, customers moved along a cafeteria-style line, with servers behind the counter customizing each order; there was room for seating or customers could have orders readied for take-out. The interior of the Dulles Circle ShopHouse resembled Chipotle interiors—sparse and a bit industrial, with an attention to such environmentally green detail as high-efficiency lighting. Much of the dining area was constructed with recycled materials, including dark maple treated to look like teak.

## COMPETITION

Chipotle competed with national and regional fast-casual, quick-service, and casual dining restaurant chains, as well as locally owned restaurants and food-service establishments. The number, size, and strength of competitors varied by region, local market area, and a particular restaurant's location within a given community. Competition among the various types of restaurants and food service establishments was based on such factors as type of food served, menu selection (including the availability of low-calorie and nutritional items), food quality and taste, speed of service, price and value, dining ambience, name recognition and reputation, convenience of location, and customer service.

Myriad dining establishments specialize in Mexican food. The leading fast-food chain in the Mexican-style food category was Taco Bell. Chipotle's two biggest competitors in the fast-casual segment were Moe's Southwest Grill and Qdoba Mexican Grill. Two smaller chains, Baja Fresh and California Tortilla, were also competitors in a small number of geographic locations.

## Taco Bell

Going into 2012, Taco Bell had 1,201 company-owned and 4,029 franchised restaurant locations in the United States, plus another 3 company-owned and 237 franchised international locations. Since 2005, the total number of Taco Bell restaurants, both domestically and internationally, had declined by about 200 units, due to more closings of underperforming locations than openings of new Taco Bell units. Same-store sales at company-owned Taco Bell restaurants in the United States declined by 2 percent in 2011, and 74 Taco Bell locations were refranchised in 2011.[7] In December, parent company Yum! Brands announced that it would reduce company ownership of Taco Bell locations from 23 percent of total locations to about 16 percent over the next two years. Yum! Brands also owned Pizza Hut, and KFC (Kentucky Fried Chicken); the company sold its A&W All American and Long John Silver's brands in December 2011.

In 2010, Taco Bell had U.S. sales of $6.9 billion at combined company-owned and franchised Taco Bell locations, compared with $6.8 billion in 2009 and $6.7 billion in 2008. Average sales at Taco Bell restaurants were $1.28 million in 2011, versus averages of

$1.29 million in 2010 and $1.26 million in 2009. The sluggish sales performance at Taco Bell restaurants, most especially those in the United States, was viewed as mainly attributable to a loss of customers to Chipotle Mexican Grill, Moe's Southwest Grill, and Qdoda Mexican Grill, all of which had more upscale menu selections and used higher-quality ingredients. During 2010–2011, Taco Bell restaurants began rolling out a new taco with a Doritos-based shell called Doritos Locos Taco, which management termed a "breakthrough product designed to reinvent the taco." Taco Bell's strategy for 2012 called for aggressive promotion of the Doritos Locos Taco, as a prelude to the upcoming menu upgrade.

A September 2011 survey by Nation's Restaurant News and consultant WD Partners found that Taco Bell scored the lowest in food quality and atmosphere among limited-service Mexican eateries, a group that included Chipotle Mexican Grill and Qdoba Mexican Grill.[8]

In March 2012, Taco Bell began introducing a new Cantina Bell menu, a group of upgraded products conceptualized by celebrity Miami chef Lorena Garcia that included such ingredients and garnishes as black beans, cilantro rice, and corn salsa.[9] The new Cantina Bell menu items had undergone extensive testing in select geographic areas. In addition to the upscaled Cantina Bell selections, Taco Bell also introduced several new breakfast selections. According to Taco Bell president, Greg Creed, it was Taco Bell's biggest new product launch ever. Taco Bell's new Cantina Bell items were priced below similar types of Chipotle products. The rollout was being supported with a new slogan and brand campaign.

The upscaled menu at Taco Bell was a competitive response to growing consumer preferences for the higher-caliber, made-to-order dishes they could get at fast-casual Mexican-food chains like Chipotle, Moe's, and Qdoba. Several fast-food hamburger chains, including McDonald's, had recently introduced upscaled hamburgers to better compete with the quality of the made-to-order burgers available at Five Guys and Smashburger locations, two up-and-coming fast-casual chains.

## Moe's Southwest Grill

Moe's Southwest Grill was founded in Atlanta, Georgia, in 2000 and acquired in 2007 by Atlanta-based FOCUS Brands, an affiliate of Roark Capital,

a private equity firm. FOCUS Brands was a global franchisor of over 3,300 Carvel Ice Cream, Cinnabon, Schlotzsky's, Moe's Southwest Grill, and Auntie Anne's locations. In 2012, there were over 420 fast-casual Moe's Southwest Grill locations in 26 states and the District of Columbia.

The menu at Moe's featured burritos, quesadillas, fajitas, tacos, nachos, rice bowls (chicken, pork, or tofu), and salads with a choice of two homemade dressings. Main dishes could be customized with a choice of 20 items that included grilled peppers, onions, and mushrooms, black olives, cucumbers, pickled jalapenos, pico de gallo (handmade fresh daily), and six salsas. There was a kids menu and vegetarian, gluten-free, and low-calorie options, as well as a selection of five side items (including queso and guacamole), two desserts (cookie or brownie), soft drinks, iced tea, and bottled water. All meals were served with chips and salsa. Moe's used high-quality ingredients, including all natural, cage-free, white breast chicken meat; steroid-free, grain-fed pulled pork; 100 percent sirloin, grass-fed steak; and organic tofu. No dishes included trans fats or msg (monosodium glutamate—a flavor enhancer) and no use was made of microwaves.

Moe's provided catering; the catering menu included a fajitas bar, a taco bar, a salad bar, mini-burrito appetizers, a box of burritos, and a selection of dips. At some locations, customer orders could be taken online.

The company and its franchisees emphasized friendly hospitable service. When customers entered a Moe's location, it was the practice for employees to do a "Welcome to Moe's!" shout-out.

## Qdoba Mexican Grill

The first Qdoba Mexican Grill opened in Denver in 1995. Rapid growth ensued and the company was acquired by Jack in the Box, Inc., a large operator and franchisor of Jack in the Box quick-service restaurants that was best known for its hamburgers. Jack in the Box had fiscal year 2011 revenues of $2.2 billion and its Jack in the Box system included 2,221 restaurants in 19 states.

As of October 2011, there were 583 Qdoba restaurants in 42 states and the District of Columbia, of which 245 were company-operated and 338 were franchise-operated. A net of 58 new Qdoba locations had opened in fiscal year 2011, up from 15 units in fiscal 2010 and 56 in fiscal 2009. Qdoba was the second largest fast-casual Mexican brand in the United States as of early 2012, based on number of restaurants. In 2011, sales revenues at all company-operated and franchise-operated Qdoba restaurant locations averaged $961,000, up from $923,000 in 2010.

Qdoba Mexican Grill billed itself as an "artisanal Mexican kitchen" where dishes were handcrafted with fresh ingredients and innovative flavors by skilled cooks. The menu included burritos, tacos, taco salads, three-cheese nachos, grilled quesadillas, tortilla soup, Mexican gumbo, chips and dips, five meals for kids, and, at select locations, a variety of breakfast burritos and breakfast quesadillas. Burritos and tacos could be customized with choices of five meats or just vegetarian ingredients. Salads were served in a crunchy flour tortilla bowl with a choice of two meats, or vegetarian, and included black bean corn salsa and fat-free picante ranch dressing.

Throughout each day at Qdoba restaurants, guacamole was prepared on site using fresh avocados, black and pinto beans were slow-simmered, shredded beef and pork were slow-roasted and adobo-marinated chicken and steak were flame-grilled. Orders were prepared in full view, with customers having multiple options to customize meals to their individual taste and nutritional preferences. Qdoba restaurants offered a variety of catering options that could be tailored to feed groups of five to several hundred. Most Qdoba restaurants operated from 10:30 a.m. to 10:00 p.m. and had seating capacity for 60 to 80 persons, including outdoor patio seating at many locations. The average check at company-operated restaurants in fiscal 2011 was $9.74.

Top management at Qdoba believed there was significant opportunity for continued growth at Qdoba, with a long-term growth potential to have 1,800 to 2,000 Qdoba units across the U.S. In fiscal 2012 (October 2011 through September 2012), management planned to open 70–90 new company and franchise restaurants.

## Restaurant Industry Statistics

Restaurant industry sales were expected to be about $632 billion in 2012 at some 970,000 food establishments in the United States. According to survey data reported in the National Restaurant Association's 2012 *Restaurant Industry Forecast,* nearly 75 percent of consumers said they were more likely to visit a

|      | Fast-Casual Unit Count | Increase over Prior Year |
|------|------------------------|--------------------------|
| **2007** | 11,013             | 11%                      |
| **2008** | 12,108             | 10%                      |
| **2009** | 12,801             | 6%                       |
| **2010** | 13,161             | 4%                       |
| **2011** | 13,643             | 7%                       |

restaurant that offered locally produced food items; a similar percentage said they were trying to eat healthier now at restaurants than they did in 2009–2010. A majority of restaurants surveyed reported that their customers were ordering healthier, more nutritious menu items.

The fast-casual segment represented only about 3 to 4 percent of the overall restaurant industry, with total sales estimated to be in the neighborhood of $22 billion in 2012. However, it was a fast-growing category, having doubled its share over the past 10 years. Fast casual was the only segment that had continued to grow in the United States during the down economy of 2008–2009 recessionary period and follow-on sluggish economic recovery in 2010–2011, largely because consumers had responded quite positively to those fast-casual restaurants that used fresh ingredients and offered made-to-order alternatives to traditional fast food.[10] While some fast casual restaurant concepts had faltered during the tough economic times, the segment as a whole benefited from fast-food consumers trading up and full-service consumers trading down.[11] According to NDP Group, the unit counts of restaurant locations classified as fast-casual had risen over the past five years (see table above).[12]

During the same five-year period, unit counts among quick-service restaurants hovered between 1 percent growth and 2 percent declines. Unit counts at midscale restaurants decreased between 1 percent and 4 percent during the period; unit counts at casual dining chains increased 2 percent in 2008, but then dropped by 2 to 3 percent in the three subsequent years.

In 2011, the average consumer made nearly 61 visits to restaurants across all categories.[13] About 61 percent of the customer traffic went to quick-service restaurants, while midscale restaurants and casual-dining chains received 10 percent and 11 percent, respectively.

## ENDNOTES

[1] See Dan Caplinger, "Has Chipotle Become the Perfect Stock?" posted at www.dailyfinance.com, February 13, 2012 and accessed February 14, 2012 and Tim Begany, "Why This Stock Could Be the Next McDonald's," posted at www.streetauthority.com on February 14, 2012 and accessed February 14, 2012.

[2] David A. Kaplan, "Chipotle's Growth Machine," *Fortune,* September 26, 2011, p. 138.

[3] Ibid.

[4] According to information posted in the careers section at www.chipotle.com, accessed February 18, 2012.

[5] Ibid.

[6] L. Wayne Hicks, "Chipotle's Farm Team grows customer loyalty," *Denver Business Journal,* September 3, 2011, posted at www.bizjournals.com/Denver and accessed on February 19, 2012.

[7] Company press release, February 6, 2012.

[8] Ibid.

[9] Leslie Patton, "Taco Bell Sees Market Share Recouped with Chipotle Menu," Bloomberg News, January 11, 2012, posted at www.bloomberg.com, accessed February 20, 2012.

[10] Valerie Killifer, "NPD: Fast Casual Only Growth Segment during Down Economy," posted at www.fastcasual.com, February 8, 2012, accessed February 21, 2012. This article utilized information from a market research report by Bonnie Riggs, "Fast Casual: A Growing Market," NPD Group, which became available in February 2012.

[11] NPD Group, press release, February 8, 2012, accessed at www.npd.com on February 21, 2012.

[12] Ibid.

[13] As cited in Valerie Killifer, "NPD: Fast Casual Only Growth Segment during Down Economy," posted at www.fastcasual.com, February 8, 2012, accessed February 21, 2012. These statistics were based on information in NPD Group's market research report "Fast Casual: A Growing Market," February 2012.

# Netflix in 2012: Can It Recover from Its Strategy Missteps?

connect

## Arthur A. Thompson
### The University of Alabama

Throughout 2010 and the first six months of 2011, Netflix was on a roll. Movie enthusiasts were flocking to become Netflix subscribers in unprecedented numbers, and shareholders were exceptionally pleased with Netflix's skyrocketing stock price. During those 18 months from January 1, 2010 through June 30, 2011, the number of domestic Netflix subscribers doubled from 12.3 million to 24.6 million, quarterly revenues climbed from $445 million to $770 million, and quarterly operating income climbed from $53 million to $125 million. Netflix's swift growth in the U.S. and its promising potential for expanding internationally pushed the company's stock price to an all-time high of $304.79 on July 13, 2011, up from a close of $55.19 on December 31, 2009. Already solidly entrenched as the biggest and best-known Internet subscription service for watching TV shows and movies, the only question in mid-2011 seemed to be how big and pervasive Netflix's service might one day become in the larger world market for renting movies and TV episodes.

Then, over the next four months, Netflix announced a series of strategy changes and new initiatives that tarnished the company's reputation and sent the company's stock price into a tailspin:

- In mid-July 2011, Netflix announced a new pricing plan that effectively raised the monthly subscription price by 60 percent for customers who were paying $9.99 per month for the ability to (1) receive an unlimited number of DVDs each month (delivered and returned by mail with one title out at a time), and (2) watch an unlimited number of movies and TV episodes streamed over the Internet. The new arrangement called for a total separation of unlimited DVDs and unlimited streaming to better reflect the different costs associated with the two delivery methods and to give members a choice: a DVD-only plan, a streaming-only plan, or the option to subscribe to both. The monthly subscription price for the unlimited streaming plan was set at $7.99 a month. The monthly subscription price for DVDs only—one out at a time—was also set at $7.99 a month. If customers wanted both unlimited streaming and unlimited DVDs, they had to sign up for both plans and pay a total of $15.98 a month ($7.99 + $7.99)—Netflix said it was discontinuing all plans that included both streaming and DVDs by mail. For new Netflix members, the changes were effective immediately. For existing members, the new pricing started for charges on or after September 1, 2011.

Customer reaction was decidedly negative. Unhappy subscribers posted thousands of comments on Netflix's site and Facebook page. Over the next eight weeks, Netflix's stock price dropped steadily to around $210–$220 per share, partly because of rumors that perhaps as many as 600,000 Netflix customers had canceled their subscriptions.

The stock price slide was exacerbated by media reports that Starz, a premium movie channel offered by many multichannel TV providers, had broken off talks with Netflix regarding renewal of the contract whereby Starz supplied Netflix with certain Starz-controlled movies and TV shows that Netflix could then provide either on DVDs or via streaming to its subscribers. The substance of the breakdown in negotiations centered on the much higher price that Starz was asking Netflix to pay to renew its rights to distribute Starz content to Netflix subscribers—Starz was rumored to have demanded as much as $300 million annually to renew its license with Netflix, versus the $30 million annually that Netflix had been paying.[1] (Netflix's licensing agreement with Starz later expired in March 2012, and the content was removed from its library of offerings to subscribers.)

- On September 18, 2011, in an attempt at damage control, Netflix CEO Reed Hastings in a post on the Netflix blog at http://blog.netflix.com/ apologetically said that the basis for the new pricing had been poorly communicated and personally took the blame for the miscue. He elaborated on the rationale behind the new pricing plans and then, in something of a bombshell, went on to reveal that Netflix was separating its DVD-by-mail subscription service and its unlimited streaming subscription service into two businesses operating at different websites. Hastings said the DVD-by-mail service would be renamed Qwikster, with its own website (www.qwikster.com) and its own billing. Current Netflix subscribers who wanted DVDs by mail would have to go to www.qwikster.com and sign up for the plan. He indicated that the Qwikster website would be operational in a matter of weeks—see Exhibit 1 for the full text of the post by Hastings.

## EXHIBIT 1   Reed Hastings's Blog Posting, September 18, 2011

### An Explanation and Some Reflections

I messed up. I owe everyone an explanation.

It is clear from the feedback over the past two months that many members felt we lacked respect and humility in the way we announced the separation of DVD and streaming, and the price changes. That was certainly not our intent, and I offer my sincere apology. I'll try to explain how this happened.

For the past five years, my greatest fear at Netflix has been that we wouldn't make the leap from success in DVDs to success in streaming. Most companies that are great at something – like AOL dialup or Borders bookstores – do not become great at new things people want (streaming for us) because they are afraid to hurt their initial business. Eventually these companies realize their error of not focusing enough on the new thing, and then the company fights desperately and hopelessly to recover. Companies rarely die from moving too fast, and they frequently die from moving too slowly.

When Netflix is evolving rapidly, however, I need to be extra-communicative. This is the key thing I got wrong.

In hindsight, I slid into arrogance based upon past success. We have done very well for a long time by steadily improving our service, without doing much CEO communication. Inside Netflix I say, "Actions speak louder than words," and we should just keep improving our service.

But now I see that given the huge changes we have been recently making, I should have personally given a full justification to our members of why we are separating DVD and streaming, and charging for both. It wouldn't have changed the price increase, but it would have been the right thing to do.

So here is what we are doing and why:

Many members love our DVD service, as I do, because nearly every movie ever made is published on DVD, plus lots of TV series. We want to advertise the breadth of our incredible DVD offering so that as many people as possible know it still exists, and it is a great option for those who want the huge and comprehensive selection on DVD. DVD by mail may not last forever, but we want it to last as long as possible.

I also love our streaming service because it is integrated into my TV, and I can watch anytime I want. The benefits of our streaming service are really quite different from the benefits of DVD by mail. We feel we need to focus on rapid improvement as streaming technology and the market evolve, without having to maintain compatibility with our DVD by mail service.

So we realized that streaming and DVD by mail are becoming two quite different businesses, with very different cost structures, different benefits that need to be marketed differently, and we need to let each grow and operate independently. It's hard for me to write this after over 10 years of mailing DVDs with pride, but we think it is necessary and best: In a few weeks, we will rename our DVD by mail service to "Qwikster".

We chose the name Qwikster because it refers to quick delivery. We will keep the name "Netflix" for streaming.

*(Continued)*

**EXHIBIT 1**  (*Concluded*)

Qwikster will be the same website and DVD service that everyone is used to. It is just a new name, and DVD members will go to qwikster.com to access their DVD queues and choose movies. One improvement we will make at launch is to add a video games upgrade option, similar to our upgrade option for Blu-ray, for those who want to rent Wii, PS3 and Xbox 360 games. Members have been asking for video games for many years, and now that DVD by mail has its own team, we are finally getting it done. Other improvements will follow. Another advantage of separate websites is simplicity for our members. Each website will be focused on just one thing (DVDs or streaming) and will be even easier to use. A negative of the renaming and separation is that the Qwikster.com and Netflix.com websites will not be integrated. So if you subscribe to both services, and if you need to change your credit card or email address, you would need to do it in two places. Similarly, if you rate or review a movie on Qwikster, it doesn't show up on Netflix, and vice-versa.

There are no pricing changes (we're done with that!). Members who subscribe to both services will have two entries on their credit card statements, one for Qwikster and one for Netflix. The total will be the same as the current charges.

Andy Rendich, who has been working on our DVD service for 12 years, and leading it for the last 4 years, will be the CEO of Qwikster. Andy and I made a short welcome video. (You'll probably say we should avoid going into movie making after watching it.) We will let you know in a few weeks when the Qwikster.com website is up and ready. It is merely a renamed version of the Netflix DVD website, but with the addition of video games. You won't have to do anything special if you subscribe to our DVD by mail service.

For me the Netflix red envelope has always been a source of joy. The new envelope is still that distinctive red, but now it will have a Qwikster logo. I know that logo will grow on me over time, but still, it is hard. I imagine it will be the same for many of you. We'll also return to marketing our DVD by mail service, with its amazing selection, now with the Qwikster brand.

Some members will likely feel that we shouldn't split the businesses, and that we shouldn't rename our DVD by mail service. Our view is with this split of the businesses, we will be better at streaming, and we will be better at DVD by mail. It is possible we are moving too fast – it is hard to say. But going forward, Qwikster will continue to run the best DVD by mail service ever, throughout the United States. Netflix will offer the best streaming service for TV shows and movies, hopefully on a global basis. The additional streaming content we have coming in the next few months is substantial, and we are always working to improve our service further.

I want to acknowledge and thank our many members that stuck with us, and to apologize again to those members, both current and former, who felt we treated them thoughtlessly.

Both the Qwikster and Netflix teams will work hard to regain your trust. We know it will not be overnight. Actions speak louder than words. But words help people to understand actions.

Respectfully yours,

Reed Hastings, Co-Founder and CEO, Netflix

*Source:* Posting at Netflix Blog, http://blog.netflix.com/, September 18, 2011, accessed March 6, 2012.

Hastings's announcement about Netflix's strategy to split the DVDs-by-mail business from the Internet streaming business and to create Qwikster sparked a second furor from already disgruntled subscribers and further adverse investor reaction (the stock price plunged from around $208 per share to about $115 per share over the next three weeks). Netflix's strategy to split the DVDs-by-mail business from the Internet streaming business drew harsh criticism from Wall Street analysts and business commentators; virtually all knowledgeable industry observers expressed amazement that Netflix executives would even contemplate such a move.

- On October 10, 2011, three weeks after Hastings disclosed the plan to divide Netflix into two

standalone businesses, Netflix sent personal e-mails to all U.S. subscribers stating that it was scrapping its Qwikster proposal and that U.S. members would continue to use one website, one account, and one password for their movie and TV watching enjoyment under the Netflix brand. Simultaneously, Netflix issued a press release and posted statements on the Netflix blog at http://blog.netflix.com/ saying it was abandoning the Qwikster strategy. In the blog, Reed Hastings said, "It is clear that for many of our members two websites would make things more difficult. So we are going to keep Netflix as one place to go for streaming and DVDs."

- On October 24, 2011, Netflix announced that in early 2012 it would begin offering unlimited TV shows and movies instantly streamed over the Internet to some 26 million households in the United Kingdom and Ireland—20 million of these households had high-speed broadband Internet service and thus could stream movies to their TVs, computers, or other devices. This move represented the third strategic initiative to expand Netflix's international reach. Netflix began streaming to members in Canada in 2010, and in September 2011 it initiated streaming services to 43 countries in Latin America and the Caribbean; there were four times as many households with high-speed broadband service in these 43 countries as there were in Canada. In all three cases, Netflix estimated that it would take about two years after the initial launch to attract sufficient subscribers to generate a positive "contribution profit"—Netflix defined "contribution profit (loss)" as revenues less cost of revenues and marketing expenses; cost of revenues included subscription costs and order fulfillment costs.

In announcing the company's entry into Latin America and the Caribbean, Netflix said it was establishing a single low monthly price of 99 pesos for subscribers in Mexico and a price of US$7.99 for customers in the 42 countries in Central America, South America, and the Caribbean. In Brazil, Netflix content was available in Portuguese; in eight other South American countries and all of the Central America countries, Netflix content was made available in Spanish; in the Caribbean, Netflix was available in English and Spanish. As part of its September entry into Latin America and the Caribbean, Netflix had entered into regional license agreements to obtain movies and TV shows in Spanish and Portuguese from a large variety of major motion picture and television studios, including Walt Disney Studios, Paramount Studios, Sony Pictures Television, NBCUniversal International Television, CBS Television, MGM, Lionsgate, Summit, Relativity, BBC Worldwide, TV Bandeirantes, Televisa, Telemundo, TV Azteca, TV Globo, Caracol, Telefe, and RCTV.

Also, on October 24, Netflix announced that the number of domestic subscribers dropped by a net of 810,000 during the third quarter of 2011, thus resulting in operating profits, a net income, and earnings per share that were below Wall Street estimates and investor expectations. Internationally, the company said it had reached 1 million subscribers in Canada and that member counts in Latin America and the Caribbean should exceed 500,000 by year-end 2011. However, Netflix's contribution losses from international operations jumped from $9.3 million in the second quarter of 2011 to $23.3 million in the third quarter of 2011, owing to increased expenses associated with the startup of operations in Latin America and the Caribbean.

On the day following the release of Netflix's third quarter financial results, the company's stock price dropped from $118.84 to close at $77.37.

- On November 21, 2011, Netflix announced that it had raised $400 million in new capital by (1) selling 2.86 million shares of common stock to certain mutual funds and accounts managed by T. Rowe Price Associates for $70 per share (which generated proceeds of $200 million) and (2) selling a $200 million aggregate principal amount of Zero Coupon Convertible Senior Notes due December 1, 2018 to a private party. Any time after six months, Netflix had the option of converting the Zero Coupon Notes into shares of Netflix common stock at an initial conversion rate of 11.6533 shares of common stock per $1,000 principal amount, subject to the satisfaction of certain conditions. Netflix executives said that the company did not intend to spend any of the newly raised capital. Rather, the company intended to use the capital as a safety net since the company's cash on hand and future cash flows from operations would likely be squeezed in upcoming quarters by the ongoing need to:

  - Make cash payments for additions to its library of titles available for streaming.
  - Absorb the expected contribution losses from international operations over the next five to seven quarters.

In the weeks following the announcement of the $400 million in new financing, Netflix's stock price dropped to as low as $62.37 and traded in the range of $65 to $71 for most all of December 2011.

Financial statement data for Netflix for 2000–2011 are shown in Exhibits 2 and 3.

## INDUSTRY ENVIRONMENT

Since 2000, the introduction of new technologies and electronics products had rapidly multiplied consumer opportunities to view movies. It was commonplace

## EXHIBIT 2   Netflix's Consolidated Statements of Operations, 2000–2011 (in millions, except per share data)

| | 2000 | 2005 | 2007 | 2009 | 2010 | 2011 |
|---|---|---|---|---|---|---|
| Revenues | $ 35.9 | $682.2 | $1,205.3 | $1,670.3 | $2,162.6 | $3,205.6 |
| Cost of revenues: | | | | | | |
| Subscription costs | 24.9 | 393.8 | 664.4 | 909.5 | 1,154.1 | 1,789.6 |
| Fulfillment expenses | 10.2 | 72.0 | 121.3 | 169.8 | 203.2 | 250.3 |
| Total cost of revenues | 35.1 | 465.8 | 786.2 | 1,079.3 | 1,357.4 | 2,039.9 |
| Gross profit | 0.8 | 216.4 | 419.2 | 591.0 | 805.3 | 1,164.7 |
| Operating expenses | | | | | | |
| Technology and development | 16.8 | 35.4 | 71.0 | 114.5 | 163.3 | 259.0 |
| Marketing | 25.7 | 144.6 | 218.2 | 237.7 | 293.8 | 402.6 |
| General and administrative | 7.0 | 35.5 | 52.4 | 51.3 | 64.5 | 117.9 |
| Other | 9.7 | (2.0) | (14.2) | (4.6) | — | 9.0 |
| Total operating expenses | 59.2 | 213.4 | 327.4 | 399.1 | 521.6 | 788.8 |
| Operating income | (58.4) | 3.0 | 91.8 | 191.9 | 283.6 | 376.1 |
| Interest and other income (expense) | (0.2) | 5.3 | 20.1 | 0.3 | (15.9) | (16.5) |
| Income before income taxes | — | 8.3 | 110.9 | 192.2 | 267.7 | 359.5 |
| Provision for (benefit from) income taxes | — | (33.7) | 44.3 | 76.3 | 106.8 | 133.4 |
| Net income | $ (58.5) | $ 42.0 | $ 66.7 | $ 115.9 | $ 160.8 | $ 226.1 |
| Net income per share: | | | | | | |
| Basic | $(20.61) | $0.79 | $0.99 | $2.05 | $3.06 | $4.28 |
| Diluted | (20.61) | 0.64 | 0.97 | 1.98 | 2.96 | 4.16 |
| Weighted average common shares outstanding: | | | | | | |
| Basic | 2.8 | 53.5 | 67.1 | 56.6 | 52.5 | 52.8 |
| Diluted | 2.8 | 65.5 | 68.9 | 58.4 | 54.3 | 54.4 |

*Note:* Totals may not add due to rounding.

*Source:* Company 10-K reports for 2003, 2006, and 2009.

## EXHIBIT 3   Selected Balance Sheet and Cash Flow Data for Netflix, 2000–2011 (in millions of $)

| | 2000 | 2005 | 2007 | 2009 | 2010 | 2011 |
|---|---|---|---|---|---|---|
| **Selected Balance Sheet Data:** | | | | | | |
| Cash and cash equivalents | $ 14.9 | $212.3 | $177.4 | $134.2 | $194.5 | $ 508.1 |
| Short-term investments | — | — | 207.7 | 186.0 | 155.9 | 290.0 |
| Current assets | n.a. | 243.7 | 432.4 | 416.5 | 637.2 | 1,830.9 |
| Net investment in content library | n.a. | 57.0 | 128.4 | 146.1 | 362.0 | 1,966.6 |
| Total assets | 52.5 | 364.7 | 679.0 | 679.7 | 982.1 | 3,069.2 |
| Current liabilities | n.a. | 137.6 | 208.9 | 226.4 | 388.6 | 1,225.1 |
| Working capital* | (1.7) | 106.1 | 223.5 | 190.1 | 248.6 | 605.8 |
| Stockholders' equity | (73.3) | 226.3 | 429.8 | 199.1 | 290.2 | 642.8 |
| **Cash Flow Data:** | | | | | | |
| Net cash provided by operating activities | $(22.7) | $157.5 | $277.4 | $325.1 | $276.4 | $ 317.7 |
| Net cash used in investing activities | (25.0) | (133.2) | (436.0) | (246.1) | (116.1) | (265.8) |
| Net cash provided by (used in) financing activities | 48.4 | 13.3 | (64.4) | (84.6) | (100.0) | 261.6 |

* Defined as current assets minus current liabilities.

*Sources:* Company 10-K reports for 2003, 2005, 2007, 2008, 2009, and 2011.

in 2012 for movies to be viewed at theaters, on air-line flights, in hotels, from the rear seats of motor vehicles equipped with video consoles, in homes, or most anywhere on a laptop PC or handheld device like an Apple iPhone, iPad, or iPod touch. Home viewing was possible on PCs, televisions connected to a digital video disc (DVD) player, and video game consoles. As of 2012, more than 90 percent of U.S. households had DVD players connected to their TVs, enabling them to play movie DVDs. Households with big-screen high-definition TVs and a Blu-ray player could rent a Blu-ray DVD and enjoy a significantly higher picture quality. In recent years, millions of households had upgraded to high-speed or broadband Internet service and purchased Blu-ray DVD devices, video game consoles, and/or televisions with built-in connectivity to the Internet, enabling them to view content streamed over the Internet. However, heading into 2012, it was clear that the 134 million U.S. households with high-speed Internet service and Internet-connected Blu-ray players, video game consoles, TVs, computers, tablets, and/or smartphones were rapidly shifting from renting physical DVDs to watching movies and TV episodes streamed over the Internet.

Increasing numbers of devices had recently appeared in electronics stores (or become available from cable, satellite, and fiber-optic TV providers) that enabled TVs to be connected to the Internet and receive streamed content from online providers with no hassle. These devices made it simple for households to order streamed movies with just a few clicks instead of traveling to a video rental store or waiting for a disk to be delivered through the mail. In 2012, more than 700 different devices were capable of streaming content from Netflix.

Consumers could obtain or view movie DVDs and TV episodes through a wide variety of distribution channels and providers. The options included:

- Watching movies on assorted cable channels included in the TV and entertainment packages provided by traditional cable providers (such as Time Warner, Comcast, Cox, and Charter), direct broadcast satellite providers (such as DIRECTV and DISH Network), or fiber-optics providers (like AT&T and Verizon that had installed thousands of miles of fiber-optic cable that enabled them to simultaneously provide TV packages, telephone, and Internet services to customers).

- Subscribing to any of several movie-only channels (such as HBO, Showtime, and Starz) through a cable, satellite, or fiber-optics provider.

- Using a TV remote to order movies instantly streamed directly to a TV on a pay-per-view basis (generally referred to as "video-on-demand" or VOD). Cable, satellite, and fiber-optic providers of multichannel TV packages were promoting their VOD services and making more movie titles available to their customers. In 2011, roughly 40 million U.S. households (15 percent) spent about $1.3 billion on VOD movie rentals.[2]

- Purchasing DVDs from such retailers as Walmart, Target, Best Buy, Toys "R" Us, and Amazon.com. DVD sales, however, had declined for the past three years, partially a reflection of growing consumer preferences to rent rather than purchase DVDs of movies and TV episodes.

- Renting DVDs from Blockbuster and other local retail stores or from standalone rental kiosks like Redbox and Blockbuster Express. Physical-disc rentals at traditional brick-and-mortar locations had been trending downward for five to eight years, but the downward spiral accelerated in 2010–2011. Blockbuster's share of physical disc rentals dropped from 23 percent in 2010 to 17 percent in 2011.[3] The chief beneficiary of declining rentals at brick-and-mortar movie rental locations was Redbox. Since 2007, when Redbox first began deploying its distinctive red vending machine kiosks, Redbox's share of physical-disc DVD and Blu-ray movie rentals in the U.S. had mushroomed to 37 percent as of 2011 (up from 25 percent in 2010).

- Renting DVDs online from Netflix, Blockbuster, and several other subscription services that either mailed DVDs directly to subscribers' homes or streamed the content to subscribers via broadband Internet connections. In 2011, Netflix had about a 30 percent share of the physical DVD rental market and about a 56 percent share of streaming rentals.[4]

- Utilizing the rental or download services of such providers as Apple's iTunes store, Amazon Instant Video, Hulu.com, VUDU.com, Best Buy Cinema Now, Sony PlayStation Network, and Google's YouTube.

- Most recently, a new class of user interface apps had become available that enabled subscribers to the services of multichannel TV providers (like cable or satellite operators) to watch certain TV shows, movies, and other programs at their convenience rather than at scheduled broadcast times. This service—called TV Everywhere—gave subscribers the option to watch programs on Internet-connected TVs and computers, iPads, iPhones, Android phones, and other devices. HBO's TV Everywhere application—called HBO GO—enabled HBO subscribers to have anytime, anywhere access to all HBO shows, hit movies, and other programs through participating multichannel TV providers. In 2012, most multichannel TV providers and the owners of most channels carried on cable and satellite networks were exploring TV Everywhere options and packages for interested viewers.

- Pirating files of movies and other content from Internet sources via the use of illegal file-sharing software. Piracy was widely thought to be a contributing factor to declining sales of movie DVDs. In 2011–2012, movie studios were becoming increasingly concerned that digital piracy could become a tidal wave.[5] Much of Netflix's streaming library was rumored to be available through online piracy.

In recent years, movie studios had released filmed entertainment content for distribution to movie DVD retailers and to companies renting movie DVDs about 17 weeks after a film first began showing in theaters. After about three months in theaters, movie studios usually released first-run films to pay-per-view and video-on-demand (VOD) providers (prior to the last several years, the release window had been about six months). However, in October 2011, a Kevin Spacey film was released in theaters and through both Netflix and Time Warner Cable on the same day; the movie grossed $3.5 million at theaters and the studio realized more than $5 million each from Netflix and Time Warner Cable.[6] Premium TV channels like HBO, Starz, Cinemax, and Showtime were next in the distribution window, typically getting access to premium films one year after initial theater showings. Movie studios released films for viewing to basic cable and network TV some two to three years after theatrical release. TV episodes were often made available for Internet viewing shortly after the original air date.

Recently, however, some movie studios had experimented with shortened release periods, including making new release titles available to video-on-demand providers or for online purchase on the same date DVDs could be sold by retailers. Other movie studios had implemented or announced their intention to implement policies preventing movie rental providers

from renting movie DVDs until 30 to 60 days following the date DVD titles could be sold by retailers. For example, in January 2012, Warner Home Entertainment increased the availability date for rental DVDs top kiosks and subscription-by-mail services to 58 days. Movie studios and TV networks were expected to continue to experiment with the timing of the releases to various distribution channels and providers, in an ongoing effort to discover how best to maximize revenues.

## Market Trends in Home Viewing of Movies

The wave of the future in the market for renting movies and TV content was unquestionably in streaming movies and TV shows to Internet-connected TVs, computers, and mobile devices. Streaming had the advantage of allowing household members to order and instantly watch the movies and TV programs they wanted to see. Renting a streamed movie could be done either by utilizing the services of Netflix, Blockbuster Online, Amazon Instant Video, Apple's iTunes, and other streaming video providers or by using a TV remote to place orders with a cable, satellite, or fiber-optics provider to instantly watch a movie from a list of several hundred selections that changed periodically. With a few exceptions, rental prices for pay-per-view and VOD movies ranged from $1 to $6, but the rental price for popular recently released movies was usually $3.99 to $5.99. During 2011, several movie studios had experimented with charging up to $30 for films released to pay-per-view and VOD providers for showing after eight weeks in theaters, but disappointingly small viewer response to such high-priced rentals quickly put an end to this strategy.[7] In 2012, many in-home movie viewers saw unlimited Internet streaming from subscription services as a better value than pay-per-view—the rental costs for two pay-per-view movies usually exceeded the $7.99 monthly price for unlimited streaming currently being charged by Netflix.

Several strategic initiatives to promote increased use of streaming video were underway in 2012.

- The owners of Hulu—Providence Equity Partners, The Walt Disney Company (owner of the ABC network), News Corp. (the parent of Fox Broadcasting and Fox Entertainment) and Comcast (the owner of NBCUniversal)—had for several years offered a free online video service at **www.hulu.com** where viewers could watch a selection of hit TV shows and movies from the libraries of ABC, NBC, Fox Broadcasting, Walt Disney Studios, Universal Studios, Fox Entertainment, and a few others; the revenues to support the free Hulu site came from advertisers whose commercials were inserted into all of the free programs. But in mid-2011, three years after creating the Hulu site, the owners became reluctant to continue giving their content away for free and began an effort to sell the venture. In October 2011, the sales process was abandoned; Google, the DISH Network, Amazon, and Yahoo were rumored to have contemplated or made offers to acquire Hulu. Shortly thereafter, Hulu began actively promoting an advertising-supported unlimited streaming service called Hulu Plus where, for $7.99 per month, subscribers could watch a much larger selection of premium movies and primetime TV shows interspersed with commercials.

- Time Warner Cable, Comcast, Charter, DISH Network, DIRECTV, HBO, Showtime, and others were in the early stages of promoting their TV Everywhere concept and program offerings that enabled customers to watch certain TV shows free at any time on any Internet-connected device (including computers and such mobile devices as iPads and smartphones) as long as they were paying subscribers. For example, DIRECTV had created a device called Nomad to help subscribers watch their recorded programs anywhere; Nomad allowed subscribers to synchronize their smartphone, laptop, or tablet with recorded content on their DVRs and watch the recorded programs anywhere, anytime. DISH Network had introduced a "Sling Adapter" that—in conjunction with an Internet-connected DVR and a free DISH remote access app downloaded onto a mobile device—enabled customers to watch TV programs at their convenience on any Internet-connected device. However, for TV Everywhere to reach its full potential, each cable, satellite, and fiber-optic multichannel TV provider had to negotiate agreements for online rights to each channel's programming. As of early 2012, just a few multichannel TV providers had secured online rights to as many as 15 channels, but this was expected to be temporary.
- Google and Apple were rolling out new versions of their Google TV and Apple TV products to try to win traction with consumers. Google had partnered with LG, Vizio, and Samsung to introduce TVs equipped with Google TV and was rapidly

expanding its library of apps optimized for Google TV, all in an attempt to facilitate easy consumer discovery of content that was available for streaming to TVs and/or Android devices. In addition, Google had invested in a new subsidiary called Google Fiber that was actively exploring plans to enter the Internet service and/or TV provider marketplaces by offering a one-gigabit-per-second Internet service coupled with an on-demand TV service that enabled customers to watch what they wanted when they wanted without ever having to record anything. In March 2012, Google filed applications with the Missouri Public Service Commission and the Kansas Corporation Commission for approval to offer a video service to subscribers in the Kansas City area—the proposal called for Google to use national and regional programming collection points to send IPTV (a television-over-Internet technology) across its private fiber-optic network (Google Fiber) to subscribers in Kansas City. It remained to be seen whether Google could secure broadcast rights from the owners of various TV channels and Hollywood movie studios to lure customers; however, Google's YouTube was spending hundreds of millions of dollars funding new TV channels that were scheduled to be available online and could be a part of Google's TV package. Time Warner Cable was the dominant TV provider in Kansas City, while Direct TV, DISH Network, and AT&T's U-verse had smaller customer bases.

Apple TV was a tiny box that enabled users to play high-definition content from iTunes, Netflix, YouTube, and live sports events (professional baseball, hockey, and basketball) on TVs, or to stream content to TVs from an iPad, iPhone, or iPod touch, or to stream music and photos from computers to TVs. In March 2012, Netflix and Apple implemented an agreement whereby Apple TV users could sign up for Netflix services directly through their Apple TV device, using their iTunes account.

IHS Screen Digest Research had forecast that streaming content would exceed 3.4 billion views in 2012.[8] It also expected that movie viewing online in 2012 would exceed combined viewing on DVDs and Blu-ray devices for the first time.[9]

## Competitive Intensity

The movie rental business was intensely competitive in 2012. Local brick-and-mortar stores that rented DVD discs were in the throes of a death spiral, as a growing number of their customers switched either to obtaining their DVDs at Redbox vending kiosks or utilizing Internet streaming services of one kind or another. Blockbuster, once a movie rental powerhouse with over $4.5 billion in annual rental revenues and more than 9,000 company-owned and franchised stores in a host of countries, was a shadow of its former self in 2012. After losing over $4 billion during the 2002–2010 period, closing thousands of store locations, and launching several unsuccessful strategic attempts to rejuvenate revenues and return to profitability, Blockbuster filed for Chapter 11 bankruptcy protection in September 2010. Following a bankruptcy court auction, DISH Network emerged in April 2011 as the owner of Blockbuster's operations in the United States and certain foreign countries for a winning bid valued at $321 million. From the acquisition date of April 26, 2011 through December 31, 2011, Blockbuster operations contributed $975 million in revenue and $4 million in net income to DISH Network's consolidated results of operations. Going into 2012, Blockbuster was operating some 1,500 retail stores in the United States, but DISH Network management had announced that it expected to close over 500 domestic Blockbuster stores during the first half of 2012 as a result of weak store-level financial performance and that additional stores might also need to be closed. For the time being, Blockbuster was offering movies and video games for sale and rental through its retail stores, the blockbuster.com website (via a DVDs-by-mail subscription service), and pay-per-view VOD service. In addition, DISH Network subscribers could access Blockbuster@Home to obtain movies, video games, and TV shows through Internet streaming, mail and in-store exchanges, and online downloads.

Movie Gallery, once the second-largest movie rental chain, filed for Chapter 11 bankruptcy protection in February 2010 and, shortly thereafter, opted to liquidate its entire movie rental business and close 1,871 Movie Gallery, 545 Hollywood Video, and 250 Game Crazy store locations. Within months, Movie Gallery ceased to exist.

The big winner in renting DVD discs was Redbox. Redbox had entered the movie rental business in 2007 with a vending machine–based strategy whereby Redbox self-service DVD kiosks were placed in leading supermarkets, drug stores, mass merchants like Walmart, convenience stores, and fast-food restaurants (McDonald's). Customers could rent new-release movie DVDs for $1 per day (the price was raised to $1.20 per day in fall 2011). Retailers with Redbox kiosks were paid a percentage of the rental revenues. Going into 2012, Redbox had deployed 35,400 of its vending machine kiosks in 29,300 locations in every state of the United States and in Puerto Rico. In February 2012, Redbox agreed to acquire about 9,000 Blockbuster-branded DVD kiosks operated by NCR Corp. Redbox and Netflix (with its DVDs-by-mail subscription option) were positioned to dominate the physical DVD rental segment for the foreseeable future.

The main battle in the movie rental marketplace was in the VOD and Internet streaming segments where several classes of competitors employing a variety of strategies were maneuvering to win the viewing time of consumers, capture enough revenue to be profitable, and become one of the market leaders. Competitors offering pay-per-view and VOD rentals were popular options for households and individuals that rented movies occasionally (once or at most twice per month), since the rental costs tended to be less than either the monthly subscription prices for unlimited streaming or the monthly fees to access premium movie channels like HBO, Starz, Cinemax, and Showtime. However, competitors offering unlimited Internet streaming plans tended to be the most economical and convenient choice for individuals and households that watched an average of three or more titles per month and for individuals that wanted to be able to watch movies or TV shows on mobile devices.

Netflix was the clear leader in Internet streaming in 2012, with over 23 million streaming subscribers that watched an average of 30 hours of video monthly and some 60,000 titles that could be viewed on an Internet-connected device.[10] But Netflix had numerous ambitious rivals that saw huge revenue and profit opportunities in using online technology to provide movies, TV programming, and other entertainment content to all types of Internet-connected devices on an anywhere, anytime basis.

Netflix's two most important subscription-based instant streaming rivals included:

- *Hulu Plus*—The subscription fee for Hulu Plus was $7.99 per month for unlimited streaming, and new subscribers got a one-week free trial. All Hulu Plus content included advertisements as a means of helping keep the monthly subscription price low. The Hulu Plus library of offerings included all current season episodes of popular TV shows, over 15,000 back season episodes of 380 + TV shows, and over 425 movies, many in high-definition.

- *Amazon Prime Instant Video*—This service entailed becoming an Amazon Prime member for a fee of $79 per year (after a one-month free trial). All Amazon Prime members were entitled to free two-day shipping on *all Amazon orders,* unlimited commercial-free streaming of 17,000 movies and TV programs, one free Kindle book rental each month, and assorted other perks. In March 2012, there were an estimated 3.5 to 5 million Amazon Prime members. New Amazon Prime members were entitled to a one-month free trial. While Amazon had originally created its Amazon Prime membership program as a means of providing unlimited two-day shipping to customers that frequently ordered merchandise from Amazon and liked to receive their orders quickly, in 2012 it was clear that Amazon was also endeavoring to brand Amazon Prime as a standalone streaming service at a subscription price below that of Netflix. In addition, Amazon competed with Netflix's DVDs-by-mail subscription service and with VOD and pay-per-view providers via its Amazon Instant Video offering, which enabled any visitor to the Amazon website to place an online order to instantly watch on a pay-per-view basis any of the 42,000 movies or TV shows in Amazon's rental library.

In February 2010, Walmart announced its intention to distribute movies over the Internet and had acquired VUDU, a leading provider of digital technologies that enabled online delivery of entertainment content. In 2012, VUDU was the largest home entertainment retailer in the United States with the capability to stream about 20,000 movie titles (including some 4,000 HD titles with Dolby Surround Sound) to Internet-connected TVs, Blu-ray players, computers, iPads and other tablets, and video game consoles (Xbox 360 and PlayStation 3). Movies were available the same day they were released on DVD or Blu-ray discs and could be purchased or rented without a subscription; the rental fee was $2 per night for two nights. First-time users were eligible for free VUDU movie credits that could be used for a one-month trial period. In April 2012, Walmart initiated an exclusive in-store disc-to-digital service powered by VUDU technology which enabled people to bring their DVD and Blu-ray collections from partnering movie studios (Paramount, Sony, Fox, Universal, and Warner Bros.) to a Walmart Photo Center and have digital copies of the DVDs placed in a personal VUDU account. Then, VUDU account holders could log on to VUDU.com and view their movies any time, any place on more than 300 different Internet-connected devices.

The growing rush among multichannel TV providers to offer subscribers attractive TV Everywhere packages signaled a widespread belief that using Internet streaming to enable subscribers to watch certain TV shows or movies free at any time on any Internet-connected device was the best long-term solution for competing effectively with Netflix's Internet streaming service. In 2012, most every major network broadcaster, multichannel TV provider, and premium movie channel was investing in Internet apps for all types of Internet-connected TVs, laptops, video game consoles, tablets, and smartphones and otherwise positioning themselves to offer attractive TV Everywhere packages. HBO with its HBO GO offering (www.hbogo.com) and Showtime with its Showtime Anytime offering (www.showtimeanytime.com) were both trying to gain more viewing hours with their subscribers. Pricing for TV Everywhere offerings was simple—users just entered an authentication code verifying their subscription status at the appropriate website. Subscribers then clicked on whichever offering interested them to initiate instant streaming to their device.

According to market research done by The NPD Group, 15 percent of U.S. consumers aged 13 and older used pay-TV VOD services from their multichannel cable, satellite, and fiber-optic providers in the 12 months ending August 2011; this translated into 40 million users and rental revenues of $1.1 billion.[11] However, there were four million fewer VOD users who paid additional fees to watch movies from these same providers in August 2011 compared to August 2010. This was attributed to the growing number of attractive VOD offerings from rival online VOD providers such as iTunes, Amazon Instant Video, VUDU, and others that instantly streamed rentals over the Internet. The NPD Group estimated that Internet streaming accounted for one out of every six VOD rentals in 2011 and that the share of Internet-streamed VOD rentals was likely to continue to grow, chiefly because many consumers saw the prices of Internet-streamed rentals as a better value and believed such providers had more movie-title selections.[12]

## NETFLIX'S BUSINESS MODEL AND STRATEGY

Since launching the company's online movie rental service in 1999, Reed Hastings, founder and CEO of Netflix, had been the chief architect of Netflix's subscription-based business model and strategy that had transformed Netflix into the world's largest online entertainment subscription service and revolutionized the way that many people rented movies and previously broadcast TV shows. Hastings's goals for Netflix were simple: Build the world's best Internet movie service, keep improving Netflix's offerings and services faster than rivals, attract growing numbers of subscribers every year, and grow long-term earnings per share. Hastings was a strong believer in moving early and fast to initiate strategic changes that would help Netflix outcompete rivals, strengthen its brand image and reputation, and fortify its position as industry leader.

## Netflix's Subscription-Based Business Model

Netflix employed a subscription-based business model. Members could choose from a variety of subscription plans whose prices and terms had varied over the years. Originally, all of the subscription plans were based on obtaining and returning DVDs by mail, with monthly prices dependent on the number of titles out at a time. But as more and more households began to have high-speed Internet connections, Netflix began bundling unlimited streaming with each of its DVD-by-mail subscription options, with the long-term intent of encouraging subscribers to switch to watching instantly streamed movies rather than using DVD discs delivered and returned by mail. The DVDs-by-mail part of the business had order fulfillment costs and postage costs that were bypassed when members opted for instant streaming.

**The DVD-by-Mail Option**   Subscribers who opted to receive movie and TV episode DVDs by mail went to Netflix's website, selected one or more movies from its DVD library of over 120,000 titles, and received the movie DVDs by first-class mail generally within one business day—more than 97 percent of Netflix's subscribers lived within one-day delivery of the company's 50 distribution centers (plus 50 other shipping points) located throughout the United States. During the 2004–2010 period, Netflix had aggressively added more distribution centers and shipping points in order to provide members with one-business-day delivery on DVD orders. Subscribers could keep a DVD for as long as they wished, with no due dates, no late fees, no shipping fees, and no pay-per-view fees. Subscribers returned DVDs via the U.S. Postal Service in a prepaid return envelope that came with each movie order. The address on the return envelope was always the closest distribution center/shipping point so that returned DVDs could quickly

be returned to inventory and used to fill incoming orders from subscribers.

Exhibit 4 shows Netflix's various subscription plan options during 2010–2012. The most popular DVD-by-mail plans were those with one, two, or three titles out at a time.

**The Streaming Option**   Netflix launched its Internet streaming service in January 2007, with instant-watching capability for 2,000 titles on personal computers. Very quickly, Netflix invested aggressively to enable its software to instantly stream content to a growing number of "Netflix-ready" devices, including Sony's PlayStation 3 consoles, Microsoft's Xbox 360, Nintendo's Wii, Internet-connected Blu-ray players and TVs, TiVo DVRs, and special Netflix players made by Roku and several other electronics manufacturers. At the same time, it began licensing increasing amounts of digital content that could be instantly streamed to subscribers. Initially, Netflix took a "metered" approach to streaming, in essence offering an hour per month of instant watching on a PC for every dollar of a subscriber's monthly subscription plan. For example, subscribers on the $16.99 per month plan, which provides unlimited DVD rentals with three discs out at a time, received 17 hours a month of movies and TV episodes watched instantly on their PCs while those on the $4.99 limited plan were entitled to 5 hours of instant streaming. In January 2009, Netflix switched to an unlimited streaming option on all of its monthly subscription plans for unlimited DVD rentals; the limited plan continued to have a monthly streaming limit. Netflix had about 6,000 movie titles available for streaming as of January 2009 and about 20,000 titles in mid-2010.

Then in July 2011, Netflix announced that effective September 1, 2011 it would no longer offer a single subscription plan including both DVD-by-mail and streaming in the United States. Domestic subscribers who wished to receive DVDs-by-mail and also watch streamed content had to elect both a DVD-by-mail subscription plan and a streaming subscription plan. By December 31, 2011, Netflix had a total of 21.7 million domestic streaming subscribers (including 1.52 million who were in their free-trial period) and 11.2 million domestic DVD-by-mail subscribers (including 210,000 who were in their free-trial period); almost 6.6 million Netflix members had both a streaming subscription and a DVD-by-mail subscription.

All new Netflix subscribers received a free one-month trial. At the end of the free trial period,

**EXHIBIT 4**  Netflix's Subscription Plans, 2010–2012

| | Monthly Subscription Price | | |
|---|---|---|---|
| **Subscription Plan Choices** | **June 2010** | **Nov. 22, 2010 through June 2011** | **September 2011 through 2012** |
| **Unlimited DVD Plans:** | | | |
| 1 title out at a time | $8.99 plus unlimited streaming | $9.99 plus unlimited streaming | $7.99 |
| 2 titles out at a time | $13.99 plus unlimited streaming | $14.99 plus unlimited streaming | $11.99 |
| 3 titles out at a time | $16.99 plus unlimited streaming | $19.99 plus unlimited streaming | $15.99 |
| 4 titles out at a time | $23.99 plus unlimited streaming | $27.99 plus unlimited streaming | $21.99 |
| 5 to 8 titles out at a time | $29.99–$47.99 plus unlimited streaming | $34.99–$53.99 plus unlimited streaming | $27.99–$43.99 |
| **Unlimited streaming (no DVDs)** | Not available | $7.99 | $7.99 |
| **Unlimited streaming plus DVDs** | | | |
| Unlimited streaming plus 1 DVD title out at a time | — | — | $15.98 |
| Unlimited streaming plus 2 DVD titles out at a time | — | — | $19.98 |
| Unlimited streaming with 3–8 DVDs | | | $23.98–$51.98 |
| **Limited plan:** | | | |
| • 1 DVD title out at a time | $4.99 | $4.99 | $4.99 |
| • A maximum of 2 DVD rentals per month | | | |
| • 2 hours of video streaming to a PC or Apple Mac per month (this plan did not allow members to stream movies to TVs via a Netflix-ready device) | | | |
| • Limited streaming selection | | | |

*Source:* Company records and postings at www.netflix.com.

members automatically began paying the monthly fee, unless they canceled their subscription. All paying subscribers were billed monthly in advance. Payments were made by credit card or debit card. Subscribers could cancel at any time.

Exhibit 5 shows trends in Netflix's subscriber growth in the United States. Exhibit 6 shows quarterly trends in Netflix subscriptions and profitability by market segment.

New subscribers were drawn to try Netflix's online movie rental service because of (1) the wide selection, (2) the extensive information Netflix provided about each movie in its rental library (including critic reviews, member reviews, online trailers, and subscriber ratings), (3) the ease with which they could find and order movies, (4) Netflix's policies of

no late fees and no due dates on DVD rentals (which eliminated the hassle of getting DVDs back to local rental stores by the designated due date), (5) the convenience of being provided a postage-paid return envelope for mailing DVDs back to Netflix, and (6) the convenience of ordering and instantly watching movies streamed to their TVs or computers with no additional pay-per-view charge.

Management believed that Netflix's subscriber base consisted of three types of customers: those who liked the convenience of home delivery and/or instant streaming, bargain hunters who were enthused about being able to watch many movies for an economical monthly price, and movie buffs who wanted the ability to choose from a very wide selection of films and TV shows.

## EXHIBIT 5  Domestic Subscriber Data for Netflix, 2000–2011

| | 2000 | 2005 | 2007 | 2009 | 2010 | Jan. 1 – June 30, 2011 | July 1 – Dec. 31, 2011 |
|---|---|---|---|---|---|---|---|
| Total subscribers at beginning of period | 107,000 | 2,610,000 | 6,316,000 | 9,390,000 | 12,268,000 | 19,501,000 | 24,594,000 |
| Gross subscriber additions during period | 515,000 | 3,729,000 | 5,340,000 | 9,322,000 | 15,648,000 | 11,614,000 | 9,930,000 |
| Subscriber cancellations during the period | 330,000 | 2,160,000 | 4,177,000 | 6,444,000 | 8,415,000 | 6,521,000 | 10,129,000 |
| Total subscribers at end of period | 292,000 | 4,179,000 | 7,479,000 | 12,268,000 | 19,501,000 | 24,594,000 | 24,395,000 |
| Net subscriber additions during the period | 185,000 | 1,569,000 | 1,163,000 | 2,878,000 | 7,233,000 | 5,093,000 | (199,000) |
| Free trial subscribers at end of period | n.a. | 153,000 | 153,000 | 376,000 | 1,566,000 | 1,331,000 | 1,537,000 |
| Subscriber acquisition cost | $49.96 | $38.78 | $40.86 | $25.48 | $18.21 | $14.70 | $15.41 |
| Average monthly revenue per paying subscriber | n.a. | $17.94 | $14.95 | $13.30 | $12.20 | $11.49 | $12.35 |

n.a. = not available.

*Sources:* Netflix's 10-K Reports, 2010, 2009, 2005, and 2003 and Netflix Quarterly Report for the period ending June 30, 2011, posted in the investors relations section at www.netflix.com, accessed March 16, 2012.

## EXHIBIT 6  Quarterly Trends in Netflix Subscriptions and Profitability, by Market Segment, Quarter 3, 2011 through Quarter 1, 2012 (in 000s)

| | Three Months Ended | | |
|---|---|---|---|
| | September 30, 2011 | December 31, 2011 | March 31, 2012 |
| **Domestic Streaming** | | | |
| Free subscriptions at end of period | 937 | 1,518 | 1,388 |
| Paid subscriptions at end of period | 20,511 | 20,153 | 22,022 |
| Total subscriptions at end of period | 21,448 | 21,671 | 23,410 |
| Revenue | n.a. | $476,334 | $ 506,645 |
| Cost of revenues and marketing expenses | n.a. | 424,224 | 440,157 |
| Contribution profit | | $ 52,110 | $  66,508 |
| **International Streaming** | | | |
| Free subscriptions at end of period | 491 | 411 | 646 |
| Paid subscriptions at end of period | 989 | 1,447 | 2,409 |
| Total subscriptions at end of period | 1,480 | 1,858 | 3,065 |
| Revenue | $ 22,687 | $ 28,988 | $  43,425 |
| Cost of revenues and marketing expenses | 46,005 | 88,731 | 146,108 |
| Contribution profit | $ (23,318) | $ (59,743) | $(102,683) |
| **Domestic DVDs-by-Mail** | | | |
| Free subscriptions at end of period | 115 | 126 | 131 |
| Paid subscriptions at end of period | 13,813 | 11,039 | 9,958 |
| Total subscriptions at end of period | 13,928 | 11,039 | 10,089 |
| Revenue | | $370,253 | $ 319,701 |
| Cost of revenues and marketing expenses | | 176,488 | 173,568 |
| Contribution profit | | $193,765 | $ 146,133 |

*(Continued)*

## EXHIBIT 6    *(Concluded)*

| | Three Months Ended | | |
| --- | --- | --- | --- |
| | September 30, 2011 | December 31, 2011 | March 31, 2012 |
| **Consolidated Operations** | | | |
| Free unique subscribers at end of period* | 1,437 | 1,948 | 2,056 |
| Paid unique subscribers at end of period* | 23,832 | 24,305 | 27,083 |
| Total unique subscribers at end of period* | 25,269 | 26,253 | 29,139 |
| Revenue | $821,839 | $875,575 | $ 869,791 |
| Cost of revenues and marketing expenses | 625,725 | 689,443 | 759,833 |
| Contribution profit | 196,114 | 186,132 | 109,958 |
| Other operating expenses | 99,272 | 124,260 | 111,893 |
| Operating income | 96,842 | 61,872 | (1,935) |
| Other income (expense) | (3,219) | (5,037) | (5,090) |
| Provision for income taxes | 31,163 | 21,616 | (2,441) |
| Net income | $ 62,460 | $ 35,219 | $    (4,584) |

*Note:* Netflix defined "contribution profit (loss)" as revenues less cost of revenues and marketing expenses. Cost of revenue includes expenses related to the acquisition and licensing of content (streaming content license agreements, DVD direct purchases and DVD revenue sharing agreements with studios, distributors and other content suppliers), as well as content delivery costs related to providing streaming content and shipping DVDs to subscribers (which includes the postage costs to mail DVDs to and from our paying subscribers, the packaging and label costs for the mailers, all costs associated with streaming content over the Internet, the costs of operating and staffing shipping centers and customer service centers, DVD inventory management expenses, and credit card fees).

*Since some Netflix members in the United States subscribed to both streaming and DVD-by-mail plans, they were counted as a single unique subscriber to avoid double counting the same subscriber.

n.a. = not applicable. During July and August of the third quarter of 2011, Netflix's domestic streaming content and DVD-by-mail operations were combined. Subscribers in the United States were able to receive both streaming content and DVDs under a single hybrid plan. Accordingly, revenues were generated and marketing expenses were incurred in connection with the subscription offerings as a whole. Therefore, the company did not allocate revenues or marketing expenses for the domestic streaming and domestic DVD segments prior to the fourth quarter of 2011.

*Source:* Netflix records posted in the Financial Statements portion of the investor relations section at www.netflix.com, accessed March 19, 2012.

## Netflix's Strategy

Netflix had a multipronged strategy to build an ever-growing subscriber base that included:

- Providing subscribers with a comprehensive selection of DVD titles.

- Acquiring new content by building and maintaining mutually beneficial relationships with entertainment video providers.

- Making it easy for subscribers to identify movies and TV shows they were likely to enjoy and to put them in a queue for either instant streaming or delivery by mail.

- Giving subscribers a choice of watching streaming content or receiving quickly delivered DVDs by mail.

- Spending aggressively on marketing to attract subscribers and build widespread awareness of the Netflix brand and service.

- Promoting rapid transition of U.S. subscribers to streaming delivery rather than mail delivery.

- Expanding internationally.

**A Comprehensive Library of Movies and TV Episodes**    Since its early days, Netflix's strategy had been to offer subscribers a large and diverse selection of DVD titles. It had been aggressive in seeking out attractive new titles to add to its offerings. Because of this, its library of offerings had grown from some 55,000 titles in 2005 to about 120,000 titles in 2012, although the number of titles available for streaming was only about 30,000 as mid-2012 approached. The lineup included everything from the latest available Hollywood releases to releases several decades old to movie classics to independent films to hard-to-locate documentaries to TV shows and how-to videos, as well as a growing collection of cartoons and movies for children 12 and under. Netflix's DVD library far outdistanced the selection available in local brick-and-mortar movie rental stores and the 200 to 400 titles available in Redbox vending machines, but it was on a par with the number of titles available at Amazon. In mid-2012, Netflix's streaming library contained more titles than any other streaming service.

**New Content Acquisition**    Over the years, Netflix had spent considerable time and energy establishing strong ties with various entertainment video providers and leveraging these ties to both expand its content library and gain access to new releases as early as possible—the time frame that Netflix gained access to films after their theatrical release was an important item of negotiation for Netflix (in 2011, Netflix was able to negotiate access to certain films produced by Lionsgate within one year of their initial theatrical release for showing to members in the UK and Ireland). Also, in 2011, Netflix had successfully negotiated *exclusive* rights to show a number of titles produced by several studios.

In August 2011, Netflix introduced a new "Just for Kids" section on its website that contained a large selection of kid-friendly movies and TV shows. In March 2012, all of the Just for Kids selections became available for streaming on PlayStation 3 game consoles. As of early March 2012, over 1 billion hours of Just for Kids programming had been streamed to Netflix members.

New content was acquired from movie studios and distributors through direct purchases, revenue-sharing agreements, and licensing agreements to stream content. Netflix acquired many of its new-release movie DVDs from studios for a low upfront fee in exchange for a commitment for a defined period of time either to share a percentage of subscription revenues or to pay a fee based on content utilization. After the revenue-sharing period expired for a title, Netflix generally had the option of returning the title to the studio, purchasing the title, or destroying its copies of the title. On occasion, Netflix also purchased DVDs for a fixed fee per disc from various studios, distributors, and other suppliers. Netflix had about 140,000 titles in its DVD library as of April 2012.

In the case of movie titles and TV episodes that were delivered to subscribers via the Internet for instant viewing, Netflix generally paid a fee to license the content for a defined period of time, with the total fees spread out over the term of the license

agreement (so as to match up content payments with the stream of subscription revenues coming in for that content). Following the expiration of the license term, Netflix either removed the content from its library of streamed offerings or negotiated an extension or renewal of the license agreement. Netflix greatly accelerated its acquisition of new streaming content in 2010 and 2011, increasing its streaming library to around 60,000 titles, up from about 17,000 titles in 2009. Netflix's payments to movie studios for streaming rights in 2010–2011 exceeded its payments for DVD distribution rights—see Exhibit 7. In 2010–2011, Netflix's rapidly growing subscriber base gave movie studios and the network broadcasters of popular TV shows considerably more bargaining power to negotiate higher prices for the new content that Netflix sought to acquire for its content library. Netflix management was fully aware of its weakening bargaining position in new content acquisition, and the higher prices it was having to pay to secure streaming rights largely accounted for why the company's contribution profits from streaming were lower than from DVD rentals—see Exhibit 6. However, Netflix executives expected that long-term growth in the number of streaming subscribers would enable the company to earn attractive profits on its streaming business, despite the increased costs of acquiring attractive new content.

Netflix had incurred obligations to pay $3.91 billion for streaming content as of December 31, 2011, up from $1.12 billion as of December 31, 2010. Some of these obligations did not appear on the company's year-end 2011 balance sheet because they did not meet content library asset recognition criteria (either the fee was not known or reasonably determinable for a specific title or the fee was known but the title was not yet available for streaming to subscribers). Certain of Netflix's new licensing agreements also had variable terms and included renewal provisions that were solely at the option of the content provider. The expected timing of Netflix's streaming content payments was as follows:[13]

| | |
|---|---|
| Less than one year | $    797.6 mil |
| Due after 1 year and through 3 years | 2,384.4 |
| Due after 3 years and through 5 years | 650.5 |
| Due after 5 years | 74.7 |
| Total streaming obligations | $3,907.2 mil |

**EXHIBIT 7**  Netflix's Quarterly Expenditures for Additions to Content Library, 2009–2011

| | Expenditures for Additions to DVD Library (in 000s) | Expenditures for Additions to Streaming Content Library (in 000s) | Total Expenditures for New Content (in 000s) |
|---|---|---|---|
| **2009** | | | |
| Quarter 1 | $ 46,499 | $ 22,091 | $ 68,590 |
| Quarter 2 | 43,224 | 9,343 | 52,567 |
| Quarter 3 | 46,273 | 9,998 | 56,271 |
| Quarter 4 | 57,048 | 22,785 | 79,833 |
| Annual Total | $193,044 | $ 64,217 | $ 257,261 |
| **2010** | | | |
| Quarter 1 | $ 36,902 | $ 50,475 | $ 87,377 |
| Quarter 2 | 24,191 | 66,157 | 90,348 |
| Quarter 3 | 29,900 | 115,149 | 145,049 |
| Quarter 4 | 32,908 | 174,429 | 207,337 |
| Annual Total | $123,901 | $ 406,210 | $ 530,111 |
| **2011** | | | |
| Quarter 1 | $ 22,119 | $ 192,307 | $ 214,426 |
| Quarter 2 | 19,065 | 612,595 | 631,660 |
| Quarter 3 | 20,826 | 539,285 | 560,111 |
| Quarter 4 | 23,144 | 976,545 | 999,689 |
| Annual Total | $ 85,154 | $2,320,732 | $2,405,886 |

*Source:* Company cash flow data, posted in the investor relations section at **www.netflix.com**, accessed March 16, 2012.

**Netflix's Convenient and Easy-to-Use Movie Selection Software**  Netflix had developed proprietary software technology that allowed members to easily scan a movie's length, appropriateness for various types of audiences (G, PG, or R), primary cast members, genre, and an average of the ratings submitted by other subscribers (based on 1 to 5 stars). With one click, members could watch a short preview if they wished. Most importantly perhaps was a personalized 1- to 5-star recommendation for each title that was based on a subscribers' own ratings of movies previously viewed, movies that the member had placed on a list for future streamed viewing and/or mail delivery), and the overall or average rating of all subscribers.

Subscribers often began their search for movie titles by viewing a list of several hundred personalized movie title "recommendations" that Netflix's software automatically generated for each member. Each member's list of recommended movies was the product of Netflix-created algorithms that organized the company's entire library of titles into clusters of similar movies and then sorted the movies in each cluster from most liked to least liked based on over 3 billion ratings provided by subscribers. In 2010–2011, Netflix added new movie ratings from subscribers to its database at a rate of about 20 million per week. Those subscribers who rated similar movies in similar clusters were categorized as like-minded viewers. When a subscriber was online and browsing through the movie selections, the software was programmed to check the clusters the subscriber had rented/viewed in the past, determine which movies the customer had yet to rent/view in that cluster, and recommended only those movies in the cluster that had been highly rated by viewers. Viewer ratings determined which available titles were displayed to a subscriber and in what order. When streaming members came upon a title they wanted to view, that title could, with a single click, be put on their "instant queue"—a list for future viewing. A member's instant queue was immediately viewable with one click whenever the member went to Netflix's website. With one additional click, any title on a member's instant queue could be activated for immediate viewing. In spring 2011, a number of the world's leading consumer electronics companies began placing a Netflix button on their remotes for operating newly purchased TVs, Blu-ray disc players, and other devices that had built-in Internet connections—the button provided Netflix subscribers with a one-click connection to their instant queue. Clicking on a remote with a Netflix button resulted in all of the titles in a subscriber's instant queue appearing on the TV screen within a few seconds; streaming was instantly initiated by clicking on whichever title the subscriber wished to watch. In the case of members with DVD-by-mail subscriptions, members browsing the title library on Netflix's website could with one click place a title on their list (or queue) to receive it by mail. DVD subscribers specified the order in which titles in their personal queue were to be mailed out and could alter the lists or the mailing order at any time. It was also possible to reserve a copy of upcoming releases. Netflix management saw the movie recommendation tool as a quick and personalized means of helping subscribers identify titles they were likely to enjoy.

Netflix management believed that over 50 percent of the titles selected by subscribers came from the recommendations generated by its proprietary software. The software algorithms were thought to be particularly effective in promoting selections of smaller, high-quality films to subscribers who otherwise might not have discovered them in the company's massive and ever-changing collection. On average, about 85 percent of the titles in Netflix's content library were rented each quarter, an indication of the effectiveness of the company's recommendation software in steering subscribers to movies of interest and achieving broader utilization of the company's entire library of titles.

## A Choice of Mail Delivery vs. Streaming

Up until 2007–2008 when streaming technology had advanced to the point that made providing video-on-demand a viable option, Netflix concentrated its efforts on speeding the time it took to deliver subscriber orders via mail delivery. The strategy was to establish a nationwide network of distribution centers and shipping points with the capability to deliver DVDs ordered by subscribers within one business day. To achieve quick delivery and return capability, Netflix created sophisticated software to track the location of each DVD title in inventory and determine the fastest way of getting the DVD orders to subscribers.

When a subscriber placed an order for a specific DVD, the system first looked for that DVD at the shipping center closest to the customer. If that center didn't have the DVD in stock, the system then checked for availability at the next closest center. The search continued until the DVD was found, at which point the regional distribution center with the ordered DVD in its inventory was provided with the information needed to initiate the order fulfillment and shipping process. If the DVD was unavailable anywhere in the system, it was wait-listed. The software system then moved to the customer's next choice and the process started all over. And no matter where the DVD was sent from, the system knew to print the return label on the prepaid envelope to send the DVDs to the shipping center closest to the customer to reduce return mail times and permit more efficient use of Netflix's DVD inventory. No subscriber orders were shipped on holidays or weekends.

By early 2007, Netflix had 50 regional distribution centers and another 50 shipping points scattered across the U.S., giving it a one-business-day delivery capability for 95 percent of its subscribers and, in most cases, also enabling one-day return times. As of 2010, additional improvements in Netflix's distribution and shipping network had resulted in a one-business-day delivery capability for 98 percent of Netflix's subscribers.

In 2007, when entertainment studios became more willing to allow Internet delivery of their content (since recent technological advances prevented streamed movies from being pirated), Netflix moved quickly to better compete with the growing numbers of video-on-demand providers by adding the feature of unlimited streaming to its regular monthly subscription plans. The market for Internet delivery of media content consisted of three segments: the rental of Internet delivered content, the download-to-own segment, and the advertising-supported online delivery segment (mainly, YouTube and Hulu). Netflix's objective was to be the clear leader in the rental segment via its instant watching feature.

Giving subscribers the option of watching DVDs delivered by mail or instantly watching movies streamed to subscribers' computers or TVs had considerable strategic appeal to Netflix in two respects. One, giving subscribers the option to order and instantly watch streamed content put Netflix in a position to compete head to head with the growing numbers of video-on-demand providers. Second, providing streamed content to subscribers had the attraction of being cheaper than (1) incurring the postage expenses on DVD orders and returns, (2) having to obtain and manage an ever-larger inventory of DVDs, and (3) covering the labor costs of additional distribution center personnel to fill a growing volume of DVD orders and handle increased numbers of returned DVDs. But streaming content to subscribers was not cost-free; it required server capacity, software to authenticate orders from subscribers, and a system of computers containing copies of the content files placed at various points in a network so as to maximize bandwidth and allow subscribers to access a copy of the file on a server near the subscriber. Having subscribers accessing a central server ran the risk of an Internet transmission bottleneck. Netflix also utilized third-party content delivery networks to help it efficiently stream movies and TV episodes in high volume to Netflix subscribers over the Internet. According to one report, Netflix incurred a cost of about 5 cents to stream a movie to a subscriber compared to costs of about $1 in roundtrip mailing and labor fees for a DVD.[14]

Netflix executives believed that the strategy of combining streaming and DVDs-by-mail into a single monthly subscription price during the 2007 to September 2011 period enabled Netflix not only to offer members an attractively large selection of movies for one low monthly price but also to enjoy a competitive advantage vis-à-vis rivals as compared to providing a postal-delivery-only or Internet-delivery-only subscription service. Furthermore, Netflix management believed the company's combination postal-delivery/streaming service delivered compelling customer value and customer satisfaction by eliminating the hassle involved in making trips to local movie rental stores to choose and return rented DVDs.

In March 2012, six months after instituting separate plans for streaming and DVDs-by-mail, Netflix instituted as yet unannounced and somewhat subtle changes at its website. A support page appeared at www.netflix.com that sent people registering for a free trial subscription to "dvd.netflix.com" if they wanted to sign up for a DVD-by-mail-only account.[15] In addition, Netflix began redirecting DVD-by-mail customers to a separate web page when they tried to rate movies on Netflix's main site, and DVD-by-mail-only subscribers that searched for movie titles were only shown titles that were also available for streaming rather than the heretofore full library of DVD titles.[16] Furthermore, ratings and recommendations by DVD and streaming customers were separated.

**Marketing and Advertising**    Netflix used multiple marketing channels to attract subscribers, including online advertising (paid search listings, banner ads, text on popular sites such as AOL and Yahoo, and permission-based e-mails), radio stations, regional and national television, direct mail, and print ads. The costs of free monthly trials were treated as a marketing expense. It also participated in a variety of cooperative advertising programs with studios through which Netflix received cash consideration in return for featuring a studio's movies in its advertising. In recent years, Netflix had worked closely with the makers of Netflix-ready electronics devices to expand the number of devices on which subscribers could view Netflix-streamed content; these expenses were all considered marketing expenses and sometimes took the form of payments to various consumer electronics partners for their efforts to produce and distribute these devices.

Management had boosted marketing expenditures of all kinds (including paid advertising) from $25.7 million in 2000 (16.8 percent of revenues) to $142.0 million in 2005 (20.8 percent of revenues) to $218.2 million in 2007 (18.1 percent of revenues). When the recession hit in late 2007 and 2008, management trimmed 2008 marketing expenditures to $199.7 million (14.6 percent of revenues) as a cost containment measure, but in 2009 marketing expenditures resumed their upward trend, climbing to $237.7 million (14.2 percent of revenues). Marketing expenses rose even more dramatically to $298.8 million in 2010 and to $402.6 million in 2011 owing to:

- Increased adverting efforts, particularly in the newly entered countries of Canada, Latin America, the United Kingdom, and Ireland.
- Increased costs of free trial subscriptions.
- Increased payments to the company's consumer electronics partners.

Advertising campaigns of one type or another were underway more or less continuously, with the lure of one-month free trials usually being the prominent ad feature. Advertising expenses totaled approximately $205.9 million in 2009, $181.4 million in 2008, and $207.9 million in 2007—ad expenses for 2011 and 2010 were not publicly reported.

**Transitioning to Internet Delivery of Content**    Netflix's core strategy in 2012 was to grow its streaming subscription business domestically and globally. Since launching streaming to

Internet-connected devices in 2007, the company had continuously improved the streaming experience of subscribers in three major ways:

- Expanding the size of its streaming content library, currently about 60,000 titles.
- Working with consumer electronics partners to increase the number of Internet-connected devices that could be used to view Netflix-streamed content.
- Improving the ease with which subscribers could navigate Netflix's website to locate and select content they wanted to watch.

The result had been rapidly growing consumer acceptance of, and interest in, the delivery of TV shows and movies directly over the Internet. Netflix subscribers watched over 2 billion hours of streaming video in the fourth quarter of 2011, an average of approximately 30 hours per member per month (which equated to a cost of $0.27 per hour of viewing, given the current $7.99 subscription price).[17] During this same period, the company realized a contribution profit of $52.1 million on its domestic streaming business segment (see Exhibit 6).

Going forward, Netflix executives expected that the number of members with DVD-by-mail subscriptions would decline, as subscribers migrated from DVD-by-mail plans to Internet streaming plans and as subscribers with both DVD-by-mail and streaming subscriptions opted for streaming-only subscriptions. An ever-smaller fraction of new subscribers was expected to opt for the DVD-by-mail plan. Management saw no need to proactively encourage or try to accelerate the decline in domestic DVD-by-mail subscriptions beyond the actions already taken—rather the strategy was to simply let subscribers choose whichever plan or plans they wished, since the company had ample ability to provide a satisfying experience to both DVD and streaming subscribers. Netflix management projected that the number of domestic DVD subscribers would decline from just over 11.0 million at the end of 2011 to about 9.5 million at the end of March 2012, with smaller sequential declines in future quarters. Early indications were that the number of Netflix streaming subscribers in the United States would rise by about 1.7 million in the first quarter of 2012.

In the near term, the falloff in revenues from declining domestic DVD subscriptions was projected to be offset by revenue gains from ongoing growth in the numbers of domestic streaming subscribers. Domestic DVD contribution margins were expected

to remain healthy despite shrinking volume, due to the lower postage costs and order fulfillment costs associated with declines in the number of DVD discs being ordered by DVD-by-mail subscribers.

In March 2012, there were reports that Netflix was in exploratory discussions with multichannel TV providers about offering its streaming content as an add-on option alongside such premium movie channels as HBO, Showtime, and Starz.[18] One benefit from such a strategic approach was said to be the likelihood that customers who purchased Netflix through a multichannel TV provider would be more likely to remain a subscriber. Anywhere from 30 to 70 percent of Netflix's subscribers canceled their subscriptions each year (see Exhibit 3)—the percentage of existing subscribers that canceled their subscriptions was referred to as the "churn rate." For Netflix to grow its subscriber base in upcoming years, it had to overcome its churn rate by attracting enough new subscribers to more than offset subscriber cancellations. The appeal of offering Netflix through multichannel TV providers was that pay-television channels had a customer churn rate of only 20 to 25 percent. At an investor event in San Francisco in late February 2012, Reed Hastings said that partnering with cable companies to offer Netflix streaming as an add-on option was a natural progression for the company.[19]

## International Expansion Strategy

Making Netflix's streaming service available to growing numbers of households and individuals outside the United States was a central element of Netflix's long-term strategy to grow revenues and profits. Netflix executives were fully aware that international expansion would temporarily depress overall company profitability since it took roughly two years to build a sufficiently large subscriber base in newly entered country markets to have sufficient revenues to cover all the associated costs. The biggest cost to enter new countries was the expense of obtaining licenses from movie studios and the owners of TV shows to stream their content to subscribers in these countries. The second biggest cost was related to the incremental advertising and marketing expenses needed to attract new subscribers and grow subscription revenues fast enough to achieve profitability within the targeted two-year time frame.

In 2011, Netflix's international streaming segment (Canada and Latin America) reported a contribution loss of $103.1 million. Top management had projected that the added international expenses of expanding service to the UK and Ireland in January 2012 would result in total international contribution losses for Canada, Latin America, United Kingdom, and Ireland of between $108 million and $118 million in Quarter 1 of 2012.

Netflix planned to continue to invest in expanding its streaming content libraries in Latin America, the United Kingdom, and Ireland throughout 2012 and beyond, just as it had done since launching its service in Canada. According to CEO Reed Hastings and CFO David Wells, a bigger content library:[20]

> improves the consumer experience, builds strong word of mouth and positive brand awareness, and drives additional acquisition [of new subscribers], all elements of a strong foundation for long-term success.

Nonetheless, Netflix's entry into Latin America presented unique challenges not encountered in the other international markets. The concept of on-demand streaming video (outside of piracy and YouTube) was not something most Latin American households were familiar with, which required Netflix to do more work in driving consumer understanding and acceptance of the company's streaming service. Moreover, in Latin America, a smaller fraction of households had fewer Internet-connected TVs, Blu-ray players, and other devices that readily connected to Netflix's service. Plus, in many locations there was an underdeveloped Internet infrastructure, relatively low credit card usage among households and individuals, and consumer payment challenges for ecommerce. Many Latin American banks turned down all ecommerce debit card transactions due to fraud risk.

# NETFLIX'S PERFORMANCE PROSPECTS IN 2012

Management's latest forecast for 2012 called for modest quarterly losses throughout 2012 and a loss for the whole year, due entirely to the sizable contribution losses in the international segment. However, continued growth in the number of domestic streaming subscribers was expected to produce contribution margins of 10–12 percent during 2012, comfortably above the company's long-term domestic streaming target of 8 percent, and in line with the 10.9 percent domestic streaming contribution margin in the fourth quarter of 2011. Netflix management said that until

the company returned to global profitability, it did not intend to launch additional international expansion.

## Highlights of Netflix's Performance in Quarter 1 of 2012

For the first three months of 2012, Netflix reported revenues of $869.8 million (21.0 percent higher than the revenues of $718.6 million in the first quarter of 2011) and a net loss of $4.6 million (versus net income of $60.2 million in the first quarter of 2011). The net loss for the quarter stemmed from contribution losses of $102.7 million in the international streaming segment; however, Netflix added 1 million more paying international subscribers during Quarter 1 and had another 600,000 international subscribers enrolled in free trials. International streaming revenues were $43.4 million in the first quarter, versus revenues of $29.0 million for the fourth quarter of 2011 and $12.3 million for the first quarter of 2012.

In the United States, the total number of streaming subscribers (including free-trial subscribers) rose from 21.7 million at the end of the fourth quarter of 2011 to 23.4 million at the end of the first quarter of 2012. Total paying subscribers jumped by 1.85 million during the quarter (from 20.15 million as of December 31, 2011 to 22.0 million as of March 31, 2012). Not surprisingly, the number of domestic DVD subscribers dropped by almost 1.1 million during the quarter to a total of 10.1 million as of March 31. Nonetheless, the customer count exceeded management's expectations, and contribution profits from this segment were $146.1 million—seven million of the DVD subscribers were also streaming subscribers. Viewing per member was at a record high level during the quarter.

Reed Hastings indicated that Netflix would likely add a net of 7 million domestic streaming subscribers during 2012 (about the same number added in 2010) and end the year with approximately 27.2 million domestic streaming customers. He also said that:

- It would take longer than eight quarters after initial entry for the company's operations in Latin America, the UK, and Ireland to reach sustained profitability, owing to ongoing investments in content improvements and somewhat slower-than-expected growth in membership.

- The company expected to return to global profitability in the second quarter of 2012 because of increasing contribution profits in domestic streaming, slow erosion of contribution profits in the domestic DVD segment, and narrowing contribution losses in the international streaming segment. Netflix had positive free cash flow of $2 million during the first three months of 2012.

- Given the strong response to the launch of the company's service in the UK, the company planned to enter another European market in Q4 of 2012. Quickly investing the growing profits from the company's domestic business in additional global expansion had two key advantages: (1) entering foreign markets ahead of other streaming rivals made it easier for Netflix to build a profitable subscriber base and (2) having growing numbers of subscribers in a growing number of countries enabled Netflix to more quickly reach the global scale needed to license global content rights economically.

Initial investor reaction to all this was decidedly negative. In the week following the April announcement of Netflix's first-quarter results, full-year expectations, and future plans, Netflix's stock price—which had climbed to $129 per share in mid-February before falling back to the $105–$110 range in mid-April—dropped about $25 per share and then over the next 10 days slid further, trading as low as $72.49.

## ENDNOTES

[1] Michael Liedtke, "Netflix's Online Gaps Likely to Continue," *Associated Press,* April 9, 2012, accessed April 16, 2012 at www.sltrib.com/sltrib/money/538815.

[2] NPD Group press release, February 16, 2012, accessed March 13, 2012 at www.npd.com.

[3] NPD Group press release, January 19, 2012, accessed March 13, 2012 at www.npd.com.

[4] Ibid.

[5] See Daniel Frankel, "Analyst to Studios: It's Time to Force Early VOD on Theater Chains," posted at www.paidcontent.org, accessed March 12, 2012.

[6] Frankel, "Analyst to Studios: It's Time to Force Early VOD on Theater Chains."

[7] See, for example, Bret Lang, "Lionsgate Tests Early VOD Waters with Taylor Lautner's 'Abduction,'" *The Wrap,* posted at www.thewrap.com, August 10, 2011, accessed March 12, 2012 and also Frankel, "Analyst to Studios: It's Time to Force Early VOD on Theater Chains."

[8] According to information in Amanda Alix, "Is Netflix Trying to Pull Another Qwikster?" *The Motley Fool,* posted March 29, 2012 at www.fool.com and accessed on March 30, 2012.

[9] William Launder, "Online Movie Viewing to Outpace DVD, Blu-ray Views this Year," *The Wall Street Journal,* posted at http://online.wsj.com on March 23, 2012, accessed March 30, 2012.

[10] Michael Liedtke, "Netflix's Online Gaps Likely to Continue," *Associated Press,* April 9, 2012, accessed April 16, 2012 at www.sltrib.com/sltrib/money/538815.

[11] NPD Group press release, February 16, 2012, accessed March 13, 2012 at www.npd.com.

[12] Ibid.

[13] Netflix's 2011 10-K Report, p. 62.

[14] Michael V. Copeland, "Reed Hastings: Leader of the Pack," *Fortune,* December 6, 2010, p. 128.

[15] Amanda Alix, "Is Netflix Trying to Pull Another Qwikster?" *The Motley Fool,* posted March 29, 2012 at www.fool.com and accessed on March 30, 2012.

[16] Ibid.

[17] Letter to Shareholders, January 25, 2012, p. 1; posted in the investor relations section at www.netflix.com, accessed March 28, 2012.

[18] Angela Moscaritolo, "Report: Netflix Looking to Partner with Cable Companies," *PC Magazine,* posted at www.PCMag.com on March 7, 2012, accessed March 7, 2012; and John Jannarone, "Netflix Risks Tangle with Cable," *The Wall Street Journal,* March 29, 2012, p. C12.

[19] Moscaritolo, "Report: Netflix Looking to Partner with Cable Companies."

[20] Letter to Shareholders, January 25, 2012, p. 6; posted in the investor relations section at www.netflix.com, accessed March 28, 2012.

# Equal Exchange: Trading Fairly and Making a Profit

**Joanna Kaminski**
Manhattan College

**Samantha Marchese**
Manhattan College

**Cara Vullo**
Manhattan College

It was the start of the workweek on a rainy day in Spring 2011. Rink Dickinson glanced at his watch. He abruptly cleared the paperwork off his desk, got up from his chair, and made his way out of his office. He nearly walked into Rob Everts who was also headed toward the conference room. After 25 years in business, 10 of which were spent as the only fair trade company in the coffee industry, Equal Exchange's tremendous success seemed to have come to a screeching halt. That was why Dickinson and Everts, co-executive directors of the fair trade co-operative, were on their way to hold yet another meeting with a few of the co-operative's veteran worker-owners. Hopefully, this would be one of the last meetings before a final decision was made about what Equal Exchange (EE) would do next.

In the conference room, Rob Everts addressed five EE veteran worker-owners as he began the meeting with a recap of the co-operative's current situation:

> If we exclude the impact of price increases, for a second year in a row, revenues have grown only 2 percent. This is difficult to imagine compared to the double-digit growth we have been familiar with for the previous 15 years.

Unfortunately, the recent recession had caused business to take a turn for the worst. EE, however, was not alone. Many companies around the world suffered from setbacks that were far worse than EE's slowdown in revenue growth. The economy tanked and customers cut back significantly. At the same time, competition had skyrocketed, leaving more and more options for consumers to choose from. In fact, the fair trade movement had gotten such a tremendous response that EE now competed with over 300 other coffee roasters who had jumped into the fair trade niche.

Rob explained one of the difficulties EE experienced because of the increased competition:

> Over the past few years, consumers have begun to show a strong desire to purchase products from local businesses.

This was a new demand that EE, the Massachusetts-based co-operative, could not satisfy in all communities around the country. It required a local presence in too many regions in all 50 states. The "buy local" ethic had increased competition from local roasters, as consumers began to prefer supporting local firms rather than those shipping their goods in from other states or regions.

Rink Dickinson spoke up about another issue:

> Now, more than ever, there is a major push by companies to offer a wide variety of green, organic, and wholesome food products. There are so many new initiatives developing, it may be possible that fair trade products will not stand out so much anymore. Consumers, for example, may not be able to tell the difference between coffee that is labeled, 'Fair Trade Certified,' and coffee that is labeled, 'Rainforest Alliance Certified.'

The group talked for a while longer. The co-executive directors and veteran worker-owners had just two more weeks until they would present their ideas for the co-operative's future. What would EE do next?

Written under the supervision of Dr. Janet Rovenpor, Manhattan College with support from a School of Business Louis F. Capalbo research grant.

We wish to thank Rodney North, the Answer Man, Rob Everts, Co-Executive Director, and Daniel Fireside, Capital Coordinator, for allowing us to interview them during an on-site visit.

# EQUAL EXCHANGE'S HISTORY

Three entrepreneurs—Rink Dickinson, Jonathan Rosenthal, and Michael Rozyne—founded EE on May 1, 1986. The men had met while working together at the New England Food Co-operative Organization (NEFCO), a natural food distributor, which bought fruits and vegetables from local farmers at above-market prices and sold them to grocers and groups of consumers interested in fresh, regionally grown produce.[1] The entrepreneurs wanted to foster similar business relationships with farmers outside the U.S. Their vision was to change the way food was grown, bought, and sold around the world.[2]

With $100,000 in startup funds and a 2,000-square-foot room in Boston's South End, EE started to purchase coffee beans from small-scale farmers at above-market prices in Latin America.[3] Initially, EE relied on other roasters and packers to prepare the premium coffee beans. It sold to natural food grocers, gourmet shops, restaurants, and nonprofit organizations. The company's founders wanted to help farmers get a better, more stable price and, at the same time, take advantage of the growing consumer demand for higher-quality "specialty" coffee.

In its first year of operation, EE ran into a problem. The U.S. government imposed an embargo on all products, including coffee, which were being imported from Nicaragua. The Reagan administration wanted to weaken the Nicaraguan economy and pressure the socialist Sandinista government to implement reforms and sever its ties with the Soviet Union. EE found a loophole in these trade policies by partnering with a Dutch trade organization so that the Nicaraguan beans could be shipped to Amsterdam, roasted there, and then be legally imported to the U.S. as a "Product of The Netherlands." The Nicaraguan coffee was called, "Café Nica."

In 1990, EE adopted a worker-owned co-operative structure. This legal structure ensured that the worker-owners, as a body, would always be the ultimate decision-makers in the organization. After working at EE for a year, an employee purchased one share of Class A voting stock and became a "worker-owner." He or she could run for the board of directors, vote on by-laws changes and other strategic decisions, and like more conventional owners share in the profits and losses. As Dickinson explained, "We were trying to take the best elements of a non-profit, a co-op, and even a for-profit and combine them. We felt that governance should be with the folks that did the work."[4]

Equal Exchange expanded rapidly. In five years, it reached a mark of $1 million in annual sales. In the late 1980s, it moved to Stoughton, a suburb of Boston. To accommodate continued growth in 1995, EE moved again, from Stoughton to Canton, Massachusetts, and opened a new office in Madison, Wisconsin. In 1998, another office and warehouse was opened in Hood River, Oregon, to better serve the critical West Coast customer base. As sales continued to increase and as new facilities were opened, EE also expanded its product offerings. In 1998, the co-op introduced a new line of fair trade teas.

In 1999, the leadership of the company shifted. Jonathan Rosenthal had been asked to resign over an apparent disagreement about EE's future direction.[5] Michael Rozyne left to launch a new fair trade enterprise, Red Tomato. The employee-led board of directors named Rink Dickinson as a co-executive director of EE. It also promoted Rob Everts, organizing manager and alumnus of the United Farm Workers in California, to become the other co-executive director (a role comparable to a CEO).

EE continued to succeed in the 2000s. In 2001, it reached another annual sales milestone by breaking the $10 million mark. The total number of worker-owners also hit a new record of 33. In 2002, EE introduced the first fair trade–certified hot cocoa mix in the U.S. In fiscal year 2005, sales grew from $16.5 million to $20.7 million and net income (before taxes) was $991,255.[6] It had become the largest employee-owned coffee roaster in the world.

2006 was the 20th anniversary of EE. It had imported a total of 26 million pounds of coffee into the U.S.[7] and sold products sourced from 38 different co-operatives in 20 countries. It had 70 worker-owners and had raised capital on favorable terms from 400 investors.[8] Also in 2006, EE became a minority investor, along with Red Tomato and AgroFair, in a fair trade banana company, known as Oké USA and led by EE co-founder, Jonathan Rosenthal.

In fiscal year 2007, annual sales increased by almost $6 million. EE ran a program called, "Faces of fair trade: Uniting the Global and Local." The organization brought together farmers from around the world to meet during fair trade month.[9] Continuing

## EXHIBIT 1    The Equal Exchange History Timeline

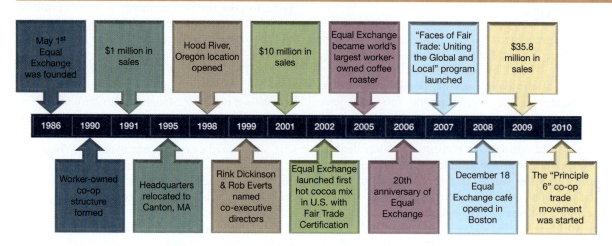

*Source:* Equal Exchange's Annual Reports.

a long EE tradition of "going to origin," tea product manager, Deepauk Khandelwal, and producer relations coordinator, Phyllis Robinson, made a trip to Sri Lanka in 2007 to visit tea-trading partners. Loose-leaf teas were added to the product offerings of EE and the tea program grew 15 percent in just one year.[10]

In 2008, EE stepped up its efforts to diversify. It increased its investment in Oké USA by acquiring a majority stake. As part of its 2008–2011 Strategic Plan, EE opened a café in Boston. This café was EE's second and followed the success of an earlier, smaller café in Seattle. Despite the worldwide economic recession, EE remained profitable in fiscal years 2008 and 2009. By the end of 2009, EE had more than 90 worker-owners with 10 more first-year staff being readied for ownership status.

In 2010, EE launched a new program called, "Principle Six." It involved six U.S. food co-ops who worked with EE to build a food system that shifted power to small, local farmers and food purveyors, and to co-operatively structured or non-profit food companies.[11] The purpose of this program was to educate consumers about the people and the organizations behind the food they ate and to persuade them of the benefits of a food economy that was not dominated by a small number of large corporations. The six co-ops— Seward Community Co-op, Bloomingfoods Co-op, Brattleboro Food Co-op, The Merc Co-op, Davis Food Co-op, and Willy Street Grocery Co-op—utilized online tools, newsletter articles, and point-of-sale materials to introduce the program to their shoppers.

Throughout the 25 years of EE's existence, worker-owners demonstrated an entrepreneurial spirit, encouraged inspired change and developed expertise in the fair trade food and beverage industry. A handful of key managers played a tremendous role in the company's success and influenced EE's business model. They were important building blocks to EE's development. Exhibit 1 lists key events and milestones for EE that occurred between 1986 and 2010.

## BIOGRAPHIES OF KEY MANAGERS

Rink Dickinson was one of the three original founders of EE. He had developed a compassion for the plight of the common man while growing up in the inner city of Detroit and the "Springsteen" area of New Jersey. He acquired a love for organic food during his time working with farmers and food co-operatives across New England in the 1980s. After holding various titles, such as co-founder, board chair, and director of sales, he was named EE's co-executive director, along with Rob Everts, in 1999.

Jonathan Rosenthal was also a co-founder of EE. He grew up in Baltimore, Maryland, and was surrounded by racism from a young age. He vowed to promote social justice and fight inequality.[12] It was while working at NEFCO that Rosenthal met Dickinson and Rozyne. Rosenthal left EE and founded Oké USA, the first fair trade tropical fruit company in the

U.S. He turned management of the business over to EE in 2008. Rosenthal became a consultant at Just Works where he provided services in strategic planning and visioning, leadership and board planning, retreat and meeting facilitation, and especially fair trade project design and implementation.[13]

Michael Rozyne, the third co-founder of EE, attended Bowdoin College in Maine. His first exposure to fair trade occurred when he was a foreign exchange student in Bombay, India, in 1974.[14] In the late 1970s, Rozyne was the marketing manager for Estabrook Farm in Maine. From 1981 to 1985, Rozyne was a head buyer and marketing manager for NEFCO. In 1986, he became marketing director at EE. In 1995, Rozyne took a sabbatical from EE. He wanted to explore ways to promote fair trade among local farmers in the northeastern U.S. In 1996, he founded a non-profit organization, Red Tomato, which helped small family farms that grew fresh fruits and vegetables to sell to local New England supermarkets accustomed to sourcing their produce from Florida and California.[15]

Everts, who was not one of the original founders, joined EE in 1997. He had been a worker advocate for his entire career. Everts grew up in Mill Valley, California. In the mid-1970s, he joined Cesar Chavez and the United Farm Workers union. Then, in 1987, he teamed up with Neighbor-to-Neighbor, a social justice organization. In 1992, he led a boycott of Folgers, a coffee brand owned by Procter & Gamble. The group felt that Procter & Gamble's purchases of coffee beans from El Salvador helped support a repressive government. Following the boycott's success, Everts worked with a union of hotel workers in Boston, and then moved to Costa Rica to work as a consultant for UNICEF and other non-government organizations. Two years after joining EE, in 1999, Everts became a co-executive director along with Rink Dickinson.[16]

# THREE SOLUTIONS TO THREE PROBLEMS

EE's mission, as articulated in its 2009 Annual Report, was: "To build long-term trade partnerships that are economically just and environmentally sound, to foster mutually beneficial relationships between farmers and consumers and to demonstrate, through our success, the contribution of worker co-operatives and fair trade to a more equitable, democratic and sustainable world." Rodney North, EE's information officer (or "Answer Man"),[17] noted that its founders created the mission to confront three problems, which they believed EE could address.

## First Problem: The Exploitation of Farmers

The first problem concerned poor farmers living in developing nations who were typically offered low prices for their coffee, tea, and cocoa. The farmers were often illiterate, did not own a truck, and had no way of finding out what the prices for their agricultural products were on the world's commodities exchanges. They had no choice but to sell to brokers who could arrange for the transportation and processing of their goods.[18] The brokers often offered pre-harvest loans to farmers, but in return, the farmers were required to sell their crops to them at very low prices. The brokers were often called "coyotes," because they exploited their greater advantages and profited unfairly from these transactions.[19] They were motivated to buy low and sell high, no matter what the cost to farmers.

In contrast, EE wanted farmers to be paid more, not less. So, it sought out fair trade–registered co-operatives that enabled small-scale farmers to pool their resources, increase their power in the marketplace and share the costs of upgrading their operations. These farmers, and their co-op managers, were trained in how to acquire information on market trends and in how to cultivate high-quality crops.[20] EE paid a guaranteed stable minimum price directly to democratically run farmer co-operatives and paid even more per pound for coffee grown with sustainable methods. EE's customers were willing to pay higher prices for flavorful fair trade coffee.

Fair Trade Labeling Organization (FLO) International set the minimum prices for non-organic and organic fair trade Arabica coffee. Between 1994 and 2004, the minimum price was $1.26 per pound for non-organic coffee beans and $1.41 per pound for certified organic coffee beans.[21] In 2010, the minimum price was raised to $1.40 per pound and $1.70 per pound, respectively. Poor rainfall and underinvestment in coffee plots had caused lower than expected coffee harvests. This created increased competition for high-quality coffee beans.[22]

FLO also raised the fair trade social premium, from 10 cents per pound to 20 cents per pound.[23] Farmers could decide how to invest the social premium in their local communities. It could go toward building roads, health clinics, or schools. As one farmer in El Salvador put it, "We used to live in homes made of corn husks. Now we have better work, better schools, homes of adobe, and a great brotherhood of decision-makers."[24]

Fair Trade companies, like EE, always paid farmers the minimum price per pound for coffee, along with the social premium, even when coffee prices in the world's commodities exchanges dropped below the fair trade minimum price. Historically, this occurred several times. In October 2001, for example, market prices fell to a 30-year low of 45 cents per pound due to an oversupply of coffee. Market prices fell again in fall 2008 when the global financial crisis began. When coffee prices in the commodities exchanges rose above the fair trade minimum price, farmers received the higher price plus the additional social premium. A comparison of fair trade and New York coffee prices per pound between October 1989 and October 2011 is presented in Exhibit 2.

EE worked with financial institutions to give farmers pre-harvest loans with affordable 8 to 9 percent short-term interest rates. Brokers typically offered loans at much higher rates of 25 percent.[25] EE also guaranteed a quarter of each pre-harvest loan. It thus shared the risks associated with misfortunes, such as hurricanes, that could destroy a co-operative's crops. EE bought the coffee beans once a year, as soon as they were harvested (even though this tied up its capital in inventory). Other companies bought the beans much later, only when they really needed them. In contrast, EE wanted to purchase the beans earlier so as to relieve the farmer co-ops of the inventory carrying costs. Farmers saw the benefits in selling their coffee beans to EE. As

## EXHIBIT 2   Comparison of Fair Trade and New York Prices in the Arabica Coffee Market, October 1989–October 2011

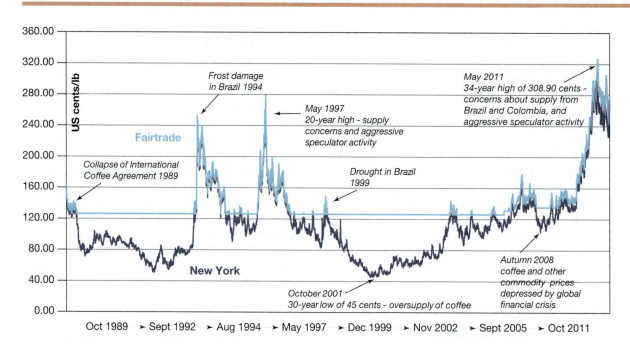

NB Fairtrade price = Fairtrade Minimum Price* of 140 cents/lb + 20 cents/lb Fairtrade Premium.**
When the New York price is 140 cents or above, the Fairtrade Price = New York price + 20 cents.
*Fairtrade Minimum Price was increased on 1 June 2008 & 1 April 2011. **Fairtrade Premium was increased on 1 June 2007 & 1 April 2011.
The New York price is the daily settlement price of the 2nd position Coffee C Futures contract at ICE Futures U.S.
©Fairtrade Foundation

Source: Fairtrade Foundation; this graph was retrieved November 11, 2001 at www.fairtrade.org.uk.

Todd Caspersen, the company's purchasing director, asserted, "The direct relationships with the actual producers, combined with our financing support, provide us with more consistent quality and a stable supply base."[26]

## Second Problem: Unsatisfactory Working Conditions in the U.S.

According to Rodney North, the founders of EE identified a second problem. This related to unsatisfactory working conditions in the U.S. Many employees did not like their jobs, worked long hours, and complained about a lack of recognition from their superiors. Families needed to have two breadwinners in order to maintain a decent quality of life, but this left parents scrambling to find childcare. Morale was low and employees, even those who held managerial level positions, complained that they were not engaged in meaningful work. Employees had little job security and faced extensive layoffs during times of industry consolidation and economic recession.

This view was consistent with the results of a 2010 poll by the Conference Board of 5,000 U.S. households, which found that job satisfaction was at its lowest level in two decades.[27] A forum, monitored by Professor James Heskett at the Harvard Business School, asked its readers to respond to the survey results.[28] Charles Wegrzyn, a student, suggested that employee job satisfaction had plunged because of "incredible pressure from the economic side," "incredible instability," and a resulting "dog-eat-dog attitude."[29] Other comments were equally insightful. Akhil Aggarwal, an IT and Telecom consultant, mentioned a "lack of personalized focus on employees and more on business and profitability."[30] John Alexander from Interpro Inc. said, "When workers see senior management face no responsibility for poor performance and continue to get highly paid, it's no wonder there is widespread dissatisfaction."[31]

In an interview, Rodney North gave EE's perspective, saying that "many, maybe most, workplaces are pretty feudal in character. Workers are treated more like furniture or equipment than human beings. In fact, sometimes equipment is treated better. Workers have no right to speak up, to information, to elect their leaders, and so on."[32] EE wanted to cultivate excellent working relationships with its employees. Its managers believed that a democratic work environment in which employees shared responsibility for decision making would lead to higher levels of job satisfaction, morale, and productivity. It made sure that the pay gap between the highest-paid manager and the lowest-paid employee was reasonable. In its fourth year, 1990, EE became a 100 percent worker-owned co-operative.

## Third Problem: Lack of Consumer Awareness

The third and final problem was that the typical consumer was unaware of the realities of the farmers who grew their food. Many consumers were not familiar with the backstory behind their products. Food marketing was focused on price, brand image, and quality. These were the attributes that consumers cared about the most. Managers at EE realized that there was a need to educate consumers on unfair trade practices and empower them to make more informed product choices. By creating a more knowledgeable consumer, one consumer at a time, EE would be able to raise general public awareness of the plight of low-income farmers and of the fair trade movement.

EE sought to reconnect consumers with the farmers who grew their food. When consumers saw a brand-name product in the supermarket, EE wanted them to realize that there was often a person toiling away for little pay behind it. By raising such awareness, the company hoped to direct consumers towards products for which farmers got paid higher prices so they could better support their ways of life.

EE managed quality control of its product lines ensuring that its customers received fine products at affordable prices. Imported coffee beans, for example, were carefully screened for color, shape, size and taste; 10 to 15 percent of the coffee beans sampled in the laboratory were rejected.[33] EE sold its products under a fair trade label that assured consumers that its coffee producers were treated well and followed sustainable farming practices.

The three solutions to these problems, according to North, were fair trade, worker co-operatives, and consumer education. Through fair trade, poor farmers were able to reap more of the benefits of their hard work. A worker-owned co-operative structure created a leveled field where workers could become owners and share in decision-making. The company's employees were all advocates, as were many of EE's fans. They worked passionately to spread EE's mission, to make big changes in the world.

# EQUAL EXCHANGE'S WORKER CO-OPERATIVE MODEL

Part of EE's mission was to demonstrate how a worker co-operative could contribute to a "more equitable, democratic and sustainable world." The U.S. Federation of Worker Cooperatives defined a worker co-operative as "a business entity that is owned and controlled by the people who work in it."[34] Among some business entities organized as worker co-operatives were (a) the Mondragon co-operatives, a network of 256 enterprises in Spain's Basque region, with 84,000 worker-owners and over $19 billion in annual revenue, (b) Rainbow Grocery, a successful San Francisco natural foods supermarket founded in 1975 and with 200 worker-owners, and (c) Union Cab, a Madison, Wisconsin, taxi company with over 200 members and a fleet of 65 vehicles.

EE believed strongly in creating better, healthier relationships with the Earth, with farmers, its workers, and with the consumer. Worker-owners enjoyed many rights and responsibilities and democratically controlled the workplace. The firm's governance structure was based on four core rights:[35]

- The right to vote (one vote per employee, not per share)
- The right to serve as leader (e.g., as a director on the board)
- The right to information (e.g., access to financial information and meeting minutes)
- The right to speak one's mind

At EE, a co-executive director, a roaster, a packer, and a customer service representative were equal, with one share and one vote per person. They had the right to speak their minds on key issues and participate in decision-making. Worker-owners, for example, determined whether or not to invest the millions necessary for coffee roasting equipment. They went on real estate scouting trips and decided where to locate the new headquarters.[36] Based on their feedback, EE relocated in 2004 to West Bridgewater, Massachusetts, the fourth home in its history.

Worker-owners elected members of the board of directors. They filled six of the nine board positions. The remaining three positions were reserved for outside directors.[37] The board of directors was responsible for hiring and supervising management and for approving budgets and personnel policies. The two top managers together constituted the Office of Executive Directors (OED). They reported to, but did not sit on, the board. One of the many tools EE used to maintain democracy in its company was the governance matrix.[38] This matrix was used daily to determine what decisions needed to be made and which worker-owners would play a deciding role. All worker-owners in the company voted upon major strategic decisions.

EE was a for-profit business but instead of top-level managers reaping all the financial gains, 40 percent of the company's profits (after taxes and dividends to outside shareholders) were distributed in equal shares to all worker-owners.[39] The company maintained a top-to-bottom pay ratio of 4-1. According to a report by United For a Fair Economy, the CEO pay ratio to average worker's pay was 344-to-1 in 2008.[40]

Turnover at EE was less than 10 percent a year.[41] In its most recent *Guide to HR Benchmarks 2010*, IOMA reported that separations as a percentage of total number of employees overall was 16.2 percent in the U.S.; two years earlier, it was 24.1 percent.[42] Mr. Haid, an HR expert from Right Management, calculated that turnover typically costs a company approximately half of the position's annual salary to recruit a new person for that job.[43]

Becoming a part of the company was not easy. Applying for a position with EE involved more than one interview and other requirements, such as an application essay. A newly appointed employee went through a yearlong probationary period in which he or she attended training sessions to learn about the company and its practices and culture. When this period was over, the existing worker-owners voted to approve or reject the employee's petition to join the co-op. If accepted, the employee would then purchase his or her one share of company stock and voting rights.[44] Thus, new hires were motivated to work hard and perform well so they could join a unique organization that had developed an advanced governance system based on democratic principles.

EE was one of the founding members of the U.S. Federation of Worker Cooperatives. A representative delivered a presentation at every conference. The Federation's members shared best practices and advanced worker-owned, worker-managed, and worker-governed workplaces through cooperative education, advocacy, and development.

# EQUAL EXCHANGE'S MARKETING STRATEGIES

EE wanted to change traditional purchasing habits and make consumers more aware of where products came from and who was responsible for making them. At the same time, it wanted to encourage consumers to buy more Fair trade products. To get its message out, EE developed advertisements, implemented public education campaigns, partnered with religious organizations, and created a school fundraising program. EE also offered a wide variety of fair trade products.

## Advertising

EE was effective in creating messages about the origins of products and where consumer dollars went. Here are some examples:

**Packaging and Labels**   EE's logo and labels suggested that consumers could have a great cup of coffee or bar of chocolate while feeling good about themselves. The wrapper on its Organic Very Dark Chocolate featured a man in South America picking cocoa beans from a tree. The words "from small farmers with love" appeared.

**Website**    Through EE's website, consumers were able to connect to the farmers who grew the products they bought. There was a feature on the website that enabled a consumer to enter the "best by" date on a product they purchased to find out about the farmers who grew it, where it came from, and to see people who loved and cared about what they do.

**Public Awareness**    EE partnered with fair trade advocacy organizations, such as Global Exchange, to create a nationwide public education campaign, "Reverse Trick-or-Treating." The campaign was intended to make the public aware of child slavery on cocoa farms in such countries as the Ivory Coast. It also wanted to let people know about poverty in cocoa growing countries and the environmental damage that could result from unsustainable cocoa farming practices.[45] When children went door to door on Halloween, the children gave the members of each household a card with a mini fair trade organic chocolate bar attached. The information card is shown in Exhibit 3.

**EXHIBIT 3**    Information Card for "Reverse Trick-or-Treating"

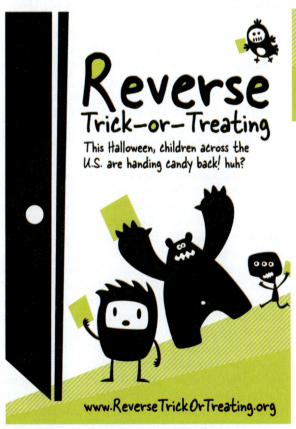

*Source:* http://envirothink.wordpress.com/2011/10/10/a-unique-halloween-event—reverse-trick-or-treating/.

## Interfaith Program

In 1996, EE partnered with Lutheran World Relief to create something that later became known as the Interfaith Program. Together, they raised relief funds for farmers in Nicaragua who were hit hard by Hurricane Mitch in 1998. The program offered wholesale prices on coffee, tea, and cocoa to religious organizations, who could then serve the beverages after worship and community events. EE created a new coffee, Fellowship Blend, specifically prepared for the large percolators commonly used in the facilities of religious organizations. By the seventh year of the program, over 10,000 congregations from 10 denominations in the U.S. were placing orders. By 2010, the Interfaith Program contributed to 20 percent of the co-operative's annual sales.[46] Partnerships like these helped EE generate revenues, create goodwill within communities, determine new product lines and market trends, and create awareness among consumers about fair trade products.[47]

## Fundraising

EE's Fundraising Program enabled teachers and parents to replace conventional fundraising that peddled magazine subscriptions or generic chocolate with one built around EE's organic, fair trade products. To help promote this new program, trips were arranged for select parents and school leaders to visit EE's cocoa partners in the Dominican Republic to see firsthand every step of the harvesting and processing of cacao pods. The program enabled schools to sell EE's products in their local communities and keep 40 percent of the revenues. To complement the fundraiser, EE also developed a 16-unit fair trade curriculum for schools and a Pen Pal Exchange to connect children in the U.S. with the children of cacao farmers abroad.

## Product Variety

Coffee was EE's primary product and the engine behind its success. In 2010, its line consisted of regular, decaffeinated, espresso, organic, and flavored organic coffees that were available in bulk and packaged form. There were 80 different choices and five different package sizes from 1.5 oz to 5 lbs. Its regular 12-oz bag of coffee was priced at around $9.00–$9.75 (suggested retail price).[48] Latest available figures showed that EE imported approximately 6 million pounds of coffee in 2009.[49]

Besides coffee, EE also purchased fairly traded tea, cocoa, and other foods from 15 small farmer co-ops in nine countries. Its line of flavored teabags was priced at $4.50/box of 20 tea bags.[50] EE sold hot cocoa mix, drinking chocolate, baking cocoa powder, and its popular chocolate bars across the U.S. In 2006, 979,882 chocolate bars were sold, a 57 percent increase from the year prior.[51] In 2007, EE extended its product line by introducing nuts and berries from U.S. farmers, initiating what would be called, "domestic fair trade." The "domestic" line featured 5-oz packages of Organic Tamari Roasted Almonds, Roasted Salted Pecans, and Organic Dried Sweetened Cranberries. A year later, bananas were introduced to EE's product portfolio.

EE had a vast mixture of products to offer to its consumers, which ranged in price. The products were available in cafés, co-operatives, supermarkets, and natural food stores throughout the U.S. They were also available for purchase online through its "Retail Web Store."[52] Creating awareness and using well-devised marketing campaigns to distribute EE's products proved to be successful strategies. Other measures of the company's achievements were indicated by each year's financial performance. The geographic distribution of EE's sales in the United States in 2010 is shown in Exhibit 4.

## EQUAL EXCHANGE'S FINANCIAL PERFORMANCE

Since importing its first coffee container in 1986, EE had become the leading fair trade brand of food and beverages in the U.S.[53] This helped the co-operative achieve a trend of double-digit revenue growth. However, the recession that struck the U.S. changed the outlook for business. The financial data for the fiscal years of 2006 through 2010 demonstrated EE's growth and showed whether the co-operative was able to weather the economic downturn.

Exhibit 5 demonstrates EE's growth of sales from fiscal year 2006 to fiscal year 2010. In 2006, success in many areas defined much of EE's 14 percent increase in revenues, which translated into an additional $2.86 million in annual sales. In particular, sales were exceptionally strong in the West Coast region. Another key contributor to sales was EE's chocolate products, which were a hit in 2006 because the quality chocolate market was seeing growing demand, or a "renaissance," as EE called it, similar to what occurred with specialty coffee 20 years prior. While this was occurring, EE simultaneously expanded its chocolate line to products such as organic dark chocolate, organic mint chocolate, and organic chocolate syrup. This expansion allowed the company to ride the growing demand for quality chocolate.[54] EE also introduced three new tea bagged products, which helped increase tea sales 35 percent.[55]

## EXHIBIT 4 Equal Exchange's U.S. Sales by State, 2010

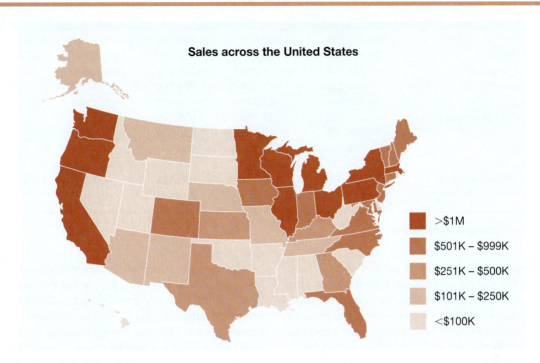

Sales across the United States

- >$1M
- $501K – $999K
- $251K – $500K
- $101K – $250K
- <$100K

*Source:* Equal Exchange's 2010 Annual Report.

## EXHIBIT 5 Equal Exchange Sales Growth

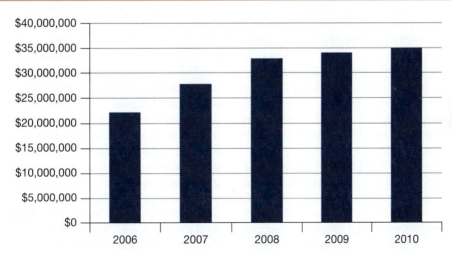

*Source:* Equal Exchange's annual reports.

The fiscal year of 2007 ended with revenue growth of almost $6 million, a 24 percent increase from 2006.[56] In that year, EE improved its sales efforts by opening a new office in Minnesota, a key market. Roasting capacity was tripled. Altogether, these moves helped grow revenues another $5.7 million.[57] Although this provided another year of steady revenue growth, as displayed in Exhibit 5, the income statement showed one variation from the other years of focus. In fiscal year 2007, EE was presented with an increased Costs of Goods

## EXHIBIT 6    Equal Exchange's Income Statement, 2006–2010

| | 2010 | 2009 | 2008 | 2007 | 2006 |
|---|---|---|---|---|---|
| Sales | $36,525,856 | $35,832,510 | $34,440,241 | $29,370,480 | $23,639,456 |
| Cost of sales | 23,659,316 | 23,075,260 | 22,446,593 | 18,866,940 | 14,164,991 |
| Operating expense | 11,234,758 | 10,771,023 | 9,535,120 | 8,646,241 | 7,946,163 |
| Other expense | 308,830 | 619,094 | 990,388 | 759,068 | 575,880 |
| Total cost | 35,202,904 | 34,465,377 | 32,972,101 | 28,272,249 | 22,687,034 |
| Net income before taxes | 1,322,952 | 1,367,133 | 1,468,140 | 1,098,231 | 952,422 |
| Taxes | 578,000 | 593,000 | 600,000 | 435,000 | 415,000 |
| Net income | $    744,952 | $    744,133 | $    868,140 | $    663,231 | $    537,422 |
| Shareholder dividends | $    324,721 | $    253,599 | $    282,959 | $    213,888 | $    173,147 |
| Annual retained earnings (reinvested in the business) | $    420,231 | $    520,534 | $    585,181 | $    449,343 | $    364,275 |

*Source:* Equal Exchange's annual reports.

Sold, amounting to roughly 64 percent of total sales. However, this did not come without good reason. That year, EE paid small farmers a higher price than usual. Since this was something the co-operative had planned and the smaller margins that resulted were expected, EE was able to plan for, and successfully reduce, operating expenses by 2.2 percent as a percentage of sales (see the data in Exhibit 6). This decrease let the company experience profitability in 2007 that was steady with the company's goals. The year ended with $29.4 million in revenue and a net income of $663,231.[58]

The next fiscal year, 2008, began the economic downturn that altered the dynamic of business. Nonetheless, EE's revenues grew by 17 percent to $34.4 million. The continued growth came in different forms. Among all of EE's products, the chocolate sector experienced the most significant growth: 39 percent.[59] EE also expressed satisfaction with the growth in the Interfaith Program, natural food co-ops, grocery stores, and the company's private label.[60] Another contributing factor was a result of EE's celebration of Fair Trade Month in October. The co-operative created display units for grocery stores that featured all EE products in one central location. These were displayed in 62 stores. EE experienced sales growth throughout the nation because of this and other clever sales strategies.[61] However, as the economic outlook remained grim, EE was tremendously vulnerable to the recession that seemed to be pulling so many companies under. How did EE fare in those troubling times?

In 2009, the co-operative benefited from price increases that had been employed midway through 2008. Revenues grew 4 percent to $35.8 million.[62] This growth was not as large as that of previous years, and it became clear that double-digit revenue growth might have come to an end. An effect of the downturn can be seen in EE's balance sheet (shown in Exhibit 7). An inventory reduction was present in 2009 compared to previous years. This was mostly because, for the first time ever, EE did not purchase nearly as much green coffee as in the past. However, because of the narrow 4 percent increase in revenue, an acceptable level of profitability was achieved, a net income $774,133.[63] The recession did not burden the co-operative entirely. In 2009, it raised over $2 million in preferred stock, the highest ever achieved in EE history. Not only was this an improvement to the balance sheet, but it also allowed EE to begin 2010 in a strong cash position.[64]

For any fair trade company trying to make a difference in the lives of farmers, 2010 was a difficult year as coffee and chocolate prices continued to rise. EE was faced with a difficult challenge of helping farmers during this time, providing customers with stable prices, and maintaining a profit margin consistent with the co-operative's goals. Sales totaled $36,525,856. This growth of roughly 2 percent was relatively flat for the second year in a row. The growth experienced was due in part to the notable increases in EE's direct sales to food co-operatives. This is something the co-operative did to avoid the use of distributors.[65]

# INVESTING IN EQUAL EXCHANGE

EE's promise to provide consumers with reasonably priced, good quality food, all while fairly paying the farmers who produced the goods was quite unlike

# EXHIBIT 7   Equal Exchange's Balance Sheet, 2006–2010

|  | 2010 | 2009 | 2008 | 2007 | 2006 |
|---|---|---|---|---|---|
| **Current Assets** | | | | | |
| Cash | $ 657,124 | $ 376,667 | $ 212,717 | $ 381,497 | $ 480,150 |
| Accounts receivable | 2,304,912 | 2,185,768 | 2,227,843 | 1,973,098 | 1,569,117 |
| Notes receivable | 267,538 | 324,996 | 88,628 | 34,174 | 10,500 |
| Inventories | 8,224,913 | 8,293,729 | 10,839,429 | 8,193,630 | 6,983,311 |
| Prepaid expenses and other current assets | 447,077 | 415,139 | 928,227 | 766,611 | 282,652 |
| Prepaid income taxes | — | — | — | — | 98,886 |
| Deferred income tax asset | 151,000 | 115,000 | 145,000 | 77,000 | 75,000 |
| Total Current Assets | 12,052,564 | 11,711,299 | 14,441,844 | 11,426,010 | 9,499,616 |
| Property, plant, and equipment, net | 6,653,683 | 7,017,564 | 7,473,243 | 7,311,901 | 6,497,284 |
| Other Assets | 649,031 | 416,594 | 460,777 | 482,308 | 292,387 |
| Total Assets | 19,355,278 | 19,145,457 | 22,375,864 | 19,220,219 | 16,289,287 |
| **Current Liabilities** | | | | | |
| Notes Payable – Lines of Credit | 567,952 | 624,928 | 5,164,438 | 4,022,153 | 3,006,846 |
| Current portion of capital lease obligations | | 432,124 | 447,679 | 420,470 | 250,328 |
| Current portion of long-term debt | 121,793 | 550,639 | 1,639,829 | 319,677 | 200,001 |
| Accounts payable and accrued expenses | 1,385,692 | 1,089,703 | 940,158 | 1,079,240 | 1,219,767 |
| Patronage rebates payable | 147,000 | 421,875 | 255,255 | 418,205 | 228,036 |
| Total Current Liabilities | 2,222,437 | 3,119,269 | 9,216,885 | 6,919,808 | 5,566,818 |
| **Long-Term Liabilities** | | | | | |
| Capital lease obligations, net of current portion | — | 693,092 | 1,125,216 | 1,572,897 | 866,058 |
| Long-term debt, net of current portion | 3,228,784 | 3,190,008 | 2,875,097 | 3,259,969 | 3,238,671 |
| Deferred income taxes | 900,000 | 770,000 | 637,000 | 404,000 | 292,000 |
| Total Long-Term Liabilties | 4,128,784 | 4,653,100 | 4,637,313 | 5,236,866 | 4,386,729 |
| Total Liabilities | 6,351,221 | 7,772,369 | 13,854,198 | 12,156,674 | 9,963,547 |
| **Stockholders' Equity** | | | | | |
| Preferred stock | 9,156,382 | 7,978.429 | 5,680,390 | 4,829,986 | 4,564,605 |
| Common stock | 313,343 | 282,683 | 260,903 | 232,555 | 222,165 |
| Less: Common stock subscriptions receivable | (60,682) | (62,807) | (73,876) | (68,064) | (80,755) |
| Retained earnings | 3,595,014 | 3,174,783 | 2,654,249 | 2,069,068 | 1,619,725 |
| Total Stockholders' Equity | 13,004,057 | 11,373,088 | 8,521,666 | 7,063,545 | 6,325,740 |
| Total Liabilities & Stockholders' Equity | $19,355,278 | $19,145,457 | $22,375,864 | $19,220,219 | $16,289,287 |

*Source:* Equal Exchange's annual reports.

most other companies. Where did EE find the capital and financing to pursue this deep commitment to social justice? This is where the fair trade co-operative's unique business model was brought into play.

As a for-profit worker co-operative, EE had shareholders that were both inside and outside of the company. This helped EE raise capital for its activities in numerous ways. A major source of financing was preferred stock offerings of Class B shares to outside investors. These shares were offered at a fixed price of $27.50. Shareholders were obligated to commit to a five-year holding period and understood that their investment granted them no voting rights. The shares had a targeted dividend rate of 5 percent of the stock's face value; however, that rate sometimes varied depending upon the company's annual performance.[66]

This type of stock could have only been bought from and sold to EE. For that reason, and because the stock was sold at a fixed price, capital gains could not be achieved with EE's stock. Instead, shareholders became long-term investors who were satisfied with yearly gains of 5 percent or so, plus the knowledge that their investments were making a substantial social impact.

An additional, smaller flow of capital came in the form of Class A shares of common stock, also known as membership shares. These shares were only sold to EE employees after they had worked at the co-operative for one year. Employees were only allowed to buy one share each, which granted them one vote. This vote was used on major company issues or to elect the company's board of directors. These shares had an original selling price of $2,000, adjusted annually for inflation. The share price as of 2010 was $3,250. Dividends were not paid on these shares. Instead, Class A shares entitled workers to a share of any profits or losses.

Purchasing stock was not the only option given to those interested in supporting EE and fair trade. EE teamed up with Eastern Bank and provided an EE Certificate of Deposit (CD), which was an alternative to a conventional CD. The minimum purchase for an EE CD was $500 and the term was three years. All of the money that was collected from EE CDs was pooled and made available to the co-operative as a line of credit with a lower rate of interest than the co-operative would otherwise find. Like a conventional CD, consumers deposited their money, earned the typical rate, and collected their money back with interest three years later. However, these CDs also greatly differed from conventional CDs. Instead of the money accumulating into a general fund that could be used for any purpose, EE used the money in the loan to fund its growth in fair trade. The typical EE CD investment was enough for EE to buy the harvest of one more coffee-farming family. This allowed people to use their money to help EE further pursue its commitment to social justice.[67] However, there was more risk involved than a typical CD, which was insured by the FDIC. With the EE CD, a depositor would still be protected if Eastern Bank failed, but not if EE was unable to repay its line of credit. This made it theoretically possible for a depositor to lose money.[68] EE had never defaulted on a loan.[69]

Another significant means to equity was retained earnings. Every year in which EE was profitable, 7 percent of its net income was donated to non-profit organizations. The remaining 60 percent was reinvested in the company so that it could continue to grow. The remaining 40 percent was distributed to the company's worker-owners, with half paid out to them

in cash and half placed in Class B shares which they could sell at the fixed price of $27.50/share one year after leaving the company. The money held in these holding accounts remained on the books of EE for use if needed.

In addition, EE included a "no exit" clause in its by-laws. This stated that if EE were to ever be sold, the co-op would have to give away to another fair trade organization all the net proceeds that remained after paying vendors, creditors and shareholders. This provided assurances that EE would never have an incentive to sell out.[70] Worker-owners could not reap a large windfall but would only receive back exactly what they had put in. It also ensured that EE's outside Class B shareholders, whose share values were fixed at the original $27.50 price, would not feel cheated in the event that a cash-rich buyer paid a premium purchase price for the company.

# THE FAIR TRADE INDUSTRY

The fair trade movement had a social agenda of promoting sustainable development, treating farmers justly, and educating consumers. Conventional trade was seen as being exploitative; poor, uneducated farmers often got underpaid for their crops while consumers were buying products that were frequently sprayed with toxic pesticides and were made from nonrenewable resources. Fair trade proponents sought to create true, win–win partnerships between producers and consumers. Both parties to a transaction would have their needs satisfied. Farmers could get fair prices for their crops, survive during difficult times and be better able to support their families. Consumers would get fine, high-quality products and feel good about their purchases. Most fair trade certifiers and membership organizations also opposed the common business goal of maximizing profits. Instead, they promoted the notion that a business could be successful when putting people first.

To have its products fair trade –certified, each participating business needed to pay a licensing fee to Fair Trade USA and follow certain guidelines.[71] Licensees were able to market their products as "Fair Trade" by placing the Fair Trade USA logo on their packaging. Since 2009, new fair trade certifiers have entered the U.S. market, but operate in a similar fashion. Fair trade certifiers agreed on eight basic principles:[72]

1. Long-term direct trading relationships
2. Prompt payment of fair prices and wages
3. No child, forced or otherwise exploited labor

4. Workplace non-discrimination, gender equity, and freedom of association

5. Safe working conditions and reasonable work hours

6. Investment in community development projects

7. Environmental sustainability

8. Traceability and transparency

## Brief History of the Fair Trade Industry

The fair trade movement began in 1946 when Edna Ruth Byler, a volunteer for Mennonite Central Committee, visited Puerto Rico. She discovered that women artisans had the ability to make beautiful lace products but that they lived in poverty. Byler began to import needlecrafts to the U.S. and to send money back directly to the women. She helped establish SELFHELP Crafts of the World, which changed its name to Ten Thousand Villages in 1996.[73] Ten Thousand Villages expanded to become one of the world's largest fair trade organizations. It sold products from struggling artisans in Asia, Africa, Latin America, and the Middle East through a network of over 390 retail outlets in North America.

In 1988, Solidaridad, a Dutch development agency, launched the first fair trade certification system. It was named, "Max Havelaar," after a fictional Dutch character who had opposed the exploitation of coffee pickers in the Dutch colonies.[74] The first "Fair Trade" coffee from Mexico was introduced into supermarkets in the Netherlands. In 1989, International Fair Trade Association, which later became the WFTO, was established as the first global fair trade network.[75] 1997 was the year when the Fair Trade Labeling Organization (FLO) was formed. In 1998, Fair Trade USA (originally under the name, "TransFair USA") was established and became the leading third-party certifier of fair trade practices and products in the U.S.

Fair Trade continued to expand and develop to the present day. In its 2010 Almanac, Fair Trade USA reported that there were over 9,500 fair trade–certified consumer products being offered by 700 industry partners in more than 600,000 retail locations.[76] Paul Rice, the president and CEO of Fair Trade USA, said that in 2010 the fair trade retail sales market was $1.4 billion in the U.S. and $3 billion in Europe.[77]

## Fair Trade Food and Beverage Products

The importation of fair trade–certified products into the U.S. began slowly. According to Fair Trade USA, imports of fair trade–certified coffee rose from 2,052,242 pounds in 1999 to 108.9 million pounds in 2010—see Exhibit 8.[78] The green coffee beans were supplied by 194 fair trade–certified producers in

**EXHIBIT 8**   Imports of Fair Trade–Certified Products in the U.S. in Pounds, 1998–2010

| Year | Coffee | Tea | Cocoa | Grains | Sugar | Produce | Vanilla/ Spices | Flowers | Honey | Wine |
|------|--------|-----|-------|--------|-------|---------|-----------------|---------|-------|------|
| 1998 | 76,059 | | | | | | | | | |
| 1999 | 2,052,242 | | | | | | | | | |
| 2000 | 4,249,534 | | | | | | | | | |
| 2001 | 6,669,308 | 65,261 | | | | | | | | |
| 2002 | 9,747,571 | 86,706 | 14,050 | | | | | | | |
| 2003 | 19,239,017 | 95,669 | 178,888 | | | | | | | |
| 2004 | 32,974,400 | 180,310 | 727,576 | | | 8,814,171 | | | | |
| 2005 | 44,585,323 | 517,500 | 1,036,696 | 73,824 | 271,680 | 7,384,202 | | | | |
| 2006 | 64,774,431 | 629,985 | 1,814,391 | 390,848 | 3,581,563 | 6,176,907 | 197,145 | | | |
| 2007 | 66,339,389 | 1,134,993 | 1,951,400 | 436,456 | 8,657,427 | 8,030,482 | 149,460 | 650,832 | | |
| 2008 | 87,772,966 | 1,372,261 | 3,847,759 | 317,652 | 8,696,172 | 25,492,767 | 44,165 | 9,835,028 | 266,385 | 257,959 |
| 2009 | 108,373,041 | 1,372,157 | 2,629,411 | 1,275,805 | 11,307,547 | 50,272,722 | 149,344 | 9,544,329 | 919,130 | 530,446 |
| 2010 | 108,928,751 | 1,899,259 | 4,392,674 | 1,437,005 | 18,146,124 | 51,055,320 | 293,739 | 9,544,329 | 919,130 | 530,446 |
| Total | 555,782,033 | 7,344,101 | 16,592,846 | 3,931,589 | 50,660,514 | 157,226,571 | 833,853 | 29,570,048 | 1,436,177 | 2,239,13 |
| Growth 2009-10 | 1% | 38% | 67% | 13% | 60% | 2% | 97% | 0% | 267% | −63% |

Source: Fair Trade USA 2011 Almanac.

**EXHIBIT 9**   Fair Trade Product Labels

| Category | Examples |
|---|---|
| 3rd Party Inspection and Certification | |
| Membership Organizations | |
| Brand Programs | |

Source: Fair World Project, Spring 2011, accessed at http://fairworldproject.org.

Latin America, Africa, and Asia.[79] The coffee producers received a total of $10.8 million in social premiums, which could be used for community, education, health, and environmental projects.[80]

In 2002, fair trade cocoa was introduced to the U.S. fair trade category. In 2004, produce was added to the mix, growing rapidly from 8,814,171 pounds to 51,055,320 pounds by 2010.[81] Grain and sugar were the next products to come into the U.S., arriving in 2005. One year later, vanilla and spices became popular imports with an increase of 97 percent growth from 2009 to 2010.[82] The newest entries to the list of fair trade imports into the U.S. were flower, honey, and wine. Fair trade, beginning with only one product, had grown to include a large range of products from beverages to fruits to condiments and to healthy snacks.

## Validation System

It was often difficult for consumers to really know which products were fair trade and which were not. There were no laws in the U.S. restricting the use of the term "Fair Trade" on product labels. A leader in the fair trade movement grouped fair trade validation systems into three major categories: 3rd Party Inspection and Certification, Membership Organizations, and Brand Programs.[83] An example of the logos associated with each validation category are shown in Exhibit 9.

The first category represented organizations that made sure trading operations were performed according to fair trade standards. They inspected a member's growing and processing activities in the field and occasionally the paper trail of transactions. If the standards were met, the products could be labeled as fair trade–certified.

The Membership Organizations evaluated a company's overall commitment, practices, and conditions against fair trade criteria. They did not necessarily verify a company's fair trade claims through an onsite inspection. Brand Programs involved socially responsible companies that developed in-house auditing and branding programs for their own sourcing programs that possessed at least some fair trade attributes. Whole Foods, for example, offered a "Whole Trade" line of products in its stores. The fair trade practices and standards varied greatly from company to company.[84]

## FAIR TRADE INDUSTRY COMPETITION

The fair trade movement caught on in 2000 when many companies began to follow the same path as EE—more specifically, into the business of fair trade coffee. Nevertheless, when it came to rivalry, EE's values provided a much different outlook than a typical business, as Rink Dickinson explained.

> Believe it or not, we want more, not less, competition. That's because we know these farmers and their struggles. They urgently need more importers to pay a just price. So we encourage our fellow roasters to expand on the modest fair trade programs they've announced so far.[85]

Fair trade coffee was EE's primary product, accounting for 80 percent of sales in 2010.[86] At that point, there were over 300 companies in the U.S. that provided fair trade coffee.[87] EE managers admired the social mission of some of these companies and even considered those who were truly committed to fair trade to be friends. However, they were also competitors. These companies were grouped in two main categories. One class of competitors consisted of larger companies that competed in the high-end, organic coffee market, but also got involved in fair trade coffee. Typically, fair trade was not the "heart and soul" of these companies, it was a subset of the business. This type of company included specialty coffee powerhouses Starbucks and Green Mountain Coffee. As more consumers became familiar with the concept of fair trade, these companies sought to capitalize on the growing fair trade market.[88]

In 2000, Green Mountain Coffee signed an agreement with Fair Trade USA to certify the company's organic coffee as fair trade–certified. In the fiscal year 2010, approximately 27 percent of the company's coffee purchases were from fair trade sources.[89] Starbucks, the largest specialty coffee company in the U.S., began to purchase fair trade–certified coffee in 2000.[90] In 2009, Starbucks committed to doubling its purchases to 40 million pounds of fair trade coffee. Shortly after, in 2010, almost 7.9 percent of all Starbucks coffee purchases were fair trade–certified. This led the company to become the largest purchaser of fair trade coffee in the world.[91] Although fair trade coffee was still a small percentage of the total coffee market, Fair Trade USA reported that the sale of fair trade coffee in the specialty market was growing at a fast rate. In 2010, sales of all fair trade products increased 24 percent.[92]

Large specialty coffee companies were not the only fair trade rivals to EE. A second group of competitors were small, local, and regional competitors operating in different areas of the U.S. Therefore, competition within this class of businesses varied in each part of the country where EE worked.[93] For example, Just Coffee, a worker-owned coffee roaster was located in Madison, Wisconsin. Deans Beans, a privately held company, was located in Orange, Massachusetts, and provided competition in the New England region. Thanksgiving Coffee Company was a publicly held coffee roaster located in Fort Bragg, California, and serviced much of the Northern California market. Just Coffee, Deans Beans, and Thanksgiving Coffee were just a few examples of fair trade businesses like EE. With so much rivalry, where did EE stand amongst this competition?

### Equal Exchange Compared to Thanksgiving Coffee

Thanksgiving Coffee Company (TCC) was established in 1972, brewing coffee for a local hotel. It was TCC's intent to make a positive contribution to the local community. Thus, the company developed the motto, "Not Just a Cup, but a Just Cup." In 2000, the company was licensed to sell fair trade coffee by Fair Trade USA. In 1996, TCC had its initial public offering of shares of common stock, and at that time was almost exactly the same size as EE. The company sold over 100 varieties of coffee as well as many complementary products, such as coffee makers, books, and mugs. TCC also had a bakery that was located in Mendocino, California.[94] Sales from the bakery accounted for 12.4 percent of TCC's revenues in 2010.[95] TCC and EE shared a similar commitment to help the farmers that grew coffee, deliver a balanced price to consumers, and record a profit.

TCC was not quite as large as EE, which is shown in the company's sales figures in Exhibit 10. In fiscal year 2010, TCC reported sales of $4,153,409, of which 86.6 percent were from roasted coffee.[96] However, the bleak economic downturn posed a challenge to many companies. EE maintained a steady 2 percent growth; however, TCC's experience with the economic conditions was more challenging. This was partially because of a fire at the company's packaging, offices, tasting room, and shipping facility on July 5, 2010. This reduced the amount of TCC's sales and was a contributing factor to a 9.2 percent decrease in revenues. Additional reasons for the reduction in revenue were typical during a recession: reduced dollars per transaction, decreased sales at the company bakery because of the soaring unemployment rate, and less tourist activity.[97]

Despite the declining sales, TCC's net income for fiscal year 2010 was $157,654. This was an increase of $114,761 over the reported net income for the prior fiscal year, which was $42,893.[98] EE's net income had remained consistent, roughly 2 percent of the co-operative's net sales. The large difference in TCC's income statement was a result of the insurance advances less the assets written off, and the additional expenses incurred in operating the business subsequent to the

fire. This was reported in "other income" on TCC's income statement for 2010. Common size balance sheets for EE and TCC for 2009 and 2010 are presented in Exhibit 10.[99]

The recession affected the profitability and growth of EE and TCC. However, additional factors should be considered when evaluating the financial performance of a company. One of the most common uses for the balance sheet is to determine a company's working capital. TCC's working capital increased to $223,762 in 2010 as compared to $157,701 on December 31, 2009.[100] Working capital for EE totaled $9,030,127 in 2010, an increase of $438,097 compared to working capital of $8,592,030 in 2010.[101] In addition, TCC experienced a significant increase of cash as well, mostly because of the insurance company's advance. This made a cash amount of $191,618 available, an increase of $136,875.[102] EE's balance sheet saw a similar growth, as cash increased from $376,667 in the year of 2009 to $657,124 in the year ended December 31, 2010.[103] Common size balance sheets for EE and TCC for 2009 and 2010 are presented in Exhibit 11.

## EQUAL EXCHANGE'S NEXT STEP

It was exactly two weeks after the last meeting. Rob Everts, Rink Dickinson, and a handful of EE's veteran worker-owners found themselves in the conference room once again. If all went well, the co-op's members

**EXHIBIT 10** Common Size Income Statements for Equal Exchange and Thanksgiving Coffee Company, 2009–2010

|  | Equal Exchange | | | | Thanksgiving Coffee | | | |
|---|---|---|---|---|---|---|---|---|
|  | 2010 | Pct. | 2009 | Pct. | 2010 | Pct. | 2009 | Pct. |
| Net sales | $36,525,856 | 100.0% | $35,832,510 | 100.0% | $4,153,409 | 100.0% | $4,576,718 | 100.0% |
| Cost of sales | 23,659,316 | 64.8 | 23,075,260 | 64.4 | 2,609,685 | 62.8 | 2,761,117 | 60.3 |
| Gross profit | 12,866,540 | 35.2 | 12,757,250 | 35.6 | 1,543,724 | 37.2 | 1,815,601 | 39.7 |
| Operating expenses | 11,234,758 | 30.8 | 10,771,023 | 30.1 | 1,648,480 | 39.7 | 1,727,413 | 37.7 |
| Earnings from operations | 1,631,782 | 4.5 | 1,986,227 | 5.5 | (104,756) | (2.5) | 88,188 | 1.9 |
| Other income (expense) | (308,830) | (0.8) | (619,094) | (1.7) | 263,210 | 6.3 | (44,495) | (0.10) |
| Income before taxes | 1,322,952 | 3.6 | 1,367,133 | 3.8 | 158,454 | 3.8 | 43,693 | 0.10 |
| Income tax expense | (484,000) | (1.3) | (430,000) | (1.2) | (800) | (0.02) | (800) | (0.02) |
| Net Income | $    744,952 | 2.0% | $    774,133 | 2.2% | $ 157,654 | 3.8% | $    42,893 | 0.9% |

*Source:* Equal Exchange's annual reports and Thanksgiving Coffee Form 10-K.

**EXHIBIT 11**  Common Size Balance Sheets for Equal Exchange and Thanksgiving Coffee Company, 2009–2010

| | Equal Exchange | | | | Thanksgiving Coffee | | | |
| --- | --- | --- | --- | --- | --- | --- | --- | --- |
| | 2010 | Pct. | 2009 | Pct. | 2010 | Pct. | 2009 | Pct. |
| Cash | $   657,124 | 3.4% | $   376,667 | 2.0% | $ 191,618 | 15.1% | $ 54,743 | 5.5% |
| Other current assets | 11,395,440 | 58.9 | 11,334,632 | 59.2 | 664,478 | 52.5 | 580,774 | 58.3 |
| Property, plant, and equipment | 6,653,683 | 34.4 | 7,017,564 | 36.7 | 403,608 | 31.9 | 342,728 | 34.4 |
| Other assets | 649,031 | 3.4 | 416,594 | 2.2 | 6,412 | 0.5 | 18,074 | 1.8 |
| Total assets | 19,355,278 | 100.0 | 19,145,457 | 100.0 | 1,266,116 | 100.0 | 996,319 | 100.0 |
| Current liabilities | 2,222,437 | 11.5 | 3,119,269 | 16.3 | 632,335 | 50.0 | 477,816 | 48.0 |
| Long-term debt | 4,128,784 | 21.3 | 4,653,100 | 24.3 | 177,701 | 14.0 | 220,077 | 22.1 |
| Total liabilities | 6,351,221 | 32.8 | 7,772,369 | 40.6 | 810,036 | 64.0 | 697,893 | 70.1 |
| Stockholders' equity | 13,004,057 | 67.2 | 11,373,088 | 59.4 | 456,080 | 36.0 | 298,426 | 30.0 |
| Total liabilities and stockholders' equity | $19,355,278 | 100.0% | $19,145,457 | 100.0% | $1,266,116 | 100.0% | $996,319 | 100.0% |

*Source:* Equal Exchange's annual reports and Thanksgiving Coffee's 2010 Form 10-K.

would leave with a final verdict made about EE's next step. However, coming to this decision would not be so simple.

The discussions that took place during previous meetings helped Rob, Rink, and the worker-owners form many different options. The managers presented their compelling arguments throughout the morning and looked for feedback from the rest of the group. Those in the meeting focused on what others had said and diligently took notes, conscious of the crucial decision that lay ahead.

> EE has experienced a significant amount of success for many years. The recession, which will eventually come to an end, has been burdensome on everyone. Meanwhile, we are not even sure of what all of our new competition may bring. The hype may die down soon and we may very well easily retain our position as the strongest competitor in the industry.

With that said, it was understood that some worker-owners believed it was in the best interest of EE to simply continue to do exactly what the co-op had been doing. This would mean that the co-op would hold off on making any changes and would instead continue to remain predominantly in the coffee sector. This had accounted for roughly 80 percent of EE's total sales. Hopefully, business would soon return to normal, which would allow the co-operative to once again enjoy double-digit revenue growth.

There was no denying that the return of EE's past success would be ideal. However, some employees were concerned that this would not be the case. This apprehension led to the next suggestion.

> What if EE added more products, and even began to offer services?

EE had nearly gone as far as the co-operative could go in the coffee sector. Although the co-op had expanded into new products, such as chocolate and tea, there were still various fairly traded goods that EE did not offer. There was also the possibility of offering products that had never been introduced to the fair trade industry before. Additionally, EE had the opportunity to expand its business into services. This would be consistent with the company's mission, such as eco-tourism to coffee or cacao growing zones to support those communities. Another prospective idea would be consulting on "best practices," like the company's co-operative model.

Some worker-owners thought otherwise. They felt that maybe EE should use this opportunity to take a step back and reorganize the co-operative internally. By now, the number of employees had increased to 110. The reorganization would include creating different groups that would each focus on a specific aspect of the business. The worker-owners would assess their needed resources and make autonomous decisions about how to expand based on outside market data. These units would be responsible for better preparing EE to overcome the many market obstacles that had developed in each of the sectors in which it operated.

At this point, three suggestions had been made for Equal Exchange's future. All of these would help shape the fair trade co-operative's next direction. It was now up to the co-directors and worker-owners to vote upon which option would present the best opportunity for continued success.

## ENDNOTES

1 As the result of a merger, New England Food Co-operative Organization was renamed Northeast Co-operatives. It was acquired by United Natural Foods in 2002.
2 "A Vision of Fairness to Farmers," *Equal Exchange: About Our Co-op.* Retrieved August 25, 2011 from http://www.equalexchange.coop/story.
3 J. G. Macdonald, "Fair Trade: How To Brew Justice," *Time,* December 11, 2005.
4 "C.B.J. Shares a Cup with Mr. Coffee, Rink Dickinson," *Cooperative Business Journal,* March/April 2007: 6.
5 J. R. Whitman, "The Worker Cooperative Life Cycle," Babson-Equal Exchange Cooperative Curriculum, March 6, 2011. Retrieved July 7, 2011, from http://cooperative-curriculum.wikispaces.com/file/view/The+Worker+Cooperative+Life+Cycle-Whitman.pdf/207807218/The%20Worker%20Cooperative%20Life%20Cycle-Whitman.pdf.
6 R. Everts and R. Dickinson, "A Vision for the Future," *Equal Exchange 2005 Annual Report:* 2, accessed at www.equalexchange.coop on October 23, 2012.
7 R. Everts and R. Dickinson, "A Movement Has Taken Hold," *Equal Exchange 2006 Annual Report:* 2, accessed at www.equalexchange.coop on October 23, 2012.
8 "Our Story," *Equal Exchange 2006 Annual Report:* 4, accessed at www.equalexchange.coop on October 23, 2012.
9 D. Johnson, "Bringing Fair Trade Home" *Equal Exchange 2007 Annual Report:* 4.
10 P. Robinson, "Farmer Partner: SOFA" *Equal Exchange 2007 Annual Report:* 5, accessed at www.equalexchange.coop on October 23, 2012.
11 Rodney North, "The Answer Man". EE's Head of PR. Direct quote.
12 H. MacNeil, "The Insightful Tea: Reflections on My Conversation with Jonathan Rosenthal," *Chasing Miracles,* March 9, 2009. Retrieved August 19, 2011 from http://chasingmiracles.tumblr.com/search/rosenthal.
13 Just Works Consulting: http://www.just-works.com/.
14 "The Worker Cooperative Life Cycle" (2011), op. cit.
15 http://www.ibiblio.org/farming-connection/fffconf/pdfs/Michael%20Rozyne.pdf.
16 Equal Exchange Press Kit, Executive Bios. http://www.equalexchange.coop/executive-bios.
17 Michael Blanding, "Meet the New Boss(es)" *Boston Magazine,* September 2007.
18 E. Weise, "Fair Trade Sweetens Pot," *USA Today,* February 8, 2005. Retrieved August 25, 2011 from http://www.usatoday.com/life/lifestyle/2005-02-08-chocolate_x.htm.

19 K. E. McKones-Sweets, "Lessons from a Coffee Supply Chain," *Supply Chain Management Review,* October, 2004.
20 Ibid.
21 Ibid.
22 "New Premium, Minimum Price and Trade Standards in Fairtrade Coffee," Fairtrade Foundation, March 17, 2010. Retrieved August 22, 2011 from http://www.fairtrade.org.uk/press_office/press_releases_and_statements/march_2011/new_premium_minimum_price_and_trade_standards_in_fairtrade_coffee.aspx.
23 Ibid.
24 M. Kelly, "Three Progressive Companies Leading the Way to a New Century," *Sonoma County Independent,* December 30, 1999 – January 5, 2000. Retrieved July 25, 2011 from http://www.metroactive.com/papers/sonoma/12.30.99/corporate-9952.html.
25 "Lessons From a Coffee Supply Chain," 2004, op. cit., p. 56.
26 Ibid.
27 "U.S. Job Satisfaction Rates Hit 20-Year Low," *Quality Progress,* vol. 43 (February 2010): 13. Retrieved August 19, 2011 from ABI/INFORM.
28 "What Do You Think? Why Are Fewer and Fewer U.S. Employees Satisfied with Their Jobs?" Harvard Business School, April 2, 2010. Retrieved August 19, 2011 from http://hbswk.hbs.edu/item/6404.html.
29 Ibid.
30 Ibid.
31 Ibid.
32 E. Polk, "An Interview on Fair Trade with Rodney North from Equal Exchange," press release, Justmeans.com, October 5, 2008. Retrieved August 25, 2011 from http://www.justmeans.com/press-releases/An-Interview-on-Fair-Trade-with-Rodney-North-from-Equal-Exchange/3240.html.
33 L. Conley, "Trade Secrets," *Fast Company,* November 1, 2004. Retrieved June 8, 2011 from http://www.fastcompany.com/magazine/88/trade-secrets.html.
34 "What Is a Worker Cooperative?" U.S. Federation of Worker Cooperatives, June 2007. Retrieved November 25, 2011 from http://www.usworker.coop/system/files/What%20is%20WC_1.pdf.
35 http://www.equalexchange.coop/worker-owned.
36 R. Rayasam, "Equal Exchange Serves Up a Cup of Cooperation," *U.S. News & World Report,* April 24, 2008. Retrieved August 27, 2011 from http://money.usnews.com/money/careers/articles/2008/04/24/equal-exchange-serves-up-a-cup-of-cooperation.

37 Notes taken on April 12, 2011 during Rodney North's PowerPoint Presentation, "Equal Exchange as a Social Enterprise," at Manhattan College, Riverdale, New York.
38 "Meet the New Boss(es)," (007), opt. cit.
39 Notes taken on April 12, 2011 during Rodney North's PowerPoint Presentation, "Equal Exchange as a Social Enterprise."
40 http://www.faireconomy.org/issues/ceo_pay.
41 K. Schuett, "Going Beyond Fair Trade: Equal Exchange's Democratic Business Structure Ensures Mission-Driven Growth," *Organic Processing Magazine,* November/December 2010. Retrieved July 7, 2011 from http://www.organicprocessing.com/opnovdec10/opnd10Enterprise.htm.
42 As reported in "The Truth About Turnover and Retention Now," *HR Focus,* vol. 86 (September 2009): 1.
43 Joe Light, "More Workers Start to Quit," *The Wall Street Journal,* May 26, 2010, p. D6. Retrieved November 22, 2011 from ABI/INFORM.
44 "Meet the New Boss(es)," (2007), op. cit.
45 "Reverse-Trick-or-Treating: Thousands of Children to Give Back Quarter Million Halloween 'Treats' in U.S. and Canada," *PR Newswire,* October 15, 2008. Retrieved August 25, 2011 from ABI/INFORM.
46 "Going Beyond Fair Trade," (2010), op. cit.
47 "Our Story: A Vision of Fairness to Farmers," *Equal Exchange 2006 Annual Report:* 4, accessed at www.equalexchange.coop on October 23, 2012.
48 "Fair Trade Coffee," *Equal Exchange Fairly Traded Coffee, Tea, Chocolate & Snacks.* Retrieved July 18, 2011 from http://www.equalexchange.coop/coffee.
49 "Fast Facts," *Equal Exchange Fairly Traded Coffee, Tea, Chocolate & Snacks.* Retrieved July 18, 2011 from http://www.equalexchange.coop/fast-facts.
50 "Fair Trade Organic Tea," *Equal Exchange Fairly Traded Coffee, Tea, Chocolate & Snacks.* Retrieved July 18, 2011 from http://www.equalexchange.coop/organic-tea.
51 D. Goodrich, "Our Products: Chocolate," *Equal Exchange 2006 Annual Report:* 6.
52 "Products," *Equal Exchange Fairly Traded Coffee, Tea, Chocolate & Snacks.* Retrieved July 18, 2011 from http://www.equalexchange.coop/product-info.
53 "Fast Facts," http://www.equalexchange.com.
54 R. Everts and R. Dickinson, "A Movement Has Taken Hold," *Equal Exchange 2006 Annual Report:* 2, accessed at www.equalexchange.coop on October 23, 2012.
55 D. Goodrich, "Our Products: Chocolate."

56 W. Nell, "A Big Year for Small Farmers," *Equal Exchange 2006 Annual Report:* 3.

57 A. Williamson, "Report from the Board," *Equal Exchange 2006 Annual Report:* 15, accessed at www.equalexchange.coop on October 23, 2012.

58 B. Albert, "Financial Report," *Equal Exchange 2006 Annual Report:* 15, accessed at www.equalexchange.coop on October 23, 2012.

59 R. Everts and R. Dickinson, "Building a Co-operative Global Network," *Equal Exchange 2008 Annual Report:* 1, accessed at www.equalexchange.coop on October 23, 2012.

60 L. Miller, "A Year that Increased Sales and Built Connections," *Equal Exchange 2008 Annual Report:* 2, accessed at www.equalexchange.coop on October 23, 2012.

61 L. Miller, "Natural Food Team Goes Direct," *Equal Exchange 2008 Annual Report:* 2, accessed at www.equalexchange.coop on October 23, 2012.

62 R. Everts and R. Dickinson, "Letter from the Office of Executive Directors," *Equal Exchange 2009 Annual Report:* 1, accessed at www.equalexchange.coop on October 23, 2012.

63 B. Albert, "A Shifting Financial Focus," *Equal Exchange 2009 Annual Report:* 4, accessed at www.equalexchange.coop on October 23, 2012.

64 R. Everts and R. Dickinson, "Letter from the Office of Executive Directors," *Equal Exchange 2009 Annual Report:* 1, accessed at www.equalexchange.coop on October 23, 2012.

65 R. Everts and R. Dickinson, "Rising Commodity Prices, Slight Growth," *Equal Exchange 2010 Annual Report:* 1, accessed at www.equalexchange.coop on October 23, 2012.

66 "Audited Financial Statements and Supplementary Data," accessed at www.equalexchange.coop on October 23, 2012.

67 "The Equal Exchange CD – Invest in Fair Trade," accessed at www.equalexchange.coop on October 23, 2012.

68 "Equal Exchange CD," http://Easternbank.com.

69 "The Equal Exchange CD – Invest in Fair Trade," http://Equalexchange.coop.

70 M. Maphalala, "The Rabble Rousers at Equal Exchange," Retrieved July 18, 2011 from http://Smallfarmersbigchange.coop.

71 On September 28, 2011, Fair Trade USA lowered its fees for coffee roasters in order to make Fair Trade more accessible to companies of all sizes.

72 "Reference Guide to Fair Trade Certifiers and Membership Organizations," *Fair World Project,* Free Publication: Issue 2, Spring 2011: 4.

73 "Our History: Roots of a Global Movement," Ten Thousand Villages, 2009, http://www.tenthousandvillages.com/php/about.us/about.history.php.

74 "Fairtrade Labelling International History," 2011. http://www.fairtrade.org.uk/what_is_fairtrade/history.aspx.

75 "Fair Trade Timeline," *Fair World Project,* Free Publication: Issue 2, Spring 2011: 3. Contributed by the Fair Trade Resource Network Web: http://www.ftrn.org.

76 "Fair Trade Certified Organic Imports Skyrocket," *Fair Trade USA Press Release,* April 25, 2011. Retrieved July 18, 2011 from http://www.transfairusa.org/press-room/press_release/fair-trade-certified-organic-imports-skyrocket.

77 D. Kaplan, "Q&A: Fair Trade USA Has Growing Influence," *McClatchy-Tribune Business News,* April 30, 2011. Retrieved July 15, 2011 from ABI/INFORM.

78 A. Schwartz, "Why Fair Trade Imports Rise Even as Buyers Shun Other Eco-Friendly Products," *Fast Company.* Retrieved July 18, 2011 from http://www.fastcompany.com/1750178/fair-trade-sales-rise-even-while-buyers-shun-other-eco-friendly-products.

79 "Coffee: Fair Trade Certified Producers that Export Green Coffee into the U.S. and World Market, by Region and Country, 2010," *Fair Trade USA 2011 Almanac:* 18.

80 Ibid.

81 Ibid.

82 Ibid.

83 "Reference Guide to Fair Trade Certifiers and Membership Organizations," *Fair World Project,* Free Publication: Issue 2, Spring 2011: 4.

84 N. Abufarha and G. Leson, "How Do You Know It's Really Fair Trade?" *Fair Trade for a Better World,* 2010. Retrieved July 18, 2011 from http://www.fairworldproject.org/index.php?c=intro&m=logos.

85 "Fair Trade Coffee Pioneers Welcome Competitors to Their Niche," *Equalexchange.coop,* September 21, 2000.

86 R. North. Presentation at Manhattan College. April 12, 2011.

87 "Thanksgiving Coffee, Inc. Form 10-K"

88 R. Everts. Conference call. July 8, 2011.

89 "Green Mountain Form10-K," accessed at www.sec.gov on October 23, 2012.

90 "Responsibly Grown Coffee," posted at www.starbucks.com and accessed October 23, 2012.

91 "Coffee Purchasing & Farmer Support," posted at www.starbucks.com and accessed October 23, 2012.

92 "Mainstream Consumers Drive Fair Trade Certified Sales up 24 Percent," posted at www.fairtradeusa.org/press-room/press_release/mainstream-consumers-drive-fair-trade-certified-sales-24-percent-0 and accessed on March 7, 2011.

93 R. Everts. Conference call. July 8, 2011.

94 "Thanksgiving Coffee, Inc. Form 10-K," accessed at www.sec.gov on October 23, 2012.

95 "Thanksgiving Coffee, Inc. Form 10-K," accessed at www.sec.gov on October 23, 2012.

96 Ibid.

97 "Thanksgiving Coffee, Inc. Form 10-K," accessed at www.sec.gov on October 23, 2012.

98 "Thanksgiving Coffee, Inc. Form 10-K," accessed at www.sec.gov on October 23, 2012.

99 Ibid.

100 Ibid.

101 "Equal Exchange Audited Financial Statements, 2010 & 2009," accessed at www.equalexchange.coop on October 23, 2012.

102 "Thanksgiving Coffee, Inc. Form 10-K," accessed at www.sec.gov on October 23, 2012.

103 "Equal Exchange Audited Financial Statements, 2010 & 2009," accessed at www.equalexchange.coop on October 23, 2012.

# Google's Strategy in 2012

## John E. Gamble
University of South Alabama

Google was the leading Internet search firm in 2012, with a nearly 67 percent market share in search from home and work computers and a 95 percent share in searches performed from mobile devices. Google's business model allowed advertisers to bid on search terms that would describe their product or service on a cost-per-impression (CPI) or cost-per-click (CPC) basis. Google's search-based ads were displayed near Google's search results and generated advertising revenues of more than $36.5 billion in 2011. The company also generated revenues of about $1.4 billion in 2010 from licensing fees charged to businesses that wished to install Google's search appliance on company intranets and from a variety of new ventures. New ventures were becoming a growing priority with Google management since the company dominated the market for search based ads and sought additional opportunities to sustain its extraordinary growth in revenues, earnings, and net cash provided by operations.

In 2012, Google was pursuing a cloud computing initiative that was intended to change the market for commonly used business productivity applications such as word processing, spreadsheets, and presentation software from the desktop to the Internet. Information technology analysts believed that the market for such applications—collectively called cloud computing—could grow to $95 billion by 2013. Google had also entered into alliances with Intel, Sony, DISH Network, Logitech, and other firms to develop the technology and products required to launch Google TV. Google TV was launched in the U.S. in 2011 and would allow users to search live network and cable programming; streaming videos from providers such as Netflix, Amazon Video On Demand, and YouTube; and recorded programs on a DVR. The company also launched its Google$^+$ social networking site in 2011 to capture additional advertising opportunities.

Perhaps the company's most ambitious strategic initiative in 2012 was its acquisition of Motorola Mobility for $12.5 billion, which put it in the hardware segment of the smartphone and tablet computer industries. Analysts following the transaction saw the move to acquire Motorola Mobility as a direct attempt to mimic Apple's strategy used for the iPhone and iPad that tightly integrated hardware and software for its most profitable and fastest growing products. Google had launched its Android operating system for mobile phones in 2008 and allowed wireless phone manufacturers such as LG, HTC, and Nokia to produce Internet-enabled phones boasting features similar to those available on Apple's iPhone. By 2012, Android was the leading smartphone platform with a 50.9 percent market share.

While Google's growth initiatives seemed to take the company into new industries and thrust it into competition with companies ranging from Facebook to Microsoft to Applet, its CEO, Eric Schmidt, saw the new ventures as natural extensions of the company's mission to "organize the world's information and make it universally accessible and useful."[1]

In April 2012, he explained the company's wide-ranging strategic initiatives by commenting "In some ways we have run the company as to let 1,000 flowers bloom, but once they do bloom you want to put together a coherent bouquet."[2]

## COMPANY HISTORY

The development of Google's search technology began in January 1996 when Stanford University computer science graduate students Larry Page and Sergey Brin collaborated to develop a new search engine. They named the new search engine BackRub because of its ability to rate websites for relevancy by examining the number of back links pointing to the website. The approach for assessing the relevancy of websites to a particular search query used by other websites at the time was based on examining and counting metatags and keywords included on various websites. By 1997, the search accuracy of BackRub had allowed it to gain a loyal following among Silicon Valley Internet users. Yahoo co-founder David Filo was among the converted, and in 1998 he convinced Brin and Page to leave Stanford to focus on making their search technology the backbone of a new Internet company.

BackRub would be renamed Google, which was a play on the word *googol*—a mathematical term for a number represented by the numeral 1 followed by 100 zeroes. Brin and Page's adoption of the new name reflected their mission to organize a seemingly infinite amount of information on the Internet. In August 1998, a Stanford professor arranged for Brin and Page to meet at his home with a potential angel investor to demonstrate the Google search engine. The investor, who had been a founder of Sun Microsystems, was immediately impressed with Google's search capabilities but was too pressed for time to hear much of their informal presentation. The investor stopped the two during the presentation and suggested, "Instead of us discussing all the details, why don't I just write you a check?"[3] The two partners held the investor's $100,000 check, made payable to Google Inc., for two weeks while they scrambled to set up a corporation named Google Inc. and open a corporate bank account. The two officers of the freshly incorporated company went on to raise a total of $1 million in venture capital from family, friends, and other angel investors by the end of September 1998.

Even with a cash reserve of $1 million, the two partners ran Google on a shoestring budget, with its main servers built by Brin and Page from discounted computer components and its four employees operating out of a garage owned by a friend of the founders. By year-end 1998, Google's beta version was handling 10,000 search queries per day and *PC Magazine* had named the company to its list of "Top 100 Web Sites and Search Engines for 1998."

The new company recorded successes at a lightning-fast pace, with the search kernel answering more than 500,000 queries per day and Red Hat agreeing to become the company's first search customer in early 1999. Google attracted an additional $25 million in funding from two leading Silicon Valley venture capital firms by mid-year 1999 to support further growth and enhancements to Google's search technology. The company's innovations in 2000 included wireless search technology, search capabilities in 10 languages, and a Google Toolbar browser plug-in that allowed computer users to search the Internet without first visiting a Google-affiliated web portal or Google's home page. Features added through 2004 included Google News, Google Product Search, Google Scholar, and Google Local. The company also expanded its index of web pages to more than 8 billion and increased its country domains to more than 150 by 2004. Google also further expanded its products for mobile phones with a short message service (SMS) feature that allowed mobile phone users to send a search request to Google as a text message. After submitting the search request to 466453 (google), a mobile phone user would receive a text message from Google providing results to his or her query.

## The Initial Public Offering

Google's April 29, 2004, initial public offering (IPO) registration became the most talked-about planned offering involving an Internet company since the dot-com bust of 2000. The registration announced Google's intention to raise as much as $3.6 billion from the issue of 25.7 million shares through an unusual Dutch auction. Among the 10 key tenets of Google's philosophy (presented in Exhibit 1) was "You can make money without doing evil."[4] The choice of a Dutch auction stemmed from this philosophy, since Dutch auctions allowed potential investors to place bids for shares regardless of size. The choice of a Dutch auction was also favorable to Google since it involved considerably lower investment banking and underwriting fees and few or no commissions for brokers.

At the conclusion of the first day of trading, Google's shares had appreciated by 18 percent to make Brin and Page each worth approximately $3.8 billion. Also, an estimated 900 to 1,000 Google employees were worth at least $1 million, with 600 to 700 holding at least $2 million in Google stock. On average, each of Google's 2,292 staff members held approximately $1.7 million in company stock, excluding the holdings of the top five executives. Stanford University also enjoyed a $179.5 million windfall from its stock holdings granted for its early investment in Brin and Page's search engine. Some of Google's early contractors and consultants also profited handsomely from forgoing fees in return for stock options in the company. One

## EXHIBIT 1   The 10 Principles of Google's Corporate Philosophy

**1. Focus on the user and all else will follow.**

From its inception, Google has focused on providing the best user experience possible. While many companies claim to put their customers first, few are able to resist the temptation to make small sacrifices to increase shareholder value. Google has steadfastly refused to make any change that does not offer a benefit to the users who come to the site:

- The interface is clear and simple.
- Pages load instantly.
- Placement in search results is never sold to anyone.
- Advertising on the site must offer relevant content and not be a distraction.

By always placing the interests of the user first, Google has built the most loyal audience on the web. And that growth has come not through TV ad campaigns, but through word of mouth from one satisfied user to another.

**2. It's best to do one thing really, really well.**

Google does search. With one of the world's largest research groups focused exclusively on solving search problems, we know what we do well, and how we could do it better. Through continued iteration on difficult problems, we've been able to solve complex issues and provide continuous improvements to a service already considered the best on the web at making finding information a fast and seamless experience for millions of users. Our dedication to improving search has also allowed us to apply what we've learned to new products, including Gmail, Google Desktop, and Google Maps.

**3. Fast is better than slow.**

Google believes in instant gratification. You want answers and you want them right now. Who are we to argue? Google may be the only company in the world whose stated goal is to have users leave its website as quickly as possible. By fanatically obsessing on shaving every excess bit and byte from our pages and increasing the efficiency of our serving environment, Google has broken its own speed records time and again.

**4. Democracy on the web works.**

Google works because it relies on the millions of individuals posting websites to determine which other sites offer content of value. Instead of relying on a group of editors or solely on the frequency with which certain terms appear, Google ranks every web page using a breakthrough technique called PageRank™. PageRank evaluates all of the sites linking to a web page and assigns them a value, based in part on the sites linking to them. By analyzing the full structure of the web, Google is able to determine which sites have been "voted" the best sources of information by those most interested in the information they offer.

**5. You don't need to be at your desk to need an answer.**

The world is increasingly mobile and unwilling to be constrained to a fixed location. Whether it's through their PDAs, their wireless phones or even their automobiles, people want information to come to them.

**6. You can make money without doing evil.**

Google is a business. The revenue the company generates is derived from offering its search technology to companies and from the sale of advertising displayed on Google and on other sites across the web. However, you may have never seen an ad on Google. That's because Google does not allow ads to be displayed on our results pages unless they're relevant to the results page on which they're shown. So, only certain searches produce sponsored links above or to the right of the results. Google firmly believes that ads can provide useful information if, and only if, they are relevant to what you wish to find.

Advertising on Google is always clearly identified as a "Sponsored Link." It is a core value for Google that there be no compromising of the integrity of our results. We never manipulate rankings to put our partners higher in our search results. No one can buy better PageRank. Our users trust Google's objectivity and no short-term gain could ever justify breaching that trust.

**7. There's always more information out there.**

Once Google had indexed more of the HTML pages on the Internet than any other search service, our engineers turned their attention to information that was not as readily accessible. Sometimes it was just a matter of integrating new databases, such as adding a phone number and address lookup and a business directory. Other efforts required a bit more creativity, like adding the ability to search billions of images and a way to view pages that were originally created as PDF files. The popularity of PDF results led us to expand the list of file types searched to include documents produced in a dozen formats such as Microsoft Word, Excel and PowerPoint. For wireless users, Google developed a unique way to translate HTML formatted files into a format that could be read by mobile devices. The list is not likely to end there as Google's researchers continue looking into ways to bring all the world's information to users seeking answers.

*(Continued)*

**EXHIBIT 1**    *(Concluded)*

> **8. The need for information crosses all borders.**
> Though Google is headquartered in California, our mission is to facilitate access to information for the entire world, so we have offices around the globe. To that end we maintain dozens of Internet domains and serve more than half of our results to users living outside the United States. Google search results can be restricted to pages written in more than 35 languages according to a user's preference. We also offer a translation feature to make content available to users regardless of their native tongue and for those who prefer not to search in English, Google's interface can be customized into more than 100 languages.
>
> **9. You can be serious without a suit.**
> Google's founders have often stated that the company is not serious about anything but search. They built a company around the idea that work should be challenging and the challenge should be fun. To that end, Google's culture is unlike any in corporate America, and it's not because of the ubiquitous lava lamps and large rubber balls, or the fact that the company's chef used to cook for the Grateful Dead. In the same way Google puts users first when it comes to our online service, Google Inc. puts employees first when it comes to daily life in our Googleplex headquarters. There is an emphasis on team achievements and pride in individual accomplishments that contribute to the company's overall success. Ideas are traded, tested and put into practice with an alacrity that can be dizzying. Meetings that would take hours elsewhere are frequently little more than a conversation in line for lunch and few walls separate those who write the code from those who write the checks. This highly communicative environment fosters a productivity and camaraderie fueled by the realization that millions of people rely on Google results. Give the proper tools to a group of people who like to make a difference, and they will.
>
> **10. Great just isn't good enough.**
> Always deliver more than expected. Google does not accept being the best as an endpoint, but a starting point. Through innovation and iteration, Google takes something that works well and improves upon it in unexpected ways. Google's point of distinction however, is anticipating needs not yet articulated by our global audience, then meeting them with products and services that set new standards. This constant dissatisfaction with the way things are is ultimately the driving force behind the world's best search engine.

*Source:* Google.com.

such contractor was Abbe Patterson, who took options for 4,000 shares rather than a $5,000 fee for preparing a PowerPoint presentation and speaking notes for one of Brin and Page's first presentations to venture capitalists. After two splits and four days of trading, her 16,000 shares were worth $1.7 million.[5] The company executed a second public offering of 14,159,265 shares of common stock in September 2005. The number of shares issued represented the first eight digits to the right of the decimal point for the value of $\pi$ (pi). The issue added more than $4 billion to Google's liquid assets.

Exhibit 2 tracks the performance of Google's common shares between August 19, 2004 and June 2012.

## Google Feature Additions between 2005 and 2012

Google used its vast cash reserves to make strategic acquisitions that might lead to the development of new Internet applications offering advertising opportunities. Google Earth was launched in 2005 after the company acquired Keyhole, a digital mapping company, in 2004. Google Earth and its companion software Google Maps allowed Internet users to search and view satellite images of any location in the world. The feature was enhanced in 2007 with the addition of street-view images taken by traveling Google camera cars. Digital images, webcam feeds, and videos captured by Internet users could be linked to locations displayed by Google Maps. Real estate listings and short personal messages could also be linked to Google Maps locations. In 2010, Google further enhanced Google Maps with the inclusion of an Earth View mode that allowed users to view 3D images of various locations from the ground level. Other search features added to Google between 2005 and 2010 that users found particularly useful included Book Search, Music Search, Video Search, and the expansion of Google News to include archived news articles dating to 1900.

Google also expanded its website features beyond search functionality to include its Gmail software, a web-based calendar, web-based document, and spreadsheet applications, its Picasa web photo albums, and a

## EXHIBIT 2    Performance of Google's Stock Price, August 19, 2004, to June 2012

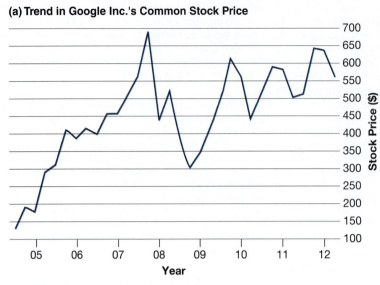

**(a) Trend in Google Inc.'s Common Stock Price**

**(b) Performance of Google Inc.'s Stock Price versus the S&P 500 Index**

translation feature that accommodated 51 languages. The company also released services for mobile phone uses such as Mobile Web Search, Blogger Mobile, Gmail, Google News, and Maps for Mobile. A complete list of Google services and tools for computers and mobile phones in 2012 is presented in Exhibit 3.

## GOOGLE'S BUSINESS MODEL

Google's business model had evolved since the company's inception to include revenue beyond the

licensing fees charged to corporations needing search capabilities on company intranets or websites. The 2000 development of keyword-targeted advertising expanded its business model to include revenues from the placement of highly targeted text-only sponsor ads adjacent to its search results. Google was able to target its ads to specific users based on the user's browsing history. The addition of advertising-based revenue allowed Google to increase annual revenues from $220,000 in 1999 to more than $86 million in 2001. A summary of Google's financial performance

**EXHIBIT 3**   Google's Services and Tools in 2012

| Search Features | |
|---|---|
| | **Alerts**<br>Get email updates on the topics of your choice |
| | **Blog Search**<br>Find blogs on your favorite topics |
| | **Books**<br>Search the full text of books |
| | **Checkout**<br>Complete online purchases more quickly and securely |
| | **Google Chrome**<br>A browser built for speed, stability and security |
| | **Custom Search**<br>Create a customized search experience for your community |
| | **Desktop**<br>Search and personalize your computer |
| | **Directory**<br>Search the web, organized by topic or category |
| | **Earth**<br>Explore the world from your computer |
| | **Finance**<br>Business info, news, and interactive charts |
| | **GOOG-411**<br>Find and connect with businesses from your phone |
| | **Google Health**<br>Organize your medical records online |
| | **iGoogle**<br>Add news, games and more to your Google homepage |
| | **Images**<br>Search for images on the Web |
| | **Maps**<br>View maps and directions |
| | **News**<br>Search thousands of news stories |
| | **Patent Search**<br>Search the full text of US Patents |

*(Continued)*

**EXHIBIT 3**   *(Continued)*

| Search Features | |
|---|---|
| | **Product Search**<br>Search for stuff to buy |
| | **Scholar**<br>Search scholarly papers |
| | **Toolbar**<br>Add a search box to your browser |
| | **Trends**<br>Explore past and present search trends |
| | **Videos**<br>Search for videos on the Web |
| | **Web Search**<br>Search billions of Web pages |

| Google Tools and Web Applications | |
|---|---|
| | **Code**<br>Developer tools, APIs and resources |
| | **Labs**<br>Explore Google's technology playground |
| | **Blogger**<br>Share your life online with a blog—it's fast, easy, and free |
| | **Calendar**<br>Organize your schedule and share events with friends |
| | **Docs**<br>Create and share your online documents, presentations, and spreadsheets |
| | **Google Mail**<br>Fast, searchable email with less spam |
| | **Groups**<br>Create mailing lists and discussion groups |
| | **Knol**<br>Share what you know |
| | **Orkut**<br>Meet new people and stay in touch with friends |
| | **Picasa**<br>Find, edit and share your photos |

*(Continued)*

**EXHIBIT 3**   *(Concluded)*

| Google Tools and Web Applications |
|---|
| **Reader** |
| Get all your blogs and news feeds fast |
| **Sites** |
| Create Web sites and secure group wikis |
| **SketchUp** |
| Build 3D models quickly and easily |
| **Talk** |
| IM and call your friends through your computer |
| **Translate** |
| View Web pages in other languages |
| **YouTube** |
| Watch, upload and share videos |

| Google Mobile Applications |
|---|
| **Maps for mobile** |
| View maps, your location and get directions on your phone |
| **Search for mobile** |
| Search Google wherever you are |

*Source:* Google.com.

for selected years between 2001 and 2011 is presented in Exhibit 4. The company's balance sheets for 2010 and 2011 are presented in Exhibit 5.

## Google Search Appliance

Google's search technology could be integrated into a third party's website or intranet if search functionality was important to the customer. Google's Site Search allowed enterprises ranging from small businesses to public companies to license Google's search appliance for use on their websites for as little as $100 per year. The Google Search Appliance was designed for use on corporate intranets to allow employees to search company documents. The Search Appliance included a variety of security features to ensure that only employees with proper authority were able to view restricted documents. The Google Mini Search Appliance was designed for small businesses with 50,000 to 300,000 documents stored on local PCs

and servers. The Google Mini hardware and software package could be licensed online (at **www.google. com/enterprise/mini**) at prices ranging from $2,990 to $9,900, depending on document count capability. Google's more robust search appliance had a document count capability of up to 30 million documents and was designed for midsized to global businesses. Licensing fees for the Google Search appliance ranged from $30,000 to $600,000, depending on document count capability.

## AdWords

Google AdWords allowed advertisers, either independently through Google's automated tools or with the assistance of Google's marketing teams, to create text-based ads that would appear alongside Google search results. AdWords users could evaluate the effectiveness of their advertising expenditures with Google through the use of performance reports

**EXHIBIT 4   Financial Summary for Google, 2001, 2005–2011 ($ millions, except per share amounts)**

| | 2011 | 2010 | 2009 | 2008 | 2007 | 2006 | 2005 | 2001 |
|---|---|---|---|---|---|---|---|---|
| **Revenues** | $37,905 | $29,321 | $23,651 | $21,796 | $16,594 | $10,605 | $6,139 | $86 |
| Costs and expenses: | | | | | | | | |
| Cost of revenues | 13,188 | 10,417 | 8,844 | 8,622 | 6,649 | 4,225 | 2,577 | 14 |
| Research and development | 5,162 | 3,762 | 2,843 | 2,793 | 2,120 | 1,229 | 600 | 17 |
| Sales and marketing | 4,589 | 2,799 | 1,984 | 1,946 | 1,461 | 850 | 468 | 20 |
| General and administrative | 2,724 | 1,962 | 1,667 | 1,803 | 1,279 | 76 | 387 | 25 |
| Contribution to Google Foundation | | | | | | | 90 | — |
| Charge related to the resolution of Department of Justice investigation | 500 | — | | — | — | | — | — |
| Total costs and expenses | 26,163 | 18,940 | 15,338 | 15,164 | 11,510 | 7,055 | 4,121 | 75 |
| Income (loss) from Operations | 11,742 | 10,381 | 8,312 | 6,632 | 5,084 | 3,550 | 2,017 | 11 |
| Impairment of equity Investments | | | | (1,095) | | | | — |
| Interest income (expense) and other, net | 584 | 415 | 69 | 316 | 590 | 461 | 124 | (1) |
| Income (loss) before income taxes | 12,326 | 10,796 | 8,381 | 5,854 | 5,674 | 4,011 | 2,142 | 10 |
| Provision for income taxes | 2,589 | 2,291 | 1,861 | 1,627 | 1,470 | 934 | 676 | 3 |
| Net income (loss) | $ 9,737 | $ 8,505 | $ 6,520 | $ 4,227 | $ 4,204 | $ 3,077 | $1,465 | $ 7 |
| Net income (loss) per share: | | | | | | | | |
| Basic | $30.62 | $26.69 | $20.62 | $13.46 | $13.53 | $10.21 | $5.31 | $0.07 |
| Diluted | $29.76 | $26.31 | $20.41 | $13.31 | $13.29 | $9.94 | $5.02 | $0.04 |
| Number of shares used in per share calculations: | | | | | | | | |
| Basic | 323 | 319 | 316 | 314 | 311 | 301 | 276 | 95 |
| Diluted | 396 | 323 | 319 | 318 | 316 | 310 | 292 | 187 |
| Net cash provided by operating activities | $14,565 | $11,081 | $ 9,316 | $ 7,853 | $ 5,775 | $ 3,581 | $2,459 | N/A |
| Cash, cash equivalents, and marketable securities | 44,626 | 34,975 | 24,485 | 15,846 | 14,219 | 11,244 | 8,034 | N/A |
| Total assets | 72,574 | 57,851 | 40,497 | 31,768 | 25,336 | 18,473 | 10,272 | N/A |
| Total long-term liabilities | 5,516 | 1,614 | 1,745 | 1,227 | 611 | 129 | 107 | N/A |
| Total stockholders' equity | 58,145 | 46,241 | 36,004 | 28,239 | 22,690 | 17,040 | 9,419 | N/A |

*Source:* Google, Form S-1, filed April 29, 2004; Google, 2009, 2010, and 2011 10-K reports.

**EXHIBIT 5**  Google's Balance Sheets, 2010–2011 ($ millions, except per share amounts)

| | 2011 | 2010 |
|---|---|---|
| **Assets** | | |
| Current assets: | | |
|     Cash and cash equivalents | $ 9,983 | $13,630 |
|     Marketable securities | 34,643 | 21,345 |
|     Accounts receivable, net of allowance of $133 and $101 | 5,427 | 4,252 |
|     Receivable under reverse repurchase agreements | 745 | 750 |
|     Deferred income taxes, net | 215 | 259 |
|     Prepaid revenue share, expenses, and other assets | 1,745 | 1,326 |
|     Total current assets | 52,758 | 41,562 |
| Prepaid revenue share, expenses, and other assets, non-current | 499 | 442 |
| Deferred income taxes, net, non-current | 0 | 265 |
| Non-marketable equity securities | 790 | 523 |
| Property and equipment, net | 9,603 | 7,759 |
| Intangible assets, net | 1,578 | 1,044 |
| Goodwill | 7,346 | 6,256 |
|     Total assets | $72,574 | $57,851 |
| **Liabilities and Stockholders' Equity** | | |
| Current liabilities: | | |
|     Accounts payable | $    588 | $     483 |
|     Short-term debt | 1,218 | 3,465 |
|     Accrued compensation and benefits | 1,818 | 1,410 |
|     Accrued expenses and other current liabilities | 1,370 | 961 |
|     Accrued revenue share | 1,168 | 885 |
|     Securities lending payable | 2,007 | 2,361 |
|     Deferred revenue | 547 | 394 |
|     Income taxes payable, net | 197 | 37 |
|     Total current liabilities | 8,913 | 9,996 |
| Long-term debt | 2,986 | 0 |
| Deferred revenue, long-term | 44 | 35 |
| Income taxes payable, long-term | 1,693 | 1,200 |
| Deferred income taxes, net, non-current | 287 | 0 |
| Other long-term liabilities | 506 | 379 |
| Commitments and contingencies | | |
| Stockholders' equity: | | |
|     Convertible preferred stock, $0.001 par value, 100,000 shares authorized; no shares issued and outstanding | 0 | 0 |
|     Class A and Class B common stock and additional paid-in capital, $0.001 par value per share: 9,000,000 shares authorized; 321,301 (Class A 250,413, Class B 70,888) and par value of $321 (Class A $250, Class B $71) and 324,895 (Class A 257,553, Class B 67,342) and par value $325 (Class A $258, Class B $67) shares issued and outstanding | 20,264 | 18,235 |
|     Accumulated other comprehensive income | 276 | 138 |
|     Retained earnings | 37,605 | 27,868 |
|     Total stockholders' equity | 58,145 | 46,241 |
|     Total liabilities and stockholders' equity | $72,574 | $57,851 |

*Source:* Google, 2011 10-K report.

that tracked the effectiveness of each ad. Google also offered a keyword targeting program that suggested synonyms for keywords entered by advertisers, a traffic estimator that helped potential advertisers anticipate charges, and multiple payment options that included charges to credit cards, debit cards, and monthly invoicing.

Larger advertisers were offered additional services to help run large, dynamic advertising campaigns. Such assistance included the availability of specialists with expertise in various industries to offer suggestions for targeting potential customers and identifying relevant keywords. Google's advertising specialists helped develop ads for customers that would increase click-through rates and purchase rates. Google also offered its large advertising customers bulk posting services that helped launch and manage campaigns including ads using hundreds or thousands of keywords.

Google's search-based ads were priced using an auction system that allowed advertisers to bid on keywords that would describe their product or service. Bids could be made on a cost-per-impression (CPI) or cost-per-click (CPC) basis. Most Google advertisers placed bids based on CPC frequency rather than how many times an ad was displayed by Google. Google's auction pricing model assigned each bidder a Quality Score, which was determined by the advertiser's past keyword click-through rate and the relevance of the ad text. Advertisers with high Quality Scores were offered lower minimum bids than advertisers with poor quality scores.

Google allowed users to pay a CPC rate lower than their bid price if their bid was considerably more than the next highest bid. For example, an advertiser who bid $0.75 per click for a particular keyword would be charged only $0.51 per click if the next highest bid was only $0.50. The AdWords discounter ensured that advertisers paid only 1 cent more than the next highest bid, regardless of the actual amount of their bid.

## AdSense

Google's AdSense program allowed web publishers to share in the advertising revenues generated by Google's text ads. The AdSense program served content-relevant Google text ads to pages on Google Network websites. For example, an Internet user reading an article about the state of the economy at **Reuters.com** would see Google text ads by investment magazines and companies specializing in home business opportunities. Google Network members shared in the advertising revenue whenever a site visitor clicked a Google ad displayed on their sites. The more than 1 million Google Network members did not pay a fee to participate in the program and received about 60 percent of advertising dollars generated from the ads. Google's AdSense program also allowed mobile phone operators to share in Google revenues if text and image ads were displayed on mobile handsets. Owners of dormant domain names, web-based game sites, video sites, and news feed services could also participate in the AdSense program. The breakdown of Google's revenues by source for 2005 through 2011 is presented in Exhibit 6.

## Other Revenue Sources

The company's 2006 acquisition of YouTube allowed it to receive advertising revenues for ads displayed during Internet videos, while its 2008 acquisition

## EXHIBIT 6    Google's Revenues by Source, 2004–2010 ($ millions)

| | 2011 | 2010 | 2009 | 2008 | 2007 | 2006 | 2005 |
|---|---|---|---|---|---|---|---|
| Advertising revenues: | | | | | | | |
| Google websites | $26,145 | $19,444 | $15,722 | $14,414 | $10,625 | $ 6,333 | $3,377 |
| Google Network websites | 10,386 | 8,792 | 7,166 | 6,715 | 5,788 | 4,160 | 2,688 |
| Total advertising revenues | 36,531 | 28,236 | 22,889 | 21,129 | 16,413 | 10,493 | 6,065 |
| Licensing and other revenues | 1,374 | 1,085 | 762 | 667 | 181 | 112 | 74 |
| Net revenues | $37,905 | $29,321 | $23,651 | $21,796 | $16,594 | $10,605 | $6,139 |

*Source:* Google, 2007, 2009, 2010, and 2011 10-K reports.

of DoubleClick allowed the company to generate advertising revenues through banner ads. The company's 2008 launch of Google Checkout generated fees of as much as 2 percent of the transaction amount for purchases made at participating e-retailer sites. Google's business model was further expanded in 2008 to include licensing fees paid by users of its web-based Google Apps document and spreadsheet software.

## GOOGLE'S STRATEGY AND COMPETITIVE POSITION IN 2012

### Google's Strategies to Dominate Internet Advertising

Google's multiple acquisitions since its 2004 IPO, and its research and development activities, were directed at increasing the company's dominance in Internet advertising. The addition of Google Maps, local search, airline travel information, weather, Book Search, Gmail, Blogger, and other features increased traffic to Google sites and gave the company more opportunities to serve ads to Internet users. Also, the $3.1 billion acquisition of Double-Click in 2008 allowed Google to diversify its Internet advertising beyond search ads to include banner ads. Google's revenues from banner ads were estimated at approximately $3 billion in 2011. Also, while You-Tube advertising revenues had proven challenging through 2010, Google recorded an estimated $1.3 billion in revenue from banner ads displayed on YouTube videos in 2011. However, not all of Google's acquisitions and innovations had resulted in meaningful contributions to the company's revenues. The company abandoned its Knol open-source encyclopedia and Wave productivity tool in 2012, and its Orkut social networking site had proven to be an abject failure.

Google made a second attempt at developing a social networking site in 2011 when it launched Google$^+$. Like Facebook, users could maintain profiles, post comments, link to content from other Internet sites, and keep online photo albums. Google$^+$ also worked on mobile devices, and allowed users to participate in multiperson video chats. In January 2012, Google$^+$ had 100 million users, who were logged on an average of 3.3 minutes per month, compared to Facebook's 850 million users, who spent about 7.5 hours per month updating their pages. The company believed that Google$^+$ would grow to challenge Facebook since Google$^+$ account information could be linked with Google's other products and services. For example, Google$^+$ users who used Google to search for a friend with a common name could pull up information on the exact individual linked to their Google$^+$ account.

Google's strategy to dominate Internet advertising also entailed becoming the number one search engine used not only in the United States but also around the world. In 2011, Google's search-based ads could be delivered to Internet users in 41 different languages. Nearly 50 percent of the company's 2011 revenues and traffic were generated from outside the United States, and the percentage of sales from outside the United States was expected to grow as Google entered emerging markets like Russia and China. China was a particularly attractive market for Google since it had more Internet users (300 + million) than any other country in the world. However, Google's 2006 entry into China was accompanied by challenges, including strong competition from local search provider Baidu and requirements by the Chinese government to censor search results that were critical of the government. Google complied with government censorship requirements until early 2010, when cyberattacks originating in China stole proprietary computer code from Google and information from the Gmail accounts of several Chinese human rights activists. Google first responded to the hacking incidents by stating that it would withdraw from the Chinese search market and then shifted to a strategy of redirecting users of its censored Google.cn site in China to its uncensored Hong Kong search site, Google.com.hk. The Chinese government was able to block search results from Google's Hong Kong site, but the new policy ended Google's involvement in China's censorship practices. To avoid breaking Chinese law prohibiting the distribution of information not authorized by the government, Google agreed in June 2010 to stop the automatic redirects to its Hong Kong site. Instead, it presented Google.cn users with a link to Google.com.hk. In 2012, 78 percent of Internet searches in China were performed by Baidu, while Google held a 17 percent share of searches in that country. A breakdown of Google's revenues and long-lived assets by geographic region for 2007 through 2011 is presented in Exhibit 7.

## EXHIBIT 7   Google's Revenues and Long-Lived Assets by Geographic Region, 2007–2011 (in millions)

| Revenues | Year Ended December 31 | | | | |
|---|---|---|---|---|---|
| | 2011 | 2010 | 2009 | 2008 | 2007 |
| United States | $17,560 | $14,056 | $11,194 | $10,636 | $ 8,698 |
| United Kingdom | 4,057 | 3,329 | 2,986 | 3,038 | 2,531 |
| Rest of the world | 16,288 | 11,936 | 9,471 | 8,122 | 5,365 |
| Total revenues | $37,905 | $29,321 | $23,651 | $21,796 | $16,594 |

| Long-Lived Assets | As of December 31 | | | | |
|---|---|---|---|---|---|
| | | 2009 | 2008 | 2007 | 2006 |
| United States | $15,963 | $ 9,432 | $ 9,783 | $ 7,335 | $ 5,071 |
| Rest of the world | 3,853 | 1,898 | 1,807 | 712 | 363 |
| Total long-lived assets | $19,816 | $11,330 | $11,589 | $ 8,047 | $ 5,434 |

*Source:* Google, 2007, 2009, and 2011 10-K reports.

## Mobile Search and Google's Emerging Rivalry with Apple in Smartphones and Tablet Computers

In 2011, more than 5 billion people worldwide and 234 million Americans ages 13 and older owned and used mobile phones. More than 35 percent of Americans and a growing percentage worldwide accessed the Internet from mobile devices, and a rapidly growing number of mobile phone users were exchanging basic mobile phones for smartphones. Smartphones like Apple's iPhone could connect to the networks of wireless carriers to make phone calls, access the Internet, or run various Internet applications. Between March 2011 and June 2011, the number of smartphone users in the U.S. had grown by 10 percent to reach 82.2 million.

Apple Inc. built its early reputation in the 1980s and 1990s on its innovative Mac computer lines, but in 2010, only $17.5 billion of its net sales of $65.2 billion came from the sale of computers. In 2011, Apple was the world's largest seller of smartphones, tablet computers, and personal media players with market shares of 19.1 percent, 85 percent, and 73 percent, respectively. In 2011, the iPhone accounted for $47.1 billion of its total sales of $108.2 billion. The iPad contributed revenues of $20.3 billion and iPod and related music products accounted for sales of more than $13 billion in 2011. The company's hefty profit margins on its electronic devices allowed it to record a net income of almost $26 billion in 2011. Apple's performance accelerated in 2012, with the company setting revenue and profit records during the second quarter of 2012. The record sales and earnings were driven largely by the iPhone, which saw a year-over-year revenue increase of 88 percent and iPad, which increased by 151 percent from the same period in 2011. The company's strong performance allowed its stock price to increase so much that it became the most valuable company in the world in 2011, as measured by market capitalization. Apple's market capitalization hit $600 billion in April 2012—a mark only achieved by one other company in history: Microsoft, in 1999, when its valuation reached $619. Microsoft's market capitalization in April 2012 stood at $260 billion. A summary of Apple's financial performance between 2007 and 2011 is presented in Exhibit 8.

Google's introduction of its Android operating system for smartphones in 2008 allowed it to increase its share of mobile searches from about 60 percent to approximately 95 percent in 2012. Android was not a phone but an operating system that Google made available free of charge to any phone manufacturer wishing to market mobile devices with Internet capability. Android's core applications matched most

**EXHIBIT 8** Financial Summary for Apple Inc., 2007–2011 ($ millions)

| | Fiscal Year Ended June 30 | | | | |
|---|---|---|---|---|---|
| | **2011** | **2010** | **2009** | **2008** | **2007** |
| Net sales | $108,249 | $65,225 | $42,905 | $37,491 | $24,006 |
| Operating income | 33,790 | 18,385 | 11,740 | 8,327 | 4,409 |
| Net income | 25,922 | 14,013 | 8,235 | 6,119 | 3,496 |
| Cash, cash equivalents, and marketable securities | $ 81,570 | $51,011 | $33,992 | $24,490 | $15,386 |
| Total assets | 116,371 | 75,183 | 47,501 | 36,171 | 24,878 |
| Long-term obligations | 10,100 | 5,531 | 3,502 | 1,745 | 687 |
| Stockholders' equity | 76,615 | 47,791 | 31,640 | 22,297 | 14,531 |

*Source:* Apple Inc. 2008, 2010, and 2011 10-K report.

**EXHIBIT 9** U.S. Smartphone Platform Market Share Rankings, Selected Periods, September 2009–May 2011

| Smartphone Platform | September 2009 | May 2010 | May 2011 | May 2012 |
|---|---|---|---|---|
| Google Android | 2.5% | 13.0% | 38.1% | 50.9% |
| Apple iPhone | 24.1 | 24.4 | 28.6 | 31.9 |
| RIM (BlackBerry) | 42.6 | 41.7 | 24.7 | 11.4 |
| Microsoft Windows for Mobile | 19.0 | 13.2 | 5.8 | 4.0 |
| Palm | 8.3 | 4.8 | 2.4 | 1.1 |
| Others | 3.5 | 2.9 | 2.4 | 0.7 |
| Total | 100.0% | 100.0% | 100.0% | 100.0% |

*Source:* ComScore.com.

features of Apple's iPhone. By 2010, all major mobile phone providers had added smartphone models running Android software to its lineup of handsets, and despite Google's late entry into the market, Android's market share had increased from zero in 2008 to almost 51 percent in May 2012—see Exhibit 9.

Similar to its relationship with mobile phone manufacturers, Google allowed mobile apps developers to use the Android operating system free of licensing fees. The worldwide market for mobile apps was estimated at $17.5 billion by 2012. In 2012, approximately 600,000 free and paid smartphone and tablet computer apps were available at Google Play. The number of apps available at Google Play was very similar to the number of apps for iPhones and iPads available at Apple's App Store in 2012. In 2010, Google briefly marketed its own Nexus One smartphone, which was produced by HTC and was compatible with all major wireless carrier 3G and 4G networks. However, its $12.5 billion acquisition of Motorola Mobility in 2012

would allow it to design and market its own line of smartphones and tablet computers. Google launched its first internally developed tablet computer in June 2012. The $199 Nexus 7 included a 7-inch screen and a camera and was designed to display books and other media available through the company's Google Play service. In 2011, Apple's iPad held a 68 percent share of the market for tablet computers, while Android-based tablet computers accounted for 29 percent of the market.

## Google's Strategic Offensive to Control the Desktop

Google's senior management believed that, in the very near future, most computer software programs used by businesses would move from local hard drives or intranets to the Internet. Many information technology analysts agreed that cloud computing would become a common software platform and could grow to a $95 billion market by 2013. Moving software applications to the cloud offered many possible benefits to corporate users, including lower software acquisition costs, lower computing support costs, and easier collaboration among employees in different locations. The beta version of Google Apps was launched in 2006 as a free word processing and spreadsheet package for individuals, but was relaunched in 2008 as a competing product to Microsoft Office. Google Apps was hosted on computers in Google's data centers and included Gmail, a calendar, instant messaging, word processing, spreadsheets, presentation software, and file storage space. Google Apps could be licensed by corporate customers at $50 per user per year. The licensing fee for the Microsoft Office and Outlook package was typically $350 per user per year. Industry analysts estimated Google Apps users at about 25 million and paid subscribers at about 1.5 million in 2010. Microsoft estimated Microsoft Office users at about 500 million in 2010. Even though Google Apps had not yet recorded any meaningful revenues as of 2012, Microsoft had launched its own cloud-based productivity package called Office 365 to defend against Google's entry into the productivity software market.

Google's Chrome browser, which was launched in September 2008, and Chrome operating system (OS) launched in July 2009 were developed specifically to accommodate cloud computing applications. The bare-bones Chrome browser was built on a multiprocessor design that would allow users to operate spreadsheets, word processing, video editing, and other applications on separate tabs that could be run simultaneously. Each tab operated independently so that if one tab crashed, other applications running from Google's data centers were not affected. The Chrome browser also provided Google with a defense against moves by Microsoft to make it more difficult for Google to deliver relevant search-based ads to Internet users. Microsoft's Internet Explorer 8 allowed users to hide their Internet address and viewing history, which prevented Google from collecting user-specific information needed for ad targeting. Mozilla's Firefox browser employed a similar feature that prevented third parties from tracking a user's viewing habits. The clean-running Chrome OS was an open-source operating system specifically designed as a platform for cloud computing applications. Google had entered into agreements with Acer, Hewlett-Packard, and Lenovo to begin producing netbooks that would use the Chrome OS and Chrome browser to access

## EXHIBIT 10  Worldwide Browser Market Share Rankings, Selected Periods, September 2008–June 2012

| Browser | September 2008 | June 2010 | June 2011 | June 2012 |
|---|---|---|---|---|
| Internet Explorer | 67% | 53% | 42% | 32% |
| Chrome | 1 | 9 | 22 | 32 |
| Firefox | 26 | 31 | 28 | 25 |
| Safari | 3 | 4 | 5 | 7 |
| Opera | 2 | 2 | 2 | 2 |
| Others | 1 | 1 | 1 | 2 |
| Total | 100% | 100% | 100% | 100% |

*Source:* gs.statcounter.com.

the cloud-based Google Apps productivity software. Worldwide market share statistics for the leading browsers for selected periods between September 2008 and June 2012 are presented in Exhibit 10.

## Google's Initiatives to Expand Search to Television

In mid-2010, Google entered into an alliance with Intel, Sony, Logitech, Best Buy, DISH Network, and Adobe to develop Google TV. Google TV would be built on the Android platform and would run the Chrome browser software to search live network and cable programming; streaming videos from providers such as Netflix, Amazon Video On Demand, and YouTube; and recorded programs on a DVR. Google TV users would also be able to use their televisions to browse the Web and run cloud-based applications such as Google Apps. DISH Network satellite service customers could use Google TV's features with the addition of a Logitech set-top box or Sony Internet TV.

Google acquired On2 Technologies, which was the leading developer of video compression technology, in February 2010 in a $124 million stock and cash transaction. The acquisition of On2 was expected to improve the video streaming capabilities of Google TV. Google also lobbied the Obama administration for Federal Communications Commission "Net neutrality" rules that would require Internet providers to manage traffic in a manner that would not restrict high-bandwidth services such as Internet television. The company was also testing an ultrafast broadband network in several cities across the United States that was as much as 100 times faster than what was offered by competing Internet providers. Google management had stated that the company did not intend to launch a nationwide Internet service, but did want to expose consumers to Internet applications and content that would be possible with greater bandwidth and faster transmission speeds.

# GOOGLE'S INTERNET RIVALS

Google's ability to sustain its competitive advantage among search companies was a function of its ability to maintain strong relationships with Internet users, advertisers, and websites. In 2012, Google was the world's most-visited Internet site, with more than 900 million unique Internet users going to Google sites each month to search for information. Google management believed its primary competitors to be Microsoft and Yahoo. A comparison of the percentage of Internet searches among websites offering search capabilities for selected periods between July 2006 and May 2012 is shown in Exhibit 11.

**EXHIBIT 11**   U.S. Search Engine Market Share Rankings, Selected Periods, July 2006–May 2012

| Search Entity | Percent of Searches | | | | |
|---|---|---|---|---|---|
| | July 2006 | June 2009 | May 2010 | July 2011 | May 2012 |
| Google Sites | 43.7% | 65.0% | 63.7% | 65.1% | 66.7% |
| Microsoft Sites | 12.8 | 8.4 | 12.1 | 14.4 | 15.4 |
| Yahoo Sites | 28.8 | 19.6 | 18.3 | 16.1 | 13.4 |
| Ask.com | 5.4 | 3.9 | 3.6 | 2.9 | 3.0 |
| AOL | 5.9 | 3.1 | 2.3 | 1.5 | 1.5 |
| Others | 3.4 | n.m. | n.m. | n.m. | n.m |
| Total | 100.0% | 100.0% | 100.0% | 100.0% | 100.0% |

n.m. = not material

*Source:* ColScore.com.

## Microsoft Online Services

Microsoft Corporation recorded fiscal 2011 revenues and a net income of approximately $70 billion and $23.2 billion, respectively, through the sales of computer software, consulting services, video game hardware, and online services. Windows 7 and Microsoft Office accounted for more than one-half of the company's 2011 revenues and nearly all of its operating profit. The company's online services business recorded sales of nearly $2.5 billion and an operating loss of almost $2.6 billion during fiscal 2011. Microsoft's online services business generated revenues from banner ads displayed at the company's MSN Web portal and its affiliated websites, search-based ads displayed with Bing results, and subscription fees from its MSN dial-up service. Microsoft's websites made the company the second-most-visited Internet destination worldwide in 2011, with approximately 900 million unique visitors each month. A financial summary for Microsoft Corporation and its Online Services Division is provided in Exhibit 12.

Microsoft's search business was launched in November 2004 as Live Search to compete directly with Google and slow whatever intentions Google might have to threaten Microsoft in its core operating system and productivity software businesses. Microsoft's concern with threats posed by Google arose shortly after Google's IPO, when Bill Gates noticed that many of the Google job postings on its site were nearly identical to Microsoft job specifications. Recognizing that the position announcements had more to do with operating-system design than search, Gates e-mailed key Microsoft executives, warning, "We have to watch these guys. It looks like they are building something to compete with us."[6] Gates later commented that Google was "more like us than anyone else we have ever competed with."[7]

Gates speculated that Google's long-term strategy involved the development of web-based software applications comparable to Word, Excel, PowerPoint, and other Microsoft products. Microsoft's strategy to compete with Google was keyed to making Live Search more effective than Google at providing highly relevant search results. Microsoft believed that any conversion of Google users to Live Search would reduce the number of PC users who might ultimately adopt Google's Web-based word processing, spreadsheet, and presentation software packages. In 2008, Microsoft paid more than $100 million to acquire Powerset, which was the developer of a semantic search engine.

**EXHIBIT 12** Financial Summary for Microsoft Corporation and Microsoft's Online Services Business Unit, 2007–2011 ($ millions)

| Financial Summary for Microsoft Corporation | 2011 | 2010 | 2009 | 2008 | 2007 |
|---|---|---|---|---|---|
| Revenue | $69,943 | $62,484 | $58,437 | $60,420 | $51,112 |
| Operating income | 27,161 | 24,098 | 20,363 | 22,492 | 18,524 |
| Net income | 23,150 | 18,760 | 14,569 | 17,681 | 14,065 |
| Cash, cash equivalents, and short-term investments | $52,772 | $36,788 | $31,447 | $23,662 | $23,411 |
| Total assets | 108,704 | 86,113 | 77,888 | 72,793 | 63,171 |
| Long-term obligations | 22,847 | 13,791 | 11,296 | 6,621 | 8,320 |
| Stockholders' equity | 57,083 | 46,175 | 39,558 | 36,286 | 31,097 |

| Financial Summary for Microsoft's Online Services Business Unit | 2011 | 2010 | 2009 | 2008 | 2007 |
|---|---|---|---|---|---|
| Revenue | $ 2,528 | $ 2,201 | $ 2,121 | $ 3,214 | $ 2,441 |
| Operating income (loss) | (2,557) | (2,337) | (1,641) | (1,233) | (617) |

*Source:* Microsoft, 2007, 2009, 2011, and 2012 annual reports.

Semantic search technology offered the opportunity to surpass the relevancy of Google's search results since semantic search evaluated the meaning of a word or phrase and considered its context when returning search results. Even though semantic search had the capability to answer questions stated in common language, semantic search processing time took several seconds to return results. The amount of time necessary to conduct a search had caused Microsoft to limit Powerset's search index to only articles listed in Wikipedia. Microsoft's developers were focused on increasing the speed of its semantic search capabilities so that its search index could be expanded to a greater number of Internet pages. The company's developers also incorporated some of Powerset's capabilities into its latest-generation search engine, Bing, which was launched in June 2009. Banner ads comprised the bulk of Microsoft's online advertising revenues, since its Bing search engine accounted for only 14.4 percent of online searches in July 2011. Even though the market for display ads was only about one-half the size of the search ad market in 2009, the advertising spending on banner ads was expected to double by 2012 to reach $15 billion.

Microsoft was also moving forward with its own approach to cloud computing. The company's Windows Live service allowed Internet users to store files online at its password-protected SkyDrive site. SkyDrive's online file storage allowed users to access and edit files from multiple locations, share files with co-workers who might need editing privileges, or make files available in a public folder for wide distribution. Azure was Microsoft's most ambitious cloud computing initiative and was intended to allow businesses to reduce computing costs by allowing Microsoft to host its operating programs and data files. In addition to reducing capital expenditures for software upgrades and added server capacity, Azure's offsite hosting provided data security in the event of natural disasters such as fires or hurricanes.

## Yahoo

Yahoo was founded in 1994 and was the third-most-visited Internet destination worldwide in 2012, with nearly 500 million unique visitors each month. Facebook was the second-most-visited website, with more than 700 million unique visitors each month in 2012. Almost any information available on the Internet could be accessed through Yahoo's web portal. Visitors could access content categorized by Yahoo or set up an account with Yahoo to maintain a personal calendar and e-mail account, check the latest news, check local weather, obtain maps, check TV listings, watch a movie trailer, track a stock portfolio, maintain a golf handicap, keep an online photo album, or search personal ads or job listings.

Yahoo also hosted websites for small businesses and Internet retailers and had entered into strategic partnerships with 20 mobile phone operators in the

United States and Europe to provide mobile search and display ads to their customers. Yahoo accounted for less than 5 percent of searches performed on mobile phones in 2012. Yahoo's broad range of services allowed it to generate revenues from numerous sources—it received fees for banner ads displayed at Yahoo.com, Yahoo! Messenger, Yahoo! Mail, Flickr, or mobile phone customers; it received listing fees at Yahoo! Autos, Cars.com, and Yahoo! Real Estate; it received revenues from paid search results at Yahoo! Search; it shared in travel agency booking fees made at Yahoo! Travel; and it received subscription fees from its registered users at Rivals.com, Yahoo! Games, Yahoo! Music, and Yahoo! Personals.

Yahoo's relationship with Google dated to 2000 and, since that time, had oscillated between cooperative and adversarial. Yahoo was among Google's earliest customers for its search appliance, but Yahoo began to distance itself from Google in 2002 when it began acquiring companies with developed search technologies. Yahoo replaced Google with its own search capabilities in February 2004. Yahoo later levied a patent infringement charge against Google that resulted in a settlement that gave Google ownership of the technology rights in return for 2.7 million shares of Google stock. Yahoo attempted to renew its relationship with Google in 2008 in hopes of reversing a decline in profitability and liquidity that began in 2006. After averting a hostile takeover by Microsoft in June 2008, Yahoo reached an agreement with Google that would allow Yahoo to host Google search ads. The partnership would provide Yahoo with an estimated $800 million in additional revenues annually, most of which would go directly to its bottom line. However, Google withdrew from the agreement in November 2008 after receiving notification from the U.S. Justice Department that the alliance would possibly violate antitrust statutes. Shortly after being notified that Google was withdrawing from the deal, Yahoo's chief managers told business reporters that the company was "disappointed that Google has elected to withdraw from the agreement rather than defend it in court."[8] In July 2009, Microsoft and Yahoo finally came to an agreement that would make Microsoft Bing Yahoo's imbedded search engine for a period of 10 years. A summary of Yahoo's financial performance between 2007 and 2011 is presented in Exhibit 13.

## ISSUES CONCERNING GOOGLE'S PERFORMANCE AND BUSINESS ETHICS IN 2012

During its first quarter of fiscal 2012, Google had been able to achieve year-over-year revenue growth of 24 percent. Commenting on the company's early 2012 successes, CEO Larry Page said the company "saw tremendous momentum from the big bets we've made in products like Android, Chrome, and YouTube. We are still at the very early stages of what technology can do to improve people's lives and we have enormous opportunities ahead."[9]

The company's strategic priorities in 2012 focused on expanding its share of mobile search and smartphone platforms, expanding into the design and sale of smartphone handsets, making Google$^{+}$ a

## EXHIBIT 13  Financial Summary for Yahoo, 2007–2011 ($ thousands)

|  | 2011 | 2010 | 2009 | 2008 | 2007 |
|---|---|---|---|---|---|
| Revenues | $4,984,199 | $6,324,651 | $6,460,315 | $7,208,502 | $6,969,274 |
| Income from operations | 800,341 | 772,524 | 386,692 | 12,963 | 695,413 |
| Net income | 1,048,827 | 1,231,663 | 597,992 | 418,921 | 639,155 |
| Cash and cash equivalents | $1,562,390 | $1,526,427 | $1,275,430 | $2,292,296 | $1,513,930 |
| Marketable debt securities | 967,527 | 2,102,255 | 3,242,574 | 1,229,677 | 849,542 |
| Working capital | 2,245,175 | 2,719,676 | 2,877,044 | 3,040,483 | 937,274 |
| Total assets | 14,928,104 | 14,928,104 | 14,936,030 | 13,689,848 | 12,229,741 |
| Long-term liabilities | 994,078 | 705,822 | 699,666 | 715,872 | 384,208 |
| Total stockholders' equity | 12,541,067 | 12,558,129 | 12,493,320 | 11,250,942 | 9,532,831 |

*Source:* Yahoo, 2007, 2009, 2010, and 2011 10-K reports.

strong competitor to Facebook, pushing forward with its plans to become the dominant provider of cloud computing solutions, increasing search advertising revenues from markets outside the United States, and extending search to television. Some analysts believed the company's priorities should also include the development of semantic search capabilities, while others were concerned that the company had strayed from its 10 Principles—specifically, Principle 6, "You can make money without doing evil."

The company agreed to a $500 million legal settlement with the U.S. Justice Department to avoid prosecution on charges that it accepted hundreds of millions of dollars in illegal ads from unlicensed online Canadian pharmacies selling controlled substances in the U.S. Among the most disturbing aspects of the case against Google related to the Justice Department's assertion that Larry Page knew of the practice and had allowed it for years. In commenting about the case, Rhode Island U.S. Attorney Peter Neronha stated "We simply know it from the documents we reviewed, the witnesses that we interviewed, that Larry Page knew what was going on."[10]

The company agreed to a $22.5 million fine levied by the FTC for bypassing Apple Safari web browser privacy settings to place tracking files on users of Apple computers, iPhones, and iPads. Also, the company was under investigation by authorities in Canada, Australia, Germany, Italy, the United Kingdom, and Spain over its Street View data collection practices between 2008 and 2010. Data collected from home Wi-Fi signals by Google included e-mails, usernames, passwords, and other private data. In 2010, Google co-founder Sergey Brin said the company "screwed up" by collecting personal data through wireless networks in an attempt to improve its mapping system.[11]

In 2012, the FCC concluded that Google did not violate U.S. wiretapping laws, but that it did obstruct the investigation, and so was fined $25,000.

Also, the company's lobbying efforts to encourage the FCC to institute policies to promote Net neutrality had drawn the scrutiny of the U.S. House Oversight Committee. The primary concern of the House Oversight Committee involved communications between the company and its former head of public policy and government affairs, Andrew McLaughlin, who had been appointed to the position of White House Deputy Chief Technology Officer. Ethics rules created by an executive order signed by President Obama barred all White House officials from communicating with lobbyists or a company potentially affected by pending policy matters. A Freedom of Information Act (FOIA) request by a consumer group found that McLaughlin regularly communicated with Google executives to discuss the administration's push to have the Internet regulated by the Federal Communications Commission to promote Net neutrality. McLaughlin's e-mails could be obtained under the FOIA since all White House e-mail accounts were required to be archived under federal law. The House Oversight Committee was particularly disturbed by McLaughlin's alleged use of a personal Gmail account to avoid having his communications with Google executives archived and subject to FOIA requests.

Some analysts believed that pressure to achieve the revenue and earnings growth necessary to maintain Google's lofty stock price may have caused Google management to make decisions that pushed the bounds of its corporate philosophy. It remained to be determined if Google's strategies could sustain its growth and stock performance in a manner that would adhere to the company founders' early beliefs.

## ENDNOTES

[1] Google, www.google.com/corporate/, accessed July 13, 2010.

[2] As quoted in Brad Stone, "The Education of Larry Page," Bloomberg Businessweek, April 15, 2012, pp. 12–14.

[3] Quoted in Google's Corporate Information, www.google.com/corporate/history.html.

[4] Google, "Our Philosophy," www.google.com/corporate/tenthings.html.

[5] "For Some Who Passed on Google Long Ago, Wistful Thinking," The Wall Street Journal Online, August 23, 2004.

[6] Quoted in "Gates vs. Google," Fortune, April 18, 2005.

[7] Ibid.

[8] Quoted in "With Google Gone, Will Microsoft Come Back to Yahoo?" Fortune, November 5, 2008.

[9] As quoted in "Google Announces First Quarter 2012 Results and Proposal for New Class of Stock," Google Press Release, April 12, 2012.

[10] Quoted in "New Heat for Google CEO," The Wall Street Journal Online, August 27, 2011.

[11] Quoted in "Google Faces European Probes on Wi-Fi Data," The Wall Street Journal Online, May 20, 2010; and "Google Loses Bid to Dismiss Street View Suit Over Privacy-Violation Claims," Bloomberg Online, June 30, 2011.

# Apple Inc. in 2012: Can It Sustain Its Growth and Defend against New Competitive Threats?

connect

**John E. Gamble**
University of South Alabama

**Lou Marino**
The University of Alabama

Despite the loss of Steve Jobs as CEO in 2011 and sluggish economic conditions in the United States, Apple Inc. had been able to sustain its impressive growth into 2012. The company set record quarterly revenues and profits during its second quarter of 2012, which resulted in its stock price catapulting to a level that made it the world's most valuable company as measured by market capitalization. In fact, only Microsoft's market capitalization of $619 billion on December 30, 1999 was greater than Apple's $600 billion-plus market capitalization on April 10, 2012. The record growth in revenues and profits came primarily from volume increases in the sale of iPhones and iPads, which increased by 88 percent and 151 percent, respectively, from the same period in 2011. The sales of Mac computers increased by 7 percent from the second quarter of 2011 to reach 4 million units. The only sales disappointment for the company was a 15 percent year-over-year decline in iPod sales. The company sold 7.7 million iPods during the second quarter of 2012.

The company's record-setting performance was a relief to those who worried that the company would struggle after the illness-forced resignation of Steve Jobs in August 2011 and then his death on October 5, 2011. Steve Jobs had battled a variety of health issues including pancreatic cancer since 2004 and had taken medical leaves of absence from his CEO position in 2004, 2009, and earlier in 2011, but despite his absence, he had been able to provide inspiration for the company's hottest new products such as the iPhone, iPad, and iPod. During all three medical leaves, Apple's chief operating officer, Tim Cook, took the helm of the company. He oversaw the successful launch of the company's most successful new products while also revamping the company's supply chain and improving overall operating efficiency. Tim Cook's successful performance during Steve Jobs' absences led to his appointment as successor to Jobs as CEO of Apple Inc.

But many challenges faced the new CEO and his chief managers in 2012. The company had yet to reverse the general decline in iPod unit sales and Apple was facing a serious competitive threat in the smartphone market. Continuing growth in iPhone sales was critical to the company's financial performance, since iPhone sales accounted for $47.2 billion of the company's 2011 revenues of $108.1 billion. Apple's iPad tablet computers were the company's second-largest contributor to total revenues, with sales of more than $20.4 billion during 2011.

Samsung had surged to the top of the smartphone market in late 2011 by introducing the Galaxy and other models that utilized Google's Android operating system to match the key features of the iPhone. In 2012, Android was the most widely used operating system platform for smartphones in the United States with a 50.9 percent share of the market. Google's $12.5 billion of Motorola Mobility in 2012 provided it with the resources needed to expand beyond software and enter the market for smartphone handsets and tablet computers. Google introduced its first hardware product, the Nexus 7 tablet computer in June 2012. Dell, HP, and other computer manufacturers were also rolling out new tablet computers to compete against the iPad. With competitive rivalry heating up and technological change accelerating, Apple's new managers would be forced to work creatively and expeditiously to sustain the company's success achieved under Steve Jobs.

# STEVE JOBS' STRATEGIC LEADERSHIP AT APPLE

Stephen Wozniak and Steve Jobs founded Apple Computer in 1976 when they began selling a crudely designed personal computer called the Apple I to Silicon Valley computer enthusiasts. Two years later, the partners introduced the first mass-produced personal computer (PC), the Apple II, which eventually sold more than 10,000 units. While the Apple II was relatively successful, the next revision of the product line, the Macintosh (Mac), would dramatically change personal computing through its user-friendly graphical user interface (GUI), which allowed users to interact with screen images rather than merely type text commands.

The Macintosh that was introduced in 1984 was hailed as a breakthrough in personal computing, but it did not have the speed, power, or software availability to compete with the PC that IBM had introduced in 1981. One of the reasons the Macintosh lacked the necessary software was that Apple put very strict restrictions on the Apple Certified Developer Program, which made it difficult for software developers to obtain Macs at a discount and receive informational materials about the operating system.

With the Mac faring poorly in the market, founder Steve Jobs became highly critical of the company's president and CEO, John Sculley, who had been hired by the board in 1983. Finally, in 1985, as Sculley was preparing to visit China, Jobs devised a boardroom coup to replace him. Sculley found out about the plan and canceled his trip. After Apple's board voted unanimously to keep Sculley in his position, Jobs, who was retained as chairman of the company but stripped of all decision-making authority, soon resigned. During the remainder of 1985, Apple continued to encounter problems and laid off one-fifth of its employees while posting its first-ever quarterly loss.

Despite these setbacks, Apple kept bringing innovative products to the market, while closely guarding the secrets behind its technology. In 1987, Apple released a revamped Macintosh computer that proved to be a favorite in K–12 schools and with graphic artists and other users needing excellent graphics capabilities. However, by 1990, PCs running Windows 3.0 and Word for Windows were preferred by businesses and consumers and held a commanding 97+ percent share of the market for personal computers.

In 1991, Apple released its first-generation notebook computer, the PowerBook and, in 1993, Apple's board of directors opted to remove Sculley from the position of CEO. The board chose to place the chief operating officer, Michael Spindler, in the vacated spot. Under Spindler, Apple released the PowerMac family of PCs in 1994, the first Macs to incorporate the PowerPC chip, a very fast processor co-developed with Motorola and IBM. Even though the PowerMac family received excellent reviews by technology analysts, Microsoft's Windows 95 matched many of the capabilities of the Mac OS and prevented the PowerMac from gaining significant market share. In January 1996, Apple asked Spindler to resign and chose Gil Amelio, former president of National Semiconductor, to take his place.

During his first 100 days in office, Amelio announced many sweeping changes for the company. He split Apple into seven distinct divisions, each responsible for its own profit or loss, and he tried to better inform the developers and consumers of Apple's products and projects. Amelio acquired NeXT, the company Steve Jobs had founded upon his resignation from Apple in 1985. Steve Jobs was rehired by Apple as part of the acquisition. In 1997, after recording additional quarterly losses, Apple's board terminated Amelio's employment with the company and named Steve Jobs interim CEO.

Under Jobs' leadership, Apple introduced the limited-feature iMac in 1998 and the company's iBook line of notebook computers in 1999. The company was profitable in every quarter during 1998 and 1999, and its share price reached an all-time high in the upper $70 range. Jobs was named permanent CEO of Apple in 2000, and in 2001 oversaw the release of the iPod. The iPod recorded modest sales until the 2003 launch of iTunes—the online retail store where consumers could legally purchase individual songs. By July 2004, 100 million songs had been sold and iTunes had a 70 percent market share among all legal online music download services. The tremendous success of the iPod helped transform Apple from a struggling computer company into a powerful consumer electronics company.

By 2005, consumers' satisfaction with the iPod had helped renew interest in Apple computers, with its market share in personal computers growing from a negligible share to 4 percent. The company also exploited consumer loyalty and satisfaction with the iPod to enter the market for smartphones with the 2007 launch of the iPhone. The brand loyalty

**EXHIBIT 1** Summary of Apple Inc.'s Financial Performance, 2007–2011 ($ in millions, except share amounts)

| | 2011 | 2010 | 2009 | 2008 | 2007 |
|---|---|---|---|---|---|
| Net sales | $108,249 | $65,225 | $42,905 | $37,491 | $24,006 |
| Costs and expenses | | | | | |
| Cost of sales | 64,431 | 39,541 | 25,683 | 24,294 | 15,852 |
| Research and development | 2,429 | 1,782 | 1,333 | 1,109 | 782 |
| Selling, general, and administrative | 7,599 | 5,517 | 4,149 | 3,761 | 2,963 |
| Total operating expenses | 10,028 | 7,299 | 5,482 | 4,870 | 3,745 |
| Operating income | 33,790 | 18,385 | 11,740 | 8,327 | 4,409 |
| Other income and expenses | 415 | 155 | 326 | 620 | 599 |
| Income before provision for income taxes | 34,205 | 18,540 | 12,066 | 8,947 | 5,008 |
| Provision for income taxes | 8,283 | 4,527 | 3,831 | 2,828 | 1,512 |
| Net income | $ 25,922 | $14,013 | $ 8,235 | $ 6,119 | $ 3,496 |
| Earnings per common share: | | | | | |
| Basic | $28.05 | $15.41 | $9.22 | $6.94 | $4.04 |
| Diluted | $27.68 | $15.15 | $9.00 | $6.78 | $3.93 |
| Cash dividends declared per common share | $0.00 | $0.00 | $0.00 | $0.00 | $0.00 |
| Shares used in computing earnings per share: | | | | | |
| Basic | 924,258 | 909,461 | 893,016 | 881,592 | 864,595 |
| Diluted | 936,645 | 924,712 | 907,005 | 902,139 | 889,292 |
| Total cash, cash equivalents, and marketable securities | $ 81,570 | $51,011 | $33,992 | $24,490 | $15,386 |
| Total assets | 116,371 | 75,183 | 47,501 | 36,171 | 24,878 |
| Total long-term obligations | 10,100 | 5,531 | 3,502 | 1,745 | 687 |
| Total liabilities | 39,756 | 27,392 | 15,861 | 13,874 | 10,347 |
| Total shareholders' equity | 76,615 | 47,791 | 31,640 | 22,297 | 14,531 |

*Sources:* Apple Inc., 2008, 2010, and 2011 10-K reports.

developed through the first iPod, and then the iPhone, made the company's 2010 launch of the iPad a roaring success with 3.3 million units sold during its first three months on the market. Much of Apple's turnaround could be credited to Steve Jobs, who had idea after idea for how to improve the company and turn its performance around. He not only consistently pushed for innovative new ideas and products but also enforced several structural changes, including ridding the company of unprofitable segments and divisions.

The success of the turnaround could also be attributed to the efforts of Tim Cook, Apple's chief operating officer, who oversaw the company's operations at various times between 2004 and 2011. Tim Cook was first asked to act as the company's chief manager in 2004 when Steve Jobs was recovering from pancreatic cancer surgery, later in 2009 when Jobs took a six-month medical leave for a liver transplant,

and again in early 2011 when Jobs left the company for another medical leave. Jobs' illness eventually forced his resignation shortly before his death on October 5, 2011. While Jobs had been the inspiration for the company's hottest new products such as the iPhone, iPad, and iPod, analysts and key Apple managers viewed Cook as an "operational genius." While COO and acting CEO, Tim Cook was responsible for overhauling Apple's supply chain system and transforming it into one of the lowest-cost electronics manufacturers.[1] Prior to coming to Apple in 1998, Tim Cook was a rising star among Compaq Computer's management team.

A summary of Apple's financial performance for fiscal years 2007 through 2010 is provided in Exhibit 1. The company's net sales by operating segment and product line and unit sales by product line for 2008 through 2010 are provided in Exhibit 2.

**EXHIBIT 2**    Apple, Inc.'s Net Sales by Operating Segment, Net Sales by Product, and Unit Sales by Product, 2009–2011 ($ in millions)

|  | 2011 | Change | 2010 | Change | 2009 |
|---|---|---|---|---|---|
| **Net Sales by Operating Segment:** | | | | | |
| Americas net sales | $ 38,315 | 56% | $24,498 | 29% | $18,981 |
| Europe net sales | 27,778 | 49% | 18,692 | 58% | 11,810 |
| Japan net sales | 5,437 | 37% | 3,981 | 75% | 2,279 |
| Asia-Pacific net sales | 22,592 | 174% | 8,256 | 160% | 3,179 |
| Retail net sales | 14,127 | 44% | 9,798 | 47% | 6,656 |
| Total net sales | $108,249 | 66% | $65,225 | 52% | $42,905 |
| **Net Sales by Product:** | | | | | |
| Desktops[a] | $ 6,439 | 4% | $ 6,201 | 43% | $ 4,324 |
| Portables[b] | 15,344 | 36% | 11,278 | 18% | 9,535 |
| Total Mac net sales | $ 21,783 | 25% | $17,479 | 26% | $13,859 |
| iPod | 7,453 | (10)% | 8,274 | 2% | 8,091 |
| Other music-related products and services[c] | 6,314 | 28% | 4,948 | 23% | 4,036 |
| iPhone and related products and services[d] | 47,057 | 87% | 25,179 | 93% | 13,033 |
| iPad and related products and services[e] | 20,358 | 311% | 4,958 | n.m. | 0 |
| Peripherals and other hardware[f] | 2,330 | 28% | 1,814 | 23% | 1,475 |
| Software, service, and other sales[g] | 2,954 | 15% | 2,573 | 7% | 2,411 |
| Total net sales | $108,249 | 66% | $65,225 | 52% | $42,905 |
| **Unit Sales by Product:** | | | | | |
| Desktops[a] | 4,669 | 1% | 4,627 | 45% | 3,182 |
| Portables[b] | 12,066 | 34% | 9,035 | 25% | 7,214 |
| Total Mac unit sales | 16,735 | 22% | 13,662 | 31% | 10,396 |
| iPod unit sales | 42,620 | (15)% | 50,312 | −7% | 54,132 |
| iPhone units sold | 72,293 | 81% | 39,989 | 93% | 20,731 |
| iPad units sold | 32,394 | 334% | 7,458 | n.m. | 0 |

n.m.: Not meaningful

[a]Includes iMac, Mac mini, Mac Pro, and Xserve product lines.

[b]Includes MacBook, MacBook Pro, iBook, and PowerBook product lines.

[c]Consists of iTunes Store sales, iPod services, and Apple-branded and third-party iPod accessories.

[d]Includes revenue recognized from iPhone sales, carrier agreements, and Apple-branded and third-party iPhone accessories.

[e]Includes revenue recognized from iPad sales, services, and Apple-branded and third-party iPad accessories.

[f]Includes sales of displays, wireless connectivity and networking solutions, and other hardware accessories.

[g]Includes sales of Apple-branded operating system and application software, third-party software, and Mac and Internet services.

[h]Derived by dividing total product-related net sales by total product-related unit sales.

*Source:* Apple Inc., 2011 10-K report.

# OVERVIEW OF THE PERSONAL COMPUTER INDUSTRY

The personal computer industry was relatively consolidated, with five sellers accounting for 76.3 percent of the U.S. shipments and 59.2 percent of worldwide shipments in 2011 (see Exhibit 3). Prior to the onset of the U.S. recession that began in 2008, the PC industry was expected to grow at a rate of 5–6 percent, to reach $354 billion by 2012. However, the effects of the recession caused a dramatic decline in revenues and unit shipments in the United States between 2007 and 2008. The PC market began to improve by 2009 as U.S. businesses replaced aging computers and demand in some

**EXHIBIT 3   U.S. and Global Market Shares of Leading PC Vendors, 2000, 2007–2011**

**A. U.S. Market Shares of the Leading PC Vendors, 2000 and 2007–2011**

| 2010 Rank | Vendor | 2011 Shipments (in 000s) | 2011 Market Share | 2010 Shipments (in 000s) | 2010 Market Share | 2009 Shipments (in 000s) | 2009 Market Share | 2008 Shipments (in 000s) | 2008 Market Share | 2007 Shipments (in 000s) | 2007 Market Share | 2000 Shipments (in 000s) | 2000 Market Share |
|---|---|---|---|---|---|---|---|---|---|---|---|---|---|
| 1 | Hewlett-Packard[1] | 18,595 | 26.1% | 19,488 | 25.9% | 18,781 | 26.9% | 16,218 | 24.7% | 16,759 | 23.9% | 5,630 | 11.5% |
| 2 | Dell | 15,898 | 22.3 | 17,352 | 23.1 | 17,099 | 24.5 | 19,276 | 29.4 | 19,645 | 28.0 | 9,645 | 19.7 |
|  | Compaq[1] | — |  | — |  | — |  | — |  | — |  | 7,761 | 15.9 |
| 3 | Apple | 7,649 | 10.7 | 6,586 | 8.8 | 5,579 | 8.0 | 5,158 | 7.9 | 4,081 | 5.8 | n.a. | n.a. |
| 4 | Toshiba | 6,695 | 9.4 | 6,624 | 8.8 | 5,379 | 7.7 | 3,788 | 5.8 | 3,509 | 5.0 | n.a. | n.a. |
| 5 | Acer[2] | 5,575 | 7.8 | 8,012 | 10.7 | 7,983 | 11.4 | 6,106 | 9.3 | 3,860 | 5.5 | n.a. | n.a. |
|  | Others | 16,897 | 23.7 | 17,038 | 22.7 | 15,008 | 21.5 | 15,026 | 22.9 | 22,235 | 31.7 | 18,959 | 38.8 |
|  | All vendors | 71,309 | 100.0% | 75,101 | 100.0% | 69,829 | 100.0% | 65,571 | 100.0% | 70,088 | 100.0% | 48,900 | 100.0% |

**B. Worldwide Market Shares of the Leading PC Vendors, 2000 and 2007–2011**

| 2010 Rank | Vendor | 2011 Shipments (in 000s) | 2011 Market Share | 2010 Shipments (in 000s) | 2010 Market Share | 2009 Shipments (in 000s) | 2009 Market Share | 2008 Shipments (in 000s) | 2008 Market Share | 2007 Shipments (in 000s) | 2007 Market Share | 2000 Shipments (in 000s) | 2000 Market Share |
|---|---|---|---|---|---|---|---|---|---|---|---|---|---|
| 1 | Hewlett-Packard[1] | 62,334 | 17.7% | 64,213 | 18.5% | 59,942 | 20.3% | 54,293 | 18.9% | 50,526 | 18.8% | 10,327 | 7.4% |
| 2 | Dell | 44,282 | 12.6 | 43,403 | 12.5 | 38,416 | 13.1 | 42,388 | 14.7 | 39,993 | 14.9 | 14,801 | 10.6 |
|  | Compaq[1] | — |  | — |  | — |  | — |  | — |  | 17,399 | 12.5 |
| 3 | Lenovo/IBM[2] | 44,007 | 12.5 | 34,182 | 9.9 | 24,887 | 8.5 | 21,870 | 7.6 | 20,224 | 7.5 | 9,308 | 6.7 |
| 4 | Acer[3] | 37,169 | 10.6 | 42,430 | 12.3 | 38,377 | 13.0 | 31,377 | 10.9 | 21,206 | 7.9 | n.a. | n.a |
| 5 | ASUS | 20,741 | 5.9 | n.a. | n.a. | n.a. | n.a. | n.a. | n.a. | n.a. | n.a. | n.a. | n.a. |
|  | Others | 143,862 | 40.7 | 142,874 | 41.3 | 132,586 | 45.1 | 137,638 | 47.9 | 137,011 | 50.9 | 87,222 | 62.8% |
|  | All vendors | 352,395 | 100.0% | 346,198 | 100.0% | 294,208 | 100.0% | 287,566 | 100.0% | 268,960 | 100.0% | 139,057 | 100.0% |

n.a. = not available; sales and market shares for these companies in the years where *n.a.* appears are included in the "Others" category because the company was not in the top five in shipments or market share.

[1]Compaq was acquired by Hewlett-Packard in May 2002.

[2]Lenovo, a Chinese computer company, completed the acquisition of IBM's PC business in 2005. The numbers for Lenovo/IBM for 2000 reflect sales of IBM-branded PCs only. In 2007, Lenovo rebranded all IBM PCs as Lenovo.

[3]Acer acquired Gateway in 2007 and Packard Bell in 2008. Data for Acer includes shipments for Gateway starting in Q4 2007 and shipments for Packard Bell starting in Q1 2008, and only Acer data for prior periods.

*Source:* International Data Corporation.

developing countries accelerated. However, worldwide PC shipments declined by 0.2 percent during the first quarter of 2012, with only Asia/Pacific (excluding Japan) maintaining healthy demand. The European debt crisis dampened demand slightly in the region, while demand in Japan and the United States fell more seriously. Demand for PCs in Japan had fallen by 7 percent during 2011, and the 5 percent decline in industry revenues in the U.S. during 2011 represented the second worst year in history for the U.S. PC industry. Modest single-digit growth in emerging markets allowed China to become the world's largest market for PCs during the second quarter of 2011. The United States remained the largest global market for PCs for the entire 2011 calendar year. While the poor growth in worldwide PC shipments was attributable to economic reasons, the rise in popularity of tablet computers had also affected PC sales. Tablet computers, such as the iPad, had yet to become widely adopted by businesses, but were commonly becoming replacements for laptops and PCs among consumers. The market for tablet computers increased from 17 million units in 2010 to 69 million units in 2011 to an estimated 106 million units in 2012.

## APPLE'S COMPETITIVE POSITION IN THE PERSONAL COMPUTER INDUSTRY

Apple's proprietary operating system and strong graphics-handling capabilities differentiated Macs from PCs, but many consumers and business users who owned PCs were hesitant to purchase a Mac because of Apple's premium pricing and because of the learning curve involved with mastering its proprietary operating system. The company's market share in the United States had improved from 4.7 percent in 2006 to 8.8 percent in 2010 primarily because of the success of the iPod and iPhone. These products created a halo effect whereby some consumers (but not business users) switched to Apple computers after purchasing an iPod, iPhone, or iPad. The company hoped to benefit even more from this effect by designing the Mac OS X operating system to emulate the look and functionality of its iOS operating system used for its mobile devices.

Apple's computer product line consisted of several models in various configurations. Its desktop lines included the Mac Pro (aimed at professional and business users); the iMac (targeted toward consumer, educational, and business use); and Mac mini (made specifically for consumer use). Apple had two notebook product lines: MacBook Pro (for professional and advanced consumer users) and MacBook Air (designed for education users and consumers). All Apple computers were priced at a steep premium compared to PCs and laptops offered by Dell, HP, and other rivals. In July 2012, Mac Pro pricing started at $2,499, iMac and MacBook Pro pricing began at $1,199, the MacBook Air was offered from $999, and Mac mini pricing started at $599.

## APPLE'S ENTRY INTO THE MARKET FOR TABLET COMPUTERS

Apple entered the market for tablet computers with its April 3, 2010, launch of the iPad. Tablet computers had been on the market since the late 1990s, but only Apple's version had gained any significant interest from consumers and business users. Previous-generation tablet computers required the use of a stylus to launch applications and enter information. Most users found the stylus interface to be an annoyance and preferred to use a smartphone or laptop when portability was required. Dell, Acer, Hewlett-Packard, and RIM had all raced to get touch-screen tablet computers to market but were unable to do so until very late 2010 and early 2011 because of the technological differences between tablet computers and PCs. Tablet computers were technologically similar to smartphones and shared almost no components with PCs. HP acquired Palm for $1.2 billion in May 2010 to accelerate its entry into tablet computers. However, most PC manufacturers chose to utilize smartphone microprocessors and Google's Android operating system in their tablet computer models. By mid-2012, Apple held a 68 percent share of the market for tablet computers.

Apple's iPad 2 that was launched in March 2011 contained a dual-core processor that was far more powerful than the first-generation iPad and most competing tablet computers. The third-generation iPad, launched in March 2012, utilized a quad core graphics chip, a 5 megapixel camera capable of capturing photos and 1080p HD video, and an ultra-high-resolution 9.7-inch display. The 3.1 million pixel display of the third-generation iPad had twice the number of pixels of the iPad 2 and one million more pixels than an HD TV. Apple's latest iPad retailed from $499 for the 16GB model to $829 for the 64GB model. With the launch of

**EXHIBIT 4**   Hewlett-Packard Personal Systems Group, Net Revenue, 2007–2011 ($ millions)

| Product | 2011 | 2010 | 2009 | 2008 | 2007 |
|---|---|---|---|---|---|
| Notebooks | $21,824 | $22,545 | $20,210 | $22,657 | $17,650 |
| Desktop PCs | 15,370 | 15,478 | 12,864 | 16,626 | 15,889 |
| Workstations | 1,805 | 1,786 | 1,261 | 1,902 | 1,721 |
| Other | 575 | 932 | 970 | 1,110 | 1,149 |
| Total | $39,574 | $40,741 | $35,305 | $42,295 | $36,409 |

*Sources:* Hewlett-Packard, 2007, 2010, and 2011 10-K reports.

the new iPad, pricing on the iPad 2 was reduced to as low as $399.

Basic e-readers such as Amazon's $79 Kindle were not considered direct competitors to the iPad since dedicated reading devices could not browse the Internet, view videos, play music, or perform other media tasks. Also, as of 2012, no Android-based tablet computer had proven to be a worthy rival to Apple's iPad. Some technology sector observers believed that Google's $199 Nexus 7 tablet computer might challenge the iPad, but would likely be a more direct rival of other Android-based tablets such as the $199 Kindle Fire.

## APPLE'S RIVALS IN THE PERSONAL COMPUTER INDUSTRY

### Hewlett-Packard

Hewlett-Packard (HP) was broadly diversified across segments of the computer industry with business divisions focused on information technology consulting services, large enterprise systems, software, personal computers, printers and other imaging devices, and financial services. The company's Personal Systems Group (PSG), which manufactured and marketed HP and Compaq desktop computers and portable computers, was its largest division, accounting for revenues of almost $40 billion in 2011. HP recorded total net revenues of $127 billion in 2011, with information technology services contributing $36 billion, imaging and printing devices contributing nearly $25.8 billion, and enterprise systems accounting for about $22.2 billion. The company's software business units accounted for sales of nearly $3.2 billion and its financial services unit contributed net revenue of about $3.6 billion in 2011.

PSG revenues declined by nearly 3 percent between 2010 and 2011, primarily because of soft demand and strong price competition in the market for desktop PCs and notebook computers. During 2011, the company's sales of desktop PCs and notebook computers to consumers declined by 15 percent, but improved overall by 2.3 percent because of increased demand for PCs, notebooks, and workstations by businesses. Even with the increased demand in the commercial segment, HP's average selling price declined by 5 percent between 2010 and 2011 because of strong price competition among PC sellers. There had been discussion within the company in 2011 that its Personal Systems Group should be divested because of its weak operating profit margins relative to its other business units. HP's shipments of PCs during the first quarter of 2012 declined by 16 percent compared to the same period in 2011. Exhibit 4 provides the revenue contribution by PSG product line for 2007 through 2011.

### Dell Inc.

Dell Inc. was the world's second-largest seller of personal computers, with revenues of about $62.1 billion for the fiscal year ending January 2012. Exhibit 5 presents Dell's revenues by product category for fiscal 2009 through fiscal 2012. Tough economic conditions, declining demand for PCs by consumers, and growing price competition in the PC industry had significantly affected Dell's financial performance, with its revenues declining from $61.1 billion in fiscal 2008 to $52.9 billion in fiscal 2010. In addition, Dell's net earnings fell from $2.9 billion in fiscal 2008 to $2.5 billion in fiscal 2009 to $1.4 billion in fiscal 2010. In fiscal 2011, the company's revenues and net income had improved to $61.5 billion and $2.6 billion, respectively, as the technology sector of the economy

**EXHIBIT 5**  Dell's Revenues by Product Category, Fiscal 2009–Fiscal 2012 ($ millions)

| Product Category | Fiscal 2012 | Fiscal 2011 | Fiscal 2010 | Fiscal 2009 |
|---|---|---|---|---|
| Servers and networking | $ 8,336 | $ 7,609 | $ 6,032 | $ 6,512 |
| Storage | 1,943 | 2,295 | 2,192 | 2,667 |
| Services | 8,322 | 7,673 | 5,622 | 5,351 |
| Software and peripherals | 10,222 | 10,261 | 9,499 | 10,603 |
| Mobility | 19,104 | 18,971 | 16,610 | 18,604 |
| Desktop PCs | 14,144 | 14,685 | 12,947 | 17,364 |
| Total net revenue | $62,071 | $61,494 | $52,904 | $61,101 |

*Source:* Dell Inc., 2011 and 2012 10-K reports.

began to improve. The improvement strengthened further in fiscal 2012 with Dell's net income improving to nearly $3.5 billion. The company offered a wide range of desktop computers and portables, ranging from low-end, low-priced models to state-of-the-art, high-priced models. The company also offered servers; workstations; peripherals such as printers, monitors, and projectors; and Wi-Fi products. Dell also offered an Android-based Streak tablet computer line and a Windows Phone 7 smartphone in 2012. The company's shipments of PCs declined by 16 percent between the first quarter of 2011 and the first quarter of 2012 because of aggressive pricing by certain rivals. Lenovo's deep price discounts had yielded a 36 percent volume gain between the first quarter of 2012 and the first quarter of 2012.

## APPLE'S COMPETITIVE POSITION IN THE PERSONAL MEDIA PLAYER INDUSTRY

Although Apple didn't introduce the first portable digital music player, the company held a 78 percent market share in digital music players in 2011, and the name iPod had become a generic term used to describe digital media players. When Apple launched its first iPod, many critics did not give the product much of a chance for success, given its fairly hefty price tag of $399. However, the iPod's sleek styling, ease of use, and eventual price decreases allowed it to develop such high levels of customer satisfaction and loyalty that rivals found it difficult to gain traction in the marketplace.

The most popular portable players in 2012 not only played music but also could be connected to Wi-Fi networks to play videos, access the Internet, view photos, or listen to FM high-definition radio. The iPod Touch was the best-selling media player in 2012 with more than 300 million units sold by year-end 2011. Even though many competing MP3 players compared favorably to Apple's iPod models, none of Apple's key rivals in the media player industry had been able to achieve a market share greater than 5 percent in 2012. Most consumers did not find many convincing reasons to consider any brand of media player other than Apple.

In 2012, Apple offered four basic styles in the iPod product line: the iPod shuffle, iPod nano, iPod Touch, and iPod classic. Apple also sold an Apple TV device that would allow users to play iPod content, including over 15,000 movies and more than 90,000 TV episodes purchased at iTunes on their televisions. The Apple TV device also allowed users to watch streaming movies and other content provided by Netflix, YouTube, Vimeo, or other Internet sources.

## ITUNES

Aside from the iPod's stylish design and ease of use, another factor that contributed to the popularity of the iPod was Apple's iPod/iTunes combination. In 2011, more than 50 million customers visited the iTunes Store to purchase and download music, videos, movies, and television shows that could be played on iPods, iPhones, or Apple TV devices. Also in 2011, Apple's iTunes Store recorded its 18 billionth download since its launch in 2003. Additionally, iTunes was the world's most popular online movie store, with customers purchasing and renting more than 50,000 movies each day.

The success of the iPod/iTunes combination gave iTunes a 65 percent share of the U.S. digital music market in 2011. Since downloads accounted for more than 50 percent of all music sales in the United States, iTunes' commanding share of the digital music sales also gave it a 23 percent share of total U.S. music sales. Amazon.com was the second-largest seller of digital music in the United States with 12 percent market share, while new entrant Google Play hoped to capture the majority of music sales to users of Android-based mobile phones.

## APPLE'S COMPETITIVE POSITION IN THE MARKET FOR SMARTPHONES

The first version of the iPhone was released on June 29, 2007, and had a multitouch screen with a virtual keyboard, a camera, and a portable media player (equivalent to the iPod) in addition to text messaging and visual voice mail. It also offered Internet services including e-mail, web browsing (using access to Apple's Safari web browser), and local Wi-Fi connectivity. More than 270,000 first-generation iPhones were sold during the first 30 hours of the product's launch. The iPhone was named *Time* magazine's Invention of the Year in 2007.

The iPhone 3G was released in 70 countries on July 11, 2008, and was available in the United States exclusively through AT&T Mobility. The iPhone 3G combined the functionality of a wireless phone and an iPod, and allowed users to access the Internet wirelessly at twice the speed of the previous version of the iPhone. Apple's new phone also featured a built-in global positioning system (GPS) and, in an effort to increase adoption by corporate users, was compatible with Microsoft Exchange.

The iPhone 3GS was introduced on June 19, 2009, and included all of the features of the iPhone 3G but could also launch applications and render web pages twice as fast as the iPhone 3G. The iPhone 4 was launched on June 24, 2010 and included video-calling capabilities (only over a Wi-Fi network), a 5-megapixel camera including flash and zoom, 720p video recording, a longer-lasting battery, and a gyroscopic motion sensor to enable an improved gaming experience. The iPhone 4 sold more than 1.7 million units within three days of its launch. The iPhone 4S sold more than four million units within the first three days of its October 14, 2011, launch. The 4S utilized Apple's dual-core A5 microprocessor, 1080p HD video recording, and Siri, Apple's intelligent assistant that responded to voice requests. By 2011, Apple had expanded its carrier network beyond AT&T to include Verizon, Sprint, and C-Spire in the United States and a variety of carriers in Europe and Asia. Industry observers expected a late-2012 release date for the iPhone 5.

## APP STORE

Like the iPod/iTunes combination, the 550,000 iPhone applications and 170,000 iPad applications available at Apple's App Store helped the company build strong competitive positions in the markets for smartphones and tablet computers. In 2012, more than 25 billion iPhone and iPad apps had been downloaded from the App Store. With more than 1 billion downloads per month and a 90 percent revenue share of the mobile software market, Apple had been able to pay more than $3.4 billion to app developers. Users of Apple's iPods, iPhones, iPads, or Macs could also use the company's iMatch or iCloud services that integrated apps, iBooks, and iTunes purchased at the App Store to all devices owned by the individual. The iCloud service also allowed users to share calendars and contacts, wirelessly push photographs to all devices, and back up data from Apple devices.

## DEMAND AND COMPETITION IN THE SMARTPHONE MARKET

Worldwide shipments of smartphones increased from 1.7 billion units in 2009 to 4.9 billion units in 2011. Although the worldwide market for mobile phones declined 1.5 percent between the first quarter of 2011 and the first quarter of 2012, the global market for smartphones experienced a year-over-year increase of 42.5 percent. Developing countries such as China offered the greatest growth opportunities but also presented challenges to smartphone producers. For example, there were 700 million mobile phone users in China, but popular-selling models were quickly counterfeited, it was difficult to develop keyboards that included the thousands of commonly used characters in the Chinese language, and most consumers preferred inexpensive feature phones over smartphones.

**EXHIBIT 6**    The Top Five Worldwide Smartphone Vendors, Their Shipment Volumes, and Market Shares, 2009 to First Quarter 2012

| Q2 2011 Rank | Vendor | Q1 2012 | | 2011 | | 2010 | | 2009 | |
|---|---|---|---|---|---|---|---|---|---|
| | | Shipments (in millions) | Market Share | Shipments (in millions) | Market Share | Shipments (in millions) | Market Share | Shipments (in millions) | Market Share |
| 1 | Samsung | 42.2 | 29.1% | 94.0 | 19.1% | 22.9 | 7.5 | 5.5 | 3.2% |
| 2 | Apple | 35.1 | 24.2 | 93.2 | 19.0 | 47.5 | 15.6% | 25.1 | 14.5 |
| 3 | Nokia | 11.9 | 8.2 | 77.3 | 15.7 | 100.1 | 32.9 | 67.7 | 39.0 |
| 4 | Research in Motion | 9.7 | 6.7 | 51.1 | 10.4 | 48.8 | 16.0 | 34.5 | 19.9 |
| 5 | HTC | 6.9 | 4.8 | 43.5 | 8.9 | 21.7 | 7.1 | 8.1 | 4.7 |
| | Others | 39.1 | 27.0 | 132.3 | 26.9 | 63.7 | 20.3 | 32.6 | 18.8 |
| | All vendors | 144.9 | 100.0% | 491.4 | 100.0% | 304.7 | 100.0% | 173.5 | 100.0% |

*Source:* International Data Corporation.

Nevertheless, many analysts expected China to account for 10 percent of worldwide smartphone shipments within the near term. Apple began selling the iPhone 4 in China in 2010 through its partnership with China Telecom, the country's second-largest wireless provider and its network of 25 flagship stores located in the country's largest cities. The iPhone 4S became available in China in January 2012—making it available in 90 countries within three months of its initial launch.

With the market for smartphones growing rapidly and supporting high average selling prices, competition was becoming more heated. Google's entry into the market with its Android operating system had allowed vendors such as HTC, Motorola, and Samsung to offer models that matched many of the features of the iPhone—so much so, that in August 2012 a jury awarded Apple more than $1 billion in a copyright infringement case against Samsung. In fact, Android's strong capabilities had made it the number-one smartphone platform in the United States with a 50.9 percent market share in May 2012. Apple's iPhone platform accounted for a 31.9 percent share of smartphones in the United States in May 2012. Android-based Samsung smartphones were the best-selling brand of smartphones in 2011 and the first quarter of 2012. Android's quick rise to the top spot among smartphone platforms led to the August 2011 announcement by Google that the company would enter the handset segment of the smartphone industry and the tablet computer business through the $12.5 billion acquisition of Motorola Mobility. Google's $199 Nexus 7 tablet computer that was launched in June 2012 was its first new hardware product introduced after the Motorola Mobility acquisition. Exhibit 6 presents shipments and market shares for the leading smartphone producers between 2009 and the second quarter of 2012.

## APPLE'S PERFORMANCE IN 2012

As of mid-2012, Apple's outstanding performance had not been impeded by the loss of Steve Jobs as CEO and the inspiration of its most important and innovative products. The company's quarterly revenue for the second quarter of 2012 of $39.2 billion was 59 percent higher than in the same period in 2011 and its quarterly profit of $11.6 billion represented a 94 percent year-over-year increase. The company's quarterly shipments of 4 million Macs was 7 percent greater than in the second quarter of 2011, its sales of 11.8 million iPads was a 151 percent improvement of the same period in 2011, and its iPhone sales of 35.1 million units was 88 percent more than were shipped during the second quarter of 2012. Unit sales for the iPod fell to 7.7 million, which was a 15 percent decline from the second quarter of 2011.

The biggest concerns for the company going into the third quarter of 2012 were how Google's entry into the market for smartphone handsets and tablet computers would impact the company's sales of iPhones and iPads. Clearly, iPad and iPhone sales were the largest contributors to the company's 2011 and early-2012 performance, and a steady stream of future innovative products would be necessary to support Apple's lofty stock price. Even though Tim Cook was successfully leading the company after the death of Steve Jobs, it was Jobs who had been widely recognized as the visionary force behind the development of the iPod, iPhone, and iPad. Cook had yet to preside over the development of such groundbreaking products that could give rise to new markets that would be dominated by Apple.

There was little doubt that Google intended to exploit its status as the number-one smartphone platform to end Apple's dominance over the markets for smartphones and tablet computers. While the Nexus 7 had done little to affect iPad sales since its June 2012 launch, Google's Android operating system had allowed Samsung to leapfrog over Apple to become the largest seller of smartphones in 2011 and early-2012. Most of Samsung's market share gains came at the expense of RIM, Nokia, and HTC, since Apple's share increased as well, but it seemed clear that Google and its Android partners seemed resolute in the strategic intent of attacking Apple in its key markets.

## ENDNOTES

[1] Yukari Iwatani Kane and Nick Wingfield, "Apple's Deep Bench Faces Challenges," *The Wall Street Journal Online*, August 24, 2011.

# The State Fair of Virginia[1]

## W. Glenn Rowe
The University of Western Ontario

## Karin Schnarr
The University of Western Ontario

At the November 21, 2011 meeting, members of the State Fair of Virginia, Inc. (SFVA) board of directors had a very difficult decision to make. Although revenues from the recently held state fair had been good, the organization was in an extremely precarious financial position. For the first time in over 150 years, the board might have to shut down the fair for good.

In 2003, SFVA decided to sell its existing site and purchase a new property to house the fair and other events. The new site, the Meadow Farm in Caroline Country, Virginia, was attractive because of its historic significance as a horse farm famous for being the birthplace of Secretariat, winner of the 1973 Triple Crown, and as the training facility for Riva Ridge, winner of the Kentucky Derby and Belmont Stakes in 1972. In 2007, the organization borrowed $83 million[2] against a $42 million investment portfolio in order to develop its new fairgrounds which opened in 2009. However, the unprecedented collapse of the financial markets in the United States in 2008, combined with a poor economy and terrible weather for the new

fairground's first two years, resulted in a situation where, in late 2011, the organization did not bring in enough in income and donations to cover the loan payments

Lenders were demanding an immediate solution while not offering one themselves. The board realized that they had no choice but to consider strategic options including applying for Chapter 11 bankruptcy, which would give them time to try to restructure their debt, or shutting down immediately.

The board knew that by the end of this meeting they had to determine how they would proceed. SVFA was out of time.

## THE STATE FAIR OF VIRGINIA: A HISTORY

While the SFVA was officially founded in 1906, the fair had been operating almost continually since 1854. It was formed with the goal of keeping cherished ideals and experiences alive in the Commonwealth of Virginia. It did this by offering events and year-round activities that showcased the potential of Virginia's rural heritage.

SFVA was a privately held, not-for-profit organization that operated the state fair independent of the state government and that received no operating support from state or local governments. SFVA operated three main events annually:

### State Fair of Virginia

While historical records indicated that a fair was held in Richmond, Virginia, as early as the 1700s, it was officially founded in 1854 and incorporated in 1906. The fair was an 11-day event held each year during the months of September and October. Curry A. Roberts, SFVA president and chief executive officer (CEO), described the fair:

> SFVA is much more than just one event and we're so much more than midway rides and fried candy bars. Each year we provide a venue for tens of thousands of youth and families to showcase their farm animals, enter apple pies and Brunswick stews in food competitions, and display quilts, paintings and handmade crafts.[3]

In 2009, the fair moved from the Richmond Raceway Complex (Richmond Raceway) in Richmond, Virginia, to a 348-acre site at the Meadow Event Park located in Doswell, Virginia. It did so voluntarily to take advantage of the development potential of the new site, even though the operators of the Richmond Raceway would have let them continue to hold the fair at that site. The first two years of the fair at the new site were a disappointment due to poor weather. However, in 2011, attendance at the fair was up to 269,000 with a 32 percent increase in paid attendance over 2010.

## Strawberry Hill Races

Founded in 1895, the Strawberry Hill Races (named for the farm that originally occupied the location of the former SFVA fairgrounds on Strawberry Hill) were a series of steeplechase horse races held the third Saturday of April. SFVA took over the operation of the Races in 1973, feeling that the event was compatible with the organization's mission to support agriculture and, with it, Virginia's equine industry. In 2001, the races were moved to Colonia Downs in New Kent County, Virginia, the state's first thoroughbred racetrack.[4]

## Meadow Highland Games and Celtic Festival

Held annually in October, this two-day event founded in 1995 included a heavy athletics competition (with a caber toss and Scottish hammers); a Celtic market; and competitions for highland dance, Irish and Scottish fiddle, and harp and pipe and drum. It was held at the Meadow Event Park.[5]

To garner additional revenue, SFVA rented out the Meadow Event Park for over 120 events every year including trade shows, weddings, and horse shows. This facility rental positively impacted the long-term financial viability of the property and had the advantage of not being impacted by adverse weather. A timeline and history of the main events of the SFVA are provided in Exhibit 1.

## THE NOT-FOR-PROFIT SECTOR

In the United States, a not-for-profit organization is one that is incorporated under a state not-for-profit corporation statute and falls under section 501(c)3

---

**EXHIBIT 1    Important Dates in the History of the State Fair of Virginia**

| | |
|---|---|
| **1854:** | Virginia State Agricultural Society is established and holds the first state fair at present-day Monroe Park in Richmond. |
| **1859:** | The fair moves to West Broad Street near the present-day Science Museum of Virginia. It is suspended from 1861 to 1866 because of the Civil War. |
| **1906:** | Virginia State Fair Association organizes to revive the fair after a 10-year absence. |
| **1946:** | The association reorganizes as Atlantic Rural Exposition Inc. and moves the fair to Strawberry Hill in rural Henrico County. The site eventually is shared through a lease with Richmond International Raceway (RIR). |
| **1999:** | Atlantic Rural Exposition sells Strawberry Hill complex to RIR for $47 million. It plans to move the fair to the Varina area of eastern Henrico County in 2001. |
| **2002:** | Atlantic Rural Exposition abandons plans to relocate in Henrico and looks at the Meadow Farm in Caroline County as a possible home. The farm is best known as the birthplace of Secretariat, who won the Triple Crown in 1973. |
| **2003:** | Atlantic Rural Exposition buys Meadow Farm site for $5.3 million, with hopes of relocating by 2006. The Atlantic Rural Exposition is renamed The State Fair of Virginia Inc. |
| **2008:** | Fair breaks ground on an $81 million complex called the Meadow Event Park. |
| **Sept. 24, 2009:** | Fair opens at Meadow Farm. |

*Source: Richmond Times-Dispatch,* March 11, 2012, http://www2.timesdispatch.com/news/2012/mar/11/tdmain12-important-dates-in-history-of-state-fair—ar-1756472/, accessed on March 23, 2012.

or 501(c)4 of the U.S. Internal Revenue Service code. This captures a broad group of organizations, associations and groups that perform a variety of services and activities. Many not-for-profit organizations are exempt from federal corporate income tax, and donors are able to deduct their contributions on their personal income tax forms. However, while not-for-profits are actually able to make a profit, they are legally restricted in what they are able to do with those profits. Net cash flows are only to be used for current and future activities rather than being distributed back to shareholders or management through financial incentives (e.g., dividends). Assets are held in trust by the board of directors in order to maintain them for the benefit of the community. In 2007, the not-for-profit sector contributed 7.2 percent to the U.S. GDP, with an average 5 percent contribution to national GDP worldwide.[6]

## Dissolution of Not-For-Profits

In the United States, insolvent not-for-profit organizations usually just close their doors and file a plan of dissolution with the charity regulator in their state. Many small not-for-profit organizations do not formally dissolve; at some point, they just stop filing the necessary tax forms, which results in involuntary or automatic dissolution. The IRS also revokes tax-exempt status for recognized groups that fail to file for three consecutive years. When not-for-profit organizations dissolve, their assets must be distributed to an exempt charitable purpose as approved by the IRS. Generally, to obtain federal tax-exempt status, a new organization must make a commitment that if (or when) it closes down, it will pass along any remaining assets to other tax-exempt organizations with similar missions. Most not-for-profit organizations outline in their bylaws or charter what this purpose will be. However, if it is not specified, it can also go to the federal government or to a state or local government for a public purpose. The assets cannot be given to a not-for-profit organization's members or private individuals for any purpose.[7]

When not-for-profit organizations have loans they cannot repay and need a way to deal with creditors, they can seek bankruptcy protection under Chapter 11 of the federal bankruptcy code (see Exhibit 10). This provides them with a way to get relief from creditors, obtain emergency financing, renegotiate leases and draw up a reorganization plan to let them emerge as financially viable. Some not-for-profits, however, have resorted to Chapter 7 of the code (see Exhibit 11), under which organizations liquidate their assets in order to pay back creditors under the guidance of a court-appointed trustee.

## Mission of Not-for-Profit Organizations

While not-for-profit organizations have financial requirements, their mission is frequently service-related, whether to members or to individuals accessing their services. The often altruistic service-based nature of not-for-profits does not make them less complex as organizational forms and management entities; they face a number of challenges not experienced in the for-profit sector. Not-for-profit management teams have to balance paid staff with volunteers and plan programs and deliver services based on unknown levels of demand from clients and uncertain levels of financial support from donations and public organizations.

## Governance of Not-for-Profit Organizations

From a corporate governance perspective, a board of directors (or board of trustees) governs non-profit organizations. These boards function in a similar way to boards of for-profit organizations; however, board members are volunteers and are not paid for their time. This can make it challenging to recruit experienced board members. The board has authority over the organization, including the organization's executive director/CEO and is usually involved in human resource decisions for the senior team and providing input into and approving the organization's strategic plan.

## SFVA'S MISSION

The mission of SFVA was, through its events, to celebrate their Commonwealth's heritage, to heed their roots in agriculture, to advance their youth through scholarships, to encourage friendly competition, and to foster multicultural celebrations in a fun, safe atmosphere.[8]

As a non-profit organization, SFVA dedicated approximately 80 percent of its revenues to its overall mission of supporting youth, agriculture, and education.[9] A significant portion was dedicated to fund its scholarship and youth education programs. The State Fair of Virginia Scholarship Program awarded scholarships based on 33 sanctioned state fair competition areas. Winners were allowed to use their scholarship winnings to attend any accredited post-secondary institution. Since its inception in 1989, the State Fair of Virginia

## EXHIBIT 2   Biography of SFVA Chief Executive Officer

Curry A. Roberts has served as the president and CEO of SFVA since 2004. A native of Bedford County, Virginia, he holds a degree in political science from Virginia Tech. He was named Outstanding Young Alumnus from Virginia Tech in 1989. Curry currently serves on the Board of Directors of Southern States Cooperative, Virginia Public Safety Foundation, and is a member of the Omnicron Delta Kappa National Leadership Honor Society. He has been active on the Board of Directors of the National Meat Association and the Virginia Tech Alumni Association, as well as the Board of visitors of Virginia State University. He had served as a Board member for the SFVA prior to becoming the CEO and president.

*Source:* 2010 Annual Report for The State Fair of Virginia, compiled for The Community Foundation Serving Richmond & Central Virginia.

Scholarship Program had awarded 2,439 scholarships and dedicated over $1.8 million to youth education.[10]

# SFVA'S OPERATING STRUCTURE

SFVA was a privately held, not-for-profit corporation that was tax exempt under IRS code section 501 (c) (3). It was independent of the state government and received no state or local operating support. As such, it was one of only a handful of state fairs in the United States structured to operate without public funding.

To be tax-exempt under section 501(c)(3) of the Internal Revenue Service Code, the SFVA had to be organized and operated exclusively for exempt purposes as set forth in the code; they qualified as a publicly supported charity that focused on education. The earnings of the organization were not allowed to be used for the benefit of any private shareholder or individual. In addition, the SFVA was restricted from being an "action" organization, in that it could not attempt to influence legislation as a substantial part of its activities and it was not able to participate in any campaign for or against political candidates.[11]

Most of the organization's activities were exempt from state and federal income taxes because of its mission to promote youth, agriculture, and education. However, other activities were potentially subject to income taxes. Additionally, products sold at the state fair and other events held at the Meadow Event Park were subject to 4.5 percent sales and use taxes, of which a part would go to Caroline County. In total, and including real estate taxes, the Meadow Event Park generated approximately $221,000 in revenue annually for Caroline County.[12]

In 2012, SFVA employed 21 people on a year-round basis. A biography of Curry Roberts, the president and CEO, is provided in Exhibit 2. The names and positions of the five most senior employees are provided in Exhibit 3. In addition, SFVA employed

## EXHIBIT 3   SFVA Senior Staff

| Name | Title |
| --- | --- |
| Curry A. Roberts | President |
| Michael Fritzsche | Senior Director, Marketing |
| John Bryan | Senior Director, Risk Management |
| David King | Senior Director, Development |
| Jodi Bufford | Senior Finance Director/ Treasurer |

*Source:* The State Fair of Virginia, Inc., IRS Form 990: Return of Organization Exempt from Income Tax, 2010.

between 12 and 20 hourly employees, particularly during the three major events it hosted every year. SFVA's staff was supplemented by volunteers who assisted with its events.

# SFVA'S CORPORATE GOVERNANCE

SFVA was streamlined in February 2004 to include a maximum 25-member, voluntary board of directors representing all regions of Virginia. Members of the board were appointed for three-year terms, with the possibility of serving an additional term, and received no financial compensation for sitting on the board. The board held six meetings annually where they established policy and direction for the corporation and approved strategic plans and annual operational and capital budgets. Numerous oversight committees and councils were selected from the volunteer ranks, including the SFVA board of directors.[13]

In November 2011, the board consisted of 20 members from across Virginia. The chairman was G. William "Billy" Beale, who was a director and CEO of Union First Market Bankshares, Inc. in Virginia. The other members of the board are outlined in Exhibit 4, and biographies of a few board members are provided in Exhibit 5.

## EXHIBIT 4    SFVA Board of Directors (2010)

| Name | Institution/Affiliation |
|---|---|
| G. William Beale (chairperson) | Union Bankshares Corp. |
| John Adams | Bowman Companies |
| Frank Atkinson | McGuire Woods Consulting LLP |
| Richard Chichester | Community volunteer |
| Dixie Dalton | Virginia Tech |
| T. Dowdy | Dowdy & Associates |
| M. Gilpin | Attorney |
| Britton Glisson | Markel Insurance Co. |
| Bruce Hazelgrove | NewMarket Corp. |
| Richard Johnson | The Wilton Companies |
| Patricia Loughridge | Loughridge Appraisals Ltd. Inc. |
| Jennifer McClellan | VA House of Delegates |
| William Mistr | Community volunteer |
| Julien Patterson | Omniplex World Services |
| Charles Payne | Hirschler Fleischer |
| Shelly Poole | Community volunteer |
| Lyle Pugh | L&M Farms |
| Christine Tillman | Hanover County Department of Social Services |
| Clinton Turner | Community volunteer |
| William Washington | PNGJ Enterprises |

*Source:* 2010 Annual Report for The State Fair of Virginia compiled for The Community Foundation Serving Richmond & Central Virginia.

## EXHIBIT 5    Biographies of Select SFVA Board Members

G. William Beale, 61, has been the CEO of Union First Market Bankshares Corporation (formerly, Union Bankshares Corp.) since July 1993. He served as the president and CEO of Union Bank and Trust Company from 1991 to 2004. He has been a Director of Union Bankshares Corp. and Union Bank and Trust Company since 1990. He is a graduate of The Citadel, majoring in business, and attended the graduate school of banking at Southern Methodist University.

John B. Adams, Jr., 66, serves as president and CEO of Bowman Companies, Inc., primarily a family real estate holding company. He is also chair of the Board of Fauquier Bankshares, Inc. and is a Director of Universal Corporation, a publicly traded company headquartered in Richmond, Virginia, where he also serves on the financial and audit committees.

Frank Atkinson is chairman of McGuireWoods Consulting LLC and a partner in McGuireWoods LLP. His practice focuses on state and local government relations, economic development, privatization and public-private partnerships, higher education and elections and voting rights. He also has extensive experience as an attorney in the areas of constitutional, election and education law and commercial and constitutional litigation.

Rich Johnson is the president and CEO of the Wilton Companies, a fully integrated real estate company engaged in the acquisition, development, ownership, management, and leasing of multi-family and commercial real estate properties. Prior to Wilton, Johnson was chairman and CEO of Southern Title Insurance Corporation and, subsequently, founder and president of Southern Financial Corporation, which became part of the Wilton Companies. During his tenure at Southern Financial Corporation, Johnson was involved with the acquisition, development, ownership, and management of commercial real estate properties, as well as the disposition of various portfolios of surplus commercial properties in excess of $100 million dollars.

Charles "Charlie" W. Payne, Jr. is a partner and attorney at Hirschler Fleischer. Payne is part of the business section of the firm and is located in the firm's Fredericksburg, Virginia office. He is a native of the Fredericksburg area and prides himself on the business development services he provides to the local community. Payne's practice areas include corporate and general business law, public-private partnerships, zoning and land use, commercial real estate, and federal and state government relations. He routinely represents corporations, real estate developers, contractors, not-for-profit foundations, banks, government contractors, medical practitioners, and economic development authorities.

## EXHIBIT 6  Secured Creditors

| Name of Creditor | Type of Debt | Amount |
|---|---|---|
| United States Department of Agriculture | Direct loans | $ 9.553 million |
| The Lender Group* | Taxable economic development bonds | 25.800 million |
| AgFirst Farm Credit Bank | Tax exempt bond | 49.790 million |
| Total | | $85.143 million |

\* The Lender Group consisted of ArborOne, Regions Bank, Farm Credit Bank of Texas, AG Texas, Farm Credit Services of Grand Forks, Capital Farm Credit, AgStar Financial Services, Farm Credit Services of Mid-America, Ag Credit, Carolina Farm Credit, Valley Farm Credit, Farm Credit of the Virginias, and Farm Credit of Southwest Florida, Southwest Georgia.

*Source:* http://www2.timesdispatch.com/mgmedia/file/462/state-fair-bankruptcy-documents/, accessed on January 13, 2012.

A number of SFVA board members had extensive legal, real estate, and financial experience, in some cases with not-for-profit organizations.

# HISTORY OF SFVA'S PROPERTY ACQUISITIONS AND DIVESTITURES

## Strawberry Hill Fairground

In 1998, SFVA's predecessor, Atlantic Rural Exposition, divested its Strawberry Hill Fairground complex by selling it to Richmond International Raceway for $47 million. $42 million was put into an investment portfolio that was professionally managed by Smith Barney. The goal was for the gains from this fund to cover two-thirds of the SFVA's debt service (principal and interest).

## The Meadow Farm

In July 2003, SFVA acquired a historic site, the Meadow Farm, located in Doswell, Virginia, for $5.3 million. The Meadow Farm consisted of 360 acres and was a nationally significant horse farm. It was famous for being both the birthplace of Secretariat, winner of the 1973 Triple Crown, and the training facility for Riva Ridge, winner of the Kentucky Derby and Belmont Stakes in 1972.

## The Meadow Event Park

The Meadow Event Park, at the Meadow Farm, was completed in 2009. It included several facilities as well as a mile of property along the North Anna River, 10 acres of wetlands, and a 143-horse-stall complex with four show rings. The buildings included a 63,354-square-foot exhibition hall, a 6,984-square-foot multipurpose facility and a 13,000-square-foot renovated mansion for special events such as weddings and conventions. Market studies indicated that more than 700,000 people would visit the Meadow Event Park for a variety of events each year.[14]

# SFVA CAPITAL STRATEGY

Using the $42 million investment portfolio as leverage, SFVA took out loans with a group of lenders (the Lender Group) for about $85 million. The plan was for the portfolio's income to cover at least two-thirds of the debt service for the first five years if not longer.

SFVA's principal debt obligations consisted of four components: taxable economic development bonds (taxable bonds); tax exempt Industrial Development Authority of the County of Caroline bonds (tax exempt bonds); three direct loans from the U.S. Department of Agriculture (USDA); and a notional amount swap with Morgan Keegan and Deutsche Bank. The proceeds of the taxable bonds, the tax exempt bonds and the USDA loans were used to develop the Meadow Event Park. Exhibit 6 provides a breakdown of the amounts for each of these creditors.

## The Taxable Economic Development Bonds

Six series of taxable economic development bonds totaling $25.80 million were issued on December 21, 2007. All of the series mature on December 1, 2037. Three of the series (2007A, 2007C, 2007E) were guaranteed by the USDA. Each series was secured by a cash-funded debt service reserve fund, a first parity lien on the SFVA's real property, and a security interest in all of its personal property, including its investment portfolio. The taxable bonds were held by a consortium of farm credit banks and Regions Bank. The bond series numbers and amounts are detailed in Exhibit 7.

**EXHIBIT 7**   Breakdown of the Taxable Economic Development Bonds

| Series Number | Amount |
|---|---|
| 2007A* | $ 8,640,000 |
| 2007B | 960,000 |
| 2007C* | 10,080,000 |
| 2007D | 1,120,000 |
| 2007E* | 4,500,000 |
| 2007F | 500,000 |
| Total | $25,800,000 |

* Guaranteed by the USDA.

*Source:* http://www2.timesdispatch.com/mgmedia/file/461/state-fair-bankruptcy-filing/, accessed on January 13, 2012.

## The Tax Exempt Bonds

The Industrial Development Authority of the County of Caroline, Virginia, also issued $49,790,000 of variable rate demand economic development revenue bonds (Meadow Event Park), on December 21, 2007. There were two bond series, 2007G ($33,670,000) and 2007H ($16,120,000), and each would mature on December 1, 2037.

The obligation of SFVA to repay the tax exempt bonds was through two promissory notes for the same amounts as the bonds. They were originally secured by a direct pay letter of credit issued by Regions Bank, later replaced by one issued on November 19, 2009 by AgFirst Farm Credit Bank, which was to expire on December 21, 2011. AgFirst would sell any tax exempt bonds it was obligated to buy to the Lender Group. The obligation of SFVA to repay the tax exempt bonds was secured on a parity basis with the same collateral that secured the taxable bonds with two exceptions: the debt service reserve funds and the investment portfolio only secured the taxable bonds.

## USDA Loans

SFVA held three USDA direct loans in the principal amounts of $4.999 million, $1.554 million, and $3 million. The first two loans were secured by cash-funded debt service funds of $262,447.50 and $86,477.50, respectively. All three loans were secured by a parity first lien on the SFVA's real property.

## Notional Amount Swap

SFVA was party to a $33.670 million notional amount swap with Morgan Keegan Financial Products, Inc. and Deutsche Bank AG as the swap counterparty. In notional amount swaps, each party agrees to pay either a fixed or floating rate denominated in a particular currency to a counterparty. The fixed or floating rate is multiplied by a notional principal amount; for SFVA it was $33.670 million. This notional amount is typically not exchanged between counterparties but is only used to calculate the amount of the cash flows. As an example, Party A is currently paying a floating rate but wants to pay a fixed rate. Party B is currently paying a fixed rate but wants to pay a floating rate. By entering into an interest rate swap, the net result is that each party can "swap" their existing obligation for their desired obligation. However, a third party (such as Morgan Keegan Financial Products, Inc.) can act as a financial intermediary.

The swap was to terminate on August 1, 2014, and SFVA was to pay a fixed rate of 3.70 percent. Regularly scheduled swap payments were secured by a parity first lien on SFVA's real and personal property.

## Additional Unsecured Debt

In addition, SFVA had unsecured debt to numerous trade creditors who provided goods and services in connection with the events SFVA put on every year. By November 2011, this trade debt and accrued liabilities totaled approximately $995,900.00. A list of the top 20 unsecured creditors is presented in Exhibit 8.

## SFVA'S CAPITAL INVESTMENT STRATEGY

The strategic decision to create and borrow against a $42 million investment fund would turn out to be disastrous for SFVA. In 2007, the Lender Group presented SFVA with the current structure of its finances. The main underpinning of the debt repayment structure was the $42 million investment portfolio with a forecasted average annual earning rate of 8 percent over a 10-year horizon. The SFVA board of directors approved and adopted this capital structure, as presented by the Lender Group.

SFVA set a fundraising goal of $12 million from both public and private sources. While an ambitious target, SFVA had not held a major capital campaign since 1946 and had significant early success. As of late

**EXHIBIT 8**    Consolidated List of Creditors Holding the 20 Largest Unsecured Claims

| Name of Creditor | Nature of Claim | Amount of Claim |
|---|---|---|
| SMG (facilities manager for the Meadow Event Park) | Trade debt | $ 287,407.91 |
| Siddall, Inc. (advertising and promotion) | Trade debt | 235,032.50 |
| Department of State Police | Trade debt | 92,259.22 |
| Extreme Clean U.S.A., Inc. | Trade debt | 73,350.77 |
| Lafayette Tent & Awning, Co. | Trade debt | 70,969.00 |
| Topside Tent & Party Rental | Trade debt | 45,152.28 |
| Sunbelt Rentals, Inc. | Trade debt | 40,918.46 |
| Pelican Paper Co., Inc. | Trade debt | 27,649.74 |
| Chocklett Press | Trade debt | 19,663.36 |
| Nationwide Golf Car, Inc. | Trade debt | 17,150.00 |
| Marsh | Trade debt | 15,725.05 |
| Morgan Keegan & Company, Inc. | Financing debt | 12,353.71 |
| Elevation, LLC | Trade debt | 11,787.62 |
| James River Equipment | Trade debt | 10,000.00 |
| GW Sound | Trade debt | 9,816.00 |
| Regalia Manufacturing Co. | Trade debt | 7,776.39 |
| Virginia Golf Cars, Inc. | Trade debt | 6,240.00 |
| Atlee Landscaping | Trade debt | 6,000.00 |
| Van's Welding & Maintenance | Trade debt | 5,200.00 |
| Dunbar Armored | Trade debt | 4,245.42 |

*Source:* http://www2.timesdispatch.com/mgmedia/file/462/state-fair-bankruptcy-documents, accessed on January 13, 2012.

2011, SFVA had raised $9.3 million against its goal, with 75 per cent of the amount obtained by 2008.

## ECONOMIC DOWNTURN

In the fall of 2008, the economic crisis that hit the United States, and then the rest of the world, resulted in a rapid decline in the financial markets. This had an extremely negative impact on the value of SFVA's investment fund, resulting in a level well below the $35 million minimum set forth in the financial agreement with the Lender Group.

In February 2009, SFVA met with the entire Lender Group and USDA to review the situation and discuss potential ways to restructure until the portfolio recovered. SFVA suggested deferment of certain debt payments until operations at the Meadow Farm began in 2009. The Lender Group gave SFVA only one option: SFVA was required to immediately take its then approximately $26 million portfolio to a cash position; reduce the scope of the project at the Meadow Farm by $2 million to free up funds for debt

service during construction; negotiate a new investment strategy before the funds could be reinvested; and seek a $10 million grant or sub debt from USDA to cushion the portfolio loss.

Although SFVA's professional fund manager strongly disagreed with the proposed course of action, SFVA was left with little choice. SFVA complied with the Lender Group's requirements to take the portfolio to cash after receiving assurances that SFVA could get assistance from USDA. Even with the $2 million reduction in the project budget, SFVA completed the project on schedule and was able to open the state fair at its new location in 2009. However, the $10 million in sub debt from USDA did not happen. Instead, USDA offered only a bridge working capital loan with a seven-year amortization schedule, of which the first two years were interest only.

SFVA accepted the working capital loan from USDA and then moved to reinvest the now $26 million portfolio in a 45 percent equity and 55 percent fixed income securities with the approval of the Lender Group. SFVA pointed out to the Lender

Group at the time that by selling at the bottom of the stock market, being restricted from reinvest until the market had recovered nearly 40 percent of its value, and not being able to restructure its debt, SFVA would find it difficult to meet the debt service required in the deal when the portfolio was valued at $42 million.

# ADVICE OF EXTERNAL CONSULTANTS

SFVA struggled not only with weather and typical startup issues throughout 2009 and 2010 but also with both fundraising and facility rental efforts due to the significant hit taken by the overall U.S. economy. After the 2010 state fair, which suffered from six out of 11 days of rain, SFVA began drawing the portfolio down below previously agreed-to minimums. Knowing that this could not continue and that its debt structure was not sustainable, SFVA met with ArborOne who represented the Lender Group (see Exhibit 6) and USDA in the late winter of 2011. Both acknowledged that a major restructuring was needed. While offering no solutions, they approved further draws from the portfolio as long as SFVA engaged two outside consultants (AECOM and Rod Markin Consulting) to provide studies to review operations and suggest improvements, as well as update previous forecasts for event attendance and facility rental.

The AECOM study was completed in August 2011 and, while concurring that the economy had negatively impacted SFVA's efforts at facility rental, predicted continued growth over the next three years. The second study by Rod Markin Consulting focused on SFVA's operations. It found that SFVA compared favourably with peer fairs but could reduce certain areas of expense and restructure certain relationships to enhance operations by a minimum of $650,000 in 2012. These reports were shared with the Lender Group when received.

The success of the 2011 state fair gave hope to SFVA that things were looking up. The 2011 state fair had been the most successful since 2007 and clearly a major improvement over the previous two fairs held in SFVA's new location. With much better weather, paid attendance increased by 44,000 people over the previous year, and revenue was positively impacted.

# SFVA'S FINANCIALS

The financial performance of SFVA had been turbulent since its investment portfolio had been impacted by the global financial crisis in 2008. An analysis of the organization's financial statements (Exhibit 9) clearly demonstrated the decline in revenues due to the decline in investment income. The global financial meltdown also made fundraising more difficult for the SFVA as evidenced in the reduction of revenues attributable to contributions and grants.

## EXHIBIT 9    SFVA Financial Performance, 2006–2010

| Fiscal Year | 2010 | 2009 | 2008 | 2007 | 2006 |
|---|---|---|---|---|---|
| Revenue | | | | | |
| Contributions and grants | $ 833,623 | $ 1,182,595 | $ 1,987,895 | $ 3,730,593 | $ 1,666,060 |
| Program service revenue | 4,987,964 | 5,359,350 | 5,091,920 | 5,280,699 | 4,401,958 |
| Investment income | 1,102,545 | (6,462,833) | (1,237,055) | 26,300,561 | 4,378,617 |
| Other revenue | (321,169) | (505,361) | 48,529 | 23,759 | 37,808 |
| Total revenue | 6,602,963 | (426,249) | 5,891,289 | 35,335,612 | 10,484,443 |
| Expenses | | | | | |
| Grants and similar amounts paid | 241,284 | 253,715 | 256,402 | 81,802 | 94,515 |
| Benefits paid to or for members | 0 | 0 | 0 | 0 | 0 |
| Salaries, other compensation, employee benefits | 2,149,783 | 2,087,841 | 2,152,120 | 2,376,731 | 2,494,410 |
| Professional fundraising fees | 0 | 0 | 0 | 0 | 274,841 |
| Other expenses | 11,650,499 | 8,448,889 | 7,990,109 | 7,897,100 | 5,817,718 |
| Total expenses | 14,041,566 | 10,790,445 | 10,298,631 | 10,3355,633 | 8,681,484 |
| Net income (loss) | ($ 7,428,603) | ($11,216,694) | ($ 4,507,342) | $24,979,979 | $ 1,802,959 |

*(Continued)*

**EXHIBIT 9** *(Concluded)*

| Fiscal Year | 2010 | 2009 | 2008 | 2007 | 2006 |
|---|---|---|---|---|---|
| Net Assets or Fund Balances | | | | | |
| Current assets | $ 1,545,252 | $ 2,950,645 | $ 3,876,546 | $12,221,425 | $ 2,372,019 |
| Total assets | 108,006,687 | 111,131,158 | 115,189,690 | 120,409,477 | 42,611,691 |
| Current liabilities | 4,612,805 | 1,826,730 | 1,130,102 | 723,532 | 515,924 |
| Total liabilities | 91,226,640 | 89,081,567 | 86,796,455 | 77,648,207 | 13,669,935 |
| Net assets | $16,780,047 | $22,049,591 | $28,393,235 | $42,761,270 | $56,281,626 |

*Source:* The State Fair of Virginia, Inc., IRS Form 990: Return of Organization Exempt from Income Tax, Years 2006–2010.

## THREAT OF BANKRUPTCY

In October and early November 2011, SFVA worked towards providing a new three-year financial forecast to the Lender Group. However, the success of the 2011 state fair in early October 2011 was not enough to change the financial direction of the organization in the eyes of the Lender Group.

At a meeting on November 14, 2011 with ArborOne, USDA, the SFVA's financial advisor, and the SFVA board and management, ArborOne offered no assurance that a deal could be reached to restructure, nor would it permit further draws from the now $20 million investment portfolio. USDA concurred and also offered no solution as to what SFVA could expect if the organization could not restructure the debt before depleting its cash balances. Most of SFVA's cash on hand was expected to be drawn over the next two to three months by debt service payments, on which interest rates would increase because the tax exempt bonds would convert to bank bonds at a much higher interest rate.

Although SFVA fully explained the cash situation and argued that it made no sense for SFVA to deplete its remaining cash to support a debt structure that could not be sustained, ArborOne, as the representative of the Lender Group, made no proposal and provided no assurances of support; in fact, it had no suggestions whatsoever concerning restructuring despite the obvious inability of SFVA to make debt service payments. While professing that it wanted to reach a solution outside of bankruptcy, ArborOne again outlined no strategy for how to restructure the debt or how SFVA could operate until an agreement was reached. SFVA proposed a six-month forbearance period and asked that it be allowed to utilize up to $1 million for operational needs while negotiating its restructuring in good faith.

SFVA was further challenged in that any restructuring required the unanimous consent of lenders, a higher bar than the traditional level of 50 percent of the lenders holding two-thirds of the debt. Arbor One did not respond favourably to SFVA's proposal. Consequently, SFVA would not be able to make its December 1, 2011 scheduled interest payment without endangering near-term operations.

## SCHOLARSHIPS IN JEOPARDY

The board also worried that the scholarships awarded to high school students could be in jeopardy.[15] SFVA had $1 million in a fund for scholarships with $400,000 from this fund held in trust for scholarships already awarded. Even though SFVA felt they had used clear language that segregated the scholarship assets from other money pledged as collateral for its loans, they worried lenders would try to seize those funds.

## STRATEGIC OPTIONS FOR SFVA

With no additional financing available from USDA or the existing Lender Group and with time running out, the board of directors of SFVA considered a number of strategic options.

1. Find another funding source: SFVA could approach the state government or find an angel donor in the broader community.
2. Commercially develop the site: SFVA could explore opportunities for rezoning with Caroline County officials in order to commercialize parts of the site.
3. Engage the public: SFVA could launch a public relations campaign to save the fair.
4. Try to restructure (Chapter 11): SFVA could declare Chapter 11 bankruptcy. Exhibit 10 provides details of the Chapter 11 bankruptcy process.

# EXHIBIT 10 Summary of Chapter 11 Bankruptcy Proceedings

In the United States, Chapter 11 of the Title 11 of the U.S. Bankruptcy Code provides a process for reorganization so that an organization can keep its business alive and pay creditors over time. Bankruptcy cases are the exclusive jurisdiction of the federal courts.

**Filing of Petition**

A Chapter 11 case begins with the filing of a petition with the bankruptcy court serving the area where the debtor lives or operates. Unless the court orders otherwise, the debtor also must file with the court the following: schedules of assets and liabilities; a schedule of current income and expenditures; a schedule of executory contracts and unexpired leases; and, a statement of financial affairs.

**Stay of Creditor Action**

As with cases under other chapters of the Bankruptcy Code, a stay of creditor actions against the Chapter 11 debtor automatically goes into effect when the bankruptcy petition is filed. The automatic stay provides a period of time in which all judgment, collection activities, foreclosures and repossessions of property are suspended and may not be pursued by the creditors on any debt or claim that arose before the filing of the bankruptcy petition.

**Debtor in Possession**

Upon filing a voluntary petition for relief under Chapter 11, the debtor automatically assumes an additional identity as the "debtor in possession." The term refers to a debtor that keeps possession and control of its assets while undergoing a reorganization under Chapter 11, without the appointment of a case trustee. A debtor will remain a debtor in possession until the debtor's plan of reorganization is confirmed, the debtor's case is dismissed or converted to Chapter 7, or a Chapter 11 trustee is appointed. The appointment or election of a trustee occurs only in a small number of cases. Generally, the debtor, as "debtor in possession," operates the business and performs many of the functions that a trustee performs in cases under other chapters.

Generally, a written disclosure statement and a plan of reorganization must be filed with the court. The disclosure statement is a document that must contain information concerning the assets, liabilities and business affairs of the debtor sufficient to enable a creditor to make an informed judgment about the debtor's plan of reorganization. The contents of the plan must include a classification of claims and must specify how each class of claims will be treated under the plan. Creditors whose claims are "impaired," i.e., those whose contractual rights are to be modified or who will be paid less than the full value of their claims under the plan, vote on the plan by ballot. After the disclosure statement is approved by the court and the ballots are collected and tallied, the court will conduct a confirmation hearing to determine whether to confirm the plan.

**Creditors' Committees**

Creditors' committees can play a major role in Chapter 11 cases. The committee is appointed by the U.S. trustee and ordinarily consists of unsecured creditors who hold the seven largest unsecured claims against the debtor. Among other things, the committee consults with the debtor in possession on administration of the case, investigates the debtor's conduct and operation of the business and participates in formulating a plan. A creditors' committee can be an important safeguard to the proper management of the business by the debtor in possession.

**Plan of Reorganization**

The debtor files a plan of reorganization during the first 120-day period after the petition is filed. In addition, the debtor has 180 days after the petition date to obtain acceptances of its plan. In practice, debtors typically seek extensions of both the plan filing and plan acceptance deadlines at the same time so that any order sought from the court allows the debtor two months to seek acceptances after filing a plan before any competing plan can be filed.

A Chapter 11 plan must designate classes of claims and interests for treatment under the reorganization. Generally, a plan will classify claim holders as secured creditors, unsecured creditors entitled to priority, general unsecured creditors and equity security holders. In a Chapter 11 case, a liquidating plan is permissible. Such a plan often allows the debtor in possession to liquidate the business under more economically advantageous circumstances than a Chapter 7 liquidation. It also permits the creditors to take a more active role in fashioning the liquidation of the assets and the distribution of the proceeds than in a Chapter 7 case.

**Approval of Reorganization Plan**

An entire class of claims is deemed to accept a plan if the plan is accepted by creditors that hold at least two-thirds in amount and more than one-half in number of the allowed claims in the class (Section 1126(c) of the Bankruptcy Code). When competing plans are presented that meet the requirements for confirmation, the court must consider the preferences of the creditors and equity security holders in determining which plan to confirm.

Any party in interest may file an objection to confirmation of a plan. The Bankruptcy Code requires the court, after notice, to hold a hearing on confirmation of a plan. If no objection to confirmation has been filed, the Bankruptcy

*(Continued)*

## EXHIBIT 10 *(Concluded)*

Code allows the court to determine whether the plan has been proposed in good faith and according to law. In order to confirm the plan, the court must find that the plan is feasible; it is proposed in good faith; and the plan and the proponent of the plan are in compliance with the Bankruptcy Code. In order to satisfy the feasibility requirement, the court must find that confirmation of the plan is not likely to be followed by liquidation (unless the plan is a liquidating plan) or the need for further financial reorganization.

### Conversion to Other Bankruptcy Actions

A debtor in a case under Chapter 11 has a one-time absolute right to convert the Chapter 11 case (reorganization) to a case under Chapter 7 (liquidation).

*Source:* U.S. Court, http://www.uscourts.gov/FederalCourts/Bankruptcy/BankruptcyBasics/Chapter11.aspx, accessed on March 23, 2012.

## EXHIBIT 11  Summary of Chapter 7 Bankruptcy Proceedings

In the United States, Chapter 7 of the Title 11 of the U.S. Bankruptcy Code provides a process for the liquidation of assets under the bankruptcy laws of the United States. To qualify for relief under Chapter 7 of the Bankruptcy Code, the debtor may be an individual, a partnership or a corporation or other business entity.

Under Chapter 7 provisions, a business ceases operations and a trustee is appointed with broad powers to oversee the business's financial affairs. Generally, the trustee gathers and sells the debtor's nonexempt assets and distributes the proceeds to pay holders of claims (creditors) in accordance with the provisions of the Bankruptcy Code. Part of the debtor's property may be subject to liens and mortgages that pledge the property to other creditors. In addition, the Bankruptcy Code will allow the debtor to keep certain "exempt" property; however, the trustee will liquidate the debtor's remaining assets.

### Stay of Creditor Action

Filing a petition under Chapter 7 "automatically stays" (stops) most collection actions against the debtor or the debtor's property. But filing the petition does not stay certain types of actions, and the stay may be effective only for a short time in some situations. As long as the stay is in effect, creditors generally may not initiate or continue lawsuits, garnishee wages or even make telephone calls demanding payments.

### Bankruptcy Estate

Commencement of a bankruptcy case creates an "estate." The estate technically becomes the temporary legal owner of all of the debtor's property. It consists of all legal or equitable interests of the debtor in property as of the commencement of the case, including property owned or held by another person if the debtor has an interest in the property. Generally speaking, the debtor's creditors are paid from nonexempt property of the estate.

A Chapter 7 case begins with the debtor filing a petition with the bankruptcy court serving the area where the individual lives or where the business debtor is organized or has its principal place of business or principal assets. In addition to the petition, the debtor must also file with the court the following: schedules of assets and liabilities, a schedule of current income and expenditures, a statement of financial affairs and a schedule of executory contracts and unexpired leases. Debtors must also provide the assigned case trustee with a copy of the tax return or transcripts for the most recent tax year as well as tax returns filed during the case (including tax returns for prior years that had not been filed when the case began).

### Payment of Claims

Section 726 of the Bankruptcy Code governs the distribution of the property of the estate. Under §726, there are six classes of claims and each class must be paid in full before the next lower class is paid anything. The debtor is only paid if all other classes of claims have been paid in full.

*Source:* U.S. Courts, http://www.uscourts.gov/FederalCourts/Bankruptcy/BankruptcyBasics/Chapter7.aspx, accessed on March 23, 2012.

5. Walk away: SFVA could just shut its doors and walk away from the situation.
6. Shut down (dissolution, or Chapter 7): SFVA could just give up and legally dissolve and terminate the organization. Exhibit 11 provides details of the Chapter 7 bankruptcy process.

## DECISION TIME FOR SFVA

Time was up for the SFVA. At their November 21, 2011 meeting, the board had to make a final decision about the fate of their organization. They had a number of serious options on the table, but they wondered if any of them would work and whether there were other solutions they were overlooking. Any option they chose would have to satisfy the Lender Group. In addition, the board felt they had an obligation to try to pay back the dozens of unsecured creditors.

The board knew they owed it to the hundreds of thousands of people who attended events at the Meadow Event Park every year to explore every strategy, no matter how extreme.

After 154 years, could the fair really be over for good?

## ENDNOTES

[1] This case was written on the basis of public sources only, including two court files taken from The State Fair of Virginia, Inc. (Case No. 11-3, 2011, United States Bankruptcy Court for the Eastern Division of Virginia, Richmond Division). These files were sourced from: http://www2.timesdispatch.com/mgmedia/file/461/state-fair-bankruptcy-filing/, accessed on January 13, 2012; and http://www2.timesdispatch.com/mgmedia/file/462/state-fair-bankruptcy-documents/, accessed on January 13, 2012. Consequently, the interpretation and perspectives presented in this case are not necessarily those of The State Fair of Virginia or any of its employees.
[2] All funds in U.S. dollars unless specified otherwise.
[3] RVA News, December 1, 2011, http://rvanews.com/news/state-fair-of-virginia-files-for-chapters-11-bankruptcy/53754, accessed on January 13, 2012.

[4] http://www.strawberryhillraces.com/tradition, accessed on March 3, 2012.
[5] http://www.meadowceltic.com/, accessed on March 3, 2012.
[6] L. M. Salamon, M. A. Haddock, S. W. Sokolowski, and H. S. Tice. (2007). Measuring Civil Societies and Volunteering: Initial Findings from the UN Handbook on Non-profit Institutions. Working paper No. 23. Baltimore: John Hopkins University Center for Civil Studies, 2007, p. 4.
[7] IRS Publication 557: Tax Exempt Status for Your Organization, p. 27. http://www.irs.gov/pub/irs-pdf/p557.pdf, accessed on March 23, 2012.
[8] http://www.facebook.com/StateFairVA?sk=info, accessed on March 3, 2012.
[9] http://www.co.caroline.va.us/meadow-farmqanda.pdf., accessed on March 3, 2012.

[10] http://www.statefair.com/scholarships, accessed on March 3, 2012.
[11] http://www.irs.gov/charities/charitable/article/0,,id=96099,00.html, accessed on March 23, 2012.
[12] Caroline County Press Release, March 9, 2012, http://www.co.caroline.va.us/sfpr3912.pdf, accessed on March 23, 2012.
[13] http://www.co.caroline.va.us/meadow-farmqanda.pdf, accessed on March 3, 2012.
[14] 2010 Annual Report for The State Fair of Virginia compiled for The Community Foundation Serving Richmond & Central Virginia.
[15] NBC12, Feb. 17, 2012, http://www.nbc12.com/story/16963220/nbc12-investigates-fair-scholarships-in-trouble, accessed on March 23, 2012.

# Eastman Kodak in 2012: Will Its Post-Bankruptcy Strategy Be Successful?

McGraw Hill connect

**John E. Gamble**
University of South Alabama

**R. Ray Gehani**
University of Akron

Eastman Kodak's decades-long struggle in making the conversion from film to digital technologies came to a dismal conclusion in January 2012 when the company filed for reorganization under Chapter 11 bankruptcy. Since 1920, Kodak had a near monopoly in the film and photography industry and was among the world's best-known brands because of its role in preserving memories from everyday occasions, birthday parties, holidays, and weddings. The company recorded stellar annual profits and cash flows for more than 50 years, but began to suffer in the 1990s when its rival, Fujifilm of Japan, launched an aggressive price war against Kodak. The company's troubles escalated further during the decade as consumers made a rapid migration to digital cameras and abandoned film and the need for photofinishing. The shift to digital technology directly impacted Eastman Kodak's two cash cows, film and film processing. Unable to respond successfully to the rapid consumer shift to digital cameras, Kodak was forced to close numerous manufacturing facilities and reduce its global workforce from a peak of 145,300 in 1988 to 18,800 at the time of the bankruptcy filing.

Kodak's profitability and cash flow problems were in full swing throughout the 2000s, with Kodak recording only one profitable year between 2004 and 2011, experiencing annual declines in liquidity, and experiencing a steady fall in its stock price from a high of $94 in 1997 to 37 cents per share just days before the Chapter 11 bankruptcy announcement. Even though Kodak's profitability and solvency had been decimated by the time bankruptcy became its only remaining option, its predicament was not unforeseen by the company's managers. Kodak had built the first digital camera in 1975 and held thousands of patents on technology used in the design of most digital cameras and camera phones in use in 2012. *The Economist* noted a 1979 report circulated among senior executives at Kodak that detailed the strengths of digital image capture and how the photography market would shift permanently from film to digital by 2010.[1]

Kodak confronted the challenge of a declining core business by the mid-1990s with its spinoff of its photography chemicals operations in 1993 and the launch of its DC-40 line of digital cameras targeted to consumers in 1995. Like Fujifilm, which shifted its focus from film to new chemical markets, Eastman Chemical was able to achieve success by strengthening and broadening its research and product development capabilities to enter new markets. Eastman Chemical earned $652 million on revenue of $7.4 billion in 2011 and its shareholders had seen a 100 percent appreciation in the company's stock price since the 1993 spinoff. Kodak divested its digital camera business unit just shortly after the bankruptcy filing, having never achieved any meaningful market share or profitability through the sale of digital cameras and picture frames. In 2012, the company's strategy was focused on transforming the company into a consumer and commercial inkjet printing company that could compete with Hewlett-Packard, Samsung, Seiko Epson, and others. In late-2011, Kodak was the fifth-largest printer brand with an estimated 5 percent market share. The company planned for the reorganization to be complete by 2013 and that capital necessary for the conversion would be available through a $950 debtor-in-possession financing agreement and as much as $2.6 billion from patent licensing fees and settlements of patent-infringement cases against Apple, HTC, and Research in Motion.

At the conclusion of the first quarter of 2012, the company's results were mixed with its selling, general, and administrative (SG&A) expenses declining by $84 million compared to the same period in 2011 and its liquidity improving by $500 million after $600 million in new net financing. However, its loss from continuing operations before interest expense, reorganization expense, and income taxes of $348 million for the quarter was $102 million greater than in the same period for 2011. Commenting on the company's situation at this time, Kodak CEO Antonio Perez stated, "During the quarter, we took decisive steps—including filing for Chapter 11 and exiting unprofitable businesses—to accelerate our transformation and emerge in 2013 as a profitable, sustainable business."[2]

## COMPANY HISTORY

The Eastman Kodak Company's foundation dates to 1884 when George Eastman established the Eastman Dry Plate and Film Company to manufacture and market flexible photographic film. The flexible film could be rolled and loaded into cameras to allow for multiple shots before reloading. George Eastman followed his invention of flexible film with the 1900 introduction of a portable Kodak Brownie camera that could be loaded with a 100-exposure roll of film. The Brownie camera made it easy for amateur photographers to take photographs and expanded the market for cameras and film beyond professional photographers. Kodak introduced upgraded models of the Brownie camera through 1966 and had sold tens of millions of the low-priced cameras by 1970 when the Brownie was discontinued. The Brownie was replaced by the Kodak Instamatic, which was launched in 1963 and had sold more than 50 million units by 1970.

Before Eastman's retirement in 1925, Kodak made many innovations in cameras and film, including the introduction of the first daylight-loading camera in 1891 and the invention of x-ray film and a coated motion picture film in 1896. The company later introduced Kodachrome color film for amateur photographers in 1935, the first home movie camera in 1936, the first slide projector in 1937, the Kodak 2620 color printer in 1966, and developed the world's first digital camera in 1975.

During its roaring growth of the 1980s, multiple takeover threats for Kodak came from T. Boone Pickens Jr., Ivan Boesky, and others. The senior executives at Kodak under CEO and chairman Colby Chandler attempted to protect the company by rapidly increasing its size through leveraged acquisitions of unrelated businesses such as Sterling Pharmaceuticals and Atex, a newspaper software supplier. With these acquisitions, Kodak's long-term debt grew to $7 billion. The projected growth in sales from diversification, however, did not materialize, as Eastman Kodak did not possess the core capabilities needed for success in most of these unrelated technological areas. The majority of Kodak's acquired unrelated businesses proved to be terribly unprofitable over time.

While Kodak's top management was focused on identifying acquisition candidates and consummating mergers, Kodak's primary photographic rival, Fujifilm, steadily increased its film market share in the United States from 0 to 12 percent. In addition, digital imaging technology was becoming an emerging threat to the traditional products of the photography industry. Potential weaknesses in Kodak's highly profitable business model based on selling and processing photographic film first became evident in 1981 when Sony launched its Mavica line of digital cameras. This digital innovation eliminated the need for photo processing and offered the additional advantage of allowing images to be stored, manipulated (enlarged and cropped), and electronically transmitted.

Rather than put further investment into its own digital camera technology, Kodak launched a compact disk-film camera in 1982. The miniaturized photographic film was loaded on a "View Master" like disc, which allowed the camera to be about the same size as a digital camera. However, customers complained that the disk-film camera and its miniaturized film produced grainy pictures. After investing substantial resources in the compact disk camera and failing to gain any excitement among consumers, Kodak abandoned the disk-film camera in 1988. Even though Kodak's compact camera had been a failure in the marketplace and Fuji continued to gain competitive strength in the market for 35mm film, photographic film continued to generate ample profits and cash flow for Kodak. In 1994, photographic film accounted for 45 percent of Kodak's revenues and 75 percent of its profits.

Because of the company's strong profit margins from photographic film, Kodak did not introduce its first digital camera until 1995—20 years after it had pioneered digital camera technology. However, neither its $1,000 first-generation DC-40 digital camera nor its second-generation DC-25 achieved any success in the digital camera marketplace. The company introduced the $219 pocket-sized DC-20 digital camera in 1996 that became a better seller than the DC-40 or DC-25, but a full-fledged price war in the film market with Fuji forced Kodak's earnings to a meager $5 million in 1997. Kodak's CEO at the time, George

Fisher, responded to the price war with Fujifilm with a restructuring plan to reduce operating expenses by $1 billion in 1999 through the elimination of 20,000 employees. The restructuring plan allowed Kodak's earnings to rebound to $1.4 billion by 1999, despite a 2 percent growth rate in photographic film revenues. Digital camera sales accounted for only $20 million of Kodak's 1999 revenues of approximately $14 billion.

Kodak tightened its focus on digital imaging in 2000 when Daniel Carp became CEO of the company. He directed Kodak's resources on digital imaging technology with an investment of more than $3 billion in digital cameras, online photo manipulation services, inkjet printers, photo printing kiosks, inks, and photographic quality printer paper. Sales of digital products had increased to $400 million in 2001, but not enough to offset the ongoing decline of the photographic film industry. Kodak's total revenues for the year had declined to $13.2 billion in 2001 and its net earnings had fallen to only $76 million. Carp planned to reverse the company's decline in revenues by pushing film and single-use cameras in emerging markets such as China, while cutting expenses through a further reduction in the company's headcount. By 2003, Kodak's revenue and net earnings had inched up slightly to $13.3 billion and $238 million, respectively. The company announced an additional workforce reduction to further reduce costs. Most importantly though, revenues for the company's digital imaging business in 2003 had increased to $4 billion and the unit had become profitable for the first time.

## CEO Antonio Perez Era (2005– )

In 2005, Carp was replaced as CEO by Antonio Perez who had joined Kodak in 2003 as president and chief operating officer. Prior to his arrival at Kodak, Perez spent 25 years at Hewlett-Packard managing the rapid growth of its printer business. The stock market cheered the new appointment of Perez as CEO, with its stock gaining four percent on the announcement. Among Perez's first actions as CEO was summoning the company's top executives to the Kodak Tower's second-floor conference room where he told them, *"You have to burn the boats"*—invoking the statement of Spanish conquistador Herman Cortez after discovering Latin America.[3] In other words, there was no going back to Kodak's long-held practice of initiating change only after an extensive protracted analysis. In a 1983 *Fortune* article that discussed Kodak's difficulties in developing digital products, a former executive with the company summarized its culture

and decision-making process by saying, "The people at Kodak are hardworking but bureaucratic. They do not understand the competitive nature of computer technology. You sometimes have to react to the marketplace on a weekly basis. At Kodak, if you came up with an idea, it would be five years before you saw the product."[4] Perez emphasized his imperative for the rapid development and launch of new digital products by promising investors that Kodak's operating earnings from digital products would increase by four times to more than $275 million by 2006—improving at a faster rate than the profits from film were projected to fall.

One of the first new digital products launched after Perez became CEO was Kodak's EasyShare-One digital camera. EasyShareOne users could wirelessly upload photos, order prints, and send picture e-mails. The accompanying EasyShare printer dock made printing pictures at home easy for consumers. EasyShare users could also store and view images with Kodak's EasyShare Picture Viewer. In 2010, Kodak's digital cameras remained distant runner-ups in the industry to Canon, Nikon, and Panasonic in the point and shoot and subcompact categories, but held 3 of the top 10 spots in the superzoom category. Kodak did not have a competitive model in the high-performance single lens reflex (SLR) category. Kodak had the seventh best-selling digital picture frame model in 2010. However, Kodak was the number-one online photofinishing processor in 2010.

Increasing digital revenues was also accomplished under Antonio Perez through licensing Kodak's patented technology to others in the industry and those in related industries. For example, Kodak had entered into a 10-year strategic cross-licensing and marketing relationship with Motorola to integrate Kodak photo sensors into Motorola mobile phones. The agreement between the two companies would also make Motorola phones compatible with Kodak printer docks, online services, and retail kiosks.

The strategic plan developed by Perez would retain the photographic film business as long as there were consumers willing to buy film, but the number of U.S. households owning film cameras in 2008 had declined to 46 percent from 55 percent in 2007, and 66 percent in 2006. But even worse, the number of households purchasing film fell to an estimated 38 percent in 2008. And only an estimated 27 percent of U.S. households processed photographic film, with an average of 3.4 rolls of film or one-time-use cameras used in 2008.

Perez's plan also included the divestiture of businesses not likely to be first or second in their respective industries. The company's health care business, which produced mammography imaging equipment, was among its significant divestitures after 2005. The restructuring resulted in a three-segment structure that included (1) consumer digital imaging, (2) film, photofinishing, and entertainment, and (3) a graphic communications group. The film, photofinishing, and entertainment group included consumer film and disposable cameras, motion picture film, film for aerial photographs, film for industrial purposes such as circuit board manufacturing, photographic paper and photochemicals, and event imaging solutions for theme parks and other venues selling souvenir photographs. The company's consumer digital imaging group included its retail printing kiosks, retail photo labs and supplies, consumer inkjet printers, digital cameras and frames, and Gallery online photo sharing service. Among Kodak's most notable products in its graphics communications business was its commercial inkjet printers and Nexpress, Flexcel NX, and Prosper commercial printing press equipment. Eastman Kodak's statements of operations for 2007–2010 are presented in Exhibit 1. The company's balance sheets for 2010 and 2011 are shown in Exhibit 2. Exhibits 3 and 4 present the company's net sales by business segment and its earnings before interest, other income, and taxes by business segment for 2007 through 2011.

# Eastman Kodak's 2012 Bankruptcy Filing

The long-term decline of Eastman Kodak Company's business prospects finally resulted in a Chapter 11 bankruptcy filing in January 2012. The company believed that reorganization under Chapter 11 bankruptcy would allow it to protect its working capital while completing its transformation to digital products, which was expected to result in $3.4 billion in restructuring costs. Digital products accounted for 75 percent of Eastman Kodak's revenues in 2011, but had so far failed to generate meaningful cash flows. The company had secured $950 million debtor-in-possession financing to provide sufficient liquidity to fund its operations during the reorganization, which would focus on divesting less attractive business units, generating revenues from its portfolio of digital capture patents, reducing its pension expense in a manner that would treat employees fairly, and further eliminating

## EXHIBIT 1    Eastman Kodak's Statements of Operations, 2007–2011 (in millions)

| | 2011 | 2010 | 2009 | 2008 | 2007 |
|---|---|---|---|---|---|
| Net sales | $6,022 | $7,167 | $7,609 | $9,416 | $10,301 |
| Cost of sales | 5,135 | 5,221 | 5,850 | 7,247 | 7,757 |
| Gross profit | 887 | 1,946 | 1,759 | 2,169 | 2,544 |
| Selling, general, and administrative expenses | 1,159 | 1,275 | 1,298 | 1,606 | 1,778 |
| Research and development | 274 | 318 | 351 | 478 | 549 |
| Restructuring and rationalization costs | 121 | 70 | 226 | 140 | 543 |
| Other operating income (expenses), net | (67) | 619 | (88) | 766 | (96) |
| Loss from continuing operations before interest, income taxes, and others, net | (600) | (336) | (28) | (821) | (230) |
| Interest expense | 156 | 149 | 119 | 108 | 113 |
| Net loss on early debt extinguishment | — | 102 | — | — | — |
| Other income (charges), net | (2) | 26 | 30 | 55 | 87 |
| Loss from continuing operations before income taxes | (758) | (561) | (117) | (874) | (256) |
| Provision (benefit) for income taxes | 9 | 114 | 115 | (147) | (51) |
| Loss from continuing operations | (767) | (675) | (232) | (727) | (205) |
| Earnings from discontinued operations, net of income taxes | 3 | (12) | 17 | 285 | 881 |
| Extraordinary item, net of tax | — | — | 6 | — | — |
| Net income (loss) | $ (764) | $ (687) | $ (209) | $ (442) | $ 676 |

*Source:* Eastman Kodak Company 2011 Annual Report.

**EXHIBIT 2   Eastman Kodak's Consolidated Balance Sheets, 2010–2011 (in millions, except share and per share data)**

| | As of December 31, | |
| --- | --- | --- |
| | 2011 | 2010 |
| **ASSETS** | | |
| Cash and cash equivalents | $  861 | $1,624 |
| Receivables, net | 1,103 | 1,196 |
| Inventories, net | 607 | 746 |
| Deferred income taxes | 58 | 120 |
| Other current assets | 74 | 100 |
| Total current assets | 2,703 | 3,786 |
| Property, plant, and equipment | 895 | 1,037 |
| Goodwill | 277 | 294 |
| Other long-term assets | 803 | 1,109 |
| Total assets | $4,678 | $6,226 |
| **LIABILITIES AND SHAREHOLDERS' EQUITY** | | |
| Accounts payables, others/trade | $  706 | $  959 |
| Short-term borrowings and current portion of long-term debt | 152 | 50 |
| Accrued income taxes | 40 | 343 |
| Other current liabilities | 1,252 | 1,468 |
| Total current liabilities | 2,150 | 2,820 |
| Long-term debt, net of current portion | 1,363 | 1,195 |
| Pension and other post-retirement liabilities | 3,053 | 2,661 |
| Other long-term liabilities | 462 | 625 |
| Total liabilities | 7,028 | 7,301 |
| Shareholders' equity (Deficit) | | |
| Common stock, $2.50 par value, 950,000,000 shares authorized; 391,292,760 shares issued as of December 31, 2011 and 2010; 271,379,883 and 268,898,978 shares outstanding as of December 31, 2011 and 2010 | 978 | 978 |
| Additional paid-in capital | 1,108 | 1,105 |
| Retained earnings | 4,071 | 4,969 |
| Accumulated other comprehensive income (loss) | (2,666) | (2,135) |
| Shareholders' equity | 3,491 | 4,917 |
| Treasury stock at cost | (5,843) | (5,994) |
| Total Eastman Kodak Company shareholders' (deficit) equity | (2,352) | (1,077) |
| Noncontrolling interests | 2 | 2 |
| Total shareholders' equity (deficit) | (2,350) | (1,075) |
| Total liabilities and shareholders' equity | $4,678 | $6,226 |

*Source:* Eastman Kodak Company 2011 Annual Report.

**EXHIBIT 3   Eastman Kodak's Net Sales by Business Segment, 2007–2011**

| Business Segment | 2011 | 2010 | 2009 | 2008 | 2007 |
| --- | --- | --- | --- | --- | --- |
| **Consumer Digital Imaging Group** | | | | | |
| Total | $1,739 | $2,739 | $2,619 | $3,088 | $ 3,247 |
| Inside USA | 864 | 1,781 | 1,618 | 1,811 | 2,011 |
| Outside USA | 875 | 958 | 1,001 | 1,277 | 1,235 |

*(Continued)*

**EXHIBIT 3**    *(Continued)*

| Business Segment | 2011 | 2010 | 2009 | 2008 | 2007 |
|---|---|---|---|---|---|
| **Film Photofinishing and Entertainment Group** | | | | | |
| Total | $1,547 | $1,762 | $2,257 | $2,987 | $ 3,632 |
| Inside USA | 456 | 542 | 508 | 835 | 1,054 |
| Outside USA | 1,091 | 1,220 | 1,749 | 2,152 | 2,578 |
| **Graphic Communications Group** | | | | | |
| Total | $2,736 | $2,681 | $2,726 | $3,334 | $ 3,413 |
| Inside USA | 738 | 810 | 831 | 1,036 | 1,178 |
| Outside USA | 1,998 | 1,871 | 1,895 | 2,298 | 2,235 |
| **All Other** | | | | | |
| Total | — | — | $    4 | $    7 | $    9 |
| Inside USA | — | — | 5 | 7 | 10 |
| Outside USA | — | — | (1) | — | (1) |
| **Consolidated Sales** | | | | | |
| Total | $6,022 | $7,167 | $7,606 | $9,416 | $10,301 |
| Inside USA | 2,058 | 3,131 | 2,962 | 3,689 | 4,254 |
| Outside USA | 3,964 | 4,036 | 4,644 | 5,727 | 6,047 |

*Source:* Eastman Kodak Company 2011 Annual Report.

**EXHIBIT 4**    Eastman Kodak's Earnings before Interest, Other Income, and Taxes by Business Segment, 2007–2011

| Business Segment | 2011 | 2010 | 2009 | 2008 | 2007 |
|---|---|---|---|---|---|
| Consumer Digital Imaging Group | $(349) | $ 278 | $(10) | $(177) | $(17) |
| Film, Photofinishing & Entertainment Group | 34 | 91 | 187 | 196 | 281 |
| Graphic Communications Group | (191) | (95) | (107) | (31) | 104 |
| All Other | — | (1) | (16) | (17) | (25) |
| Total | $(506) | $273 | $ 54 | $ (29) | $343 |

*Source:* Eastman Kodak Company 2011 Annual Report.

non-value adding costs. The company had generated revenues of more than $3 billion from its digital capture patent portfolio between 2003 and 2010 and expected gains of up to an additional $2.6 billion during the restructuring from patent licensing fees and from settlements of its patent-infringement cases against Apple, HTC, and Research in Motion.

At the time of the announcement of the bankruptcy filing, CEO Antonio Perez stated, "We have already effectively exited certain traditional operations, closing 13 manufacturing plants and 130 processing labs, and reducing our workforce by 47,000 since 2003. Now we must complete the transformation by further addressing our cost structure and effectively monetizing non-core IP assets. We look forward to working with our stakeholders to emerge a lean, world-class, digital imaging and materials science company."[5]

# EASTMAN KODAK'S BUSINESS OPERATIONS IN 2012

Within weeks of the bankruptcy filing, the company announced that it would divest its digital camera and digital picture frame businesses. The move would require a $30 million restructuring charge in 2012, but would reduce operating expenses by $100 million annually. The exit from digital cameras and picture frames allowed Kodak to reorganize its three major business units into two segments—commercial and

## EXHIBIT 5   Eastman Kodak's Operating Structure in 2012

| Commercial (2011 revenues of $3.4 billion) | Consumer (2011 revenues of $2.6 billion) |
|---|---|
| **Graphics, Entertainment, and Commercial Film**<br>• Commercial prepress printing equipment and consumables and services<br>• Film for the entertainment industry<br>• Industrial films for aerial photographs and circuit board production<br>**Digital and Functional Printing**<br>• Digital printing presses and consumables and services<br>**Enterprise Services and Solutions**<br>• Enterprise document scanners, software, and services | **Retail Systems Solutions**<br>• Kodak instant picture kiosks, retail photo labs, supplies, and software<br>**Consumer Inkjet**<br>• Office and home inkjet printers<br>**Intellectual Property**<br>• Over 10,000 worldwide patents supporting Kodak products and licensing portfolios<br>**Consumer Film**<br>• Film and disposable cameras<br>**Gallery**<br>• Online photo sharing, photo books, and other merchandise<br>**Paper and Output Systems**<br>• Photographic paper, photochemicals, and output systems<br>**Event Imaging Solutions**<br>• Photography for theme park rides and other photo souvenir events |

consumer. Business units included in the commercial segment were (1) graphics, entertainment, and commercial film, (2) digital and functional printing, and (3) enterprise services and solutions. The consumer segment included seven businesses—(1) retail systems solutions, (2) consumer inkjet, (3) paper and output systems, (4) event imaging solutions, (5) Gallery, (6) intellectual property, and (7) consumer film. Exhibit 5 provides an overview of products offered by each business unit in the two segments.

The reorganization was designed to allow the company to exploit any competitive advantage resulting from its materials science research and digital imaging expertise. In 2012, the company had market leading positions in photographic film, consumer digital printing kiosks, retail photo labs and consumables, and digital printing plates used in commercial printing presses. The company expected the expertise in these businesses could be transferred to its growing consumer inkjet printer, document scanning equipment, software and services, and digital printing press businesses.

## Eastman Kodak's Business Strategy in 2012

**Kodak's Strategy in Its Commercial Segment**   Kodak's new organizational structure made commercial products the largest segment of its

operations with 2011 sales of $3.4 billion. The company was the worldwide leader in film used in the motion picture industry and for special industrial applications, such as aerial photography and circuit board production. Entertainment imaging produced ample free cash flows that could be used to support growth in Kodak's other businesses, but operated in a declining industry. Sales of film for motion pictures was expected to decline by 75 percent between 2012 and 2015 as motion picture studios further shifted to digital technology and attempted to lower production costs. A reduction in the number of movie-goers and falling DVD sales had led to an overall decline in profitability for motion picture studios since the early 2000s. The projected decline in motion picture film sales for the 2012–2015 period followed an actual decline in sales of motion picture film of more than 50 percent between 2009 and 2012. While only 20 percent of the world's first-run movie theater screens utilized digital cinema technology in 2009, between 40 and 50 percent had been converted by 2011 and between 80 and 90 percent were expected to be converted to digital cinema technology by 2015. The company's sales of entertainment film had declined from $913 million in 2009 to $541 million in 2011.

The company's managers believed that digital prepress printing devices and consumables offered substantial growth opportunities for Kodak. The worldwide market for digital prepress plates and services was expected to grow at a 4 percent annual rate between 2010 and 2015 to reach $22 billion. The company held number-one positions in prepress output devices and consumables and saw both as profit and cash generators through 2015. However, Kodak's net sales of prepress solutions had declined from $1.67 billion in 2009 to $1.56 billion in 2011. Kodak believed that opportunities for growth in digital prepress products existed in markets for both established and emerging printing applications. Kodak's sales of industrial films for aerial photographs and circuit board production were not of a sufficient size to significantly impact the profitability of the graphics, entertainment, and commercial film business unit.

The company also saw an opportunity for growth in digital and functional printing. Traditional printing markets such as direct mail pieces, catalogs, promotional materials, books, and packaging had all grown at rates ranging from 10 to 42 percent between 2009 and 2012. The company's high-volume roll-fed color presses, sheet-fed production presses, and consumables such as printheads, ink, and toner, were all highly regarded in the industry. Kodak's Prosper printing presses and components offered magazine-quality production, a broad range of applications, and the industry's highest-speed inkjet printing and lowest running cost. Although the company's commercial printing presses were among the industry's best, the company's financial struggles had made some buyers reluctant to purchase Kodak presses, which could cost as much as $1.8 million. A Los Angeles printing company owner explained, "I was really nervous about what was going to happen [at Kodak]. We looked at HP and they were a lot more stable."[6] In fact, rivals such as Canon and Ricoh had developed tactics aimed at exploiting Kodak's image problems to help build global market shares in the industry of 25 and 20 percent, respectively. While printing press consumables such as ink and supplies and printing press servicing contracts offered healthy profit margins, Kodak's small installed base of digital printing presses had prevented the division from earning profits as of 2011.

The company's enterprise services and solutions business targeted government, financial institutions, pharmaceutical manufacturers, and retailers needing document management equipment and services. Users of Kodak's high-speed document scanners were also able to use the company's workflow software to make documents readily available on company intranets for archival and decision-making purposes. The business unit's revenues approximated $600 million each year between 2009 and 2011. Even though the unit had seen no significant growth since 2009, Kodak management believed services under development, such as document security services, would generate revenue increases in what was generally considered a declining industry. While industry-wide sales of scanners were estimated by Kodak at $900 million in 2012 and sales of document management software was estimated at $500 million, the company estimated that industry-wide enterprise document management services revenues could grow by as much as 14 percent annually to exceed $15 billion by 2015.

**Kodak's Strategy in Its Consumer Segment**   Kodak's retail systems solutions group was ranked number one in picture printing, with more than 100,000 instant picture kiosks installed in about 65,000 retail locations around the world in 2012. Over 160 million kiosk sessions per year were conducted by about 80 million consumers to instantly print pictures from digital media. The company also had the industry's largest installed base of dry labs and thermal printers that allowed consumers to create prints, photo books, personal greeting cards, posters, and collages from digital images. While traditional photofinishing services for $4 \times 6$ prints were expected to decline by 5.2 percent annually between 2010 and 2015, Kodak expected the market for photo books and photo merchandise to grow at annual rates of 13.4 percent and 11.4 percent, respectively, between 2010 and 2015.

The company had great expectations for its consumer inkjet business unit, which competed in a $43 billion global retail market. As of 2011, Kodak was ranked fifth in the consumer inkjet printer industry with a 5 percent market share behind Hewlett-Packard, Canon, Seiko Epson, and Brother International. However, Kodak's management believed that its innovative business model would allow it to quickly build a large enough installed base of inkjet printers to generate substantial volume in sales of ink cartridges. Whereas, leading printer makers priced printers at near break-even and then earned hefty profit margins on the sale of printer ink, Kodak's business model was based on charging premium prices for its printers and selling ink cartridges at a below-market price. On average, Kodak consumer inkjet printers were priced about 14 percent above comparable models offered by HP in 2011. An executive at HP discounted the viability of Kodak's pricing plan by commenting that "Customer buying behavior is pretty well established" and continued that Kodak's "ability to charge a premium has been challenged significantly."[7]

The company also expected to generate significant revenues from its efforts to monetize its intellectual property. The company possessed over 10,000 worldwide patents that not only gave rise to the development of some of its most important products, but were also the technological foundation for products produced by others. For example, its digital capture technology was used by the makers of almost all mobile phones. Kodak had generated more than $3 billion in patent licensing fees between 2003 and 2010, with $1.9 billion of that received between 2008 and 2010. Future licensing agreements and pending litigation with Apple, HTC, and Research in Motion was expected to generate as much as $2.6 billion for Kodak.

While Kodak was number one in photofinishing solutions, its photofinishing paper and output systems revenues had declined from $836 million in 2009 to $722 million in 2011 as consumers took fewer pictures using film-based cameras. For the same reason, the company's worldwide sales of consumer film had declined from about $500 million in 2009 to $250 million in 2011. Revenues from its event imaging solutions business and its Gallery online photo sharing and photo merchandise business did not amount to a noteworthy percentage of the consumer group's overall revenues in 2011.

## EASTMAN KODAK'S PERFORMANCE IN 2012

During the company's first quarter in bankruptcy, Antonio Perez and Kodak's management team had successfully reduced selling, general, and administrative (SG&A) expenses by $84 million compared to SG&A at the end of the first quarter of fiscal 2011. The company's liquidity had also improved by the end of the first quarter of 2012 with its cash balance increasing by $500 million from the same period in fiscal 2011 after $600 million in net new financing. The company's quarterly revenues of $965 million were 27 percent below the $1,322 million recorded during the same period in 2011. The decline in revenues reflected Kodak's exit from digital cameras and frames, the continued decline in the usage of film and film processing, and a $61 million revenue reduction associated with a tax refund sharing agreement with intellectual property licensees. The reduction was the result of a $122 million tax refund granted by the Korean government and recorded during the quarter. The consumer segment recorded a $164 million loss during the first quarter of 2012, which was $23 million less than the collection of businesses recorded in the first quarter of 2011. The $64 million loss recorded by the commercial segment was $3 million less than the loss recorded by Kodak's commercial businesses in the first quarter of 2011. The company's loss from continuing operations before interest expense, reorganization expense, and income taxes was $348 million for the quarter compared to $246 million for the same period in 2011.

Perez summed up the company's first three months of 2012 by commenting that "Kodak is focusing on opportunities, reducing costs, and fine-tuning the balance between liquidity and growth to enable the enterprise to emerge from its Chapter 11 restructuring in 2013 as a leaner, stronger, and sustainable business."[8]

## ENDNOTES

1 Larry Keeley, "The Kodak Lie," *Fortune Online Edition,* January 16, 2012.
2 As quoted in "Kodak's 1st Quarter Results Show Improvement in Segment Profitability and Reduced Operating Costs," *Eastman Kodak Press Release,* April 27, 2012.
3 Brad Stone, "What's Kodak's Strategy?" *Newsweek,* January 16, 2006.
4 As quoted in "Embattled Kodak Enters the Electronic Age, *Fortune,* originally published

in 1983 and reprinted in the January 8, 2012 online edition.
5 As quoted in "Eastman Kodak Company and Its U.S. Subsidiaries Commence Voluntary Chapter 11 Business Reorganization," *Eastman Kodak Company Press Release,* January 19, 2012.
6 As quoted in "Kodak Tries to Bring Its Digital Revival into Focus," *Bloomberg Businessweek Online,* September 1, 2011.

7 Ibid.
8 As quoted in "Kodak's 1st Quarter Results Show Improvement in Segment Profitability and Reduced Operating Costs," *Eastman Kodak Press Release,* April 27, 2012.

# Nucor Corporation in 2012: Using Economic Downturns as an Opportunity to Grow Stronger

McGraw Hill connect

## Arthur A. Thompson
The University of Alabama

In 2012, Nucor Corp., with a production capacity approaching 27 million tons, was the largest manufacturer of steel and steel products in North America and ranked as the 11th-largest steel company in the world based on tons shipped in 2011. It was regarded as a low-cost producer, and it had a sterling reputation for being a global leader in introducing innovative steel-making technologies throughout its operations. Nucor began its journey from obscurity to a steel industry leader in the 1960s. Operating under the name of Nuclear Corporation of America in the 1950s and early 1960s, the company was a maker of nuclear instruments and electronics products. After suffering through several money-losing years and facing bankruptcy in 1964, Nuclear Corporation of America's board of directors opted for new leadership and appointed F. Kenneth Iverson as president and CEO. Shortly thereafter, Iverson concluded that the best way to put the company on sound footing was to exit the nuclear instrument and electronics business and rebuild the company around its profitable South Carolina–based Vulcraft subsidiary that was in the steel joist business—Iverson had been the head of Vulcraft prior to being named president. Iverson moved the company's headquarters from Phoenix, Arizona, to Charlotte, North Carolina, in 1966, and proceeded to expand the joist business with new operations in Texas and Alabama. Then, in 1968, top management decided to integrate backward into steelmaking, partly because of the benefits of supplying its own steel requirements for producing steel joists and partly because Iverson saw opportunities to capitalize on newly emerging technologies to produce steel more cheaply. In 1972, the company adopted the name Nucor Corporation, and Iverson initiated a long-term strategy to grow Nucor into a major player in the U.S. steel industry.

By 1985 Nucor had become the seventh largest steel company in North America, with revenues of $758 million, six joist plants, and four state-of-the-art steel mills that used electric arc furnaces to produce new steel products from recycled scrap steel. Nucor was regarded as an excellently managed company, an accomplished low-cost producer, and one of the most competitively successful manufacturing companies in the country.[1] A series of articles in *The New Yorker* related how Nucor, a relatively small American steel company, had built an enterprise that led the whole world into a new era of making steel with recycled scrap steel. NBC did a business documentary that used Nucor to make the point that American manufacturers could be successful in competing against low-cost foreign manufacturers.

During the 1985–2000 period, Nucor continued to construct additional steel-making capacity, adopt trailblazing production methods, and expand its lineup of steel products. By 2000, Nucor was the second-largest steel producer in the U.S. and charging to overtake long-time leader United States Steel. Nucor's sales in 2000 exceeded 11 million tons annually and revenues were nearly $4.8 billion. Nucor continued its long-term growth strategy during 2006–2011, constructing additional plants and acquiring other (mostly troubled) steel facilities at bargain basement prices, enabling it to enter new product segments and offer customers a diverse variety of steel shapes and steel products. Heading into 2012, Nucor was solidly entrenched as the largest steel producer in North America (based on production capacity) with 23 plants having the capacity to produce 27 million tons of assorted steel shapes (steel bars, sheet steel, steel plate, and structural steel) and additional steel manufacturing facilities with the capacity to make 4.7 million tons of steel joists, steel decking, cold finish bars, steel buildings, steel mesh, steel grating, steel fasteners, and fabricated steel reinforcing products. The company had 2011 revenues of $20.0 billion and net profits of $778.2 million, well below its pre-recession peak in 2008 of $23.7 billion in revenues and $1.8 billion in net profits.

With the exception of three quarters in 2009 and one quarter in 2010 (when the steel industry in the United States was in the midst of a deep economic downturn and the demand for steel was unusually weak), Nucor had earned a profit in every quarter of every year since 1966—a truly remarkable accomplishment in a mature and cyclical business where it was common for industry members to post losses when demand for steel sagged. As of April 2012, Nucor had paid a dividend for 156 consecutive quarters and had raised the base dividend it paid to stockholders every year since 1973 when the company first began paying cash dividends (in years when earnings and cash flows permitted, it was Nucor's practice to pay a supplemental year-end dividend in addition to the base quarterly dividend). Exhibit 1 provides highlights of Nucor's growth since 1970.

Standard & Poor's, in a January 9, 2012 report titled "North American Metals and Mining Companies, Strongest to Weakest," ranked Nucor #1 for credit rating and credit outlook among a universe of 68 companies, in large part because of the company's strong competitive position and profit performance relative to peer companies in the steel industry.

## NUCOR IN 2012

Ken Iverson, the architect of Nucor's climb to prominence in the steel industry, was regarded by many as a "model company president." Under Iverson, who served as Nucor's CEO until late 1998, Nucor was known for its aggressive pursuit of innovation and technical excellence, rigorous quality systems, strong emphasis on employee relations and workforce productivity, cost-conscious corporate culture, and its ability to achieve low costs per ton produced. The company had a very streamlined organizational structure, incentive-based compensation systems, and steel mills that were among the most modern and efficient in the United States. Iverson proved himself a master in crafting and executing a low-cost leadership strategy, and he made a point of making sure that he

## EXHIBIT 1    Nucor's Growing Presence in the Market for Steel, 1968–2011

| Year | Total Tons Sold to Outside Customers | Average Price per Ton | Net Sales (in millions) | Earnings before Taxes (in millions) | Pretax Earnings per Ton | Net Earnings (in millions) |
|------|------|------|------|------|------|------|
| 1970 | 207,000 | $245 | $ 50.8 | $ 2.2 | $10 | $ 1.1 |
| 1975 | 387,000 | 314 | 121.5 | 11.7 | 30 | 7.6 |
| 1980 | 1,159,000 | 416 | 482.4 | 76.1 | 66 | 45.1 |
| 1985 | 1,902,000 | 399 | 758.5 | 106.2 | 56 | 58.5 |
| 1990 | 3,648,000 | 406 | 1,481.6 | 111.2 | 35 | 75.1 |
| 1995 | 7,943,000 | 436 | 3,462.0 | 432.3 | 62 | 274.5 |
| 2000 | 11,189,000 | 425 | 4,756.5 | 478.3 | 48 | 310.9 |
| 2001 | 12,237,000 | 354 | 4,333.7 | 179.4 | 16 | 113.0 |
| 2002 | 13,442,000 | 357 | 4,801.7 | 227.0 | 19 | 162.1 |
| 2003 | 17,473,000 | 359 | 6,265.8 | 70.0 | 4 | 62.8 |
| 2004 | 19,109,000 | 595 | 11,376.8 | 1,725.9 | 96 | 1,121.5 |
| 2005 | 20,465,000 | 621 | 12,701.0 | 2,027.1 | 104 | 1,310.3 |
| 2006 | 22,118,000 | 667 | 14,751.3 | 2,692.4 | 129 | 1,757.7 |
| 2007 | 22,940,000 | 723 | 16,593.0 | 2,253.3 | 104 | 1,471.9 |
| 2008 | 25,187,000 | 940 | 23,663.3 | 2,790.5 | 116 | 1,831.0 |
| 2009 | 17,576,000 | 637 | 11,190.3 | (470.4) | (28) | (293.6) |
| 2010 | 22,019,000 | 720 | 15,844.6 | 194.9 | 9 | 134.1 |
| 2011 | 23,044,000 | 869 | 20,023.6 | 1,169.9 | 53 | 778.2 |

Source: Company records posted at www.nucor.com, accessed April 8, 2012.

practiced what he preached when it came to holding down costs. The offices of executives and division general managers were simply furnished. There were no company planes and no company cars, and executives were not provided with company-paid country club memberships, reserved parking spaces, executive dining facilities, or other perks. To save money on his own business expenses and set an example for other Nucor managers, Iverson flew coach class and took the subway when he was in New York City.

When Iverson left the company in 1998 following disagreements with the board of directors, he was succeeded briefly by John Correnti and then Dave Aycock, both of whom had worked in various roles under Iverson for a number of years. In 2000, Daniel R. DiMicco, who had joined Nucor in 1982 and risen up through the ranks to executive vice president, was named president and CEO. DiMicco was Nucor's chairman and CEO in 2012. Like his predecessors, DiMicco continued to pursue a rapid growth strategy, expanding the company production capabilities via both acquisition and new plant construction and boosting tons sold from 11.2 million in 2000 to 25.2 million in 2008 before the financial crisis in the fourth quarter of 2008 and the subsequent economic fallout caused tons sold in 2009 to plunge to 17.6 million tons and revenues to nosedive from $23.7 billion in 2008 to $11.2 billion in 2009. Nucor's business was still in the recovery stages in 2010–2011 (see Exhibit 2).

In the 12 years of Dan DiMicco's leadership, Nucor was quite opportunistic in initiating actions to strengthen its competitive position during periods when the demand for steel was weak and then to capitalize on these added strengths in periods of strong market demand for steel products and significantly boost financial performance. According to Dan DiMicco:[2]

> Our objective is to deliver improved returns at every point in the economic cycle. We call it delivering higher highs and higher lows. In the last major economic slump, from 2001 through 2003, Nucor had total net earnings of $339.8 million. During the even deeper slump of 2009 through 2011, Nucor earned $618.7 million, an increase of 82 percent. The most recent peak to peak earnings grew from $310.9 million in 2000 to $1.83 billion in 2008, an increase of 489 percent.
>
> Nucor uses each economic downturn as an opportunity to grow stronger. We use the good times to prepare for the bad, and we use the bad times to prepare for the good. Emerging from downturns stronger than we enter them is how we build long-term value for

our stockholders. We get stronger because our team is focused on continual improvement and because our financial strength allows us to invest in attractive growth opportunities throughout the economic cycle.

Nucor's top executives expected the full benefits of the $7 billion in investments made from 2007 through 2011 (plus whatever amounts the company invested in 2012 and 2013) to lead to significantly higher revenues and profits when healthy economic conditions and strong market demand for steel products reappeared.

## Nucor's Ever-Growing Product Line, 1967–2012

Over the years, Nucor had expanded progressively into the manufacture of a wider and wider range of steel shapes and steel products, enabling it in 2012 to offer steel users the broadest product lineup of any North American steel producer. Steel shapes and steel products were considered commodities. While some steel-makers had plants where production quality was sometimes inconsistent or on occasions failed to meet customer-specified metallurgical characteristics, most steel plants turned out products of comparable metallurgical quality—one producer's reinforcing bar was essentially the same as another producer's reinforcing bar, a particular type and grade of sheet steel made at one plant was essentially identical to the same type and grade of sheet steel made at another plant. The commodity nature of steel products forced steel producers to be very price competitive, with the market price of each particular steel product being driven by demand-supply conditions for that product.

**Steel Products**  Nucor's first venture into steel in the late 1960s, via its Vulcraft division, was principally one of fabricating steel joists and joist girders from steel that was purchased from various steel-makers. Vulcraft expanded into the fabrication of steel decking in 1977. The division expanded its operations over the years and, as of 2012, Nucor's Vulcraft division was the largest producer and leading innovator of open-web steel joists, joist girders, and steel deck in the United States. It had seven plants with an annual capacity of 715,000 tons that made steel joists and joist girders and six plants with 530,000 tons of capacity that made steel deck; in 2010–2011 about 90 percent of the steel needed to make these products was supplied by various Nucor steel-making plants. Vulcraft's

## EXHIBIT 2   Five-Year Financial and Operating Summary, Nucor Corporation, 2007–2011 ($ in millions, except per share data and sales per employee)

| FOR THE YEAR | 2011 | 2010 | 2009 | 2008 | 2007 |
|---|---|---|---|---|---|
| Net sales | $20,023.6 | $15,844.6 | $11,190.3 | $23,663.3 | $16,593.0 |
| Costs, expenses and other: | | | | | |
|   Cost of products sold | 18,075.0 | 15,001.0 | 11,035.9 | 19,612.3 | 13,462.9 |
|   Marketing, administrative, and other expenses | 520.6 | 391.4 | 351.3 | 714.1 | 553.1 |
|   Equity in losses of minority-owned enterprises | 10.0 | 32.1 | 82.3 | 36.9 | 24.6 |
|   Impairment of non-current assets | | | | 105.2 | |
|   Interest expense, net | 166.1 | 153.1 | 134.7 | 90.5 | 5.5 |
|     Total | 18,771.8 | 15,577.5 | 11,604.3 | 20,559.0 | 14,046.2 |
| Earnings (loss) before income taxes and non-controlling interests | 1,251.8 | 267.1 | (414.0) | 3,104.4 | 2,546.8 |
| Provision for (benefit from) income taxes | 390.8 | 60.8 | (176.8) | 959.5 | 781.4 |
| Net earnings (loss) | 861.0 | 206.3 | (237.2) | 2,144.9 | 1,765.4 |
| Less earnings attributable to minority ownership in unconsolidated enterprises | 82.8 | 72.2 | 56.4 | 13.9 | 293.5 |
| Net earnings (loss) attributable to Nucor stockholders | $    778.2 | $    134.1 | $   (293.6) | $ 1,831.0 | $ 1,471.9 |
| Net earnings (loss) per share: | | | | | |
|   Basic | $2.45 | $0.42 | $(0.94) | $5.99 | $4.96 |
|   Diluted | 2.45 | 0.42 | (0.94) | 5.98 | 4.94 |
| Dividends declared per share | $1.4525 | $1.4425 | $1.41 | $1.91 | $2.44 |
| Percentage of net earnings to net sales | 3.9% | 0.8% | −2.6% | 7.7% | 8.9% |
| Return on average stockholders' equity | 10.7% | 1.8% | −3.8% | 28.1% | 29.4% |
| Capital expenditures | $450.6 | $345.3 | $390.5 | $1,019.0 | $520.3 |
| Acquisitions (net of cash acquired) | 4.0 | 64.8 | 32.7 | 1,826.0 | 1,542.7 |
| Depreciation | 522.6 | 512.1 | 494.0 | 479.5 | 403.2 |
| Sales per employee (000s) | 974 | 777 | 539 | 1,155 | 1,085 |
| **AT YEAR END** | | | | | |
| Cash, cash equivalents, and short-term investments | $ 2,563.3 | $ 2,479.0 | $ 2,242.0 | $ 2,355.1 | $ 1,576.4 |
| Current assets | 6,708.1 | 5,861.2 | 5,182.2 | 6,397.5 | 5,073.2 |
| Current liabilities | 2,396.1 | 1,504.4 | 1,227.1 | 1,854.2 | 1,582.0 |
| Working capital | 4,312.0 | 4,356.8 | 3,995.1 | 4,543.3 | 3,491.2 |
| Cash provided by operating activities | 1,032.6 | 873.4 | 1,173.2 | 2,502.1 | 1,953.3 |
| Current ratio | 2.8 | 3.9 | 4.2 | 3.5 | 3.2 |
| Property, plant, and equipment | $ 3,755.6 | $ 3,852.1 | $ 4,013.8 | $ 4,131.9 | $ 3,233.0 |
| Total assets | 14,570.4 | 13,921.9 | 12,571.9 | 13,874.4 | 9,826.1 |
| Long-term debt (including current maturities) | 4,280.2 | 4,280.2 | 3,086.2 | 3,266.6 | 2,250.3 |
| Stockholders' equity | 7,474.9 | 7,120.1 | 7,390.5 | 7,929.2 | 5,112.9 |
| Percentage of long-term debt to total capital* | 35.7% | 36.9% | 28.9% | 28.3% | 29.4% |
| Shares outstanding (000s) | 316,749 | 315,791 | 314,856 | 313,977 | 287,993 |
| Employees | 20,800 | 20,500 | 20,400 | 21,700 | 18,000 |

*Total capital is defined as stockholders' equity plus long-term debt.

*Source:* Nucor's 2011 Annual Report, p. 39.

joist, girder, and decking products were used mainly for roof and floor support systems in retail stores, shopping centers, warehouses, manufacturing facilities, schools, churches, hospitals, and, to a lesser extent, multi-story buildings and apartments. Customers for these products were principally nonresidential construction contractors.

In 1979, Nucor began fabricating cold finished steel products. These consisted mainly of cold drawn and turned, ground, and polished steel bars or rods of various shapes—rounds, hexagons, flats, channels, and squares—made from carbon, alloy, and leaded steels based on customer specifications or end-use requirements. Cold finished steel products were used in tens of thousands of products, including anchor bolts, hydraulic cylinders, farm machinery, air conditioner compressors, electric motors, motor vehicles, appliances, and lawn mowers. Nucor sold cold finish steel directly to large-quantity users in the automotive, farm machinery, hydraulic, appliance, and electric motor industries and to steel service centers that in turn supplied manufacturers needing only relatively small quantities. In 2011, Nucor Cold Finish was the largest producer of cold finished bar products in North America and had facilities in Missouri, Nebraska, South Carolina, Utah, Wisconsin, and Ontario, Canada. It obtained most of its steel from Nucor's mills that made steel bar. This factor, along with the fact that all of Nucor's cold finished facilities employed the latest technology and were among the most modern in the world, resulted in Nucor Cold Finish having a highly competitive cost structure. It maintained sufficient inventories of cold finish products to fulfill anticipated orders.

Nucor produced metal buildings and components throughout the United States under several brands: Nucor Building Systems, American Buildings Company, Kirby Building Systems, Gulf States Manufacturers, and CBC Steel Buildings. In 2012, the Nucor Buildings Group had 11 metal buildings plants with an annual capacity of approximately 465,000 tons. Sales were 232,000 tons in 2011, a decrease of 3 percent from 239,000 tons in 2010. Nucor's Buildings Group began operations in 1987 and currently had the capability to supply customers with buildings ranging from less than 1,000 square feet to more than 1,000,000 square feet. Complete metal building packages could be customized and combined with other materials such as glass, wood, and masonry to produce a cost-effective, aesthetically pleasing building built to a customer's particular requirements. The

buildings were sold primarily through an independent builder distribution network. The primary markets served were commercial, industrial, and institutional buildings, including distribution centers, automobile dealerships, retail centers, schools, warehouses, and manufacturing facilities. Nucor's Buildings Group obtained a significant portion of its steel requirements from the Nucor bar and sheet mills.

Another Nucor division produced steel mesh, grates, and fasteners. Various steel mesh products were made at three facilities in the United States and one in Canada that had combined annual production capacity of about 248,000 tons. Steel and aluminum bar grating, safety grating, and expanded metal products were produced at several North American locations that had combined annual production capacity of 103,000 tons. Nucor Fastener, located in Indiana, began operations in 1986 with the construction of a $25 million plant. At the time, imported steel fasteners accounted for 90 percent of the U.S. market because U.S. manufacturers were not competitive on cost and price. Iverson said "We're going to bring that business back; we can make bolts as cheaply as foreign producers." Nucor built a second fastener plant in 1995, giving it the capacity to supply about 20 percent of the U.S. market for steel fasteners. Currently, these two facilities had annual capacity of over 75,000 tons and produced carbon and alloy steel hex head cap screws, hex bolts, structural bolts, nuts and washers, finished hex nuts, and custom-engineered fasteners that were used for automotive, machine tool, farm implement, construction, military, and various other applications. Nucor Fastener obtained much of the steel for making these products from Nucor mills that made steel bars and maintained sufficient inventories of its various products to meet anticipated demand from customers in the United States and Canada.

Beginning in 2007, Nucor—through its newly acquired Harris Steel subsidiary—began fabricating, installing, and distributing steel reinforcing bars (rebar) for highways, bridges, schools, hospitals, airports, stadiums, office buildings, high-rise residential complexes, and other structures where steel reinforcing was essential to concrete construction. Harris Steel had over 70 fabrication facilities in the United States and Canada, with each facility serving the surrounding local market. Since acquiring Harris Steel, Nucor had more than doubled its rebar fabrication capacity to 1,695,000 tons annually. Two new rebar facilities had been added in 2011, and total fabricated rebar sales in 2011 were 1,074,000 tons, up 9 percent over the 981,000 tons sold in 2010. Much of the steel used in making fabricated rebar products was obtained from Nucor steel plants that made steel bar. Fabricated reinforcing products were sold only on a contract bid basis.

**Steel-making**   In 1968, Nucor got into basic steel-making, building a mill in Darlington, South Carolina, to manufacture steel bars. The Darlington mill was one of the first plants of major size in the U.S to use electric arc furnace technology to melt scrap steel and cast molten metal into various shapes. Electric arc furnace technology was particularly appealing because the labor and capital requirements to melt steel scrap and produce crude steel were far lower than those at conventional integrated steel mills where raw steel was produced using coke ovens, basic oxygen blast furnaces, ingot casters, and multiple types of finishing facilities to make crude steel from iron ore, coke, limestone, oxygen, scrap steel, and other ingredients. By 1981, Nucor had four steel mills making carbon and alloy steels in bars, angles, and light structural shapes. Since then, Nucor had undertaken extensive capital projects to keep these facilities modernized and globally competitive. In 2000–2011, Nucor aggressively expanded its market presence in steel bars and by 2012 had 13 bar mills located across the United States that produced concrete reinforcing bars, hot-rolled bars, rods, light shapes, structural angles, channels and guard rails in carbon and alloy steels. These 13 plants had total annual capacity of approximately 9.1 million tons. Four of the 13 mills made hot-rolled special-quality bars manufactured to exacting specifications. Nucor had plans to invest an additional $290 million in three of the special-quality bar mills that would add the capability to produce 1 million additional tons annually by early 2014. The products of the 13 bar mills had wide usage and were sold primarily to customers in the agricultural, automotive, construction, energy, furniture, machinery, metal building, railroad, recreational equipment, shipbuilding, heavy truck, and trailer industries. In addition, the company's newly renovated wire rod and bar mill in Kingman, Arizona, had the ability to increase its production from 200,000 tons annually to 500,000 tons annually with very little additional investment, thus putting the company in a strong position to serve wire rod and rebar customers in the southwestern U.S. market. Nucor executives expected that the added capacity at the three special bar quality mills and at the Kingman plant would be an important source of growth in upcoming years.

In the late 1980s, Nucor entered into the production of sheet steel at a newly constructed plant in Crawfordsville, Indiana. Flat-rolled sheet steel was used in the production of motor vehicles, appliances, steel pipe and tubes, and other durable goods. The Crawfordsville plant was the first in the world to employ a revolutionary thin slab casting process that substantially reduced the capital investment and costs to produce flat-rolled sheet steel. Thin-slab casting machines had a funnel-shaped mold to squeeze molten steel down to a thickness of 1.5–2.0 inches, compared to the typically 8- to 10-inch thick slabs produced by conventional casters. It was much cheaper to then build and operate facilities to roll thin-gauge sheet steel from 1.5- to 2-inch thick slabs than from 8- to 10-inch thick slabs. When the Crawfordsville plant first opened in 1989, it was said to have costs $50 to $75 per ton below the costs of traditional sheet steel plants, a highly significant cost advantage in a commodity market where the going price at the time was $400 per ton. *Forbes* magazine described Nucor's pioneering use of thin slab casting as the most substantial, technological, industrial innovation in the past 50 years.[3] By 1996, two additional sheet steel mills that employed thin slab casting technology were constructed, and a fourth mill was acquired in 2002, giving Nucor the capacity to produce 11.3 million tons of sheet-steel products annually as of 2012. Nucor also operated two Castrip sheet production facilities, one built in 2002 at the Crawfordsville plant and a second built in Arkansas in 2009. These facilities used the breakthrough strip casting technology that involved the direct casting of molten steel into a final shape and thickness without further hot or cold rolling. The process allowed for lower capital investment, reduced energy consumption, smaller scale plants, and improved environmental impact (because of significantly lower emissions).

Also in the late 1980s, Nucor added wide-flange steel beams, pilings, and heavy structural steel products to its lineup of product offerings. Structural steel products were used in buildings, bridges, overpasses, and similar such projects where strong weight-bearing support was needed. Customers included construction companies, steel fabricators, manufacturers, and steel service centers. To gain entry to the structural steel segment, in 1988 Nucor entered into a joint venture with Yamato-Kogyo, one of Japan's major producers of wide-flange beams, to build a new structural steel mill in Arkansas; a second mill was built on the same site in the 1990s that made the Nucor-Yamato venture in Arkansas the largest structural beam facility in the Western Hemisphere. In 1999, Nucor started operations at a third structural steel mill in South Carolina. The mills in Arkansas and South Carolina both used a special continuous casting method that was quite cost-effective. Going into 2012, Nucor had the capacity to make 3.7 million tons of structural steel products annually.

Starting in 2000, Nucor began producing steel plate of various thicknesses and lengths that was sold to manufacturers of heavy equipment, ships, barges, bridges, rail cars, refinery tanks, pressure vessels, pipe and tube, wind towers, and similar products. Steel plate was made at two mills in Alabama and North Carolina that had combined capacity of about 2.9 million tons. In early 2011, Nucor started operations at a newly constructed 125,000-ton heat treating facility at the plate mill in North Carolina. Heat treated steel plate was used in applications requiring higher strength, abrasion resistance, and toughness.

All of Nucor's steel mills used electric arc furnaces, whereby scrap steel and other metals were melted and the molten metal then poured into continuous casting systems. Sophisticated rolling mills converted the billets, blooms, and slabs produced by various casting equipment into rebar, angles, rounds, channels, flats, sheet, beams, plate, and other finished steel products. Nucor's steel mill operations were highly automated, typically requiring fewer operating employees per ton produced than the mills of rival companies. High worker productivity at all Nucor steel mills resulted in labor costs roughly 50 percent lower than the labor costs at the integrated mills of companies using union labor and conventional blast furnace technology. Nucor's value chain (anchored in using electric arc furnace technology to recycle scrap steel) involved far fewer production steps, far less capital investment, and considerably less labor than the value chains of companies with integrated steel mills that made crude steel from iron ore.

Exhibit 3 shows Nucor's sales by product category for 1990–2011. The breadth of Nucor's product line made it the most diversified steel producer in North America, and all of its steel mills were among the most modern and efficient mills in the United States. The company had market leadership in several product categories—it was the largest U.S. producer of steel bars, structural steel, steel reinforcing bars, steel joists and girders, steel deck, and cold-finished steel products bars. And Nucor was among the leading producers of sheet steel, steel plate, steel fasteners, metal building systems, light gauge steel framing, and rebar fabrication.

The average capacity utilization rates at Nucor's steel mills were 70 percent in 2010 and 74 percent in 2011; the average capacity utilization rates at Nucor's steel products facilities were 54 percent in 2010 and 57 percent in 2011.

**Pricing and Sales**  In 2011, approximately 86 percent of the production by Nucor's steel mills segment was sold to external customers. The balance of the company's steel mill production went to supply the steel needs of the company's joist, deck, rebar fabrication, fastener, metal buildings, and cold finish operations.

The commodity nature of steel products meant that the prices a company could command were driven by prevailing market demand-supply conditions which changed more or less continually. The big majority of Nucor's steel sales were to customers who placed orders monthly based on their immediate upcoming needs; sales were made at the prevailing spot market price, as determined by current market demand–supply conditions. As a consequence, Nucor's average sales prices per ton varied considerably from quarter to quarter (see Exhibit 4). Nucor's strategy was to quote the same payment terms to all customers and for customers to pay all shipping charges.

Nucor marketed the output of its steel mills and steel products facilities mainly through an in-house sales force; there were salespeople located at most every Nucor production facility. In 2011, approximately 50 percent of Nucor's sheet steel sales were to contract customers (versus 40 percent in 2010 and 30 percent in 2009). These contracts for sheet steel were usually for periods of 6 to 12 months and permitted price adjustments to reflect changes in prevailing raw material costs. The other 50 percent of Nucor's sheet steel production and virtually all of the company's plate, structural, and bar steel was sold to customers who typically placed orders monthly based on their immediate upcoming needs; sales were made at the prevailing spot market price, as determined by current market demand-supply conditions. Nucor's steel mills maintained inventory levels deemed adequate to fill the expected incoming orders from customers.

Nucor sold steel joists and joist girders, and steel deck on the basis of firm, fixed-price contracts that, in most cases, were won in competitive bidding against rival suppliers. Longer-term supply contracts for these items that were sometimes negotiated with customers contained clauses permitting price adjustments to reflect changes in prevailing raw materials costs. Steel joists,

**EXHIBIT 3   Nucor's Sales of Steel and Steel Products, by Product Category, 1990–2011**

Tons Sold to Outside Customers (in thousands)

| Year | Steel Mill Products | | | | | Finished Steel Products | | | | Total Tons |
| | Sheet Steel (2011 capacity of ~11.3 million tons) | Steel Bars (2011 capacity of ~9.1 million tons) | Structural Steel (2011 capacity of ~3.7 million tons) | Steel Plate (2011 capacity of ~2.9 million tons) | Total (2011 capacity of ~27 million tons) | Steel Joists (2011 capacity of ~715,000 tons) | Steel Deck (2011 capacity of ~530,000 tons) | Cold Finished Steel (2011 capacity of ~860,000 tons) | Rebar Fabrication and Other Products* | |
|---|---|---|---|---|---|---|---|---|---|---|
| 2011 | 7,500 | 4,680 | 2,338 | 2,278 | 16,796 | 288 | 312 | 494 | 5,154 | 23,044 |
| 2010 | 7,434 | 4,019 | 2,139 | 2,229 | 15,821 | 276 | 306 | 462 | 5,154 | 22,019 |
| 2009 | 5,212 | 3,629 | 1,626 | 1,608 | 12,075 | 264 | 310 | 330 | 4,596 | 17,576 |
| 2008 | 7,505 | 5,266 | 2,934 | 2,480 | 18,185 | 485 | 498 | 485 | 4,534 | 25,187 |
| 2007 | 8,266 | 6,287 | 3,154 | 2,528 | 20,235 | 542 | 478 | 449 | 1,236 | 22,940 |
| 2006 | 8,495 | 6,513 | 3,209 | 2,432 | 20,649 | 570 | 398 | 327 | 174 | 22,118 |
| 2005 | 8,026 | 5,983 | 2,866 | 2,145 | 19,020 | 554 | 380 | 342 | 169 | 20,465 |
| 2004 | 8,078 | 5,244 | 2,760 | 1,705 | 17,787 | 522 | 364 | 271 | 165 | 19,109 |
| 2003 | 6,954 | 5,530 | 2,780 | 999 | 16,263 | 503 | 353 | 237 | 117 | 17,473 |
| 2002 | 5,806 | 2,947 | 2,689 | 872 | 12,314 | 462 | 330 | 226 | 110 | 13,442 |
| 2001 | 5,074 | 2,687 | 2,749 | 522 | 11,032 | 532 | 344 | 203 | 126 | 12,237 |
| 2000 | 4,456 | 2,209 | 3,094 | 20 | 9,779 | 613 | 353 | 250 | 194 | 11,189 |
| 1995 | 2,994 | 1,799 | 1,952 | — | 6,745 | 552 | 234 | 234 | 178 | 7,943 |
| 1990 | 420 | 1,382 | 1,002 | — | 2,804 | 443 | 134 | 163 | 104 | 3,648 |

*Includes steel fasteners (steel screws, nuts, bolts, washers, and bolt assemblies), steel mesh, steel grates, metal building systems, light gauge steel framing, and scrap metal.

*Source:* Company records posted at www.nucor.com, accessed April 9, 2012.

**EXHIBIT 4**  Nucor's Average Quarterly Sales Prices for Steel Products, by Product Category, 2011–2012

| Period | Sheet Steel | Steel Bars | Structural Steel | Steel Plate | Average of All Steel Mill Products | Average of All Steel Products* |
|--------|------------|-----------|-----------------|------------|-----------------------------------|-------------------------------|
| **2011** | | | | | | |
| Qtr 1 | $755 | $779 | $831 | $880 | $789 | $1,274 |
| Qtr 2 | 894 | 803 | 923 | 1,029 | 891 | 1,361 |
| Qtr 3 | 800 | 811 | 901 | 1,021 | 847 | 1,381 |
| Qtr 4 | 744 | 796 | 891 | 946 | 806 | 1,395 |
| **2012** | | | | | | |
| Qtr 1 | 780 | 823 | 866 | 929 | 824 | 1,413 |
| Qtr 2 | 770 | 795 | 905 | 922 | 812 | 1,416 |

*An average of the steel prices for steel deck, steel joists and girders, steel buildings, cold finished steel products, steel mesh, fasteners, fabricated rebar, and other steel products.

*Source:* Company records posted at www.nucor.com, accessed April 23, 2012.

girders, and deck were manufactured to customers' specifications and shipped immediately; Nucor's plants did not maintain inventories of steel joists, girders, or steel deck. Nucor also sold fabricated reinforcing products only on a construction contract bid basis. However, cold finished steel, steel fasteners, steel grating, wire, and wire mesh were all manufactured in standard sizes, with each facility maintaining sufficient inventories of its products to fill anticipated orders; most all sales of these items were made at the prevailing spot price.

## Strategy

Starting in 2000, Nucor embarked on a five-part growth strategy that involved new acquisitions, new plant construction, continued plant upgrades and cost reduction efforts, international growth through joint ventures, and greater control over raw materials costs.

**Strategic Acquisitions**  Beginning in the late 1990s, Nucor management concluded that growth-minded companies like Nucor might well be better off purchasing existing plant capacity rather than building new capacity, provided the acquired plants could be bought at bargain prices, economically retrofitted with new equipment if need be, and then operated at costs comparable to (or even below) those of newly constructed state-of-the-art plants. At the time, the steel industry worldwide had far more production capacity than was needed to meet market demand, forcing many companies to operate in the red. Nucor had not made any acquisitions since about 1990, and a team of five people was assembled in 1998 to explore

acquisition possibilities that would strengthen Nucor's customer base, geographic coverage, and lineup of product offerings.

For almost three years, no acquisitions were made. But then the economic recession that hit Asia and Europe in the late 1990s reached the United States in full force in 20002001. The September 11, 2001 terrorist attacks further weakened steel purchases by such major steel-consuming industries as construction, automobiles, and farm equipment. Many steel companies in the U.S. and other parts of the world were operating in the red. Market conditions in the U.S. were particularly grim. Between October 2000 and October 2001, 29 steel companies in the U.S., including Bethlehem Steel Corp. and LTV Corp., the nation's third- and fourth-largest steel producers respectively, filed for bankruptcy protection. Bankrupt steel companies accounted for about 25 percent of U.S. capacity. *The Economist* noted that of the 14 steel companies tracked by Standard & Poor's, only Nucor was indisputably healthy. Some experts believed that close to half of the U.S. steel industry's production capacity might be forced to close before conditions improved; about 47,000 jobs in the U.S. steel industry had vanished since 1997.

One of the principal reasons for the distressed market conditions in the U.S. was a surge in imports of low-priced steel from foreign countries. Outside the U.S., weak demand and a glut of capacity had driven commodity steel prices to 20-year lows in 1998. Globally, the industry had about 1 billion tons of annual capacity, but puny demand had kept production levels in the 750 to 800 million tons per year range during

1998–2000. A number of foreign steel producers, anxious to keep their mills running and finding few good market opportunities elsewhere, began selling steel in the U.S. market at cut-rate prices in 1997–1999. Nucor and other U.S. companies reduced prices to better compete and several filed unfair trade complaints against foreign steelmakers. The U.S. Department of Commerce concluded in March 1999 that steel companies in six countries (Canada, South Korea, Taiwan, Italy, Belgium, and South Africa) had illegally dumped stainless steel in the United States, and the governments of Belgium, Italy, and South Africa further facilitated the dumping by giving their steel producers unfair subsidies that at least partially made up for the revenue losses of selling at below-market prices. Congress and the Clinton Administration opted to not impose tariffs or quotas on imported steel, which helped precipitate the number of bankruptcy filings. However, the Bush Administration was more receptive to protecting the U.S. steel industry from the dumping practices of foreign steel companies. In October 2001, the U.S. International Trade Commission (ITC) ruled that increased steel imports of semi-finished steel, plate, hot-rolled sheet, strip and coils, cold-rolled sheet and strip, and corrosion-resistant and coated sheet and strip were a substantial cause of serious injury, or threat of serious injury, to the U.S. industry. In March 2002, the Bush Administration imposed tariffs of up to 30 percent on imports of selected steel products to help provide relief from Asian and European companies dumping steel in the U.S. at ultra-low prices.

Even though market conditions were tough for Nucor, management concluded that oversupplied steel industry conditions and the number of beleaguered U.S. companies made it attractive to expand Nucor's production capacity via acquisition. Starting in 2001, the company proceeded to make a series of acquisitions:

- In 2001, Nucor paid $115 million to acquire substantially all of the assets of Auburn Steel Company's 400,000-ton steel bar facility in Auburn, New York. This acquisition gave Nucor expanded market presence in the Northeast and was seen as a good source of supply for a new Vulcraft joist plant being constructed in Chemung, New York.
- In November 2001, Nucor announced the acquisition of ITEC Steel Inc. for a purchase price of $9 million. ITEC Steel had annual revenues of $10 million and produced load bearing light gauge steel

framing for the residential and commercial market at facilities in Texas and Georgia. Nucor was impressed with ITEC's dedication to continuous improvement and intended to grow ITEC's business via geographic and product line expansion. ITEC Steel's name was changed to Nucon Steel Commercial Corporation in 2002.

- In July 2002, Nucor paid $120 million to purchase Trico Steel Company, which had a 2.2 million ton sheet steel mill in Decatur, Alabama. Trico Steel was a joint venture of LTV (which owned a 50 percent interest), and two leading international steel companies—Sumitomo Metal Industries and British Steel. The joint venture partners had built the mill in 1997 at a cost of $465 million, but Trico was in Chapter 11 bankruptcy proceedings at the time of the acquisition and the mill was shut down. The Trico mill's capability to make thin sheet steel with a superior surface quality added competitive strength to Nucor's strategy to gain sales and market share in the flat-rolled sheet segment. By October 2002, two months ahead of schedule, Nucor had restarted operations at the Decatur mill and was shipping products to customers.
- In December 2002, Nucor paid $615 million to purchase substantially all of the assets of Birmingham Steel Corporation, which included four bar mills in Alabama, Illinois, Washington, and Mississippi. The four plants had a capacity of approximately 2 million tons annually. The purchase price also included approximately $120 million in inventory and receivables, the assets of Port Everglade Steel Corp., the assets of Klean Steel, Birmingham Steel's ownership interest in Richmond Steel Recycling, and a mill in Memphis, Tennessee, that was not currently in operation. Top executives believed the Birmingham Steel acquisition would broaden Nucor's customer base and build profitable market share in bar steel products.
- In August 2004, Nucor acquired a cold rolling mill in Decatur, Alabama, from Worthington Industries for $80 million. This 1 million ton mill, which opened in 1998, was located adjacent to the previously acquired Trico mill and gave Nucor added ability to service the needs of sheet steel buyers located in the southeastern U.S.
- In June 2004, Nucor paid a cash price of $80 million to acquire a plate mill owned by Britain-based Corus Steel that was located in Tuscaloosa, Alabama. The Tuscaloosa mill, which currently had a capacity

of 700,000 tons that Nucor management believed was expandable to 1 million tons, was the first U.S. mill to employ a special technology that enabled high-quality wide steel plate to be produced from coiled steel plate. The mill produced coiled steel plate and plate products that were cut to customer-specified lengths. Nucor intended to offer these niche products to its commodity plate and coiled sheet customers.

- In February 2005, Nucor completed the purchase of Fort Howard Steel's operations in Oak Creek, Wisconsin; the Oak Creek facility produced cold finished bars in size ranges up to 6-inch rounds and had approximately 140,000 tons of annual capacity.

- In June 2005, Nucor purchased Marion Steel Company located in Marion, Ohio, for a cash price of $110 million. Marion operated a bar mill with annual capacity of about 400,000 tons; the Marion location was within close proximity to 60 percent of the steel consumption in the United States.

- In May 2006, Nucor acquired Connecticut Steel Corporation for $43 million in cash. Connecticut Steel's bar products mill in Wallingford had annual capacity to make 300,000 tons of wire rod and rebar and approximately 85,000 tons of wire mesh fabrication and structural mesh fabrication, products that complemented Nucor's present lineup of steel bar products provided to construction customers.

- In late 2006, Nucor purchased Verco Manufacturing Co. for approximately $180 million; Verco produced steel floor and roof decking at one location in Arizona and two locations in California. The Verco acquisition further solidified Vulcraft's market leading position in steel decking, giving it total annual capacity of over 500,000 tons.

- In January 2007, Nucor acquired Canada-based Harris Steel for about $1.07 billion. Harris Steel had 2005 sales of Cdn$1.0 billion and earnings of Cdn $64 million. The company's operations consisted of (1) Harris Rebar which was involved in the fabrication and placing of concrete reinforcing steel and the design and installation of concrete post-tensioning systems; (2) Laurel Steel which manufactured and distributed wire and wire products, welded wire mesh, and cold finished bar; and (3) Fisher & Ludlow which manufactured and distributed heavy industrial steel grating, aluminum grating, and expanded metal. In Canada, Harris Steel had 24 reinforcing steel fabricating plants, two steel grating distribution centers, and one cold finished bar and wire processing plant; in the U.S., it had 10 reinforcing steel fabricating plants, two steel grating manufacturing plants, and three steel grating manufacturing plants. Harris had customers throughout Canada and the United States and employed about 3,000 people. For the past three years, Harris had purchased a big percentage of its steel requirements from Nucor. Nucor management opted to operate Harris Steel as an independent subsidiary.

- Over several months in 2007 following the Harris Steel acquisition, Nucor through its new Harris Steel subsidiary acquired rebar fabricator South Pacific Steel Corporation, Consolidated Rebar, Inc., a 90 percent equity interest in rebar fabricator Barker Steel Company, and several smaller transactions—all aimed at growing its presence in the rebar fabrication marketplace.

- In August 2007, Nucor acquired LMP Steel & Wire Company for a cash purchase price of approximately $27.2 million, adding 100,000 tons of cold drawn steel capacity.

- In October 2007, Nucor completed the acquisition of Nelson Steel, Inc. for a cash purchase price of approximately $53.2 million, adding 120,000 tons of steel mesh capacity.

- In the third quarter of 2007, Nucor completed the acquisition of Magnatrax Corporation, a leading provider of custom-engineered metal buildings, for a cash purchase price of approximately $275.2 million. The Magnatrax acquisition enabled Nucor's Building System Group to become the second-largest metal building producer in the United States.

- In August 2008, Nucor's Harris Steel subsidiary acquired Ambassador Steel Corporation for a cash purchase price of about $185.1 million. Ambassador Steel was a one of the largest independent fabricators and distributors of concrete reinforcing steel—in 2007, Ambassador shipped 422,000 tons of fabricated rebar and distributed another 228,000 tons of reinforcing steel. Its business complemented that of Harris Steel and represented another in a series of moves to greatly strengthen Nucor's competitive position in the rebar fabrication marketplace.

- Another small rebar fabrication company, Free State Steel, was acquired in late 2009, adding to Nucor's footprint in rebar fabrication.

By 2005–2006, steel industry conditions worldwide had improved markedly. Prices in the U.S. were about

50 percent higher than in 2000 and Nucor's sales and earnings were robust in 2005–2008 (see Exhibit 1). But Nucor's performance slumped badly when the sudden financial crisis and economic downturn that hit in the fourth quarter of 2008 spilled over into 2009 and caused the demand for steel to plummet—Nucor's utilization of its steel mill capacity fell to 54 percent in 2009 from 91 percent in the first three quarters of 2008. Operating rates at Nucor's steel mills recovered modestly to 70 percent in 2010 and 74 percent in 2011. Market conditions in the steel industry remained challenging in 2012 in light of the slow economic recovery, making the 2009–2012 period one of the longest and deepest economic slumps in several decades.

## The Commercialization of New Technologies and New Plant Construction

The second element of Nucor's growth strategy was to continue to be a technology leader and to be opportunistic in constructing new plant capacity that would enable the company to expand its presence in attractive new or existing market segments. From its earliest days, Nucor had been an early and aggressive investor in two types of steel-making breakthroughs:

- *Disruptive technological innovations*—production processes and equipment that would give Nucor a commanding market advantage and thus be disruptive to the efforts of competitors in matching Nucor's cost competitiveness and/or product quality.

- *Leapfrog technological innovations*—production processes and equipment that would enable Nucor to overtake competitors in terms of product quality, cost per ton, or market share.

One of Nucor's biggest and most recent successes in pioneering new technology had been at its Crawfordsville facilities where Nucor had the world's first installation of direct strip casting of carbon sheet steel—a process called Castrip®. After several years of testing and process refinement at Crawfordsville, Nucor announced in 2005 that the Castrip process was ready for commercialization; Nucor had exclusive rights to Castrip technology in the U.S. and Brazil. The process, which had proven to be quite difficult to bring to commercial reality, was a major technological breakthrough for producing flat-rolled, carbon, and stainless steels in very thin gauges; it involved far fewer process steps to cast metal at or very near customer-desired thicknesses and shapes. The Castrip process drastically reduced capital outlays for equipment and produced savings on operating expenses as well—major expense savings included being able to use lower-quality scrap metal and 90 percent less energy to process liquid metal into hot-rolled steel sheets. A big environmental benefit of the Castrip process was cutting greenhouse gas emissions by up to 80 percent. Nucor's Castrip facility at Crawfordsville had the capacity to produce 500,000 tons annually. In 2006, Nucor built a second Castrip facility on the site of its structural steel mill in Arkansas.

Nucor's growth strategy also included investing in the construction of new plant capacity whenever management spotted opportunities to strengthen its market presence:

- In 2006, Nucor announced that it would construct a new $27 million facility to produce metal buildings systems in Brigham City, Utah. The new plant, Nucor's fourth building systems plant, had capacity of 45,000 tons and gave Nucor national market reach in building systems products.

- In 2006, Nucor initiated construction of a $230 million state-of-the-art steel mill in Memphis, Tennessee, with annual capacity to produce 850,000 tons of special quality steel bars. Management believed this mill, together with the company's other special bar quality mills in Nebraska and South Carolina, would give Nucor the broadest, highest-quality, and lowest-cost SBQ product offering in North America.

- In 2009, Nucor opened an idle and newly renovated $50 million wire rod and bar mill in Kingman, Arizona, that had been acquired in 2003. Production of straight-length rebar, coiled rebar, and wire rod began in mid-2010; the plant had initial capacity of 100,000 tons, with the ability to increase annual production to 500,000 tons.

- A new $150 million galvanizing facility located at the company's sheet steel mill in Decatur, Alabama, began operations in mid-2009. This facility gave Nucor the ability to make 500,000 tons of 72-inch wide galvanized sheet steel, a product used by motor vehicle and appliance producers and in various steel frame and steel stud buildings. The galvanizing process entailed dipping steel in melted zinc at extremely high temperatures; the zinc coating protected the steel surface from corrosion.

- Construction and installation of new vacuum degassers at Nucor's Hickman, Arkansas, sheet mill and Hertford County, North Carolina, plate mill were expected to begin operating in 2012, enabling these mills to produce increased volumes of higher-grade sheet steel.

- Construction of a heat treating facility at the company's recently opened steel plate mill in Hertford County, North Carolina, began in 2011. The heat treat line had estimated annual capacity of 125,000 tons and the ability to produce heat-treated plate from 3/16 of an inch through 2 inches thick.

- In January 2012, Nucor announced that it would invest $290 million for projects to be completed at the company's special bar quality mills in Memphis, Tennessee, Norfolk, Nebraska, and Darlington, South Carolina steel mills that would expand its production capacities by a combined one million tons. The planned capital expenditures included putting in place state-of-the-art quality inspection capabilities that would enable these plants to produce bar and wire rod for the most demanding engineered bar applications. Nucor expected to complete these projects by year-end 2013.

### The Drive for Plant Efficiency and Low-Cost Production

A key part of Nucor's strategy was to make ongoing capital investments to improve efficiency and production costs at each and every facility it operated. From its earliest days in the steel business, Nucor had built state-of-the-art facilities in the most economical fashion possible and then made it standard company practice to invest in plant modernization and efficiency improvements as technology advanced and new cost-saving opportunities emerged. Nucor management made a point of staying on top of the latest advances in steel making around the world, diligently searching for emerging cost-effective technologies it could adopt or adapt in its facilities. Executives at Nucor had a longstanding commitment to provide the company's workforce with the best technology available to get the job done safely and in an environmentally responsible manner. When Nucor acquired plants, it immediately began getting them up to Nucor standards—a process it called "Nucorizing." This included increasing operational efficiency by reducing the amount of time, space, energy, and manpower it took to produce steel or steel products and paying close attention to worker safety and environmental protection practices.

Nucor management also stressed continual improvement in product quality and cost at each one of its production facilities. Most all of Nucor's production locations were ISO 9000 and ISO 14000 certified. The company had a "BESTmarking" program aimed at being the industry-wide best performer on a variety of production and efficiency measures. Managers at all Nucor plants were accountable for demonstrating that their operations were competitive on both product quality and cost vis-à-vis the plants of rival companies. One trait of Nucor's corporate culture was the expectation that plant-level managers would be persistent in implementing methods to improve product quality and keep costs per ton low relative to rival plants.

Examples of Nucor's latest efforts to upgrade and fully modernize the operations of its production facilities included a three-year bar mill modernization program and adding vacuum degassers to its four sheet steel mills. The addition of the vacuum degassers not only improved Nucor's ability to produce some of the highest-quality sheet steel available but also resulted in expanded capacity at low incremental cost. Nucor's capital expenditures for new technology, plant improvements, and equipment upgrades in 2004–2011 are shown in Exhibit 5; capital expenditures in 2012–2013 were expected to be close to $1 billion.

Nucor management viewed the task of optimizing its manufacturing operations as a continuous process. According to CEO Dan DiMicco:[4]

> We talk about "climbing a mountain without a peak" to describe our constant improvements. We can take pride in what we have accomplished, but we are never satisfied.

### Global Growth via Joint Ventures

In 2007, Nucor management decided it was time to begin building an international growth platform. The company's strategy to grow its international revenues had two elements:

### EXHIBIT 5    Nucor's Capital Expenditures for New Technology, Plant Improvements, and Equipment Upgrades, 2000–2011

| Year | Capital Expenditures (in millions) | Year | Capital Expenditures (in millions) |
|------|------|------|------|
| 2000 | $415.0 | 2006 | $ 338.4 |
| 2001 | 261.0 | 2007 | 520.4 |
| 2002 | 244.0 | 2008 | 1,019.0 |
| 2003 | 215.4 | 2009 | 390.5 |
| 2004 | 285.9 | 2010 | 345.3 |
| 2005 | 331.5 | 2011 | 440.5 |

- Establishing foreign sales offices and exporting U.S.-made steel products to foreign markets. Because about 60 percent of Nucor's steel-making capacity was located on rivers with deep water transportation access, management believed that the company could be competitive in shipping U.S.-made steel products to customers in a substantial number of foreign markets.
- Entering into joint ventures with foreign partners to invest in steel-making projects outside North America. Nucor executives believed that the success of this strategy element was finding the right partners to grow with internationally.

Nucor opened a Trading Office in Switzerland and proceeded to establish international sales offices in Mexico, Brazil, Colombia, the Middle East, and Asia. The company's Trading Office bought and sold steel and steel products that Nucor and other steel producers had manufactured. In 2010, approximately 11 percent of the shipments from Nucor's steel mills were exported. Customers in South and Central America presented the most consistent opportunities for export sales, but there was growing interest from customers in Europe and other locations.

In January 2008, Nucor entered into a 50/50 joint venture with the European-based Duferco Group to establish the production of beams and other long products in Italy, with distribution in Europe and North Africa. A few months later, Nucor acquired 50 percent of the stock of Duferdofin-Nucor S.r.l. for approximately $667 million (Duferdofin was Duferco's Italy-based steel-making subsidiary). Duferdofin-Nucor operated a steel melt shop and bloom/billet caster in San Zeno, Italy, with an annual capacity of 1.1 million tons and three rolling mills in Pallanzeno in the Piedmont region and Giammoro, Sicily, with combined capacity of 1.1 million tons. Total production in the joint venture's fiscal year ended September 30, 2008 was approximately 1,080,000 tons. A new merchant bar mill with annual capacity of 495,000 tons was in the final stages of construction at the Giammoro plant and began production in 2009. Duferdofin Nucor also operated a 60,000-ton trackshoes/cutting edges mill. The customers for the products produced by Duferdofin Nucor were primarily steel service centers and distributors located both in Italy and throughout Europe. So far, the joint venture project had not lived up to the partners' financial expectations because all of the plants made construction-related products. The European construction industry had been hard hit by the economic events of 2008–2009 and the construction-related demand for steel products in Europe was very slowly creeping back toward pre-crisis levels. The two joint venture partners had agreed to consider investing in additional projects in future years.

In early 2010, Nucor invested $221.3 million to become a 50/50 joint venture partner with Mitsui USA to form NuMit LLC—Mitsui USA was the largest wholly owned subsidiary of Mitsui & Co., Ltd., a diversified global trading, investment, and service enterprise headquartered in Tokyo, Japan. NuMit LLC owned 100 percent of the equity interest in Steel Technologies LLC, an operator of 25 sheet steel processing facilities throughout the United States, Canada, and Mexico. The NuMit partners agreed that Nucor's previously announced plans to construct a greenfield flat-rolled processing center in Monterrey, Mexico, would be implemented by Steel Technologies.

**Raw Materials Strategy**  Scrap metal and scrap substitutes were Nucor's single biggest cost—all of Nucor's steel mills used electric arc furnaces to make steel products from recycled scrap steel, scrap iron, pig iron, hot briquetted iron (HBI), and direct reduced iron (DRI). On average, it took approximately 1.1 tons of scrap and scrap substitutes to produce a ton of steel—the proportions averaged about 70 percent scrap steel and 30 percent scrap substitutes. Nucor was the biggest user of scrap metal in North America, and it also purchased millions of tons of pig iron, HBI, DRI, and other iron products annually—top-quality scrap substitutes were especially critical in making premium grades of sheet steel, steel plate, and special bar quality steel at various Nucor mills. Scrap prices were driven by market demand–supply conditions and could fluctuate significantly (see Exhibit 6). Rising scrap prices adversely impacted the company's costs and ability to compete against steel-makers that made steel from scratch using iron ore, coke, and traditional blast furnace technology.

Nucor's raw materials strategy was aimed at achieving greater control over the costs of all types of metallic inputs (both scrap metal and iron-related substitutes) used at its steel plants. A key element of this strategy was to backward-integrate into the production of 6,000,000 to 7,000,000 tons per year of high-quality scrap substitutes (chiefly pig iron and direct reduced iron) at either its own wholly owned and operated plants or at plants jointly owned by Nucor and other partners—integrating backward into supplying a big fraction of its own iron requirements held

**EXHIBIT 6**  Nucor's Costs for Scrap Steel and Scrap Substitute, 2000–2011

| Period | Average Cost of Scrap and Scrap Substitute per Ton Used | Period | Average Cost of Scrap and Scrap Substitute per Ton Used |
|---|---|---|---|
| **2000** | $120 | **2010** Quarter 1 | $318 |
| **2001** | 101 | Quarter 2 | 373 |
| **2002** | 110 | Quarter 3 | 354 |
| **2003** | 137 | Quarter 4 | 359 |
| **2004** | 238 | **Full-Year Average** | 351 |
| **2005** | 244 | | |
| **2006** | 246 | **2011** Quarter 1 | 424 |
| **2007** | 278 | Quarter 2 | 444 |
| **2008** | 438 | Quarter 3 | 449 |
| **2009** | 303 | Quarter 4 | 441 |
| | | **Full-Year Average** | 439 |

*Source:* Nucor's annual reports for 2011, 2009, 2007, and information posted in the investor relations section at www.nucor.com, accessed October 25, 2006 and April 12, 2012.

the promise of raw material savings and less reliance on outside iron suppliers. The costs of producing pig iron and direct reduced iron (DRI) were not as subject to steep swings as was the price of scrap steel.

Nucor's first move to execute its long-term raw materials strategy came in 2002 when it partnered with The Rio Tinto Group, Mitsubishi Corporation, and Chinese steel maker Shougang Corporation to pioneer Rio Tinto's HIsmelt® technology at a new plant to be constructed in Kwinana, Western Australia. The HIsmelt technology entailed converting iron ore to liquid metal or pig iron and was both a replacement for traditional blast furnace technology and a hot metal source for electric arc furnaces. Rio Tinto had been developing the HIsmelt technology for 10 years and believed the technology had the potential to revolutionize iron-making and provide low-cost, high-quality iron for making steel. Nucor had a 25 percent ownership in the venture and had a joint global marketing agreement with Rio Tinto to license the technology to other interested steel companies. The Australian plant represented the world's first commercial application of the HIsmelt technology; it had a capacity of over 880,000 tons and was expandable to 1.65 million tons at an attractive capital cost per incremental ton. Production started in January 2006. However, the joint venture partners opted to permanently close the HIsmelt plant in December 2010 because the project, while technologically acclaimed, proved to be financially unviable. Nucor's loss in the joint venture partnership amounted to $94.8 million.

In April 2003, Nucor entered a joint venture with Companhia Vale do Rio Doce (CVRD) to construct and operate an environmentally friendly $80 million pig iron project in northern Brazil. The project, named Ferro Gusa Carajás, utilized two conventional mini-blast furnaces to produce about 418,000 tons of pig iron per year, using iron ore from CVRD's Carajás mine in northern Brazil. The charcoal fuel for the plant came exclusively from fast-growing eucalyptus trees in a cultivated forest in northern Brazil owned by a CVRD subsidiary. The cultivated forest removed more carbon dioxide from the atmosphere than the blast furnace emitted, thus counteracting global warming—an outcome that appealed to Nucor management. Nucor invested $10 million in the project and was a 22 percent owner. Production of pig iron began in the fourth quarter of 2005; the joint venture agreement called for Nucor to purchase all of the plant's production.

Nucor's third raw-material sourcing initiative came in 2004 when it acquired an idled direct reduced iron (DRI) plant in Louisiana, relocated all of the plant assets to Trinidad (an island off the coast of South America near Venezuela), and expanded the project to a capacity of nearly 2 million tons. The plant used a proven technology that converted iron ore pellets into direct reduced iron. The Trinidad site was chosen because it had a long-term and very cost-attractive supply of natural gas (large volumes of natural gas were consumed in the plant's production process), along with favorable logistics for receiving iron ore and shipping direct reduced iron to Nucor's steel mills in the United States. Nucor entered into contracts with natural gas suppliers to purchase natural gas in amounts needed to operate the Trinidad through 2028. Production began in January 2007. Nucor personnel at the Trinidad plant had recently achieved world-class product quality levels in making DRI; this achievement allowed Nucor to use an even larger percentage of DRI in producing the most demanding steel products. In 2011, construction was underway to increase the Trinidad DRI plant's annual capacity to approximately 2,200,000 tons

In September 2010, Nucor announced plans to build a $750 million DRI facility with an annual capacity of 2.5 million tons on a 4,000-acre site in St. James Parish, Louisiana. This investment moved Nucor two-thirds of the way toward its long-term objective of being able to supply 6 to 7 million tons of its requirements for high-quality scrap substitutes. However, the new DRI facility was the first phase of a multiphase plan that included a second 2.5-million-ton DRI facility, a coke plant, a blast furnace, an iron ore pellet plant, and a steel mill. Permits for both DRI plants were received from the Louisiana Department of Environmental Quality in January 2011. Construction of the first DRI unit at the St. James site began in 2011, and production startup was scheduled for mid-2013. Because producing DRI was a natural gas–intensive process, Nucor had entered into a long-term, onshore natural gas working interest drilling program with one of North America's largest producers of natural gas to help offset the company's exposure to future increases in the price of natural gas consumed by the DRI facility in St. James Parish. All natural gas from Nucor's working interest drilling program was being sold to outside parties.

In February 2008, Nucor acquired The David J. Joseph Company (DJJ) and related affiliates for a cash purchase price of approximately $1.44 billion, the largest acquisition in Nucor's history. DJJ was one of the leading scrap metal companies in the United States, with 2007 revenues of $6.4 billion. It processed about 3.5 million tons of scrap iron and scrap steel annually at some 35 scrap yards and brokered over 20 million tons of iron and steel scrap and over 500 million pounds of non-ferrous materials in 2007. The DJJ Mill and Industrial Services business provided logistics and metallurgical blending operations and offered onsite handling and trading of industrial scrap. The DJJ Rail Services business owned over 2,000 railcars dedicated to the movement of scrap metals and offered complete railcar fleet management and leasing services. All of these businesses had strategic value to Nucor in helping gain control over its scrap metal costs. Nucor was familiar with DJJ and its various operations because it had obtained scrap from DJJ since 1969. Within months of completing the DJJ acquisition (which was operated as a separate subsidiary), the DJJ management team acquired four other scrap processing companies. A fifth scrap processor was acquired in 2010. Since becoming a Nucor subsidiary, DJJ had added approximately 1.1 million tons of scrap processing capacity and 27 locations through five acquisitions and the opening of three new scrapyards. This gave Nucor total annual scrap processing capacity of almost 5 million tons and, because of DJJ's railcar fleet, the ability to improve the cost and speed with which scrap could be delivered to its steel mills. DJJ obtained scrap from industrial plants, the manufacturers of products that contained steel, independent scrap dealers, peddlers, auto junkyards, demolition firms, and other sources. In 2011, approximately 12 percent of the ferrous and non-ferrous metals and scrap substitute tons processed and sold by DJJ were sold to external customers, and the remainder was delivered to various Nucor steel mills.

## Nucor's Newest Strategic Initiative: Shifting Production from Lower-End Steel Products to Value-Added Products

In 2010–2012, Nucor shifted a growing percentage of the production tonnage at its steel mills and steel products facilities to "value-added products" that could command higher prices and yield better profit margins than could be had by producing lower-end or commodity steel products. Examples included:

- The new galvanizing capability at the Decatur, Alabama, mill that enabled Nucor to sell 500,000 tons of corrosion-resistant, galvanized sheet steel for high-end applications.

- The ability to supply customers with an additional 200,000 tons per year of cut-to-length and tempered steel plate due to expanding the cut-to-length capabilities at the Tuscaloosa, Alabama, mill.

- Shipping 250,000 tons of new steel plate and structural steel products in 2010 that were not offered in 2009, and further increasing shipments of these same new products to 500,000 tons in 2011.

- Being able to supply customers with 125,000 tons of new products annually because of the new heat-treat facility at the Hertford plate mill in North Carolina.

- Being able to upgrade the caliber of sheet steel and steel plate produced at the Hickman and Hertford mills because of the investments made in vacuum degassers.

Similar product offering upgrades were underway at Nucor's special bar quality, cold-finished, and fastener facilities.

In 2010–2011, approximately 55 percent of Nucor's steel mill shipments were to customers who bought multiple types of products from the company.

## Nucor's Commitment to Being a Global Leader in Environmental Performance

Every Nucor facility was evaluated for actions that could be taken to promote greater environmental sustainability. Measurable objectives and targets relating to such outcomes as the reduced use of oil and grease, more efficient use of electricity, and site-wide recycling were in place at each plant. Computerized controls on large electric motors and pumps and energy-recovery equipment to capture and reuse energy that otherwise would be wasted had been installed throughout Nucor's facilities to lower energy usage—Nucor considered itself to be among the most energy-efficient steel companies in the world. All of Nucor's facilities had water-recycling systems. Nucor even recycled the dust from its electric arc furnaces because scrap metal contained enough zinc, lead, chrome, and other valuable metals to recycle into usable products; the dust was captured in each plant's state-of-the-art bag house air pollution control devices and then sent to a recycler that converted the dust into zinc oxide, steel slag, and pig iron. All of Nucor's steelmaking operations had ISO 14001 certified Environmental Management Systems in place in 2011.

Nucor's sheet mill in Decatur, Alabama, used a measuring device called an opacity monitor, which gave precise, minute-by-minute readings of the air quality that passed through the bag house and out of the mill's exhaust system. While rival steel producers had resisted using opacity monitors (because they documented any time a mill's exhaust was out of compliance with its environmental permits, even momentarily), Nucor's personnel at the Decatur mill viewed the opacity monitor as a tool for improving environmental performance. They developed the expertise to read the monitor so well that they could pinpoint in just a few minutes the first signs of a problem in any of the nearly 7,000 bags in the bag house—before those problems resulted in increased emissions. Their early-warning system worked so well that the division had applied for a patent on the process, with an eye toward licensing it to other companies.

## Organization and Management Philosophy

Nucor had a simple streamlined organizational structure to allow employees to innovate and make quick decisions. The company was highly decentralized, with most day-to-day operating decisions made by group or plant-level general managers and their staff. Each group or plant operated independently as a profit center and was headed by a general manager, who in most cases also had the title of vice president. The group manager or plant general manager had control of the day-to-day decisions that affected the group or plant's profitability.

The organizational structure at a typical plant had three management layers:

- General Manager
- Department Manager
- Supervisor/Professional
- Hourly Employee

Group managers and plant managers reported to one of five executive vice presidents at corporate headquarters. Nucor's corporate staff was exceptionally small, consisting of only 100 people in 2011, the philosophy being that corporate headquarters should consist of a small cadre of executives who would guide a decentralized operation where liberal authority was delegated to managers in the field. Each plant had a sales manager who was responsible for selling the products made at that particular plant; such staff functions as engineering, accounting, and personnel management were performed at the group/plant level. There was a minimum of paperwork and bureaucratic systems. Each group/plant was expected to earn about a 25 percent return on total assets before corporate expenses, taxes, interest, or profit-sharing. As long as plant managers met their profit targets, they were allowed to operate with minimal restrictions and interference from corporate headquarters. There was a very friendly spirit of competition from one plant to the next to see which facility could be the best performer, but since all of the vice-presidents and general managers shared the same bonus systems, they functioned pretty much as a team despite operating their facilities individually. Top executives did not hesitate to replace group or plant managers who consistently struggled to achieve profitability and operating targets.

## Workforce Compensation Practices

Nucor was a largely nonunion "pay for performance" company with an incentive compensation system that rewarded goal-oriented individuals and did not put a maximum on what they could earn. All employees, except those in the recently acquired Harris Steel and DJJ subsidiaries that operated independently from the rest of Nucor, worked under one of four basic compensation plans, each featuring incentives related to meeting specific goals and targets:

1. *Production Incentive Plan*—Production line jobs were rated on degree of responsibility required and assigned a base wage comparable to the wages paid by other manufacturing plants in the area where a Nucor plant was located. But in addition to their base wage, operating and maintenance employees were paid weekly bonuses based on the number of tons by which the output of their production team or work group exceeded the "standard" number of tons. All operating and maintenance employees were members of a production team that included the team's production supervisor, and the tonnage produced by each work team was measured for each work shift and then totaled for all shifts during a given week. If a production team's weekly output beat the weekly standard, team members (including the team's production supervisor) earned a specified percentage bonus for each ton produced above the standard—production bonuses were paid weekly (rather than quarterly or annually) so that workers and supervisors would be rewarded immediately for their efforts. The standard rate was calculated based on the capabilities of the equipment employed (typically at the time plant operations began), and no bonus was paid if the equipment was not operating (which gave maintenance workers a big incentive to keep a plant's equipment in good working condition)—Nucor's philosophy was that when equipment was not operating everybody suffered and the bonus for downtime ought to be zero. Production standards at Nucor plants were seldom raised unless a plant underwent significant modernization or important new pieces of equipment were installed that greatly boosted labor

productivity. It was common for production incentive bonuses to run from 50 to 150 percent of an employee's base pay, thereby pushing compensation levels up well above those at other nearby manufacturing plants. Worker efforts to exceed the standard and get a bonus did not so much involve working harder as it involved good teamwork and close collaboration in resolving problems and figuring out how best to exceed the production standards.

2. *Department Manager Incentive Plan*—Department managers earned annual incentive bonuses based primarily on the percentage of net income to dollars of assets employed for their division. These bonuses could be as much as 80 percent of a department manager's base pay.

3. *Professional and Clerical Bonus Plan*—A bonus based on a division's net income return on assets was paid to employees that were not on the production worker or department manager plan.

4. *Senior Officers Incentive Plan*—Nucor's senior officers did not have employment contracts and did not participate in any pension or retirement plans. Their base salaries were set at approximately 90 percent of the median base salary for comparable positions in other manufacturing companies with comparable assets, sales, and capital. The remainder of their compensation was based on Nucor's annual overall percentage of net income to stockholder's equity (ROE) and was paid out in cash and stock. Once Nucor's ROE reached a threshold of not less than 3 percent or more than 7 percent (as determined annually by the compensation committee of the board of directors), senior officers earned a bonus equal to 20 percent of their base salary. If Nucor's annual ROE was 20 percent or higher, senior officers earned a bonus equal to 225 percent of their base salary. Officers could earn an additional bonus up to 75 percent of their base salary based on a comparison of Nucor's net sales growth with the net sales growth of members of a steel industry peer group. There was also a long-term incentive plan that provided for stock awards and stock options. The structure of these officer incentives was such that bonus compensation for Nucor officers fluctuated widely—from close to zero (in years like 2003 when industry conditions were bad and Nucor's performance was sub-par) to 400 percent (or more) of their base salary (when Nucor's performance was excellent, as had been the case in 2004–2008).

Nucor management had designed the company's incentive plans for employees so that bonus calculations involved no discretion on the part of a plant/division manager or top executives. This was done to eliminate any concerns on the part of workers that managers or executives might show favoritism or otherwise be unfair in calculating or awarding incentive awards.

There were two other types of extra compensation:

- *Profit Sharing*—Each year, Nucor allocated 10 percent of its operating profits to profit-sharing bonuses for all employees (except senior officers). Depending on company performance, the bonuses could run anywhere from 1 percent to over 20 percent of pay. Twenty percent of the bonus amount was paid to employees in the following March as a cash bonus and the remaining 80 percent was put into a trust for each employee, with each employee's share being proportional to their earnings as a percent of total earnings by all workers covered by the plan. An employee's share of profit-sharing became vested after one full year of employment. Employees received a quarterly statement of their balance in profit sharing.
- *401(k) Plan*—Both officers and employees participated in a 401(k) plan where the company matched from 5 percent to 25 percent of each employee's first 7 percent of contributions; the amount of the match was based on how well the company was doing.

In 2012, an entry-level worker at a Nucor plant could expect to earn about $47,000 to $50,000 annually (including bonuses). Total compensation for Nucor's plant employees in 2011 was in the range of $70,000 to $100,000 annually. It was common for worker compensation at Nucor plants to be double or more the average earned by workers at other manufacturing companies in the states where Nucor's plants were located. At Nucor's new $450 million plant in Hertford County, North Carolina, where jobs were scarce and poverty was common, Nucor employees earned three times the local average manufacturing wage. Nucor management philosophy was that workers ought to be excellently compensated because the production jobs were strenuous and the work environment in a steel mill was relatively dangerous.

Employee turnover in Nucor mills was extremely low; absenteeism and tardiness were minimal. Each employee was allowed four days of absences and could also miss work for jury duty, military leave, or the death of close relatives. After this, a day's absence cost a worker their entire performance bonus pay for that week, and being more than a half-hour late to work on a given day resulted in no bonus payment for the day. When job vacancies did occur, Nucor was flooded with applications from people wanting to get a job at Nucor; plant personnel screened job candidates very carefully, seeking people with initiative and a strong work ethic.

# Employee Relations and Human Resources

Employee relations at Nucor were based on four clear-cut principles:

1. Management is obligated to manage Nucor in such a way that employees will have the opportunity to earn according to their productivity.
2. Employees should feel confident that if they do their jobs properly, they will have a job tomorrow.
3. Employees have the right to be treated fairly and must believe that they will be.
4. Employees must have an avenue of appeal when they believe they are being treated unfairly.

The hallmarks of Nucor's human resources strategy were its incentive pay plan for production exceeding the standard and the job security provided to production workers—despite being in an industry with strong down-cycles, Nucor had made it a practice not to lay off workers. Instead, when market conditions were tough and production had to be cut back, workers were assigned to plant maintenance projects, cross-training programs, and other activities calculated to boost the plant's performance when market conditions improved.

Nucor took an egalitarian approach to providing fringe benefits to its employees; employees had the same insurance programs, vacation schedules, and holidays as upper level management. However, certain benefits were not available to Nucor's officers. The fringe benefit package at Nucor included:

- *Medical and Dental Plans*—The company had a flexible and comprehensive health benefit program for officers and employees that included wellness and health care spending accounts.
- *Tuition Reimbursement*—Nucor reimbursed up to $3,000 of an employee's approved educational expenses each year and up to $1,500 of a spouse's educational expenses for two years.

- *Service Awards*—After each five years of service with the company, Nucor employees received a service award consisting of five shares of Nucor stock.
- *Scholarships and Educational Disbursements*— Nucor provided the children of every employee (except senior officers) with college funding of $3,000 per year for four years to be used at accredited academic institutions. As of 2011, Nucor had paid out over $61 million.
- *Other benefits*—Long-term disability, life insurance, vacation.

Most of the changes Nucor made in work procedures and in equipment came from employees. The prevailing view at Nucor was that the employees knew the problems of their jobs better than anyone else and were thus in the best position to identify ways to improve how things were done. Most plant-level managers spent considerable time in the plant, talking and meeting with frontline employees and listening carefully to suggestions. Promising ideas and suggestions were typically acted upon quickly and implemented—management was willing to take risks to try worker suggestions for doing things better and to accept the occasional failure when the results were disappointing. Teamwork, a vibrant team spirit, and a close worker–management partnership were much in evidence at Nucor plants.

Nucor plants did not utilize job descriptions. Management believed job descriptions caused more problems than they solved, given the teamwork atmosphere and the close collaboration among work group members. The company saw formal performance appraisal systems as a waste of time and added paperwork. If a Nucor employee was not performing well, the problem was dealt with directly by supervisory personnel and the peer pressure of work group members (whose bonuses were adversely affected).

Employees were kept informed about company and division performance. Charts showing the division's results in return-on-assets and bonus payoff were posted in prominent places in the plant. Most all employees were quite aware of the level of profits in their plant or division. Nucor had a formal grievance procedure, but grievances were few and far between. The corporate office sent all news releases to each division where they were posted on bulletin boards. Each employee received a copy of Nucor's annual report; it was company practice for the cover of the annual report to consist of the names of all Nucor employees.

All of these practices had created an egalitarian culture and a highly motivated workforce that grew out of former CEO Ken Iverson's radical insight: that employees, even hourly clock punchers, would put forth extraordinary effort and be exceptionally productive if they were richly rewarded, treated with respect, and given real power to do their jobs as best they saw fit.[5] There were countless stories of occasions when managers and workers had gone beyond the call of duty to expedite equipment repairs (in many instances even using their weekends to go help personnel at other Nucor plants solve a crisis); the company's workforce was known for displaying unusual passion and company loyalty even when no personal financial stake was involved. As one Nucor worker put it, "At Nucor, we're not 'you guys' and 'us guys.' It's all of us guys. Wherever the bottleneck is, we go there, and everyone works on it."[6]

It was standard procedure for a team of Nucor veterans, including people who worked on the plant floor, to visit with their counterparts as part of the process of screening candidates for acquisition.[7] One of the purposes of such visits was to explain the Nucor compensation system and culture face-to-face, gauge reactions, and judge whether the plant would fit into "the Nucor way of doing things" if it was acquired. Shortly after making an acquisition, Nucor management moved swiftly to institute its pay-for-performance incentive system and to begin instilling the egalitarian Nucor culture and idea-sharing. Top priority was given to looking for ways to boost plant production using fewer people and without making substantial capital investments; the take-home pay of workers at newly acquired plants typically went up rather dramatically. At the Auburn Steel plant, acquired in 2001, it took Nucor about six months to convince workers that they would be better off under Nucor's pay system; during that time Nucor paid people under the old Auburn Steel system but posted what they would have earned under Nucor's system. Pretty soon, workers were convinced to make the changeover—one worker saw his pay climb from $53,000 in the year prior to the acquisition to $67,000 in 2001 and to $92,000 in 2005.[8]

**New Employees** Each plant/division had a "consul" responsible for providing new employees with general advice about becoming a Nucor teammate and serving as a resource for inquiries about how things were done at Nucor, how to navigate the division and company, and how to resolve issues that might come up.

**EXHIBIT 7**  Worldwide Production of Crude Steel, with Compound Average Growth Rates, 1975–2011

| Year | World Crude Steel Production (millions of tons) | Compound Average Growth Rates in World Crude Steel Production | |
|---|---|---|---|
| | | Period | Percentage Rate |
| 1975 | 707 | 1975–1980 | 2.2% |
| 1980 | 788 | 1980–1985 | 0.1 |
| 1985 | 791 | 1985–1990 | 1.4 |
| 1990 | 847 | 1990–1995 | −0.5 |
| 1995 | 827 | 1995–2000 | 2.4 |
| 2000 | 933 | 2000–2005 | 6.2 |
| 2001 | 936 | 2005–2010 | 4.4 |
| 2002 | 995 | 2010–2011 | 4.4 |
| 2003 | 1,067 | | |
| 2004 | 1,178 | | |
| 2005 | 1,258 | | |
| 2006 | 1,372 | | |
| 2007 | 1,481 | | |
| 2008 | 1,462 | | |
| 2009 | 1,356 | | |
| 2010 | 1,559 | | |
| 2011 | 1,680 | | |

*Source:* World Steel Association, *Steel Statistical Yearbook, various years,* accessed at www.worldsteel.org on April 23, 2012.

Nucor provided new employees with a personalized plan that set forth who would give them feedback about how well they were doing and when and how this feedback would be given; from time to time, new employees met with the plant manager for feedback and coaching. In addition, there was a new employee orientation session that provided a hands-on look at the plant/division operations; new employees also participated in product group meetings to provide exposure to broader business and technical issues. Each year, Nucor brought all recent college hires to the Charlotte headquarters for a forum intended to give the new hires a chance to network and provide senior management with guidance on how best to leverage their talent.

# THE WORLD STEEL INDUSTRY

Both 2010 and 2011 were record years for global production of crude steel, with worldwide production reaching 1,559 million tons in 2010 and 1,680 million tons in 2011 (see Exhibit 7). Steel-making capacity worldwide was approximately 2,090 million tons in 2011, resulting in a 2011 capacity utilization rate of 80 percent versus just over 75 percent in 2010. Worldwide demand for steel mill products had grown about 5.5 percent annually since 2000 (well above the 1.1 percent growth rate from 1975 to 2000), but there had been periods of both strong and weak demand during the 2000–2011 time frame (see Exhibit 7). The six biggest steel-producing countries in 2011 were:

| Country | Total Production of Crude Steel | Percent of Worldwide Production |
|---|---|---|
| China | 752 million tons | 45.9% |
| Japan | 118 million tons | 7.2% |
| United States | 95 million tons | 5.8% |
| India | 79 million tons | 4.8% |
| Russia | 76 million tons | 4.6% |
| South Korea | 75 million tons | 4.6% |

**EXHIBIT 8**   Top 15 Steel Companies Worldwide, Based on Crude Steel Production, 2010

| 2010 Rank | Company (Headquarters) | Crude Steel Production (in millions of tons) | |
|---|---|---|---|
| | | 2005 | 2010 |
| 1. | ArcelorMittal (Luxembourg) | 120.9 | 98.2 |
| 2. | Baosteel (China) | 25.0 | 37.0 |
| 3. | POSCO (South Korea) | 33.6 | 35.4 |
| 4. | Nippon Steel (Japan) | 35.3 | 35.0 |
| 5. | JFE (Japan) | 32.9 | 31.1 |
| 6. | Jiangsu Shagang (China) | n.a. | 23.2 |
| 7. | Tata Steel (India) | n.a. | 23.2 |
| 8. | United States Steel (USA) | 21.3 | 22.3 |
| 9. | Ansteel (China) | 13.1 | 22.1 |
| 10. | Gerdau (Brazil) | 15.1 | 18.7 |
| 11. | Nucor (USA) | 20.3 | 18.3 |
| 12. | Severstal (Russia) | 15.0 | 18.2 |
| 13. | Wuhan (China) | 14.3 | 16.6 |
| 14. | ThyssenKrupp (Germany) | 18.2 | 16.4 |
| 15. | Evraz (Russia) | 15.3 | 16.3 |
| 14. | Gerdau (Brazil) | 15.1 | 16.1 |
| 15. | Severstal (Russia) | 15.0 | 14.1 |

*Source:* World Steel Association, www.worldsteel.org, accessed on November 6, 2006 and April 25, 2012.

Exhibit 8 shows the world's 15 largest producers of steel in 2010.

## Steel-making Technologies

Steel was produced either by integrated steel facilities or "mini-mills" that employed electric arc furnaces. Integrated mills used blast furnaces to produce hot metal typically from iron ore pellets, limestone, scrap steel, oxygen, assorted other metals, and coke (coke was produced by firing coal in large coke ovens and was the major fuel used in blast furnaces to produce molten iron). Melted iron from the blast furnace process was then run through the basic oxygen process to produce liquid steel. To make flat rolled steel products, liquid steel was either fed into a continuous caster machine and cast into slabs or else cooled in slab form for later processing. Slabs were further shaped or rolled at a plate mill or hot strip mill. In making certain sheet steel products, the hot strip mill process was followed by various finishing processes, including pickling, cold-rolling, annealing, tempering, galvanizing, or other coating procedures. These various

processes for converting raw steel into finished steel products were often distinct steps undertaken at different times and in different onsite or offsite facilities rather than being done in a continuous process in a single plant facility—an integrated mill was thus one which had multiple facilities at a single plant site and could therefore not only produce crude (or raw) steel but also run the crude steel through various facilities and finishing processes to make hot-rolled and cold-rolled sheet steel products, steel bars and beams, stainless steel, steel wire and nails, steel pipes and tubes, and other finished steel products. The steel produced by integrated mills tended to be purer than steel produced by electric arc furnaces since less scrap was used in the production process (scrap steel often contained non-ferrous elements that could adversely affect metallurgical properties). Some steel customers required purer steel products for their applications.

Mini-mills used an electric arc furnace to melt steel scrap or scrap substitutes into molten metal which was then cast into crude steel slabs, billets, or blooms in a continuous casting process. As was the case at integrated mills, the crude steel was then run through various facilities and finishing processes to make hot-rolled and cold-rolled sheet steel products, steel bars and beams, stainless steel, steel wire and nails, steel pipes and tubes, and other finished steel products. Mini-mills could accommodate short production runs and had relatively fast product change-over times. The electric arc technology employed by mini-mills offered two primary competitive advantages: capital investment requirements that were 75 percent lower than those of integrated mills and a smaller workforce (which translated into lower labor costs per ton shipped).

Initially, companies that used electric arc furnace technology were able to only make low-end steel products (such as reinforcing rods and steel bars). But when thin-slab casting technology came on the scene in the 1980s, mini-mills were able to compete in the market for flat-rolled carbon sheet and strip products; these products sold at substantially higher prices per ton and thus were attractive market segments for mini-mill companies. Carbon sheet and strip steel products accounted for about 50 to 60 percent of total steel production and represented the last big market category controlled by the producers employing basic oxygen furnace and blast furnace technologies. Thin-slab casting technology, which had been developed by SMS Schloemann-Siemag AG of Germany, was pioneered in the U.S. by Nucor at its plants in Indiana and elsewhere. Other mini-mill companies in the U.S. and across the world were quick to adopt thin-slab casting technology because the low capital costs of thin-slab casting facilities, often coupled with lower labor costs per ton, gave mini-mill companies a cost and pricing advantage over integrated steel producers, enabling them to grab a growing share of the global market for flat-rolled sheet steel and other carbon steel products. Many integrated producers also switched to thin-slab casting as a defensive measure to protect their profit margins and market shares.

In 2011–2012, about 70 percent of the world's steel mill production was made at large integrated mills and about 29 percent was made at mills that used electric arc furnaces. In the United States, however, roughly 60 percent of the steel was produced at mills employing electric arc furnaces and 40 percent at mills using blast furnaces and basic oxygen processes. Large integrated steel mills using blast furnaces, basic oxygen furnaces, and assorted casting and rolling equipment typically had the ability to manufacture a wide variety of steel mill products but faced significantly higher energy costs and were often burdened with higher capital and fixed operating costs. Electric-arc furnace mill producers were challenged by increases in scrap prices but tended to have lower capital and fixed operating costs compared with the integrated steel producers.

The global marketplace for steel was considered to be relatively mature and highly cyclical as a result of ongoing ups and downs in the world economy or the economies of particular countries. However, in 2010–2012, the world steel market was divided into "two separate worlds." In those places like Europe, the United States, and Japan where recovery from the 2008–2009 financial crisis and economic recession was slow, the demand for steel was weak and there was abundant excess steel-making capacity. In fast-developing areas of the world—like Asia (especially China and India) and many countries in Latin America and the Middle East—the demand for steel was strong and often exceeded the capacity of local steelmakers, many of which were adding new capacity.

In general, competition within the global steel industry was intense and expected to remain so. Companies with excess production capacity were active in seeking to increase their exports of steel to foreign markets. During the 2005–2011 period, the biggest steel-exporting countries were China, Japan, South Korea, Russia, the Ukraine, and Germany; the biggest steel-importing countries during this same time were France, Germany, Italy, the United States, China, and South Korea. China, Germany, and South Korea were both big exporters and big importers because they had more capacity to make certain types and grades of steel than was needed inside their borders (and thus local steelmakers sought to export supplies to other countries) but lacked sufficient internal capacity to supply local steel users with other types and grades of steel.

**Industry Consolidation**   In both the U.S. and across the world, industry downturns had resulted in numerous mergers and acquisitions. Some of the mergers/acquisitions were the result of a financially and managerially strong company seeking to acquire a high-cost or struggling steel company at a bargain price and then pursue cost reduction initiatives to make newly acquired steel mill operations more cost competitive. Other mergers/acquisitions reflected the strategies of growth-minded steel companies looking to expand both their production capacity and geographic market presence.

# NUCOR AND COMPETITION IN THE MARKET FOR STEEL IN THE UNITED STATES

Nucor competed in the markets for a wide variety of finished steel products and unfinished steel products, plus the markets for scrap steel and scrap substitutes. Nucor executives considered all these markets to be highly competitive and populated with many domestic and foreign firms. Competition for steel mill products and finished steel products (like steel joists, steel deck, steel mesh, fasteners, cold-finished items, and fabricated rebar) was centered on price and the ability to meet customer delivery requirements.

Most recently, Nucor had experienced mounting competitive pressures in the market for sheet steel in the United States, largely because of significant increases in rivals' production capacity. Since the beginning of 2010, domestic sheet capacity had increased by approximately 5,000,000 tons as a result of the opening of a very large sheet facility in Alabama owned by ThyssenKrupp, capacity additions at several existing sheet mills, and the reopening of a previously shuttered sheet mill in Maryland.

However, Nucor considered that one of its most formidable competitive threats in the U.S. market came from foreign steelmakers who were intent on exporting some of their production to the United States. Many foreign steel producers had costs on a par with or even below those of Nucor, although their competitiveness in the U.S. market varied significantly according to the prevailing strength of their local currencies versus the U.S. dollar. But the unique challenge that Nucor faced from foreign steel-makers was that many were often able to undercut the prices of domestic steel producers because they received various types of subsidies from their own governments, either directly or indirectly through government-owned enterprises or government-owned or controlled financial institutions in their countries. Many Chinese steel-makers were government-owned in whole or in part, and, in the opinion of Nucor executives, benefited from their government's manipulation of foreign currency exchange rates as well as from the receipt of government subsidies. According to Dan DiMicco, who was a frequent spokesman for the domestic steel industry in voicing complaints against the below-market prices of foreign steel producers and calling upon government policymakers to enforce global trade agreements and address the jobs crisis in the United States:[9]

> Artificially cheap exports by some of our major foreign competitors to the United States and elsewhere reduce our net sales and adversely impact our financial results. Direct steel imports in 2010 accounted for a 21 percent share of the U.S. market despite significant unused domestic steelmaking capacity. Aggressive enforcement of trade rules by the World Trade Organization (WTO) to limit unfairly traded imports remains uncertain, although it is critical to our ability to remain competitive. We have been encouraged by recent actions the United States government has taken before the WTO to challenge some of China's trade practices as violating world trade rules, and we continue to believe that assertive enforcement of world trade rules must be one of the highest priorities of the United States government.

In Nucor's 2011 10-K report, management said:[10]

> China's unfair trade practices seriously undermine the ability of the Company and other domestic producers to compete on price when left unchallenged. That country's artificially lowered production costs have significantly contributed to the exodus of manufacturing jobs from the United States. When such a flight occurs, Nucor's customer base is diminished, thereby providing us with fewer opportunities to supply steel to those shuttered businesses. Rigorous trade law enforcement is critical to our ability to maintain our competitive position against foreign producers that engage in unlawful trade practices.

Foreign imports accounted for approximately 22 percent of the U.S. steel market in 2011. In 2011 and the first three months of 2012, foreign steel producers were selling an average of 2.2 million tons of steel products per month to customers in the United States. Nearly 100,000 tons per month of these imported steel products were coming from steel-makers in China. In the first three months of 2012, steel imports from Turkey jumped to an average of 178,000 tons per month, up sharply from an average of about 58,000 tons per month in 2011. A big fraction of the remaining import tonnage came from steel-makers in Europe, Asia, and Brazil.

Exhibit 9 shows shipments, exports, and imports of steel mill products in the United States for 2000–2011 (not included are statistics relating to the shipments, exports, and imports of such finished steel products as steel joists, steel deck, cold finished items, fabrication rebar, and steel fasteners). The average

**EXHIBIT 9**    Apparent Consumption of Steel Mill Products in the United States, 2000–2010 (in millions of tons)

| Year | U.S. Shipments of Steel Mill Products | U.S. Exports of Steel Mill Products | U.S. Imports of Steel Mill Products | Apparent U.S. Consumption of Steel Mill Products* |
|------|------|------|------|------|
| 2000 | 109.1 | 6.5 | 38.0 | 140.6 |
| 2001 | 99.1 | 6.4 | 30.8 | 123.5 |
| 2002 | 100.7 | 6.2 | 33.3 | 127.8 |
| 2003 | 103.0 | 8.5 | 23.8 | 118.3 |
| 2004 | 109.6 | 8.6 | 36.0 | 137.0 |
| 2005 | 104.4 | 10.4 | 33.2 | 127.2 |
| 2006 | 108.4 | 10.5 | 46.4 | 144.3 |
| 2007 | 107.9 | 10.8 | 30.5 | 127.6 |
| 2008 | 100.5 | 13.2 | 27.1 | 114.4 |
| 2009 | 64.0 | 10.2 | 16.9 | 70.7 |
| 2010 | 88.5 | 13.0 | 24.8 | 100.3 |

*Apparent U.S. consumption equals total shipments minus exports plus imports.

*Source:* World Steel Association, *Steel Statistical Yearbook,* 2011. Accessed at www.worldsteel.org, April 24, 2012.

capacity utilization rate of U.S. steel mills was at a historically unprecedented low of 52 percent in 2009. Since then, the average capacity utilization rate had improved to 70 percent in 2010 and 75 percent in 2011. These rates, though improved, still compared unfavorably to the capacity utilization rates of 87 percent in 2007 and 81 percent in 2008. Domestic demand for steel and steel products was expected to improve slowly in 2012, making it unlikely that 2012 capacity utilization rates would increase significantly.

## NUCOR'S TWO LARGEST DOMESTIC COMPETITORS

Consolidation of the industry into a smaller number of larger and more efficient steel producers had heightened competitive pressures for Nucor and most other steelmakers. Nucor had two major rivals in the United States—the USA division of ArcelorMittal and United States Steel. ArcelorMittal USA competed chiefly in carbon steel product categories, with much of its production going to customers in the automotive, trucking, off-highway, agricultural equipment, and railway industries. It also was a supplier to companies in the appliance, office furniture, electrical motor, packaging, and industrial machinery sectors, as well as to steel service centers. In 2011, ArcelorMittal USA

operated about 20 facilities, including large integrated steel mills, plants that used electric arc furnaces, and rolling and finishing plants. Its facilities were considered to be modern and efficient. The company's shipments of steel products in North America (the United States and Canada) totaled 21.7 million tons in 2011 and 19.5 million tons in 2010. ArcelorMittal's earnings before interest, taxes, depreciation, amortization (EBITDA) in North America were $1.7 billion in 2011 and $754 million in 2010. ArcelorMittal's worldwide operations had sales revenues of $94.0 billion and net earnings of $2.3 billion in 2011 and sales revenues of $78.0 billion and net earnings of $2.9 billion in 2010.[11]

U.S. Steel had net sales of $19.9 billion in 2011 and $17.4 billion in 2010, down from a peak of $23.8 billion in 2008; the company reported net losses of $53 million in 2011 and $482 million in 2010, far below its peak earnings of $2.1 billion in 2008. Its steel shipments from mills in North America were 17.3 million tons in 2011 and 16.8 million tons in 2010 (the company's integrated steel mills in Slovakia and Serbia shipped 4.9 million tons in 2011 and 5.5 million tons in 2010—however, all of the company's operations in Serbia were sold to the Republic of Serbia for $1 dollar on January 31, 2012, resulting in a loss of approximately $400 million). At year-end 2011, U.S. Steel had approximately 24,000 employees in North America and 19,000 employees in Europe. In North America, the company operated 23 steel-making facilities in the United States, 4 in Canada, and 2 in Mexico that produced sheet steel, steel pipe and other tubular products, steel plate, and tin mill products. Principal customers included steel service centers and companies in the transportation (including automotive), construction, container, appliance, electrical equipment, oil, gas, and petrochemical sectors, as well as manufacturers that bought steel mill products for conversion into a variety of finished steel products. U.S. Steel exported 736,000 tons of its steel mill products in 2011, 746,000 tons in 2010, and 390,000 tons in 2009. U.S. Steel had a labor cost disadvantage versus Nucor and ArcelorMittal USA, partly due to the lower productivity of its unionized workforce and partly due to its retiree pension costs.

## ENDNOTES

[1] Tom Peters and Nancy Austin, *A Passion for Excellence: The Leadership Difference* (New York: Random House, 1985) and "Other Low-Cost Champions," *Fortune,* June 24, 1985.

[2] Nucor's 2011 Annual Report, p. 4.

[3] According to information posted at www.nucor.com, accessed October 11, 2006.

[4] Nucor's 2008 Annual Report, p. 5.

[5] Nanette Byrnes, "The Art of Motivation," *BusinessWeek,* May 1, 2006, p. 57.

[6] Ibid., p. 60.

[7] Ibid.

[8] Ibid.

[9] Nucor's 2010 Annual Report, p. 22.

[10] Company 10-K report, 2011, p. 6.

[11] Company annual report, 2011.

# Tata Motors: Can It Become a Global Contender in the Automobile Industry?

McGraw Hill connect

**David L. Turnipseed**
University of South Alabama

**John E. Gamble**
University of South Alabama

Tata Motors, Ltd. was India's leading automobile company by revenue and was the number-one commercial vehicle manufacturer and the number-three passenger vehicle manufacturer in India in 2012. It was also the world's fourth-largest medium- and large-sized bus manufacturer, and the fourth-largest truck manufacturer in the world. Tata's passenger car portfolio ranged from the world's least expensive four-wheel automobile, the Nano, to luxury automobile brands Jaguar and Land Rover. The company manufactured vehicles in India, the United Kingdom, Thailand, South Africa, Morocco, South Korea, and Spain. As of 2012, Tata employed over 1,400 engineers and scientists in six research and development centers in India, Italy, the UK, and South Korea.

Although Tata Motors was a very successful competitor in India and many international markets, poor macroeconomic conditions, increasing competition, and a variety of other strategic issues had created challenges that would need to be addressed by the division's top management. The possible elimination of diesel subsidies by the Indian government might possibly affect the demand for its diesel-powered vehicles sold in India. Also, the company's managers needed to consider how to expand the market for its low-priced Nano, which had required substantial investment during its development. In addition, the company needed to capture the benefits of its recent acquisitions of Jaguar and Land Rover and expand the market for its commercial vehicles outside of India.

## THE HISTORY OF TATA MOTORS

Tata Motors was a division of the Tata Group, which was India's largest corporation, owning more than 90 companies spanning seven business sectors (chemicals, information technology and communications, consumer products, engineering, materials, services, and energy). In 2012, the corporation had operations in over 80 countries and had gross revenues of $83.5 billion in 2011. Nearly 60 percent of the Tata Group's revenues were generated from outside of India. The Tata Group was a powerful symbol of India's emergence as a world economic power and was India's largest private-sector employer with over 425,000 employees. A financial summary for the Tata Group for fiscal 2010 and fiscal 2011 is presented in Exhibit 1.

Tata Motors' history began in 1945 when Tata Engineering and Locomotive Company began manufacturing locomotives and engineering products. In 1948, Tata began production of steam road rollers, in

**EXHIBIT 1** Financial Summary for the Tata Group, Fiscal 2010–Fiscal 2011* (in billions of U.S. dollars)

| | Fiscal 2011 | Fiscal 2010 | % Change |
|---|---|---|---|
| Total revenue | $83.3 | $67.4 | 23.6% |
| Sales | 82.2 | 65.6 | 25.3 |
| Total assets | 68.9 | 52.8 | 30.5 |
| International revenues | 48.3 | 38.4 | 25.8 |
| Profit after tax | 5.8 | 1.74 | 233.3 |

*Fiscal period April–March.
Exchange rate: 1 USD = Rs45.57 for 2011 and 1 USD = Rs47.41 for 2010.

*Source:* www.tata.com.

collaboration with UK manufacturer, Marshall Sons. In 1954, the company entered into a 15-year collaborative agreement with Daimler Benz AG, Germany to manufacture medium-sized commercial vehicles. The company began producing hydraulic excavators in collaboration with Japan's Hitachi in 1985. The first independently designed light commercial vehicle, the Tata 407 "pickup" was produced in 1986, followed by the Tata 608 light truck. Tata Engineering began manufacturing passenger cars in 1991 and entered into a joint agreement with Cummins Engine Co. to manufacture high horsepower and low-emission diesel engines for cars and trucks in 1993.

In 1994, the company began a joint venture with Daimler–Benz/Mercedes-Benz to manufacture Mercedes Benz passenger cars in India. Also that year, Tata signed a joint venture agreement with Tata Holset Ltd., UK to manufacture turbochargers for the Cummins engines. India's first sports utility vehicle, the Tata Safari, was launched in 1998 and its independently designed Indica V2 became the number one car in its segment in India in 2001. Also during 2001, Tata exited its joint venture with Daimler Chrysler and entered into a product agreement with UK-based MG Rover in 2002.

Tata Engineering changed its name to Tata Motors Limited in 2003 and in that year the company produced its three millionth vehicle. The next year, Tata Motors and South Korea's Daewoo Commercial Vehicle Co. Ltd. entered into a joint venture that produced and marketed heavy-duty commercial trucks in South Korea. Tata Motors acquired 21 percent interest in Spanish bus manufacturer Hipo Carrocera SA in 2005 and began production of several new vehicles, including small trucks and SUVs.

Tata Motors produced their four millionth vehicle in 2006, and in that year began a joint venture with Brazil's Marcopolo to manufacture buses for India and foreign markets, expanded Tata Daewoo's product line to include LNG-powered tractor-trailer trucks, and established three joint ventures with Fiat. The company formed a joint venture with Thonburi Automotive Assembly Plant Co. in Thailand to manufacture, assemble, and market pickup trucks. In 2007, Tata sold all its interest in Tata-Holset to Cummins, Inc.

In 2008, Tata purchased the iconic British brands Land Rover and Jaguar and began selling passenger cars and pickup trucks in the D.R. Congo and announced its "People's Car," named the Nano. The Nano hit the market in 2009 at a base price of about $2,250, and won India's Car of the Year award. Tata

began exporting the Nano to South Africa, Kenya, and developing countries in Asia and Africa. In that year, Tata purchased the remaining 79 percent of Hipo Carrocera and purchased a 50.3 percent interest in Miljø Grenland/Innovasjon, a Norwegian firm specializing in electric vehicle technology. Also, Tata entered into an agreement with Motor Development International (MDI) from Luxembourg to develop an air-powered car. In 2010, the Tata Nano Europa was set up for sale in developed economies, especially country markets in Europe.

Tata celebrated its 50th year in international business in 2011. During that year, the company announced the opening of a commercial vehicle assembly plant in South Africa and a Land Rover assembly plant in India. Two long-distance busses, the Tata Divo Luxury Coach and the Tata Starbus Ultra, were introduced, and two new SUVs—the Tata Sumo Gold and the Range Rover Evoque went on the market. Also in 2011, upscale Tata Manza and the Prima heavy truck were launched in South Africa.

During 2011, Tata won two prestigious awards, helping bring the company to global prominence. The Jaguar c-x75 won the Louis Vuitton award in Paris, and the Range Rover Evoque won Car Design of the Year. The new Pixel, Tata's city car concept for Europe, was displayed at the 81st Geneva Motor Show and its Tata 407 light truck celebrated its silver anniversary in 2011, selling 7 out of every 10 vehicles in the light commercial vehicle (LCV) category. The company began exporting the Nano to Sri Lanka, and launched the Tata Magic IRIS, a four-to-five seater four-wheel passenger carrier (top speed of 34 MPH) for public transportation. Also in that year, the Tata Ace Zip, a small "micro truck" for deep-penetration goods transport on the poor roads of rural India, and the new Tata Indica eV2, the most fuel-efficient car in India, were introduced.

Continuing its innovative operations, Tata signed an agreement of cooperation in 2012 with Malaysia's DRB-HICOM's Defense Technologies: Tata also introduced its Anti-Terrorist Indoor Combat Vehicle concept at DEFEXPO-India. The company brought out three new vehicles at the 2012 Auto Expo: Tata Safari Storme, a large SUV; Tata Ultra, a light commercial vehicle (truck); and the Tata LPT 3723, a medium duty truck and India's first five-axle rigid truck. The air-powered car developed with (MDI) from Luxembourg is showing promise and could serve a large market niche that wants ultra-economical transportation.

Tata Motor's joint ventures, subsidiaries, and associated companies are presented in Exhibit 2.

## EXHIBIT 2    Tata Motors Joint Ventures, Subsidiaries, and Associate Companies in 2012

| Subsidiaries, JVs, and Associates |
| --- |
| Jaguar Land Rover |
| Tata Daewoo Commercial Vehicle Company Ltd (TDCV) |
| Tata Marcopolo Motors Ltd (TMML) |
| Tata Hispano Motors Carrocera S. A. |
| Tata Motors (Thailand) Limited (TMTL) |
| Tata Motors (SA) Proprietary Ltd (TMSA) |
| TML Drivelines Limited |
| Telco Construction Equipment Co. Ltd. (Telcon) |
| TAL Manufacturing Solutions Ltd. (TAL) |
| Tata Motors European Technical Centre plc. (TMETC) |
| Tata Technologies Ltd. (TTL) and its subsidiaries |
| TML Distribution Company Limited (TDCL) |
| Concorde Motors (India) Ltd. (Concorde) |
| Tata Motors Finance Limited |
| Tata Motors Insurance Broking & Advisory Services Ltd (TMIBASL) |
| TML Holdings Pte. Ltd. (TML) |
| Sheba Properties Ltd. (Sheba) |

Source: Tata Motors Annual Report, 2012.

Consolidated income statements and balance sheets for Tata Motors are presented in Exhibits 3 and 4, respectively.

# MACROECONOMIC CONDITIONS IN INDIA IN 2012

As of 2012, India was the seventh-largest nation in area, with about one-third the land size of the United States. It was the second most populous country on earth with 1.2 billion people (versus the U.S. with 313 million). The average age in India was 26.2 years (36.9 in the U.S.), and the population growth was 1.3 percent per year (0.89 percent in the U.S.); however, 25 percent were below the poverty line in 2011. The Indian GDP (purchasing power parity) in 2011 ranked fourth in the world, at about $4.5 trillion. Indian per capita GDP was about $3,700 in 2011 (versus $48,000 in the U.S.) and was growing at about 7.2 percent per year (the 26th highest growth rate in the world).

India's economy recovered well from the global recession, primarily because of strong domestic demand, with economic growth over 8 percent. However, in 2011, this growth slowed due to the lack of progress on economic reforms, high interest rates, and continuing high inflation. The Indian government

## EXHIBIT 3    Tata Motors' Consolidated Summarized Income Statements, Fiscal 2011–Fiscal 2012* (in crore rupees or ten million rupees)

|  | Year Ending March 31, 2012 | Year Ending March 31, 2011 |
| --- | --- | --- |
| **Income** | | |
| Revenue from operations | 170,677.58 | 126,414.24 |
| Less: Excise duty | 5,023.09 | 4,286.32 |
|  | 165,654.49 | 122,127.92 |
| Other income | 661.77 | 429.46 |
|  | 166,316.26 | 122,557.38 |
| **Expenditures** | | |
| Cost of material consumed | 100,797.44 | 70,453.73 |
| Purchase of products for sale | 11,205.86 | 10,390.84 |
| Changes in inventories of furnished goods, work-in-progress, and products for sale | (2,535.72) | (1,836.19) |
| Employee cost/benefits expense | 12,298.45 | 9,342.67 |
| Finance cost | 2,982.22 | 2,385.27 |
| Depreciation and amortization expense | 5,625.38 | 4,655.51 |
| Product development expense / engineering expenses | 1,389.23 | 997.55 |
| Other expenses | 28,453.97 | 21,703.09 |
| Expenditure transferred to capital and other accounts | (8,265.98) | (5,741.25) |

(Continued)

**EXHIBIT 3** *(Concluded)*

|  | Year Ending March 31, 2012 | Year Ending March 31, 2011 |
|---|---|---|
| **Total expenses** | 151,950.85 | 112,351.22 |
| Profit/(loss) before tax | 14,365.41 | 10,206.16 |
| Exchange loss/(gain) (net) including on revaluation of foreign currency borrowings, deposits and loan | 654.11 | (231.01) |
| Goodwill impairment and other costs | 177.43 | — |
| **Profit before tax** | 13,533.87 | 10.437.17 |
| Tax expense/(credit) | (40.04) | 1,261.38 |
| **Profit after tax from continuing operations (3–4)** | 13,573.91 | 9,220.79 |
| Share of profit from associates (net) | 24.92 | 101.35 |
| Minority interest | (82.33) | (48.52) |
| **Profit for the year** | 13,516.50 | 9,273.62 |

*Fiscal period April–March.

*Source:* Tata Motors Annual Report, 2012.

**EXHIBIT 4**  Tata Motors' Consolidated Summarized Balance Sheets, Fiscal 2011–Fiscal 2012* (in crore rupees or ten million rupees)

|  | Year Ending March 31, 2012 | Year Ending March 31, 2011 |
|---|---|---|
| **Assets** | | |
| Fixed assets | 56,212.50 | 43,221.05 |
| Goodwill | 4,093.74 | 3,584.79 |
| Noncurrent investments | 1,391.54 | 1,336.79 |
| Deferred tax assets (net) | 4,539.33 | 632.34 |
| Long-term loans and advances | 13,657.95 | 9,818.30 |
| Other noncurrent assets | 574.68 | 332.27 |
| Foreign currency monetary item translation difference account (net) | 451.43 | — |
| Current assets | 64,461.47 | 42,088.82 |
| Total assets | 145,382.64 | 101,014.18 |
| Liabilities | | |
| Long-term borrowings | 27,962.48 | 17,256.00 |
| Other long-term liabilities | 2,458.58 | 2,292.72 |
| Long-term provisions | 6,071.38 | 4,825.64 |
| Net worth | | |
|     Share capital | 634.75 | 637.71 |
|     Reserves and surplus | 32,515.18 | 18,533.76 |
| Minority interest | 307.13 | 246.60 |
| Deferred tax liabilities (net) | 2,165.07 | 2,096.13 |
| Current liabilities | 73,268.07 | 55,125.62 |
| Total liabilities | 145,382.64 | 101,014.18 |

*Fiscal period April–March.

*Source:* Tata Motors Annual Report, 2012.

subsidized several fuels (including diesel, which is a component in its inflation index), and as crude prices remained high, the fuel subsidy expenditures caused an increasing fiscal deficit and current account deficit. In 2010, 2011, and continuing into 2012, India suffered from numerous serious corruption scandals that sidetracked legislative work, and little economic reform occurred as a result.

Despite the scandals, poor infrastructure, a lack of non-agricultural employment, limited access to education, and the rapid migration of the population to unprepared urban centers, growth over the next three to five years is projected to approach 7 percent. This growth would result from India's young population (average age 26.5 years), which has a low dependency ratio and high savings (household savings were about 30 percent of annual income) and investment rates. The Reserve Bank of India suggested that inflation, which had been between 7 and 10 percent since 2009, peaked and then dropped to 6.6 percent in early 2012. The inflationary situation was not likely to show further improvement in 2013 because of increases in energy prices. There was the very real probability of spikes in crude oil processes resulting from the unstable political situation in the Middle East. Between 2011 and 2012, the rupee became cheaper by about 12 percent, relative to the U.S. dollar, giving Indian exporters a competitive advantage.

Education was highly valued in India and the Indian workforce was well-educated, which allowed India to become a major provider of engineering, design, and information technology services. Despite pressing problems such as significant overpopulation, environmental degradation, extensive poverty, and widespread corruption, rapid economic development was fueling India's rise on the world stage.

# THE INDIAN AUTOMOTIVE INDUSTRY

The Indian automobile industry was dominated by Maruti (an Indian subsidiary of Suzuki), Hyundai, and Tata. Mahindra was a distant fourth in the industry. The Indian automobile industry was rapidly growing in 2012 and benefitted from four significant factors: urbanization, growth in road infrastructure, increasing disposable income (resulting from an increase in the income level and a decrease in income tax), and a rapidly growing population.

## EXHIBIT 5    Sales of Commercial Vehicles in Selected Country Markets, 2010 and 2011

| Country | 2011 | 2010 | Growth (%) |
|---------|------|------|-----------|
| India | 882,557 | 725,531 | +22 |
| China | 3,933,550 | 4,367,678 | −10 |
| USA | 5,687,427 | 5,031,439 | +13 |
| Japan | 1,240,129 | 1,318,558 | −6 |
| Canada | 1,144,410 | 1,101,112 | +4 |

Source: "India tops commercial vehicles sales chart," *Economic Times*, March 30, 2012.

India had 10 of the 30 fastest growing urban areas in the world. By 2050, over 700 million people were forecasted to move to India's urban centers. The country had the third-highest amount of road miles in the world, and an estimated 5.2 billion rupees would be spent on national highways, as well as state and rural roads, between 2010 and 2014.

Commercial vehicle sales in India grew at the fastest rate of all countries, including China, in 2011. India was the world's fastest growing truck and bus market for the second consecutive year. Sales of commercial vehicles, primarily trucks, buses, and light cargo vehicles, grew by 22 percent between 2010 and 2011. Exhibit 5 presents sales of commercial vehicles for the five largest country markets in 2010 and 2011.

The Indian automobile industry had evolved during three relatively unique periods: protectionism (until the early 1990s), economic liberalism (early 1990s–2007), and then a period of globalization. The protectionist years were characterized by a closed economy with high duties and sales taxes. The automobile industry at that time was a seller's market with long waits for automobiles.

The period of economic liberalism that began in the early 1990s included the deregulation of industries, the privatization of state-owned businesses, and reduced controls on foreign trade and investment, which increased the entry of foreign businesses. This period triggered economic growth which averaged over 7 percent annually between 1997 and 2011. During the economic liberalization period, automobile financing greatly expanded and the automobile market became more competitive.

Indian auto sales reached record levels in the first quarter of 2012, as consumers increased their purchasing—primarily of diesel vehicles—due to

**EXHIBIT 6**   Average Household Disposable Income in India, 1985–2005 (Actual) and 2005–2025 (Forecasted) (in thousands of Indian rupees)

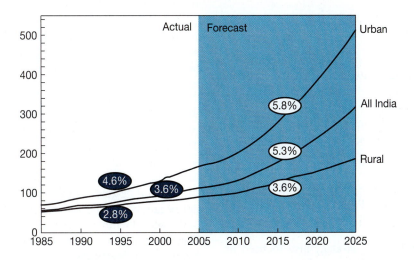

*Circled figures represent compound annual growth rates.

*Source:* McKinsey Global Institute.

concerns that the government would raise taxes on diesel vehicles in the next fiscal year. Increased loan rates and higher fuel prices in 2011 reduced the demand for cars; however, the boom in diesel sales lifted overall sales to a new high of 211,402 autos in April 2012. The demand for diesel vehicles grew to 45 percent of total demand, up from 30 percent in 2010. Diesel was more fuel-efficient than gas, and the Indian government instituted controls on the price of diesel because of its impact on inflation. In the first quarter of 2012, diesel was 40 percent cheaper than gasoline.

Several trends impacted the Indian passenger car industry: household income level, especially in the middle income segment, which accounted for the largest number of auto sales, was expected to have significant

growth. This was predicted to increase the demand for passenger cars. Exhibit 6 presents the actual and projected disposable income in India from 1985 to 2025.

Ongoing national urban and rural highway projects through 2014 would increase national and state highways by 110,000 kilometers (68,350 miles) and rural roads by 411,000 kilometers (255,000 miles). This large increase in roads was also expected to increase the demand for cars, especially the more affordable models targeting rural customers. The almost certainty of increasing fuel prices would force successful automakers to focus on increasing fuel efficiency and to search for alternative fuels, which was one of Tata's competencies. Exhibit 7 presents domestic unit sales for various types of vehicles in India for fiscal 2005 through fiscal 2011.

**EXHIBIT 7**   Domestic Vehicle Unit Sales in India, Fiscal 2005–Fiscal 2011 (in thousands)

| Category | 2005 | 2006 | 2007 | 2008 | 2009 | 2010 | 2011 |
|---|---|---|---|---|---|---|---|
| Passenger Vehicles | 1,061 | 1,143 | 1,379 | 1,549 | 1,552 | 1,951 | 2,520 |
| Commercial Vehicles | 318 | 351 | 467 | 490 | 384 | 532 | 676 |
| Three Wheelers | 307 | 359 | 403 | 364 | 349 | 440 | 526 |
| Two Wheelers | 6,209 | 7,052 | 7,872 | 7,249 | 7,437 | 9,370 | 11,790 |
| Total | 7,897 | 8,906 | 10,123 | 9,654 | 9,724 | 12,295 | 15,513 |

*Source:* Society of Indian Automobile Manufacturers, 2012.

# TATA MOTORS' BUSINESS STRATEGY IN 2012

## Tata Motors' Strategy in Passenger Cars

Tata Motors' strategy for its passenger car division was keyed to leveraging its broad product line and concentrating on all-around value, including fuel efficiency. The company offered compact-sized Indica and mid-sized Indigo passenger cars for sales primarily in India, although the company exported passenger cars to parts of Europe and Africa. The company's passenger cars were powered by 1.2-to-1.4-liter gasoline and diesel engines, and the lineup also included the electric-powered Indica Vista. The division also produced the widely publicized Nano micro-sized car.

The passenger vehicle strategy also focused on aggressive growth of new vehicle sales, service locations, and growth in the used-car business through *Tata Assured*. Tata management believed that a better sales and service network would enhance customer care and increase sales. The Jaguar and Land Rover brands were targeted for international growth in the key markets of China, Russia, and Brazil. Tata Motors' passenger vehicle strategy included exporting the Nano to markets throughout the developing world, where there was a sizeable number of lower- and middle-income consumers needing basic transportation.

## The "People's Car"—Tata Nano

In 2009, even though India's population was the second-largest on earth and its economy was rapidly growing, there were only 12 cars per thousand people (compared to 56 per thousand in China, 178 per thousand in Brazil, and 439 per thousand in the United States). In contrast, there were over seven million scooters and motorcycles sold in India that year. The two-wheeled vehicle sales were the result of India's large population, high urban density, and the low income level. Tata Motors recognized the huge market for very-low-cost motorized transportation that was being filled by scooters and motorcycles.

The middle-class household income in India started at about $4,500 in 2007. Tata believed that a car costing about $2,500 would be able to take advantage of the very large market that was being served only by two-wheel vehicles. In 2007, about 7.75 million

Indians owned automobiles; however, more than 17 million others had the financial ability to purchase an automobile. Tata Motors' management believed that the potential market for automobiles priced under $3,000 could grow to about 30 million consumers in India. Tata Motors created the Tata Nano to capture such demand for low-cost automobiles and switch a large portion of the demand for two-wheeled vehicles to the Nano.

Ratan Tata, the chairman of Tata Motors' board, viewed the Nano as the "People's car." Mr. Tata once remarked about the many families riding on scooters: The father would drive with a child standing in front of him; the mother seated behind him and holding a baby. The Nano was intended to be the means to keep Indian middle-class families from transporting the entire family on one scooter. The Nano was widely anticipated in India, and it was anticipated that the Nano might have an effect on the used-car market because of its low price.

Tata Motors began the Nano design with a comprehensive study of the potential customer, their needs, wants, and purchasing ability. In a unique pricing approach, the company set the base price at $2,500, which was the price Tata thought its customers could pay, and worked backward into the design. The base price at introduction was about $2,000 U.S.; however, it quickly went up to $2,300, and by 2012, the price was about $2,600. A typical 2012 Nano model is presented in Exhibit 8.

The base Nano model had a 625cc two-cylinder engine which produced a top speed of 65 miles per

## EXHIBIT 8    The 2012 Tata Nano

*Source:* NationalTurk.com, 2012.

hour and offered gas mileage of nearly 50 miles per gallon. The small engine was well-matched to the driving conditions in urban markets in India, which were characterized by crowded streets with an average speed of less than 20 miles per hour. The base Nano model did not include air conditioning, nor a radio or CD player, and access to the trunk was through the interior—there was no trunk door on the outside of the vehicle. Every possible cost saving was implemented: There were only three lug nuts on the wheels, no airbags, one windshield wiper, and the speedometer was in the middle of the dash rather than behind the steering wheel, which saved on parts and reduced cost. A supplier of suspension parts used a hollow steel tube to replace the solid steel tube normally used so as to save on steel costs.

The Nano was manufactured using a module design, which allowed components to be built separately and shipped to a location where they could be assembled. Tata Motors created a geographically dispersed network of Nano dealers in developing countries such as Brazil, China, Malaysia, Nepal, Bangladesh, Nigeria, Myanmar, and Indonesia. Tata Motors distribution network also included dealers in the Middle East, South Africa, and the African continent.

Despite very high expectations, Nano sales were less than expected after its introduction. Sales for calendar year 2010 were 59,576. For fiscal year 2011, sales rose to 70,432. Sales then rose by 6 percent in 2012 to 74,527. Analysts estimated that approximately 200,000 to 250,000 Nanos per year would need to be sold for Tata Motors to achieve an acceptable return on its $400 million investment in the Nano's development.

The potential of a low-price car in the global automobile marketplace was widely recognized, and there were several potential competitors with plans to enter the market. There were rumors in the industry that GM was working with Wuling Automotive in China to design and produce a car that would directly compete with the Nano. Ford opened its second plant in India in 2011, and had invested over $2 billion in its manufacturing facilities in India. Ford's new Figo offered features close to those of American cars at a price of slightly over $7,000 for the base model. Volkswagen also opened a manufacturing plant in India and was selling its base VW Polo for $8,495, which was well-equipped compared to the Nano and the Ford's Figo. France's Renault also offered an economical car, the Pulse, which was very well-equipped, for about $7,850. In turn, Nissan sold their Micra for about $7,650, Maruti offered the Ritz for $7,500, and Chevrolet put out the Beat, which is priced at $8,030.

## Commercial Vehicles

Tata's commercial vehicle strategy focused on providing a wide range of products that offered the lowest cost of ownership for truck users in developing countries. Tata's strategy was to continuously evaluate their entire commercial product range with the intent of offering a very strong combination of existing products and new commercial platforms and products. Tata Motors offered small commercial vehicles that could be used for local deliveries, light pickup trucks, and light commercial vehicles capable of carrying larger payloads. The company also produced a full line of large buses and coaches, as well as medium and heavy commercial vehicles suitable for long-haul trucking.

Growth in international markets was a strategic priority, which Tata planned to address by combining the efforts of Tata Motors Limited, Hispano (Spain), Tata Motors Thailand, and Tata Daewoo Commercial Vehicles, and expanding its international manufacturing (Tata opened an assembly plant in South Africa in 2011). Tata's commercial vehicle strategy also included plans to refurbish commercial vehicles, sell annual maintenance contracts, and provide parts and services to the defense department in India.

Tata's strategy included a commitment to quality and the lowest total cost of ownership. This was to be achieved by their in-depth knowledge of the Indian market and leveraging their development and design capabilities. The company planned an increased customer-centric operation, which was to be accomplished by a focus on customer services throughout the entire product life cycle, the use of Customer Relationship Technology, and an increase in the availability of customer financing.

## Jaguar and Land Rover

The Jaguar and Land Rover (JLR) brands were in a separate division within Tata Motors and had a significantly different target market than Tata-branded passenger cars. Tata Motors' strategy for JLR was to capitalize on growth opportunities in the premium market segments with the two globally recognized brands. The strategy included achieving additional synergy and benefits with the support of Tata Motors. There were plans for substantial investment in new JLR technologies and products, more competitive powertrain combinations, and new body styles. Revenues for the JLR division had increased from 36,245 crore rupees in fiscal 2009 to 103,635 crore

**EXHIBIT 9**    Total Unit Sales by Brand and Geographic Region for Tata Motors'
Jaguar/Land Rover Division

| Sales by Region | Fiscal 2011 | First Nine Months of Fiscal 2012 |
|---|---|---|
| United Kingdom | 24.0% | 19.1% |
| North America | 21.6 | 19.4 |
| China | 11.0 | 16.3 |
| Europe | 22.4 | 22.4 |
| Russia | 4.8 | 5.2 |
| Rest of the world | 16.2 | 17.6 |
| Total | 100.0% | 100.0% |
| *Sales by brand* | | |
| Jaguar | 52,993 | 39,921 |
| Land Rover | 190,628 | 176,491 |
| | 243,621 | 216,412 |

*Source:* Tata Motors Ltd, Road Show Presentation, 2012.

rupees in fiscal 2012. The division's EBITDA had improved from a loss of 63 crore rupees in fiscal 2009 to a profit of 17,035 crore rupees in fiscal 2012. The division's rise in sales and profitability was largely a result of the growing popularity of its Land Rover brand, which included the Defender, LR2, LR4, Range Rover Evoque, Range Rover Sport, and Range Rover models. Land Rover sales accounted for 82.8 percent of the luxury division's unit sales in 2012. Exhibit 9 presents total unit sales and the change in geographic distribution of JLR sales by brand in 2011, along with the first nine months of 2012.

## TATA MOTORS' SITUATION GOING INTO 2013

Tata Motors Group had a successful fiscal 2012, with net revenues increasing by 36 percent and profits after tax increasing by 46 percent. Tata Motors' domestic commercial vehicle segment experienced a 19 percent increase in sales with light commercial vehicles achieving a market share in its segment of 59.6 percent and medium heavy commercial vehicles obtaining a market share in its segment of the Indian market of 62.2 percent.

Tata's domestic passenger car grew about 4 percent in 2012—which was the same rate as industry growth. The company increased prices for its passenger cars by an average of about 3.3 percent. The customers' preference for diesel over gas engines helped Tata because of its large line of diesel passenger cars.

During 2012, passenger car exports continued to grow with Bangladesh and Sri Lanka becoming Tata Motors' largest export markets. Exports to countries in Africa also grew at a healthy pace.

The Jaguar / Land Rover segment of Tata continued its very strong growth. Sales for the Jaguar/Land Rover division increased by 29.1 percent in 2012, being bolstered by the new Range Rover Evoque, which was launched in September 2011. The Evoque had won over 100 international awards for styling, quality, and performance. The Jaguar XF included an optional 2.2 diesel engine, which made it the most fuel-efficient Jaguar. Tata signed a joint venture agreement with Chery Automotive Co., Ltd., a Chinese automobile manufacturer, to design, manufacture, and sell Jaguars in the Chinese market, pending Chinese regulatory approval. Also, the company had begun purchasing selected subassemblies such as automatic transmissions from suppliers in China and planned to construct a new engine plant in Wolverhampton, UK, that would manufacture low-emission engines.

The Tata Group believed that future growth for its subsidiaries would come from both investments in the growing Indian economy and opportunities in international markets. Tata Motors' management believed that the Indian passenger car industry would experience strong growth over the next 10 years, growing faster than the top five markets (U.S., China, Japan, Germany, and Brazil) and become the third-largest passenger car market (after the U.S. and China) by 2021. The company believed that the introduction of a national goods and services tax to replace the present VAT administered by the separate states would be favorable for the automobile industry. Also, Tata Motors' management expected that the increase in CNG fueling centers and increasing GDP growth would further improve growth in the market. There was a question about how the U.S. market might fit into the company's plans. Jaguar and Land Rover were popular brands in the U.S., but the majority of American consumers had never heard of Tata, and was unaware that Jaguar and Land Rover were owned by an Indian company. There were no other Tata Motors vehicles sold in the United States. Although, Tata Motors had showcased the Nano to the American market at the 2010 Detroit auto show, it would need significant upgrades to meet U.S. safety requirements. Adapting the Nano to meet these safety requirements would add over $2,500 to the cost of the car, bringing the base model price up over $5,000.

In addition to the safety and cost issues, the Nano might not match the needs and wants of American auto consumers. The Nano was a very basic car, and the cars sold in the U.S. competed vigorously with numerous convenience and comfort features. However, some analysts believed the Nano would be a good alternative to used cars for consumers seeking basic transportation. The Nano might also be attractive to consumers living in large, congested cities.

Of course, rising interest rates, significant increases in oil prices, or a slowdown in GDP would hurt passenger car sales. Also, if the Indian government accelerated the implementation of domestic emission standards equal to those of the U.S., the domestic passenger car industry in India would likely suffer. Many opportunities existed in the industry, but the costs of mistakes could be very high in the global automobile industry. Tata Motors' managers would be required to carefully evaluate the domestic and global opportunities and the emerging opportunities and determine the best course for the company.

# 7-Eleven in Taiwan: Adaptation of Convenience Stores to New Market Environments

## Aihwa Chang
### National Chengchi University

## Shih-Fen Chen
### The University of Western Ontario

In early February 2011, a group of Taiwanese businesspeople were on holiday in the United States to celebrate the lunar New Year. They took a shuttle bus from Los Angeles International Airport to their hotel in the city. As they drove past a 7-Eleven store, the group erupted into applause: A Taiwanese store in the United States! The collective acclaim showed how completely Taiwanese consumers had identified with the American convenience store chain and its logo.

## 7-ELEVEN WORLDWIDE

7-Eleven Inc. was the world's largest operator, franchisor and licensor of convenience stores, with annual sales of more than $62 billion.[1] The company had pioneered the concept of convenience stores in the United States, where it had 7,200 stores. This concept was also extended to several countries in North America, Europe, and Asia, including more than 36,400 franchises outside the United States, the largest of which were located in Asia. Beyond the borders of the United States, Japan had the single largest number of stores in the 7-Eleven chain, followed by Thailand, Taiwan, and South Korea (see Exhibit 1: 7-Eleven Franchises Worldwide – January 2011).

### EXHIBIT 1  7-Eleven Franchises Worldwide–January 2011

| Territory | Date First Store Opened | Number of Locations |
|---|---|---|
| United States | 1927 | 7,200 |
| Canada | 1969 | 467 |
| Mexico | 1971 | 1,286 |
| Japan | 1974 | 13,590 |
| Australia | 1977 | 531 |
| Sweden | 1978 | 185 |
| Taiwan | 1980 | 4,783 |
| China | 1981 | 1,505 |
| Singapore | 1983 | 556 |
| Philippines | 1984 | 631 |
| Malaysia | 1984 | 1,305 |
| Norway | 1986 | 167 |
| South Korea | 1989 | 4,755 |
| Thailand | 1989 | 6,206 |
| Denmark | 1993 | 195 |
| Beijing PRC | 2004 | 121 |
| Shanghai PRC | 2009 | 81 |
| Indonesia | 2009 | 42 |
| Total | | 43,606 |

*Sources:* http://corp.7-eleven.com/AboutUs/DomesticLicensing and http://corp.7-eleven.com/AboutUs/International Licensing, accessed November 20, 2011.

College of Commerce
National Chengchi University

Richard Ivey School of Business
The University of Western Ontario

Professor Aihwa Chang (College of Commerce, National Chengchi University) and Professor Shih-Fen Chen (Richard Ivey School of Business, University of Western Ontario) wrote this case solely to provide material for class discussion. The authors do not intend to illustrate either effective or ineffective handling of a managerial situation. The authors may have disguised certain names and other identifying information to protect confidentiality.

## Founding in the United States

7-Eleven was founded in 1927 as the Southland Ice Company in Dallas, Texas. It started by selling ice blocks that were used to refrigerate food in homes. The first stores were known as Tote'm stores because customers "toted" away the ice blocks.

An enterprising employee at one of the stores began offering milk, bread and eggs on Sundays, when the regular grocery stores were closed for the weekend. Customers found the service very convenient. The store picked up on the cue and opened for extended hours during weekdays. It was thus that the business of convenience stores originated in the United States, pioneered by Tote'm.

Tote'm changed its name to 7-Eleven in 1946, when the stores were open from 7 A.M. to 11 P.M. daily. During the 1950s, 7-Eleven started moving beyond the Dallas market into other regions of Texas and also into Florida and Washington, DC.

The move to stay open 24 hours started by accident in 1962, at a store in Austin, Texas, located close to the university campus. On a Saturday night after a football game, the store was so busy that its employees lost track of time and did not bring down the shutters. As an experiment, the store manager opened the store 24 hours a day, seven days a week. It worked and soon caught on with the rest of the 7-Eleven stores in the United States; the extended hours remained unchanged, as a defining characteristic of 7-Eleven.

7-Eleven's new store hours (24/7) were popular for several reasons. More than 10 million people in the United States were awake at 3 A.M., 7 million of whom were gainfully employed in some kind of work.[2] In fact, the American work routine was changing. Late-night or early morning schedules were becoming common, and factories were running three full shifts, leading to several categories of American workers who were staying up later, getting up earlier, and needing a convenient place to shop.

## Concept of Convenience Stores

7-Eleven had articulated its mission as: "Meeting the needs of convenience-oriented customers by providing a broad selection of fresh, high-quality products and services at everyday fair prices, speedy transactions and a clean, friendly shopping environment."[3]

The concept of convenience stores, developed by 7-Eleven, was shaping the way Americans shopped; in turn, American buying behaviour and the American landscape were both shaping the identity of convenience stores. As a matter of habit, Americans shopped at big-box stores and supermarkets for all their weekly or monthly supplies. Convenience stores served as sources for supplementary shopping, for picking up daily-use items that had run out. Convenience stores were thus stuck in a warp. They could not gain top-of-mind recall among American consumers; they seemed destined to stay on the fringes.

## Standardization of Business Format

The evolution of 7-Eleven Inc. was based on three distinctive features of the American landscape.

First, the stores in the 7-Eleven chain were separated from one another by long distances because the United States was geographically the third-largest country in the world, spread across 9.83 million square kilometres. Second, areas where people congregated, such as street corners, became the natural sites for 7-Eleven locations, which, for similar reasons, veered toward gas stations in the United States. 7-Eleven was, in fact, known as a gas station retailer. Third, the 7-Eleven stores were largely located in U.S. rural areas, where population density was low. As a result, customers invariably drove to a store. Almost every 7-Eleven store, therefore, had sufficient space for parking. Drive-thrus were normal, even among 7-Eleven stores located in metropolitan cities such as New York.

Other core elements of the basic business format related not only to the store logo and store location but also to each store's product offerings and merchandising. These core elements, such as the floor plan, were uniform across the 7-Eleven chain (see Exhibit 2: Standard Floor Plan of the U.S. 7-Eleven Stores).

In the United States, new 7-Eleven franchisees commonly constructed a store on a free-standing space. The process of putting the physical structure together from scratch ensured conformity with the guidebook norms the U.S. head office provided to a new franchisee. One norm was that the total store area should be between 2,400 and 3,000 square metres. The franchisee could, however, choose from among several standard formats (e.g., $40 \times 60$ metres, $80 \times 30$ metres; $55 \times 45$ metres, and so on). Another norm pertaining to the floor plan stated the positioning of each of the store's physical components (e.g., retail shelves, refrigerators, microwave ovens and the cash counter).

Franchisees also received general instructions on which categories and subcategories of products, as

**EXHIBIT 2**    Standard Outside Appearance and Floor Plan
of the U.S. 7-Eleven Stores

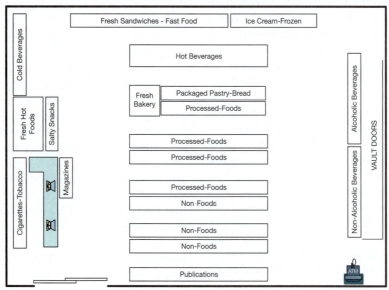

*Source:* Company files.

defined by the head office, should be stocked in the store. The definitions were part of the Product Maintenance Agreement (PMA) that the head office entered into with large vendors for stocking its own-managed stores. Since the PMAs were usually with loss leaders (which guaranteed customer traffic at the store and ensured sales of products with higher margins), they were equally applicable to franchised stores. The head office would also suggest the names of local suppliers

from whom the franchised stores could source products covered by a PMA.

The chain's Operation Field Consultants (OFCs) visited the various franchised stores under their watch to ensure, on an ongoing basis, the uniformity of 7-Eleven stores' layout, floor plan, and merchandising. The OFCs generally played mentoring roles, including suggesting how franchisees could incorporate best practices from other stores.

## International Expansion

The concept of convenience stores had evolved in countries outside the United States along the same lines as it had evolved in the United States. Convenience stores served as a source of supplementary purchases of essential items that could be readily consumed by shoppers. The format established in the United States could be replicated in any part of the world.

In 1969, 7-Eleven opened its first store outside the United States, in Canada. It soon entered a new country every two to three years, by using the franchising route, even outside the United States. In an industry in which domestic players prevailed and proliferated in every country, 7-Eleven was making progress wherever it opened stores. It seemed to have understood the pulse of the customer in every foreign market better than the homegrown convenience stores.

7-Eleven Inc. sought, from its franchisees worldwide, consistency in the colour separations of its signage, the presentation of the corporate logo and the arrangement of the store interiors, while leaving to the franchisee the choice of the location. 7-Eleven Inc. was usually guarded, however, about enforcing any directives on the product range for three reasons: customers in a convenience store were largely from the local community, their needs would be largely local and the products they were buying would also likely be largely local. It was in the product offerings that local nuances came into play.

The global expansion of 7-Eleven was progressing so rapidly that the number of stores outside the United States was soon nearly four times the number of stores within the United States. The chain had begun its foray into the Asian region by entering Japan in 1974. In 1980, it opened the first store in Taiwan, through a franchise deal with President Chain Store Corp. (PCSC), the distribution arm of a Taiwanese foods conglomerate, Uni-President Enterprises Corporation Group (UPEC).

## CONVENIENCE STORES INDUSTRY IN TAIWAN

Taiwan, an island nation in East Asia, had, at 616 persons per square kilometre, the second highest population density in the world, surpassed only by Bangladesh. The capital city, Taipei, was Taiwan's most crowded metropolis with 9,737 persons per square kilometre.[4]

The country had evolved, for over half a century, as both a democracy and a capitalist economy. It was known as one of Asia's economic tigers (see Exhibit 3: Comparison of United States and Taiwan). Traditionally, 70 percent of the growth in Taiwanese GDP came from exports, particularly of electronics and machinery. Until

## EXHIBIT 3   Comparison of United States and Taiwan

|  | USA | TAIWAN |
| --- | --- | --- |
| Land area | 9,826,675 square kilometres | 35,980 square kilometres |
| Terrain | Vast plains in central area, Hills in the East, Mountains in the West | Rugged mountains in the East, Flat plains in the West |
| Natural hazards | Hurricanes along the coast | Typhoons, earthquakes |
| Comparatives | About half the size of Russia; Slightly larger than China; European Union | Slightly smaller than the American states Maryland and Delaware combined |
| Population | 307.7 million | 23.07 million |
| Population growth rate | 0.96% | 0.19% |
| Age structure of the population | Ages 0–14: 20.1% | Ages 0–14 years: 15.6% |
|  | Ages 15–64: 66.8% | Ages 15–64 years: 73.4% |
|  | Ages 65-plus: 13.1% | Ages 65-plus 10.9% |
| Ethnic groups | White: 79.96% | Taiwanese: 84% |
|  | Black: 12.85% | Mainland Chinese: 14% |
|  | Asian: 4.43% | Indigenous: 2% |

*(Continued)*

**EXHIBIT 3**    *(Continued)*

| | USA | TAIWAN |
|---|---|---|
| **Internet users** | 245.0 million | 16.1 million |
| **Main urban centres** | New York (19.0 million) | Taipei (2.6 million) |
| | Los Angeles (12.9 million) | Kashsiung (1.5 million) |
| | Chicago (9.13 million) | Taichung (1.0 million) |
| | | Tainan (0.7 million) |

*Source:* Central Intelligence Agency, "Taiwan," *The World Factbook*, https://www.cia.gov/library/publications/the-world-factbook/geos/tw.html, accessed October 20, 2011.

about 2000, Taiwan was a low-cost, offshore destination for manufacturers in North America and Europe.

Over a long period of time, the rates of inflation were low in Taiwan, coupled with high growth rates. The government's steady liberalization of the economy had increased local competition, which, in turn, had helped to hold down prices. Food prices comprised a large proportion of the consumer price index basket in Taiwan, and trends in international and domestic food prices had a considerable impact on the overall rate of inflation.

Retail trade in Taiwan was valued at $116.85 billion in 2010 and formed about 14 percent of the country's GDP.[5] Almost every major global retailer had its presence in Taiwan, including hypermarket chain Carrefour, restaurant chain Pizza Hut and coffee chain Starbucks. Retail sales were an important metric of private consumption, which the government was tracking monthly.

Taiwan's high population density was a natural platform for the growth of not only retailing but also the convenience store industry. The concept of convenience stores had been pioneered by PCSC, a few years before it launched the first franchised store under the 7-Eleven logo in Taiwan in 1980. PCSC had first entered into the business of convenience stores in May 1979, when it launched 14 President Chain stores island-wide.

Some characteristics of Taiwanese society were central to the evolution of the convenience store industry in Taiwan. In the United States and Canada, property zoning was horizontal, marked by a clear segregation of offices, residential buildings, commercial centres and shopping malls across geographical spaces known as blocks. In Taiwan, the zoning was vertical, characterized by individual high-rise buildings that accommodated offices, apartments, stores, service centres, convenience stores and even workshops. In one building, the first floor housed a storefront bank, the second floor was a beauty salon and the floors above were residential apartments. In another building, the first floor was a car dealer, and the second floor housed a clinic plus a pharmacy centre and the rest of the building comprised offices and service centres. In some buildings, the basement would accommodate a restaurant or a supermarket, in addition to a parking lot. Explained James Hsieh, chief operating officer, PCSC:

> The advantage of vertical zoning is that there would always be people entering or exiting the high-rise. For a retailing business, footfalls are crucial. They are opportunities for making a profit. Consider a place like Manhattan in New York. Outside office hours, the place is deserted. You won't see a vacuum of such a kind in Taiwan. There is a flow of potential customers 24/7.

Some unique Taiwanese traits were conducive to the growth of the convenience stores industry. Taiwanese consumers had an obsession with immediacy; they did not like to wait, as evidenced by the way they sailed through the traffic in Taipei. Convenience stores were thus aligned with this need for instant gratification. Taiwanese entrepreneurs were drawn intuitively toward business models around franchising, which gave them freedom to manage their own destiny. They were also quite friendly and greeting a customer came naturally to a store owner in Taiwan.

Taiwan had many street vendors serving low-cost, tasty but not entirely hygienic food. These family-managed businesses had succeeded because they were nimble, focused and carried no frills. They had thrived because of the high density of footfalls in the streets of Taiwan. This situation was an ideal opportunity for a convenience store seeking a niche as a provider of low-cost, tasty, and hygienic food.

**EXHIBIT 4   Convenience Stores in Taiwan**

| Chain Store | 2010 | 2009 | 2008 | 2007 |
|---|---|---|---|---|
| 7-Eleven | 4,750 | 4,750 | 4,800 | 4,705 |
| Family Mart | 2,576 | 2,401 | 2,326 | 2,228 |
| Hi-Life | 1,247 | 1,245 | 1,239 | 1,296 |
| OK | 837 | 837 | 830 | 818 |
| Total | 9,410 | 9,233 | 9,195 | 9,047 |

*Source:* Company files.

By May 2010, Taiwan had a total of 9,410 convenience stores, giving it the highest density of convenience stores in the world. The stores were each a six-minute walk apart, and each served a community of approximately 2,500 people. Of the total number of stores, 14.3 percent were company-owned, while franchise stores accounted for 85.7 percent of the total.[6]

7-Eleven had the largest number of convenience stores in Taiwan at 4,750 (see Exhibit 4: Convenience Stores in Taiwan). Family Mart, which had its origins in Japan, owned the second-largest number of convenience stores at 2,576. Family Mart made its first acquisition in the Taiwanese convenience store industry in 1997, when it took over 157 Nikomart stores, a competitor at the time. Hi-Life, the third-largest chain with 1,247 stores, had opened its first store in 1988.

# 7-ELEVEN IN TAIWAN

UPEC, the parent company of PCSC, was a home-grown business enterprise founded in 1967 by Wu Hsiu-Chi, a Taiwanese entrepreneur, in Tainan, a city in southern Taiwan. After beginning with the manufacture of flour and animal feeds on a capital investment of about NT$16 million (roughly US$400,000 at that time), the start-up company later diversified into making pork noodles and rice noodles. UPEC had several production plants that covered six major business areas: Provisions, Dairy and Beverages, Instant Foods, General Foods, Consumer Health and Logistics.

UPEC was driven by the vision of being "No. 1 in Taiwan, Top around the Globe." It was founded on the principles of what, in local lingo, was referred to as "Three Goods plus One Fairness": good quality, good credibility, good service plus fair price.

In April 1978, UPEC set up PCSC to serve, initially, its captive needs of distribution. Over the next decade, PCSC acquired skills in managing the supply chain for various business divisions of the group. Setting up its own President Chain stores in May 1979 was a logical extension of the competencies it had built up in distribution. In less than six months after launching President Chain stores, PCSC had begun talks with the 7-Eleven's U.S. office, which culminated in the launch of 7-Eleven stores in Taiwan.

The first 7-Eleven store opened in Taipei in February 1980. The bright, neat and well-lit environment of the store made an impact because of its sharp contrast to local stores, which were cramped, musty and dark. It was so clean that several customers assumed they had to take their shoes off before entering the store!

According to Hsieh, the growth of 7-Eleven in Taiwan since 1980 could be divided into three distinct phases of about a decade each: imitation, localization and innovation. Each stage summed up the managerial focus at PCSC at the time. All three stages connected seamlessly with one another.

## Phase One: Imitation

As PCSC was the sole franchisor for the whole of Taiwan, it was keen on falling in line with the 7-Eleven mould, rather than breaking away from it. At this imitation stage, its immediate priority was to establish a good working relationship with the American partner. The first decade, 1980 to 1990, was thus characterized by PCSC's conformity with the tried and tested U.S. model.

Taiwan's scarcity of freestanding sites in cities limited the opportunities to build new stores from the ground up. As a result, it was difficult to conform to the U.S. model of stores of standard size, format, and floor plan. The average store area of the Taiwanese 7-Eleven stores was also smaller, at 700 square metres, one-quarter of the area of a U.S. store (see Exhibit 5: 7-Eleven's Irregular Store Layout in Taiwan).

During this phase, PCSC had retained the 7-Eleven stores under its control. It had not taken the franchising route to the next level by opening these locations up to other Taiwanese franchisees. The captive model had helped reinforce the spirit of conformity within the group.

This period, however, witnessed three minor "mistakes" on the part of PCSC in setting up the franchise, as recalled by Hsieh.

First, it had opened 7-Eleven stores mainly in the residential communities, within city centres, which meant the target consumers were housewives; however, price was a main concern for these women and 7-Eleven was positioned in Taiwan as a chain of high-end convenience stores. Second, stores had opened simultaneously

**EXHIBIT 5    7-Eleven's Irregular Store Layout in Taiwan**

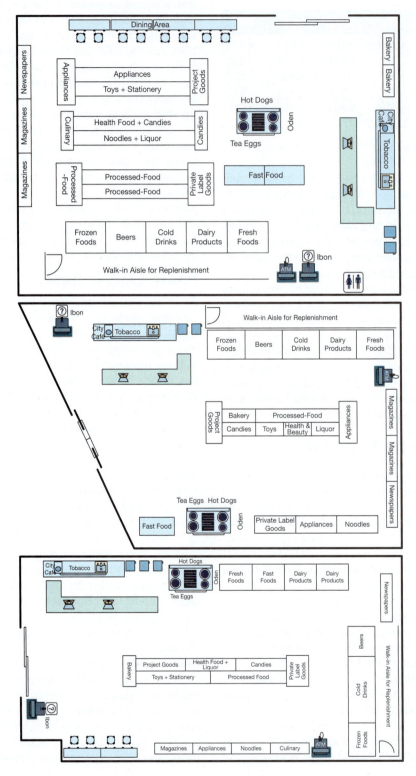

*Source:* Company files.

across Taiwan, particularly in the north, the central area and in the south, which had spread the group resources thin. Third, rather than renting space, PCSC was buying premises, which had led to high upfront costs.

Given these initial issues, 7-Eleven's expansion into Taiwan was smooth without major setbacks. By December 1990, PCSC had become the largest retailer in Taiwan with revenues of NT$10.8 billion (approximately US$366 million).

## Phase Two: Localization

The second decade marked the beginnings of the realization that the "mistakes" of the first decade needed to be undone. PCSC started to loosen up some of the established systems and structures, principally those that pertained to ownership, location, and merchandise.

PCSC had owned its stores for the first 10 years. It was now no longer buying stores' properties but was instead renting the premises from various landlords. The company was also franchising its stores in addition to opening its own stores. This approach meant less capital outflow, less managerial time spent in monitoring operations, more rapid growth, and greater flexibility in the choice of sites and store locations. This approach also led to greater decentralization in operations because of the leeway given to the franchisees in making decisions at the store level.

The new franchisees were setting up stores not in residential communities but in city centres in high-density locations, such as railway stations. PCSC itself was moving its owned stores in cities such as Taipei to corner sites (see Exhibit 6: 7-Eleven Stores at City Centres and Street Corners in Taipei). The move into city centres also meant that the stores no longer needed to appeal to price-sensitive housewives but now needed to appeal to a different demographic group, young urban professionals. PCSC appealed to the younger generation by promoting American products such as the Slurpy, backed by advertising in the local media. The margin from a single Slurpy was higher than the margin from a dozen infant formulas.

Merchandise offered an opportunity both to conform and deviate. 7-Eleven Taiwan stores retained the U.S. model by selling fast foods, frozen foods,

## EXHIBIT 6    7-Eleven Stores at City Centres and Street Corners in Taipei

*Source:* Company files.

drinks, instant noodles, newspapers, magazines and cigarettes. These products were basic to modern living and were recurring purchases. The stores stopped stocking less frequent purchases such as pots, pans, plates, saucers, and hardware. Instead, they served hot dogs, which were common in the United States and catching on in Taiwan.

Simultaneously, PCSC had begun taking steps to provide a local flavour in its stores. It started selling *tea egg*, a local breakfast dish prepared from spices, sauces, eggs, and tea leaves. The new products were catching on with local customers. Recalled Hseih:

> The U.S. office had apprehensions about our selling tea egg, which has a certain fragrance. The Americans thought it was "smelly" and, thus, in their view, could cause allergies for customers. But tea egg is not only a local delicacy but a brisk selling product. When revenue considerations ultimately prevailed, we knew that we could begin to experiment at the ground level.

7-Eleven stores in Taiwan also offered *baozi* (breakfast buns cooked originally in large bamboo steamers), which could be warmed up at the point of sale; *luwei* (simmered vegetable potpourri), which could be cut and weighed to order at the store; and *fantuan* (glutinous rice, usually in triangle form, packed around meat, fish, or veggies, and then wrapped in seaweed leaf and packaged in plastic). Besides, the stores sold *biandang*, a hot, microwaved meal that customers could grab at any time of the day. This packaged offering was in direct competition to the traditional *biandang* sold by street vendors.

The success in marketing local foods led to the decision to extend the concept of customer convenience in two ways: moving beyond selling packaged foods to selling fresh foods, and selling products that could be consumed immediately rather than held for stock. PCSC changed the store profile and increased the convenience factor. All these decisions together helped undo the "mistakes" of the first decade.

By mid-1995, PCSC had opened its 1,000th store and had accomplished an island-wide network through store expansion into eastern Taiwan. In July 2000, PCSC signed a perpetual agreement with 7-Eleven Inc., which not only underscored the confidence of the American partner but also set the stage for a new decade of business transformation.

## Phase Three: Innovations

The period beginning in 2000 saw PCSC reinforce the concept of customer convenience not only at the level of operations, as it had thus far, but also at the level of technology. The former involved thinking outside of the box to come up with untested but workable ideas around products and services offered at the store; the latter involved leveraging the existing resources of the UPEC group as a whole to improve the productivity of the 7-Eleven chain in Taiwan.

There was a limit to how far the concept of convenience stores could evolve in Taiwan on the basis of product offerings alone. PCSC was therefore looking for ways other than merchandise to find its basis of differentiation. It found a window of opportunity in the bourgeoning information technology (IT) sector. Soon, IT laid the foundations of a mindset, in which, as long as the basics—such as the store logo and the concept of customer convenience—remained intact, the chain would be open to any out-of-the-box thinking (see Exhibit 7: Service Innovations of the Taiwanese 7-Eleven Stores).

IT laid the foundation for ibon, an e-commerce kiosk connected to a cloud server (see Exhibit 8: 7-Eleven Taiwan – ibon). This IT platform enabled each 7-Eleven store to become a distribution channel of digitized services in its own right. The nature and number of transactions that customers could do on the ibon platform seemed endless.

For example, customers could walk into a 7-Eleven store in Taiwan to reserve tickets for domestic travel by air and high-speed rail, book tickets for movies and operas, pay credit card bills, and download documents from e-mails and print them (in colour, if required). The ibon kiosk also enabled payment of personal taxes, vehicle licence fees, driver's licence fees, parking tickets, and speeding fines. Consumers could also pay their gas, electricity, water, and phone bills at ibon, which served as an automated teller machine (ATM) to withdraw money.

The biggest advantage of ibon was that it increased footfalls (which could then generate collateral purchases). Licence renewal was an example of a category that increased footfalls. Taiwan had approximately 20 million scooters and 10 million cars. The driving licences were renewable every six years, amounting to an average of 5 million requests for licence renewals annually. Of those renewals, 30 percent, or approximately 1.5 million, were processed at 7-Eleven stores. Thus, licence renewals alone attracted approximately 4,500 footfalls every day.

Service offerings were another area that opened up infinite possibilities for PCSC changing the conventional nature of its 7-Eleven stores. The basic idea was to increase revenue not only through footfalls but also through a fee for some of the services.

**EXHIBIT 7**   Service Innovations of the Taiwanese 7-Eleven Stores

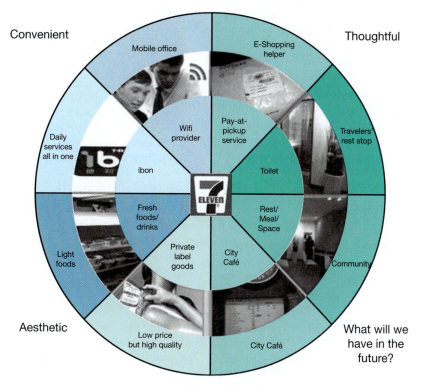

*Source:* Carat Media Weekly Newsletter, *2011/07/11–2011/07/17, no. 594.*

**EXHIBIT 8**   7-Eleven Taiwan

*Source:* Company files.

## Pre-ordering

Pre-ordering was among the first fee-based services introduced. PCSC executives realized, in late 1990s, that Taiwanese people were devoting progressively less time to regular shopping due to longer working hours. The trend was particularly evident in seasonal shopping for occasions such as Valentine's Day and Mother's Day. PCSC came up with a novel idea, wherein customers could order their purchases by phone and pick up the goods on payment at the 7-Eleven store of their choice on a day and time that suited them. Pre-ordering soon covered a wide range of unconventional items, such as foods from five-star restaurants.

## Delivery and Pick Up

The e-commerce platform installed at each 7-Eleven store was being used as a conduit for delivery and pick up of any product that was outside the realm of the store. The most popular use of this service was for the purchase of books. The store would not sell the books but any customer could walk into the store and use ibon to order a book through Amazon, the global online book distributor. The customer could then designate a specific 7-Eleven store for Amazon to deliver the book. The store would receive the book from the courier on behalf of the customer for pick-up at a convenient time.

The other popular delivery/pick-up service was laundry. Customers could drop their laundry at a 7-Eleven store on their way to work. At a fixed time each day, a dry cleaner would collect the laundry. The laundered clothes would then be returned to the store, either for customers to pick up in the evening or for delivery to the customers by the 7-Eleven trucks.

7-Eleven also facilitated buyers and sellers who used auction sites. For example, a seller could leave a purchased auction item at a 7-Eleven store in Taipei city for pick-up at another 7-Eleven store in Tainan city. The 7-Eleven transportation network would send the item from Taipei to Tainan, where the buyer, after making the payment, could pick it up. The money would be transferred, electronically, from Tainan to Taipei for the seller to collect.

## Telecom

7-Eleven stores sold prepaid phone cards, in addition to monthly phone plans. The store had its own brand called 7-Mobile. It was part of the telecom services provided by Uni-President which was competing with the much bigger, state-owned Chunghwa Telecom, for cellular services. Said Hsieh:

> 7-Mobile has carved out its own niche in the face of state monopoly. It has its own advantage in the sense that Chunghwa Telecom (the leading mobile phone operator in Taiwan) does not sell foods and beverages. At NT$140 per month for two years (less than US$5), we also offer a low threshold price. The calls within the same telecom network are free. We have secured a licence from National Communications Commission, the country's official regulator of the telecom sector, but 7-Eleven uses the infrastructure and airtime of Far East Tone, a mobile phone service wholesaler, which preempts us from the need to invest in cellular base stations. 7-Mobile is a private brand telecom service.

Ninety-five percent of 7-Eleven stores in Taiwan had Wi-Fi access points, which allowed anyone with a wireless card (from either Chunghwa Telecom or 7-Mobile) to have free access to the Internet from their cellphone in most 7-Eleven stores.

## i-Cash

The Taiwanese 7-Eleven stores sold i-Cash cards, pre-paid cards available in a range of denominations of the local currency, the New Taiwan dollar. These cards removed the need to carry cash as they could be used like a debit card at any point of purchase. i-Cash could also be used to make purchases at one 7-Eleven store for delivery to another person at any other 7-Eleven store anywhere in Taiwan. The cards could also be used by parents to pay for purchases made either by their school-aged children or by their older children who were away at college. Young urban professionals also used the cards to pay for purchases made by their retired parents.

PCSC had also collaborated with EasyCard Corp, a Taiwanese provider of touch-and-go integrated circuit (IC) cards, which could be used by customers to gain entry to metro services, bus services, designated parks, stores, and government agencies. The i-Cash-EasyCard, as the joint offering was called, had become a popular e-wallet for small daily purchases in Taiwan. It was convenient because it eliminated fumbling for the correct change at payment counters.

## Coffee Counter

The decision to move into fresh foods was extended in 2004 to the launch of fresh coffee, branded as City Café, in Taiwan's 7-Eleven stores. Coffee was almost an addiction among Taiwanese people, who wanted it in cold weather or hot weather, with breakfast or lunch, with a sandwich or a rice bowl. City Café had changed Taiwan's coffee landscape, triggering not only the offering of coffee from fast-food chains such as McDonald's and other convenience stores such as Family Mart and Hi-Life but also the launch of independent, stand-alone coffee chains such as Starbucks and 85°C.

According to estimates made by the Fair Trade Commission, an official agency of Taiwan in charge of competition policy, approximately 530,000 cups of coffee were sold every day at convenience stores in Taiwan. Up to 400,000 of those cups of coffee were sold by 7-Eleven stores alone.[7]

## Seating Areas

Another example of innovating to local needs was the services that 7-Eleven targeted to seniors. Double-income families were on the rise in Taiwan, creating a social vacuum for seniors, whose numbers were also increasing. Seniors needed to find ways to occupy their time because their children were away at work all day. Some 7-Eleven stores designated a small seating area for seniors, where they could linger, mingle, chat with each other, exercise together and generally feel good and included in their community. 7-Eleven developed and sold special products for the seniors, such as low-calorie and high-fibre snacks. The designated seating areas in the stores were also used as a children's after-school waiting room. The children could colour drawings and do homework before being picked up by their parents on their way home.

## Taxi Services

7-Eleven stores in Taiwan had a provision for calling for a taxi service for handicapped persons. These people then received a discount in cab fare from 7-Eleven in cooperation with the Social Affairs Bureau of the Taiwanese government. People with hearing problems could use the store's ibon, for free, to call a cab. The store also kept a log book to help in the retrieval of personal belongings lost by such customers while in the cab. A unique service offered by the Taiwanese 7-Eleven stores provided assistance to customers who had drunk too much alcohol to drive home. The store would arrange for two drivers—one to take them home and the other to drive their car home. Explained Hsieh:

> The Taiwanese society is changing in many ways. The needs of its people are changing. The concept of convenience is also changing. What we are doing at 7-Eleven must change accordingly. The two basic questions we ask ourselves regularly are: "How can we help customers manage their daily chores? How can we help them cope with their day-to-day inconveniences?" Customers should walk in to a 7-Eleven store and be free to say, "This is my personal store. I can do whatever I want here."

By January, 2011, 7-Eleven had 4,783 stores in Taiwan (see Exhibit 9: 7-Eleven Stores and Market

## EXHIBIT 9    7-Eleven Stores and Market Share in Taiwan

*Source:* Company files.

Share in Taiwan). For 2011, PCSC had generated a revenue of NT$138.9 billion and a net income of NT$6.1 billion (see Exhibit 10: President Chain Store Corp. Income Statements, 2000–2011). For the year, it had assets of NT$ 69.8 billion (see Exhibit 11: President Chain Store Corp. Balance Sheets, 2000–2011).[8] According to Hsieh, the growing view was that "people in Taiwan could live without the government but they could not live without 7-Eleven."

## INFRASTRUCTURE OF HQ

The six major businesses of UPEC—Provisions, Dairy and Beverages, Instant Foods, General Foods, Consumer Health, and Logistics—covered a wide range of products, which, in turn, required a network of collection and distribution hubs for both procurement (the back end) and sales (the front end). As a result, the group had developed an in-house infrastructure.

One major competitive advantage of 7-Eleven Taiwan was its being part of a conglomerate (see Exhibit 12: UPEC Infrastructure Companies). In leveraging the internal network to meet the needs of its stores, both owned and franchised, 7-Eleven in Taiwan was able to move its focus in capturing value from the inside of the store (during the localization phase of growth) to its external environment (during the innovative phase of its growth).

The first step in this regard was PCSC's decision to use the group's own logistics business, rather than private vendors, to deliver inventory to the 7-Eleven stores. PCSC had been relying on private vendors because its own transportation needs were limited by the size of the Taiwanese market. The shift to internal services reduced the number of delivery trucks that each 7-Eleven store needed to monitor from about 30 to 8, generating immediate efficiency in the supply chain. The sharing of resources was soon expanded to other areas, such as cash flow and information systems management.

PCSC had 27 warehouses in Taiwan and eight fresh food preparation centres. By 10 a.m. each day, the latter took orders from individual stores for Bentos (single portion dishes served in take-out boxes), dumplings, and sandwiches, which had an expiry limit of 24 hours. The fleet was deployed for delivery by 10 p.m. through Computer Aided Planning and Scheduling (CAPS), which would tie up all routes and schedules. PCSC was using its own fleet of vehicles for delivery. Each vehicle, in turn, was franchised. The system helped reduce the costs of supervision and encouraged entrepreneurship within the group.

The infrastructure support preempted the need for a storage area in each store, which represented a major saving in space (which was in short supply in Taiwan) and in recurring expenses (such as rent). Said Hsieh:

> The good thing is that it is easy for a 7-Eleven store in Taiwan to relocate. It is not because the store is smaller in size than a U.S. store. It is because, unlike the U.S. store, our entire infrastructure is outside the store. It has reduced the cost of relocation and improved our responsiveness. It is like the way the nomads keep moving to where the pasture is. We are like retail nomads. We can pack up and go where the growth is.

7-Eleven was the first convenience store in Taiwan to use EOS (Electronic Ordering System) to not only regulate its inventory but link the cashier at each store with the head office. PCSC was also continuously implementing new technologies. In 1995, it improved the prevailing EOS with Point of Sales (POS) systems and, within two years, introduced Graphic Ordering Terminals to further improve the requisitioning and ordering processes at each store, while the employees were working on the store floor. The Mobile Office platform launched in 2000 enabled the company to get closer to the OFCs, franchisees and, thereby, the end customers.

The decade beginning in 2000 was a time when the Internet euphoria was beginning to fade and global skepticism surrounded the promise and the potential of the virtual world. But, for UPEC, e-commerce was emerging as a potential opportunity to pool group synergies. Explained Hsieh:

> We entered the e-commerce market from the last mile unlike the normal practice of doing so from the first mile. The basic trigger came from two factors. The first was the recognition that the Taiwanese market was small; so small, in fact, that it was impossible to build scale from a single business. The second was the fact that the parent company, UPEC, was a conglomerate. It was focused on foods but, within it, was not only hugely diversified but fully integrated. There was thus untapped potential for leverage within group companies, by which each could add value to the other while getting value in turn.

The services provided by the head office to the chain stores included purchasing, warehousing, and transportation, and delivery. The centralization of these three activities had not only generated cost savings for the group but had also led to better utilization of resources. Individual stores could send their requisitions for supplies to the head office rather than to different vendors. Bulk purchases had led to

**EXHIBIT 10** President Chain Store Corp. Income Statements, 2000–2011 (in millions of NT$)

| Year* | 2011 | 2010 | 2009 | 2008 | 2007 | 2006 | 2005 | 2004 | 2003 | 2002 | 2001 | 2000 |
|---|---|---|---|---|---|---|---|---|---|---|---|---|
| Operating revenues | 138,960 | 169,917 | 148,278 | 145,899 | 141,982 | 132,945 | 119,941 | 95,275 | 90,063 | 81,050 | 70,863 | 57,282 |
| Cost of sales | (92,571) | (115,961) | (100,138) | (99,256) | (98,324) | (93,042) | (83,225) | (66,486) | (63,104) | (56,578) | (49,475) | (39,923) |
| Gross profit | 46,389 | 53,956 | 48,140 | 46,643 | 43,658 | 39,903 | 36,716 | 28,789 | 26,959 | 24,472 | 21,388 | 17,359 |
| Operating expenses | (39,536) | (46,305) | (42,027) | (40,889) | (38,606) | (34,783) | (31,887) | (25,403) | (23,554) | (21,690) | (19,329) | (15,117) |
| Operating income | 6,853 | 7,651 | 6,113 | 5,754 | 5,051 | 5,120 | 4,829 | 3,386 | 3,405 | 2,782 | 2,059 | 2,242 |
| Non-operating income | 1,055 | 1,475 | 1,755 | 647 | 1,433 | 1,112 | 874 | 899 | 1,034 | 682 | 769 | 799 |
| Non-operating expenses | (450) | (1,235) | (2,316) | (1,494) | (1,185) | (700) | (641) | (397) | (419) | (331) | (559) | (606) |
| Income before income tax | 7,458 | 7,891 | 5,552 | 4,907 | 5,299 | 5,532 | 5,062 | 3,888 | 4,020 | 3,133 | 2,269 | 2,435 |
| Income tax expense | (1,377) | (1,522) | (1,146) | (1,304) | (1,497) | (1,491) | (1,215) | (765) | (260) | (538) | (539) | (649) |
| Net income | 6,081 | 6,368 | 4,406 | 3,603 | 3,802 | 4,041 | 3,847 | 3,123 | 3,760 | 2,595 | 1,730 | 1,786 |

*Year end for 2011 was September 30, 2011; Year end for all other years was December 31.

*Source:* Company annual reports.

**EXHIBIT 11**  President Chain Store Corp. Balance Sheets, 2000–2011 (in millions of NT$)

| Year* | 2011 | 2010 | 2009 | 2008 | 2007 | 2006 | 2005 | 2004 | 2003 | 2002 | 2001 | 2000 |
|---|---|---|---|---|---|---|---|---|---|---|---|---|
| ASSETS | | | | | | | | | | | | |
| Current assets | 36,938 | 36,454 | 34,137 | 30,091 | 24,657 | 18,298 | 15,216 | 7,542 | 9,032 | 6,375 | 8,528 | 5,254 |
| Long-term investments | 10,197 | 11,236 | 12,344 | 13,879 | 14,078 | 14,482 | 13,619 | 12,155 | 10,734 | 10,933 | 5,979 | 6,164 |
| Fixed assets (net) | 17,956 | 16,697 | 15,509 | 15,479 | 14,686 | 12,448 | 12,102 | 11,802 | 10,025 | 9,316 | 8,447 | 5,919 |
| Other assets | 4,735 | 4,701 | 4,704 | 4,279 | 3,859 | 4,007 | 4,018 | 2,421 | 2,498 | 2,433 | 1,710 | 631 |
| Total | 69,826 | 69,088 | 66,694 | 63,728 | 57,280 | 49,235 | 44,955 | 33,920 | 32,289 | 29,057 | 24,664 | 17,968 |
| LIABILITIES & EQUITY | | | | | | | | | | | | |
| Current liabilities | 38,906 | 37,039 | 34,205 | 32,143 | 28,694 | 26,847 | 21,948 | 13,993 | 13,574 | 11,885 | 9,704 | 6,912 |
| Long-term debt | 4,564 | 5,527 | 7,662 | 10,079 | 7,640 | 2,090 | 4,069 | 3,385 | 2,663 | 3,395 | 3,184 | 1,204 |
| Other liabilities | 3,190 | 3,125 | 3,033 | 2,720 | 2,536 | 2,284 | 2,083 | 1,550 | 1,440 | 1,288 | 1,176 | 1,054 |
| Total liabilities | 46,660 | 45,691 | 44,900 | 44,942 | 38,870 | 31,221 | 28,100 | 18,928 | 17,677 | 16,568 | 14,064 | 9,170 |
| Equity | 23,166 | 23,397 | 21,794 | 18,786 | 18,410 | 18,014 | 16,855 | 14,992 | 14,612 | 12,489 | 10,600 | 8,798 |
| Total | 69,826 | 69,088 | 66,694 | 63,728 | 57,280 | 49,235 | 44,955 | 33,920 | 32,289 | 29,057 | 24,664 | 17,968 |

* Year end for 2011 was September 30, 2011; Year end for all other years was December 31.

*Source:* Company annual reports

## EXHIBIT 12   Uni-President Enterprises Corporation Group Infrastructure Companies

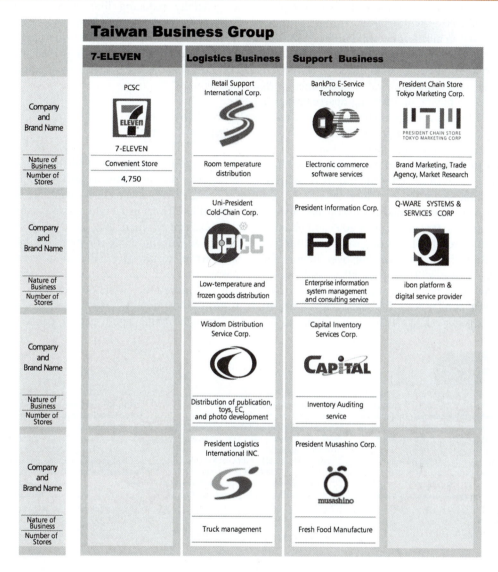

*Source:* Company files.

economies of scale. The 27 warehouses across Taiwan served as feeder lines to 7-Eleven stores. Some warehouses specialized in product categories, such as fresh foods, which required specially built freezers. Some catered only to the popular home delivery service, known locally as *Takkayubin*.

PCSC was most innovative in its transportation activities. The group's fleet of 3,000 vehicles and 5,000 drivers operated in two shifts. The drivers were franchisees and, thus, were entrepreneurs in their own

right. Each individual driver was responsible for keeping the vehicle clean and in running condition and for ensuring timely deliveries. Each driver had a fixed route and, thus, had guaranteed work every month.

## FUTURE DEVELOPMENTS

One of PCSC's priorities, in terms of future developments, was to draw on group-wide synergies to further improve its competitive position in the Taiwanese market. In the immediate context, PCSC was working on two major goals.

The ongoing service innovations at 7-Eleven Taiwan stores would be built increasingly on the platform of shared services within UPEC. On the domestic front, PCSC was in talks with Taiwan Railway Administration, which was managing passenger and freight traffic by rail, for the sale of its tickets at its stores. PCSC was also planning to provide its customers with such services as buying and renting apartments and automobiles. In this context, according to Hsieh, the next generation of 7-Eleven stores "would look dramatically different from what they look today."

On the international front, PCSC had secured the licence from 7-Eleven Japan for full franchise rights in Shanghai. China was considered the next growth frontier for 7-Eleven Taiwan. It had already opened Shanghai's first 7-Eleven store in February 2009 and planned to open 300 stores in China's largest city within five years. PCSC had chosen Shanghai over Beijing for the launch because, with its small alleys and streets, which encouraged people to walk rather than drive, Shanghai was similar to a Taiwanese city. 7-Eleven also had 6,000 stores in Thailand, half of them in the city of Bangkok. It planned to add another 1,000 stores in Thailand by 2013.

In the larger context, 7-Eleven Taiwan had aimed at generally reducing life's inconveniences to the Taiwanese people. It was a broad mandate that placed no limit to the extent to which 7-Eleven Taiwan could expand and diversify its offerings. "Whatever bothers customers," according to Hsieh, "is our business opportunity."

## EPILOGUE

Shortly after visiting the United States, the same group of Taiwanese businesspeople were travelling to Shanghai. Having realized, while in Los Angeles, that 7-Eleven was in fact an all-American enterprise, they exclaimed when they saw a 7-Eleven store in Shanghai: One more U.S. company in China! But, they were wrong again. The 7-Eleven store they had just passed was, in fact, a store that had been franchised, not by 7-Eleven Inc. in the United States, but by PCSC from Taiwan, their own homegrown business icon. 7-Eleven Taiwan had gone global.

## ENDNOTES

[1] 7-Eleven Stores Pty. Ltd., "Why 7-Eleven," http://7elevenfranchise.com.au/why-7-eleven, accessed November 20, 2011. All dollar amounts shown in U.S. dollars unless otherwise indicated.

[2] 7-Eleven Inc., "About Us," http://corp.7-eleven.com/, accessed August 6, 2011.

[3] 7-Eleven Stores Pty. Ltd., "Why 7-Eleven," http://7elevenfranchise.com.au/why-7-eleven, accessed September 12, 2011.

[4] Taiwan Government Information Office, "People: Taiwan's Population Distribution," http://www.gio.gov.tw/taiwan-website/5-gp/yearbook/2002/chpt02-1.htm, accessed November 25, 2011.

[5] "Taiwan Retail Sales Forecast to Hit Record High This Year," Taipei Times, December 26, 2010, http://www.taipeitimes.com/News/biz/archives/2010/12/26/2003491871, accessed November 25, 2011.

[6] http://www.taipeitimes.com/News/biz/archives/2009/07/10/2003448311, accessed August 06, 2011.

[7] Lydia Lin, "Convenience Chains Fined for Coffee Price-Fixing," The China Post, November 3, 2011, http://www.chinapost.com.tw/taiwan-business/2011/11/03/321803/Convenience-chains.htm, accessed January 5, 2012.

[8] US $1 = NT$29.4898, http://fx-rate.net/USD/, as on February 29, 2011.

# The Walt Disney Company: Its Diversification Strategy in 2012

**John E. Gamble**

University of South Alabama

The Walt Disney Company was a broadly diversified media and entertainment company with a business lineup that included theme parks and resorts, motion picture production and distribution, cable television networks, the ABC broadcast television network, eight local television stations, and a variety of other businesses that exploited the company's intellectual property. The company's revenues increased from $35.5 billion in fiscal 2007 to $40.9 billion in fiscal 2011, and its share price had consistently outperformed the S&P 500 since 2003. While struggling somewhat in the mid-1980s, the company's performance had been commendable in almost every year since Walt Disney created Mickey Mouse in 1928. Disney CEO Robert Iger commented on the company's performance since becoming its chief manager in 2005, as well as on its situation in 2012 during an investor's conference in May of 2012.[1]

> I inherited a great company seven years ago, obviously a strong brand in Disney and a strong business in ESPN. As I look back on the seven years, what I think I'm most proud of is that I made a strong company stronger with the acquisition of some very, very valuable and important brands for the company—notably, Pixar and Marvel. And the company today is extremely brand-focused. It's where we invest most of our capital. And those brands are not only stronger in the United States than they were before, but they are stronger globally.
>
> With that in mind, the company is also more diversified in terms of the territories that it does business in. So, while we are still predominantly a U.S.-based company, meaning well more than 50 percent of our bottom-line profits are generated from the U.S., we're far more global than we ever have been. And we've planted some pretty important seeds to make the international side of our business even bigger in the years ahead—notably, in some of the big emerging markets but also in some of the more developed markets outside the U.S.
>
> We also adopted, I think, just at the right time, seven years ago, a technology-friendly approach, believing that nothing the company was going to do was going to stand in the way of technology and its developments. And, rather than watch technology throw threat after threat at us and disrupt our very valuable business models, we decided to embrace it and use it to not only enhance the quality of our product and the connection we have to our customers and make the company more efficient but, ultimately, to reach more people in more ways. And I'm pleased to say that that has definitely worked.
>
> The other thing that I think is very notable about the company is that, as many businesses as we are in, and as many territories as we operate in, the company is managed in a very cohesive fashion. The credit really belongs to a senior management team that knows where the value is created at the company, is invested in The Walt Disney Company and not in [their] individual business, and [strives for] coordination between the businesses . . . is a real distinguishing factor or attribute of our company. And it sets us apart from many companies in the world, and it certainly sets us apart from all media companies.[2]

As the company entered its fourth quarter of 2012, it was coming off of a record-setting third quarter, but faced several strategic issues. The company had invested nearly $15 billion in capital in its businesses during the past five years, including a 43 percent investment in a $4.5 billion theme park in China, the construction of two new 340-meter ships for its Disney Cruise Line, and the acquisitions of Pixar and Marvel. The company had also funded an aggressive share buyback plan that had placed demands on its cash reserves. In addition, not all of the company's business units were providing sufficient returns on invested capital and some business units competed in challenging industry environments. Going into 2013, Iger and Disney's management team planned to evaluate the corporation's diversification strategy.

# COMPANY HISTORY

Walt Disney's venture into animation began in 1919 when he returned to the United States from France, where he had volunteered to be an ambulance driver for the American Red Cross during World War I. Disney volunteered for the American Red Cross only after being told he was too young to enlist for the United States Army. Upon returning after the war, Disney settled in Kansas City, Missouri, and found work as an animator for Pesman Art Studio. Disney, and fellow Pesman animator, Ub Iwerks, soon left the company to found Iwerks-Disney Commercial Artists in 1920. The company lasted only briefly, but Iwerks and Disney were both able to find employment with a Kansas City company that produced short animated advertisements for local movie theaters. Disney left his job again in 1922 to found Laugh-O-Grams, where he employed Iwerks and three other animators to produce short animated cartoons. Laugh-O-Grams was able to sell its short cartoons to local Kansas City movie theaters, but its costs far exceeded its revenues—forcing Disney to declare bankruptcy in 1923. Having exhausted his savings, Disney had only enough cash to purchase a one-way train ticket to Hollywood, California, where his brother, Roy, had offered a temporary room. Once in California, Roy began to look for buyers for a finished animated-live action film he retained from Laugh-O-Grams. The film was never distributed, but New York distributors Margaret Winkler and Charles Mintz were impressed enough with the short film that they granted Disney a contract in October 1923 to produce a series of short films that blended cartoon animation with live action motion picture photography. Disney brought Ub Iwerks from Kansas City to Hollywood to work with Disney Brothers Studio (later to be named Walt Disney Productions) to produce the Alice Comedies series that would number 50-plus films by the series end in 1927. Disney followed the Alice Comedies series with a new animated cartoon for Universal Studios. After Disney's *Oswald the Lucky Rabbit* cartoons quickly became a hit, Universal terminated Disney Brothers Studio and hired most of Disney's animators to continue producing the cartoon.

In 1928, Disney and Iwerks created Mickey Mouse to replace Oswald as the feature character in Walt Disney Studios cartoons. Unlike with Oswald, Disney retained all rights over Mickey Mouse and all subsequent Disney characters. Mickey Mouse and his girlfriend, Minnie Mouse, made their cartoon debuts later in 1928 in the cartoons, *Plane Crazy, The Gallopin' Gaucho,* and *Steamboat Willie. Steamboat Willie* was the first cartoon with synchronized sound and became one of the most famous short films of all time. The animated film's historical importance was recognized in 1998 when it was added to the National Film Registry by the United States Library of Congress. Mickey Mouse's popularity exploded over the next few decades with a Mickey Mouse Club being created in 1929, new accompanying characters such as Pluto, Goofy, Donald Duck, and Daisy Duck being added to Mickey Mouse cartoon storylines, and Mickey Mouse appearing in Walt Disney's 1940 feature length film, *Fantasia.* Mickey Mouse's universal appeal reversed Walt Disney's series of failures in the animated film industry and became known as the mascot of Disney Studios, Walt Disney Productions, and The Walt Disney Company.

The success of The Walt Disney Company was sparked by Mickey Mouse, but Disney Studios also produced several other highly successful animated feature films including *Snow White and the Seven Dwarfs* in 1937, *Pinocchio* in 1940, *Dumbo* in 1941, *Bambi* in 1942, *Song of the South* in 1946, *Cinderella* in 1950, *Treasure Island* in 1950, and *Peter Pan* in 1953, *Sleeping Beauty* in 1959, and *One Hundred and One Dalmatians* in 1961. What would prove to be Disney's greatest achievement began to emerge in 1954 when construction began on his Disneyland Park in Anaheim, California. Walt Disney's Disneyland resulted from an idea that Disney had many years earlier while sitting on an amusement park bench watching his young daughters play. Walt Disney thought that there should be a clean and safe park that had attractions that both parents and children alike would find entertaining. Walt Disney spent years planning the park and announced the construction of the new park to America on his *Disneyland* television show that was launched to promote the new $17 million park. The park was an instant success when it opened in 1955 and recorded revenues of more than $10 million during its first year of operation. After the success of Disneyland, Walt Disney began looking for a site in the eastern United States for a second Disney park. He settled on an area near Orlando, Florida in 1963 and acquired more than 27,000 acres for the new park by 1965.

Walt Disney died of lung cancer in 1966, but upon his death, Roy O. Disney postponed retirement to become president and CEO of Walt Disney Productions and oversee the development of Walt Disney World Resort. Walt Disney World Resort opened in October 1971—only two months before Roy O. Disney's death in December 1971. The company was led by Donn Tatum from 1971 to 1976. Tatum had been with Walt Disney Productions since 1956 and led the further development of Walt Disney World Resort and began the planning of EPCOT in Orlando and Tokyo Disneyland. Those two parks were opened during the tenure of Esmond Cardon Walker, who had been an executive at the company since 1956 and chief operating officer since Walt Disney's death in 1966. Walker also launched The Disney Channel before his retirement in 1983. Walt Disney Productions was briefly led by Ronald Miller, who was the son-in-law of Walt Disney. Miller was ineffective as Disney chief executive officer and was replaced by Michael Eisner in 1984.

Eisner formulated and oversaw the implementation of a bold strategy for Walt Disney Studios, which included the acquisitions of ABC, ESPN, Miramax Films, and the Anaheim Angels, and the Fox Family Channel, the development of Disneyland Paris, Disney-MGM Studios in Orlando, Disney California Adventure Park, Walt Disney Studios theme park in France, and Hong Kong Disneyland, and the launch of the Disney Cruise Line, the Disney Interactive game division, and the Disney Store retail chain. Eisner also restored the company's reputation for blockbuster animated feature films with the creation of *The Little Mermaid* in 1989, *Beauty and the Beast* in 1991, *Aladdin* in 1992, and *The Lion King* in 1994. Despite Eisner's successes, his tendencies toward micromanagement and skirting board approval for many of his initiatives and his involvement in a long-running

derivatives suit led to his removal as chairman in 2004 and his resignation in 2005.

The Walt Disney Company's CEO in 2012, Robert (Bob) Iger, became a Disney employee in 1996 when the company acquired ABC. Iger was president and CEO of ABC at the time of its acquisition by The Walt Disney Company and remained in that position until made president of Walt Disney International by Alan Eisner in 1999. Bob Iger was promoted to president and chief operating officer of The Walt Disney Company in 2000 and was named as Eisner's replacement as CEO in 2005. Iger's first strategic moves in 2006 included the $7.4 billion acquisition of Pixar animation studios and the purchase of the rights to Disney's first cartoon character, Oswald the Lucky Rabbit, from NBCUniversal. In 2007, Robert Iger commissioned two new 340-meter ships for the Disney Cruise Lines that would double its fleet size from two ships to four. The new ships ordered by Iger were 40 percent larger than Disney's two older vessels and entered service in 2011 and 2012. Iger also engineered the acquisition of Marvel Entertainment in 2009, which would enable the Disney production motion pictures featuring Marvel comic book characters such as Iron Man, the Incredible Hulk, Thor, Spider-Man, and Captain America. All of the movies produced by Disney's Marvel unit had performed exceptionally well at the box office, with *The Avengers,* which was released in May 2012, recording worldwide box office receipts of more than $1 billion. Disney's Miramax film production company and Dimension film assets were divested by Iger in 2010 for $663 million. A financial summary for The Walt Disney Company for 2007 through 2011 is provided in Exhibit 1. Exhibit 2 tracks the performance of The Walt Disney Company's common shares between August 2002 and August 2012.

## EXHIBIT 1   Financial Summary for The Walt Disney Company, Fiscal 2007–Fiscal 2011 (in millions)

| | 2011[1] | 2010[2] | 2009[3] | 2008[4] | 2007[5][6] |
|---|---|---|---|---|---|
| Revenues | $40,893 | $38,063 | $36,149 | $37,843 | $35,510 |
| Income from continuing operations | 5,258 | 4,313 | 3,609 | 4,729 | 4,851 |
| Income from continuing operations attributable to Disney | 4,807 | 3,963 | 3,307 | 4,427 | 4,674 |
| Per common share | | | | | |
| Earnings from continuing operations attributable to Disney | | | | | |
| Diluted | $2.52 | $2.03 | $1.76 | $2.28 | 2.24 |
| Basic | 2.56 | 2.07 | 1.78 | 2.34 | 2.33 |
| Dividends | 0.40 | 0.35 | 0.35 | 0.35 | 0.31 |

*(Continued)*

**EXHIBIT 1**    (*Continued*)

| | 2011[1] | 2010[2] | 2009[3] | 2008[4] | 2007[5][6] |
|---|---|---|---|---|---|
| **Balance sheets** | | | | | |
| Total assets | $72,124 | $69,206 | $63,117 | $62,497 | $60,928 |
| Long-term obligations | 17,717 | 16,234 | 16,939 | 14,889 | 14,916 |
| Disney shareholders' equity | 37,385 | 37,519 | 33,734 | 32,323 | 30,753 |
| **Statements of cash flows** | | | | | |
| Cash provided by operations | $ 6,994 | $ 6,578 | $ 5,319 | $ 5,685 | $ 5,519 |
| *Investing activities* | | | | | |
| Investments in parks, resorts, and other property | (3,559) | (2,110) | (1,753) | (1,578) | (1,566) |
| Proceeds from dispositions | 564 | 170 | 185 | 14 | 1,530 |
| Acquisitions | (184) | (2,493) | (176) | (660) | (608) |
| *Financing activities* | | | | | |
| Dividends | (756) | (653) | (648) | (664) | (637) |
| Repurchases of common stock | (4,993) | (2,669) | (138) | (4,453) | (6,923) |
| *Supplemental cash flow information* | | | | | |
| Interest paid | 377 | 393 | 485 | 555 | 551 |
| Income taxes paid | 2,341 | 2,170 | 1,609 | 2,768 | 2,796 |

[1] The fiscal 2011 results include restructuring and impairment charges that rounded to $0.00 per diluted share and gains on the sales of Miramax and BASS ($0.02 per diluted share), which collectively resulted in a net adverse impact of $0.02 per diluted share. See the discussion of the per share impacts in Item 7.

[2] During fiscal 2010, the Company completed a cash and stock acquisition for the outstanding capital stock of Marvel for $4.2 billion (see Note 4 to the Consolidated Financial Statements for further discussion). In addition, results include restructuring and impairment charges ($0.09 per diluted share), gains on the sales of investments in two television services in Europe ($0.02 per diluted share), a gain on the sale of the *Power Rangers* property ($0.01 per diluted share), and an accounting gain related to the acquisition of The Disney Store Japan ($0.01 per diluted share). Including the impact of rounding, these items collectively resulted in a net adverse impact of $0.04 per diluted share.

[3] The fiscal 2009 results include restructuring and impairment charges ($0.17 per diluted share), a non-cash gain in connection with the AETN/Lifetime merger ($0.08 per diluted share) and a gain on the sale of their investment in two pay television services in Latin America ($0.04 per diluted share). Including the impact of rounding, these items collectively resulted in a net adverse impact of $0.06 per diluted share.

[4] The fiscal 2008 results include an accounting gain related to the acquisition of the Disney Stores North America and a gain on the sale of movies.com (together $0.01 per diluted share), the favorable resolution of certain income tax matters ($0.03 per diluted share), a bad debt charge for a receivable from Lehman Brothers ($0.03 per diluted share) and an impairment charge ($0.01 per diluted share). These items collectively had no net impact on earnings per share.

[5] During fiscal 2007, the Company concluded the spin-off of the ABC Radio business and thus reports ABC Radio as discontinued operations for all periods presented.

[6] The fiscal 2007 results include gains from the sales of E! Entertainment and Us Weekly (together $0.31 per diluted share), the favorable resolution of certain income tax matters ($0.03 per diluted share), an equity-based compensation plan modification charge ($0.01 per diluted share), and an impairment charge ($0.01 per diluted share). These items collectively resulted in a net benefit of $0.32 per diluted share.

*Source:* The Walt Disney Company 2008 and 2011 10-Ks.

# THE WALT DISNEY COMPANY'S CORPORATE STRATEGY AND BUSINESS OPERATIONS IN 2012

In 2012, The Walt Disney Company was broadly diversified into theme parks, hotels and resorts, cruise ships, cable networks, broadcast television networks, television production, television station operations, live action and animated motion picture production and distribution, music publishing, live theatrical productions, children's book publishing, interactive media, and consumer products retailing. The company's corporate strategy was centered on (1) creating high-quality family content, (2) exploiting technological innovations to make entertainment experiences more memorable, and (3) international expansion. The company's 2006 acquisition of Pixar and 2009 acquisition of Marvel were executed to enhance the resources and capabilities of its core animation business with the addition of new animation skills and characters. The company's 2010 acquisition

**EXHIBIT 2**   Performance of The Walt Disney Company's Stock Price, August 2002 to August 2012

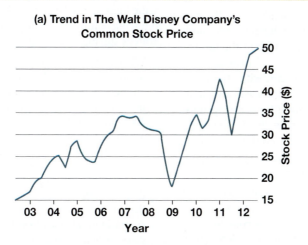

(a) Trend in The Walt Disney Company's Common Stock Price

(b) Performance of The Walt Disney Company's Stock Price versus the S&P 500 Index

of Playdom gave the company new online gaming capabilities, and its 2011 acquisition of UTV was engineered to facilitate its international expansion efforts. When asked about the company's recent acquisitions during a media, cable, and telecommunications conference in May 2012, Disney chief financial officer Jay Rasulo made the following comments:[3]

> Our acquisition strategy is pretty clear. Either we are buying IP that is under-exploited, underused by the owners . . . Or we're buying capabilities to reach consumers in new places or in new ways.
>
> Marvel, like Pixar, was primarily an IP acquisition. We knew there was buried treasure there. The company was doing well to exploit it, but it was doing it largely through third parties.
>
> We decided to make our big play on *Avengers* . . . It's done $1.3 billion as of today in the worldwide box office. Hasn't even opened in Japan yet. So it's definitely

still got some running room. And in addition to the box office, it's hitting in consumer products. There's a social game. It's just exactly what we envisioned when we purchased [Marvel].

> If you look at the other end of the spectrum . . . Playdom did not own a lot of IP but had a capability in social gaming that we simply did not have. Certainly we could have built it, but it would have taken a long time. Social gaming, as you all know, was taking off and continues to rise like a rocket. And we wanted to jumpstart ourselves into that space, so we bought that company with the idea of using both IP we had and the creation of new IP to get into the social space.
>
> UTV . . . is sort of a geographic. We want to grow in India. We want to grow in China. We want to grow in Russia and in Turkey, the big four and the ten after. But you need an entry strategy. And with UTV, we became the largest studio, an owner of nine television networks, and a bigger and more grounded distribution

network for the Disney IP than we have in that market. Our ambition in India is clear. We want to be the family brand of India.

Disney's corporate strategy also called for sufficient capital to be allocated to its core theme parks and resorts business to sustain its advantage in the industry. The company expanded the range of attractions at its Disney California Adventure park with the addition of the $75 million World of Color water and light show in 2010 and the $200 million Radiator Springs outdoor race track in Cars Land in 2012. Bob Iger, Disney's chairman and CEO, discussed the company's approach to allocating financial resources during an investors' conference in May 2012:[4]

Well, first of all, it begins with an overall evaluation of how we deploy capital across the company. So, if the theme park group comes to us with a proposal to renovate Fantasyland in Florida, we obviously look at it in a very discrete fashion, meaning what are the likely returns on that specific capital investment. But we look at it against the whole capital expenditure needs of the company over a given year, or over a given period of time.

So, if you look back in the seven years since I've been CEO, we've actually deployed capital in multiple ways. We've just increased our dividend. We've purchased a fair amount of our stock. We have now 103 Disney Channels worldwide, which took capital to do that. And, of course, we've invested more in our parks and resorts, which includes our theme parks.

Once we decide what kind of capital we believe we might be willing to invest over a period of time as a company, we take a very, very hard look at the specific opportunity or the specific request.

The Walt Disney Company's corporate strategy also attempted to capture synergies existing between its business units. Two of the company's highest grossing films, *Pirates of the Caribbean: On Stranger Tides* and *Cars 2* were also featured at the company's Florida and California theme parks. Disney had also made much of its content available digitally, including its WatchESPN services for Internet, smartphone, and table computer users, its growing list of Disney Publishing e-book offerings, and family content available through its Disney.com/YouTube partnership.

Disney's international expansion efforts were largely directed at exploiting opportunities in emerging markets. In 2012, the Disney Channel reached 75 percent of viewers in China and Russia and was available in more than 100 countries, compared to 19 countries in 2002. Disney opened a Toy Story Land attraction at Hong Kong Disneyland in 2011 and had two more lands planned for the Hong Kong resort. The company was also developing the Shanghai Disney Resort that would include two themed hotels, attractions, and the largest interactive Magic Kingdom-style castle built at any Disney park. Bob Iger also made the following comments about the company's international strategy during the May 2012 investors' conference:[5]

When we talk about growing internationally for instance, we know that we've had opportunities to invest in that business to, essentially, increase our footprint internationally. So the opening of Hong Kong Disneyland in 2005 and the expansion of Hong Kong Disneyland that's already underway—in fact, we're opening three new lands. One's already open, one is opening this summer, and then there's a third to come later in the year.

And then, of course, Shanghai Disneyland—and that's one where I think is probably the best opportunity the company's had since Walt Disney bought land in central Florida in the 1960s. This is a 7.5-square-kilometer piece of land sitting in Pudong, right in the heart of Shanghai. 330 million live within three hours commuting distance to this park. We stood on a tower overlooking a cleared piece of property recently. I couldn't believe its size. But I'm certain that it will fulfill its potential in what is the world's most populous country in the world.

In 2012, the company's business units were organized into five divisions: Media networks, parks and resorts, studio entertainment, consumer products, and interactive media.

## Media Networks

The Walt Disney Company's media networks business unit included its domestic and international cable networks, the ABC television network, television production, and U.S. domestic television stations. The company's television production was limited to television programming for ABC and its eight local television stations were all ABC affiliates. Six of Disney's eight domestic television stations were located in the ten largest U.S. television markets. In all, ABC had 238 affiliates in the United States. When asked about Disney's ABC-related businesses, Bob Iger suggested that the businesses made positive contributions to the company's overall performance.[6]

The television studio, ABC, the network, and the eight stations that we own are a nicely profitable business for us and should continue to be nicely profitable. One of the reasons they're profitable is that, by using the studio and the network to support the creation of pretty high-quality, intellectual property or filmed entertainment, we've taken advantage of what has been a real growth market globally in the consumption of American-based filmed entertainment.

We think we have distinctive, local news brands. Our stations tend to be—most of them are number one in the market. If they're not number one, they're number two. And they tend to rely on a very strong local news brand.

Exhibit 3 provides the market ranking for Disney's local stations and its number of subscribers and ownership percentage of its cable networks. The exhibit also provides a brief description of its ABC

## EXHIBIT 3   The Walt Disney Company's Media Networks, 2011

| Cable Networks | Estimated Subscribers (in millions)[1] | Ownership % |
|---|---|---|
| *ESPN*[2] | | |
| ESPN | 99 | 80.0 |
| ESPN2 | 99 | 80.0 |
| ESPNEWS | 73 | 80.0 |
| ESPN Classic | 33 | 80.0 |
| ESPNU | 72 | 80.0 |
| *Disney Channels Worldwide* | | |
| Disney Channel–Domestic | 99 | 100.0 |
| Disney Channels–International[3] | 141 | 100.0 |
| Disney Junior[3] | 58 | 100.0 |
| Disney XD – Domestic | 78 | 100.0 |
| Disney XD – International[3] | 91 | 100.0 |
| *ABC Family* | 98 | 100.0 |
| *SOAPnet* | 74 | 100.0 |
| *A&E/Lifetime* | | |
| A&E[2] | 99 | 42.1 |
| Lifetime Television | 99 | 42.1 |
| HISTORY | 99 | 42.1 |
| Lifetime Movie Network | 82 | 42.1 |
| The Biography Channel | 65 | 42.1 |
| History International | 64 | 42.1 |
| Lifetime Real Women[3] | 18 | 42.1 |

*Broadcasting*

ABC Television Network (238 local affiliates reaching 99% of U.S. television households)

*Television Production*

ABC Studios and ABC Media Productions (daytime, primetime, late night, and news television programming)

*Domestic Television Stations*

| Market | TV Station | Television Market Ranking[4] |
|---|---|---|
| New York, NY | WABC-TV | 1 |
| Los Angeles, CA | KABC-TV | 2 |
| Chicago, IL | WLS-TV | 3 |
| Philadelphia, PA | WPVI-TV | 4 |
| San Francisco, CA | KGO-TV | 6 |
| Houston, TX | KTRK-TV | 10 |
| Raleigh-Durham, NC | WTVD-TV | 24 |
| Fresno, CA | KFSN-TV | 55 |

[1]Estimated U.S. subscriber counts according to Nielsen Media Research as of September 2011, except as noted below.

[2]ESPN and A&E programming is distributed internationally through other networks discussed below.

[3]Subscriber counts are not rated by Nielsen and are based on internal management report.

[4]Based on Nielsen Media Research, U.S. Television Household Estimates, January 1, 2011.

*Source:* The Walt Disney Company 2011 10-K.

broadcasting and television production operations. The division also included Radio Disney, which aired family-oriented radio programming on 34 terrestrial radio stations (31 of which were owned by Disney) in the United States. Radio Disney was also available on SiriusXM satellite radio, iTunes Radio Tuner and Music Store, XM/DIRECTV, and on mobile phones. Radio Disney was also broadcast throughout most of South America on Spanish-language terrestrial radio stations. The company's 2011 acquisition of UTV would expand the division's television broadcasting and production capabilities to India.

Among the most significant challenges to Disney's media networks division was the competition for viewers, which impacted advertising rates and revenues. Not only did the company compete against other broadcasters and cable networks for viewers, it also competed against other types of entertainment that consumers might enjoy. For example, consumers might prefer to watch a DVD, play video games, or browse the Internet rather than watch television. The effect of the Internet on broadcast news had been significant and the growth of streaming services had the potential to affect the advertising revenue potential of all of Disney's media businesses. However, Bob Iger believed that technology provided great opportunities for Disney.[7]

> It's no longer just a television market. . . it's a media world. And it's rich. And it's no longer just in the home; it's everywhere. It's in school, in your car, walking down the street. You name it, you can consume media. And it's not just filmed entertainment, it's casual games and surfing websites and social networking.

We're launching a TV everywhere app for the Disney Channel. This is like the WatchESPN app that we launched a while back, an app that will enable kids or anyone, for that matter, to watch the Disney Channel and its programs on a mobile device using our app, provided they are subscribers of a multichannel service. . . . And I know that the adoption rate for the ESPN app has been great. It's a fantastic product. And, we're going to launch. . . ABC, ABC Family, and so on.

In summarizing his thoughts about the opportunities for Disney's media programming, Iger concluded,[8]

> We believe that high-quality, branded entertainment is going to continue to deliver real value to our shareholders, not just the value that we've delivered in the past but growth in a world that enables more and more distribution of that product and more consumption of it. Every one of our brands is in high demand by any new platform. You can't launch a platform today without some good content on it, and we're very well-positioned, probably better than anybody in the business, in that regard.

Operating results for Disney's media networks division for fiscal 2009 through fiscal 2011 is presented in Exhibit 4.

## Parks and Resorts

The Walt Disney Company's parks and resorts division included the Walt Disney World Resort in Orlando, the Disneyland Resort in California, the Aulani Disney Resort and Spa in Hawaii, the Disney Vacation Club, and the Disney Cruise Line. The company

## EXHIBIT 4    Operating Results for Walt Disney's Media Networks Business Unit, Fiscal 2009–Fiscal 2011 (in millions)

|  | 2011 | 2010 | 2009 |
|---|---|---|---|
| **Revenues** | | | |
| Affiliate fees | $8,790 | $8,082 | $7,407 |
| Advertising | 7,598 | 7,028 | 6,566 |
| Other | 2,326 | 2,052 | 2,236 |
| Total revenues | 18,714 | 17,162 | 16,209 |
| Operating expenses | 10,376 | 9,888 | 9,464 |
| Selling, general, administrative, and other | 2,539 | 2,358 | 2,341 |
| Depreciation and amortization | 237 | 222 | 206 |
| Equity in the income of investees | (584) | (438) | (567) |
| Operating Income | $6,146 | $5,132 | $4,765 |

*Source:* The Walt Disney Company 2011 10-K.

also owned a 51 percent interest in Disneyland Paris, a 47 percent interest in Hong Kong Disneyland Resort, and a 43 percent interest in Shanghai Disney Resort. Disney also licensed the operation of Tokyo Disney Resort in Japan. Revenue for the division was primarily generated through park admission fees, hotel room charges, merchandise sales, food and beverage sales, sales and rentals of vacation club properties, and fees charged for cruise vacations.

Revenues from hotel lodgings and food and beverage sales were a sizeable portion of the division's revenues. For example, at the 25,000-acre Walt Disney World Resort alone, the company operated 17 resort hotels with approximately 22,000 rooms. An 18th hotel with 2,000 rooms would be added at the Walt Disney World Resort in 2012. Walt Disney World Resort also included the 120-acre Downtown Disney retail, dining, and entertainment complex where visitors could dine and shop during or after park hours. Walt Disney World Resort in Orlando also included four championship golf courses, full-service spas, tennis courts, sailing facilities, water skiing, two water parks, and a 220-acre sports complex that was host to over 200 amateur and professional events each year.

Walt Disney's 461-acre resort in California included two theme parks—Disneyland and Disney California Adventure—along with three hotels and its Downtown Disney retail, dining, and entertainment complex. Disney California Adventure was opened in 2001 adjacent to the Disneyland property and included four lands—Golden State, Hollywood Pictures Backlot, Paradise Pier, and Bug's Land. The park was initially built to alleviate overcrowding at Disneyland and was expanded with the addition of World of Color in 2010 and Cars Land in 2012 to strengthen its appeal with guests. Rasulo discussed the history and shortcomings of Disney California Adventure in 2012.[9]

We were starting to see rejection from Disneyland because it was simply too crowded every day. And we built [Disney California Adventure] both to expand the resort in terms of its offering, but also to pull people away from Disneyland.

Well, the concept wasn't strong enough. It didn't have a great nighttime appeal, so the stays over there were very short, and the people would come back to Disneyland in the evening and accentuate the problem. Now you will see a totally renewed park with a real strong concept called Cars Land, built around the movie *Cars*. It's 12 acres. It's compelling. It's one of the biggest attractions we've ever done with a land around it. And we've already seen World of Color increase attendance at the resort.

Disney held a 51 percent ownership stake in Disneyland Paris and its seven hotels, convention center, shopping, dining, and entertainment complex, and 27-hole golf facility. The company had a 47 percent ownership interest in Hong Kong Disneyland Resort, which included two hotels. A staged expansion of Hong Kong Disneyland, that included three new lands—Toy Story Land, Grizzly Gulch, and Mystic Point—was expected to be completed by 2013. Disney received royalties from the operation of Tokyo Disney Resort, which was owned and operated by Oriental Land Company, a Japanese corporation in which Disney had no ownership interest. Disney would have a 43 percent ownership interest in Shanghai Disney Resort, which would be a $4.5 billion project including Shanghai Disneyland, two themed hotels, a retail, dining, and entertainment complex, and an outdoor recreational area. The resort in China was expected to open in 2016.

The company also offered timeshare sales and rentals in 11 resort facilities through its Disney Vacation Club. The Disney Cruise Line operated ships out of Port Canaveral, Florida, and Los Angeles. Disney's cruise activities were developed to appeal to the interests of children and families. Its Port Canaveral cruises included a visit to Disney's Castaway Cay, a 1,000-acre private island in the Bahamas. The popularity of Disney's cruise vacations allowed its original two-ship fleet to be booked to full capacity year-round. Bob Iger commented on the business's strong performance while addressing investors in May 2012:[10]

The cruise ships [were] a solid business in that we had mid-teen returns on invested capital in two legacy ships that had been built in the 1990s. We believe that we had a quality product, that there was definitely room for us to add capacity, and that the market was there for us to expand in it. And we built two ships, the *Dream*, which launched in early 2011, and the *Fantasy*, which launched a couple of months ago. Again, a very specific look at return on invested capital for the two new ships. Interestingly enough, our four ships are about 90 percent booked for the year. The *Dream*, which we sailed, as I mentioned, [in] early 2011, was accretive, bottom line, the first full quarter of operation. The same thing will be true for the *Fantasy*. And it's just an incredible, high-quality product.

The division's operating results for fiscal 2009 through fiscal 2011 are presented in Exhibit 5.

## Studio Entertainment

The Walt Disney Company's studio entertainment division produced live-action and animated motion

**EXHIBIT 5**   **Operating Results for Walt Disney's Parks and Resorts Business Unit, Fiscal 2009–Fiscal 2011 (in millions)**

|  | 2011 | 2010 | 2009 |
|---|---|---|---|
| Revenues |  |  |  |
| Domestic | $9,302 | $8,404 | $8,442 |
| International | 2,495 | 2,357 | 2,225 |
| Total revenues | 11,797 | 10,761 | 10,667 |
| Operating expenses | 7,383 | 6,787 | 6,634 |
| Selling, general, administrative, and other | 1,696 | 1,517 | 1,467 |
| Depreciation and amortization | 1,165 | 1,139 | 1,148 |
| Operating Income | $1,553 | $1,318 | $1,418 |

*Source:* The Walt Disney Company 2011 10-K.

pictures, pay-per-view and DVD home entertainment, musical recordings, and *Disney on Ice* and *Disney Live!* live performances. The division's motion pictures were produced and distributed under the Walt Disney Pictures, Pixar, and Marvel banners. The division also distributed motion pictures under the Touchstone Pictures banner. Bob Iger summarized the division's strategy with the following comments.[11]

> The strategy for our motion picture group, or our studio, is very clear. We are likely to make two animated films a year, a Pixar and a Disney. There will be some times over the next five years that you could see two Pixar films in one year and a Disney. But, basically, you're looking at two a year. We intend to make, probably, two Marvel films a year going forward, and that slate is pretty defined over the next three to four years. And then, somewhere in the neighborhood of six to eight, probably closer to six, Disney-branded live action films. . .We're not in the business of making 20 films a year or more than that. We are only in the business of making those branded films—Disney, Pixar, and Marvel. We believe that our returns on investment in those branded movies are likely to be better than the overall industry. And, when we have success with a Disney, Pixar, or a Marvel film, we can leverage it much more broadly and deeply and for a longer period of time than we can in any other film that we might make.

Most motion pictures typically incurred losses during the theatrical distribution of the film because of production costs and the cost of extensive advertising campaigns accompanying the launch of the film. Profits for many films did not occur until the movie became available on DVD or Blu-ray disks for home entertainment, which usually began three to six months after the film's theatrical release. Revenue was also generated when a movie moved to pay-per-view (PPV) / video-on-demand (VOD) two months after the release of the DVD and when the motion picture became available on subscription premium cable channels such as HBO about 16 months after PPV/VOD availability. Broadcast networks such as ABC could purchase telecast rights to movies later as could basic cable channels such as Lifetime, Hallmark Channel, and ABC Family. Premium cable channels such as Showtime and Starz might also purchase telecast rights to movies long after their theatrical release. Telecast right fees decreased as the length of time from initial release increased. Also, the decline in DVD sales and rentals had affected industry revenues as motion pictures moved to lower-revenue-generating telecasts more quickly. The operating results for The Walt Disney Company's Studio Entertainment division for fiscal 2009 through fiscal 2011 is presented in Exhibit 6.

## Consumer Products

The company's consumer products division included the company's Disney Store retail chain and businesses specializing in merchandise licensing and children's book and magazine publishing. In 2011, the company owned and operated 208 Disney Stores in North America, 103 stores in Europe and 46 stores in Japan. Its publishing business included comic books, various children's book and magazine titles available in print and ebook format, and smartphone and tablet computer apps designed for children. The company's bestselling apps in 2011 were Disney Princess Dress-Up and Cars 2. Licensing revenues were generated from the use of Disney's portfolio of characters by manufacturers of toys, apparel, home décor, stationery, footwear, and

**EXHIBIT 6**   **Operating Results for Walt Disney's Studio Entertainment Business Unit, Fiscal 2009–Fiscal 2011 (in millions)**

|  | 2011 | 2010 | 2009 |
|---|---|---|---|
| Revenues |  |  |  |
| Theatrical distribution | $1,733 | $2,050 | $1,325 |
| Home entertainment | 2,435 | 2,666 | 2,762 |
| Television distribution and other | 2,183 | 1,985 | 2,049 |
| Total revenues | 6,351 | 6,701 | 6,136 |
| Operating expenses | 3,136 | 3,469 | 3,210 |
| Selling, general, administrative, and other | 2,465 | 2,450 | 2,687 |
| Depreciation and amortization | 132 | 89 | 60 |
| Equity in the income of investees | — | — | (4) |
| Operating Income | $ 618 | $ 693 | $ 175 |

*Source:* The Walt Disney Company 2011 10-K.

consumer electronics. In 2011, Disney was the largest licensor of character-based merchandise in the world. The division's sales were primarily affected by seasonal shopping trends and changes in consumer disposable income. An overview of the division's operating results for fiscal 2009 through fiscal 2011 is presented in Exhibit 7.

## Interactive Media

Disney's interactive media business unit produced video games for handheld game devices, game consoles, and smartphone platforms. The division also developed games and other content for Disney.com and Disney's websites for its parks and resorts and studio entertainment division. The interactive media division had found it difficult to compete in the highly seasonal video game industry and had suffered losses each year between fiscal 2009 and fiscal 2011. In addition, the division's sales were affected dramatically by the timing of new console releases and the popularity of its game titles. In 2010, the company acquired Playdom, Inc., a company that developed online games for social networking sites to help speed the company's product development capabilities in that area. In summing up the division's performance and future prospects, CEO Iger stated:[12]

> We have an interactive division that includes games and a number of our Disney-branded websites. We've lost money in that space. The division overall is small when you compare it with the other big divisions of

**EXHIBIT 7**   **Operating Results for Walt Disney's Consumer Products Business Unit, Fiscal 2009–Fiscal 2011 (in millions)**

|  | 2011 | 2010 | 2009 |
|---|---|---|---|
| Revenues |  |  |  |
| Licensing and publishing | $1,933 | $1,725 | $1,584 |
| Retail and other | 1,116 | 953 | 841 |
| Total revenues | 3,049 | 2,678 | 2,425 |
| Operating expenses | 1,334 | 1,236 | 1,182 |
| Selling, general, administrative, and other | 794 | 687 | 597 |
| Depreciation and amortization | 105 | 78 | 39 |
| Equity in the income of investees | — | — | 2 |
| Operating Income | $ 816 | $ 677 | $ 609 |

*Source:* The Walt Disney Company 2011 10-K.

the company and it will continue to be relatively small. We've said that we're targeting 2013 as a year of profitability. It's about time, because we've invested a fair amount . . . Our goal now and our strategy is to diversify our gaming efforts. Some modest investment on the console front, very Disney-branded and Marvel-branded, some investment on the mobile front, and investment on the social games front.

Operating results for Disney's Interactive Media division for fiscal 2009 through fiscal 2011 are presented in Exhibit 8. The company's consolidated statements of income for fiscal 2009 through fiscal 2011 are presented in Exhibit 9. The Walt Disney Company's balance sheets for fiscal 2010 and fiscal 2011 are presented in Exhibit 10.

**EXHIBIT 8   Operating Results for Walt Disney's Interactive Media Business Unit, Fiscal 2009–Fiscal 2011 (in millions)**

| | 2011 | 2010 | 2009 |
|---|---|---|---|
| Revenues | | | |
| Game sales and subscriptions | $ 768 | $ 563 | $ 565 |
| Advertising and other | 214 | 198 | 147 |
| Total revenues | 982 | 761 | 712 |
| Operating expenses | 732 | 581 | 623 |
| Selling, general, administrative, and other | 504 | 371 | 336 |
| Depreciation and amortization | 54 | 43 | 50 |
| Equity in the income of investees | — | — | 2 |
| Operating Loss | $(308) | $(234) | $(295) |

*Source:* The Walt Disney Company 2011 10-K.

**EXHIBIT 9   Consolidated Statements of Income for The Walt Disney Company, Fiscal 2009–Fiscal 2011 (in millions, except per share data)**

| | 2011 | 2010 | 2009 |
|---|---|---|---|
| Revenues | $40,893 | $38,063 | $36,149 |
| Costs and expenses | 33,112 | 31,337 | 30,452 |
| Restructuring and impairment charges | 55 | 270 | 492 |
| Add: Other income | 75 | 140 | 342 |
| Net interest expense | 343 | 409 | 466 |
| Add: Equity in the income of investees | 585 | 440 | 577 |
| Income before income taxes | 8,043 | 6,627 | 5,658 |
| Income taxes | 2,785 | 2,314 | 2,049 |
| Net Income | 5,258 | 4,313 | 3,609 |
| Less: Net Income attributable to noncontrolling interests | 451 | 350 | 302 |
| Net Income attributable to The Walt Disney Company (Disney) | $ 4,807 | $ 3,963 | $ 3,307 |
| Earnings per share attributable to Disney: | | | |
| Diluted | $2.52 | $2.03 | $1.76 |
| Basic | $2.56 | $2.07 | $1.78 |
| Weighted average number of common and common equivalent shares outstanding: | | | |
| Diluted | 1,909 | 1,948 | 1,875 |
| Basic | 1,878 | 1,915 | 1,856 |

*Source:* The Walt Disney Company 2011 10-K.

**EXHIBIT 10** Consolidated Balance Sheets for The Walt Disney Company, Fiscal 2010–Fiscal 2011 (in millions, except per share data)

|  | October 1, 2011 | October 2, 2010 |
|---|---|---|
| ASSETS | | |
| Current assets | | |
|   Cash and cash equivalents | $ 3,185 | $ 2,722 |
|   Receivables | 6,182 | 5,784 |
|   Inventories | 1,595 | 1,442 |
|   Television costs | 674 | 678 |
|   Deferred income taxes | 1,487 | 1,018 |
|   Other current assets | 634 | 581 |
|   Total current assets | 13,757 | 12,225 |
| Film and television costs | 4,357 | 4,773 |
| Investments | 2,435 | 2,513 |
| Parks, resorts, and other property, at cost | | |
|   Attractions, buildings, and equipment | 35,515 | 32,875 |
|   Accumulated depreciation | (19,572) | (18,373) |
|  | 15,943 | 14,502 |
| Projects in progress | 2,625 | 2,180 |
| Land | 1,127 | 1,124 |
|  | 19,695 | 17,806 |
| Intangible assets, net | 5,121 | 5,081 |
| Goodwill | 24,145 | 24,100 |
| Other assets | 2,614 | 2,708 |
|   Total assets | $72,124 | $69,206 |
| LIABILITIES AND EQUITY | | |
| Current liabilities | | |
|   Accounts payable and other accrued liabilities | $ 6,362 | $ 6,109 |
|   Current portion of borrowings | 3,055 | 2,350 |
|   Unearned royalties and other advances | 2,671 | 2,541 |
|   Total current liabilities | 12,088 | 11,000 |
| Borrowings | 10,922 | 10,130 |
| Deferred income taxes | 2,866 | 2,630 |
| Other long-term liabilities | 6,795 | 6,104 |
| Commitments and contingencies | | |
| Equity | | |
| Preferred stock, $.01 par value | | |
| Authorized—100 million shares, Issued—none | — | — |
| Common stock, $.01 par value | | |
| Authorized—4.6 billion shares, Issued—2.7 billion shares | 30,296 | 28,736 |
| Retained earnings | 38,375 | 34,327 |
| Accumulated other comprehensive loss | (2,630) | (1,881) |
|  | 66,041 | 61,182 |
| Treasury stock, at cost, 937.8 million shares at October 1, 2011 and 803.1 million shares at October 2, 2010 | (28,656) | (23,663) |
| Total Disney Shareholder's equity | 37,385 | 37,519 |
| Noncontrolling interests | 2,068 | 1,823 |
| Total Equity | 39,453 | 39,342 |
|   Total liabilities and equity | $72,124 | $69,206 |

*Source:* The Walt Disney Company 2011 10-K.

# THE WALT DISNEY COMPANY'S THIRD QUARTER 2012 PERFORMANCE AND ITS FUTURE PROSPECTS

The Walt Disney Company recorded record earnings per share during its first nine months of fiscal 2012 with its media networks division achieving an 8 percent period-over-period increase in operating profit, its parks and resorts division seeing a 24 percent increase in operating profits, its studio entertainment division operating profit increasing by 28 percent, and its consumer electronics operating profit increasing by 10 percent between the first nine months of 2011 and the same period in 2012. The operating loss for Disney's interactive division decreased from $214 million for the nine months ended July 2, 2011 to $140 million for the nine months ending June 30, 2012. Disney CEO Bob Iger summarized the company's position at mid-2012.[13]

I can say I look back at the last year and breaking ground in Shanghai, launching two new cruise ships, opening up *Cars Land* in a couple of weeks, buying a media company in India, buying a network in Russia to brand the Disney Channel, all big—and buying our stock back and increasing our dividend and, I think, proving to the world that the Marvel acquisition was a strong acquisition. So it's been, I'll call it a rich and aggressive time, one that we feel good about in terms of the impact on our bottom line, both current and future. And we'll continue to look opportunistically. We obviously have demonstrated that we're not averse to allocating capital in multiple directions.

## ENDNOTES

[1] As quoted by Bob Iger, Chairman and Chief Executive Officer of The Walt Disney Company, during the Sanford C. Bernstein Strategic Decisions Conference, May 30, 2012.

[2] Ibid.

[3] As quoted by Jay Rasulo, Senior Executive Vice President and Chief Financial Officer of The Walt Disney Company, during the Nomura U.S. Media, Cable, and Telecom Summit, May 30, 2012.

[4] As quoted by Bob Iger, Chairman and Chief Executive Officer of The Walt Disney Company, during the Sanford C. Bernstein Strategic Decisions Conference, May 30, 2012.

[5] Ibid.

[6] Ibid.

[7] Ibid.

[8] Ibid.

[9] As quoted by Jay Rasulo, Senior Executive Vice President and Chief Financial Officer of The Walt Disney Company, during the Nomura U.S. Media, Cable, and Telecom Summit, May 30, 2012.

[10] As quoted by Bob Iger, Chairman and Chief Executive Officer of The Walt Disney Company, during the Sanford C. Bernstein Strategic Decisions Conference, May 30, 2012.

[11] Ibid.

[12] Ibid.

[13] Ibid.

# Kraft Foods Inc.: Will the Spinoff of Its North American Grocery Business Lead to Increased Shareholder Value?

## John E. Gamble
### University of South Alabama

Kraft Foods Inc. was the world's second-largest processed foods company in 2012, with annual revenues of more than $54 billion in 2011. The company's global lineup of brands included Maxwell House, Oreo, Cadbury, Chips Ahoy!, Honey Maid, Dentyne, Velveeta, Cheez Whiz, Oscar Mayer, and Kraft. In all, the company had 12 brands, with annual revenues exceeding $1 billion each, and approximately 80 brands that generated annual revenues of more than $100 million each. The company was organized by geographic region and product sector. The majority of Kraft Foods' brands held number-one market shares in their product categories, which created strong business units in North America, Europe, and developing markets.

Even though Kraft Foods' business units produced strong profits, slow growth in the processed foods industry in North America and parts of Europe had restricted the company's ability to deliver increases in shareholder value. In fact, the trading range of the company's shares in 2011 was relatively unchanged from that in 2007 when it became an independent company after a spinoff by the Altria Group (formerly Philip Morris). Some of the lackluster growth in its share price could be attributed to the economic slowdown that began in 2007 and inflationary forces that began in 2010, but the company's upper management and its board believed the underlying cause of its poor market performance was a corporate strategy that was not sufficiently focused on growth. A summary of Kraft Foods Inc.'s financial performance between 2007 and 2011 is presented in Exhibit 1.

The company's board announced in August 2011 that Kraft Foods Inc. would spin off its North American grocery business, with the transaction to be completed by year-end 2012. The restructuring would create a high-growth global snacks business and a high-margin North American grocery business. The new snacks-oriented company would include all of Kraft Foods' business units and brands in Europe and developing markets, plus its U.S. snacks business, and would be named Mondelez International. Mondelez (pronounced mohn-dah-Leez) was a newly coined word that drew upon *mundus,* the Latin root for the word "world," and "delez," which was meant as an expression for "delicious." The creators of the name added "International" to capture the global nature of the business. The remainder of the company's Kraft Foods North American business unit would become known as Kraft Foods Group upon completion of the spinoff.

Kraft Foods Inc.'s chairman and CEO Irene Rosenfeld suggested that the planned spinoff and restructuring would unleash the company's potential to create value for shareholders. "The Kraft brand is a perfect fit for the North American grocery business and gives it a wonderful platform on which to build an exciting future," she commented. "For the new global snacks company, we wanted to find a new name that could serve as an umbrella for our iconic brands, reinforce the truly global nature of this business and build on our higher purpose—to 'make today delicious.' Mondelez perfectly captures the idea of a 'delicious world' and will serve as a solid foundation for the strong relationships we want to create with our consumers, customers, employees and shareholders."[1]

Going into late 2012, the company's sales volume had stalled, but steady price increases for its best-known products and ongoing efforts to control expenses had produced an increase in operating profits of nearly

# EXHIBIT 1   Financial Summary for Kraft Foods Inc., 2007–2011 (in millions, except per share amounts)

| Year Ended December 31: | 2011 | 2010 | 2009 | 2008 | 2007 |
|---|---|---|---|---|---|
| Net revenues | $54,365 | $49,207 | $38,754 | $40,492 | $34,580 |
| Cost of sales | 35,350 | 31,305 | 24,819 | 27,164 | 22,848 |
| Operating income | 6,657 | 5,666 | 5,183 | 3,576 | 3,939 |
| *Operating margin* | *12.20%* | *11.5%* | *13.4%* | *8.8%* | *11.4%* |
| Interest and other expense, net | 1,885 | 2,024 | 1,237 | 1,240 | 604 |
| Earnings from continuing operations before income taxes | 4,772 | 3,642 | 3,946 | 2,336 | 3,335 |
| Provision for income taxes | 1,225 | 1,147 | 1,136 | 658 | 992 |
| Earnings from continuing operations | 3,547 | 2,495 | 2,810 | 1,678 | 2,343 |
| Earnings and gain from discontinued operations, net of income taxes | – | 1,644 | 218 | 1,215 | 381 |
| Net earnings | 3,547 | 4,139 | 3,028 | 2,893 | 2,724 |
| Noncontrolling interest | 20 | 25 | 7 | 9 | 3 |
| Net earnings attributable to Kraft Foods | $ 3,527 | $ 4,114 | $ 3,021 | $ 2,884 | $ 2,721 |
| **Basic EPS attributable to Kraft Foods:** | | | | | |
| Continuing operations | $2.00 | $1.44 | $1.90 | $1.11 | $1.47 |
| Discontinued operations | – | 0.96 | 0.14 | 0.81 | 0.24 |
| Net earnings attributable to Kraft Foods | $2.00 | $2.40 | $2.04 | $1.92 | $1.71 |
| **Diluted EPS attributable to Kraft Foods:** | | | | | |
| Continuing operations | $1.99 | $1.44 | $1.89 | $1.10 | $1.46 |
| Discontinued operations | – | 0.95 | 0.14 | 0.8 | 0.24 |
| Net earnings attributable to Kraft Foods | $1.99 | $2.39 | $2.03 | $1.90 | $1.70 |
| Weighted-average shares-basic | 1,765 | 1,715 | 1,478 | 1,505 | 1,591 |
| Weighted-average shares-diluted | 1,772 | 1,720 | 1,486 | 1,515 | 1,600 |
| Net cash provided by operating activities | $4,520 | $3,748 | $5,084 | $4,141 | $3,571 |
| Capital expenditures | 1,771 | 1,661 | 1,330 | 1,367 | 1,241 |
| Depreciation | 1,260 | 1,229 | 905 | 963 | 873 |
| **As of December 31:** | | | | | |
| Inventories, net | $5,706 | $5,310 | $3,775 | $3,881 | $4,238 |
| Property, plant, and equipment, net | 13,813 | 13,792 | 10,693 | 9,917 | 10,778 |
| Total assets | 93,837 | 95,289 | 66,714 | 63,173 | 68,132 |
| Long-term debt | 23,095 | 26,859 | 18,024 | 18,589 | 12,902 |
| Total debt | 26,931 | 28,724 | 18,990 | 20,251 | 21,009 |
| Total long-term liabilities | 40,064 | 43,454 | 29,251 | 29,773 | 23,574 |
| Total Kraft Foods shareholders' equity | 35,217 | 35,834 | 25,876 | 22,295 | 27,407 |

*(Continued)*

## EXHIBIT 1   *(Concluded)*

| Year Ended December 31: | 2011 | 2010 | 2009 | 2008 | 2007 |
|---|---|---|---|---|---|
| Total equity | 35,328 | 35,942 | 25,972 | 22,356 | 27,445 |
| Shares outstanding at year end | 1,768 | 1,748 | 1,478 | 1,469 | 1,534 |
| Book value per common share outstanding | $19.92 | $20.50 | $17.51 | $15.18 | $17.87 |
| Dividends declared per share | 1.16 | 1.16 | 1.16 | 1.12 | 1.04 |
| Dividends as a % of basic/diluted EPS | 58.0%/58.3% | 48.3%/48.5% | 56.9%/57.1% | 58.3%/58.9% | 60.8% / 61.2% |
| Common stock closing price at year end | $37.36 | $31.51 | $27.18 | $26.85 | $32.63 |
| Common stock price—high/low | $37.93/$30.21 | $32.67/$27.09 | $29.84/$20.81 | $34.97/$24.75 | $37.20/$29.95 |
| Price/earnings ratio—basic/diluted | 19/19 | 13/13 | 13/13 | 14/14 | 19/19 |
| Number of employees | 126,000 | 127,000 | 97,000 | 98,000 | 103,000 |

*Source:* Kraft Foods Inc. 2011 10-K.

10 percent for the first six months of 2012. While dividing the company to produce a high-margin North American processed food company and a separate high-growth international snacks company might prove to lead to higher returns for shareholders, it was uncertain if a mere division of Kraft Foods Inc. would accelerate growth in revenues and profits for either new company.

## COMPANY HISTORY

Kraft Food's marquee brands all had rich histories that began with the efforts of entrepreneurs who were inspired to launch new businesses that could provide consumers with value and support for their families. The history of the namesake Kraft company began in Chicago in 1903 when J. L. Kraft began purchasing cheese from a wholesale market and reselling it to local merchants. J. L. Kraft began his venture with a single horse-drawn wagon but, by 1914, the company's sales grew to such a level that Kraft engaged the help of his brothers to purchase a cheese factory. The Kraft Cheese Company's sales continued to increase throughout the 1920s and 1930s with the introduction of new products such as Velveeta processed cheese, Miracle Whip salad dressing, and Kraft macaroni and cheese dinner. The majority of the brands included in Kraft Foods' business lineup in 2012 had similar growth trajectories during the early-1900s, with Maxwell House and Jacobs coffee brands, Nabisco-branded cookies

and crackers, Planters peanuts, Kool-Aid drink mix, JELL-O desserts, and Oscar Mayer meats all becoming market-leading national brands by the 1930s.

Kraft Foods' possession of such brands resulted from a series of mergers and acquisitions dating to 1928 when the Kraft Cheese Company merged with Phenix Cheese Corporation, the maker of Philadelphia cream cheese. The proliferation of brands owned by Kraft accelerated in 1988 when Philip Morris Companies purchased Kraft for $12.9 billion. Philip Morris' acquisition of Kraft was part of a corporate strategy focused on diversifying the company beyond its well-known cigarette business, which included the Marlboro, Virginia Slims, Parliament, and Basic brands. At the time of the acquisition of Kraft, Philip Morris had already acquired brands such as Oscar Mayer, Tang, JELL-O, Crystal Light, and Post cereals through the 1985 acquisition of General Foods for $5.6 billion. The addition of the company's Nabisco brands came about through Philip Morris' $18.9 billion acquisition of that company in 2000. Kraft Foods' return to independence began in 2001, when Philip Morris (renamed Altria Group in 2003) began the divestiture of its non-tobacco related businesses to protect those business assets from tobacco litigation. Phillip Morris first sold an 11 percent interest in the company through a 2001 initial public offering (IPO) and then spun off its remaining interest in the company through a tax-free dividend to Altria Group shareholders in 2007.

# KRAFT FOODS' CORPORATE STRATEGY AS AN INDEPENDENT COMPANY

Philip Morris' June 2001 IPO of Kraft Foods netted about $8 billion that the company used to repay about one-half of the $15 billion borrowed to acquire Nabisco in 2000. The IPO was the second-largest in history at the time and created the second-largest processed food company in the world. Only Nestlé's sales of about $50 billion in 2000 exceeded Kraft Foods' revenues of $33.9 billion in 2000. By the time the Altria Group had spun off its remaining interest in Kraft Foods in 2007, the company remained the second-largest processed foods company, with worldwide sales of $34.6 billion in 2006. Immediately after the spinoff from Philip Morris, Kraft Foods acquired Groupe Danone's European cracker and cookie business for $7.6 billion. In 2008, Kraft Foods spun off its Post cereals business as a tax-free distribution to shareholders. Post cereals included brands such as Honey Bunches of Oats, Pebbles, Shredded Wheat, Selects, Grape Nuts, and Honeycomb and recorded sales of $1.1 billion in 2007. Kraft Foods sold its North American pizza business to Nestlé in 2010 for $3.7 billion. Kraft's frozen pizza brands included the DiGiorno, Tombstone, and Jack's brands in the United States and the Delissio brand in Canada. The company's divested pizza business also produced and distributed California Pizza Kitchen–branded frozen pizzas under license. Also in 2010, Kraft Foods spent $18. 5 billion to acquire United Kingdom-based Cadbury, which was the maker of Cadbury chocolates, Halls cough drops, Clorets breath-freshening gum, and Trident, Dentyne, and Stride chewing gum.

By 2011, Kraft Foods remained the world's second-largest food company, but had increased revenues to $54.4 billion through its acquisition of Cadbury and via organic growth. Kraft's business operations spanned more than 80 countries and included 220 manufacturing and processing facilities and 228 distribution centers in the United States, Europe, Latin America, and the Asia Pacific region. The company also operated 15 new product development centers in North America, Europe, Latin America, and China. Because of the nature of the company's products and varying government regulations governing food products, each region where Kraft Foods competed required dedicated facilities for the manufacture of its products. Also, most types of food products manufactured by Kraft Foods involved processes that required dedicated facilities. For example, the processes involved in the manufacture and packaging of crackers were quite different from those involved in the production of chocolates or cheese.

Beyond restructuring their business lineup, Kraft Foods' corporate strategy as an independent company involved addressing weaknesses in its core businesses. The company's product development processes at the time of the spinoff had become stale and insular, and as a result, Kraft Foods had not created any successful new products in years. Also, in 2006, the company's divisions operated under a highly centralized structure that aggressively managed costs—even at the expense of such competitively important activities as advertising support, new product development, and quality assurance. By 2009, the company had replaced 80 percent of its management in leadership positions, changed its organizational structure to fix accountability at the business unit level, and had boosted advertising and promotions by $600 million.

The series of divestitures and acquisitions executed between 2007 and 2010 were directed at improving the company's geographic mix, sector mix, and channel mix to increase its number of products in attractive country markets, product sector categories, and distribution channels. Specifically, the company expanded its percentage of cookies and confectionery products (a high-margin growth product sector) from 29 percent of sales in 2006 to 50 percent of sales in 2010. Also, the restructuring resulted in sales in rapidly growing developing markets increasing from 13 percent of sales in 2006 to 28 percent of sales in 2010. The company also shifted its channel mix to double its percentage of sales in convenience store channels from 10 percent to 20 percent to avoid its dependence on the consolidating supermarket industry that was comprised primarily of large, powerful buyers.

The restructuring moves gave Kraft Foods more than 80 brands with annual revenues of over $100 million each and 12 brands with more than $1 billion each in annual revenues. In addition, the majority of Kraft Foods' brands in 2012 held number-one positions in their respective product categories. The strength of the overall business lineup allowed Kraft Foods to lead the processed foods industry in terms of EPS growth in 2011. Exhibit 2 presents Kraft Foods' brands by business segment in 2011.

The company's planned spinoff of its North American grocery business in late-2012 would result in Kraft Foods Group, Inc. retaining U.S. Beverages, U.S. Cheese, U.S. Convenience Meals, U.S. Grocery, and Canada and N.A. Foodservice. The newly created

**EXHIBIT 2**  **Kraft Foods' Brands by Business Segment Prior to Its Planned Spinoff of Its North American Grocery Business**

| Kraft Foods North America |
| --- |

**U.S. Beverages**

Beverages:   *Maxwell House, Gevalia, Maxwell House International* and *Yuban* coffees; *Tassimo* hot beverage system; *Capri Sun* (under license) and *Kool-Aid* packaged juice drinks; *Kool-Aid, Crystal Light, Tang,* and *Country Time* powdered beverages; and *MiO* liquid concentrate.

**U.S. Cheese**

Cheese:   *Kraft* and *Cracker Barrel* natural cheeses; *Philadelphia* cream cheese; *Kraft* grated cheeses; *Polly-O* and *Athenos* cheese; *Velveeta* and *Cheez Whiz* processed cheeses; *Kraft* and *Deli Deluxe* processed cheese slices; and *Breakstone's* and *Knudsen* cottage cheese and sour cream.

**U.S. Convenient Meals**

Convenient Meals:   *Oscar Mayer* cold cuts, hot dogs and bacon; *Lunchables* lunch combinations; *Boca* soy-based meat alternatives; and *Claussen* pickles.

**U.S. Grocery**

Grocery:   *JELL-O* dry-packaged desserts; *Cool Whip* whipped topping; *JELL-O* refrigerated gelatin and pudding snacks; *Jet-Puffed* marshmallows; *Kraft* and *Miracle Whip* spoonable dressings; *Kraft* and *Good Seasons* salad dressings; *A.1.* steak sauce; *Kraft* and *Bull's-Eye* barbecue sauces; *Grey Poupon* premium mustards; *Planters* peanut butter; *Shake N' Bake* coatings; and *Baker's* chocolate and baking ingredients.

Convenient Meals:   *Kraft* and *Kraft Deluxe* macaroni and cheese dinners; *Stove Top* stuffing mix; *Taco Bell Home Originals* (under license) meal kits; and *Velveeta* shells and cheese dinners.

**U.S. Snacks**

Biscuits:   *Oreo, Chips Ahoy!, Newtons, Nilla, Nutter Butter, LU* and *SnackWell's* cookies; *Ritz, Premium, Triscuit, Wheat Thins, Cheese Nips, Flavor Originals, Honey Maid* grahams, *Teddy Grahams* crackers, *Nabisco* 100 Calorie Packs; *Planters* nuts and trail mixes; *Handi-Snacks* two-compartment snacks; and *Back to Nature* granola, cookies, crackers, nuts, and fruit and nut mixes.

Confectionery:   *Toblerone, Trident, Halls, Stride, Dentyne, Sour Patch Kids, Swedish Fish, Maynards, Bubbas, Chiclets, Milka* bars, and *Clorets.*

**Canada & N.A. Foodservice**   Canada & N.A Foodservice products span all Kraft Foods North America segments and sectors. Canadian brand offerings include *Nabob* coffee, *Kraft* peanut butter and *Peek Freans* biscuits, as well as a range of products bearing brand names similar to those marketed in the U.S. The N.A. Foodservice business sells primarily branded products, including *Maxwell House* coffee, *Oreo* cookies, *A.1.* steak sauce, and a broad array of *Kraft* sauces, dressings, and cheeses.

| Kraft Foods Europe |
| --- |

Biscuits:   *Oreo, Digestive, Tuc, Mikado* (under license), *Ourson, Petit Déjeuner, Cracotte, Belin, Heudebert, Grany, Petit Écolier, Oro, Fonzies, Prince/Principe, Belvita, LU, Pepito, Vitalinea* (under license), *Milka, Cote d'Or, Chips Ahoy!, Liga, Ritz, Fontaneda, Cipster, PiM's, Granola, Napolitain, Paille D'Or,* and *Pelletier* biscuits.

Confectionery:   *Milka, Marabou, Cote D'Or, Toblerone, Freia, Suchard, Lacta, Pavlides, Mirabell, Terry's, Daim / Dime, Twist, Cadbury Dairy Milk, Roses, Creme Egg, Twirl, Flake, Crunchie, Heroes / Favourites, Wispa, Mini Eggs, Green and Black's, Buttons, Milk Tray, Double Decker, Moro / Boost, Timeout, Trident, Hollywood, Stimorol, Halls, Bassetts, Maynards, Trebor, Carambar, Poulain, La Pie Qui Chante, V6, TNCC, Cadbury Eclairs, Malabar, Bubbas, Bubblicious,* and *La Vosgienne.*

Beverages:   *Jacobs, Gevalia, Carte Noire, Jacques Vabre, Kaffee HAG, Grand' Mère, Kenco, Saimaza, Maxwell House, Onko,* and *Splendid* coffees; *Tassimo* hot beverage system; and *Suchard Express, O'Boy* and *Cadbury* chocolate drinks.

Cheese:   *Dairylea, Sottilette, Osella* and *El Caserío* cheeses; and *Philadelphia* cream cheese.

*(Continued)*

**EXHIBIT 2**    *(Concluded)*

| Kraft Foods Europe | |
| --- | --- |
| Grocery: | *Kraft* pourable and spoonable salad dressings; *Miracle Whip* spoonable dressings; *Royal* dry-packaged desserts; and *Mirácoli* sauces. |
| Convenient Meals: | *Lunchables* lunch combinations; *Mirácoli* pasta dinners and sauces; and *Simmenthal* canned meats. |

| Kraft Foods Developing Markets | |
| --- | --- |
| Biscuits: | *Oreo, Chips Ahoy!, Ritz, Club Social, Express, Kraker Bran, Honey Bran, Aveny Bran, Marbu, Variedad, Pacific, Belvita, Cerealitas, Lucky, Trakinas, Tuc, Mikado* (under license), *Ourson, Petit Déjeuner, Cracotte, Bolshevik, Prichuda, Jubilee, Major, Merendina, Jacob's, Chipsmore, Biskuat / Tiger, Milka, Hi Calcium Soda, Pépito, PiM's/Delicje, LU, Barny / Gyoeri Edes, Prince/Principe, Utrenne/Jo Regge, U'Guan, Premium, San, Jai Gai* and *Newtons* biscuits; and *Estrella, Twisties, Cheezels, Chachos, Kar, Lux* and *Planters* nuts and salted snacks. |
| Confectionery: | *Milka, Toblerone, Lacta, Côte d'Or, Terrabusi, Kent, Kan, Alpen Gold, Korona, Poiana, Svoge, Vozdushny, Figaro, Prince Polo / Siesta, Sport / Smash / Jazz / Moreni, Cadbury Dairy Milk, Picnic, 5 Star, Cadbury Heroes / Favourites, Flake, Crunchie, Perk, Old Gold, Freddo, Cherry Ripe, Moro / Boost, Roses, Trident, Halls, Clorets, Bubbas, Dirol, Chiclets, Eclairs, Beldent, Dentyne, Recaldent, Xylicrystal, Falim, TNCC, Tom Tom, Bournville, 3-Bit, Pascall, Chappies, First, Stride, Stimorol.* |
| Beverages: | *Tang, Bournvita, Clight, Kool-Aid, Fresh, Frisco, Cadbury* and *Capri Sun* beverages; *Jacobs, Maxwell House,* and *Carte Noire* coffees. |
| Cheese: | *Kraft, Velveeta,* and *Eden* processed cheeses; *Philadelphia* cream cheese; *Kraft* natural cheese; and *Cheez Whiz* processed cheese spread. |
| Grocery: | *Royal* dry packaged desserts; *Kraft* spoonable and pourable salad dressings; *Miracle Whip* spoonable dressings; *JELL-O* dessert toppings; *Kraft* peanut butter; and *Vegemite* yeast spread. |
| Convenient Meals: | *Kraft* macaroni and cheese dinners; *Velveeta* boxed dinners; *Lunchables* lunch combinations; and *Oscar Mayer* cold cuts. |

*Source:* Kraft Foods Inc. 1011 10-K.

Mondelez International would retain the company's U.S. snacks business unit and all of the operations and brands included in its Kraft Foods Europe and Kraft Foods Developing Markets business units. The company's revenues by business segment and consumer sector for 2011 are presented in Exhibit 3.

## KRAFT FOODS' BUSINESS SEGMENT PERFORMANCE IN 2011

Kraft Foods' corporate strategy was directed at building a globally dominant snacks business, leveraging its heritage foods brands, and creating a performance-driven corporate culture that would bring about profitable growth capable of generating attractive returns for shareholders. The company also expected to reduce overhead and administrative costs to provide for additional investments in marketing and innovation. Also,

the company was focused on achieving synergies existing between its business units, especially with recent acquisitions. Kraft Foods expected that the integration of Cadbury's operations would result in cost savings of $750 million by 2012 and would also create revenue synergies from marketing and product development innovations. Resource allocation decisions for Kraft Foods' business segments were based upon the opportunities and past operating performance of each unit.

All of Kraft Foods business segments competed in industries that were characterized by strong competitive rivalry that required strong distribution and marketing skills to attract consumer demand and ensure product availability in supermarkets, discount clubs, mass merchandisers, convenience stores, drug stores, and retail food locations serviced by its food distribution operations. Brand building, consumer health and wellness, and advertising and promotions were all critical to success in the industry. In fact, Kraft Foods' ability to compete against lower-priced branded and

**EXHIBIT 3   Kraft Foods' Percentage of Revenues by Business Segment and Consumer Sector, 2011**

| Business Segment | Consumer Segment | | | | | | Business Segment Percentage of Total Kraft Foods |
| --- | --- | --- | --- | --- | --- | --- | --- |
| | Biscuits | Confectionery | Beverages | Cheese | Grocery | Convenient Meals | |
| Kraft Foods North America: | | | | | | | |
| U.S. Beverages | – | – | 31.1% | – | – | – | 5.5% |
| U.S. Cheese | – | – | – | 49.4% | – | – | 7.0% |
| U.S. Convenient Meals | – | – | – | – | – | 62.8% | 6.1% |
| U.S. Grocery | – | 1.0% | – | – | 52.9% | 22.5% | 6.6% |
| U.S. Snacks | 42.8% | 6.9% | – | 0.8% | 1.1% | – | 11.6% |
| Canada & N.A. Foodservice | 7.5% | 4.5% | 6.1% | 21.6% | 22.0% | 7.2% | 9.5% |
| Total Kraft Foods North America | 50.3% | 12.4% | 37.2% | 71.8% | 76.0% | 92.5% | 46.3% |
| Kraft Foods Europe | 21.7% | 37.4% | 32.6% | 15.3% | 8.7% | 5.1% | 24.6% |
| Kraft Foods Developing Markets | 28.0% | 50.2% | 30.2% | 12.9% | 15.3% | 2.4% | 29.1% |
| Total Kraft Foods | 100.0% | 100.0% | 100.0% | 100.0% | 100.0% | 100.0% | 100.0% |
| Consumer Sector Percentage of Total Kraft Foods | 22.1% | 28.5% | 17.8% | 14.2% | 7.7% | 9.7% | 100.0% |

*Source:* Kraft Foods Inc. 2011 10-K.

store-brand products was a function of its ability to successfully differentiate its products from lower-priced alternatives. Also, differentiation was essential to retaining shelf space as the retail grocery industry consolidated and provided retailers with greater leverage in negotiations with food manufacturers. The company's successful differentiation of its products had also allowed it to achieve organic revenue growth of 6.0 percent in 2011 through net price increases.

The company's processed foods divisions had experienced cost increases as inflationary forces had led to higher prices for commodities used in the manufacture of its products such as coffee, cocoa, oils, nuts, and sugar. For example, Kraft Foods' commodity costs in 2010 were $1 billion higher than in 2009 and increased an additional $2.6 billion between 2010 and 2011. However, Kraft Foods' price increases made possible by its strong product differentiation had more than offset the increased cost of commodity inputs in 2011. Also, the production of Kraft Foods' products was regulated by the U.S. Food and Drug Administration in the United States, and similar organizations in the 170 countries where its products were sold. In addition, the company's packaging practices were regulated by governmental agencies in the United States and the European Union.

**Kraft Foods North America**   In 2011, Kraft Foods North America's U.S. Beverages business unit experienced declining revenues and segment operating profit because of the loss of its licensing agreement with Starbucks that allowed it to roast, package, and distribute Starbucks-branded premium coffees in supermarkets and other retail grocery locations and because of the decline in shipments of its mainstream Maxwell House and Gevalia coffee brands. However, Maxwell House was the number-one brand of packaged coffee sold in the United States, with a 20 percent market share and sales that were 1.3 times that of its nearest competitor. Although coffee sales had declined in 2011, the segment's sales of MiO liquid concentrate, Capri Sun, Kool-Aid, and Tassimo coffee improved from 2010 to 2011. For the most part, all of Kraft Foods' U.S. beverage brands competed in slowing declining product categories, although the premium specialty coffee segment offered attractive growth and profitability. The loss of Starbucks branded packaged coffee left Kraft Foods without a viable brand in this segment in 2012.

Kraft Foods U.S. Cheese division also competed in a slow-growing food category, but had been able to achieve growth in revenues and operating profit through price increases. However, the company's Philadelphia brand was the number-one brand of cream cheese sold in the United States with a 37 percent market share and recorded 2011 sales that were

280 percent greater than the sales of the nearest competitor. Volume sales of U.S. Convenience Meals such as bacon, hot dogs, cold cuts, and Lunchables combination meals were also declining slowly in 2011, but the division had also been able to achieve growth in revenues and operating profit through price increases that averaged about 6 percent during the year. Volume sales of spoonable dressings, ready-to-eat desserts, barbecue sauces, and dessert toppings were declining by as much as 3 percent per year, but the U.S. Grocery division's revenues and operating profits had increased during 2011 as a result of price increases and higher sales of Kraft macaroni and cheese dinners. A 5 percent price increase in the company's U.S. Snacks division also helped the division achieve revenue and operating income growth in 2011, despite lower shipments of crackers and only modest volume growth in the cookie segment. Nabisco was the leading brand of crackers and cookies with a worldwide market share of 16 percent and had revenues in 2011 that were 1.7 times larger than its nearest competitor.

## Kraft Foods Europe and Kraft Foods Developing Markets

The only business unit within Kraft Foods' North America segment to compete in an attractively growing section of the food industry was its Canada and N.A. Foodservice unit. The Kraft business unit that delivered Kraft- and Cadbury-branded products to restaurants, cafeterias, and other dining establishments experienced a nearly 10 percent increase in revenues in 2011 and an almost 20 percent increase in revenues in 2010. The division's increase in revenues was partly attributable to the addition of Cadbury's brands, as well as net pricing increases of about 5 percent in 2011 and 2 percent in 2010. Another factor contributing to its growth was the increase in the number of meals eaten away from home in Canada and the United States.

The Kraft Foods Europe business segment also experienced strong revenue and operating growth in 2010 and 2011 as a result of the Cadbury acquisition, net price increases, and growth in demand for cheese, crackers and cookies, and chocolate in Europe. The company held a number-one position in the $335 billion snack foods industry in Europe, which was growing 1.4 times faster than the overall European processed foods industry. While growth in the processed foods industry in Europe was attractive, developing markets in Latin America and Asia offered the most attractive growth opportunities for Kraft Foods, Nestlé, and other food companies in 2011. Revenues and operating profits for the Kraft Foods Developing Markets business segment grew rapidly between 2009 and 2011 as consumer demand for processed foods increased and markets supported price increases that approached 10 percent in 2011. However, high inflation and rapid currency devaluations in some developing markets resulted in a $115 million exchange rate loss for the division in 2010. A financial summary providing revenues, operating profit, total assets, depreciation expense, and capital expenditures for Kraft Foods' business segments for 2009 through 2011 is provided in Exhibit 4. Exhibit 5 presents Kraft Foods' revenues by product type and geographic region for 2009 through 2011.

## EXHIBIT 4  Financial Summary for Kraft Foods' Business Segments, 2009–2011 (in millions)

|  | 2011 | 2010 | 2009 |
|---|---|---|---|
| **Net revenues** |  |  |  |
| Kraft Foods North America: |  |  |  |
| U.S. Beverages | $ 3,006 | $ 3,212 | $ 3,057 |
| U.S. Cheese | 3,810 | 3,528 | 3,605 |
| U.S. Convenient Meals | 3,328 | 3,131 | 3,029 |
| U.S. Grocery | 3,563 | 3,398 | 3,453 |
| U.S. Snacks | 6,329 | 6,001 | 4,964 |
| Canada & N.A. Foodservice | 5,152 | 4,696 | 3,922 |
| Kraft Foods Europe | 13,356 | 11,628 | 8,768 |
| Kraft Foods Developing Markets | 15,821 | 13,613 | 7,956 |
| Net revenues | $54,365 | $49,207 | $38,754 |

*(Continued)*

## EXHIBIT 4   (Continued)

| | 2011 | 2010 | 2009 |
|---|---|---|---|
| **Earnings from continuing operations before income taxes** | | | |
| Operating income: | | | |
| Kraft Foods North America: | | | |
| U.S. Beverages | $    450 | $    564 | $    511 |
| U.S. Cheese | 629 | 598 | 667 |
| U.S. Convenient Meals | 319 | 268 | 234 |
| U.S. Grocery | 1,240 | 1,164 | 1,146 |
| U.S. Snacks | 847 | 845 | 723 |
| Canada & N.A. Foodservice | 682 | 582 | 462 |
| Kraft Foods Europe | 1,406 | 1,115 | 785 |
| Kraft Foods Developing Markets | 2,053 | 1,577 | 936 |
| Unrealized gains / (losses) on hedging activities | (100) | 67 | 203 |
| Certain U.S. pension plan costs | (206) | (179) | (165) |
| General corporate expenses | (438) | (724) | (293) |
| Amortization of intangibles | (225) | (211) | (26) |
| Operating income | 6,657 | 5,666 | 5,183 |
| Interest and other expense, net | (1,885) | (2,024) | (1,237) |
| Earnings from continuing operations before income taxes | $  4,772 | $  3,642 | $  3,946 |
| **Total assets** | | | |
| Kraft Foods North America: | | | |
| U.S. Beverages | $  2,837 | $  2,513 | $  2,382 |
| U.S. Cheese | 4,156 | 4,633 | 4,589 |
| U.S. Convenient Meals | 2,151 | 2,064 | 3,063 |
| U.S. Grocery | 5,142 | 5,574 | 5,565 |
| U.S. Snacks | 20,587 | 20,895 | 16,418 |
| Canada & N.A. Foodservice | 6,989 | 7,207 | 5,051 |
| Kraft Foods Europe | 24,525 | 24,261 | 16,073 |
| Kraft Foods Developing Markets | 24,559 | 25,738 | 11,087 |
| Unallocated assets | 2,891 | 2,404 | 2,486 |
| Total assets | $93,837 | $95,289 | $66,714 |
| **Depreciation expense** | | | |
| Kraft Foods North America: | | | |
| U.S. Beverages | $      66 | $      73 | $      69 |
| U.S. Cheese | 80 | 67 | 66 |
| U.S. Convenient Meals | 83 | 61 | 67 |
| U.S. Grocery | 86 | 88 | 82 |
| U.S. Snacks | 126 | 139 | 127 |
| Canada & N.A. Foodservice | 128 | 110 | 83 |
| Kraft Foods Europe | 354 | 355 | 237 |
| Kraft Foods Developing Markets | 337 | 320 | 157 |
| Total continuing operations | 1,260 | 1,213 | 888 |
| Discontinued operations | — | 16 | 17 |
| Total depreciation expense | $  1,260 | $  1,229 | $    905 |
| **Capital expenditures** | | | |
| Kraft Foods North America: | | | |
| U.S. Beverages | $    121 | $      88 | $      82 |
| U.S. Cheese | 72 | 88 | 72 |
| U.S. Convenient Meals | 88 | 109 | 135 |

(Continued)

## EXHIBIT 4  *(Concluded)*

|  | 2011 | 2010 | 2009 |
|---|---:|---:|---:|
| U.S. Grocery | 74 | 76 | 85 |
| U.S. Snacks | 235 | 245 | 190 |
| Canada & N.A. Foodservice | 90 | 112 | 94 |
| Kraft Foods Europe | 378 | 334 | 292 |
| Kraft Foods Developing Markets | 713 | 607 | 319 |
| Total continuing operations | 1,771 | 1,659 | 1,269 |
| Discontinued operations | — | 2 | 61 |
| Total capital expenditures | $ 1,771 | $ 1,661 | $ 1,330 |

*Source:* Kraft Foods Inc. 2011 10-K.

## EXHIBIT 5  Kraft Foods' Revenues by Product Category, 2009–2011 (in millions)

|  | Kraft Foods North America | Kraft Foods Europe | Kraft Foods Developing Markets | Total |
|---|---:|---:|---:|---:|
| *2011* | | | | |
| Biscuits | $ 6,046 | $ 2,598 | $ 3,366 | $12,010 |
| Confectionery | 1,916 | 5,785 | 7,774 | 15,475 |
| Beverages | 3,598 | 3,158 | 2,917 | 9,673 |
| Cheese | 5,535 | 1,182 | 995 | 7,712 |
| Grocery | 3,188 | 363 | 642 | 4,193 |
| Convenient Meals | 4,905 | 270 | 127 | 5,302 |
| Total net revenues | $25,188 | $13,356 | $15,821 | $54,365 |
| *2010* | | | | |
| Biscuits | $ 5,646 | $ 2,323 | $ 2,806 | $10,775 |
| Confectionery | 1,807 | 5,234 | 6,666 | 13,707 |
| Beverages | 3,741 | 2,511 | 2,536 | 8,788 |
| Cheese | 5,089 | 982 | 904 | 6,975 |
| Grocery | 3,088 | 334 | 579 | 4,001 |
| Convenient Meals | 4,595 | 244 | 122 | 4,961 |
| Total net revenues | $23,966 | $11,628 | $13,613 | $49,207 |
| *2009* | | | | |
| Biscuits | $ 5,628 | $ 2,330 | $ 2,446 | $10,404 |
| Confectionery | 301 | 2,446 | 1,891 | 4,638 |
| Beverages | 3,545 | 2,390 | 2,094 | 8,029 |
| Cheese | 4,980 | 972 | 844 | 6,796 |
| Grocery | 3,136 | 369 | 566 | 4,071 |
| Convenient Meals | 4,440 | 261 | 115 | 4,816 |
| Total net revenues | $22,030 | $ 8,768 | $ 7,956 | $38,754 |

*Source:* Kraft Foods Inc. 2011 10-K.

# KRAFT FOODS' CORPORATE RESTRUCTURING IN 2012

In August 2011, Kraft Foods' board of directors approved the spinoff of its North American grocery business to shareholders, with the transaction expected to be completed by year-end 2012. Under the terms of the proposal, each Kraft Foods Inc. shareholder would receive one share of the newly created Kraft Foods Group for every three shares of Kraft Foods Inc. owned by the shareholder. At the time of the spinoff, Kraft Foods Inc. would change its name to Mondelez

International, Inc. and its ticker symbol would become MDLZ. The KFT ticker symbol would be retired after the transaction. Shares of the newly formed Kraft Foods Group would trade under the ticker symbol KRFT.

The restructuring would create a high-growth global snacks business and a high-margin North American grocery business. Kraft Foods Group would begin its operations with about $19 billion in 2011 revenues and would retain all of the company's business operations and brands in North America, with the exception of the U.S. Snacks business unit. Products such as Kraft macaroni and cheese diner, Capri Sun, Philadelphia cream cheese, and Miracle Whip salad dressing all competed in slow-growth food categories, but offered attractive profit margins. The strategy at Kraft Foods Group would be directed at reducing costs to further enhance margins and achieving modest growth through selective new product introductions. Kraft Foods Group was expected to pay attractive dividends to shareholders.

Mondelez International would begin its operations with about $35 billion in 2011 revenues and would include the U.S. Snacks divisions and all Kraft Foods businesses in Europe and developing markets in Eastern Europe, Asia/Pacific, Middle East/Africa, and South America. It was expected that the new company could achieve industry-leading growth by competing in high-growth categories with ample opportunities for product innovation. Mondelez would focus on its powerful, iconic global brands such as Cadbury, Milka, Toblerone, Oreo, LU, Tassimo, and Jacobs in all international markets, while selectively promoting regional brands with strong growth potential outside the region. The company was expected to pay modest dividends, but make substantial investments in product development and promotional campaigns. Kraft Foods Inc.'s income statements for the three years prior to the planned restructuring are presented in Exhibit 6. The company's balance sheets for 2010 and 2011 are shown in Exhibit 7.

## EXHIBIT 6   Kraft Foods Inc. Income Statements, 2009–2011 (in millions, except per share amounts)

|  | 2011 | 2010 | 2009 |
| --- | --- | --- | --- |
| Net revenues | $54,365 | $49,207 | $38,754 |
| Cost of sales | 35,350 | 31,305 | 24,819 |
| Gross profit | 19,015 | 17,902 | 13,935 |
| Selling, general, and administrative expenses | 12,140 | 12,001 | 8,784 |
| Asset impairment and exit costs | (7) | 18 | (64) |
| Losses on divestitures, net | — | 6 | 6 |
| Amortization of intangibles | 225 | 211 | 26 |
| Operating income | 6,657 | 5,666 | 5,183 |
| Interest and other expense, net | 1,885 | 2,024 | 1,237 |
| Earnings from continuing operations before income taxes | 4,772 | 3,642 | 3,946 |
| Provision for income taxes | 1,225 | 1,147 | 1,136 |
| Earnings from continuing operations | 3,547 | 2,495 | 2,810 |
| Earnings and gain from discontinued operations, net of income taxes | — | 1,644 | 218 |
| Net earnings | 3,547 | 4,139 | 3,028 |
| Noncontrolling interest | 20 | 25 | 7 |
| Net earnings attributable to Kraft Foods | $ 3,527 | $ 4,114 | $ 3,021 |
| Per share data: | | | |
| Basic earnings per share attributable to Kraft Foods: | | | |
| Continuing operations | $2.00 | $1.44 | $1.90 |
| Discontinued operations | — | $0.96 | $0.14 |
| Net earnings attributable to Kraft Foods | $2.00 | $2.40 | $2.04 |
| Diluted earnings per share attributable to Kraft Foods: | | | |

(Continued)

## EXHIBIT 6   (*Concluded*)

|  | 2011 | 2010 | 2009 |
|---|---|---|---|
| Continuing operations | $1.99 | $1.44 | $1.89 |
| Discontinued operations | — | $0.95 | $0.14 |
| Net earnings attributable to Kraft Foods | $1.99 | $2.39 | $2.03 |
| Dividends declared | $1.16 | $1.16 | $1.16 |

*Source:* Kraft Foods Inc. 2011 10-K.

## EXHIBIT 7   Kraft Foods Inc. Balance Sheets, 2010–2011 (in millions)

|  | 2011 | 2010 |
|---|---|---|
| **ASSETS** | | |
| Cash and cash equivalents | $ 1,974 | $ 2,481 |
| Receivables (net of allowances of $143 in 2011 and $246 in 2010) | 6,361 | 6,539 |
| Inventories, net | 5,706 | 5,310 |
| Deferred income taxes | 912 | 898 |
| Other current assets | 1,249 | 993 |
| Total current assets | 16,202 | 16,221 |
| Property, plant, and equipment, net | 13,813 | 13,792 |
| Goodwill | 37,297 | 37,856 |
| Intangible assets, net | 25,186 | 25,963 |
| Prepaid pension assets | 31 | 86 |
| Other assets | 1,308 | 1,371 |
| TOTAL ASSETS | 93,837 | 95,289 |
| **LIABILITIES** | | |
| Short-term borrowings | 182 | 750 |
| Current portion of long-term debt | 3,654 | 1,115 |
| Accounts payable | 5,525 | 5,409 |
| Accrued marketing | 2,863 | 2,515 |
| Accrued employment costs | 1,365 | 1,292 |
| Other current liabilities | 4,856 | 4,812 |
| Total current liabilities | 18,445 | 15,893 |
| Long-term debt | 23,095 | 26,859 |
| Deferred income taxes | 6,738 | 7,984 |
| Accrued pension costs | 3,597 | 2,382 |
| Accrued postretirement health care costs | 3,238 | 3,046 |
| Other liabilities | 3,396 | 3,183 |
| TOTAL LIABILITIES | 58,509 | 59,347 |
| Commitments and contingencies | | |
| **EQUITY** | | |
| Common stock, no par value (1,996,537,778 shares issued in 2011 and 2010) | | |
| Additional paid-in capital | 31,318 | 31,231 |
| Retained earnings | 18,012 | 16,619 |
| Accumulated other comprehensive losses | (6,637) | (3,890) |
| Treasury stock, at cost | (7,476) | (8,126) |
| Total Kraft Foods Shareholders Equity | 35,217 | 35,834 |
| Noncontrolling interest | 111 | 108 |
| TOTAL EQUITY | 35,328 | 35,942 |
| TOTAL LIABILITIES AND EQUITY | $93,837 | $95,289 |

*Source:* Kraft Foods Inc. 2011 10-K.

# KRAFT FOODS' PERFORMANCE IN LATE-2012

Kraft Foods Inc.'s results for the first half of 2012 were mixed, with revenues for the first half of the year declining by 0.3 percent, but operating EPS increasing by 9.6 percent compared to the same period in 2011. Continued pricing increases in North America and Europe contributed to organic net revenue increases in the two regions, although volume sales in both regions declined during the first six months of 2012 when compared to the first six months of 2011. The company's revenues and volume sales in developing markets increased at a steady rate during the first six months of 2012. Kraft Foods' CFO David Brearton was satisfied with the company's performance as it entered the second half of 2012, stating that the company's first-half results were "on track with our previous annual guidance of organic net revenue growth of approximately 5 percent and operating EPS growth of at least 9 percent on a constant currency basis." He continued optimistically with the comment, "As we look forward, we're confident that we're launching two industry-leading companies, each with a great future."[2]

## ENDNOTES

[1] As quoted in *Kraft Foods Inc. Press Release,* March 21, 2012.

[2] As quoted in *Kraft Foods Inc. Press Release,* August 2, 2012.

# Robin Hood

Joseph Lampel
City University London

It was in the spring of the second year of his insurrection against the High Sheriff of Nottingham that Robin Hood took a walk in Sherwood Forest. As he walked he pondered the progress of the campaign, the disposition of his forces, the Sheriff's recent moves, and the options that confronted him.

The revolt against the Sheriff had begun as a personal crusade. It erupted out of Robin's conflict with the Sheriff and his administration. However, alone Robin Hood could do little. He therefore sought allies, men with grievances and a deep sense of justice. Later he welcomed all who came, asking few questions and demanding only a willingness to serve. Strength, he believed, lay in numbers.

He spent the first year forging the group into a disciplined band, united in enmity against the Sheriff and willing to live outside the law. The band's organization was simple. Robin ruled supreme, making all important decisions. He delegated specific tasks to his lieutenants. Will Scarlett was in charge of intelligence and scouting. His main job was to shadow the Sheriff and his men, always alert to their next move. He also collected information on the travel plans of rich merchants and tax collectors. Little John kept discipline among the men and saw to it that their archery was at the high peak that their profession demanded. Scarlock took care of the finances, converting loot to cash, paying shares of the take, and finding suitable hiding places for the surplus. Finally, Much the Miller's son had the difficult task of provisioning the ever-increasing band of Merry Men.

The increasing size of the band was a source of satisfaction for Robin, but also a source of concern. The fame of his Merry Men was spreading, and new recruits were pouring in from every corner of England. As the band grew larger, their small bivouac became a major encampment. Between raids the men milled about, talking and playing games. Vigilance was in decline, and discipline was becoming harder to enforce. "Why," Robin reflected, "I don't know half the men I run into these days."

The growing band was also beginning to exceed the food capacity of the forest. Game was becoming scarce, and supplies had to be obtained from outlying villages. The cost of buying food was beginning to drain the band's financial reserves at the very moment when revenues were in decline. Travelers, especially those with the most to lose, were now giving the forest a wide berth. This was costly and inconvenient to them, but it was preferable to having all their goods confiscated.

Robin believed that the time had come for the Merry Men to change their policy of outright confiscation of goods to one of a fixed transit tax. His lieutenants strongly resisted this idea. They were proud of the Merry Men's famous motto: "Rob the rich and give to the poor." "The farmers and the townspeople," they argued, "are our most important allies. How can we tax them, and still hope for their help in our fight against the Sheriff?"

Robin wondered how long the Merry Men could keep to the ways and methods of their early days. The Sheriff was growing stronger and becoming better organized. He now had the money and the men and was beginning to harass the band, probing for its weaknesses. The tide of events was beginning to turn against the Merry Men. Robin felt that the campaign must be decisively concluded before the Sheriff had a chance to deliver a mortal blow. "But how," he wondered, "could this be done?"

Robin had often entertained the possibility of killing the Sheriff, but the chances for this seemed increasingly remote. Besides, killing the Sheriff might satisfy his personal thirst for revenge, but it would not improve the situation. Robin had hoped that the perpetual state of unrest and the Sheriff's failure to collect taxes would lead to his removal from office. Instead, the Sheriff used his political connections to obtain reinforcement. He had powerful friends at court and was well regarded by the regent, Prince John.

Prince John was vicious and volatile. He was consumed by his unpopularity among the people, who wanted the imprisoned King Richard back. He also lived in constant fear of the barons, who had first given him the regency but were now beginning to dispute his claim to the throne. Several of these barons had set out to collect the ransom that would release King Richard the Lionheart from his jail in Austria. Robin was invited to join the conspiracy in return for future amnesty. It was a dangerous proposition. Provincial banditry was one thing, court intrigue another. Prince John had spies everywhere, and he was known for his vindictiveness. If the conspirators' plan failed, the pursuit would be relentless and retributions swift.

The sound of the supper horn startled Robin from his thoughts. There was the smell of roasting venison in the air. Nothing was resolved or settled. Robin headed for camp promising himself that he would give these problems his utmost attention after tomorrow's raid.

# Dilemma at Devil's Den

### Allan R. Cohen
Babson College

### Kim Johnson
Babson College

My name is Susan, and I'm a business student at Mt. Eagle College. Let me tell you about one of my worst experiences. I had a part-time job in the campus snack bar, The Devil's Den. At the time, I was 21 years old and a junior with a concentration in finance. I originally started working at the Den in order to earn some extra spending money. I had been working there for one semester and became upset with some of the happenings. The Den was managed by contract with an external company, College Food Services (CFS). What bothered me was that many employees were allowing their friends to take free food, and the employees themselves were also taking food in large quantities when leaving their shifts. The policy was that employees could eat whatever they liked free of charge while they were working, but it had become common for employees to leave with food and not to be charged for their snacks while off duty as well.

I felt these problems were occurring for several reasons. For example, employee wages were low, there was easy access to the unlocked storage room door, and inventory was poorly controlled. Also, there was weak supervision by the student managers and no written rules or strict guidelines. It seemed that most of the employees were enjoying freebies, and it had been going on for so long that it was taken for granted. The problem got so far out of hand that customers who had seen others do it felt free to do it whether they knew the workers or not. The employees who witnessed this never challenged anyone because, in my opinion, they did not care and they feared the loss of friendship or being frowned upon by others. Apparently, speaking up was more costly to the employees than the loss of money to CFS for the unpaid food items. It seemed obvious to me that the employees felt too secure in their jobs and did not feel that their jobs were in jeopardy.

The employees involved were those who worked the night shifts and on the weekends. They were students at the college and were under the supervision of another student, who held the position of manager. There were approximately 30 student employees and 6 student managers on the staff. During the day there were no student managers; instead, a full-time manager was employed by CFS to supervise the Den. The employees and student managers were mostly freshmen and sophomores, probably because of the low wages, inconvenient hours (late weeknights and weekends), and the duties of the job itself. Employees were hard to come by; the high rate of employee turnover indicated that the job qualifications and the selection process were minimal.

The student managers were previous employees chosen by other student managers and the full-time CFS day manager on the basis of their ability to work and on their length of employment. They received no further formal training or written rules beyond what they had already learned by working there. The student managers were briefed on how to close the

snack bar at night but still did not get the job done properly. They received authority and responsibility over events occurring during their shifts as manager, although they were never actually taught how and when to enforce it! Their increase in pay was small, from a starting pay of just over minimum wage to an additional 15 percent for student managers. Regular employees received an additional nickel for each semester of employment.

Although I only worked seven hours per week, I was in the Den often as a customer and saw the problem frequently. I felt the problem was on a large enough scale that action should have been taken, not only to correct any financial loss that the Den might have experienced but also to help give the student employees a true sense of their responsibilities, the limits of their freedom, respect for rules, and pride in their jobs. The issues at hand bothered my conscience, although I was not directly involved. I felt that the employees and customers were taking advantage of the situation whereby they could "steal" food almost whenever they wanted. I believed that I had been brought up correctly and knew right from wrong, and I felt that the happenings in the Den were wrong. It wasn't fair that CFS paid for others' greediness or urges to show what they could get away with in front of their friends.

I was also bothered by the lack of responsibility of the managers to get the employees to do their work. I had seen the morning employees work very hard trying to do their jobs, in addition to the jobs the closing shift should have done. I assumed the night managers did not care or think about who worked the next day. It bothered me to think that the morning employees were suffering because of careless employees and student managers from the night before.

I had never heard of CFS mentioning any problems or taking any corrective action; therefore, I wasn't sure whether they knew what was going on, or if they were ignoring it. I was speaking to a close friend, Mack, a student manager at the Den, and I mentioned the fact that the frequently unlocked door to the storage room was an easy exit through which I had seen different quantities of unpaid goods taken out. I told him about some specific instances and said that I believed that it happened rather frequently. Nothing was ever said to other employees about this, and the only corrective action was that the door was locked more often, yet the key to the lock was still available upon request to all employees during their shifts.

Another lack of strong corrective action I remembered was when an employee was caught pocketing cash from the register. The student was neither suspended nor threatened with losing his job (nor was the event even mentioned). Instead, he was just told to stay away from the register. I felt that this weak punishment happened not because he was a good worker but because he worked so many hours and it would be difficult to find someone who would work all those hours and remain working for more than a few months. Although a customer reported the incident, I still felt that management should have taken more corrective action.

The attitudes of the student managers seemed to vary. I had noticed that one in particular, Bill, always got the job done. He made a list of each small duty that needed to be done, such as restocking, and he made sure the jobs were divided among the employees and finished before his shift was over. Bill also stared down employees who allowed thefts by their friends or who took freebies themselves; yet I had never heard of an employee being challenged verbally, nor had anyone ever been fired for these actions. My friend Mack was concerned about theft, or so I assumed, because he had taken some action about locking the doors, but he didn't really get after employees to work if they were slacking off.

I didn't think the rest of the student managers were good motivators. I noticed that they did little work themselves and did not show much control over the employees. The student managers allowed their friends to take food for free, thereby setting bad examples for the other workers, and allowed the employees to take what they wanted even when they were not working. I thought their attitudes were shared by most of the other employees: not caring about their jobs or working hard, as long as they got paid and their jobs were not threatened.

I had let the "thefts" continue without mention because I felt that no one else really cared and may even have frowned on me for trying to take action. Management thus far had not reported significant losses to the employees so as to encourage them to watch for theft and prevent it. Management did not threaten employees with job loss, nor did they provide employees with supervision. I felt it was not my place to report the theft to management, because I was just an employee and I would be overstepping the student managers. Also, I was unsure whether management would do anything about it anyway—maybe they did not care. I felt that talking to the student managers or other employees would be useless, because they were either abusing the rules themselves or clearly aware of what was going on and just ignored it. I felt that others may have frowned on me and made it uncomfortable for me to continue working there. This would be very difficult for me, because I wanted to become a student manager the next semester and did not want to create any waves that might have prevented me from doing so. I recognized the student manager position as a chance to gain some managerial and leadership skills, while at the same time adding a great plus to my résumé when I graduated. Besides, as a student manager, I would be in a better position to do something about all the problems at the Den that bothered me so much.

What could I do in the meantime to clear my conscience of the freebies, favors to friends, and employee snacks? What could I do without ruining my chances of becoming a student manager myself someday? I hated just keeping quiet, but I didn't want to make a fool of myself. I was really stuck.

# Starbucks in 2012: Evolving into a Dynamic Global Organization

**Arthur A. Thompson**
The University of Alabama

Since its founding in 1987 as a modest nine-store operation in Seattle, Washington, Starbucks had become the premier roaster and retailer of specialty coffees in the world, with over 17,400 store locations in more than 55 countries as of April 2012 and annual sales that were expected to exceed $13 billion in fiscal 2012. But the sudden and sharp economic downturn that plagued much of the world's economy in late 2008 and all of 2009 hit Starbucks hard. Declining sales at Starbucks stores prompted management to close 800 underperforming stores in the United States and an additional 100 stores in other countries, reduce the number of planned new store openings, trim its workforce by about 6,700 employees, and institute a rigorous cost containment program. On the heels of these retrenchment moves, the company's founder and CEO, Howard Schultz, launched a series of sweeping transformation initiatives to elevate the customer experience at Starbucks stores, including:

- Conducting a special retraining program for all store employees aimed at reigniting their emotional attachment to customers (a longstanding tradition at Starbucks stores), and refocusing their attention on the details of delivering superior customer service and pleasing customers. Starbucks stores were closed worldwide for three hours to allow all employees to go through the hands-on training exercise.
- Sharing best practices across all stores worldwide.
- Refreshing menu offerings at Starbucks stores.
- Introducing improved and more environmental-friendly designs for future Starbucks stores.
- Providing additional resources and tools for store employees, including laptops, an Internet-based software for scheduling work hours for store employees, and a new point-of-sale system for all stores in the United States, Canada, and the United Kingdom.
- Insisting that the entire Starbucks organization put renewed emphasis on product innovation and differentiation.
- Reinstituting efforts to add more retail stores and expand the Starbucks global footprint.

Starbucks' robust recovery and performance in fiscal years 2010–2011 suggested that Schultz's efforts were successful and that Starbucks was once again poised to deliver sustained growth in revenues and profits. In describing Starbucks' performance for the second quarter of fiscal 2012, Howard Schultz said:[1]

> Starbucks record Q2 performance demonstrates the strength of our business, the increasing power and global relevance of our brand, and the success of our unique Blueprint for Profitable Growth business strategy. In Q2 we expanded our retail presence, recorded our seventh consecutive quarter of over 20% sales growth in China, introduced new products into multiple channels, and more than offset high legacy commodity costs through increased efficiencies. I could not be more excited or more optimistic about the future of our company as we pursue disciplined, profitable growth all around the world.

On the strength of Starbucks recent performance, executives announced that the company was accelerating new store growth in fiscal 2012 to approximately 1,000 net new stores globally. Exhibit 1 provides an overview of Starbucks performance during fiscal years 2007–2011.

**EXHIBIT 1**  Financial and Operating Summary for Starbucks Corporation, Fiscal Years 2007–2011 ($ in millions, except for per-share amounts)

| | Oct. 2, 2011 | Oct. 3, 2010 | Sep 27, 2009 | Sep 28, 2008 | Sep 30, 2007 |
|---|---|---|---|---|---|
| **INCOME STATEMENT DATA** | | | | | |
| Net revenues: | | | | | |
| Company-operated stores | $ 9,632.4 | $ 8,963.5 | $8,180.1 | $ 8,771.9 | $7,998.3 |
| Licensed stores | 1,007.5 | 875.2 | 795.0 | 779.0 | 660.0 |
| Consumer products, foodservice, and other | 1,060.5 | 868.7 | 799.5 | 832.1 | 753.2 |
| Total net revenues | $11,700.4 | $10,707.4 | $9,774.6 | $10,383.0 | $9,411.5 |
| Cost of sales, including occupancy costs | $ 4,949.3 | $ 4,458.6 | 4,324.9 | 4,645.3 | 3,999.1 |
| Store operating expenses | 3,665.1 | 3,551.4 | 3,425.1 | 3,745.3 | 3,215.9 |
| Other operating expenses | 402.0 | 293.2 | 264.4 | 330.1 | 294.2 |
| Depreciation and amortization expenses | 523.3 | 510.4 | 534.7 | 549.3 | 467.2 |
| General and administrative expenses | 636.1 | 569.5 | 453.0 | 456.0 | 489.2 |
| Restructuring charges | 0.0 | 53.0 | 332.4 | 266.9 | — |
| Total operating expenses | 10,175.8 | 9,436.1 | 9,334.5 | 9,992.7 | 8,465.6 |
| Income from equity investees and other | 203.9 | 148.1 | 121.9 | 113.6 | 108.0 |
| Operating income | 1,728.5 | 1,419.4 | 562.0 | 503.9 | 1,053.9 |
| Net earnings attributable to Starbucks | $ 1,245.7 | $ 945.6 | $ 390.8 | $ 315.5 | $ 672.6 |
| Net earnings per common share—diluted | $1.62 | $1.24 | $0.52 | $0.43 | $0.87 |
| **BALANCE SHEET DATA** | | | | | |
| Current assets | $3,794.9 | $2,756.5 | $2,035.8 | $1,748.0 | $1,696.5 |
| Current liabilities | 2,973.1 | 2,703.6 | 1,581.0 | 2,189.7 | 2,155.6 |
| Total assets | 7,360.4 | 6,385.9 | 5,576.8 | 5,672.6 | 5,343.9 |
| Short-term borrowings | — | — | — | 713 | 710.3 |
| Long-term debt (including current portion) | 549.5 | 549.4 | 549.5 | 550.3 | 550.9 |
| Shareholders' equity | 4,384.9 | 3,674.7 | $3,045.7 | $2,490.9 | $2,284.1 |
| **OTHER FINANCIAL DATA** | | | | | |
| Net cash provided by operating activities | $1,612.4 | $1,704.9 | $1,389.0 | $1,258.7 | $1,331.2 |
| Capital expenditures (additions to property, plant, and equipment) | 531.9 | 440.7 | 445.6 | 984.5 | 1,080.3 |
| **STORE INFORMATION** | | | | | |
| Stores open at year-end | | | | | |
| United States | | | | | |
| Company-operated stores | 6,705 | 6,707 | 6,764 | 7,238 | 6,793 |
| Licensed stores | 4,082 | 4,424 | 4,364 | 4,329 | 3,891 |
| International | | | | | |
| Company-operated stores | 2,326 | 2,182 | 2,198 | 2,093 | 1,831 |
| Licensed stores | 3,890 | 3,545 | 3,309 | 3,020 | 2,496 |
| Percentage change in sales at company-operated stores open 13 months or longer | | | | | |
| United States | 8% | 7% | (6)% | (5)% | 4% |
| International | 5% | 6% | (2)% | 2% | 7% |
| Worldwide average | 7% | 7% | (5)% | (3)% | 5% |

*Source:* 2011, 2009, and 2007 10-K reports.

# COMPANY BACKGROUND

## Starbucks Coffee, Tea, and Spice

Starbucks got its start in 1971 when three academics, English teacher Jerry Baldwin, history teacher Zev Siegel, and writer Gordon Bowker—all coffee aficionados—opened Starbucks Coffee, Tea, and Spice in touristy Pikes Place Market in Seattle. The three partners shared a love for fine coffees and exotic teas and believed they could build a clientele in Seattle that would appreciate the best coffees and teas. They each invested $1,350 and borrowed another $5,000 from a bank to open the Pikes Place store. Customers were encouraged to learn how to grind the beans and make their own freshly brewed coffee at home. The store did not offer fresh-brewed coffee sold by the cup, but tasting samples were sometimes available. Initially, Zev was the only paid employee. He wore a grocer's apron, scooped out beans for customers, extolled the virtues of fine, dark-roasted coffees, and functioned as the partnership's retail expert. The other two partners kept their day jobs, but came by at lunch or after work to help out. During the startup period, Jerry kept the books and developed a growing knowledge of coffee; Gordon served as the "magic, mystery, and romance man."[2] The store was an immediate success, with sales exceeding expectations, partly because of interest stirred by a favorable article in the *Seattle Times*. Initially, Starbucks ordered its coffee bean supplies from a specialty coffee retailer in Berkeley, California, but toward the end of the first year, the partners purchased a used roaster from Holland, set up roasting operations in a nearby ramshackle building, and came up with their own blends and flavors.

By the early 1980s, the company had four Starbucks stores in the Seattle area and had been profitable every year since opening its doors. But then Zev Siegel experienced burnout and left the company to pursue other interests. Jerry Baldwin took over day-to-day management of the company and functioned as chief executive officer; Gordon remained involved as an owner, but devoted most of his time to his advertising and design firm, a weekly newspaper he had founded, and a microbrewery that he was launching known as the Redhook Ale Brewery.

## Howard Schultz Enters the Picture

In 1981, Howard Schultz, vice president and general manager of U.S. operations for a Swedish maker of stylish kitchen equipment and coffeemakers, decided to pay Starbucks a visit. He was curious why Starbucks was selling so many of his company's products. When he arrived at the Pikes Place store, a solo violinist was playing Mozart at the door (his violin case open for donations). Schultz was immediately taken by the powerful and pleasing aroma of the coffees, the wall displaying coffee beans, and the rows of coffeemakers on the shelves. As he talked with the clerk behind the counter, the clerk scooped out some Sumatran coffee beans, ground them, put the grounds in a cone filter, poured hot water over the cone, and shortly handed Schultz a porcelain mug filled with freshly brewed coffee. After only taking three sips of the brew, Schultz was hooked. He began asking questions about the company, the coffees from different parts of the world, and the different ways of roasting coffee.

Later, when he met with Jerry Baldwin and Gordon Bowker, Schultz was struck by their knowledge about coffee, their commitment to providing customers with quality coffees, and their passion for educating customers about the merits of dark-roasted coffees. Baldwin told Schultz, "We don't manage the business to maximize anything other than the quality of the coffee."[3] The company purchased only the finest Arabica coffees and put them through a meticulous dark-roasting process to bring out their full flavors. Jerry explained that the cheap robusta coffees used in supermarket blends burned when subjected to dark roasting. He also noted that the makers of supermarket blends preferred lighter roasts because it allowed higher yields (the longer a coffee was roasted, the more weight it lost).

Schultz was also struck by the business philosophy of the two partners. It was clear that Starbucks stood not just for good coffee, but also for the dark-roasted flavor profiles that the founders were passionate about. Top quality, fresh-roasted, whole-bean coffee was the company's differentiating feature and a bedrock value. It was also clear to Schultz that Starbucks was strongly committed to educating its customers to appreciate the qualities of fine coffees. The company depended mainly on word-of-mouth to get more people into its stores, then built customer loyalty cup by cup as buyers gained a sense of discovery and excitement about the taste of fine coffee.

On his return trip to New York, Howard Schultz could not stop thinking about Starbucks and what it would be like to be a part of the enterprise. Schultz recalled, "There was something magic about it, a passion and authenticity I had never experienced in business."[4] By the time he landed at Kennedy Airport, he knew in his heart he wanted to go to work for Starbucks. Shortly thereafter, Schultz asked Baldwin whether there was any way he could fit into Starbucks. But it took a year, numerous meetings at which Schultz presented his ideas about the tremendous potential of expanding the Starbucks enterprise outside Seattle and exposing people all over America to Starbucks coffee, and a lot of convincing to get Baldwin, Bowker, and their silent partner from San Francisco to agree to hire him, chiefly because they were nervous about bringing in an outsider, especially a high-powered New Yorker, who had not grown up with the values of the company. Then, in spring 1982, following another round of meetings and discussions with the three owners, Schultz was offered the job of heading marketing and overseeing Starbucks' retail stores. In September 1982, Howard Schultz took over his new responsibilities at Starbucks.

## Starbucks and Howard Schultz: The 1982–1985 Period

In his first few months at Starbucks, Schultz spent most of his time in the four Seattle stores—working behind the counters, tasting different kinds of coffee, talking with customers, getting to know store personnel, and learning the retail aspects of the coffee business. By December, Jerry Baldwin concluded Schultz was ready for the final part of his training, that of actually roasting the coffee. Schultz spent a week getting an education about the colors of different coffee beans, listening for the telltale second pop of the beans during the roasting process, learning to taste the subtle differences among the various roasts, and familiarizing himself with the roasting techniques for different beans.

Schultz overflowed with ideas for the company. However, his biggest inspiration and vision for Starbucks' future came during the spring of 1983 when the company sent him to Milan, Italy, to attend an international housewares show. While walking from his hotel to the convention center, he spotted an espresso bar and went inside to look around. The cashier beside the door nodded and smiled. The "barista" behind the counter greeted Schultz cheerfully and began pulling a shot of espresso for one customer and handcrafting a foamy cappuccino for another, all the while conversing merrily with patrons standing at the counter. Schultz thought the barista's performance was "great theater."

Just down the way on a side street, he went in an even more crowded espresso bar where the barista, which he surmised to be the owner, was greeting customers by name; people were laughing and talking in an atmosphere that plainly was comfortable and familiar. In the next few blocks, he saw two more espresso bars. That afternoon, Schultz walked the streets of Milan to explore more espresso bars. Some were stylish and upscale; others attracted a blue-collar clientele. Most had few chairs and it was common for Italian opera to be playing in the background. What struck Schultz was how popular and vibrant the Italian coffee bars were. Energy levels were typically high and they seemed to function as an integral community gathering place. Each one had its own unique character, but they all had a barista that performed with flair and there was camaraderie between the barista and the customers.

Schultz remained in Milan for a week, exploring coffee bars and learning as much as he could about the Italian passion for coffee drinks. Schultz was particularly struck by the fact that there were 1,500 coffee bars in Milan, a city about the size of Philadelphia, and a total of 200,000 in all of Italy. In one bar, he heard a customer order a "caffe latte" and decided to try one himself—the barista made a shot of espresso, steamed a frothy pitcher of milk, poured the two together in a cup, and put a dollop of foam on the top. Schultz liked it immediately, concluding that lattes should be a feature item on any coffee bar menu even though none of the coffee experts he had talked to had ever mentioned coffee lattes.

Schultz's 1983 trip to Milan produced a revelation: the Starbucks stores in Seattle completely missed the point. There was much more to the coffee business than just selling beans and getting people to appreciate grinding their own beans and brewing fine coffee in their homes. What Starbucks needed to do was serve fresh brewed coffee, espressos, and cappuccinos in its stores (in addition to beans and coffee equipment) and try to create an American version of the Italian coffee bar culture. Going to Starbucks should be an experience, a special treat, a place to meet friends and visit. Recreating the authentic Italian coffee bar culture in the U.S. could be Starbucks' differentiating factor.

## Schultz Becomes Frustrated

On Schultz's return from Italy, he shared his revelation and ideas for modifying the format of Starbucks' stores with Baldwin and Bowker, but they strongly resisted, contending that Starbucks was a retailer, not a restaurant or coffee bar. They feared serving drinks would put them in the beverage business and diminish the integrity of Starbucks' mission as a purveyor of fine coffees. They pointed out that Starbucks had been profitable every year and there was no reason to rock the boat in a small, private company like Starbucks. It took Howard Schultz nearly a year to convince Jerry Baldwin to let him test an espresso bar. Jerry relented when Starbucks opened its sixth store in April 1984. It was the first store designed to sell beverages and it was the first store located in downtown Seattle. Schultz asked for a 1,500-square-foot space to set up a full-scale Italian-style espresso bar, but Jerry agreed to allocating only 300 square feet in a corner of the new store. The store opened with no fanfare as a deliberate experiment to see what happened. By closing time on the first day, some 400 customers had been served, well above the 250-customer average of Starbucks' best performing stores. Within two months the store was serving 800 customers per day. The two baristas could not keep up with orders during the early morning hours, resulting in lines outside the door onto the sidewalk. Most of the business was at the espresso counter, while sales at the regular retail counter were only adequate.

Schultz was elated at the test results, expecting that Baldwin's doubts about entering the beverage side of the business would be dispelled and that he would gain approval to pursue the opportunity to take Starbucks to a new level. Every day he went into Baldwin's office to show him the sales figures and customer counts at the new downtown store. But Baldwin was not comfortable with the success of the new store, believing that it felt wrong and that espresso drinks were a distraction from the core business of marketing fine Arabica coffees at retail.[5] While he didn't deny that the experiment was succeeding, Baldwin didn't want to go forward with introducing beverages in other Starbucks stores, although to avoid a total impasse Baldwin finally did agree to let Schultz put espresso machines in the back of one or two other Starbucks stores.

Over the next several months, Schultz made up his mind to leave Starbucks and start his own company. His plan was to open espresso bars in high-traffic downtown locations, serve espresso drinks and coffee by the cup, and try to emulate the friendly, energetic atmosphere he had encountered in Italian espresso bars. Baldwin and Bowker, knowing how frustrated Schultz had become, supported his efforts to go out on his own and agreed to let him stay in his current job

and office until definitive plans were in place. Schultz left Starbucks in late 1985.

## Schultz's Il Giornale Venture

With the aid of a lawyer friend who helped companies raise venture capital and go public, Schultz began seeking out investors for the kind of company he had in mind. Ironically, Jerry Baldwin committed to investing $150,000 of Starbucks' money in Schultz's coffee bar enterprise, thus becoming Schultz's first investor. Baldwin accepted Schultz's invitation to be a director of the new company and Gordon Bowker agreed to be a part-time consultant for six months. Bowker proposed that the new company be named Il Giornale Coffee Company (pronounced il-jor-nahl'-ee), a suggestion that Howard accepted. In December 1985, Bowker and Schultz made a trip to Italy where they visited some 500 espresso bars in Milan and Verona, observing local habits, taking notes about décor and menus, snapping photographs, and videotaping baristas in action.

By the end of January 1986, Schultz had raised about $400,000 in seed capital, enough to rent an office, hire a couple of key employees, develop a store design, and open the first store. But it took until the end of 1986 to raise the remaining $1.25 million needed to launch at least eight espresso bars and prove that Schultz's strategy and business model were viable. Schultz made presentations to 242 potential investors, 217 of which said "no." Many who heard Schultz's hour-long presentation saw coffee as a commodity business and thought that Schultz's espresso bar concept lacked any basis for sustainable competitive advantage (no patent on dark roast, no advantage in purchasing coffee beans, no way to bar the entry of imitative competitors). Some noted that coffee couldn't be turned into a growth business—consumption of coffee had been declining since the mid-1960s. Others were skeptical that people would pay $1.50 or more for a cup of coffee, and the company's unpronounceable name turned some off. Nonetheless, Schultz maintained an upbeat attitude and displayed passion and enthusiasm in making his pitch. He ended up raising $1.65 million from about 30 investors; most of the money came from nine people, five of whom became directors.

The first Il Giornale store opened in April 1986. It measured 700 square feet and was located near the entrance of Seattle's tallest building. The décor was Italian and there were Italian words on the menu. Italian opera music played in the background. The baristas wore white shirts and bow ties. All service was stand up—there were no chairs. National and international papers were hung on rods on the wall. By closing time on the first day, 300 customers had been served—mostly in the morning hours. But while the core idea worked well, it soon became apparent that several aspects of the format were not appropriate for Seattle. Some customers objected to the incessant opera music, others wanted a place to sit down; many people did not understand the Italian words on the menu. These "mistakes" were quickly fixed, but an effort was made not to compromise the style and elegance of the store. Within six months, the store was serving more than 1,000 customers a day. Regular customers had learned how to pronounce the company's name. Because most customers were in a hurry, it became apparent that speedy service was essential.

Six months after opening the first store, a second store was opened in another downtown building. In April 1987, a third store was opened in Vancouver, British Columbia, to test the transferability of the company's business concept outside Seattle. Schultz's goal was to open 50 stores in five years and he needed to dispel his investors' doubts about geographic expansion early on to achieve his growth objective. By mid-1987, sales at each of the three stores were running at a rate equal to $1.5 million annually.

## Il Giornale Acquires Starbucks

In March 1987, Jerry Baldwin and Gordon Bowker decided to sell the whole Starbucks operation in Seattle—the stores, the roasting plant, and the Starbucks name. Schultz knew immediately that he had to buy Starbucks; his board of directors agreed. Schultz and his newly hired finance and accounting manager drew up a set of financial projections for the combined operations and a financing package that included a stock offering to Il Giornale's original investors and a line of credit with local banks. Within weeks, Schultz had raised the $3.8 million needed to buy Starbucks. The acquisition was completed in August 1987. The new name of the combined companies was Starbucks Corporation. Howard Schultz, at the age of 34, became Starbucks' president and CEO.

## STARBUCKS AS A PRIVATE COMPANY: 1987–1992

The following Monday morning, Howard returned to the Starbucks offices at the roasting plant, greeted all the familiar faces, and accepted their congratulations.

Then, he called the staff together for a meeting on the roasting plant floor: [6]

> All my life I have wanted to be part of a company and a group of people who share a common vision. . . . I'm here today because I love this company. I love what it represents. . . . I know you're concerned. . . . I promise you I will not let you down. I promise you I will not leave anyone behind. . . . In five years, I want you to look back at this day and say "I was there when it started. I helped build this company into something great."

Schultz told the group that his vision was for Starbucks to become a national company with values and guiding principles that employees could be proud of. He aspired for Starbucks to become the most respected brand name in coffee and for the company to be admired for its corporate responsibility. He indicated that he wanted to include people in the decision-making process and that he would be open and honest with them. For Schultz, building a company that valued and respected its people, that inspired them, and that shared the fruits of success with those who contributed to the company's long-term value was essential, not just an intriguing option. He made the establishment of mutual respect between employees and management a priority.

The business plan Schultz had presented investors called for the new 9-store company to open 125 stores in the next five years—15 the first year, 20 the second, 25 the third, 30 the fourth, and 35 the fifth. Revenues were projected to reach $60 million in 1992. But the company lacked experienced management. Schultz had never led a growth effort of such magnitude and was just learning what the job of CEO was all about, having been the president of a small company for barely two years. Dave Olsen, a Seattle coffee bar owner who Schultz had recruited to direct store operations at Il Giornale, was still learning the ropes in managing a multistore operation. Ron Lawrence, the company's controller, had worked as a controller for several organizations. Other Starbucks employees had only the experience of managing or being a part of a six-store organization.

Schultz instituted a number of changes in the first several months. To symbolize the merging of the two companies and the two cultures, a new logo was created that melded the designs of the Starbucks logo and the Il Giornale logo. The Starbucks stores were equipped with espresso machines and remodeled to look more Italian than old-world nautical. Il Giornale green replaced the traditional Starbucks brown. The result was a new type of store—a cross between a retail coffee bean store and an espresso bar/café—that is now Starbucks' signature.

By December 1987, the mood at Starbucks was distinctly upbeat, with most all employees buying into the changes that Schultz was making and trust was beginning to build between management and employees. New stores were on the verge of opening in Vancouver and Chicago. One Starbucks store employee, Daryl Moore, who had started working at Starbucks in 1981 and who had voted against unionization in 1985, began to question the need for a union with his fellow employees. Over the next few weeks, Moore began a move to decertify the union. He carried a decertification letter around to Starbucks' stores, securing the signatures of employees who no longer wished to be represented by the union. He got a majority of store employees to sign the letter and presented it to the National Labor Relations Board. The union representing store employees was decertified. Later, in 1992, the union representing Starbucks' roasting plant and warehouse employees was also decertified.

## Market Expansion Outside the Pacific Northwest

Starbucks' entry into Chicago proved far more troublesome than management anticipated. The first Chicago store opened in October 1987 and three more stores were opened over the next six months. Customer counts at the stores were substantially below expectations. Chicagoans did not take to dark-roasted coffee as fast as Schultz had anticipated. It was more expensive to supply fresh coffee to the Chicago stores out of the Seattle warehouse (the company solved the problem of freshness and quality assurance by putting freshly roasted beans in special FlavorLock bags that utilized vacuum packaging techniques with a one-way valve to allow carbon dioxide to escape without allowing air and moisture in). Rents were higher in Chicago and so were wage rates. The result was a squeeze on store profit margins. Gradually, customer counts improved, but Starbucks lost money on its Chicago stores until, in 1990, prices were raised to reflect higher rents and labor costs, more experienced store managers were hired, and a critical mass of customers caught on to the taste of Starbucks products.

Portland, Oregon, was the next market entered, and Portland coffee drinkers took to Starbucks products quickly. Store openings in Los Angeles and San Francisco soon followed. L.A. consumers embraced Starbucks quickly and the *Los Angeles Times* named

Starbucks the best coffee in America before the first store opened.

Starbucks' store expansion targets proved easier to meet than Schultz had originally anticipated and he upped the numbers to keep challenging the organization. Starbucks opened 15 new stores in fiscal 1988, 20 in 1989, 30 in 1990, 32 in 1991, and 53 in 1992—producing a total of 161 stores, significantly above his original 1992 target of 125 stores.

From the outset, the strategy was to open only company-owned stores; franchising was avoided so as to keep the company in full control of the quality of its products and the character and location of its stores. But company-ownership of all stores required Starbucks to raise new venture capital to cover the cost of new store expansion. In 1988, the company raised $3.9 million; in 1990, venture capitalists provided an additional $13.5 million; and in 1991, another round of venture capital financing generated $15 million. Starbucks was able to raise the needed funds despite posting losses of $330,000 in 1987, $764,000 in 1988, and $1.2 million in 1989. While the losses were troubling to Starbucks' board of directors and investors, Schultz's business plan had forecast losses during the early years of expansion. At a particularly tense board meeting where directors sharply questioned Schultz about the lack of profitability, Schultz said:[7]

> Look, we're going to keep losing money until we can do three things. We have to attract a management team well beyond our expansion needs. We have to build a world-class roasting facility. And we need a computer information system sophisticated enough to keep track of sales in hundreds and hundreds of stores.

Schultz argued for patience as the company invested in the infrastructure to support continued growth well into the 1990s. He contended that hiring experienced executives ahead of the growth curve, building facilities far beyond current needs, and installing support systems laid a strong foundation for rapid profitable growth later on down the road. His arguments carried the day with the board and with investors, especially since revenues were growing approximately 80 percent annually and customer traffic at the stores was meeting or exceeding expectations.

Starbucks became profitable in 1990. Profits had increased every year since 1990 except for fiscal year 2000 (because of $58.8 million in investment write-offs in four **dot.com** enterprises) and for fiscal year 2008 (when the sharp global economic downturn hit the company's bottom line very hard—see Exhibit 1).

# STARBUCKS STORES: DESIGN, AMBIENCE, AND EXPANSION OF LOCATIONS

## Store Design

Starting in 1991, Starbucks created its own in-house team of architects and designers to ensure that each store would convey the right image and character. Stores had to be custom-designed because the company didn't buy real estate and build its own freestanding structures. Instead, each space was leased in an existing structure, making each store differ in size and shape. Most stores ranged in size from 1,000 to 1,500 square feet and were located in office buildings, downtown and suburban retail centers, airport terminals, university campus areas, and busy neighborhood shopping areas convenient for pedestrian foot traffic and/or drivers. A few were in suburban malls. Four store templates—each with its own color combinations, lighting scheme, and component materials—were introduced in 1996; all four were adaptable to different store sizes and settings (downtown buildings, college campuses, neighborhood shopping areas).

But as the number of stores increased rapidly during the 2000–2003 period, greater store diversity and layout quickly became necessary. Some stores were equipped with special seating areas to help make Starbucks a desirable gathering place where customers could meet and chat or simply enjoy a peaceful interlude in their day. Flagship stores in high-traffic, high-visibility locations had fireplaces, leather chairs, newspapers, couches, and lots of ambience. Increasingly, the company began installing drive-through windows at locations where speed and convenience were important to customers and utilizing kiosks in supermarkets, building lobbies, and other public places.[8] As of 2012, about 25 percent of Starbucks locations in the U.S. were equipped with drive-thru windows.

A new global store design strategy was introduced in 2009. Core design characteristics included the celebration of local materials and craftsmanship, a focus on reused and recycled elements, the exposure of structural integrity and authentic roots, the absence of features that distracted from an emphasis on coffee, seating layouts that facilitated customer gatherings, an atmosphere that sought to engage all five customer senses (sight, smell, sound, hearing, and feel), and flexibility to meet the needs of many customer types.[9] Each new store was to be a reflection of the environment in which it operated and be environmentally friendly. In 2010, Starbucks began an effort to achieve LEED (Leadership in Energy and Environmental Design) Certification for all new company-owned stores (a LEED-certified building had to incorporate green building design, construction, operations, and maintenance solutions).[10] Exhibit 2 shows the diverse nature of Starbucks' stores.

To better control average store opening costs, the company centralized buying, developed standard contracts and fixed fees for certain items, and consolidated work under those contractors who displayed good cost control practices. The retail operations group outlined exactly the minimum amount of equipment each core store needed, so that standard items could be ordered in volume from vendors at 20 to 30 percent discounts, then delivered just in time to the store site either from company warehouses or the vendor. Modular designs for display cases were developed. The layouts for new and remodeled stores were developed on a computer, with software that allowed the costs to be estimated as the design evolved. All this cut store opening and remodeling costs significantly and shortened the process to about 18 weeks.

## Store Ambience

Starbucks management viewed each store as a billboard for the company and as a contributor to building the company's brand and image. The company went to great lengths to make sure the store fixtures, the merchandise displays, the colors, the artwork, the banners, the music, and the aromas all blended to create a consistent, inviting, stimulating environment that evoked the romance of coffee and signaled the company's passion for coffee. To try to keep the coffee aromas in the stores pure, smoking was banned, and employees were asked to refrain from wearing perfumes or colognes. Prepared foods were kept covered so customers would smell coffee only. Colorful banners and posters were used to keep the look of the Starbucks stores fresh and in keeping with seasons and holidays. All these practices reflected a conviction that every detail mattered in making Starbucks stores a welcoming and pleasant "third place" (apart from home and work) where people could meet friends and family, enjoy a quiet moment alone with a newspaper or book, or simply spend quality time relaxing—and most importantly, have a satisfying experience.

Starting in 2002, Starbucks began providing Internet access capability and enhanced digital

**EXHIBIT 2**   Scenes from Starbucks Stores

entertainment to patrons at over 1,200 Starbucks locations. The objective was to heighten the "third place" Starbucks experience, entice customers into perhaps buying a second latte or espresso while they caught up on e-mail, listened to digital music, put the finishing touches on a presentation, or surfed the Internet. Since then, wireless Internet service had been added at all company-operated store locations in the United States and at growing numbers of locations worldwide.

## Store Expansion Strategy

In 1992 and 1993, Starbucks began concentrating its store expansion efforts on locations with favorable demographic profiles that also could be serviced and supported by the company's operations infrastructure. For each targeted region, Starbucks selected a large city to serve as a "hub"; teams of professionals were located in hub cities to support the goal of opening 20 or more stores in the hub within two years. Once a number of stores were opened in a hub, then additional stores were opened in smaller surrounding "spoke" areas in the region. To oversee the expansion process, Starbucks had zone vice presidents that oversaw the store expansion process in a geographic region and that were also responsible for instilling the Starbucks culture in the newly opened stores.

More recently, Starbucks strategy in major metropolitan cities had been to blanket major cities with stores, even if some stores cannibalized a nearby store's business. While a new store might draw 30 percent of the business of an existing store two or so blocks away, management believed a "Starbucks everywhere" strategy cut down on delivery and management costs, shortened customer lines at individual stores, and increased foot traffic for all the stores in an area. In 2002, new stores generated an average of $1.2 million in first-year revenues, compared to $700,000 in 1995 and only $427,000 in 1990. The steady increases in new-store revenues were due partly to growing popularity of premium coffee drinks, partly to Starbucks' growing reputation, and partly to expanded product offerings. But the strategy of saturating big metropolitan areas with stores ended up cannibalizing sales of existing stores to such an extent that average sales per store in the United States dropped under $1,000,000 annually in 2008–2009 and pushed store operating margins down from 14.3 percent in fiscal 2007 to 6.0 percent in fiscal 2008 and 7.5 percent in fiscal 2009. Because Starbucks' long-term profitability target for its retail stores in the United States was an operating profit margin in the high teens, Starbucks' management cut the number of metropolitan locations when it closed 900 underperforming Starbucks locations in 2008–2009 (some 75 percent of the closed stores were within three miles of another Starbucks store).

Despite the mistake of over-saturating portions of some large metropolitan areas with stores, Starbucks was regarded as having the best real estate team in the coffee bar industry and a core competence in identifying good retailing sites for its new stores. The company's sophisticated methodology enabled it to identify not only the most attractive individual city blocks but also the exact store location that was best. It also worked hard at building good relationships with local real estate representatives in areas where it was opening multiple store locations.

**Licensed   Starbucks   Stores**   In   1995, Starbucks began entering into licensing agreements for store locations in areas where it did not have the ability to locate its own outlets. Two early licensing agreements were with Marriott Host International to operate Starbucks retail stores in airport locations and with Aramark Food and Services to put Starbucks stores on university campuses and other locations operated by Aramark. Very quickly, Starbucks began to make increased use of licensing, both domestically and internationally. Starbucks preferred licensing to franchising because it permitted tighter controls over the operations of licensees.

Starbucks received a license fee and a royalty on sales at all licensed locations and supplied the coffee for resale at these locations. All licensed stores had to follow Starbucks' detailed operating procedures and all managers and employees who worked in these stores received the same training given to managers and employees in company-operated Starbucks stores. As of April 2012, Starbucks had 4,161 licensed stores in the United States and 4,124 licensed stores internationally.

**International Expansion**   In markets outside the continental United States, Starbucks had a two-pronged store expansion strategy: either open company-owned-and-operated stores or else license a reputable and capable local company with retailing know-how in the target host country to develop and operate new Starbucks stores. In most countries, Starbucks utilized a local partner/licensee to help it recruit talented individuals, set up supplier relationships, locate suitable store sites, and cater to local market conditions. Starbucks looked for partners/licensees that had strong retail/restaurant experience, had values and a corporate culture compatible with Starbucks, were committed to good customer service, possessed talented management and strong financial resources, and had demonstrated brand-building skills. In those foreign countries where business risks were deemed relatively high, most if not all Starbucks stores were licensed rather than being company-owned and operated.

Exhibit 3 shows the speed with which Starbucks had expanded its network of company-operated and licensed retail stores during the period from 1987 through April 2012.

## EXHIBIT 3  Company-Operated and Licensed Starbucks Stores

### A.  Number of Starbucks Store Locations Worldwide, Fiscal Years 1987–2011 and April 1, 2012

| End of Fiscal Year* | Company-Operated Store Locations | | Licensed Store Locations | | Worldwide Total |
| --- | --- | --- | --- | --- | --- |
| | United States | International | United States | International | |
| 1987 | 17 | 0 | 0 | 0 | 17 |
| 1990 | 84 | 0 | 0 | 0 | 84 |
| 1995 | 627 | 0 | 49 | 0 | 676 |
| 2000 | 2,446 | 530 | 173 | 352 | 3,501 |
| 2005 | 4,918 | 1,263 | 2,435 | 1,625 | 10,241 |
| 2006 | 5,728 | 1,521 | 3,168 | 2,023 | 12,440 |
| 2007 | 6,793 | 1,831 | 3,891 | 2,496 | 15,011 |
| 2008 | 7,238 | 2,093 | 4,329 | 3,020 | 16,680 |
| 2009 | 6,764 | 2,141 | 4,364 | 3,366 | 16,635 |
| 2010 | 6,707 | 2,126 | 4,424 | 3,601 | 16,858 |
| 2011 | 6,705 | 2,326 | 4,082 | 3,890 | 17,003 |
| April 1, 2012 | 6,714 | 2,421 | 4,161 | 4,124 | 17,420 |

### B.  International Starbucks Store Locations, April 1, 2012

| International Locations of Company-operated Starbucks Stores | | International Locations of Licensed Starbucks Stores | | | |
| --- | --- | --- | --- | --- | --- |
| | | **Americas** | | **Europe/Africa/Middle East** | |
| Canada | 851 | Canada | 295 | Turkey | 162 |
| United Kingdom | 603 | Mexico | 342 | United Kingdom | 138 |
| China | 330 | Other | 113 | United Arab Emirates | 98 |
| Germany | 153 | | | Spain | 75 |
| Thailand | 146 | **Asia-Pacific** | | Saudi Arabia | 63 |
| Other | 333 | Japan | 955 | Kuwait | 67 |
| | | South Korea | 415 | Russia | 56 |
| Total | 2,416 | Taiwan | 264 | Greece | 46 |
| | | China | 247 | Other | 194 |
| | | Philippines | 190 | | |
| | | Malaysia | 125 | | |
| | | Indonesia | 122 | Licensed Total Worldwide | 4,124 |
| | | Other | 157 | | |

*Starbucks' fiscal year ends on the Sunday closest to September 30.

*Source:* Company 10-K reports, various years, and company records posted in the investor relations section at www.starbucks.com, accessed May 4, 2012.

Starbucks' long-term profitability target for its international operations was an operating profit margin in the mid-to-high teens. But the international store margins in recent years had been below the target: 8.1 percent in fiscal 2007, 5.2 percent in fiscal 2008, 4.8 percent in fiscal 2009, 9.8 percent in fiscal 2010, and 13.3 percent in fiscal 2011.

## STARBUCKS' STRATEGY TO EXPAND ITS PRODUCT OFFERINGS AND ENTER NEW MARKET SEGMENTS

In the mid-1990s, Howard Schultz began a long-term strategic campaign to expand Starbucks product offerings beyond its retail stores and to pursue sales of Starbucks products in a wider variety of distribution channels and market segments. The strategic objectives were to capitalize on Starbucks growing brand awareness and brand-name strength and create a broader foundation for sustained long-term growth in revenues and profits.

The first initiative involved the establishment of an in-house specialty sales group to begin marketing Starbucks coffee to restaurants, airlines, hotels, universities, hospitals, business offices, country clubs, and select retailers. Early users of Starbucks coffee included Horizon Airlines, a regional carrier based in Seattle, and United Airlines. There was much internal debate at Starbucks about whether it made sense for Starbucks coffee to be served on all United flights (since there was different coffee-making equipment on different planes) and the possible damage to the integrity of the Starbucks brand if the quality of the coffee served did not measure up. It took seven months of negotiations for Starbucks and United to arrive at a mutually agreeable way to handle quality control on United's various types of planes. The specialty sales group then soon won accounts at Hyatt, Hilton, Sheraton, Radisson, and Westin hotels, resulting in packets of Starbucks coffee being in each room with coffee-making equipment. Later, the specialty sales group began working with leading institutional foodservice distributors, including SYSCO Corporation and US Foodservice, to handle the distribution of Starbucks products to hotels, restaurants, office coffee distributors, educational and healthcare institutions, and other such enterprises. In fiscal 2009, Starbucks generated revenues of $372.2 million from providing whole bean and ground coffees and assorted other Starbucks products to some 21,000 foodservice accounts.

The second initiative came in 1994 when PepsiCo and Starbucks entered into a joint venture arrangement (now called the North American Coffee Partnership) to create new coffee-related products in bottles or cans for mass distribution through Pepsi channels. Howard Schultz saw the venture with PepsiCo as a major paradigm shift with the potential to cause Starbucks' business to evolve in heretofore unimaginable directions. The joint venture's first new product, a lightly flavored carbonated coffee drink, was a failure. Then, at a meeting with Pepsi executives, Schultz suggested developing a bottled version of Frappuccino, a new cold coffee drink Starbucks began serving at its retail stores in the summer of 1995 that quickly became a big hot weather seller. Pepsi executives were enthusiastic. Sales of Frappuccino ready-to-drink beverages reached $125 million in 1997 and achieved a national supermarket penetration of 80 percent. Sales of ready-to-drink Frappuccino products began in 2005 in Japan, Taiwan, and South Korea, chiefly through agreements with leading local distributors; the ready-to-drink beverage market in these countries represented more than $10 billion in annual sales.[11] In 2007, the PepsiCo–Starbucks partnership introduced a line of chilled Starbucks Doubleshot® espresso drinks in the United States. Also in 2007, PepsiCo and Starbucks entered into a second joint venture agreement called the International Coffee Partnership (ICP) for the purpose of introducing Starbucks-related beverages in country markets outside of North America; one of ICP's early moves was to begin marketing Frappuccino in China.[12] In 2010, sales of Frappuccino products worldwide reached $2 billion annually.[13] In 2008, Starbucks partnered with Suntory to begin selling chilled ready-to-drink Doubleshot® drinks in Japan. In 2010, Starbucks partnered with Arla Foods to begin selling Doubleshot products and Starbucks Discoveries chilled cup coffees in retail stores across the United Kingdom (as well as in Starbucks retail stores in the United Kingdom).

In October 1995, Starbucks partnered with Dreyer's Grand Ice Cream to supply coffee extracts for a new line of coffee ice cream made and distributed by Dreyer's under the Starbucks brand. Starbucks coffee-flavored ice cream became the number-one-selling super-premium brand in the coffee segment in mid-1996. In 2008, Starbucks discontinued its arrangement with Dreyer's and entered into an exclusive agreement with Unilever to manufacture, market, and distribute Starbucks-branded ice creams in the United States and Canada. Unilever was the global leader in ice cream with annual sales of about $6 billion; its ice cream brands included Ben & Jerry's, Breyers, and Good Humor. There were seven flavors of Starbucks ice cream and two flavors of novelty bars being marketed in 2010.

In 1997, a Starbucks store manager who had worked in the music industry and selected the music Starbucks played as background in its stores suggested that Starbucks begin selling the background music on tapes (and later on CDs as they become the preferred format). The Starbucks tapes/CDs proved a significant seller. Later, Starbucks began offering customers the option of downloading music from the company's 200,000-plus song library and, if they wished, having the downloaded songs burned onto a CD for purchase. In 2008, Starbucks, in partnership with Apple's iTunes, began offering a Pick of the Week music card at its stores in the United States that allowed customers to download each week's music selection at iTunes.[14] In 2012, Starbucks was continuing to offer CDs with handpicked music and new CDs featuring particular artists; the CDs were typically priced at $12.95.

In 1998, Starbucks licensed Kraft Foods to market and distribute Starbucks whole bean and ground coffees in grocery and mass merchandise channels across the United States. Kraft managed all distribution, marketing, advertising, and promotions and paid a royalty to Starbucks based on a percentage of net sales. Product freshness was guaranteed by Starbucks' FlavorLock packaging, and the price per pound paralleled the prices in Starbucks' retail stores. Flavor selections in supermarkets were more limited than the varieties at Starbucks stores. The licensing relationship with Kraft was later expanded to include the marketing and distribution of Starbucks coffees in Canada, the United Kingdom, and other European countries. Going into 2010, Starbucks coffees were available in some 33,500 grocery and warehouse clubs in the United States and 5,500 retail outlets outside the United States; Starbucks revenues from these sales were approximately $370 million in fiscal 2009.[15] During fiscal 2011, Starbucks discontinued its distribution arrangement with Kraft and instituted its own in-house organization to handle direct sales of packaged coffees to supermarkets and to warehouse club stores (chiefly Costco, Sam's Club, and BJ's Warehouse).

In 1999, Starbucks purchased Tazo Tea for $8.1 million. Tazo Tea, a tea manufacturer and distributor

based in Portland, Oregon, was founded in 1994 and marketed its teas to restaurants, food stores, and tea houses. Starbucks proceeded to introduce hot and iced Tazo Tea drinks in its retail stores. As part of a long-term campaign to expand the distribution of its lineup of super-premium Tazo teas, Starbucks expanded its agreement with Kraft to market and distribute Tazo teas worldwide. In August 2008, Starbucks entered into a licensing agreement with a partnership formed by PepsiCo and Unilever (Lipton Tea was one of Unilever's leading brands) to manufacture, market, and distribute Starbucks' super-premium Tazo Tea ready-to-drink beverages (including iced teas, juiced teas, and herbal-infused teas) in the United States and Canada—in 2012, the Pepsi/Lipton Tea partnership was the leading North American distributor of ready-to-drink teas. In fiscal 2011, when Starbucks broke off its arrangement with Kraft and created its own in-house organization to handle direct sales of Starbucks coffees to supermarkets and warehouse clubs, it also broke off its arrangement with Kraft for distribution of Tazo tea and began selling Tazo teas directly to supermarkets (except for Tazo Tea ready-to-drink beverages).

In 2001, Starbucks introduced the Starbucks Card, a reloadable card that allowed customers to pay for their purchases with a quick swipe of their card at the cash register and also to earn and redeem rewards. Cardholders were entitled to free select syrups, milk options and refills on tea or brewed coffee during a store visit, and Gold Level members earned a free drink after 15 purchases at participating Starbucks stores. The company's My Starbucks Rewards™ program had 3.5 million members in late 2011. In addition, in 2011 close to 25 million payments at Starbucks stores were being made on cell phones equipped with the Starbucks Card Apps for iPhones and Android-based smartphones.

In 2003, Starbucks spent $70 million to acquire Seattle's Best Coffee, an operator of 540 Seattle's Best coffee shops, 86 Seattle's Best Coffee Express espresso bars, and marketer of some 30 varieties of Seattle's Best whole bean and ground coffees. The decision was made to operate Seattle's Best as a separate subsidiary. Very quickly, Starbucks expanded its licensing arrangement with Kraft Foods to include marketing, distributing, and promoting the sales of Seattle's Best coffees and by 2009, Seattle's Best coffees were available nationwide in supermarkets and at more than 15,000 foodservice locations (college campuses, restaurants, hotels, airlines, and cruise lines). A new Seattle's Best line of ready-to-drink iced lattes was introduced in April 2010 in major grocery and convenience stores in the western United States; the manufacture, marketing, and distribution of the new Seattle's Best beverages was managed by PepsiCo as part of the long-standing Starbucks–PepsiCo joint venture for ready-to-drink Frappuccino products. In 2010, Starbucks introduced new distinctive red packaging and a red logo for Seattle's Best Coffee, boosted efforts to open more franchised Seattle's Best cafés, and expanded the availability of Seattle's Best coffees to 30,000 distribution points, including 7,250 Burger King outlets in the U.S., 9,000 Subway locations, and some 299 AMC movie theaters in five countries. During fiscal 2011, the licensing agreement with Kraft to handle sales and distribution of Seattle's Best coffee products was terminated and responsibility for the sales and distribution of these products was transitioned to the same in-house sales force that handled direct sales and distribution of Starbucks-branded coffees and Tazo tea products to supermarkets and warehouse clubs. The Seattle's Best subsidiary generated revenues of approximately $150 million in fiscal 2010 and $175 million in fiscal 2011.

In 2008, Starbucks introduced a new coffee blend called Pike Place™ Roast that would be brewed every day, all day, in every Starbucks store.[16] Before then, Starbucks rotated coffees through its brewed lineup, sometimes switching them weekly, sometimes daily. While some customers liked the ever-changing variety, the feedback from a majority of customers indicated a preference for a consistent brew that customers could count on when they came into a Starbucks store. Pike Place™ Roast was brewed in smaller batches in 30-minute intervals to ensure that customers were provided the freshest coffee possible. The new Pike Place™ Roast was created by Starbucks master roasters and coffee quality team using input from nearly 1,000 customers—it was smoother than Starbucks other signature dark roast coffee varieties. In January 2012, after eight months of testing over 80 different recipe and roast iterations, Starbucks introduced three blends of lighter-bodied and milder-tasting Starbucks Blonde Roast® coffees to better appeal to an estimated 54 million coffee drinkers in the U.S. who said they liked flavorful, lighter coffees with a gentle finish. The Blonde Roast blends were available as a brewed option in Starbucks stores in the U.S. and in packaged form in Starbucks stores and supermarkets. Because the majority of coffee sales in supermarkets were in the light and medium roast categories, Starbucks management saw its new Blonde Roast coffees blends as being a $1 billion market opportunity in the U.S. alone.

In fall 2009, Starbucks introduced Starbucks VIA® Ready Brew, packets of roasted coffee in an instant form, in an effort to attract a bigger fraction of on-the-go and at-home coffee drinkers. VIA was made with a proprietary microground technology that Starbucks claimed represented a breakthrough.[17] Simply adding a packet of VIA to a cup of hot or cold water produced an instant coffee with a rich, full-bodied taste that closely replicated the taste, quality, and flavor of traditional freshly brewed coffee. Starbucks stores held a four-day Starbucks VIA Taste Challenge promotion where customers were invited to compare the difference between Starbucks VIA and fresh-brewed Starbucks coffee. During the 2009 holiday season, Starbucks VIA Ready Brew was one of the top-selling coffee products at Amazon.com. Encouraged by favorable customer response, Starbucks expanded the distribution of VIA to some 25,000 grocery, mass merchandise, and drugstore accounts, including Kroger, Safeway, Walmart, Target, Costco, and CVS. Instant coffee made up a significant fraction of the coffee purchases in the United Kingdom (80 percent), Japan (53 percent), Russia (85 percent), and other countries where Starbucks stores were located—in both the UK and Japan, sales of instant coffee exceeded $4 billion annually. Globally, the instant and single-serve coffee category was a $23 billion market. In early 2010, Starbucks introduced VIA in all of the Starbucks stores in the UK and Japan.[18] By the end of fiscal 2011, VIA products were available at 70,000 locations and generated total sales of $250 million.

In fall 2011, Starbucks began selling Starbucks-branded coffee K-Cup® Portion Packs for the Keurig® Single-Cup Brewing system in its retail stores; the Keurig Brewer was produced and sold by Green Mountain Coffee Roasters. Starbucks entered into a strategic partnership with Green Mountain to manufacture the Starbucks-branded portion packs and also to be responsible for marketing, distributing, and selling them to major supermarket chains, drugstore chains, mass merchandisers and wholesale clubs, department stores, and specialty retailers throughout the United States and Canada. The partnership made good economic sense for both companies. Green Mountain could manufacture the single-cup portion packs in the same plants where it was producing its own brands of single-cup packs and then use its own internal resources and capabilities to market, distribute, and sell Starbucks-branded single-cup packs alongside its own brands of single-cup packs. It was far cheaper for Starbucks to pay Green Mountain to handle these functions than to build its own manufacturing plants and put its own in-house resources in place to market, distribute, and sell Starbucks single-cup coffee packs. Both partners expected their arrangement would help accelerate growth of the single-cup serving segment of the coffee market. Initially, the Starbucks single-cup packs were available in five blends of coffee and two blends of Tazo tea. Single-cup coffee packs represented a $3 billion market and the premium single-cup segment was the fastest growing part of the coffee market in the United States; globally, single-cup coffee constituted 8 percent of total coffee revenue. Just two months after launch, shipments of Starbucks-branded single-cup portion packs had exceeded 100 million units and the packs were available in about 70 percent of the targeted retailers; company officials estimated that Starbucks had achieved an 11 percent dollar share of the market for single-cup coffee packs in the United States.[19]

In March 2012, Starbucks announced that it would begin selling its first at-home premium single cup espresso and brewed coffee machine, the Verismo™ system by Starbucks, at select Starbucks store locations, online, and upscale specialty stores in late 2012. The Verismo system was a high-pressure system with the capability to brew both coffee and Starbucks-quality espresso beverages, from lattes to americanos, consistently and conveniently one cup at a time; sales of the Verismo single-cup machine put Starbucks into head-to-head competition with Nestlé's Nespresso machine and, to a lesser extent, Green Mountain's popular lineup of low-pressure Keurig brewers. Howard Schultz said that the move to begin sales of its own brewing system and single-serve coffee packs was "not about any disappointment with Green Mountain; it's about controlling our own destiny."[20] The global market for premium at-home espresso/coffee machines was estimated at $8 billion.[21] The introduction of the Verismo was the last phase of Starbucks' strategic plan to have coffee products covering all aspects of the single-cup coffee segment—instant coffees (with its VIA offerings), single portion coffee packs for single-cup brewers, and single-cup brewing machines.

Also in March 2012, Starbucks and Green Mountain announced the expansion of their strategic partnership to include the manufacturing, marketing, distribution, and sale of Starbucks-branded Vue™ packs for use in Green Mountain's recently introduced Keurig Vue Brewer that used Keurig Vue packs to brew coffee, tea, hot cocoa, and iced beverages. The expanded partnership called for Green Mountain initially to distribute the Starbucks Vue coffee packs to specialty retailers, department stores, and

mass merchandisers in the U.S. as well as sell them on Green Mountain's consumer direct website.

In response to customer requests for more wholesome food and beverage options and also to bring in business from non-coffee drinkers, Starbucks in 2008 altered its menu offerings in stores to include fruit cups, yogurt parfaits, skinny lattes, banana walnut bread (that was nearly 30 percent real banana), a 300-calorie farmer's market salad with all-natural dressing, and a line of 250-calorie "better-for-you" smoothies.[22] In 2009–2011, the company continued to experiment with healthier, lower-calorie selections and reformulated its recipes to include whole grains and dried fruits and to cut back on or eliminate the use of artificial flavorings, dyes, high-fructose corn syrup, and artificial preservatives. As of May 2012, retail store menus included an assortment of pastries and bakery selections, prepared breakfast and lunch sandwiches and wraps, a selection of bistro boxes (cheese and fruit, tuna salad, sliced chicken and hummus, chicken lettuce wraps), oatmeal, salads, parfaits, juices, and bottled water—at most stores in North America, food items could be warmed. Most recently, Starbucks had announced that it would soon add beer, wine, and complementary food offerings to its menu to help its stores become an attractive and relaxing after-work destination.

Starbucks overall sales mix in its retail stores in fiscal 2011 was 75 percent beverages, 19 percent food, 2 percent coffee-making equipment and other merchandise, and 3 percent whole bean, ground, and instant coffees.[23] However, the product mix in each store varied, depending on the size and location of each outlet. Larger stores carried a greater variety of whole coffee beans, gourmet food items, teas, coffee mugs, coffee grinders, coffee-making equipment, filters, storage containers, and other accessories. Smaller stores and kiosks typically sold a full-line of coffee beverages, a limited selection of whole bean and ground coffees and Tazo teas, and a few coffee-drinking accessories. Moreover, menu offerings at Starbucks stores were typically adapted to local cultures—for instance, the menu offerings at stores in North America included a selection of muffins, but stores in France had no muffins and instead featured locally made French pastries.

## Starbucks' Consumer Products Group

In 2010, Starbucks formed a new Consumer Products Group (CPG) to be responsible for sales of Starbuck products sold in all channels other than Starbucks company-operated and licensed retail stores and to manage the company's partnerships and joint ventures with PepsiCo, Unilever, Green Mountain Coffee Roasters, and others. Exhibit 4 shows the recent performance of the Consumer Products Group. Starbucks executives considered that the sales opportunities for Starbucks products in distribution channels outside Starbucks retail stores were quite attractive from the standpoint of both long-term growth and profitability.

In the first quarter of fiscal 2012, Starbucks expanded the CPG's portfolio of product offerings by spending $30 million to acquire Evolution Fresh, Inc., a maker of super-premium juices that were sold mostly at Whole Foods Market, the biggest organic and natural foods supermarket chain in North America. The strategic purpose of this acquisition was not only to use Starbucks sales and marketing resources to grow the sales of Evolution Fresh and capture a bigger share of the $3.4 billion super-premium juice segment but also to begin a long-term campaign to pursue growth opportunities in the $50 billion health and wellness sector of the U.S. economy. Starbucks opened its first Evolution Fresh retail store in Bellevue, Washington, in March 2012; more openings of Evolution Fresh stores were planned for later in 2012 and beyond. Starbucks also began selling Evolution Fresh juices in supermarket channels in March 2012.

## Advertising

Starbucks spent sparingly on advertising, preferring instead to build the brand cup by cup with customers and depend on word of mouth and the appeal of its storefronts. Advertising expenditures were $141.4

### EXHIBIT 4 Performance of Starbucks' Consumer Products Group, Fiscal Years 2009–2011 (in millions)

| Consumer Products Group operations | Fiscal Year | | |
|---|---|---|---|
| | 2011 | 2010 | 2009 |
| Total net revenues | $860.5 | $707.4 | $674.4 |
| Operating income | $273.0 | $261.4 | $281.8 |
| Operating income as a percent of total net revenues | 31.7% | 37.0% | 41.8% |

*Source:* 2011 10-K Report, p. 76.

million in fiscal 2011, $176.2 million in fiscal 2010, $126.3 million in fiscal 2009, $129.0 million in fiscal 2008, and $103.5 million in 2007. Starbucks stepped up advertising efforts in 2008 to combat the strategic initiatives of McDonald's and several other fast-food chains to begin offering premium coffees and coffee drinks at prices below those charged by Starbucks. In 2009, McDonald's reportedly spent more than $100 million on television, print, radio, billboard, and online ads promoting its new line of McCafé coffee drinks. Starbucks countered with the biggest advertising campaign the company had ever undertaken.[24]

## Vertical Integration

Howard Schultz saw Starbucks as having a unique strategy compared to the strategies pursued by its many coffeehouse competitors. He observed:[25]

> People sometimes fail to realize that almost unlike any retailer or restaurant, we are completely vertically integrated. We source coffee from 30 countries. We have a proprietary roasting process. We distribute to company owned stores, and finally serve the coffee. Others are resellers of commodity-based coffees.

# HOWARD SCHULTZ'S EFFORTS TO MAKE STARBUCKS A GREAT PLACE TO WORK

Howard Schultz deeply believed that Starbucks' success was heavily dependent on customers having a very positive experience in its stores. This meant having store employees who were knowledgeable about the company's products, who paid attention to detail in preparing the company's espresso drinks, who eagerly communicated the company's passion for coffee, and who possessed the skills and personality to deliver consistent, pleasing customer service. Many of the baristas were in their 20s and worked part-time, going to college on the side or pursuing other career activities. The challenge to Starbucks, in Schultz's view, was how to attract, motivate, and reward store employees in a manner that would make Starbucks a company that people would want to work for and that would generate enthusiastic commitment and higher levels of customer service. Moreover, Schultz wanted to send all Starbucks employees a message that would cement the trust that had been building between management and the company's workforce.

## Instituting Health Care Coverage for All Employees

One of the requests that employees had made to the prior owners of Starbucks was to extend health care benefits to part-time workers. Their request had been turned down, but Schultz believed that expanding health care coverage to include part-timers was something the company needed to do. His father had recently passed away with cancer and he knew from having grown up in a family that struggled to make ends meet how difficult it was to cope with rising medical costs. In 1988, Schultz went to the board of directors with his plan to expand the company's health care coverage to include part-timers who worked at least 20 hours per week. He saw the proposal not as a generous gesture but as a core strategy to win employee loyalty and commitment to the company's mission. Board members resisted because the company was unprofitable and the added costs of the extended coverage would only worsen the company's bottom line. But Schultz argued passionately that it was the right thing to do and wouldn't be as expensive as it seemed. He observed that if the new benefit reduced turnover, which he believed was likely, then it would reduce the costs of hiring and training—which equaled about $3,000 per new hire. He further pointed out that it cost $1,500 a year to provide an employee with full benefits. Part-timers, he argued, were vital to Starbucks, constituting two-thirds of the company's workforce. Many were baristas who knew the favorite drinks of regular customers; if the barista left, that connection with the customer was broken. Moreover, many part-time employees were called upon to open the stores early, sometimes at 5:30 or 6 a.m.; others had to work until closing, usually 9 p.m. or later. Providing these employees with health care benefits, he argued, would signal that the company honored their value and contribution.

The board approved Schultz's plan and part-timers working 20 or more hours were offered the same health coverage as full-time employees starting in late 1988. Starbucks paid 75 percent of an employee's health care premium; the employee paid 25 percent. Over the years, Starbucks extended its health coverage to include preventive care, prescription drugs, dental care, eye care, mental health, and chemical dependency. Coverage was also offered for unmarried partners in a committed relationship. Since most Starbucks employees were young and comparatively healthy, the company had been able to provide broader coverage while keeping monthly payments relatively low.

## A Stock Option Plan for Employees

By 1991, the company's profitability had improved to the point where Schultz could pursue a stock option plan for all employees, a program he believed would have a positive, long-term effect on the success of Starbucks.[26] Schultz wanted to turn every Starbucks employee into a partner, give them a chance to share in the success of the company, and make clear the connection between their contributions and the company's market value. Even though Starbucks was still a private company, the plan that emerged called for granting stock options to every full-time and part-time employee in proportion to their base pay. In May 1991, the plan, dubbed Bean Stock, was presented to the board. Though board members were concerned that increasing the number of shares might unduly dilute the value of the shares of investors who had put up hard cash, the plan received unanimous approval. The first grant was made in October 1991, just after the end of the company's fiscal year in September; each partner was granted stock options worth 12 percent of base pay. When the Bean Stock program was initiated, Starbucks dropped the term employee and began referring to all of its people as "partners" because every member of the Starbucks workforce became eligible for stock option awards after six months of employment and 500 paid work hours.

Starbucks went public in June 1992, selling its initial offering at a price of $17 per share. Starting in October 1992 and continuing through October 2004, Starbucks granted each eligible employee a stock option award with a value equal to 14 percent of base pay. Beginning in 2005, the plan was modified to tie the size of each employee's stock option awards to three factors: (1) Starbucks' success and profitability for the fiscal year, (2) the size of an employee's base wages, and (3) the price at which the stock option could be exercised. Since becoming a public company, Starbucks stock had split 2-for-1 on five occasions; the stock traded at an all-time high of $62 per share in April 2012. As of October 2, 2011, Starbucks partners held 45.3 million shares in stock option awards that had a weighted average contractual life of 6.4 years; these shares had a weighted average exercise price of $18.57 and an aggregate value of $848 million.[27]

# Starbucks' Stock Purchase Plan for Employees

In 1995, Starbucks implemented an employee stock purchase plan that gave partners who had been employed for at least 90 days an opportunity to purchase company stock through regular payroll deductions. Partners who enrolled could devote anywhere from 1 to 10 percent of their base earnings (up to an annual maximum of $25,000) to purchasing shares of Starbucks stock. After the end of each calendar quarter, each participant's contributions were used to buy Starbucks stock at a discount of 5 percent of the closing price on the last business day of each calendar quarter (the discount was 15 percent until March 2009).

Since inception of the plan, some 24.8 million shares had been purchased by partners; roughly 30 percent of Starbucks partners participated in the stock purchase plan during the 2000–2011 period.

# The Workplace Environment

Starbucks management believed its competitive pay scales and comprehensive benefits for both full-time and part-time partners allowed it to attract motivated people with above-average skills and good work habits. An employee's base pay was determined by the pay scales prevailing in the geographic region where an employee worked and by the person's job, skills, experience, and job performance. About 90 percent of Starbucks' partners were full-time or part-time baristas, paid on an hourly basis. After six months of employment, baristas could expect to earn $8.50 to $9.50 per hour. In 2009, experienced full-time baristas in the company's U.S. stores earned an average of about $37,800; store managers earned an average of $44,400.[28] Voluntary turnover at Starbucks was 13 percent in 2009.[29] Starbucks executives believed that efforts to make the company an attractive, caring place to work were responsible for its relatively low turnover rates. Starbucks received 225,000 job applications in 2008 and 150,000 job applications in 2009.

Surveys of Starbucks partners conducted by *Fortune* magazine in the course of selecting companies for inclusion on its annual list of the "100 Best Companies to Work For" indicated that full-time baristas liked working at Starbucks because of the camaraderie, while part-timers were particularly pleased with the health insurance benefits (those who enrolled in Starbucks' most economical plan for just routine health care paid only $6.25 per week).[30] Starbucks had been named to *Fortune*'s list in 1998, 1999, 2000, and every year from 2002 through 2012.

Starbucks' management utilized annual "Partner View" surveys to solicit feedback from its workforce, learn their concerns, and measure job satisfaction. The 2002 survey revealed that many employees viewed the benefits package as only "average," prompting the company to increase its match of 401(k) contributions for those who had been with the company more than three years and to have these contributions vest immediately. In a survey conducted in fiscal 2008, 80 percent of Starbucks' partners reported being satisfied.[31]

Schultz's approach to offering employees good compensation and a comprehensive benefits package was driven by his belief that sharing the company's success with the people who made it happen helped everyone think and act like an owner, build positive long-term relationships with customers, and do things in an efficient way. Schultz's rationale, based on his father's experience of going from one low-wage, no-benefits job to another, was that if you treat your employees well, that is how they will treat customers.

Exhibit 5 summarizes Starbucks' fringe benefit package.

# Employee Training and Recognition

To accommodate its strategy of rapid store expansion, Starbucks put in systems to recruit, hire, and train baristas and store managers. Starbucks' vice president for human resources used some simple guidelines in screening candidates for new positions, "We want passionate people who love coffee. . . . We're looking for a diverse workforce, which reflects our community. We want people who enjoy what they're doing and for whom work is an extension of themselves."[32]

Every partner/barista hired for a retail job in a Starbucks store received at least 24 hours training in their first two to four weeks. The topics included classes on coffee history, drink preparation, coffee knowledge (four hours), customer service (four hours), and retail skills, plus a four-hour workshop on "Brewing the Perfect Cup." Baristas spent considerable time learning about beverage preparation—grinding the beans, steaming milk, learning to pull perfect (18- to 23-second) shots of espresso, memorizing the recipes of all the different drinks, practicing making the different drinks, and learning how to customize drinks to customer specifications. There

## EXHIBIT 5   Starbucks' Fringe Benefit Program, 2012

- Medical insurance
- Sick time
- Dental and vision care
- Paid vacations (up to 120 hours annually for hourly workers with 5 or more years of service at retail stores and up to 200 hours annually for salaried and non-retail hourly employees with 10 or more years of service)
- Seven paid holidays
- One paid personal day every six months for salaried and non-retail hourly partners
- A 30 percent discount on purchases of beverages, food, and merchandise at Starbucks stores
- Mental health and chemical dependency coverage
- 401(k) retirement savings plan—the company matched 100 percent on the first 3 percent of eligible pay that a participant contributed, plus 50 percent of the next 2 percent of eligible pay contributed OR 100 percent on the first 6 percent of eligible pay a participant contributed. Starbucks matching contributions to the 401(k) plans worldwide totaled $45.5 million in fiscal 2011 and $23.5 million in fiscal 2010.
- Short- and long-term disability
- Stock purchase plan—eligible employees could buy shares at a 5 percent discount through regular payroll deductions of between 1 and 10 percent of base pay.
- Life insurance
- Short- and long-term disability insurance
- Accidental death and dismemberment insurance
- Adoption assistance
- Financial assistance program for partners that experience a financial crisis
- Stock option plan (Bean stock); shares were granted to eligible partners based on the company's performance and how many shares the company's board of directors made available.
- Pre-tax payroll deductions for commuter expenses
- Free coffee and tea products each week
- Tuition reimbursement program

*Source:* Information in the Careers section at **www.starbucks.com**, accessed May 3, 2012 and Starbucks 2011 10-K Report, p. 69.

were sessions on cash register operations, how to clean the milk wand on the espresso machine, explaining the Italian drink names to unknowing customers, selling home espresso machines, making eye contact with customers and interacting with them, and taking personal responsibility for the cleanliness of the store. And there were rules to be memorized: milk must be steamed to at least 150 degrees Fahrenheit but never more than 170 degrees; every espresso shot not pulled within 23 seconds must be tossed; never let coffee sit in the pot more than 20 minutes; always compensate dissatisfied customers with a Starbucks coupon that entitles them to a free drink.

Management trainees attended classes for 8 to 12 weeks. Their training went much deeper, covering not only coffee knowledge and information imparted to baristas but also going into the details of store operations, practices and procedures as set forth in the company's operating manual, information systems, and the basics of managing people. Starbucks' trainers were all store managers and district managers with onsite experience. One of their major objectives was to ingrain the company's values, principles, and culture and to pass on their knowledge about coffee and their passion about Starbucks.

When Starbucks opened stores in a new market, it sent a Star team of experienced managers and baristas to the area to lead the store opening effort and to conduct one-on-one training following the company's formal classes and basic orientation sessions at the Starbucks Coffee School in San Francisco. From time to time, Starbucks conducted special training programs, including a coffee masters program for store employees, leadership training for store managers, and career programs for partners in all types of jobs.

To recognize partner contributions, Starbucks had created a partner recognition program consisting of 18 different awards and programs. Examples included Coffee Master awards, Certified Barista awards, Spirit of Starbucks awards for exceptional achievement by a partner, a Manager of the Quarter for store manager leadership, Green Apron Awards for helping create a positive and welcoming store environment, Green Bean Awards for exceptional support of the company's environmental mission, and Bravo! awards for exceeding the standards of Starbucks customer service, significantly increasing sales, or reducing costs.

# STARBUCKS' VALUES, BUSINESS PRINCIPLES, AND MISSION

During the early building years, Howard Schultz and other Starbucks senior executives worked to instill some key values and guiding principles into the Starbucks culture. The cornerstone value in their effort "to build a company with soul" was that the company would never stop pursuing the perfect cup of coffee by buying the best beans and roasting them to perfection. Schultz was adamant about controlling the quality of Starbucks products and building a culture common to all stores. He was rigidly opposed to selling artificially flavored coffee beans—"we will not pollute our high-quality beans with chemicals"; if a customer wanted hazelnut-flavored coffee, Starbucks would provide it by adding hazelnut syrup to the drink, rather than by adding hazelnut flavoring to the beans during roasting. Running flavored beans through the grinders left chemical residues behind that altered the flavor of beans ground afterward.

Starbucks' management was also emphatic about the importance of employees paying attention to what pleased customers. Employees were trained to go out of their way, and to take heroic measures if necessary, to make sure customers were fully satisfied. The theme was "just say yes" to customer requests. Further, employees were encouraged to speak their minds without fear of retribution from upper management—senior executives wanted employees to be vocal about what Starbucks was doing right, what it was doing wrong, and what changes were needed. The intent was for employees to be involved in and contribute to the process of making Starbucks a better company.

## Starbucks' Mission Statement

In early 1990, the senior executive team at Starbucks went to an offsite retreat to debate the company's values and beliefs and draft a mission statement. Schultz wanted the mission statement to convey a strong sense of organizational purpose and to articulate the company's fundamental beliefs and guiding principles. The draft was submitted to all employees for review and several changes were made based on employee comments. The resulting mission statement and guiding principles are shown in Exhibit 6. In 2008, Starbucks partners from all across the company met for several months to refresh the mission statement and rephrase the underlying guiding principles; the revised mission statement and guiding principles are also shown in Exhibit 6.

# STARBUCKS' COFFEE PURCHASING STRATEGY

Coffee beans were grown in 70 tropical countries and were the second most traded commodity in the world after petroleum. Most of the world's coffee was grown by some 25 million small farmers, most of whom lived on the edge of poverty. Starbucks personnel traveled regularly to coffee-producing countries, building relationships with growers and exporters, checking on agricultural conditions and crop yields, and searching out varieties and sources that would meet Starbucks' exacting standards of quality and flavor. The coffee purchasing group, working with Starbucks personnel in roasting operations, tested new varieties and blends of green coffee beans from different sources. Sourcing from multiple geographic areas not only allowed Starbucks to offer a greater range of coffee varieties to customers but also spread its risks regarding weather, price volatility, and changing economic and political conditions in coffee-growing countries.

Starbucks' coffee sourcing strategy had three key elements:

- Make sure that the prices Starbucks paid for green (unroasted) coffee beans was high enough to ensure that small farmers were able to cover their production costs and provide for their families.
- Utilize purchasing arrangements that limited Starbucks exposure to sudden price jumps due to weather, economic and political conditions in the growing countries, new agreements establishing export quotas, and periodic efforts to bolster prices by restricting coffee supplies.
- Work directly with small coffee growers, local coffee-growing cooperatives, and other types of coffee suppliers to promote coffee cultivation methods that protected biodiversity and were environmentally sustainable.

## EXHIBIT 6   Starbucks' Mission Statement, Values, and Business Principles

| Mission Statement, 1990 – October 2008 |
| --- |

Establish Starbucks as the premier purveyor of the finest coffee in the world while maintaining our uncompromising principles as we grow.

The following six guiding principles will help us measure the appropriateness of our decisions:

- Provide a great work environment and treat each other with respect and dignity.
- Embrace diversity as an essential component in the way we do business.
- Apply the highest standards of excellence to the purchasing, roasting, and fresh delivery of our coffee.
- Develop enthusiastically satisfied customers all of the time.
- Contribute positively to our communities and our environment.
- Recognize that profitability is essential to our future success.

| Mission Statement, October 2008 – Present |
| --- |

Our Mission: To inspire and nurture the human spirit—one person, one cup, and one neighborhood at a time.

Here are the principles of how we live that every day:

**Our Coffee**

It has always been, and will always be, about quality. We're passionate about ethically sourcing the finest coffee beans, roasting them with great care, and improving the lives of people who grow them. We care deeply about all of this; our work is never done.

**Our Partners**

We're called partners, because it's not just a job, it's our passion. Together, we embrace diversity to create a place where each of us can be ourselves. We always treat each other with respect and dignity. And we hold each other to that standard.

**Our Customers**

When we are fully engaged, we connect with, laugh with, and uplift the lives of our customers—even if just for a few moments. Sure, it starts with the promise of a perfectly made beverage, but our work goes far beyond that. It's really about human connection.

**Our Stores**

When our customers feel this sense of belonging, our stores become a haven, a break from the worries outside, a place where you can meet with friends. It's about enjoyment at the speed of life—sometimes slow and savored, sometimes faster. Always full of humanity.

**Our Neighborhood**

Every store is part of a community, and we take our responsibility to be good neighbors seriously. We want to be invited in wherever we do business. We can be a force for positive action—bringing together our partners, customers, and the community to contribute every day. Now we see that our responsibility—and our potential for good—is even larger. The world is looking to Starbucks to set the new standard, yet again. We will lead.

**Our Shareholders**

We know that as we deliver in each of these areas, we enjoy the kind of success that rewards our shareholders. We are fully accountable to get each of these elements right so that Starbucks—and everyone it touches—can endure and thrive.

*Source:* Company documents and postings at www.starbucks.com, accessed May 15, 2012.

## Pricing and Purchasing Arrangements

Commodity-grade coffee was traded in a highly competitive market as an undifferentiated product. However, high-altitude Arabica coffees of the quality purchased by Starbucks were bought on a negotiated basis at a substantial premium above commodity coffee. The prices of the top-quality coffees sourced by Starbucks depended on supply and demand conditions at the time of the purchase and were subject to considerable volatility due to weather, economic and political conditions in the growing countries, new agreements establishing export quotas, and periodic efforts to bolster prices by restricting coffee supplies.

Starbucks bought coffee using fixed-price and price-to-be-fixed purchase commitments, depending on market conditions, to secure an adequate supply of quality green coffee. Price-to-be-fixed contracts were purchase commitments whereby the quality, quantity, delivery period, and other negotiated terms were agreed upon, but the date at which the base price component of commodity grade coffee was to be fixed was as yet unspecified. For these types of contracts, either Starbucks or the seller had the option to select a date on which to "fix" the base price of commodity grade coffee prior to the delivery date. As of October 2, 2011, Starbucks had a total of $1.0 billion in purchase commitments, of which $193 million represented the estimated cost of price-to-be-fixed contracts. All price-to-be-fixed contracts as of October 2, 2011 gave Starbucks the right to fix the base price component of commodity-grade coffee. Management believed that its purchase agreements as of October 2, 2011 would provide an adequate supply of green coffee through fiscal 2012.[33]

## Starbucks' Ethical Sourcing Practices for Coffee Beans

Starbucks was committed to buying green coffee beans that were responsibly grown and came from sources that guaranteed small coffee growers received prices for their green coffee beans sufficiently high enough to allow them to pay fair wages to their workers and earn enough to reinvest in their farms and communities, develop the business skills needed to compete in the global market for coffee, and afford basic health care, education, and home improvements. The company's supplies of green coffee beans were chiefly grown on tens of thousands of small family farms (less than 30 acres) located in low-income countries in Central America, East Africa, and Asia.

Since 1998, Starbucks had partnered with Conservation International's Center for Environmental Leadership to develop specific guidelines (called Coffee and Farmer Equity [C.A.F.E.] Practices) covering four areas: product quality, the price received by farmers/growers, safe and humane working conditions (including compliance with minimum wage requirements and child labor provisions), and environmentally responsible cultivation practices.[34] Some 100,000 small coffee bean farms employing more than

1 million workers were operating according to C.A.F.E. Practices in 2010. Numerous other small coffee growers were members of cooperatives that were associated with one of the 25 members of Fair Trade International that (1) helped small farmers get fair prices for their products and develop market opportunities, (2) set international Fair Trade standards, and (3) oversaw companies that wanted to market their products as Fair Trade–certified. Increasingly, many small farmers were growing their coffees "organically" without the use of pesticides, herbicides, or chemical fertilizers; organic cultivation methods resulted in clean ground water and helped protect against degrading of local ecosystems, many of which were fragile or in areas where biodiversity was under severe threat.

Top management at Starbucks had set a goal that by 2015 all of the green coffee beans purchased from growers would be C.A.F.E. Practice certified, Fair Trade certified, organically certified, or certified by some other equally acceptable third party. In 2011, 86 percent of Starbucks purchases of green coffee beans were C.A.F.E. Practices–verified sources and about 8 percent were from Fair Trade–certified sources. Starbucks was among the world's largest purchasers of Fair Trade–certified coffee beans, and it marketed Fair Trade–certified coffees at most of its retail stores and through other locations that sold Starbucks coffees.

Starbucks' Tazo tea operation was a member of the Ethical Tea Partnership and worked with other tea buyers to improve conditions for workers on tea estates. Through the CHAI (Community Health and Advancement Initiative) project, a joint partnership with Mercy Corps, Starbucks supported tea-growing communities with health services and economic development.

**Small Farmer Support Programs**    Because many of the tens of thousands of small family farms with less than 30 acres that grew coffees purchased by Starbucks often lacked the money to make farming improvements and/or cover all expenses until they sold their crops, Starbucks provided funding to organizations that made loans to small coffee growers. In 2010, $14.6 million was loaned to nearly 56,000 farmers who grew green coffee beans for Starbucks in 10 countries; in 2011, $14.7 million was loaned to over 45,000 farmers who grew green coffee beans for Starbucks in 7 countries. Starbucks goal was to increase funding to $20 million by 2015. In addition, the company funded Starbucks Farmer Support Centers in Central America, East Africa, and Asia where

Starbucks agronomists and quality experts helped local coffee farmers implement environmentally responsible growing practices, improve the quality and size of their harvests, and ultimately earn better prices.

# COFFEE ROASTING OPERATIONS

Starbucks considered the roasting of its coffee beans to be something of an art form, entailing trial-and-error testing of different combinations of time and temperature to get the most out of each type of bean and blend. Recipes were put together by the coffee department, once all the components had been tested. Computerized roasters guaranteed consistency. Highly trained and experienced roasting personnel monitored the process, using both smell and hearing, to help check when the beans were perfectly done—coffee beans make a popping sound when ready. Starbucks' standards were so exacting that roasters tested the color of the beans in a blood-cell analyzer and discarded the entire batch if the reading wasn't on target. After roasting and cooling, the coffee was immediately vacuum-sealed in bags that preserved freshness for up to 26 weeks. As a matter of policy, however, Starbucks removed coffees on its shelves after three months and, in the case of coffee used to prepare beverages in stores, the shelf life was limited to seven days after the bag was opened.

Starbucks had roasting plants in Kent, Washington; York, Pennsylvania; Minden, Nevada; Charleston, South Carolina; and The Netherlands. In addition to their roasting capability, these plants also had additional space for warehousing and shipping coffees. In keeping with Starbucks' corporate commitment to reduce its environmental footprint, the state-of-the-art roasting plant built in South Carolina in 2009 had been awarded LEED Silver Certification for New Construction by the U.S. Green Building Council. Twenty percent of materials used in the construction of the building were from recycled content and over 75 percent of the waste generated during construction was recycled. In addition, the facility utilized state-of-the-art light and water fixtures and was partly powered by wind energy. Some of the green elements in the South Carolina plant were subsequently implemented in the other roasting plants as part of the company's initiative to achieve LEED Certification for all company-operated facilities by the end of 2010.[35]

# STARBUCKS' CORPORATE SOCIAL RESPONSIBILITY STRATEGY

Howard Schultz's effort to "build a company with soul" included a long history of doing business in ways that were socially and environmentally responsible. A commitment to do the right thing had been central to how Starbucks operated since Howard Schultz first became CEO in 1987, and one of the core beliefs at Starbucks was that "the way to build a great, enduring company is to strike a balance between profitability and a social conscience." The specific actions comprising Starbucks' social responsibility strategy had varied over the years but the intent of the strategy was consistently one of contributing positively to the communities in which Starbucks had stores, being a good environmental steward, and conducting its business in ways that earned the trust and respect of customers, partners/employees, suppliers, and the general public.

In 2008–2012, Starbucks' corporate social responsibility strategy had four main elements:

1. *Ethically sourcing all of its products*—This included promoting responsible growing practices for the company's coffees and teas (and the cocoa contained in the beverages it served) and striving to buy the manufactured products and services it needed from suppliers who had a demonstrated commitment to social and environmental responsibility. Company personnel purchased paper products with high levels of recycled content and unbleached fiber. Suppliers were encouraged to provide the most energy-efficient products within their category and eliminate excessive packaging; Starbucks had recently instituted a set of Supplier Social Responsibility Standards covering the suppliers of all the manufactured goods and services used in the company's operations. No genetically modified ingredients were used in any food or beverage products that Starbucks served, with the exception of milk (U.S. labeling requirements did not require milk producers to disclose the use of hormones aimed at increasing the milk production of dairy herds).

In 2011, Starbucks audited 129 supplier factories and found 38 that failed its zero-tolerance standards. Purchases from 26 of these factories were discontinued for standards issues, although purchases from 14 previously dropped factories were later resumed when they achieved compliance. Since initiating audits of supplier compliance in 2006, Starbucks had conducted more than 500 factory assessments and continued to work with more than 100 of these factories on programs to improve their standards. Also in 2011, Starbucks became a member of the Global Social Compliance Program, a business-driven effort to promote the continuous improvement of environmental and working conditions at supplier factories worldwide.

2. *Community involvement and corporate citizenship*—
   Active engagement in community activities and display of good corporate citizenship had always been core elements in the way Starbucks conducted its business. Starbucks stores and employees regularly volunteered for community improvement projects and initiatives that would have a meaningful impact on the localities in which Starbucks had a presence. The company had a goal of getting Starbucks partners and customers to contribute more than 1 million hours of community service annually by 2015; service contributions totaled 246,000 hours in 2008, 186,000 hours in 2009, 191,000 hours in 2010, and 442,000 hours in 2011. In addition, Starbucks had a goal of annually engaging 50,000 young people to help meet needs and solve problems they saw in their neighborhoods. Toward this end, Starbucks made a series of Youth Action Grants each year to involve young people in community improvement projects—these Youth Action Grants totaled $2.1 million in fiscal 2009 and $1.6 million in fiscal 2010. To celebrate the 40th anniversary of the opening of the first Starbucks Coffee store at Pike Place in Seattle, during fiscal 2011 the company sponsored a special global month of service in which more than 60,000 people in 30 countries volunteered for over 150,000 service hours and completed 1,400 community-service projects. Starbucks held its second global month of service in April 2012.

3. *Environmental stewardship*—Initiatives here included a wide variety of actions to increase recycling, reduce waste, be more energy efficient, use renewable energy sources, conserve water resources, make all company facilities as green as possible by using environmentally friendly building materials and energy efficient designs, and engage in more efforts to address climate change. Beginning in January 2011, all new company-owned retail stores globally were built to achieve LEED certification.

In 2008, Starbucks set a goal of reducing water consumption by 25 percent in company-owned stores by 2015, and after two years had implemented proactive measures that had decreased water use by almost 22 percent. Also in 2008, Starbucks undertook actions to purchase renewable energy equivalent to 50 percent of the electricity used in its North American company-owned stores; that goal was achieved during 2009, at which point Starbucks set a goal to increase its renewable energy purchases to 100 percent of the energy used in all company-owned stores worldwide. The Environmental Protection Agency named Starbucks as one of the Top Five Green Power Purchasers in the U.S. in 2010 and 2011. Starbucks had a program in place to achieve a 25 percent reduction in energy use by 2015. In 2011, nearly 80 percent of company-owned Starbucks stores in North America were recycling cardboard boxes and other back-of-store items; efforts were underway to have front-of-store recycling bins in place in all company-owned locations in North America by 2015 (however, Starbucks faced significant challenges in implementing recycling at its 17,000-plus stores worldwide because of wide variations in municipal recycling capabilities). Since 1985, Starbucks had given a $0.10 discount to customers who brought reusable cups and tumblers to stores for use in serving the beverages they ordered—in 2011, some 34.1 million beverages were served in customers' containers. The company's goal was to serve 5 percent of the beverages made in its stores in reusable containers by 2015. Stores participated in Earth Day activities each year with in-store promotions and volunteer efforts to educate employees and customers about the impacts their actions had on the environment. Starbucks was a founding member of the Business for Innovative Climate and Energy Policy coalition, where it worked with other companies to advocate stronger clean energy and climate policies.

4. *Charitable contributions*—The Starbucks Foundation, set up in 1997, oversaw a major portion of the company's philanthropic activities; it received the majority of its funding from Starbucks Coffee Company and private donations. In 2010, the Starbucks Foundation made more than 100 grants to nonprofit organizations totaling $5.4 million, including $1 million to the American Red Cross efforts for the Haiti earthquake relief effort; the Foundation

made 145 grants totaling $13.5 million to various nonprofit organizations in fiscal 2011. The 2011 grants included financial support to the American Red Cross for ongoing relief to U.S. communities experiencing severe tornado damage, floods, and other natural disasters; the Japan Earthquake Relief Fund; communities in the tea-growing regions of Darjeeling, India; and Save the Children for efforts to improve education, health, and nutrition in both Guatemala and Indonesia. In 2010, Starbucks Corporation made charitable contributions totaling $10.3 million in cash and $6.7 million in in-kind contributions toward community-building programs. In 2011, it made cash contributions of $30.5 million and in-kind contributions of $17.3 million. For a number of years, Starbucks had made donations to the Global Fund and Product (RED)™ to provide medicine to people in Africa with AIDS; so far Starbucks had made contributions equaling more than 18 million doses of medicine daily. In years past, Starbucks had made a $5 million, five-year commitment to long-term relief and recovery efforts for victims of hurricanes Rita and Katrina and committed $5 million to support educational programs in China.[36]

Water, sanitation, and hygiene education programs in water-stressed countries were supported through the Starbucks Foundation's Ethos Water Fund. For each bottle of Ethos water purchased at Starbucks stores, Starbucks donated $0.05 ($0.10 in Canada) to the Ethos Water Fund. Since 2005, the Fund had made $6 million in grants, benefitting more than 420,000 people around the world. (Starbucks had acquired Ethos Water for $8 million in 2005 and sold Ethos-branded bottled water in its stores. The production, distribution, and marketing of Ethos water products was handled by PepsiCo, as part of its longstanding joint venture with Starbucks.)

In 2012, Starbucks was named to *Corporate Responsibility Magazine*'s list of the 100 Best Corporate Citizens for 2010, the 12th time that Starbucks had been named to the magazine's list. The 100 Best Corporate Citizens List was based on more than 360 data points of publicly available information in seven categories: Environment, Climate Change, Human Rights, Philanthropy, Employee Relations, Financial Performance, and Governance. Over the years, Starbucks had received over 25 awards from a diverse group of organizations for its philanthropic, community service, and environmental activities.

# TOP MANAGEMENT CHANGES: CHANGING ROLES FOR HOWARD SCHULTZ

In 2000, Howard Schultz decided to relinquish his role as CEO, retain his position as chairman of the company's board of directors, and assume the newly created role of chief strategic officer. Orin Smith, a Starbucks executive who had been with the company since its early days, was named CEO. Smith retired in 2005 and was replaced as CEO by Jim Donald who had been president of Starbucks' North American division. In 2006, Donald proceeded to set a long-term objective of having 40,000 stores worldwide and launched a program of rapid store expansion in an effort to achieve that goal.

But investors and members of Starbucks' board of directors (including Howard Schultz) became uneasy about Donald's leadership of the company when the company's stock price drifted downward through much of 2007, customer traffic in Starbucks stores in the U.S. began to erode in 2007, new store openings worldwide were continuing at the rate of six per day, and Donald kept pressing for increased efficiency in store operations at the expense of good customer service. Schultz had lamented in an internal company e-mail in 2007 (which was leaked to the public) that the company's aggressive growth had led to "a watering down of the Starbucks experience."[37] In January 2008, the Starbucks board asked Howard Schultz to return to his role as CEO and lead a major restructuring and revitalization initiative.

# HOWARD SCHULTZ'S CAMPAIGN TO REINVIGORATE STARBUCKS, 2008–2011

Immediately upon his return as Starbucks CEO, Schultz revamped the company's executive leadership team and changed the roles and responsibilities of several key executives.[38] Believing that Starbucks in recent years had become less passionate about customer relationships and the coffee experience that had fueled the company's success, Schultz hired a former Starbucks executive to fill the newly created position of chief creative officer responsible for elevating the in-store experience of customers and achieving new levels of innovation and differentiation. He then proceeded to launch a series of actions to recast Starbucks into the company he envisioned it ought to be, push the company to new plateaus of differentiation and innovation, and prepare for renewed global expansion of Starbucks retail store network. This transformation effort, which instantly became the centerpiece of his return as company CEO, had three main themes: strengthen the core, elevate the experience, and invest and grow. Schultz's cost containment and efficiency campaign produced gratifying results—the productivity of Starbucks employees in U.S. company-operated retail stores increased from an average of 9.8 transactions per labor hour in fiscal 2008 to 11.3 transactions per labor hour in fiscal 2011.[39] In addition, the percentage change in sales at company-operated retail stores open at least 13 months had risen from –9 percent in Q1 of fiscal 2009 to +4 percent in Q1 of fiscal 2010 to +9 percent in Q3 of fiscal 2010 and then remained in the range of +7 to +9 percent every quarter through Q2 of fiscal 2012.

In 2010, as part of Schultz's "invest and grow" aspect of transforming Starbucks, the company began formulating plans to open "thousands of new stores" in China over time.[40] Japan had long been Starbucks biggest foreign market outside North America, but Howard Schultz said that, "Asia clearly represents the most significant growth opportunity on a go-forward basis."[41] Schultz also indicated that Starbucks was anxious to begin opening stores in India and Vietnam, two country markets that Starbucks believed were potentially lucrative. During fiscal 2011, Starbucks opened its 500th store in mainland China but, as of April 2012, no stores had yet opened in either Vietnam or India. Top management expected that China would remain the focal point of the company's global expansion efforts and become its largest market outside of the United States, with more than 1,500 stores by 2015.

## STARBUCKS' FUTURE PROSPECTS

Starbucks reported strong performance for its first two quarters of fiscal 2012:

- Revenues were $6.6 billion, up 16 percent over the first six months of fiscal 2011.
- Operating income was $986.4 million, up 12 percent compared to the first half of fiscal 2011.

- Earnings per share were $0.90, up 14 percent over the prior year.
- Sales at all company-operated retail stores open 13 months or longer rose 8 percent during the first two quarters of fiscal 2012.
- In the second quarter, sales growth at company-operated stores in China open at least 13 months exceeded 20 percent for the seventh consecutive quarter.

In addition, top management provided the following updated performance targets for full-year 2012:

- Opening a net of 500 new stores in the Americas, with licensed stores comprising approximately one-half of the new additions.
- Opening a net of 400 new stores in the China/ Asia Pacific region (including 200 in China), with licensed stores comprising approximately two-thirds of the new additions.
- Maintaining its plan to open a net of 100 new stores in Europe, the Middle East, Russia, and Africa (EMEA), with licensed stores comprising approximately two-thirds of the new stores.
- Achieving revenue growth in the low teens, driven by mid-single-digit comparable store sales growth, 1,000 net new store openings, and continued strong growth in the Consumer Products Group segment.
- Achieving earnings per share of $1.81 to $1.84, representing a 19 to 21 percent increase over fiscal 2011 EPS of $1.52. EPS growth was expected to be approximately 25 to 29 percent in the second half of fiscal 2012.

Management also indicated that it expected to encounter higher commodity costs of approximately $230 million in fiscal 2012, with the majority of this already reflected in the results for the first half of the year. Capital expenditures for fiscal 2012 were expected to be about $900 million.

In January 2012, Howard Schultz said:[42]

Starbucks future has never been brighter. Our foundation never more solid. We are remarkably well positioned to pursue our diversified, multichannel, multibrand business model.

He believed that Starbucks was firing on all cylinders and ready to take full advantage of the many global opportunities that lay ahead.[43]

## ENDNOTES

1 Company press release, April 26, 2012.

2 Howard Schultz and Dori Jones Yang, *Pour Your Heart Into It* (New York: Hyperion, 1997), p. 33.

3 Ibid., p. 34.

4 Ibid., p. 36.

5 Ibid., pp. 61–62.

6 Ibid., pp. 101–102.

7 Ibid., p. 142.

8 2009 Annual Report, p. 3, and Starbucks webcast, March 8, 2012.

9 "Starbucks Plans New Global Store Design," *Restaurants and Institutions,* June 25, 2009, accessed at www.rimag.com on December 29, 2009.

10 Starbucks Global Responsibility Report for 2009, p. 13.

11 Company press releases, May 31, 2005 and October 25, 2005.

12 Company press release, November 1, 2007.

13 As stated by Howard Schultz in an interview with *Harvard Business Review* editor-in-chief Adi Ignatius; the interview was published in the July–August 2010 issue of the *Harvard Business Review,* pp. 108–115.

14 "Starbucks and iTunes Bring Complimentary Digital Music and Video Offerings with Starbucks Pick of the Week," *Starbucks.com,* April 15, 2008, http://news.starbucks.com/article_display.cfm?article_id=93, accessed June 8, 2010.

15 2009 Annual Report, p. 5.

16 Company press release, April 7, 2008.

17 Company press release, February 19, 2009.

18 Company press release, April 13, 2010.

19 Company press release, January 26, 2012.

20 Starbucks webcast, March 8, 2012; also quoted in Christelle Agboka, "Verisimo to Give Starbucks an Edge in Single-Cup Coffee Market," posted at www.reportlinker.com on March 14, 2012, accessed May 17, 2012.

21 Starbucks management presentation at UBS Global Consumer Conference, March 14, 2012; accessed at www.starbucks.com on May 18, 2012.

22 Company press release, July 14, 2008.

23 2009 Annual Report, p. 4.

24 Claire Cain Miller, "New Starbucks Ads Seek to Recruit Online Fans," *The New York Times,* May 18, 2009, accessed at www.nytimes.com on January 3, 2010.

25 Andy Server, "Schultz' Plan to Fix Starbucks," *Fortune,* January 18, 2008, accessed at www.fortune.com on June 21, 2010.

26 As related in Schultz and Yang, *Pour Your Heart Into It,* pp. 131–136.

27 2011 10-K Report, p. 67.

28 As cited in Fortune's 2010 list of the "100 Best Companies to Work For," http://money.cnn.com/magazines/fortune/bestcompanies/2010/snapshots/93.html, accessed June 9, 2010.

29 Ibid.

30 Company news release, May 21, 2009, accessed at www.starbucks.com on June 14, 2010.

31 Starbucks 2008 Global Responsibility Report.

32 Kate Rounds, "Starbucks Coffee," *Incentive,* Vol. 167, No. 7, p. 22.

33 2011 10-K Report, p.6.

34 Information posted in the corporate responsibility section at www.starbucks.com, accessed on June 18, 2010.

35 Company press release, February 19, 2009.

36 Company press release, January 18, 2010.

37 As reported in "Shakeup at Starbucks," www.cbsnews.com, January 7, 2008, accessed June 16, 2010.

38 Transcript of Starbucks Earnings Conference Call for Quarters 1 and 3 of fiscal year 2008, posted at http://seekingalpha.com and accessed June 16, 2010.

39 Starbucks management presentation at UBS Global Consumer Conference, March 14, 2012, accessed at www.starbucks.com on May 18, 2012.

40 Mariko Sanchanta, "Starbucks Plans Major China Expansion," *The Wall Street Journal,* April 13, 2010, accessed at http://online.wsj.com on June 10, 2010.

41 Ibid.

42 Letter to the shareholders, Starbucks 2011 Annual Report, p. 2.

43 Company press release, January 26, 2012.

# Herman Miller Inc. in 2012: An Ongoing Case of Reinvention and Renewal

**Frank Shipper**
Salisbury University

**Karen Manz**
Author and Researcher

**Steven B. Adams**
Salisbury University

**Charles C. Manz**
University of Massachusetts

Herman Miller was widely recognized as the leader in the office furniture industry and had built a reputation for innovation in products and processes since D. J. De Pree became president over 90 years ago. Herman Miller was one of only four companies and the only non-high-technology enterprise named to *Fortune*'s "Most Admired Companies" and "The 100 Best Companies to Work For" lists and also to *FastCompany*'s "Most Innovative Companies" list in both 2008 and 2010. The three high-technology organizations selected for these lists were Microsoft, Cisco, and Google. Unlike most firms, especially those in mature industries and most of its office furniture rivals, Herman Miller had pursued a path distinctively marked by reinvention and renewal.

This path had served it well over the decades. It survived the Great Depression early in its history and multiple recessions in the 20th century. In the early part of the 21st century, it recovered from the dot-com bust. In 2012, Herman Miller once again was facing turbulent and uncertain economic conditions. Would its propensity for using innovation to reinvent and renew its business once again allow the company to flourish and grow? How far and how fast might the company be able to push its annual revenues above the 2011 level of $1.6 billion?

## COMPANY BACKGROUND

Herman Miller's roots went back to 1905 and the Star Furniture Company, a manufacturer of traditional-style bedroom suites in Zeeland, Michigan. In 1909, it was renamed Michigan Star Furniture Company and hired Dirk Jan De Pree as a clerk. De Pree became president in 1919 and four years later convinced his father-in-law, Herman Miller, to purchase the majority of shares; De Pree renamed the company Herman Miller Furniture Company in recognition of Miller's support.

In 1927, De Pree committed himself to treating "all workers as individuals with special talents and potential." This occurred after he visited the family of a millwright who had died unexpectedly. During the visit, the widow read some poetry. Upon asking the widow who the poet was, De Pree was surprised to learn it was the millwright. This led him to wonder whether the millwright was a worker who wrote poetry or a poet who worked as a millwright. This story was part of Herman Miller's corporate culture, which continued to generate respect for all employees and fueled the quest to tap the diversity of gifts and skills held by all.

In 1930, the United States was in the Great Depression and Herman Miller was in financial trouble. As De Pree was looking for a way to save the company, Gilbert Rhode, a designer from New York, approached him and told him about his design philosophy. Rhode then asked for an opportunity to design a bedroom suite for a fee of $1,000. When De Pree reacted negatively to such a fee, Rhode suggested an alternative payment plan—a 3 percent royalty on the furniture sold—to which De Pree agreed, figuring that there was nothing to lose.

Many sources were helpful in providing material for this case, most particularly employees at Herman Miller who generously shared their time and viewpoints about the company to help ensure that the case accurately reflected the company's practices and culture. They provided many resources, including internal documents and stories of their personal experiences.

A few weeks later, De Pree received the first designs from Rhode. Again, he reacted negatively. In response, Rhode wrote De Pree a letter explaining his design philosophy: "[First,] utter simplicity: no surface enrichment, no carvings, no moldings, [and second,] furniture should be anonymous. People are important, not furniture. Furniture should be useful." Rhode's designs were antithetical to traditional designs, but De Pree saw merit in them and set Herman Miller on a course of designing and selling furniture that reflected a way of life.

In 1942, Herman Miller produced its first office furniture—a Gilbert Rhode design referred to as the Executive Office Group. Rhode died two years later, and De Pree began a search for a new design leader. After reading an article in *Life* magazine about designer George Nelson, De Pree hired Nelson as Herman Miller's first design director.

In 1946, De Pree hired Charles and Ray Eames, a husband-and-wife design team based in Los Angeles. In the same year, Charles Eames's designs were featured in the first one-man furniture exhibit at New York's Museum of Modern Art. Some of his designs became part of the museum's permanent collection.

In 1950, Herman Miller, under the guidance of Dr. Carl Frost, a professor at Michigan State University, became the first company in the state of Michigan to implement a Scanlon Plan, a productivity incentive program devised by labor expert Joseph N. Scanlon. Underlying the Scanlon Plan were the "principles of equity and justice for everyone in the company." Two major functional elements of Scanlon Plans were the use of committees for sharing ideas on improvements and a structure for sharing increased profitability. The relationship between Frost and Herman Miller continued for at least four decades.

During the 1950s, Herman Miller introduced a number of new furniture designs, including those by Alexander Girard, Charles and Ray Eames, and George Nelson. Specifically, the company introduced the first molded fiberglass chairs and the Eames lounge chair and ottoman (see Exhibit 1). The Eames designs were introduced on NBC's *Home Show* with Arlene Francis, a precursor to the *Today* show. Also in the 1950s, Herman Miller began its first overseas foray, selling its products in the European market.

In 1962, D. J. De Pree became chairman of the board and his son, Hugh De Pree, became president and chief executive officer. D. J. De Pree had served for more than 40 years as the president of Herman Miller.

**EXHIBIT 1   Eames Lounge Chair and Ottoman**

During the 1960s, Herman Miller introduced many new designs for both home and office. The most notable design was the Action Office System, the world's first open-plan modular office arrangement of movable panels and attachments. By the end of the 1960s, Herman Miller had formed a subsidiary in England with sales and marketing responsibility throughout England and the Scandinavian countries. The company also established dealers in South and Central America, Australia, Canada, Europe, Africa, the Near East, and Japan.

In 1970, Herman Miller went public and made its first stock offering. The stock certificate was designed by the Eames office staff. The company entered the health/science market in 1971 and introduced the Ergon chair, its first design based on scientific observation and ergonomic principles, in 1976. In 1979, in conjunction with the University of Michigan, Herman Miller established the Facility Management Institute, which pioneered the profession of facility management. The company continued to expand overseas and introduce new designs throughout the 1970s.

By 1977, more than half of Herman Miller's 2,500 employees worked outside the production area. The Scanlon Plan therefore needed to be overhauled, since it had been designed originally for a production workforce. In addition, employees worked at multiple U.S. and overseas locations. In 1978, an ad hoc committee of 54 people from nearly every segment of the company was elected to examine the need for changes and to make recommendations. By January 1979, the committee had developed a final draft. The plan established a new organization structure based on work teams, caucuses, and councils. All employees were given an opportunity to discuss the new plan in small group settings. On January 26, 1979, 96 percent of the employees voted to accept the new plan.

After 18 years as president and CEO, Hugh De Pree stepped down; his younger brother, Max De Pree, became chairman and chief executive officer in 1980. In 1981, Herman Miller took a major initiative to become more efficient and environmentally friendly. Its Energy Center generated both electrical and steam power to run its 1-million-square-foot facility by burning waste.

In 1983, Herman Miller established a plan whereby all employees became shareholders. This initiative occurred approximately 10 years before congressional incentives fueled employee stock ownership plan (ESOP) growth.

In 1984, Herman Miller introduced the Equa chair, a second chair based on ergonomic principles; many other designs followed in the 1980s. In 1987, the first non–De Pree family member, Dick Ruch, became chief executive officer.

By the end of the decade, *Time* magazine had recognized the Equa chair as a Design of the Decade. Also, in 1989, Herman Miller established its Environmental Quality Action Team, whose purpose was to "coordinate environmental programs worldwide and involve as many employees as possible."

In 1990, Herman Miller became a founding member of the Tropical Forest Foundation and was the only furniture manufacturer to belong. That same year, it discontinued using endangered rosewood in its award-winning Eames lounge chair and ottoman, and substituted cherry and walnut from sustainable sources. It also became a founding member of the U.S. Green Building Council in 1994. Some of the buildings at Herman Miller were used to establish Leadership in Energy and Environmental Design (LEED) standards. Because of its environmental efforts, Herman Miller received awards from *Fortune* magazine and the National Wildlife Federation in the 1990s.

Also in the 1990s, Herman Miller again introduced some groundbreaking designs. In 1994, it introduced the Aeron chair (see Exhibit 2), which almost immediately was added to the New York Museum of Modern Art's permanent design collection. In 1999, the Aeron chair won the Design of the Decade Award from *BusinessWeek* and the Industrial Designers |Society of America.

In 1992, J. Kermit Campbell became Herman Miller's fifth CEO and president. He was the first person from outside the company to hold either position. In 1995, Campbell resigned and Mike Volkema was

**EXHIBIT 2**    The Herman Miller Aeron Chair

promoted to CEO. Volkema, just 39 years old, had been with a company called Meridian for seven years before Herman Miller acquired it in 1990, so when he became CEO he had been with either Herman Miller or its subsidiary for 12 years. At the time, the industry was in a slump and Herman Miller was being restructured. Sales were approximately $1 billion annually.

In 1994, the company launched a product line called Herman Miller for the Home to focus on the residential market. It reintroduced some of its modern classic designs from the 1940s, 1950s, and 1960s as well as new designs. In 1998, it set up a specific website (www.hmhome.com) to tap into this market.

The company took additional marketing initiatives to focus on small and midsize businesses. It established a network of 180 retailers to focus on small businesses and made a 3-D design computer program available to midsize customers. In addition, its order entries were digitally linked among the company and its suppliers, distributors, and customers to expedite orders and improve their accuracy.

## THE FIRST DECADE OF THE 21ST CENTURY

The first decade of the 21st century started off spectacularly for Herman Miller, with record profits and sales in 2000 and 2001. The company offered an employee stock option plan (ESOP) in July 2000, and *Time* magazine selected the Eames molded plywood chair a Design of the Century. Sales had more than doubled in the six years that Mike Volkema had been CEO.

Then the dot-com bubble burst and the terrorist attacks of September 11, 2001, shook the U.S. economy. Herman Miller's sales dropped by 34 percent, from more than $2.2 billion in 2001 to less than $1.5 billion in 2002. In the same two years, the company saw a decline in profits from a positive $144 million to a negative $56 million. In an interview for *FastCompany* magazine in 2007, Volkema said, "One night I went to bed a genius and woke up the town idiot."

Although sales continued to drop in 2003, Herman Miller returned to profitability in that year. To do so, Herman Miller had to drop its long-held tradition of lifelong employment; approximately 38 percent of the workforce was laid off, and an entire plant in Georgia was closed. Mike Volkema and Brian Walker, then president of Herman Miller North America, met with all the workers to tell them what was happening and why it had to be done. One of the workers being laid off was so moved by Volkema and Walker's presentation that she told them she felt sorry for them having to personally lay off workers.

To replace the tradition of lifelong employment, Volkema, with input from many others, developed what the company referred to as "the new social contract." He explained it as follows:

> We are a commercial enterprise, and the customer has to be on center stage, so we have to first figure out whether your gifts and talents have a match with the needs and wants of this commercial enterprise. If they don't, then we want to wish you the best, but we do need to tell you that I don't have a job for you right now.

As part of the implementation of the social contract, the company redesigned benefit plans such as educational reimbursement and 401(k) plans to be more portable. This was done to decrease the cost of changing jobs for employees whose gifts and talents no longer matched customer needs.

Herman Miller's sales and profits began to climb from 2003 to 2008. In 2008, even though sales were not at an all-time high, the company's profits had reached a record level. Walker became president in 2003 and CEO in 2004. Volkema became chairman of the board in 2004.

Then Herman Miller was hit by the recession of 2009. Sales dropped by 19 percent, from approximately $2.0 billion in 2008 to approximately $1.6 billion in 2009. In the same years, profits dropped from $152 million to $68 million. In March 2009, Mark Schurman, director of external communications at Herman Miller, predicted that the changes made to recover from the 2001–2003 recession would help the company weather the recession that began in late 2007.

# HERMAN MILLER IN 2012

Herman Miller had codified its long-practiced organizational values and published them on its website on a page titled "What We Believe." Those beliefs, listed as follows, were intended as a basis for uniting all employees, building relationships, and contributing to communities:

- **Curiosity & Exploration:** These are two of our greatest strengths. They lie behind our heritage of research-driven design. How do we keep our curiosity? By respecting and encouraging risk, and by practicing forgiveness. You can't be curious and infallible. In one sense, if you never make a mistake, you're not exploring new ideas often enough. Everybody makes mistakes: we ought to celebrate honest mistakes, learn from them, and move on.

- **Engagement:** For us, it is about being owners—actively committed to the life of this community called Herman Miller, sharing in its success and risk. Stock ownership is an important ingredient, but it's not enough. The strength and the payoff really come when engaged people own problems, solutions, and behavior. Acknowledge responsibility, choose to step forward and be counted. Care about this community and make a difference in it.

- **Performance:** Performance is required for leadership. We want to be leaders, so we are committed to performing at the highest level possible. Performance isn't a choice. It's up to everybody at Herman Miller to perform at his or her best. Our own high performance—however we measure it—enriches our lives as employees, delights our customers, and creates real value for our shareholders

- **Inclusiveness:** To succeed as a company, we must include all the expressions of human talent and potential that society offers. We value the whole person and everything each of us has to offer, obvious or not so obvious. We believe that every person should have the chance to realize his or her potential regardless of color, gender, age, sexual orientation, educational background, weight, height, family status, skill level—the list goes on and on. When we are truly inclusive, we go beyond toleration to understanding all the qualities that make people who they are, that make us unique, and most important, that unite us.

- **Design:** Design for us is a way of looking at the world and how it works—or doesn't. It is a method for getting something done, for solving a problem. To design a solution, rather than simply devising one, requires research, thought, sometimes starting over, listening, and humility. Sometimes design results in memorable occasions, timeless chairs, or really fun parties. Design isn't just the way something looks; it isn't just the way something works, either.

- **Foundations:** The past can be a tricky thing—an anchor or a sail, a tether or a launching pad. We value and respect our past without being ruled by it. The stories, people, and experiences in Herman Miller's past form a unique foundation. Our past teaches us about design, human compassion, leadership, risk taking, seeking out change and working together. From that foundation, we can move forward together with a common language, a set of owned beliefs and understandings. We value our rich legacy more for what it shows us we might become than as a picture of what we've been.

- **A Better World:** This is at the heart of Herman Miller and the real reason why many of us come to work every day. We contribute to a better world by pursuing sustainability and environmental wisdom. Environmental advocacy is part of our heritage and a responsibility we gladly bear for future generations. We reach for a better world by giving time and money to our communities and causes outside the company; through becoming a good corporate citizen worldwide; and even in the (not so) simple act of adding beauty to the world. By participating in the effort, we lift our spirits and the spirits of those around us.

- **Transparency:** Transparency begins with letting people see how decisions are made and owning the decisions we make. So when you make a decision, own it. Confidentiality has a place at Herman Miller, but if you can't tell anybody about a decision you've made, you've probably made a poor choice. Without transparency, it's impossible to have trust and integrity. Without trust and integrity, it's impossible to be transparent

All employees were expected to live these values.

## Management

Mike Volkema remained chairman of the board in 2012, and Brian Walker was president and CEO. Walker's compensation was listed by *Bloomberg Businessweek* as $693,969 in 2011. The magazine listed compensation for CEOs at four competitors as ranging from $778,000 to $973,000. Walker and four other top executives at Herman Miller took a 10 percent pay cut in January 2009 and, along with all salaried workers, another 10 percent cut in March 2009. The production workers were placed on a work schedule that consisted of nine days in two weeks, effectively cutting their pay by 10 percent as well. That the executives would take a pay cut before salaried workers, and one twice as much as that required by workers, was just one way human compassion was practiced at Herman Miller. However, most employees' pay cuts and furloughs were ended in June 2010 when the company's financial performance began to improve.

By U.S. Securities and Exchange Commission (SEC) regulations, a publicly traded company had to have a board of directors. By Herman Miller's corporate policy, the majority of the 14 members of the board had to be independent. To be judged independent, the individual as a minimum had to meet the NASDAQ National Market requirements for independent directors (NASDAQ Stock Market Rule 4200). In addition, the individual could not have any "other material relationship with the company or its affiliates or with any executive officer of the company or his or her affiliates." Moreover, according to company documents, any "transaction between the Company and any executive officer or director of the Company (including that person's spouse, children, stepchildren, parents, stepparents, siblings, parents-in-law, children-in-law, siblings-in-law and persons sharing the same residence) must be disclosed to the Board of Directors and is subject to the approval of the Board of Directors or the Nominating and Governance Committee unless the proposed transaction is part of a general program available to all directors or employees equally under an existing policy or is a purchase of Company products consistent with the price and terms of other transactions of similar size with other purchasers." Furthermore, "It is the policy of the Board that all directors, consistent with their responsibilities to the stockholders of the company as a whole, hold an equity interest in the company. Toward this end, the Board requires that each director will have an equity interest after one year on the Board, and within five years the Board encourages the directors to have shares of common stock of the company with a value of at least three times the amount of the annual retainer paid to each director." In other words, board members were held to standards consistent with Herman Miller's corporate beliefs and its ESOP program.

Although Herman Miller had departments, the most frequently referenced work unit was the team. Paul Murray, director of environmental health and safety, explained the relationship between the team and the department as follows:

> At Herman Miller, *team* has just been the term that has been used since the Scanlon Plan and the De Prees brought that into Herman Miller. And so I think that's why we use that almost exclusively. The department— as a department, we help facilitate the other teams. And so they aren't just department driven.

Teams were often cross-functional. Membership on a team was based on the employee's ability to contribute to that team. As Gabe Wing, lead chemical engineer for the company's Design for the Environment division, described it,

> You grab the appropriate representative who can best help your team achieve its goal. It doesn't seem to be driven based on title. It's based on who has the ability to help us drive our initiatives towards our goal.

Teams were often based on product development. When the product had been developed, the members of that team were redistributed to new projects. New projects could come from any level in the organization. One way in which leadership was shared at Herman Miller was through the concept of "talking up and down the ladder." Workers at all levels were encouraged to put forth new ideas. Herman Miller environmental specialist Rudy Bartels said,

> If they try something . . . they have folks there that will help them and be there for them. . . . That requires a presence of one of us or an e-mail or just to say, "Yeah, I think that's a great idea." That's how a lot . . . in the organization works.

Because Herman Miller workers felt empowered, a new manager could run into some startling behavior. Paul Murray recalled,

> I can remember my first day on the job. I took my safety glasses off . . . and an employee stepped forward and said, "Get your safety glasses back on." At [Company X, Company Y],[1] there was no way they would have ever talked to a supervisor like that, much less their supervisor's manager. It's been a fun journey when the workforce is that empowered.

The company's beliefs were also reinforced through the Employee Gifts Committee and the Environmental Quality Action Team. True to Herman Miller's practice of shared leadership, the Employee Gifts Committee distributed funds and other resources based on employee involvement. Jay Link, manager of corporate giving, explained the program as follows:

> Our first priority is to honor organizations where our employees are involved. We believe that it's important that we engender kind of a giving spirit in our employees, so if we know they're involved in organizations, which is going to be where we have a manufacturing presence, then our giving kind of comes alongside organizations that they're involved with. So that's our first priority.

In addition, all Herman Miller employees could work 16 paid hours a year with a charitable organization of their choice. The company set goals for the number of employee volunteer hours contributed annually to its communities. Progress toward meeting those goals was reported to the CEO.

The Environmental Affairs Team, formed in 1988 with the authorization of Max De Pree, had responsibility for such activities as recycling solid waste and designing products from sustainable resources. One of the team's successes was in the reduction of solid waste taken to landfills. In 1991, Herman Miller was sending 41 million pounds of solid waste to landfills. That figure was down to 24 million pounds by 1994 and to 3.6 million pounds by 2008. Such improvements were both environmentally friendly and cost-effective.

Herman Miller's beliefs carried over to the family and the community. Gabe Wing related, "I've got the worst lawn in my neighborhood. That's because I don't spread pesticides on it, and I don't put fertilizer down." He went on to say that he and his wife had to make a difficult decision in the summer of 2009 because Herman Miller had a policy "to avoid PVC [polyvinyl chloride] wherever possible." In restoring their home, they chose fiber cement board over PVC siding even though the fiber cement board was considerably more costly. Wing said, "Seven years ago, I didn't really think about it."

Rudy Bartels was involved in a youth soccer association that raised money to buy uniforms by collecting newspapers and aluminum cans. Bartels said, "When I'll speak they'll say, 'Yeah, that's Rudy. He's Herman Miller. You should—you know we're gonna have to do this.'"

The company's beliefs carried over to all functional areas of the business. Some of them were obviously beneficial, and some were simply the way Herman Miller chose to conduct its business.

## Marketing

Herman Miller products were sold internationally through wholly owned subsidiaries in countries including Canada, France, Germany, Italy, Japan, Mexico, Australia, Singapore, China, India, and the Netherlands. Its products were offered through independent dealerships. The customer base was spread over 100 countries.

Herman Miller used so-called green marketing to sell its products. For example, the Mirra chair—introduced in 2003 with PostureFit Technology (see Exhibit 3)—was developed from its inception to be environmentally friendly. The Mirra was made of 45 percent recycled materials, and 96 percent of its materials were, in turn, recyclable. In addition, assembly of the chairs used 100 percent renewable energy. In 2003, *Architectural Record* and *Environmental Building News* named the Mirra chair among their lists of "Top 10 Green Products." Builders who used Herman Miller products in their buildings could earn points toward Leadership in Energy and Environmental Design (LEED) certification.

In addition, Herman Miller engaged in cooperative advertising with strategic partners. For example, at Hilton Garden Inns, some rooms were equipped with Herman Miller's Mirra chairs. On the desk in the room was a card that explained how to adjust the chair for comfort and listed a Hilton Garden Inn website where the chair could be purchased.

## Production/Operations

Herman Miller was globally positioned in terms of manufacturing operations. In the United States, its manufacturing operations were located in Michigan, Georgia, and Wisconsin. In Europe, it had considerable manufacturing presence in the United Kingdom, its largest market outside the United States. In Asia, it had manufacturing operations in Ningbo, China.

Herman Miller used a system of lean manufacturing techniques collectively referred to as the Herman Miller Performance System (HMPS)—see Exhibit 4. THE HMPS strove to maintain efficiencies and cost savings by minimizing the amount of inventory on hand through a just-in-time process. Some suppliers

### EXHIBIT 3   An Example of Cooperative Advertising

### EXHIBIT 4   The Herman Miller Production System

delivered parts to Herman Miller production facilities five or six times per day.

Production was order-driven, with direct materials and components purchased as needed to meet demand. The standard lead time for the majority of the company's products was 10 to 20 days. As a result, the rate of inventory turnover was high. These combined factors could cause inventory levels to appear relatively low in relation to sales volume. A key element of Herman Miller's manufacturing strategy was to limit fixed production costs by outsourcing component parts from strategic suppliers. This strategy had allowed the company to increase the variable nature of its cost structure while retaining proprietary control over those production processes that it believed provided a competitive advantage. Because of this strategy, manufacturing operations were largely assembly-based.

The success of the HMPS was the result of much hard work. For example, in 1996, business at the Herman Miller subsidiary Integrated Metals Technology (IMT), which supplied the parent company with pedestals, was not going well. IMT's prices were high, its lead time was long, and its quality was in the 70 percent range. Leaders at IMT decided to hire the Toyota Supplier Support Center, the consulting arm of automaker Toyota. By inquiring, analyzing, and "enlisting help and ideas of everyone," IMT made significant improvements. For example, quality defects in parts per million decreased from approximately 9,000 in 2000 to 1,500 in 2006. Concurrently, on-time shipments improved from 80 percent to 100 percent, and safety incidents per 100 employees dropped from 10 to 3 per year.

Herman Miller's organizational values were incorporated into the environmentally friendly design of the Greenhouse, Herman Miller's main production facility in Michigan. For example, the Greenhouse took advantage of natural light and landscaping to grow native plants without the use of fertilizers, pesticides, or irrigation. After the facility was opened, aggressive paper wasps found the design to their liking. Employees and guests were stung, frequently. Rather than using pesticides to kill the wasps, the company sought a solution that would be in keeping with its beliefs. Through research, it learned that honeybees and paper wasps were incompatible. Therefore, the company located 600,000 honeybees in 12 hives on the property. In addition to driving away the wasps, the introduction of the honeybees resulted (via pollination) in a profusion of wildflowers around the facility and, subsequently, the production of a large amount of honey. Guests to the home office were given a four-ounce bottle of the honey, symbolizing Herman Miller's corporate beliefs.

## Human Resource Management

Human resource management was considered a strength for Herman Miller. It was routinely listed on *Fortune*'s "100 Best Companies to Work For" list, including in 2010, and it had approximately 278 applicants for every job opening. In 2009, during the ongoing economic downturn, Herman Miller cut its workforce by more than 15 percent, reduced the pay of the remaining workforce by at least 10 percent, and suspended 401(k) contributions. According to the February 8, 2010, issue of *Fortune*, employees praised management for "handling the downturn with class and doing what is best for the collective whole." *Fortune* also estimated voluntary turnover at Herman Miller to be less than 2 percent. On June 1, 2010, the 10 percent time and pay cuts that the company began in the spring of 2009 were discontinued due to Herman Miller's quick turnaround.

Herman Miller practiced what Hugh De Pree had once called "Business as Unusual." That policy appeared to pay off in both good times and tough ones. Herman Miller shared the gains as well as the pains with its employees, especially in regard to compensation.

Pay was geared to firm performance and took many forms at Herman Miller. All employees received a base pay and, in addition, participated in a profit-sharing program whereby they received stock according to the company's annual financial performance. Employees were immediately enrolled in this plan upon joining Herman Miller, and immediately vested. Profit sharing was based on corporate performance. As one employee explained:

> The problem we see is you get to situations where project X corporately had a greater opportunity for the entirety of the business, but it was difficult to tell these folks that they needed to sacrifice in order to support the entirety of the business when they were being compensated specifically on their portion of the business. So you would get into some turf situations. So we ended up moving to a broader corporate EVA [economic value added] compensation to prevent those types of turf battles.

The company offered an employee stock purchase plan (ESPP) through payroll deductions at a 15 percent discount from the market price. Also, all employees were offered a 401(k) plan; until it was suspended in 2009 due to the recession, the company had offered a matching plan in which employees received a 50 percent match for the first 6 percent of their salaries they contributed to the 401(k). Through the profit-sharing plan and the ESPP, the employees owned approximately 8 percent of the outstanding stock.

Furthermore, all employees were offered a retirement income plan whereby the company deposited into an account 4 percent of compensation, on which interest was paid quarterly. Employees were immediately eligible to participate in this plan upon joining Herman Miller, but were required to participate for five years before being vested. Additionally, a length-of-service bonus was paid after five years of employment. Finally, the company paid a universal annual bonus to all employees based on the company's performance against economic value added (EVA) objectives. EVA was a calculation of the company's net operating profits, after tax, minus a charge for the cost of shareholder capital. The annual EVA bonus came in addition to the other compensation programs, including profit sharing, with the same calculation used to determine both employee and executive bonus potential.

Thus, most forms of compensation at Herman Miller were at least partially, if not wholly, contingent on corporate performance. One employee summed up pay as follows, "You can dip into Herman Miller's pocket several times based on the performance of the company."

Other benefits also took many forms at Herman Miller. As in many other organizations, employees were given a range of benefits. Standard benefits included health insurance, dental insurance, vision care plans, prescription plans, flexible spending accounts, short- and long-term disability plan, life insurance, accidental death and disability insurance, and critical illness/personal accident/long-term care. The company also offered extensive wellness benefits, including fitness facilities or subsidized gym memberships, health services, employee assistance programs, wellness programs/classes, and health risk assessments. Some benefits, however, were quite different from those found in other organizations. For example, the company offered a $100 rebate on a bike purchase, which it justified as "part of our comprehensive program designed for a better world around you." Other benefits included the following:

- 100 percent tuition reimbursement.
- Employee product purchase discounts.
- Flexible schedules, including job-sharing, compressed workweek, and telecommuting options.
- Concierge services, including directions to travel locations, dry cleaning, greeting cards, and take-home meals.
- On-site services, including massage therapy, cafeterias, banking, health services, fitness centers, fitness classes, and personal trainers.

All benefits were available also to domestic partners.

When appropriate, Herman Miller promoted people within the organization. Education and training were seen as key to preparing employees to take on new responsibilities. For example, environmental specialist Rudy Bartels, as well as multiple vice presidents, began their careers at Herman Miller on the production floor.

Three other benefits were unique to Herman Miller. First, every family that gave birth to or adopted a child received a Herman Miller rocking chair. Second, every employee who retired after 25 years with the company and was 55 or older received an Eames lounge chair. Third, Herman Miller had no executive retreat, but it did have an employee retreat, the Marigold Lodge, on Lake Michigan. This retreat was available to employees for corporate-related events, such as retirement parties and other celebrations, and some of those events included invited family and guests.

## Finance

During normal economic times, financial management at Herman Miller would have been considered conservative. Through 2006, the company's leverage ratio was below the industry average and its times-interest-earned ratio was over twice the industry average. Due to the drop-off in business during the recession, the debt-to-equity ratio rose precipitously, from 1.18 in 2006 to 47.66 in 2008. To improve this ratio, the company sold more than 3 million shares of stock in fiscal 2009.[2] In the four previous fiscal years, Herman Miller had been repurchasing shares. The debt-to-equity ratio was reduced to 3.81 by the end of 2009. To improve short-term assets, dividends per share were cut by approximately 70 percent and capital expenditures were reduced to zero in 2009. Exhibits 5 and 6

**EXHIBIT 5**   Herman Miller's Consolidated Balance Sheets, Fiscal Years 2006–2011 ($ millions, except share and per-share data)

| | Fiscal Years Ending | | | | | |
| --- | --- | --- | --- | --- | --- | --- |
| | May 28, 2011 | May 29, 2010 | May 30, 2009 | May 31, 2008 | June 2, 2007 | June 3, 2006 |
| **Assets** | | | | | | |
| Current assets: | | | | | | |
| Cash and cash equivalents | $148.6 | $134.8 | $192.9 | $155.4 | $ 76.4 | $ 106.8 |
| Short-term investments | — | — | — | 15.7 | 15.9 | 15.2 |
| Marketable securities | 11.1 | 12.1 | 11.3 | — | — | — |
| Accounts receivable | 193.1 | 144.7 | 148.9 | 209.0 | 188.1 | 173.2 |
| Less allowances in each year | 4.5 | 4.4 | 7.3 | 5.6 | 4.9 | 5.0 |
| Inventories, net | 66.2 | 57.9 | 37.3 | 55.1 | 56.0 | 47.1 |
| Prepaid expenses and other | 59.2 | 45.2 | 60.5 | 58.0 | 48.3 | 47.9 |
| Total current assets | 478.1 | 394.7 | 450.9 | 493.2 | 384.7 | 390.2 |
| Property and equipment: | | | | | | |
| Land and improvements | 19.9 | 19.4 | 18.8 | 19.0 | 18.9 | 20.9 |
| Buildings and improvements | 149.5 | 147.6 | 137.4 | 139.4 | 137.2 | 139.1 |
| Machinery and equipment | 531.0 | 546.4 | 552.0 | 547.4 | 543.3 | 523.8 |
| Construction in progress | 13.0 | 10.7 | 9.8 | 17.4 | 17.6 | 23.5 |
| Gross property & equipment | 713.4 | 724.1 | 718.0 | 723.2 | 717,0 | 707.3 |
| Less: accumulated depreciation | (544.3) | (548.9) | (538.8) | (526.9) | (520.4) | (504.0) |
| Net property and equipment | 169.1 | 175.2 | 179.2 | 196.3 | 196.6 | 203.3 |
| Goodwill and indefinite-lived intangibles | 133.6 | 132.6 | 72.7 | 40.2 | 39.1 | 39.1 |
| Other amortizable intangibles, net | 24.3 | 25.0 | 11.3 | — | — | — |
| Other assets | 9.3 | 43.1 | 53.2 | 53.5 | 45.8 | 35.4 |
| Total assets | $814.4 | $770.6 | $767.3 | $783.2 | $666.2 | $668.0 |
| **Liabilities and Shareholders' Equity** | | | | | | |
| Current liabilities: | | | | | | |
| Unfunded checks | $ 6.4 | $ 4.3 | $ 3.9 | $ 8.5 | $ 7.4 | $ 6.5 |
| Current maturities of long-term debt | — | 100.0 | 75.0 | — | 3.0 | 3.0 |
| Accounts payable | 112.7 | 96.3 | 79.1 | 117.9 | 110.5 | 112,3 |
| Accrued liabilities | 153.1 | 112.4 | 124.2 | 184.1 | 163.6 | 177.6 |
| Total current liabilities | 272.2 | 313.0 | 282.2 | 310.5 | 284.5 | 299.4 |
| Long-term debt, less current maturities | 250.0 | 201.2 | 302.4 | 375.5 | 173.2 | 175.8 |
| Other liabilities | 87.2 | 176.3 | 174.7 | 73.8 | 52.9 | 54.2 |
| Total liabilities | 609.4 | 690.5 | 759.3 | 759.8 | 510.6 | 529.4 |
| Minority interest | — | — | — | — | .3 | .2 |

*(Continued)*

## EXHIBIT 5    *(Continued)*

| | Fiscal Years Ending | | | | | |
| --- | --- | --- | --- | --- | --- | --- |
| | May 28, 2011 | May 29, 2010 | May 30, 2009 | May 31, 2008 | June 2, 2007 | June 3, 2006 |
| Shareholders' equity: | | | | | | |
| Preferred stock, no par value (10,000,000 shares authorized, none issued) | — | — | — | — | — | — |
| Common stock, $0.20 par value | 11.6 | 11.4 | 10.8 | 11.1 | 12.6 | 13.2 |
| Additional paid-in capital | 82.0 | 55.9 | 5.9 | – | – | – |
| Retained earnings | 218.2 | 152.4 | 129.2 | 76.7 | 197.8 | 192.2 |
| Accumulated other comprehensive loss | (104.2) | (136.2) | (134.1) | (60.1) | (51.6) | (63.3) |
| Key executive deferred compensation | (2.6) | (3.4) | (3.8) | (4.3) | (3.5) | (3.7) |
| Total shareholders' equity | 205.0 | 80.1 | 8.0 | 23.4 | 155.3 | 138.4 |
| Total liabilities and shareholders' equity | $814.4 | $770.6 | $767.3 | $783.2 | $666.2 | $668.0 |

*Source:* Herman Miller, 10-K reports, various years.

show the company's financial statements for fiscal years 2006–2011.

For fiscal 2008, 15 percent of Herman Miller's revenues and 10 percent of its profits were from non–North American countries. In 2007, non–North American countries accounted for 16.5 percent of revenues and approximately 20 percent of Herman Miller's profits.

Financially, Herman Miller held true to its beliefs. Even in downturns, it invested in research and development (R&D). In the dot-com downturn, it invested tens of millions of dollars in R&D. Inside Herman Miller, this investment project was code-named Purple.

In the December 19, 2007, issue of *FastCompany* magazine, Clayton Christensen, Harvard Business School professor and author of *The Innovator's Dilemma,* commented on the Purple project, saying, "Barely one out of 1,000 companies would do what [Herman Miller] did. It was a daring bet in terms of increasing spending for the sake of tomorrow while cutting back to survive today."

## The Accessories Team

Herman Miller's Accessories Team was an outgrowth of project Purple. One of the goals of this project was

to stretch beyond the normal business boundaries. Office accessories was one area in which Herman Miller had not been historically involved, even though office accessories were a big part of what independent dealers sold. According to Mark Schurman, director of external communications at Herman Miller, once the company identified accessories as a potential growth area, "Robyn [Hofmeyer] was tapped to put together a team to really explore this as a product segment that we could get more involved with."

In 2006, Hofmeyer established the Accessories Team by recruiting Larry Kallio to be the head engineer and Wayne Baxter to lead sales and marketing. Together, they assembled a flexible team to launch a new product in 16 months. They recruited people with different disciplines needed to support that goal. Over the next two years, they remained a group of six. Some people started with the team to develop a particular product and, as it got through that piece of work, then went on to different roles within the company. During its first eight months, the Accessories Team met twice a week for half a day. Twenty months out, it met only once a week.

The group acted with a fair amount of autonomy, but it did not want complete autonomy. "We don't want to be out there completely on our own because

**EXHIBIT 6   Herman Miller's Consolidated Statements of Operations, Fiscal Years 2006–2011 ($ millions, except per-share data)**

| | Fiscal Years Ending | | | | | |
| --- | --- | --- | --- | --- | --- | --- |
| | May 28, 2011 | May 29, 2010 | May 30, 2009 | May 31, 2008 | June 2, 2007 | June 3, 2006 |
| Net sales | $1,649.2 | $1,318.8 | $1,630.0 | $2,012.1 | $1,918.9 | $1,737.2 |
| Cost of sales | 1,111.1 | 890.3 | 1102.3 | 1,313.4 | 1,273.0 | 1,162.4 |
| Gross margin | 538.1 | 428.5 | 527.7 | 698.7 | 645.9 | 574.8 |
| Operating expenses: | | | | | | |
| Selling, general, and administrative | 366.0 | 317.7 | 330.8 | 395.8 | 395.8 | 371.7 |
| Restructuring expenses | 3.0 | 16.7 | 28.4 | 5.1 | – | |
| Design and research | 45.8 | 40.5 | 45.7 | 51.2 | 52.0 | 45.4 |
| Total operating expenses | 414.8 | 374.9 | 404.9 | 452.1 | 447.8 | 417.1 |
| Operating earnings | 123.3 | 53.6 | 122.8 | 246.6 | 198.1 | 157.7 |
| Other expenses (income): | | | | | | |
| Interest expense | 19.9 | 21.7 | 25.6 | 18.8 | 13.7 | 14.0 |
| Interest and other investment income | (1.5) | (4.6) | (2.6) | (3.8) | (3.1) | (4.9) |
| Other, net | 2.4 | 1.7 | .9 | 1.2 | 1.5 | 1.0 |
| Net other expenses | 20.8 | 18.8 | 23.9 | 16.2 | 1.0 | 10.1 |
| Earnings before income taxes and minority interest | 102.5 | 34.8 | 98.9 | 230.4 | 187.0 | 147.6 |
| Income tax expense | 31.7 | 6.5 | 31.0 | 78.2 | 57.9 | 47.7 |
| Minority interest, net of income tax | —— | —— | (.1) | (0.1) | —— | 0.7 |
| Net earnings | $    70.8 | $    28.3 | $    68.0 | $  152.3 | $  129.1 | $    99.2 |
| Earnings per share—basic | $    1.24 | $    0.51 | $    1.26 | $    2.58 | $    2.01 | $    1.40 |
| Earnings per share—diluted | $    1.06 | $    0.43 | $    1.25 | $    2.56 | $    1.98 | $    1.45 |

*Source:* Herman Miller, 10-K reports, various years.

we have such awesome resources here at Herman Miller," Robyn Hofmeyer explained. When different disciplines were needed for a particular product, the group reached out to other areas in the company and found people who could allocate some of their time to support that product.

Wayne Baxter described what happened on the team as follows:

We all seem to have a very strong voice regarding almost any topic; it's actually quite fun and quite dynamic. We all have kind of our roles on the team, but I think other than maybe true engineering, we've all kind of tapped into other roles and still filled in to help each other as much as we could.

Another member of the Accessories Team described the group's decision making as follows:

If we wanted to debate and research and get very scientific, we would not be sitting here talking about the things that we've done, we'd still be researching them. In a sense, we rely upon our gut a lot, which I think is, at the end of the day just fine because we have enough experience. We're not experts, but we're also willing to take risks and we're also willing to evolve.

Thus, leadership and decision making was shared both within the Accessories Team and across the organization. Ideas and other contributions to the success of the team were accepted from all sources.

Out of this process grew Herman Miller's Thrive Collection. The name was chosen to indicate the focus on the individual and the idea of personal comfort, control, and ergonomic health. Thrive Collection products included the Ardea Personal Light, the Leaf

Personal Light, the Flo Monitor Arm, and C2 Climate Control. All of these were designed for improving the individual's working environment. Continuing Herman Miller's tradition of innovative design, the Ardea Personal Light earned both Gold and Silver honors from the International Design Excellence Awards (IDEA) in June 2010.

## THE INDUSTRY

Office equipment (classified by Standard & Poor's Research Insight as Office Services & Supplies) was an economically volatile industry. The office furniture segment of the industry was hit hard by the recession. Industry sales decreased by approximately 26.5 percent from 2008 to 2009. Herman Miller's sales dropped 19 percent during that period. Herman Miller's stock market value of more than $1 billion at the end of 2009 represented 7.3 percent of the total stock market value of the industry. The value of Herman Miller's shares had increased to more than $1.4 billion by 2011—representing 10.8 percent of the industry's total stock market value. According to Hoover's, Herman Miller's top three competitors were Haworth, Steelcase, and HNI Corporation.

The industry had been impacted by a couple of trends. First, telecommuting had decreased the need of large companies to have office equipment for all employees. At some companies, such as Oracle, a substantial percentage of employees telecommuted—for example, the majority of JetBlue reservation clerks telecommuted. Second, more employees were spending more hours in front of computer screens than ever before. Due to this trend, the need for ergonomically correct office furniture had increased. Such furniture helped decrease fatigue and injuries like carpal tunnel syndrome. Finally, as with most industries, the cost of raw materials and competition from overseas had had an impact on office furniture. These trends tended to impact low-cost office furniture producers more than they impacted the high-quality producers.

## THE FUTURE

In a June 24, 2010, press release, Herman Miller's CEO, Brian Walker, stated:

> One of the hallmarks of our company's history has been the ability to emerge from challenging periods with transformational products and processes. I believe our commitment to new products and market development over the past two years has put us in a position to do this once again. Throughout this period, we remained focused on maintaining near-term profitability while at the same time investing for the future. The award-winning new products we introduced last week at the NeoCon tradeshow are a testament to that focus, and I am incredibly proud of the collective spirit it has taken at Herman Miller to make this happen.

While the company's performance had steadily improved through year-end 2011, executives at Herman Miller faced two particular questions: (1) Will the strategies that have made Herman Miller an outstanding and award-winning company continue to provide it with the ability to reinvent and renew itself? And (2) Will disruptive global, economic, and competitive forces compel it to change its business model?

## ENDNOTES

[1] The names of the two Fortune 500 companies were deleted by the authors.

[2] Herman Miller's fiscal year ends on May 30 of the following calendar year.

# Henkel: Building a Winning Culture

## Robert Simons
### Harvard Business School

## Natalie Kindred
### Harvard Business School

*Development Roundtable. Düsseldorf, Germany, December 2011:*[a]

"We have too many in the 'T' category. We can't have more than 10%."

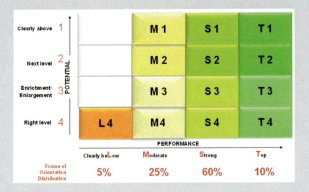

"What about Ashur Al Diri?"

"No. I would like to keep him as a 'T2.' He's our top sales manager in the region. As you know, Egypt is in turmoil—and he's managed to keep up both volume and margins. He is a real winner. I think he'll be ready to move up to the next management level within a year."

"What has he done that so impresses you . . . ?"

"Ashur has been very entrepreneurial in the face of unprecedented political turmoil. He's changed distribution routes, figured out new trade allowances to boost volume, and put more focus on high-margin brands. He's been extremely fast in coming up with new approaches as circumstances change. The ideas are always there."

"O.K. I think we can agree on 'T2.' What about Borzou Benzekri in Tunisia? Is he doing as well with the instability there?"

"No. I could go along with rating him 'M3.' He's solid, but his business is underperforming its potential. I think there are other things he could have done to seize the initiative. In my opinion, he focuses too much on effort and excuses. I keep telling him that excuses don't count. Only results matter when you're in this kind of a competitive race."

"I'm speaking to Kasper this afternoon. He knows him. Do you want me to get his input . . . ?"

In 2008, Kasper Rorsted was appointed CEO of Henkel AG & Co KGaA (Henkel). The 46-year-old father of four was the company's youngest-ever CEO and the first born outside Germany or Austria. A native of Denmark, Rorsted studied economics at the International Business School in Copenhagen before beginning his career in U.S.-based technology companies. In 1989, at age 27, he took his first

Kasper Rorsted
Source: Company documents.

**HARVARD|BUSINESS|SCHOOL**

9-112-060

Professor Robert Simons and Research Associate Natalie Kindred, Global Research Group, prepared this case. HBS cases are developed solely as the basis for class discussion. Cases are not intended to serve as endorsements, sources of primary data, or illustrations of effective or ineffective management.

sales management position at Digital Equipment, where he was younger than all but two of his 20 direct reports: "After about six months, I had to lay somebody off. I remember I was sleeping very poorly for almost a week. He had a family. But I had to start having honest conversations with people about how they performed, and that taught me a lesson. I've always been friendly, but never been friends anymore."[1]

In 1995, Rorsted joined computer company Compaq, where he rose to vice president and general manager of its Europe, Middle East, and Africa (EMEA) business. Seven years later, when Hewlett Packard (HP) acquired Compaq, Rorsted continued to lead HP's EMEA division with responsibility for 40,000 people and $30 billion in revenues. However, following a disappointing quarter in 2004, HP CEO Carly Fiorina—who had championed the Compaq acquisition—fired several former Compaq executives, including Rorsted. Within a month, Rorsted had a dozen job offers, but decided to take the single offer that was not from a high-tech firm: "I decided I would take the job offer from Henkel—a consumer goods and adhesives company—because there was a clear path I could see to the CEO job."[2]

As part of a three-year succession plan to replace retiring CEO Ulrich Lehner, Rorsted joined Henkel in 2005 as executive vice president of human resources, purchasing, information technology, and infrastructure services. As an industry outsider he faced a steep learning curve: "I had to start from scratch again. . . . It was a reminder of just how important it is to ask questions and listen."[3]

From the start, Rorsted's management style was distinct. He rarely used e-mail, preferring face-to-face interaction. He took six-week-long trips to key operating markets, including the U.S. and Asia. He constantly pushed for efficiency and set ambitious targets, most notably a set of financial goals he announced in 2008 upon becoming Henkel's new CEO.

## HENKEL UNTIL 2008

Fritz Henkel founded what would become modern-day Henkel in 1876 to manufacture a new laundry detergent. By the 1920s, Henkel, based in Düsseldorf, had grown into a leading German detergent producer and had diversified into glues. Following Fritz Henkel's death in 1930, shares of the company were distributed to his three children. After World War II, which saw most of Henkel's infrastructure destroyed, the company—still privately held—reopened several plants and started selling personal care products in addition to detergents and adhesives. In 1965, Henkel sponsored the

first-ever advertisement on German television with its *Persil* flagship detergent brand. In the subsequent years, Henkel expanded its product portfolio and geographic footprint through numerous acquisitions. In 1985, it raised capital to support continuing expansion by offering non-voting shares to the public. By 2008, sales had grown to €4 billion across 125 countries: the majority from the EMEA region (64%), followed by North America (19%), Asia-Pacific (11%), and Latin America (6%). Although only 20% of its 55,000 employees were based in Germany, the company preserved its German, family-owned roots: most members of the executive team were German and the Henkel family retained an active role on the company's shareholder committee.

Henkel was organized into three major business units. Adhesive Technologies (48% of overall sales) sold sealants and surface treatments to industrial customers in various industries, including electronics, transportation and construction, as well as to consumers. Laundry and Home Care (30% of sales) sold detergents and related home care products. The Cosmetics/Toiletries unit (22% of sales) produced and marketed personal care products such as shampoos, hair coloring, skin creams, deodorants, and toothpastes. (See Exhibit 1 for a comparison of Henkel's and selected competitors' financial performance, Exhibit 2 for performance by Henkel business units, and Exhibit 3 for major Henkel brands and products.)

Although all three businesses operated in highly competitive industries, the dynamics of each business differed greatly. With brands such as *Loctite* and *Pritt* glue sticks (Henkel invented the world's first glue stick), Henkel was the industry leader in the adhesives business, competing with companies such as 3M, which operated in 60 countries and had 2008 sales of €18.1 billion. But Henkel was a relatively small player in the laundry and personal care markets where its major brands—*Dial* soap, *Schwarzkopf hair* care products, and *Persil* laundry detergent—competed against global brands from much larger competitors Procter & Gamble (operating in 180 countries with sales of €50.4 billion), Unilever (150 countries; €40.5 billion sales), and L'Oreal (130 countries; €17.5 billion sales).[4]

### 2012 Goal: 14% EBIT Margin

In 2008, when Rorsted took over as CEO, Henkel was reporting comfortable growth and profits: €14 billion in sales, an increase of 8% over the previous year, and an EBIT margin of 10.3%. But many analysts—and even some Henkel executives—perceived

## EXHIBIT 1   Key Financials of Henkel and Selected Competitors, 2000–2010

| | 2000 | 2001 | 2002 | 2003 | 2004 | 2005 | 2006 | 2007 | 2008 | 2009 | 2010 |
|---|---|---|---|---|---|---|---|---|---|---|---|
| **Total Revenue (€ millions)** | | | | | | | | | | | |
| P&G | 41,733 | 46,312 | 40,749 | 37,764 | 42,215 | 46,845 | 53,650 | 55,387 | 50,364 | 54,710 | 64,283 |
| Unilever | 47,582 | 51,514 | 48,270 | 42,693 | 38,566 | 38,401 | 39,642 | 40,187 | 40,523 | 39,823 | 44,262 |
| 3M | 17,778 | 18,027 | 15,573 | 14,465 | 14,780 | 17,869 | 17,372 | 16,751 | 18,084 | 16,134 | 19,883 |
| L'Oreal | 12,671 | 13,740 | 14,288 | 14,029 | 13,641 | 14,533 | 15,790 | 17,063 | 17,542 | 17,473 | 19,496 |
| Henkel | 12,779 | 9,410[a] | 9,656 | 9,436 | 10,592 | 11,974 | 12,740 | 13,074 | 14,131 | 13,573 | 15,092 |
| **Sales Growth (%)** | | | | | | | | | | | |
| P&G | 4.8 | −1.8 | 2.5 | 7.8 | 18.5 | 10.4 | 20.2[c] | 12.1 | 6.9 | −6.2 | 2.9 |
| Unilever | 16.1 | 8.3 | −6.3 | −11.6 | −9.7 | −0.4 | 3.2 | 1.4 | 0.8 | −1.7 | 11.1 |
| 3M | 6.2 | −4.0 | 1.7 | 11.6 | 9.8 | 5.8 | 8.3 | 6.7 | 3.3 | −8.5 | 15.3 |
| L'Oreal | 17.9 | 8.4 | 4.0 | −1.8 | −2.8 | 6.5 | 8.7 | 8.1 | 2.8 | −0.4 | 11.6 |
| Henkel | 12.5 | 2.2 | 2.6[a] | −2.3 | 12.3[b] | 13.0 | 6.4 | 2.6 | 8.1 | −3.9 | 11.2 |
| **EBIT Margin (%)** | | | | | | | | | | | |
| P&G | 14.9 | 12.1 | 16.6 | 18.1 | 19.1 | 18.5 | 19.4 | 20.2 | 20.4 | 20.0 | 20.3 |
| Unilever | 11.1 | 11.2 | 11.8 | 13.1 | 14.9 | 13.2 | 13.6 | 14.5 | 14.3 | 14.7 | 15.0 |
| 3M | 17.2 | 13.6 | 18.7 | 20.9 | 22.9 | 22.9 | 20.2 | 21.8 | 20.7 | 20.8 | 22.2 |
| L'Oreal | 12.0 | 11.5 | 12.1 | 12.6 | 15.0 | 15.9 | 16.1 | 16.5 | 15.5 | 14.8 | 15.7 |
| Henkel[d] | 7.4 | 6.4 | 6.9 | 7.5 | 9.4 | 9.7 | 10.2 | 10.3 | 10.3 | 10.0 | 12.3 |

*Source:* Compiled from Capital IQ and company documents, citing Bloomberg.

*Note:* Data are year-end December 31 except P&G (year-end June 30). Revenues for 3M and P&G were converted from USD to Euros via Capital IQ using fiscal year-end rates. Sales growth for 3M and P&G was calculated using reporting currency (USD), and may not match sales growth as calculated from the Euro-denominated revenue figures given in the table.

[a] Including the divestment of chemicals business Cognis, 2001 revenues were €13,060 and 2002 sales growth was 226.06%.

[b] Reflects the acquisition of Dial in 2004.

[c] Reflects the acquisition of Gillette in late 2005.

[d] Henkel's EBIT margin (2008–2010) is adjusted for one-time charges/gains and restructuring charges.

## EXHIBIT 2   Henkel Financials by Business Line, 2010 (€ millions unless otherwise noted)

| | Laundry & Home Care | Cosmetics/ Toiletries | Adhesive Technologies | Corporate | Henkel Group |
|---|---|---|---|---|---|
| Sales | 4,319 | 3,269 | 7,306 | 199 | 15,092 |
| Sales growth 2006–2010 | 4.9% | 14.1% | 32.6% | — | 18.5% |
| Proportion of Henkel sales | 29% | 22% | 48% | 1% | 100% |
| Operating profit (EBIT) | 542 | 411 | 878 | −108[a] | 1,723 |
| Adj'd return on sales (EBIT margin)[b] | 13.0% | 13.3% | 12.8% | — | 12.3% |
| Return on capital employed (%) | 21.2% | 20.1% | 12.5% | — | 14.9% |
| Size of world market | 94,000 | 135,000 | 47,000 | | |

*Source:* Compiled from company documents.

[a] Including restructuring charges of € 14 million disclosed for the last time under Corporate, arising from integration of the National Starch businesses.

[b] EBIT margins for the individual business units were greater than the Group margin because of the effect of costs in the corporate sector (e.g., human resources, information technology, corporate communications, and finance).

**EXHIBIT 3    Selected Henkel Products and Brands by Business Segment**

Laundry and Home Care

Beauty and Personal Care

Adhesive Technologies

*Source:* Company documents.

Henkel as a complacent player that lacked a strong competitive spirit. One company official notoriously called Henkel, "the happy underperformer: always #2 or #3."

Moreover, by the second half of 2008, the impact of the global financial crisis and subsequent economic slowdown was having an effect in Henkel's key markets. In personal care and beauty products, consumers cut back on spending, traded down to lower-priced brands and focused on basic products, foregoing discretionary purchases. To offset rising raw material costs, Henkel increased prices on many products. Such steps, combined with the slowing economy, caused volume growth in all of Henkel's business units to fall in the second half of 2008.

Faced with falling demand and corporate complacency, Rorsted vowed to transform Henkel into a leaner, more performance-driven company. In his opinion, "staying where we are is no longer an option. We either move up or move down: we either become relevant or we will be made irrelevant."

To catalyze the organization and signal his commitment to change, Rorsted called a press conference in November 2008 to announce a set of ambitious four-year financial goals for sales growth, EBIT margin and EPS.

Nov. 6, 2008, 4:29 a.m. (Market Watch, *The Wall Street Journal*)

> *FRANKFURT—Burdened by integration and restructuring charges, consumer goods and adhesives producer Henkel (HEN.XE) Thursday reported a 58% drop in third-quarter net profit and lowered its 2008 earnings guidance. The company, which has about 55,000 employees, confirmed it expects 2008 organic revenue growth of between 3% to 5% from EUR13 billion last year. At 0816 GMT, Henkel shares traded down EUR0.59, or 2.5%. Henkel shares have fallen about 39% since the start of the year.*
>
> *Henkel also defined financial targets for 2012 and said it expects average organic sales growth of 3% to 5%, an adjusted EBIT margin of 14%, and average growth in adjusted earnings per preferred share of above 10%.*
>
> *An analyst said the reduced earnings outlook for 2008 isn't good and while the financial targets for 2012 look encouraging, "we don't have a clue on how they can be reached." He adds it remains to be seen if the targets are based on strategy or are simply wishful thinking.*

Business reporters and analysts echoed the skepticism of *The Wall Street Journal* report. "The listeners of the London analyst conference could not believe their ears," said one report; "14 percent seems too ambitious," asserted another; "As for the recently announced 2012 margin target of 14%, we frankly think it has little credibility," stated a third.[5]

## Building a Winning Culture

Rorsted knew that the ambitious financial goals—which promised improving sales growth and profitability in declining markets—could only be achieved by transforming the complacent spirit within Henkel into what he called a "winning culture." This concept would underpin three new strategic priorities: (1) Achieve our full business potential, (2) focus more on our customers, and (3) strengthen our global team. (See Exhibit 4.)

Throughout 2008 and 2009, Rorsted and his management team worked to consistently communicate the new strategic priorities to Henkel's employees and to translate them into actions in each business unit. To "achieve our full business potential," Rorsted focused on optimizing Henkel's portfolio by devoting extra resources to top-performing brands and high-potential markets. In 2008, Henkel made its largest-ever acquisition, paying €3.7 billion for the adhesives and electronic materials businesses of the National Starch and Chemical Company, thereby consolidating its worldwide leadership position in adhesives.

**EXHIBIT 4**  Henkel's "Winning Culture" Concept and Financial Targets for 2012

*Source:* Company documents.

In North America, Henkel invested heavily in its *Dial* brand, moving it from fifth in its category to one of the top brands in the body wash market. At the same time, the company divested underperforming activities or non-strategic brands, including the Adhesive unit's water-treatment business and numerous consumer brands. Rorsted noted:

> To be more competitive, you have to make tough decisions about every aspect of the business. We are concentrating on brands and countries where we are in a leading position or able to generate sustainable growth. If we lack the ability to win in a market or can't get there in a reasonable time, we leave. For example, we decided to exit our laundry and home care business in China—where we could not see a growth strategy—and focus on adhesives and cosmetics where we see strong potential. In total, we have gone from 900 brands to less than 500, and there's still more work to do.

Henkel executives also searched for cost efficiencies in administration and procurement through process standardization and automation, as well as improvements in capacity utilization at their various production sites.

## 2009 TO 2012: FROM PROMISE TO REALITY

Rorsted had intentionally undertaken the plant closings, divestitures, and administrative consolidation before embarking on the more sensitive cultural transformation needed for Henkel to achieve its 2012 goals. "We tackled the 'hard' things before attempting the 'soft' ones," he explained. "For the first part, I expected that people in the organization would feel uncomfortable, but we had to implement these changes to secure our future. We closed 60 plants worldwide and shifted functions such as purchasing, finance, and human resources into centralized shared-services offices in Slovakia, Mexico, and the Philippines. For the second part I needed to have everybody on board . . . I needed emotional buy-in."

The cultural overhaul—"building a winning culture"—comprised two major initiatives: (1) redefining Henkel's vision and values, and (2) implementing a new performance management system to strengthen management capabilities and increase accountability.

## Vision and Values

"A Brand Like a Friend" was Henkel's corporate tagline. But this no longer seemed to fit Henkel's new strategy for two reasons. First, its consumer focus did not resonate with the industrial adhesives business which had grown to be Henkel's largest business. Second, the tagline did not, in Rorsted's view, communicate the new competitive culture he wanted to create. "It is not about being friendly," he stated. "We want to be winners in every market in which we compete."

Rorsted realized that to sharpen Henkel's focus on its financial goals and priorities, the company required more clarity in the values that would guide the tough choices needed to transform it into a winning competitor. Henkel had a longstanding list of 10 values that included goals (e.g., "we aspire to excellence in quality"), work principles ("we communicate openly and actively"), and history ("we preserve the tradition of an open family company"). (See Exhibit 5 for a list of these 10 values.) Although these aspirations could be found in company reports, internal signage, and on the back of business cards, few employees—even at the highest levels—could remember them. The values "were everywhere but had little meaning," one

executive explained, adding that he could not think of a single situation when they were a factor in key decisions.

Rorsted believed that core values should provide the foundation for tough decisions. To identify potential themes for the new values, in June 2009 Henkel surveyed 134 executives in the top executive team and the next management layer. Based on these results, Rorsted held workshops with the Henkel management board to discuss what the new vision and values should be. Concurrently, Simone Bagel-Trah, a fifth-generation member of the Henkel family who served as chairwoman of both Henkel's shareholders' committee and supervisory board, worked with the Henkel family to get their input on defining the new values. (In addition to her role at Henkel, Bagel-Trah, who held a Ph.D. in microbiology, was partner and director of Antiinfectives Intelligence, a Bonn, Germany-based microbiological research company.)

In January 2010, the Henkel board of directors approved a new vision—"A global leader in brands and technologies"—and five new values:

1. We put our CUSTOMERS at the center of what we do.
2. We value, challenge and reward our PEOPLE.
3. We drive excellent sustainable FINANCIAL performance.
4. We are committed to leadership in SUSTAINABILITY.
5. We build our future on our FAMILY business foundation.

To underscore the importance of customers in Henkel's new values, Rorsted banned the use of the word "customer" to describe any internal unit within Henkel.

Senior executives next endeavored to communicate the new vision and values to Henkel's 48,000 employees. In July 2010, the company launched a "360-degree" communication campaign using Henkel's intranet, posters, employee magazine (*Henkel Life*) and town hall meetings in all major countries. Starting September 24, 2010 ("Henkel Day," marking the founding of the company), Vision & Values workshops were facilitated by line-managers in over 60 countries. In these three- to four-hour sessions, managers used materials from a toolkit to discuss with their teams how the new values could be linked to their day-to-day work and to develop concrete action plans to build a winning culture. Examples of actions from the workshops—with assigned accountability

## EXHIBIT 5   Henkel's Pre-2010 Values

- We are customer driven
- We develop superior brands and technologies
- We aspire to excellence in quality
- We strive for innovation
- We embrace change
- We are successful because of our people
- We are committed to shareholder value
- We are dedicated to sustainability and corporate social responsibility
- We communicate openly and actively
- We preserve the tradition of an open family company

*Source:* Company documents.

and due dates—included designing new "meet-your-customer" programs, instituting new ROI measures to improve resource allocation, increasing the visibility of sustainability targets, and recognizing entrepreneurial behavior with a new "Entrepreneurial Award." Over a period of six months, more than 5,000 of these workshops took place.

To allow employees to visualize how the new values would affect the company's success, the tool-kits included two imagined news-stories "from the future"—one celebrating Henkel's realization of its 2012 goals (see Exhibit 6 for an aspirational slide used in company presentations); the other describing the company's failure to meet them—allowing employees to understand the negative consequences to the company's competitiveness and prestige.

These and other internal communications efforts were managed by Henkel's 120-strong corporate communications team, led by Carsten Tilger. "It was extremely important that the workshops were run by business managers, not human resources or communications," said Tilger. "When we launched a 'soft' initiative in the past, executives would ask HR to handle it for them. Leaders were not used to discussing vision and values in terms of our competitive success. Our new approach turned out to be very successful."

Henkel's new culture was also reflected in the new company tagline, "Excellence is our Passion," used in corporate branding for both internal and external audiences. The new slogan was launched in early 2011 after the finalization of the Vision & Values workshops: "We wanted the employees to see their own contribution, and be able to put action behind the words. The workshops were key to achieving this goal," stated Tilger.

Felix Werner, a country manager in Henkel's Adhesives business, was stunned when he was fired. His financial performance had been predictably good, and he had successfully restructured the business in a difficult market. But as his business had flourished, his senior colleagues had become increasingly upset about his attitude. He was not a team player: he had been reluctant to participate in the new DRT performance management process; he did not want his business controllers reporting to group HQ; he resisted moving his support functions to the new shared-services units; and he wanted his business to be a brand that was distinct from Henkel. When informed of the decision to terminate his employment, Felix was told that the executive board members were not willing to work with someone who did not embrace Henkel's new strategy and values.

## Performance Management

Kathrin Menges was the newly promoted global head of human resources responsible for implementing Henkel's new performance management system. Menges had started her career as a high school teacher in East Germany. After the fall of the Berlin Wall in 1989, she moved to Berlin and began a business career in banking and consumer products. She attended Harvard's Advanced Management Program in 2010 after taking the new role as head of human resources. In 2011, after 12 years with the company, Menges was appointed to the Henkel management board.

According to Menges, Henkel historically had a culture of long employee tenure: "Many employees have been with Henkel for 20, 30, even 40 years," she said. "The company has been able to show stable performance over many years, so people were generally content with the way things were."

"We used to set rather easy individual targets," added Rorsted. "From 2004 to 2008, 95% of employees hit their earnings even though the company as a whole didn't reach its goals even once. It created a perception at the company that everyone is great, and yet the company as a whole was losing."

Rorsted sought to overturn this attitude of complacency through a new performance management system. "Our new system signals that being a 'happy

**EXHIBIT 6    Henkel Poster Promoting 2012 Goals**

*Source:* Company documents.

underperformer' isn't good enough anymore," said Rorsted. "We are no longer striving for second place."

**Evaluation Grid**   In 2009, Henkel introduced a new performance management system for its four layers of management (approximately 9,000 employees). Under the new system, each employee was assigned a rating representing (1) his or her performance (a reflection of past work) and (2) potential (future advancement prospects). The ratings were summarized in a four-by-four grid, with a vertical "potential" scale using numerical grades and a horizontal "performance" scale using letter grades (see Exhibit 7 for the grid). On the "performance" scale, employees were graded as either "L" (low: consistently fails to meet minimum performance requirements), "M" (moderate: meets many but not all performance requirements), "S" (strong: fully meets all performance requirements), or "T" (top: exceeds performance requirements and achieves exceptional results). For "potential," employees received a grade of one through four: "1" signaled significant advancement potential and "4" meant that the employee was already performing at the limits of his or her ability and was unlikely to advance.

For example, a "T1" rating would be assigned to a top performer with significant advancement potential. An "S3" rating would fall to an employee with strong performance who is most likely an expert in his field, but has little advancement potential.

> Hannah Hofmann, a quality engineer in Henkel's laundry business, announced that she was resigning. She would be taking a position with a government agency in Berlin. Hannah had been rated "S4" in the most recent DRT performance evaluation. She had been classified as "S" (strong) because she was considered technically competent and fully met the requirements of her job. Hannah had trouble getting on with people and was considered difficult to work with. As a result, she was rated a "4" (lowest) for future leadership potential in the company. Without significant personal change, she was unlikely to advance further within Henkel.

**Development Roundtable**   Rankings were assigned in a collaborative forum called the "Development Roundtable" (DRT). DRTs were meetings of managers—usually a group head and his or her direct reports, along with a moderator from the human resources department—in which they evaluated their direct reports, spending roughly five to 10 minutes discussing each individual. The performance evaluation grid scores served as the basis for DRT discussions.

**EXHIBIT 7**   Henkel Employee Evaluation Grid and Frame of Orientation

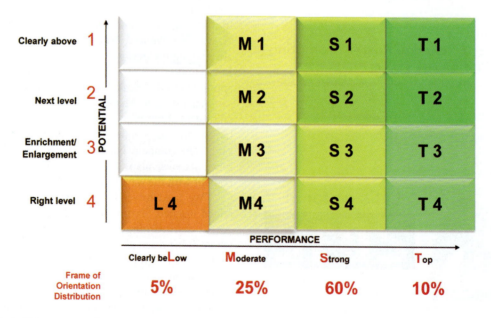

*Source:* Adapted from company documents.

In the typical DRT session (see the first page of this case), the moderator first announced the name and position of the employee to be evaluated, and then the employee's direct manager provided an overview of the employee's performance and suggested grades for performance and potential. Next, other attendees could ask the manager questions about the employee and offer their perspective on his or her performance and rating. While some evaluations ended in quick consensus, others led to lively debate. At times of disagreement, the final decision rested with the most senior executive in attendance. The typical DRT meeting covered roughly 20 to 30 employees and lasted up to a full day. About 400 DRT sessions were held each year across the company. Once all DRT sessions concluded, managers met with their reports one-on-one to discuss their rating and individual development plans.

**Frame of Orientation** The DRT process flowed bottom-up, beginning at the country level, then to region and global levels. Throughout the process, Henkel tracked the percentage of employees in each performance category. To compel managers to make tough choices and differentiate employees, Henkel created a ranking system—known as the "frame of orientation"—along the performance scale. Annually, in each department and company-wide, 5% of employees had to receive an "L" rating; 25% "M" ratings; 60% "S" ratings; and 10% "T" ratings.

As indicated in the dialogue at the beginning of this case, the grades awarded to employees "on the fence" (e.g., between "strong" and "moderate" performance) had to be adjusted to meet this distribution. For example, if a DRT meeting ended with no employees in the "L" category, the DRT participants would revisit moderate performers, compare them to each other, and move the lowest performing of the group to the "L" category to properly reflect the difference in performance.

According to Menges, this system fundamentally changed the way feedback was given at Henkel: "In the past nobody was low performing and managers were appreciative of everybody." She continued:

> Managers often delivered very positive feedback face-to-face, saving their criticism for confidential meetings when the employee was not present. We realized we needed to be fair and objective, but more critical. It's not that people were never let go in the past. But when they were, they would be shocked because they had never received a bad review. We realized it's better to be honest with people, tell them how they are really doing, and give them a chance to improve.

The distribution system also created a way to calibrate the relative performance of employees in comparable roles across different geographies and to identify high-potential leaders who might otherwise be invisible to Henkel executives. For the bottom of the distribution, the ranking mandated the delivery of negative reviews to low performers. This was especially important in countries where delivering negative feedback to subordinates ran counter to cultural norms.

The new evaluation system spurred many employees to improve their performance, moving up in the ratings over time. Other employees struggled to adjust to the sudden accountability and transparency. "It creates tension because people who were told they were great throughout their career are suddenly being told they're not so great anymore," said Rorsted.

> Robert Wilson, a third-level manager in the purchasing department in the U.S., reluctantly agreed to resign. Robert had worked for Henkel for six years and had, most recently, participated in efforts to standardize purchasing solutions across Henkel's various businesses. Robert was passionate about hobbies outside of Henkel. However, as a Henkel employee, he showed little enthusiasm and generally did the minimum amount of work required. Nevertheless, over the years, his various supervisors have never given him clear critiques of his performance. Under the new appraisal systems, Robert had been classified as an "M3" performer, meaning that he just met expectations and had low prospects for advancement. In 2011, his performance was downgraded to "L" (low), signaling that he was in the bottom 5% of the employee distribution in his unit. Keeping his job would require a significant increase in commitment and effort.

## Bonus Compensation

Under the new system, bonuses were linked to overall company financial performance, team performance (e.g., a business unit), and individual performance.

**Group Performance** Each year, Henkel set two or three key performance indicators (KPIs) at the company level (e.g., adjusted EBIT margin, organic sales growth). Performance against each KPI was measured on a scale of 0% to 200%, where 0% indicated no progress, 100% meant the targets were achieved, and a maximum of 200% recognized that targets had been substantially surpassed. Scores for each KPI were averaged to create an overall group score.

**Team Performance** The process was similar at the team level where targets were based on specific business unit targets or local market targets. Each business was measured against one to three KPIs (e.g., EBIT margin, sales growth), again on a scale of 0% to 200%.

Company scores (30% weight) and team performance scores (70% weight) were then added together. If both Henkel overall and the relevant business unit exactly met their KPIs, the resulting combined score would be 100%.

**Individual Performance**  Individual performance was calculated using two inputs, each weighted 50%:

**(a)** Performance on two equally weighted individual KPIs (e.g., successful new product launch, project progress). Performance on each KPI was measured on a scale of 0% to 150%, with 0% representing no progress, 100% (full achievement of targets), and 150% (substantially surpassed targets).

**(b)** Performance rating from the DRT process: a "T" rating yielded a score of 150%, "S" (100%), "M" (75%), and "L" (25%).

To illustrate, an employee who scored 100% on her two individual KPIs and earned a "T" (150%) rating from the DRT process would have an overall individual score of 125% ([100 + 150] ÷ 2).

**Bonus Payout**  Each manager was eligible for a target bonus based on his or her job grade/management level (e.g., 25% of base salary). To determine an individual's bonus payout, the [group + team] score was multiplied by the individual's performance score. The product of this calculation was then applied to the target bonus. For example, an employee who worked in a business that scored 150% on [group + team] performance and scored 150% on individual performance would receive 225% (150% × 150%) of her target bonus. An "L" ranked employee in the same business might receive only 37.5% (150% × 25%) of his or her bonus potential.

**Additional Payout Linked to 2012 Goals**
As an added incentive, the bonuses awarded to Henkel's top managers—around 3,000 people—would be doubled in 2012 if the company met its financial targets.

# A ROUNDTABLE DISCUSSION WITH HENKEL EXECUTIVES

The case writers met with Henkel executives to record their thoughts on Henkel's journey to build a "winning culture." Present were:

| Executive | Position |
|---|---|
| Simone Bagel-Trah (age 42) | Chairwoman, Supervisory Board, and Shareholders' Committee |
| Kasper Rorsted (49) | Chief Executive Officer |
| Lothar Steinebach (63) | EVP, Finance/Purchasing /IT/Legal |
| Hans Van Bylen (50) | EVP, Cosmeticsv/Toiletries |
| Jan-Dirk Auris (43) | EVP, Adhesive Technologies |
| Bruno Piacenza (46) | EVP, Laundry & Home Care |
| Kathrin Menges (47) | EVP, Human Resources |
| Carsten Tilger (44) | SVP, Corporate Communications |
| Ashraf El Afifi (41) | SVP, Laundry & Home Care, President MEA |

*How important were the targets that Kasper announced in 2008 to building a winning culture?*

[Jan-Dirk] "We always set long-term targets, but they never seemed to be our first priority. Some teams would plan annual targets which they could achieve within 10 months. Because of this type of behavior, we never achieved the full potential of the company. Now, the tension is unprecedented. We have set what I call 'vicious targets.' The 14% EBIT margin is just a number, but this number will transform the company in the way we set our ambitions and how we go after them."

[Kathrin] "Every year we raise the bar. A person who received an 'S' last year won't necessarily earn an 'S' next year for the same performance. They need to keep improving. This has really changed behavior. There is more clarity about what good performance is and people are really starting to pay attention."

[Lothar] "I agree. With the new vision, values, and performance management system, we all speak the same language."

*How do core values fit into your change agenda?*

[Kasper] "The new values formed the foundation from which we could undertake other changes. If you just focus on financial performance, you lose people. The cultural element provided signposts. You can't forge change without providing some stability."

*Were values developed bottom-up or top-down?*

[Carsten] "The values were created during the management board workshops taking into account input from the family shareholders. Then, we included everyone in the company in the roll-out. We asked every employee to put the values into their own words and build personal action plans. This way everyone felt invested in the changes. It was also critical that this happened in real teams, led by operating managers."

*How easy is it for people to relate to the new values?*

[Ashraf] "You have to translate the values in ways that people on the front lines can relate to. Take our financial value. Some employees in the region—who may be earning €200 to €300 a month—say to me, 'What does this have to do with us?' Then I explain how important their roles are to the company and how they can contribute to Henkel's results."

"The customer value was the easiest to translate. In the Middle East, there are a lot of start-ups which are often family run, and people understand the importance of customers. For example, Egypt has 300,000 small retailers where laundry products are sold in single-use sachets. If you talk to a worker on the line who is filling these sachets, you can talk in terms of quality. Workers understand that better quality means customers will like the product more and buy more. Helping them and helping us."

*What about the 'family' value? How do they relate to this?*

[Simone] "As chairwoman of the supervisory board and shareholders' committee, I also represent the family—the majority of the voting shareholders. To us, the value 'building on a family business foundation' implies entrepreneurship and accountability. My wish is that every employee should feel like an entrepreneur—taking risks, making changes, and moving at a fast pace. The employee should be able to decide and feel like we do as owners. In emerging markets, being owned by a family is a plus—it builds trust. But it doesn't mean that our business is a big family. It means accountability."

[Bruno] "Let me echo that. A company is not a family. In a performance-oriented company, like in sports, you select the best players, offer training and support to them, and then they need to be accountable and perform. If you want to build the best team, you must have high expectations. You cannot tolerate continued weak performance."

*Have you changed what you measure?*

[Kathrin] "Kasper loves to quote Steve Jobs: 'simplicity is the highest form of sophistication.' In the past, performance awards were based on a multitude of objectives and projects. Bonus payouts were linked to complex scorecards. We ended up with a very complex system of KPIs. We have really tried to simplify things. Instead of 20 KPIs on a scorecard, we now have three measures. We had 10 values; now we have five. At the same time, we have also substantially widened the measures for which we hold people accountable. For example, everyone now has some type of customer-focused measure in their targets."

"When it comes time for evaluation, we now focus on proof: the first thing we talk about is quantity and quality of output. This is a big change from when we used to assess people on activities and efforts, but not results. Next, we focus on the individual's ability to be customer-oriented in their work. Finally, we look at leadership qualities such as people management. All of this rolls up into our assessment of their future potential."

*Has this changed behavior?*

[Kasper] "The new performance management system has encouraged stronger teamwork, more collaboration, and significantly more innovation as people respond to the need to deliver results. Let me give you an example of the kind of innovation that arises from this heightened level of accountability. In 2008, managers in our cosmetics business realized that our targets might be at risk because our high-end hair products were under increasing price pressure. When these products are sold in professional salons, consumers pay premium prices for the quality and service. So we developed a new 'professional performance' brand offering the same quality that could previously only be purchased at the hairdresser—but sold at the retail store. Today, a range of products under this brand has been launched successfully in more than 30 countries and generates several hundred million euros in sales. Without the new targets and performance pressures, I doubt this innovation would have occurred."

[Kathrin] "I also can give you any number of examples of people who have improved their performance as a result of the new system. They are not only innovating more . . . in many cases, individuals are now routinely seeking feedback from their peers to ensure that they are on track with their improvement plans."

[Ashraf] "Let me second that. When you attended our DRT meetings, you got some sense of the type of entrepreneurial behavior we are looking to recognize and promote. Our new performance orientation has had a huge payoff in terms of competitiveness, growth, and profitability. For example, we were able to perform very strongly in the past years with a CAGR[b] for Henkel in MEA of more than 12%, which is more than three times the average CAGR of the global laundry and home care industry in the same period. This is why the role of emerging markets is so important."

[Bruno] "Being part of a winning culture also brings psychological benefits. No one wants to be on a losing team. We are now playing in the same league as our top international competitors in terms of market share growth, revenue growth, and net profit growth. Winning is highly motivational and we are starting to see the payoffs. We recently attracted a top person from P&G: with our new values, people want to be part of the story. We are now an attractive place to be."

*Weren't some people threatened by this approach?*

[Kasper] "We are trying to transform the company. In 2008, we said that we would get EBIT margins up to 14% by 2012. Not one analyst believed we could do it. By 2010 we had EBIT up from 10% to 12%, so people could see that it was possible. And we are now providing guidance for a 13% margin target for 2011. We are not backing down, even with the current financial crisis. I keep reminding everyone, 'the target is the target.'"

"We are looking for people who are innovative and entrepreneurial. Our new culture does not appeal to everyone, and a number of people have left. But the organization as a whole has accepted it because we have made more cuts at the top than at the middle. Everyone who didn't want to play under the new rules was asked to leave. Around 50% of our top 180 executives, including the management board, have changed in the past three years; the majority of the new people, more than 75%, were appointed from within. A lot of young people got promoted to take on new responsibility—and this has injected new vitality into the organization."

[Kathrin] "The people who parted ways shared two traits: they were not able or willing to adapt to the speed of change, or they were not able to communicate to their teams and implement what we are trying to do. The business controller who just wants to be a number cruncher cannot survive in our new culture where they are expected to be an advisor and partner to the business."

[Carsten] "Of course, some people did not want 'to get it.' Let me give you an example. To bring the concept of a 'winning culture' to life for our employees and those whom we might like to hire, we developed

a series of ads showing Henkel employees who were excited by their work. We rolled these out with our new tagline, 'Excellence is our Passion.' The ads were intended to be eye-catching and humorous [see Exhibit 8 for examples]. In one, a smiling female executive says eagerly, 'Yes! It's 6 A.M.' In another, a beaming manager sits outside during a coffee break under the caption, 'Breaks are Boring.' We were a little surprised when some people called in to complain that, under German law, breaks are a right, and these ads were improper. But let me add: our target group—ambitious job-seekers—got the joke and really liked it."

*How do you identify the people who can thrive in this new environment?*

[Kathrin] "We have defined clear criteria for performance and potential assessment. We consider not only quantity and quality of results, but also if an employee is a good team player, acts in a customer-oriented way, and is a good leader. Those in the 'T' category—the top 10%—have to clearly exceed our requirements. These are our gold medal players. We limit the size of this category because you don't give two gold medals in sports. And if you earned the gold medal in one year, this doesn't mean you will receive it automatically the year after—next year it might go to somebody who tried harder. This way you keep up the winning spirit."

[Hans] "Also, our new processes have increased the visibility of people dramatically. Senior managers now work hard to get to know top performers. When I am travelling abroad, I make it a point to meet personally with the most talented managers independent of their seniority level. The DRT meetings make these high performers clearly visible to me and other senior management. I follow up regularly and build a relationship with these often-young managers through multiple meetings. As board members, we act as role models. When we are seen reaching out to identify high performers and getting to know them, managers at lower levels will follow in our footsteps."

*What do you say to people who don't want to work so hard?*

[Lothar] "Anyone who aspires to a leadership position in a winning company needs to understand that they have to work hard to achieve their goal. The business must come first. Not everyone is willing to accept this reality. Before you appoint someone to a position of leadership, you have to challenge them

**EXHIBIT 8    Henkel Employer Branding Posters**

*Source:* Company documents.

to see how they cope with the extra work, the stress, and the successes and failures that accompany stretch goals and high performance expectations."

[Hans] "At the same time, we are responsible for ensuring business processes that foster motivation without fatigue. The foundation of such a process is the balance of creativity and discipline. Creativity provides freedom to blossom; accountability provides the discipline to ensure effectiveness and efficiency. With a fast and transparent decision process, we clearly define accountability and responsibility, so that we avoid fatigue and stimulate motivation."

*Do you believe that these changes have indeed created a winning culture?*

[Kasper] "The first step was restructuring and establishing the right mindset. Keeping our financial targets stable when the financial crisis happened—and

actually achieving them—has hugely added to our credibility, both internally and externally. We have been consistent, clear, and credible."

"And a huge piece of this transformation effort has been reducing and eliminating—from lowering the number of KPIs and values to cutting underperforming products, businesses, and people. But we must continue communicating the idea that the need to constantly improve—the pressure to perform and adapt—isn't going to stop. Leaders of winning businesses must constantly inspire and motivate people to do more."

[Simone] "This is something I pay a lot of attention to . . . getting the pulse of the organization. I travel a lot speaking with different employee groups: I have recently been to the Global Finance conference and to our new Middle East headquarters in Dubai. I know nearly all of the top 180 leaders in the company. When I see them, alone or in small groups, I often ask, 'What is

the difference between Henkel and other companies?'
I have received very positive feedback on our vision
and values in these discussions. That makes me proud
and shows me that the Henkel spirit is alive and well."

## Postscript

March 8, 2012. Düsseldorf. Henkel Press Release:

**Henkel delivers sales and earnings at record levels**

- Sales increase of 3.4 percent to 15,605 million euros

- Adjusted operating profit: plus 9.0 percent to 2,029 minion euros
- Adjusted EBIT margin: plus 0.7 percentage points to 13.0 percent
- CEO Kasper Rorsted stated, "For 2012, the economic environment remains challenging. . . . However, we consider Henkel to be well-positioned. . . . We expect to increase our adjusted EBIT margin to 14 percent and improve adjusted earnings per preferred share by at least 10 percent."

## ENDNOTES

[a] Names, functions, and countries in the examples throughout this case have been disguised to preserve anonymity.
[1] Adam Bryant, "No Need to Hit the 'Send' Key. Just Talk to Me," *New York Times,* August 28, 2010, accessed December 2011.
[2] Ibid.

[3] Ibid.
[4] Compiled via Capital IQ and Procter & Gamble, 2008 Annual Report (Cincinnati, Procter & Gamble, 2008), pp. ii, 39; Unilever, 2008 Annual Report (Rotterdam, Unilever, 2008), pp. 22, 81; L'Oreal, 2008 Annual Report (Paris, L'Oreal, 2008), p. 1; 3M, 2008 Annual Report

(St. Paul, 3M, 2008), pp. 4, 8, accessed January 2012. Procter & Gamble and 3M sales converted from USD to Euros via Capital IQ, using fiscal year-end exchange rates.
[5] Reported in company documents.
[b] Compound Annual Growth Rate.

# Bayonne Packaging, Inc.

## Roy D. Shapiro
### Harvard Business School

## Paul E. Morrison
### Boston University

Cold grey light came through the window of John Milliken's cubicle in the Production office of Bayonne Packaging at 6:30 AM on Monday, January 2, 2012. The new VP of Operations, Milliken had arrived a half-hour before the first shift started on his first day of work at Bayonne to review reports that had been prepared for him, and to begin his tour of the factory and interviews with key Manufacturing and other personnel. When he had been hired in mid-December, the president, Dave Rand, had asked him to analyze Bayonne's operations swiftly and present his recommendations by the end of the week.

## COMPANY AND INDUSTRY BACKGROUND

Bayonne Packaging, Inc., was a $43 million company located in Bayonne, N.J., a sub-chapter S corporation founded 48 years earlier by Rand's father. The board was composed of family members, a local banker, and outside counsel. Bayonne was a "specialty packaging" paper converter that produced customized, complex-design packaging that was used by industrial customers for promotional materials, software, luxury beverages, and gift food and candy. Except for a few low-volume operations such as laminating and gold- or silver-foil finishing, Bayonne provided all the necessary services from design assistance through final delivery of the package. Bayonne's sales force worked closely with customers to develop the artwork and package design, culminating in a proof for customer approval. Bayonne then created the printing plates and die, sheeted the paper from roll stock, printed the artwork on 4- and 6-color presses, die-cut the printed sheets into "blanks,"[1] and folded and glued the blanks into the final product, which was typically finished at this point and ready to be shipped to the customer or a contents fulfillment house. In some cases Bayonne provided additional finishing work if needed such as attaching string-and-button fasteners, Velcro dots, or other attachments.

The paper packaging industry grew rapidly in the 1980s and early 1990s as consumer goods companies sought to make a greater impact with their promotional materials or moved their promotional budget from print media and broadcast forms to the package itself at the point of purchase. In addition, the explosive growth of software packaging, which featured expensively printed large "boxes," provided additional customer market segments that were often willing to spend freely to make a quick impact in a crowded marketplace. Bayonne had grown from just over $10 million in sales in 1982 to $32 million in 2001. The company then faced new challenges with the bursting of the dot-com bubble and the subsequent migration of software sales and distribution from CDs to the Internet. Bayonne survived by diversifying into new markets where the company could apply its great

strength in innovative and difficult package design and the ability to fold and glue the complex blanks.

President Rand had asked Milliken to focus on three problem areas: cost, quality, and delivery. At the end of November 2011 Rand had fired the previous long-serving VP of Operations. Rand told Milliken, "Our sales are up—we have to run two shifts now. But we ran a loss for the first time last year since 2001. [See Exhibit 1 for income statements.] We're getting more and more complaints about quality, and, what might be even worse for our customers, we're delivering late more often. I understand we're a job shop and there's usually a tradeoff between keeping your costs down, getting good quality, and hitting your delivery promises—but lately it seems we can't even hit two out of the three. What started to go so wrong for us? Your predecessor couldn't explain it to me, and his 'plan' of 'We'll just have to try harder' told me he had no idea what to do. I hope you can do better."

# TOURING THE FACTORY IN JANUARY 2012

John Milliken graduated in 2001 from Rensselaer Polytechnic Institute with a BS in Mechanical Engineering. For the past five years he had been the Operations Manager of a small packaging firm serving the northern New Jersey pharmaceuticals industry, so he came to Bayonne familiar with the general manufacturing processes Bayonne used to design and deliver customized small-unit packaging. During the hiring process he met most of the management at Bayonne and also the factory supervisors on both shifts, and had asked for several reports to be prepared for him when he came to work in January. Digging into the pile, Milliken focused on October 2011 since that was Bayonne's highest-volume month and, as October 31 closes the fiscal year, it would show him complete and audited 12-month financial statements for the company. He reviewed the Income Statement, keeping in mind Bayonne's practice—a common one—of recognizing revenue when it billed the customer, and it billed when it shipped product. Milliken then turned to a production report that listed standard setup and run times, as well as scheduled production and standard hours for October in key work centers (Exhibit 2). A second report showed "good pieces in/ out" for the month (Exhibit 3). The last report presented the daily and cumulative dollar volumes shipped in October, net of customer returns (Exhibit 4). He also had his own chart showing the usual flow of orders through the plant's departments (Exhibit 5).

## Quality Control

Milliken left his office and crossed the factory floor to the Quality Control office to find QC Manager Fran Schuler inside. They chatted about the procedures for the start of each shift, then Milliken asked where the main problems arose.

Schuler told him that quality problems were concentrated in Fold & Glue with either missing glued lines or excess glue. Schuler showed him a report from October, their worst month of fiscal 2011, indicating that 6% of products were found defective due to glue problems and were scrapped, with a further 1% of shipped product rejected by the customer due to glue problems. There were also some problems in Finishing—a much lower volume department—primarily due to orders shipping with some or all pieces missing an attachment like a button or zipper. If the customer returned these they could usually be reworked rather than scrapped.

"What's your staffing, and your procedures for preventing or finding defects?" asked Milliken. "The supervisor signs off on the first good piece the operator runs," said Schuler. "That goes in the Work Order Jacket." The Work Order Jacket traveled with the job; it listed the routing, the standard setup and run times, any special instructions, and ship-to information. It also held the customer's signed proof along with samples signed by operators, supervisors, and QC at each operation.

Schuler told him that QC had one inspector on each shift covering the Composition, Sheet, Print, and Die-cut departments, and a second for Fold & Glue, Finishing, and the shipping dock. The inspectors went from machine to machine checking two pieces every hour during the production run, and performed a final inspection of material before it shipped out. Schuler said, "In Shipping we check the product against the proof in the Work Order Jacket, and against any special instructions like special packing or ship-to. Usually it takes about 15 minutes to do an order. Of course we might not have the Work Order Jacket at that point if it's been partialed since the jacket gets filed up in the Production office after the first shipment." If an order was running late it was sometimes possible to rush a "partial" quantity of the whole order to satisfy part of the customer need, with the rest of the order completed and shipped later.

**EXHIBIT 1** Income Statements for Bayonne Packaging, 2009–Oct. 2011 ($000)

| | Oct. 2011 | | Sept. 2011 | | Aug. 2011 | | Nov. – Aug. 2011 | | 2010 | | 2009 | |
|---|---|---|---|---|---|---|---|---|---|---|---|---|
| Gross Sales | $5,140,467 | 101.5% | $4,438,500 | 100.8% | $3,075,860 | 100.7% | $30,758,666 | 100.9% | $37,071,038 | 100.6% | $35,069,202 | 100.5% |
| Less: Customer Rejects | (75,455) | –1.5% | (33,834) | –0.8% | (21,531) | –0.7% | (276,828) | –0.9% | (222,426) | –0.6% | (175,346) | –0.5% |
| Net Sales | 5,065,012 | 100.0% | 4,404,666 | 100.0% | 3,054,329 | 100.0% | 30,481,838 | 100.0% | 36,848,612 | 100.0% | 34,893,856 | 100.0% |
| COGS: | | | | | | | | | | | | |
| Shipped Material | 3,285,673 | 64.9% | 2,704,465 | 61.4% | 1,820,380 | 59.6% | 17,770,912 | 58.3% | 20,782,617 | 56.4% | 19,296,302 | 55.3% |
| (Scrap) | 597,671 | 11.8% | 405,229 | 9.2% | 268,781 | 8.8% | 2,529,993 | 8.3% | 2,616,251 | 7.1% | 2,163,419 | 6.2% |
| Regular DL | 525,748 | 10.4% | 396,420 | 9.0% | 271,835 | 8.9% | 2,499,511 | 8.2% | 2,874,192 | 7.8% | 2,547,251 | 7.3% |
| OT DL | 116,495 | 2.3% | 74,879 | 1.7% | 12,217 | 0.4% | 173,746 | 0.6% | 294,789 | 0.8% | 265,193 | 0.8% |
| IL, supervisory | 29,884 | 0.6% | 25,107 | 0.6% | 15,272 | 0.5% | 134,120 | 0.4% | 125,285 | 0.3% | 139,575 | 0.4% |
| Other Mfg OH | 40,520 | 0.8% | 57,261 | 1.3% | 51,924 | 1.7% | 548,673 | 1.8% | 736,972 | 2.0% | 732,771 | 2.1% |
| Total COGS | 4,595,992 | 90.7% | 3,663,360 | 83.2% | 2,440,409 | 79.9% | 23,656,955 | 77.6% | 27,430,107 | 74.4% | 25,144,513 | 72.1% |
| Gross Profit | 469,020 | 9.3% | 741,305 | 16.8% | 613,920 | 20.1% | 6,824,884 | 22.4% | 9,418,505 | 25.6% | 9,749,343 | 27.9% |
| Selling Expense | 419,383 | 8.3% | 277,494 | 6.3% | 167,988 | 5.5% | 1,493,610 | 4.9% | 1,547,642 | 4.2% | 1,817,970 | 5.2% |
| Admin. Expense | 415,331 | 8.2% | 259,875 | 5.9% | 186,314 | 6.1% | 2,011,801 | 6.6% | 2,284,614 | 6.2% | 2,128,525 | 6.1% |
| Total Selling and Admin. | 834,714 | 16.5% | 537,369 | 12.2% | 354,302 | 11.6% | 3,505,411 | 11.5% | 3,832,256 | 10.4% | 3,946,495 | 11.3% |
| Net Profit Before Tax | (365,694) | –7.2% | 203,936 | 4.6% | 259,618 | 8.5% | 3,319,472 | 10.9% | 5,586,250 | 15.2% | 5,802,848 | 16.6% |

## EXHIBIT 2    October Scheduled Orders, Standard Setup and Run Time (minutes)

| | Standard Times[a] | | | | | Standard Hours | | |
|---|---|---|---|---|---|---|---|---|
| Machine or Work Center | Setup | Run | Number Mach. | Sheets/ Pcs Scheduled | Orders Sched. | Total Setup Hrs | Total Run Hrs | Total Hrs Per Mach. |
| Composition (plates)[b] | 40 | 2 | 1 | 1,438 | 310 | 207 | 48 | 255 |
| Jagenburg sheeter (sheets) | 20 | 0.0033 | 1 | 3,185,032 | 310 | 103 | 175 | 279 |
| Heidelberg press (sheets) | 50 | 0.0083 | 2 | 3,162,737 | 310 | 258 | 438 | 348 |
| Bobst die-cut (sheets)[c] | 30 | 0.0075 | 2 | 3,108,971 | 310 | 155 | 389 | 272 |
| Int. Royal/Queen F&G (pieces)[d] | 180 | 0.0023 | 3 | 6,209,329 | 77 | 231 | 238 | 156 |
| Int. Staude F&G (pieces) | 40 | 0.015 | 4 | 2,242,039 | 233 | 155 | 561 | 179 |
| Int. 3A window/ patch (pieces)[e] | 100 | 0.011 | 2 | 782,274 | 88 | 147 | 143 | 145 |
| Finishing (pieces)[f] | 30 | 0.1 | N/A | 687,601 | 28 | 14 | 1,146 | N/A |

*Note:* October 2011 had 347 scheduled work hours net of breaks, including half-day Saturdays.

[a] "Standard Times" were estimates of setup and run time per job, derived from times recorded in Work Order Jackets from previous, similar jobs.
[b] In Composition, Setup time is per order while Run time is per plate. Approx. 2/3 of the orders were for 4-color (4 plate) printing; the rest were for 6-color.
[c] Changing dies took 2-3 hours but the standards assumed that four to six or more different orders using the same die would be "ganged" or run together on a single setup. Since Cost Estimating could not know—when routing any individual order—how many orders it might be ganged with at Die-cutting, Estimating simply routed each order for 30 minutes.
[d] Blanks could run on a Royal/ Queen or a Staude, but no order ran on both.
[e] 30 of the 3A orders ran on the Royal/ Queens, the remaining 58 on the Staudes.
[f] Finishing was labor-intensive piece-work. Bayonne was able to vary the labor as needed, and so effectively could apply as much capacity as it needed.

## EXHIBIT 3    Material Flow through Operations, October 2011

| Machine/Work Center | Pieces In[a] | Pieces Out |
|---|---|---|
| Sheet | 9,555,097 | 9,488,211 |
| Print | 9,488,211 | 9,326,912 |
| Die-cut | 9,326,912 | 9,233,643 |
| Royal/Queen | 6,209,329 | 5,588,396 |
| Staude | 2,242,039 | 2,085,096 |
| 3A | 782,274 | 768,193 |
| Finishing | 687,601 | 675,335 |
| Total pieces shipped: | | 8,441,686 |

[a] Material scheduled at Sheet, Print, Die-cut has been converted from sheets to pieces, sheets averaged 3 pieces

## Sales Management

Milliken next spoke with VP Sales Alex Wascov and asked him about his biggest concerns. "On-time delivery," said Wascov. "We're selling a piece of an expensive promotional campaign. The customer has bought ads, Internet, direct marketing mailings, point-of-purchase display units and coupons, commission payments to the retail channel so they'll push the product, people handing out samples on the street—you name it. It's all scheduled to hit, to have impact, on a specific date. If our product isn't there, the customer goes nuts. We have orders as small as 1,000 pieces, but we sell some of those for a high price per piece—they're just as important to the customer. In October, since you ask, we were late more than 20% of the time. Two years ago I hit the roof if it was 5% in a month. The factory doesn't agree with me on this, they take a bow for being "on time" if they get a partial out. But that's nowhere near good enough for the customer. You try getting the customer to give us a second look if we've been late once. I'm telling you, it's getting worse not better, year after year." Milliken nodded. "The second biggest problem is the boxes popping open with not enough glue or no glue at all. Sometimes there's too much glue laid on so it bleeds out, it looks bad or you can't open it because it's stuck so bad. Don't get me wrong—we have a beautiful product, great designs, classy printing. But the glue problems are real, or

## EXHIBIT 4  Value of Actual Shipments in October (dollars)

| Date | Daily (in $) | Cumulative (in $) | Orders Shipped[a] | Late | Partialed |
|------|---|---|---|---|---|
| 1-Oct | 189,380 | 189,380 | 15 | 4 | 3 |
| 3-Oct | (3,405) | 185,976 | 6 | 2 | 1 |
| 4-Oct | 140,208 | 326,184 | 5 | 0 | 1 |
| 5-Oct | 3,674 | 329,858 | 7 | 1 | 2 |
| 6-Oct | 76,914 | 406,772 | 9 | 1 | 2 |
| 7-Oct | 366,641 | 773,413 | 12 | 2 | 3 |
| 8-Oct | 7,711 | 781,124 | 11 | 0 | 1 |
| 10-Oct | (23,639) | 757,485 | 9 | 1 | 2 |
| 11-Oct | 163,777 | 921,262 | 12 | 2 | 1 |
| 12-Oct | 243,332 | 1,164,594 | 9 | 0 | 2 |
| 13-Oct | 56,747 | 1,221,341 | 7 | 0 | 2 |
| 14-Oct | 208,154 | 1,429,495 | 15 | 1 | 4 |
| 15-Oct | 113,677 | 1,543,172 | 12 | 1 | 2 |
| 17-Oct | 134,586 | 1,677,758 | 8 | 0 | 1 |
| 18-Oct | 204,803 | 1,882,562 | 6 | 0 | 1 |
| 19-Oct | (5,080) | 1,877,482 | 15 | 1 | 3 |
| 20-Oct | 211,883 | 2,089,365 | 12 | 0 | 2 |
| 21-Oct | 456,738 | 2,546,103 | 18 | 2 | 4 |
| 22-Oct | 184,201 | 2,730,304 | 14 | 1 | 3 |
| 24-Oct | 192,185 | 2,922,489 | 16 | 3 | 3 |
| 25-Oct | 191,585 | 3,114,074 | 15 | 3 | 4 |
| 26-Oct | 284,708 | 3,398,782 | 19 | 4 | 7 |
| 27-Oct | 338,036 | 3,736,819 | 17 | 5 | 6 |
| 28-Oct | 222,682 | 3,959,501 | 22 | 8 | 12 |
| 29-Oct | 419,952 | 4,379,453 | 28 | 12 | 15 |
| 31-Oct | 685,559 | 5,065,012 | 34 | 19 | 20 |
| Total pieces shipped: | | 8,441,686 | | | |
|  |  |  | 353 | 73 | 107 |

[a]Counts each partial separately

sometimes the product is just missing some Finishing piece. Delivery is the big issue, though."

Milliken asked why customers sometimes wanted to "move up" or expedite a due date to receive product sooner than they had originally been promised, assuming schedule was part of a coordinated marketing project. Wascov said that, first, some customers had learned or heard that Bayonne on-time delivery was not to be trusted. Second, the customer may have originally wanted the material sooner but someone had settled for the standard date, and then later come back to get what they really wanted. Third, some other component of the marketing project might become available earlier than anticipated, giving the customer hope that all of the pieces, including Bayonne's,

could come together sooner. Fourth, sometimes the customer was putting together the project for some other company that wanted more lead-time—for example, it was not uncommon for retail channels to demand that promotional materials be staged sooner than originally promised.

Hoping to switch away from this litany of woe, Milliken asked, "Other than the problems, how is Bayonne doing?" Wascov looked immediately happier. "Great!" he said. "We're grabbing into new markets, getting aggressive about taking customers we've never had before. This year for the first time we've had some big, solid hits, like up to two-hundred thousand piece orders in candies, pretty much a whole new product for us. Same thing with those little corporate gift sets. I told

## EXHIBIT 5   Flow of Orders through Production Department

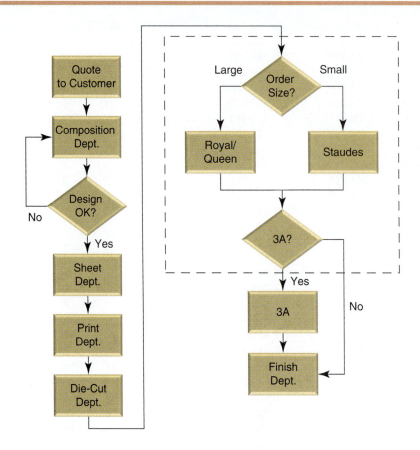

my sales people to do what it takes, price aggressively to the market, and boy they surely did. Dave Rand complains about the margins, but he doesn't complain about getting the volume. The designers had to learn a few new tricks, and the Fold and Glue operators too, plus we got into some FDA requirements about coatings, adhesives, and liners, but the amount of business we're pulling in is great. If we could just get a track record for delivering on time we can win a lot more customers too, especially with the kinds of products we haven't touched before, just over the river. You know how much promotional material money there is in Manhattan?!"

## Composition, Sheeting, Printing, and Die-Cut

By mid-afternoon Milliken had worked his way through most of Bayonne's factory work centers. First he toured the Composition Department, where both printing and package designs were developed and

finalized, printing plates made, and die-cutting dies ordered. From there Milliken passed through the Sheet Department, where the Jagenburg sheeter turned roll stock into sheets of paper stacked on skids to be printed. In the Print Department he watched 4- and 6-color Heidelberg presses print the sheets. He finished this part of his tour in the Die-Cut Department, where Bobst die-cutters cut the printed sheets into blanks—the flat cut-out shapes of printed paper ready to be folded and glued into finished product. He was led through these areas by Sean Quinn, the manager for these departments. Quinn had a supervisor within each department on both shifts reporting to him.

Watching the assistant sheeter operator expertly maneuver the clamp truck to fetch and stack up rolls of paper, Milliken asked Quinn how they scheduled the sheeter and the Heidelberg printers, and how often a lack of stock caused delays.

Quinn told him that he scheduled the sheeter by what needed to be printed in the following day or two.

## EXHIBIT 6A Bobst Die-Cut Machine

## EXHIBIT 6B International Queen Fold and Glue Machine

They rarely stocked out of because they kept enough variety on hand, and their supplier, International Paper, could restock from their warehouse in Montvale, New Jersey, within a day or two in almost all cases.

Quinn scheduled printing by due dates, which were either the standard ones originally promised to the customer (typically three weeks from signed proof, depending on the number of operations and the size of the order), rush orders sold from the start with shorter-than-standard lead times or, about twice a day, dates expedited after the order was placed.

In Quinn's office looking out a window at pallets of printed sheets waiting to be die-cut into blanks, Milliken asked how the Bobst die-cutters were scheduled. "As much as we can by having the same die," Quinn said. "We sell enough of the same package designs so we can gang orders.[2] Jerry, the cost estimator, knows that when Order Entry routes the orders they give us 30 minutes as a standard setup time—they know it really takes two or three hours if you have to change over a Bobst die, but they figure on me ganging. I juggle the orders I have in the department and that generally allows me to gang six or eight orders on a setup. If I didn't gang, I couldn't get enough run time to stay on schedule." Milliken asked how long Quinn usually held an order waiting for more to come in to the department for ganging. Quinn said it was usually about a week, sometimes as much as two.

While he talked, Quinn illustrated his scheduling by pointing to a board where small magnetic clips each held a piece of paper with a Work Order number

and its die number. Most were placed neatly in columns under the two Bobst machine numbers, lined up in the order to be run. Pushed off to one side of the board was a jumble of clips with orders that had not yet been scheduled to run. Milliken studied the jumble for a moment. Each order appeared to have a different die number. Milliken asked Quinn about the schedule that was generated twice weekly by the computerized scheduling system. "It's useless," Quinn said bluntly. Milliken asked him why. Quinn said, "The biggest reason being, between rush orders and ganging the orders to keep the machines running, I couldn't afford time-wise to do what the printout says. Apart from that, what the schedule tells you is, excuse me, garbage. It says you have an order when you've never seen it, or that you still have an order that you know you finished and got out of here. That doesn't have to happen too many times before you just don't worry about the printout."

## Fold & Glue

Milliken's next stop was the Fold & Glue Department, where the die-cut blanks were turned into finished product. The department had four kinds of machines: two International Queens and one International Royal, which were high-speed machines but complex to setup; four International Staudes, which were slow machines but easier to setup, best used for low-volume jobs; and two International 3A machines which were "window/patch" machines, using rotating cylinders which attached clear plastic "windows" and also tear-strips on envelope-style products.

Milliken asked department manager Rick Gomes about his problems. Gomes told him, "The department runs pretty good, but we get a lot of problems that are not our fault. Sean Quinn sends me a lot of orders that are one or two days from the due date, or even late already. So we have to run them as soon as possible, but there are already orders ahead of them here lined up. So I can't gang orders like he can. With those, and the rush orders too, I have to break into runs, get the order done, and then go back to the first order I broke into—so that makes for partials." "What about the glue problems?" asked Milliken. "Getting the hot melt glue guns synchronized to the belts and swords[3] is the tough thing about a setup," said Gomes. "If you do the setup quick and dirty, it runs slow—but I can't run slow with our volume. Usually we get it alright, but sometimes not. Let me show you here on this Queen." Milliken was familiar with fold & glue machines, but he stood with Gomes looking at the 35' straight-line machine and nodded while Gomes talked over the noise. "The feed takes the blank from the stack here we get from Die-cut, lays it down flat, then the fingers grab and move it. At the first glue gun a line of glue gets laid down, then the swords pick up the tabs, fold them over and lay them down. They go between the top and bottom belts, which squeeze the fold while the glue sets, for the first fold. On this order, that happens again at the second guns. Getting it running at 22,000 to 27,000-an-hour like this with the swords, belts and guns synched, not too little, not too much, and not folding off—it's not easy. The Staudes are quick to setup. They're great for little jobs, but they run slow, of course."

Milliken looked at a hot melt glue gun closely. The tiny glue orifice in the brass nozzle was open, with some hardened residue around it. The fitting from the glue canister was tightened on with an automobile-style hose clamp. He touched the nozzle and it shifted slightly. "How often do you change the filter?" he asked. Gomes said, "When it's needed-we can tell."

Milliken asked, "How do you decide between the Royal and Queens or the Staudes where to run orders?" Gomes said, "If we could do what we wanted we'd run orders of 60,000 or more on the Queens or the Royal, and anything less on the Staudes. 'Course, a lot of times we can't do that." Milliken asked about the shop floor schedule. Gomes said, "Just personally, I don't look at it. By the time I get orders, I'm just going by what's getting expedited and due dates. Whatever fire is hottest, I'm putting it out."

They watched a grizzled operator setting up the Royal, banging forcefully on a sword adjustment with a steel mallet. The part didn't move. The operator swung the mallet harder and the part jumped about an inch. "What's your maintenance schedule?" asked Milliken. "Well, operators are responsible for clean-up at the end of shift, and checking oil and grease points at the start. If something breaks down, Maintenance is good about getting right on it. We've got a pretty good supply of spare parts there in the cage."

## Scheduling

The Finishing Department manager was out sick so Milliken decided to tour there the next day. Back in the Production office Milliken sat down with Jim Worthen, the plant scheduler, and asked him about his job.

Worthen told Milliken that his job was to do whatever it took to deliver on time. The plant held a daily production meeting every morning where the main topic was what had gone wrong the previous day, the status of large, important orders, and what the department managers would do to deliver on time any newly expedited orders. Worthen indicated that generally they did not tell Sales if an order was going to be late. He said, "We're supposed to but a lot of times we don't know for sure until the end because we're hoping to get a partial out on time. If you tell Sales ahead of time an order is going to be late, Wascov just starts hammering us and calling up Dave Rand and the rep starts screaming. It creates a lot of unnecessary work—and then they bump something else, so the ripple effect is just more jobs late. Of course, they don't blame themselves for that, do they?"

Milliken asked, "When you partial, do you break orders in half or have a little part and a bigger part usually? And do you break into more than two pieces?" Worthen said, "It's always just the first and second piece, and they're just about always the same size—it's easier that way to justify doing all the additional setups if the partials don't have tiny numbers."

Milliken said, "Sean Quinn and Rick Gomes say they can't use the schedule. Why is that?" Worthen told him that much of the shop floor reporting was missing or wrong, forcing Worthen to spend several hours each day trying to scrub the data using information on work order pieces completed in each operation which the operators recorded by hand in the Work Order Jackets.

Milliken asked why the data reported through the shop floor computer terminals was so inaccurate.

Worthen told him that operators recorded pieces completed in the Work Order Jacket and their start and stop times on setup and run. The Estimator used that data for estimating standard times, and Payroll got attendance data when the operators swiped their bar-coded ID cards through the terminals. Milliken knew that operators got a 30-minute meal break in the middle of their 8-hour shift. Roll stock use at the sheeter, plates in Comp, and ink in Print were recorded by different, manual systems, and the experienced operators there maintained their own local inventory records to make sure that they did not run short. As a result, no one felt a real need for accurate terminal-based shop floor production reporting.

Milliken asked what rules the computer-based scheduling system used. Worthen told him that the computer recalculated and printed a new schedule twice a week for two "buckets"—the machine capacity in hours available in each work center in the Monday-Tuesday-Wednesday and the Thursday-Friday-Saturday (half-day) buckets. The system added up the standard setup and run hours for every order released to the plant and "filled the buckets" by scheduling orders by priority.

Priority was set by the "critical ratio". The ratio's numerator was the number of hours between the calculation date and the due date, and the denominator was the total standard setup and run hours for all remaining operations plus 48 hours for each remaining operation. The lower the ratio, the higher the priority. Worthen added, "My rule of thumb is that if the critical ratio when the job starts is lower than 2, I have to watch that job, it's born in trouble."

While Worthen was explaining this, Milliken sketched his understanding of the rules with an example (see Exhibit 7). He showed this to Worthen, who nodded and remarked, "Nobody ever got that before the first time I told him."

Milliken asked, "Has this extra two days at each work center for scheduling purposes, in addition to the work time there, got something to do with partials, like the orders really turn into two orders on their way through?" Worthen said, "No, it's a bunch of things that cause orders to just sit around and not get worked on; I'm just telling you that in my experience, anything less than a two ratio is almost always late."

Milliken asked, "Who has authority to expedite orders?" Worthen said, "Well, Dave Rand of course. Wascov gets on the horn to him, or he would call John McNulty [Milliken's predecessor] directly to get orders expedited. Since John's gone, Wascov's been calling me. Quinn and Gomes complain, and Joe Pensiero in Finishing actually gets it worst of all since he's dead last after any other delays. But the system actually works pretty good. If an order gets expedited after it's out on the floor, we give it to Neil Rand. He takes the Work Order right through whatever is left and makes sure it happens, puts it on a machine right away with no delays, wherever it's routed. Red carpet treatment." Worthen grinned. "Of course Neil's worked all over the factory since he was a kid—he's actually a good setup man himself in Fold & Glue. His orders are never late unless we hand it to him already past due—so of course Wascov is always trying to get expedites authorized." Milliken asked politely, "Neil is a family member?" "Yeah," said Worthen. "He's Dave's uncle. He wasn't ever really executive material, but he's a great guy; everybody loves him."

Back in Milliken's office the mid-afternoon January sun was already sinking. Aware that President Rand wanted his recommendations by the end of the week, Milliken pulled out a fresh pad of paper and started organizing his thoughts. He had quite a few questions to answer, among them:

1. Why were delivery, cost, and quality *all* tanking last October? It seemed like a good month to analyze because he had fairly complete data for it, and it probably showed Bayonne operating under its greatest stress.

## EXHIBIT 7   Example of a Scheduling Critical Ratio

| Operation | Standard Setup and Run Hours |
|---|---|
| Comp | 3 |
| Sheet | 2 |
| Print | 6 |
| Die-cut | 3 |
| Fold & Glue | 8 |
| Total hours: | 22 setup and run + (5 ops × 48 hours each) = 262 |
| Today: | January 2.     Due date: January 25. Hours: 23 × 24 = 552 |
| Critical ratio: | 552/262 = 2.11 |

2. The plant had seemed relatively busy as he walked through, though he knew that operators and supervisors tended to look that way while the boss was touring. Still, given Bayonne's delivery performance, he wondered if capacity were adequate, or if some or even most of the work centers would be over-stretched even with better management than he had observed. How did the quality problems play into this? Were orders being run on the right machines? Could he quantify the effect of the runs being broken into by the expediting and partialing?

3. What was the practical effect of the informal system Bayonne used to schedule the order in which jobs were run? The computer system was obviously useless right now, but would it be worth trying to fix the data and then get adherence to the scheduling system?

## ENDNOTES

[1] "Blanks" are die-cut paper shapes ready to be folded and glued into the final product. To create blanks from printed sheets, the die-cutter sliced through the paper to cut out the shape, and made other, more shallow impressions to create the creases for folding.

[2] Orders were "ganged" when they were similar enough in some setup characteristic so that several orders could be run sequentially after a single setup. In die-cutting, if several orders had the same paper thickness, blank shape, and crease lines, they could normally all use the same die and be run on a single setup.

[3] "Swords" were long thin smoothly curving metal pieces. When the side or tab on a blank lying flat and traveling down the length of the machine at high speed touched the sword, the sword guided it up and folded it over along an indented fold line pressed into the blank by the die-cutting operation.

# Rhino Sales, Hunting, and Poaching in South Africa, 2012

## A. J. Strickland
The University of Alabama

## William E. Mixon
The University of Alabama, 2011
MBA graduate

Dr. Markus Hofmeyr, head of Veterinary Wildlife Services for South African National Parks (SAN-Parks), returned from another South African rhino capture with his team. They had captured their 252n rhino for the year before the rainy season set in—heat and rain made it almost impossible to capture rhino. As Hofmeyr and his team were winding down another successful year, given that each rhino captured was worth between $30,000–$40,000, he began to reflect on next year's game capture. Hofmeyr faced the daunting question of how to continue to supplement the funding for SANParks' Park Development Fund. Over the years, the budget for his Kruger National Park unit had been reduced, and pressure for "self-funding" of Kruger National Park was increasing. An even more nagging issue was the increase in rhino poaching. Each rhino poached meant less funds to support the Wildlife Services within the confines of Kruger National Park, and an unwelcome decline in the park's rhino population.

Much of the funding for Kruger's operations had long been provided by the South African national government in the form of an annual grant. That began to change in 2010–2011, however, when budget constraints prompted the government to discontinue annual grants starting in 2015. The South African government shifted its strategy toward building a new South Africa, with emphasis on greater funding of education, job creation through infrastructure expansions, better health care for all South Africans, and economic growth. Funding cuts outside of these priority areas threatened the ability of the Veterinary Wildlife Services organization to continue delivering normal veterinary and operational services—services that were beneficial to all park wildlife and the habitat in which the wildlife had roamed for centuries. Kruger National Park's 2011 financials are shown in Exhibit 1. Rhino anti-poaching for infrastructure (mostly mobile units) was $275,000. Kruger National Parks used $10 million of its income and grant monies to support anti-poaching efforts.

## KRUGER NATIONAL PARK

Kruger National Park was established in South Africa in 1898 to protect the fast-dwindling wildlife areas. By the turn of the century, it was estimated that white rhinos were extinct in Kruger. The first translocation of white rhinos to Kruger National Park occurred in 1961, and a total of 345 white rhinos had been relocated from the parks in Kwa Zulu Natal by the mid-1970s. In 2007, an assessment by the African Rhino Specialist Group estimated that 15,000 white rhino and 1,500 black rhino existed in South Africa. Even though poaching took a toll on the rhino population, Kruger National Park still had the largest rhino population in the world (see Exhibit 2).

Kruger National Park covered 7,722 square miles (20,000 square kilometers) of conservation area, with eight gates that controlled the flow of traffic into the park. Since its establishment, it has become known for its unrivaled wildlife diversity and easy viewing, and for its world leadership in advanced environmental management techniques, research, and policies. Many viewed Kruger as the best national park in all of Africa in all aspects—management, infrastructure, and, of course, biodiversity. Kruger was the flagship of South Africa's 22 national parks and contained a

## EXHIBIT 1    Kruger National Park's Financials, 2011 (in US Dollars)

| Income | 2011 Budget | 2011 Actual | Difference | Percent |
|---|---|---|---|---|
| Entrance Fees | $12,747,116.99 | $12,510,576.81 | $  (236,540.18) | 1.86% |
| Land Rental for Private Safari Camps | 5,580,005.61 | 5,596,111.82 | 16,106.20 | −0.29% |
| Tourist Store Sales (Curios and Grocery) | 1,417,142.39 | 2,130,975.33 | 713,832.94 | −50.37% |
| Visitor Lodging, Meals, etc. | 48,556,177.40 | 47,642,362.92 | (913,814.48) | 1.88% |
| Other Income | 2,204,721.12 | 2,252,037.08 | 47,315.95 | −2.15% |
| Total Income | 70,505,163.52 | 70,163,722.30 | (341,441.21) | 0.48% |
| Expenses | | | | |
| Human Resource Cost | 31,405,562.04 | 33,657,115.36 | 2,251,553.32 | −7.17% |
| Maintenance | 3,965,834.12 | 3,679,202.07 | (286,632.05) | 7.23% |
| Depreciation | 1,376,719.79 | 1,314,277.70 | (62,442.10) | 4.54% |
| Operating Costs | 16,741,731.02 | 18,966,906.06 | 2,225,175.04 | −13.29% |
| Finance Cost | 144,005.76 | 85,360.12 | (58,645.64) | 40.72% |
| Total Expenses | 53,633,852.73 | 57,702,861.30 | 4,069,008.57 | −7.59% |
| Net Profit | $16,871,310.78 | $12,460,861.00 | $(4,410,449.78) | 26.14% |

*Note:* 1 U.S. Dollar = 6.77 Rands as of July 18, 2011.

*Source:* Kruger National Park Statistics.

## EXHIBIT 2    Estimated Population of Rhino in South Africa

| Year | 2007 | 2011 |
|---|---|---|
| White Rhino | 15,000 | 19,500 |
| Black Rhino | 1,500 | 1,900 |

*Source:* Kruger National Park Statistics.

variety of species: 336 trees, 49 fish, 34 amphibians, 114 reptiles, 507 birds, and 147 mammals. Over time, the park developed into a tourist attraction because of the wildlife and beautiful scenery representative of South Africa's Lowveld region. Tourist operations were quite large, with the park offering 21 rest camps, 7 private lodge concessions, and 11 private safari lodges. Lodges that were previously private were operated in partnership between communities and private companies, which provided concessions for parcels of land. The concessions were placed on tender, and areas were allocated for 25- to 30-year leases, during which operational activities linked with tourism were allowed. At the end of the period, the fixed assets became the property of Kruger, which could decide to extend the lease or retender the concession. An integral part of Kruger National Park's conservation effort was game capture. Traditionally, capturing game allowed Kruger National Park to reintroduce certain species to previously uninhabited areas of the park, as well as introduce rhino to the other national parks in South Africa and neighboring countries.

Game capture also enabled the park to better manage rare species by placing them in breeding enclosures. In some instances, game capture was used to reduce populations where that goal was impeded by natural regulatory mechanisms. Traditional game capture evolved into an income-generating operation as the demand for rhino increased.

## Income Generation from Game Capture

The sale of wildlife for income generation was accepted and supported by South Africa's National Environmental Management Act (2004). Kruger officials maximized income from wildlife sales by concentrating on selling high-value species. The two species sold without clearly required ecological reasons for their sale were white rhinos from Kruger National Park and disease-free buffalos from other parks. The only condition required when an animal was sold was that its removal could not negatively impact the populations from which it came. In 2011, approximately

# EXHIBIT 3    Flow Chart of Sales Transactions

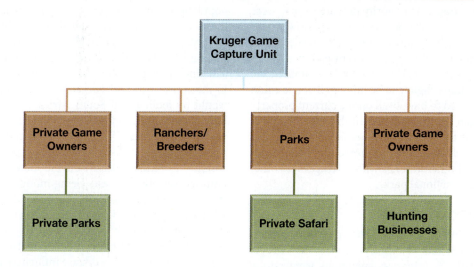

700 rhinos were sold across all of South Africa. Kruger National Park claimed 252 of these transactions, with additional sales coming from other South Africa parks and the private sector. A flow chart of sales transactions is shown in Exhibit 3. Rhinos were sold at prices averaging $37,000 for adult females, $52,000 for adult bulls, and lesser prices for younger animals depending on size. The price for rhino bulls was linked to the horn size. Many wildlife biologists and other experts feared that the rhinos sold at auction would eventually fall prey to private game hunters. Hunting and rhino breeding for future sales or hunting was driving up rhino prices. Hunting values ranged from $3,600 per horn inch to $4,500/inch for long-horned rhino. SANParks accepted hunting as a legal form of wildlife utilization, but did not support unethical put-and-take hunting practices because it was very difficult to determine what happened to a rhino after leaving SANParks. SANParks was not responsible for enforcing hunting regulations on wildlife; instead, this responsibility was delegated to each respective South African province. However, many provinces were understaffed, which weakened the regulation of hunting activities.

The most common method for selling rhino outside of Kruger National Park was through provincial and private sector auctions. In 2011, 45 auctions accounted for most rhino sales outside the South African National Park system (SANParks). During 2011, 252 rhino on a direct tender were captured in the bush and sold at three auctions held by SANParks, generating revenues of $7,033,400. These revenues were used to supplement the conservation budget for SANParks' park development fund. The buyers of the live rhino were dealers who specialized in wild game or private owners who bought directly from SANParks. Rhino were typically either sold to a private game reserve for tourist viewing or hunting. Rhino were also sold or donated by SANParks to neighboring countries. Rhinos purchased in the private sector were sometimes sold internationally to zoos, or to buyers who dealt in wild game.

Typically, white rhinos were sold more often than black rhinos, since black rhinos were rarer and much more aggressive. SANParks had sold only two black rhino bulls; the other black rhinos moved from Kruger were donated as part of conservation efforts to reestablish them in countries where they had gone extinct. The private sector bought black rhinos from Kwa Zulu Natal Wildlife, where the remaining black rhinos survived with white rhinos at the turn of the twentieth century. Kwa Zulu Natal moved from completely selling black rhinos to retaining full ownership of the adults and partial ownership of the offspring. Offspring were placed into a custodianship program that split the rights between two or more parties. North West Province sold black rhinos, as did the privately owned enterprises. Black rhinos were more difficult to introduce and had a higher intraspecies mortality rate from fighting. The tendency to fight made black rhinos a riskier investment than white rhinos, which bred and coexisted much better than black rhinos. The majority of white rhinos were purchased in cow/calf combinations, which were not hunted. White rhino bulls were much likelier to be purchased for hunting than white rhino cows. However, most provinces had regulations that limited the number of rhinos eligible to be hunted. Before a rhino was killed, it had to have lived on the current property for more than two years; however, this regulation was very difficult to enforce. Park Services had an active and critical role in striving to protect the populations of rhinos and other animals within Kruger and other South African national parks.

## Park Services

Veterinary Wildlife Services (VWS) provided a variety of operational and veterinary services for Kruger National Park. Veterinarian operations were critical to the conservation of wildlife within and outside the park. The service's operations included wildlife capture, holding and translocation, park development, species conservation management, wildlife sales, animal exchanges and contractual commitments, regional cooperation, and research. VWS aims and objectives and responsibilities are shown in Exhibit 4. Game capture operations began in the 1980s for Kruger National Park; Kruger had also operated game capture in other parks. In the 1990s, a second unit was established for operations outside of Kruger. Both units were combined to form the VWS department in 2002, ensuring that the service was serving SANParks' objectives and not just those of Kruger National Park. The current strategy of VWS was to provide ethical and professional services relating to capture, holding, translocation, and research pertaining to wildlife. Kruger National Park aimed to "provide ethical and professional services relating to capture, holding, translocation and research pertaining to wildlife."[1] Some of the values and functions associated with VWS are shown in Exhibit 5.

## SANParks' Game Capture Organization

SANParks' Game Capture Unit had branch offices in three locations in South Africa: Kruger, Kimberley, and Port Elizabeth. The capture, translocation, and reestablishment functions of VWS are shown in Exhibit 6.

Population growth, sex and age structure, spatial use, natural dispersal, resource distribution, and population dynamics were considered when making the decision to sell an animal to a private buyer. According to SANParks' Chief Executive, Dr. David Mabunda, "SANParks, by selling or donating rhino, is assisting in the process of re-colonization of the range in the country and outside. It should be noted that it would be foolhardy if South Africa were to have its only rhino population residing in the Kruger, because we run the danger of losing them should there be a major outbreak of disease or rampant poaching. We would be sitting ducks." Bovine tuberculosis and anthrax were two diseases being monitored by VWS in efforts to better understand how to contain them, which in turn would lead to better decisions about disease management where required. Intervention was not always needed in wildlife populations, but an understanding of how a disease influences population dynamics was. VWS disease management services are shown in Exhibit 7. In addition to these concerns, SANParks concerned itself with the park's capability to assess and evaluate financial implications and the risks imposed to the white rhino population of Kruger National Park by intense localized removals and emerging diseases.[2]

## CAPTURING A RHINO

The rhino capture process involved the use of state-of-the-art equipment accompanied by a team of experts A game capture team included a helicopter pilot, veterinarian, operational coordinator, veterinarian technician, five capture staff personnel, and two drivers for the translocation and crane trucks. Expenses associated with rhino capture are shown in Exhibit 8.

Once a rhino was located, the capture process consisted of darting it with a drug combination from a helicopter. The fast-acting drug combination made the whole capture process less dangerous to the capture unit by rendering the rhino unconscious for evaluation before relocation. Once the rhino was unconscious, a team from the game capture unit moved in to examine it. The game capture unit conducted a medical examination of the rhino by taking blood samples to test for any signs of disease. At this point in the game capture process, three radio-frequency identification (RFID) microchips were tagged on the rhino for identification

**EXHIBIT 4**   Aims, Objectives, and Responsibilities of SANParks' Veterinary Wildlife Services

**SANParks' Strategic and Organizational Objectives**

Prioritization of services according to resources, ethical and legal constraints

Optimal utilization of resources

Development and training of the wildlife profession

Recognition that SANParks concerns itself with populations rather than individuals

The leveraging of information and skills developed in SANParks to the benefit of the SADC region

The recognition of the importance of the wildlife, and ecological, socio-interfaces

Coordination of research on wildlife diseases and their impact on human livelihoods, wildlife itself, and livestock

Implementation of wildlife capture and translocation programs

Reintroducing populations into national parks

Enhancing the conservation status of rare and threatened species

Controlling over-abundant wildlife populations to avert the threats of habitat degradation and loss of biodiversity

Generating revenue for SANParks through wildlife sales

Enhancing breeding projects involving valuable and rare species

Building capacity in the veterinary and wildlife capture fields, particularly in persons from historically disadvantaged population groups

**EXHIBIT 5**    Veterinary Wildlife Values and Functions

Service to scientific services and park management with regard to implementing veterinary aspects of removals and introductions into our parks, collar fitting, sample taking and any other activities that require handling of wildlife

Disease monitoring, management and surveillance (including sample taking, storing and distribution aid research)

Development of current veterinary aspects of capture, translocation and animal husbandry techniques

Veterinary support to species management related to approved plans (e.g., predator management plans)

Conservation medicine (implementing and integrating disease and ecological principles in our function)

Veterinary research relevant to the service delivery component of VWS

Liaison and education at the appropriate national and international level

**EXHIBIT 6**    Capture, Translocation, and Reestablishment Functions of Veterinary Wildlife Services

Operational capture, care and translocation of wildlife species aligned with SANParks requirements

Import species and disease free breeding projects

Coordination of game sales

Transfrontier development

International translocations

Coordination of capture by external entities

## EXHIBIT 7  Disease Management Services

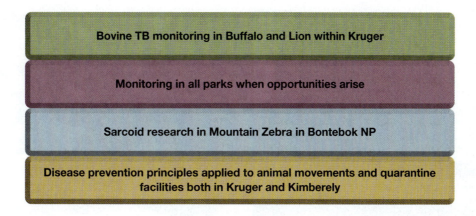

Bovine TB monitoring in Buffalo and Lion within Kruger

Monitoring in all parks when opportunities arise

Sarcoid research in Mountain Zebra in Bontebok NP

Disease prevention principles applied to animal movements and quarantine facilities both in Kruger and Kimberely

## EXHIBIT 8  Selected Operating Expenses of Rhino Capture (in US Dollars)

| Game Capture Operating Expenses | Cost per Rhino | Cost per Hour | Cost per Day | Cost per Year | Unit Cost |
|---|---|---|---|---|---|
| Helicopter | N/A | $800 | N/A | N/A | N/A |
| Transportation of rhino | $300 | N/A | N/A | $11,000 | N/A |
| Truck | N/A | N/A | $ 300 | N/A | N/A |
| Boom | N/A | N/A | $ 300 | N/A | N/A |
| Capture team | N/A | $200 | $1,400 | N/A | N/A |
| RFID microchip | $ 50 | N/A | N/A | N/A | $17 |

*Source:* Kruger National Park Statistics.

purposes. Inserting an RFID microchip involved drilling into the horn, which is made of keratin, a material similar to that which human hair and fingernails are composed of. Photos of the game capture process are shown in Exhibit 9.

Park officials used tagging as a method to better understand the rhinos' movement within their landscape. South African law mandated the tagging of any rhino darted as well. Park officials were also looking at ways to place tracking devices on rhinos to increase the capability of understanding rhino movements within their landscape. Prevention was the main emphasis of the rhino poaching counteroffensive in Kruger. It was thought that these potential tracking devices would help deter poaching, but the main deterrent was gaining information from informants on possible plans for rhino poaching.

After the evaluation and tagging process, a partial antidote was administered to partially wake up the rhino but keep it in a semi-anesthetized state. Partial antidotes were necessary to protect the game capture team while walking the rhino into the transportation crate. After the rhino was successfully loaded into a transportation crate, a boom truck lifted the crate onto the translocation truck. A boom truck was needed since an average rhino weighed 3,300 pounds (1,500 kilograms). Typically, the average distance traveled by a rhino captured from Kruger National Park was 50 miles (80 kilometers), at a cost of $300 per rhino per 16 miles.

# EXHIBIT 9    The Game Capture Process

Game capture personnel drill a hole in the rhino's horn to insert the RFID microchip.

The game capture unit follows the helicopter in pursuit of a rhino.

Game capture personnel inspect the sedated rhino.

The dart shot from the helicopter is inspected by game capture personnel.

Boom trucks are needed to load the rhino.

Game capture unit personnel inspect the sedated rhino.

Game capture personnel load the rhino for translocation.

**EXHIBIT 10** Dr. Markus Hofmeyr
Standing above *Bomas*
(Holding Pens)

The next translocation process was maintenance in holding facilities (see Exhibit 10). Rhinos were placed in *bomas* (holding pens). *Bomas* allowed a rhino to become accustomed to a new habitat by slowly facilitating a passive release. Once released, the rhino was typically still confined to a larger pen or fenced-in area, depending on the buyer's intentions. It was estimated that 50 percent of the bulls transferred to private hunting companies were killed within two years, at a price of $8,000 per inch of rhino horn.

## Rhino Hunting

A typical rhino hunt could cost $55,400 per hunter. In 2011, South Africa generated an estimated $8.2 billion in revenues from tourist attractions, equal to about 10.2 percent of South Africa's total Gross Domestic Product; of that amount, hunting accounted for about 70 percent.[3] The cost of booking a rhino hunt varied depending on the safari company, as detailed in Exhibit 11. Most safari companies required a deposit

**EXHIBIT 11**  Selected Company Safari Expenses and Trip Details

| Africa Sport Hunting Safaris |
|---|

**Services Offered**

- First-class rifle and bow hunting
- Ethical, professional hunters
- Personal attention to all our clients
- Family and photographic tours
- Specialized, well-maintained vehicles
- Luxury accommodation
- Excellent cuisine
- Dedicated staff

**Firearms and Calibers**

- Rhino legal minimum .375 caliber and 3–9 × 40 variable-power telescope
- Ammunition recommended minimum of 40 full metal jacket/solids in addition to soft point bullets

**Travel Information**

- Valid passport required

**Trophy Handling**

- All animals will be skinned by our very experienced skinners, as well as marked, salted, and dried prior to being sent to a taxidermist. All documentation will be handled by Africa Sport Hunting Safaris.

**Clothing and Other Requirements**

- Three sets of hunting clothing: long pants (zip-offs), long sleeve shirts, socks, and underwear
- Hunting boots/shoes—comfortable
- Casual/running shoes
- Sweater/warm jacket
- Flip flops / sweat suit

*(Continued)*

## EXHIBIT 11 *(Continued)*

| Africa Sport Hunting Safaris |
| --- |

– Cap / wide-brimmed hat

– Casual clothes

– Adjust your clothing to the time of year your hunt takes place.

– Winter: May–August (35–70°F)

– Summer: September–April ( 50–90°F)

**Personal**

– Personal medical kit

– Sunblock—minimum 30 SPF

– Mosquito repellent

– Pair of sunglasses

– Toiletries

**Additional Equipment**

– Small day pack

– Flashlight with spare batteries

– Binoculars

– Camera with spare film and batteries

– Pocket knife

**Accommodation: Luxury Thatched Chalets with a True African Ambience**

– Private rooms with ensuite bathrooms

– Running hot and cold water

– Electricity with converters

– Flush toilets

**Food and Beverages**

– Traditional South African cuisine. For dietary requirements such as diabetes and high cholesterol, please make arrangements on booking of the safari.

**Additional Services**

– Facials and full body massages

– Manicures and pedicures

– Day excursions

| South African Hunting Areas Price List Limpopo Province 2010 | Price (in US dollars) |
| --- | --- |
| – White Rhino | $55,000 |
| – White Rhino (Green-Hunt) | $13,000 |
| **Daily Rate: South Africa** | |
| – Dangerous Game | $   800 |
| – Plains Game | |
| – 1 Hunter × 1 Professional Hunter: | $   400 |
| – 2 Hunter × 1 Professional Hunter: | $   300 |
| – All non-hunters are welcome at: | $   200 |
| **Included in Daily Rate** | |
| – Pick up and drop off at Polokwane International Airport | |

*(Continued)*

– Hunting licenses and fees

– Transportation to and from hunting concessions

– Field preparation of trophies

– Professional hunters, trackers, skinners, and camp staff

– Fully equipped hunting vehicles

– Luxury accommodation and meals

– Drinks and beverages in moderation

– Daily laundry services

**Excluded from Daily Rates**

– Flights: international and domestic

– Charter flights where applicable

– All animals shot and wounded will be charged per price list

– Dipping, packing, taxidermy cost

– Non-hunting, traveling days at $150 per day

– Accommodation before and after hunt

– Any additional tours or excursions

**Methods of Payment Accepted**

– U.S. currency

– Traveler's checks

– Wire transfers

– Credit cards

– Personal checks with prior approval

**Members Of:**

– Professional Hunters Association South Africa

– Accredited Tour Guides

– Safari Club International

– North American Hunters Association

– National Rifle Association

## Chattaronga Safaris

**Daily Fees Hunter**

| | |
|---|---|
| 1 | $400 |
| 2 | $350 |
| 3 | $300 |
| 4 | $300 |
| Observer | $200 |

**Included Tariffs**

– Accommodation including full board

– Liquor and beverages served in camp

– Full-time service of experienced professional hunter

– Trained staff

– Trackers

– Skinners

*(Continued)*

## EXHIBIT 11   (*Continued*)

| Chattaronga Safaris | |
|---|---|
| – Field preparation of trophies | |
| – All transportation within hunting areas | |
| – All hunting licenses | |
| – Pickup and drop off at international airport: Limpopo-Polokwane, Kwa-Zulu Natal-Johannesburg, Mpumalanga-Johannesburg | |
| **Excluded Tariffs** | |
| – International and domestic flights | |
| – Traveling day (non-hunting days) at $180 per day | |
| – Trophy fees of animal shot or wounded | |
| – Rifle hire (firearms may be rented at $80 per day) | |
| – Ammunition is available at cost | |
| – Dipping, packing, taxidermy, and shipping | |
| – Air charters and accommodation before and after safari | |
| – Tips for staff, telephone calls, and curio purchases | |
| **Rhino Safari** | |
| 7 Day 1 × 1 | $60,000 |
| Includes representative 20" fake horn (because it is not standard practice to cut off the horn of a rhino) | |

| Dumukwa | |
|---|---|
| **Daily Rates** | |
| 1 hunter/1 professional hunter | $    400 |
| 2 hunters/1 professional hunter | $    300 |
| Non-hunters/observers | $    200 |
| Rhino dart | $ 8,500 |
| 5 day 1 × 1 Hunt | |
| **Included in Daily Rates** | |
| – Full accommodation, meals, and use of camp facilities | |
| – All liquid refreshments including wine, beer, bottled water, and sodas | |
| – Daily laundry | |
| – Service of professional hunter with his team of skinners and trackers | |
| – Field preparation of trophies | |
| – Transport of raw trophies to local taxidermist for the area you hunt in | |
| – All transportation during the safari, including from and to the airport | |
| – 14 percent value added tax (VAT) on all packages | |
| **Excluded in Daily Rates** | |
| – Internet, faxes, and telephone calls | |
| – Airfare | |
| – Hotel accommodation before and after the contracted safari | |
| – Dipping and packing or mounting of trophies | |
| – Shipping of trophies back to your country | |
| – Optional hire of firearms | |

(*Continued*)

## EXHIBIT 11 (Concluded)

| Zingeli Safaris |
|---|

**Included in Daily Rates**

– Full board and lodging with traditional catering

– South African wines and beer in moderation, and soft drinks

– Experienced professional hunter and trained staff

– Trackers and skinners

– Field preparation, salting and packing

– Transportation of trophies to reliable and qualified taxidermist who will follow your instructions and fulfill the necessary requirements

– Use of hunting vehicle

– Laundry services

– Transportation to the ranch and return to Johannesburg International Airport or charter plane

**Excluded in Daily Rates**

– Air travel before, during, and after the contracted period of the safari

– Accommodation and travel charges incurred before and after the contracted period of the safari

– Trophy fees for animals taken or wounded

– Value added tax (VAT) 14 percent on daily rates

– Air charters

– Gratuities to professional hunters and staff

– Preparation, packing, documentation, and export of trophies from South Africa

of 50 percent of the basic cost of a safari, which was fully refundable up until three months of the contracted safari date. Accommodations varied depending on packages offered by each safari company and were considered comparable to those of any other tourist attraction in the world. Some safari companies offered photo safaris and wedding packages, in addition to hunting services, to further generate revenue for operations.

Typically, each safari company recommended certain equipment and clothing for hunters to bring along with them. This list varied by season since temperatures could range from 30°F in the winter to 90°F in the wet summer season. Expenses also varied according to the specific details of a trip, such as length of stay, trophy fees, number of hunters and observers, and the daily rate charged per hunter. Airfare to and from South Africa also varied depending on how far in advance travel arrangements were made and whether the flight was direct. Typically, coach seating ranged from $800 to $1,100, whereas

first-class prices could easily approach $3,000. Rifles, bows, and darting weapons were offered in some packages, but rifles could be imported into South Africa under strict guidelines and regulations. However, hunters were not allowed to import automatic or semiautomatic weapons.

Some companies charged high trophy fees and low daily rates, in contrast to low trophy fees and high daily rates. Trophy fees varied according to the specific animal wounded or killed and were typically not paid until the end of the safari. Daily rates depended on the services offered and could include or exclude a number of amenities necessary to hunt in South Africa. In general, some safari companies offered a lower daily rate as a marketing tool to increase their customer base; a large trophy fee reflected the fact that a safari company's profits depended on a successful hunt by the customer. As Zingeli Safaris stated in its brochure, "If you don't get your animal we lose; this is your guarantee that we will do our best to find you your dream trophy!"

Customers incurred taxidermist fees, in addition to trophy fees, if they desired to have something tangible to take home.

## Poaching

Strong demand for rhino horn in emerging markets such as Asia and India have made selling rhino horn highly profitable. The black market price for rhino horn was $10,700/lb in 2011. Adult rhino horns ranged from 2.5 pounds to 9.0 pounds, depending on a rhino's age and horn growth.

Businesses with ties to political insiders were entering the market to supply and sell rhino horn. The market for raw rhino horn was mainly driven by demand coming from cultural beliefs, combined with increasing national and personal wealth in China, India, and Vietnam, which have created a strong foundation for demand of raw rhino horn. Asians believed that rhino horn was a very beneficial aphrodisiac, and Indians desired rhino horn daggers. These beliefs and desires were strong enough to produce prices high enough to entice the illegal killing of rhinos in South Africa without regard to such law enforcers as the SANParks Environmental Crimes Unit, South African Police Service, and park rangers.

### EXHIBIT 12    Number of Poached Rhinos in South Africa, by Province, 2010 through April 20, 2012

| SA | 2010 | 2011 | 2012 (April 20) |
|---|---|---|---|
| **Kruger Nat'l Park** | 146 | 252 | **111** |
| **Other Nat'l Parks** | 0 | 6 | **3** |
| Gauteng (GP) | 15 | 9 | 0 |
| Mpumalanga (MP) | 52 | 74 | 25 |
| Eastern Cape (EC) | 17 | 31 | 3 |
| Limpopo (LP) | 57 | 21 | 17 |
| North West (NW) | 4 | 11 | 3 |
| Free State (FS) | 3 | 4 | 0 |
| Natal (KZN) | 38 | 34 | 18 |
| Western Cape (WC) | 0 | 6 | 1 |
| Northern Cape (NC) | 1 | 0 | 0 |
| **TOTAL** | 333 | 448 | 181 |

*Source:* Kruger National Park Statistics.

### EXHIBIT 13    Poachers Cut the Horn off this Rhino and Left It to Die.

Poachers were well equipped with highly sophisticated transportation, including helicopters and the latest military weaponry available in the region. They were able to strike fast within even the most protected game conservation areas. Poaching was even a problem in Kruger National Park, home to what some considered the best anti-poaching unit in South Africa. In 2011 alone, there were 252 rhinos poached in Kruger and 448 poached in South Africa as a whole—see Exhibit 12 for the numbers of rhino poached by province for the years 2010 and 2011, and partial year 2011.

Poachers were ruthless in the slaughtering of rhinos. They typically cut off a rhino's horns after darting it with a deadly poison (see Exhibit 13). Poachers also darted rhinos with an immobilizing antidote that sometimes left the rhino helpless in the wild to be eaten by other game. SANParks Chief Executive Officer Dr. David Mabunda called poachers as "dangerous criminals" whose exploits were not limited to rhino, but included human trafficking, arms smuggling, prostitution, and drug trafficking.

"Poachers must beware," Mabunda said in a statement announcing a $250,000 funding boost, in addition to the $768,000 allocated to train and prepare the SANParks Environmental Crimes Unit and South African Police Service. Fifty-seven rangers equipped with night vision goggles and high-powered motorbikes were dispatched to guard highly poached areas of the park day and night. Said Mabunda, "This war we plan on winning." In

## EXHIBIT 14 Number of Arrested Poachers

| South Africa – Arrests | 2010 | 2011 | 2012 (April 20) |
|---|---|---|---|
| KNP (KNP) | 67 | 82 | 29 |
| Gauteng (GP) | 10 | 16 | 11 |
| Mpumalanga (MP) | 16 | 73 | 38 |
| Eastern Cape (EC) | 7 | 2 | 0 |
| Limpopo (LP) | 36 | 34 | 7 |
| North West (NW) | 2 | 21 | 15 |
| Free State (FS) | 0 | 0 | 6 |
| KZN (KZN) | 25 | 4 | 6 |
| Western Cape (WC) | 2 | 0 | 0 |
| Northern Cape (NC) | 0 | 0 | 1 |
| Total | 165 | 232 | 113 |

addition to the funding boost, consideration was being given to using military personnel to guard the porous border near Kruger National Park. Elisabeth McLellan, a species expert with the World Wildlife Foundation (WWF), was quoted as saying, "The situation is bad for rhino worldwide, in terms of poaching." Conservationists were facing an environment that had evolved into an industry, as world trade had reached a 15-year high for illegal rhino horn trading. See Exhibit 14 for the success in arresting rhino poachers.

Kenyan authorities at Jomo Kenyatta International Airport recently seized a 662-pound load of elephant tusk and rhino horn, believed to have come from South Africa. It was speculated that the cache, valued at approximately $2 million, was destined for China. Industry experts suggested that the high value placed on elephant tusk and rhino horn by consumers was driving poaching activities. As Kruger Park struggled to deter poachers, another front began to arise as animal activists condemned Kruger's sales transaction process.

## Animal Supermarket

Kruger National Park was determined to win the war against poaching, but determination alone wasn't enough to protect the rhino. Primary-market transactions involved buyers that protected the rhino—such as other national parks, private game farms, game dealers, and photography safari business owners—but secondary markets from the sale of captured rhinos had also developed. Hunters had become the most numerous buyers in the secondary market, which wasn't aligned with Kruger National Park's mission. Animal rights activists dubbed the sale of animals at Kruger National Park an "animal supermarket." Many believed that the commercial trade posed a greater threat than poaching did. Many also felt it was fundamentally wrong to herd animals from a popular wildlife reserve and sell them in efforts at "conservation." Wildlife activists accused SANParks of misusing the park by serving as nothing more than a private game breeder, and experts feared that the vast majority of the rhinos sold by SANParks would fall into the hands of private hunters.

## SANParks' Justification for Selling Rhino

SANParks officials were guided in their decision to sell wildlife by Clause 55(2) (b) of the Protected Areas Act, No. 57 of 2003 (as amended), which stated that "SANParks may, in managing national parks sell, exchange or donate any animal, plant, or other organism occurring in a park, or purchase, exchange or otherwise acquire any indigenous species which it may consider desirable to reintroduce into a specific park." SANParks believed that it was critical to its conservation efforts to maintain the sale of animals to private entities. For years, SANParks had sold animals to fund conservation efforts, and in many cases the park had traded animals to obtain other species. Also, SANParks screened animals and buyers to ensure that animals were released not arbitrarily, but to buyers with the proper permits and intentions. Decisions to sell or donate wildlife were scientifically determined according to population dynamics, sex and age structure, spatial use, natural dispersal, and resource distribution.

SANParks' strategy was shaped by the following objectives: population control, broadening of the range for populations, spreading the risk of managing wildlife, making the populations more resilient and viable, and fundraising for specific conservation and land-expansion programs. The responsibilities of SANParks' conservation biologists are shown in Exhibit 15: The catch-22 facing SANParks was how to effectively communicate that selling rhino is for the greater good.

**EXHIBIT 15**  The Responsibilities of Conservation Biologists

Identifying key research themes necessary for national parks to achieve their conservation objectives

Conducting research on key themes

Coordinating research projects conducted by external scientific institutions in national parks

Integrating best available biodiversity data into park management through interactions with external researchers and research institutions

Maintaining inventories of biodiversity in national parks, including species checklists for vertebrates and higher plants and the mapping of landscape, geology, soil, and vegetation

Averting threats to biodiversity in national parks, including overabundance of certain wildlife populations, invasive alien plant and animal species, pollutants, human development, excessive resource exploitation or other factors

Ensuring that development within parks takes place in a manner that does not compromise biodiversity conservation

Working to conserve rare and threatened species

Providing scientific inputs on the rehabilitation of degraded landscapes

Providing scientific inputs on biodiversity aspects of park management plans and activities

Building capacity in conservation biology and related sciences, particularly in persons from historically disadvantaged population groups.

## ENDNOTES

[1] Sam Ferreira & Travis Smith Scientific Services, SANParks, Skukuza, South Africa.

[2] Ibid.

[3] *Wildlife Research Magazine.*

# The Upper Big Branch Mine Disaster

McGraw Hill connect

## Anne T. Lawrence
### San Jose State University

On Monday, April 5, 2010, just before 3 o'clock in the afternoon, miners at Massey Energy Corporation's Upper Big Branch coal mine in southern West Virginia were in the process of a routine shift change. Workers on the evening shift were climbing aboard "mantrips," low-slung electric railcars that would carry them into the sprawling, three mile–wide drift mine, cut horizontally into the side of a mountain. Many day shift workers inside the mine had begun packing up and were preparing to leave, and some were already on their way to the portals. At one of the mine's main "longwalls," one thousand feet below the surface, a team of four highly experienced miners was operating a shearer, a massive machine that cut coal from the face with huge rotating blades. The shearer had been shut down for part of the day because of mechanical difficulties, and the miners were making one last pass before the evening shift arrived to take their places.

Suddenly, a spark thrown off as the shearer's blades cut into hard sandstone ignited a small pocket of flammable methane gas. One of the operators immediately switched off the high-voltage power to the machine. Seconds later, the flame reached a larger pocket of methane, creating a small fireball. Apparently recognizing the danger, the four miners on the longwall crew began running for the exit opposite the fire. They had traveled no more than 400 feet when coal dust on the ground and in the air ignited violently, setting off a wave of powerful explosions that raced through the mine's seven miles of underground tunnels. When it was over, three minutes later, 29 miners (including all 4 members of the longwall crew) were dead, and two were seriously injured. Some had died from injuries caused by the blast itself, others from carbon monoxide suffocation as the explosion sucked the oxygen out of the mine. It was the worst mining disaster in the United States in almost 40 years.

An evening shift miner who had just entered the mine and boarded a mantrip for the ride to the coal face later told investigators what he had experienced:

> All of a sudden you heard this big roar, and that's when the air picked up. I'd say it was probably 60-some miles per hour. Instantly black. It took my hardhat and ripped it off my head, it was so powerful.

This miner and the rest of his group abandoned the mantrip and ran for the entrance, clutching each other in the darkness. On the outside, stunned and shaken, they turned to the most senior member of their crew for an explanation. "Boys. . ., I've been in the mines a long time," the veteran miner said. "That [was] no [roof] fall. . . The place blew up."[1]

## MASSEY ENERGY CORPORATION

At the time of the explosion, Massey Energy Corporation, the owner and operator of the Upper Big Branch mine, was one of the leading coal producers in the United States. The company, which specialized in the production of high-grade metallurgical coal, described itself as "the most enduring and successful coal company in central Appalachia," where it owned one-third of the known coal reserves. Massey extracted 37 million tons of coal a year, ranking it sixth among U.S. producers in tonnage. The company sold its coal to more than a hundred utility, metallurgical, and industrial customers (mostly on long-term contracts) and exported to 13 countries. In 2009, Massey earned $227 million on revenue of $2.7 billion. The company and its subsidiaries employed 5,800 people in 42 underground and 14 surface mines and several coal processing facilities in West Virginia, Kentucky, and Virginia.

Massey maintained that it brought many benefits to the nation as a whole and to the Appalachian region. The coal industry in the United States, of which Massey was an important part, provided the fuel for about half of the electricity generated in the United States, lessening the country's reliance on imported oil. The company provided thousands of relatively well-paying jobs in a region that had long been marked by poverty and unemployment. Economists estimated that for every job in the coal industry, around three and a half jobs were created elsewhere. The company donated to scholarship programs, partnered with local schools, and provided emergency support during natural disasters, such as severe flooding in West Virginia in May 2009. "We recognize that it takes healthy and viable communities for our company to continue to grow and succeed," Massey declared in its 2009 report to shareholders.

But critics saw a darker side of Massey. The company was one of the leading practitioners of mountaintop removal mining, in which explosives were used to blast away the tops of mountains to expose valuable seams of coal. The resulting waste was frequently dumped into adjacent valleys, polluting streams, harming wildlife, and contaminating drinking water. In 2008, Massey paid $20 million to resolve violations of the Clean Water Act, the largest-ever settlement under that law. In an earlier incident, toxic mine sludge spilled from an impoundment operated by the company in Martin County, Kentucky, contaminating hundreds of miles of the Big Sandy and Ohio rivers, necessitating a $50 million cleanup. Worker safety was also a concern. An independent study found that Massey had the worst fatality rate of any coal company in the United States. For example, in the decade leading up to the Upper Big Branch disaster, Peabody Coal (the industry leader in tons produced) had one fatality for every 296 million tons of coal mined; Massey's rate was one fatality per 18 million tons—more than 16 times as high.

## Donald L. Blankenship

At the time of the Upper Big Branch mine disaster, the chief executive officer and undisputed boss of Massey Energy was Don Blankenship. A descendant of the McCoy family of the famous warring clans, the Hatfields and the McCoys, Blankenship was raised by a single mother in a trailer in Delorme, a railroad depot in the coal fields of West Virginia. His mother supported the family by working six days a week, 16 hours a day, running a convenience store and gas station. Michael Shnayerson, who wrote about Blankenship in his book, *Coal River,* reported that the executive had absorbed from his mother the value of hard work—as well as contempt for others who might be less fortunate. "Anyone who didn't work as hard as she did deserved to fail," Shnayerson wrote. "Sympathy appeared to play no part in her reckonings."[2]

Blankenship graduated from Marshall University in Huntington, West Virginia, with a degree in accounting. As a college student, he worked briefly in a coal mine to earn money for tuition. In 1982, at age 32, he returned to the coal fields to join Massey Energy, taking a job as an office manager for a subsidiary called Rawls. Soon after, Massey announced it intended to spin off its subsidiaries as separate companies and reopen them as nonunion operations. The United Mine Workers, the union that then represented many Massey workers, struck the company. Jeff Goodell, a journalist who profiled Blankenship in *Rolling Stone,* described the young manager's technique for defeating the union at Rawls:

> Blankenship erected two miles of chain link fence around the facility, brought in dogs and armed guards, and ferried nonunion workers through the union's blockades. The strike, which lasted more than a year, grew increasingly violent—strikers took up baseball bats against the workers trying to take their jobs, and a few even fired shots at the scabs. A volley of bullets zinged into Blankenship's office and smashed into an old TV. . . . For years afterward, Blankenship kept the TV with a bullet hole through it in his office as a souvenir.[3]

The union's defeat at Massey (by 2010, only about one percent of Massey's workers were union members, all of them in coal preparation plants rather than mines) contributed to the overall decline of the United Mine Workers in the coal fields. In the 1960s, unions represented nearly 90 percent of the nation's mine workers; by 2010, they represented just 19 percent.

Blankenship quickly moved through the management ranks. In 1990, only eight years after he joined the company, he became president and chief operating officer of the Massey Coal Company, and in 1992 was promoted to CEO and chairman. (The company was renamed Massey Energy in 2000 when it separated from its parent, Fluor Corp.) By some measures, he was a successful CEO. Between 2001, the first full year of Massey's independent operation, and 2009, annual revenue increased from $1.2 billion to $2.7 billion. During this period, employment rose from around 3,700 to 5,800. Blankenship more than doubled the

## EXHIBIT 1    Don Blankenship, Total Compensation, 2007–2009

| Year | Salary | Bonus | Stock Awards | Option Awards | Incentive Plan | Change in Pension Value | Other(*) | Total Compensation |
|------|--------|-------|--------------|---------------|----------------|------------------------|----------|---------------------|
| 2009 | $ 933,369 | $300,000 | $3,869,819 | $      0.0 | $11,549,156 | $573,618 | $609,875 | $17,835,837 |
| 2008 | 1,000,000 | 300,000 | 390,000 | 2,160,000 | 6,022,447 | 691,415 | 357,129 | 11,020,991 |
| 2007 | 1,000,000 | 300,000 | 604,800 | 1,700,000 | 5,257,576 | 111,794 | 386,480 | 9,361,000 |

*Notes:* "Other" includes personal use of company cars, aircraft (the Challenger 601 corporate jet), housing, and related costs and services.

*Source:* Massey Energy 2010 Proxy, "Compensation Discussion and Analysis" and "Compensation of Named Executive Officers."

company's coal reserves, mainly through acquisitions of smaller firms. Massey shareholders, like all investors, were buffeted by the extreme volatility of the stock market during the 2000s. Nevertheless, an investor who purchased $10,000 worth of Massey stock in December, 2004, would have a holding valued at $12,800 in December, 2010—a rate of return close to that of the coal industry as a whole during this period.[4]

As CEO, Blankenship developed a reputation as a hands-on, detail-oriented manager. He lived in the coal fields and ran the company out of a double-wide trailer in Belfry, Kentucky, just over the West Virginia line. He signed off on all hires, all the way down to janitors. One manager expressed amazement when he learned that the CEO would have to approve a tankful of gasoline for his truck. Managers were required to fax production figures to Blankenship every half hour. Red phones connected mine managers directly to the CEO. "If the report was late or the numbers weren't good, or the mine was shut down for any reason," Shnayerson reported, "the red phone would ring. The terrified manager would pick it up to hear Mr. B demanding to know why the numbers weren't right."[5] Blankenship told an interviewer, "People talk about character being what you do when no one else is looking. But the truth of the matter is character is doing that which is unpopular if it's right, even if it causes you to be vilified."[6]

As CEO, Blankenship maintained a laser focus on productivity. In 2005, he sent a memo titled "RUNNING COAL" to all Massey underground mine superintendents which stated:

If any of you have been asked by your group presidents, your supervisors, engineers, or anyone else to do anything other than run coal (i.e., build overcasts, do construction jobs, or whatever) you need to ignore them and run coal. This memo is necessary only because we seem not to understand that coal pays the bills.

A week later, after this memo had been widely circulated, he followed up with another one which referred to the company's S-1, P-2 (safety first, production second) program. He wrote: "By now each of you should know that safety and S-1 is our first responsibility. Productivity and P-2 are second."

## Executive Compensation

Blankenship was well compensated for running Massey. As shown in Exhibit 1, his total compensation in 2009 was almost $18 million; this was up from $11 million in 2008 and $9 million in 2007. Blankenship's base salary in all three years was close to $1 million. By far the greatest proportion of his total pay came from a performance-based incentive system established by Massey's board of directors. In its filings with the SEC, the board described its philosophy of compensation this way:[7]

We compensate our named executive officers in a manner that is meant to attract and retain highly qualified and gifted individuals and to appropriately incentivize and motivate the named executive officers to achieve continuous improvements in company-wide performance for the benefit of our stockholders.[8]

Accordingly, the compensation committee of the board established an incentive plan for Massey's CEO. (Similar plans were in place for other senior executives as well.) The plan set specific performance measures for "areas over which Mr. Blankenship was responsible and positioned to directly influence outcome." These areas, and the proportion of his incentive compensation based on them, are shown in Exhibit 2.

By one estimate, in the 10 years leading up to the disaster Blankenship received a total of $129 million in compensation from Massey.[9] "I don't care what people think," he once said during a talk to a gathering of Republican Party leaders in West Virginia, speaking of himself in the third person. "At the end of the day,

## EXHIBIT 2   Incentive Compensation Plan for Massey Energy's CEO, 2009

The calculation of incentive plan compensation was based on achievement of specific targets in these areas:

| | |
|---|---|
| EBIT (earnings before interest and taxes) | 15% |
| Produced tons | 15% |
| Continuous miner productivity (feet/shift) | 5% |
| Surface mining productivity (tons/man-hour) | 5% |
| Environmental violations (% reduction) | 10% |
| Fulfillment of contracts | 15% |
| Nonfatal days lost due to injury and accident (% reduction) | 10% |
| Identification of successors | 5% |
| Employee retention | 15% |
| Diversity of members | 5% |

*Note:* A "continuous miner" is a large machine that extracts coal underground.

*Source:* Massey Energy 2010 Proxy.

Don Blankenship is going to die with more money than he needs."[10]

## Government Regulation of Mining Safety and Health

Coal mining had always been a hazardous occupation. Methane gas, an odorless and colorless byproduct of decomposing organic matter that was often present alongside coal, was highly flammable. Methane explosions had contributed to the deaths of more than 10,000 miners in the United States since 1920. To mine safely, methane levels had to be constantly monitored, and ventilation systems had to be effective enough to remove it from the mine. Coal dust itself—whether on the floor or other surfaces, or suspended in the air—was also highly flammable. The standard practice was to apply layers of rock dust (crushed limestone) over the coal dust to render it inert. In addition to the ever-present danger of fire, miners had long contended with the threat of collapsing roofs and walls, dangerous mechanical equipment, and suffocation. Miners often developed coal workers' pneumoconiosis, commonly called black lung, a chronic, irreversible disease caused by breathing coal dust. (Black lung was preventable with proper coal dust control.)

Health and safety in the mining industry had long been regulated at both the federal and state levels. Over the years, lawmakers had periodically strengthened government regulatory control, mostly in response to mining disasters.

- In 1910, following an explosion at the Monongah mine in West Virginia in which 362 men died, Congress established the *U.S. Bureau of Mines* to conduct research on the safety and health of miners.

- The Federal Coal Mine Health and Safety Act, known as the *Coal Act*—which passed in 1969 after the death of 78 miners at the Consol Number 9 mine in Farmington, West Virginia—greatly increased federal enforcement powers. This law established fines for violations and criminal penalties for "knowing and willful" violations. It also provided compensation for miners disabled by black lung disease.

- The 1977 *Mine Act* further strengthened the rights of miners and established the Mine Safety and Health Administration, MSHA (pronounced "Em-shah") to carry out its regulatory mandates. The law required at least four full inspections of underground mines annually.

- In 2006, after yet another string of mine tragedies focused public attention on the dangers of mining, Congress passed the Mine Improvement and New Emergency Response Act, known as the *MINER Act*. This law created new rules to help miners survive underground explosions and accidents. [11]

States like West Virginia that had significant mining industries also had their own regulatory rules and agencies.

Although MSHA was empowered to inspect mines unannounced and to fine operators for violations, the agency had limited authority to shut down a mine if a serious problem was present or if the operator refused to pay its fines. Criminal violations of mine safety laws were normally considered misdemeanors rather than felonies.

Over time, fatalities in the industry had declined. At the turn of the twentieth century, around 300 to 400 miners died every year in the nation's coal mines; by the 1980s, this number had dropped to less than 50. Injuries and illnesses had also dropped. In part, these declines reflected tougher government regulations. They also reflected the rise of surface mining (mostly in the Western United States), which tended to be safer, and the emergence of new technologies that mechanized the process of underground mining. The unionization of the mining industry had also given workers a greater voice and the right to elect safety representatives in many workplaces.

# THE UPPER BIG BRANCH MINE

Massey had bought the Upper Big Branch mine in 1993 from Peabody Coal. It was a particularly valuable property because its thick coal seam produced the high-grade metallurgic coal favored by utilities and the steel industry. Two hundred employees worked there on three, round-the-clock shifts. In 2009, Upper Big Branch produced 1.2 million tons of coal, about 3 percent of Massey's total. The mine, like all of those operated by Massey, was non-union.

The regulatory record revealed a widespread pattern of safety violations at the Upper Big Branch mine and an increasingly contentious relationship between its managers and government regulators. As shown in Exhibit 3, government inspectors had issued an increasing number of violations over time, with a sharp spike upward the year before the disaster. These data also showed that around 2006, management had begun to contest regulatory penalties rather than pay them. The state investigation reported the story that at one point Massey's vice president for safety—an attorney—"took a violation written by an inspector, looked at her people, and said, 'Don't worry, we'll litigate it away.'" Appealing the citations not only allowed the company to delay or avoid paying, it also blocked tougher sanctions, such as shutting down the mine.

Miners testified that they were intimidated or disciplined if they complained about safety. When one foreman told his men not to run coal until a ventilation problem was fixed, he was suspended for three days for "poor work performance." Another miner, who was killed in the blast, had told his wife that a manager had told him when he complained about conditions, "If you can't go up there and run coal, just bring your [lunch] bucket outside and go home." The father of a young miner who was still a trainee when he was killed at Upper Big Branch related his son's experience to investigators. The young man had told his father that when he had expressed concerns about safety to his supervisor, he was told, "If you're going to be that scared of your job here, you need to rethink your career."[12] Miners who were hurt on the job were told not to report their injuries, so an NFDL (non-fatal day lost) would not be recorded. A former Massey miner who testified before a Senate committee explained, "If you got hurt, you were told not to fill out the lost-time accident paperwork. The company would just pay guys to sit in the bathhouse or to stay at home if they got hurt."[13]

Investigators found that the company had kept two sets of books at UBB, one for its own record keeping and the other to show inspectors. "If a coal mine wants to keep two sets of books, that's their business," the administrator for MSHA later commented. "They can keep five sets of books if they want. But they're required to record the hazards in the official set of books."[14] Conditions that were recorded in the company's own books—but not the official set—included sudden methane spikes, inoperative safety equipment, and other dangers.

The mine also had a system in place, set up by its chief of security, to warn underground managers that an inspector was on the way—a clear violation of the law. A miner who survived the explosion later told Congress, "The code word would go out we've got a man [government inspector] on the property . . . When the word goes out, all effort is made to correct the deficiencies."[15] A surviving miner testified:

> Nobody shuts one of Don Blankenship's mines down. It has never happened. Everyone knows when mine inspectors are coming, you clean things up for a few minutes, make it look good, then you go back to the business of running coal. That's how things work at Massey. When inspectors write a violation, the company lawyers challenge it in court. It's just all a game. Don Blankenship does what he wants.[16]

## EXHIBIT 3 Safety and Health Citations, Upper Big Branch Mine, Assessed Penalties and Amount Paid, 2000–2009

| Year | Number of Citations | Assessed Penalty | Amount Paid |
|------|------|------|------|
| 2000 | 240 | $55,325 | $55,325 |
| 2001 | 398 | 48,761 | 48,761 |
| 2002 | 221 | 64,726 | 64,726 |
| 2003 | 175 | 41,934 | 41,405 |
| 2004 | 238 | 48,371 | 48,371 |
| 2005 | 143 | 32,577 | 32,576 |
| 2006 | 173 | 191,249 | 84,411 |
| 2007 | 271 | 253,984 | 61,745 |
| 2008 | 197 | 239,566 | 105,965 |
| 2009 | 515 | 897,325 | 292,953 |

*Source:* MSHA data, reported in the appendices of *Industrial Homicide: Report on the Upper Big Branch Mine Disaster.*

After the disaster, Blankenship stated, "Violations are unfortunately a normal part of the mining process. There are violations in every coal mine in America, and UBB was a mine that had violations."

## Causes of the Disaster

In the months following the tragedy at Upper Big Branch, three separate investigations—conducted by the federal MSHA, a commission established by the governor of West Virginia, and the United Mine Workers—examined the causes of the fatal explosion. All came to the same conclusion: that a spark from the longwall shearer had ignited a pocket of methane, which had then set off a series of explosions of volatile coal dust that had raced through the mine. Such events could only have happened in the presence of serious, systematic safety violations. Among the problems cited by the investigators were these:

- *Rock Dust.* Investigators found that the company had failed to meet government standards for the application of rock dust. As a result, explosive coal dust had built up on surfaces and in the air throughout the mine.

   The state commission reported that the Upper Big Branch mine had only two workers assigned to rock dusting, and they typically worked at the task only three days a week and were frequently called away to do other jobs. Moreover, their task was often impossible because the mine's single dusting machine, which was about 30 years old, was broken most of the time. Federal investigators later determined that more than 90 percent of the area of the mine where the explosion occurred was inadequately rock dusted at the time of the explosion. They also found that the area of the longwall where the explosion began had not been rock dusted a single time since production started there in September 2009. The presence of large amounts of floating coal dust in the mine was also suggested by medical evidence. Seventy-one percent of the autopsied victims showed clinical signs of black lung disease, caused by breathing airborne coal dust. Nationally, the rate of black lung disease in underground coal miners is around 3 percent.

- *Ventilation.* Investigators found that the Upper Big Branch Mine did not have sufficient ventilation to provide the miners with fresh, breathable air, and to remove coal dust as well as methane and other dangerous gases.

Upper Big Branch, like many mines, used a so-called push-pull system in which large fans at the portal blew fresh air into the mine, and a fan on the other end pulled air out. The state investigation found that this system did not work very well at Upper Big Branch. The fans were powerful enough, but the plan was not properly engineered.

> The push-pull ventilation system at Upper Big Branch . . . had a design flaw: its fans were configured so that air was directed in a straight line even though miners worked in areas away from the horizontal path. As a result, air had to be diverted from its natural flow pattern into the working sections. . . . Because these sections were located on different sides of the natural flow pattern, multiple diversionary controls had to be constructed and frequently were in competition with one another.[17]

Poor ventilation had likely caused methane to build up near the longwall shearer, providing the fuel for the initial fireball, investigators found.

- *Equipment Maintenance.* Investigators concluded that water sprays on the longwall shearer were not functioning properly, and as a result were unable to extinguish the initial spark.

   After the disaster, investigators closely studied the longwall shearer where the initial fire had started. They found that several of the cutting teeth on the rotating blades (called "bits") had worn flat and lost their carbide tips, so they were likely to create sparks when hitting sandstone. The investigators also examined the water nozzles on the shearer, which normally sprayed water onto the coal face during operation to cool the cutting bits, extinguish sparks, and push away any methane that might have leaked into the area. They found that seven of the nozzles were either missing or clogged. Tests found that the longwall shearer did not have adequate water pressure to keep the surface wet and cool. As a result, any small sparks thrown off during the mining process could not be extinguished.

In short, a series of interrelated safety violations had combined to produce a preventable tragedy. The United Mine Workers called the disaster "industrial homicide" and called for the criminal prosecution of Massey's managers.

For its part, Massey had a completely different interpretation of the causes of the events of April 5. An investigation commissioned by the company and headed by Bobby R. Inman, its lead independent director, said that the explosion was caused by a sudden, massive inundation of natural gas through a crack in the mine's floor—an Act of God that the company could not have anticipated or prevented. The company report stated:

> . . . the scientific data that [Massey] has painstakingly assembled over the last year with the assistance of a team of nationally renowned experts so far compels at least five conclusions. *First,* a massive inundation of natural gas caused the UBB explosion and coal dust did not contribute materially to the magnitude or severity of the blast; *second,* although an ignition source may never be determined, the explosion likely originated in the Tailgate 21 entries, but certainly not as a result of faulty shearer maintenance; *third,* [the

company] adequately rock dusted the mine prior to the explosion such that coal dust could not have played a causal role in the accident; *fourth,* the mine's underground ventilation system provided significantly more fresh air than required by law and there is no evidence that ventilation contributed to the explosion; and *fifth,* MSHA has conducted a deeply flawed accident investigation that has been predicated, in part, upon secrecy, protecting its own self-interest, witness intimidation, obstruction of [company] investigators, and retaliatory citations.[18]

In a conversation with stock analysts six months after the disaster, Blankenship stated that he had a "totally clear conscience" and that he did not believe Massey had "contributed in any way to the accident."[19]

## ENDNOTES

[1] Governor's Independent Investigation Panel, *Report to the Governor,* p. 26. This account of the disaster is based on a reconstruction of the events of April 5, 2010, by federal and state investigators and by the United Mine Workers Union.
[2] Michael Shnayerson, *Coal River: How a Few Brave Americans Took on a Powerful Company—and the Federal Government—to Save the Land They Love* (New York, Farrar, Straus, and Giroux: 2008), p. 155.
[3] Jeff Goodell, "The Dark Lord of Coal Country," *Rolling Stone,* December 9, 2010.
[4] Massey, 2009 Annual Report, "Shareholder Information," p. 23.
[5] Michael Shnayerson, quoted in United Mine Workers of America, *Industrial Homicide: Report on the Upper Big Branch Mine Disaster,* p. 80.
[6] Jim Snyder, "Q&A with Don Blankenship," November 16, 2009, http://thehill.com.
[7] At the time of the UBB disaster, Massey was governed by a nine-person board of directors

chaired by Blankenship. The other members were Baxter Phillips, Jr., Massey's President; Stanley Suboleski, formerly Massey's Chief Operating Officer and later Commissioner of the Federal Mine Safety and Health Review Commission under President George W. Bush; Lady Judge, an attorney and former commissioner of the Securities and Exchange Commission; Bobby R. Inman, a retired naval admiral and former director of the National Security Agency; James Crawford, a former coal industry executive; Robert Fogelsong, President and Executive Director of the Appalachian Leadership and Education Foundation; Richard Gabrys, formerly Vice Chairman of Deloitte and Touche; and Dan Moore, a retired banker. In 2009, directors earned $39,600 in cash and $90,000 in stock, plus $2,000 for each meeting attended, plus extra compensation for special duties (e.g., lead director). (Massey, Form 8-K, November, 2009.)
[8] Massey Energy, 2010 Proxy, p. 25.

[9] David Roberts, "Grist" [blog], April 9, 2010, www.grist.org.
[10] Goodell, op. cit.
[11] "History of Mine Safety and Health Legislation," Mine Safety and Health Administration, www.msha.gov.
[12] UMW, op. cit., p. 81.
[13] Ibid., p. 78.
[14] *The New York Times,* "Mine Owners Misled Inspectors, Investigators Say," June 29, 2011.
[15] UMW, op. cit., p. 77.
[16] Jeff Goodell, op. cit.
[17] Governor's Independent Investigation Panel, op. cit., p. 61.
[18] http://www.usmra.com/download/MasseyUBBReport.pdf.
[19] *The Charleston Gazette,* "CEO Says Massey Has 'Clear Conscience' over Upper Big Branch," October 27, 2010.

# Frog's Leap Winery in 2011—the Sustainability Agenda

## Armand Gilinsky
### Sonoma State University

There's an old saying in the wine industry that goes, "In order to make a small fortune you need to start out with a *large* one." Unfortunately, I'd never heard of that "rule" before I started out. I came here to the Napa Valley 27 years ago with $40 in my pocket, sold my motorcycle for $5,000 to start a winery, and now I owe $22 million to the bank. And I still haven't been able to buy back my motorcycle, because the current loan covenants with the bank do not permit me to ride, so I'm not sure that I am a success story, really.

—John Williams, founder and CEO, Frog's Leap Winery[1]

From the autumn of 1999 to late spring 2011, most Napa Valley premium wineries were embracing modernity—launching websites, using viral marketing, developing wine clubs, and shifting distribution channels from on-premises accounts to direct sales. John Williams, the co-founder, owner, and CEO/winemaker of Frog's Leap Winery in Rutherford, California, had followed suit by making modest investments in these marketing programs. Williams nevertheless remained skeptical that these changes would dictate *his* winery's future. In May 2011, Williams reflected upon his heritage as the son of upstate New York dairy farmers and his 35 years' working in the wine industry since graduation from Cornell University. Williams not only displayed his normally irreverent humor, but also acknowledged that he had quietly developed the industry's most sophisticated environmental management system.[2] Environmental management systems (EMS) had risen in importance for wine businesses, as they confronted survival threats from the natural world, such as rising energy prices, water scarcity, mounting concerns about chemical exposure, and climate change.[3] Yet Williams wondered aloud: "How could Frog's Leap, which has grabbed the 'low-hanging fruit' of environmental management, become even more sustainable?" See Exhibit 1 for a timeline of events in Frog's Leap's evolution.

## NAPA VALLEY AND THE PREMIUM WINE INDUSTRY

Napa Valley was a prominent American Viticultural Area (AVA) in California's North Coast wine-producing region, which encompassed Lake, Napa, Mendocino, and Sonoma counties. [See "Glossary of Common Wine Industry Terminology" at the end of this case.] Since 1999, the number of premium wineries in the North Coast had grown from 329 to 1,250.[4] Of that number, nearly 92 percent could be classified as small or "boutique" wineries—that is, those producing fewer than 50,000 cases per year. The number of boutique wineries increased dramatically during the 12-year period, from 249 to 1,133. By contrast, midsized wineries (those producing between 50,000–499,999 cases per year) and large wineries (those producing more than 499,999 cases per year) grew more modestly in number during the same period, from 80 to 117.

In the year following the height of the global economic downturn of 2008 and 2009, the premium wine industry witnessed a small but significant rebound in growth. Mid-priced and high-priced

## EXHIBIT 1  Evolution of Frog's Leap Winery

| Year | Major Events |
|------|--------------|
| 1884 | Welcoming building built as the Adamson Winery |
| 1972 | As undergraduate at Cornell, John Williams obtains internship at Taylor Wine Company, falls in love with wine as a result |
| 1975 | While touring Napa Valley with a friend, John meets Larry Turley at Larry's newly bought farmstead; returns in summer to begin graduate work in enology at UC Davis; starts working part-time at Stag's Leap Wine Cellars (under Warren Winiarski); makes (and consumes) with Turley the first unofficial Frog's Leap vintage, a fizzy Chardonnay |
| 1980 | John returns to Napa Valley to become head winemaker at Spring Mountain, marries Julie Johnson; first Frog's Leap vintage, a Cabernet Sauvignon, is (somewhat unofficially) crushed |
| 1981 | John Williams forms Frog's Leap Winery in Napa with Larry Turley; winery is bonded; winery makes its first Sauvignon Blanc and Zinfandel |
| 1984 | Julie Williams becomes Frog's Leap's first employee |
| 1985 | John leaves Spring Mountain to work full-time at Frog's Leap |
| 1989 | Frog's Leap certifies its first organic vineyard |
| 1992 | First Frog's Leap Merlot (1990) is released |
| 1993 | Larry and John agree to create separate wineries; John and Julie buy Frog's Leap from Larry and begin to look for new home for winery; Larry starts Turley Wine Cellars on original Frog's Leap site (the Frog Farm) |
| 1994–1995 | John and Julie purchase defunct Adamson Winery from Freemark Abbey and restart Frog's Leap at the "Red Barn" ranch in Rutherford |
| 1999 | First appearance of winery's Rutherford label (1996 vintage); underground barrel *chai* (barrel hall) next to the Red Barn completed; John and Julie are divorced; Julie starts her own winery, Tres Sabores |
| 2002 | At urging of John, Rutherford Dust Society begins Napa River Restoration project; debut of winery's Syrah and La Grenouille Rouganté, a dry rosé |
| 2005 | Photovoltaic system goes live after installation of 1,020 panels at the Red Barn vineyard; original green mailbox at winery entrance is removed and road signage to winery added |
| 2006 | Frog's Leap completes 10-year plan for winery and opens new LEED certified hospitality and administrative offices; Red Barn rebuilt |
| 2009 | Frog's Leap creates wine club, "Fellowship of the Frog" and begins developing "wine by the glass program" by packaging wines for delivery to restaurants in half kegs |

*Sources:* Casewriters' research; Beer, J. (2007), *Organically Sublime, Sustainably Ridiculous: The First Quarter Century of Frog's Leap,* Kennett Square, PA: Union Street Press.

## EXHIBIT 2  U.S. Premium Wine Industry—Key Financial Data, 2002–2010

|  | 2002 | 2003 | 2004 | 2005 | 2006 | 2007 | 2008 | 2009 | 2010 |
|--|------|------|------|------|------|------|------|------|------|
| Annual Sales Growth | 5.2% | 17.6% | 25.5% | 19.4% | 21.2% | 22.3% | 2.0% | −3.8% | 10.8% |
| Gross Margin | 51.5% | 50.2% | 51.5% | 52.8% | 54.5% | 57.1% | 55.3% | 52.4% | 53.7% |
| Pretax Profit | 3.2% | 6.3% | 7.6% | 12.6% | 11.3% | 16.3% | 9.5% | 2.2% | 6.7% |

*Source:* Silicon Valley Bank, *2011–12 State of the Wine Industry,* April 2011, p. 11.

wines led that growth. See Exhibit 2 for data comprising the U.S. premium wine industry's percent sales growth, margins, and pretax profits from 2002–2010. Exhibit 3 presents volume and value changes for various price points of wines during 2010.

## CONSUMER SEGMENTS FOR PREMIUM WINES

The U.S. surpassed both France and Italy in 2008 as the world's largest consumer of wine by dollar value. In 2010, U.S. wine consumption in terms of volume reached an

## EXHIBIT 3 U.S. Wine Industry—Price Segment Data, December 31, 2009–December 31, 2010

| Price Segment | Last 52 Wks $ Share | Value % Change | | Volume % Change | |
| --- | --- | --- | --- | --- | --- |
| | | Last 52 Wks | Last 26 Wks | Last 52 Wks | Last 26 Wks |
| Total table wine | | +4.5% | +4.8% | +3.2% | +3.5% |
| $ 0–$ 2.99 | 8.4 | −1.3 | −2.5 | −2.4 | −2.6 |
| $ 3–$ 5.99 | 29.3 | +4.4 | +4.2 | +4.8 | +4.9 |
| $ 6–$ 8.99 | 20.2 | −3.4 | −3.3 | −1.0 | −0.9 |
| $ 9–$11.99 | 20.8 | +10.0 | +10.5 | +12.4 | +12.5 |
| $12–$14.99 | 10.0 | +7.8 | +8.1 | +10.3 | +10.2 |
| $15–$19.99 | 6.2 | +7.0 | +9.4 | +7.7 | +10.3 |
| >$20 | 5.0 | +11.4 | +11.8 | +9.2 | +11.0 |
| | 100.0% | | | | |

*Source:* The Nielsen Companies, in Silicon Valley Bank, *2011–12 State of the Wine Industry,* April 2011, p. 4.

all-time peak of 2.54 gallons per resident over 21. In that same year, 25- to 44-year-olds emerged as the largest segment of wine consumers, supplanting the "Baby Boom" generation that had led much of the industry's growth during the prior 30 years. Consumer demographics of the U.S. wine industry in 2010 is shown in Exhibit 4.

Trends in consumer health awareness also had a considerable impact on U.S. wine consumption. The

## EXHIBIT 4 Consumer Demographics Data for the U.S. Wine Industry in 2010

| | Unemployment Rate | % of Population | % of Wine Drinking Population |
| --- | --- | --- | --- |
| **Race/Ethnicity** | | | |
| White | 8.5% | 68.9% | 78.5% |
| Hispanic | 13.0% | 13.4% | 8.9% |
| African-American | 15.8% | 10.8% | 7.3% |
| **Age** | | | |
| 21–24 | 15.3% | 7.4% | 4.0% |
| 25–34 | 10.1% | 18.7% | 13.6% |
| 35–44 | 7.8% | 19.6% | 16.3% |
| 45–54 | 7.5% | 20.6% | 22.0% |
| 55+ | 6.9% | 33.7% | 44.1% |
| **Education** | | | |
| High school diploma | 15.3% | 19.2% | 10.2% |
| Some college | 10.6% | 28.4% | 20.2% |
| College grad | 4.9% | 24.3% | 39.9% |

*Source:* The Nielsen Companies, in Silicon Valley Bank, *2011–12 State of the Wine Industry,* April 2011, p. 13.

"Baby Boomers" increasingly desired to stave off aging and infirmity by incorporating better nutrition and wellness into their lives. The postulated positive health aspects of drinking red wine in moderation contributed to increasing wine sales across all age groups.

So-called "green" consumers comprised an emerging demographic segment called LOHAS (Lifestyles of Health and Sustainability). This segment sought a better world for themselves and their children. LOHAS consumers were savvy, sophisticated, ecologically and economically aware and believed that society had reached a watershed moment in history because of increasing public scrutiny of corporations' environmental and ethical practices.[5] The LOHAS consumer focused on health and fitness, the environment, personal development, sustainable living, and social justice. The segment was estimated at about 38 million people, or 17 percent of the U.S. adult population, with a spending power of $209 billion annually.[6] Among all ages of consumers, younger consumers, aged 14–24, were reported to be the most concerned about issues such as climate change and environmental protection, and were the major drivers of growth in the LOHAS segment. See Exhibit 5 for demographic data on "green" consumers versus all consumers.

Yet considerable confusion remained among wine consumers of all ages regarding organic wine versus wine made from organically grown grapes. Organic wine was fermented and aged without sulfites, regardless of how the grapes were grown. Wine made from organically grown grapes might or might not have sulfites added to preserve shelf life. The two products were considerably different in origin, composition, and potential shelf lives.[7] Furthermore, wines labeled as organic or biodynamic were typically placed in a separate section away from other mainstream brands in supermarkets and specialist shops. Nevertheless, U.S. sales of certified organic wine and those made with organic grapes reached $80 million in 2006, and rose to nearly $130 million in 2008, an increase of 28 percent over 2004, according to the Organic Trade Association.[8]

## SUSTAINING THE CALIFORNIA WINE INDUSTRY

After a period of unprecedented and sustained growth from 2002–2007, wine producers sought an edge to differentiate their brands and also to reduce costs during the 2008–2009 industry downturn. Many wineries faced financial difficulties due to market saturation. Almost all 6,785 wineries across the U.S. (of which 3,306 were in California) faced downward pressure on prices and margins. Some industry observers opined that wine producers faced a newly "hyper-competitive" trading environment: the rate of new brand introductions slowed in 2009 and 2010, in a period when wholesalers and distributors of wine were struggling to sell off a backlog of wine inventory and thus were less receptive to taking on new wines to sell.[9]

Barbara Banke was co-proprietor of Jackson Family Wines in Santa Rosa, California (Sonoma County), a wine business known for its Kendall-Jackson, Hartford Family, Matanzas Creek, and Cardinale brands. Banke listed sustainability as one of the greatest challenges the wine industry faced in 2011:

> We've had a reduction in the workforce last year, and we focused on controlling our costs and not investing so much capital. We have a constant battle to get the recognition we deserve with all the work we've done on sustainability. The industry is very green—and yet that's something that's not widely known. The California wine industry should work on enhancing its reputation for sustainability.[10]

To many in the wine industry, sustainability was defined as the "triple bottom line," meaning that producers needed to measure the impacts of their

## EXHIBIT 5   Profile of the "Green" Consumer

|  | All Consumers | "Green" Consumers |
|---|---|---|
| Average age | 44 | 40 |
| Gender |  |  |
|   Female | 51% | 54% |
|   Male | 49% | 46% |
| Ethnicity |  |  |
|   Caucasian/other | 75% | 62% |
|   Hispanic | 13% | 21% |
|   African-American | 11% | 16% |
| College educated | 25% | 31% |
| Median household income | $58,700 | $65,700 |

Source: Brooks, S. (2009), "The Green Consumer," *Restaurant Business,* September, pp. 20–21.

# EXHIBIT 6  Overview of the California Sustainable Winegrowing Program

Wine Institute and the California Association of Wine Growers (CAWG) partnered to design and launch the Sustainable Winegrowing Program (SWP) in 2002. The California Sustainable Winegrowing Alliance (CSWA) was incorporated a year later to continue implementing this program.

**Mission**

The long-term mission for the SWP includes:

- Establishing voluntary high standards of sustainable practices to be followed and maintained by the entire California wine community;

- Enhancing grower-to-grower and vintner-to-vintner education on the importance of sustainable practices and how self-governance improves the economic viability and future of the wine community; and

- Demonstrating how working closely with neighbors, communities, and other stakeholders to maintain an open dialogue addresses concerns, enhances mutual respect, and accelerates positive results.

**Vision**

The vision of the SWP is the sustainability of the California wine community for future generations. In the context of winegrowing, the program defines sustainability as wine grape growing and winemaking practices that are sensitive to the environment (Environmentally Sound), responsive to the needs and interest of society at-large (Socially Equitable), and economically feasible to implement and maintain (Economically Feasible). The combination of these three principles is often referred to as the three E's of sustainability. These important principles are translated into information and education about specific practices that are documented in the program's comprehensive Code workbook and are conveyed during the program's targeted education events that are aimed to encourage the adoption of improvements over time.

**SWP Voluntary Participation Data, 2004 and 2009**

| Vineyard Data Comparison | 2004 | 2009 | |
|---|---|---|---|
| Number of Distinct Vineyard Organizations | 813 | 1,237 | |
| Total Vineyard Acres Farmed by the 1,237 Organizations | 223,971 | 358,121 | *(68.1% of 526,000 total statewide acres)* |
| Number of Vineyard Acres Assessed by the 1,237 Organizations | 137,859 | 241,325 | *(45.9% of 526,000 total statewide acres)* |
| Number of Vineyard Organizations that Submitted Assessment Results | 614 | 868 | *(70.2% of 1,237 total organizations)* |
| Total Vineyard Acres from 868 Organizations Assessed and Submitted | 124,576 | 206,899 | *(39.3% of 526,000 total statewide acres)* |
| Winery Data Comparison | 2004 | 2009 | |
| Number of Distinct Winery Organizations | 128 | 329 | |
| Total Winery Cases Produced by 329 Organizations | 145.6M | 150M | *(62.5% of 240 million total statewide cases)* |
| Number of Winery Cases Assessed by 329 Organizations | 126.6M | 141.5M | *(59% of 240 million total statewide cases)* |
| Number of Winery Organizations that Submitted Assessment Results | 86 | 173 | *(52.6% of 329 total organizations)* |
| Total Winery Cases from 173 Organizations Assessed and Submitted | 96.8M | 134.6M | *(56.1% of 240 million total statewide cases)* |

*Sources:* California Wine Community, Sustainability Report 2009, pp. 6–7; Brodt, S. and Thrupp, A. (2009, July), "Understanding Adoption and Impacts of Sustainable Practices in California Vineyards," California Sustainable Winegrowing Alliance, pp. 5–8, www.sustainablewinegrowing.org.

activities upon "people, planet, and profit"—that is, how it created social, environmental, and economic value. That the wine industry was greening was borne out by a report issued by the California Sustainable Winegrowing Alliance in 2009.[11] Some 1,237 California vineyard and 329 winery owners voluntarily participated in the Sustainable Winegrowing Program (SWP), despite widespread perceptions that sustainable farming practices increased the cost of production and lowered crop yields. Information about the SWP is shown in Exhibit 6. According to the Napa Valley Vintners Association, Napa Valley boasted 404 premium wineries, of which 60 were classified as "Green" or "Sustainable" in some fashion. See Exhibit 7 for more information on the 60 "Green" wineries in Napa in 2011.

## EXHIBIT 7  "Green" Wineries in Napa Valley in 2011

| | Winery Name | Annual Case Production (est.) | Certified Napa Green *Land* (1) | Certified Napa Green *Winery* (2) | Sustainable Practices (3) |
|---|---|---|---|---|---|
| 1 | Araujo Estate Wines | 5,000–49,999 | X | X | X |
| 2 | Artesa | 50,000–499,999 | X | | X |
| 3 | Beaulieu Vineyard | 500,000+ | X | | X |
| 4 | Beringer Vineyards | 500,000+ | X | X | X |
| 5 | Boeschen Vineyards | <1,000 | | X | X |
| 6 | Bouchaine Vineyards | 5,000–49,999 | X | | X |
| 7 | CADE Winery | 5,000–49,999 | | X | X |
| 8 | Cain Vineyard & Winery | 5,000–49,999 | X | | X |
| 9 | Cakebread Cellars | 50,000–499,999 | X | X | X |
| 10 | Chateau Boswell Winery | 1,000–4,999 | X | X | X |
| 11 | Chateau Montelena | 5,000–49,999 | | X | X |
| 12 | Clark-Claudon Vineyards | 1,000–4,999 | X | | X |
| 13 | Clos Du Val | 50,000–499,999 | X | X | X |
| 14 | Clos Pegase | 5,000–49,999 | X | | X |
| 15 | CONSTANT | 1,000–4,999 | | X | X |
| 16 | Cuvaison Estate Wines | 50,000–499,999 | X | X | X |
| 17 | Duckhorn Vineyards | 50,000–499,999 | X | | X |
| 18 | Etude | 5,000–49,999 | X | X | X |
| 19 | Franciscan Estate | 50,000–499,999 | X | X | |
| 20 | Frog's Leap | 50,000–499,999 | X | X | X |
| 21 | Gargiulo Vineyards | 1,000–4,999 | X | | |
| 22 | HALL | 5,000–49,999 | X | | X |
| 23 | HdV Wines - Hyde de Villaine | 1,000–4,999 | X | | X |
| 24 | Heitz Wine Cellars | 5,000–49,999 | X | | X |
| 25 | Hess Collection Winery, The | 500,000+ | X | X | X |
| 26 | Honig Vineyard & Winery | 5,000–49,999 | X | | X |
| 27 | Jericho Canyon Vineyard | 1,000–4,999 | X | X | X |
| 28 | Joseph Phelps Vineyards | 50,000–499,999 | X | | X |
| 29 | Judd's Hill | 1,000–4,999 | | X | X |
| 30 | Krupp Brothers | 5,000–49,999 | X | | X |
| 31 | Ladera Vineyards | 5,000–49,999 | X | | X |
| 32 | Larkmead Vineyards | 5,000–49,999 | | X | X |
| 33 | Long Meadow Ranch Winery | 5,000–49,999 | X | | X |
| 34 | Markham Vineyards | 50,000–499,999 | X | | X |
| 35 | Merryvale Vineyards | 50,000–499,999 | X | X | X |

*(Continued)*

**EXHIBIT 7**   *(Continued)*

| | Winery Name | Annual Case Production (est.) | Certified Napa Green *Land* (1) | Certified Napa Green *Winery* (2) | Sustainable Practices (3) |
|---|---|---|---|---|---|
| 36 | Mumm Napa | 50,000–499,999 | | X | X |
| 37 | Opus One | 5,000–49,999 | X | X | X |
| 38 | Ovid Napa Valley | <1,000 | | X | X |
| 39 | Parry Cellars | 5,000–49,999 | X | | X |
| 40 | Peju | <1,000 | X | | X |
| 41 | Quintessa | 5,000–49,999 | X | | X |
| 42 | Robert Craig Winery | 5,000–49,999 | | X | X |
| 43 | Robert Mondavi Winery | 50,000–499,999 | X | | X |
| 44 | Saintsbury | 50,000–499,999 | X | | X |
| 45 | Salvestrin | 1,000–4,999 | X | | X |
| 46 | Schramsberg Vineyards | 50,000–499,999 | X | X | |
| 47 | Silver Oak Cellars | 5,000–49,999 | X | | |
| 48 | Silverado Vineyards | 50,000–499,999 | X | | X |
| 49 | Spottswoode Estate Vineyard & Winery | 1,000–4,999 | X | X | X |
| 50 | St. Supéry Estate | 50,000–499,999 | X | | X |
| 51 | Stag's Leap Wine Cellars (4) | 50,000–499,999 | X | X | X |
| 52 | Stags' Leap Winery (5) | 50,000–499,999 | X | | |
| 53 | Sterling Vineyards | 50,000–499,999 | X | X | X |
| 54 | Stony Hill Vineyard | 5,000–49,999 | X | | X |
| 55 | Trefethen Family Vineyards | 50,000–499,999 | X | X | X |
| 56 | Trinchero Napa Valley | 500,000+ | X | | X |
| 57 | V. Sattui Winery | 50,000–499,999 | X | | X |
| 58 | Volker Eisele Family Estate | 50,000–499,999 | X | | |
| 59 | White Rock Vineyards | 1,000–4,999 | X | | X |
| 60 | William Hill Estate Winery | 50,000–499,999 | X | | X |

*Notes:*

(1) The **Certified Napa Green *Land*** program was a third-party certified, voluntary program for Napa vintners and grape growers. The program sought to restore, protect, and enhance the regional watershed and included restoration of wildlife habitat, healthy riparian environments, and sustainable agricultural practices. As of 2011, approximately 45,000 acres were enrolled in this program and more than 19,000 acres were certified.

(2) Founded in 2007, the **Certified Napa Green *Winery*** designation was developed by the Napa Valley Vintners Association in coordination with the County's Department of Environmental Management (DEM), and was based on the Association of Bay Area Government's (ABAG) Green Business Program. ABAG's winery-specific checklist included: water conservation, energy conservation, pollution prevention, and solid waste reduction.

(3) The Napa Valley Vintners Association defined **Sustainable practices** as environmentally sound, economically viable, and socially responsible winegrowing methods. Examples of sustainable practices that pertained to resource conservation and/or effective vineyard management included:

- Cover crops
- Reduced tillage
- Reduced risk pesticides
- Use only organic inputs
- Erosion control measures
- Hedgerows/habitat management
- Installing bird boxes
- Integrated pest management (monitoring of pests and beneficial plants, reduced-risk materials, leaf-pulling)

*(Continued)*

## EXHIBIT 7 (Concluded)

- Energy conservation
- Weather station
- Renewable energy (solar, biofuels)
- Creek and river restoration

(4) Founder Warren Winiarski sold Stag's Leap Winery in 2007 to a joint venture between Chateau Ste. Michelle (Washington state) and Marchesi Antinori (Italy). Notably, Stag's Leap's Cabernet Sauvignon won a gold medal in the famous Paris wine tasting in 1978, an event that suddenly put Napa on the map as a global wine producer. Warren Winiarski was John Williams's first employer in the Napa wine industry.

(5) Often misspelled and confused with Stag's Leap Winery, Stags' Leap was purchased by Beringer Wine Estates in 1999, and is currently owned by Treasury Wine Estates, a recent spinoff of Foster's Group (Australia).

*Sources:* Napa Valley Vintners Association Green Wineries Program, http://www.napavintners.com/wineries/napa_green_wineries.asp, accessed May 23, 2011, company websites, *Wines and Vines.*

Frog's Leap had hosted a Sustainable Wine Growers conference each year since 2006. The purpose of these conferences was to share information and best practices. Attendance had grown from 10 to over 250 California wineries (out of 329 members of the California Sustainable Winegrowing Alliance) in just five years. At the 2010 conference, Ted Hall, owner of Long Meadow Ranch, an organic Napa vineyard located in the Mayacamas Mountains above the valley, said:

> There is only one reason we farm organically, and that's because it results in higher quality and lower costs. Organic growing could double the life of a vineyard, perhaps to 40 years. That should be considered in calculating its costs. The fundamental objective of organic farming is to create a healthy plant. We're trying to create a plant that is balanced and appropriate for its site, slope and conditions. A healthy plant can produce fantastic flavors at full physiological ripeness without practices like water stress and long hang-time that can weaken the plant. You have to take a systems approach to organic growing. You can't just substitute organic pesticides or fertilizers for conventional chemicals. As much as we like to believe when we tell the rest of the world about the value of the Napa Valley appellation, not every piece of [Napa vineyard] property is suitable for growing quality grapes [organically] at a reasonable cost.[12]

A 2011 survey of 98 U.S. wine producers found that wineries appeared highly aware of sustainability issues and recognized the importance of caring for the environment.[13] Notably, about one-third of the respondents had increased investment in EMS during the recent recession. However, although many reportedly had adopted some sustainable practices such as organic and biodynamic cultivation, energy-efficient production, and dry farming, the *perceived* benefits of going beyond those practices to the adoption of a formal EMS program remained unclear. There was a perception of a cost advantage benefit to a formal EMS program, but not necessarily a differentiation benefit, with the possible exception of an increased ability to enter new market segments.

# FROG'S LEAP IN 2011

Frog's Leap commenced production with 653 cases of Sauvignon Blanc in 1981. By 2010, the winery produced 62,000 cases of predominantly red wines. Varietal brands included white wines made from Sauvignon Blanc ($18 retail) and Chardonnay grapes ($26), and red wines from Zinfandel ($27), Merlot ($34), two wines made from Cabernet Sauvignon ($42 and $70), and Petite Sirah ($35). Frog's Leap also sold the amusingly named Frogenbeerenauslese ($25), a 100 percent Riesling, and La Grenouille Rougante ($14), a rosé blend made from Gamay and a touch of Riesling. In addition, the winery produced its own olive oil and honey.[14]

Staff headcount at Frog's Leap grew 100 percent over 12 years, from 25 to 50 personnel. Most of the new hires were fieldworkers. Other employees included those in its tasting room, such as Shannon Oren, Tasting Room Assistant. In 2011, three managers reported to John Williams. Paula Moschetti, after five years' service as enologist for the firm, was promoted to Assistant Winemaker. Jonah Beer, former director of sales for Stag's Leap Wine Cellars, was hired as Director of Sales, Marketing, and Public Relations in

August 2003, and soon after became the winery's first General Manager. Upon the retirement of Gary Gates, Frog's Leap's longtime financial consultant, the firm hired Doug DeMerritt as its Chief Financial Officer. DeMerritt had served in a similar capacity at another Napa winery, Duckhorn Vineyards, from 2002 until that company's acquisition by a private equity firm in August 2007.

From 1999 to 2010, Frog's Leap purchased 100 acres of vineyards in the surrounding Rutherford area in Napa Valley, effectively doubling its acreage under production in an area where land for vineyards was valuable and seldom available for purchase. Wine case production grew comparatively more modestly, from 59,000 cases to 62,000 cases. Williams commented,

> The true growth of Frog's Leap over the last 10 years has been the acquisition and planting of vineyards, which has reduced our income, increased our debt, and added significantly to our operating costs in the short term BUT has guaranteed a high-quality source of grapes for the future—a future which seems to be heading in the direction of grape supply shortage and rising prices.

Company net sales grew from $7 million in 1999 to $12 million in 2010. Frog Leap's portfolio of premium wines was sold primarily via what was called the "Three-tier distribution" chain in the alcoholic beverages industry. Resellers included wine specialists and selected supermarkets (off-premises accounts) or restaurants and hotels (on-premises accounts). Approximately 80 percent of 2010 company net sales in the U.S. were to resellers. Exports, primarily to Japan, accounted for about 7 to 8 percent of company net sales. The remainder was sold to consumers from Frog's Leap's tasting room and hospitality center, opened in 2006, and its "Fellowship of the Frog" wine club, created in 2009. Direct sales to consumers, where permitted by state laws regarding the sale of alcohol, had become increasingly important to wineries during the 2008–2010 recession to reduce backlogged inventories of wine. Direct sales to consumers also generated higher gross profit margins for wineries than sales to resellers, as wineries could charge consumers full retail prices (or provide a slight discount for wine club members), whereas wines to resellers typically sold at 50 percent off the retail price, in order to provide markup incentives for moving products along the chain.

Although Frog's Leap's reputation in the wine industry had begun with a 1982 review by Terry Robards in *The New York Times* ("Frog's Leap: A Prince of a Wine"), Williams subsequently paid little attention to ratings of his wines by popular wine critics. While many winemakers and winery owners depended on high ratings by wine critics to drive consumer demand, Williams commented on the fact that only two of his wines had ever been reviewed:

> . . . we built our brand on Frog's Leap and fun. We started developing a loyal following that reduced our reliance on establishing our brand through traditional channels. I've made wine for 27 years, and I think [that] only two of our wines have ever been reviewed by Robert Parker [editor of *Wine Advocate*]. That's just fine with me. I don't have to worry about reviews that fail to recognize the brilliance of our wines, because our customers will go out and buy the wine because they love it no matter what other people say. The love of our brand evolved out of our approach, and it has allowed me to be freer as a winemaker, and more edgy in my winemaking.[15]

## A PHILOSOPHY OF SUSTAINABILITY

Frog's Leap adhered to pre-1970s Napa Valley winemaking traditions, such as dry farming. Dry farming involved growing grape vines without using drip irrigation systems. Growing grapes without drip irrigation resulted in minimal water use and a more European style and wine flavor profile, with far lower alcohol content and fruitiness than the wines that had been produced by other Napa Valley wineries since 1970.

Other EMS practices adopted by Frog's Leap over the years included organic and biodynamic growing techniques. According to Williams, both techniques primarily involved building soil health through the use of cover crops and compost. Healthy, living soils produced healthy, living plants that naturally resisted disease. Natural-based soil fertility worked to regulate the vigor of the grapevine and naturally conferred its health and balance to the fruit, and thus to the fermenting wine, thereby avoiding many of the problems he would otherwise have had to confront in the wine cellar at a later stage of the production process.

Creating its own source of compost was another money saver for Frog's Leap. Field workers gathered the major byproducts of winemaking (like stems and pomace, or grape skins), added in all the coffee grounds, garden waste, and vegetable or fruit scraps from the kitchen, covered the pile, and let it turn into compost. Temperature readings indicated when and how often the compost pile needed to be turned. Frog's Leap saved money by not paying someone to haul the waste away, which was in keeping with the tenets of sustainable farming.

Why did Frog's Leap convert its grape production to organic and biodynamic and develop an EMS? According to Paula Moschetti, Assistant Winemaker,

It's what we believe. We know that it not only produces better quality wine, but it just makes sense for the quality of life for the employees; it makes sense for giving back to society; it makes sense for the environment. Like everybody says, "Respect where the grapes are grown." We try to optimize that, but also to not take wine too seriously. We want to make great, world-class wine, but with a sense of humor, a tongue-in-cheek attitude. And I think people really respond to that.[16]

Meanwhile, Frog's Leap moved towards energy self-sufficiency via investments in geothermal and solar power. Williams would not disclose the cost of the geothermal system, but it was known to be one of the relatively few such systems in California. Cost of the solar power system, installed in February 2005, was $1.2 million, offset by a $600,000 cash rebate from the local power utility company. That system generated sufficient electricity to power 150 homes, and any excess power generated was sold back to the public utility. Jonah Beer, General Manager, described some of the cost advantages provided by Frog's Leap's energy systems:

There is virtually no cost to operate the geothermal heating and cooling system . . . and the cost payback is only about six years. It comes with a 30-year warranty for the pumps, and the wells have a lifetime warranty. The exchanger itself is 70 percent more efficient at its job because it only has to do one thing. Plus, our pumps use the electricity from our own solar power. The savings from solar is very obvious; what's amazing is that everyone *isn't* doing it. While the upfront cost estimate was $1.2 million, Pacific Gas & Electric (PG&E) gave [us] a $600,000 cash rebate upfront, and [our] bank gave [us] a loan on the rest. As far as payback goes, we're actually paying less on the loan per month than we were paying on our electric bill. We're cash flow positive, and we'll be paid back in seven years. The system has a 25-year warranty. So we get 18 years of free electricity. Even if you don't care about green at all, it's kind of silly not to do it. [Our] system produces 450,000 KW-hours of electricity, which will save $CO_2$ emissions equal to not driving four million miles.[17]

In 2006, Frog's Leap opened the industry's first LEED-certified wine tasting and office facility, primarily from recycled building materials. LEED was an acronym for *L*eadership in *E*nergy and *E*nvironmental *D*esign. Buildings attained LEED certification from the U.S. Green Business Council. Lower operation costs were typically associated with a LEED building: approximately 30 to 40 percent less energy use and 40 percent less water. Application for LEED certification of an existing property could cost upward of $10,000, depending upon the size of the building, the number of rooms, and the level of certification sought.[18]

Frog's Leap provided full-time, year-round employment and benefits for winery personnel, who were mostly immigrant laborers. According to Williams:

The Mexican workforce has been wonderful for us, and we try to return that favor. The workers don't have to be laid off after pruning in January until tying canes in May, or from leafing until harvest. In between, our workers can prune trees, turn compost, bottle Sauvignon Blanc, harvest broccoli, rack and wash barrels, thin pears and apples, bottle Merlot, etc. They work full time—and get paid, three-week vacations, 401(k) plans and health benefits. We also have fewer safety issues, because they're well-trained and experienced. They're an engaged and highly motivated workforce. Are there higher overall labor costs? How can you really measure your labor costs? The workers get stable wages, they don't have to worry about housing and health care and where their kids go to school. They're a community of workers. There are fewer problems with documentation, better health, less crime and use of the community's safety net.[19]

While other winery operators remained dubious about the cost/benefit trade-off of investing in EMS and providing full-time employment to immigrant workers, Frog's Leap remained mostly profitable during the 2009–10 recession.[20] To generate incremental cash flows, Frog's Leap augmented its sales via conventional distribution channels by an innovative "wine-by-the-glass" program using kegs (instead of bottles) of wine, and by initiating direct-to-consumer programs, including a tasting room, and the "Fellowship of the Frog" wine club. Exhibit 8 presents Frog's Leap's income statements for 2000–01 and 2009–10. The company's balance sheets for 2000–01 and 2009–10 are presented in Exhibit 9. Williams commented:

Over the long term, we have seen that our methods are viable. This is not just an experiment. [From a cash flow perspective] we are a thriving business with above average margins and below average operating expenses.

**EXHIBIT 8**  Frog's Leap Winery Statements of Income, 2000–2001 and 2009–2010 (dollar amounts in thousands)

|  | 2000 | % of Sales | 2001 | % of Sales | 2009 | % of Sales | 2010 | % of Sales |
|---|---|---|---|---|---|---|---|---|
| Cases sold | 61,000 |  | 54,000 |  | 53,000 |  | 62,000 |  |
| Sales | $9,638 | 100% | $9,180 | 100% | $10,017 | 100% | $12,152 | 100% |
| Cost of goods sold | 4,514 | 46.8% | 4,050 | 44.1% | 4,346 | 43.4% | 4,960 | 40.8% |
| Gross profit | 5,124 | 53.2% | 5,130 | 55.9% | 5,671 | 56.6% | 7,192 | 59.2% |
| Operating expenses: |  |  |  |  |  |  |  |  |
| Sales & marketing | 1,580 | 16.4% | 1,615 | 17.6% | 2,853 | 28.5% | 3,337 | 27.5% |
| General & administrative | 1,200 | 12.5% | 1,300 | 14.2% | 1,678 | 16.8% | 1,483 | 12.2% |
| Depreciation & amortization | 675 | 7.0% | 900 | 9.8% | 1,250 | 12.5% | 1,100 | 9.1% |
| Total operating expenses | 2,780 | 28.8% | 2,915 | 31.8% | 4,531 | 45.2% | 4,820 | 39.7% |
| Operating income | 2,344 | 24.3% | 2,215 | 24.1% | 1,140 | 11.4% | 2,372 | 19.5% |
| Interest expense | 450 | 4.7% | 875 | 9.5% | 1,420 | 14.2% | 1,420 | 11.7% |
| Earnings before taxes | $1,894 | 19.7% | $1,340 | 14.6% | $ (280) | −2.8% | $ 952 | 7.8% |

*Source:* Frog's Leap Winery. Some data have been disguised by the company, but the relationships are accurate.

**EXHIBIT 9**  Frog's Leap Winery Balance Sheets, 2000–2001 and 2009–2010 (dollar amounts in thousands)

|  | 2000 | % of Total Assets | 2001 | % of Total Assets | 2009 | % of Total Assets | 2010 | % of Total Assets |
|---|---|---|---|---|---|---|---|---|
| **ASSETS** |  |  |  |  |  |  |  |  |
| Current assets |  |  |  |  |  |  |  |  |
| Cash | $ 130 | 0.7% | $ 80 | 0.4% | $ 10 | 0.0% | $ 20 | 0.1% |
| Accounts receivable | 400 | 2.1% | 550 | 2.6% | 1,650 | 4.1% | 1,950 | 5.0% |
| Inventory | 6,500 | 33.5% | 7,560 | 35.5% | 12,010 | 30.1% | 11,550 | 29.5% |
| Prepaid and other expenses | 125 | 0.6% | 250 | 1.2% | 320 | 0.8% | 325 | 0.8% |
| Total current assets | 7,155 | 36.9% | 8,440 | 39.6% | 13,990 | 35.0% | 13,845 | 35.4% |
| Property, plant and equipment | 15,250 | 78.6% | 16,150 | 75.8% | 36,750 | 92.1% | 37,100 | 94.9% |
| Less: Accumulated depreciation & amort. | 3,150 | 16.2% | 3,450 | 16.2% | 10,925 | 27.4% | 11,950 | 30.6% |
| net property, plant and equipment | 12,100 | 62.4% | 12,700 | 59.6% | 25,825 | 64.7% | 25,150 | 64.3% |
| Other assets | 150 | 0.8% | 175 | 0.8% | 100 | 0.3% | 110 | 0.3% |
| Total assets | $19,405 | 100.0% | $21,315 | 100.0% | $39,915 | 100.0% | $39,105 | 100.0% |
| **LIABILITIES & CAPITAL** |  |  |  |  |  |  |  |  |
| Current liabilities |  |  |  |  |  |  |  |  |
| Notes payable | $ 3,150 | 16.2% | $ 4,370 | 20.5% | $ 2,450 | 6.1% | $ 2,425 | 6.2% |
| Accounts payable and accruals | 2,610 | 13.5% | 1,470 | 6.9% | 2,325 | 5.8% | 2,150 | 5.5% |
| Current portion of LTD | 540 | 2.8% | 960 | 4.5% | 890 | 2.2% | 950 | 2.4% |
| Total current liabilities | 6,300 | 32.5% | 6,800 | 31.9% | 5,665 | 14.2% | 5,525 | 14.1% |

*(Continued)*

## EXHIBIT 9 *(Concluded)*

| | 2000 | % of Total Assets | 2001 | % of Total Assets | 2009 | % of Total Assets | 2010 | % of Total Assets |
|---|---|---|---|---|---|---|---|---|
| Long-term debt | 5,030 | 25.9% | 7,040 | 33.0% | 20,400 | 51.1% | 19,500 | 49.9% |
| Total liabilities | 11,330 | 58.4% | 13,840 | 64.9% | 26,065 | 65.3% | 25,025 | 64.0% |
| Shareholder equity | 8,075 | 41.6% | 7,475 | 35.1% | 13,850 | 34.7% | 14,080 | 36.0% |
| Total liabilities and equity | $19,405 | 100.0% | $21,315 | 100.0% | $39,915 | 100.0% | $39,105 | 100.0% |

*Source:* Frog's Leap Winery. Some data have been disguised by the company, but the relationships are accurate.

## EXHIBIT 10 Financial Ratios and Benchmarks for Frog's Leap Peer Wineries, 2000–2001 and 2009–2010

| | 2000 | 2001 | 2009 | 2010 |
|---|---|---|---|---|
| Growth Rate, Cased Goods Revenue | | −14.1% | | +2.9% |
| Current Ratio (x) | 2.11x | 1.76x | 1.91x | 2.29x |
| Quick Ratio (x) | 0.49x | 0.30x | 0.22x | 0.08x |
| Working Capital ($000) | $4,203 | $3,941 | $ 6,063 | $ 8,518 |
| Cased Goods Revenues/Net Working Capital (x) | 1.67x | 1.53x | 1.84x | 1.35x |
| Account Receivable Days (365) | 95.3 | 91.1 | 39.8 | 14.8 |
| Inventory Days | 575 | 805 | 1,118 | 1,533 |
| Tangible Net Worth (TNW, $000) | $4,499 | $4,361 | $12,863 | $13,597 |
| Total Liabilities to TNW (x) | 0.9x | 1.3x | 1.6x | 1.7x |
| Senior Liabilities/TNW + Subordinate Debt (x) | 0.9x | 1.3x | 1.4x | 1.4x |
| Gross Profit Margin (%) | 45.70% | 45.30% | 67.20% | 70.00% |
| Sales & Marketing Expenses/Sales (% of sales) | 9.50% | 12.20% | 10.90% | 9.80% |
| Net Margin (Return on sales, %) | 14.70% | 5.70% | 9.10% | 9.70% |
| EBITDA ($000) | $1,528 | $ 799 | $ 3,964 | $ 4,269 |
| EBITDA, Less Distributions or Dividends ($000) | $ 218 | $ 325 | $ 3,502 | $ 4,062 |
| Debt Service Coverage (x) | 6.4x | 3.9x | 2.0x | 2.4x |
| Total Interest / Total Senior Debt (%) | 7.50% | 4.90% | 6.80% | 6.00% |
| Conventional ROE (%) | 22.70% | 7.80% | 7.90% | 8.20% |
| Operating Return on Assets (%) | 11.90% | 3.50% | 3.00% | 3.10% |

*Source:* Casewriter's research, based on data provided by Silicon Valley Bank that were compiled from anonymous wineries similar in size to Frog's Leap. For more highly aggregated financial data, see: Jordan, D. J., Aguilar, D., and Gilinsky, A. (2010), "Benchmarking Northern California Wineries," *Wine Business Monthly,* October, 60–67.

Our cost here for making a bottle of wine is equal to or less than the industry average.[21]

For purposes of comparison, Exhibit 10 provides financial ratios and benchmarks compiled by Silicon Valley Bank based on actual data from several anonymous wineries similar in size to Frog's Leap during the 2000–2001 and 2009–2010 time periods.

A reporter for the *San Francisco Chronicle* opined, "Frog's Leap could be the poster child for a new generation of Napa wineries: beautifully appointed, genteel, terroir-oriented and dedicated to a green agenda."[22]

## OPEN OTHER END

Early in Frog's Leap's history, John Williams had managed to persuade the U.S. Alcohol Tobacco Tax and Trade Bureau (known in the industry as the TTB), which has to approve all bottle labeling, that it was not frivolous to mark the bottom of his wine bottles with a sage precaution: "Open Other End." The word "Ribbit" was printed on the cork of every bottle of Frog's Leap wine.

Humorous presentations aside, Williams remained serious about sustaining growth of his business while remaining at the same level of production output. "How can we continue to grow sales and profits while remaining a small winery production-wise? I know that some business people are trained to think outside of the box, but first I want to know *where* the box is and what is *in* the box before I think about what's outside," he quipped in May 2011.

One option for sustaining Frog's Leap's growth was to pursue other EMS projects. Williams maintained that Frog's Leap still had a long way to go to become a truly sustainable winery:

> We're not 100 percent there. We're not even close. But we've done a lot of interesting things, and a lot of the big projects are behind us. Now we're into some of the more fun and challenging ideas that will help us take our philosophy further: Healthier field workers; healthier, longer living vineyards; enriched soil fertility; less erosion; lessened environmental contamination; greater trust with our consumers; and even considerably higher wine quality, converting farm equipment to biodiesel and reducing employee car use by commuting. Startups are going to be more expensive. There's no getting around it. However, if you take the long view of it, once you get past 10 years, the costs are less, and you've got a vineyard that will outlast everyone else's.[23]
>
> Over time, it has developed that every decision at Frog's Leap is weighed at least in some measure by its social and ecological costs and benefits. We believe that these are the kinds of questions all businesses will have to ask and answer if we wish [to have] a sustainable future. . .[24]

Williams felt that pursuing any new sustainability projects in the near-to-medium term would have highly uncertain associated costs and benefits. Building out the direct-to-consumer sales channels (tasting room and wine club) was another option under consideration, but might come at the expense of taking attention away from distributors. A longer-term question about sustainability was also nagging at him: Frog's Leap's debt load. Williams and his former wife, Julie (who now owned another winery, Trés Sabores), had three sons who would presumably take over the business someday:

> Right now my kids think my legacy is $22 million of debt (laughs). You know I don't really think about my

legacy too often. I'm happy about growing grapes and making wine and having fun doing it. But I believe our winery has changed the dialogue about the healthy growing of grapes, conservation of soil, and natural resources. I hope to be remembered for that.[25]

Williams's eldest son was working for another winery, his middle child was starting business school in fall 2011, and his youngest was preparing to start law school. Now entering his mid-50s, Williams wondered aloud how to "position the business to be successful for the next 10–20 years, after which time the transition to that next generation would *inevitably* begin."

# GLOSSARY OF COMMON WINE INDUSTRY TERMINOLOGY

**American Viticultural Area (AVA)**—A designated "viticultural area" (e.g., Napa Valley, Sonoma, Central Coast) that must produce 85 percent of the grapes processed for bottling and sale. For a specified vineyard name, a particular vineyard must grow 95 percent of the grapes, and all grapes used must be from the AVA.

**Appellation**—Similar to an AVA, the term appellation is used by other wine-producing nations to demarcate a legally defined and specific region where wine grapes are grown. A wine claiming to be sourced from a named boundary (e.g., Côtes du Rhône in France, Chianti in Italy, or Rioja in Spain) must be comprised of at least 75 percent of the grapes grown within that boundary.

**Biodynamics**—Biodynamics, a growing agricultural movement both in the U.S. and internationally, is based on a series of lectures given in the 1920s by Austrian philosopher Rudolf Steiner. The movement views the vineyard (or farm) as an ecological whole—not just the vines, but also the soil, insects, and other local flora and fauna. Like organic farmers, biodynamic growers are interested in naturally healthy plants, and in enriching their soil without artificial fertilizers or pesticides. Where biodynamics differs from classic organics, however, is in the belief that agriculture can be aligned to the spiritual forces of the cosmos. This may mean harvesting grapes when the moon is passing in front of a certain constellation, or sometimes by creating a homeopathic mixture that, when sprayed on the vines, will—in theory—help the grapes ripen and improve their flavors.

**Brand**—The name of the product. This can be a made-up name, the name of the actual producer, a virtual winery, or it could be a restaurant or grocery store chain that contracts with a winery for a "special label" purchase.

**Chai**—A barrel *chai* is a wine shed, or other storage place above ground, used for storing casks; common in Bordeaux. Usually different types of wine are kept in separate sheds. The New World counterpart to the *chai* may be called the barrel hall. In Bordeaux, the person in charge of vinification and ageing of all wine made at an estate, or the *chais* of a *négociant*, is titled a *Maître de Chai*.

**Dry farming**—For most of the history of agriculture, grape growers dry-farmed their lands, and they still do in many wineries in Europe. Then, in the 1970s, drip irrigation conquered the world. A farming practice as old as agriculture itself fell to the wayside as wells were drilled, streams tapped, and pipes and hoses were run through thousands of acres of vineyards and orchards. By no coincidence, water supplies have now entered an era of decline in California, where land is subsiding in many regions as the aquifers below are emptied. Above ground, many small streams have drained into the earth; they may still flow—just underground. Dry-farmed wines, many sources say, are better, as grapevines, working under stressed conditions, produce smaller grapes than watered vines. The result is a greater quantity of tannin-rich skins and seeds to volume of juice, which can render denser, richer wines. For a dry farmer, the challenge is to lock the winter and spring rainfall in the soil for the duration of the dry season.

**Economy wine**—Regardless of where they are produced, table wines that retail for less than $3.00 per 750ml bottle are deemed to be in the generic, economy, or "jug" wine category.

**Organic grapes**—Organically grown grapes follow a broad definition of organic farming issued by the U.S. Department of Agriculture: "Organic farming is a production system which avoids or largely excludes the use of synthetically compounded fertilizers, pesticides, growth regulators, and livestock feed additives. To the maximum extent feasible, organic farming systems rely on crop rotations, crop residues, animal manures, legumes, green manures, off farm organic wastes and aspects of biological pest control to maintain soil productivity and tilth, to supply plant nutrients and to control insects, weeds and other pests . . .

The concept of soil as a 'living system' is central to this definition." Wines made from organically grown grapes must be referred to as "wines made from organic grapes" (or organically grown grapes), as they are allowed to contain up to 100 ppm of added sulfites.

**Organic wine**—Organic wine is defined by the U.S. Department of Agriculture as "a wine made from organically grown grapes *and* without any added sulfites."

**Premium wine**—Wines selling for more than $3.00 per bottle are considered to be in the premium wine category. Most bottled wines in the premium category show a vintage date on their labels—that is, the product is made with at least 95 percent of grapes harvested, crushed, and fermented in the calendar year shown on the label and also uses grapes from an appellation of origin (i.e., Napa Valley, Central Coast, Willamette Valley). Several market segments within the premium category are based on retail price points, typically double the wholesale value of a bottle or case of wine. *Impact Databank, Review & Forecast of the Wine Industry,* classifies wines "Sub-Premium" as those that retail for $3.00 to $6.00 per bottle; the "Premium" category retail for $7.00 to $9.99; the "Super-Premium" category retail for $10.00 to $13.99 per bottle, while the "Deluxe" segment are wines commanding a retail price above $14.00. Motto Kryla Fisher, a Napa Valley wine consulting firm, further refines the "Deluxe" segment into sub-segments: "Ultra Premium" wines, priced from $14.00 to $29.99, and "Luxury" wines, that retail in excess of $30.00 per bottle.

**Three-tier distribution**—Myriad state laws and regulations restricting the sale of alcoholic beverages generally require wineries to use a "three-tier" distribution system (winery to distributor to retailer to consumer). However, distributor consolidation (through termination or acquisition) increased substantially since the May 16, 2005 *Granholm v. Heald* U.S. Supreme Court decision, prohibiting discrimination between in-state products and products from out of state, and that subsequently served to increase liberalization of shipping wine across some state lines, direct from producers to consumers.

**Varietal**—A type of grape (i.e., Merlot, Cabernet Sauvignon, Zinfandel, Chardonnay, etc.). To declare a "varietal" on the label, at least 75 percent of the wine must consist of that variety of grape. Some wineries use almost 100 percent of the same varietal. Some blend a principal varietal (the one named on the label) with wines made from other varieties of the same color for better flavor balance. Others blend in "filler" varieties, which usually go unlisted, to get the most out of their supply of then-popular varieties, which are the ones touted on the label. If the label mentions a varietal, it will always be in conjunction with an appellation to inform consumers of the source of the varietal grape.

**Vintage**—The year in which the harvest of the wine grapes occurs. By law, grapes grown in a declared vintage year (harvest year) must account for 95 percent of the wine if the label declares a vintage year.

*Source:* Casewriters' research; MDM Distribution.

## ENDNOTES

[1] Originally quoted in Rainsford, P. (1999), "Frog's Leap Winery" (video case presented to the North American Case Research Association conference in Santa Rosa, California). Williams updated this quotation during interviews at Frog's Leap Winery in May and September 2011; Jonah Beer, Doug DeMerritt, and Shannon Oren also agreed to be interviewed on camera for the video case.

[2] Intardonato, J. (2007, June 15), "Frog's Leap Pursues Their Green Vision," *Wine Business Monthly online,* http://www.winebusiness. com/wbm/?go=getArticle&dataId=48589, accessed April 10, 2011.

[3] Hertsgaard, M. (2010), "Grapes of Wrath," *Mother Jones,* July/August, pp. 37–39.

[4] Wines and Vines (1999, 2004, 2009), *Wines and Vines Annual Directory,* San Francisco, CA.

[5] Ekberg, P. (2006), "The Keyword Is LOHAS," *Japan Spotlight,* Japan Economic Foundation (JEF), March 1, 146.

[6] As cited by Brooks, S. (2009), "The Green Consumer," *Restaurant Business,* September, pp. 20–21.

[7] Delmas, M. A. and Grant, L. E. (2008, March), "Eco-labeling Strategies: The Eco-Premium Puzzle in the Wine Industry," *AAWE working paper* no. 13; Guthey, G. T. and Whiteman, G. (2009), "Social and Ecological Transitions: Winemaking in California," *E:CO,* Vol. 11, No. 3, pp. 37–48.

[8] Delmas, M. A. and Grant, L. E., *op. cit.*

[9] Penn, C. (2011, February 15) "Review of the Industry: Outlook and Trends," *Wine Business Monthly,* p. 70.

[10] *Ibid.*

[11] Brodt, S. and Thrupp, A. (2009, July), "Understanding Adoption and Impacts of Sustainable Practices in California Vineyards," California Sustainable Winegrowing Alliance, www.sustainablewinegrowing.org, accessed April 12, 2011.

[12] Franson, P. (2010), "Organic Grapegrowing for Less," *Wines & Vines,* July 28, http:// www.winesandvines.com/template.cfm?sect ion=news&content=76728, accessed April 10, 2011.

[13] Atkin, T., Gilinsky, A., and Newton, S. K. (2011), "Sustainability in the Wine Industry: Altering the Competitive Landscape?" Paper presented to the 6th Academy of Wine Business Research conference, June 9–11, Bordeaux, France.

[14] Saekel, K. (2009, May 13), "Napa Frog's Leap Comes with a Bit of Whimsy," *San Francisco Chronicle,* http://www.seattlepi. com/default/article/Napa-winery-Frog-s-Leap-comes-with-a-bit-of-whimsy-1303945.php, accessed April 10, 2011.

[15] As quoted in Cutler, L. (2008, February 15), "Industry Roundtable: Humor in the Wine Trade," *Wine Business Monthly online,* http://www.winebusiness.com/wbm/?go=ge tArticle&dataId=54456, accessed April 10, 2011.

[16] Brenner, D. (2006), "Paula Moschetti," *Women of the Vine,* Hoboken, NJ: John Wiley & Sons, p. 168.

[17] Intardonato, J., *op. cit.*

[18] For more on LEED certified buildings in Northern California, see: http://www.mland-man.com/gbuildinginfo/leedbuildings.shtml (updated every 8 weeks, accessed 5/25/2011).

[19] Franson, P. (2010), "Winegrowers Cash in on Other Crops," *Wines & Vines,* May 25, http:// www.winesandvines.com/template.cfm?sect ion=news&content=74538&htitle=Winegr owers%20Cash%20in%20on%20Other%20 Crops, accessed April 10, 2011.

[20] Hertsgaard, *op. cit.;* Guthey, G. T. and Whiteman, G. *op. cit.*

[21] Intardonato, J., *op. cit.*

[22] Saekel, K., *op. cit.*

[23] As quoted by Saekel, K., *op. cit.*

[24] As quoted by Daniel, L. (2011, November 1), "Grapegrower Interview: John Williams: Winegrowing from the Roots Up," http:// www.allbusiness.com/agriculture-forestry/ agriculture-animal-farming/16738095-1. html#ixzz1kPJtKSHF, accessed January 26, 2012.

[25] Walters, C. (2010, May 3), "How Organic and Biodynamic Viticulture Will Change the Way You Think: An Interview with Frog's Leap Owner and Winemaker John Williams," *Indigo Wine Blog,* http://indigowinepress. com/2010/05/how-organic-and-biodynamic-viticulture-will-change-the-way-you-think-an-interview-with-frogs-leap-owner-and-winemaker-john-williams/, accessed January 29, 2011.

# Guide to Case Analysis

*I keep six honest serving men*
*(They taught me all I knew);*
*Their names are What and Why and When;*
*And How and Where and Who.*

*Rudyard Kipling*

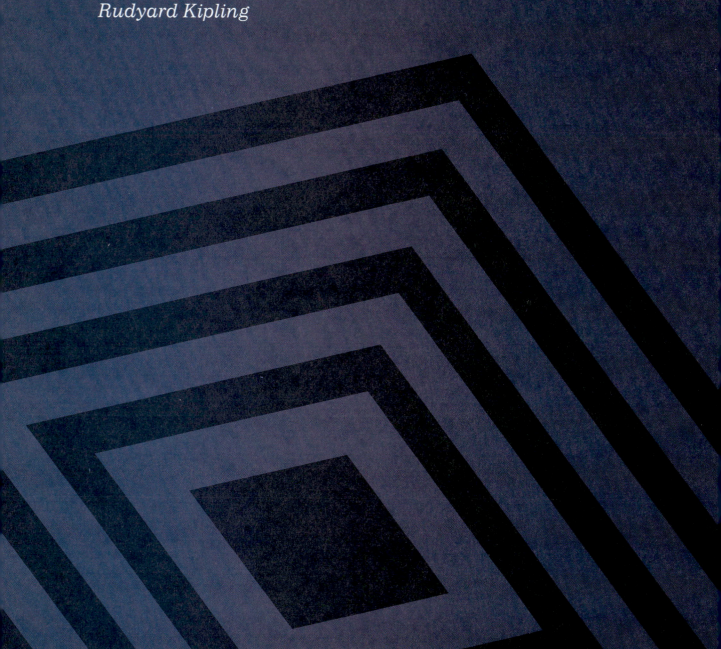

I n most courses in strategic management, students use cases about actual companies to practice strategic analysis and to gain some experience in the tasks of crafting and implementing strategy. A case sets forth, in a factual manner, the events and organizational circumstances surrounding a particular managerial situation. It puts readers at the scene of the action and familiarizes them with all the relevant circumstances. A case on strategic management can concern a whole industry, a single organization, or some part of an organization; the organization involved can be either profit seeking or not-for-profit. The essence of the student's role in case analysis is to *diagnose* and *size up* the situation described in the case and then to *recommend* appropriate action steps.

# WHY USE CASES TO PRACTICE STRATEGIC MANAGEMENT?

> A student of business with tact
> Absorbed many answers he lacked.
> But acquiring a job,
> He said with a sob,
> "How does one fit answer to fact?"

The foregoing limerick was used some years ago by Professor Charles Gragg to characterize the plight of business students who had no exposure to cases.[1] The facts are that the mere act of listening to lectures and sound advice about managing does little for anyone's management skills and that the accumulated managerial wisdom cannot effectively be passed on by lectures and assigned readings alone. If anything had been learned about the practice of management, it is that a storehouse of ready-made textbook answers does not exist. Each managerial situation has unique aspects, requiring its own diagnosis, judgment, and tailor-made actions. Cases provide would-be managers with a valuable way to practice wrestling with the actual problems of actual managers in actual companies.

The case approach to strategic analysis is, first and foremost, an exercise in learning by doing. Because cases provide you with detailed information about conditions and problems of different industries and companies, your task of analyzing company after company and situation after situation has the twin benefit of boosting your analytical skills and exposing you to the ways companies and managers actually do things. Most college students have limited managerial backgrounds and only fragmented knowledge about companies and real-life strategic situations. Cases help substitute for on-the-job experience by (1) giving you broader exposure to a variety of industries, organizations, and strategic problems; (2) forcing you to assume a managerial role (as opposed to that of just an onlooker); (3) providing a test of how to apply the tools and techniques of strategic management; and (4) asking you to come up with pragmatic managerial action plans to deal with the issues at hand.

## Objectives of Case Analysis

Using cases to learn about the practice of strategic management is a powerful way for you to accomplish five things:[2]

1. *Increase your understanding of what managers should and should not do in guiding a business to success.*
2. *Build your skills in sizing up company resource strengths and weaknesses and in conducting strategic analysis in a variety of industries and competitive situations.*
3. *Get valuable practice in identifying strategic issues that need to be addressed, evaluating strategic alternatives, and formulating workable plans of action.*
4. *Enhance your sense of business judgment, as opposed to uncritically accepting the authoritative crutch of the professor or "back-of-the-book" answers.*
5. *Gaining in-depth exposure to different industries and companies, thereby acquiring something close to actual business experience.*

If you understand that these are the objectives of case analysis, you are less likely to be consumed with curiosity about "the answer to the case." Students who have grown comfortable with and accustomed to textbook statements of fact and definitive lecture notes are often frustrated when discussions about a case do not produce concrete answers. Usually, case discussions produce good arguments for more than one course of action. Differences of opinion nearly always exist. Thus, should a class discussion conclude without a strong, unambiguous consensus on what to do, don't grumble too much when you are not told what the answer is or what the company actually did. Just remember that in the business world answers don't come in conclusive black-and-white terms. There are nearly always several feasible courses of action and approaches, each of which may work out satisfactorily. Moreover, in the business world, when one elects a particular course of action, there is no peeking at the back of a book to see if you have chosen the best thing to do and no one to turn to for a probably correct answer. The best test of whether management action is "right" or "wrong" is *results*. If the results of an action turn out to be "good," the decision to take it may be presumed "right." If not, then the action chosen was "wrong" in the sense that it didn't work out

Hence, the important thing for you to understand about analyzing cases is that the managerial exercise of identifying, diagnosing, and recommending is aimed at building your skills of business judgment. Discovering what the company actually did is no more than frosting on the cake—the actions that company managers actually took may or may not be "right" or best (unless there is accompanying evidence that the results of their actions were highly positive.

The point is this: *The purpose of giving you a case assignment is not to cause you to run to the library or surf the Internet to discover what the company actually did but, rather, to enhance your skills in sizing up situations and developing your managerial judgment about what needs to be done and how to do it.* The aim of case analysis is for you to become actively engaged in diagnosing the business issues and managerial problems posed in the case, to propose workable solutions, and to explain and defend your assessments—this is how cases provide you with meaningful practice at being a manager.

## Preparing a Case for Class Discussion

If this is your first experience with the case method, you may have to reorient your study habits. Unlike lecture courses where you can get by without preparing intensively for each class and where you have latitude to work assigned readings and reviews of lecture notes into your schedule, a case assignment requires conscientious preparation before class. You will not get much out of hearing the class discuss a case you haven't read, and you certainly won't be able to contribute anything yourself to the discussion. What you have got to do to get ready for class discussion of a case is to study the case, reflect carefully on the situation presented, and develop some reasoned thoughts. Your goal in preparing the case should be to end up with what you think is a sound, well-supported analysis of the situation and a sound, defensible set of recommendations about which managerial actions need to be taken.

To prepare a case for class discussion, we suggest the following approach:

1. *Skim the case rather quickly to get an overview of the situation it presents.* This quick overview should give you the general flavor of the situation and indicate the kinds of issues and problems that you will need to wrestle with. If your instructor has provided you with study questions for the case, now is the time to read them carefully.

2. *Read the case thoroughly to digest the facts and circumstances.* On this reading, try to gain full command of the situation presented in the case. Begin to develop some tentative answers to the study questions your instructor has provided. If your instructor has elected not to give you assignment questions, then start forming your own picture of the overall situation being described.

3. *Carefully review all the information presented in the exhibits.* Often, there is an important story in the numbers contained in the exhibits. Expect the information in the case exhibits to be crucial enough to materially affect your diagnosis of the situation.

4. *Decide what the strategic issues are.* Until you have identified the strategic issues and problems in the case, you don't know what to analyze, which tools and analytical techniques are called for, or otherwise how to proceed. At times the strategic issues are clear—either being stated in the case or else obvious from reading the case. At other times you will have to dig them out from all the information given; if so, the study questions will guide you.

5. *Start your analysis of the issues with some number crunching.* A big majority of strategy cases call for some kind of number crunching—calculating assorted financial ratios to check out the company's financial condition and recent performance, calculating growth rates of sales or profits or unit volume, checking out profit margins and the makeup of the cost structure, and understanding whatever revenue-cost-profit relationships are present. See Table 1 for a summary of key financial ratios, how they are calculated, and what they show.

6. *Apply the concepts and techniques of strategic analysis you have been studying.* Strategic analysis is not just a collection of opinions; rather, it entails applying the concepts and analytical tools described in Chapters 1 through 13 to cut beneath the surface and produce sharp insight and understanding. Every case assigned is strategy related and presents you with an opportunity to usefully apply what you have learned. Your instructor is looking for you to demonstrate that you know how and when to use the material presented in the text chapters.

7. *Check out conflicting opinions and make some judgments about the validity of all the data and*

## TABLE 1    Key Financial Ratios: How to Calculate Them and What They Mean

| Ratio | How Calculated | What It Shows |
|---|---|---|
| **Profitability Ratios** | | |
| 1. Gross profit margin | $$\frac{\text{Sales} - \text{Cost of goods sold}}{\text{Sales}}$$ | Shows the percentage of revenues available to cover operating expenses and yield a profit. Higher is better and the trend should be upward. |
| 2. Operating profit margin (or return on sales) | $$\frac{\text{Sales} - \text{Operating expenses}}{\text{Sales}}$$ or $$\frac{\text{Operating income}}{\text{Sales}}$$ | Shows the profitability of current operations without regard to interest charges and income taxes. Higher is better and the trend should be upward. |
| 3. Net profit margin (or net return on sales) | $$\frac{\text{Profits after taxes}}{\text{Sales}}$$ | Shows after-tax profits per dollar of sales. Higher is better and the trend should be upward. |
| 4. Total return on assets | $$\frac{\text{Profits after taxes} + \text{Interest}}{\text{Total assets}}$$ | A measure of the return on total monetary investment in the enterprise. Interest is added to after-tax profits to form the numerator since total assets are financed by creditors as well as by stockholders. Higher is better and the trend should be upward. |
| 5. Net return on total assets (ROA) | $$\frac{\text{Profits after taxes}}{\text{Total assets}}$$ | A measure of the return earned by stockholders on the firm's total assets. Higher is better, and the trend should be upward. |
| 6. Return on stockholder's equity (ROE) | $$\frac{\text{Profits after taxes}}{\text{Total stockholders' equity}}$$ | Shows the return stockholders are earning on their capital investment in the enterprise. A return in the 12–15% range is "average," and the trend should be upward. |
| 7. Return on invested capital (ROIC)—sometimes referred to as return on capital employed (ROCE) | $$\frac{\text{Profits after taxes}}{\text{Long-term debt} + \text{Total stockholders' equity}}$$ | A measure of the return shareholders are earning on the long-term monetary capital invested in the enterprise. A higher return reflects greater bottom-line effectiveness in the use of long-term capital, and the trend should be upward. |
| 8. Earnings per share (EPS) | $$\frac{\text{Profits after taxes}}{\text{Number of shares of common stock outstanding}}$$ | Shows the earnings for each share of common stock outstanding. The trend should be upward, and the bigger the annual percentage gains, the better. |
| **Liquidity Ratios** | | |
| 1. Current ratio | $$\frac{\text{Current assets}}{\text{Current liabilities}}$$ | Shows a firm's ability to pay current liabilities using assets that can be converted to cash in the near term. Ratio should definitely be higher than 1.0; ratios of 2 or higher are better still. |
| 2. Working capital | Current assets − Current liabilities | Bigger amounts are better because the company has more internal funds available to (1) pay its current liabilities on a timely basis and (2) finance inventory expansion, additional accounts receivable, and a larger base of operations without resorting to borrowing or raising more equity capital. |
| **Leverage Ratios** | | |
| 1. Total debt-to-assets ratio | $$\frac{\text{Total debt}}{\text{Total assets}}$$ | Measures the extent to which borrowed funds have been used to finance the firm's operations. Low fractions or ratios are better—high fractions indicate overuse of debt and greater risk of bankruptcy. |
| 2. Long-term debt-to-capital ratio | $$\frac{\text{Long-term debt}}{\text{Long-term debt} + \text{Total stockholders' equity}}$$ | An important measure of creditworthiness and balance sheet strength. Indicates the percentage of capital investment which has been financed by creditors and bondholders. Fractions or ratios below .25 or 25% are usually quite satisfactory since monies invested |

*(Continued)*

**TABLE 1**        (*Continued*)

| Leverage Ratios (*Continued*) | | |
|---|---|---|
| | | by stockholders account for 75% or more of the company's total capital. The lower the ratio, the greater the capacity to borrow additional funds. Debt-to capital ratios above 50% and certainly above 75% indicate a heavy and perhaps excessive reliance on debt, lower creditworthiness, and weak balance sheet strength. |
| 3. Debt-to-equity ratio | $$\frac{\text{Total debt}}{\text{Total stockholders' equity}}$$ | Should usually be less than 1.0. High ratios (especially above 1.0) signal excessive debt, lower creditworthiness, and weaker balance sheet strength. |
| 4. Long-term debt-to-equity ratio | $$\frac{\text{Long-term debt}}{\text{Total stockholders' equity}}$$ | Shows the balance between debt and equity in the firm's *long-term* capital structure. Low ratios indicate greater capacity to borrow additional funds if needed. |
| 4. Times-interest-earned (or coverage) ratio | $$\frac{\text{Operating income}}{\text{Interest expenses}}$$ | Measures the ability to pay annual interest charges. Lenders usually insist on a minimum ratio of 2.0, but ratios above 3.0 signal better creditworthiness. |

| Activity Ratios | | |
|---|---|---|
| 1. Days of inventory | $$\frac{\text{Inventory}}{\text{Cost of goods sold} \div 365}$$ | Measures inventory management efficiency. Fewer days of inventory are usually better. |
| 2. Inventory turnover | $$\frac{\text{Cost of goods sold}}{\text{Inventory}}$$ | Measures the number of inventory turns per year. Higher is better. |
| 3. Average collection period | $$\frac{\text{Accounts receivable}}{\text{Total sales revenues} \div 365}$$ or $$\frac{\text{Accounts receivable}}{\text{Average daily sales}}$$ | Indicates the average length of time the firm must wait after making a sale to receive cash payment. A shorter collection time is better. |

| Other Important Measures of Financial Performance | | |
|---|---|---|
| 1. Dividend yield on common stock | $$\frac{\text{Annual dividends per share}}{\text{Current market price per share}}$$ | A measure of the return that shareholders receive in the form of dividends. A "typical" dividend yield is 2–3%. The dividend yield for fast-growth companies is often below 1% (maybe even 0); the dividend yield for slow-growth companies can run 4–5%. |
| 2. Price-earnings ratio | $$\frac{\text{Current market price per share}}{\text{Earnings per share}}$$ | P-e ratios above 20 indicate strong investor confidence in a firm's outlook and earnings growth; firms whose future earnings are at risk or likely to grow slowly typically have ratios below 12. |
| 3. Dividend payout ratio | $$\frac{\text{Annual dividends per share}}{\text{Earnings per share}}$$ | Indicates the percentage of after-tax profits paid cut as dividends. |
| 4. Internal cash flow | After tax profits + Depreciation | A quick and rough estimate of the c business is generating after payment of operating expenses, interest, and taxes. Such amounts can be used for dividend payments or funding capital expenditures. |
| 5. Free cash flow | After tax profits + Depreciation − Capital expenditures − Dividends | A quick and rough estimate of the cash a company's business is generating after payment of operating expenses, interest, taxes, dividends, and desirable reinvestments in the business. The larger a company's free cash flow, the greater is its ability to internally fund new strategic initiatives, repay debt, make new acquisitions, repurchase shares of stock, or increase dividend payments. |

*information provided.* Many times cases report views and contradictory opinions (after all, people don't always agree on things, and different people see the same things in different ways). Forcing you to evaluate the data and information presented in the case helps you develop your powers of inference and judgment. Asking you to resolve conflicting information "comes with the territory" because a great many managerial situations entail opposing points of view, conflicting trends, and sketchy information.

8. *Support your diagnosis and opinions with reasons and evidence.* The most important things to prepare for are your answers to the question "Why?" For instance, if after studying the case you are of the opinion that the company's managers are doing a poor job, then it is your answer to "Why?" that establishes just how good your analysis of the situation is. If your instructor has provided you with specific study questions for the case, by all means prepare answers that include all the reasons and number-crunching evidence you can muster to support your diagnosis. If you are using study questions provided by the instructor, *generate at least two pages of notes!*

9. *Develop an appropriate action plan and set of recommendations.* Diagnosis divorced from corrective action is sterile. The test of a manager is always to convert sound analysis into sound actions—actions that will produce the desired results. Hence, the final and most telling step in preparing a case is to develop an action agenda for management that lays out a set of specific recommendations on what to do. Bear in mind that proposing realistic, workable solutions is far preferable to casually tossing out off-the-top-of-your-head suggestions. Be prepared to argue why your recommendations are more attractive than other courses of action that are open.

As long as you are conscientious in preparing your analysis and recommendations, and have ample reasons, evidence, and arguments to support your views, you shouldn't fret unduly about whether what you've prepared is "the right answer" to the case. In case analysis, there is rarely just one right approach or set of recommendations. Managing companies and crafting and executing strategies are not such exact sciences that there exists a single provably correct analysis and action plan for each strategic situation. Of course, some analyses and action plans are better than others; but, in truth, there's nearly always more than one good way to analyze a situation and more than one good plan of action.

## Participating in Class Discussion of a Case

Classroom discussions of cases are sharply different from attending a lecture class. In a case class, students do most of the talking. The instructor's role is to solicit student participation, keep the discussion on track, ask "Why?" often, offer alternative views, play the devil's advocate (if no students jump in to offer opposing views), and otherwise lead the discussion. The students in the class carry the burden for analyzing the situation and for being prepared to present and defend their diagnoses and recommendations. Expect a classroom environment, therefore, that calls for your size-up of the situation, your analysis, what actions you would take, and why you would take them. Do not be dismayed if, as the class discussion unfolds, some insightful things are said by your fellow classmates that you did not think of. It is normal for views and analyses to differ and for the comments of others in the class to expand your own thinking about the case. As the old adage goes, "Two heads are better than one." So it is to be expected that the class as a whole will do a more penetrating and searching job of case analysis than will any one person working alone. This is the power of group effort, and its virtues are that it will help you see more analytical applications, let you test your analyses and judgments against those of your peers, and force you to wrestle with differences of opinion and approaches.

To orient you to the classroom environment on the days a case discussion is scheduled, we compiled the following list of things to expect

1. Expect the instructor to assume the role of extensive questioner and listener.

2. Expect students to do most of the talking. The case method enlists a maximum of individual participation in class discussion. It is not enough to be present as a silent observer; if every student took this approach, there would be no discussion. (Thus, expect a portion of your grade to be based on your participation in case discussions.)

3. Be prepared for the instructor to probe for reasons and supporting analysis.

4. Expect and tolerate challenges to the views expressed. All students have to be willing to submit their conclusions for scrutiny and rebuttal. Each student needs to learn to state his or her views

without fear of disapproval and to overcome the hesitation of speaking out. Learning respect for the views and approaches of others is an integral part of case analysis exercises. But there are times when it is OK to swim against the tide of majority opinion. In the practice of management, there is always room for originality and unorthodox approaches. So while discussion of a case is a group process, there is no compulsion for you or anyone else to cave in and conform to group opinions and group consensus.

5. Don't be surprised if you change your mind about some things as the discussion unfolds. Be alert to how these changes affect your analysis and recommendations (in the event you get called on).

6. Expect to learn a lot in class as the discussion of a case progresses; furthermore, you will find that the cases build on one another—what you learn in one case helps prepare you for the next case discussion.

There are several things you can do on your own to be good and look good as a participant in class discussions:

Although you should do your own independent work and independent thinking, don't hesitate before (and after) class to discuss the case with other students. In real life, managers often discuss the company's problems and situation with other people to refine their own thinking.

- In participating in the discussion, make a conscious effort to contribute, rather than just talk. There is a big difference between saying something that builds the discussion and offering a long-winded, off-the-cuff remark that leaves the class wondering what the point was.

- Avoid the use of "I think," "I believe," and "I feel"; instead, say, "My analysis shows —" and "The company should do _____ because _____." Always give supporting reasons and evidence for your views; then your instructor won't have to ask you "Why?" every time you make a comment.

- In making your points, assume that everyone has read the case and knows what it says. Avoid reciting and rehashing information in the case—instead, use the data and information to explain your assessment of the situation and to support your position.

- Bring the printouts of the work you've done on Case-Tutor or the notes you've prepared (usually two or three pages' worth) to class and rely on them

extensively when you speak. There's no way you can remember everything off the top of your head—especially the results of your number crunching. To reel off the numbers or to present all five reasons why, instead of one, you will need good notes. When you have prepared thoughtful answers to the study questions and use them as the basis for your comments, *everybody* in the room will know you are well prepared, and your contribution to the case discussion will stand out.

## Preparing a Written Case Analysis

Preparing a written case analysis is much like preparing a case for class discussion, except that your analysis must be more complete and put in report form. Unfortunately, though, there is no ironclad procedure for doing a written case analysis. All we can offer are some general guidelines and words of wisdom—this is because company situations and management problems are so diverse that no one mechanical way to approach a written case assignment always works.

Your instructor may assign you a specific topic around which to prepare your written report. Or, alternatively, you may be asked to do a comprehensive written case analysis, where the expectation is that you will (1) *identify* all the pertinent issues that management needs to address, (2) perform whatever *analysis* and *evaluation* is appropriate, and (3) propose an *action plan* and *set of recommendations* addressing the issues you have identified. In going through the exercise of identify, evaluate, and recommend, keep the following pointers in mind.[3]

**Identification**     It is essential early on in your paper that you provide a sharply focused diagnosis of strategic issues and key problems and that you demonstrate a good grasp of the company's present situation. Make sure you can identify the firm's strategy (use the concepts and tools in Chapters 1–8 as diagnostic aids) and that you can pinpoint whatever strategy implementation issues may exist (again, consult the material in Chapters 9–11 for diagnostic help). Consult the key points we have provided at the end of each chapter for further diagnostic suggestions. Consider beginning your paper with an overview of the company's situation, its strategy, and the significant problems and issues that confront management. State problems/issues as clearly and precisely as you can. Unless it is necessary to do so for emphasis, avoid recounting facts and history about the company (assume your professor has read the case and is familiar with the organization).

### Analysis and Evaluation

This is usually the hardest part of the report. Analysis is hard work! Check out the firm's financial ratios, its profit margins and rates of return, and its capital structure, and decide how strong the firm is financially. Table 1 contains a summary of various financial ratios and how they are calculated. Use it to assist in your financial diagnosis. Similarly, look at marketing, production, managerial competence, and other factors underlying the organization's strategic successes and failures. Decide whether the firm has valuable resource strengths and competencies and, if so, whether it is capitalizing on them.

Check to see if the firm's strategy is producing satisfactory results and determine the reasons why or why not. Probe the nature and strength of the competitive forces confronting the company. Decide whether and why the firm's competitive position is getting stronger or weaker. Use the tools and concepts you have learned about to perform whatever analysis and evaluation is appropriate. Work through the case preparation exercise on Case-Tutor if one is available for the case you've been assigned.

In writing your analysis and evaluation, bear in mind four things:

1. You are obliged to offer analysis and evidence to back up your conclusions. Do not rely on unsupported opinions, over-generalizations, and platitudes as a substitute for tight, logical argument backed up with facts and figures.

2. If your analysis involves some important quantitative calculations, use tables and charts to present the calculations clearly and efficiently. Don't just tack the exhibits on at the end of your report and let the reader figure out what they mean and why they were included. Instead, in the body of your report cite some of the key numbers, highlight the conclusions to be drawn from the exhibits, and refer the reader to your charts and exhibits for more details.

3. Demonstrate that you have command of the strategic concepts and analytical tools to which you have been exposed. Use them in your report.

4. Your interpretation of the evidence should be reasonable and objective. Be wary of preparing a one-sided argument that omits all aspects not favorable to your conclusions. Likewise, try not to exaggerate or overdramatize. Endeavor to inject balance into your analysis and to avoid emotional rhetoric. Strike phrases such as "I think," "I feel," and "I believe" when you edit your first draft and write in "My analysis shows," instead.

### Recommendations

The final section of the written case analysis should consist of a set of definite recommendations and a plan of action. Your set of recommendations should address all of the problems/issues you identified and analyzed. If the recommendations come as a surprise or do not follow logically from the analysis, the effect is to weaken greatly your suggestions of what to do. Obviously, your recommendations for actions should offer a reasonable prospect of success. High-risk, bet-the-company recommendations should be made with caution. State how your recommendations will solve the problems you identified. Be sure the company is financially able to carry out what you recommend; also check to see if your recommendations are workable in terms of acceptance by the persons involved, the organization's competence to implement them, and prevailing market and environmental constraints. Try not to hedge or weasel on the actions you believe should be taken.

By all means state your recommendations in sufficient detail to be meaningful—get down to some definite nitty-gritty specifics. Avoid such unhelpful statements as "the organization should do more planning" or "the company should be more aggressive in marketing its product." For instance, if you determine that "the firm should improve its market position," then you need to set forth exactly how you think this should be done. Offer a definite agenda for action, stipulating a timetable and sequence for initiating actions, indicating priorities, and suggesting who should be responsible for doing what.

In proposing an action plan, remember there is a great deal of difference between, on the one hand, being responsible for a decision that may be costly if it proves in error and, on the other hand, casually suggesting courses of action that might be taken when you do not have to bear the responsibility for any of the consequences.

A good rule to follow in making your recommendations is: *Avoid recommending anything you would not yourself be willing to do if you were in management's shoes.* The importance of learning to develop good managerial judgment is indicated by the fact that, even though the same information and operating data may be available to every manager or executive in an organization, the quality of the judgments about what the information means and which actions need to be taken does vary from person to person.[4]

It goes without saying that your report should be well organized and well written. Great ideas amount to little unless others can be convinced of their merit—this takes tight logic, the presentation of convincing evidence, and persuasively written arguments.

## Preparing an Oral Presentation

During the course of your business career it is very likely that you will be called upon to prepare and give a number of oral presentations. For this reason, it is common in courses of this nature to assign cases for oral presentation to the whole class. Such assignments give you an opportunity to hone your presentation skills.

The preparation of an oral presentation has much in common with that of a written case analysis. Both require identification of the strategic issues and problems confronting the company, analysis of industry conditions and the company's situation, and the development of a thorough, well-thought out action plan. The substance of your analysis and quality of your recommendations in an oral presentation should be no different than in a written report. As with a written assignment, you'll need to demonstrate command of the relevant strategic concepts and tools of analysis and your recommendations should contain sufficient detail to provide clear direction for management. The main difference between an oral presentation and a written case is in the delivery format. Oral presentations rely principally on verbalizing your diagnosis, analysis, and recommendations and visually enhancing and supporting your oral discussion with colorful, snappy slides (usually created on Microsoft's Power-Point software).

Typically, oral presentations involve group assignments. Your instructor will provide the details of the assignment—how work should be delegated among the group members and how the presentation should be conducted. Some instructors prefer that presentations begin with issue identification, followed by analysis of the industry and company situation analysis, and conclude with a recommended action plan to improve company performance. Other instructors prefer that the presenters assume that the class has a good understanding of the external industry environment and the company's competitive position and expect the presentation to be strongly focused on the group's recommended action plan and supporting analysis and arguments. The latter approach requires cutting straight to the heart of the case and supporting each recommendation with detailed analysis and persuasive reasoning. Still other instructors may give you the latitude to structure your presentation however you and your group members see fit.

Regardless of the style preferred by your instructor, you should take great care in preparing for the presentation. A good set of slides with good content and good visual appeal is essential to a first-rate presentation. Take some care to choose a nice slide design, font size and style, and color scheme. We suggest including slides covering each of the following areas:

- An opening slide covering the "title" of the presentation and names of the presenters.
- A slide showing an outline of the presentation (perhaps with presenters' names by each topic).
- One or more slides showing the key problems and strategic issues that management needs to address.
- A series of slides covering your analysis of the company's situation.
- A series of slides containing your recommendations and the supporting arguments and reasoning for each recommendation—one slide for each recommendation and the associated reasoning will give it a lot of merit.

You and your team members should carefully plan and rehearse your slide show to maximize impact and minimize distractions. The slide show should include all of the pizzazz necessary to garner the attention of the audience, but not so much that it distracts from the content of what group members are saying to the class. You should remember that the role of slides is to help you communicate your points to the audience. Too many graphics, images, colors, and transitions may divert the audience's attention from what is being said or disrupt the flow of the presentation. Keep in mind that visually dazzling slides rarely hide a shallow or superficial or otherwise flawed case analysis from a perceptive audience. Most instructors will tell you that first-rate slides will definitely enhance a well-delivered presentation, but that impressive visual aids, if accompanied by weak analysis and poor oral delivery, still add up to a substandard presentation.

## Researching Companies and Industries via the Internet and Online Data Services

Very likely, there will be occasions when you need to get additional information about some of the assignee cases, perhaps because your instructor has asked you to do further research on the industry or company or because you are simply curious about what has happened to the company since the case was written. These days, it is relatively easy to run down recent industry developments and to find out whether a company's strategic and financial situation has improved, deteriorated, or changed little since the conclusion of the case. The amount of information about companies and industries available on the Internet and through online data services is formidable and expanding rapidly.

It is a fairly simple matter to go to company websites, click on the investor information offerings and press release files, and get quickly to useful information. Most company websites allow you to view or print the company's quarterly and annual reports, its 10K and 10Q filings with the Securities and Exchange Commission, and various company press releases of interest. Frequently, a company's website will also provide information about its mission and vision statements, values statements, codes of ethics, and strategy information, as well as charts of the company's stock price. The company's recent press releases typically contain reliable information about what of interest has been going on—new product introductions, recent alliances and partnership agreements, recent acquisitions, summaries of the latest financial results, tidbits about the company's strategy, guidance about future revenues and earnings, and other late-breaking company developments. Some company web pages also include links to the home pages of industry trade associations where you can find information about industry size, growth, recent industry news, statistical trends, and future outlook. Thus, an early step in researching a company on the Internet is always to go to its website and see what's available.

## Online Data Services
Lexis-Nexis, Bloomberg Financial News Services, and other online subscription services available in many university libraries provide access to a wide array of business reference material. For example, the web-based Lexis-Nexis Academic Universe contains business news articles from general news sources, business publications, and industry trade publications. Broadcast transcripts from financial news programs are also available through Lexis-Nexis, as are full-text 10-Ks, 10-Qs, annual reports, and company profiles for more than 11,000 U.S. and international companies. Your business librarian should be able to direct you to the resources available through your library that will aid you in your research.

## Public and Subscription Websites with Good Information
Plainly, you can use a search engine such as Google or Yahoo! or MSN to find the latest news on a company or articles written by reporters that have appeared in the business media. These can be very valuable in running down information about recent company developments. However, keep in mind that the information retrieved by a search engine is "unfiltered" and may include sources that are not reliable or that contain inaccurate or misleading information. Be wary of information provided by authors who are unaffiliated with reputable organizations or publications and articles that were published in off-beat sources or on websites with an agenda. Be especially careful in relying on the accuracy of information you find posted on various bulletin boards. Articles covering a company or issue should be copyrighted or published by a reputable source. If you are turning in a paper containing information gathered from the Internet, you should cite your sources (providing the Internet address and date visited); it is also wise to print web pages for your research file (some web pages are updated frequently).

*The Wall Street Journal, Bloomberg Businessweek, Forbes, Barron's,* and *Fortune* are all good sources of articles on companies. The online edition of *The Wall Street Journal* contains the same information that is available daily in its print version of the paper, but the WSJ website also maintains a searchable database of all *The Wall Street Journal* articles published during the past few years. *Fortune* and *Bloomberg Businessweek* also make the content of the most current issue available online to subscribers as well as provide archives sections that allow you to search for articles published during the past few years that may be related to a particular keyword.

The following publications and websites are particularly good sources of company and industry information:

Securities and Exchange Commission EDGAR database (contains company 10-Ks, 10-Qs, etc.)
http://www.sec.gov/edgar/searchedgar/companysearch
Google Finance
http://finance.google.com
CNN Money
http://money.cnn.com
Hoover's Online
http://hoovers.com
*The Wall Street Journal Interactive Edition*
www.wsj.com
*Bloomberg Businessweek*
www.businessweek.com and www.bloomberg.com

*Fortune*
   www.fortune.com
MSN Money Central
   http://moneycentral.msn.com
Yahoo! Finance
   http://finance.yahoo.com/

Some of these Internet sources require subscriptions in order to access their entire databases.

You should/always explore the investor relations section of every public company's website. In today's world, these websites typically have a wealth of information concerning a company's mission, core values, performance targets, strategy, recent financial performance, and latest developments (as described in company press releases).

**Learning Comes Quickly** With a modest investment of time, you will learn how to use Internet sources and search engines to run down information on companies and industries quickly and efficiently. And it is a skill that will serve you well into the future. Once you become familiar with the data available at the different websites mentioned above and learn how to use a search engine, you will know where to go to look for the particular information that you want. Search engines nearly always turn up too many information sources that match your request rather than too few. The trick is to learn to zero in on those most relevant to what you are looking for. Like most things, once you get a little experience under your belt on how to do company and industry research on the Internet, you will find that you can readily find the information you need.

## The Ten Commandments of Case Analysis

As a way of summarizing our suggestions about how to approach the task of case analysis, we have we like to call "The Ten Commandments of Case Analysis." They are shown in Table 2. If you observe all or even most of these commandments faithfully as you prepare a case either for class discussion or for a written report, your chances of doing a good job on the assigned cases will be much improved. Hang in there, give it your best shot, and have some fun exploring what the real world of strategic management is all about.

**TABLE 2    The Ten Commandments of Case Analysis**

| To be observed in written reports and oral presentations, and while participating in class discussions. |
| --- |
| 1. Go through the case twice, once for a quick overview and once to gain full command of the facts. Then take care to explore the information in every one of the case exhibits. |
| 2. Make a complete list of the problems and issues that the company's management needs to address. |
| 3. Be thorough in your analysis of the company's situation (make a minimum of one to two pages of notes detailing your diagnosis). |
| 4. Look for opportunities to apply the concepts and analytical tools in the text chapters—all of the cases in the book have very definite ties to the material in one or more of the text chapters!!!! |
| 5. Do enough number crunching to discover the story told by the data presented in the case. (To help you comply with this commandment, consult Table 1 in this section to guide your probing of a company's financial condition and financial performance.) |
| 6. Support any and all off-the-cuff opinions with well-reasoned arguments and numerical evidence. Don't stop until you can purge "I think" and "I feel" from your assessment and, instead, are able to rely completely on "My analysis shows." |
| 7. Prioritize your recommendations and make sure they can be carried out in an acceptable time frame with the available resources. |
| 8. Support each recommendation with persuasive argument and reasons as to why it makes sense and should result in improved company performance. |
| 9. Review your recommended action plan to see if it addresses all of the problems and issues you identified. Any set of recommendations that does not address all of the issues and problems you identified is incomplete and insufficient. |
| 10. Avoid recommending any course of action that could have disastrous consequences if it doesn't work out as planned. Therefore be as alert to the downside risks of your recommendations as you are to their upside potential and appeal. |

# ENDNOTES

[1] Charles I. Gragg, "Because Wisdom Can't Be Told," in *The Case Method at the Harvard Business School,* ed. M. P. McNair (New York: McGraw-Hill, 1954), p. 11.

[2] Ibid., pp. 12–14; and D. R. Schoen and Philip A. Sprague, "What Is the Case Method?" in *The Case Method at the Harvard Business School,* ed. M. P. McNair, pp. 78–79.

[3] For some additional ideas and viewpoints, you may wish to consult Thomas J. Raymond, "Written Analysis of Cases," in *The Case Method at the Harvard Business School,* ed. M. P. McNair, pp. 139–63. Raymond's article includes an actual case, a sample analysis of the case, and a sample of a student's written report on the case.

[4] Gragg, "Because Wisdom Can't Be Told," p. 10.

# PHOTO CREDITS

**Chapter 1**

page 6: © David Paul Morris/Bloomberg via Getty Images; page 11: © PR NEWSWIRE / AP

**Chapter 2**

page 26: © 2010, Zappos.com, Inc.; page 30: Joe Raedle/Getty Images; page 39: © Jason Reed/Reuters/Corbis; Jay Mallin/Bloomberg via Getty Images

**Chapter 3**

page 73: © Bloomberg via Getty Images; © Bloomberg via Getty Images

**Chapter 4**

page 100: © KP MacLane/Brian Woodcock

**Chapter 5**

page 127: © Bloomberg via Getty Images; page 137: © Willie Davis/Aravind Eye Foundation; page 138: © Martin Klimek/ZUMApress.com

**Chapter 6**

page 153: © PRNewsFoto/Gilt Groupe/AP; page 157: © Amazon.com; page 161 © Bloomberg via Getty Images; page 166: © American Apparel

**Chapter 7**

page 192: © Bloomberg via Getty Images; page 205: © Julie Dermansky/Julie Dermansky/Corbis; page 208: © Bloomberg via Getty Images

**Chapter 8**

page 248: © AP Photo/Mike Derer; page 250: © Bloomberg via Getty Images

**Chapter 9**

page 259: © Bloomberg via Getty Images; page 267 © PRNewsFoto/Novo Nordisk/AP; page 273: © Bloomberg via Getty Images

**Chapter 10**

page 294: © Proctor and Gamble; page 298: © Toyota; page 303 © Apple Inc.

**Chapter 11**

page 326: © Paulo Fridman/Corbis; page 333: © Bloomberg via Getty Images; page 336: © Bloomberg via Getty Images

**Chapter 12**

page 345: © PRNewsFoto/W. L. Gore & Associates/AP

# COMPANY INDEX

## O

## U

# NAME INDEX

# SUBJECT INDEX